Microsoft

Microsoft Excel 2016 Data Analysis and Business Modeling

Wayne L. Winston

PHI Learning Private Limited

Delhi-110092
2019

This Indian Reprint—₹ 795.00
(Original U.S. Edition—₹ 3410.00)

MICROSOFT EXCEL 2016 DATA ANALYSIS AND BUSINESS MODELING
by Wayne L. Winston

ISBN-978-81-203-5335-0

Published by Asoke K. Ghosh, PHI Learning Private Limited, Rimjhim House, 111, Patparganj Industrial Estate, Delhi-110092 and Printed by Rajkamal Electric Press, Plot No. 2, Phase IV, HSIDC, Kundli-131028, Sonepat, Haryana.

Contents at a glance

	Introduction	*xxi*
CHAPTER 1	Basic spreadsheet modeling	1
CHAPTER 2	Range names	9
CHAPTER 3	Lookup functions	21
CHAPTER 4	The INDEX function	29
CHAPTER 5	The MATCH function	33
CHAPTER 6	Text functions	39
CHAPTER 7	Dates and date functions	55
CHAPTER 8	Evaluating investments by using net present value criteria	63
CHAPTER 9	Internal rate of return	69
CHAPTER 10	More Excel financial functions	75
CHAPTER 11	Circular references	89
CHAPTER 12	IF statements	95
CHAPTER 13	Time and time functions	113
CHAPTER 14	The Paste Special command	119
CHAPTER 15	Three-dimensional formulas and hyperlinks	125
CHAPTER 16	The auditing tool	131
CHAPTER 17	Sensitivity analysis with data tables	139
CHAPTER 18	The Goal Seek command	151
CHAPTER 19	Using the Scenario Manager for sensitivity analysis	157
CHAPTER 20	The COUNTIF, COUNTIFS, COUNT, COUNTA, and COUNTBLANK functions	163
CHAPTER 21	The SUMIF, AVERAGEIF, SUMIFS, and AVERAGEIFS functions	171
CHAPTER 22	The OFFSET function	177
CHAPTER 23	The INDIRECT function	191
CHAPTER 24	Conditional formatting	199
CHAPTER 25	Sorting in Excel	227
CHAPTER 26	Tables	235
CHAPTER 27	Spin buttons, scroll bars, option buttons, check boxes, combo boxes, and group list boxes	251
CHAPTER 28	The analytics revolution	263

CHAPTER 29	An introduction to optimization with Excel Solver	269
CHAPTER 30	Using Solver to determine the optimal product mix	273
CHAPTER 31	Using Solver to schedule your workforce	285
CHAPTER 32	Using Solver to solve transportation or distribution problems	291
CHAPTER 33	Using Solver for capital budgeting	297
CHAPTER 34	Using Solver for financial planning	305
CHAPTER 35	Using Solver to rate sports teams	311
CHAPTER 36	Warehouse location and the GRG Multistart and Evolutionary Solver engines	317
CHAPTER 37	Penalties and the Evolutionary Solver	327
CHAPTER 38	The traveling salesperson problem	333
CHAPTER 39	Importing data from a text file or document	337
CHAPTER 40	Validating data	343
CHAPTER 41	Summarizing data by using histograms and Pareto charts	351
CHAPTER 42	Summarizing data by using descriptive statistics	365
CHAPTER 43	Using PivotTables and slicers to describe data	383
CHAPTER 44	The Data Model	429
CHAPTER 45	Power Pivot	439
CHAPTER 46	Power View and 3D Maps	451
CHAPTER 47	Sparklines	465
CHAPTER 48	Summarizing data with database statistical functions	471
CHAPTER 49	Filtering data and removing duplicates	481
CHAPTER 50	Consolidating data	495
CHAPTER 51	Creating subtotals	501
CHAPTER 52	Charting tricks	507
CHAPTER 53	Estimating straight-line relationships	543
CHAPTER 54	Modeling exponential growth	551
CHAPTER 55	The power curve	555
CHAPTER 56	Using correlations to summarize relationships	561
CHAPTER 57	Introduction to multiple regression	567
CHAPTER 58	Incorporating qualitative factors into multiple regression	575
CHAPTER 59	Modeling nonlinearities and interactions	585
CHAPTER 60	Analysis of variance: One-way ANOVA	593
CHAPTER 61	Randomized blocks and two-way ANOVA	599
CHAPTER 62	Using moving averages to understand time series	609

CHAPTER 63	Winters method	613
CHAPTER 64	Ratio-to-moving-average forecast method	619
CHAPTER 65	Forecasting in the presence of special events	623
CHAPTER 66	An introduction to probability	631
CHAPTER 67	An introduction to random variables	641
CHAPTER 68	The binomial, hypergeometric, and negative binomial random variables	647
CHAPTER 69	The Poisson and exponential random variable	655
CHAPTER 70	The normal random variable and Z-scores	659
CHAPTER 71	Weibull and beta distributions: Modeling machine life and duration of a project	669
CHAPTER 72	Making probability statements from forecasts	675
CHAPTER 73	Using the lognormal random variable to model stock prices	679
CHAPTER 74	Introduction to Monte Carlo simulation	683
CHAPTER 75	Calculating an optimal bid	693
CHAPTER 76	Simulating stock prices and asset-allocation modeling	699
CHAPTER 77	Fun and games: Simulating gambling and sporting-event probabilities	709
CHAPTER 78	Using resampling to analyze data	717
CHAPTER 79	Pricing stock options	721
CHAPTER 80	Determining customer value	735
CHAPTER 81	The economic order quantity inventory model	741
CHAPTER 82	Inventory modeling with uncertain demand	747
CHAPTER 83	Queuing theory: The mathematics of waiting in line	753
CHAPTER 84	Estimating a demand curve	759
CHAPTER 85	Pricing products by using tie-ins	765
CHAPTER 86	Pricing products by using subjectively determined demand	771
CHAPTER 87	Nonlinear pricing	777
CHAPTER 88	Array formulas and functions	785
CHAPTER 89	Recording macros	803
	Index	*815*

Contents

Introduction . . . . *xxi*

Chapter 1 Basic spreadsheet modeling 1

Answers to this chapter's questions. 1

Problems. 8

Chapter 2 Range names 9

How can I create named ranges? 9

Using the Name box to create a range name 10

Creating named ranges by using the Create From Selection option. 11

Creating range names by using the Define Name option 12

The Name Manager. 13

Answers to this chapter's questions. 14

Remarks 18

Problems. 19

Chapter 3 Lookup functions 21

Syntax of the lookup functions. 21

VLOOKUP syntax 21

HLOOKUP syntax 22

Answers to this chapter's questions. 22

Problems. 25

Chapter 4 The INDEX function 29

Syntax of the INDEX function 29

Answers to this chapter's questions. 29
Problems. 31

Chapter 5 The MATCH function 33

Syntax of the MATCH function 33
Answers to this chapter's questions. 35
Problems. 38

Chapter 6 Text functions 39

Text function syntax 40
The LEFT function. 41
The RIGHT function 41
The MID function. 41
The TRIM function 41
The LEN function 41
The FIND and SEARCH functions. 41
The REPT function 41
The CONCATENATE and & functions 42
The REPLACE function. 42
The VALUE function. 42
The UPPER, LOWER, and PROPER functions 42
The CHAR function 42
The CLEAN function 43
The SUBSTITUTE function. 43
Answers to this chapter's questions. 43
Extracting data by using the Convert Text To Columns Wizard . . .47
Problems. 51

Chapter 7 Dates and date functions 55

Answers to this chapter's questions. 56
Problems. 61

Chapter 8 Evaluating investments by using net present value criteria **63**

Answers to this chapter's questions. 64

Problems. 68

Chapter 9 Internal rate of return **69**

Answers to this chapter's questions. 70

Problems. 73

Chapter 10 More Excel financial functions **75**

Answers to this chapter's questions. 75

CUMPRINC and CUMIPMT functions 80

Problems. 83

Chapter 11 Circular references **89**

Answers to this chapter's questions. 89

Problems. 92

Chapter 12 IF statements **95**

Answers to this chapter's questions. 96

Problems. 108

Chapter 13 Time and time functions **113**

Answers to this chapter's questions. 114

Problems. 118

Chapter 14 The Paste Special command **119**

Answers to this chapter's questions. 119

Problems. 123

Chapter 15 Three-dimensional formulas and hyperlinks **125**

Answers to this chapter's questions. 125

Problems 128

Chapter 16 The auditing tool **131**

Answers to this chapter's questions. 134

Problems. 138

Chapter 17 Sensitivity analysis with data tables **139**

Answers to this chapter's questions. 140

Problems. 146

Chapter 18 The Goal Seek command **151**

Answers to this chapter's questions. 151

Problems. 154

Chapter 19 Using the Scenario Manager for sensitivity analysis **157**

Answer to this chapter's question 157

Remarks 161

Problems. 161

Chapter 20 The COUNTIF, COUNTIFS, COUNT, COUNTA, and COUNTBLANK functions **163**

Answers to this chapter's questions. 165

Remarks 168

Problems. 168

Chapter 21 The SUMIF, AVERAGEIF, SUMIFS, and AVERAGEIFS functions **171**

Answers to this chapter's questions. 172

Problems. 175

Chapter 22 The OFFSET function **177**

Answers to this chapter's questions. 178

Remarks 187

Problems. 187

Chapter 23 The INDIRECT function **191**

Answers to this chapter's questions. 192

Problems. 198

Chapter 24 Conditional formatting **199**

Answers to this chapter's questions. 201

Problems. 222

Chapter 25 Sorting in Excel **227**

Answers to this chapter's questions. 227

Problems. 234

Chapter 26 Tables **235**

Answers to this chapter's questions. 235

Problems. 248

Chapter 27 Spin buttons, scroll bars, option buttons, check boxes, combo boxes, and group list boxes **251**

Answers to this chapter's questions. 252

Problems. 261

Chapter 28 The analytics revolution **263**

Answers to this chapter's questions. 263

Chapter 29 An introduction to optimization with Excel Solver **269**

Problems. 272

Chapter 30 Using Solver to determine the optimal product mix **273**

Answers to this chapter's questions. 273

Problems. 282

Chapter 31 Using Solver to schedule your workforce 285

Answers to this chapter's question 285

Problems.....288

Chapter 32 Using Solver to solve transportation or distribution problems 291

Answer to this chapter's question 291

Problems.....294

Chapter 33 Using Solver for capital budgeting 297

Answer to this chapter's question 297

Handling other constraints.....300

Solving binary and integer programming problems.....301

Problems.....302

Chapter 34 Using Solver for financial planning 305

Answers to this chapter's questions.....305

Problems.....309

Chapter 35 Using Solver to rate sports teams 311

Answer to this chapter's question 312

Why is our model not a linear Solver model?.....314

Problems.....314

Chapter 36 Warehouse location and the GRG Multistart and Evolutionary Solver engines 317

Understanding the GRG Multistart and Evolutionary Solver engines 317

How does Solver solve linear model problems?.....317

How does the GRG Nonlinear engine solve nonlinear optimization models? 318

How does the Evolutionary Solver engine tackle nonsmooth optimization problems? 321

Answer to this chapter's questions 321

Problems...326

Chapter 37 Penalties and the Evolutionary Solver 327

Answers to this chapter's questions.....................................327

Using conditional formatting to highlight each employee's ratings.....................................330

Problems...330

Chapter 38 The traveling salesperson problem 333

Answers to this chapter's questions.....................................333

Problems...336

Chapter 39 Importing data from a text file or document 337

Answers to this chapter's question 337

Problems...341

Chapter 40 Validating data 343

Answers to this chapter's questions.....................................343

Remarks...347

Problems...348

Chapter 41 Summarizing data by using histograms and Pareto charts 351

Answers to this chapter's questions.....................................351

Problems...362

Chapter 42 Summarizing data by using descriptive statistics 365

Answers to this chapter's questions.....................................366

Using conditional formatting to highlight outliers 371

Problems...380

Chapter 43 Using PivotTables and slicers to describe data **383**

Answers to this chapter's questions. 384

Remarks about grouping 412

Problems. 424

Chapter 44 The Data Model **429**

Answers to this chapter's questions. 429

Problems. 437

Chapter 45 Power Pivot **439**

Answers to this chapter's questions. 440

Problems. 449

Chapter 46 Power View and 3D Maps **451**

Questions answered in this chapter. 452

Problems. 464

Chapter 47 Sparklines **465**

Answers to this chapter's questions. 465

Problems. 469

Chapter 48 Summarizing data with database statistical functions **471**

Answers to this chapter's questions. 473

Problems. 478

Chapter 49 Filtering data and removing duplicates **481**

Answers to this chapter's questions. 483

Problems. 494

Chapter 50 Consolidating data **495**

Answer to this chapter's question 495

Problems. 499

Chapter 51 Creating subtotals **501**

Answers to this chapter's questions. 501

Problems. 505

Chapter 52 Charting tricks **507**

Answers to this chapter's questions. 508

Problems. 540

Chapter 53 Estimating straight-line relationships **543**

Answers to this chapter's questions. 544

Problems. 549

Chapter 54 Modeling exponential growth **551**

Answers to this chapter's question 551

Problems. 554

Chapter 55 The power curve **555**

Answer to this chapter's question 557

Problems. 559

Chapter 56 Using correlations to summarize relationships **561**

Answer to this chapter's question 563

Filling in the correlation matrix 564

Using the CORREL function 565

Relationship between correlation and R-squared 565

Correlation and regression toward the mean. 566

Problems. 566

Chapter 57 Introduction to multiple regression **567**

Answers to this chapter's questions. 567

Chapter 58 Incorporating qualitative factors into multiple regression 575

Answers to this chapter's questions. 575

Chapter 59 Modeling nonlinearities and interactions 585

Answers to this chapter's questions. 585

Problems for Chapters 57 through 59. 589

Chapter 60 Analysis of variance: One-way ANOVA 593

Answers to this chapter's questions. 594

Problems. 597

Chapter 61 Randomized blocks and two-way ANOVA 599

Answers to this chapter's questions. 600

Problems. 607

Chapter 62 Using moving averages to understand time series 609

Answers to this chapter's question 609

Problem 611

Chapter 63 Winters method 613

Time-series characteristics. 613

Parameter definitions. 613

Initializing Winters method. 614

Estimating the smoothing constants. 615

Remarks 617

Problems. 617

Chapter 64 Ratio-to-moving-average forecast method 619

Answers to this chapter's questions. 619

Problem 622

Chapter 65 Forecasting in the presence of special events **623**

Answers to this chapter's questions. 623

Problems. 630

Chapter 66 An introduction to probability **631**

Answers to this chapter's questions. 631

Problems. 637

Chapter 67 An introduction to random variables **641**

Answers to this chapter's questions. 641

Problems. 645

Chapter 68 The binomial, hypergeometric, and negative binomial random variables **647**

Answers to this chapter's questions. 648

Problems. 653

Chapter 69 The Poisson and exponential random variable **655**

Answers to this chapter's questions. 655

Problems. 658

Chapter 70 The normal random variable and Z-scores **659**

Answers to this chapter's questions. 659

Problems. 666

Chapter 71 Weibull and beta distributions: Modeling machine life and duration of a project **669**

Answers to this chapter's questions. 669

Problems. 673

Chapter 72 Making probability statements from forecasts **675**

Answers to this chapter's questions. 675

Problems. 677

Chapter 73 Using the lognormal random variable to model stock prices **679**

Answers to this chapter's questions 679

Remarks 682

Problems 682

Chapter 74 Introduction to Monte Carlo simulation **683**

Answers to this chapter's questions 683

The impact of risk on your decision 689

Confidence interval for mean profit 690

Problems 690

Chapter 75 Calculating an optimal bid **693**

Answers to this chapter's questions 693

Problems 696

Chapter 76 Simulating stock prices and asset-allocation modeling **699**

Answers to this chapter's questions 699

Problems 707

Chapter 77 Fun and games: Simulating gambling and sporting-event probabilities **709**

Answers to this chapter's questions 709

Problems 715

Chapter 78 Using resampling to analyze data **717**

Answer to this chapter's question 717

Problems 719

Chapter 79 Pricing stock options **721**

Answers to this chapter's questions 722

Problems 732

Chapter 80 Determining customer value **735**

Answers to this chapter's questions. 735

Problems. 739

Chapter 81 The economic order quantity inventory model **741**

Answers to this chapter's questions. 741

Problems. 745

Chapter 82 Inventory modeling with uncertain demand **747**

Answers to this chapter's questions. 748

The back-order case 748

The lost-sales case 749

Problems. 752

Chapter 83 Queuing theory: The mathematics of waiting in line **753**

Answers to this chapter's questions. 753

Problems. 757

Chapter 84 Estimating a demand curve **759**

Answers to this chapter's questions. 759

Problems. 763

Chapter 85 Pricing products by using tie-ins **765**

Answer to this chapter's question 765

Problems. 768

Chapter 86 Pricing products by using subjectively determined demand **771**

Answer to this chapter's questions 771

Problems. 774

Chapter 87 Nonlinear pricing **777**

Answers to this chapter's questions. 777

Problems. 784

Chapter 88 Array formulas and functions **785**

Answers to this chapter's questions. 786

Problems. 800

Chapter 89 Recording macros **803**

Answers to this chapter's questions. 803

Problems. 812

Index *815*

Introduction

Whether you work for a Fortune 500 corporation, a small company, a government agency, or a not-for-profit organization, if you're reading this introduction, the chances are you use Microsoft Excel in your daily work. Your job probably involves summarizing, reporting, and analyzing data. It might also involve building analytic models to help your employer increase profits, reduce costs, or manage operations more efficiently.

Since 1999, I've taught thousands of analysts at organizations such as Abbott Labs, Booz Allen Hamilton consulting, Bristol-Myers Squibb, Broadcom, Cisco Systems, Deloitte Consulting, Drugstore.com, eBay, Eli Lilly, Ford, General Electric, General Motors, Intel, Microsoft, MGM Hotels, Morgan Stanley, NCR, Owens Corning, Pfizer, Proctor & Gamble, PWC, Sabre, Schulmberger, Tellabs, 3M, the US Army, the US Department of Defense, the US Navy, and Verizon how to use Excel more efficiently and productively in their jobs. Students have often told me that the tools and methods I teach in my classes have saved them hours of time each week and provided them with new and improved approaches for analyzing important business problems.

I've used the techniques described in this book in my own consulting practice to solve many business problems. For example, I have used Excel to help the Dallas Mavericks and New York Knickerbockers NBA basketball teams evaluate referees, players, and lineups. During the last 20 years, I have also taught Excel business modeling and data analysis classes to MBA students at Indiana University's Kelley School of Business and the University of Houston's Bauer College of Business. (As proof of my teaching excellence, I have won more than 45 teaching awards and have won the school's overall MBA teaching award six times.) I would like to also note that 95 percent of MBA students at Indiana University took my spreadsheet modeling class even though it was an elective.

The book you have in your hands is an attempt to make these successful classes available to everyone. Here is why I think the book will help you learn how to use Excel more effectively:

- The materials have been tested while teaching thousands of analysts working for Fortune 500 corporations and government agencies.
- I've written the book as though I am talking to the reader. I hope this approach transfers the spirit of a successful classroom environment to the written page.

- I teach by example, which makes concepts easier to master. These examples are constructed to have a real-world feel. Many of the examples are based on questions sent to me by employees of Fortune 500 corporations.

For the most part, I lead you through the approaches I take in Excel to set up and answer a wide range of data analysis and business questions. You can follow along with my explanations by referring to the sample worksheets that accompany each example. However, I have also included template files for the book's examples on the companion website (*http://aka.ms/ExcelData2016/downloads*). If you want to, you can use these templates to work directly with Excel and complete each example on your own.

Generally, the chapters in this book are short and organized around a single concept. You should be able to master the content of most chapters with at most two hours of study. By looking at the questions that begin each chapter, you'll gain an idea about the types of problems you'll be able to solve after mastering a chapter's topics.

In addition to learning about Excel formulas, you will learn some important math in a fairly painless fashion. For example, you'll learn about statistics, forecasting, optimization models, Monte Carlo simulation, inventory modeling, and the mathematics of waiting in line. You will also learn about some recent developments in business thinking, such as real options, customer value, and mathematical pricing models.

At the end of each chapter, I've provided a group of practice problems (more than 800 in total) that you can work through on your own. Many of these problems are based on actual situations faced by business analysts at Fortune 500 companies. These problems will help you fully understand the information in each chapter. Answers to all problems are included in files you can download from the book's companion website.

Most of all, learning should be fun. If you read this book, you will learn how to predict US presidential elections, how to set football point spreads, how to determine the probability of winning at craps, and how to determine the probability of a specific team winning an NCAA tournament. These examples are interesting and fun, and they also teach you a lot about solving business problems with Excel.

> **Note** To follow along with this book, you must have Excel 2016. Previous versions of this book can be used with Excel 2003, Excel 2007, Excel 2010, or Excel 2013.

What's new in this edition

This edition of the book contains the following changes:

- An introductory chapter (Chapter 1) on basic spreadsheet modeling, which should better enable the reader who is an Excel novice to understand the rest of the book. In particular, Chapter 1 discusses the concept of absolute and relative addressing in formulas (you need to understand $ signs!) and the order of operations used in Excel formulas.
- A discussion (in Chapter 52) of Excel 2016's exciting new charts.
- Chapter 66 contains an introduction to probability (including Bayes' theorem) that should be helpful to instructors who use the book in a quantitative methods class.
- Chapter 89 shows the reader how to record time-saving macros.
- More than 100 new problems have been added.

What you should know before reading this book

To follow the examples in this book, you do not need to be an Excel guru. Basically, the two key actions you should know how to do are the following:

- **Enter a formula** You should know that formulas must begin with an equals sign (=). You should also know the basic mathematical operators. For example, you should know that an asterisk (*) is used for multiplication, a forward slash (/) is used for division, and the caret key (^) is used to raise a quantity to a power.
- **Work with cell references** You should know that when you copy a formula that contains a cell reference such as $A$4 (an absolute cell reference, which is created by including the dollar signs), the formula still refers to cell A4 in the cells you copy it to. When you copy a formula that contains a cell reference such as $A4 (a mixed cell address), the column remains fixed, but the row changes. Finally, when you copy a formula that contains a cell reference such as A4 (a relative cell reference), both the row and the column of the cells referenced in the formula change.

These ideas are thoroughly described in Chapter 1.

How to use this book

As you read along with the examples in this book, you can take one of two approaches:

- You can open the template file that corresponds to the example you are studying and complete each step of the example as you read the book. You will be surprised how easy this process is and amazed with how much you learn and retain. This is the approach I use in my corporate classes.
- Instead of working in the template files, you can follow my explanations as you look at the final version of each sample file.

Downloads

This book features a companion website that makes available to you all the sample files you can use in the book's examples (both the final Excel workbooks and the starting templates you can work with on your own). The workbooks and templates are organized in folders named for each chapter. The answers to all chapter-ending problems in the book are also included with the sample files. Each answer file is named so that you can identify it easily. For example, the file containing the answer to Problem 2 in Chapter 10 is named S10_2.xlsx.

To work through the examples in this book, you need to copy the book's sample files to your computer. These practice files can be downloaded from the book's download page, located at:

http://aka.ms/ExcelData2016/downloads

Display the page in your web browser, and follow the instructions for downloading the files.

Acknowledgments

I am eternally grateful to Jennifer Skoog and Norm Tonina, who had faith in me and first hired me to teach Excel classes for Microsoft finance. Jennifer in particular was instrumental in helping design the content and style of the classes on which the book is based. Keith Lange of Eli Lilly, Pat Keating and Doug Hoppe of Cisco Systems, and Dennis Fuller of the US Army also helped me refine my thoughts on teaching data analysis and modeling with Excel.

Project editor John Pierce is by far the best editor I have ever had, and he did a great job of keeping me (and the book) on schedule. Ed Price was also the most thorough and best technical editor I have ever had. I am grateful to my many students at the organizations where I've taught and students at the Indiana University Kelley School of Business and University of Houston Bauer College of Business. Many of them have taught me things I did not know about Excel.

Alex Blanton, formerly of Microsoft Press, championed this project at the start and shared my vision of developing a user-friendly text designed for use by business analysts.

Finally, my lovely and talented wife, Vivian, and my wonderful children, Jennifer and Gregory, put up with my long weekend hours at the keyboard.

Errata, updates, & book support

We've made every effort to ensure the accuracy of this book and its companion content. You can access updates to this book—in the form of a list of submitted errata and their related corrections—at:

http://aka.ms/ExcelData2016/errata

If you discover an error that is not already listed, please submit it to us at the same page.

If you need additional support, email Microsoft Press Book Support at *mspinput@microsoft.com*.

Please note that product support for Microsoft software and hardware is not offered through the previous addresses. For help with Microsoft software or hardware, go to *http://support.microsoft.com*.

Free ebooks from Microsoft Press

From technical overviews to in-depth information on special topics, the free ebooks from Microsoft Press cover a wide range of topics. These ebooks are available in PDF, EPUB, and Mobi for Kindle formats, ready for you to download at:

http://aka.ms/mspressfree

Check back often to see what is new!

We want to hear from you

At Microsoft Press, your satisfaction is our top priority, and your feedback our most valuable asset. Please tell us what you think of this book at:

http://aka.ms/tellpress

We know you're busy, so we've kept it short with just a few questions. Your answers go directly to the editors at Microsoft Press. (No personal information will be requested.) Thanks in advance for your input!

Stay in touch

Let's keep the conversation going! We're on Twitter: *http://twitter.com/MicrosoftPress*

CHAPTER 1

Basic spreadsheet modeling

Questions answered in this chapter:

- How can I efficiently determine each of my employee's weekly wages?
- How can I efficiently determine how much a bakery owes each supplier?
- How can I predict the number of customers a new health club will have in 10 years?
- What does "Please excuse my dear Aunt Sally" (PEMDAS) have to do with writing correct Excel formulas?
- How can my local coffee shop determine how changes in price and unit cost affect profit?

A friend of mine, Dennis Fuller, told me "the spreadsheet is the canvas for the business analyst." None of us can paint a masterpiece like Van Gogh's *Starry Night*, but if we master Excel we can start with a blank spreadsheet and create our own masterpiece that enables us to model virtually any situation. For many people, the barrier to entry in becoming proficient at Excel is in understanding how Excel formulas work. In this chapter, we will develop several simple spreadsheet models that should get you ready to master the complexities of Excel.

Answers to this chapter's questions

How can I efficiently determine each of my employee's weekly wages?

In the file Wagestemp.xlsx (in the Templates folder), shown in Figure 1-1, you are given the hours worked this week and hourly salary for several employees. You want to determine the amount paid to each employee, as well as total hours worked and average hourly wage.

D22

	B	C	D	E	F
1					
2					
3	Employee	Hours	Wage Per Hour	Weekly Salary	
4	Luka Abrus	49	$ 10.00	$ 490.00	=C4*D4
5	Terry Adams	36	$ 13.00	$ 468.00	=C5*D5
6	David Ahs	43	$ 14.00	$ 602.00	=C6*D6
7	Kim Akers	35	$ 10.00	$ 350.00	=C7*D7
8	Ties Arts	38	$ 9.00	$ 342.00	=C8*D8
9	Kamil Amerih	38	$ 14.00	$ 532.00	=C9*D9
10	Amy Alberts	42	$ 11.00	$ 462.00	=C10*D10
11	Matt Berg	39	$ 9.00	$ 351.00	=C11*D11
12	Totals	320			
13		=SUM(C4:C11)			
14			Average Salary	$ 449.63	
15				=AVERAGE(E4:E11)	

FIGURE 1-1 Calculating weekly payroll.

To calculate Luka's weekly salary, you need to multiply the value in cell C4 by the value in cell D4. So you enter in cell E4 the formula =C4*D4.

You could move to cell E5 and enter the formula =C5*D5 to compute Terry's salary, but Excel's Copy command allows you to easily compute the weekly salary for every employee, even if there are 1,000,000 employees. (Excel 2007 and later have 1,048,576 rows!) Simply move to cell E4 and use the keystroke combination Ctrl+C to copy the formula. Then select the range E5:E11 and use either the keystroke combination Ctrl+V or the Enter key to add the formula to the range E5:E11. You could also copy the formula in E4 to the range E5:E11 by pointing at the tiny square in the lower-right corner of E4 and, after observing the cursor change to a thin black crosshair, press the left mouse button and drag the formula to the range E5:E11. In each cell where the formula is copied, Excel will multiply the two values to the left of the cell in column E. Note that we will often use Excel's FORMULATEXT function (which debuted in Excel 2013) to make our formulas show up in the spreadsheet. For example, entering the formula =FORMULATEXT(E4) in cell F4 shows the cell E4 formula.

You could also compute in cell C12 (as I did in the file Wagesfinal.xlsx) the total hours worked this week with the formula =SUM(C4:C11). In cell E14, I computed the average salary per employee with the formula =AVERAGE(E4:E11).

How can I efficiently determine how much a bakery owes each supplier?

In the file Bakery1temp.xlsx, you are given the price per pound that a bakery paid each of six suppliers for sugar, butter, and flour. Determine the amount paid to each supplier for sugar, flour, and butter. Also determine the total amount paid.

As shown in Figure 1-2, in cell E23 we compute the cost paid to Supplier 1 for sugar by multiplying the cost per pound that Supplier 1 charged for sugar by the amount of sugar bought from Supplier 1. To do this, we use the formula =E5*E14.

To compute the cost paid to each supplier for each product, we can use any of the following approaches:

- Select cell E23 and, after pressing Ctrl+C, select the range E23:G28 and press Ctrl+V.
- Select cell E23 and, after pressing Ctrl+C, select the range E23:G28 and then press the Enter key.
- Select cell E23 and, after the cursor changes to the crosshair, drag the formula to F23:G23. Then drag the range E23:G23 to E24:G28.

	C	D	E	F	G	H	I	J
4			Sugar	Butter	Flour			
5		Supplier 1	$ 0.32	$ 1.57	$ 0.11			
6		Supplier 2	$ 0.35	$ 1.54	$ 0.10			
7		Supplier 3	$ 0.25	$ 1.54	$ 0.21			
8		Supplier 4	$ 0.29	$ 1.24	$ 0.10			
9		Supplier 5	$ 0.35	$ 1.30	$ 0.18			
10		Supplier 6	$ 0.27	$ 1.42	$ 0.15			
11								
12		**Quantity**						
13			Sugar	Butter	Flour			
14		Supplier 1	364	391	220			
15		Supplier 2	387	245	314			
16		Supplier 3	290	211	200			
17		Supplier 4	340	265	330			
18		Supplier 5	261	345	246			
19		Supplier 6	365	232	390			
20								
21		**Cost**						
22			Sugar	Butter	Flour	Total		
23	=E5*E14	Supplier 1	$ 116.48	$ 613.87	$ 24.20	$ 754.55	=SUM(E23:G23)	
24		Supplier 2	$ 135.45	$ 377.30	$ 31.40	$ 544.15	=SUM(E24:G24)	
25		Supplier 3	$ 72.50	$ 324.94	$ 42.00	$ 439.44	=SUM(E25:G25)	
26		Supplier 4	$ 98.60	$ 328.60	$ 33.00	$ 460.20	=SUM(E26:G26)	
27		Supplier 5	$ 91.35	$ 448.50	$ 44.28	$ 584.13	=SUM(E27:G27)	
28		Supplier 6	$ 98.55	$ 329.44	$ 58.50	$ 486.49	=SUM(E28:G28)	
29		Total	$ 612.93	$ 2,422.65	$ 233.38			
30			=SUM(E23:E28)	=SUM(F23:F28)	=SUM(G23:G28)			

FIGURE 1-2 Computing bakery costs: different prices for each supplier.

To find the total amount paid to each supplier, enter in H23 the formula =SUM(E23:G23) and copy this formula to H24:H28. Entering the formula =SUM(E23:E28) in cell E29 and copying this formula to F29:H29 computes the total amount paid for each product.

A quicker way to create our totals is to select the range H23:H28 and (after holding down the Ctrl key) select the range E30:G30. Then simply click the AutoSum button in the Editing group on the Home tab of the ribbon, as shown in Figure 1-3.

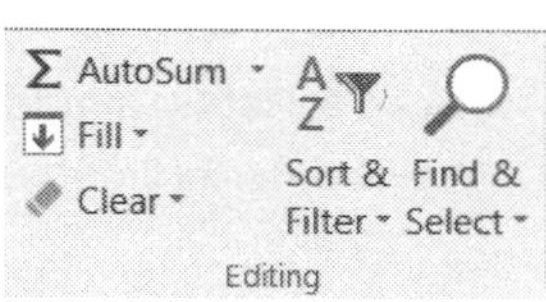

FIGURE 1-3 Use the AutoSum button to total a set of numbers.

The AutoSum command guesses (not always correctly, so be careful!) the range of cells you want to sum in order to fill the selected cells. In this case, AutoSum might save you five seconds!

In the file Bakery2temp.xlsx, shown in Figure 1-4, we now assume that each supplier charges the same price for all products. Again compute the total amount paid to each supplier for each product and the total amount the bakery pays each supplier.

	C	D	E	F	G	H
9						
10						
11			**Price**			
12			$0.40	$1.20	$0.12	
13		**Quantity**	Sugar	Butter	Flour	
14		Supplier 1	364	391	220	
15		Supplier 2	387	245	314	
16		Supplier 3	290	211	200	
17		Supplier 4	340	265	330	
18		Supplier 5	261	345	246	
19		Supplier 6	365	232	390	
20						
21		**Cost**				
22			Sugar	Butter	Flour	Total
23	=E$12*E14	Supplier 1	$ 145.60	$ 469.20	$ 26.40	$ 641.20
24	=E$12*E15	Supplier 2	$ 154.80	$ 294.00	$ 37.68	$ 486.48
25	=E$12*E16	Supplier 3	$ 116.00	$ 253.20	$ 24.00	$ 393.20
26	=E$12*E17	Supplier 4	$ 136.00	$ 318.00	$ 39.60	$ 493.60
27	=E$12*E18	Supplier 5	$ 104.40	$ 414.00	$ 29.52	$ 547.92
28	=E$12*E19	Supplier 6	$ 146.00	$ 278.40	$ 46.80	$ 471.20
29		Total	$ 802.80	$2,026.80	$ 204.00	

FIGURE 1-4 Computing bakery costs: all supplier prices are the same.

Proceeding as before, the naïve reader might enter into cell E23 the formula E12*E14 and copy this formula to the range E23:G28. Unfortunately, in rows 24 through 28, the row references 12 and 14 will both change. As the formula is copied, we want the 14 to change but not the 12, because we always need to pull the unit cost for each product from row 12. To accomplish this goal, we place a $ sign before the 12. This is called *absolute addressing* or *locking the row.* When a row is preceded with the dollar sign in a formula and the formula is copied, the row number remains unchanged. Therefore, we enter in cell E23 the formula =E$12*E14.

An easy way to insert dollar signs in a formula is to use the F4 key. If you select part of a formula and repeatedly hit F4, Excel cycles through adding a dollar sign to the row and column, then just the row, then just the column, and finally shows no dollar sign.

How can I predict the number of customers a new health club will have in 10 years?

Our answer is in file Chapter1customer.xlsx, shown in Figure 1-5. Here we need to set up a model from scratch. Spreadsheet models have inputs or assumptions that we use to calculate desired outputs. In a basic customer estimation input model, we need three inputs:

- The number of customers at the beginning of Year 1.
- Churn rate: the fraction of starting customers (excluding new customers) who quit each year.

- The number of new customers obtained each year.

We entered values for these inputs in C2:C4. It's important that spreadsheet inputs should be separated from spreadsheet outputs and never hard-coded in Excel formulas. Separating spreadsheet inputs from outputs makes it easy to determine how changing the inputs affects the spreadsheet outputs.

	B	C	D	E	F	G	H	I
1								
2	Start	100						
3	Newperyear	20						
4	Churnrate	0.15						
5								
6								
7	Year	Start customers	New Customers	Quits	End Customers	Start Formulas	Quit Formulas	End Formulas
8	1	100	20	15	105	=C2	=$C$4*C8	=C8+D8-E8
9	2	105	20	15.75	109.25	=F8	=$C$4*C9	=C9+D9-E9
10	3	109.25	20	16.39	112.8625	=F9	=$C$4*C10	=C10+D10-E10
11	4	112.8625	20	16.93	115.933125	=F10	=$C$4*C11	=C11+D11-E11
12	5	115.93313	20	17.39	118.543156	=F11	=$C$4*C12	=C12+D12-E12
13	6	118.54316	20	17.78	120.761683	=F12	=$C$4*C13	=C13+D13-E13
14	7	120.76168	20	18.11	122.64743	=F13	=$C$4*C14	=C14+D14-E14
15	8	122.64743	20	18.4	124.250316	=F14	=$C$4*C15	=C15+D15-E15
16	9	124.25032	20	18.64	125.612768	=F15	=$C$4*C16	=C16+D16-E16
17	10	125.61277	20	18.84	126.770853	=F16	=$C$4*C17	=C17+D17-E17

FIGURE 1-5 Predicting customers by setting up a model with inputs and outputs.

The key to our customer estimation model is in the following relationships:

- (Ending Year t Customers) = (Start Year t Customers) + (New Year t Customers) – (Year Customer quits).
- (Start Year t+1 Customers) = (End Year t Customers)
- Start Year 1 Customers = Value in Cell C2.

Another key to solving this problem is in knowing what we need to track during each year:

- Start customers
- New customers
- Quitting customers
- Ending customers

In cell C8, we compute the number of Year 1 starting customers with the formula =C2. Next, in column D, we reenter the number of new customers from each year by copying from D8 to D9:D17 the formula =$C$3 or C$3.

Note that the numeral 3 must be preceded with the dollar sign; otherwise, when the formula in D8 is copied, the 3 would change, giving incorrect results. Preceding the letter C with a dollar sign is a matter of choice because we are not copying the formula across a column.

The number of customers quitting each month is the starting customers multiplied by the churn rate. Therefore, in column E we compute the number of customers that quit each month by copying from E8 to E9:E18 the formula =$C$4*C8 or C$4*C8. Note here that the numeral 8 does not use the dollar sign because when it's copied, we want 8 to change to 9, 10, and so on.

The ending value for customers for each month is obtained by adding starting customers and new customers and then subtracting quitting customers. Copying from F8 to F9:F18 the formula =C8+D8-F8 computes each month's ending customers.

For months 2–10, starting customers will equal the previous month's ending customers, so copy from C9 to C10:C17 the formula =F8. We find (don't worry about the fraction) that after 10 years, our health club will have around 127 customers.

The astute reader might argue that we really do not know the churn rate and number of new customers each year. She is absolutely right. We should perform a sensitivity analysis to determine how changes in each year's new customers and the annual churn rate change the number of Year 10 ending customers. In Chapter 17, you will learn how to use data tables to perform such a sensitivity analysis.

What does "Please excuse my dear Aunt Sally" (PEMDAS) have to do with writing correct Excel formulas?

Complex Excel formulas often involve a variety of complex mathematical operations, such as exponentiation, multiplication, and division. Excel follows the PEMDAS (or Please excuse my dear Aunt Sally) order of operations rules when evaluating formulas:

- First perform any operations within parentheses.
- Next perform any exponentiations, working from left to right.
- Perform any multiplication and divisions, working from left to right.
- Perform any additions and subtractions, working from left to right.

As an example, Excel would evaluate the formula =3+6*(5+4)/3-7 in the following order.

- 3+6*9/3 – 7 (parentheses removed)
- 3 + 54/3 – 7 (multiplication)
- 3 + 18 – 7 (division)
- 21 – 7 (addition)
- 14 (subtraction)

As another example, suppose we need to take the square root of the annual percentage increase in sales of our products (see file PEMDAStemp.xlsx and Figure 1-6).

	D	E	F	G	H	I
3	This Year	Next Year	Square Root of Improvement	Wrong	Right Formula	Wrong Formula
4	100	150	0.707106781	5	=((E4-D4)/D4)^0.5	=(E4-D4)/D4^0.5
5	200	2000	3	127.279	=((E5-D5)/D5)^0.5	=(E5-D5)/D5^0.5
6	80	400	2	35.7771	=((E6-D6)/D6)^0.5	=(E6-D6)/D6^0.5

FIGURE 1-6 An example of PEMDAS.

In F4, we entered the correct formula, =((E4-D4)/D4)^0.5, and copied the formula to F5:F6. This formula causes Excel to compute the percentage (expressed as a fraction) increase in sales (.5) and *then* to take the square root. The final answer .707 (the square root of .5) is correct. Note the ^ sign (over the 6) is the key used to raise numbers to a power.

In G4, we entered an incorrect formula, =(E4-D4)/D4^.5.

This formula first computes E4-D4 = 50 and then computes the square root of D4 (10). Then our final (incorrect) result is 50/10 = 5.

How can my local coffee shop determine how changes in price and unit cost affect profit?

The key to understanding how alterations of price affect profit is the proper estimation of a demand curve. A demand curve shows how changes in price change product demand. Let's assume daily demand for cups of coffee is given by 100-15*Price in dollars. (See Chapters 84 through 86 for a further discussion of demand curve estimation.) In the file Coffee.xlsx (see Figure 1-7), we show how daily profit varies as the unit cost and price of a cup of coffee vary.

	E	F	G	H	I	J	K	L
1								
2	Demand=100-15*price			Profit=(Price-Unit Cost)*Demand				
3								
4	Demandslope	15						
5	Demandintercept	100						
6								
7								
8		Price						
9	Cost	$2.00	$2.50	$3.00	$3.50	$4.00	$4.50	$5.00
10	$0.50	$105.00	$125.00	$137.50	$142.50	$140.00	$130.00	$112.50
11	$1.00	$70.00	$93.75	$110.00	$118.75	$120.00	$113.75	$100.00
12	$1.50	$35.00	$62.50	$82.50	$95.00	$100.00	$97.50	$87.50
13	$2.00	$0.00	$31.25	$55.00	$71.25	$80.00	$81.25	$75.00
14								
15								
16		=($F$5-$F$4*F$9)*(F$9-$E10)						

FIGURE 1-7 Demand dependence on price and unit cost.

We assume the unit cost of a cup of coffee varies between $0.50 and $2.00 and the price of a cup of coffee varies between $2.00 and $5.00. To determine profit for each price/unit-cost combination, all we need to do is enter in F10 the formula =($F$5-$F$4*F$9)*(F$9-$E10) and copy the formula from F10 to F10:L13. Our references to F5 and F4 are absolute because we do not want the row or column to change as we copy our formulas. Our reference to price (cell F9) requires using dollar signs (or locking the row) because we always need the price pulled from row 9. Our reference to unit cost (E10) requires the column to use the dollar sign because we always need the unit cost pulled from column E.

We find, for example, that if the unit cost is $1.50 and we charge $4.00, our profit is $100:

```
(100-4*15)*(4-1.5) = $100.
```

Note for each unit cost, the price that maximizes profit is highlighted. You will learn in Chapter 24 how conditional formatting is used to create this nifty highlighting.

Problems

1. In my class, I give five homework assignments, each worth 25 points, and three exams, each worth 100 points. I currently compute a student's final grade by giving 75 percent of the weight to exams and 25 percent to homework. Set up a spreadsheet to calculate the final grade for a student that allows you to change the weight given to exams.

2. A person's body mass index (BMI) is computed as $BMI=703*Weight/Height^2$. Set up a spreadsheet to compute a person's BMI.

3. The Fibonacci sequence is defined as follows: $F_0 = 0$, $F_1 = 1$ and for n larger than 1, $F_{N+1} = F_N + F_{N-1}$. Set up a spreadsheet to compute the Fibonacci sequence. Show that for large N, the ratio of successive Fibonacci numbers approaches the Golden Ratio (1.61).

4. The famous butterfly effect states that if a butterfly flaps its wings in Tahiti, that small event might cause a hurricane to hit Texas. Suppose that weather at time t is always between 0 and 1 and is governed by $x_{t+1}=4*x_t*(1-x_t)$. For $x_t = 0.3$ and $x_t=.3000001$, determine $x_1, x_2, \ldots x_{50}$. How do your calculations illustrate the butterfly effect?

5. A lake is currently stocked with 12,230 fish. Each year, the number of births per fish is 1.2 and number of deaths per fish is 0.7. Show that if 6,115 fish per year are harvested, the number of fish in the lake will stay constant.

6. The Gini index is a commonly used measure of a nation's income inequality. If the income of n people is listed in increasing order (x_1= smallest income, x_n = largest income), then the Gini index is defined by the formula

$$G = \frac{n+1}{n} - \frac{2\sum_1^n (n+1-i)x_i}{n\sum_1^n x_i}$$

Set up a spreadsheet that determines the Gini index for a group of five people.

CHAPTER 2

Range names

Questions answered in this chapter:

- I want to sum the sales in Arizona, California, Montana, New York, and New Jersey. Can I use a formula to compute total sales in a form such as AZ+CA+MT+NY+NJ instead of SUM(A21:A25) and still get the right answer?
- What does a formula like Average(A:A) do?
- What is the difference between a name with workbook scope and one with worksheet scope?
- I really am getting to like range names. I have started defining range names for many of the workbooks I have developed at the office. However, the range names do not show up in my formulas. How can I make recently created range names show up in previously created formulas?
- How can I paste a list of all range names (and the cells they represent) into my worksheet?
- I am computing projected annual revenues as a multiple of last year's revenue. Is there a way to have the formula look like (1+growth)*last year?
- For each day of the week, we are given the hourly wage and hours worked. Can we compute total salary for each day with the formula wages*hours?

You have probably worked with worksheets that use formulas such as SUM(A5000:A5049). With a formula such as this, you have to find out what's contained in cells A5000:A5049. If cells A5000:A5049 contain sales in each US state, wouldn't the formula SUM(USSales) be easier to understand? In this chapter, I'll teach you how to name individual cells or ranges of cells. I'll also show you how to use range names in formulas.

How can I create named ranges?

You can choose from three ways to create named ranges:

- By entering a range name in the Name box.
- By clicking Create From Selection in the Defined Names group on the Formulas tab.
- By clicking Name Manager or Define Name in the Defined Names group on the Formulas tab.

Using the Name box to create a range name

The Name box (shown in Figure 2-1) is located directly above the label for column A. (To see the Name box, you need to display the Formula bar.) To create a range name in the Name box, simply select the cell or range of cells that you want to name, click the Name box, and then type the range name you want to use. Press Enter, and you've created the range name. Clicking the arrow beside the Name box displays the range names defined in the current workbook. You can display all the range names in a workbook by pressing the F3 key to open the Paste Name dialog box. When you select a range name from the Name box, Excel selects the cells corresponding to that range name. This enables you to verify that you've chosen the cell or range that you intended to name. Range names are not case sensitive.

FIGURE 2-1 You can create a range name by selecting the cell range you want to name and then typing the range name in the Name box.

For example, suppose you want to name cell F3 *east* and cell F4 *west*. See Figure 2-2 and the file Eastwest.xlsx. Simply select cell F3, type **east** in the Name box, and then press Enter. Then select cell F4, type **west** in the Name box, and press Enter. If you now reference cell F3 in another cell, you see *=east* instead of *=F3*. This means that whenever you see the reference east in a formula, Excel will insert whatever is in cell F3.

	E	F
1		
2		
3	east	5
4	west	10

FIGURE 2-2 Naming cell F3 *east* and cell F4 *west.*

Suppose you want to assign the name *data* to a rectangular range of cells (such as A1:B4). Simply select the cell range A1:B4, type **data** in the Name box, and press Enter. Now a formula such as =AVERAGE(data) would average the contents of cells A1:B4. (See the file Data.xlsx and Figure 2-3.)

F9

	A	B	C	D
1	1	2		
2	3	2		
3	1	1		
4	2	-1		
5			1.375	
6		cell C5	=AVERAGE(data)	
7		contains		

FIGURE 2-3 Naming range A1:B4 data.

Sometimes you want to name a range of cells made up of several noncontiguous rectangular ranges. For example, in Figure 2-4 and the file Noncontigtemp.xlsx, we might want to assign the name *noncontig* to the range consisting of cells B3:C4, E6:G7, and B10:C10. To assign this name, select any one of the three rectangles making up the range (I chose B3:C4). Hold down the Ctrl key, and then select the other two ranges (E6:G7 and B10:C10). Now release the Ctrl key, type the name **noncontig** in the Name box, and press Enter. Using *noncontig* in any formula will now refer to the contents of cells B3:C4, E6:G7, and B10:C10. For example, entering the formula =AVERAGE(noncontig) in cell E11 yields 4.75 (because the 12 numbers in our range add up to 57 and 57/12=4.75).

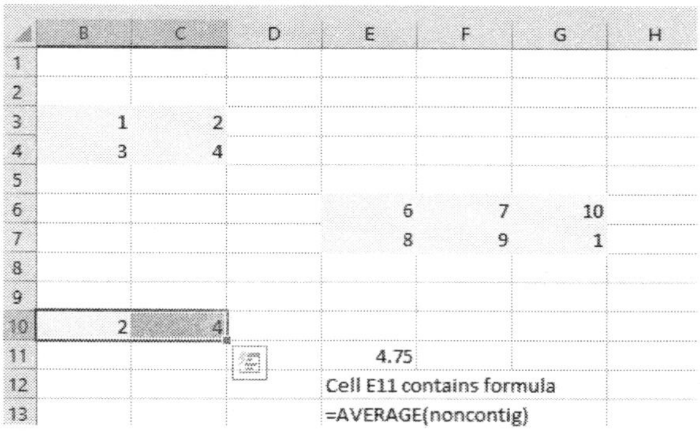

	B	C	D	E	F	G	H
1							
2							
3	1	2					
4	3	4					
5							
6				6	7	10	
7				8	9	1	
8							
9							
10	2	4					
11				4.75			
12				Cell E11 contains formula			
13				=AVERAGE(noncontig)			

FIGURE 2-4 Naming a noncontiguous range of cells.

Creating named ranges by using the Create From Selection option

The worksheet Statestemp.xlsx contains sales during March for each of the 50 US states. Figure 2-5 shows a subset of this data. We would like to name each cell in the range B6:B55 using the correct state abbreviation. To do this, select the range A6:B55, and click Create From Selection in the Defined Names group on the Formulas tab of the ribbon (see Figure 2-6). Then select the Left Column check box, as indicated in Figure 2-7, and click OK.

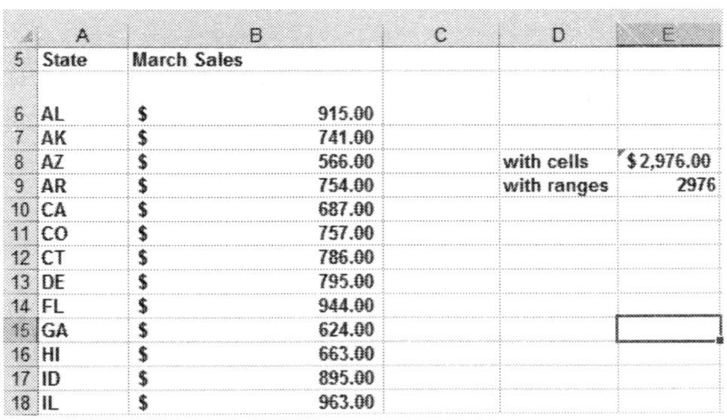

	A	B	C	D	E
5	State	March Sales			
6	AL	$ 915.00			
7	AK	$ 741.00			
8	AZ	$ 566.00		with cells	$2,976.00
9	AR	$ 754.00		with ranges	2976
10	CA	$ 687.00			
11	CO	$ 757.00			
12	CT	$ 786.00			
13	DE	$ 795.00			
14	FL	$ 944.00			
15	GA	$ 624.00			
16	HI	$ 663.00			
17	ID	$ 895.00			
18	IL	$ 963.00			

FIGURE 2-5 By naming the cells that contain state sales with state abbreviations, you can use the abbreviation rather than the cell's column letter and row number when you refer to the cell.

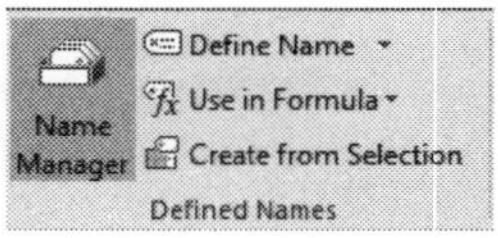

FIGURE 2-6 The Create From Selection option.

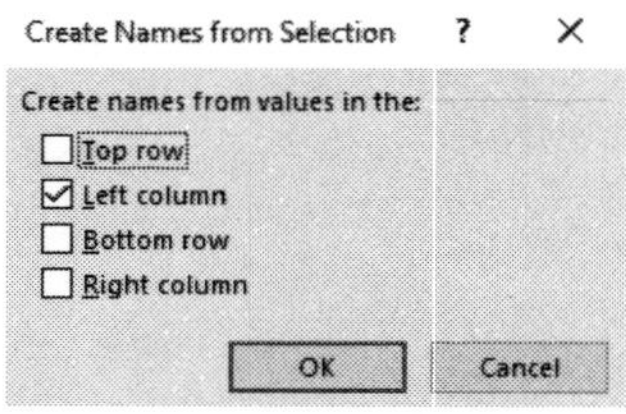

FIGURE 2-7 Options for creating names from specific row and column positions.

Excel now knows to associate the names in the first column of the selected range with the cells in the second column of the selected range. Thus, B6 is assigned the range name AL, B7 is named AK, and so on. Note that creating these range names in the Name box would have been incredibly tedious! Click the arrow beside the Name box to verify that these range names have been created.

Creating range names by using the Define Name option

In the Defined Names group on the Formulas tab, click Define Name from the menu shown earlier in Figure 2-6. The New Name dialog box shown in Figure 2-8 opens.

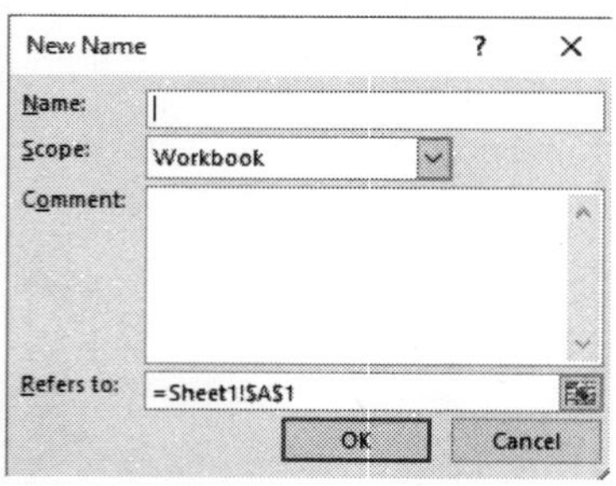

FIGURE 2-8 The New Name dialog box before creating any range names.

Suppose you want to assign the name *range1* (range names are not case sensitive) to the cell range A2:B7. Simply type **range1** in the Name box, and then specify the range A2:B7 in the Refers To area. The New Name dialog box will now look like Figure 2-9. Click OK, and you're done.

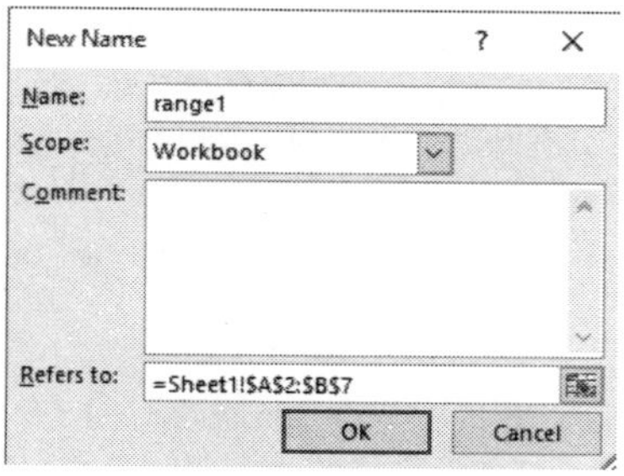

FIGURE 2-9 The New Name dialog box after creating a range name.

If you open the Scope list, you can select the option Workbook or any worksheet in your workbook. I'll discuss this decision later, so for now just choose the default scope of Workbook. You can also add comments for any of your range names.

The Name Manager

If you now click the arrow by the Name box, the name *range1* (and any other ranges you have created) appears in the Name box. In Excel 2016 there is an easy way to edit or delete your range names. Simply open the Name Manager by selecting the Formulas tab and then clicking Name Manager from the Defined Names group. You will now see a list of all range names. For example, for the file States.xlsx, the Name Manager dialog box will look like Figure 2-10.

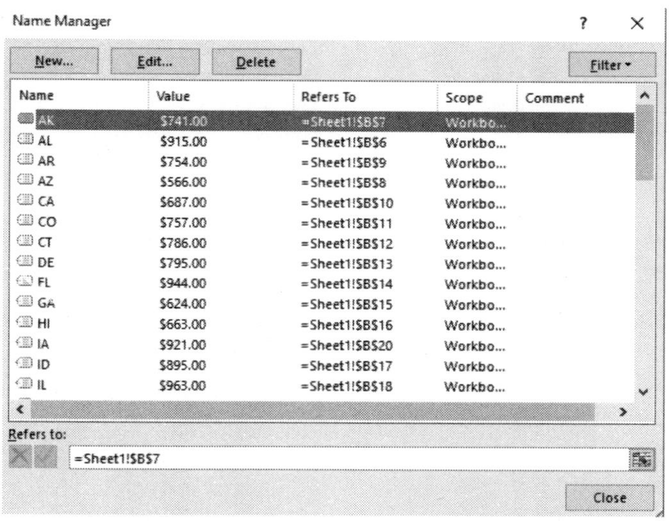

FIGURE 2-10 The Name Manager dialog box for States.xlsx.

To edit any range name, simply double-click the range name or select the range name and click Edit. Then, in the Edit Name dialog box, you can change the name of the range, the cells the range refers to, or the scope of the range.

To delete any subset of range names, first select the range names you want to delete. If the range names are listed consecutively, simply select the first range name in the group you want to delete, hold down the Shift key, and select the last range name in the group. If the range names are not listed consecutively, you can select any range name you want to delete and then hold down the Ctrl key while you select the other range names for deletion. Then press the Delete key to delete the selected range names.

Now let's look at some specific examples of how to use range names.

Answers to this chapter's questions

I want to sum the sales in Arizona, California, Montana, New York, and New Jersey. Can I use a formula to compute total sales in a form such as AZ+CA+MT+NY+NJ instead of SUM(A21:A25) and still get the right answer?

Let's return to the file States.xlsx, in which we assigned each state's abbreviation as the range name for the state's sales. If you want to compute total sales in Alabama, Alaska, Arizona, and Arkansas, you could clearly use the formula SUM(B6:B9). You could also point to cells B6, B7, B8, and B9, and the formula would be entered as =AL+AK+AZ+AR. The latter formula is, of course, much easier to understand.

As another illustration of how to use range names, look at the file Historicalinvesttemp.xlsx, shown in Figure 2-11, which contains annual percentage returns on stocks, T-bills, and 10-year bonds. (Some rows are hidden in this figure; the data ends in row 89.)

	A	B	C	D	E
1	*Year*	*Stocks*	*Tbills*	*Bonds10*	
2	1928	43.81%	3.08%	0.84%	Average Stock Returns
3	1929	-8.30%	3.16%	4.20%	0.114121591
4	1930	-25.12%	4.55%	4.54%	=AVERAGE(Stocks)
5	1931	-43.84%	2.31%	-2.56%	
6	1932	-8.64%	1.07%	8.79%	
7	1933	49.98%	0.96%	1.86%	
86	2012	15.89%	0.05%	2.97%	
87	2013	32.15%	0.07%	-9.10%	
88	2014	13.52%	0.05%	10.75%	
89	2015	1.36%	0.21%	1.28%	

FIGURE 2-11 Historical investment data.

After selecting the cell range B1:D89 and clicking Create From Selection from the Formulas tab, I created names in the top row of the range. The range B2:B89 is named *Stocks*, the range C2:C89 *Tbills*, and the range D2:D89 *Bonds10*. After typing **=AVERAGE(** in a cell, but before you type in the range, you can press F3 and the Paste Name dialog box appears, as shown in Figure 2-12.

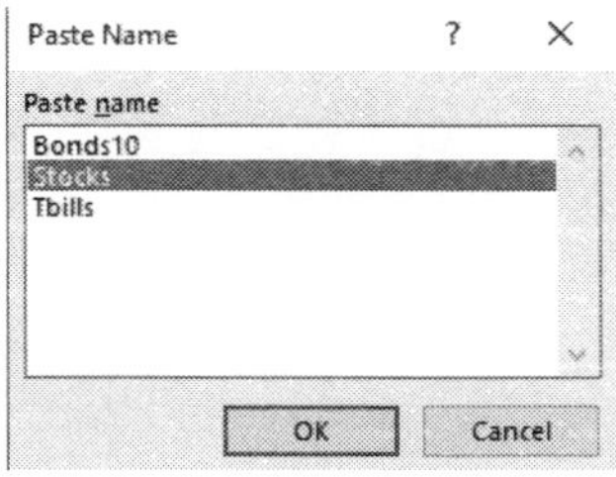

FIGURE 2-12 You can add a range name to a formula by using the Paste Name dialog box.

Now you can select Stocks in the Paste Name list and click OK (this is what was done in cell E3). After entering the closing parenthesis, the formula, =AVERAGE(Stocks), computes the average return on stocks (11.41 percent). The beauty of this approach is that even if you don't remember where the data is, you can work with the stock return data anywhere in the workbook!

I would be remiss if I did not mention the exciting AutoComplete capabilities of Excel 2016. If you begin typing **=Average(T,** Excel shows you a list of range names and functions that begin with T. You can simply double-click Tbills to complete the entry of the range name and then type the closing parenthesis.

What does a formula like Average(A:A) do?

If you use a column name (in the form A:A, C:C, and so on) in a formula, Excel treats an entire column as a named range. For example, entering the formula =AVERAGE(A:A) will average all numbers in column A. Using a range name for an entire column is very helpful if you frequently enter new data into a column. For example, if column A contains monthly sales of a product, as new sales data is entered each month, our formula computes an up-to-date monthly sales average. I caution you, however, that if you enter the formula =AVERAGE(A:A) in column A, you will get a circular reference message because the value of the cell containing the average formula depends on the cell containing the average. You will learn how to resolve circular references in Chapter 11, "Circular references." Similarly, entering the formula =AVERAGE(1:1) will average all numbers in row 1.

What is the difference between a name with workbook scope and one with worksheet scope?

The file Sheetnames.xlsx will help you understand the difference between range names that have workbook scope and range names that have worksheet scope. When you create names with the Name box, the names have workbook scope. For example, suppose you use the Name box to assign the name *sales* to the cell range E4:E6 in Sheet3, and these cells contain the numbers 1, 2, and 4, respectively. Then, if you enter a formula such as =SUM(sales) in any worksheet, you obtain an answer of 7 because the Name box creates names with workbook scope. Anywhere in the workbook where you refer to the name *sales* (which has workbook scope), the name refers to cells E4:E6 of Sheet3.

Now suppose that you type 4, 5, and 6 in cells E4:E6 of Sheet1, and 3, 4, and 5 in cells E4:E6 of Sheet2. Next you open the Name Manager, give the name *jam* to cells E4:E6 of Sheet1, and define the scope of this name as Sheet1. Then you move to Sheet2, open the Name Manager, and give the name *jam* to cells E4:E6, and define the scope of this name as Sheet2. The Name Manager dialog box now looks like Figure 2-13.

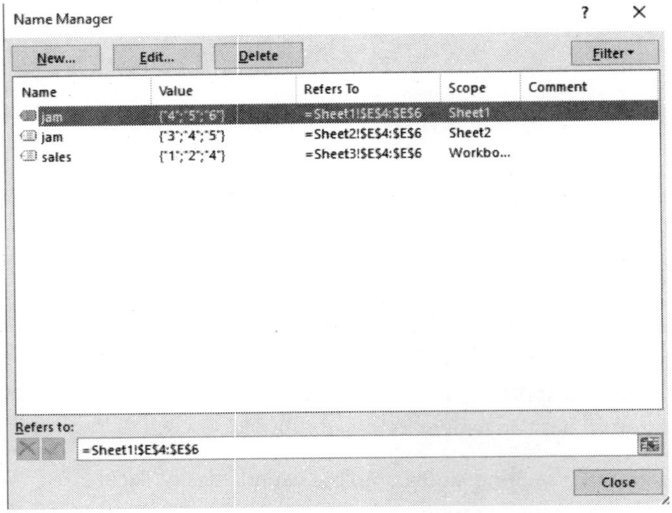

FIGURE 2-13 The Name Manager dialog box with worksheet and workbook names.

Now, what if you enter the formula =SUM(jam) in each sheet? In Sheet 1, =SUM(jam) will total cells E4:E6 of Sheet1. Because those cells contain 4, 5, and 6, you obtain 15. In Sheet2, =SUM(jam) will total cells E4:E6 of Sheet2, yielding 3 + 4 + 5 = 12. In Sheet3, however, the formula =SUM(jam) will yield a #NAME? error because there is no range named *jam* defined in Sheet3. If you enter anywhere in Sheet3 the formula =SUM(Sheet2!jam), Excel will recognize the worksheet-level name that represents cell range E4:E6 of Sheet2 and yield a result of 3 + 4 + 5 = 12. Thus, prefacing a worksheet-level name by its sheet name, followed by an exclamation point (!), allows you to refer to a worksheet-level range in a worksheet other than the sheet in which the range is defined.

I really am getting to like range names. I have started defining range names for many of the workbooks I have developed at the office. However, the range names do not show up in my formulas. How can I make recently created range names show up in previously created formulas?

Let's look at the file Applynames.xlsx. See Figure 2-14.

	E	F
3	price	$5.00
4	demand	8500
5	unitcost	$4.00
6	fixedcost	$3,000.00
7	profit	$5,500.00

FIGURE 2-14 How to apply range names to formulas.

I entered the price of a product in cell F3 in Sheet 1, and product demand of =10000–300*F3 in cell F4. The unit cost and fixed cost are entered in cells F5 and F6, respectively, and profit is computed in cell F7 with the formula =F4*(F3–F5)–F6. I used Formulas, Create From Selection, and chose the Left Column option to name cell F3 *price*, cell F4 *demand*, cell F5 *unit cost*, cell F6 *fixed cost*, and cell F7 *profit*. We would like these range names to show up in the cell F4 and cell F7 formulas. To apply the range names, first select the range where you want the range names applied (in this case, F4:F7). Now go to the Defined Names group on the Formulas tab, click the Define Name arrow, and then click Apply Names. Highlight the names you want to apply, and then click OK. Note that cell F4 now contains the formula =10000–300*price and cell F7 contains the formula =demand*(price–unitcost)–fixedcost, as you wanted.

By the way, if you want the range names to apply to the entire worksheet, simply select the entire worksheet by clicking the Select All triangular button at the intersection of the column and row headings.

How can I paste a list of all range names (and the cells they represent) into my worksheet?

Press F3 to display the Paste Name box, and then click the Paste List button. A list of range names and the cells each corresponds to will be pasted into your worksheet, beginning at the current cell location.

I am computing projected annual revenues as a multiple of last year's revenue. Is there a way to have the formula look like (1+growth)*last year?

The file Last year.xlsx contains the solution to this problem. As shown in Figure 2-15, we want to compute revenues for 2014–2021 that grow at 10 percent per year off a base level of $300 million in 2014.

	A	B	C
3	growth	0.1	
4			
5		revenue	
6	2014	$ 300.00	
7	2015	$ 330.00	=lastyear*(1+growth)
8	2016	$ 363.00	
9	2017	$ 399.30	
10	2018	$ 439.23	
11	2019	$ 483.15	
12	2020	$ 531.47	
13	2021	$ 584.62	

FIGURE 2-15 Creating a range name for last year.

To begin, we use the Name box to name cell B3 *growth*. Now comes the neat part! Move the cursor to B7 and bring up the New Name dialog box by clicking Define Name in the Defined Names group on the Formulas tab. Then fill in the New Name dialog box as shown in Figure 2-16, which shows how, with the cursor in cell B7, we can create a range name *lastyear* that always refers to the cell one row above the current cell.

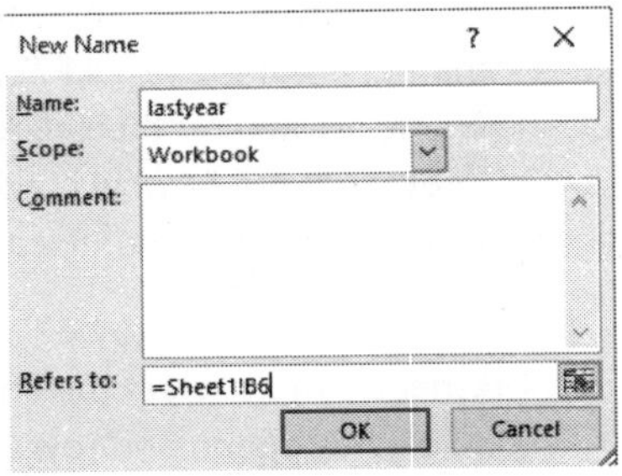

FIGURE 2-16 Creating a range name to pick up last year's sales.

Because we are in cell B7, Excel interprets this range name to always refer to the cell above the current cell. Of course, this would not work if the cell reference B6 contains any dollar signs. Now if we enter in cell B7 the formula =lastyear*(1+growth) and copy it to the range B8:B13, each cell will contain the formula we want and will multiply 1.1 by the contents of the cell directly above the active cell.

For each day of the week we are given the hourly wage and hours worked. Can we compute total salary for each day with the formula wages*hours?

As shown in Figure 2-17 (see the file Namedrows.xlsx), row 12 contains daily wage rates, and row 13 contains hours worked each day.

	E	F	G	H	I	J	K	L
11		Monday	Tuesday	Wednesd	Thursday	Friday	Saturday	Sunday
12	wage	$ 5.00	$ 6.00	$ 7.00	$ 8.00	$ 9.00	$ 15.00	$ 15.00
13	hours	55	65	75	65	77	88	36
14	payroll	$ 275.00	$ 390.00	$ 525.00	$ 520.00	$ 693.00	$ 1,320.00	$ 540.00

FIGURE 2-17 Using range names to refer to different rows.

You can simply select row 12 (by clicking on the 12) and use the Name box to enter the name *wage*. Then select row 13 and use the Name box to enter the name *hours*. If you now enter in cell F14 the formula wage*hours and copy this formula to the range G14:L14, you can see that in each column Excel finds the wage and hours values and multiplies them.

Remarks

- Excel does not allow you to use the letters *r* and *c* by themselves as range names.
- If you use Create From Selection to create a range name and your name contains spaces, Excel inserts an underscore (_) to fill in the spaces. For example, the name Product 1 is created as Product_1.
- Range names cannot begin with numbers or look like a cell reference. For example, 3Q and A4 are not allowed as range names. Because Excel has more than 16,000 columns, a range name such as cat1 is not permitted because there is a cell CAT1. If you try to name a cell CAT1, Excel tells you the name is invalid. Probably your best alternative is to name the cell cat1_.

- The only symbols allowed in range names are periods (.) and underscores (_).

Problems

1. The file Stock.xlsx contains monthly stock returns for General Motors and Microsoft. Name the ranges containing the monthly returns for each stock and compute the average monthly return on each stock.
2. Open a worksheet and name the range containing the cells A1:B3 and A6:B8 as Red.
3. Given the latitude and longitude of any two cities, the file Citydistances.xlsx computes the distance between the two cities. Define range names for the latitude and longitude of each city and ensure that these names show up in the formula for total distance.
4. The file Sharedata.xlsx contains the numbers of shares you own of each stock and the price of each stock. Compute the value of the shares of each stock with the formula shares*price.
5. Create a range name that averages the last five years of sales data. Assume annual sales are listed in a single column.

CHAPTER 3

Lookup functions

Questions answered in this chapter:

- How do I write a formula to compute tax rates based on income?
- Given a product ID, how can I look up the product's price?
- Suppose that a product's price changes over time. I know the date the product was sold. How can I write a formula to compute the product's price?

Syntax of the lookup functions

Lookup functions enable you to "look up" values from worksheet ranges. Microsoft Excel 2016 allows you to perform both vertical lookups (by using the VLOOKUP function) and horizontal lookups (by using the HLOOKUP function). In a vertical lookup, the lookup operation starts in the first column of a worksheet range. In a horizontal lookup, the operation starts in the first row of a worksheet range. Because the majority of formulas using lookup functions involve vertical lookups, I'll concentrate on VLOOKUP functions.

VLOOKUP syntax

The syntax of the VLOOKUP function is as follows. The brackets (**[ ]**) indicate optional arguments.

```
VLOOKUP(lookup value,table range,column index,[range lookup])
```

- *Lookup value* is the value that you want to look up in the first column of the table range.
- *Table range* is the range that contains the entire lookup table. The table range includes the first column, in which you try to match the lookup value, and any other columns in which you want to look up formula results.
- *Column index* is the column number in the table range from which the value of the lookup function is obtained.
- *Range lookup* is an optional argument. The point of *range lookup* is to allow you to specify an exact or approximate match. If the *range lookup* argument is True or omitted, the first column of the table range must be in ascending numerical order. If the *range lookup* argument is True or omitted and an exact match for the lookup value is found in the first column of the table

range, Excel bases the lookup on the row of the table in which the exact match is found. If the *range lookup* argument is True or omitted and an exact match does not exist, Excel bases the lookup on the largest value in the first column that is less than the lookup value. If the *range lookup* argument is False and an exact match for the lookup value is found in the first column of the table range, Excel bases the lookup on the row of the table in which the exact match is found. If no exact match is obtained, Excel returns an #N/A (Not Available) response. In Chapter 12, you will learn how to use the IFERROR function to eliminate #N/A responses. Note that a *range lookup* argument of 1 is equivalent to True, whereas a *range lookup* argument of 0 is equivalent to False.

HLOOKUP syntax

In an HLOOKUP function, Excel tries to locate the lookup value in the first row (not the first column) of the table range. For an HLOOKUP function, use the VLOOKUP syntax and change *column* to *row.*

Let's explore some interesting examples of lookup functions.

Answers to this chapter's questions

How do I write a formula to compute tax rates based on income?

The following example shows how a VLOOKUP function works when the first column of the table range consists of numbers in ascending order. Suppose that the tax rate depends on income, as shown in the following table.

Income level	Tax rate
$0–$9,999	15%
$10,000–$29,999	30%
$30,000–$99,999	34%
$100,000 and over	40%

To see an example of how to write a formula that computes the tax rate for any income level, open the file Lookup.xlsx, shown in Figure 3-1.

	A	B	C	D	E	F	G
1							
2							
3			Lookup Tables				
4							
5				Income	Tax rate		Lookup=D6:E9
6				0	0.15		
7				10000	0.3		
8				30000	0.34		
9				100000	0.4		
10							
11					TRUE	FALSE	
12				Income	Rate		
13				-1000	#N/A	#N/A	
14				30000	0.34	0.34	
15				29000	0.3	#N/A	
16				98000	0.34	#N/A	
17				104000	0.4	#N/A	

FIGURE 3-1 Using a lookup function to compute a tax rate. The numbers in the first column of the table range are sorted in ascending order.

I began by entering the relevant information (tax rates and break points) in cell range D6:E9. I named the table range D6:E9 *lookup*. I recommend that you always name the cells you're using as the table range. If you do so, you need not remember the exact location of the table range, and when you copy any formula involving a lookup function, the lookup range will always be correct. To illustrate how the lookup function works, I entered some incomes in the range D13:D17. By copying from E13:E17 the formula VLOOKUP(D13,Lookup,2,True), I computed the tax rate for the income levels listed in D13:D17.

Let's examine how the lookup function worked in cells E13:E17. Note that because the column index in the formula is 2, the answer always comes from the second column of the table range.

- In D13, the income of –$1,000 yields #N/A because –$1,000 is less than the lowest income level in the first column of the table range. If you want a tax rate of 15 percent associated with an income of –$1,000, simply replace the 0 in D6 by a number that is –1,000 or smaller.
- In D14, the income of $30,000 exactly matches a value in the first column of the table range, so the function returns a tax rate of 34 percent.
- In D15, the income level of $29,000 does not exactly match a value in the first column of the table range, which means the lookup function stops at the largest number less than $29,000 in the first column of the range—$10,000 in this case. This function returns the tax rate in column 2 of the table range opposite $10,000, or 30 percent.
- In D16, the income level of $98,000 does not yield an exact match in the first column of the table range. The lookup function stops at the largest number less than $98,000 in the first column of the table range. This returns the tax rate in column 2 of the table range opposite $30,000—34 percent.
- In D17, the income level of $104,000 does not yield an exact match in the first column of the table range. The lookup function stops at the largest number less than $104,000 in the first column of the table range, which returns the tax rate in column 2 of the table range opposite $100,000—40 percent.

In F13:F17, I changed the value of the *range lookup* argument from True to False and copied from F13 to F14:F17 the formula VLOOKUP(D13,Lookup,2,False). Cell F14 still yields a 34 percent tax rate because the first column of the table range contains an exact match to $30,000. All the other entries in F13:F17 display #N/A because none of the other incomes in D13:D17 have an exact match in the first column of the table range.

Given a product ID, how can I look up the product's price?

Often, the first column of a table range does not consist of numbers in ascending order. For example, the first column of the table range might list product ID codes or employee names. In my experience teaching thousands of financial analysts, I've found that many people don't know how to deal with lookup functions when the first column of the table range does not consist of numbers in ascending order. In these situations, you need to remember only one simple rule: use False as the value of the *range lookup* argument.

Here's an example. In the file Lookup.xlsx (see Figure 3-2), you can see the prices for five products, listed by their product ID code. How do you write a formula that takes a product ID code and returns the product price?

	H	I	J
7			
8			
9			Lookup2=H11:I15
10	Product ID	Price	
11	A134	$ 3.50	
12	B242	$ 4.20	
13	X212	$ 4.80	
14	C413	$ 5.00	
15	B2211	$ 5.20	
16			
17	ID	Price	
18	B2211	3.5	
19	B2211	5.2	

FIGURE 3-2 Looking up prices from product ID codes. When the table range isn't sorted in ascending order, enter False as the last argument in the lookup function formula.

Many people would enter the formula as I have in cell I18: VLOOKUP(H18,Lookup2,2). However, note that when you omit the fourth argument (the *range lookup* argument), the value is assumed to be True. Because the product IDs in the table range Lookup2 (H11:I15) are not listed in alphabetical order, an incorrect price ($3.50) is returned. If you enter the formula VLOOKUP(H18,Lookup2,2,False) in cell I18, the correct price ($5.20) is returned, as shown in cell I19.

You would also use False in a formula designed to find an employee's salary by using the employee's last name or ID number.

By the way, you can see in Figure 3-2 that columns A–G are hidden. To hide columns, you begin by selecting the columns you want to hide. Click the Home tab on the ribbon. In the Cells group, click Format, point to Hide & Unhide (under Visibility), and then click Hide Columns.

Suppose that a product's price changes over time. I know the date the product was sold. How can I write a formula to compute the product's price?

Suppose the price of a product depends on the date the product was sold. How can you use a lookup function in a formula that will pick up the correct product price? More specifically, suppose the price of a product is as shown in the following table.

Date sold	Price
January–April 2005	$98
May–July 2005	$105
August–December 2005	$112

Let's write a formula to determine the correct product price for any date on which the product is sold in the year 2005. For variety, we'll use an HLOOKUP function. I've placed the dates for when the price changes in the first row of the table range. See the file Datelookup.xlsx, shown in Figure 3-3.

	A	B	C	D
1				
2	Date	1/1/2005	5/1/2005	8/1/2005
3	Price	98	105	112
4				
5			Lookup:B2:D3	
6				
7		Date	Price	
8		1/4/2005	98	
9		5/10/2005	105	
10		9/12/2005	112	
11		5/1/2005	105	
12				

FIGURE 3-3 Using an HLOOKUP function to determine a price that changes depending on the date it's sold.

I copied from C8 to C9:C11 the formula HLOOKUP(B8,lookup,2,TRUE). This formula tries to match the dates in column B with the first row of the range B2:D3. At any date between 1/1/05 and 4/30/05, the lookup function stops at 1/1/05 and returns the price in B3; for any date between 5/01/05 and 7/31/05, the lookup stops at 5/1/05 and returns the price in C3; and for any date on or later than 8/01/05, the lookup stops at 8/01/05 and returns the price in D3.

Problems

1. The file Hr.xlsx gives employee ID codes, salaries, and years of experience. Write a formula that takes a given ID code and yields the employee's salary. Write another formula that takes a given ID code and yields the employee's years of experience.

2. The file Assign.xlsx gives the assignment of workers to four groups. The suitability of each worker for each group (on a scale from 0 to 10) is also given. Write a formula that gives the suitability of each worker for the group to which the worker is assigned.

3. You are thinking of advertising Microsoft products on a sports telecast. As you buy more ads, the price of each ad decreases as shown in the following table.

Number of ads	Price per ad
1–5	$12,000
6–10	$11,000
11–20	$10,000
21 and higher	$9,000

For example, if you buy 8 ads, you pay $11,000 per ad, but if you buy 14 ads, you pay $10,000 per ad. Write a formula that yields the total cost of purchasing any number of ads.

4. You are thinking of advertising Microsoft products on a popular TV music program. You pay one price for the first group of ads, but as you buy more ads, the price per ad decreases as shown in the following table.

Ad number	Price per ad
1–5	$12,000
6–10	$11,000
11–20	$10,000
21 or higher	$9,000

For example, if you buy 8 ads, you pay $12,000 per ad for the first 5 ads and $11,000 for each of the next 3 ads. If you buy 14 ads, you pay $12,000 for each of the first 5 ads, $11,000 for each of the next 5 ads, and $10,000 for each of the last 4 ads. Write a formula that yields the total cost of purchasing any number of ads. Hint: You probably need at least three columns in your table range, and your formula might involve two lookup functions.

5. The annual rate your bank charges you to borrow money for 1, 5, 10, or 30 years is shown in the following table.

Duration of loan	Annual loan rate
1 year	6%
5 years	7%
10 years	9%
30 years	10%

If you borrow money from the bank for any duration from 1 through 30 years that's not listed in the table, your rate is found by interpolating the appropriate number between the rates given in the table. For example, let's say you borrow money for 15 years. Because 15 years is one quarter of the way between 10 years and 30 years, the annual loan rate would be calculated as follows: .25*.09 + .75*.10.

Write a formula that returns the annual interest rate on a loan for any period between 1 and 30 years.

6. The distance between any two US cities (excluding cities in Alaska and Hawaii) can be approximated by the following formula:

$$69 * \sqrt{(\text{lat1} - \text{lat2})^2 + (\text{long1} - \text{long2})^2}$$

The file Citydata.xlsx contains the latitude and longitude of selected US cities. Create a table that gives the distance between any two of the listed cities.

7. In the file Pinevalley.xlsx, the first worksheet contains the salaries of several employees at Pine Valley University, the second worksheet contains the age of the employees, and the third worksheet contains the years of experience. Create a fourth worksheet that contains the salary, age, and experience for each employee.

8. The file Lookupmultiplecolumns.xlsx contains information about several sales made at an electronics store. A salesperson's name will be entered in B17. Write an Excel formula that can be copied from C17 to D17:F17 that will extract that salesperson's radio sales to C17, TV sales to D17, printer sales to E17, and CD sales to F17.

9. The file Grades.xlsx contains student's grades on an exam. Suppose the curve is as follows:

Score	Grade
Below 60	F
60–69	D
70–79	C
80–89	B
90 and above	A

Use Excel to return each student's letter grade on this exam.

10. The file Employees.xlsx contains the ranking each of 35 workers has given (on a 0–10 scale) to three jobs. The file also gives the job to which each worker is assigned. Use a formula to compute each worker's ranking for the job to which the worker is assigned.

11. Suppose one dollar can be converted to 1,000 yen, 5 pesos, or 0.7 euros. Set up a spreadsheet in which the user can enter an amount in US dollars and a currency, and the spreadsheet converts dollars to the entered currency.

12. The file Qb2013.xlsx gives NFL quarterback (QB) statistics for the 2013 season. Write formulas in cells J2 and K2 that return the QB's TDs and interceptions when you type a QB's name in cell I2.

13. The file NBAplayers.xlsx gives the age and salary for several NBA players. Enter formulas in cells J5:K50 that return each player's age and salary.

14. Column F of the file Hardware.xlsx gives product codes for hardware products, and Column G gives the price of each product. Columns M–O list the quantity and price a hardware store paid for various products. Determine the total cost of the hardware store's purchases.

CHAPTER 4

The INDEX function

Questions answered in this chapter:

- I have a list of distances between US cities. How do I write a function that returns the distance between, for example, Seattle and Miami?
- Is there a way I can write a formula that references the entire column containing the distances between each city and Seattle?

Syntax of the INDEX function

The INDEX function allows you to return the entry in any row and column within an array of numbers. The most commonly used syntax for the INDEX function is the following:

```
INDEX(Array,Row Number,Column Number)
```

To illustrate, the formula INDEX(A1:D12,2,3) returns the entry in the second row and third column of the array A1:D12. This entry is the one in cell C2.

Answers to this chapter's questions

I have a list of distances between US cities. How do I write a function that returns the distance between, for example, Seattle and Miami?

The file INDEX.xlsx (see Figure 4-1) contains the distances between eight US cities. The range C10:J17, which contains the distances, is named *distances*.

	A	B	C	D	E	F	G	H	I	J
1										
2										
3										
4		Boston-Denver	1991			T Dist to Seattle	15221			
5		Seattle- Miami	3389							
6										
7										
8										
9			Boston	Chicago	Dallas	Denver	LA	Miami	Phoenix	Seattle
10	1	Boston	0	983	1815	1991	3036	1539	2664	2612
11	2	Chicago	983	0	1205	1050	2112	1390	1729	2052
12	3	Dallas	1815	1205	0	801	1425	1332	1027	2404
13	4	Denver	1991	1050	801	0	1174	2100	836	1373
14	5	LA	3036	2112	1425	1174	0	2757	398	1909
15	6	Miami	1539	1390	1332	2100	2757	0	2359	3389
16	7	Phoenix	2664	1729	1027	836	398	2359	0	1482
17	8	Seattle	2612	2052	2404	1373	1909	3389	1482	0

FIGURE 4-1 You can use the INDEX function to calculate the distance between cities.

Suppose that you want to enter in a cell the distance between Boston and Denver. Because distances from Boston are listed in the first row of the array named *distances*, and distances to Denver are listed in the fourth column of the array, the appropriate formula is INDEX(distances,1,4). The results show that Boston and Denver are 1,991 miles apart. Similarly, to find the (much longer) distance between Seattle and Miami, you would use the formula INDEX(distances,6,8). Seattle and Miami are 3,389 miles apart.

Imagine that the Seattle Seahawks NFL team is embarking on a road trip in which they play games in Phoenix, Los Angeles , Denver, Dallas, and Chicago. At the conclusion of the road trip, the Seahawks return to Seattle. Can you easily compute how many miles they travel on the trip? As you can see in Figure 4-2, you simply list the cities the Seahawks visit (8-7-5-4-3-2-8) in the order they are visited, starting and ending in Seattle, and copy from D21 to D26 the formula INDEX(distances,C21,C22). The formula in D21 computes the distance between Seattle and Phoenix (city number 7), the formula in D22 computes the distance between Phoenix and Los Angeles, and so on. The Seahawks will travel a total of 7,112 miles on their road trip. Just for fun, I used the INDEX function to show that the Miami Heat travel more miles during the NBA season than any other team.

	C	D
19	**Road Trip!!**	
20	City	Distance
21	8	1482
22	7	398
23	5	1174
24	4	801
25	3	1205
26	2	2052
27	8	
28	Total	7112

FIGURE 4-2 Distances for a Seattle Seahawks road trip.

Is there a way I can write a formula that references the entire column containing the distances between each city and Seattle?

The INDEX function makes it easy to reference an entire row or column of an array. If you set the row number to 0, the INDEX function references the listed column. If you set the column number to 0, the INDEX function references the listed row in the array. To illustrate, suppose you want to total the distances from each listed city to Seattle. You could enter either of the following formulas:

```
SUM(INDEX(distances,8,0))

SUM(INDEX(distances,0,8))
```

The first formula totals the numbers in the eighth row (row 17) of the *distances* array; the second formula totals the numbers in the eighth column (column J) of the *distances* array. In either case, you find that the total distance from Seattle to the other cities is 15,221 miles, as you can see in Figure 4-1.

Problems

1. Use the INDEX function to compute the distance between Los Angeles and Phoenix and the distance between Denver and Miami.
2. Use the INDEX function to compute the total distance from Dallas to the other seven cities listed in Figure 4-1.
3. Jerry Jones and the Dallas Cowboys are embarking on a road trip that takes them to Chicago, Denver, Los Angeles, Phoenix, and Seattle. How many miles will they travel on this road trip?
4. The file Product.xlsx contains monthly sales for six products. Use the INDEX function to compute the sales of Product 2 in March. Use the INDEX function to compute total sales during April.
5. The file NBAdistances.xlsx shows the distance between any pair of NBA arenas. Suppose you begin in Atlanta, visit the arenas in the order listed, and then return to Atlanta. How far would you travel?
6. Use the INDEX function to solve Problem 10 of Chapter 3, "Lookup functions." Here is the problem again: The file Employees.xlsx contains the ranking that each of 35 workers has given (on a 0–10 scale) to three jobs. The file also gives the job to which each worker is assigned. Use a formula to compute each worker's ranking for the job to which the worker is assigned.

CHAPTER 5

The MATCH function

Questions answered in this chapter:

- Given monthly sales for several products, how do I write a formula that returns the sales of a product during a specific month? For example, how much of Product 2 did I sell during June?
- Given a list of baseball players' salaries, how do I write a formula that yields the player with the highest salary? How about the player with the fifth-highest salary?
- Given the annual cash flows from an investment project, how do I write a formula that returns the number of years required to pay back the project's initial investment cost?

Syntax of the MATCH function

Suppose you have a worksheet with 5,000 rows containing 5,000 names. You need to find the name *John Doe*, which you know appears somewhere (and only once) in the list. Wouldn't you like to know a formula that would return the row number in which that name is located? The MATCH function enables you to find within a given array the first occurrence of a match to a given text string or number. You should use the MATCH function instead of a lookup function in situations in which you want the position of a number in a range rather than the value in a particular cell. This is the syntax of the MATCH function:

```
Match(lookup value,lookup range,[match type])
```

In the explanation that follows, we'll assume that all cells in the lookup range are located in the same column. In this syntax, the following is true:

- *Lookup value* is the value you're trying to match in the lookup range.
- *Lookup range* is the range you're examining for a match to the lookup value. The lookup range must be a row or a column.
- *Match type=1* requires the lookup range to consist of numbers listed in ascending order. The MATCH function then returns the row location in the lookup range (relative to the top of the lookup range) that contains the largest value in the range that is less than or equal to the lookup value.

- *Match type=–1* requires the lookup range to consist of numbers listed in descending order. The MATCH function returns the row location in the lookup range (relative to the top of the lookup range) that contains the last value in the range that is greater than or equal to the lookup value.

- *Match type=0* returns the row location in the lookup range that contains the first exact match to the lookup value. (I discuss how to find the second or third match in Chapter 20, "The COUNTIF, COUNTIFS, COUNT, COUNTA, and COUNTBLANK functions.") When no exact match exists and match type=0, Excel returns the error message #N/A. Most MATCH function applications use match type=0, but if match type is not included, match type=1 is assumed. Thus, use match type=0 when the cell contents of the lookup range are unsorted. This is the situation you usually face.

The file Matchex.xlsx, shown in Figure 5-1, contains three examples of the MATCH function's syntax.

	A	B	C	D	E	F	G
1							
2							
3							
4		Boston			-5		6
5		Chicago			-4		5
6		Dallas			-3		4
7		Denver			-1		3
8		LA			3		-1
9		Miami			4		-3
10		Phoenix			5		-4
11		Seattle			6		-5
12				last number<=0	4	last number>=-4	7
13	Boston	1					
14	Phoenix	7					
15	Pho*	7					

FIGURE 5-1 Using the MATCH function to locate the position of a value in a range.

In cell B13, the formula MATCH("Boston",B4:B11,0) returns 1 because the first row in the range B4:B11 contains the value *Boston*. Text values must be enclosed in quotation marks (""). In cell B14, the formula MATCH("Phoenix",B4:B11,0) returns 7 because cell B10 (the seventh cell in B4:B11) is the first cell in the range that matches *Phoenix*. In cell E12, the formula MATCH(0,E4:E11,1) returns 4 because the last number that is less than or equal to 0 in the range E4:E11 is in cell E7 (the fourth cell in the lookup range). In cell G12, the formula MATCH(–4,G4:G11,–1) returns 7 because the last number that is greater than or equal to –4 in the range G4:G11 is –4, contained in cell G10 (the seventh cell in the lookup range).

The MATCH function can also work with an inexact match. For example, the formula in cell B15, MATCH("Pho*",B4:B11,0), returns 7. The asterisk is treated as a wildcard, which means that Excel searches for the first text string in the range B4:B11 that begins with *Pho*. Incidentally, this same technique can be used with a lookup function. For example, in the price lookup exercise in Chapter 3, "Lookup functions," the formula VLOOKUP("x*",lookup2,2) would return the price of product X212 ($4.80).

If the lookup range is contained in a single row, Excel returns the relative position of the first match in the lookup range, moving from left to right. As shown in the following examples, the MATCH function is often very useful when it is combined with other Excel functions, such as VLOOKUP, INDEX, or MAX.

Answers to this chapter's questions

Given monthly sales for several products, how do I write a formula that returns the sales of a product during a specific month? For example, how much of Product 2 did I sell during June?

The file Productlookup.xlsx (shown in Figure 5-2) lists the sales of four NBA bobblehead dolls from January through June. How can you write a formula that computes the sales of a given product during a specific month? The trick is to use one MATCH function to find the row in which the given product is located, and another MATCH function to find the column in which the given month is located. You can then use the INDEX function to return the product sales for the month.

	A	B	C	D	E	F	G
1							
2							
3		January	February	March	April	May	June
4	Curry	831	685	550	965	842	804
5	Kobe	719	504	965	816	639	814
6	MJ	916	906	851	912	964	710
7	Durant	844	509	991	851	742	817
8							
9	Product	Month	Row # of product	Column # of month	Product Sales		
10	Kobe	June	2	6	814		

FIGURE 5-2 The MATCH function can be used in combination with functions such as INDEX and VLOOKUP.

I named the range B4:G7, which contains sales data for the dolls, as *Sales*. I entered the product I want to know about in cell A10 and the month in cell B10. In C10, I used the formula MATCH(A10,A4:A7,0) to determine which row number in the range *Sales* contains sales figures for the Kobe doll. Then, in cell D10, I use the formula MATCH(B10,B3:G3,0) to determine which column number in the range *Sales* contains June sales. Now that I have the row and column numbers that contain the sales figures we want, I can use the formula INDEX(Sales,C10,D10) in cell E10 to yield the piece of sales data that's needed. For more information on the INDEX function, see Chapter 4, "The INDEX function."

Given a list of baseball players' salaries, how do I write a formula that yields the player with the highest salary? How about the player with the fifth-highest salary?

The file Baseball.xlsx (see Figure 5-3) lists the salaries paid to 401 major league baseball players during the 2001 season. The data is not sorted by salary, and we want to write a formula that returns the name of the player with the highest salary, as well as the name of the player with the fifth-highest salary.

To find the name of the player with the highest salary, proceed as follows:

- Use the MAX function to determine the value of the highest salary.
- Use the MATCH function to determine the row that contains the player with the highest salary.
- Use a VLOOKUP function (keying off the data row containing the player's salary) to look up the player's name.

I named the range C12:C412, which includes the players' salaries, *salaries*. I named the range used in our VLOOKUP function (range A12:C412) *lookup*.

	A	B	C	D
6		name	Alex Rodriguez	dl-Derek Jeter
7			highest	5th highest
8		player position	345	232
9		amount	22000000	12600000
10				
11		name	salary	
12	1	dl-Mo Vaughn	13166667	
13	2	Tim Salmon	5683013	
14	3	Garret Anderson	4500000	
15	4	Darin Erstad	3450000	
16	5	Troy Percival	3400000	
17	6	Ismael Valdes	2500000	
18	7	Pat Rapp	2000000	
19	8	Glenallen Hill	1500000	
20	9	Troy Glaus	1250000	
21	10	Shigetoshi Hasegaw	1150000	
22	11	Scott Spiezio	1125000	
23	12	Orlando Palmeiro	900000	
24	13	Alan Levine	715000	
25	14	Mike Holtz	705000	
26	15	Jorge Fabregas	500000	
27	16	Benji Gil	350000	

FIGURE 5-3 This example uses the MAX, MATCH, and VLOOKUP functions to find and display the highest value in a list.

In cell C9, I find the highest player salary ($22 million) with the formula MAX(salaries). Next, in cell C8, I use the formula MATCH(C9,salaries,0) to determine the "player number" of the player with the highest salary. I used match type=0 because the salaries are not listed in either ascending or descending order. Player number 345 has the highest salary. Finally, in cell C6, I use the function VLOOKUP(C8,lookup,2) to find the player's name in the second column of the lookup range. Not surprisingly, we find that Alex Rodriguez was the highest paid player in 2001.

To find the name of the player with the fifth-highest salary, you need a function that yields the fifth-largest number in an array. The LARGE function does that job. The syntax of the LARGE function is LARGE(cell range,k). When the LARGE function is entered this way, it returns the *k*th-largest number in a cell range. Thus, the formula LARGE(salaries,5) in cell D9 yields the fifth-largest salary ($12.6 million). Proceeding as before, we find that Derek Jeter is the player with the fifth-highest salary. The function SMALL(salaries,5) would return the fifth-lowest salary.

Given the annual cash flows from an investment project, how do I write a formula that returns the number of years required to pay back the project's initial investment cost?

The file Payback.xlsx, shown in Figure 5-4, illustrates the projected cash flows for an investment project over the next 15 years. We assume that in Year 1, the project required a cash outflow of $100 million. During Year 1, the project generated a cash inflow of $14 million. We expect cash flows to grow at 10 percent per year. How many years will pass before the project pays back its investment?

The number of years required for a project to pay back an investment is called the *payback period.* In high-tech industries, the payback period is often used to rank investments. You'll learn in Chapter 8, "Evaluating investments by using net present value criteria," that payback is flawed as a measure of investment quality because it ignores the value of money over time. For now, let's concentrate on how to determine the payback period for our simple investment model.

	A	B	C	D	E
1	Year 1 cash flow	14			Payback Period
2	Growth	0.1			6
3	Initial Investment	-100			
4	Year	Annual Cash flow	Cumulative cash flow		
5	0	-100	-100		
6	1	14	-86		
7	2	15.4	-70.6		
8	3	16.94	-53.66		
9	4	18.634	-35.026		
10	5	20.4974	-14.5286		
11	6	22.54714	8.01854		
12	7	24.801854	32.820394		
13	8	27.2820394	60.1024334		
14	9	30.01024334	90.11267674		
15	10	33.01126767	123.1239444		
16	11	36.31239444	159.4363389		
17	12	39.94363389	199.3799727		
18	13	43.93799727	243.31797		
19	14	48.331797	291.649767		
20	15	53.1649767	344.8147437		

FIGURE 5-4 Using the MATCH function to calculate an investment's payback period.

To determine the payback period for the project, proceed as follows:

- In column B, compute the cash flows for each year.
- In column C, compute the cumulative cash flows for each year.

Now you can use the MATCH function (with match type=1) to determine the row number of the first year in which the cumulative cash flow is positive. This calculation gives you the payback period.

I gave the cells in B1:B3 the range names listed in A1:A3. Year 0 cash flow (–Initial_investment) is entered in cell B5. Year 1 cash flow (Year_1_cf) is entered in cell B6. Copying from B7 to B8:B20 the formula B6*(1+Growth) computes the cash flow for Years 2 through 15.

To compute the Year 0 cumulative cash flow, I used the formula B5 in cell C5. For later years, you can calculate cumulative cash flow by using a formula such as Year t cumulative cash flow = Year t–1 cumulative cash flow + Year t cash flow. To implement this relationship, simply copy from C6 to C7:C20 the formula =C5+B6.

To compute the payback period, use the MATCH function (with match type=1) to compute the last row of the range C5:C20 containing a value less than 0. This calculation always gives you the payback period. For example, if the last row in C5:C20 that contains a value less than 0 is the sixth row in the range, that means the seventh value marks the cumulative cash flow for the first year the project is paid back. Because our first year is Year 0, the payback occurs during Year 6. Therefore, the formula in cell E2, MATCH(0,C5:C20,1), yields the payback period (six years). If any cash flows after Year 0 are negative, this method fails and yields an error message because the range of cumulative cash flows would not be listed in ascending order. Using the IFERROR function (discussed in Chapter 12), you could ensure that cell E2 returns a text message (such as "No payback year exists") when no payback year exists.

Problems

1. Using the distances between US cities given in the file Index.xlsx, write a formula using the MATCH function to determine (based on the names of the cities) the distance between any two of the cities.
2. The file Matchtype1.xlsx lists in chronological order the dollar amounts of 30 transactions. Write a formula that yields the first transaction for which the total volume to date exceeds $10,000.
3. The file Matchthemax.xlsx gives the product ID codes and unit sales for 265 products. Use the MATCH function in a formula that yields the product ID code of the product with the largest unit sales.
4. The file Buslist.xlsx gives the amount of time between bus arrivals (in minutes) at 45th Street and Park Avenue in New York City. Write a formula that, for any arrival time after the first bus, gives the amount of time you have to wait for a bus. For example, if you arrive 12.4 minutes from now, and buses arrive 5 minutes and 21 minutes from now, you wait 21–12.4=8.6 minutes for a bus.
5. The file Salesdata.xlsx contains the number of computers in a store sold by each salesperson. Create a formula that returns the units sold by a given salesperson.
6. Suppose the VLOOKUP function has been removed from Excel. Explain how you could still make useful calculations by using the MATCH and INDEX functions?
7. In the file Baseballproblem7.xlsx, you are given major league team statistics. You will enter a team's name in cell I2 and a statistic in cell J2. Write a formula in cell K2 that returns the value of the statistic for the selected team.
8. The file Footballproblem8.xlsx shows statistics on NFL quarterbacks. Suppose we enter a QB's name in cell G3 and a statistic in cell H3. Write a formula that returns in cell I3 the QB's statistic.

CHAPTER 6

Text functions

Questions answered in this chapter:

- I have a worksheet in which each cell contains a product description, a product ID, and a product price. How can I put all the product descriptions in column A, all the product IDs in column B, and all the prices in column C?
- Every day I receive data about total US sales, which is computed in a cell as the sum of East, North, and South regional sales. How can I extract East, North, and South sales to separate cells?
- At the end of each school semester, my students evaluate my teaching performance on a scale from 1 to 7. I know how many students gave me each possible rating score. How can I easily create a bar graph of my teaching evaluation scores?
- I have downloaded numerical data from the Internet or a database. When I try to do calculations with the data, I always get a #VALUE error. How can I solve this problem?
- I like text functions, but is there an easy way (not involving text functions) to extract first or last names from data, create an email list from a list of names, or perform other routine operations on text data?
- What are Unicode characters?

When someone sends you data or you download data from the Web, it often isn't formatted the way you want. For example, in sales data you download, dates and sales amounts might be in the same cell, but you need them to be in separate cells. How can you manipulate data so that it appears in the format you need? The answer is to become good at using the Microsoft Excel text functions. In this chapter, I'll show you how to use the following Excel text functions:

- LEFT
- RIGHT
- MID
- TRIM
- LEN
- FIND

- SEARCH
- REPT
- CONCATENATE
- REPLACE
- VALUE
- UPPER
- LOWER
- PROPER
- CHAR
- CLEAN
- SUBSTITUTE

I'll also show you can use the new Flash Fill feature to magically manipulate your data so that it looks the way you want. Finally, you will learn about the vast set of Unicode characters available in Excel 2016.

Text function syntax

The file Textfunctions.xlsx, shown in Figure 6-1, includes examples of text functions. You'll see how to apply these functions to a specific problem later in the chapter, but let's begin by seeing what each of the text functions does. Then we'll combine the functions to perform some fairly complex manipulations of data.

	A	B	C	D	E
1	Reggie	Miller			
2					
3	Reggie Miller	Left 4	Regg		
4		Right 4	ller		
5		Trim spaces	Reggie Miller		
6		Number of characters	15		
7		Number of characters in trimmed result	13		
8		5 characters starting at space 2	eggie		
9		Find first space	7		
10		Find first r (case sensitive)	15		
11		Find first r (not case sensitive)	1		
12		Combining first and Last Name	Reggie Miller	Reggie Miller	
13		Replace gg with nn	Rennie Miller		
14	Text 31	Number 31			
15	31	31			
16		Change to lower case	reggie miller		
17		Change to Upper case	REGGIE MILLER	I LOVE EXCEL 2016!	
18		Change to Proper case	Reggie Miller		
19		Replace all spaces by *	I*LOVE*EXCEL*2016!		
20		Replace only third space by *	I LOVE EXCEL*2016!		

FIGURE 6-1 Examples of text functions.

The LEFT function

The function LEFT(text,k) returns the first *k* characters in a text string. For example, cell C3 contains the formula LEFT(A3,4). Excel returns *Regg*.

The RIGHT function

The function RIGHT(text,k) returns the last *k* characters in a text string. For example, in cell C4, the formula RIGHT(A3,4) returns *ller*.

The MID function

The function MID(text,k,m) begins at character *k* of a text string and returns the next *m* characters. For example, the formula MID(A3,2,5) in cell C8 returns characters 2–6 from cell A3, the result being *eggie*.

The TRIM function

The function TRIM(text) removes all spaces from a text string except for single spaces between words. For example, in cell C5, the formula TRIM(A3) eliminates two of the three spaces between *Reggie* and *Miller* and yields *Reggie Miller*. The TRIM function also removes spaces at the beginning and end of the cell.

The LEN function

The function LEN(text) returns the number of characters in a text string (including spaces). For example, in cell C6, the formula LEN(A3) returns *15* because cell A3 contains 15 characters. In cell C7, the formula LEN(C5) returns *13*. Because the trimmed result in cell C5 has two spaces removed, cell C5 contains two fewer characters than the original text in A3.

The FIND and SEARCH functions

The function FIND(text_to_find,actual_text,k) returns the location at or after character *k* of the first character of *text to find* in *actual text*. FIND is case sensitive. SEARCH has the same syntax as FIND, but it is not case sensitive. For example, the formula FIND("r",A3,1) in cell C10 returns *15*, the location of the first lowercase *r* in the text string *Reggie Miller*. (The uppercase *R* is ignored because FIND is case sensitive.) Entering SEARCH("r",A3,1) in cell C11 returns *1* because SEARCH matches *r* to either a lowercase character or an uppercase character. Entering FIND(" ",A3,1) in cell C9 returns *7* because the first space in the string *Reggie Miller* is the seventh character.

The REPT function

The REPT function allows you to repeat a text string a specified number of times. The syntax is REPT(text,number_of_times). For example REPT("|",3) produces the output |||.

The CONCATENATE and & functions

The function CONCATENATE(text1,text2, . . .,text30) can be used to join as many as 30 text strings into a single string. The & operator can be used instead of CONCATENATE. For example, entering in cell C12 the formula A1&" "&B1 returns *Reggie Miller.* Entering in cell D12 the formula CONCATENATE(A1," ",B1) yields the same result.

The REPLACE function

The function REPLACE(old_text,k,m,new_text) begins at character *k* of *old text* and replaces the next *m* characters with *new text*. For example, in cell C13, the formula REPLACE(A3,3,2,"nn") replaces the third and fourth characters (*gg*) in cell A3 with *nn*. This formula yields *Rennie Miller.*

The VALUE function

The function VALUE(text) converts a text string that represents a number to a number. For example, entering in cell B15 the formula VALUE(A15) converts the text string *31* in cell A15 to the numerical value *31*. You can identify the value *31* in cell A15 as text because it is left justified. Similarly, you can identify the value *31* in cell B15 as a number because it is right justified.

The UPPER, LOWER, and PROPER functions

The function UPPER(text) changes text to all uppercase. For example, in cell C16 the formula LOWER(C12) changes the capital letters to lowercase and yields *reggie miller.* In cell C17, the formula UPPER(C16) changes all letters to uppercase and yields *REGGIE MILLER.* Finally, in cell C18 the formula PROPER(C17) restores the proper case and yields *Reggie Miller.*

The CHAR function

The function CHAR(number) yields (for a number between 1 and 255) the ASCII character identified with that number. For example, CHAR(65) yields *A*, CHAR(66) yields *B*, and so on. The file ASCIIcharacters.xlsx contains a list of ASCII characters. A partial listing is shown in Figure 6-2.

	C	D
39	36	$
40	37	%
41	38	&
42	39	'
43	40	(
44	41	)
45	42	*
46	43	+
47	44	,
48	45	-
49	46	.
50	47	/
51	48	0
52	49	1
53	50	2
54	51	3
55	52	4
56	53	5
57	54	6
58	55	7
59	56	8
60	57	9

FIGURE 6-2 Partial list of ASCII characters.

The CLEAN function

As you can see in Figure 6-2, certain characters, such as character number 10 (which represents a line feed), are invisible. Applying the CLEAN function to a cell will remove some, but not all, of the invisible (or nonprinting) ASCII characters. The CLEAN function will not remove, for example, CHAR(160), which is a nonbreaking space. Later in this chapter, we will examine how to remove troublesome characters such as CHAR(160) from a cell.

The SUBSTITUTE function

The SUBSTITUTE function is used to replace specific text in a cell when you do not know the position of the text. The syntax of the SUBSTITUTE function is SUBSTITUTE(cell,old_text,new_text,instance_number). The last argument is optional. If it's omitted, every occurrence of *old_text* in the cell is replaced by *new_text*. If the last argument is included (say with a value of *n*), then only the *n*th instance of *old_text* is replaced by *new_text*. To illustrate the use of the SUBSTITUTE function, suppose we want to replace the spaces in cell D17 by asterisks. First we enter in cell C19 the formula SUBSTITUTE(D17," ","*"). This replaces each space with an * and yields *I*LOVE*EXCEL*2016!*. Entering in cell C20 the formula SUBSTITUTE(D17," ","*",3) replaces only the third space with an * and yields *I LOVE EXCEL*2016!*.

Answers to this chapter's questions

You can see the power of text functions by using them to solve some actual problems that were sent to me by former students working for Fortune 500 corporations. Often, the key to solving a problem is to combine multiple text functions into a single formula.

I have a worksheet in which each cell contains a product description, a product ID, and a product price. How can I put all the product descriptions in column A, all the product IDs in column B, and all the prices in column C?

In this example, the product ID is always defined by the first 12 characters, and the price is always indicated in the last 8 characters (with two spaces following the end of each price). The solution, contained in the file Lenora.xlsx (and shown in Figure 6-4), uses the LEFT, RIGHT, MID, VALUE, TRIM, LEN, and CONCATENATE functions.

It's always a good idea to begin by trimming excess spaces, which you can do by copying from B4 to B5:B12 the formula TRIM(A4). The only excess spaces in column A turn out to be the two spaces inserted after each price. To see this, put the cursor in cell A4 and press F2 to edit the cell. If you move to the end of the cell, you will see two blank spaces. The results of using the TRIM function are shown in column B of Figure 6-3. To prove that the TRIM function removed the two extra spaces at the end of cell A4, you can use the formulas =LEN(A4) and =LEN(B4) to show that cell A4 contains 52 characters and cell B4 contains 50 characters.

	A	B
1	length of A4	length of B4
2	52	50
3	Untrimmed	Trimmed
4	32592100AFES CONTROLLERPENTIUM/100,(2)1GB H 304.00	32592100AFES CONTROLLERPENTIUM/100,(2)1GB H 304.00
5	32592100JCP9 DESKTOP UNIT 225.00	32592100JCP9 DESKTOP UNIT 225.00
6	325927008990 DESKTOP WINDOWS NT 4.0 SERVER 232.00	325927008990 DESKTOP WINDOWS NT 4.0 SERVER 232.00
7	325926008990 DESKTOP WINDOWS NT 4.0 WKST 232.00	325926008990 DESKTOP WINDOWS NT 4.0 WKST 232.00
8	325921008990 DESKTOP, DOS OS 232.00	325921008990 DESKTOP, DOS OS 232.00
9	325922008990 DESKTOP, WINDOWS DESKTOP OS 232.00	325922008990 DESKTOP, WINDOWS DESKTOP OS 232.00
10	325925008990 DESKTOP, WINDOWS NT OS 232.00	325925008990 DESKTOP, WINDOWS NT OS 232.00
11	325930008990 MINITOWER, NO OS 232.00	325930008990 MINITOWER, NO OS 232.00
12	32593000KEYY MINI TOWER 232.00	32593000KEYY MINI TOWER 232.00

FIGURE 6-3 Using the TRIM function to trim away excess spaces.

To capture the product ID, you need to extract the 12 leftmost characters from column B. To do this, copy from C4 to C5:C12 the formula LEFT(B4,12). This formula extracts the 12 leftmost characters from the text in cell B4 and the following cells, yielding the product ID, as you can see in Figure 6-4.

	B	C	D	E	F
1	length of B4				
2	50				
3	Trimmed	Product ID	Price	Product Description	Concatenation
4	32592100AFES CONTROLLERPENTIUM/100,(2)1GB H 304.00	32592100AFES	304	CONTROLLERPENTIUM/100,(2)1GB H	32592100AFES CONTROLLERPENTIUM/100,(2)1GB H 304
5	32592100JCP9 DESKTOP UNIT 225.00	32592100JCP9	225	DESKTOP UNIT	32592100JCP9 DESKTOP UNIT 225
6	325927008990 DESKTOP WINDOWS NT 4.0 SERVER 232.00	325927008990	232	DESKTOP WINDOWS NT 4.0 SERVER	325927008990 DESKTOP WINDOWS NT 4.0 SERVER 232
7	325926008990 DESKTOP WINDOWS NT 4.0 WKST 232.00	325926008990	232	DESKTOP WINDOWS NT 4.0 WKST	325926008990 DESKTOP WINDOWS NT 4.0 WKST 232
8	325921008990 DESKTOP, DOS OS 232.00	325921008990	232	DESKTOP, DOS OS	325921008990 DESKTOP, DOS OS 232
9	325922008990 DESKTOP, WINDOWS DESKTOP OS 232.00	325922008990	232	DESKTOP, WINDOWS DESKTOP OS	325922008990 DESKTOP, WINDOWS DESKTOP OS 232
10	325925008990 DESKTOP, WINDOWS NT OS 232.00	325925008990	232	DESKTOP, WINDOWS NT OS	325925008990 DESKTOP, WINDOWS NT OS 232
11	325930008990 MINITOWER, NO OS 232.00	325930008990	232	MINITOWER, NO OS	325930008990 MINITOWER, NO OS 232
12	32593000KEYY MINI TOWER 232.00	32593000KEYY	232	MINI TOWER	32593000KEYY MINI TOWER 232

FIGURE 6-4 Using text functions to extract the product ID, price, and product description from a text string.

To extract the product price, we know that the price occupies the last six digits of each cell, so we need to extract the rightmost six characters from each cell. I copied from cell D4 to D5:D12 the formula VALUE(RIGHT(B4,6)). I used the VALUE function to turn the extracted text into a numerical value. If you don't convert the text to a numerical value, you can't perform mathematical operations on the prices.

Extracting the product description is much trickier. By examining the data, you can see that if we begin our extraction with the thirteenth character and continue until we are six characters from the end of the cell, we can get the data we want. Copying from E4 to E5:E12 the formula MID(B4,13,LEN(B4)–6–12) does the job. LEN(B4) returns the total number of characters in the trimmed text. This formula (MID for Middle) begins with the thirteenth character and then extracts the number of characters equal to the total number less the 12 characters at the beginning (the product ID) and the six characters at the end (price). This subtraction leaves only the product description.

Now suppose you are given the data with the product ID in column C, the price in column D, and the product description in column E. Can you put these values together to recover our original text?

Text can easily be combined by using the CONCATENATE function. Copying from F4 to F5:F12 the formula CONCATENATE(C4,E4,D4) recovers our original (trimmed) text, which you can see in Figure 6-4.

The concatenation formula starts with the product ID in cell C4. Next, you add the product description from cell E4. Finally, you add the price from cell D4. You have now recovered the entire text describing each computer. Concatenation can also be performed by using the & sign. You could recover the original product ID, product description, and price in a single cell with the formula C4&E4&D4. Note that cell E4 contains a space before the product description and a space after the product description. If cell E4 did not contain these spaces, you could use the formula C4&" "&E4&" "&D4 to insert the necessary spaces. Note that the space between each pair of quotation marks results in the insertion of a space.

If the product IDs do not always contain 12 characters, this method of extracting the information fails. You could, however, extract the product IDs by using the FIND function to discover the location of the first space. Then you could obtain the product ID by using the LEFT function to extract all characters to the left of the first space. The example in the next section shows how this approach works.

If the price does not always contain precisely six characters, extracting the price would be a little tricky. See Problem 15 for an example of how to extract the last word in a text string.

Every day I receive data about total US sales, which is computed in a cell as the sum of East, North, and South regional sales. How can I extract East, North, and South sales to separate cells?

This problem was sent to me by an employee in the Microsoft finance department. She receives a worksheet each day containing formulas such as =50+200+400, =5+124+1025, and so on. She needs to extract each number into a cell in its own column. For example, she wants to extract the first number (East sales) in each cell to column C, the second number (North sales) to column D, and the third number (South sales) to column E. What makes this problem challenging is that we don't know the exact location of the character at which the second and third numbers start in each cell. In cell A3, North sales begin with the fourth character. In cell A4, North sales begin with the third character.

The data for this example is in the file Salesstripping.xlsx, shown in Figure 6-5. You can identify the locations of the different regions' sales as follows:

- East sales are represented by every character to the left of the first plus sign (+).
- North sales are represented by every character between the first and second plus signs.
- South sales are represented by every character to the right of the second plus sign.

By combining the FIND, LEFT, LEN, and MID functions, you can easily solve this problem as follows:

- Use the Edit, Replace command to replace each equal sign (=) with a space. To remove the equal signs, select the range A3:A6. Then, on the Home tab in the Editing group, click Find & Select, and then click Replace. In the Find What field, enter an equal sign and insert a space in the Replace With field. Then click Replace All. This converts each formula into text by replacing the equal sign by a space.
- Use the FIND function to locate the two plus signs in each cell.

	A	B	C	D	E	F	G
1	Extracting Sales in Three Regions						
2	East+North+South	First +	Second +	East	North	Total Length	South
3	10+300+400	3	7	10	300	10	400
4	4+36.2+800	2	7	4	36.2	10	800
5	3+23+4005	2	5	3	23	9	4005
6	18+1+57.31	3	5	18	1	10	57.31

FIGURE 6-5 Extracting East, North, and South sales with a combination of the FIND, LEFT, LEN, and MID functions.

Begin by finding the location of the first plus sign for each piece of data. By copying from B3 to B4:B6 the formula FIND("+",A3,1), you can locate the first plus sign for each data point. To find the second plus sign, begin one character after the first plus sign, copying from C3 to C4:C6 the formula FIND("+",A3,B3+1).

To find East sales, you can use the LEFT function to extract all the characters to the left of the first plus sign, copying from D3 to D4:D6 the formula LEFT(A3,B3-1). To extract North sales, use the MID function to extract all the characters between the two plus signs. Begin one character after the first plus sign and extract the number of characters equal to (Position of 2nd plus sign)–(Position of 1st plus sign) – 1. If you leave out the –1, you'll get the second plus sign. (Go ahead and check this.) So, to get North sales, copy from E3 to E4:E6 the formula MID(A3,B3+1,C3–B3–1). Refer back up to the "Text function syntax" section to review each argument taken by the functions.

To extract South sales, use the RIGHT function to extract all the characters to the right of the second plus sign. South sales will have the number of characters equal to (Total characters in cell) – (Position of 2nd plus sign). Compute the total number of characters in each cell by copying from F3 to F4:F6 the formula LEN(A3). Finally, you can obtain South sales by copying from G3 to G4:G6 the formula RIGHT(A3,F3-C3).

Extracting data by using the Convert Text To Columns Wizard

There is an easy way to extract East, North, and South sales (and data similar to this example) without using text functions. Simply select cells A3:A6, and then, on the Data tab on the ribbon, in the Data Tools group, click the Text To Columns option. Select Delimited, click Next, and then fill in the dialog box as shown in Figure 6-6.

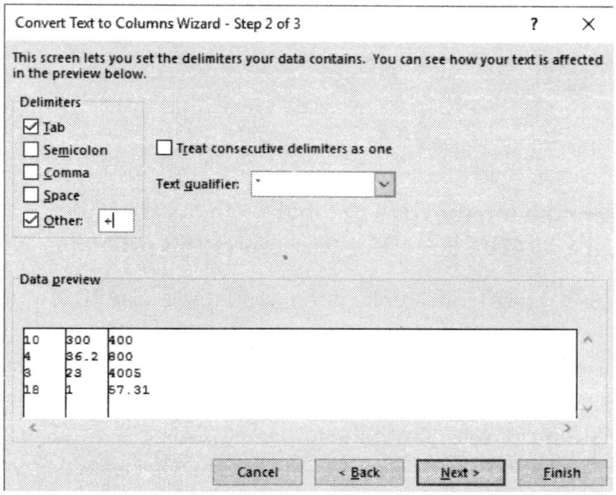

FIGURE 6-6 Using the Convert Text To Columns Wizard.

Entering the plus sign in the Delimiters area (check Other) directs Excel to separate each cell into columns, breaking at each occurrence of the plus sign. Note that options are provided for breaking data at tabs, semicolons, commas, or spaces. Now click Next, select the upper-left corner of your destination range (in the example, I chose cell A8), and click Finish. The result is shown in Figure 6-7.

	A	B	C	D
8	10	300	400	
9	4	36.2	800	
10	3	23	4005	
11	18	1	57.31	
12				

FIGURE 6-7 Results of using the Convert Text To Columns Wizard.

At the end of each school semester, my students evaluate my teaching performance on a scale from 1 to 7. I know how many students gave me each possible rating score. How can I easily create a bar graph of my teaching evaluation scores?

The file Repeatedhisto.xlsx contains my teaching evaluation scores (on a scale from 1 through 7). Two people gave me scores of 1, three people gave me scores of 2, and so on. Using the REPT function, you can easily create a graph to summarize this data. Simply copy from D4 to D5:D10 the formula =REPT("|",C4). This formula places in column D as many "|" characters as the entry in column C. Figure 6-8 makes clear the preponderance of good scores (6s and 7s) and the relative rarity of poor scores (1s and 2s). Repeating a character such as | enables you to easily mimic a bar graph or histogram. See

Chapter 41, "Summarizing data by using histograms and Pareto charts," for further discussion of how to create histograms with Excel.

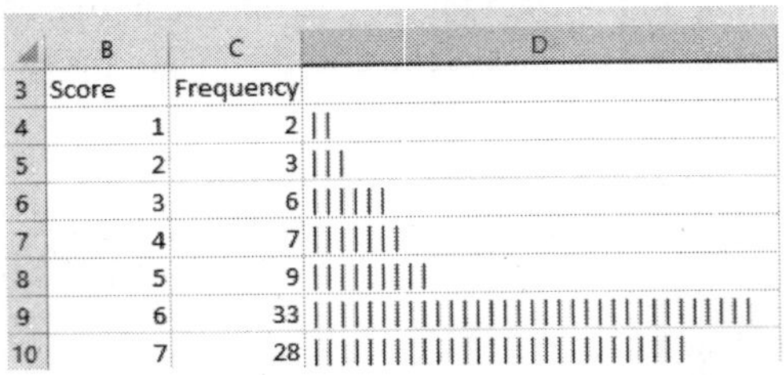

FIGURE 6-8 Using the REPT function to create a frequency graph.

I have downloaded numerical data from the Internet or a database. When I try to do calculations with the data, I always get a #VALUE error. How can I solve this problem?

In the file Cleanexample.xlsx (see Figure 6-9), I have concatenated the unprintable CHAR(10) and CHAR(160) in front of the number 33 in cells E5 and H6, respectively. In cells E8 and H8, we apply the VALUE function in an attempt to transform the contents of E5 and H6 into numbers, but the result is the #VALUE error, which indicates that Excel cannot figure out that we want to treat these cells as numbers. In cell E11, we "cleaned" the contents of cell E5 with the formula CLEAN(E5). In cell E12, we see the numerical value 33, so the formula VALUE(E11) meets with success after we cleaned CHAR(10). However, in cell H10 we attempted to clean the contents of cell H6 with the formula CLEAN(H6). In cell H11, the formula VALUE(H10) meets with failure because the CLEAN function does not remove CHAR(160). We can, however, use the SUBSTITUTE function to replace CHAR(160) with an empty space, and all is well. In cell H14, we use the formula FIND(CHAR(160),H10) to verify that CHAR(160) is present in cell H10. We find that the first character in cell H10 was CHAR(160); if the FIND function returned an error, we would know that CHAR(160) was not present in cell H10. In cell H15, the formula SUBSTITUTE(H6,CHAR(160),"") replaces all occurrences of CHAR(160) with an empty space. In cell H16, the formula VALUE(H15) yields the number 33, so we can now perform mathematical operations on the contents of cell H15.

	E	F	G	H	I	J
4	char 10					
5	33			char 160		
6				33		
7						
8	#VALUE!			#VALUE!		
9				CLEAN?		
10	cleaned			33		
11	33			#VALUE!		
12	33			CLEAN and VALUE DO NOT WORK		
13				SUBSTITUTE		
14			FIND CHAR 160	1		
15			SUBSTITUTE	33		
16			VALUE	33		
17				160		

FIGURE 6-9 Using the CLEAN and SUBSITUTE functions to remove unprintable characters.

I like text functions, but is there an easy way (not involving text functions) to extract first or last names from data, create an email list from a list of names, or perform other routine operations on text data?

Flash Fill uses sophisticated pattern-recognition technology to mimic many tasks that were previously performed with text functions. The file Flashfill.xlsx contains the following examples of Flash Fill in action:

- Extracting first and last names (in the First And Last worksheet).
- Creating email addresses for UXYZ University by appending @UXYZ.edu to a person's last name (in the Email worksheet).
- Extracting the dollar and cents amounts from a list of prices (in the Dollar And Centers worksheet).

Using the Flash Fill feature lets you go to a column near your data, and in the row containing the first row of data, type in an example of what you want to accomplish. Usually, if you press the Enter key and then Ctrl+E, Flash Fill will correctly anticipate your wishes and fill in the remaining cells. Sometimes, however it takes more than one example for Flash Fill to get things right.

As shown in Figure 6-10, we want to extract each person's first and last name in columns E and F. In the First And Last worksheet, simply type Tricia in cell E6 and press Enter. Then press Ctrl+E, and Excel fills in each person's first name in E7:E13. Similarly, if we type Lopez in F6 and press the Enter key and then Ctrl+E, Flash Fill enters each person's last name in F7:F13.

	D	E	F
5	Full	First	Last
6	Tricia Lopez	Tricia	Lopez
7	Will Wong	Will	Wong
8	Jack Spratt	Jack	Spratt
9	Vivian Hibbits	Vivian	Hibbits
10	Jose Gomez	Jose	Gomez
11	April Chou	April	Chou
12	Tanya Walters	Tanya	Walters
13	James Jones	James	Jones

FIGURE 6-10 Flash Fill automatically fills in the first and last names.

As shown in Figure 6-11, we want to create an email address for each person by appending *@UXYZ.edu* to each person's last name. We begin by typing Lopez@UXYZ.edu in cell E6 of the Email worksheet. After pressing the Enter key, we press Ctrl+E, and then Flash Fill magically creates email addresses in the range E7:E13.

	D	E
5	Name	Email
6	Tricia Lopez	Lopez@UXYZ.edu
7	Will Wong	Wong@UXYZ.edu
8	Jack Spratt	Spratt@UXYZ.edu
9	Vivian Hibbits	Hibbits@UXYZ.edu
10	Jose Gomez	Gomez@UXYZ.edu
11	April Chou	Chou@UXYZ.edu
12	Tanya Walters	Walters@UXYZ.edu
13	James Jones	Jones@UXYZ.edu

FIGURE 6-11 Creating email addresses with Flash Fill.

As shown in Figure 6-12, we want to extract the dollar and cents amount of the prices shown in the cell range D6:D11 of the worksheet Dollars And Cents. To begin, type 6 in cell E6 and press the Enter key. After you press Ctrl+E, the correct dollar amounts are filled in E7:E11. Similarly, if we enter 56 in F6 and hit the Enter key followed by Ctrl+E, Flash Fill fills in the correct cents amounts in F7:F11.

	D	E	F
5	Price	Dollars	Cents
6	$6.56	6	56
7	$7.43	7	43
8	$9.86	9	86
9	$15.43	15	43
10	$173.32	173	32
11	$4.21	4	21

FIGURE 6-12 Using Flash Fill to extract dollars and cents.

Flash Fill can make mistakes, especially when the data is not extremely consistent. Also (unlike formulas involving text functions), the results from Flash Fill are not dynamic and will not update if the original data is changed.

If you want to, you can disable Flash Fill by selecting Options from the File menu on the ribbon; under Advanced, navigate to the Editing Options section of the dialog box and clear Automatically Flash Fill.

What are Unicode characters?

The Unicode character set consists of around 120,000 characters, including many symbols used by scientists and characters from many languages. Each Unicode character has a code number. (The best reference to Unicode characters appears to be *http://www.alanwood.net/unicode/*.)

You can discover, for example, that the Greek alphabet (important to Greeks and scientists!) has character numbers around 900 (see the file Unicodefinal.xlsx and Figure 6-13). You can find the character associated with a code number by using the function UNICHAR(code number). For example, the formula =UNICHAR(F67) returns the Greek letter μ, because the code number for μ is 956. You can also find the code number for a given character by using the function UNICHAR(character). For example, the formula =UNICODE(G67) returns the code number for μ (956).

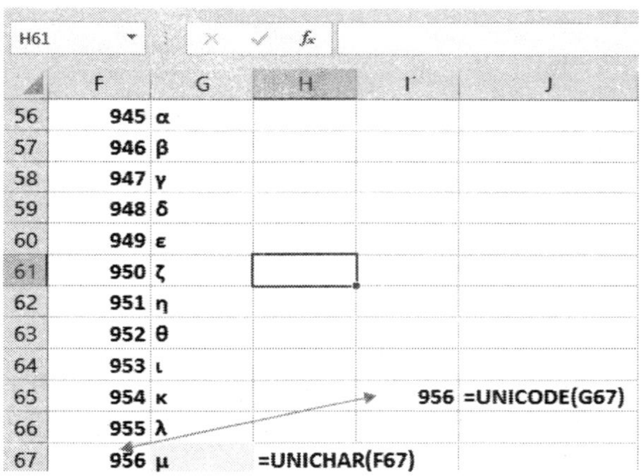

FIGURE 6-13 Examples of using the UNICODE and UNICHAR functions.

Problems

1. Cells B2:B5 of the workbook Showbiz.xlsx contain the fictitious addresses of some of our favorite people. Use text functions to extract each person's name to one column and each person's street address to another.

2. The workbook IDprice.xlsx contains the product ID and prices for various products. Use text functions to put the product IDs and prices in separate columns. Then use the Convert Text To Columns command on the Data tab on the ribbon to accomplish the same goal.

3. The workbook Quarterlygnpdata.xlsx contains quarterly GNP data for the United States (in billions of 1996 dollars). Extract this data to three separate columns in which the first column contains the year, the second column contains the quarter number, and the third column contains the GNP value.

4. The file Textstylesdata.xlsx contains information about the style, color, and size for a variety of shirts. For example, the first shirt is style 100 (indicated by digits between the colon and the

hyphen). Its color is 65, and its size is L. Use text functions to extract the style, color, and size of each shirt.

5. The file Emailproblem.xlsx gives first and last names of several new Microsoft employees. To create an email address for each employee, you need to follow the first letter of the employee's first name by the employee's last name and add *@microsoft.com* to the end. Use text functions to efficiently create the email addresses.

6. The file Lineupdata.xlsx gives the number of minutes played by five-player combinations (lineups). (Lineup 1 played 10.4 minutes, and so on.) Use text functions to put this data into a form suitable for numerical calculations; for example, transform 10.4m into the number 10.4.

7. The file Reversenames.xlsx gives the first names, middle names or initials, and last names of several people. Transform these names so that the last name appears first, followed by a comma, followed by the first and middle names. For example, transform *Gregory William Winston* into *Winston, Gregory William.*

8. The file Incomefrequency.xlsx contains the distribution of starting salaries for MBA graduates of Faber College. Summarize this data by creating a frequency graph.

9. Recall that CHAR(65) yields the letter *A*, CHAR(66) yields the letter *B*, and so on. In a new workbook, use these facts to efficiently populate cells B1:B26 with the sequence *A*, *B*, *C*, and so on through *Z*.

10. The file Capitalizefirstletter.xlsx contains various song titles or phrases, such as "The rain in Spain falls mainly in the plain." Ensure that the first letter of each song title is capitalized.

11. The file Ageofmachine.xlsx contains data in the following form:

    S/N: 160768, vib roller,84" smooth drum,canopy Auction: 6/2–4/2005 in Montgomery, Alabama

    Each row refers to a machine purchase. Determine the year of each purchase.

12. When downloading corporate data from the Security and Exchange Commission's EDGAR site, you often obtain data for a company that looks something like this:

    Cash and Cash Equivalents $31,848 $ 31,881

    How would you efficiently extract the Cash and Cash Equivalents for each company?

13. The file Lookuptwocolumns.xlsx gives the model, year, and price for each of a series of cars. Set up formulas that enable you to enter the model and year of a car and return its price.

14. The file Moviedata.xlsx contains the names of several movies followed by the number of copies of the movie DVD purchased by a local video store. Extract the title of each movie from this data.

15. The file Moviedata.xlsx contains the names of several movies followed by the number of copies of the movie DVD purchased by a local video store. For each movie, extract the number of copies purchased from this data. Hint: You probably want to use the SUBSTITUTE function. The syntax of the SUBSTITUTE function is SUBSTITUTE(text,old_text,new_text,instance_

number). If *instance_number* is omitted, every occurrence of *old_text* in *text* is replaced by *new_text*. If *instance_number* is given, only that occurrence of *old_text* is replaced by *new_text*. For example, SUBSTITUTE(A4,1,2) would replace each *1* in cell A4 with a *2*, but SUBSTITUTE(A4,1,2,3) would replace only the third occurrence of a *1* in cell A4 with a *2*.

16. The file Problem16data.xlsx contains the number of people who responded 1–5 on a marketing questionnaire (1 = Very unlikely to buy product, ..., 5 = Very likely to buy product). Summarize this data graphically by using the asterisk symbol. To make your summary look more appealing, you can go to the Home tab on the ribbon and choose Orientation in the Alignment group and make the text vertical. Then right-click the row number, and increase the row height. Finally, in the Alignment group, choose Wrap Text so that you make the text of your graph vertical.

17. The file Problem17data.xlsx contains people's names (such as *Mr. John Doe*). Use text functions to extract each person's title and first name to separate columns.

18. The file Weirddata.xls contains three numbers imported from an Internet site. When you try adding the numbers, you will see the total is incorrect. Modify the data so that the SUM function can obtain the correct sum of the three numbers. Hint: Use the FIND function to find out which invisible character is present!

19. Use Flash Fill to change the names in the worksheet Flashfilltemplate.xlsx (in the Templates folder) to lowercase.

20. Use Flash Fill to extract the number from each row in the file Movienumbers.xlsx.

21. For the data in Movienumbers.xlsx, use Flash Fill to create a column that inserts the number in the movie title at the end of the phrase *The number in the title of this movie is.*

22. Each row of the file Problem22data.xlsx gives the name of a city, state, and population of the city. Use text functions to extract the state to a separate column.

23. The file Problem23data.xlsx gives the name of a quarterback (QB) followed by the player's QB rating, followed by the number of completed passes thrown by the QB. Use text functions to extract each QB's number of completed passes.

24. In each row of the file Problem24data.xlsx you will find a city's zip code, city name, state (always Texas!), latitude, and longitude. Use formulas to extract the name of the city in each row. You may assume that each zip code is five characters long. Hint: the FIND function is case sensitive.

25. Each row of the file Problem25data.xlsx contains between the hyphen and comma a QB's number of completions. Use text function to extract each QB's number of completions.

CHAPTER 7

Dates and date functions

Questions answered in this chapter:

- When I enter dates in Excel, I often see a number such as 37625 rather than a date such as 1/4/2003. What does this number mean, and how do I change it to a normal date?
- Can I use a formula to automatically display today's date?
- How do I determine a date that is 50 workdays after another date? What if I want to exclude holidays?
- How do I determine the number of workdays between two dates?
- I have 500 different dates entered in an Excel worksheet. How do I write formulas to extract from each date the month, year, day of the month, and day of the week?
- I am given the year, month, and day of the month for a date. Is there an easy way to recover the actual date?
- My business has purchased and sold machines. For some, I have the date the machine was purchased and the date the machine was sold. Can I easily determine how many months we kept these machines?
- How can I place a static (unchanging) date in a worksheet?

To illustrate the most commonly used month-day-year formats in Microsoft Excel 2016, let's suppose today is January 4, 2004. You can enter this date as any of the following:

- 1/4/2004
- 4-Jan-2004
- January 4, 2004
- 1/4/04

If you use only two digits to represent a year, and the digits are 30 or higher, Excel assumes the digits represent years in the twentieth century; if the digits are lower than 30, Excel assumes they represent years in the twenty-first century. For example, 1/1/29 is treated as January 1, 2029, but 1/1/30 is treated as January 1, 1930. Each year, the year treated as dates in the twenty-first century increases by one.

Answers to this chapter's questions

When I enter dates into Excel, I often see a number such as *37625* rather than a date such as 1/4/2003. What does this number mean, and how do I change it to a normal date?

The way Excel treats calendar dates is sometimes confusing to the novice. The key is understanding that Excel can display a date in a variety of month-day-year formats, or it can display a date in serial format. A date in serial format, such as *37625*, is simply a positive integer that represents the number of days between the given date and January 1, 1900. Both the current date and January 1, 1900 are included in the count. For example, Excel displays January 3, 1900, in serial format as the number *3*, which means there are three days between January 1, 1900, and January 3, 1900 (including both days).

> **Note** Excel assumes that 1900 was a leap year containing 366 days. In reality, 1900 contained only 365 days. For some fascinating information on the origin of this bug, see *www.joelonsoftware.com/items/2006/06/16.html.*

Figure 7-1 shows the worksheet named *Serial Format* in the file Dates.xlsx. Suppose you are given the dates shown in cells D5:D14 in serial format. For example, the value *37622* in cell D5 indicates a date that is 37,622 days after January 1, 1900 (including both January 1, 1900, and day 37,622). To display these serial dates in the month-day-year format, copy them to E5:E14. Select the cell range E5:E14, right-click the selection, and click Format Cells. (At any time, by the way, you can bring up the Format Cells dialog box by pressing Ctrl+1.) Now select the date format you want from the list shown in Figure 7-2. The dates in E5:E14 will be displayed in date format, as you can see in Figure 7-1. If you want to format dates in the serial number format, select E5:E14, right-click the selection, and choose Format Cells, General.

	D	E
4	Dates	Reformatted
5	37622	1/1/2003
6	37623	1/2/2003
7	37624	1/3/2003
8	37625	1/4/2003
9	37626	1/5/2003
10	37627	1/6/2003
11	37628	1/7/2003
12	37629	1/8/2003
13	37630	1/9/2003
14	37631	1/10/2003

FIGURE 7-1 Use the Format Cells command to change dates from serial number format to month-day-year format.

Simply changing the date format of a cell to General will yield the date in serial format. Another way to obtain the date in serial format is to use the DATEVALUE function and enclose the date in quotation marks. For example, in the Date Format worksheet of the file Dates.xlsx, cell I5 contains the formula DATEVALUE("1/4/2003"). Excel yields 37625, which is the serial format for January 4, 2003.

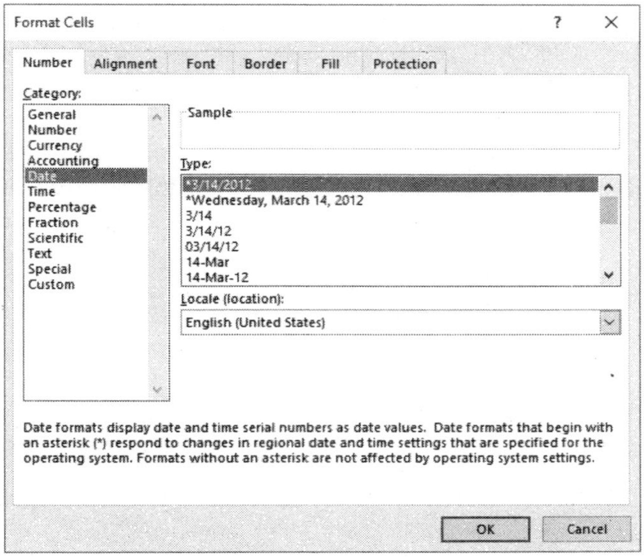

FIGURE 7-2 A list of date formats in the Format Cells dialog box.

Can I use a formula to automatically display today's date?

Displaying today's date with a formula is easy, as you can see by looking at cell C13 of the Date Format worksheet from the file Dates.xlsx, as shown in Figure 7-3. Entering the TODAY() function in a cell will display today's date. I created this screenshot on June 15, 2016.

	B	C	D	E	F	G	H	I
1								
2								
3								
4			Year	Month	Day	Day of Week	Putting date together	Serial Number
5	1/4/2003	1/4/2003	2003	1	4	7	1/4/2003	37625
6	2/1/1901	2/1/1901	1901	2	1	6	2/1/1901	398
7	4-Jan-2003	4-Jan-03	2003	1	4	7	1/4/2003	
8	January 4, 2003	4-Jan-03	2003	1	4	7	1/4/2003	
9	1/4/03	4-Jan-03	2003	1	4	7	1/4/2003	
10		3-Jan-01	1900	1	0	7	1/0/1900	3
11								
12								
13	Today's date	6/15/2016	50 workdays from start date	excluding holidays				
14	Start date	1/3/2003	3/14/2003	3/17/2003				
15	Later date	8/4/2003						
16					Holidays			
17	Workdays between (excluding	150			7/4/2003			
18	Workdays between (no holidays)	152			1/20/2003			

FIGURE 7-3 Examples of date functions.

How do I determine a date that is 50 workdays after another date? What if I want to exclude holidays?

The function WORKDAY(start_date,#days,[holidays]) displays the date that is the number of workdays indicated by *#days* after a given start date. (A workday is a nonweekend day.) *Holidays* is an optional argument for the function that allows you to exclude from the calculation any dates that are listed in a cell range. Thus, entering the formula WORKDAY(C14,50) in cell D14 of the Date Format worksheet tells us that 3/14/2003 is 50 workdays after 01/03/2003. If we believe that the only two holidays that matter are Martin Luther King Day and Independence Day, we can change the formula to WORKDAY(C14,50,F17:F18), which is in cell E14. With this addition, Excel does not count 01/20/2003 in its calculations, making 03/17/2003 the fiftieth workday after 01/03/2003. Note that instead of referring to the holidays in other cells, you can enter them directly in the WORKDAY formula with the serial number of each holiday enclosed in { }. For example, WORKDAY(38500,10,{38600,38680,38711}) would find the tenth workday after the date with serial number 38500, ignoring Labor Day, Thanksgiving, and Christmas of 2005.

The function WORKDAY.INTL was introduced in Excel 2010. This function allows you to choose your own definition of a *workday*. The syntax is WORKDAY.INTL(start_date,days,weekend, [holidays]). The third argument lets you specify the definition of a day off. You can use the following codes to specify the definition of a day off:

1 or omitted	Saturday, Sunday
2	Sunday, Monday
3	Monday, Tuesday
4	Tuesday, Wednesday
5	Wednesday, Thursday
6	Thursday, Friday
7	Friday, Saturday
11	Sunday only
12	Monday only
13	Tuesday only
14	Wednesday only
15	Thursday only
16	Friday only
17	Saturday only

For example, in sheet Date Format of the file Date.xlsx, I computed in cell C27 (see Figure 7-4) the date 100 workdays after 3/14/2011, with Sunday and Monday as days off, with the formula WORKDAY.INTL(C23,100,2). In cell C28, I computed the date 100 workdays after 3/14/2011 when only Sunday is a day off by using the formula WORKDAY.INTL(C23,100,11). You can also enter the definition of *days off* with a string of seven ones and zeroes, where a one indicates a day off and the first entry in the string is Monday, the second is Tuesday, and so on. Thus, in cells D26 and D27 I duplicated our previous results with the formulas WOR KDAY.INTL(C23,100,"1000001") and WORKDAY.INTL(C23,100,"0000001"), respectively.

How do I determine the number of workdays between two dates?

The key to solving this problem is to use the NETWORKDAYS function. The syntax for this function is NETWORKDAYS(start_date,end_date,[holidays]), where *holidays* is an optional argument identifying a cell range that lists the dates you want to count as holidays. The NETWORKDAYS function returns the number of working days between *start_date* and *end_date*, excluding weekends and any listed holidays. As an illustration of the NETWORKDAYS function, look at cell C18 in the Date Format worksheet of the file Dates.xlsx, which contains the formula NETWORKDAYS(C14,C15). This formula yields the number of working days between 1/3/2003 and 8/4/2003, which is 152. The formula NETWORKDAYS(C14,C15,F17:F18) in cell C17 yields the number of workdays between 1/3/2003 and 8/4/2003, excluding Martin Luther King Day and Independence Day. The answer is 152–2=150.

The function NETWORKDAYS.INTL was introduced in Excel 2010. Like the WORKDAYS.INTL function, NETWORKDAYS.INTL allows you to customize the definition of a weekend. For example, in cell C31 of the worksheet Date Format of the file Dates.xlsx, I computed the number of workdays (373) between 3/14/2011 and 8/16/2012, when Sunday and Monday are days off, with the formula NETWORKDAYS.INTL(C23,C24,2). (See Figure 7-4.) In cell D31, I computed the same result with the formula NETWORKDAYS.INTL(C23,C24,"1000001").

	B	C	D
21	**International Functions**		
22			
23	Start Date	3/14/2011	
24	End Date	8/16/2012	
25			
26	**100 workdays later**		
27	Sunday Monday as weekend	7/30/2011	7/30/2011
28	Sunday as weekend	7/8/2011	7/8/2011
29			
30	**Days Between Start and End Date**		
31	Sunday Monday as weekend	373	373
32	Sunday as weekend	448	448

FIGURE 7-4 Examples of international date functions.

I have 500 different dates entered in an Excel worksheet. How do I write formulas that will extract from each date the month, year, day of the month, and day of the week?

The Date Format worksheet of the file Dates.xlsx (see Figure 7-3) lists several dates in the cell range B5:B10. In B5 and B7:B9, I used four different formats to display January 4, 2003. In columns D:G, I extracted the year, month, day of the month, and day of the week for each date. By copying from D5 to D6:D10 the formula YEAR(B5), I extracted the year for each date. By copying from E5 to E6:E10 the formula MONTH(B5), I extracted the month (1=January, 2=February, and so on) portion of each date. By copying from F5 to F6:F10 the formula DAY(B5), I extracted the day of the month for each date. Finally, by copying from G5 to G6:G10 the formula WEEKDAY(B5,1), I extracted the day of the week for each date.

When the last argument of the WEEKDAY function is 1, then 1=Sunday, 2=Monday, and so on. When the last argument is 2, then 1=Monday, 2=Tuesday, and so on. When the last argument is 3, then 0=Monday, 1=Tuesday, and so on.

I am given the year, month, and day of the month for a date. Is there an easy way to recover the actual date?

The DATE function, whose arguments are DATE(year,month,day), returns the date with the given year, month, and day of the month. In the Date Format worksheet, copying from cell H5 to cells H6:H10 the formula DATE(D5,E5,F5) recovers the dates we started with.

My business has purchased and sold machines. For some, I have the date the machine was purchased and the date the machine was sold. Can I easily determine how many months we kept these machines?

The DATEDIF function can easily determine the number of complete years, months, or days between two dates. In file Datedif.xlsx (see Figure 7-5), you can see that a machine was bought on 10/15/2016 and was sold on 4/10/2018. How many complete years, months, or days was the machine kept? The syntax of the DATEDIF function is DATEDIF(startdate,enddate,time unit). If the unit is written as *"y"*, you get the number of complete years between the start and end dates; if the unit is written as *"m"*, you get the number of complete months between the start and end dates; and if the unit is written as *"d"*, you get the number of complete days between the start and end dates. Thus, entering DATEDIF(D4,D5,"y") in cell D6 shows that the machine was kept for one full year. Entering the formula DATEDIF(D4,D5,"m") in cell D7 shows the machine was kept for 17 complete months. Entering the formula DATEDIF(D4,D5,"d") in cell D7 shows the machine was kept for 543 complete days. By the way, the DATEDIF function is not listed in the function wizard.

	C	D	E
4	bought	10/15/2016	
5	sold	4/10/2018	
6	years	1	=DATEDIF(D4,D5,"y")
7	months	17	=DATEDIF(D4,D5,"m")
8	days	542	=DATEDIF(D4,D5,"d")

FIGURE 7-5 Using the DATEDIF function.

How can I place a static (unchanging) date in a worksheet?

Entering =TODAY() in a cell always returns today's date. If we create a workbook, we might want the date we create it to always appear in the workbook. The keystroke combination Ctrl+; (the semicolon) will place today's date in a cell, and unlike with the =TODAY() function, the date will never change. The workbook shown in Figure 7-6 (see Staticdate.xls) was created June 16, 2016, and that date will always show up in cell F6.

	F	G	H	I
5				
6	6/16/2016	With F6 selected I used		
7		the keystroke combination		
8		Control+;		

FIGURE 7-6 Use the keystroke combination Ctrl+; to create a static date.

Problems

1. What is the serial format for January 25, 2006?
2. What is the serial format for February 14, 1950?
3. To what actual date does a serial format of *4526* correspond?
4. To what actual date does a serial format of *45000* correspond?
5. Determine the day that occurs 74 workdays after today's date (including holidays).
6. Determine the day that occurs 74 workdays after today's date (including holidays but excluding the current year's Christmas, New Year's Day, and Independence Day).
7. How many workdays (including holidays) are there between July 10, 2005 and August 15, 2006?
8. How many workdays (including holidays but excluding Christmas, New Year's Day, and Independence Day) are there between July 10, 2005 and August 15, 2006?

The file Datep.xlsx contains several hundred dates. Use this file for the next set of problems.

9. Determine the month, year, day of the month, and day of the week for each date.
10. Express each date in serial format.
11. A project begins December 4, 2005. The project consists of three activities: Activities 1, 2, and 3. Activity 2 can start the day after Activity 1 finishes. Activity 3 can start the day after Activity 2 finishes. Set up a worksheet that accepts as inputs the duration (in days) of the three activities and then produces both the month and year during which each activity is completed.
12. We bought a stock July 29, 2005 and sold it December 30, 2005. The stock exchange is closed Labor Day, Christmas, and Thanksgiving. Create a list of dates when the stock market was open during the time we owned the stock.
13. The file Machinedates.xlsx contains dates on which several machines were bought and sold. Determine how many months and years each machine was kept.
14. Given any date, find a way to have Excel compute the day of the week of the first day of the date's month.
15. Given any date, find a way to have Excel compute the last day of the date's month. Hint: DATE(2005,13,1), surprisingly, returns 1/1/2006.
16. Given any date, how can you compute which day of the year it is? For example, what day of the year will 4/15/2020 be? Hint: The formula DATE(2020,1,0) will return the serial number for day 0 of January 2020, and Excel will treat this as December 31, 2019.

17. In Fredonia, employees have Tuesday and Wednesday off. What date is 200 workdays after 5/3/2013?

18. In Lower Ampere, employees have Friday and Saturday off. Also Valentine's Day is a holiday. How many workdays are there between 1/10/2014 and 5/31/2015?

19. Suppose the first quarter of each year is January–March, the second quarter is April–June, and so on. Write a formula that returns for a given date the first day of the quarter.

20. Using the definitions of quarters given in Problem 19, write a formula that computes for any given date the last day of the previous quarter.

21. Set up a spreadsheet in which a person can enter his or her date of birth and the spreadsheet returns the person's actual age.

22. Memorial Day is always the last Monday in May. Set up a spreadsheet in which you can enter the year and the spreadsheet determines the date of Memorial Day.

23. Create a spreadsheet that always lists the next 50 workdays (assuming no holidays and that Monday-Friday are the workdays).

24. Greg Winston works for the federal government, and in 2016 he gets 10 federal holidays off. (Look up the dates of these holidays on the Internet.) Greg also gets every other Friday off, as well as weekends starting with 1/8/2016. Create a list of all the days Greg works in 2016.

CHAPTER 8

Evaluating investments by using net present value criteria

Questions answered in this chapter:

- What is net present value (NPV)?
- How do I use the Excel NPV function?
- How can I compute NPV when cash flows are received at the beginning of a year or in the middle of a year?
- How can I compute NPV when cash flows are received at irregular intervals?

Consider the following two investments, whose cash flows are listed in the file NPV.xlsx and shown in Figure 8-1:

- Investment 1 requires a cash outflow of $10,000 today and $14,000 two years from now. One year from now, this investment will yield $24,000.
- Investment 2 requires a cash outflow of $6,000 today and $1,000 two years from now. One year from now, this investment will yield $8,000.

Which is the better investment? Investment 1 yields total cash flow of $0, whereas Investment 2 yields a total cash flow of $1,000. At first glance, Investment 2 appears to be better. But wait a minute. Most of the cash outflow for Investment 1 occurs two years from now, while most of the cash outflow for Investment 2 occurs today. Spending $1 two years from now doesn't seem as costly as spending $1 today, so maybe Investment 1 is better than it first appears. To determine which investment is better, you need to compare the values of cash flows received at different points in time. That's where the concept of net present value proves useful.

	A	B	C	D	E	F
1						
2						
3		r	0.2			
4	NPV	Time	0	1	2	Total cf
5	277.7778	Inv 1 CF	-10000	24000	-14000	0
6	-27.7778	Inv 2 CF	-6000	8000	-1000	1000
7		PV Inv 1	-10000	20000	-9722.22	
8		PV Inv 2	-6000	6666.667	-694.444	
9						
10		**PV beginning of Year**				
11		Inv 1	$277.78	$277.78		
12		Inv 2	($27.78)	($27.78)		
13		**PV End of Year**				
14		Inv 1	$231.48			
15		Inv 2	($23.15)			
16		**PV Middle of year**				
17		Inv 1	$253.58			
18		Inv 2	($25.36)			

FIGURE 8-1 To determine which investment is better, you need to calculate the net present value.

Answers to this chapter's questions

What is net present value?

The net present value (NPV) of a stream of cash flow received at different points in time is simply the value measured in today's dollars. Suppose you have $1 today and you invest this dollar at an annual interest rate of r percent. This dollar will grow to $1+r$ dollars in the first year, $(1+r)^2$ dollars in two years, and so on. You can say, in some sense, that $1 today equals $\$(1+r)$ a year from now and $\$(1+r)^2$ two years from now. In general, you can say that $1 today is equal to $\$(1+r)^n$ n years from now. As an equation, this calculation can be expressed as follows:

$1 now=$\$(1+r)^n$ received n years from now

If you divide both sides of this equation by $(1+r)^n$, you get the following important result:

$1/(1+r)^n$ now=$1 received n years from now

This result tells you how to compute (in today's dollars) the NPV of any sequence of cash flows. You can convert any cash flow to today's dollars by multiplying the cash flow received n years from now (n can be a fraction) by $1/(1+r)^n$.

You then add up the value of the cash flows (in today's dollars) to find the investment's NPV. Let's assume r is equal to 0.2. You could calculate the NPV for the two investments we're considering, as follows:

$$= \text{Investment1NPV} = -10{,}000 + \frac{24{,}000}{(1+0.20)^1} + \frac{-14{,}000}{(1+0.20)^2} = \$277.78$$

$$= \text{Investment2NPV} = -6{,}000 + \frac{8{,}000}{(1+0.20)^1} + \frac{-1{,}000}{(1+0.20)^2} = \$-27.78$$

On the basis of NPV, Investment 1 is superior to Investment 2. Although total cash flow for Investment 2 exceeds the total cash flow for Investment 1, Investment 1 has a better NPV because a greater proportion of Investment 1's negative cash flow comes later, and the NPV criterion gives less weight to cash flows that come later. If you use a value of .02 for *r*, Investment 2 has a larger NPV because when *r* is very small, later cash flows are not discounted as much, and NPV returns results similar to those derived by ranking investments according to the total cash flow.

> **Note** I randomly chose the interest rate r=0.2, skirting the issue of how to determine an appropriate value of *r*. You need to study finance for at least a year to understand the issues involved in determining an appropriate value for *r*. The appropriate value of *r* used to compute NPV is often called the company's cost of capital. Suffice it to say that most US companies use an annual cost of capital between 0.1 (10 percent) and 0.2 (20 percent). If the annual interest rate is chosen according to accepted finance practices, projects with NPV>0 increase the value of a company, projects with NPV<0 decrease the value of a company, and projects with NPV=0 keep the value of a company unchanged. A company should (if it had unlimited investment capital) invest in every available investment having positive NPV.

To determine the NPV of Investment 1 in Excel, I first assigned the range name *r_* to the interest rate (located in cell C3). (As pointed out in Chapter 2, when you try to name a cell *r*, Excel names the cell *r_*.) I then copied the Time 0 cash flow from C5 to C7. I determined the NPV for Investment 1's Year 1 and Year 2 cash flows by copying from D7 to E7 the formula D5/(1+r_)^D$4. The caret symbol (^), located over the number 6 on the keyboard, raises a number to a power. In cell A5, I computed the NPV of Investment 1 by adding the NPV of each year's cash flow with the formula SUM(C7:E7). To determine the NPV for Investment 2, I copied the formulas from C7:E7 to C8:E8 and from A5 to A6.

How do I use the Excel NPV function?

The Excel NPV function uses the syntax NPV(rate,range of cells). This function determines the NPV for the given rate of the cash flows in the range of cells. The function's calculation assumes that the first cash flow is one period from now. In other words, entering the formula NPV(r_,C5:E5) will not determine the NPV for Investment 1. Instead, this formula (entered in cell C14) computes the NPV of the following sequence of cash flows: –$10,000 a year from now, $24,000 two years from now, and –$14,000 three years from now. Let's call this Investment 1 (End of Year). The NPV of Investment 1 (End of Year) is $231.48. To compute the actual cash NPV of Investment 1, I entered the formula C7+NPV(r_,D5:E5) in cell C11. This formula does not discount the Time 0 cash flow at all (which is correct because the Time 0 cash flow is already in today's dollars), but it first multiplies the cash flow in D5 by 1/1.2 and then multiplies the cash flow in E5 by 1/1.22.

The formula in cell C11 yields the correct NPV of Investment 1, $277.78.

How can I compute NPV when cash flows are received at the beginning of a year or in the middle of a year?

To use the NPV function to compute the net present value of a project whose cash flows always occur at the beginning of a year, you can use the approach I described to determine the NPV of Investment 1: separate out the Year 1 cash flow and apply the NPV function to the remaining cash flows. Alternatively, observe that for any year *n*, $1 received at the beginning of year *n* is equivalent to $(1+*r*) received at the end of year *n*. Remember that in one year, a dollar will grow by a factor (1+*r*). Thus, if you multiply the result obtained with the NPV function by (1+*r*), you can convert the NPV of a sequence of year-end cash flows to the NPV of a sequence of cash flows received at the beginning of the year. You can also compute the NPV of Investment 1 in cell D11 with the formula (1+r_)*C14. Of course, you again obtain an NPV of $277.78.

Now suppose the cash flows for an investment occur in the middle of each year. For an organization that receives monthly subscription revenues, you can approximate the 12 monthly revenue amounts received during a given year as a lump sum received in the middle of the year. How can you use the NPV function to determine the NPV of a sequence of midyear cash flows? For any Year *n*,

$$\$\sqrt{1+r}$$

received at the end of Year *n* is equivalent to $1 received at the middle of Year *n* because in half a year, $1 will grow by the following factor:

$$\sqrt{1+r}$$

If you assume the cash flows for Investment 1 occur midyear, you can compute the NPV of the midyear version of Investment 1 in cell C17 with the formula SQRT(1+r_)*C14. You obtain a value of $253.58.

How can I compute NPV when cash flows are received at irregular intervals?

Cash flows often occur at irregular intervals, which makes computing the NPV or internal rate of return (IRR) of these cash flows more difficult. Fortunately, the Excel XNPV function makes computing the NPV of irregularly timed cash flows a snap.

The XNPV function uses the syntax XNPV(rate,values,dates). The first date listed must be the earliest, but other dates need not be listed in chronological order. The XNPV function computes the NPV of the given cash flows assuming the current date is the first date in the sequence. For example, if the first listed date is 4/08/13, the NPV is computed in April 8, 2013 dollars.

To illustrate the use of the XNPV function, look at the example for the NPV As Of First Date worksheet in the file XNPV.xlsx, which is shown in Figure 8-2. Suppose that on April 8, 2015, you paid out $900. Later, you receive the following amounts:

- $300 on August 15, 2015
- $400 on January 15, 2016
- $200 on June 25, 2016

- $100 on July 3, 2016

If the annual interest rate is 10 percent, what is the NPV of these cash flows? I entered the dates (in Excel date format) in D3:D7 and the cash flows in E3:E7. Entering the formula XNPV(A9,E3:E7,D3:D7) in cell D11 computes the project's NPV in April 8, 2015 dollars because that is the first date listed. This project would have an NPV, in April 8, 2015 dollars, of $28.64.

	A	B	C	D	E	F	G
1							
2	XNPV Function		Code	Date	Cash Flow	Time	discount factor
3			42102.00	4/8/2015	-900		1
4			42231.00	8/15/2015	300	0.353425	0.966876054
5			42384.00	1/15/2016	400	0.772603	0.92900895
6			42546.00	6/25/2016	200	1.216438	0.890529581
7			42554.00	7/3/2016	100	1.238356	0.888671215
8	Rate						
9	0.1						
10				XNPV	Direct		
11				28.63943	28.639434		

FIGURE 8-2 Using the XNPV function.

The computations performed by the XNPV function are as follows:

1. Compute the number of years after April 8, 2015 that each date occurred. (I did this in column F.) For example, August 15 is 0.3534 years after April 8, 2015.
2. Discount cash flows at the rate 1/(1+rate)years after.

   For example, the August 15, 2015 cash flow is discounted by the following amount: $(1+0.1)^{3534}$
3. Sum in cell E11 overall cash flows: (cash flow value)*(discount factor).

Suppose that today's date is actually July 8, 2013. How would you compute the NPV of our investment in today's dollars? Simply add a row with today's date and 0 cash flow and include this row in the range for the XNPV function. (See Figure 8-3 and the Today worksheet in the file XNPV.xlsx.) The NPV of the project in today's dollars is $106.99.

	A	B	C	D	E
1					
2	XNPV Function		Code	Date	Cash Flow
3			41463.00	7/8/2013	0
4			42102.00	4/8/2015	-900
5			42231.00	8/15/2015	300
6			42384.00	1/15/2016	400
7			42546.00	6/25/2016	200
8			42554.00	7/3/2016	100
9			42188.00	7/3/2015	100
10	Rate				
11	0.1				
12				XNPV	
13				106.9907	

FIGURE 8-3 NPV converted to today's dollars.

I'll close by noting that if a cash flow is left blank, the NPV function ignores both the cash flow and the period, and the XNPV function returns a #NUM error.

Problems

1. An NBA player is to receive a $1,000,000 signing bonus today and $2,000,000 one year, two years, and three years from now. Assuming r=0.10 and ignoring tax considerations, would he be better off receiving $6,000,000 today?

2. A project has the following cash flows:

Now	One year from now	Two years from now	Three years from now
–$4 million	$4 million	$4 million	–$3 million

If the company's cost of capital is 15 percent, should it proceed with the project?

3. Beginning one month from now, a customer will pay his Internet provider $25 per month for the next five years. Assuming all revenue for a year is received at the middle of a year, estimate the NPV of these revenues. Use r=0.15.

4. Beginning one month from now, a customer will pay $25 per month to her Internet provider for the next five years. Assuming all revenue for a month is received at the beginning of the month, use the XNPV function to obtain the exact NPV of these revenues. Use r=0.15.

5. Consider the following set of cash flows over a four-year period. Determine the NPV of these cash flows, if r=0.15 and cash flows occur at the end of the year.

Year	1	2	3	4
	-$600	$550	-$680	$1,000

6. Consider the following cash flows:

Date	Cash flow
12/15/01	–$1,000
1/11/02	$300
4/07/03	$600
7/15/04	$925

If today is November 1, 2001, and r=0.15, what is the NPV of these cash flows?

7. After earning an MBA, a student will begin working at an $80,000-per-year job on September 1, 2005. She expects to receive a 5 percent raise each year until she retires on September 1, 2035. If the cost of capital is 8 percent a year, determine the total present value of her before-tax earnings.

8. Consider a 30-year bond that pays $50 at the end of Years 1–29 and $1,050 at the end of Year 30. If the appropriate discount rate is 5 percent per year, what is a fair price for this bond?

CHAPTER 9

Internal rate of return

Questions answered in this chapter:

- How can I find the internal rate of return (IRR) of cash flows?
- Does a project always have a unique IRR?
- Are there conditions that guarantee a project will have a unique IRR?
- If two projects each have a single IRR, how do I use the projects' IRRs?
- How can I find the IRR of irregularly spaced cash flows?
- What is the MIRR and how do I compute it?

The net present value (NPV) of a sequence of cash flows depends on the interest rate (r) used. For example, if you consider cash flows for Projects 1 and 2 (see the worksheet IRR in the file IRR.xlsx, shown in Figure 9-1), you find that for r=0.2, Project 2 has a larger NPV, and for r=0.01, Project 1 has a larger NPV. When you use NPV to rank investments, the outcome can depend on the interest rate. It is the nature of human beings to want to boil everything in life down to a single number. The internal rate of return (IRR) of a project is simply the interest rate that makes the NPV of the project equal to 0. If a project has a unique IRR, the IRR has a nice interpretation. For example, if a project has an IRR of 15 percent, you receive an annual rate of return of 15 percent on the cash flow you invested. In this chapter's examples, you'll find that Project 1 has an IRR of 47.5 percent, which means that the $400 invested at Time 1 is yielding an annual rate of return of 47.5 percent. Sometimes, however, a project might have more than one IRR or even no IRR. In these cases, speaking about the project's IRR is useless.

	A	B	C	D	E	F	G	H	I	J	K
1		Time	1	2	3	4	5	6	7	NPV r=.2	NPV r= .01
2	Project 1		-400	200	600	-900	1000	250	230	$268.54	$918.99
3	Project 2		-200	150	150	200	300	100	80	$297.14	$741.07
4	Project 1	IRR Proj 1 No Guess	IRR Proj 2 No Guess								
5	no guess	47.5%	80.1%								
6											
7	guess	Guess Proj 1	Guess proj 2								
8	-0.9	47.5%	80.1%								
9	-0.7	47.5%	80.1%								
10	-0.5	47.5%	80.1%								
11	-0.3	47.5%	80.1%								
12	-0.1	47.5%	80.1%								
13	0.1	47.5%	80.1%								
14	0.3	47.5%	80.1%								
15	0.5	47.5%	80.1%								
16	0.7	47.5%	80.1%								
17	0.9	47.5%	80.1%								

FIGURE 9-1 Example of the IRR function.

Answers to this chapter's questions

How can I find the internal rate of return (IRR) of cash flows?

The IRR function calculates internal rate of return. The function has the syntax IRR(range of cash flows,[guess]), where *guess* is an optional argument. If you do not enter a guess for a project's IRR, Excel begins its calculations with a guess that the project's IRR is 10 percent and then varies the estimate of the IRR until it finds an interest rate that makes the project's NPV equal 0 (the project's IRR). If Excel can't find an interest rate that makes the project's NPV equal 0, Excel returns #NUM. In cell B5 of the worksheet IRR in the file IRR.xlsx, I entered the formula IRR(C2:I2) to compute Project 1's IRR. Excel returns 47.5 percent. Thus, if you use an annual interest rate of 47.5 percent, Project 1 will have an NPV of 0. Similarly, you can see that Project 2 has an IRR of 80.1 percent.

Even if the IRR function finds an IRR, a project might have more than one IRR. To check whether a project has more than one IRR, you can vary the initial guess of the project's IRR (for example, from –90 percent to 90 percent). I varied the guess for Project 1's IRR by copying from B8 to B9:B17 the formula IRR($C$2:$I$2,A8). Because all the guesses for Project 1's IRR yield 47.5 percent, I can be fairly confident that Project 1 has a unique IRR of 47.5 percent. Similarly, I can be fairly confident that Project 2 has a unique IRR of 80.1 percent.

Does a project always have a unique IRR?

In the worksheet Multiple IRR in the file IRR.xlsx (see Figure 9-2), you can see that Project 3 (cash flows of –20, 82, –60, 2) has two IRRs. I varied the guess about Project 3's IRR from –90 percent to 90 percent by copying from C8 to C9:C17 the formula IRR($B$4:$E$4,B8).

	A	B	C	D	E	F
1	Multiple IRR's					
2						
3		1	2	3	4	
4	Project 3	-20	82	-60	2	
5			plain irr	-9.6%		
6						
7		guess				
8		-0.9	-9.6%		npv at -9.6%	($0.01)
9		-0.7	-9.6%		npv at 216.1%	$0.00
10		-0.5	-9.6%			
11		-0.3	-9.6%			
12		-0.1	-9.6%			
13		0.1	-9.6%			
14		0.3	-9.6%			
15		0.5	216.1%			
16		0.7	216.1%			
17		0.9	216.1%			

FIGURE 9-2 Project with more than one IRR.

Note that when a guess is 30 percent or less, the IRR is –9.6 percent. For other guesses, the IRR is 216.1 percent. For both these interest rates, Project 3 has an NPV of 0.

In the worksheet No IRR in the file IRR.xlsx (shown in Figure 9-3), you can see that no matter what guess you use for Project 4's IRR, you receive the #NUM message. This message indicates that Project 4 has no IRR.

When a project has multiple IRRs or no IRR, the concept of IRR loses virtually all meaning. Despite this problem, however, many companies still use IRR as their major tool for ranking investments.

	A	B	C	D
1				
2		No IRR		
3				
4		0	1	2
5	Project 4	10	-30	35
6				
7		guess		
8		-0.9	#NUM!	
9		-0.8	#NUM!	
10		-0.7	#NUM!	
11		-0.6	#NUM!	
12		-0.5	#NUM!	
13		-0.4	#NUM!	
14		-0.3	#NUM!	
15		-0.2	#NUM!	
16		-0.1	#NUM!	
17		0	#NUM!	
18		0.1	#NUM!	
19		0.2	#NUM!	
20		0.3	#NUM!	
21		0.4	#NUM!	
22		0.5	#NUM!	
23		0.6	#NUM!	
24		0.7	#NUM!	
25		0.8	#NUM!	
26		0.9	#NUM!	

FIGURE 9-3 Project with no IRR.

Are there conditions that guarantee a project will have a unique IRR?

If a project's sequence of cash flows contains exactly one change in sign, the project is guaranteed to have a unique IRR. For example, for Project 2 in cells C3:I3 of the worksheet IRR, the sign of the cash flow sequence is – + + + + +. There is only one change in sign (between Time 1 and Time 2), so Project 2 must have a unique IRR. For Project 3 in cells B4:E4 of the worksheet Multiple IRR, the signs of the cash flows are – + – +. Because the sign of the cash flows changes three times, a unique IRR is not guaranteed. For Project 4 in cells B5:D5 of the worksheet No IRR, the signs of the cash flows are + – +. Because the signs of the cash flows change twice, a unique IRR is not guaranteed in this case, either. Most capital investment projects (such as building a plant) begin with a negative cash flow followed by a sequence of positive cash flows. Therefore, most capital investment projects do have a unique IRR.

If two projects each have a single IRR, how do I use the projects' IRRs?

If a project has a unique IRR, you can state that the project increases the value of the company if and only if the project's IRR exceeds the annual cost of capital. For example, if the cost of capital for a company is 15 percent, both Project 1 and Project 2 would increase the value of the company.

Suppose two projects are under consideration (both having unique IRRs), but you can undertake at most one project. It's tempting to believe that you should choose the project with the larger IRR. To illustrate that this belief can lead to incorrect decisions, look at Figure 9-4 and the Which Project worksheet in IRR.xlsx. Project 5 has an IRR of 40 percent, and Project 6 has an IRR of 50 percent. If you rank projects based on IRR and can choose only one project, you would choose Project 6. Remember, however, that a project's NPV measures the amount of value the project adds to the company. Clearly, Project 5 will (for virtually any cost of capital) have a larger NPV than Project 6. Therefore, if only one project can be chosen, Project 5 is it. IRR is problematic because it ignores the scale of the project. Whereas Project 6 is better than Project 5 on a per-dollar-invested basis, the larger scale of Project 5 makes it more valuable to the company than Project 6. IRR does not reflect the scale of a project, whereas NPV does.

	B	C	D	E
2	Project	Time 0	Time 1	IRR
3	5	-100	140	40%
4	6	-1	1.5	50%

FIGURE 9-4 IRR can lead to an incorrect choice of which project to pursue.

How can I find the IRR of irregularly spaced cash flows?

Cash flows occur on actual dates, not just at the start or end of the year. The XIRR function has the syntax XIRR(cash flow, dates, [guess]). The XIRR function determines the IRR of a sequence of cash flows that occur on any set of irregularly spaced dates. As with the IRR function, guess is an optional argument. For an example of how to use the XIRR function, look at Figure 9-5 and the worksheet XIRR of the file IRR.xlsx.

	A	B	C	D	E	F
1					Project 7	
2	XIRR Function			Date	Cash Flow	
3				Code	Date	Cash Flo
4				4/8/2011	4/8/2011	-1500
5				8/15/2011	8/15/2011	300
6				1/15/2012	1/15/2012	400
7				6/25/2012	6/25/2012	200
8				XIRR		
9				-48.69%		

FIGURE 9-5 Example of the XIRR function.

The formula XIRR(F4:F7,E4:E7) in cell D9 shows that the IRR of Project 7 is –48.69 percent.

What is the MIRR and how do I compute it?

In many situations, the rate at which a company borrows funds is different from the rate at which the company reinvests funds. IRR computations implicitly assume that the rate at which a company borrows and reinvests funds is equal to the IRR. If we know the actual rate at which we borrow money and the rate at which we can reinvest money, the modified internal rate of return (MIRR) function computes a discount rate that makes the NPV of all our cash flows (including paying back our loan and reinvesting our proceeds at the given rates) equal to 0. The syntax of MIRR is MIRR(cash_flow_values,borrowing_rate,reinvestment_rate). A nice thing about MIRR is that it is always unique. Worksheet MIRR of the file IRR.xls contains an example of MIRR. (See Figure 9-6.) Suppose you borrow $120,000 today and receive the following cash flows: Year 1: $39,000, Year 2: $30,000, Year 3: $21,000, Year 4: $37,000, Year 5: $46,000. Assume that you can borrow at 10 percent per year and reinvest your profits at 12 percent per year.

After entering these values in cells E7:E12 of worksheet MIRR, you can find the MIRR in cell D15 with the formula MIRR(E7:E12,E3,E4). Thus, this project has an MIRR of 12.61 percent. In cell D16, I computed the actual IRR of 13.07 percent.

	C	D	E	F
1				
2				
3		borrow	0.1	
4		invest	0.12	
5				
6		Year	Amt	
7		0	-120000	
8		1	39000	
9		2	30000	
10		3	21000	
11		4	37000	
12		5	46000	
13			total	
14				
15	MIRR	12.6094%		
16	IRR	13.0736%		

FIGURE 9-6 Example of the MIRR function.

I'll close by noting that if a cash flow is left blank, the IRR function ignores both the cash flow and the period. If a cash flow is left blank, the IRR function will return a #NUM error.

Problems

1. Compute all IRRs for the following sequence of cash flows:

Year 1	Year 2	Year 3	Year 4	Year 5	Year 6	Year 7
–$10,000	$8,000	$1,500	$1,500	$1,500	$1,500	–$1,500

2. Consider a project with the following cash flows. Determine the project's IRR. If the annual cost of capital is 20 percent, would you undertake this project?

Year 1	Year 2	Year 3
–$4,000	$2,000	$4,000

3. Find all IRRs for the following project:

Year 1	Year 2	Year 3
$100	–$300	$250

4. Find all IRRs for a project having the given cash flows on the listed dates.

1/10/2003	7/10/2003	5/25/2004	7/18/2004	3/20/2005	4/1/2005	1/10/2006
–$1,000	$900	$800	$700	$500	$500	$350

5. Consider the following two projects, and assume a company's cost of capital is 15 percent. Find the IRR and NPV of each project. Which projects add value to the company? If the company can choose only a single project, which project should it choose?

	Year 1	Year 2	Year 3	Year 4
Project 1	–$40	$130	$19	$26
Project 2	–$80	$36	$36	$36

6. Meg Prior is 25 years old and is going to invest $10,000 in her retirement fund at the beginning of each of the next 40 years. Assume that during each of the next 30 years Meg will earn 15 percent on her investments and during the last 10 years before she retires, her investments will earn 5 percent. Determine the IRR associated with her investments and her final retirement position. How do you know there will be a unique IRR? How would you interpret the unique IRR?

7. Give an intuitive explanation of why Project 6 (on the worksheet Which Project in the file IRR.xlsx) has an IRR of 50 percent.

8. Consider a project having the following cash flows:

Year 1	Year 2	Year 3
–$70,000	$12,000	$15,000

Try to find the IRR of this project without simply guessing. What problem arises? What is the IRR of this project? Does the project have a unique IRR?

9. For the cash flows in Problem 1, assume you can borrow at 12 percent per year and invest profits at 15 percent per year. Compute the project's MIRR.

10. Suppose today that you paid $1,000 for the bond described in Problem 9 of Chapter 8, "Evaluating investments by using net present value criteria." What would be the bond's IRR? A bond's IRR is often called the yield of the bond.

CHAPTER 10

More Excel financial functions

Questions answered in this chapter:

- You are buying a copier. Would you rather pay $11,000 today or $3,000 a year for five years?
- If at the end of each of the next 40 years, I invest $2,000 a year toward my retirement and earn 8 percent a year on my investments, how much will I have when I retire?
- I am borrowing $10,000 for 10 months with an annual interest rate of 8 percent. What are my monthly payments? How much principal and interest am I paying each month?
- I want to borrow $80,000 and make monthly payments for 10 years. The maximum monthly payment I can afford is $1,000. What is the maximum interest rate I can afford?
- If I borrow $100,000 at 8 percent interest and make payments of $10,000 per year, how many years will it take me to pay back the loan?
- I'm a CPA and often have to work with complicated methods for depreciating machinery cost. Does Excel have functions to help me compute depreciation?

When we borrow money to buy a car or house, we always wonder if we are getting a good deal. When we save for retirement, we are curious how large a nest egg we'll have when we retire. In our daily work and personal lives, financial questions similar to these often arise. Knowledge of the Excel PV, FV, PMT, PPMT, IPMT, CUMPRINC, CUMIPMT, RATE, and NPER functions makes it easy to answer these types of questions.

Answers to this chapter's questions

You are buying a copier. Would you rather pay $11,000 today or $3,000 a year for five years?

The key to answering this question is being able to value the annual payments of $3,000 per year. Assume the cost of capital is 12 percent per year. You could use the NPV function to answer this question, but the Excel PV function provides a much quicker way to solve it. A stream of cash flow that involves the same amount of cash outflow (or inflow) each period is called an annuity. Assuming that each period's interest rate is the same, you can easily value an annuity by using the Excel PV function. The PV function returns the value in today's dollars of a series of future payments, under the assumption of periodic, constant payments and a constant interest rate. The syntax of the PV function is PV(rate,#per,[pmt],[fv],[type]), where *pmt*, *fv*, and *type* are optional arguments.

> **Note** When working with Microsoft Excel financial functions, I use the following conventions for the signs of *pmt* (payment) and *fv* (future value): money received has a positive sign and money paid out has a negative sign.

- *Rate* is the interest rate per period. For example, if you borrow money at 6 percent per year and the period is a year, then *rate*=0.06. If the period is a month, then *rate*=0.06/12=0.005.
- *#per* is the number of periods in the annuity. For our copier example, *#per*=5. If payments on the copier are made each month for five years, then *#per*=60. Your rate must, of course, be consistent with *#per*. That is, if *#per* implies a period is a month, you must use a monthly interest rate; if *#per* implies a period is a year, you must use an annual interest rate.
- *Pmt* is the payment made each period. For our copier example, pmt=–$3,000. A payment has a negative sign, whereas money received has a positive sign. At least one instance of *pmt* or *fv* must be included.
- *Fv* is the cash balance (or future value) you want to have after the last payment is made. For our copier example, *fv*=0. For example, if you want to have a $500 cash balance after the last payment, then *fv*=$500. If you want to make an additional $500 payment at the end of a problem *fv*=–$500. If *fv* is omitted, it is assumed to equal 0.
- *Type* is either 0 or 1 and indicates when payments are made. When *type* is omitted or equal to 0, payments are made at the end of each period. When *type*=1, payments are made at the beginning of each period. Note that you may also write *True* instead of 1 and *False* instead of 0 in all functions discussed in this chapter.

Figure 10-1 illustrates the worksheet PV from the file Excelfinfunctions.xlsx and indicates how to solve our copier problem.

	A	B
1		
2	PMT	
3	Pay $3000 for 5 years end of year	$10,814.33
4	Pay $3000 for 5 years beginning of year	$12,112.05
5	Extra $500 payment end of year 5;end of year payments	$11,098.04

FIGURE 10-1 Example of the PV function.

In cell B3, I computed the present value of paying $3,000 at the end of each year, for five years, with a 12 percent cost of capital, by using the formula =PV(0.12,5,–3000,0,0). Excel returns an NPV of $10,814.33. By omitting the last two arguments, I obtained the same answer with the formula =PV(0.12,5,–3000). Thus, it is a better deal to make payments at the end of the year than to pay out $11,000 today.

If you make payments on the copier of $3,000 at the beginning of each year for five years, the NPV of the payments is computed in cell B4 with the formula =PV(0.12,5,–3000,0,1). Note that changing the last argument from 0 to 1 changes the calculations from end of year to beginning of year. You can see that the present value of our payments is $12,112.05. Therefore, it's better to pay $11,000 today than make payments at the beginning of the year.

Suppose you pay $3,000 at the end of each year and must include an extra $500 payment at the end of Year 5. You can now find the present value of all our payments in cell B5 by including a future value of $500 with the formula =PV(0.12,5,–3000–,500,0). Note the $3,000 and $500 cash flows have negative signs because you are paying out the money. The present value of all these payments is equal to $11,098.04.

If at the end of each of the next 40 years, I invest $2,000 a year toward my retirement and earn 8 percent a year on my investments, how much will I have when I retire?

In this situation, we want to know the value of an annuity in terms of future dollars (40 years from now) and not today's dollars. This is a job for the Excel FV (future value) function. The FV function gives the future value of an investment assuming periodic, constant payments with a constant interest rate. The syntax of the FV function is FV(rate,#per,[pmt],[pv],[type]), where *pmt, pv,* and *type* are optional arguments:

- *Rate* is the interest rate per period. In our case, *rate* equals 0.08.
- *#Per* is the number of periods in the future at which you want the future value computed. *#Per* is also the number of periods during which the annuity payment is received. In our case, *#per* equals 40.
- *Pmt* is the payment made each period. In our case, *pmt* equals –$2,000. The negative sign indicates we are paying money into an account. At least one instance of *pmt* or *pv* must be included.
- *Pv* is the amount of money (in today's dollars) owed right now. In our case, *pv* equals $0. If today we owe someone $10,000, then *pv* equals $10,000 because the lender gave us $10,000 and we received it. If today we have $10,000 in the bank, then *pv* equals –$10,000 because we must have paid $10,000 into our bank account. If *pv* is omitted, it is assumed to equal 0.
- *Type* is 0 or 1 and indicates when payments are due or money is deposited. If *type* equals 0 or is omitted, then money is deposited at the end of the period. In our case, *type* is 0 or omitted. If *type* equals 1, then payments are made or money is deposited at the beginning of the period.

In worksheet FV of file Excelfinfunctions.xlsx (see Figure 10-2), I entered in cell B3 the formula =FV(0.08,40,–2000,0,0) to find that our nest egg will be worth $518,113.04 in 40 years. Note that I entered a negative value for the annual payment. I did this because the $2,000 is paid into our account. You could obtain the same answer by entering the last two unnecessary arguments with the formula FV(0.08,40,–2000,0,0).

If deposits were made at the beginning of each year for 40 years, the formula (entered in cell B4) =FV(0.08,40,–2000,0,1) would yield the value in 40 years of our nest egg: $559,562.08.

	A	B
1		
2	FV	
3	Invest $2000 end of year for 40 years	$518,113.04
4	Invest $2000 beginning of year for 40 years	$559,562.08
5	We start with $30000 and invest $2000 per year at end of year for 40 years	$1,169,848.68

FIGURE 10-2 Example of FV function.

Finally, suppose that in addition to investing $2,000 at the end of each of the next 40 years, you initially have $30,000 to invest. If you earn 8 percent per year on your investments, how much money will you have when you retire in 40 years? You can answer this question by setting *pv* equal to –$30,000 in the FV function. The negative sign is used because you have deposited, or paid, $30,000 into your account. In cell B5 of worksheet FV, the formula =FV(0.08,40,–2000,–30000,0) yields a future value of $1,169,848.68.

I am borrowing $10,000 for 10 months with an annual interest rate of 8 percent. What are my monthly payments? How much principal and interest am I paying each month?

The Excel PMT function computes the periodic payments for a loan, assuming constant payments and a constant interest rate. The syntax of the PMT function is PMT(rate,#per,pv,[fv],[type]), where *fv* and *type* are optional arguments:

- *Rate* is the per-period interest rate of the loan. In this example, I will use one month as a period, so *rate* equals 0.08/12=0.006666667.
- *#Per* is the number of payments made. In this case, *#per* equals 10.
- *Pv* is the present value of all the payments. That is, *pv* is the amount of the loan. In this case, *pv* equals $10,000. *Pv* is positive because we are receiving the $10,000.
- *Fv* indicates the future value of the final loan balance you want to have after making the last payment. In our case, *fv* equals 0. If *fv* is omitted, Excel assumes that it equals 0. Suppose you have taken out a balloon loan for which you make payments at the end of each month, but at the conclusion of the loan you pay off the final balance by making a $1,000 balloon payment. Then *fv* equals –$1,000. The $1,000 is negative because we are paying it out.

- *Type* is 0 or 1 and indicates when payments are due. If *type* equals 0 or is omitted, then payments are made at the end of the period. I first assumed end-of-month payments, so *type* is 0 or omitted. If *type* equals 1, then payments are made or money is deposited at the beginning of the period.

In cell G1 of the worksheet PMT in the file Excelfinfunctions.xlsx (see Figure 10-3), I computed the monthly payment on a 10-month loan for $10,000, assuming an 8 percent annual interest rate and end-of-month payments with the formula =–PMT(0.08/12,10,10000,0,0). The monthly payment is $1,037.03. The PMT function by itself returns a negative value because we are making payments to the company giving us the loan.

If you want to, you can use the Excel IPMT and PPMT functions to compute the amount of interest paid each month toward the loan and the amount of the balance paid down each month. (This is called the *payment on the principal*.)

	C	D	E	F	G	H
1		rate	0.00666667	payment	$1,037.03	
2		months	10	end of month		
3		loan amount	$ 10,000.00			
4						
5	Time	Beginning balance	Monthly Payment	Principal	Interest	Ending Balance
6	1	$ 10,000.00	$1,037.03	$970.37	$66.67	$9,029.63
7	2	$9,029.63	$1,037.03	$976.83	$60.20	$8,052.80
8	3	$8,052.80	$1,037.03	$983.35	$53.69	$7,069.45
9	4	$7,069.45	$1,037.03	$989.90	$47.13	$6,079.55
10	5	$6,079.55	$1,037.03	$996.50	$40.53	$5,083.05
11	6	$5,083.05	$1,037.03	$1,003.15	$33.89	$4,079.90
12	7	$4,079.90	$1,037.03	$1,009.83	$27.20	$3,070.07
13	8	$3,070.07	$1,037.03	$1,016.56	$20.47	$2,053.51
14	9	$2,053.51	$1,037.03	$1,023.34	$13.69	$1,030.16
15	10	$1,030.16	$1,037.03	$1,030.16	$6.87	($0.00)
16						
17	NPV of payments	$10,000.00				
18				cum int months 2-4	cumprinc months 2-4	
19	payment beginning of each month	$1,030.16		-161.0125862	-2950.083682	
20	monthly payment if we make $1000 ending payment	$940.00				

FIGURE 10-3 Examples of the PMT, PPMT, CUMPRINC, CUMIPMT, and IPMT functions.

To determine the interest paid each month, use the IPMT (interest payment) function. The syntax of the IPMT function is IPMT(rate,per,#per,pv,[fv],[type]), where *fv* and *type* are optional arguments. The *per* argument indicates the period number for which you compute the interest. The other arguments mean the same as they do for the PMT function. Similarly, to determine the amount paid toward the principal each month, you can use the PPMT (principal payment) function. The syntax of the PPMT function is PPMT(rate,per,#per,pv,[fv],[type]). The meaning of each argument is the same as it is for the IPMT function. By copying from F6 to F7:F16 the formula =–PPMT(0.08/12,C6,10,10000,0,0), you can compute the amount of each month's payment that is applied to the principal. For example, during Month 1 you pay only $970.37 toward the principal. As expected, the amount paid toward the principal increases each month. The minus sign (before PPMT) is needed because the principal is paid to the company giving you the loan, and PPMT will return a negative number. By copying from G6 to G7:G16 the formula =–IPMT(0.08/12,C6,10,10000,0,0), you can compute the amount of interest paid each month. For example, in Month 1 you pay $66.67 in interest. Of course, the amount of interest paid each month decreases.

Note that each month, (Interest Paid)+(Payment Toward Principal)=(Total Payment). Sometimes the total is off by a penny because of rounding.

You can also create the ending balances for each month in column H by using the relationship (Ending Month *t* Balance)=(Beginning Month *t* Balance)–(Month *t* Payment toward Principal). Note that in Month 1, Beginning Balance equals $10,000. In column D, I created each month's beginning balance by using the relationship (for *t*=2, 3, ...10)(Beginning Month *t* Balance)=(Ending Month *t*–1 Balance). Of course, Ending Month 10 Balance equals $0 (in cell H15), as it should.

Interest each month can be computed as (Month *t* Interest)=(Interest rate)*(Beginning Month *t* Balance). For example, the Month 3 interest payment can be computed as =(0.0066667)*($8,052.80), which equals $53.69.

Of course, the NPV of all payments is exactly $10,000. I checked this in cell D17 with the formula NPV(0.08/12,E6:E15). Note the cell D17 formula is =NPV(E1,E6:E15), and the cell E1 formula is =0.08/12. (See Figure 10-3.)

If the payments are made at the beginning of each month, the amount of each payment is computed in cell D19 with the formula =–PMT(0.08/12,10,10000,0,1). Changing the last argument to 1 changes each payment to the beginning of the month. Because the lender is getting her money earlier, monthly payments are less than the end-of-month case. If you pay at the beginning of the month, the monthly payment is $1,030.16.

Finally, suppose that you want to make a balloon payment of $1,000 at the end of 10 months. If you make your monthly payments at the end of each month, the formula =–PMT(0.08/12,10,10000, –1000,0) in cell D20 computes your monthly payment. The monthly payment turns out to be $940. Because $1,000 of the loan is not being paid with monthly payments, it makes sense that your new monthly payment is less than the original end-of-month payment of $1,037.03.

CUMPRINC and CUMIPMT functions

You'll often want to accumulate the interest or principal paid during several periods. The CUMPRINC and CUMIPMT functions make this a snap.

The CUMPRINC (cumulative principal) function computes the principal paid between two periods (inclusive). The syntax of the CUMPRINC function is CUMPRINC(rate,#per,pv,start period,end period,type). *Rate*, *#per*, *pv*, and *type* have the same meanings as described previously.

The CUMIPMT (cumulative interest payment) function computes the interest paid between two periods (inclusive). The syntax of the CUMIPMT function is CUMIPMT(rate,#nper,pv,start period,end period,type). *Rate*, *#per*, *pv*, and *type* have the same meanings as described previously. For example, in cell F19 on the PMT worksheet, I computed the interest paid during months 2 through 4 ($161.01) by using the formula =CUMIPMT(0.08/12,10,10000,2,4,0). In cell G19, I computed the principal paid off in months 2 through 4 ($2,950.08) by using the formula =CUMPRINC(0.08/12,10,10000,2,4,0).

I want to borrow $80,000 and make monthly payments for 10 years. The maximum monthly payment I can afford is $1,000. What is the maximum interest rate I can afford?

Given a borrowed amount, the length of a loan, and the payment each period, the RATE function tells you the rate of the loan. The syntax of the RATE function is RATE(#per,pmt,pv,[fv],[type],[guess]), where *fv*, *type*, and *guess* are optional arguments. *#Per*, *pmt*, *pv*, *fv*, and *type* have the same meanings as previously described. *Guess* is simply a guess at what the loan rate is. Usually *guess* can be omitted. Entering in cell D9 of worksheet Rate (in the file Excelfinfunctions.xlsx) the formula =RATE(120,–1000,80000,0,0,) yields 0.7241 percent as the monthly rate. I am assuming end-of-month payments. (See Figure 10-4.)

	D	E	F	G	H
6	BORROWING $80,000				
7	120 MONTHLY PAYMENTS OF $1000 PER MONTH				
8	WHAT IS MAX RATE YOU CAN HANDLE?				
9	0.72410%	=RATE(120,-1000,80000,0,0)			
10	IF YOU CAN PAY $10,000 AT END				
11	WHAT IS MAX RATE YOU CAN HANDLE?				
12	0.818%				
13					
14					
15	$80,000.08				
16		CHECK!			
17		=PV(0.007241,120,-1000,0,0)			

FIGURE 10-4 Example of the RATE function.

In cell D15, I verified the RATE function calculation. The formula =PV(.007241,120,–1000,0,0) yields $80,000.08. This shows that payments of $1,000 at the end of each month for 120 months have a present value of $80,000.08.

If you could pay back $10,000 during month 120, the maximum rate you could handle would be given by the formula =RATE(120,–1000,80000,–10000,0,0). In cell D12, this formula yields a monthly rate of 0.818 percent.

If I borrow $100,000 at 8 percent interest and make payments of $10,000 per year, how many years will it take me to pay back the loan?

Given the size of a loan, the payments each period, and the loan rate, the NPER (number of periods) function tells you how many periods it takes to pay back a loan. The syntax of the NPER function is NPER(rate,pmt,pv,[fv],[type]), in which *fv* and *type* are optional arguments.

Assuming end-of-year payments, the formula =NPER(0.08,–10000,100000,0,0) in cell D7 of worksheet Nper (in the file Excelfinfunctions.xlsx) yields 20.91 years. (See Figure 10-5.) Thus, 20 years of payments will not quite pay back the loan, but 21 years will overpay the loan. To verify the calculation, in cells D10 and D11 I used the PV function to show that paying $10,000 per year for 20 years pays back $98,181.47, and paying back $10,000 for 21 years pays back $100,168.03.

Suppose that you are planning to pay back $40,000 in the final payment period. How many years will it take to pay back the loan? I entered in cell D14 the formula =NPER(0.08,–10000,100000, –40000,0), which shows that it will take 15.90 years to pay back the loan. Thus, 15 years of payments will not quite pay off the loan, and 16 years of payments will slightly overpay the loan.

	C	D	E
1			
2			
3		Borrow $100000 8%	
4		ANNUAL PAYMENTS OF $10,000 PER YEAR	
5		END OF YEAR PAYMENT	
6		HOW MANY YEARS?	
7		20.91237188	=NPER(0.08,-10000,100000,0,0)
8		20 YEARS WILL NOT PAY IT OFF; 21 WILL	
9		CHECK	
10	20 YEARS	$98,181.47	=PV(0.08,20,-10000,0,0)
11	21 YEARS	$100,168.03	=PV(0.08,21,-10000,0,0)
12			
13		IF WE PAY $40,000 AT END OF PROBLEM	
14		15.9012328	=NPER(0.08,-10000,100000,-40000,0)
15		15 YEARS WILL NOT PAY IT OFF; 16 YEARS WILL	

FIGURE 10-5 Example of the NPER function.

I'm a CPA and often have to work with complicated methods for depreciating machinery cost. Does Excel have functions to help me compute depreciation?

Depreciation is the reduction in the long-lived assets from use or obsolescence. The three most commonly used methods for computing depreciation are the following:

- Straight-Line depreciation (SLN)
- Sum-of-Years' Digits depreciation (SYD)
- Double-Declining-Balance depreciation (DDB)

Let's consider a new machine that is worth $15,000 and over five years will be depreciated to a final (or salvage value) of $3000. The question is how the various depreciation methods allocate $15,000 – $3000 = $12,000 of depreciation over five years.

- The Straight-Line deprecation method (SLN) simply depreciates the machine's value an equal amount (in this case $12,000/5 = $2400) during each year.
- When there are *N* total years, the Sum-of-Years' Digits method (SYD) allocates during year I a fraction (5-I+1)/(N*(N+1)/2) of the Cost – Salvage Value. (N*(N+1)/2) is the sum of the integers 1, 2, ...,*N*. In our example, 5/15 of total depreciation occurs during Year 1, 4/15 during Year 2, and so on.
- If we define Book Value = Cost – Accumulated Depreciation, then for depreciation over *N* years, the Double-Declining-Balance method (DDB) calculates depreciation during a year as 2*Book Value)/N. In our example, *N* = 5. So during each year, depreciation should equal 40 percent of the Book Value. Unfortunately, DDB as we just described may not allocate exactly an amount equal to Cost – Salvage Value to depreciation. In such cases, DDB adjusts depreciation during the last few years, so total Depreciation would equal Cost – Salvage Value. In our example, DDB allocates 0.4*$15,000 = $6000 during Year 1, 0.4*$9000 =$3600 during Year 2, and 0.4*($5400) = $2160 during Year 3. If we allocated 0.4*($3240) = $1296 to Year 4 depreciation, our total depreciation would exceed $12,000. Therefore, Year 4 Depreciation = $12,000 – ($6000+ $3600 + $2160) = $240, and Year 5 Depreciation = 0.

Fortunately, Excel has a function for each type of depreciation:

- For Straight-Line depreciation, the function SLN(Cost,Salvage_value,Years) computes each year's depreciation.
- For Sum-of-Years' Digits depreciation, the function SYD(Cost,Salvage_value,Years,i) computes depreciation during year *i*.
- For Double-Declining-Balance depreciation, the function DDB(Cost,Salvage_value,Years,i) computes Year i depreciation.

Therefore, after creating range names for cells C2:C4 based on the range B2:B4 (as shown in Figure 10-6 and the file Depreciationexamples.xlsx), we can compute depreciation for each of the three methods as follows:

- Compute Straight-Line depreciation by copying from E8 to F8:J8 the formula =SLN(Cost,Salvage_Value,Years).
- Compute Sum-of-Years' Digits depreciation by copying from E9 to F9:J9 the formula = SYD(Cost, Salvage_value,Years,E7).
- Compute Double-Declining-Balance depreciation by copying from E10 to F10:J10 the formula = DDB(Cost,Salvage_value,Years,E7).

Note that both SYD and DDB front load more of the depreciation to early years.

	B	C	D	E	F	G	H	I	J
1									
2	Cost	$15,000.00							
3	Salvage value	$3,000.00							
4	Years	5							
5									
6				Year					
7				1	2	3	4	5	Total
8	=SLN(Cost,Salvage_value,Years)		Straight-Line	$2,400.00	$2,400.00	$2,400.00	$2,400.00	$2,400.00	$12,000.00
9	=SYD(Cost,Salvage_value,Years,E7)		Sum-of-Years'-Digits	$4,000.00	$3,200.00	$2,400.00	$1,600.00	$800.00	$12,000.00
10	=DDB(Cost,Salvage_value,Years,E7)		Double-Declining-Balance	$6,000.00	$3,600.00	$2,160.00	$240.00	$0.00	$12,000.00

FIGURE 10-6 Examples of Excel depreciation functions.

Problems

Unless otherwise mentioned, all payments are made at the end of the period.

1. You have just won the lottery. At the end of each of the next 20 years, you will receive a payment of $50,000. If the cost of capital is 10 percent per year, what is the present value of your lottery winnings?
2. A *perpetuity* is an annuity that is received forever. If I rent out my house and at the beginning of each year I receive $14,000, what is the value of this perpetuity? Assume an annual 10 percent cost of capital. Hint: Use the PV function and let the number of periods be many!

3. I now have $250,000 in the bank. At the end of each of the next 20 years, I withdraw $15,000. If I earn 8 percent per year on my investments, how much money will I have in 20 years?

4. I deposit $2,000 per month (at the end of each month) over the next 10 years. My investments earn 0.8 percent per month. I would like to have $1 million in 10 years. How much money should I deposit now?

5. An NBA player is receiving $15 million at the end of each of the next seven years. He can earn 6 percent per year on his investments. What is the present value of his future revenues?

6. At the end of each of the next 20 years, I will receive the following amounts:

Years	Amounts
1–5	$200
6–10	$300
11–20	$400

   Use the PV function to find the present value of these cash flows, where the cost of capital is 10 percent. Hint: Begin by computing the value of receiving $400 a year for 20 years, and then subtract the value of receiving $100 a year for 10 years, and so on.

7. You are borrowing $200,000 on a 30-year mortgage, with an annual interest rate of 10 percent. Assuming end-of-month payments, determine the monthly payment, interest payment each month, and amount paid toward the principal each month.

8. Answer each question in Problem 7 assuming beginning-of-month payments.

9. Use the FV function to determine the value to which $100 accumulates in three years, if you are earning 7 percent per year.

10. You have a liability of $1,000,000 due in 10 years. The cost of capital is 10 percent per year. What amount of money do you need to set aside at the end of each of the next 10 years to meet this liability?

11. You are going to buy a new car. The cost of the car is $50,000. You have been offered two payment plans:

    - A 10 percent discount on the sales price of the car, followed by 60 monthly payments financed at 9 percent per year.

    - No discount on the sales price of the car, followed by 60 monthly payments financed at 2 percent per year.

    If you believe your annual cost of capital is 9 percent, which payment plan is a better deal? Assume all payments occur at the end of the month.

12. I presently have $10,000 in the bank. At the beginning of each of the next 20 years, I am going to invest $4,000 and I expect to earn 6 percent per year on my investments. How much money will I have in 20 years?

13. A balloon mortgage requires you to pay off part of a loan during a specified time period and then make a lump sum payment to pay off the remaining portion of the loan. Suppose you borrow $400,000 on a 20-year balloon mortgage and the interest rate is 0.5 percent per month. Your end-of-month payments during the first 20 years are required to pay off $300,000 of your loan, at which point you have to pay off the remaining $100,000. Determine your monthly payments for this loan.

14. An adjustable-rate mortgage (ARM) ties monthly payments to a rate index (say, the US T-bill rate). Suppose you borrow $60,000 on an ARM for 30 years (360 monthly payments). The first 12 payments are governed by the current T-bill rate of 8 percent. In years 2–5, monthly payments are set at the year's beginning monthly T-bill rate + 2 percent. Suppose the T-bill rates at the beginning of years 2–5 are as follows:

Beginning of year	T-bill rate
2	10 percent
3	13 percent
4	15 percent
5	10 percent

Determine the monthly payments during years 1–5 and each year's ending balance.

15. Suppose you have borrowed money at a 14.4 percent annual rate and you make monthly payments. If you have missed four consecutive monthly payments, how much should next month's payment be to catch up?

16. You want to replace a machine in 10 years, and you estimate the cost will be $80,000. If you can earn 8 percent annually on your investments, how much money should you put aside at the end of each year to cover the cost of the machine?

17. You are buying a motorcycle. You pay $1,500 today and $182.50 a month for three years. If the annual rate of interest is 18 percent, what was the original cost of the motorcycle?

18. Suppose the annual rate of interest is 10 percent. You pay $200 a month for two years, $300 a month for a year, and $400 for two years. What is the present value of all your payments?

19. You can invest $500 at the end of each six-month period for five years. If you want to have $6,000 after five years, what is the annual rate of return you need on your investments?

20. I borrow $2,000 and make quarterly payments for two years. The annual rate of interest is 24 percent. What is the size of each payment?

21. I have borrowed $15,000. I am making 48 monthly payments, and the annual rate of interest is 9 percent. What is the total interest paid over the course of the loan?

22. I am borrowing $5,000 and plan to pay back the loan with 36 monthly payments. The annual rate of interest is 16.5 percent. After one year, I pay back $500 extra and shorten the period of the loan to two years total. What will my monthly payment be during the second year of the loan?

23. With an adjustable-rate mortgage, you make monthly payments, depending on the interest rates at the beginning of each year. You have borrowed $60,000 on a 30-year ARM. For the first year, monthly payments are based on the current annual T-bill rate of 9 percent. In years 2–5, monthly payments will be based on the following annual T-bill rates +2 percent:

- Year 2: 10 percent
- Year 3: 13 percent
- Year 4: 15 percent
- Year 5: 10 percent

The catch is that the ARM contains a clause that ensures that monthly payments can increase a maximum of 7.5 percent from one year to the next. To compensate the lender for this provision, the borrower adjusts the ending balance of the loan at the end of each year, based on the difference between what the borrower actually paid and what he should have paid. Determine the monthly payments during years 1–5 of the loan.

24. You have a choice of receiving $8,000 each year beginning at age 62 and ending when you die, or receiving $10,000 each year beginning at age 65 and ending when you die. If you think you can earn an 8 percent annual return on your investments, which will net the largest amount?

25. You have just won the lottery and will receive $50,000 a year for 20 years. What rate of interest would make these payments the equivalent of receiving $500,000 today?

26. A bond pays a $50 coupon at the end of each of the next 30 years and pays $1,000 face value in 30 years. If you discount cash flows at an annual rate of 6 percent, what would be a fair price for the bond?

27. You have borrowed $100,000 on a 40-year mortgage with monthly payments. The annual interest rate is 16 percent. How much will you pay over the course of the loan? With four years left on the loan, how much will you still owe?

28. I need to borrow $12,000. I can afford payments of $500 per month, and the annual rate of interest is 4.5 percent. How many months will it take to pay off the loan?

29. You are considering borrowing $50,000 on a 180-month loan. The annual interest rate on the loan depends on your credit score in the following fashion:

	C	D
9	Credit Score	Annual Rate
10	740-850	8.15
11	720-739	8.45
12	700-719	8.95
13	670-699	9.725
14	640-669	11.225
15	620-639	12.475

Write a formula that gives your monthly payments as a function of your credit score.

30. You are going to borrow $40,000 for a new car. You want to determine the monthly payments and total interest paid for the following situations:

- 48-month loan, 6.85% annual rate.
- 60-month loan, 6.59% annual rate.

31. Consider a machine that costs $50,000 and will be depreciated over 10 years to a final salvage value of $5000. Determine the depreciation during each year for Straight-Line, Sum-of-Years' Digits, and Double-Declining-Balance depreciations.

CHAPTER 11

Circular references

Questions answered in this chapter:

- I often get a circular-reference message from Excel. Does this mean I've made an error?
- How can I resolve circular references?

When Microsoft Excel 2016 displays a message that your workbook contains a circular reference, it means there is a loop, or dependency, between two or more cells in a worksheet. For example, a circular reference occurs if the value in cell A1 influences the value in D3, the value in cell D3 influences the value in cell E6, and the value in cell E6 influences the value in cell A1. Figure 11-1 illustrates the pattern of a circular reference.

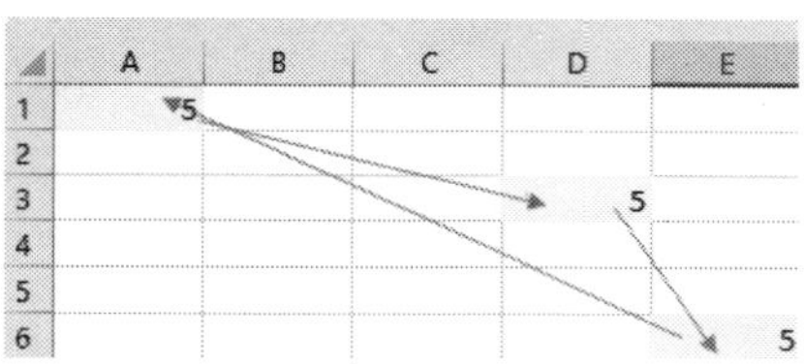

FIGURE 11-1 A loop causing a circular reference.

As you'll soon see, you can resolve circular references by selecting Enable Iterative Calculation in the Calculation Options area of the Formulas page in the Excel Options dialog box.

Answers to this chapter's questions

I often get a circular-reference message from Excel. Does this mean I've made an error?

A circular reference usually arises from a logically consistent worksheet in which several cells exhibit a looping relationship similar to that illustrated in Figure 11-1. Let's look at a simple example of a problem that cannot easily be solved in Excel without creating a circular reference.

A small company earns $1,500 in revenues and incurs $1,000 in costs. They want to give 10 percent of their after-tax profits to charity. Their tax rate is 40 percent. How much money should they give to charity? The solution to this problem is in worksheet Sheet1 in the file Circular.xlsx, shown in Figure 11-2.

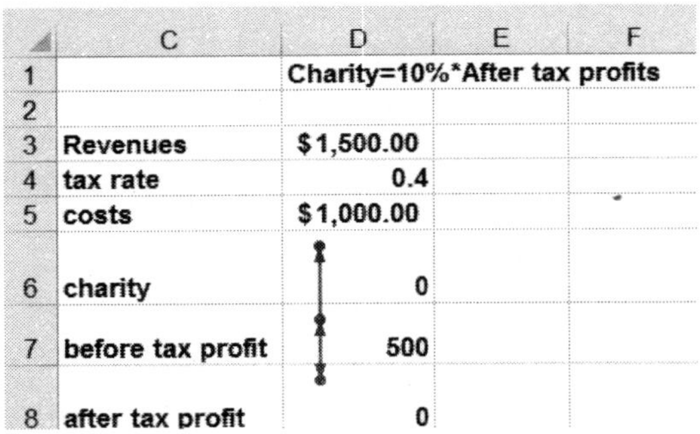

FIGURE 11-2 A circular reference can occur when you're calculating taxes.

I began by naming the cells in D3:D8 with the corresponding names in cells C3:C8. Next, I entered the firm's revenue, tax rate, and costs in D3:D5. To compute a contribution to charity as 10 percent of after-tax profit, I entered in cell D6 the formula =0.1*after_tax_profit. Then I determined before-tax profit in cell D7 by subtracting costs and the charitable contribution from revenues. The formula in cell D7 is =Revenues–Costs–Charity. Finally, I computed after-tax profit in cell D8 as =(1–tax_rate)*before_tax_profit.

Excel indicates a circular reference in cell D8 (see the bottom-left corner of the file Circular.xlsx). What's going on?

1. Charity (cell D6) influences before-tax profit (cell D7).
2. Before-tax profit (cell D7) influences after-tax profit (cell D8).
3. After-tax profit (cell D8) influences charity.

Thus, we have a loop of the form D6-D7-D8-D6 (indicated by the blue arrows in Figure 11-2), which causes the circular-reference message. The worksheet is logically correct; we have done nothing wrong. Still, you can see from Figure 11-2 that Excel is calculating an incorrect answer for charitable contributions.

How can I resolve circular references?

Resolving a circular reference is easy. Simply click the File tab at the left end of the ribbon, and then click Options to open the Excel Options dialog box. Choose Formulas in the left pane, and then select the Enable Iterative Calculation check box in the Calculation Options section, as shown in Figure 11-3. Click OK.

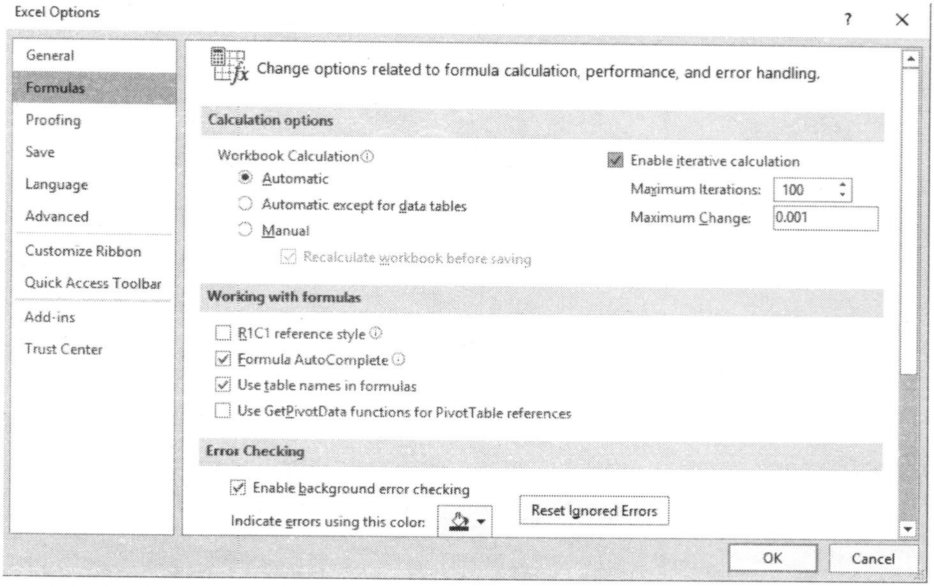

FIGURE 11-3 Use the Enable Iterative Calculation option to resolve a circular reference.

When you activate the Enable Iterative Calculation option, Excel recognizes that your circular reference has generated the following system of three equations with three unknowns:

```
Charity=0.1*(AfterTax Profit)
BeforeTax Profit=Revenue-Charity-Costs
AfterTax Profit= (1-Tax rate)*(BeforeTax Profit)
```

The three unknowns are *Charity*, *BeforeTax Profit*, and *AfterTax Profit*. When you activate the Enable Iterative Calculation option, Excel iterates (based on my experience with circular references, 100 iterations should be used) to seek a solution to all equations generated by the circular reference. From one iteration to the next, the values of the unknowns are changed by a complex mathematical procedure (Gauss-Seidel Iteration). Excel stops if the maximum change in any worksheet cell from one iteration to the next is smaller than the Maximum Change value (0.001 by default). You can reduce the Maximum Change setting to a smaller number, such as 0.000001. If you do not reduce the Maximum Change setting to a smaller number, you might find that Excel assigns a value of, for example, 5.001 to a cell that should equal 5, and this is inaccurate. Also, some complex worksheets might require more than 100 iterations before a resolution of the circularity emerges. For this example, however, the circularity is almost instantly resolved, and you can see the solution given in Figure 11-4.

	C	D	E	F
1		Charity=10%*After tax profits		
2				
3	Revenues	$1,500.00		
4	tax rate	0.4		
5	costs	$1,000.00		
6	charity	28.301887		
7	before tax profit	471.69811		
8	after tax profit	283.01887		

FIGURE 11-4 Excel runs the calculations to resolve the circular reference.

Note that the charitable contribution of $28.30 is now exactly 10 percent of the after-tax profit of $283.01. All other cells in the worksheet are now correctly computed.

Note also that Excel's iteration procedure is guaranteed to work only when solving systems of linear equations. In other situations, a solution is not always guaranteed. In the tax example, resolving the circular references requires solving a system of linear equations, so you know Excel will find the correct answer.

Here's one more example of a circular reference. In any Excel formula, you can refer to an entire column or row by name. For example, the formula AVERAGE(B:B) averages all cells in column B. The formula =AVERAGE(1:1) averages all cells in row 1. This shortcut is useful if you're continually dumping new data (such as monthly sales) into a column or row. The formula always computes average sales, and you do not need to ever change it. The problem is, of course, that if you enter this formula in the column or row that it refers to, you create a circular reference. By activating the Enable Iterative Calculation option, circular references such as these are resolved quickly.

Problems

1. Before paying employee bonuses and state and federal taxes, a company earns profits of $60,000. The company pays employees a bonus equal to 5 percent of after-tax profits. State tax is 5 percent of profits (after bonuses are paid). Federal tax is 40 percent of profits (after bonuses and state tax are paid). Determine the amount paid in bonuses, state tax, and federal tax.

2. On January 1, 2002, I have $500. At the end of each month, I earn 2 percent interest. Each month's interest is based on the average of the month's beginning and ending balances. How much money will I have after 12 months?

3. My airplane is flying the following route: Houston-Los Angeles-Seattle-Minneapolis-Houston. On each leg of the journey, the plane's fuel usage (expressed as miles per gallon) is 40–0.02*(average fuel en route). Here, average fuel en route is equal to 0.5*(initial fuel en route+final fuel en route). My plane begins in Houston with 1,000 gallons of fuel. The distance flown on each leg of the journey is as follows:

Leg	Miles
Houston to Los Angeles	1,200
Los Angeles to Seattle	1,100
Seattle to Minneapolis	1,500
Minneapolis to Houston	1,400

How many gallons of fuel remain when I return to Houston?

4. A common method used to allocate costs to support departments is the reciprocal cost allocation method. This method can easily be implemented by use of circular references. To illustrate, suppose Widgetco has two support departments: Accounting and Consulting. Widgetco also has two product divisions: Division 1 and Division 2. Widgetco has decided to allocate $600,000 of the cost of operating the Accounting department and $116,000 of the cost of operating the Consulting department to the two divisions. The fraction of accounting and consulting time used by each part of the company is as follows:

	Accounting	Consulting	Division 1	Division 2
Percentage of accounting work done for other parts of the company	0%	20%	30%	50%
Percentage of consulting work done for other parts of the company	10%	0%	80%	10%

How much of the accounting and consulting costs should be allocated to other parts of the company? You need to determine two quantities: total cost allocated to accounting and total cost allocated to consulting. Total cost allocated to accounting equals $600,000+.1*(total cost allocated to consulting), because 10 percent of all consulting work was done for the Accounting department. A similar equation can be written for the total cost allocated to consulting. You should now be able to calculate the correct allocation of both accounting and consulting costs to each other part of the company.

5. We start a year with $200 and receive $100 during the year. We also receive 10 percent interest at the end of the year, with the interest based on our starting balance. In this case, we end the year with $320. Determine the ending balance for the year if interest accrues on the average of our starting and ending balance.

CHAPTER 12

IF statements

Questions answered in this chapter:

- If I order up to 500 units of a product, I pay $3.00 per unit. If I order from 501 through 1,200 units, I pay $2.70 per unit. If I order from 1,201 through 2,000 units, I pay $2.30 per unit. If I order more than 2,000 units, I pay $2.00 per unit. How can I write a formula that expresses the purchase cost as a function of the number of units purchased?
- I just purchased 100 shares of stock at a cost of $55 per share. To hedge the risk that the stock might decline in value, I purchased 60 six-month European put options. Each option has an exercise price of $45 and costs $5. How can I develop a worksheet that indicates the six-month percentage return on my portfolio for a variety of possible future prices?
- Many stock market analysts believe that moving-average trading rules can outperform the market. A commonly suggested moving-average trading rule is to buy a stock when the stock's price moves above the average of the last 15 months and to sell a stock when the stock's price moves below the average of the last 15 months. How would this trading rule have performed against the Standard & Poor's 500 Stock Index (S&P)?
- In the game of craps, two dice are tossed. If the total of the dice on the first roll is 2, 3, or 12, you lose. If the total of the dice on the first roll is 7 or 11, you win. Otherwise, the game keeps going. How can I write a formula to determine the status of the game after the first roll?
- In most pro forma financial statements, cash is used as the plug to make assets and liabilities balance. I know that using debt as the plug would be more realistic. How can I set up a pro forma statement having debt as the plug?
- When I copy a VLOOKUP formula to determine salaries of individual employees, I get a lot of #NA errors. Then when I average the employee salaries, I cannot get a numerical answer because of the #NA errors. Can I easily replace the #NA errors with a blank space so that I can compute the average salary?
- My worksheet contains quarterly revenues for Wal-Mart. Can I easily compute the revenue for each year and place it in the row containing the first quarter's sales for that year?
- IF statements can get rather large. How many IF statements can I nest in a cell? What is the maximum number of characters allowed in an Excel formula?

The situations listed above seem to have little, if anything, in common. However, setting up Microsoft Excel 2016 models for each of these situations requires the use of an IF statement. I believe that the IF formula is the single most useful formula in Excel. IF formulas let you conduct conditional tests on values and formulas, mimicking (to a limited degree) the conditional logic provided by computing languages such as C, C++, and Java.

An IF formula begins with a condition such as A1>10. If the condition is true, the formula returns the first value listed in the formula; otherwise, we move on within the formula and repeat the process. The easiest way to show you the power and utility of IF formulas is to use them to help answer each of this chapter's questions.

Answers to this chapter's questions

If I order up to 500 units of a product, I pay $3.00 per unit. If I order from 501 through 1,200 units, I pay $2.70 per unit. If I order from 1,201 through 2,000 units, I pay $2.30 per unit. If I order more than 2,000 units, I pay $2.00 per unit. How can I write a formula that expresses the purchase cost as a function of the number of units purchased?

You can find the solution to this question on the Quantity Discount worksheet in the file named Ifstatement.xlsx. The worksheet is shown in Figure 12-1.

	A	B	C	D
1		cutoff	price	
2	cut1	500	$ 3.00	price1
3	cut2	1200	$ 2.70	price2
4	cut3	2000	$ 2.30	price3
5			$ 2.00	price4
6				
7				
8	order quantity	cost	per unit cost	
9	450	$1,350.00	$ 3.00	
10	900	$2,430.00	$ 2.70	
11	1450	$3,335.00	$ 2.30	
12	2100	$4,200.00	$ 2.00	

FIGURE 12-1 You can use an IF formula to model quantity discounts.

Suppose cell A9 contains our order quantity. You can compute an order's cost as a function of the order quantity by implementing the following logic:

- If A9 is less than or equal to 500, the cost is 3*A9.
- If A9 is from 501 through 1,200, the cost is 2.70*A9.
- If A9 is from 1,201 through 2,000, the cost is 2.30*A9.
- If A9 is more than 2,000, the cost is 2*A9.

Begin by assigning the range names in A2:A4 to cells B2:B4 and the range names in cells D2:D5 to cells C2:C5. Then you can implement this logic in cell B9 with the following formula:

```
IF(A9<=_cut1,price1*A9,IF(A9<=_cut2,price2*A9,IF(A9<=_cut3,price3*A9,price4*A9)))
```

To understand how Excel computes a value from this formula, recall that IF statements are evaluated from left to right. If the order quantity is less than or equal to 500 (*cut1*), the cost is given by price1*A9. If the order quantity is not less than or equal to 500, the formula checks to see whether the order quantity is less than or equal to 1,200. If this is the case, the order quantity is from 501 through 1,200, and the formula computes a cost of price2*A9. Next, the formula checks whether the order quantity is less than or equal to 2,000. If this is true, the order quantity is from 1,201 through 2,000, and the formula computes a cost of price3*A9. Finally, if the order cost has not yet been computed, the formula defaults to the value price4*A9. In each case, the IF formula returns the correct order cost. Note that I entered three other order quantities in cells A10:A12 and copied the cost formula to B10:B12. For each order quantity, the formula returns the correct total cost.

An IF formula containing more than one IF statement is called a *nested IF formula*.

I just purchased 100 shares of stock at a cost of $55 per share. To hedge the risk that the stock might decline in value, I purchased 60 six-month European put options. Each option has an exercise price of $45 and costs $5. How can I develop a worksheet that indicates the six-month percentage return on my portfolio for a variety of possible future prices?

Before tackling this problem, I want to review some basic concepts from the world of finance. A *European put option* allows you to sell at a given time in the future (in this case, six months) a share of a stock for the *exercise price* (in this case, $45). If the stock's price in six months is $45 or higher, the option has no value. Suppose, however, that the price of the stock in six months is below $45. Then you can make money by buying a share and immediately reselling the stock for $45. For example, if in six months the stock is selling for $37, you can make a profit of $45–$37, or $8 per share, by buying a share for $37 and then using the put to resell the share for $45. You can see that put options protect you against downward moves in a stock price. In this case, whenever the stock's price in six months is below $45, the puts start kicking in some value. This cushions a portfolio against a decrease in value of the shares it owns. Note also that the percentage return on a portfolio (assume that no dividends are paid by the stocks in the portfolio) is computed by taking the change in the portfolio's value (final portfolio value–initial portfolio value) and dividing that number by the portfolio's initial value.

With this background, let's look at how the six-month percentage return on this portfolio, consisting of 60 puts and 100 shares of stock, varies as the share price varies between $20 and $65. You can find this solution on the Hedging worksheet in the file Ifstatement.xlsx. The worksheet is shown in Figure 12-2.

The labels in A2:A7 are assigned as names to cells B2:B7. The initial portfolio value is equal to 100($55)+60($5)=$5,800, shown in cell B7 as the formula =Nshares*pricenow+putcost*Nputs. By copying from B9 to B10:B18 the formula =IF(A9<exprice,exprice–A9,0)*Nputs, I computed the final value of the puts. If the six-month price is less than the exercise price, you can value each put as exercise price–six-month price. Otherwise, each put will in six months have a value of $0. Copying from C9 to C10:C18 the formula =Nshares*A9, I compute the final value of the shares. Copying from D9 to D10:D18, the formula =((C9+B9)–startvalue)/startvalue computes the percentage return on the hedged portfolio. Copying from E9 to E10:E18, the formula =(C9–Nshares*pricenow)/(Nshares*pricenow) computes the percentage return on the portfolio if we are unhedged (that is, buy no puts).

	A	B	C	D	E
2	Nputs	60			
3	Nshares	100			
4	exprice	$ 45.00			
5	pricenow	$ 55.00			
6	putcost	$ 5.00			
7	startvalue	$5,800.00			
8	final stock price	final put value	final share value	percentage return hedged	percentage return unhedged
9	$ 20.00	$1,500.00	$2,000.00	-39.7%	-63.6%
10	$ 25.00	$1,200.00	$2,500.00	-36.2%	-54.5%
11	$ 30.00	$ 900.00	$3,000.00	-32.8%	-45.5%
12	$ 35.00	$ 600.00	$3,500.00	-29.3%	-36.4%
13	$ 40.00	$ 300.00	$4,000.00	-25.9%	-27.3%
14	$ 45.00	$ -	$4,500.00	-22.4%	-18.2%
15	$ 50.00	$ -	$5,000.00	-13.8%	-9.1%
16	$ 55.00	$ -	$5,500.00	-5.2%	0.0%
17	$ 60.00	$ -	$6,000.00	3.4%	9.1%
18	$ 65.00	$ -	$6,500.00	12.1%	18.2%

FIGURE 12-2 Hedging example that uses IF statements.

In Figure 12-2, you can see that if the stock price drops below $45, the hedged portfolio has a larger expected return than an unhedged portfolio. Also note that if the stock price does not decrease, the unhedged portfolio has a larger expected return. This is why the purchase of puts is often referred to as *portfolio insurance.*

Many stock market analysts believe that moving-average trading rules can outperform the market. A commonly suggested moving-average trading rule is to buy a stock when the stock's price moves above the average of the previous 15 months and to sell a stock when the stock's price moves below the average of the previous 15 months' price. How would this trading rule have performed against the Standard & Poor's 500 Index?

In this example, I'll compare the performance of the moving-average trading rule (in the absence of transaction costs for buying and selling stock) to a buy-and-hold strategy. The strength of a moving-average trading rule is that it helps you follow market trends. A moving-average trading rule lets you ride up with a bull market and sell before a bear market destroys you.

The data set in the file Matradingrule.xlsx contains the monthly value of the S&P 500 Index for the time period January 1871 through October 2002. To track the performance of the moving-average trading strategy, I need to track the following information each month:

- What is the average of the S&P 500 Index over the last 15 months?
- Do I own stock at the beginning of each month?
- Do I buy stock during the month?
- Do I sell stock during the month?
- What is the cash flow for the month (positive if I sell stock, negative if I buy stock, and 0 otherwise)?

The worksheet for this situation requires you to scroll down many rows. It helps to keep columns A and B, as well as the headings in row 8, visible as you scroll down. To do this, in the file

Matradingruletemp.xlsx, move the cursor to cell C9 (one row below the headings), click the View tab on the ribbon, click Freeze Panes (in the Window group) to open the Freeze Panes options, and then click the Freeze Panes option at the top of that menu, shown in Figure 12-3.

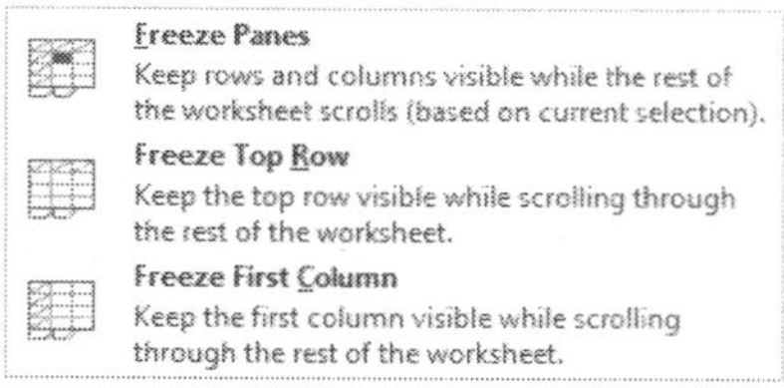

FIGURE 12-3 The Freeze Panes options.

Choosing the Freeze Panes option from the Freeze Panes drop-down menu keeps columns A and B and rows 6–8 visible as you scroll through the worksheet. For example, if you scroll down, you will always see rows 6-8. If you scroll to the right, you will always see columns A and B. The Freeze Top Row option lets you keep just the top row visible while you scroll through the rest of the worksheet. For example, if the top visible row is row 6, you see row 6 no matter how far down you scroll. If you choose the Freeze First Column option, you always see the leftmost column as you scroll through the worksheet. Selecting Unfreeze Panes from the menu returns you to the normal worksheet view.

The file Matradingrule.xlsx, shown in Figure 12-4, includes the formulas needed to track the effectiveness of a moving-average strategy. Tackling this problem requires several IF formulas, and some of the IF formulas require an AND operator. For example, I'll buy stock during a month if and only if I don't own the stock at the beginning of the month and if the current month's price is higher than the 15-month moving average for the stock's price. The first month for which I can compute a 15-month moving average is April 1872, so I begin my calculations in row 24.

	A	B	C	D	E	F	G
6		S&P				MA profit	$1,319.75
7		Comp.				Buy and hold profit	$849.45
8	Date	P	Own?	MA	Buy?	Sell?	Cash flow
18	1871.1	4.59					
19	1871.11	4.64					
20	1871.12	4.74					
21	1872.01	4.86					
22	1872.02	4.88					
23	1872.03	5.04					
24	1872.04	5.18	Yes	4.739	no	no	0
25	1872.05	5.18	Yes	4.788	no	no	0
26	1872.06	5.13	Yes	4.833	no	no	0
27	1872.07	5.1	Yes	4.868	no	no	0
28	1872.08	5.04	Yes	4.892	no	no	0
29	1872.09	4.95	Yes	4.904	no	no	0
30	1872.1	4.97	Yes	4.913	no	no	0
31	1872.11	4.95	Yes	4.929	no	no	0
32	1872.12	5.07	Yes	4.939	no	no	0
33	1873.01	5.11	Yes	4.955	no	no	0
34	1873.02	5.15	Yes	4.989	no	no	0
35	1873.03	5.11	Yes	5.023	no	no	0
36	1873.04	5.04	Yes	5.048	no	yes	5.04

FIGURE 12-4 Moving-average trading rule beats the buy-and-hold strategy.

Let's assume I first owned the stock in April 1872, so I enter **Yes** in cell C24.

- By copying from D24 to D25:D1590 the formula =AVERAGE(B9:B23), I compute the 15-month moving average for each month.

> **Note** An easy way to copy the formula from D24 to D25:D1590 is to point at the lower-right corner of cell D24 (the pointer appears as a crosshair) and then double-click the left mouse button. Double-clicking copies the formula to all the cells in the column with a value in the column to the left. This trick can also be used to copy formulas in multiple columns.

- By copying from E24 to E25:E1590 the formula =IF(AND(C24="No",B24>D24),"yes","no"), I determine for each month whether the S&P share is purchased during the month. Remember that I purchase the share only if I did not own the stock at the beginning of the month and the current value of the S&P exceeds its 15-month moving average. Notice the AND portion of the formula. It contains two conditions (more than two are allowed) separated by a comma. If both conditions are satisfied, the formula returns *Yes*; otherwise, it returns *No*. For an IF formula to recognize text, you need to place quotation marks (" ") around the text.
- By copying from F24 to F25:F1590 the formula IF(AND(C24="Yes",B24<D24),"yes","no"), I determine for each month whether the S&P share is sold. The stock is sold if and only if I owned the S&P share at the beginning of the month and the current value of the S&P share is below the 15-month moving average. April 1873 is the first month in which I sell our S&P stock.
- During any month before October 2002, if I buy a share of the S&P during the month, the cash flow is negative the value of the S&P share I bought. If I sell a share of the S&P during the month, the cash flow equals the value of the S&P. Otherwise, the cash flow is 0. During October 2002, I sell any S&P share I own to get credit for its value. Therefore, by copying from G24 to G25:G1589 the formula =IF(E24="yes",–B24,IF(F24="yes",B24,0)), I record the cash flow for all months before October 2002. Entering in cell G1590 the formula =IF(C1590="yes",B1590,0) gives me credit for selling any stock I own at the beginning of the last month.
- In cell G6, I compute total profit from the moving-average trading strategy with the formula =SUM(G24:G1590). You can see that the 15-month moving average strategy earns a profit of $1,319.75.
- The profit from buying and holding shares is simply the October 2002 S&P value minus the April 1872 S&P value. I compute the profit from the buy-and-hold strategy in cell G7 with the formula =B1590–B24.

As you can see, the buy-and-hold profit of $849.45 is far worse than the profit from the moving-average trading rule. Of course, this solution ignores the transaction costs incurred in buying and selling stocks. If transaction costs are large, this might wipe out the excess profits earned by the moving-average trading strategy.

In the game of craps, two dice are tossed. If the total of the dice on the first roll is 2, 3, or 12, you lose. If the total of the dice on the first roll is 7 or 11, you win. Otherwise, the game keeps going. How can I write a formula to determine the status of the game after the first roll?

The fact that you lose in craps if you throw a 2, 3, or 12 can be conveniently modeled by placing an OR formula within an IF formula. In cell B5 of the Craps worksheet of the file Ifstatement.xlsx, shown in Figure 12-5, I entered the formula =IF(OR(A5=2,A5=3,A5=12),"lose",IF(OR(A5=7,A5=11),"win", "keep going")). This formula is then copied from B5 to B6:B7. The formula displays *lose* if a 2, 3, or 12 is entered in cell A5. It displays *win* if a 7 or 11 is entered, and it displays *keep going* for any other value.

	A	B	C
1			
2	**Craps**		
3			
4	**Toss**	**Result**	
5	**3**	**lose**	
6	**7**	**win**	
7	**9**	**keep going**	

FIGURE 12-5 Using IF statements to model the first roll in craps.

In most pro forma financial statements, cash is used as the plug to make assets and liabilities balance. I know that using debt as the plug would be more realistic. How can I set up a pro forma statement having debt as the plug?

A pro forma statement is basically a prediction of a company's financial future. A pro forma projection requires construction of a company's future balance sheets and income statements. The balance sheet provides a snapshot of the company's assets and liabilities at any point in time. An income statement tells you how the company's financial status is changing at any point in time. Pro forma statements can help a company determine its future needs for debt and are also key parts of models that stock analysts use to determine whether a stock is properly valued. In the file Proforma.xlsx, I generated the free cash flows (FCFs) for a company for the next four years. Figure 12-6 shows the balance sheet, and Figure 12-7 shows the income statement.

	B	C	D	E	F	G	H
3	Sales growth	SG	0.02		CA/Sales		0.15
4	Initial sales	IS	1,000.00		CL/Sales		0.07
5	Interest rate on debt	IRD	0.10		NFA/Sales		0.60
6	Dividend payout	DIV	0.05		GFA/Sales		0.90
7	Tax rate	TR	0.53				
8	COGS/Sales	COGS	0.75				
9	Depreciation rate	DEP	0.10				
10	Liquid asset interest rate	LAIR	0.09				
11	Balance sheet						
12			0.00	1.00	2.00	3.00	4.00
13	Cash and marketable securities			0.00	0.00	0.00	52.56
14	Current assets		150.00	153.00	156.06	159.18	162.36
15	Gross fixed assets		900.00	1,001.33	1,115.29	1,243.29	1,386.93
16	Acc. dep.		300.00	400.13	511.66	635.99	774.68
17	Net fixed assets		600.00	601.20	603.62	607.30	612.24
18	Total assets		750.00	754.20	759.68	766.48	827.17
19							
20	Current liabilities		70.00	71.40	72.83	74.28	75.77
21	Debt		180.00	118.96	59.33	1.80	0.00
22	Stock		400.00	400.00	400.00	400.00	400.00
23	Retained earnings		100.00	163.84	227.52	290.39	351.40
24	Equity		500.00	563.84	627.52	690.39	751.40
25	Total liabilities		750.00	754.20	759.68	766.48	827.17

FIGURE 12-6 Pro forma assumptions and balance sheet.

	B	C	D	E	F	G	H
27	Income statement		0.00	1.00	2.00	3.00	4.00
28	Sales		1,000.00	1,020.00	1,040.40	1,061.21	1,082.43
29	Cost of goods sold		700.00	765.00	780.30	795.91	811.82
30	Depreciation			100.13	111.53	124.33	138.69
31	Operating income			154.87	148.57	140.97	131.92
32	Interest income			0.00	0.00	0.00	4.73
33	Interest expense			11.90	5.93	0.18	0.00
34	Income before taxes			142.97	142.64	140.79	136.65
35	Taxes			75.77	75.60	74.62	72.42
36	Net income			67.20	67.04	66.17	64.22
37							
38	Beg. retained earnings			100.00	163.84	227.52	290.39
39	Dividends			3.36	3.35	3.31	3.21
40	Ending retained earnings			163.84	227.52	290.39	351.40

FIGURE 12-7 Pro forma income statement.

Column D contains information about the company's current status (during year 0). Our basic assumptions are as follows:

- Sales growth (SG) is 2 percent per year.
- Initial sales are $1,000.
- Interest rate on debt is 10 percent.
- Dividend payout is 5 percent of net income.
- The tax rate is 53 percent.
- Cost of goods sold (COGS) is 75 percent of sales.
- Depreciation is 10 percent of gross fixed assets.
- Liquid assets earn 9 percent.

- Current assets are 15 percent of sales.
- Current liabilities are 7 percent of sales.

I assigned the names in the cell range C3:C10 to the cells in the range D3:D10. Then, during each Year *t*, basic finance and accounting imply the following relationships, which are then implemented in a series of formulas:

- Formula 12.1: Year t+1 sales=(Year t sales)*(1+SG). I computed sales during each year by copying from E28 to F28:H28 the formula =D28*(1+SG).
- Formula 12.2: Year t COGS=COGS*(Year t sales). Each year's COGS are computed by copying from E29 to F29:H29 the formula =COGS*E28.
- Formula 12.3: If Year t assets>Year t liabilities, Year *t* debt must be set equal to Year t total assets–Year t current liabilities–Year t equity. Otherwise, Year *t* debt equals 0. I computed each year's debt by copying from E21 to F21:H21 with the formula =IF(E18>E20+E24,E18–E20–E24,0). If Year *t* total assets are greater than Year *t* total liabilities, this formula sets Year *t* debt to Year t total assets–Year t current liabilities–Year t equity. This equalizes, or balances, assets and liabilities. Otherwise, you set Year *t* debt equal to 0. In this case, Year *t* cash and marketable securities are used to balance assets and liabilities.
- Formula 12.4: Year t current liabilities=(CL/Sales ratio)*(Year t sales). In E20:H20, I use the formula =$H$4*E28 to compute current liabilities for each year (copying this formula from E20 to F20:H20).
- Formula 12.5: Year t equity=Year t stock+Year t retained earnings. In E24:H24, I compute equity by copying from E24 to F24:H24 the formula =SUM(E22:E23).
- Formula 12.6: If Year t debt is greater than 0, Year t cash and marketable securities equal 0. Otherwise, Year t cash and marketable securities equal MAX(0,Year t total liabilities–Year t current assets–Year t net fixed assets). In E13:H13, I compute cash and marketable securities for each year by copying from E13 to F13:H13 the formula =IF(E21>0,0,MAX(0,E25–E14–E17)). If Year *t* debt is greater than 0, you need not use Year *t* cash and marketable securities to balance assets and liabilities. In this case, I set Year *t* cash and marketable securities equal to 0. Otherwise, I set Year *t* cash and marketable securities equal to Year t total assets–Year t current liabilities–Year t equity. This balances assets and liabilities if Year *t* assets (without cash and marketable securities) are less than Year *t* liabilities. If debt does not balance assets and liabilities, this creates liquid assets as the plug that does balance assets and liabilities.
- Formula 12.7: Year t interest expense=(Year t debt)*IRD. In E33, I compute interest expense by using the formula =IRD*E21, copying this formula again to F33:H33.
- Formula 12.8: Year t interest income=(Year t cash and marketable securities)*LAIR. In E32:H32, I compute interest income by copying from E32 to F32:H32 the formula =LAIR*E13.
- Formula 12.9: Year t operating income=Year t sales–Year t COGS–Year t depreciation. In E31:H31, operating income is computed by copying from E31 to F31:H31 the formula =E28–E29–E30.

- Formula 12.10: Year t dividends=(Year t net income)*DIV. In E39:H39, I copy from E39 to F39:H39 the formula =E36*DIV to compute dividends for each year.
- Formula 12.11: Year t+1 beginning retained earnings=Year t ending retained earnings. I compute beginning retained earnings each year in F38:H38, copying from F38 to G38:H38 the formula =E40.
- Formula 12.12: Year t end of year retained earnings=Year t beginning retained earnings+Year t net income–Year t dividends. In E40:H40, I compute each year's ending retained earnings by copying from E40 to F40:H40 the formula =E38+E36–E39.
- Formula 12.13: Year t income before taxes=Year t operating income–Year t interest expense+Year t cash income. I compute income before taxes by copying from E34 to F34:H34 the formula =E31–E33+E32.
- Formula 12.14: Year t taxes=(Year t income before taxes)*TR. I compute each year's taxes in E35:H35 by copying from E35 to F35:H35 the formula =TR*E34.
- Formula 12.15: Year t net income after taxes=(Year t income before taxes)–(Year t taxes). In E36:H36, I compute each year's net income by copying from E36 to F36:H36 the formula =E34–E35.
- Formula 12.16: Year t gross fixed assets=Year t net fixed assets+Year t accumulated depreciation. In cells E15:H15, I compute gross fixed assets for each year by copying from E15 to G15:H15 the formula =E17+E16.
- Formula 12.17: Year t depreciation=(Year t net fixed assets)*DEP. For each year, I use the formula =DEP*E15 to compute depreciation, copying the formula from E30 to F30:H30.
- Formula 12.18: Year t accumulated depreciation=Year t–1 accumulated depreciation+Year t depreciation. For each year, I use the formula =D16+E30 to compute accumulated depreciation by copying the formula from E16 to F16:H16.
- Formula 12.19: Year t net fixed assets=Year t gross fixed assets–Year t accumulated depreciation. In row 17, to compute net fixed assets, I copy from E17 to F17:H17 the formula =E15–E16.
- Formula 12.20: Year t total assets=Year t liquid assets+Year t net fixed assets+Year t cash and marketable securities. By adding liquid assets, current assets, and net fixed assets, I compute total assets by copying from E18 to F18:H18 the formula =SUM(E13,E14,E17).
- Formula 12.21: Year t total liabilities=Year t current liabilities+Year t debt+Year t equity. By copying from E25 to F25:H25 the formula =SUM(E20,E21,E24), I compute total liabilities for each period. Each year will balance because of our debt and liquid asset statements.

Formulas 12.3 and 12.6 require the use of IF statements. This worksheet will also contain circular references. (For more information about solving circular references, see Chapter 11, "Circular references.") For example, the following relationships create a circular reference:

- Year *t* cash affects Year *t* total assets.

- Year *t* total assets affect Year *t* debt.
- Year *t* debt affects Year *t* cash.

Because the worksheet contains circular references, you need to click the File tab, click Options, choose the Formulas page on the left, and select the Enable Iterative Calculation check box from the Calculations Options section. Then click OK. As explained in Chapter 11, this enables Excel to resolve circular references. Note that for each Year *t*, total assets in row 18 equal total liabilities in row 25. This shows the power of IF formulas combined with circular references.

When I copy a VLOOKUP formula to determine salaries of individual employees, I get a lot of #N/A errors. Then when I average the employee salaries, I cannot get a numerical answer because of the #N/A errors. Can I easily replace the #N/A errors with a blank space so that I can compute the average salary?

The file Errortrap.xlsx (see Figure 12-8) contains salaries and names of five employees in the cell range D3:E7 in the worksheet Sheet1. In D11:D15 I have a list of five people (some are repeated from the top set), and I compute their salary by copying from E11 to E12:E15 the formula =VLOOKUP(D11,$D3:$E$7,2,False). Unfortunately, in cells E13 and E14, Excel displays an #N/A error. (*NA* is short for "not available.") Excel returns an #N/A error value when a formula cannot return an appropriate result. Because JR and Josh have no listed salary, VLOOKUP cannot return a salary value for them. Thus, when I compute average salary in E16 with the formula =AVERAGE(E11:E15), I get an #N/A error. Many people whom I have taught go through and manually replace the #N/A errors with spaces so that their average formula will calculate properly (by ignoring the spaces). But there's a better way! The IFERROR function makes replacing errors with a character (such as a space or a 0) a snap. The syntax of IFERROR is IFERROR(value,value_if_error). Next I'll show you an example of this.

The first argument is the formula you want calculated, and the second argument is the value to insert in the cell if your formula returns an error value. (Other common error values are #DIV/0, #NAME, #NUM, #REF, and #VALUE; I'll explain these more later in the section.) Therefore, copying from F11 to F12:F15 the formula IFERROR(VLOOKUP(D11,$D$3:$E3:$E7,2,False)," ") computes the salary correctly for each actual employee and enters a blank space for people who are not actual employees. (That's why F13:F14 show as blank cells. You can verify the formulas in those cells.) The formula =AVERAGE(F11:F15) in cell F16 now correctly computes the average salary for all listed employees.

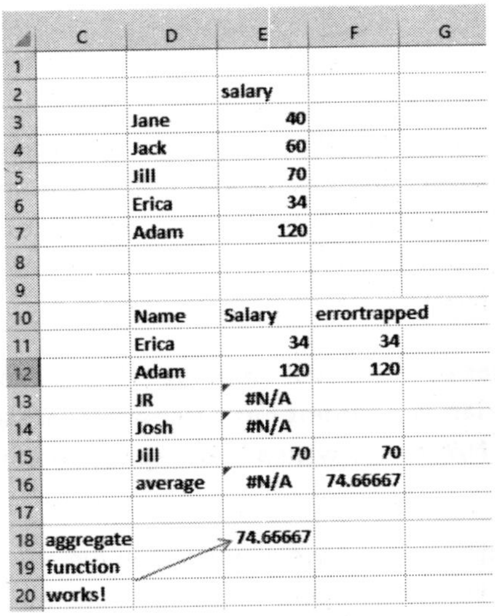

	C	D	E	F	G
1					
2			salary		
3		Jane	40		
4		Jack	60		
5		Jill	70		
6		Erica	34		
7		Adam	120		
8					
9					
10		Name	Salary	errortrapped	
11		Erica	34	34	
12		Adam	120	120	
13		JR	#N/A		
14		Josh	#N/A		
15		Jill	70	70	
16		average	#N/A	74.66667	
17					
18	aggregate		74.66667		
19	function				
20	works!				

FIGURE 12-8 Error-trapping formulas.

Beginning with Excel 2010, Excel introduced a new function, the AGGREGATE function, which allows you to perform calculations and ignore rows that contain errors. The syntax of the AGGREGATE function is AGGREGATE(function number, option, array). *Function number* is a code between 1 and 19 that gives the function involved in your calculations. For example, 1 = AVERAGE and 9 = SUM. See the Help topic on this function (obtained by clicking Help On This Function in the Function Wizard) for a complete list of available codes). *Option* gives the type of cells that should be ignored in your calculations. (See the following table.) I used Option 6 so that error values are ignored. *Array* is simply the range of cells used in your calculations. As shown in cell E18, the formula AGGREGATE(1,6,E11:E15) correctly computes the average (74.6667) of the listed salaries.

Option	Behavior
0 or omitted	Ignore nested SUBTOTAL and AGGREGATE functions
1	Ignore hidden rows and nested SUBTOTAL and AGGREGATE functions
2	Ignore error values and nested SUBTOTAL and AGGREGATE functions
3	Ignore hidden rows, error values, and nested SUBTOTAL and AGGREGATE functions
4	Ignore nothing
5	Ignore hidden rows
6	Ignore error values
7	Ignore hidden rows and error values

The file Errortypes.xlsx, shown in Figure 12-9, contains examples of other common error values.

	B	C	D	E	F	G
1	**Error Examples**					
2						
3	5	0	#DIV/0!	=C3/D3		
4						
5						
6	5	jack	#VALUE!	=c6+d6		
7			#NAME?	=sum(sales)		
8			#NUM!	=sqrt(-1)		
9		#REF!		=SUM(A1:A3);DELETED COLUMN A		

FIGURE 12-9 Examples of Excel error values.

- The following examples explore the different error values:
- In cell D3, the formula =B3/C3 yields a #DIV/0! value because you can't divide by 0.
- In cell D6, the formula =B6+C6 yields a #VALUE! error because *Jack* is not the appropriate type of data for the entered formula. (*Jack* is text.)
- In cell D7, the formula =SUM(Sales) returns a #NAME? error, indicating that the range name *Sales* referred to in the formula is not defined.
- In cell D8, the formula =SQRT(–1) results in a #NUM! error. The #NUM error results when you enter an unacceptable argument in a function. Because negative numbers do not have square roots, Excel displays the #NUM! error.
- In cell C9, I entered the formula SUM(A1:A3) and then deleted column A. This results in a #REF! error because the cells that are referred to in the formula (cells A1:A3) are no longer in the worksheet.

The IFERROR function can be used to replace any of these error values by a number or text string.

My worksheet contains quarterly revenues for Wal-Mart. Can I easily compute the revenue for each year and place it in the row containing the first quarter's sales for that year?

The file Walmartrev.xlsx contains quarterly revenues (in millions of dollars) for Wal-Mart. (See Figure 12-10.) Rows 6, 10, 14, and so on contain the revenues for the first quarter of each year. In each of these rows, I would like to compute total revenues for the year in column E. In other rows, column E should be blank. I could enter in cell E6 the formula =SUM(D6:D9) and copy this formula to E10, then E14, then E18, and so on, but there must be a better way. Using an IF statement with two neat Excel functions, (ROW and MOD), gives me an easy way to enter my formula once and then copy the formula. The function ROW(cell reference) yields the row of reference. The function =ROW(A6) yields a 6; if you are in row 6, the =ROW() function would also yield a 6. The function MOD(number,divisor) yields the remainder when *number* is divided by *divisor*. For example, MOD(9,4) yields 1, whereas MOD(6,3) yields 0. Note that I want my formula to work only in rows that leave a remainder of 2 when divided by 4. Therefore, copying from E6 to E7:E57 the formula =IF(MOD(ROW(),4)= 2,SUM(D6:D9)," ") ensures that I add up revenues for the current year only in rows that leave a remainder of 2 when divided by 4. This means that I compute annual revenues only in the first quarter of each year, which is the goal.

	B	C	D	E
3	Wal-Mart revenues			
4				
5	Year	Quarter	revenue	Annual revenues
6	1991	1	9,281	43886.76096
7	1991	2	10,340	
8	1991	3	10,628	
9	1991	4	13,639	
10	1992	1	11,649	55483.59296
11	1992	2	13,028	
12	1992	3	13,684	
13	1992	4	17,122	
14	1993	1	13,920	67344.29593
15	1993	2	16,237	
16	1993	3	16,827	
17	1993	4	20,361	
18	1994	1	17,686	82493.89093
19	1994	2	19,942	
20	1994	3	20,418	
21	1994	4	24,448	
22	1995	1	20,440	93627

FIGURE 12-10 Summarizing Wal-Mart annual revenues.

IF statements can get rather large. How many IF statements can I nest in a cell? What is the maximum number of characters allowed in an Excel formula?

In Excel 2016, you can nest up to 64 IF statements in a cell. In previous versions of Excel, you could nest a maximum of seven IF statements. In Excel 2010 (and Excel 2007), a cell can contain up to 32,000 characters.

Problems

1. Suppose the price of a product will change at dates in the future, as follows:

Date	Price
On or before February 15, 2004	$8
From February 16, 2004, through April 10, 2005	$9
From April 11, 2005, through January 15, 2006	$10
After January 15, 2006	$11

Write a formula that computes the price of the product based on the date the product is sold.

2. The Blue Yonder Airline flight from Seattle to New York has a capacity of 250 people. The airline sold 270 tickets for the flight at a price of $300 per ticket. Tickets are nonrefundable. The variable cost of flying a passenger (mostly food costs and fuel costs) is $30 per passenger. If more than 250 people show up for the flight, the flight is overbooked and Blue Yonder must pay overbooking compensation of $350 per person to each overbooked passenger. Develop a worksheet that computes Blue Yonder's profit based on the number of customers who show up for the flight.

3. A major drug company is trying to determine the correct plant capacity for a new drug. A unit of annual capacity can be built for a cost of $10. Each unit of the drug sells for $12 and incurs variable costs of $2. The drug will be sold for 10 years. Develop a worksheet that computes the company's 10-year profit given the chosen annual capacity level and the annual demand for the drug. Assume demand for the drug is the same each year. You can ignore the time value of money in this problem.

4. The same drug company is producing a new drug. The company has made the following assumptions:

   - During Year 1, 100,000 units will be sold.
   - Sales will grow for three years and then decline for seven years.
   - During the growth period, sales will grow at a rate of 15 percent per year. During the decline, sales will drop at a rate of 10 percent per year.

   Develop a worksheet that takes values for Year 1 sales, the length of the growth cycle, the length of the decline cycle, the growth rate during the growth cycle, and the rate of decrease during the decline cycle, and then computes unit sales for Years 1–11.

5. You are bidding on a construction project. The low bid gets the project. You estimate the project cost at $10,000. Four companies are bidding against you. It costs $400 to prepare the bid. Write a formula that (given the bids of your four competitors and your bid) computes your profit (or loss if you lose the bid).

6. We are bidding on a valuable painting. The high bid gets the painting. We estimate the painting's value at $10,000. Four companies are bidding against us. It costs $400 to prepare the bid. Write a formula that (given the bids of our four competitors and our bid) determines whether we get the painting.

7. A drug company believes its new drug will sell 10,000 units during 2004. They expect two competitors to enter the market. The year in which the first competitor enters, the company expects to lose 30 percent of its market share. The year in which the second competitor enters, the company expects to lose 15 percent of its market share. The size of the market is growing at 10 percent per year. Given values for the years in which the two competitors enter, develop a worksheet that computes the annual sales for the years 2004–2013.

8. A clothing store has ordered 100,000 swimsuits. It costs $22 to produce a swimsuit. They plan to sell them until August 31 at a price of $40 and then mark the price down to $30. Given values for demand through August 31 and after August 31, develop a worksheet to compute the profit from this order.

9. In a game of craps, on each roll of the dice after the first roll, the rules are as follows: If the game has not ended and the current roll matches the first roll, you win the game. If the game has not ended and the current roll is a 7, you lose. Otherwise, the game continues. Develop a worksheet that tells you (given knowledge of the first four rolls) the status of the game after four dice rolls.

10. On the S&P moving-average example, suppose we still buy shares if the current price exceeds the 15-month moving average, but we sell if the current price is less than the 5-month moving average. Is this strategy more profitable than selling when the current price is less than the 15-month moving average?

11. A European call option gives you the right to buy at a specified future date a share of stock for a given exercise price. A *butterfly spread* involves buying one call option with a low exercise price, buying one call option with a high exercise price, and selling two call options with an exercise price midway between the low and high exercise prices. Here is an example of a butterfly spread: The current stock price is $60. You buy a $54 six-month European call option for $9, buy a $66 six-month European call option for $4, and sell two $60 European call options for the price of $6. Compute the profit (in dollars, not percentage) for this transaction as a function of six-month stock prices ranging from $40–$80. When a trader purchases a butterfly spread, which type of movement in the stock price during the next six months is the trader betting on?

12. Suppose a stock is currently selling for $32. You buy a six-month European call option with an exercise price of $30 for $2.50 and sell a six-month European call option with an exercise price of $35 for $1. Compute the profit of this strategy (in dollars) as a function of a six-month stock price ranging from $25–$45. Why is this strategy called a *bull spread*? How would you modify this strategy to create a *bear spread*?

13. Let's reconsider our pro forma example. Suppose the interest rate on our debt depends on our financial well-being. More specifically, suppose that if our earnings before interest and taxes (EBIT) are negative, our interest rate on debt is 16 percent. If our interest expense is more than 10 percent of EBIT and EBIT is positive, our interest rate on debt is 13 percent. Otherwise, our interest rate is 10 percent. Modify the pro forma statement to account for this variable interest rate.

14. Do this problem independently of Problem 13. Suppose our firm wants a debt-to-equity ratio of 50 percent during each year. How would you modify the pro forma statement? Hint: You must keep each year's stock non-negative and use stock and cash or marketable securities to balance assets and liabilities.

15. Martin Luther King Day occurs on the third Monday in January. Write a formula that computes (given the year) the date of Martin Luther King Day. Hint: First determine the day of the week for January 1 of the given year.

16. Thanksgiving occurs on the fourth Thursday in November. Write a formula that computes (given the year) the date of Thanksgiving. Hint: First determine the day of the week for November 1 of the given year.

17. The first quarter of the year is January–March; the second quarter, April–June; the third quarter, July–September; and the fourth quarter, October–December. Write a formula that returns (for any given date) the quarter of the year.

18. Write a formula that returns a person's age, given his or her date of birth.

19. Labor Day is the first Monday in September. Write a formula that determines the date of Labor Day for a given year.

20. The file Nancybonds.xlsx gives the bond rating for several bonds in a previous and future month. You want to efficiently count how many bonds were downgraded. Unfortunately, each company is listed in more than one row. Assuming you have sorted the data on the company name, how would you determine the number of downgraded bonds?

21. The file Addresses.xlsx gives people's names on one line, their street address on the next line, and their city, state, and ZIP code on the following line. How could you put each person's information on one line?

22. The file FormattingDDAnum.xlsx gives a bunch of text strings, such as DDA : D in cell C4, DDA1250045 in cell C17, and so on. A cell is properly formatted if the first three characters are DDA and the last seven characters are a number 1 million or larger (with no spaces). Determine which cells are properly formatted.

23. Suppose the number of Group 1 members is listed in cell B1, the number of Group 2 members is listed in cell B2, and the number of Group 3 members is listed in cell B3. The total number of group members is always 100. Suppose that Group 1 has 50 members, Group 2 has 30 members, and Group 3 has 20 members. Efficiently place a 1 for each Group 1 member in column D, a 2 for each Group 2 member in column D, and a 3 for each Group 3 member in column D. Thus, column D should (in our example) have a 1 in D1:D50, a 2 in D51:D80 and a 3 in D81:D100.

24. The file Dividebyprice.xlsx contains units sold of each product and total revenue. Determine the average price for each product and display each average in column H. Of course, if units sold is 0, then there is no average price. Error-trap the file Dividebyprice.xlsx to ensure that all products with zero sales yield the message *No sales* instead of a #DIV!0 error.

25. The School of Fine Art has 100 lockers numbered 1–100. At present, all lockers are open. We begin by closing every locker whose number evenly divides by 3. Then we toggle (*toggling* means opening a closed locker and closing an open locker) each locker whose number is divisible by 4; then we toggle each locker whose number is divisible by 5, ...we count upwards and continue this with each number, and finally we toggle each locker whose number is divisible by 100. How many lockers are now open?

26. The file Matchlist.xlsx contains a list of people who bought your product in February and a list of people who bought it in March. Determine how many of your February customers purchased your product in March.

27. Set up a *calendar worksheet* that takes a given month and year as inputs and tells you the day of the week on which each day of the month occurs.

28. Some rows of column C of file Problem28data.xlsx contain the word *and*. Create formulas in column D that place an *X* in a row of column D if and only if column C in that row contains the word *and*.

29. Suppose you toss two 20-sided dice. The 400 possible outcomes are (1,1), (1,2),. ... (20,20). Use IF statements to systematically generate all 400 possible outcomes.

30. Using the data in the file Catsanddogs.xlsx, determine how many times the text string *cat* appears and how many times the text string *dog* occurs.

31. The file Footballdata.xlsx gives win-loss records for NFL teams during the 2015 season. Write a formula in H13 that can be copied to H14:H31 that gives the winning percentage for each team and gives no error messages.

32. At the beginning of Year 1, your auto-insurance premium for the next year is $300. If you have 0 accidents in a year your premium for the next year drops 10 percent, if you have 1 accident in a year your premium for the next year increases10 percent, and if you have 2 accidents in a year your premium for the next year increases 30 percent. Set up a spreadsheet that will determine the premium cost for Years 1–30.

33. Suppose the sales of our product depends on my price and the competitor's price as follows: If my price is at least $3 higher than the competitor's price, we sell 500 units; if my price is at least $3 lower than the competitor's price we sell 1500 units; otherwise we sell 1000 units. Assuming all prices are integers between $1 and $10 inclusively, write formulas that compute our unit sales for all possible price combinations.

34. You are to determine a company's annual revenues based on the information in cells C1:D5 of file Problem34data.xlsx. Unit sales increase at the given rate until a competitor enters; thereafter, unit sales remain constant. Each year, the product price increases by the inflation rate. Write formulas in the yellow cells that correctly determine price, unit sales, and revenue for years 1–10.

35. Cell D2 of file Problem35data.xlsx gives Year 1 Market Size. Cell D3 gives market share (the same each year), cell D4 gives product price (same each year), and D5 gives profit margin (the same each year). Cell D6 gives growth in market size during each year of growth, and D7 gives years of market growth. Write formulas that compute each year's profit and the total 10–year profit.

36. President's Day is the third Monday of February. Create a spreadsheet in which the user enters the year and the spreadsheet returns the date of President's Day.

37. You are to create formulas that return the profit made from selling a greeting card. Current information is given in cells B1:B7 of the file Problem37data.xlsx. We ordered cards at a cost of $3.50 per card. Cards sold at full-price are sold for $6. Full-price demand will be entered in cell B7. The first 40 leftover cards are sold for $2. Remaining leftover cards are sold for $0.50. Write formulas that always return the correct profit for any set of nonnegative inputs.

CHAPTER 13

Time and time functions

Questions answered in this chapter:

- How do I enter times in Excel?
- How do I enter a time and date in the same cell?
- How does Excel do computations with times?
- How can I have my worksheet always display the current time?
- How can I use the TIME function to create times?
- How can I use the TIMEVALUE function to convert a text string to a time?
- How do I extract the hour, minute, or second from a given time?
- Given work starting and ending times, how do I determine the number of hours an employee worked?
- I added up the total time an employee worked, and I never get more than 24 hours. What did I do wrong?
- How can I easily create a sequence of regularly spaced time intervals?
- How can I place a static time in a workbook?

Recall from Chapter 7, "Dates and date functions," that Microsoft Excel 2016 gives the date January 1, 1900, the serial number 1, the date January 2, 1900, the serial number 2, and so on. Excel also assigns serial numbers to times (as a fraction of a 24-hour day). The starting point is midnight, so 3:00 AM has a serial number of .125, noon has a serial number of .5, 6:00 PM has a serial number of .75, and so on. If you combine a date and time in a cell, the serial number is the number of days after January 1, 1900, plus the time fraction associated with the given time. Thus, entering January 1, 2007, in a cell yields (when formatted as General) a serial number of 39083, whereas January 1, 2007, 6:00 AM yields a serial number of 39083.25.

Answers to this chapter's questions

How do I enter times in Excel?

To indicate times, you enter a colon (:) after the hour and another colon before the seconds. For example, in file Time.xlsx (see Figure 13-1), I entered in cell C2 the time 8:30 AM as 8:30 AM. As shown in cell D2, I could also have entered 8:30 AM as simply 8:30. In cell C3, I entered 8:30 PM as 8:30 PM. As shown in cell D3, I could also have entered 8:30 PM with 24-hour military time as 20:30. In cell A4, I entered the formula =TIME(15,10,30), which yields the time 3:10:30 PM. This represents 30 seconds after 3:10 PM.

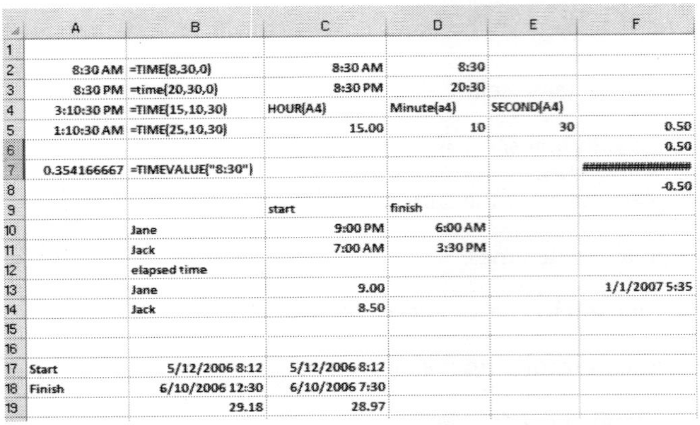

	A	B	C	D	E	F
1						
2	8:30 AM	=TIME(8,30,0)	8:30 AM	8:30		
3	8:30 PM	=time(20,30,0)	8:30 PM	20:30		
4	3:10:30 PM	=TIME(15,10,30)	HOUR(A4)	Minute(a4)	SECOND(A4)	
5	1:10:30 AM	=TIME(25,10,30)	15.00	10	30	0.50
6						0.50
7	0.354166667	=TIMEVALUE("8:30")				################
8						-0.50
9			start	finish		
10		Jane	9:00 PM	6:00 AM		
11		Jack	7:00 AM	3:30 PM		
12		elapsed time				
13		Jane	9.00			1/1/2007 5:35
14		Jack	8.50			
15						
16						
17	Start	5/12/2006 8:12	5/12/2006 8:12			
18	Finish	6/10/2006 12:30	6/10/2006 7:30			
19		29.18	28.97			

FIGURE 13-1 Examples of time formats.

How do I enter a time and date in the same cell?

Simply put a space after the date and enter the time. In cell F13 of the worksheet Sheet1 in the file Time.xlsx, I entered January 1, 2007 5:35. Of course, this represents 5:35 AM on January 1, 2007. Excel immediately reformatted this to 1/1/2007 5:35, and the Formula bar shows 1/1/2007 5:35:00 AM.

How does Excel do computations with times?

When Excel computes differences in times, the result displayed depends on the format used in the cell. Figure 13-2 displays the various Excel time formats.

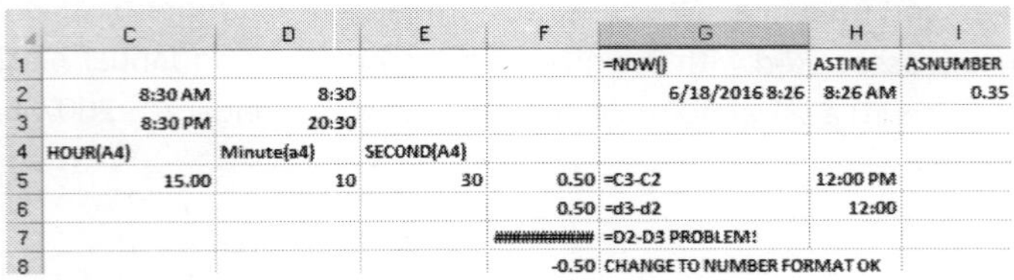

	C	D	E	F	G	H	I
1					=NOW()	ASTIME	ASNUMBER
2	8:30 AM	8:30			6/18/2016 8:26	8:26 AM	0.35
3	8:30 PM	20:30					
4	HOUR(A4)	Minute(a4)	SECOND(A4)				
5	15.00	10	30	0.50	=C3-C2	12:00 PM	
6				0.50	=d3-d2	12:00	
7				###########	=D2-D3 PROBLEM!		
8				-0.50	CHANGE TO NUMBER FORMAT OK		

FIGURE 13-2 Excel time formats.

In the file Time.xlsx (see Figure 13-2), I took the difference between 8:30 PM and 8:30 AM in cells F5 and H5 with the formula =C3–C2. If you do not change the format, Excel thinks these times are 12 hours apart and enters 12:00 PM, as shown in cell H5. In most cases, you'll want Excel to portray these times as 0.5 days apart. (Multiplying by 24, you could convert this time difference to hours.) To make Excel show 0.5 in cell F5, simply format cell F5 as a number.

In cell F7, I tried to subtract an earlier time from a later time with the formula =D2–D3. Because I did not reformat the cell, Excel displays the dreaded ##############. If you simply change the cell containing the formula to the Number format (as in cell F8), you obtain the correct time difference, –0.5 days.

Cells B17 and C17 give the start times for two jobs, whereas cells B18 and C18 give the finish times for the jobs. (See Figure 13-3.) If you want to calculate how many hours it takes to complete each job, simply copy from B19 to C19 the formula =B18–B17 and reformat the cell as Number. Thus, the first job took 29.18 days, and the second job took 28.97 days.

	A	B	C
17	Start	5/12/2006 8:12	5/12/2006 8:12
18	Finish	6/10/2006 12:30	6/10/2006 7:30
19		29.18	28.97

FIGURE 13-3 Determining the time needed to complete jobs.

How can I have my worksheet always display the current time?

The Excel formula =NOW() gives today's date and the current time. For example, in cell G2 (see Figure 13-4) of the file Time.xlsx, entering =NOW() yields 6/18/2016 8:28 because I created the screen capture at 8:28 AM on June 18, 2016. (Note that if you edit the file Time.xlsx, cell G2 will yield your current date and time.) To compute the current time, you can also enter in cell H2 or I2 the formula =NOW()–TODAY(). Cell H2 is formatted to show a time (8:28 AM), whereas cell I2 is formatted to show a number (such as 0.35 days). This represents the fact that 8:28 AM is 35 percent of the way between midnight of one day and midnight of the next day.

	G	H	I
1	=NOW()	ASTIME	ASNUMBER
2	6/18/2016 8:28	8:28 AM	0.35

FIGURE 13-4 Using the Now() and Today() functions.

How can I use the TIME function to create times?

The TIME function has the syntax TIME(hour,minute,second). Given numbers for hour, minute, and second, the TIME function returns a time of day. The TIME function never returns a value exceeding 24 hours.

In cell A2 (see Figure 13-1), the formula =TIME(8,30,0) yields 8:30 AM. In cell A3, the formula =TIME(20,30,0) yields 8:30 PM. In cell A4, the formula =TIME(15,10,30) yields 3:10:30 PM. Finally, note that in cell A5 the formula =TIME(25,10,30) treats the 25 as if it were 25–24=1 and yields 1:10:30 AM.

Of course, if the number of seconds does not show up in a cell, just go to the Time category in the Format Cells dialog box and select a time format that displays seconds.

How can I use the TIMEVALUE function to convert a text string to a time?

The function TIMEVALUE has the syntax =TIMEVALUE(timetext), where *timetext* is a text string that shows a time in a valid format. Then TIMEVALUE returns the time as a fraction between 0 and 1. (This means that the TIMEVALUE function ignores any date in *timetext*.) For example, in cell A7 of the file Time.xlsx (see Figure 13-1), the formula =TIMEVALUE("*8:30*") yields 0.354166667 because 8:30 AM is 35.4 percent of the way between midnight of one day and midnight of the next day.

How do I extract the hour, minute, or second from a given time?

The Excel HOUR, MINUTE, and SECOND functions extract the appropriate time unit from a cell containing time. For example, (as shown in Figure 13-1), entering in cell C5 the formula =HOUR(A4) yields 15.00 (3:00 PM is 15:00 military time). Entering in cell D5 the formula =Minute(A4) yields 10, whereas entering =SECOND(A4) in cell E5 yields 30.

Given work starting and ending times, how do I determine the number of hours an employee worked?

In cells C10:D11 (see Figure 13-5), I entered the times that Jane and Jack started and ended work. We want to figure out how long each of them worked. The problem is that Jane finished work the day after she started, so simple subtraction does not give the actual number of hours she worked. Copying from C13 to C14 the formula =IF(D10>C10,(D10–C10)*24,24+(D10–C10)*24) yields the correct result. Of course, I formatted these cells as the Number type. If the finish time is after the start time, subtracting the start time from the finish time and multiplying by 24 yields the hours worked. If the finish time is before the start time, then 24*(finish time–start time) yields a negative number of hours, but adding 24 hours fixes things, assuming the end of the shift was one day later. Thus, Jane worked 9 hours and Jack worked 8.5 hours.

	B	C	D
8			
9		start	finish
10	Jane	9:00 PM	6:00 AM
11	Jack	7:00 AM	3:30 PM
12	elapsed time		
13	Jane	9.00	
14	Jack	8.50	

FIGURE 13-5 Computing the length of time worked by employees.

I added up the total time an employee worked, and I never get more than 24 hours. What did I do wrong?

In cells C31:D35 in Figure 13-6, I give the number of hours (formatted as h:mm) an employee worked on each day of her workweek. In cell D36, the formula =SUM(D31:D35) is used to compute the total number of hours worked during the week. Excel yields 14:48. This is clearly wrong! With the format h:mm, Excel never yields a value exceeding 24 hours. In cell D38, I chose a format (showing 38:48:00) that allows for more than 24 hours. Then, summing up the hours worked each day yields the correct number of hours worked (38 hours and 48 minutes).

	C	D
31	mon	9:23
32	tues	8:30
33	wed	7:20
34	thur	9:40
35	fri	3:55
36	total	14:48
37	38 hours 48 min	
38	total reformatted	38:48:00

FIGURE 13-6 Determining the total hours worked during the week.

How can I easily create a sequence of regularly spaced time intervals?

Suppose a doctor takes appointments from 8:00 AM in 20 minute segments up to 5:00 PM. How can I enter in different rows the list of possible appointment times? Simply use Excel's great AutoFill feature. (See Figure 13-7.) Enter the first two times (8:00 AM and 8:20 AM) in cells L15:L16. Now select cells L15:L16, and move the cursor to the lower-right corner of cell L16 until you see the black cross. Drag the pointer down until you see 5:00 PM (the last appointment time) in the ScreenTip. From cells L15:L16, Excel has guessed (correctly) that you want to enter times that are 20 minutes apart. Of course, entering Monday in a cell and Tuesday below and using AutoFill will yield the sequence Monday, Tuesday, Wednesday,..., eventually restarting at Monday. Entering 1/1/2007 in one cell, 2/1/2007 in another cell, selecting these two cells, and using AutoFill yields a sequence of dates, like 1/1/2007, 2/1/2007, 3/1/2007, and so on.

	L
14	sequence of times
15	8:00 AM
16	8:20 AM
17	8:40 AM
18	9:00 AM
19	9:20 AM
20	9:40 AM
21	10:00 AM
22	10:20 AM
23	10:40 AM
24	11:00 AM
25	11:20 AM
26	11:40 AM
27	12:00 PM
28	12:20 PM
29	12:40 PM
30	1:00 PM

FIGURE 13-7 Entering a sequence of times.

How do I enter a static time in a cell?

Suppose you create a workbook and want the spreadsheet to always list the exact time that you created the spreadsheet. Simply go to a blank cell and use the keystroke sequence **Ctrl+Shift+;** (the semicolon key) and you will always see the time the spreadsheet was created. For example, as shown in Figure 13-8, you can see that the worksheet was created at 8:45 AM.

	D	E
3		
4		
5		8:45 AM

FIGURE 13-8 Inserting a static time in a cell.

Problems

1. Write a formula that will return a time 18 hours after the current time.
2. The file Marathon.xlsx gives marathon race times for four runners. Problems **a** through **c** refer to this data. Compute the average time of the runners.
   - **a.** How much faster was John than Jill?
   - **b.** How many total minutes did each runner take?
   - **c.** How many total seconds did each runner take?
3. The file Jobshop.xlsx gives the start time and date for several jobs and the time required to complete each job. Determine the completion time for each job.

CHAPTER 14

The Paste Special command

Questions answered in this chapter:

- How can I move the results of calculations (not the formulas) to a different part of a worksheet?
- I have a list of names in a column. How can I make the list appear in a row instead of a column?
- I've downloaded US T-bill interest rates from a website into Excel. The data displays 5 when the interest rate is 5 percent, 8 when the interest rate is 8 percent, and so on. How can I easily divide my results by 100 so that a 5 percent interest rate, for example, is displayed as 0.05?

With the Paste Special command in Microsoft Excel 2016, you can easily manipulate worksheet data. In this chapter, I'll show how you can use the Paste Special command to perform the following types of operations:

- Paste only the values in cells (not the formulas) to a different part of a worksheet.
- Transpose data in columns to rows and vice versa.
- Transform a range of numbers by adding, subtracting, dividing, or multiplying each number in the range by a given constant.

Answers to this chapter's questions

How can I move the results of calculations (not the formulas) to a different part of a worksheet?

In the Paste Special Value worksheet in the file Pastespecial.xlsx, the cell range E4:H9 contains the names, games, total points, and points per game for five 10–11-year-old basketball players from Bloomington, Indiana. In the cell range H5:H9, I used the data in cells F5:G9 to compute each child's points per game, as shown in Figure 14-1.

	E	F	G	H
4		Games	Points	Points/game
5	Dan	4	28	7.00
6	Gabe	4	28	7.00
7	Gregory	5	35	7.00
8	Christian	6	22	3.67
9	Max	6	15	2.50
10				
11				
12				
13		Games	Points	Points/game
14	Dan	4	28	7
15	Gabe	4	28	7
16	Gregory	5	35	7
17	Christian	6	22	3.66666667
18	Max	6	15	2.5

FIGURE 14-1 Using the Paste Special command to paste only values.

Suppose you want to copy this data and the calculated points per game—but not the formulas that perform the calculations—to a different cell range (E13:H18, for example). All you do is select the range E4:H9, press Ctrl+C, and then move to the upper-left corner of the range where you want to copy the data (cell E13 in this example). Next, right-click the upper-left corner cell in the target range, click Paste Special, and then fill in the Paste Special dialog box, selecting Values from the Paste section, as indicated in Figure 14-2. After you click OK, the range E13:H18 contains the data but not the formulas from the cell range E4:H9. You can check this by going to cell H16. You will see a value (7) but not the formula that was used to compute Gregory's average points per game. Note that if you use the Paste Special command, select Values, and then paste the data into the same range from which you copied the data, your formulas disappear from the worksheet.

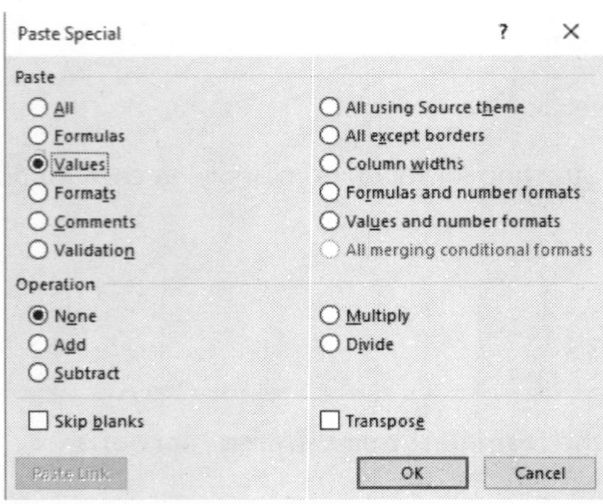

FIGURE 14-2 The Paste Special dialog box with Values selected. Selecting Values pastes only values and not any formulas.

I have a list of names in a column. How can I make the list appear in a row instead of a column?

To realign data from a row to a column (or vice versa), copy the data and then use the Paste Special command with Transpose selected. The Transpose option in the Paste Special dialog box essentially flips selected cells around so that the first row of the copied range becomes the first column of the range you paste data into, and vice versa. For an example, look at the Paste Special Transpose worksheet in the file Pastespecial.xlsx, shown in Figure 14-3.

Suppose that you want to list the players' names in one row (starting in cell E13). Simply select the range E5:E9, and then press Ctrl+C to copy the data. Right-click cell E13, click Paste Special, and select the Transpose option in the bottom section of the Paste Special dialog box. After you click OK, Excel transposes the players' names into one row.

	E	F	G	H	I	J
3						
4		Games	Points	Points/game		
5	Dan	4	28	7.00		
6	Gabe	4	28	7.00		
7	Gregory	5	35	7.00		
8	Christian	6	22	3.67		
9	Max	6	15	2.50		
10						
11						
12						
13	Dan	Gabe	Gregory	Christian	Max	
14						
15						
16						
17		Dan	Gabe	Gregory	Christian	Max
18	Games	4	4	5	6	6
19	Points	28	28	35	22	15
20	Points/game	7.00	7.00	7.00	3.67	2.50

FIGURE 14-3 Use the Transpose option in the Paste Special dialog box to transpose a row of data into a column or a column of data into a row.

Suppose you want to transpose the spreadsheet content in E4:H9 to a range beginning in cell E17. Begin by selecting the range E4:H9. Next, press Ctrl+C. Now move to the upper-left corner of the range where you want to put the transposed information (E17). Right-click and choose Paste Special, select Transpose, and then click OK. You'll see that the content of E4:H9 is transposed (turned on its side), as shown in Figure 14-3. Note that in F20:J20, Excel was smart enough to adjust the points-per-game formula so that the average for each player is now computed from data in the same column instead of the same row.

> **Note** When you select Paste Special and click Paste Link (in the lower left of the dialog box) instead of OK, the transposed cells are linked to the original cells, and changes you make to the original data are reflected in the copy. By changing the value in cell F5 to 7, the value in cell F18 becomes 7 as well, and cell F20 would display Dan's average as 4 points per game.

I've downloaded US T-bill interest rates from a website into Excel. The data displays 5 when the interest rate is 5 percent, 8 when the interest rate is 8 percent, and so on. How can I easily divide my results by 100 so that a 5 percent interest rate, for example, is displayed as 0.05?

The Paste Special Divide Before worksheet in the file Pastespecial.xlsx (see Figure 14-4) contains the annual rate of interest paid by three-month US T-bills for each month between January 1970 and February 1987. In January 1970, the annual rate on a three-month T-bill was 8.01 percent. Suppose you want to earn annual interest on $1 invested at the current T-bill rate. The formula to calculate the rate is (1+(annual rate)/100). It would be easier to compute earned interest if the column of annual interest rates were divided by 100.

	C	D	E
5			
6			
7			
8			
9	date	3mo	
10	1.1970	8.01	
11	2.1970	7.01	
12	3.1970	6.48	
13	4.1970	7.03	
14	5.1970	7.04	
15	6.1970	6.52	
16	7.1970	6.43	
17	8.1970	6.38	
18	9.1970	6.03	
19	10.1970	5.96	
20	11.1970	5.07	
21	12.1970	4.9	
22	1.1971	4.17	
23	2.1971	3.43	
24	3.1971	3.64	

FIGURE 14-4 Data for using the Divide option in the Paste Special dialog box to divide a data range by a constant.

The Operations area of the Paste Special dialog box lets you add, subtract, multiply, or divide each number in a range by a given number, providing an easy way to divide each interest rate by 100. Here we want to divide each number in column D. To begin, I enter our divisor (100). You can enter it anywhere in the worksheet. I chose F5. (See Figure 14-6.) With F5 selected, press Ctrl+C. You will see the "moving ants" animation surrounding cell F5. Next, select the range of numbers you want to modify. To select all the data in column D, click in cell D10 and press Ctrl+Shift and then the Down arrow key. This shortcut is a useful trick for selecting a "tall" cell range. (To select a "wide" set of data listed in one row, move to the first data point and then press Ctrl+Shift and the Right arrow key.) Next, right-click and choose Paste Special, and then select Divide in the Operation section of the Paste Special dialog box, as shown in Figure 14-5.

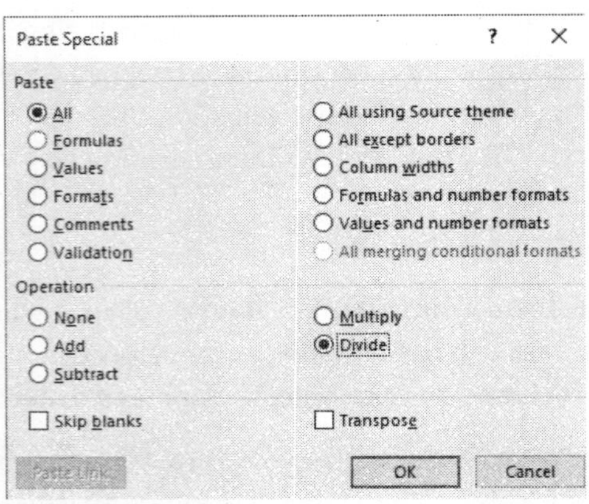

FIGURE 14-5 You can apply an option in the Operation area of the Paste Special dialog box to a range of cells.

After you click OK, Excel divides each selected number in column D by 100. The results are shown in Figure 14-6. If you had selected Add, D10 would display 108.01; if you had selected Subtract, D10 would display –91.99; and if you had selected Multiply, D10 would display 801.

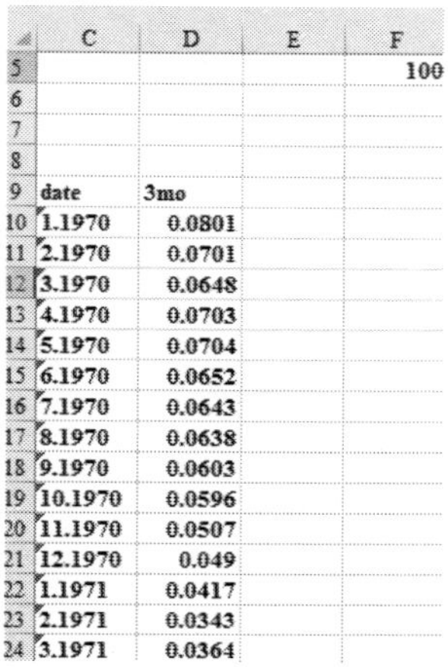

	C	D	E	F
5				100
6				
7				
8				
9	date	3mo		
10	1.1970	0.0801		
11	2.1970	0.0701		
12	3.1970	0.0648		
13	4.1970	0.0703		
14	5.1970	0.0704		
15	6.1970	0.0652		
16	7.1970	0.0643		
17	8.1970	0.0638		
18	9.1970	0.0603		
19	10.1970	0.0596		
20	11.1970	0.0507		
21	12.1970	0.049		
22	1.1971	0.0417		
23	2.1971	0.0343		
24	3.1971	0.0364		

FIGURE 14-6 Results of using the Divide option in the Paste Special dialog box.

Problems

1. The file Mavs.xlsx contains statistics for the great 2002–2003 Dallas Mavericks basketball team. Player names are listed in column A, statistical categories are listed in row 3, and statistical results are listed in rows 4–20. Change the worksheet so that all player names are listed in the same row and all statistical categories are listed in the same column.

2. Field-goal percentage, free-throw percentage, and three-point percentage are listed as decimals. For example, Steve Nash made 91.9 percent of his free throws, which is listed as 0.919. Change the worksheet so that all shooting percentages are listed as numbers, from 1 through 100.

3. The file Productpaste.xlsx contains data on quarterly sales for four products. Copy this data to another range so that quarterly sales are read across instead of down. Link your copied data to the original data so that your computation of annual sales in the copied data range will reflect changes entered in rows 5–8.

4. The file Productsalespaste.xlsx contains sales of Products X, Y, and Z (in thousands of units). Convert this sales data to sales in actual units. Hint: Remember you can use the Ctrl key (as explained in Chapter 2, "Range names") to select a noncontiguous range of cells.

CHAPTER 15

Three-dimensional formulas and hyperlinks

Questions answered in this chapter:

- Is there an easy way to set up a multiple-worksheet workbook in which each worksheet has a similar structure? Can I easily create formulas that involve cells in multiple worksheets?
- I have a 200-worksheet workbook. How can I easily navigate between worksheets?

In this chapter, you will learn how to set up workbooks in which the individual worksheets have a similar structure. In this chapter, I also discuss three-dimensional formulas, which allow you to easily write formulas to perform calculations on cells in multiple worksheets. And I show how hyperlinks can be used to easily navigate between worksheets in a multiple-worksheet workbook.

Answers to this chapter's questions

Is there an easy way to set up a multiple-worksheet workbook in which each worksheet has a similar structure? Can I easily create formulas that involve cells in multiple worksheets?

Let's suppose you want to set up a workbook that contains a separate worksheet to track sales in each region (East, South, Midwest, and West) of the United States. You also want to summarize total sales in a summary worksheet. In each worksheet, you want to track your product's price, unit cost, and units sold, as well as your fixed cost and profits. In the summary worksheet, you want to track just total profit and units sold. You want your individual region worksheets to look like Figure 15-1.

	A	B	C	D
1	East			
2				
3		Price	10	
4		Unit cost	5	
5		Units sold	35	
6		Fixed cost	100	
7		Profit	75	

FIGURE 15-1 Sales in the East region.

To set up this structure, you enter in cell C3 of each worksheet the product price, in cell C4 the unit cost, in cell C5 the units sold, and in cell C6 the fixed cost. Then, in cell C7, you would compute the

East region profit with the formula =(C3-C4)*C5-C6. Of course, you want the same structure in the worksheets for the other regions. It turns out you need to enter the headings and formula in only one worksheet, and then Excel will automatically copy them to the other region's worksheets.

To begin, open a blank workbook, which by default contains one worksheet. By clicking the New Sheet icon (the plus sign) to the right of the last-named worksheet (or by pressing Shift+F11), insert four new worksheets so that your workbook contains five worksheets. Name the first four worksheets East, South, Midwest, and West. Name the last worksheet Summary. All sales will be totaled in the Summary worksheet. (By the way, if you select Options on the File tab, on the General page of the Excel Options dialog box, you can change the number of worksheets included in a workbook by default by changing the value in the Include This Many Sheets box in the When Creating New Workbooks section.)

To set up the regional worksheets, select the first worksheet (East) and then hold down the Shift key and select the last regional worksheet (West). Now, whatever you enter in the East worksheet is duplicated in the other regional worksheets. Simply type Price in cell B3, Unit Cost in cell B4, Units Sold in cell B5, Fixed Cost in cell B6, and Profit in cell B7. Finally, enter the formula =(C3-C4)*C5-C6 in cell C7. Next, click the last sheet to leave this data entry procedure, and then click the other worksheets. You will see that each regional worksheet has the same headings in column B and the correct profit formula in cell C7.

You are now ready to use three-dimensional formulas to compute total units sold and profit. In cell C5, you will compute total units sold. Remember that you entered units sold in each region's worksheet in cell C5. Move your cursor to cell C5 in the Summary worksheet, where you want to compute total units sold. Type **=SUM(** and then move your cursor to the first cell you want to total (cell C5 of sheet East). Next, hold down the Shift key and click the last cell you want to total (cell C5 of worksheet West). Last, enter a right parentheses in the Formula bar (in the West worksheet), and you will see entered in cell C5 of the Summary sheet the formula SUM(East:West!C5). This formula is an example of a three-dimensional formula. Most Excel formulas operate in two dimensions (rows and columns.) A three-dimensional formula operates in a third dimension: across worksheets. This formula tells Excel to sum cell C5 in all worksheets, starting with the East worksheet and ending with the West worksheet. Of course, if you wanted to, you could have simply typed this formula in cell C5 of the Summary worksheet. Copy this formula from cell C5 and paste it to cell C7 of the Summary worksheet to compute our company's total profit. (See Figure 15-2.) As you can imagine, next you would enter the labels in the Summary worksheet and the values in each region's worksheet.

	A	B	C
1	Summary		
2			
3			
4			
5		Units Sold	150
6			
7		Profit	350

FIGURE 15-2 Summarizing unit sales and profit.

In the following chapters, you will learn about four other methods that can be used to summarize data from multiple worksheets or workbooks:

- Chapter 43, "Using PivotTables and slicers to describe data"
- Chapter 44, "The Data Model"
- Chapter 45, "Power Pivot"
- Chapter 50, "Consolidating data"

I have a 200-worksheet workbook. How can I easily navigate between worksheets?

One easy way to navigate between worksheets is to use hyperlinks. The workbook Hyperlinktemp.xlsx (in this chapter's Template folder) contains five worksheets. Wouldn't it be nice to place a clickable link in the first worksheet that would send you to cell A1 of each worksheet? To create a link to the International worksheet in cell A10 of the first worksheet, simply put your cursor in cell A10 and select Insert, Hyperlink (or press Ctrl+K). Then fill in the dialog box as shown in Figure 15-3.

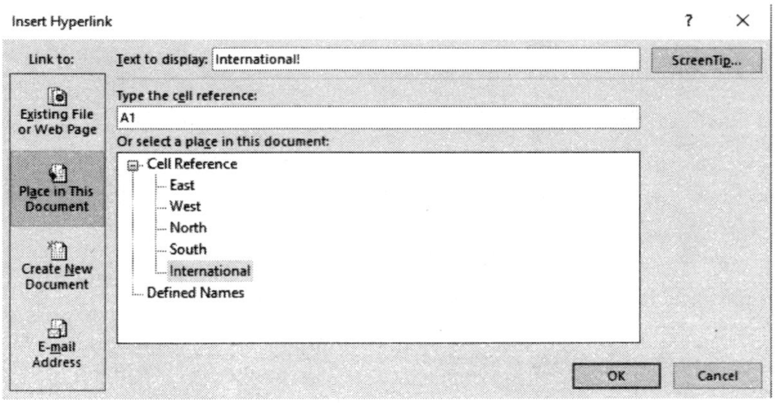

FIGURE 15-3 How to create a hyperlink.

When we click the International hyperlink in cell A10 (see Figure 15-4), we are immediately sent to cell A1 of worksheet International. In a similar fashion, we created links to cell A1 of the other worksheets. (See the file Hyperlinks.xlsx and Figure 15-4.) Note you can also easily create a hyperlink to a webpage, a location in another existing file, or an email address.

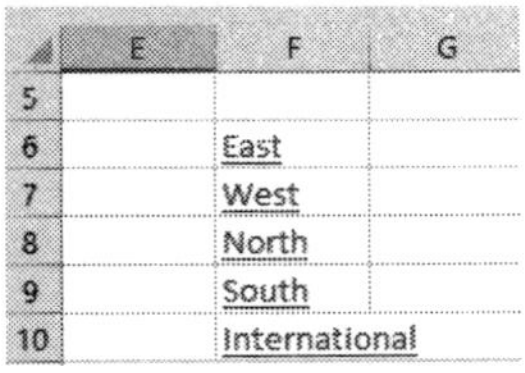

FIGURE 15-4 Hyperlinks provide a clickable link to other worksheets.

Here are several other methods that can help you navigate multiple-worksheet workbooks:

- Ctrl+Page Down takes you to the next worksheet in the workbook while Ctrl+Page Up takes you to the previous worksheet.
- If you right-click on the arrows in the lower-left side of the screen, you will see a list of worksheets in the current workbook, as shown in Figure 15-5. You can click any worksheet to go to that worksheet.
- Suppose your workbook contains many worksheets (see the file Multipleworksheetstemp.xlsx). If you are near the first worksheet and you hover over the arrows to the left of the tab for the first worksheet, then pressing Ctrl+left click sends you to the last worksheet. If you are near the last worksheet and you hover over the arrows to the left of the tab for the first worksheet, then Ctrl+left click sends you to the first worksheet in the workbook.

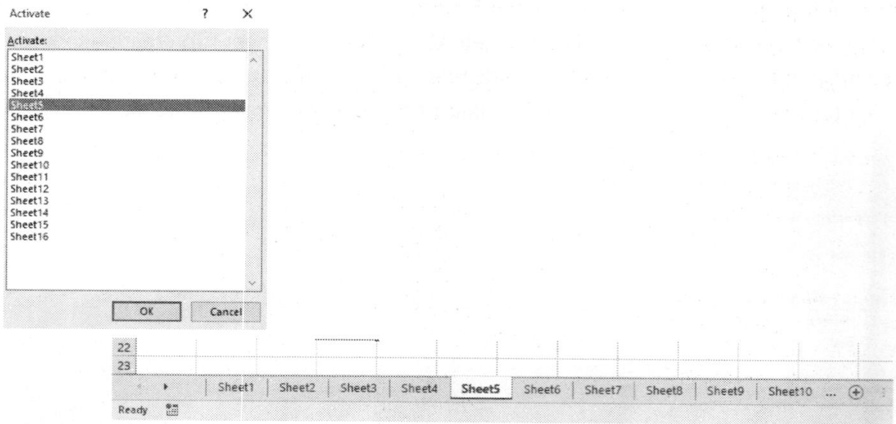

FIGURE 15-5 Right-click the arrows to find a list of worksheets.

Problems

1. You own six local coffee shops. The revenues and customer count for each coffee shop are given in the following table.

Shop	Revenues	Customer Count
1	$8,000	1,950
2	$7,000	1,800
3	$9,000	2,200
4	$8,400	2,000
5	$5,900	1,400
6	$10,100	2,500

Set up a workbook that makes it easy to enter revenue and customer count for each store, and then create a summary worksheet (using three-dimensional formulas) that computes the total weekly revenue and customer count.

2. Place hyperlinks in the file Multipleworksheetstemp.xlsx to cell A5 in worksheets Sheet 3, Sheet 5, and Sheet 7, as well as to the website Officeblog.com.

CHAPTER 16

The auditing tool

Questions answered in this chapter:

- I've just been handed a 5,000–row worksheet that computes the net present value (NPV) of a new car. In the worksheet, my financial analyst made an assumption about the annual percentage of the growth in the product's price. Which cells in the worksheet are affected by this assumption?
- I think my financial analyst made an error computing Year 1 before-tax profit. Which cells in the worksheet model were used for this calculation?
- How does the auditing tool work when I'm working with data in more than one worksheet or workbook?

When we hear the word *structure*, we often think about the structure of a building. The structure of a worksheet model refers to the way input assumptions (data such as unit sales, price, and unit cost) are used to compute outputs of interest, such as NPV, profit, or cost. The Microsoft Excel 2016 auditing tool provides an easy method for documenting the structure of a worksheet, which makes understanding the logic underlying complex worksheet models easier.

To view the auditing options in Excel, display the Formulas tab on the ribbon, and then view the Formula Auditing group, shown in Figure 16-1) In this chapter, I discuss most of these commands. I discuss the Evaluate Formula command in Chapter 22, "The OFFSET function."

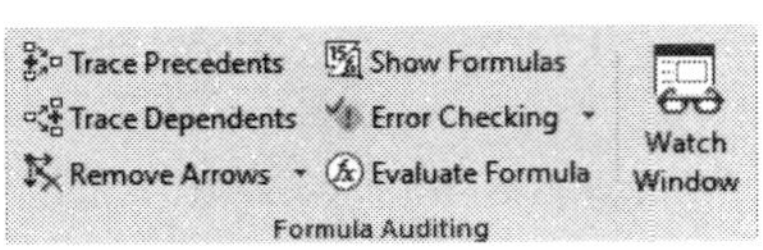

FIGURE 16-1 The Formula Auditing group on the ribbon.

Clicking Show Formulas serves as a switch that toggles the display of formulas in cells and the display of the values that result from the formulas. You can also press Ctrl+~ to toggle between showing formulas in cells and showing the formulas' results. Formulas can also be shown in a spreadsheet by using the FORMULATEXT function, which was introduced in Excel 2013. The file ISFORMULATEXT.xlsx (see Figure 16-2) illustrates the use of this function.

	A	B	C	D	E
3	x	y	Column A ISFORMULA?	Column B ISFORMULA?	FORMULATEXT
4	1	5	FALSE	TRUE	=5*A4
5	2	10	FALSE	TRUE	=5*A5
6	3	15	FALSE	TRUE	=5*A6

FIGURE 16-2 Using the ISFORMULA and FORMULATEXT functions.

In column A, we entered the numbers 1, 2, and 3. In column B, we multiplied these numbers by 5. Copying from E4 to E5:E6 the formula =FORMULATEXT(B4) results in the formulas from column B appearing in column E.

Columns C and D illustrate the use of another Excel function, ISFORMULA (added in Excel 2013). This function returns True if a cell contains a formula and False otherwise. Copying the formula =ISFORMULA(A4) from C4 to C4:D6, we see that column B contains formulas and column A does not.

The Error Checking option in the Formula Auditing group allows you to check your worksheet for errors and gives you help fixing the errors. To illustrate how Excel's Error Checking capability works, let's look again at the file Errortrap.xlsx (see Figure 16-3), which you first encountered in Chapter 12, "IF statements." (The file Errortrap.xlsx is also available in the Chapter 16 Practice Files folder, but it is an identical file.)

	C	D	E	F	G
1					
2			salary		
3		Jane	40		
4		Jack	60		
5		Jill	70		
6		Erica	34		
7		Adam	120		
8					
9					
10		Name	Salary	errortrapped	
11		Erica	34	34	
12		Adam	120	120	
13		JR	#N/A		
14		Josh	#N/A		
15		Jill	70	70	
16		average	#N/A	74.66667	
17					
18	aggregate		74.66667		
19	function				
20	works!				

FIGURE 16-3 Tracing errors.

In cell E13, you can click the Error icon's drop-down arrow to open a menu for that error. Or, in the Formula Auditing group, you can click the Error Checking drop-down arrow to display three options: Error Checking, Trace Error, and Circular References. (Our workbook contains no circular references, so the Circular References option is not available. If the workbook contained any circular references, Excel would highlight them.) If you select Error Checking, Excel will move to the first cell it finds with an error (the first error found is in cell E13), and the dialog box shown in Figure 16-4 appears. Clicking the Help On This Error option leads you to further information about the error. Show Calculation Steps allows you to step through the calculation of the formula. Ignore Error closes the dialog box. Edit In Formula Bar allows you to edit the formula. Selecting the Previous button will return you to the previously found error; Next sends you to the dialog box for the next error.

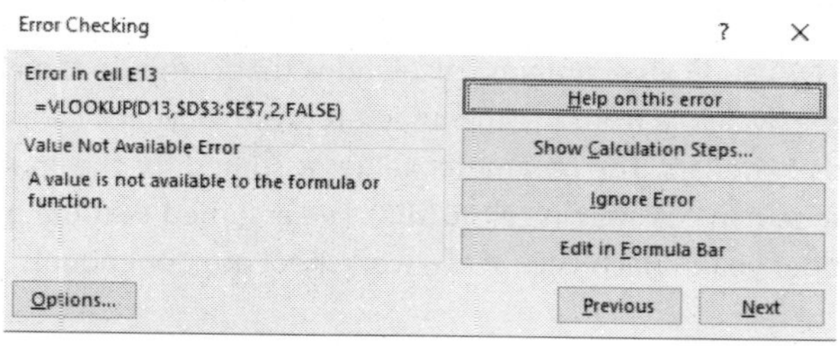

FIGURE 16-4 The Error Checking dialog box.

When you select Trace Error from the Error Checking options, if the active cell contains an error, the cells needed to compute the active cell are indicated by blue arrows or a blue rectangle. For example, back in Figure 16-3 we see that cell D13 and the cell range D3:E7 are needed to compute cell E13. (This cell generated an #N/A error.)

By opening the Watch window in the Formula Auditing group, you can select a cell or cells and then, no matter where you are in the workbook, you will see how the values of the selected cells change. For example, after selecting Watch Window, you can click Add Watch and add a formula (say to cell C3 in Sheet1) to watch one or more cells. Now, even if you are working in a different workbook, the Watch window shows you how cell C3 of Sheet1 changes.

In the Formula Auditing group, the Trace Precedents and Trace Dependents buttons locate and display precedents and dependents for worksheet cells or formulas. A *precedent* is any cell whose value is needed to compute a selected formula's value. For example, if you were analyzing a direct mail campaign, you would make assumptions about the number of letters mailed and the response rate for the mailing. Then you could compute the number of responses as response rate*letters mailed. In this case, the response rate and total letters mailed are precedents of the cell containing the formula used to compute total responses. A *dependent* is any cell containing a formula whose values can't be computed without knowledge of a selected cell. In the previous example, the cell containing the total number of responses is a dependent of the cell containing the response rate. Excel marks precedents and dependents with blue arrows when you use these formula-auditing tools. The Remove Arrows button in the Formula Auditing group clears the display of the arrows.

Now let's apply the formula-auditing tools to some practical problems.

Answers to this chapter's questions

I've just been handed a 5,000–row worksheet that computes the net present value (NPV) of a new car. In the worksheet, my financial analyst made an assumption about the annual percentage of the growth in the product's price. Which cells in the worksheet are affected by this assumption?

The Original Model worksheet in the file NPVaudit.xlsx contains calculations that compute the NPV of after-tax profits for a car expected to be available from the manufacturer for five years. (See Figure 16-5.) The price and cost are in thousands of dollars. The parameter values assumed for the analysis are given in cells C1:C8 (with assigned range names listed in cells B1:B8). I've assumed that the price of the product will increase by 3 percent per year. Which cells in the worksheet are dependents of this assumption?

	A	B	C	D	E	F
1		taxrate	0.4			
2		Year1sales	10000			
3		Sales growth	0.1			
4		Year1price	$ 9.00			
5		Year1cost	$ 6.00			
6		intrate	0.15			
7		costgrowth	0.05			
8		pricegrowth	0.03			
9	Year	1	2	3	4	5
10	Unit Sales	10000	11000	12100	13310	14641
11	unit price	$ 9.00	$ 9.27	$ 9.55	$ 9.83	$ 10.13
12	unit cost	$ 6.00	$ 6.30	$ 6.62	$ 6.95	$ 7.29
13	Revenues	$ 90,000.00	$ 101,970.00	$115,532.01	$ 130,897.77	$ 148,307.17
14	Costs	$ 60,000.00	$ 69,300.00	$ 80,041.50	$ 92,447.93	$ 106,777.36
15	Before Tax Profit	$ 30,000.00	$ 32,670.00	$ 35,490.51	$ 38,449.83	$ 41,529.81
16	Tax paid	$ 12,000.00	$ 13,068.00	$ 14,196.20	$ 15,379.93	$ 16,611.92
17	Aftertax Profits	$ 18,000.00	$ 19,602.00	$ 21,294.31	$ 23,069.90	$ 24,917.89
18						
19	NPV	$70,054.34				

FIGURE 16-5 You can use the formula-auditing tools to trace formulas in complex spreadsheets.

To answer this question, select cell C8 (the cell containing the assumption of 3 percent price growth), and then click the Trace Dependents button in the Formula Auditing group on the Formulas tab. Excel displays the set of arrows shown in Figure 16-6, pointing to the direct dependents of cell C8.

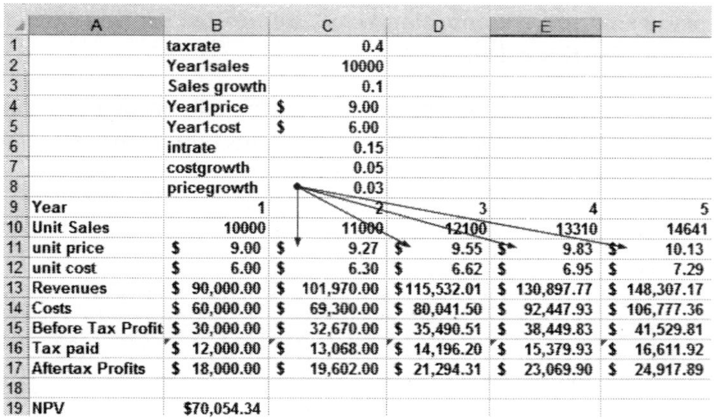

	A	B	C	D	E	F
1		taxrate	0.4			
2		Year1sales	10000			
3		Sales growth	0.1			
4		Year1price	$ 9.00			
5		Year1cost	$ 6.00			
6		intrate	0.15			
7		costgrowth	0.05			
8		pricegrowth	0.03			
9	Year	1	2	3	4	5
10	Unit Sales	10000	11000	12100	13310	14641
11	unit price	$ 9.00	$ 9.27	$ 9.55	$ 9.83	$ 10.13
12	unit cost	$ 6.00	$ 6.30	$ 6.62	$ 6.95	$ 7.29
13	Revenues	$ 90,000.00	$ 101,970.00	$115,532.01	$ 130,897.77	$ 148,307.17
14	Costs	$ 60,000.00	$ 69,300.00	$ 80,041.50	$ 92,447.93	$ 106,777.36
15	Before Tax Profit	$ 30,000.00	$ 32,670.00	$ 35,490.51	$ 38,449.83	$ 41,529.81
16	Tax paid	$ 12,000.00	$ 13,068.00	$ 14,196.20	$ 15,379.93	$ 16,611.92
17	Aftertax Profits	$ 18,000.00	$ 19,602.00	$ 21,294.31	$ 23,069.90	$ 24,917.89
18						
19	NPV	$70,054.34				

FIGURE 16-6 Tracing direct dependent cells.

When you click the Trace Dependents button once, Excel points to the cells that directly depend on the price growth assumption. In Figure 16-6, you can see that only the unit prices for Years 2–5 depend directly on this assumption. Clicking Trace Dependents repeatedly shows all the formulas whose calculations require the value for annual price growth, as shown in Figure 16-7.

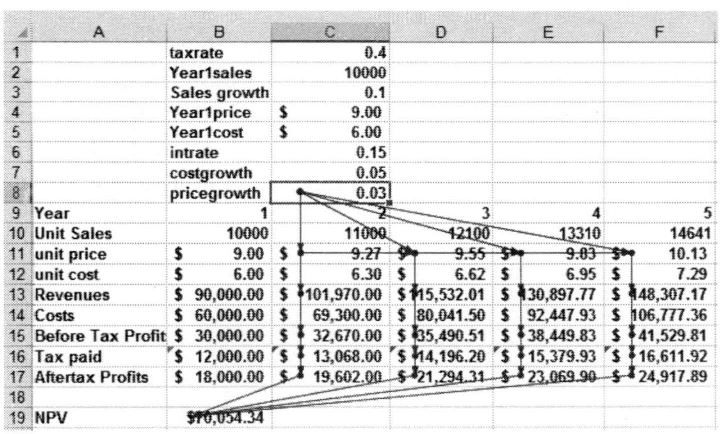

	A	B	C	D	E	F
1		taxrate	0.4			
2		Year1sales	10000			
3		Sales growth	0.1			
4		Year1price	$ 9.00			
5		Year1cost	$ 6.00			
6		intrate	0.15			
7		costgrowth	0.05			
8		pricegrowth	0.03			
9	Year	1	2	3	4	5
10	Unit Sales	10000	11000	12100	13310	14641
11	unit price	$ 9.00	$ 9.27	$ 9.55	$ 9.83	$ 10.13
12	unit cost	$ 6.00	$ 6.30	$ 6.62	$ 6.95	$ 7.29
13	Revenues	$ 90,000.00	$ 101,970.00	$ 115,532.01	$ 130,897.77	$ 148,307.17
14	Costs	$ 60,000.00	$ 69,300.00	$ 80,041.50	$ 92,447.93	$ 106,777.36
15	Before Tax Profit	$ 30,000.00	$ 32,670.00	$ 35,490.51	$ 38,449.83	$ 41,529.81
16	Tax paid	$ 12,000.00	$ 13,068.00	$ 14,196.20	$ 15,379.93	$ 16,611.92
17	Aftertax Profits	$ 18,000.00	$ 19,602.00	$ 21,294.31	$ 23,069.90	$ 24,917.89
18						
19	NPV	$70,054.34				

FIGURE 16-7 Clicking Trace Dependents repeatedly shows all the dependents of the price growth assumption.

You can see that in addition to unit price in Years 2–5, the price growth assumption affects the Years 2–5 revenue, before-tax profits, tax paid, after-tax profits, and NPV. You can remove the arrows by clicking the Remove Arrows button.

The keystroke combination Ctrl+] highlights all the direct dependents of the active cell, while the keystroke combination Ctrl+Shift+] highlights all the dependents of the active cell.

I think my financial analyst made an error in computing Year 1 before-tax profit. Which cells in the worksheet model were used for this calculation?

Now we want to find the precedents for cell B15. These precedents are the cells needed to compute Year 1 before-tax profit. Select cell B15, and then click the Trace Precedents button once. You'll see the arrows shown in Figure 16-8.

	A	B	C	D	E	F
1		taxrate	0.4			
2		Year1sales	10000			
3		Sales growth	0.1			
4		Year1price	$ 9.00			
5		Year1cost	$ 6.00			
6		intrate	0.15			
7		costgrowth	0.05			
8		pricegrowth	0.03			
9	Year	1	2	3	4	5
10	Unit Sales	10000	11000	12100	13310	14641
11	unit price	$ 9.00	$ 9.27	$ 9.55	$ 9.83	$ 10.13
12	unit cost	$ 6.00	$ 6.30	$ 6.62	$ 6.95	$ 7.29
13	Revenues	$ 90,000.00	$ 101,970.00	$115,532.01	$ 130,897.77	$ 148,307.17
14	Costs	$ 60,000.00	$ 69,300.00	$ 80,041.50	$ 92,447.93	$ 106,777.36
15	Before Tax Profit	$ 30,000.00	$ 32,670.00	$ 35,490.51	$ 38,449.83	$ 41,529.81
16	Tax paid	$ 12,000.00	$ 13,068.00	$ 14,196.20	$ 15,379.93	$ 16,611.92
17	Aftertax Profits	$ 18,000.00	$ 19,602.00	$ 21,294.31	$ 23,069.90	$ 24,917.89
18						
19	NPV	$70,054.34				

FIGURE 16-8 Direct precedents for Year 1 before-tax profit.

As you can see, the cells directly needed to compute before-tax Year 1 profit are Year 1 revenues and Year 1 cost. (Before-tax Year 1 profit equals Year 1 revenue minus Year 1 cost.) Repeatedly clicking the Trace Precedents button yields all the precedents of Year 1 before-tax profit, as shown in Figure 16-9. Here, the only input assumptions that influence the Year 1 before-tax profit are the Year 1 sales, Year 1 price, and Year 1 cost.

	A	B	C	D	E	F
1		taxrate	0.4			
2		Year1sales	10000			
3		Sales growth	0.1			
4		Year1price	$ 9.00			
5		Year1cost	$ 6.00			
6		intrate	0.15			
7		costgrowth	0.05			
8		pricegrowth	0.03			
9	Year	1	2	3	4	5
10	Unit Sales	10000	11000	12100	13310	14641
11	unit price	$ 9.00	$ 9.27	$ 9.55	$ 9.83	$ 10.13
12	unit cost	$ 6.00	$ 6.30	$ 6.62	$ 6.95	$ 7.29
13	Revenues	$ 90,000.00	$ 101,970.00	$115,532.01	$ 130,897.77	$ 148,307.17
14	Costs	$ 60,000.00	$ 69,300.00	$ 80,041.50	$ 92,447.93	$ 106,777.36
15	Before Tax Profit	$ 30,000.00	$ 32,670.00	$ 35,490.51	$ 38,449.83	$ 41,529.81
16	Tax paid	$ 12,000.00	$ 13,068.00	$ 14,196.20	$ 15,379.93	$ 16,611.92
17	Aftertax Profits	$ 18,000.00	$ 19,602.00	$ 21,294.31	$ 23,069.90	$ 24,917.89
18						
19	NPV	$70,054.34				

FIGURE 16-9 Click Trace Precedents repeatedly to show all the precedents of Year 1 before-tax profit.

How does the auditing tool work when I'm working with data in more than one worksheet or workbook?

Consider the simple worksheet model in the workbook Audittwosheets.xlsx, shown in Figure 16-10. The formula in the Profit worksheet computes a company's profit (unit sales*(price–variable cost)–fixed cost) from information contained in the Data worksheet.

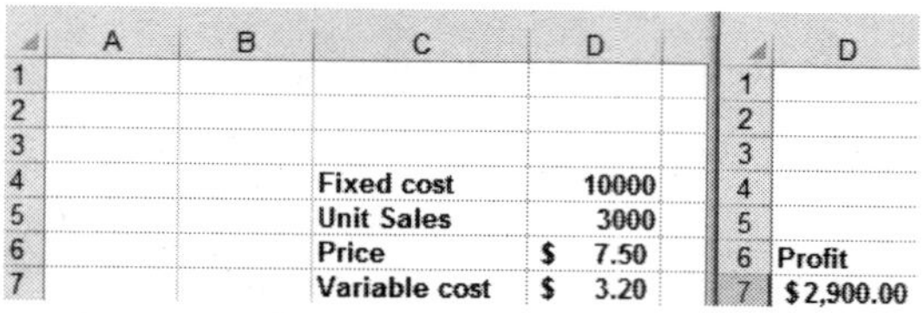

FIGURE 16-10 Data for using the formula-auditing tools on multiple worksheets.

Suppose you want to know the precedents of the profit formula. Select cell D7 in the Profit worksheet, and then click Trace Precedents in the Formula Auditing group. You'll see a dotted line, an arrow, and the worksheet icon shown in Figure 16-11.

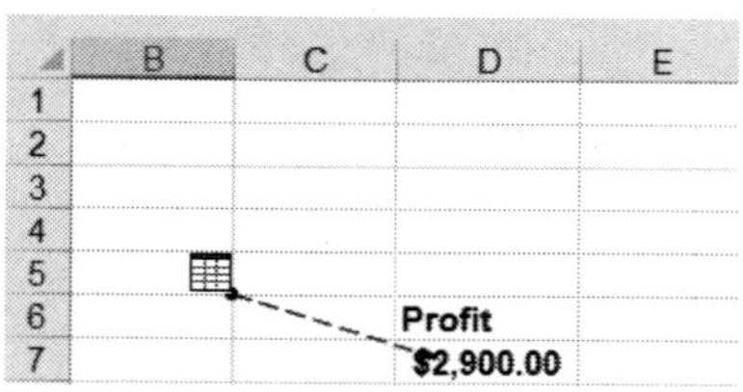

FIGURE 16-11 Results of tracing precedents with data on multiple worksheets.

The worksheet icon indicates that the precedents of the profit formula lie in another worksheet. Double-clicking the dotted line displays the Go To dialog box, shown in Figure 16-12.

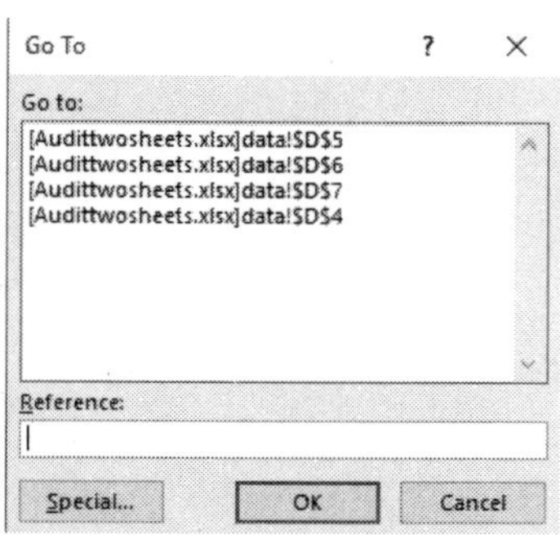

FIGURE 16-12 Using the Go To dialog box, you can audit data in multiple worksheets.

Now you can click any of the listed precedents (cells D4:D7 in the Data worksheet), and Excel will send you to the precedent you selected.

Problems

1. In the car NPV example, determine the following:
   a. The direct dependents and all the dependents of the interest rate.
   b. The direct dependents and all the dependents of the tax rate.
   c. The direct precedents and all the precedents for Year 4 unit sales.
   d. The direct precedents and all the precedents for Year 3 costs.
2. For the file Productmix.xlsx, determine the following:
   a. The precedents of profit.
   b. The dependents of the amount of Product 1 produced.

CHAPTER 17

Sensitivity analysis with data tables

Questions answered in this chapter:

- I'm thinking of starting a store in the local mall to sell gourmet lemonade. Before opening the store, I'm curious about how my profit, revenue, and variable costs will depend on the price I charge and the unit cost.
- I am going to build a new house. The amount of money I need to borrow (with a 15-year repayment period) depends on the price for which I sell my current house. I'm also unsure about the annual interest rate I'll receive when I close. How can I determine how my monthly payments will depend on the amount borrowed and the annual interest rate?
- A major Internet company is thinking of purchasing another online retailer. The retailer's current annual revenues are $100 million, with expenses of $150 million. Current projections indicate that the retailer's revenues are growing at 25 percent per year and its expenses are growing at 5 percent per year. We know projections might be in error, however, and would like to know, for a variety of assumptions about annual revenue and expense growth, the number of years before the retailer will show a profit.

Most worksheet models contain assumptions about certain parameters or inputs to the model. In our lemonade example, the inputs include:

- The price for which a glass of lemonade is sold
- The unit cost of producing a glass of lemonade
- The sensitivity of demand for lemonade to price charged
- The annual fixed cost of running a lemonade stand

Based on input assumptions, you can compute outputs of interest. For the lemonade example, the outputs of interest might include:

- Annual profit
- Annual revenue
- Annual variable cost

Despite best intentions, assumptions about input values can be in error. For example, your best guess about the variable cost of producing a glass of lemonade might be $0.45, but it's possible that your assumption is in error. Sensitivity analysis determines how a spreadsheet's outputs vary in response to changes to its inputs. For example, you might want to see how a change in product price affects yearly profit, revenue, and variable cost. A data table in Microsoft Excel 2016 lets you easily vary one or two inputs and perform a sensitivity analysis. With a one-way data table, you can determine how changing one input changes any number of outputs. With a two-way data table, you can determine how changing two inputs changes a single output. This chapter's three examples will show how easy it is to use a data table and obtain meaningful sensitivity results.

Answers to this chapter's questions

I'm thinking of starting a store in the local mall to sell gourmet lemonade. Before opening the store, I'm curious about how my profit, revenue, and variable costs will depend on the price I charge and the unit cost.

The work required for this analysis is in the file Lemonade.xlsx. (See Figures 17-1, 17-2, and 17-4.) The input assumptions are given in the range D1:D4. I assume that annual demand for lemonade (see the formula in cell D2) equals 65000–9000*price. (Chapter 84, "Estimating a demand curve," contains a discussion of how to estimate a demand curve.) I've created the names in C1:C7 to correspond to cells D1:D7.

I computed annual revenue in cell D5 with the formula =demand*price. In cell D6, I computed the annual variable cost with the formula =unit_cost*demand. Finally, in cell D7, I computed profit by using the formula =revenue–fixed_cost–variable_cost.

	C	D
1	price	$ 4.00
2	demand	29000
3	unit cost	$ 0.45
4	fixed cost	$ 45,000.00
5	revenue	$ 116,000.00
6	variable cost	$ 13,050.00
7	profit	$ 57,950.00

FIGURE 17-1 Analysis of a lemonade store.

Suppose that I want to know how changes in price (for example, from $1.00 through $4.00 in $0.25 increments) affect annual profit, revenue, and variable cost. Because I'm changing only one input, a one-way data table will solve the problem. The data table is shown in Figure 17-2.

	B	C	D	E	F
9			profit	revenue	variable cost
10	price		57950	116000	13050
11		$ 1.00	$ (14,200.00)	$ 56,000.00	$ 25,200.00
12		$ 1.25	$ (2,000.00)	$ 67,187.50	$ 24,187.50
13		$ 1.50	$ 9,075.00	$ 77,250.00	$ 23,175.00
14		$ 1.75	$ 19,025.00	$ 86,187.50	$ 22,162.50
15		$ 2.00	$ 27,850.00	$ 94,000.00	$ 21,150.00
16		$ 2.25	$ 35,550.00	$ 100,687.50	$ 20,137.50
17		$ 2.50	$ 42,125.00	$ 106,250.00	$ 19,125.00
18		$ 2.75	$ 47,575.00	$ 110,687.50	$ 18,112.50
19		$ 3.00	$ 51,900.00	$ 114,000.00	$ 17,100.00
20		$ 3.25	$ 55,100.00	$ 116,187.50	$ 16,087.50
21		$ 3.50	$ 57,175.00	$ 117,250.00	$ 15,075.00
22		$ 3.75	$ 58,125.00	$ 117,187.50	$ 14,062.50
23		$ 4.00	$ 57,950.00	$ 116,000.00	$ 13,050.00

FIGURE 17-2 A one-way data table with varying prices.

To set up a one-way data table, begin by listing input values in a column. I listed the prices of interest (ranging from $1.00 through $4.00 in $0.25 increments) in the range C11:C23. Next, I moved over one column and up one row from the list of input values, and there I listed the formulas I want the data table to calculate. I entered the formula for profit in cell D10, the formula for revenue in cell E10, and the formula for variable cost in cell F10.

Now select the table range (C10:F23). The table range begins one row above the first input; its last row is the row containing the last input value. The first column in the table range is the column containing the inputs; its last column is the last column containing an output. After selecting the table range, display the Data tab on the ribbon. In the Forecast group, click What-If Analysis, and then click Data Table. Now fill in the Data Table dialog box, as shown in Figure 17-3.

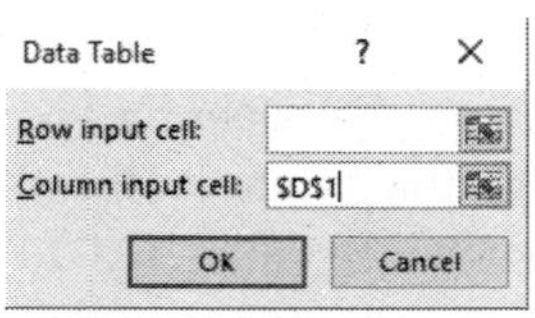

FIGURE 17-3 Creating a data table.

For the column input cell, you use the cell in which you want the listed inputs—that is, the values listed in the first column of the data table range—to be assigned. Because the listed inputs are prices, I pointed to D1 as the column input cell. After you click OK, Excel creates the one-way data table shown in Figure 17-4.

	B	C	D	E	F
1		price	$ 4.00		
2		demand	29000		
3		unit cost	$ 0.45		
4		fixed cost	$ 45,000.00		
5		revenue	$ 116,000.00		
6		variable cost	$ 13,050.00		
7		profit	$ 57,950.00		
8					
9			profit	revenue	variable cost
10	price		57950	116000	13050
11		$ 1.00	$ (14,200.00)	$ 56,000.00	$ 25,200.00
12		$ 1.25	$ (2,000.00)	$ 67,187.50	$ 24,187.50
13		$ 1.50	$ 9,075.00	$ 77,250.00	$ 23,175.00
14		$ 1.75	$ 19,025.00	$ 86,187.50	$ 22,162.50
15		$ 2.00	$ 27,850.00	$ 94,000.00	$ 21,150.00
16		$ 2.25	$ 35,550.00	$ 100,687.50	$ 20,137.50
17		$ 2.50	$ 42,125.00	$ 106,250.00	$ 19,125.00
18		$ 2.75	$ 47,575.00	$ 110,687.50	$ 18,112.50
19		$ 3.00	$ 51,900.00	$ 114,000.00	$ 17,100.00
20		$ 3.25	$ 55,100.00	$ 116,187.50	$ 16,087.50
21		$ 3.50	$ 57,175.00	$ 117,250.00	$ 15,075.00
22		$ 3.75	$ 58,125.00	$ 117,187.50	$ 14,062.50
23		$ 4.00	$ 57,950.00	$ 116,000.00	$ 13,050.00

FIGURE 17-4 The entire one-way data table with varying prices.

In the range D11:F11, profit, revenue, and variable cost are computed for a price of $1.00. In cells D12:F12, profit, revenue, and variable cost are computed for a price of $1.25, and on through the range of prices. The profit-maximizing price among all listed prices is $3.75. A price of $3.75 would produce an annual profit of $58,125.00, annual revenue of $117,187.50, and an annual variable cost of $14,062.50.

Suppose I want to determine how annual profit varies as price varies from $1.50 through $5.00 (in $0.25 increments) and unit cost varies from $0.30 through $0.60 (in $0.05 increments). Because here I'm changing two inputs, I need a two-way data table. (See Figure 17-5.) I list the values for one input down the first column of the table range (I'm using the range H11:H25 for the price values) and the values for the other input in the first row of the table range. (In this example, the range I10:O10 holds the list of unit cost values.) A two-way data table can have only one output cell, and the formula for the output must be placed in the upper-left corner of the table range. Therefore, I placed the profit formula in cell H10.

	H	I	J	K	L	M	N	O
8								
9		unit cost						
10	57950	$ 0.30	$ 0.35	$ 0.40	$ 0.45	$ 0.50	$ 0.55	$ 0.60
11	$ 1.50	$16,800.00	$14,225.00	$11,650.00	$ 9,075.00	$ 6,500.00	$ 3,925.00	$ 1,350.00
12	$ 1.75	$26,412.50	$23,950.00	$21,487.50	$19,025.00	$16,562.50	$14,100.00	$11,637.50
13	$ 2.00	$34,900.00	$32,550.00	$30,200.00	$27,850.00	$25,500.00	$23,150.00	$20,800.00
14	$ 2.25	$42,262.50	$40,025.00	$37,787.50	$35,550.00	$33,312.50	$31,075.00	$28,837.50
15	$ 2.50	$48,500.00	$46,375.00	$44,250.00	$42,125.00	$40,000.00	$37,875.00	$35,750.00
16	$ 2.75	$53,612.50	$51,600.00	$49,587.50	$47,575.00	$45,562.50	$43,550.00	$41,537.50
17	$ 3.00	$57,600.00	$55,700.00	$53,800.00	$51,900.00	$50,000.00	$48,100.00	$46,200.00
18	$ 3.25	$60,462.50	$58,675.00	$56,887.50	$55,100.00	$53,312.50	$51,525.00	$49,737.50
19	$ 3.50	$62,200.00	$60,525.00	$58,850.00	$57,175.00	$55,500.00	$53,825.00	$52,150.00
20	$ 3.75	$62,812.50	$61,250.00	$59,687.50	$58,125.00	$56,562.50	$55,000.00	$53,437.50
21	$ 4.00	$62,300.00	$60,850.00	$59,400.00	$57,950.00	$56,500.00	$55,050.00	$53,600.00
22	$ 4.25	$60,662.50	$59,325.00	$57,987.50	$56,650.00	$55,312.50	$53,975.00	$52,637.50
23	$ 4.50	$57,900.00	$56,675.00	$55,450.00	$54,225.00	$53,000.00	$51,775.00	$50,550.00
24	$ 4.75	$54,012.50	$52,900.00	$51,787.50	$50,675.00	$49,562.50	$48,450.00	$47,337.50
25	$ 5.00	$49,000.00	$48,000.00	$47,000.00	$46,000.00	$45,000.00	$44,000.00	$43,000.00

FIGURE 17-5 A two-way data table showing profit as a function of price and unit variable cost.

I select the table range (cells H10:O25) and display the Data tab. In the Forecast group, I click What-If Analysis and then click Data Table. Cell D1 (price) is the column input cell, and cell D3 (unit variable cost) is the row input cell. These settings ensure that the values in the first column of the table range are used as prices, and the values in the first row of the table range are used as unit variable costs. After clicking OK, we see the two-way data table shown in Figure 17-5. As an example, in cell K19, when we charge $3.50 and the unit variable cost is $0.40, the annual profit equals $58,850.00. For each unit cost, I've highlighted the profit-maximizing price. Note that as the unit cost increases, the profit-maximizing price increases as some of the cost increase is passed on to customers. Of course, I can guarantee only that the profit-maximizing price in the data table is within $0.25 of the actual profit-maximizing price. When you work with Excel Solver in Chapter 84, you'll learn how to determine (to the penny) the exact profit-maximizing price.

Here are some other notes on this problem:

- As you change input values in a worksheet, the values calculated by a data table change, too. For example, if you increased the fixed cost by $10,000, all the profit numbers in the data table would be reduced by $10,000.
- You can't delete or edit a portion of a data table. If you want to save the values in a data table, select the table range, copy the values, and then right-click and select Paste Special. Then choose Values from the Paste Special menu. If you take this step, however, changes to your worksheet inputs no longer cause the data table calculations to update.
- When setting up a two-way data table, be careful not to mix up your row and column input cells. A mix-up will cause nonsensical results.
- Most people set their worksheet calculation mode to Automatic. With this setting, any change in your worksheet will cause all your data tables to be recalculated. Usually, you want this, but if your data tables are large, automatic recalculation can be incredibly slow. If the constant recalculation of data tables is slowing your work down, click the File tab on the ribbon, click Options, and then click the Formulas tab in the Excel Options dialog box. Then select Automatic Except For Data Tables in the Calculation Options section. When you select Automatic Except For Data Tables, all your data tables recalculate only when you press the F9 (recalculation) key. Alternatively, you can click the Calculation Options button (in the Calculation group on the Formulas tab) and then click Automatic Except For Data Tables.

I am going to build a new house. The amount of money I need to borrow (with a 15-year repayment period) depends on the price for which I sell my current house. I'm also unsure about the annual interest rate I'll receive when I close. How can I determine how my monthly payments will depend on the amount borrowed and the annual interest rate?

The real power of data tables becomes evident when you combine a data table with one of the Excel functions. In this example, we'll use a two-way data table to vary two inputs (the amount borrowed and the annual interest rate) to the Excel PMT function and determine how the monthly payment varies as these inputs change. (The PMT function is discussed in detail in Chapter 10, "More Excel financial functions.") Our work for this example is in the file Mortgagedt.xlsx, shown in Figure 17-6.

Suppose you're borrowing money on a 15-year mortgage, where monthly payments are made at the end of each month. I've entered the amount borrowed in cell D2, the number of months in the mortgage (180) in D3, and the annual interest rate in D4. I've associated the range names in cells C2:C4 with the cells D2:D4. Based on these inputs, I compute the monthly payment in D5 with the formula =-PMT(Annual_int_rate/12,Number_of_Months,Amt_Borrowed).

	C	D	E	F	G	H	I	J
1								
2	Amt Borrowed	$400,000.00						
3	Number of Months	180						
4	Annual int rate	6%						
5	Monthly Payment	$3,375.43						
6			Annual	Interest	Rate			
7	$3,375.43	5.0%	5.5%	6.0%	6.5%	7.0%	7.5%	8.0%
8	$ 300,000.00	$2,372.38	$2,451.25	$2,531.57	$2,613.32	$2,696.48	$2,781.04	$2,866.96
9	$ 350,000.00	$2,767.78	$2,859.79	$2,953.50	$3,048.88	$3,145.90	$3,244.54	$3,344.78
10	$ 400,000.00	$3,163.17	$3,268.33	$3,375.43	$3,484.43	$3,595.31	$3,708.05	$3,822.61
11	$ 450,000.00	$3,558.57	$3,676.88	$3,797.36	$3,919.98	$4,044.73	$4,171.56	$4,300.43
12	$ 500,000.00	$3,953.97	$4,085.42	$4,219.28	$4,355.54	$4,494.14	$4,635.06	$4,778.26
13	$ 550,000.00	$4,349.36	$4,493.96	$4,641.21	$4,791.09	$4,943.56	$5,098.57	$5,256.09
14	$ 600,000.00	$4,744.76	$4,902.50	$5,063.14	$5,226.64	$5,392.97	$5,562.07	$5,733.91
15	$ 650,000.00	$5,140.16	$5,311.04	$5,485.07	$5,662.20	$5,842.38	$6,025.58	$6,211.74

FIGURE 17-6 A data table showing how mortgage payments vary as the amount borrowed and the interest rate change.

You think that the amount borrowed will range (depending on the price for which you sell your current house) between $300,000 and $650,000 and that your annual interest rate will range between 5 percent and 8 percent. In preparation for creating a data table, I entered the amounts borrowed in the range C8:C15 and possible interest rate values in the range D7:J7. Cell C7 contains the output you want to recalculate for various input combinations. Therefore, I set cell C7 equal to cell D5. Next I select the table range (C7:J15), click What-If Analysis on the Data tab (in the Forecast group), and then click Data Table. Because numbers in the first column of the table range are amounts borrowed, I enter D2 in the Column Input Cell box. Numbers in the first row of the table are annual interest rates, so I enter D4 in the Row Input Cell box. After you click OK, you see the data table shown in Figure 17-6. This table shows, for example, that if you borrow $400,000 at an annual rate of 6 percent, your monthly payments would be just over $3,375. The data table also shows that at a low interest rate (for example, 5 percent), an increase of $50,000 in the amount borrowed raises the monthly payment by around $395, whereas at a high interest rate (such as 8 percent), an increase of $50,000 in the amount borrowed raises the monthly payment by about $478.

A major Internet company is thinking of purchasing another online retailer. The retailer's current annual revenues are $100 million, with expenses of $150 million. Current projections indicate that the retailer's revenues are growing at 25 percent per year and its expenses are growing at 5 percent per year. We know projections might be in error, however, and we would like to know, for a variety of assumptions about annual revenue and expense growth, the number of years before the retailer will show a profit.

We want to determine the number of years needed to break even, using annual growth rates in revenue from 10 percent through 50 percent and annual expense growth rates from 2 percent through 20 percent. Let's also assume that if the firm cannot break even in 13 years, we'll say "cannot break even." Our work is in the file Bezos.xlsx, shown in Figure 17-7.

I chose to hide columns A and B and rows 16–18. To hide columns A and B, first select any cells in columns A and B (or select the column headings), and then display the Home tab. In the Cells group, click Format, point to Hide & Unhide, and select Hide Columns. To hide rows 16–18, select any cells in each row (or select the row headings) and repeat the previous procedure, selecting Hide Rows. Of course, the Visibility options also include Unhide Rows and Unhide Columns. If you receive a worksheet with many hidden rows and columns and want to quickly unhide all of them, you can select the entire worksheet by clicking the Select All button at the intersection of the column and row headings. Now selecting Unhide Rows and/or Unhide Columns will unhide all hidden rows and/or columns in the worksheet. If an entire worksheet is hidden, Unhide Sheet will be available, and you can select the worksheet to unhide.

In row 11, I project the firm's revenue out 13 years (based on the annual revenue growth rate assumed in E7) by copying from F11 to G11:R11 the formula =E11*(1+$E$7). In row 12, I project the firm's expenses out 13 years (based on the annual expense growth rate assumed in E8) by copying from F12 to G12:R12 the formula =E12*(1+$E$8). (See Figure 17-7.)

	C	D	E	F	G	H	O	P	Q	R
1										
2										
3										
4										
5										
6			growth							
7	Revenue	1E+08	0.25							
8	Expenses	1.50E+08	0.05							
9										
10			0	1	2	3	10	11	12	13
11		Revenues	1E+08	1.25E+08	1.56E+08	1.95E+08	9.31E+08	1.16E+09	1.46E+09	1.82E+09
12		Expenses	1.5E+08	1.58E+08	1.65E+08	1.74E+08	2.44E+08	2.57E+08	2.69E+08	2.83E+08
13		Breakeven		0	0	3	0	0	0	0
14										
15		Total	3							
19					Expense	Growth				
20			3	0.02	0.03	0.04	0.11	0.12	0.13	0.14
21			0.1	6	7	8	No BE	No BE	No BE	No BE
22		Revenue	0.11	5	6	7	No BE	No BE	No BE	No BE
23		growth	0.12	5	5	6	No BE	No BE	No BE	No BE
24			0.13	4	5	5	No BE	No BE	No BE	No BE
25			0.14	4	4	5	No BE	No BE	No BE	No BE
55			0.44	2	2	2	2	2	2	2
56			0.45	2	2	2	2	2	2	2
57			0.46	2	2	2	2	2	2	2
58			0.47	2	2	2	2	2	2	2
59			0.48	2	2	2	2	2	2	2
60			0.49	2	2	2	2	2	2	2
61			0.5	2	2	2	2	2	2	2

FIGURE 17-7 Using a data table to calculate how many years it will take to break even.

We would like to use a two-way data table to determine how varying the growth rates for revenues and expenses affects the years needed to break even. We need one cell whose value always tells us the number of years needed to break even. Because we can break even during any of the next 13 years, this might seem like a tall order.

I begin by using in row 13 an IF statement for each year to determine whether we break even during the year. The IF statement returns the number of the year if we break even during the year or 0 otherwise. I determine the year we break even in cell E15 by simply adding together all the numbers in row 13. Finally, I can use cell E15 as the output cell for a two-way data table.

I copy from cell F13 to G13:R13 the formula =IF(AND(E11<E12,F11>F12),F10,0). This formula reflects the fact that we break even for the first time during a year if, and only if, during the previous year, revenues are less than expenses and during the current year, revenues are greater than expenses. If this is the case, the year number is entered in row 13; otherwise, 0 is entered.

Now, in cell E15 I can determine the breakeven year (if any) with the following formula:

```
=IF(SUM(F13:R13)>0,SUM(F13:R13),"No BE"
```

If we do not break even during the next 13 years, the formula enters the text string *"No BE"*.

I now enter the annual revenue growth rates (10 percent through 50 percent) in the range E21:E61. I enter annual expense growth rates (2 percent to 20 percent) in the range F20:X20. I ensure that the year-of-breakeven formula is copied to cell E20 with the formula =E15. Next, I select the table range E20:X61, click What-If Analysis in the Forecast group on the Data tab, and then click Data Table. I select cell E7 (revenue growth rate) as the column input cell and cell E8 (expense growth rate) as the row input cell, and then I click OK. With these settings, I obtain the two-way data table shown in Figure 17-7.

Note, for example, that if expenses grow at 4 percent a year, a 10-percent annual growth in revenue will result in breaking even in eight years, whereas a 50-percent annual growth in revenue will result in breaking even in only two years! Also note that if expenses grow at 12 percent per year and revenues grow at 14 percent per year, we will not break even by the end of 13 years.

Problems

1. You've been assigned to analyze the profitability of Bill Clinton's autobiography. The following assumptions have been made:

   - Bill is receiving a one-time royalty payment of $12 million.
   - The fixed cost of producing the hardcover version of the book is $1 million.
   - The variable cost of producing each hardcover book is $4.
   - The publisher's net from book sales per hardcover unit sold is $15.
   - The publisher expects to sell 1 million hardcover copies.
   - The fixed cost of producing the paperback is $100,000.
   - The variable cost of producing each paperback book is $1.
   - The publisher's net from book sales per paperback unit sold is $4.
   - Paperback sales will be double hardcover sales.

   Use this information to answer the following questions.

a. Determine how the publisher's before-tax profit will vary as hardcover sales vary from 100,000 through 1 million copies.

b. Determine how the publisher's before-tax profit varies as hardcover sales vary from 100,000 through 1 million copies and the ratio of paperback to hardcover sales varies from 1 through 2.4.

2. The annual demand for a product equals $500-3p+10a^{.5}$, where *p* is the price of the product in dollars and *a* is hundreds of dollars spent on advertising the product. The annual fixed cost of selling the product is $10,000, and the unit variable cost of producing the product is $12. Determine a price (within $10) and amount of advertising (within $100) that maximizes profit.

3. Reconsider our hedging example from Chapter 12, "IF statements." For stock prices in six months that range from $20 through $65 and the number of puts purchased varying from 0 through 100 (in increments of 10), determine the percentage return on your portfolio.

4. For our mortgage example, suppose you know the annual interest rate will be 5.5 percent. Create a table that shows for amounts borrowed from $300,000 through $600,000 (in $50,000 increments), the difference in payments between a 15-year, 20-year, and 30-year mortgage.

5. Currently, you sell 40,000 units of a product for $45 each. The unit variable cost of producing the product is $5. You are thinking of cutting the product price by 30 percent. You are sure this will increase sales by an amount from 10 percent to 50 percent. Perform a sensitivity analysis to show how profit will change as a function of the percentage increase in sales. Ignore fixed costs.

6. Let's assume that at the end of each of the next 40 years, you put the same amount in your retirement fund and earn the same interest rate each year. Show how the amount of money you will have at retirement changes as you vary your annual contribution from $5,000 through $25,000 and the rate of interest varies from 3 percent through 15 percent.

7. The payback period for a project is the number of years needed for a project's future profits to pay back the project's initial investment. A project requires a $300 million investment at Time 0. The project yields profit for 10 years, and Time 1 cash flow will be between $30 million and $100 million. Annual cash flow growth will be from 5 percent through 25 percent a year. How does the project payback depend on the Year 1 cash flow and cash flow growth rates?

8. A software development company is thinking of translating a software product into Swahili. Currently, 200,000 units of the product are sold per year at a price of $100 each. Unit variable cost is $20. The fixed cost of translation is $5 million. Translating the product into Swahili will increase sales during each of the next three years by some unknown percentage over the current level of 200,000 units. Show how the change in profit resulting from the translation depends on the percentage increase in product sales. You can ignore the time value of money and taxes in your calculations.

9. The file Citydistances.xlsx gives latitude and longitude for several U.S. cities. There is also a formula that determines the distance between two cities by using a given latitude and longitude. Create a table that computes the distance between any pair of cities listed.

10. You have begun saving for your child's college education. You plan to save $5,000 per year, and want to know for annual rates of return on your investment from 4 percent through 12 percent the amount of money you will have in the college fund after saving for 10–15 years.

11. If you earn interest at percentage rate *r* per year and compound your interest *n* times per year, then in *y* years $1 will grow to $(1+(r/n))^{ny}$ dollars. Assuming a 10 percent annual interest rate, create a table showing the factor by which $1 will grow in 5–15 years for daily, monthly, quarterly, and semiannual compounding.

12. Assume I have $100 in the bank. Each year, I withdraw *x* percent (ranging from 4 percent through 10 percent) of my original balance. For annual growth rates of 3 percent through 10 percent per year, determine how many years it will take before I run out of money. Hint: You should use the IFERROR function (discussed in Chapter 12) because if my annual growth rate exceeds the withdrawal rate, I will never run out of money.

13. If you earn interest at an annual rate of *x* percent per year, then in *n* years $1 will become $(1+x)^n$ dollars. For annual rates of interest from 1 percent through 20 percent, determine the exact time (in years) in which $1 will double.

14. You are borrowing $200,000 and making payments at the end of each month. For an annual interest rate ranging from 5 percent through 10 percent and loan durations of 10, 15, 20, 25, and 30 years, determine the total interest paid on the loan.

15. You are saving for your child's college fund. You are going to contribute the same amount of money to the fund at the end of each year. Your goal is to end up with $100,000. For annual investment returns ranging from 4 percent through 15 percent and number of years investing varying from 5–15 years, determine your required annual contribution.

16. The file Antitrustdata.xlsx shows the starting and ending years for many court cases. Determine the number of court cases active during each year.

17. You can retire at age 62 and receive $8,000 per year or retire at age 65 and receive $10,000 per year. What is the difference (in today's dollars) between these two choices as you vary the annual rate at which you discount cash flows between 2 percent and 10 percent and vary age of death between 70 and 84?

18. You are thinking of opening a restaurant that will have six four-person tables. Each day that the restaurant is open, there are two lunch seatings and three dinner seatings.

    a. The restaurant will be closed on Monday.

    b. The average lunch check is $20 and you earn a 40 percent profit margin on lunch checks.

    c. The average dinner check is $40 and you earn a 50 percent profit margin on dinner checks.

    d. Assume the fixed cost of running a restaurant is $400,000 per year.

    Assuming 364 days in a year, use a data table to show how annual profit changes as percentage of seats filled at each meal varies between 10 percent and 100 percent.

19. You are investing in a new Broadway play, *Insect in the Light*. You are given the following information about the play:

    a. The fixed cost of opening the play is $5 million.

    b. The average ticket price is $100.

    c. The theatre seats 2,000 people, and there are 365 performances per year.

    Use a data table to determine how total profit generated by the play varies as the length of the play run varies between 1 and 5 years, and average occupancy rates varies between 70 percent and 90 percent.

20. Currently a magazine has 5,000 subscribers. Determine how the number of subscribers at the end of Year 6 varies as the number of new subscribers varies between 1,000 and 5,000 and the annual retention rate varies between 60 percent and 90 percent.

21. When a customer places an order from a catalog, assume a profit of $50 (not including cost of mailing the catalog) is earned. Use a data table to determine how the total profit earned from the mailing varies as the response rate to the mailing varies between 1 percent and 10 percent.

22. Today, you bought five shares of Stock 1 for $30 per share and three shares of Stock 2 for $25 per share. In a month, you will sell all your stock. Use a data table to determine how total profit varies as the change in the price of each stock varies from -$5 to $5.

CHAPTER 18

The Goal Seek command

Questions answered in this chapter:

- For a given price, how many glasses of lemonade does a lemonade store need to sell per year to break even?
- We want to pay off our mortgage in 15 years. The annual interest rate is 6 percent. The bank told us we can afford monthly payments of $2,000. How much can we borrow?
- I always had trouble with story problems in high-school algebra. Can Excel make solving story problems easier?

The Goal Seek feature in Microsoft Excel 2016 enables you to compute a value for a worksheet input that makes the value of a given formula match the goal you specify. For example, using the lemonade store example in Chapter 17, "Sensitivity analysis with data tables," suppose you have fixed overhead costs, fixed per-unit costs, and a fixed sales price. Given this information, you can use Goal Seek to calculate the number of glasses of lemonade you need to sell to break even. Essentially, Goal Seek embeds a powerful equation solver in your worksheet. To use Goal Seek, you need to provide Excel with three pieces of information:

- **Set Cell** Specifies that the cell contains the formula that calculates the information you're seeking. In the lemonade example, the Set Cell would contain the formula for profit.
- **To Value** Specifies the numerical value for the goal that's calculated in the Set Cell. In the lemonade example, because we want to determine the sales volume that represents the breakeven point, the To Value would be 0.
- **By Changing Cell** Specifies the input cell that Excel changes until the Set Cell calculates the goal defined in the To Value cell. In the lemonade example, the By Changing Cell would contain annual lemonade sales.

Answers to this chapter's questions

For a given price, how many glasses of lemonade does a lemonade store need to sell per year to break even?

The work for this section is in the file Lemonadegs.xlsx, which is shown in Figure 18-1. As in Chapter 17, I've assumed an annual fixed cost of $45,000.00 and a variable unit cost of $0.45. Let's assume a price of $3.00. And, as noted, the question is how many glasses of lemonade do I need to sell each year to break even?

	C	D
1	price	$ 3.00
2	demand	17647.05882
3	unit cost	$ 0.45
4	fixed cost	$ 45,000.00
5	revenue	$ 52,941.18
6	variable cost	$ 7,941.18
7	profit	$ -

FIGURE 18-1 Using data to set up the Goal Seek feature to perform a breakeven analysis.

To start, insert any number for demand in cell D2. In the Forecast group on the Data tab, click What-If Analysis, and then click Goal Seek. Now fill in the Goal Seek dialog box as shown in Figure 18-2.

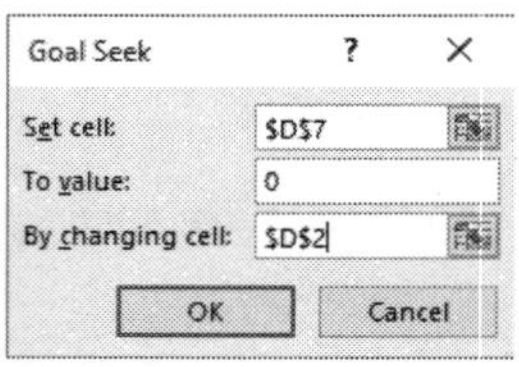

FIGURE 18-2 The Goal Seek dialog box filled in with entries for a breakeven analysis.

The dialog box indicates that I want to change cell D2 (annual demand, or sales) until cell D7 (profit) hits a value of 0. After I click OK, I get the result that's shown in Figure 18-1. If I sell approximately 17,647 glasses of lemonade per year (or 48 glasses per day), I'll break even. To find the value I'm seeking, Excel varies the demand in cell D2 (alternating between high and low values) until it finds a value that makes profit equal $0. If a problem has more than one solution, Goal Seek will still display only one answer.

We want to pay off our mortgage in 15 years. The annual interest rate is 6 percent. The bank told us we can afford monthly payments of $2,000. How much can we borrow?

You can begin to answer this question by setting up a worksheet to compute the monthly payments on a 15-year loan (let's assume payments at the end of the month) as a function of the annual interest rate and a trial loan amount. You can see the work I did in the file Paymentgs.xlsx and in Figure 18-3.

	D	E
3	Years	180
4	Annual int rate	0.06
5	Amount borrowed	$ 237,007.03
6	Monthly payment	$2,000.00

FIGURE 18-3 Using data with the Goal Seek feature to determine the amount you can borrow, based on a set monthly payment.

In cell E6, the formula =–PMT(annual_int_rate/12,years,amt._borrowed) computes the monthly payment associated with the amount borrowed, which is listed in cell E5. Filling in the Goal Seek dialog box as shown in Figure 18-4 calculates the amount borrowed that results in monthly payments equal to $2,000. With a limit of $2,000 for monthly payments, you can borrow up to $237,007.03.

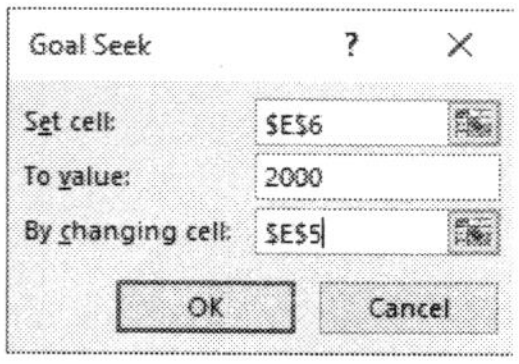

FIGURE 18-4 The Goal Seek dialog box set up to calculate the mortgage example.

I always had trouble with story problems in high-school algebra. Can Excel make solving story problems easier?

If you think back to high-school algebra, most story problems required you to choose a variable (usually it was called *x*) that solved a particular equation. Goal Seek is an equation solver, so it's perfectly suited to solving story problems. Here's a typical high-school algebra problem:

> *Maria and Edmund have a lover's quarrel while honeymooning in Seattle. Maria storms into her Mazda Miata and drives 64 miles per hour toward her mother's home in Los Angeles. Two hours after Maria leaves, Edmund jumps into his BMW in hot pursuit, driving 80 miles per hour. How many miles will each person have traveled when Edmund catches Maria?*

You can find the solution in the file Maria.xlsx, shown in Figure 18-5.

	C	D
1		
2	**Time Maria drives**	10
3	**Maria speed**	64
4	**Time Edmund drive**	8
5	**Edmund speed**	80
6	**Maria distance**	640
7	**Edmund distance**	640
8	**Difference**	0

FIGURE 18-5 Goal Seek can help you solve story problems.

The Set Cell will be the difference between the distances Maria and Edmund have traveled. You can set this to a value of 0 by changing the number of hours Maria drives. Of course, Edmund drives two fewer hours than Maria.

I entered a trial number of hours that Maria drives in cell D2. Then I assigned the range names from the cell range C2:C8 to the cells D2:D8. Because Edmund drives two fewer hours than Maria, in cell D4 I entered the formula =Time_Maria_drives–2. In cells D6 and D7, I used the fact that distance=speed*time to compute the total distance Maria and Edmund travel. The difference between the distances traveled by Edmund and Maria is computed in cell D8 with the formula =Maria_distance–Edmund_distance. Now I can fill in the Goal Seek dialog box as shown in Figure 18-6.

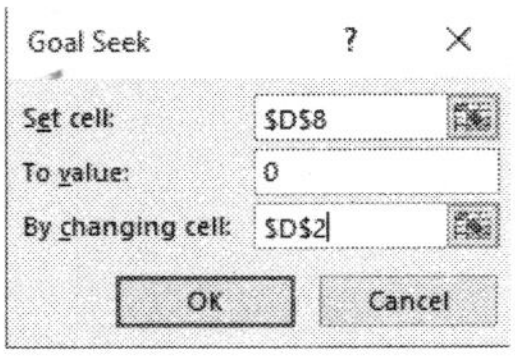

FIGURE 18-6 The Goal Seek dialog box filled in to solve an algebra story problem.

I change Maria's hours of driving (cell D2) until the difference between the miles traveled by Edmund and Maria (cell D8) equals 0. As you can see, after Maria drives 10 hours and Edmund 8 hours, they will each have driven a distance of 640 miles.

Problems

1. From Problem 1 in Chapter 17, determine how many hardcover books must be sold to break even.

2. From the car net present value (NPV) example in Chapter 16, "The auditing tool," by what rate do annual sales need to grow for total NPV to equal $1 million?

3. What value of Year 1 unit cost would increase our NPV in the car example in Chapter 16 to $1 million?

4. In our mortgage example, suppose I need to borrow $200,000 for 15 years. If my maximum payments are limited to $2,000 per month, how high an annual interest rate can I tolerate?

5. How could I use Goal Seek to determine a project's internal rate of return (IRR)?

6. At the end of each of the next 40 years, I'm going to put $20,000 in my retirement fund. What rate of return on my investments do I need so that I will have $2 million available for retirement in 40 years?

7. I expect to earn 10 percent per year on my retirement investments. At the end of each of the next 40 years, I want to put the same amount of money in my retirement portfolio. How much money do I need to put in each year if I want to have $2 million in my account when I retire?

8. Consider two projects with the following cash flows:

	Year 1	Year 2	Year 3	Year 4
Project 1	–$1,000	$400	$350	$400
Project 2	–$900	$100	$100	$1,000

For what rate of interest will Project 1 have a larger NPV? Hint: Find the interest rate that brings both projects to the same NPV.

9. I am managing a conference at my college. My fixed costs are $15,000. I must pay the 10 speakers $700 each, and the college union $300 per conference participant for food

and lodging costs. I am charging each conference participant who is not also a speaker $900, which includes the conference fee and their food and lodging costs. How many paid registrants need to attend for me to break even?

10. I am buying 40 pounds of candy. Some of the candy sells for $10 per pound, and some sells for $6 per pound. How much candy at each price should I buy to arrive at an average cost of $7 per pound?

11. Three electricians are wiring my new home. Electrician 1 by himself will need 11 days to do the job. Electrician 2 by himself will need 5 days to do the job. Electrician 3 by herself will need 9 days to do the job. If all three electricians work on the job, how long will the job take to complete?

12. To celebrate the Lewis and Clark Expedition, I am traveling 40 miles upstream and then 40 miles downstream in a canoe. The speed of the river current is 5 miles per hour. If the trip takes me 5 hours total, how fast do I travel if the river has no current?

13. In the NPV.xlsx file in Chapter 8, "Evaluating investments by using net present value criteria," we found that for high interest rates Project 1 has a larger NPV and for small interest rates Project 2 has a larger NPV. For what interest rate would the two projects have the same NPV?

14. Suppose you are borrowing $500,000 and are making annual payments for 20 years at the beginning of each year. What annual interest rate corresponds to this situation?

15. It is April 15, and so far this month we have sold $35,000 worth of merchandise. Our quota is to sell $72,500 worth of units in April. If we charge a price *p* for our product, we will sell 800-4p units during the rest of the month. What price would enable us to meet our April revenue quota?

16. The current annual interest rate is 5 percent, and you are taking out a 20-year loan with a monthly end-of-month payment. If you can afford monthly payments of $3000 per month, what is the most you can borrow?

17. Greg Winston has gone bankrupt and started a lemonade stand. He has invested $400 in lemonade equipment and sells a glass of lemonade for $4. His unit cost of producing a cup of lemonade is $2.50. How many glasses of lemonade must Greg sell to generate a profit of $300?

CHAPTER 19

Using the Scenario Manager for sensitivity analysis

Question answered in this chapter:

- I'd like to create best, worst, and most-likely scenarios for the sales of an automobile by varying the values of Year 1 sales, annual sales growth, and Year 1 sales price. Data tables for sensitivity analysis allow me to vary only one or two inputs, so I can't use a data table. Does Excel have a tool I can use to vary more than two inputs in a sensitivity analysis?

You can use the Scenario Manager to perform sensitivity analysis by varying as many as 32 input cells. With the Scenario Manager, you first define the set of input cells you want to vary. Next, you name your scenario and enter for each scenario the value of each input cell. Finally, you select the output cells (also called *result cells*) that you want to track. The Scenario Manager then creates a beautiful report containing the inputs and the values of the output cells for each scenario.

Answer to this chapter's question

I'd like to create best, worst, and most-likely scenarios for the sales of an automobile by varying the values of Year 1 sales, annual sales growth, and Year 1 sales price. Data tables for sensitivity analysis allow me to vary only one or two inputs, so I can't use a data table. Does Excel have a tool I can use to vary more than two inputs in a sensitivity analysis?

Suppose you want to create the following three scenarios related to the net present value (NPV) of a car, using the example in Chapter 16, "The auditing tool."

Scenario	Year 1 sales	Annual sales growth	Year 1 sales price
Best case	$20,000	20%	$10.00
Most likely case	$10,000	10%	$7.50
Worst case	$5,000	2%	$5.00

For each scenario, you want to look at the firm's NPV and each year's after-tax profit. The work is in the file NPVauditscenario.xlsx. Figure 19-1 shows the worksheet model (contained in the Original Model worksheet), and Figure 19-2 shows the scenario report (contained in the Scenario Summary worksheet).

	A	B	C	D	E	F
1		taxrate	0.4			
2		Year1sales	12000			
3		Sales growth	0.05			
4		Year1price	$ 7.50			
5		Year1cost	$ 6.00			
6		intrate	0.15			
7		costgrowth	0.05			
8		pricegrowth	0.03			
9	Year	1	2	3	4	5
10	Unit Sales	12000	12600	13230	13891.5	14586.075
11	unit price	$ 7.50	$ 7.73	$ 7.96	$ 8.20	$ 8.44
12	unit cost	$ 6.00	$ 6.30	$ 6.62	$ 6.95	$ 7.29
13	Revenues	$ 90,000.00	$ 97,335.00	$105,267.80	$ 113,847.13	$ 123,125.67
14	Costs	$ 72,000.00	$ 79,380.00	$ 87,516.45	$ 96,486.89	$ 106,376.79
15	Before Tax Profit	$ 18,000.00	$ 17,955.00	$ 17,751.35	$ 17,360.24	$ 16,748.88
16	Tax	$ 7,200.00	$ 7,182.00	$ 7,100.54	$ 6,944.10	$ 6,699.55
17	Aftertax Profits	$ 10,800.00	$ 10,773.00	$ 10,650.81	$ 10,416.15	$ 10,049.33
18						
19	NPV	$35,492.08				

FIGURE 19-1 The data on which the scenarios are based.

	B	C	D	E	F	G
1						
2	Scenario Summary					
3			Current Values:	Best	Most Likely	Worst
5	Changing Cells:					
6		Year1sales	12000	20000	10000	5000
7		Sales_growth	0.05	0.2	0.1	0.02
8		Year1price	$ 7.50	$ 10.00	$ 7.50	$ 5.00
9	Result Cells:					
10		$B$17	$ 10,800.00	$ 48,000.00	$ 9,000.00	$ (3,000.00)
11		$C$17	$ 10,773.00	$ 57,600.00	$ 9,405.00	$ (3,519.00)
12		$D$17	$ 10,650.81	$ 69,016.32	$ 9,741.10	$ (4,090.33)
13		$E$17	$ 10,416.15	$ 82,560.80	$ 9,980.12	$ (4,718.50)
14		$F$17	$ 10,049.33	$ 98,588.50	$ 10,087.17	$ (5,408.35)
15		$B$19	$35,492.08	$226,892.67	$32,063.83	($13,345.75)
16	Notes: Current Values column represents values of changing cells at					
17	time Scenario Summary Report was created. Changing cells for each					
18	scenario are highlighted in gray.					

FIGURE 19-2 The scenario summary report.

To begin defining the best-case scenario, while in the Original Model worksheet, display the Data tab, and then click Scenario Manager on the What-If Analysis menu in the Forecast group. Then click the Add button, and fill in the Add Scenario dialog box as shown in Figure 19-3.

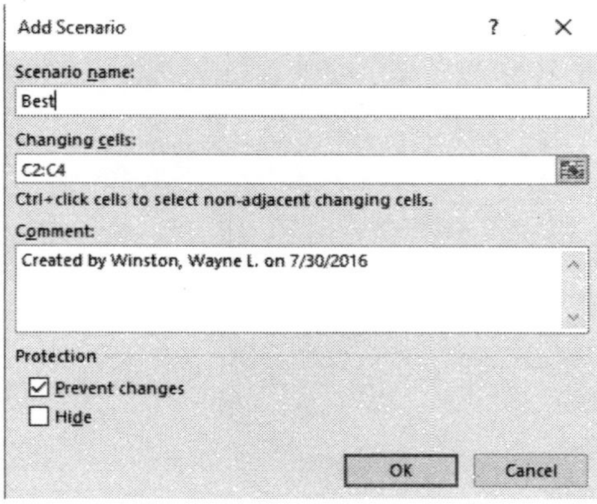

FIGURE 19-3 Data inputs for the best-case scenario.

Enter the scenario name as *Best*, and select or enter cells C2:C4 as the changing cells, which contain the values that define the scenario. After you click OK in the Add Scenario dialog box, fill in the Scenario Values dialog box with the input values that define the best case, as shown in Figure 19-4.

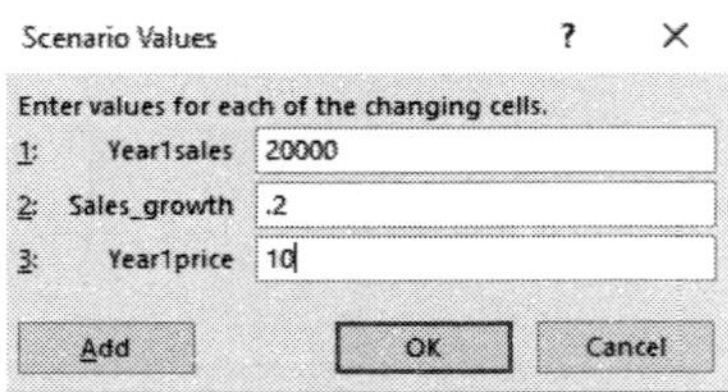

FIGURE 19-4 Defining the input values for the best-case scenario.

For the Best scenario, I entered 2000 as the value in Year1sales, 0.2 in Sales_growth, and 10 in Year1price. By clicking Add in the Scenario Values dialog box (which isn't available when you edit a scenario), you can enter the data for the most-likely and worst-case scenarios as well. After clicking Add and entering data for all three scenarios (Best, Most Likely, and Worst), click OK in the Scenario Values dialog box. The Scenario Manager dialog box, shown in Figure 19-5, lists the scenarios I created.

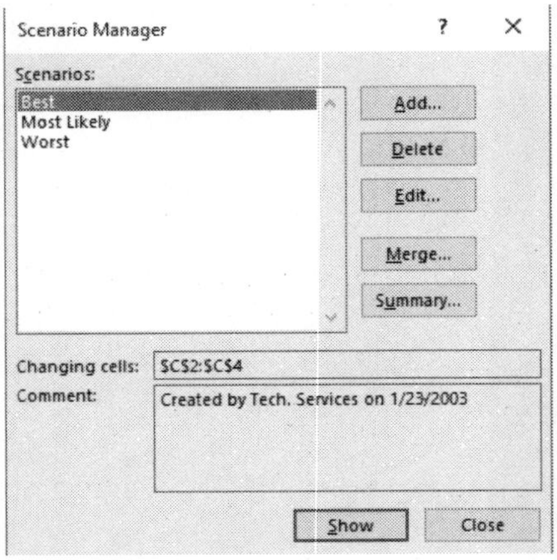

FIGURE 19-5 The Scenario Manager dialog box displays each scenario you define.

When you click Summary in the Scenario Manager dialog box, you can enter in the Result Cells box the cells that will be displayed in the scenario reports. Figure 19-6 shows how I indicated in the Scenario Summary dialog box that I want the scenario summary report to track each year's after-tax profit (cells B17:F17) as well as the total NPV (cell B19).

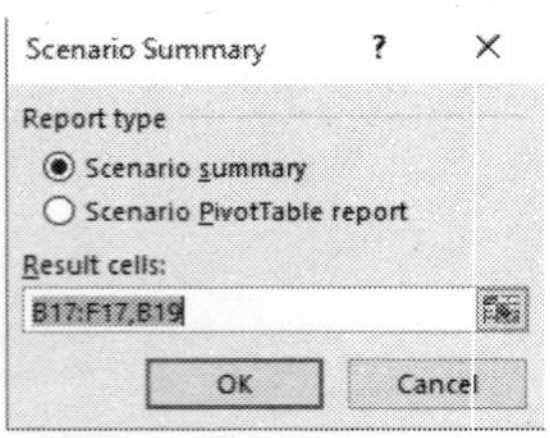

FIGURE 19-6 Using the Scenario Summary dialog box to select the result cells for the summary report.

Because the result cells come from more than one range, I separated the ranges B17:F17 and B19 with a comma. (I could also have used the Ctrl key to select and enter multiple ranges.) After you select Scenario Summary (instead of the PivotTable option) and click OK, Excel creates the beautiful Scenario Summary report pictured earlier in Figure 19-2. In the Scenario Summary worksheet, notice that Excel includes a column, labeled Current Values, for the values that were originally placed in the worksheet. The worst case loses money (a loss of $13,345.75), whereas the best case is quite profitable (a profit of $226,892.67). Because the worst-case price is less than our variable cost, the worst case loses money in each year.

Remarks

- The Scenario PivotTable Report option in the Scenario Summary dialog box presents the scenario results in a PivotTable format.
- Suppose you select a scenario in the Scenario Manager dialog box and then click the Show button. The input cells' values for the selected scenario then appear in the worksheet, and Excel recalculates all formulas. This tool is great for presenting a slide show of your scenarios.
- It's hard to create a lot of scenarios with the Scenario Manager because you need to enter each individual scenario's values. Monte Carlo simulation (see Chapter 74, "Introduction to Monte Carlo simulation") makes it easy to create many scenarios. Using the Monte Carlo simulation method, you can find information such as the probability that the NPV of a project's cash flows is nonnegative—an important measure because it is the probability that the project adds value to the company.
- Clicking the minus (–) sign (to the left of the row numbers) in row 5 of the Scenario Summary report hides the Assumption cells and shows only the results. Clicking the plus (+) sign restores the full report.
- Suppose you send a file to several people, and each adds his or her own scenarios. After each person returns the file containing the scenarios to you, you can merge all the scenarios into one workbook by opening each person's version of the workbook, and in the original workbook, clicking the Merge button in the Scenario Manager dialog box, and then selecting the workbooks containing the scenarios you want to merge. Excel merges the selected scenarios in the original workbook.

Problems

1. Delete the best-case scenario and run another scenario report.
2. Add a scenario named High Price, in which Year 1 price equals $15 and the other two inputs remain at their most-likely values.
3. For the lemonade stand example in Chapter 17, "Sensitivity analysis with data tables," use the Scenario Manager to display a report summarizing profit for the following scenarios:

Scenario	Price	Unit cost	Fixed cost
High cost/high price	$5.00	$1.00	$65,000.00
Medium cost/medium price	$4.00	$0.75	$45,000.00
Low cost/low price	$2.50	$0.40	$25,000.00

4. For the mortgage-payment example in Chapter 17, use the Scenario Manager to create a report tabulating monthly payments for the following scenarios:

Scenario	Amount borrowed	Annual rate	Number of monthly payments
Lowest payment	$300,000	4%	360
Most-likely payment	$400,000	6%	240
Highest payment	$550,000	8%	180

CHAPTER 20

The COUNTIF, COUNTIFS, COUNT, COUNTA, and COUNTBLANK functions

Questions answered in this chapter:

- Suppose I have a list of songs that were played on the radio. For each song, I know the singer, the date the song was played, and the length of the song. How can I answer questions such as these about the songs in the list?
    - How many were sung by each singer?
    - How many were not sung by Eminem?
    - How many were at least four minutes long?
    - How many were longer than the average length of all songs on the list?
    - How many were sung by singers whose last names begin with S?
    - How many were sung by singers whose last names contain exactly six letters?
    - How many were played after June 15, 2005?
    - How many were played before 2009?
    - How many were exactly four minutes long?
    - How many songs played were sung by Bruce Springsteen and were exactly four minutes long?
    - How many songs played were sung by Madonna and were three to four minutes long?
- In a more general context, how do I perform operations such as the following?
    - Count the number of cells in a range containing numbers
    - Count the number of blank cells in a range
    - Count the number of nonblank cells in a range

You often need to count the number of cells in a range that meet a given criterion. For example, if a worksheet contains information about makeup sales, you might want to count the number of sales transactions made by the salesperson named Jennifer or the number of sales transactions that occurred after June 10. The COUNTIF function lets you count the number of cells in a range that meet criteria that are defined on the basis of one row or column of the worksheet.

The syntax of the COUNTIF function is COUNTIF(range,criterion), using the following arguments:

- *Range* is the range of cells in which you want to count cells meeting a given criterion.
- *Criterion* is a number, date, or expression that determines whether to count a given cell in the range.

The syntax of the COUNTIFS function is COUNTIFS(range1,criterion1,range2,criterion2,..., range_n,criterion_n).

COUNTIFS counts the number of rows for which the *range1* entry meets *criterion1*, the *range2* entry meets *criterion2*, the range_*n* entry meets *criterion_n*, and so on. Thus, COUNTIFS allows the criteria to involve more than one column or multiple conditions in one column. Other functions that allow for multiple criteria are discussed in Chapter 21, "The SUMIF, AVERAGEIF, SUMIFS, and AVERAGEIFS functions," and Chapter 48, "Summarizing data with database statistical functions."

The key to using the COUNTIF function (and similar functions) successfully is in understanding the wide variety of criteria that Excel accepts. The types of criteria you can use are best explained through the use of examples. In addition to examples of the COUNTIF function, I'll provide examples of the COUNT, COUNTA, and COUNTBLANK functions:

- The COUNT function counts the number of cells in a range containing numbers.
- The COUNTA function counts the number of nonblank cells in a range.
- The COUNTBLANK function counts the number of blank cells in a range.

As an illustration of how to use these functions, consider a database (file Rock.xlsx) that gives the following information for each song played on radio station WKRP:

- The singer
- The date the song was played
- The length of the song

Figure 20-1 shows a subset of the data.

	D	E	F	G
4				average
5				3.483701
6	Song Number	Singer	Date	Minutes
7	1	Eminem	5/21/2004	4
8	2	Eminem	4/15/2004	2
9	3	Cher	1/28/2005	2
10	4	Eminem	1/28/2005	4
11	5	Moore	11/5/2004	2
12	6	Cher	9/18/2004	4
13	7	Spears	4/15/2004	3
14	8	Spears	3/17/2005	3
15	9	Manilow	1/16/2005	4
16	10	Eminem	4/10/2005	4
17	11	Madonna	2/15/2004	3
18	12	Eminem	1/10/2004	4
19	13	Springsteen	4/10/2005	2
20	14	Spears	4/15/2004	4
21	15	Moore	7/8/2004	3
22	16	Madonna	6/26/2004	4
23	17	Spears	5/28/2005	3
24	18	Mellencamp	7/27/2005	5
25	19	Spears	9/18/2004	5
26	20	Madonna	7/8/2004	4

FIGURE 20-1 The song database used for the COUNTIF examples.

Answers to this chapter's questions

How many songs were sung by each singer?

To begin, I selected the first row of the database, the range D6:G6. Then I selected the whole database by pressing Ctrl+Shift+Down arrow. Next, in the Defined Names group on the Formulas tab, I clicked Create From Selection, chose Top Row, and clicked OK. This names the range D7:D957 *Song Number*, the range E7:E957 *Singer*, the range F7:F957 *Date*, and the range G7:G957 *Minutes*. To determine how many songs were sung by each singer, you copy from C5 to C6:C12 the formula =COUNTIF(Singer,B5). In cell C5, this formula now displays the number of cells in the range Singer that match the value in B5 (Eminem). The database contains 114 songs sung by Eminem. Similarly, Cher sang 112 songs, and so on, as you can see in Figure 20-2. I could have also found the number of songs sung by Eminem with the formula =COUNTIF(Singer,"Eminem"). Note that you must enclose text such as Eminem in quotation marks (" "), and that criteria are not case sensitive.

	B	C
1		
2	count	9
3	counta	18
4	countblank	2
5	Eminem	114
6	Cher	112
7	Moore	131
8	Spears	129
9	Mellencamp	115
10	Madonna	133
11	Springsteen	103
12	Manilow	114
13	Total	951

FIGURE 20-2 Using COUNTIF to determine how many songs were sung by each singer.

How many songs were not sung by Eminem?

To solve this problem, you need to know that Excel interprets the character combination **<>** as *not equal to*. The formula =COUNTIF(Singer,"<>Eminem"), entered in cell C15, tells you that 837 songs in the database were not sung by Eminem, as you can see in Figure 20-3. I need to enclose <>*Eminem* in quotation marks because Excel treats the not equal to (**<>**) character combination as text and Eminem is, of course, text. You could obtain the same result by using the formula =COUNTIF(Singer,"<>"&B5), which uses the ampersand (&) symbol to concatenate the reference to cell B5 and the **<>** operator.

	B	C
15	Not by Eminem	837
16	Songs >= 4 minutes	477
17	Songs longer than average	477
18	Singer begins with S	232
19	Singer has six letters in name	243
20	Songs after 6/15/2005	98
21	Songs Before 2009	951
22	Songs exactly 4 minutes	247
23	Songs exactly 5 minutes	230
24	Springsteen songs 4 minutes	24
25	Madonna songs 3 or 4 minutes	70

FIGURE 20-3 You can combine the COUNTIF function with the not-equal-to operator (**<>**).

How many songs were at least four minutes long?

In cell C16, I computed the number of songs played that lasted at least four minutes by using the formula =COUNTIF(Minutes,">=4"). You need to enclose >=4 in quotation marks because the greater than or equal to (**>=**) character combination, like **<>**, is treated as text. You can see that 477 songs lasted at least four minutes.

How many songs were longer than the average length of all songs on the list?

To answer this question, I first computed in cell G5 the average length of a song with the formula AVERAGE(Minutes). Then, in cell C17, I computed the number of songs that last longer than the average with the formula =COUNTIF(Minutes,">"&G5). I can refer to another cell (in this case G5) in the criteria by using the & character. You can see that 477 songs lasted longer than average, which matches the number of songs lasting at least four minutes. The reason these numbers match is that I assumed the length of each song was an integer. For a song to last at least 3.48 minutes, it has to last at least four minutes.

How many songs were sung by singers whose last names begin with S?

To answer this question, I used a wildcard character, the asterisk (*****), in the criteria. An asterisk represents any sequence of characters. Thus, the formula =COUNTIF(Singer,"S*") in cell C18 picks up any song sung by a singer whose last name begins with *S*. (The criteria are not case sensitive.) Two hundred thirty-two songs were sung by singers with last names that begin with *S*. This number is simply the total of the songs sung by Bruce Springsteen and Britney Spears (103+129=232).

How many songs were sung by singers whose last names contain exactly six letters?

In this example, I used the question mark (**?**) wildcard character. The question mark matches any character. Therefore, entering the formula =COUNTIF(Singer,"??????") in cell C19 counts the number of songs sung by singers having six letters in their last name. The result is 243. Two singers have last names of six characters, Britney Spears and Eminem, who together sang a total of 243 songs (129+114=243).

How many songs were played after June 15, 2005?

The criteria you use with COUNTIF functions handle dates on the basis of a date's serial number. (A later date is considered larger than an earlier date.) The formula =COUNTIF(Date,">6/15/2005") in cell C20 tells you that 98 songs were played after June 15, 2005.

How many songs were played before 2009?

Here, we want our criteria to pick up all dates on or before December 31, 2008. I entered in cell C21 the formula =COUNTIF(Date,"<=12/31/2008"). You can see that 951 songs (which turn out to be all the songs) were played before the start of 2009.

How many songs were exactly four minutes long?

In cell C22, I computed the number of songs lasting exactly four minutes with the formula =COUNTIF(Minutes,4). This formula counts the number of cells in the range G7:G957 containing a *4*. As you can see, 247 songs lasted exactly four minutes. In a similar fashion, cell C23 shows that 230 songs lasted exactly five minutes.

How many songs played were sung by Bruce Springsteen and were exactly four minutes long?

We want to count each row where an entry in the Singer column is *Springsteen* and an entry in the Minutes column is *4*. Because this question involves more than one criteria, this is a job for the wonderful COUNTIFS function. Simply enter in cell C24 the formula =COUNTIFS(Singer,"Springsteen", Minutes,4).

This formula counts any row in which Singer is *Springsteen* and Minutes equals *4*. Bruce Springsteen sang 24 songs that were exactly four minutes long. My favorite Springsteen song is "Thunder Road," but that song is more than four minutes long. I recommend using the function wizard to enter formulas involving the COUNTIFS function. Don't forget that you can paste range names into your formula with the F3 key.

How many songs played were sung by Madonna and were three to four minutes long?

Because we are dealing with multiple criteria, this is again a job for COUNTIFS. Entering in cell C25 the formula =COUNTIFS(Singer,"Madonna",Minutes,"<=4",Minutes,">=3") counts all rows in which Madonna sang a song that was from three to four minutes long. These are exactly the rows we want to count. It turns out that Madonna sang 70 songs that were from three to four minutes long. (My favorite one is "Crazy for You!")

How do I count the number of cells in a range containing numbers?

The COUNT function counts the number of cells in a range containing a numeric value. For example, the formula =COUNT(B5:C14) in cell C2 displays 9 because nine cells (the cells in C5:C13) in the range B5:C14 contain numbers. (See Figure 20-2.)

How do I count the number of blank cells in a range?

The COUNTBLANK function counts the number of blank cells in a range. For example, the formula =COUNTBLANK(B5:C14) entered in cell C4 returns a value of 2 because two cells (B14 and C14) in the range B5:C14 are blank.

How do I count the number of nonblank cells in a range?

The COUNTA function returns the number of nonblank cells in a range. For example, the formula =COUNTA(B5:C14) in cell C3 returns 18 because 18 cells in the range B5:C14 are not blank.

Remarks

In the remainder of the book, I discuss alternative methods for answering questions involving two or more criteria (such as how many Britney Spears songs were played before June 10, 2005).

- Database statistical functions are discussed in Chapter 48, "Summarizing data with database statistical functions."
- Array formulas are discussed in Chapter 88, "Array formulas and functions."

Problems

The following questions refer to the file Rock.xlsx.

1. How many songs were not sung by Britney Spears?
2. How many songs were played before June 15, 2004?
3. How many songs were played between June 1, 2004, and July 4, 2006? Hint: Take the difference between two COUNTIF functions.
4. How many songs were sung by singers whose last names begin with *M*?
5. How many songs were sung by singers whose names contain an *e*?
6. Create a formula that always yields the number of songs played today. Hint: Use the TODAY() function.
7. For the cell range D4:G15, count the cells containing a numeric value. Count the number of blank cells. Count the number of nonblank cells.
8. How many songs sung by Barry Manilow were played in 2004?

9. How many songs at least four minutes long and sung by Mandy Moore were played in 2007 or earlier?

10. How many songs that are exactly three minutes long and sung by Britney Spears were played later than 2004?

11. The file NBA.xlsx contains the following information:

    - Columns A and B contain the name of each NBA team and a code number for each team. For example, Team 1 is Atlanta.
    - Column C contains the home team for each game.
    - Column D contains the visiting team for each game.
    - Column E contains points scored by the home team.
    - Column F contains points scored by the visiting team.

    From this data, compute the number of games played by each team.

12. The file Matchthesecond.xlsx gives a list of names. Note that some names occur more than once. You need to determine the row in which, for example, the second occurrence of the name *Dave* occurs. Set up a worksheet that allows you to enter a person's name and a positive integer (such as *n*) and returns the row in which the name occurs for the *n*th time.

13. The file Numbers.xlsx contains a set of numbers. Count how many of these numbers are between 1 and 12 inclusively.

CHAPTER 21

The SUMIF, AVERAGEIF, SUMIFS, and AVERAGEIFS functions

Questions answered in this chapter:

- I'm a sales manager for a makeup company and have summarized for each sales transaction the following information: salesperson, date of sale, units sold (or returned), and the total price received (or paid out for returns). How can I answer the following questions?
  - What is the total dollar amount of merchandise sold by each salesperson?
  - How many units were returned?
  - What is the total dollar amount of sales in or after 2005?
  - How many units of lip gloss were sold? How much revenue did lip gloss sales bring in?
  - What is the total dollar amount of sales made by someone other than a specific salesperson?
  - What is the average number of units sold in each transaction made by a specific salesperson?
  - What is the total dollar amount of lipstick sold by a specific salesperson?
  - What is the average quantity (in units) of lipstick in each sale made by a specific salesperson?
  - Among transactions involving at least 50 units, what is the average quantity of lipstick in each sale made by a specific salesperson?
  - Among transactions of more than $100, what is the total dollar amount of lipstick sold by a specific salesperson? What about transactions of less than $100?

If you want to sum all the entries in one column (or row) that match criteria that depend on another column (or row), the SUMIF function gets the job done. The syntax of the SUMIF function is SUMIF(range,criterion,[sum range]).

- *Range* is the range of cells that you want to evaluate with a criterion.

- *Criterion* is a number, date, or expression that determines whether a given cell in the *sum range* is added.
- *Sum range* is the range of cells that are added. If *sum range* is omitted, it is assumed to be the same as *range*.

The rules for criteria you can use with the SUMIF function are identical to the rules used for the COUNTIF function. For information about the COUNTIF function, see Chapter 20, "The COUNTIF, COUNTIFS, COUNT, COUNTA, and COUNTBLANK functions."

AVERAGEIF averages the range of cells that meet a criterion. The AVERAGEIF function uses the syntax AVERAGEIF(range,criterion,[average_range]).

Microsoft Excel 2016 includes three functions (introduced in Excel 2007) that you can use to flag rows that involve multiple criteria: COUNTIFS (discussed in Chapter 20), SUMIFS, and AVERAGEIFS. Other functions that you can use to do calculations involving multiple criteria are discussed in Chapter 48, "Summarizing data with database statistical functions." Array functions (see Chapter 88, "Array formulas and functions") can also be used to handle calculations involving multiple criteria.

The syntax of SUMIFS is SUMIFS(sumrange,range1,criterion1,range2,criterion2,...,rangeN, criterionN). SUMIFS sums up every entry in the *sumrange* for which *criterion1* (based on *range1*), *criterion2* (based on *range2*), ..., *criterionN* (based on *rangeN*) are all satisfied. In a similar fashion, the AVERAGEIFS function has the syntax AVERAGEIFS(sumrange,range1, criterion1,range2,criterion2, ...,rangeN,criterionN). AVERAGEIFS averages every entry in the *sumrange* for which *criterion1* (based on *range1*), *criterion2* (based on *range2*), ..., *criterionN* (based on *rangeN*) are all satisfied.

Answers to this chapter's questions

What is the total dollar amount of merchandise sold by each salesperson?

The work for the problems in this chapter is in the file Makeup2007.xlsx. Figure 21-1 shows a subset of the data.

	G	H	I	J	K	L
4	Trans Number	Name	Date	Product	Units	Dollars
5	1	Betsy	4/1/2004	lip gloss	45	$ 137.20
6	2	Hallagan	3/10/2004	foundatio	50	$ 152.01
7	3	Ashley	2/25/2005	lipstick	9	$ 28.72
8	4	Hallagan	5/22/2006	lip gloss	55	$ 167.08
9	5	Zaret	6/17/2004	lip gloss	43	$ 130.60
10	6	Colleen	11/27/2005	eye liner	58	$ 175.99
11	7	Cristina	3/21/2004	eye liner	8	$ 25.80
12	8	Colleen	12/17/2006	lip gloss	72	$ 217.84
13	9	Ashley	7/5/2006	eye liner	75	$ 226.64
14	10	Betsy	8/7/2006	lip gloss	24	$ 73.50
15	11	Ashley	11/29/2004	mascara	43	$ 130.84
16	12	Ashley	11/18/2004	lip gloss	23	$ 71.03
17	13	Emilee	8/31/2005	lip gloss	49	$ 149.59
18	14	Hallagan	1/1/2005	eye liner	18	$ 56.47
19	15	Zaret	9/20/2006	foundatio	-8	$ (21.99)
20	16	Emilee	4/12/2004	mascara	45	$ 137.39
21	17	Colleen	4/30/2006	mascara	66	$ 199.65
22	18	Jen	8/31/2005	lip gloss	88	$ 265.19
23	19	Jen	10/27/2004	eye liner	78	$ 236.15
24	20	Zaret	11/27/2005	lip gloss	57	$ 173.12
25	21	Zaret	6/2/2006	mascara	12	$ 38.08
26	22	Betsy	9/24/2004	eye liner	28	$ 86.51

FIGURE 21-1 The data we'll use for SUMIF examples.

As usual, I begin by labeling the data in columns G through L with the corresponding names in cells G4:L4. For example, the range name Product corresponds to the range J5:J1904. To compute the total amount sold by each salesperson (see Figure 21-2), I simply copy from cell B5 to B6:B13 the formula =SUMIF(Name,A5,Dollars). This formula adds up every entry in the Dollars column that contains the name *Emilee* in the Name column and shows that Emilee sold $25,258.87 worth of makeup. Of course, the formula =SUMIF(Name,"Emilee",Dollars) would yield the same result.

	A	B	C
4	Name	Dollar Volume	
5	Emilee	$ 25,258.87	
6	Hallagan	$ 28,705.16	
7	Ashley	$ 25,947.24	
8	Zaret	$ 26,741.31	
9	Colleen	$ 24,890.66	
10	Cristina	$ 23,849.56	
11	Betsy	$ 28,803.15	
12	Jen	$ 29,050.53	
13	Cici	$ 27,590.57	
14			
15			
16	Units returned	922	
17	Total dollars sold 2005 or later	$ 157,854.32	
18	Units of lip gloss sold	16333	
19	$s of lip gloss sold	$ 49,834.64	
20	$s sold not by Jen	$ 211,786.51	
21	Lipstick $s by Jen	3953	
22	avg units lipstick by Zaret	33	
23	avg units lipstick Zaretunits >=50	68	
24	Lipstick $s >=$100 Jen	3583	
25	Lipstick $s <$100 Jen	370	check
26	average units by Jen	43.548	43.548

FIGURE 21-2 Results of SUMIF computations.

How many units were returned?

In cell B16 (of the file Makeup2007.xlsx), the formula =SUMIF(Units,"<0",Units) totals every number less than 0 in the Units column (column K). The result is –922. Inserting a minus sign in front of the SUMIF formula shows that 922 units were returned. Recall that when the *sum range* argument is omitted from a SUMIF function, Excel assumes that *sum range* equals *range*. Here, the formula –SUMIF(Units,"<0") would also yield 922

What is the total dollar amount of sales in or after 2005?

In cell B17, the formula =SUMIF(Date,">=1/1/2005",Dollars) totals every entry in the Dollars column (column L) that contains a date on or after 1/1/2005 in the Date column. The formula in cell B17 shows that $157,854.32 worth of makeup was sold in 2005 or later.

How many units of lip gloss were sold? How much revenue did lip gloss sales bring in?

In cell B18, the formula SUMIF(Product,"lip gloss",Units) totals every cell in the Units column that contains the text *lip gloss* in the Product column (column J). You can see that 16,333 units of lip gloss were sold. This is the net sales amount; transactions in which units of lip gloss were returned are counted as negative sales.

In a similar fashion, in cell B19 the formula =SUMIF(Product,"lip gloss",Dollars) tells you that a net amount of $49,834.64 worth of lip gloss was sold. This calculation counts refunds associated with returns as negative revenue.

What is the total dollar amount of sales made by someone other than Jen?

In cell B20, the formula =SUMIF(Name,"<>Jen",Dollars) sums the dollar amount of all transactions that do not have Jen in the Name column. We find that salespeople other than Jen sold $211,786.51 worth of makeup.

What is the average number of units sold in each transaction made by a specific salesperson?

This is a job for the AVERAGEIF function. Enter in cell B26 the formula =AVERAGEIF(Name,"Jen",Units) to average every entry in the Units column that contains Jen in the Name column. Jen's average transaction size was 43.548 units. I verified this in cell C26 with the formula =SUMIF(Name,"Jen",Units) /COUNTIF(Name,"Jen").

What is the total dollar amount of lipstick sold by Jen?

This calculation involves two criteria (Name="Jen" and Product="lipstick"). Therefore, you need to compute the quantity you're looking for in cell B21 with the formula =SUMIFS(Dollars,Name,"Jen", Product,"lipstick"). The total dollar amount of all transactions in which Jen sold lipstick is $3,953.

What is the average quantity (in units) of lipstick in each sale made by Zaret?

This calculation requires the AVERAGEIFS function. I computed the quantity in cell B22 with the formula =AVERAGEIFS(Units,Name,"Zaret",Product,"lipstick"). For the sales transactions in which Zaret sold lipstick, the average number of units sold is 33.

Among transactions involving at least 50 units, what is the average quantity of lipstick in each sale made by Zaret?

Here again I used AVERAGEIFS, but I added a criterion to ensure that the units sold in each transaction was at least 50. In cell B23, I entered the formula =AVERAGEIF(Units,Name,"Zaret", Product,"lipstick",Units,">=50"). In all transactions in which Zaret sold at least 50 units of lipstick, the average transaction size is 68 units.

Among transactions of more than $100, what is the total dollar amount of lipstick sold by Jen? What about transactions of less than $100?

Because the criteria is Name=Jen, Product=lipstick, and some statement about the dollar size of each order, you need to use the SUMIFS function. In cell B24, I compute the total amount in transactions in which Jen sold lipstick and the dollar amount was at least $100 with the formula =SUMIFS(Dollars,Name,"Jen",Product,"lipstick",Dollars">=100"). Jen sold $3,583 worth of lipstick in such transactions. In lipstick transactions involving less than $100, you can see in cell B25 (the formula is =SUMIFS(Dollars,Name,"Jen",Product,"lipstick",Dollars,"<100") that the answer is $370. Note that $370+$3,583 equals the total revenue Jen generated from lipstick sales (computed in cell B21).

Problems

1. For each product, determine the total number of units and dollar volume sold.
2. Determine the total revenue earned before December 10, 2005.
3. Determine the total units sold by salespeople whose last names begin with C.
4. Determine the total revenue earned by people who have five letters in their names.
5. How many units were sold by people other than Colleen?
6. How many units of makeup were sold from January 15, 2004, through February 15, 2005?
7. The file NBA.xlsx contains the following information:
   - Columns A and B list the name of each NBA team and a code number for each team. For example, team 1 is Atlanta, and so on.
   - Column C lists the home team for each game.
   - Column D lists the visiting team for each game.
   - Column E lists points scored by the home team.
   - Column F lists points scored by the visiting team.

   From this data, compute for each team the average number of points the team scored per game and the average number of points the team gave up.

8. The file Toysrus.xlsx contains sales revenue (in millions of dollars) during each quarter for the years 1997–2001 and the first two quarters of 2002. Use this data to compute a seasonal index for each quarter of the year. For example, if average sales during the first quarter were 80 percent of the overall average sales per quarter, the first quarter would have a seasonal index of 0.8.

9. The file Sumifrows.xlsx contains sales data during several winter, spring, summer, and fall quarters. Determine average sales during the winter, spring, summer, and fall quarters.

10. Again using the file Makeup2007.xlsx (for questions 10–16), how much revenue was made on sales transactions involving at least 50 units of makeup?

11. How many units of lip gloss did Cici sell in 2004?

12. What is the average number of units of foundation sold by Emilee?

13. What is the average dollar size of a foundation sale made by Betsy after the end of 2004?

14. In transactions in which Ashley sold at least 40 units of lipstick, what is the total dollar amount?

15. Create a table that contains sales of each product made by each person.

16. Create a table that, when you enter a year in your worksheet, contains sales of each product by person during that year.

17. For the file Numbers.xlsx, find the total of all numbers between 5 and 15 inclusively.

18. For the file Numbers.xlsx, find the average of all numbers 10 and 25 inclusively.

19. The file Problem19data.xlsx shows each US temperature during each month of 1895–2015. For this time period, calculate the average temperature during each month of the year.

20. The file Problem20data.xlsx shows the yards gained in rushing and passing plays for NFL teams. Determine the average yards gained per play by each team in running and passing plays.

21. The file Problem21data.xlsx has statistics on NFL quarterbacks. Determine the total completions and attempts for each NFL teams. Remember some teams have more than one QB!

CHAPTER 22

The OFFSET function

Questions answered in this chapter:

- How can I create a reference to a range of cells that is a specified number of rows and columns from a cell or another range of cells?
- How can I perform a lookup operation based on the right-most column in a table range instead of the left-most column?
- I often download software product sales information listed by country/region. I need to track revenues from Iran as well as costs and units sold, but the data about Iran isn't always in the same location in the worksheet. Can I create a formula that will always pick out Iran's revenues, costs, and units sold?
- Each drug developed by my company goes through three stages of development. I have a list of the cost by month for each drug, and I also know the length in months of each development stage. Can I create formulas that compute for each drug the total cost incurred during each stage of development?
- I run a small video store. In a worksheet, my accountant has listed the name of each movie and the number of copies in stock. Unfortunately, he combined this information in one cell for each movie. How can I extract the number of copies of each movie in stock to a separate cell?
- How does Excel's Evaluate Formula feature work?
- How can I write a formula that always returns the last number in a column?
- How can I set up a range name that automatically includes new data?
- I am charting my company's monthly unit sales. Each month, I download the most recent month's unit sales. I would like my chart to update automatically. Is there an easy way to accomplish this?

The OFFSET function is used to create a reference to a range that is a specified number of rows and columns away from a cell or range of cells. Basically, to create a reference to a range of cells, you first specify a reference cell. You then indicate the number of rows and columns away from the reference cell that you want to use to create your range. For example, by using the OFFSET function, I can create a reference to a cell range that contains two rows and three columns and begins two columns to the right and one row above the current cell. You can calculate the specified number of rows and columns you move from a reference cell by using other Excel functions.

The syntax of the OFFSET function is OFFSET(reference,rows moved,columns moved,height,width), which takes the following arguments:

- *Reference* is a cell or range of cells from which the offset begins. If you specify a range of cells, the cells must be adjacent to each other. *Rows moved* is the number of rows away from the reference cell or range that you want the range reference to start (the upper-left cell in the offset range). A negative number of rows moves you up from the reference; a positive number of rows moves you down. For example, if *reference* equals C5 and *rows moved* equals –1, you move to row 4. If *rows moved* equals +1, you move to row 6. If *rows moved* equals 0, you stay at row 5.
- *Columns moved* is the number of columns away from the reference cell or range that you want the range reference to start. A negative number of columns moves you left from the reference; a positive number of columns moves you right. For example, if *reference* equals C5 and *columns moved* equals –1, you move to column B. If *columns moved* equals +1, you move to column D. If *columns moved* equals 0, you stay at column C.
- *Height* and *width* are optional arguments that give the number of rows and columns in the offset range. If *height* or *width* is omitted, the OFFSET function creates a range for which the value of *height* or *width* equals the height or width of the reference cell or range.

Answers to this chapter's questions

How can I create a reference to a range of cells that is a specified number of rows and columns from a cell or another range of cells?

The file Offsetexample.xlsx, shown in Figure 22-1, offfers some examples of the OFFSET function in action.

	A	B	C	D	E	F	G	H	I	J	K
1											
2											
3		Offset examples									
4											
5											
6		1	2	3	4			1	2	3	4
7		5	6	7	8			5	6	7	8
8		9	10	11	12			9	10	11	12
9											
10	=SUM(OFFSET(B7,-1,1,2,1))	8					=SUM(OFFSET(H6,0,1,3,2)	39			
11											
12											
13											
14		1	2	3	4						
15		5	6	7	8						
16		9	10	11	12						
17											
18	=SUM(OFFSET(E16,-2,-3,2,3))	24									

FIGURE 22-1 Using the OFFSET function.

For example, in cell B10, I entered the formula shown in cell A10: =SUM(OFFSET(B7,–1,1,2,1)). This formula begins in cell B7. It moves one row up and one column to the right, which brings us to cell C6. The formula now selects a range consisting of two rows and one column, which yields the range C6:C7. The SUM function adds the numbers in this range, which yields 2+6=8. The other two examples shown in Figure 22-1 work the same way. In the following sections, I'll show you how to apply the OFFSET function to some problems that were sent to me by former students working at major US companies.

How can I perform a lookup operation based on the right-most column in a table range instead of the left-most column?

In Figure 22-2 (see the workbook Lefthandlookup.xlsx), I listed the members of the 2002–2003 Dallas Mavericks NBA basketball team and their field-goal percentages. If I'm asked to find the player with a specific field-goal percentage, I could easily solve that problem by using a VLOOKUP function. But what I really want to do is a *left-hand lookup*, which involves finding the field-goal percentage for a player by using his name. A VLOOKUP function can't perform a left-hand lookup, but a left-hand lookup is simple if you combine the MATCH and OFFSET functions.

	B	C	D	E
4				
5		Left-hand lookup		
6			Name	FG %age
7	FG%	Player	Walt Williams	0.397
8	45.8%	Dirk Nowitzki		
9	41.8%	Michael Finley		
10	46.3%	Steve Nash		
11	39.5%	Nick Van Exel		
12	53.5%	Raef LaFrentz		
13	60.2%	Eduardo Najera		
14	51.2%	Shawn Bradley		
15	39.7%	Walt Williams		
16	44.4%	Adrian Griffin		
17	48.4%	Avery Johnson		
18	47.6%	Raja Bell		
19	66.7%	Evan Eschmeyer		
20	41.0%	Popeye Jones		
21	40.0%	Mark Strickland		
22	23.5%	Adam Harrington		

FIGURE 22-2 Performing a left-hand lookup by using the MATCH and OFFSET functions.

First, I enter the player's name in cell D7. Then I use a reference cell of B7 (the field-goal percentage column header) in the OFFSET function. To find the player's field-goal percentage, I need to move down to the row below row 7 where the player's name appears. This is a job for the MATCH function. The MATCH function portion of the formula OFFSET(B7,MATCH(D7,$C$8:$C$22,0),0) moves down to the row containing the specified player's name and then moves over 0 columns. Because the reference consists of one cell, omitting the *height* and *width* arguments of the OFFSET function ensures that the range returned by this formula is also one cell. Thus, I pick up the player's field-goal percentage. See cell E7.

I often download software product sales information listed by country/region. I need to track revenues from Iran as well as costs and units sold, but the data about Iran isn't always

in the same location in the worksheet. Can I create a formula that will always pick out Iran's revenues, costs, and units sold?

The file Asiansales.xlsx (see Figure 22-3) contains data for units sold, sales revenue, and the variable costs for software sold to several countries/regions in Asia and the Middle East. Each month, when you download the monthly financial reports, the location of each country/region in the worksheet changes, so you need formulas that always return (for a given country/region) the correct units sold, revenue, and variable cost.

	C	D	E	F
6	Country/Regior	Units solc	Revenue	Variable Cost
7	India	541	$ 4,328	$ 1,082
8	China	1000	$ 5,000	$ 2,000
9	Iran	577	$ 2,308	$ 1,731
10	Israel	454	$ 3,632	$ 1,362
11	Japan	141	$ 705	$ 423
12	Taiwan	221	$ 1,105	$ 663
13	Thailand	223	$ 1,115	$ 446
14	Indonesia	524	$ 2,620	$ 1,048
15	Malaysia	328	$ 1,968	$ 984
16	Vietnam	469	$ 2,814	$ 1,407
17	Cambodia	398	$ 1,990	$ 796
18				
19		Units solc	Revenue	Variable Cost
20	Country/Regior	1	2	3
21	Iran	577	2308	1731

FIGURE 22-3 Using the OFFSET function in calculations when working with data that isn't always in the same location in a worksheet.

By copying from D21 to E21:F21 the formula =OFFSET($C$6,MATCH ($C21,$C$7:$C$17,0),D20), you can compute the result you want. This formula sets a reference equal to cell C6 (which contains the words *Country/Region*). Then it moves over one column (to cell D20) to find the units sold and down to the row containing the country/region listed in C21. In cell E21, the reference to D20 now refers to E20, which is 2, so you move over two columns to the right of column C to find the revenue. In cell F21, the reference to D20 now refers to F20, which is 3, so you move three columns to the right of column C to find the variable cost.

Each drug developed by my company goes through three stages of development. I have a list of the cost by month for each drug, and I also know how many months each development stage took for each drug. Can I create formulas that compute for each drug the total cost incurred during each stage of development?

The file Offsetcost.xlsx contains the monthly costs incurred to develop five drugs and, for each drug, the number of months required to complete each phase. A subset of the data is shown in Figure 22-4.

	B	C	D	E	F	G	H
1		Dur Phase 1	2	3	9	12	6
2		Dur Phase 2	2	8	5	4	12
3		Dur Phase 3	2	11	4	11	15
4		Phase 1 Cost	110	313	795	1167	615
5		Phase 2 Cost	142	789	465	397	1096
6		Phase 3 Cost	234	876	401	1135	1588
7							
8							
9	Code	Month	Drug 1	Drug 2	Drug 3	Drug 4	Drug 5
10	1	Jan-98	52	135	131	121	69
11	2	Feb-98	58	120	77	60	68
12	3	Mar-98	80	58	66	52	113
13	4	Apr-98	62	56	78	61	146
14	5	May-98	130	126	98	118	94
15	6	Jun-98	104	102	64	117	125
16	7	Jul-98	121	59	115	112	137
17	8	Aug-98	107	123	56	102	77
18	9	Sep-98	80	88	110	85	93
19	10	Oct-98	51	111	72	118	89
20	11	Nov-98	74	124	82	143	66
21	12	Dec-98	76	107	99	78	66
22	13	Jan-99	97	97	129	77	142

FIGURE 22-4 Using the OFFSET function to compute development costs for Phases 1–3.

The goal is to determine for each drug the total cost incurred during each development phase. In cells D4:D6, I compute the total development costs for Phases 1–3 for Drug 1. I compute Phase 1 costs for Drug 1 by using a cell reference of D10, with *rows moved* and *columns moved* equal to 0. Setting *height* equal to the number of months in Phase 1 and *width* equal to 1 captures all Phase 1 costs. I compute the Phase 1 costs for Drug 1 in cell D4 with the formula =SUM(OFFSET(D10,0,0,D1,1)). Next, in cell D5, I compute the Phase 2 total costs for Drug 1 by using the formula =SUM(OFFSET(D10,D1,0,D2,1)). Note that I start with a cell reference of D10 (the first month of costs) and move down the number of rows equal to the length of Phase 1. This brings me to the beginning of Phase 2. Setting *height* equal to the value in cell D2 ensures that I include all the Phase 2 costs. Finally, in cell D6, I find the Phase 3 development costs for Drug 1 by using the formula =SUM(OFFSET(D10,D1+D2,0,D3,1)). In this formula, I start from the first month of sales and move down the number of rows equal to the total time needed for Phases 1 and 2. This brings me to the beginning of Phase 3, where in cell D6, I total the number of rows to capture Phase 3 costs. Then, by copying the formulas in D4:D6 to E4:H6, I can compute total costs for Phases 1–3 for Drugs 2 through 5. For example, for Drug 2, the total Phase 1 costs equal $313, the total Phase 2 costs equal $789, and the total Phase 3 costs equal $876.

I run a small video store. In a worksheet, my accountant has listed the name of each movie and the number of copies in stock. Unfortunately, he combined this information into one cell for each movie. How can I extract the number of copies of each movie in stock to a separate cell?

The worksheet Movies in the file Movies.xlsx, shown in Figure 22-5, contains the name of each movie and the number of copies in stock.

	A	B	C	D	E	F	G	H	I
1	count words	Number	Movie and Number of Copies						
2	2	40	Seabiscuit 40	Seabiscuit	40				
3	4	12	Lara Croft Tombraider 12	Laura	Croft	Tombraide	12		
4	6	36	Raiders of the Lost Ark 36	Raiders	of	the	Lost	Ark	36
5	3	5	Annie Hall 5	Annie	Hall	5			
6	2	4	Manhattan 4	Manhattan	4				
7	3	112	Star Wars 112	Star	Wars	112			
8	4	128	How to Deal 128	How	to	Deal	128		
9	4	1	The Matrix Reloaded 1	The	Matrix	Reloaded	1		
10	3	1040	Johnny English 1040	Johnny	English	1040			
11	3	12	Rosemary's Baby 12	Rosemary's	Baby	12			
12	3	1002	High Noon 1002	High	Noon	1002			

FIGURE 22-5 Movie example using the OFFSET function.

I want to extract the number of copies the video store owns of each movie to a separate cell. If the number of copies were listed to the left of a movie's title, this problem would be easy. I could use the FIND function to locate the first space and then use the LEFT function to return all the data to the left of the first space. (See Chapter 6, "Text functions," for a discussion of how to use the LEFT and FIND functions, as well as other functions you can use to work with text.) Unfortunately, this technique doesn't work when the number of copies is listed to the right of the movie title. For a one-word movie title, for example, the number of copies is to the right of the first space, but for a four-word movie title, the number of copies is to the right of the fourth space.

One way to solve this problem is to click the Data tab on the ribbon and then, in the Data Tools group, click the Text To Columns button to open the Convert Text To Columns Wizard (see instructions below), to place each word in a title and the number of copies in separate columns. You can use the COUNTA function to count the total number of words in a title, including the number of items as a word, for each movie. You can then use the OFFSET function to locate the number of items.

To begin, insert a sufficient number of columns to the right of the data to allow each word in the movies' titles and the number of items to be extracted to a separate column. I used six columns ("Raiders of the Lost Ark" requires six columns), adding columns D-I, as you can see back in Figure 22-5. Then I select the cell range C2:C12, and click Text To Columns on the Data tab. I select Delimited in the Convert Text To Columns Wizard, click Next (to move to step 2 of the wizard), and I clear Tab and select Space in the Delimiters section to use the space character as the delimiting character. Then I click Next, enter cell D2 as the destination cell, and click Finish. You can see the results in columns D through I of Figure 22-5.

Now I count the number of words (including the numbers) in each movie's cell (counting the number of items as a word) by copying from A2 to A3:A12 the formula =COUNTA(D2:I2). The results are shown back in Figure 21-5.

Finally, copying from B2 to B3:B12 the formula OFFSET(C2,0,A2), I can locate the number of copies of each movie in stock. This formula begins at the reference cell containing the movie title and moves over the number of columns equal to the number of words in the title cell. Because the reference cell contains only one cell, I can omit the *height* and *width* arguments of the OFFSET function so that the function uses only the cell containing the last "word" (the number of copies) of the title cell.

As shown in Figure 22-6 and the worksheet Flash Fill, you could use Flash Fill to extract the number of copies of each movie. I enter 40 in cell D2 and 12 in cell D3, I press the Enter key, and then I press

Ctrl+E. Note that if you try this with the Flash Fill worksheet (and not get an error), you'll want to delete cells D4:D12.

	C	D
1	Movie and Number of Copies	Number
2	Seabiscuit 40	40
3	Laura Croft Tombraider 12	12
4	Raiders of the Lost Ark 36	36
5	Annie Hall 5	5
6	Manhattan 4	4
7	Star Wars 112	112
8	How to Deal 128	128
9	The Matrix Reloaded 1	1
10	Johnny English 1040	1040
11	Rosemary's Baby 12	12
12	High Noon 1002	1002

FIGURE 22-6 Using Flash Fill to extract the number of movie copies.

How does Excel's Evaluate Formula feature work?

If you select any portion of a cell formula and then press F9, Excel displays the value created by that portion of the formula. You must press the Esc key or you lose the formula. This trick makes debugging and understanding complex formulas easier. Thus, it might be easier to understand what the OFFSET portion of the formula does if you apply this trick to any of the formulas in this chapter. For example, returning to the file Offsetcost.xlsx, cell E4 generates the total Phase 1 cost with the formula =SUM(OFFSET(E10,0,0,E1,1)). If you move the cursor over OFFSET(E10,0,0,E1,1), highlight this part of the formula, and then press F9, you will see =SUM({135,120,58}), which indicates that the OFFSET portion of the formula in cell D4 uses the correct cells (D10:D12). Be sure to press Esc to exit this procedure or you will lose your formula!

Another way to see how a complex formula works is to use the Evaluate Formula command. Click cell E4 and then click the Formulas tab on the ribbon. In the Formula Auditing group, click Evaluate Formula. (See Figure 22-7.) Click the Evaluate button three times, and Excel simplifies the formula step by step until you see the formula's final result. After clicking Evaluate twice, the formula appears as =SUM($E$10:E$12), so you know that in cell E4 you have selected the Phase 1 cells for Drug 2, which is what you wanted. If you click Evaluate a third time, you see the final result, *313*.

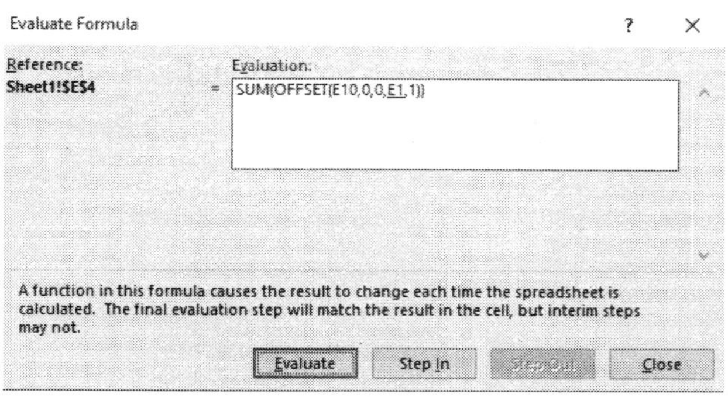

FIGURE 22-7 The Evaluate Formula dialog box.

How can I write a formula that always returns the last number in a column?

You often download new data into a worksheet. Can you write a formula that always returns sales during the most recent month? (See the file Mostrecent.xlsx and Figure 22-8.)

S26

	B	C	D	E
3			Most recent	
4			110	
5				
6	Sales			
7	20			
8	3			
9	40			
10	50			
11	60			
12	90			
13	110			

FIGURE 22-8 Finding the last number in a column.

Simply enter in cell D4 the formula =OFFSET(B6,COUNT(B:B),0,1,1).

This formula begins in cell B6 and moves down a number of rows equal to the number of numerical entries in column B. This takes you to the most recent month of sales, cell B13, which is selected because *1,1* returns only one cell. Thus cell D4 returns the value of cell B13, 110.

How can I set up a range name that automatically includes new data?

Users of Excel often add rows or columns of data to a range of data that is used to create a PivotTable or to perform another type of analysis. Usually, they simply update the range of cells referred to in their formula and then rerun the analysis. However, you can use dynamic range names and never have to update the range of data referred to in a formula or PivotTable. The range will automatically update. Here is an example.

The file Dynamicrange.xlsx shows entries from an HR database. (See Figure 22-9.)

	A	B	C	D	E	F	G
1	Name	Salary	Exp	Gender			
2	John	35500	3	M			
3	Jack	42300	4	M			
4	Jill	53426	5	F			
5	Erica	56000	6	F			
6	JR	62000	8	M			
7	Bianca	49000	10	F			
8	Francis	52000	5	M			
9	Roger	56000	7	M			
10	Maggie	42000	4				
11							448278

FIGURE 22-9 An example of a dynamic range.

Currently, the data contains nine rows and four columns of data. Wouldn't it be nice if you could create a range name that would automatically include more rows and/or columns when you add people or fields of information to the database?

To create a dynamic range, click the Formulas tab and then, in the Defined Names group, click Name Manager. Then click the New option and define a range as shown in Figure 22-10.

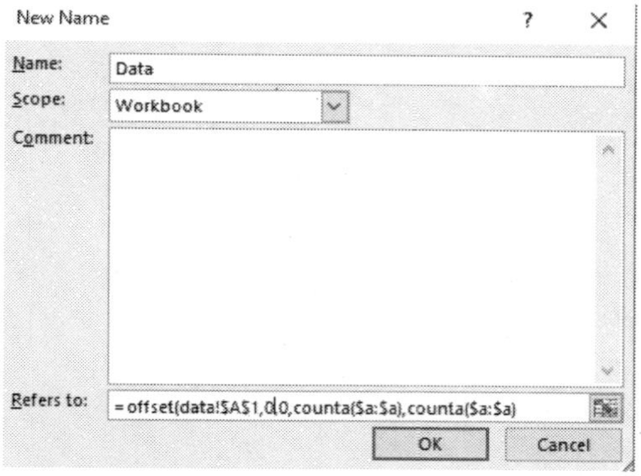

FIGURE 22-10 Creating a dynamic range.

You can select the range name Data that I created. It shows the formula =OFFSET(data!$A$1,0,0, COUNTA(data!$A:$A),COUNTA(data!$1:$1)). The range starts in the upper-left corner: cell A1. Next we move 0 rows and columns from cell A1. The selected range has *number of rows=number of nonblank entries* in column A and *number of columns=number of nonblank entries* in row 1. Thus, if you add people or data fields, the formula will automatically expand to include them. The dollar signs (**$**) are needed so that the defined range will not shift if you move around the worksheet.

To try this out, enter the formula =SUM(data) in cell G11. At present, this formula totals all numbers in the range A1:D9 and yields $448,278.

Now add to row 11 the name *Meredith*, enter in B11 a salary of $10,000, enter in E1 a variable for Mistakes (add the word *Mistakes*), and in E11 enter *1,000*. The formula =SUM(data) now includes the 10,000 and 1,000, and automatically updates to $459,278.

I am charting my company's monthly unit sales. Each month, I download the most recent month's unit sales. I would like my chart to update automatically. Is there an easy way to accomplish this?

The workbook Chartdynamicrange.xlsx (see Figure 22-11) contains the units sold of your company's product. As you can see, the units sold have been charted using an XY (Scatter) chart.

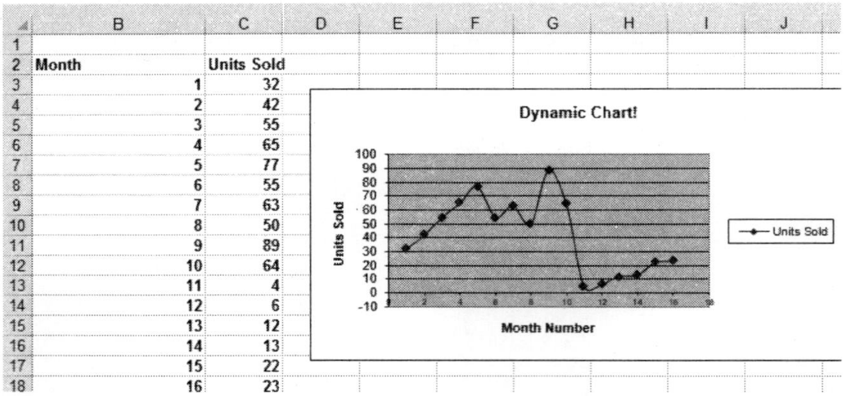

Month	Units Sold
1	32
2	42
3	55
4	65
5	77
6	55
7	63
8	50
9	89
10	64
11	4
12	6
13	12
14	13
15	22
16	23

FIGURE 22-11 Using the OFFSET function to update this chart dynamically.

Beginning in row 19, you will add and download new sales data. Is there an easy way to ensure that the chart automatically includes the new data?

The key to updating the chart is to use the OFFSET function to create dynamic range names for both the Month column and the Units Sold column. As new data is entered, the dynamic range for unit sales will automatically include all sales data, and the dynamic range for months will include each month number. After creating these ranges, you can modify the chart, replacing the data ranges used in the chart with the dynamic ranges. The chart now updates as new data is entered.

To begin, on the Formulas tab, in the Defined Names group, click Define Names to display the New Name dialog box. Create a range named *Units* by filling in the dialog box as shown in Figure 22-12.

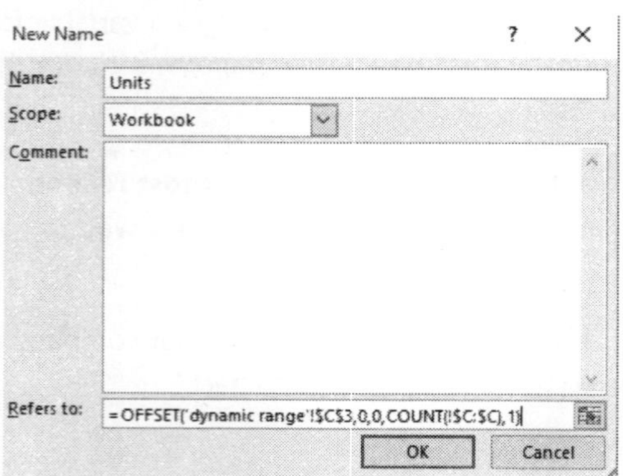

FIGURE 22-12 Creating a dynamic range name for the units sold.

Entering =OFFSET('dynamic range'!$C$3,0,0,COUNT(!$C:$C),1) in the Refers To area of the dialog box creates a range one column wide beginning in cell C3, which contains the first unit sales data point. The range will contain as many numbers as there are in column C, which is derived by the portion of the formula that reads COUNT('dynamic range'!$C:$C). As new data is entered into column C, the data is automatically included in the range named *Units*.

Next, create a dynamic range named *Month* for the months entered in column B. The formula is shown in Figure 22-13.

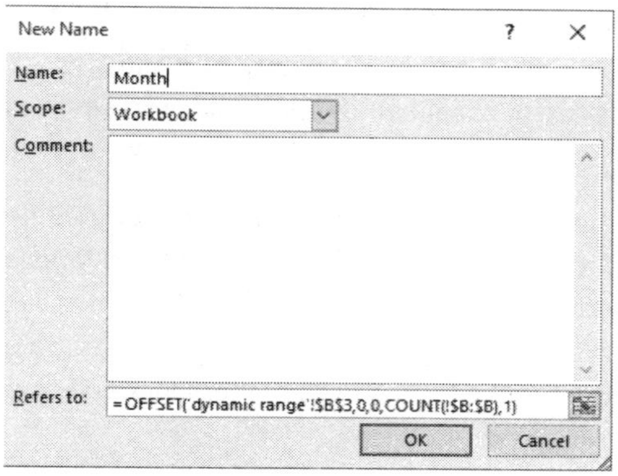

FIGURE 22-13 Using a formula to define a dynamic range named *Month*.

Now go to the chart and click any point. In the formula box, you'll see the formula =SERIES('dynamic range'!$C$2,'dynamic range'!$B$3:$B$18,'dynamic range'!$C$3:$C$18,1). This formula is Excel's version of the data originally used to set up the chart. Replace the ranges $B$3:$B$18 and $C$3:$C18 with the dynamic range names as follows:

```
SERIES('dynamicrange'!$C$2,Chartdynamicrange.xlsx!Month,Chartdynamicrange.xlsx!Units,1)
```

Of course, if a blank space is listed above any new data, this method won't work. Enter some new data in B19:C19 and below, and you'll see that it is added to the chart.

Remarks

The Excel table feature makes it easy to set things up so that charts and formulas automatically incorporate new data. See Chapter 26, "Tables," for a discussion of this feature.

Problems

1. The file Ch21p1.xlsx contains data about unit sales for 11 products during the years 1999–2003. Write a formula using the MATCH and OFFSET functions that determines the sales of a given product during a given year. Can you think of another way to solve this problem without using the MATCH and OFFSET functions?

2. A commonly suggested moving-average trading rule is to buy a stock when its price moves above the average of the last *D* months and to sell it when its price moves below the average of the last *D* months. In Chapter 12, "IF statements," I showed that for *D*=15, this trading rule outperformed the Standard & Poor's 500 by a substantial amount. By combining a one-way data table with the OFFSET function, determine the value of *D* that maximizes trading profit (excluding transactions costs). You can find pertinent data in the file Matradingrule.xlsx.

3. A commonly suggested moving-average trading rule is to buy a stock when its price moves above the average of the last *B* months and to sell it when its price moves below the average of the last *S* months. In Chapter 13, "Time and time functions," I showed that for *B*=*S*=15, this trading rule outperformed the Standard & Poor's 500 by a substantial amount. By combining a two-way data table with the OFFSET function, determine the values of *B* and *S* that maximize trading profit (excluding transactions costs). You'll find data for this problem in the file Matradingrule.xlsx.

4. The file Lagged.xlsx contains data about the number of magazine ads placed by US Army recruiting during each of 60 consecutive months. For each month, the *k*-month lagged number of ads is defined to equal the number of ads placed *k* months ago. For months 7–60, you want to compute the 1-month lagged, 2-month lagged, through 6-month lagged values of the number of ads. Use the OFFSET function to efficiently compute these lagged values.

5. The file Verizondata.xlsx gives sales of four different Verizon phones in five regions. Determine an efficient method to enter for each of the 20 region-product combinations, the region, type of phone, and sales of each phone into one row.

6. This problem is a difficult one. The file Agingdata.xlsx gives the number of insurance claims projected to be received daily and the number of insurance company workers available. Each day, a worker can process up to 30 claims. Workers process the oldest claims in the system first. In the file s22_6.xlsx from the Solution Files folder, cells H6:AL6 contain the number of claims already in the system on January 1, before new claims arrive. Set up a worksheet to track the "aging" of the claims. That is, for each day, how many 1-day old , 2-day old, ... 30-day old, and over 30-day old claims will be in the system.

7. Each row of the file DVDsales.xlsx contains monthly sales of DVDs. Write a formula to determine the sales for each DVD during its first six months on the market.

8. To obtain a golfer's handicap, you average the 10 lowest of the golfer's last 20 rounds. Then you subtract 80 and round to the nearest integer. Thus, if the 10 lowest of the last 20 rounds adds up to 864, the handicap would be 6. The file Golfdata.xlsx contains a golfer's scores. Beginning in row 24, compute the golfer's handicap after each round. Assume that if the tenth best score in the last 20 rounds occurs more than once, then all rounds including that score will be included in the handicap calculation. Note that the Excel function =ROUND(x,0) will round *x* to the nearest integer.

9. Each row of the file Carsumdata.xlsx contains sales data for a product (car, train, or plane) from January through July. Suppose you enter a month and a product into the worksheet. Write a formula that gives the total sales of that product during the given month.

10. The file Verizon.xlsx contains monthly returns on Verizon stock. Use the OFFSET function to extract all the January returns to one column, all the February returns to one column, and so on.

11. The file Casesensitive.xlsx contains product codes and product prices. Note that the product codes are case sensitive. For example, *DAG32* is not the same product as *dag32*. Write a

formula that gives the product price for any product code. Hint: You might need to use the EXACT function. The formula EXACT(cell1,cell2) yields True if cell1 and cell2 have exactly the same contents. EXACT differentiates between uppercase and lowercase letters.

12. The file Reversed.xlsx contains a column of numbers. Use the OFFSET function to reverse the numbers so that the number on bottom occurs on top, and so on.

13. The file Diagonal.xlsx contains a matrix of numbers. Determine how to put the diagonal elements of the matrix in a single column.

14. The file Yeartodate.xlsx contains a company's monthly sales from January 2008 through August 2013. Write a formula that returns for a given year and month of a year, the year's cumulative sales to date. For example, if you enter a *6* for the month and *2010* for the year, your formula should compute total sales for the period January–June 2010.

15. Show how you might create a graph of monthly sales that always displays just the last six months of sales.

16. The file Transactiondata.xlsx contains sales transactions in divisions A, B, C, D, and E of a drug company. Use the OFFSET function to modify this data so that the sales for each division appear in a single row.

CHAPTER 23

The INDIRECT function

Questions answered in this chapter:

- My worksheet formulas often contain references to cells, ranges, or both. Rather than change these references in my formulas, can I place the references in their own cells so that I can easily change my cell or range references without changing my underlying formulas?
- Each worksheet in a workbook lists monthly sales of a product in cell D1. Is there an easy way to write and copy a formula that lists each month's product sales in one worksheet?
- Suppose I total the values in the range A5:A10 with the formula SUM(A5:A10). If I insert a blank row somewhere between rows 5 and 10, my formula updates automatically to SUM(A5:A11). How can I write a formula so that when I insert a blank row between rows 5 and 10, my formula still totals the values in the original range, A5:A10?
- How can I use the INDIRECT function in a formula to recognize the range-name portion of a formula in a worksheet?
- My workbook contains sales in each country or region for each of my company's products, where each continent is listed in a different worksheet. How can I easily pool this data in a single summary worksheet?
- Is there an easy way to list all the worksheets in a workbook?

The INDIRECT function is probably one of the most difficult Microsoft Excel functions to master. Knowing how to use the INDIRECT function, however, enables you to solve many seemingly unsolvable problems. Essentially, any reference to a cell within the INDIRECT portion of a formula results in the immediate evaluation of the cell reference to equal the content of the cell. To illustrate the use of INDIRECT, look at the file Indirectsimpleex.xlsx, which is shown in Figure 23-1.

	A	B	C
1			
2			
3		Value	Indirect Reference
4	B4	6	6
5	B5	9	9

FIGURE 23-1 A simple example of the INDIRECT function.

In cell C4, I entered the formula =INDIRECT(A4). Excel returns the value 6 because the reference to A4 is immediately replaced by the text string *"B4"*, and the formula is evaluated as =B4, which yields the value 6. Similarly, entering in cell C5 the formula =INDIRECT(A5) returns the value in cell B5, which is 9.

Answers to this chapter's questions

My worksheet formulas often contain references to cells, ranges, or both. Rather than change these references in my formulas, can I place the references in their own cells so that I can easily change my cell or range references without changing my underlying formulas?

In this example, the data we'll use is contained in the file Sumindirect.xlsx, shown in Figure 23-2. The cell range B4:H16 lists monthly sales data for six products during a 12-month period.

I currently calculate total sales of each product during Months 2–12. An easy way to make this calculation is to copy from C18 to D18:H18 the formula =SUM(C6:C16). Suppose, however, that you want to change which months are totaled. For example, you might want total sales for months 3–12. You could change the formula in cell C18 to =SUM(C7:C16) and then copy this formula to D18:H18, but using this approach is problematic because you have to copy the formula in C18 to D18:H18 and, without looking at the formulas, nobody knows which rows are being added.

	B	C	D	E	F	G	H
1			Lower	Upper			
2			6	16			
3		C	D	E	F	G	H
4	Month	Prod 1	Prod 2	Prod 3	Prod 4	Prod 5	Prod 6
5	1	28	86	79	31	84	58
6	2	38	7	61	1	20	2
7	3	91	48	73	8	80	14
8	4	33	32	24	77	29	80
9	5	82	70	41	29	57	90
10	6	75	40	15	92	55	91
11	7	52	21	26	45	59	21
12	8	19	6	35	67	40	81
13	9	11	18	68	11	52	78
14	10	90	30	52	32	30	1
15	11	47	86	46	0	38	55
16	12	69	71	75	65	53	52
17							
18	Total	607	429	516	427	513	565

FIGURE 23-2 Using the INDIRECT function to change cell references in formulas without changing the formulas themselves.

The INDIRECT function provides another approach. I placed in cells D2 and E2 the starting and ending rows of our summation. Then, by using the INDIRECT function, all I need to do is change the starting and ending row references in D2 and E2, and the sums are updated to include the rows I want. Also, by looking at the values in D2 and E2, you can see at a glance which rows (months) are being added. All I need to do is copy from C18 to D18:H18 the formula =SUM(INDIRECT(C$3&$D$2& ":"&C$3&$E$2)).

If you want to see how Excel evaluates a reference to the INDIRECT function, use the following trick. Click in part of the formula (for example, C$3) and then press F9. Excel shows you the value of the selected portion of the formula. For example, C$3 evaluates to C. (Be sure to press the Esc key to return to Excel.) Every cell reference within the INDIRECT portion of this formula is evaluated to equal the contents of the cell. C$3 is evaluated as C, $D$2 is evaluated as 6, and $E$2 is evaluated as 16. With the ampersand (**&**) included as the concatenation symbol, Excel evaluates this formula as SUM(C6:C16), which is exactly whata you want. The formula in C18 returns the value 38+91+...69=607. In cell D18, the formula evaluates as SUM(D6:D16), which is the result you want. Of course, if you want to add up sales during months 4 through 6, you simply enter **8** in D2 and **10** in E2, and then the formula in C18 returns 33+82+75=190. (For information about using the ampersand to concatenate values, see Chapter 6, "Text functions.")

Each worksheet in a workbook lists monthly sales of a product in cell D1. Is there an easy way to write and copy a formula that lists each month's product sales in one worksheet?

The file Indirectmultisheet.xlsx (see Figure 23-3) contains seven worksheets. In each worksheet, cell D1 contains data about the sales of a product during a particular month. Let's suppose Sheet1 contains Month 1 sales, Sheet 2 contains Month 2 sales, and so on. For example, sales in Month 1 equals 1, in Month 2 it equals 4, and so on.

	C	D	E
7			
8			
9		Sheet#	Cell D1 entry
10	Sheet	1	1
11		2	4
12		3	0
13		4	12
14		5	15
15		6	3
16		7	4

FIGURE 23-3 Monthly sales (Months 1–7) of a product listed by using the INDIRECT function.

Now suppose you want to compile a list of each month's sales into one worksheet. A tedious approach would be to list Month 1 sales with the formula =Sheet1!D1, Month 2 sales with the formula =Sheet2!D1, and so on, until you list Month 7 sales with the formula =Sheet7!D1. If you have 100 months of data, this approach is very time consuming. A much more elegant approach is to list Month 1 sales in cell E10 of Sheet1 with the formula =INDIRECT($C$10&D10&"!D1"). Excel evaluates $C$10 as *"Sheet"*, D10 as *"1"*, and "!D1" as the text string *"!D1"*. The whole formula is evaluated as =Sheet1!D1, which yields Month 1 sales, located in cell D1 of Sheet1. Copying this formula to the range E11:E16 lists the entries in cell D1 of Sheets 2 through 7. When the formula in cell E10 is copied to cell E11, the reference to D10 changes to D11, and cell E11 returns the value located at Sheet2!D1.

Suppose I total the values in the range A5:A10 with the formula SUM(A5:A10). If I insert a blank row somewhere between rows 5 and 10, my formula updates automatically to SUM(A5:A11). How can I write a formula so that when I insert a blank row between rows 5 and 10, my formula still totals the values in the original range, A5:A10?

The worksheet named SUM(A5A10) in the file Indirectinsertrow.xlsx (shown in Figure 23-4) illustrates several ways to total the numbers in cell range A5:A10. (Note that the worksheet Row Inserted is similar but very different.) In cell A12, I entered the traditional formula SUM(A5:A10), which yields 6+7+8+9+1+2=33.

Similarly, the formula SUM($A$5:$A$10) in cell E9 yields a value of 33. As you'll soon see, however, if you insert a row between rows 5 and 10, both formulas attempt to total the cells in the range A5:A11.

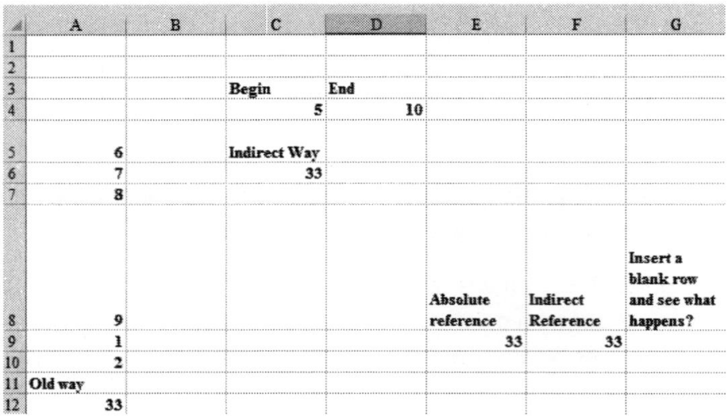

FIGURE 23-4 Showing several ways to sum the values in the cell range A5:A10.

With the INDIRECT function, you have at least two ways to total the values in the range A5:A10. In cell F9, I entered the formula SUM(INDIRECT("A5:A10")). Because Excel treats INDIRECT("A5:A10") as the text string *"A5:A10"*, if you insert a row in the worksheet, this formula still totals the entries in the cell range A5:A10.

Another way to use the INDIRECT function to total the entries in the range A5:A10 is the formula =SUM(INDIRECT("A"&C4&":A"&D4)), which is the formula entered in cell C6. Excel treats the reference to C4 as a *5* and the reference to D4 as a *10*, so this formula becomes SUM(A5:A10). Inserting a blank row between row 5 and row 10 has no effect on this formula because the reference to C4 is still treated as a *5*, and the reference to D4 is still treated as a *10*. In Figure 23-5, you can see the sums calculated by the four formulas after a blank row is inserted below row 7. You can find this data on the worksheet Row Inserted in the file Indirectinsertrow.xlsx.

As you can see, the classic SUM formulas, which do not use the INDIRECT function, have changed to add up the entries in the range A5:A11, so these formulas still yield a value of 33. The two SUM formulas that do use the INDIRECT function continue to add up the entries in the range A5:A10, so the value of 2 (now in cell A11) is no longer included in the calculated sum. The SUM formulas that use the INDIRECT function yield a value of 31.

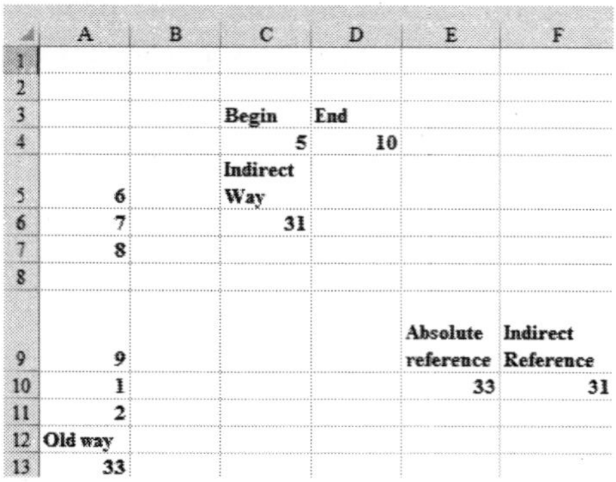

FIGURE 23-5 Results of SUM formulas after inserting a blank row in the original range.

How can I use the INDIRECT function in a formula to recognize the range-name portion of a formula in a worksheet?

Suppose you have named several ranges in a worksheet to correspond to quarterly product sales. (See Figure 23-6 and the file Indirectrange.xlsx.) For example, the range D4:E6 (named *Quarter1*) contains fictitious first-quarter sales of various Microsoft products.

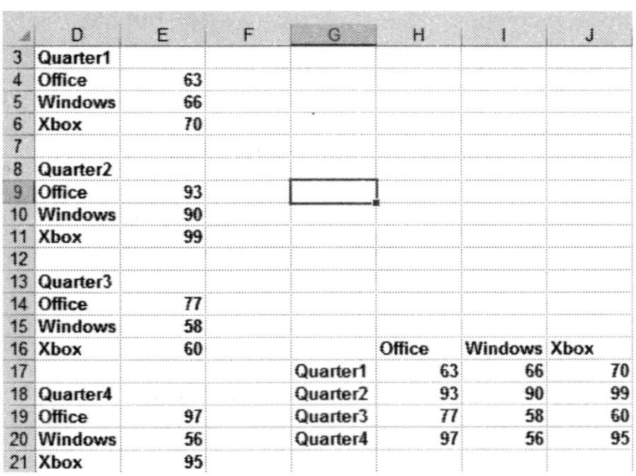

FIGURE 23-6 Use the INDIRECT function to create a reference to a range name within a formula.

It would be great to write a formula that can easily be copied and that then yields the sales of each product in each quarter in a single rectangular range of the worksheet, as shown in H17:J20. You would think you could enter in cell H17 the formula =VLOOKUP(H$16,$G17,2,FALSE) and then copy this formula to the range H17:J20. Unfortunately, Excel does not recognize $G17 as referring to the range name *Quarter1*. Rather, Excel just thinks $G17 is the text string *"Quarter1"*. The formula, therefore, returns an #NA error. To remedy this problem, simply enter in cell H17 the formula =VLOOKUP (H$16,INDIRECT($G17),2,FALSE) and then copy this formula to range H17:J20. This works perfectly! INDIRECT($G17) is evaluated as *Quarter1* and is now recognized as a range name. You have now easily generated sales of all the products during all four quarters.

My workbook contains sales in each country or region for each of my company's products, where each continent is listed in a different worksheet. How can I easily pool this data in a single summary worksheet?

Cells E7:E9 of the file Indirectconsolidate.xlsx contain the sales of cars, trucks, and planes on each continent. Each continent has its own worksheet. How can you summarize this data in a single sheet?

In the worksheet Summary, I created the summary shown in Figure 23-7.

	C	D	E	F	G	H	I
5			=LA!E7				
6			LA	NA	Asia	Africa	Europe
7	E7	Cars	100	200	500	100	80
8	E8	Trucks	150	150	400	50	120
9	E9	Planes	200	100	200	25	100

FIGURE 23-7 Using the INDIRECT function to create a summary of product sales.

I copied from cell E7 to the range E7:I9 the formula =INDIRECT(E$6&"!"&$C7). This formula creates the formula =LA!E7, which calculates car sales in Latin America. Copying this formula collects the sales for each type of product on each continent.

In the worksheet Another Summary (see Figure 23-8), I created the same table in a slightly different manner. I automated the generation of the cell addresses from which I pull the car, truck, and plane sales by copying from C7 to C8:C9 the formula =ADDRESS(ROW(),COLUMN()+2). This generates column E in the cell address and then rows 8 and 9. The function ROW() entered in a cell returns the cell's row number, and the function COLUMN() entered by itself in a cell returns the column number of the current cell (in this case 3). When entered as part of the third argument of the ADDRESS function, the term COLUMN()+2 effectively returns the column label for the cell two columns to the right of the current cell (in this case column E.) Then I copied from cell E7 to the range E7:I9 the formula =INDIRECT(E$6&"!"&$C7).

	C	D	E	F	G	H	I
5			=LA!E7				
6			LA	NA	Asia	Africa	Europe
7	$E$7	Cars	100	200	500	100	80
8	$E$8	Trucks	150	150	400	50	120
9	$E$9	Planes	200	100	200	25	100

FIGURE 23-8 Using efficiently copied cell addresses to summarize a workbook.

Is there an easy way to list all the worksheets in a workbook?

In the last example, it was easy to list the worksheet names. Suppose we had a workbook with 100 or more worksheets. If we wanted to unleash the full power of the INDIRECT function to pull data from a subset of these worksheets, we need an efficient method for listing the name of each worksheet in a workbook. To efficiently list all the worksheet names in a workbook, proceed as described in the following list. (See the workbook Worksheetnames.xlsm and Figures 23-9 and 23-10.)

- From the Formulas tab, select Define Names. Then in the New Name dialog box, create a range name. Let's call the range *Worksheet* with the formula in the Refers To field, =GET.WORKBOOK(1), as you see in Figure 23-9. GET.WORKBOOK(1) is a macro (macros are discussed in Chapter 89), so the file suffix must be *.xlsm*.
- Select a horizontal array containing as many rows as your workbook has worksheets, although in our current example, it is easy to see there are only three worksheets. If you do not know the number of worksheets in a workbook, you can use the SHEETS() function (added in Excel 2013). We enter the SHEETS() function in cell H13. The SHEETS() function returns the number of worksheets in a workbook (in this case 3). By the way, the SHEET() formula enters the number of the current worksheet in the workbook. For example, if you entered =SHEET() anywhere in the Bob worksheet, the formula would enter 1, anywhere in the Allen worksheet 2, anywhere in the Jill worksheet 3.
- In the left-hand corner of the selected range (in this case H15), type **=Worksheet** and press the key combination Ctrl+Shift+Enter. The *Worksheet* range name acts as an array formula (see Chapter 88, "Array formulas and functions," for more discussion of array formulas), so you must press Ctrl+Shift+Enter for the formula to work. In the cell range H15:J15, you now see the workbook name enclosed in square brackets followed by the worksheet names, listed in the order of the worksheets.

To return each worksheet name to a separate cell, we simply use the RIGHT and FIND functions, described in Chapter 6, "Text functions," to extract each worksheet name by pulling out all the characters to the right of the square bracket. Simply copy from H16 to I16:J16 the formula =RIGHT(I15,LEN(I15)-FIND("]",I15,1)). You now see the worksheet names listed in the range H16:J16.

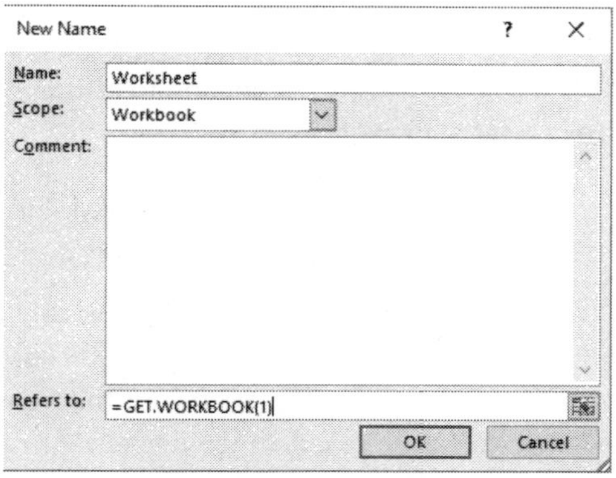

FIGURE 23-9 Creating a range name that can be used to extract worksheet names.

	H	I	J
5	Obtaining worksheet names		
6	1. Go to Define names and create a Name worksheet		
7	using =GET.WORKBOOK(1)		
8	2. Select horizontal array ofsize = number of worksheets		
9	3. Type =worksheet and then Control+shift+Enter		
10	4. Use Text functions to pull out worksheet names		
11			
12	How many worksheets?		
13	3		
14			
15	[worksheetnames.xlsm]Bob	[worksheetnames.xlsm]Allen	[worksheetnames.xlsm]Jill
16	Bob	Allen	Jill

FIGURE 23-10 Extracting worksheet names in row 16, and using the SHEET() function to pull the number of sheets.

Problems

1. The ADDRESS function yields the actual cell address associated with a row and column. For example, the formula ADDRESS(3,4) yields $D$3. What result would be obtained if you entered the formula =INDIRECT(ADDRESS(3,4))?

2. The workbook P23_2.xlsx contains data for the sales of five products in four regions (East, West, North, and South). Use the INDIRECT function to create formulas that enable you to easily calculate the total sales of any combination of consecutively numbered products, such as Products 1–3, Products 2–5, and so on.

3. The file P23_3.xlsx contains six worksheets. Sheet 1 contains Month 1 sales for Products 1–4. These sales are always listed in the range E5:H5. Use the INDIRECT function to efficiently tabulate the sales of each product by month in a separate worksheet.

4. Write a formula that will total the entries in the cell range G2:K2, even if you insert one or more columns between columns G and K.

5. The file Marketbasketdata.xlsx contains sales of various items. For each row, a 1 in columns B through K indicates a purchased item, whereas a 0 marks an item that was not purchased. In the Day Week column, a 1 means the transaction was on a Monday, a 2 means the transaction was on a Tuesday, and so on. For each item listed in K9:K14, calculate the percentage of transactions in which the item was purchased. Also calculate the fraction of transactions taking place on each day.

6. The file Verizonindirectdata.xlsx contains each employee's hours of work and employee rating for January–May. Set up a consolidation sheet that enables you to choose any person and then gather that person's hours of work during each month, along with his or her overall rating for the month.

CHAPTER 24

Conditional formatting

Questions answered in this chapter:

- How can I visually indicate whether recent temperature data is consistent with global warming?
- How does the Highlight Cells conditional formatting feature work?
- How do I check or customize my rules?
- How do data bars work?
- How does Excel 2016 treat negative data bars?
- How do color scales work?
- How do icon sets work?
- How can I color-code monthly stock returns so that every good month is indicated in one color and every bad month in another?
- Given quarterly corporate revenues, how can I indicate quarters in which revenues increased over the previous quarter in one color and quarters in which revenues decreased from the previous quarter in another color?
- Given a list of dates, how can I indicate weekend dates in a specific color?
- Our basketball coach has given each player a rating between 1 and 10 based on the player's ability to play guard, forward, or center. Can I set up a worksheet that visually indicates the ability of each player to play the position to which she's assigned?
- What does the Stop If True option in the Manage Rules dialog box do?
- How can I use the Format Painter to copy a conditional format?

Conditional formatting lets you specify formatting for a cell range on the basis of the contents of the cell range. For example, given exam scores for students, you can use conditional formatting to display in red the names of students who have a final average of at least 90 percent. Basically, when you set up conditions for formatting a range of cells, Microsoft Excel 2016 checks each cell in the range to determine whether any of the conditions you specified (such as average>90) is satisfied. Then Excel applies the format you choose for that condition to all the cells that satisfy the condition. If the content of a cell does not satisfy any of the conditions, the formatting of the cell remains unchanged. In Excel 2007, conditional formatting was completely revised and expanded. Excel 2010 added some minor improvements to conditional formatting. In this chapter, I show you how to use all the conditional formatting features included in Excel 2016.

To view the conditional formatting options, first select the range you want to format. Then, on the Home tab, in the Styles group, click the Conditional Formatting arrow (see Figure 24-1) to open a menu of conditional formatting options, as shown in Figure 24-2.

FIGURE 24-1 The Conditional Formatting command.

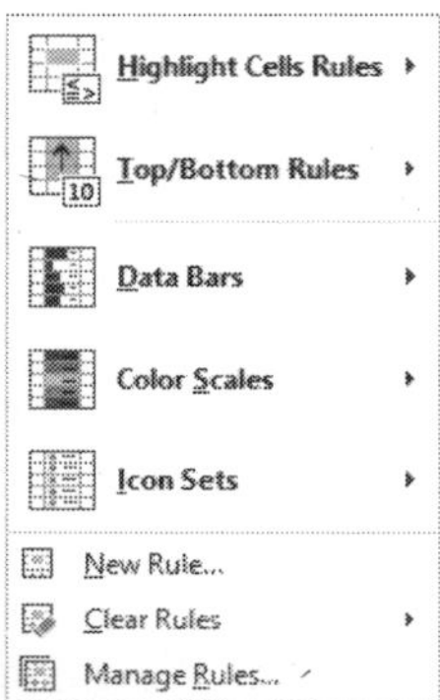

FIGURE 24-2 Conditional formatting options.

- Highlight Cells Rules allows you to assign a format to cells whose contents meet one of the following criteria:
  - Are within a specific numerical range
  - Match a specific text string
  - Are within a specific range of dates (relative to the current date)
  - Occur more than once (or only once) in the selected range
- Top/Bottom Rules allows you to assign a format to any of the following:
  - *N* largest or smallest values in a range
  - Top or bottom *n* percent of numbers in a range
  - Numbers above or below the average of all the numbers in a range
- Data Bars, Color Scales, and Icon Sets allow you to easily identify large, small, or intermediate values in the selected range. Larger data bars are associated with larger numbers. With color

scales, you might, for example, have smaller values appear in red and larger values in blue, with a smooth transition applied as values in the range increase from small to large. With icon sets, you can use as many as five symbols to identify different ranges of values. For example, you might display an arrow pointing up to indicate a large value, pointing to the right to indicate an intermediate value, and pointing down to indicate a small value.

- New Rule allows you to create your own formula to determine whether a cell should have a specific format. For example, if a cell exceeds the value of the cell above it, you could apply the color green to the cell. If the cell is the fifth-largest value in its column, you could apply the color red to the cell, and so on.
- Clear Rules allows you to delete all conditional formats you have created for a selected range or for the entire worksheet.
- Manage Rules allows you to view, edit, and delete conditional formatting rules, create new rules, or change the order in which Excel applies the conditional formatting rules you have set.

Answers to this chapter's questions

How can I visually indicate whether recent temperature data is consistent with global warming?

This question offers a perfect opportunity for applying the Top/Bottom conditional formatting rules. The file Globalwarming2016.xlsx contains for each year the annual deviation in world temperature from the 1951–1980 average Celsius temperature. (Figure 24-4 shows a subset of this data.) If global warming has occurred, you would expect the numbers in recent years to be larger than the numbers in earlier years. To determine whether recent years are warmer, let's try to highlight the 20 warmest years in red. For my examples, I first selected the range B3:B138 containing the temperatures. On the Home tab, in the Styles group, I clicked Conditional Formatting and then selected Top/Bottom Rules. Next, I selected Top 10 Items and filled in the dialog box as shown in Figure 24-3. I changed the default 10 value to 20, and I left the default highlight selection, Light Red Fill With Dark Red Text. The 20 warmest years are now highlighted in red. Note that 11 years since 1998 are among the 20 warmest. If there were no trend in temperature, you would have expected around two years since 1998 to rank in the 20 warmest years.

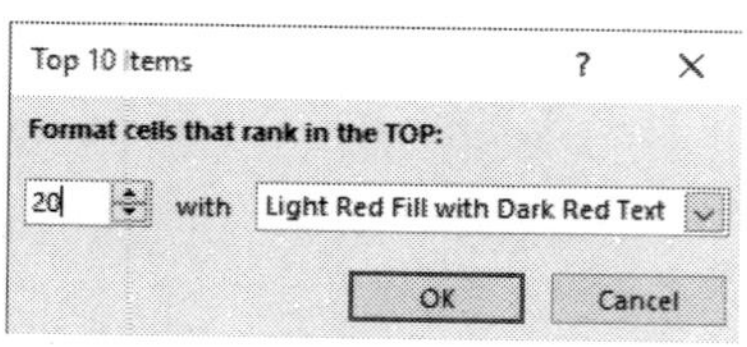

FIGURE 24-3 Highlighting the 20 highest temperatures in red.

Note Clicking the arrow shown on the right side of Figure 24-3 displays a list of options, including Custom Format. Selecting this option displays the Format Cells dialog box, which allows you to create a custom format that is applied when you click OK in both dialog boxes.

Next, I selected the range C3:C138 and went back to Top/Bottom Rules. In a similar fashion, in column F, I highlighted the top 10 percent of the temperatures in red by clicking Conditional Formatting, Top/Bottom Rules, Top 10%, retained the default settings, and then clicked OK in the Top 10% dialog box. Then I highlighted the bottom 10 percent in green by clicking Conditional Formatting, Top/Bottom Rules, Bottom 10%. Then, in the Bottom 10% dialog box, I selected the highlight setting Green Fill With Dark Green Text and clicked OK. Finally, in column D I highlighted above-average temperatures in green and below-average temperatures in red by using the Above Average and Below Average options in the Conditional Formatting drop-down menu. Note that thirteen years since 1998 rank in the warmest 10 percent of all the years. If there were no trend in world temperatures, you would expect around two of those years to rank in the top 10 percent. Also observe that all years since 1977 have above average temperatures! If temperatures showed no trend, there would be around a 50 percent chance of a year having above average temperatures, so the 1977–2015 temperatures (if there is no trend) is like tossing heads 39 consecutive times! This example shows that conditional formatting is a powerful visualization tool that can be used to demonstrate that the earth (for whatever reasons) seems to have recently become warmer.

	A	B	C	D
2	Year	Top20	Top 10% and Bottom 10%	Above and Below Average
3	1880	-0.2	-0.2	-0.2
4	1881	-0.11	-0.11	-0.11
5	1882	-0.1	-0.1	-0.1
6	1883	-0.2	-0.2	-0.2
7	1884	-0.27	-0.27	-0.27
8	1885	-0.31	-0.31	-0.31
9	1886	-0.3	-0.3	-0.3
10	1887	-0.33	-0.33	-0.33
11	1888	-0.2	-0.2	-0.2
12	1889	-0.11	-0.11	-0.11
13	1890	-0.37	-0.37	-0.37
113	1990	0.44	0.44	0.44
114	1991	0.42	0.42	0.42
115	1992	0.23	0.23	0.23
116	1993	0.24	0.24	0.24
117	1994	0.32	0.32	0.32
118	1995	0.46	0.46	0.46
119	1996	0.34	0.34	0.34
120	1997	0.48	0.48	0.48
121	1998	0.63	0.63	0.63
122	1999	0.42	0.42	0.42
123	2000	0.42	0.42	0.42
124	2001	0.55	0.55	0.55
125	2002	0.63	0.63	0.63
126	2003	0.62	0.62	0.62
127	2004	0.55	0.55	0.55
128	2005	0.69	0.69	0.69
129	2006	0.63	0.63	0.63
130	2007	0.66	0.66	0.66
131	2008	0.53	0.53	0.53
132	2009	0.64	0.64	0.64
133	2010	0.71	0.71	0.71
134	2011	0.6	0.6	0.6
135	2012	0.63	0.63	0.63
136	2013	0.65	0.65	0.65
137	2014	0.74	0.74	0.74
138	2015	0.37	0.87	0.87

FIGURE 24-4 Conditional formatting using Top/Bottom Rules.

How does the Highlights Cells conditional formatting feature work?

The file Highlightcells.xlsx (see Figure 24-5) demonstrates how the Highlight Cells feature is used. For example, suppose you want to highlight all the duplicate names in C2:C11 in red. Simply select the cell range C2:C11, click Conditional Formatting in the Styles group on the Home tab, click Highlight Cells Rules, click Duplicate Values, and then choose Light Red Fill With Dark Red Text. Click OK to apply the rule so that all names occurring more than once (John and Josh) are highlighted in red.

	C	D	E	F
1	duplicates red fill	text containing Eric red fill red text	last 7 days red then yesterday green	
2	John	John	6/1/2006	
3	Eric	Eric	6/20/2016	today()-1
4	James	James	6/16/2016	today()-5
5	John	John	5/15/2007	
6	Erica	Erica	6/14/2006	
7	JR	JR	2/3/2003	
8	Adam	Adam	5/12/2006	
9	Josh	Josh	6/17/2005	
10	Babe	Babe	8/1/2006	
11	Josh	Josh	9/2/2005	

FIGURE 24-5 Using the Highlight Cells Rules option.

Now suppose that you want to highlight in red all cells in the range D2:D11 that contain the text *Eric*. Simply select the cell range D2:D11, click Conditional Formatting, click Highlight Cells Rules, and then click Text That Contains. Enter **Eric** in the left box, and choose Light Red Fill With Dark Red Text on the right. As shown in Figure 24-5, both *Eric* and *Erica* are highlighted. (*Erica*, of course, contains the text string *Eric*). The Text Contains option is not case sensitive, so you could enter *eric* in lowercase and get the same result.

Suppose you have a list of dates (such as in E2:E11), and you want to highlight any cell that contains yesterday's date in green and any other date during the last seven days in red. (See the worksheet Right Way in the file Highlightcells.xlsx.) Assume (as in Figure 24-5) that the current date is June 21, 2016. Note that cell E3 contains the formula =TODAY()–1, so cell E3 always displays yesterday's date. Cell E4 contains the formula =TODAY()–5 and shows you the date from five days ago.

For my examples, I began by selecting the cell range I want to format (E2:E11). Next, I clicked Conditional Formatting, Highlight Cells Rules, and then chose the A Date Occurring option. In the A Date Occurring dialog box, I selected the Yesterday option with Green Fill With Dark Green Text and clicked OK. Then I clicked Conditional Formatting, Highlight Cells Rules and again chose A Date Occurring. In the A Date Occurring dialog box, this time I selected In The Last 7 Days and Light Red Fill With Dark Red Text. Formatting rules created later have precedence over rules created earlier (unless you change the order of precedence, as explained later in the chapter). This explains why yesterday's date is left formatted in red rather than green.

How do I check or customize my rules?

After creating conditional formatting rules, you can view your rules by clicking Manage Rules on the Conditional Formatting menu. For example, select the dates in E2:E11, click Conditional Formatting, click Manage Rules, and you see the rules displayed as in Figure 24-6. You can see that the Last 7 Days formatting rule will be applied before the Yesterday formatting rule.

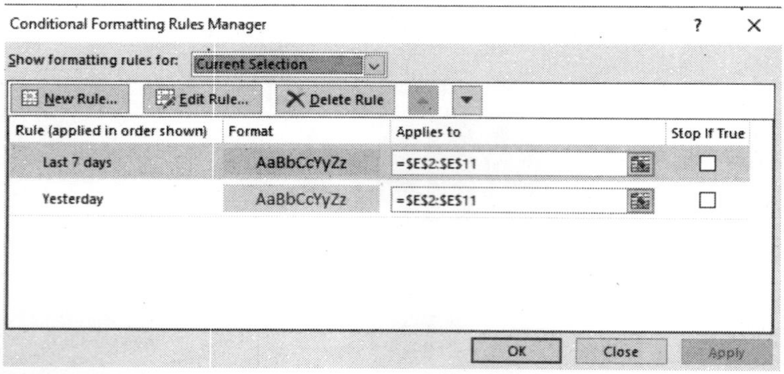

FIGURE 24-6 Conditional Formatting Rules Manager dialog box.

In the Conditional Formatting Rules Manager dialog box, you can do the following:

- Create a rule by clicking the New Rule button.
- Edit or change a rule by clicking the Edit Rule button.
- Delete a rule by selecting it and then clicking the Delete Rule button.
- Change the order of precedence by selecting a rule and then clicking the up arrow or down arrow.

To illustrate the use of the Conditional Formatting Rules Manager dialog box, I copied the previous worksheet (simply right-click the worksheet tab, click Move Or Copy, and then select the Create A Copy check box) to the Right Way worksheet of the file Highlightcells.xlsx. I selected the Yesterday rule and clicked the up arrow. The Yesterday rule now has higher precedence than the Last 7 Days rule, so E3 will be formatted green and not red. Figure 24-7 shows how the Conditional Formatting Rules Manager dialog box looks, and Figure 24-8 shows that cell E3 is green and cell E4 is red, as we wanted.

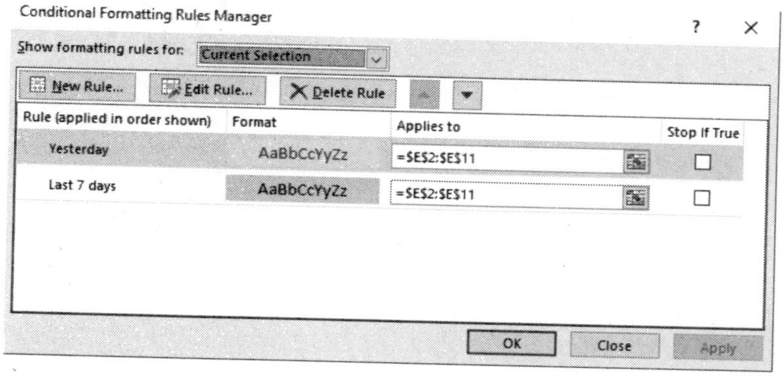

FIGURE 24-7 Showing that Yesterday now has a higher priority than Last 7 Days.

	C	D	E	F
1	duplicates red fill	text containing Eric red fill red text	yesterday green then last 7 days red	
2	John	John	6/1/2006	
3	Eric	Eric	6/20/2016	today()-1
4	James	James	6/16/2016	today()-5
5	John	John	5/15/2007	
6	Erica	Erica	6/14/2006	
7	JR	JR	2/3/2003	
8	Adam	Adam	5/12/2006	
9	Josh	Josh	6/17/2005	
10	Babe	Babe	8/1/2006	
11	Josh	Josh	9/2/2005	

FIGURE 24-8 Showing that Yesterday is now formatted in green, after the order of rules is changed.

How do data bars work?

When you have a long list of numbers, it's nice to have a visual indicator that enables you to easily identify large and small numbers. Data bars, color scales, and icon sets (all introduced in Excel 2007) are perfect tools for displaying differences in a list of numbers. The file Scalesiconsdatabars.xlsx illustrates the use of these tools.

Figure 24-9 (see the file Databars.xlsx) shows the use of data bars. For my examples, I began by applying the default data bars to the data in D6:D15. I selected the data in that range, clicked Conditional Formatting, and then clicked Data Bars. Next, in the Gradient Fill section, I chose the blue data bars to create the format shown in column D of Figure 24-9. Cells containing larger numbers contain longer blue bars. The default option is to associate the shortest data bar with the smallest number in the selected range and the longest data bar with the largest number. As you can see in column D, the size of the data bars is directly proportional to the data value; that is, the data bar for 8 is twice as large as the data bar for 4, and so on.

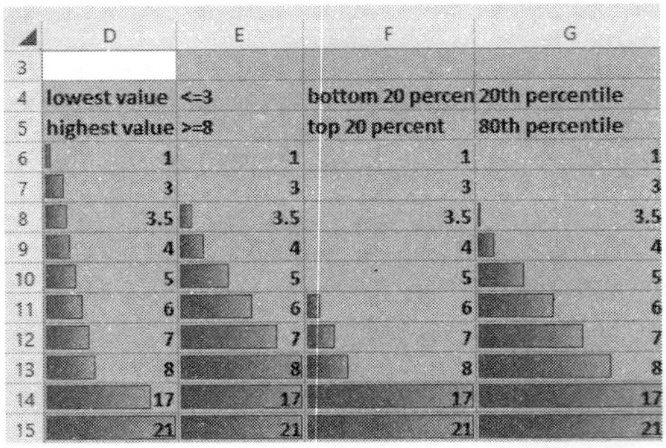

FIGURE 24-9 Visually distinguishing numeric values by using data bars.

If, after clicking Data Bars, you click More Rules, the New Formatting Rule dialog box shown in Figure 24-10 is displayed. (You can also display this dialog box by clicking Manage Rules and then clicking Edit Rule or by double-clicking a rule.) From this dialog box, you can change the criteria used to assign no data bar and the longest data bars to cells. In E6:E15, I assigned no data bar to numbers less than or equal to 3 and the longest bar to any number greater than or equal to 8. As shown in Figure 24-9, all numbers in column E that are less than or equal to 3 have no data bar, all numbers that are greater than or equal to 8 have the longest bar, and the numbers between 3 and 8 have graduated bars. Note that in the Edit Formatting Rule dialog box, you can select the Show Bar Only check box to display only the color bar and not the cell value in the conditionally formatted cells.

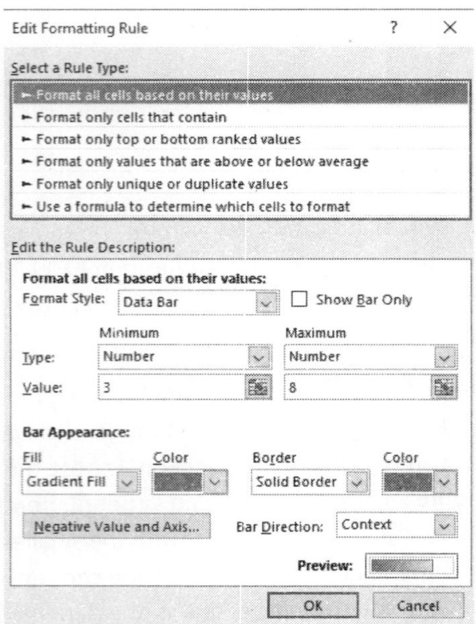

FIGURE 24-10 Customizing your data bars.

Next, in column F, I chose to assign no bar to numbers in the bottom 20 percent of the range F6:F15, and the longest bar to numbers in the top 20 percent. In other words, all numbers

<=1+.2(21–1)=5 have no data bar, and all numbers >=1+.8(21–1)=17 have the longest data bar. Figure 24-9 shows that in column F, the first five numbers have no data bar and the numbers 17 and 21 have the longest data bar.

In the cell range G6:G13, I associated no data bar with all numbers at or below the twentieth percentile of the data (3), and I associated the longest data bar with all numbers at or above the 80th percentile of the data (17). From the Bar Direction list, you can specify whether your data bars begin at the right or left border of the cell.

Excel 2016 allows solid shading for data bars and also allows you to orient data bars associated with negative values so that they run in a direction opposite to positive values. After selecting Negative Values and Axis from the Edit The Rule Description dialog box, you can move the axis from the normal position in the center of the cell and/or make the negative data bars open to the left (the default) or to the right. The file Negativedatabars.xlsx and Figure 24-11 show how solid data bars appear for a data set containing negative numbers. Note the last two columns in Figure 24-11 use the Automatic Axis setting, which allocates more space to the positive entries because they are larger in magnitude than the negative values.

	D	E	F	G	H	I
1	Left to Right Centered		Right to Left Centered			Automatic
2	Year	Sales	Year	Sales	Year	Sales
3	2000	-5	2000	-5	2000	-5
4	2001	56	2001	56	2001	500
5	2002	85	2002	85	2002	500
6	2003	-31	2003	-31	2003	-31
7	2004	-26	2004	-26	2004	-26
8	2005	-40	2005	-40	2005	-40
9	2006	85	2006	85	2006	200
10	2007	34	2007	34	2007	34
11	2008	50	2008	50	2008	50
12	2009	46	2009	-46	2009	-46
13	2010	4	2010	4	2010	4
14	2011	47	2011	47	2011	47
15	2012	-5	2012	-5	2012	-5
16	2013	44	2013	44	2013	44

FIGURE 24-11 Data bars for negative values with both solid and gradient shading.

How do color scales work?

Now let's use color scales to summarize some data sets. Like the Highlight Cells Rules option, a color scale uses cell shading to display the differences in cell values. Here I'll describe an example of a three-color scale. (The file Colorscales2016.xlsx and Figure 24-12 illustrate the use of a three-color scale. Note that I have hidden rows 19–80; to unhide them, select rows 18 and 81, right-click the selection, and then click Unhide.)

	D	E	F	G
5	Year	S&P 500	3-month T.Bill	10-year T. Bond
6	1928	43.81%	3.08%	0.84%
7	1929	-8.30%	3.16%	4.20%
8	1930	-25.12%	4.55%	4.54%
9	1931	-43.84%	2.31%	-2.56%
10	1932	-8.64%	1.07%	8.79%
11	1933	49.98%	0.96%	1.86%
12	1934	-1.19%	0.32%	7.96%
13	1935	46.74%	0.18%	4.47%
14	1936	31.94%	0.17%	5.02%
15	1937	-35.34%	0.30%	1.38%
16	1938	29.28%	0.08%	4.21%
17	1939	-1.10%	0.04%	4.41%
18	1940	-10.67%	0.03%	5.40%
81	2003	28.36%	1.03%	0.38%
82	2004	10.74%	1.23%	4.49%
83	2005	4.83%	3.01%	2.87%
84	2006	15.61%	4.68%	1.96%
85	2007	5.48%	4.64%	10.21%
86	2008	-36.55%	1.59%	20.10%
87	2009	25.94%	0.14%	-11.12%
88	2010	14.82%	0.13%	8.46%
89	2011	2.10%	0.03%	16.04%
90	2012	15.89%	0.05%	2.97%
91	2013	32.15%	0.07%	-9.10%
92	2014	13.52%	0.05%	10.75%
93	2015	1.36%	0.21%	1.28%

FIGURE 24-12 Three-color scales.

For my examples, I selected the annual returns on stocks, T-bills, and T-bonds in cells B6:D93. I then clicked Conditional Formatting, Color Scales, and then More Rules to display the Edit Formatting Rule dialog box, which I filled in as shown in Figure 24-13.

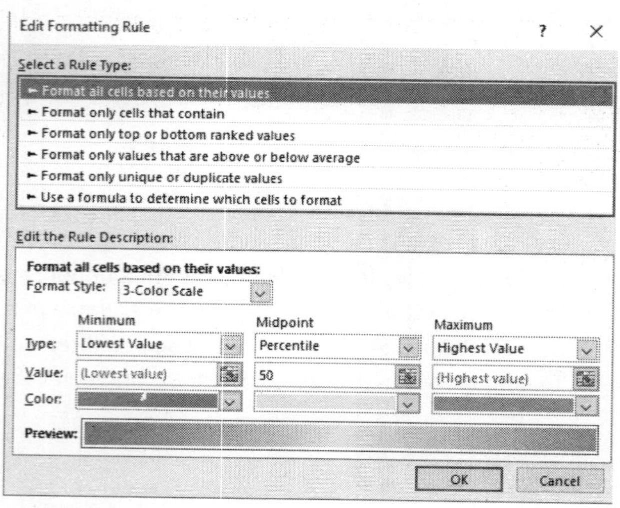

FIGURE 24-13 Customizing a three-color scale.

I chose the color red to indicate the lowest return, green to indicate the highest return, and orange to indicate the return at the midpoint. Amazingly, Excel makes small changes to the color shading of each cell based on the value in the cell. In column B of Figure 24-12, the lowest return is shaded red. Note that 1931 and 2008 (as we all know) were very poor years for stocks. As the returns approach the fiftieth percentile, the cell color gradually changes to yellow. Then, as the returns increase from the fiftieth percentile toward the largest return, the cell color changes from yellow to green. Most of the green and red cells are associated with stocks because annual stock returns are more variable than bond or T-bill returns. This variability causes large and small stock returns to occur quite frequently. Virtually all annual returns for T-bills or T-bonds are yellow because the low variability of annual returns on these investments means that intermediate returns occur most of the time.

I created some two-color scales for the file Scalesiconsdatabars.xlsx, shown in Figure 24-14. I selected the range of cells and then clicked Conditional Formatting, Color Scales. You can select the color combination you want from the given list or create your own by clicking More Rules.

For my examples, I chose a two-color scale that indicates lower values in white and higher values in dark blue:

- In the cell range D19:D28, I chose to make the lowest value white and the highest value blue. As numbers increase, the cell shading becomes darker.
- In the range E19:E28, I chose to make values less than or equal to 3 white and values greater than or equal to 8 blue. For numbers between 3 and 8, as numbers increase, the cell shading becomes darker.
- In the range F19:F28, I chose to make values in the bottom 20 percent of the range white and numbers in the top 20 percent blue. For numbers in the middle 60 percent, cell shading becomes darker as numbers increase.

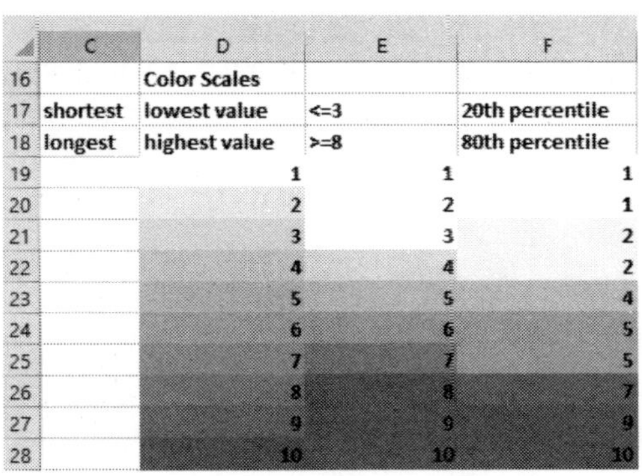

	C	D	E	F
16		Color Scales		
17	shortest	lowest value	<=3	20th percentile
18	longest	highest value	>=8	80th percentile
19		1	1	1
20		2	2	1
21		3	3	2
22		4	4	2
23		5	5	4
24		6	6	5
25		7	7	5
26		8	8	7
27		9	9	9
28		10	10	10

FIGURE 24-14 Two-color scales.

How do icon sets work?

You can also display numerical differences by using icon sets, illustrated in Figure 24-15 and the file Scalesiconsdatabars.xlsx. An icon set consists of three to five symbols. You define criteria to associate an icon with each value in a cell range. For example, you might use a down arrow for small numbers, an up arrow for large numbers, and a horizontal arrow for intermediate values. The cell range E32:F41 contains two illustrations of the use of icon sets. For each column, I used the red down arrow, the yellow horizontal arrow, and the green up arrow.

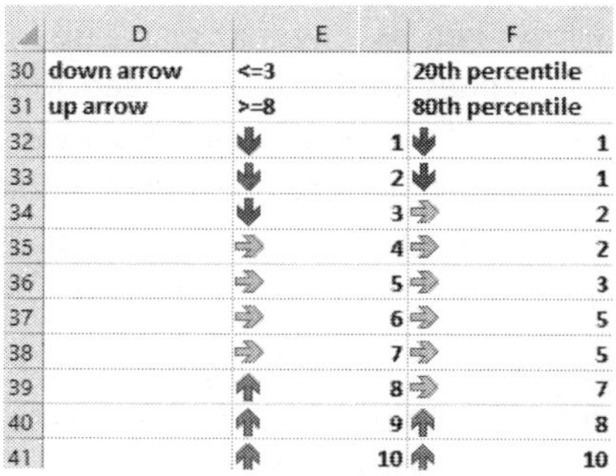

FIGURE 24-15 Using an icon set.

Here is how I assigned icons to a range of numerical values:

- After selecting the numbers in E32:E41, I clicked Conditional Formatting, Icon Sets, and then clicked More Rules and chose the 3 Arrows (Colored) icon set at the top of the Icon Styles list. In column E, I want numbers less than 4 to display a down arrow, numbers from 4 to 8 to display a horizontal arrow, and numbers 8 or larger to display an up arrow. To accomplish this goal, I set the options in the New Formatting Rule dialog box to Number in both of the Type lists, and I entered 8 in the top Value box and 4 in the bottom Value box, as shown in Figure 24-16.
- In a similar fashion, I set up a formatting rule for F31:F42 so that up arrows are placed in cells containing numbers in the eightieth percentile or above of all values (>=8), and down arrows are placed in cells containing numbers in the twentieth percentile or below of all values (<=1). In the New Formatting Rule dialog box, I selected the same icon style, I left the Type list as Percent by default, and I changed the top Value box to 80 and the bottom to 20. Figure 24-17 displays the needed formatting settings.

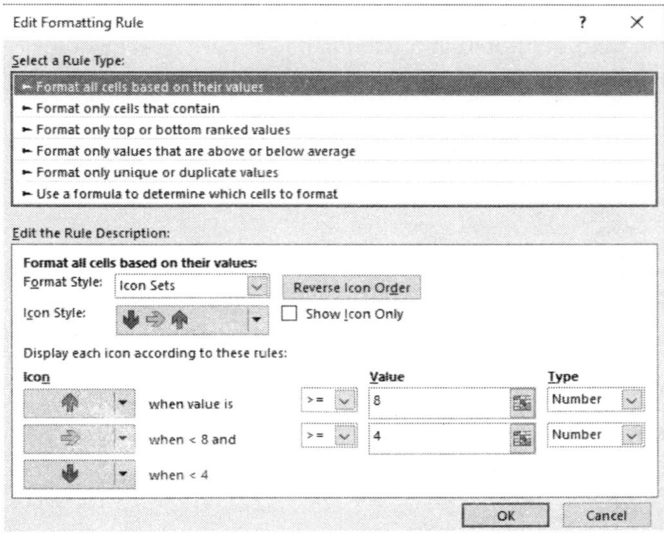

FIGURE 24-16 Assigning icons to numerical values.

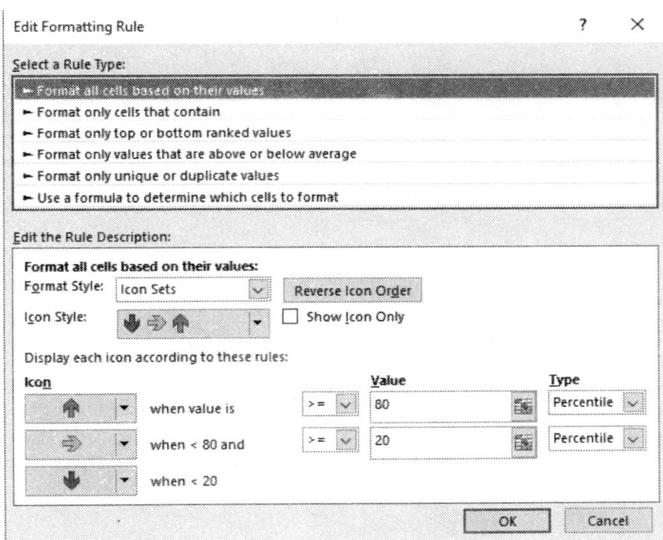

FIGURE 24-17 Assigning icons to percentile values.

Optional settings include Reverse Icon Order, which associates the icons on the left with small numbers and the icons on the right with larger numbers, and Show Icon Only, which hides the contents of the cell. In Excel 2016, you can hide a subset of icons. You can also customize icon sets. In the worksheet Customize Icons in the file Historicalinvest.xlsx, I used three icons to summarize investment returns. The top third of the returns appear with an up gray arrow, the bottom third of the returns contain a down red arrow. I hid the horizontal arrow icon for the middle third of the returns. Figure

24-18 shows the resulting icons, and Figure 24-19 shows the dialog box (accessed from Manage Rules) that I used to create this formatting. I customized the three gray arrow icon set by replacing the down gray arrow with a red arrow.

	A	B	C	D
7	Year	Stocks	T.Bills	T.Bonds
8	1928	↑ 43.81%	3.08%	↓ 0.84%
9	1929	↓ -8.30%	3.16%	4.20%
10	1930	↓ -25.12%	4.55%	4.54%
11	1931	↓ -43.84%	2.31%	↓ -2.56%
12	1932	↓ -8.64%	↓ 1.07%	↑ 8.79%
13	1933	↑ 49.98%	↓ 0.96%	↓ 1.86%
14	1934	↓ -1.19%	↓ 0.30%	↑ 7.96%
15	1935	↑ 46.74%	↓ 0.23%	4.47%
80	2000	↓ -9.03%	5.37%	↑ 16.66%
81	2001	↓ -11.85%	5.73%	5.57%
82	2002	↓ -22.10%	↑ 17.84%	3.83%
83	2003	↑ 28.68%	↓ 1.45%	1.65%
84	2004	↑ 10.88%	↑ 8.51%	↓ 1.02%
85	2005	4.91%	7.81%	↓ 1.20%
86	2006	↑ 15.79%	↓ 1.19%	2.98%
87	2007	5.49%	↑ 9.88%	4.66%
88	2008	↓ -37.00%	↑ 25.87%	1.60%
89	2009	↑ 26.46%	↓ -14.90%	↓ 0.10%

FIGURE 24-18 Customized icon set with hidden icon.

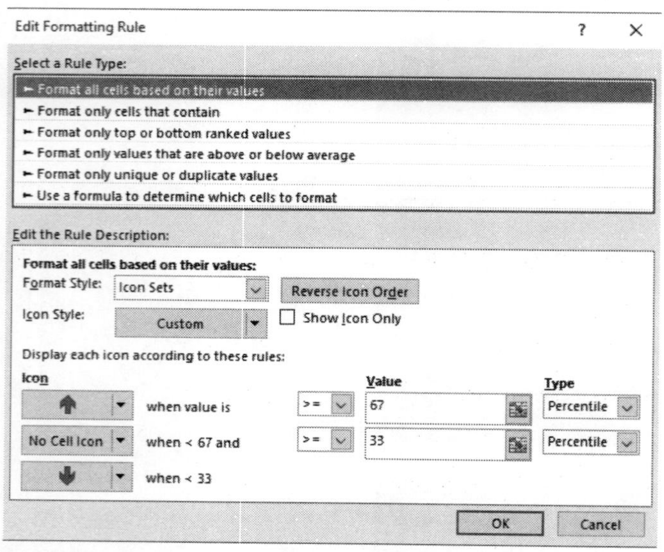

FIGURE 24-19 Dialog box for customizing and hiding icons.

How can I color-code monthly stock returns so that every good month is indicated in one color, and every bad month in another?

The file Sandp.xlsx, shown in Figure 24-20, contains monthly values and returns on the Standard & Poor's stock index. Suppose that you want to highlight in green each month in which the S&P index went up by more than 3 percent, and to highlight in red each month in which it went down more than 3 percent.

	A	B	C
6		S&P	
7		Comp.	
8	Date	P	Change
9	1871.01	4.44	
10	1871.02	4.5	0.01351
11	1871.03	4.61	0.02444
12	1871.04	4.74	0.0282
13	1871.05	4.86	0.02532
14	1871.06	4.82	-0.0082
15	1871.07	4.73	-0.0187
16	1871.08	4.79	0.01268
17	1871.09	4.84	0.01044
18	1871.1	4.59	-0.0517
19	1871.11	4.64	0.01089
20	1871.12	4.74	0.02155
21	1872.01	4.86	0.02532
22	1872.02	4.88	0.00412
23	1872.03	5.04	0.03279

FIGURE 24-20 Conditional formatting highlights returns in the S&P stock index.

I began by moving to cell C10 (the first month containing an S&P return) and then selecting all the monthly returns by pressing Ctrl+Shift+Down arrow. Next, I clicked Conditional Formatting, Manage Rules, New Rule, and selected the Format Only Cells That Contain option. Then I filled in the dialog box as shown in Figure 24-21. I selected Greater Than from the second list and entered 0.03 in the box on the right, which told Excel to format cells in the selected range that are >0.03. After clicking Format, I selected the format to use (a green fill).

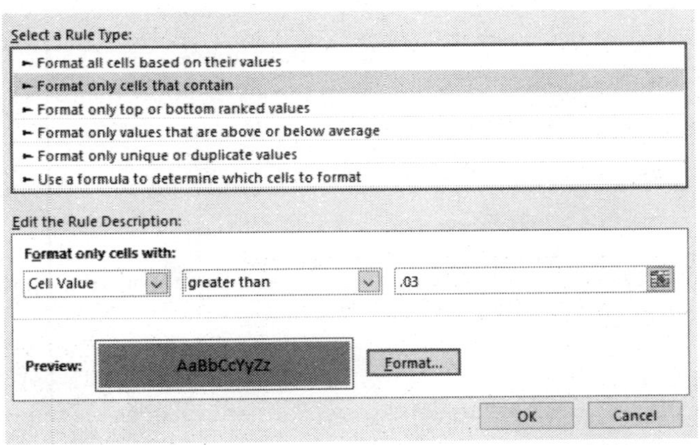

FIGURE 24-21 Applying special formatting to S&P returns greater than 3 percent.

In the Format Cells dialog box, notice that the lists for fonts and font size aren't available, so your choice of formatting can't change these attributes. The Fill tab provides the option to shade cells in a color you choose, and the Borders tab lets you create a border for cells that satisfy your conditional criteria (you can change the border colors from the Colors list). After clicking OK in the Format Cells dialog box, you return to the New Formatting Rule dialog box. Click OK. You can now click New Rule again, and in a similar fashion set things up so that all the cells containing numbers that are less than –0.03 have a red fill. (See Figure 24-22.)

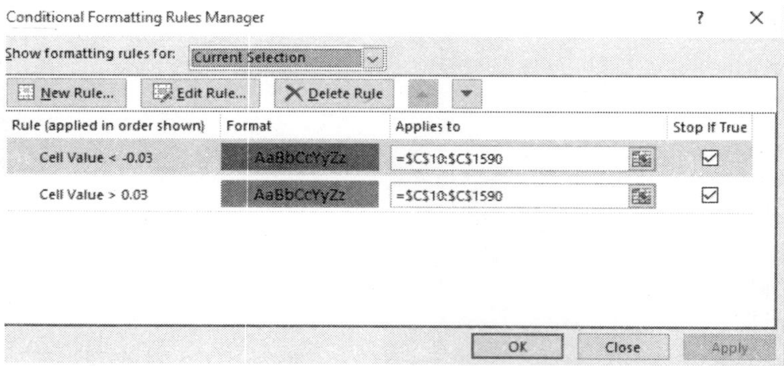

FIGURE 24-22 Coloring stock returns less than -3 percent in red and greater than 3 percent in green.

When you click OK, all months with an S&P return that's greater than 3 percent (see cell C23, for example) are displayed in green, and all months with an S&P return of less than –3 percent (see cell C18) are displayed in red. Cells in which the monthly returns don't meet either of these conditions maintain their original formatting.

Here are some useful tips concerning conditional formatting:

- To delete conditional formatting (or any format) applied to a range of cells, simply select the range of cells, click Conditional Formatting, click Clear Rules, and then click Clear Rules From Selected Cells.
- To select all the cells in a worksheet to which conditional formatting applies, press F5 to display the Go To dialog box. In the dialog box, click Special in the lower-left corner, select Conditional Formats on the lower right, and then click OK.
- If you want to edit a conditional formatting rule, click Conditional Formatting and Manage Rules, and then double-click the rule or select a rule and click Edit Rule.
- You can delete a specific conditional formatting rule by clicking Conditional Formatting, then Manage Rules, selecting the rule in question, and then clicking Delete Rule.

Notice that after both rules are defined, the red formatting rule is listed first (because it was created more recently than the green formatting rule). In the Conditional Formatting Rules Manager dialog box, rules are listed in order of precedence. In this example, it does not matter which rule is listed first because no cell can satisfy the criteria for both rules. If rules conflict, however, the rule listed first takes precedence. To change the order of conditional formatting rules, select the rule and click the up arrow to move the rule up in precedence, or the down arrow to move the rule down in precedence.

Given quarterly corporate revenues, how can I indicate quarters in which revenues increased over the previous quarter in one color, and quarters in which revenues decreased from the previous quarter in another color?

The file Amazon.xlsx contains quarterly revenues (in millions) for Amazon.com during the years 1995–2015. You can see part of this data in Figure 24-23. We want to highlight quarters in which revenues increased over the previous quarter in green and highlight quarters in which revenues decreased over the previous quarter in red.

	C	D	E
4	FiscalYear	FiscalQuarter	Revenue
5	1995	4	0.511
6	1996	1	0.875
7	1996	2	2.230
8	1996	3	4.173
9	1996	4	8.468
10	1997	1	16.005
11	1997	2	27.855
12	1997	3	37.887
13	1997	4	66.040
14	1998	1	87.361
15	1998	2	115.982
16	1998	3	153.649
17	1998	4	252.893
18	1999	1	293.643
19	1999	2	314.376
20	1999	3	355.778
21	1999	4	676.042
22	2000	1	573.889
23	2000	2	577.876
24	2000	3	637.858
25	2000	4	972.360
26	2001	1	700.356
27	2001	2	667.625
28	2001	3	639.281
29	2001	4	1115.171

FIGURE 24-23 Highlighting increased sales in green and decreased sales in red.

The Use A Formula option in the New Formatting Rule dialog box (click New Rule in the Conditional Formatting Manager dialog box) enables you to specify a formula that defines conditions that Excel checks before it applies formatting to a cell. I'll use this option in this section, but before I demonstrate the formula option, let's look at how Excel evaluates some logical functions. The work is in the file Logicalexamples.xlsx.

What happens when you type a formula such as =B3<2 in cell B4? If the value in B3 is a number smaller than 2, Excel returns the value True in cell B4; otherwise, Excel returns False. You can refer to the file Logicalexamples.xlsx, shown in Figure 24-24, for other examples like this, including combinations of AND, OR, and NOT in formulas:

- In cell B6, the formula =OR(B3<3, C3>5) returns the value True if either of the conditions B3<3 or C3>5 is true. Because the value of C3 is greater than 5, Excel returns True.
- In cell B7, the formula =AND(B3=3,C3>5) returns True if B3=3 and C3>5. Because B3 is not equal to 3, Excel returns False. In cell B8, however, the formula =AND(B3>3,C3>5) returns True because B3>3 and C3>5 are both true.

- In cell B9, the formula =NOT(B3<2) returns True because B3<2 would return False, and a not-false value becomes True.

	A	B	C
1			
2		Logical functions	
3		4	6
4	B3<2	FALSE	
5	B3>3	TRUE	
6	OR(B3<3,C3>5)	TRUE	
7	AND(B3=3,C3>5)	FALSE	
8	AND(B3>3,C3>5)	TRUE	
9	NOT(B3<2)	TRUE	

FIGURE 24-24 Logical functions.

Now let's look at how the Use A Formula option allows you to create a conditional format in a range of cells. Begin by selecting the range of cells to which you want to apply a conditional format. Then click Conditional Formatting and Manage Rules to display the Conditional Formatting Rules Manager dialog box. Click New Rule, and then select the Use A Formula To Determine Which Cells To Format option. (This is the last option; I also simply call it the *formula option*.) To use the formula option, you enter a formula (the formula must start with an equals sign) that is true if and only if you want the cell in the upper-left corner to be assigned the chosen format. Your logical formula can be copied like an ordinary formula to the remainder of the selected range, so judicious use of dollar signs ($) is needed to ensure that for each cell of the selected range the formula will be true if and only if you want your format to apply to the cell. Click Format, and then enter the formatting you want. Click OK. After clicking OK in the New Formatting Rule dialog box, your formula and formatting are copied to the whole cell range. The formatting is applied to any cell in the selected range that satisfies the condition defined in the formula.

Returning to the file Amazon.xlsx, let's focus on highlighting in green the quarters in which revenues increase. Basically, what you want to do is select the range E6:E85 (there is no prior quarter to which you can compare the revenue figure in cell E5), and then instruct Excel that if a cell's value is larger than the cell above it, highlight the cell in green. Figure 24-25 shows how to set up the rule.

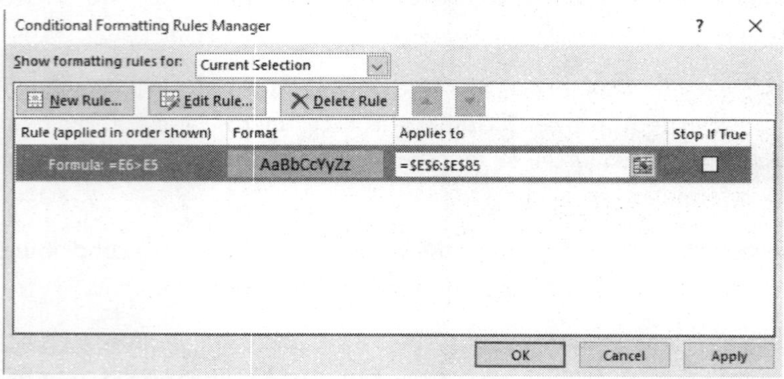

FIGURE 24-25 Conditional formatting settings that will display in green the quarters in which the revenue increased.

If you enter =E6>E5 by pointing to the appropriate cells, be sure you remove the $ signs from the formula in the Conditional Formatting dialog box, or the formula won't be copied. Probably the easiest way to insert or delete dollar signs is to use the F4 key. When you highlight a cell reference such as A3, pressing F4 includes or deletes dollars signs in the following order: A3, $A$3, A$3, $A3. Thus, if you start with $A$3, pressing F4 changes the cell reference to A$3. The formula in this example ensures that cell E6 is colored green if and only if sales in that quarter exceed the previous quarter. After clicking OK, you'll find that all quarters in which revenue increased are colored green. Notice that in cell E7, for example, the formula was copied in the usual way, becoming =E7>E6.

To add the condition for formatting cells in which revenue decreased, select the range E6:E61 again, open the Conditional Formatting Rules Manager dialog box, click New Rule, and then select the Use A Formula To Determine Which Cells To Format option. Enter the formula =E6<E5, and then click Format. On the Fill tab, change the fill color to red, and then click OK twice. The Conditional Formatting Rules Manager dialog box now appears as shown in Figure 24-26.

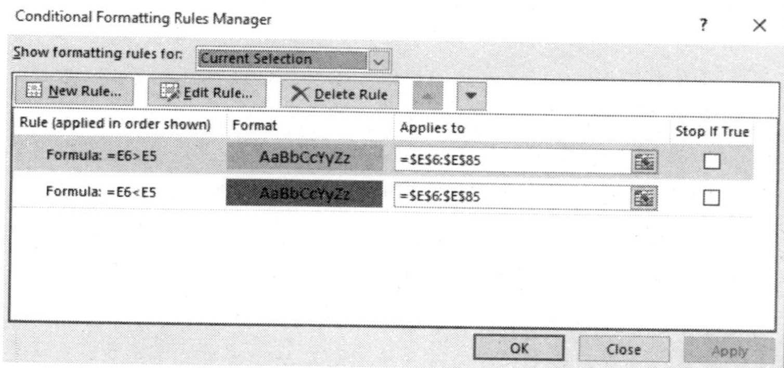

FIGURE 24-26 Conditions for displaying in green quarters during which revenue increased, and in red quarters during which revenue decreased.

You can use the formula option with color scales, data bars, and icon sets. Simply select the option when setting the criteria for your color scale, data bars, or icon sets.

Given a list of dates, how can I indicate weekend dates in a specific color?

The file Weekendformatting.xlsx (see Figure 24-27) contains several dates. I want to highlight all Saturdays and Sundays in red. To do this, I first copied the formula =WEEKDAY(C6,2) from cell D6 to D7:D69. Choosing Type=2 for the WEEKDAY function returns a 1 for each Monday, a 2 for each Tuesday, and so on, so that the function returns a 6 for each Saturday and a 7 for each Sunday.

	C	D
3		Monday =
4		
5	Date	Weekday
6	2/8/2003	6
7	1/2/2007	2
8	1/2/2005	7
9	10/25/2005	2
10	10/10/2004	7
11	10/13/2006	5
12	9/26/2006	2
13	9/25/2006	1
14	11/1/2005	2
15	11/29/2006	3
16	2/16/2005	3
17	7/27/2007	5
18	3/24/2004	3
19	10/6/2008	1
20	4/11/2007	3
21	2/3/2004	2
22	1/22/2009	4
23	10/29/2006	7
24	6/9/2005	4
25	8/16/2008	6
26	12/13/2006	3
27	3/5/2007	1
28	8/8/2008	5
29	9/1/2007	6

FIGURE 24-27 Using the WEEKDAY function to highlight weekend days in red.

I now select the range D6:D69, click Conditional Formatting, and then click Manage Rules. After clicking New Rule and the formula option, I fill in the dialog box as shown in Figure 24-28.

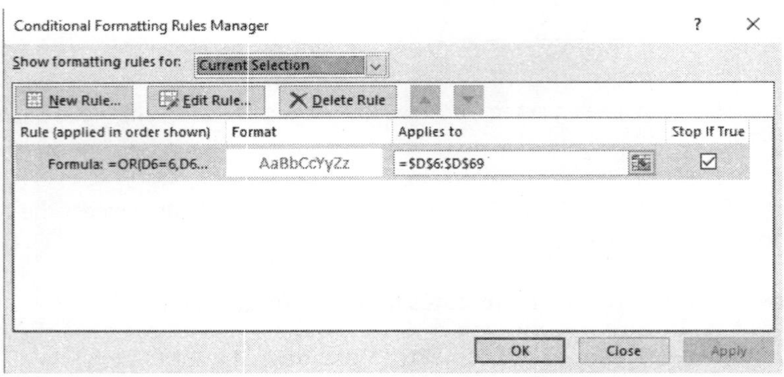

FIGURE 24-28 Setting up a rule to display weekend days in red.

After I click OK, each date for which the weekday is equal to 6 (for Saturday) or 7 (for Sunday) is colored red. The formula =OR(D6=6,D6=7) implies that a cell entry of 6 or 7 will activate the red font color. Of course, I could have used Format Only Cells That Contain and used >=6 or >5 to obtain the same formatting.

Our basketball coach has given each player a rating between 1 and 10 based on the player's ability to play guard, forward, or center. Can I set up a worksheet that visually indicates the ability of each player to play the position to which she's assigned?

The file Basketball.xlsx, shown in Figure 24-29, contains ratings given to 20 players for each position and the position (1=Guard, 2=Forward, 3=Center) played by each player. The goal here is to fill with red the cell containing the rating for each player for the position to which she's assigned.

	A	B	C	D	E	F
1			1	2	3	
2	Position played	Player	Guard rating	Forward rating	Center rating	
3	1	1	1	9	2	1=Guard
4	1	2	4	3	9	2=Forward
5	2	3	7	3	7	3=Center
6	2	4	9	8	8	
7	2	5	5	8	9	
8	3	6	2	7	2	
9	3	7	7	6	6	
10	3	8	4	4	3	
11	3	9	3	8	10	
12	3	10	6	1	4	
13	2	11	6	7	5	
14	2	12	2	6	5	
15	2	13	8	6	9	
16	1	14	1	1	3	
17	1	15	3	6	8	
18	2	16	4	10	1	
19	2	17	8	5	1	
20	2	18	1	7	7	
21	3	19	9	2	7	
22	3	20	10	3	10	

FIGURE 24-29 Rating each player's ability to play a position.

Begin by selecting the range C3:E22, which contains the players' ratings. Click Conditional Formatting and then Manage Rules. Click New Rule, and choose the formula option. Now fill in the dialog box as shown Figure 24-30.

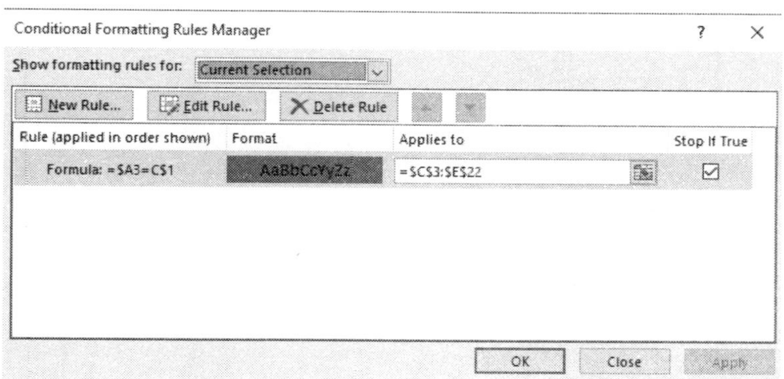

FIGURE 24-30 Setting up a rule to show player ratings in red fill.

The formula =$A3=C$1 compares the player's assigned position to the column heading (1, 2, or 3) in row 1. If the player's assigned position is set to 1 (Guard), her rating in column C, which is her guard rating, appears in red. Similarly, if the player's assigned position is set to 2, her forward rating in column D appears in red. Finally, if the assigned position is set to 3, her center rating in column E appears in red. Note that if you do not include the dollar sign with the A and the 1 in the formula, the formula will not copy down and across correctly.

I also want to note that Excel 2016 allows conditional formats created with formulas to reference data in other worksheets.

What does the Stop If True option in the Manage Rules dialog box do?

Suppose that the Stop If True option is selected for a rule. If a cell satisfies this rule, all lower-precedent rules are ignored. We will use the file Income.xlsx to illustrate the use of Stop If True. This file shows median income for each US state for years between 1984 and 2010. Suppose (as shown in Figure 24-31) that you want up arrows to mark the 10 states that have the highest median income in 2010 and want no icons to appear for any other states. The key is to use in the first rule No Format for the states with the 40 lowest median incomes and select Stop If True. Then create the desired icon set.

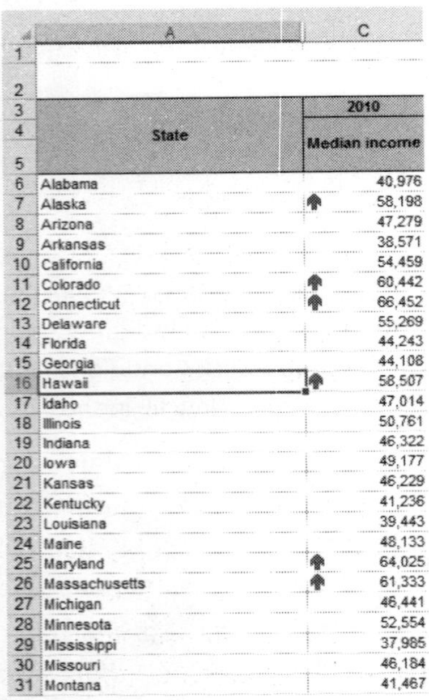

	A	C
1		
2		
3	State	2010
4		Median income
5		
6	Alabama	40,976
7	Alaska	58,198
8	Arizona	47,279
9	Arkansas	38,571
10	California	54,459
11	Colorado	60,442
12	Connecticut	66,452
13	Delaware	55,269
14	Florida	44,243
15	Georgia	44,108
16	Hawaii	58,507
17	Idaho	47,014
18	Illinois	50,761
19	Indiana	46,322
20	Iowa	49,177
21	Kansas	46,229
22	Kentucky	41,236
23	Louisiana	39,443
24	Maine	48,133
25	Maryland	64,025
26	Massachusetts	61,333
27	Michigan	46,441
28	Minnesota	52,554
29	Mississippi	37,985
30	Missouri	46,184
31	Montana	41,467

FIGURE 24-31 Using up arrows to highlight the 10 states with the largest median income.

The settings that hide the arrows for the 40 states with the lowest median 2010 incomes are shown in Figure 24-32.

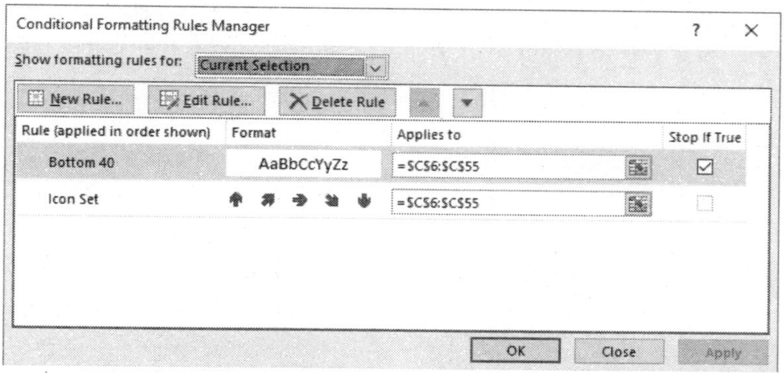

FIGURE 24-32 Settings to ensure that only top 10 median incomes are highlighted with up arrows.

The settings for the second rule are shown in Figure 24-33. Note that the top 20 percent of states is produced via the formula .2*50 = 10 states. The remaining settings are of no importance.

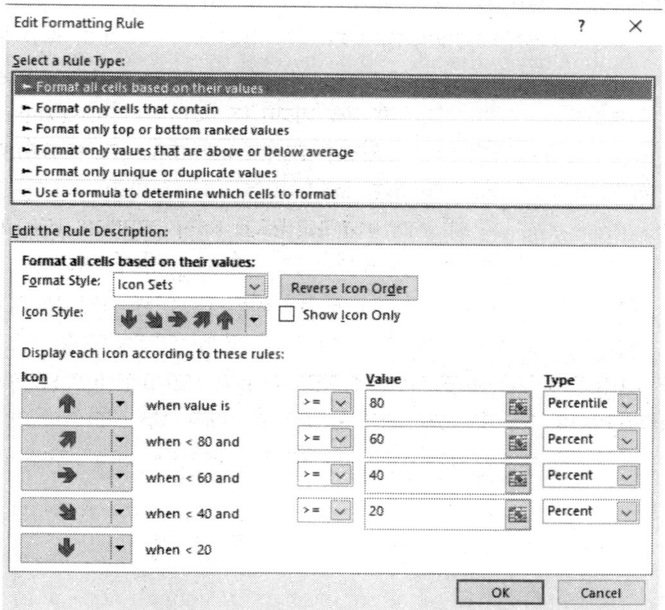

FIGURE 24-33 Settings to ensure top 10 states in median income get an up arrow.

How can I use the Format Painter to copy a conditional format?

The Format Painter (the paintbrush icon shown in Figure 24-34) enables you to apply the format (including conditional formats) from any cell or group of cells to any other group of cells. Simply select the cell or group of cells with the format you want copy and then click the Format Painter. Then use the paintbrush to select the cells where you want the format copied.

If you want to copy a format to a range that includes nonadjacent cells, double-click the Format Painter and select all the cells for which you want the format copied. To turn off the Format Painter, click the Format Painter again.

FIGURE 24-34 Format Painter icon on the Home tab.

Problems

1. Using the data in the file Sandp.xlsx, use conditional formatting in the following situations:
   - Format in bold each month in which the value of the S&P index increased, and underline each month in which the value of the S&P index decreased.
   - Highlight in green each month in which the S&P index changed by a maximum of 2 percent.
   - Highlight the largest S&P index value in red and the smallest in purple.
2. Using the data in the file Toysrusformat.xlsx, highlight in red all quarters for which revenue has increased over at least the last two quarters. Highlight all fourth-quarter revenues in blue and first-quarter revenues in red.
3. The file Test.xlsx contains exam scores for students. The top 10 students receive an A, the next 20 students receive a B, and all other students receive a C. Highlight the A grades in red, the B grades in green, and the C grades in blue. Hint: The formula =LARGE(D4:D63,10) gives you the tenth-highest grade on the test.
4. In the file Weekendformatting.xlsx, highlight all weekdays in red. Highlight in blue all days that occur in the first 10 days of the month. Which color takes precedence when both colors are applied to one cell?
5. Suppose each worker in Microsoft's finance department has been assigned to one of four groups. The supervisor of each group has rated each worker on a 0–10 scale, and each worker has rated his satisfaction with each of the four groups. (See the file Satissuper.xlsx.) Based on the group to which each worker is assigned, highlight the supervisor rating and the worker satisfaction rating for each worker.
6. The file Varianceanalysis.xlsx contains monthly profit forecasts and monthly actual sales. The sales variance for a month equals:

$$\frac{actualsales - predictedsales}{predictedsales}$$

Highlight in red all the months with a favorable variance of at least 20 percent, and highlight in green all the months with an unfavorable variance of more than 20 percent.

7. For our drug cost example (see file Offsetcost.xlsx from Chapter 22, "The OFFSET function," format the worksheet so that all Phase 1 costs are displayed in red, all Phase 2 costs are displayed in green, and all Phase 3 costs are displayed in purple.

8. The file Names.xlsx contains a list of names. Highlight all the duplicates in green and all the names containing *Ja* in red.

9. The file Duedates.xlsx contains due dates for various invoices. Highlight in red all invoices due by the end of the next month.

10. In the file Historicalinvest.xlsx, set up conditional formatting with three icons so that 10 percent of returns have an up arrow, 10 percent have a down arrow, and 80 percent have a horizontal arrow.

11. The file Nbasalaries.xlsx contains salaries of NBA players in millions of dollars. Set up data bars to summarize this data. Players making less than $1 million should have the shortest data bar, and players making more than $15 million should have longest data bar.

12. Set up a three-color scale to summarize the NBA salary data. Change the color of the bottom 10 percent of all the salaries to green and the top 10 percent to red.

13. Use five icons to summarize the NBA player data. Create break points for icons at $3 million, $6 million, $9 million, and $12 million.

14. How could you set things up so that no icons are shown for players who have salaries between $7 million and $8 million? Hint: Use the Stop If True option.

15. The file Fractiondefective.xlsx contains the percentage of defective units produced daily. A day's production is considered acceptable if 2 percent or less of the items produced are defective. Highlight all the acceptable days with a green flag. In another worksheet, highlight all the acceptable days with a red flag. Hint: Use the Stop If True option to ensure that no icon occurs in any cell containing a number less than 2.

16. The file Globalwarming2011.xlsx contains average world temperatures in degrees Celsius for the years 1881–2011. Use color scales to ensure lower temperatures should be blue, intermediate temperatures should be yellow, and higher temperatures should be red.

17. Suppose you are saving for your child's college fund. You are going to contribute the same amount of money to the fund at the end of each year. Your goal is to end up with $100,000. For annual investment returns ranging from 4 percent to 15 percent, and number of years investing varying from 5 to 15 years, determine your required annual contribution. Suppose you are able to save $10,000 per year. Use conditional formatting to highlight for each annual return rate the minimum number of years needed to accumulate $100,000.

18. The file Amazon.xlsx contains quarterly revenues for Amazon.com. Use conditional formatting to ensure that the sales during each quarter are highlighted in a different color.

19. Set up conditional formatting that colors the cell range A1:H8 like a checkerboard, with alternating white and black coloring. Hint: The ROW() function gives the row number of a cell, and the COLUMN() function gives the column number of a cell.

20. When students take Vivian's accounting exam, they are told to enter their email aliases on a Scantron. Often, they make mistakes. Vivian has a list of the actual email aliases for the students in the class. She would like to highlight in yellow the email aliases entered by students that are not true aliases. This will help her easily correct them. The file Scantrons.xlsx contains the necessary data. Help Vivian out!

21. The file Top5.xlsx contains the revenues each year of 50 companies. For each year, highlight the companies that have the five largest revenues. Hint: The formula =LARGE(B1:B50,5) would return the fifth largest number in the range B1:B50.

22. The file Threetimes.xlsx contains a list of names. Highlight in red each name that appears at least three times.

23. The file GNP.xlsx contains records of the quarterly US gross national product. Take advantage of the fact that data bars handle negative values to summarize quarterly GNP percentage growth rates.

24. Using the data in the file Globalwarming2011temp.xlsx (from the Templates folder), highlight the years (not the temperatures) in which the temperature is above average.

25. The file Accountsums.xlsx (see Figure 24-35) shows weekly salaries in thousands of dollars (listed in chronological order) paid to several top-notch consultants. For example, Britney made $91,000 during the first week and made $57,000 during the last week. Follow these steps:

- Use the formula option to highlight each person's name in yellow.
- Use the formula option to highlight each person's first week of salary in orange.

	A	B	C
3			
4		Britney	
5			79
6			73
7			70
8			82
9			54
10			60
11			53
12			98
13			55
14			70
15			51
16			78
17			64
18			100
19			93
20		Lindsay	
21			65
22			91

FIGURE 24-35 Data for problem 25.

26. The file Shading.xlsx contains 27 quarters of sales. Shade alternate rows in green and yellow. Then, alternate shading with four rows in green and four rows in yellow, and so on.

27. The file Problem27data.xlsx contains names of several people. A name will be entered in cell E2. Use conditional formatting to highlight each occurrence of the person's name.

28. The file Problem28data.xlsx contains information about voters in 20 congressional districts. In cell I2, we will enter the number of a congressional district. Your job is to set up a format that will highlight all rows of data involving the district listed in cell I2.

29. In the file Problem29data.xlsx, columns E-I contain the following information. Use conditional formatting to highlight each row of data for days the stock was sold. Show the following data:

    - Opening price of a stock.
    - Did we own stock at beginning of a day?
    - Did we sell the stock that day?
    - Did we own the stock at the end of the day?

30. The file Problem30data.xlsx contains statistics for 2014 NFL quarterbacks. In cell J21, I will enter a number of Yards *x*. Use Conditional formatting to highlight all information for all quarterbacks who have YDs>=x. For example, if we enter *4500* in cell J2, then any QB with YDS>=4500 should have all their information highlighted.

CHAPTER 25

Sorting in Excel

Questions answered in this chapter:

- How can I sort sales transaction data so that transactions are sorted first by salesperson, then by product, then by units sold, and finally in chronological order from oldest to most recent?
- I have always wanted to sort my data based on cell color or font color. Is this possible in Excel 2016?
- I love the great icon sets described in Chapter 24, "Conditional formatting." Can I sort my data based on the icon in the cell?
- My worksheet includes a column containing the month in which each sale occurred. When I sort by this column, I get either April (first month alphabetically) or October (last month alphabetically) on top. How can I sort by this column so that January transactions are on top, followed by February, and so on?
- Can I sort data without using the Sort dialog box?
- I often have to type a list of cities in which my company has business offices. Can I create a Customer list that allows me to type the first city on the list and then drag the cursor down and automatically fill in the remaining cities?

Almost every user of Microsoft Excel has at one time or another sorted columns of data alphabetically or by numerical value. Let's look at some examples of how wonderful and powerful sorting is in Excel 2016.

Answers to this chapter's questions

How can I sort sales transaction data so that transactions are sorted first by salesperson, then by product, then by units sold, and finally in chronological order from oldest to most recent?

JAC is a small company that sells makeup. The Makeup worksheet in the Makeupsorttemp.xlsx file in the Templates folder for this chapter (see Figure 25-1) contains the following sales transaction information:

- Transaction number
- Name of salesperson

- Date of transaction
- Product sold
- Units sold
- Dollars received
- Location of transaction

	E	F	G	H	I	J	K
3	Trans Number	Name	Date	Product	Units	Dollars	Location
4	1	Betsy	4/1/2004	lip gloss	45	$ 137.20	south
5	2	Hallagan	3/10/2004	foundatio	50	$ 152.01	midwest
6	3	Ashley	2/25/2005	lipstick	9	$ 28.72	midwest
7	4	Hallagan	5/22/2006	lip gloss	55	$ 167.08	west
8	5	Zaret	6/17/2004	lip gloss	43	$ 130.60	midwest
9	6	Colleen	11/27/2005	eye liner	58	$ 175.99	midwest
10	7	Cristina	3/21/2004	eye liner	8	$ 25.80	midwest
11	8	Colleen	12/17/2006	lip gloss	72	$ 217.84	midwest
12	9	Ashley	7/5/2006	eye liner	75	$ 226.64	south
13	10	Betsy	8/7/2006	lip gloss	24	$ 73.50	east
14	11	Ashley	11/29/2004	mascara	43	$ 130.84	east
15	12	Ashley	11/18/2004	lip gloss	23	$ 71.03	west
16	13	Emilee	8/31/2005	lip gloss	49	$ 149.59	west

FIGURE 25-1 Sales transaction data before sorting.

I want to sort the data so that the following occurs:

- Transactions are listed alphabetically by salesperson. I want to sort in the usual A-to-Z order so that all of Ashley's transactions are first and all of Zaret's transactions are last.
- Each person's transactions are sorted by product. Thus, Ashley's eyeliner transactions will be followed by Ashley's foundation transactions and so on.
- For each salesperson and product, transactions are listed by number of units sold (in descending order).
- If a salesperson makes two or more sales of the same product for the same number of units, transactions are listed in chronological order.

In versions of Excel before Excel 2007, it was difficult to sort on more than three criteria. Now Excel allows you to apply up to 64 criteria in one sort. To sort the sales data, I first need to select the data (cell range E3:K1894). Two easy ways to select this data are as follows:

- Position the cursor in the upper-left corner of the data (cell E3), and then press Ctrl+Shift+Right arrow followed by Ctrl+Shift+Down arrow.
- Position the cursor anywhere in the cell range and press Ctrl+Shift+*.

Next, on the Data tab on the ribbon, in the Sort & Filter group, I click Sort to display the Sort dialog box, as shown in Figure 25-2.

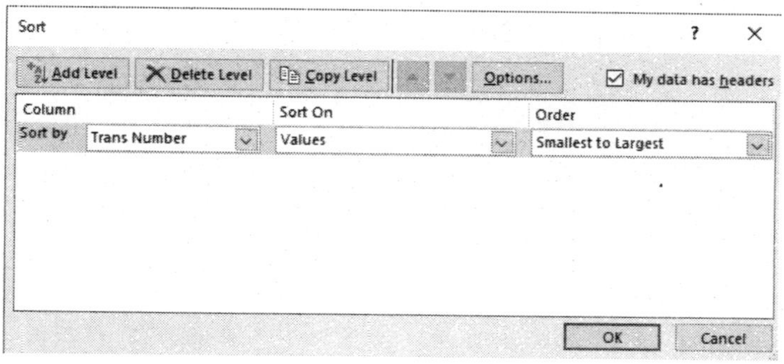

FIGURE 25-2 The Sort dialog box ready to be filled in.

Because row 3 contains headings for the data columns, I select the My Data Has Headers check box in the upper right. Now I select the following four criteria in the order shown:

1. Sort by the Name column so that values (this means cell contents) are in A-to-Z order. In the Column list of the top Sort By level, I select Name. In the Sort On list, I leave the default Values selected. The Order list defaults to A To Z because I selected Name in the Sort By list, and I leave that setting.

2. Sort by the Product column so that values are in A-to-Z order. I click Add Level to add a Then By level under the Sort By level. I select Product from the Column list, leave Values in the Sort On list, and leave A To Z in the Order list.

3. Sort by the Units column so that values are in order from largest to smallest. I click Add Level and then, for the new level, select Units from the Column list, leave Values in the Sort On list, and select Largest To Smallest in the Order list.

4. Sort by the Date column so that values are in chronological order from oldest to newest. I add a level, select Date in the Column list, and leave the default Oldest To Newest in the Order list.

The dialog box now looks like Figure 25-3.

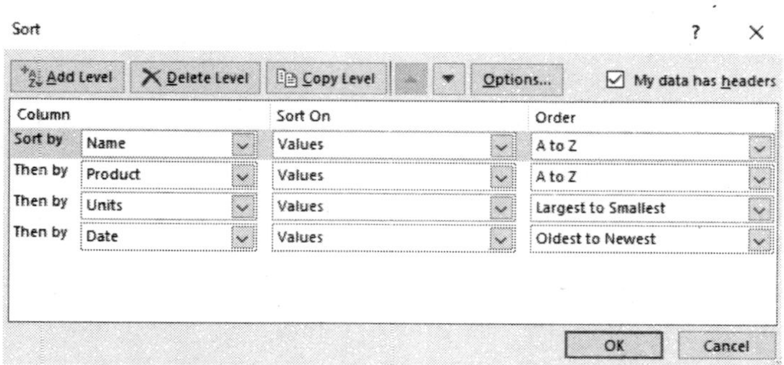

FIGURE 25-3 The Sort dialog box set up for the sales sorting example.

I click OK to implement my sort settings. The final result of our sort is shown in Figure 25-4.

	E	F	G	H	I	J	K
3	Trans Number	Name	Date	Product	Units	Dollars	Location
4	785	Ashley	4/10/2005	eye liner	92	$ 278.34	east
5	1879	Ashley	8/18/2006	eye liner	90	$ 271.85	midwest
6	1685	Ashley	11/5/2005	eye liner	88	$ 265.96	south
7	1737	Ashley	3/28/2006	eye liner	88	$ 265.53	east
8	1579	Ashley	6/6/2004	eye liner	87	$ 262.85	east
45	1858	Ashley	7/7/2005	foundation	95	$ 286.83	south
46	1491	Ashley	7/18/2005	foundation	93	$ 281.34	south
199	555	Ashley	11/14/2006	mascara	-1	$ (1.28)	south
200	1245	Ashley	11/16/2005	mascara	-10	$ (27.09)	south
201	1290	Betsy	7/7/2005	eye liner	95	$ 286.61	east
202	1777	Betsy	12/19/2005	eye liner	95	$ 286.41	midwest
203	855	Betsy	1/23/2005	eye liner	94	$ 284.42	south
204	1609	Betsy	4/10/2005	eye liner	94	$ 283.46	east
205	1483	Betsy	7/29/2005	eye liner	94	$ 284.31	midwest
206	735	Betsy	5/2/2005	eye liner	91	$ 274.96	west
207	1509	Betsy	4/30/2006	eye liner	83	$ 251.40	midwest
208	91	Betsy	8/18/2006	eye liner	83	$ 251.18	south
209	872	Betsy	9/20/2006	eye liner	79	$ 239.06	south
210	487	Betsy	1/23/2005	eye liner	75	$ 227.10	west
211	100	Betsy	10/3/2005	eye liner	74	$ 224.23	west

FIGURE 25-4 Sorted sales transaction data.

Note that all of Ashley's transactions are listed first, with eyeliner followed by foundation, and so on. Eyeliner transactions are listed from the largest number of units sold to the smallest. In the case of a tie (see the Units column in rows 6 and 7), the transactions are listed in chronological order. In Figure 25-3, you can see that Excel first sorts by your first level (Name), then the second (Product), and so on.

Using the Sort dialog box, you can easily add sort criteria (Add Level), delete sort criteria (Delete Level), copy the settings that define a level of the sort (Copy Level), or specify whether your data has headers (if you don't select this option, the Column options are named by the column letters, such as *Column E*). By selecting Options, you can make the sort operation case sensitive or even sort data for which each data item is listed in a different column (instead of the more common situation in which each case is in a different row).

I have always wanted to sort my data based on cell color or font color. Is this possible in Excel 2016?

In Excel 2016, sorting on a cell or font color is simple. Consider the Makeup worksheet in the Makeupsorttemp.xlsx file. Several names in column F are highlighted in different colors. For example, Cici in cell F620 is highlighted in red, and Colleen in cell F833 is highlighted in yellow. Suppose you want the names with green fill on top, followed by yellow, and then by red, with the rest of the rows on the bottom. To sort the Name column by color, simply select the range you want to sort (E3:K1894), click Sort in the Data tab, and click Add Level. After selecting the Name column, click the Sort On setting, and select Cell Color (selecting Font Color sorts by font color). For the first level, select green from the Order list, and leave the default On Top setting. Then add two more levels; select yellow for the second level, and select red for the third level. The completed dialog box is shown in Figure 25-5. Click OK to complete the sort. The resulting sort is shown in the Colors worksheet of the Makeupsort.xlsx file found in the Practice Files folder for this chapter and is shown in Figure 25-6.

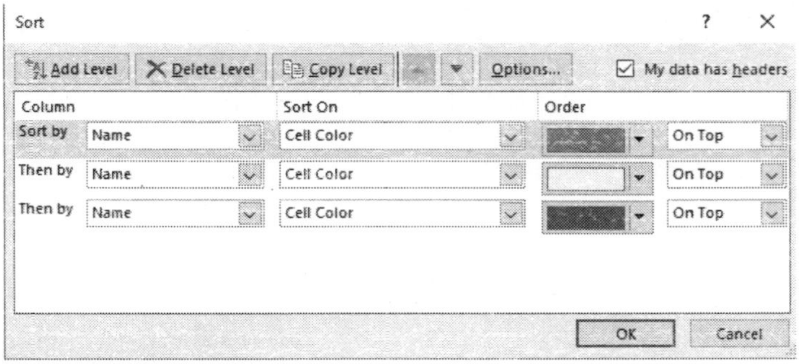

FIGURE 25-5 The Sort dialog box set up to sort by color.

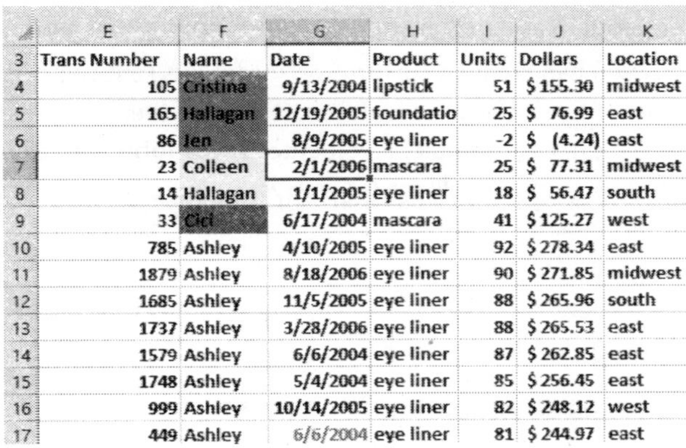

	E	F	G	H	I	J	K
3	Trans Number	Name	Date	Product	Units	Dollars	Location
4	105	Cristina	9/13/2004	lipstick	51	$ 155.30	midwest
5	165	Hallagan	12/19/2005	foundatio	25	$ 76.99	east
6	86	Jen	8/9/2005	eye liner	-2	$ (4.24)	east
7	23	Colleen	2/1/2006	mascara	25	$ 77.31	midwest
8	14	Hallagan	1/1/2005	eye liner	18	$ 56.47	south
9	33	Cici	6/17/2004	mascara	41	$ 125.27	west
10	785	Ashley	4/10/2005	eye liner	92	$ 278.34	east
11	1879	Ashley	8/18/2006	eye liner	90	$ 271.85	midwest
12	1685	Ashley	11/5/2005	eye liner	88	$ 265.96	south
13	1737	Ashley	3/28/2006	eye liner	88	$ 265.53	east
14	1579	Ashley	6/6/2004	eye liner	87	$ 262.85	east
15	1748	Ashley	5/4/2004	eye liner	85	$ 256.45	east
16	999	Ashley	10/14/2005	eye liner	82	$ 248.12	west
17	449	Ashley	6/6/2004	eye liner	81	$ 244.97	east

FIGURE 25-6 Results of sorting by color.

I love the great icon sets described in Chapter 24, "Conditional formatting." Can I sort my data based on the icon in the cell?

To sort by icon, simply select Cell Icon from the Sort On list in the Sort dialog box (in the Data tab, click Sort). Then, in the Order list, choose the icon you want on top for the first level, and add a new level for each icon you want to sort.

My worksheet includes a column containing the month in which each sale occurred. When I sort by this column, I get either April (first month alphabetically) or October (last month alphabetically) on top. How can I sort by this column so that January transactions are on top, followed by February, and so on?

The Dates worksheet in the Makeupsorttemp.xlsx file contains a list of months. (See Figure 25-7.) I would like to sort the months so that they appear in chronological order beginning with January. I begin by selecting the range D6:D15, clicking Sort on the Data tab, and then sorting column D by values. When selecting the order, I select Custom List and then, in the Custom Lists dialog box, I select the option beginning with *January, February, March* (near the bottom of Custom Lists on the left). Note that you could also have sorted by the day of the week. I click OK to finish the selection and return to the Sort dialog box. The completed dialog box is shown in Figure 25-8, with the resulting sort shown in Figure 25-9.

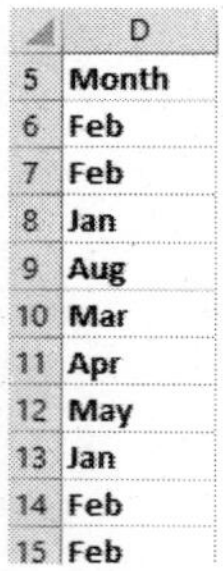

FIGURE 25-7 The months to be sorted.

Note that in the Custom Lists dialog box you can create a custom sort-order list. First select New List. Then, under List Entries, type the entries in the order you want to sort by, and then click Add. Your new list is now included as a menu selection. For example, if you enter **Jack**, **John**, and **Alan** in List Entries (on different lines or separated by commas), all entries with *Jack* would be listed first, followed by *John* listings, with *Alan* listings at the end.

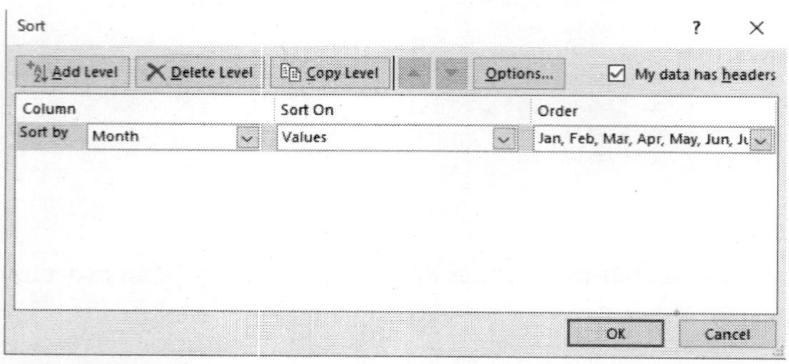

FIGURE 25-8 The Sort dialog box set up to sort by month.

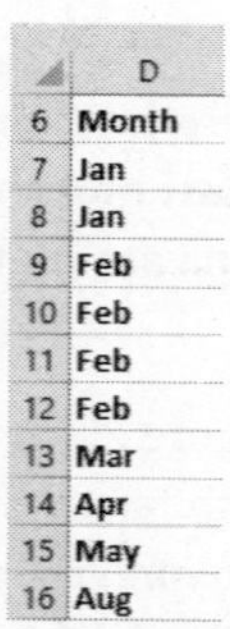

FIGURE 25-9 Sorting the months in chronological order.

Can I sort data without using the Sort dialog box?

Sometimes, sorting data without using the Sort dialog box is more convenient. To illustrate how this is done, suppose again that you want to sort the sales transaction data in the Makeup worksheet in the Makeupsort.xlsx file so that transactions are sorted first by salesperson, then by product, then by units sold, and finally in chronological order from the oldest to the most recent. To begin, select the least important column to sort on first, which is the date column (G3:G1894). Next, in the Sort & Filter group on the Data tab, click the Sort A To Z button (see the button in the upper left of Figure 25-10), and in the Sort Warning dialog box, with the Expand The Selection option selected, click Sort, so that all the columns are sorted. The Sort A To Z button sorts numerical data so that the smallest numbers or oldest dates are on top and sorts text so that A precedes B, and so on.

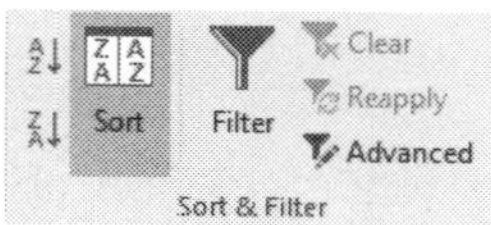

FIGURE 25-10 The Sort & Filter buttons.

As you'd expect, the Sort Z To A button sorts numerical data so that the largest numbers or most recent dates are on top and sorts text data so that Z precedes Y.

Next, sort by the second least important column (Units) Z To A, because you want larger sales on top. Then sort from A to Z by Product, and finally from A to Z by salesperson. These steps achieve the same results as shown previously in Figure 25-4.

I often have to type a list of cities in which my company has business offices. Can I create a Customer list that allows me to type the first city on the list and then drag the cursor down and automatically fill in the remaining cities?

Suppose your company has business offices in the cities shown in Figure 25-11 (see the file Listtemp.xlsx from this chapter's Templates folder).

	G
6	Sao Paulo
7	Shanghai
8	New York City
9	Palo Alto
10	Seattle
11	Lagos
12	London
13	Sydney

FIGURE 25-11 List of cities to be used in creating a custom list.

To create a Custom List, proceed as follows:

- Click the File tab on the ribbon, click Options near the bottom of the left pane, click Advanced in the left pane of the Excel Options dialog box, scroll down, and, then in the bottom of the General section, click the Edit Custom List button.

- You will see the Custom Lists dialog box in Figure 25-12. Click in the Import List From Cells box (near the bottom), select the range (G6:G13) containing the list, and then click Import. You will see your list of cities join the collection of built-in custom lists on the left. Click OK to close the Custom Lists dialog box, and then click OK to close the Excel Options dialog box.

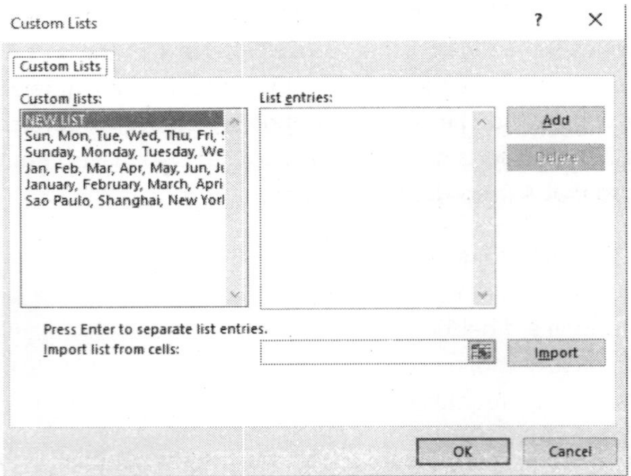

FIGURE 25-12 The custom list of cities has been created.

Now if you type **Sao Paulo** in any cell, hover over the square in the bottom-right corner of the cell, and drag the cursor down, you will see the cities listed in the order Sao Paulo, Shanghai, and so on. If you drag the cursor down far enough, the list will repeat. Of course, if you want to drag down copies of Sao Paulo, just type **Sao Paulo** in two cells and then drag down the two cells.

Problems

1. In the Makeupsort.xlsx file, sort the sales data alphabetically by location, then by product type, then by name, then by date of sale, and finally by units sold.
2. The Sortday.xlsx file contains hours worked on different days of the week. Sort the data so that the Monday data is followed by the Tuesday data, and so on.
3. The Sorticons.xlsx file contains annual investment returns with an up arrow used to indicate good years, a horizontal arrow used to indicate average years, and a red arrow used to indicate bad years. Sort the data by the icons in the Stock column with the up arrows on top, followed by the horizontal arrows, and then the red arrows.
4. The file Makeupsortfont.xlsx contains our makeup data with certain dates shown in blue, red, or brown font. Sort the data so that the brown dates are on top, followed by the red dates, and then the blue dates.

CHAPTER 26

Tables

Questions answered in this chapter:

- I have entered in a worksheet the number of units sold and total revenue for each salesperson, and I can easily compute the average price per unit for each salesperson. How can I create a nice format that is automatically copied if I enter new data? Also, is there an easy way to automatically copy my formulas when new data is added?
- I have entered in my worksheet several years of natural gas prices, and I created a nice line chart displaying the monthly variation in prices. Can I set things up so that when I add new gas price data, my chart automatically updates?
- For each sales transaction, I have the salesperson, date, product, location, and size of the transaction. Can I easily summarize, for example, the total lipstick sales in the East made by Jen or Colleen?
- How do table slicers (added in Excel 2013) help us "slice and dice" data in an Excel Table?
- How can I easily refer to portions of a table in other parts of my workbook?
- Do conditional formats automatically apply to new data added to a table?

When most of us use Microsoft Excel, we often enter new data. Then we manually update our formulas, formats, and charts. What a drag! The Excel table capabilities make this drudgery a thing of the past.

Answers to this chapter's questions

I have entered in a worksheet the number of units sold and total revenue for each salesperson, and I can easily compute the average price per unit for each salesperson. How can I create a nice format that is automatically copied if I enter new data? Also, is there an easy way to automatically copy my formulas when new data is added?

The file Tableexampletemp.xlsx in the Templates folder for this chapter (see Figure 26-1) contains the units sold and revenue data for each of six salespersons. You know that new data will be added, beginning in row 12. Also, in column H, you would like to calculate the average price (Units/Revenue) earned by each salesperson. You would like to create an attractive format for the data and have the formula for average price copied down automatically as new data is added.

	E	F	G
5	Name	Units	Revenue
6	John	814	39886
7	Adam	594	26136
8	Dixie	528	13200
9	Tad	806	20956
10	Erica	826	27258
11	Gabrielle	779	28044

FIGURE 26-1 The data for creating a table.

Creating a table allows your analysis and formatting to be automatically updated when you add data. Begin by selecting the current range of data (E5:G11), including the headers. Next, click Table on the Insert tab of the ribbon, or press Ctrl+T. After selecting the My Table Has Headers check box (it might be selected by default) and clicking OK, you will see that the table range (E5:G11) is formatted beautifully. This formatting will continue automatically whenever new data is entered into the table. When you are working in a table, many styles and options are available on the Design tab. (See Figure 26-2.) The Design Tab is visible only when the active cell is within a table. You can select a formatting style that will be applied as new data is added to the table.

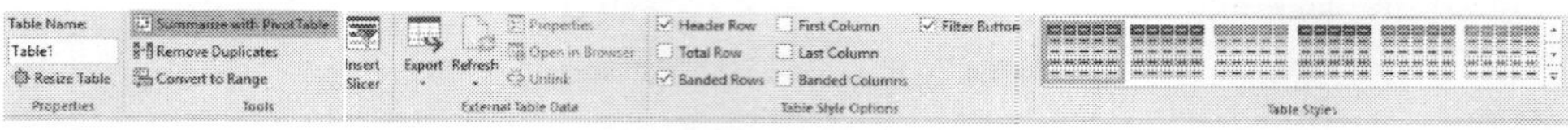

FIGURE 26-2 The table design options.

Note that the column headings have arrows, as you can see in Figure 26-3. These arrows work as filters that can be used to sort or filter the table. (More on filtering later in this chapter.)

	E	F	G	H
5	Name	Units	Revenue	Unit price
6	John	814	39886	49
7	Adam	594	26136	44
8	Dixie	528	13200	25
9	Tad	806	20956	26
10	Erica	826	27258	33
11	Gabrielle	779	28044	36
12	Amanda	400	5000	12.5

FIGURE 26-3 Formatted table with filters.

The cells in the selected table (excluding the headers) are given the name *Table1* by default. I changed the name to *Sales* in the Properties group on the Design tab. If you click the Formulas tab and then click Name Manager (in the Defined Names group), you can see that range E6:G11 is named *Sales*. The beauty of this range concept (and the table) is that the range dynamically expands to include new rows added to the bottom of the table and new columns added to the right of the table. In Chapter 22, "The OFFSET function," I used the OFFSET function to create a dynamic range, but table capabilities make the creation of a dynamic range a snap.

Suppose that in D15 you want to compute the total revenue. Begin by typing **=SUM(S**. Excel then offers you the option to automatically complete the entry with the table range *Sales*. I implemented AutoComplete by double-clicking the range name. You can also implement AutoComplete by selecting Sales (by clicking it once or pressing the Down arrow key) and pressing the Tab key. Then, when you see =*SUM(Sales* and type an opening bracket ([ ), Formula AutoComplete offers the option to complete the formula with column headings from the Sales table. You can complete your formula as =SUM(Sales[Revenue]) and calculate the total revenue as $155,480, as you can see in Figure 26-4. You will see an example of selecting the entries in the AutoComplete box that begin with number signs (**#**) later in this chapter.

	C	D	E	F	G	H
5			Name	Units	Revenue	Unit price
6			John	814	39886	49
7			Adam	594	26136	44
8			Dixie	528	13200	25
9			Tad	806	20956	26
10			Erica	826	27258	33
11			Gabrielle	779	28044	36
12						
13						
14						
15	revenue	155480				

FIGURE 26-4 The total revenue for the original data.

If new rows of data are added, the data in these rows is automatically accounted for in the formula. To illustrate this idea, you can add new data in row 12: Amanda sold 400 units for $5,000, as shown in Figure 26-5. Note that total revenue has increased by $5,000 to $160,480.

The formatting has been extended to row 12 as well, and the total revenue formula has been updated to include Amanda's data. Even if data is added within the table (instead of at the bottom), everything will be updated in a consistent fashion.

	C	D	E	F	G	H
5			Name	Units	Revenue	Unit price
6			John	814	39886	49
7			Adam	594	26136	44
8			Dixie	528	13200	25
9			Tad	806	20956	26
10			Erica	826	27258	33
11			Gabrielle	779	28044	36
12			Amanda	400	5000	12.5
13						
14						
15	revenue	160480				

FIGURE 26-5 New data added to the table in row 12.

Now suppose that you want to compute in column H the price per unit earned by each salesperson. Simply type **Unit Price** in H5 as the column heading, and then in cell H6 type **=Sales[**. In the AutoComplete list, double-click Revenue and type a closing bracket (]).. The formula is now =SALES[Revenue]. Type a slash (**/**), and use Formula AutoComplete to complete the formula as =SALES[Revenue]/Sales[Units]. An amazing thing happens. Excel automatically copies the formula down to the bottom of the table in cell H12, as shown in Figure 26-6. If you go to any cell in column H, the formula appears as [@Revenue]/[@Units]. Of course, =[@Revenue]/[@Units] is a lot easier to understand than =G6/F6. This formula can be interpreted as taking whatever is in the current row in the Revenue column and dividing it by whatever is in the current row in the Units column.

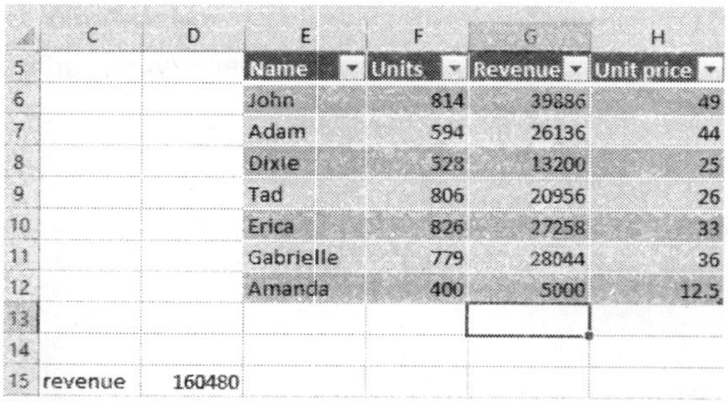

	C	D	E	F	G	H
5			Name	Units	Revenue	Unit price
6			John	814	39886	49
7			Adam	594	26136	44
8			Dixie	528	13200	25
9			Tad	806	20956	26
10			Erica	826	27258	33
11			Gabrielle	779	28044	36
12			Amanda	400	5000	12.5
13						
14						
15	revenue	160480				

FIGURE 26-6 Automatically copying the unit price formula.

If you click anywhere in a table, the Table Tools Design tab appears on the ribbon and offers choices (see Figure 26-2), including the following:

- **Change Table Name** Can be used to rename a table. I changed the name from *Table1* (the default) to *Sales*. Found in the Properties group.
- **Resize Table** Adds or subtracts rows and/or columns to the defined table range. Found in the Properties group.
- **Remove Duplicates** Removes rows that contain duplicates. For example, selecting only the Name column in the Remove Duplicates dialog box ensures that a name will not occur more than once. Checking both the Names and Units columns ensures that no rows in the table will match both Name and Units, and so on. Found in the Tools group.
- **Convert to Range** Converts the table range to normal cells and removes the table structure. Found in the Tools group.
- **Header Row** If selected, displays the header row. If cleared the header row is not displayed. Found in the Table Style Options group.
- **Total Row** I discuss the total row later in this chapter.
- **First Column** If selected, applies a special format to the first column of the table.
- **Last Column** If selected, assigns a special format to the last column of the table.
- **Banded Rows** If selected, gives the even-numbered rows in the table a different format than odd-numbered rows.
- **Banded Columns** If selected, gives odd-numbered columns in the table a format different from even-numbered columns.
- **Table Styles** Select from any of the table formats shown in this group. Of course, if the table expands or contracts, the format will adjust appropriately.

I have entered in my worksheet several years of natural gas prices, and I created a nice line chart displaying the monthly variation in prices. Can I set things up so that when I add new gas price data, my chart automatically updates?

In the file Gasprices507.xlsx, the worksheet Original contains natural gas prices per thousand feet from July 2002 through December 2004. (See Figure 26-7.) As I previously described, you can select B5:C34 (containing months and prices) and press Ctrl+T to create a table from this range. Then you can create a line graph to display this data by clicking Insert Line Or Area Chart in the Charts group on the Insert tab and selecting the fourth type of line graph, Line With Markers. The line graph I created is shown in Figure 26-8.

	A	B	C
4		month	gas price
5		Jul-02	3.278
6		Aug-02	2.976
7		Sep-02	3.268
8		Oct-02	3.686
9		Nov-02	4.126
10		Dec-02	4.140
11		Jan-03	4.988
12		Feb-03	5.660
13		Mar-03	9.133
14		Apr-03	5.146
15		May-03	5.123
16		Jun-03	5.945
17		Jul-03	5.291
18		Aug-03	4.693
19		Sep-03	4.927
20		Oct-03	4.430
21		Nov-03	4.459
22		Dec-03	4.860
23		Jan-04	6.150
24		Feb-04	5.775
25		Mar-04	5.150
26		Apr-04	5.365
27		May-04	5.935
28		Jun-04	6.680
29		Jul-04	6.141
30		Aug-04	6.048
31		Sep-04	5.062
32		Oct-04	5.723
33		Nov-04	7.626
34		Dec-04	7.976

FIGURE 26-7 Gas price data: 2002–2004.

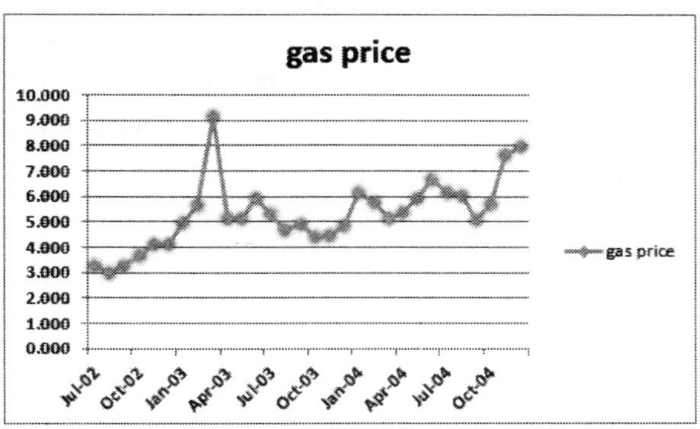

FIGURE 26-8 Gas price line graph data from 2002–2004.

Next, I copied this worksheet (by right-clicking the worksheet name, clicking Move Or Copy Sheet, and then clicking Make A Copy) and added gas prices through July 2006. (The data now extends to row 53.) I named the new worksheet *Newdata*. Note that the line graph in this worksheet automatically updates to include the new data. (See Figure 26-9.)

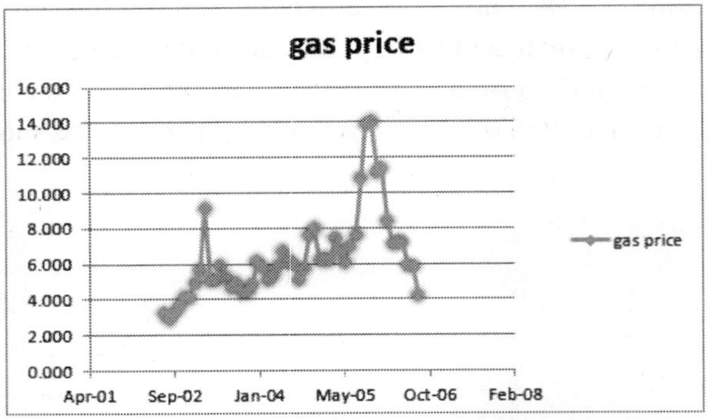

FIGURE 26-9 Gas price line graph, displaying 2002–2006 data.

This example illustrates that if you create a table of your data before creating a chart, new data will automatically be included in the chart.

For each sales transaction, I have the salesperson, date, product, location, and size of the transaction. Can I easily summarize, for example, the total lipstick sales in the East made by Jen or Colleen?

The file Tablemakeuptemp.xlsx contains sales transactions. (See Figure 26-10.) For each transaction, I have the following information: transaction number, name, date, product, number of units sold, dollars, and location. If I format this data as a table, I can add a total row for the Units and Dollars columns and then use the filter arrows to make the total row include the subset of transactions I want. To begin, click anywhere within the data and create a table by pressing Ctrl+T. The Create Table dialog box has E3:K1894 selected. Click OK. Note that if you scroll through the table, the header row remains visible. With a cell selected in the table, select the Total Row check box in the Table Style Options group on the Design tab. By default, Excel will enter the total number of rows in the table in cell K1895, which you can delete. Click the cells I1895 (the Units column) and J1895 (the Dollars column), click the arrow to the right of each cell, and then click Sum. This totals all the entries in the columns I and J of the table. Thus, currently the total revenue is $239,912.67, and 78,707 units were sold. (See Figure 26-11 and the file Tablemakeuptotals.xlsx.)

	E	F	G	H	I	J	K
3	Trans Number	Name	Date	Product	Units	Dollars	Location
4	1	Betsy	38078	lip gloss	45	137.2045583	south
5	2	Hallagan	38056	foundation	50	152.0073031	midwest
6	3	Ashley	38408	lipstick	9	28.71948312	midwest
7	4	Hallagan	38859	lip gloss	55	167.0753225	west
8	5	Zaret	38155	lip gloss	43	130.6028724	midwest
9	6	Colleen	38683	eye liner	58	175.9909741	midwest
10	7	Cristina	38067	eye liner	8	25.80069218	midwest
11	8	Colleen	39068	lip gloss	72	217.8396539	midwest
12	9	Ashley	38903	eye liner	75	226.6423269	south
13	10	Betsy	38936	lip gloss	24	73.50234217	east
14	11	Ashley	38320	mascara	43	130.8353684	east
15	12	Ashley	38309	lip gloss	23	71.03436769	west
16	13	Emilee	38595	lip gloss	49	149.5927969	west
17	14	Hallagan	38353	eye liner	18	56.47199923	south
18	15	Zaret	38980	foundation	-8	-21.99304472	east
19	16	Emilee	38089	mascara	45	137.3903759	east
20	17	Colleen	38837	mascara	66	199.6543347	south
21	18	Jen	38595	lip gloss	88	265.1875515	midwest
22	19	Jen	38287	eye liner	78	236.1469779	south
23	20	Zaret	38683	lip gloss	57	173.1152946	midwest

FIGURE 26-10 Makeup sales data.

	E	F	G	H	I	J	K
1884	1890	Cici	38518	foundation	16	49.7539874	east
1885	1891	Betsy	38452	foundation	39	119.1888319	east
1886	1892	Cici	38771	mascara	92	278.4349111	west
1887	1893	Cici	38199	foundation	20	61.92385747	midwest
1888	1894	Colleen	38122	lip gloss	60	181.8703479	east
1889	1895	Emilee	38683	eye liner	15	47.16102233	east
1890	1896	Ashley	38397	foundation	36	109.8425992	east
1891	1897	Colleen	38661	lip gloss	46	140.4088994	west
1892	1898	Zaret	38001	lipstick	72	217.8358862	west
1893	1899	Hallagan	39024	eye liner	28	85.65682953	south
1894	1900	Cristina	38881	eye liner	54	164.4873342	midwest
1895	Total				78707	39912.6741	1891

FIGURE 26-11 Total revenue and units sold.

To make the totals reflect only the lipstick sales in the East made by either Ashley or Hallagan, click the arrow in cell F3 (to the right of the Name header). Clear the Select All box so that no names are selected. Then select the check boxes for Ashley and Hallagan (see Figure 26-12), and click OK. Next, click the Product arrow and select the lipstick check box, and then click the Location arrow and select the East check box. Use the same approach to show only lipstick in the Product column and only East in the Location column. You now see all the data fitting the filtering criteria in Figure 26-13 and in the file Tablemakeuptotals.xlsx in this chapter's Program Files folder. You'll see that Ashley and Hallagan sold 564 units of lipstick in the East for a total of $1,716.56. This table filtering feature makes it a snap to easily compute totals for any subset of rows in an Excel worksheet. If you want, you can also copy the rows involving Ashley or Hallagan selling lipstick in the East and paste them elsewhere.

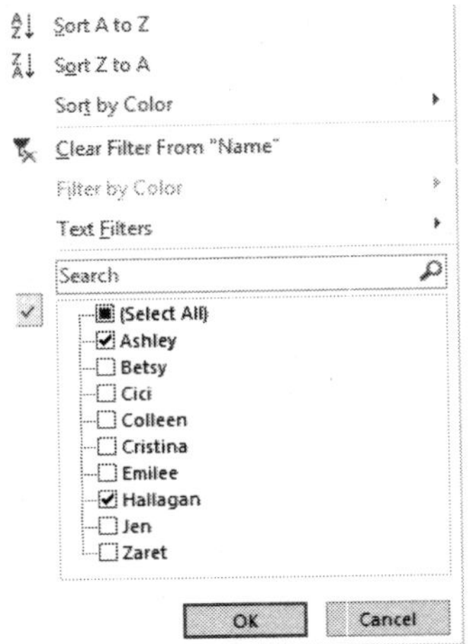

FIGURE 26-12 Filtering on names from the table.

	E	F	G	H	I	J	K
1							
2							
3	Trans Number	Name	Date	Product	Units	Dollars	Location
282	288	Ashley	38606	lipstick	-8	-21.9125458	east
565	571	Hallagan	38925	lipstick	60	182.2924607	east
670	676	Hallagan	38023	lipstick	8	25.63945706	east
702	708	Ashley	38375	lipstick	71	215.1433462	east
968	974	Ashley	39002	lipstick	72	218.0571538	east
1142	1148	Ashley	38727	lipstick	42	127.8685805	east
1173	1179	Ashley	38452	lipstick	70	211.6914545	east
1186	1192	Hallagan	38023	lipstick	40	122.5516179	east
1282	1288	Ashley	38320	lipstick	84	254.1193721	east
1332	1338	Ashley	38969	lipstick	50	152.3101916	east
1423	1429	Hallagan	38441	lipstick	24	73.61606446	east
1469	1475	Ashley	38705	lipstick	51	155.1847283	east
1895	Total				564	1716.561881	12

FIGURE 26-13 Filtered subtotals for units and revenue.

How do table slicers (added in Excel 2013) help us "slice and dice" data in an Excel Table?

In Excel 2010, slicers were introduced to simplify the filtering of PivotTables (see Chapter 43, "Using PivotTables and slicers to describe data" for details.) Starting in Excel 2013, slicers can be used to filter tables. The advantage of slicers is that you can easily see the filters that define the visible rows and the totals calculations. To create filters for our makeup example (see the file Tablemakeuptotals.xlsx), simply click inside the table and then, from the Insert tab, select Slicer from the Filters group. To create slicers for the Name, Product, and Location columns, simply select them as shown in Figure 26-14.

FIGURE 26-14 Creating slicers for the Name, Product, and Location columns.

The slicers are shown in Figure 26-15. When working with a slicer, you can select filters by using the Shift key to select adjacent items and the Ctrl key to select nonadjacent items. Our slicers filter all the sales involving Ashley selling lipstick in the East. Note the totals row and visible rows are identical to Figure 26-13. Clicking a slicer's funnel clears the filter for that column in the table.

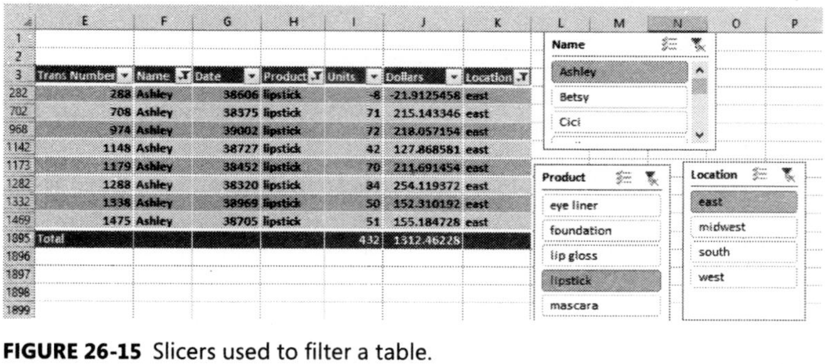

FIGURE 26-15 Slicers used to filter a table.

When you click inside a slicer, you can easily resize the slicer if you hold down the Ctrl key. You can also click the Slicer Tools Options tab on the ribbon. Then you can modify many features of the slicer, including the slicer style, slicer caption name, the number of columns, and the slicer's size.

Computing totals based on table slicers is tricky. Consider the file Sumwithslicerstemp.xlsx (from this chapter's Templates folder). Annual sales in the United States and overseas are given. A subset of the data (months March through September are hidden) is shown in Figure 26-16. I would like to use slicers to select any subset of years and select US and/or international sales and compute the total sales for that subset of data. To begin, I attempted to sum all the sales in the table by entering in cell Q15 the formula =SUM(Table1[[January]:[December]]). A total revenue of $14,977,000 is obtained. Next I inserted slicers for Year and Type and select INT and 2010–2011.

As shown in Figure 26-17, I still get a total of $14,977,000. This cannot be right! The problem is that Excel is not ignoring the hidden rows. If I enter in cell P4 the formula =AGGREGATE(9,5,Table1[[January]:[December]]), then, when I select INT sales and the Years 2010–2011 with slicers, I obtain the correct sales total $1,506,000. The first argument of *9* in the AGGREGATE function indicates that I need to compute a Sum, and the second argument of *5* tells Excel to ignore the rows hidden by my slicer selection.

	A	B	C	D	L	M	N
14							
15	Year	Type	January	February	October	November	December
16	2010	US	$177,000	$107,000	$128,000	$190,000	$113,000
17	2010	INT	$74,000	$71,000	$66,000	$51,000	$70,000
18	2011	US	$149,000	$128,000	$171,000	$172,000	$183,000
19	2011	INT	$63,000	$75,000	$55,000	$61,000	$67,000
20	2012	US	$184,000	$103,000	$110,000	$126,000	$127,000
21	2012	INT	$67,000	$58,000	$55,000	$52,000	$64,000
22	2013	US	$109,000	$173,000	$196,000	$122,000	$110,000
23	2013	INT	$74,000	$51,000	$62,000	$75,000	$70,000
24	2014	US	$112,000	$136,000	$123,000	$123,000	$149,000
25	2014	INT	$51,000	$74,000	$64,000	$58,000	$65,000
26	2015	US	$113,000	$181,000	$176,000	$165,000	$185,000
27	2015	INT	$59,000	$57,000	$72,000	$67,000	$65,000

FIGURE 26-16 Summing a table with slicers.

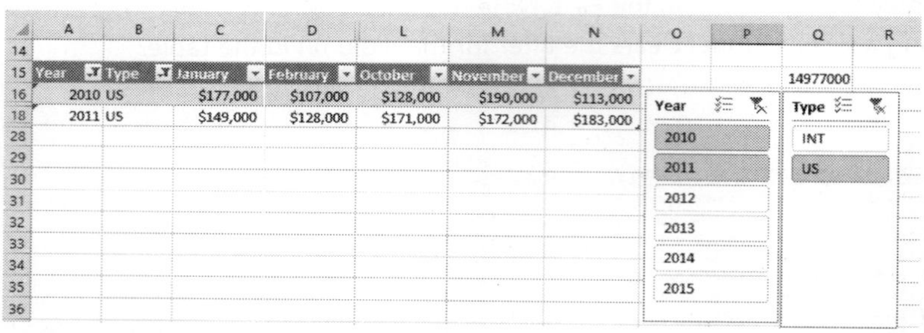

FIGURE 26-17 Using slicers to total the revenue.

How can I easily refer to portions of a table in other parts of my workbook?

The file Tablestructure.xlsx shows many examples of how you can refer to parts of a table when you are working outside the table's range. These references are often called *structured references*. (See Figure 26-18.) When you enter a table name into a formula, AutoComplete makes the column names and the following table specifiers available for selection:

- **Table Name** All cells in the table, excluding the header and total rows.
- **#All** All the cells in the table, including the total row (if any).
- **#Data** All the cells in the table, except for the first row and the total row.
- **#Headers** Just the header row.

- **#Totals** Just the total row. If there is no total row, this returns an empty cell range.
- **@/#This Row** All table entries in the current row. Starting in Excel 2010, the at symbol (@) replaced [#This Row] for signifying all the cells in the row.

A *column reference* includes all the cells in a table column, excluding the header and total row entries (if any).

Here are some examples of how table specifiers can be used in formulas (see the worksheet Original in the file Tablestructure.xlsx):

- In cell C15, the formula =COUNTA(Table1[#All]) yields 55 because the table contains 55 entries.
- In cell C16, the formula =COUNTA(Table1) yields 45 because the header and total rows are not counted. In cell C17, the formula =COUNTA(Table[#Data]) yields 45 because the cell range D5:H13 is referenced.
- In cell C18, the formula =COUNTA(Table1[#Headers]) yields 5 because only the header row (D4:H4) is referenced.
- In cell C19, the formula =SUM(Table1[Q1]) yields 367 because the formula sums the entries in E5:E13.
- In cell C20, the formula =SUM(Table1[#Totals]) sums all the entries in the total row and yields 1,340, which is the total sum of all the table entries.
- In cell C21, the formula =SUM(Table1[[#Data],[Q1]:[Q3]]) sums all the data entries that are in columns Q1:Q3, inclusively (cells E5:G13). Thus, column names separated by a colon include all the data entries between and including the column name before the colon and the column name after the colon.
- In cell B8, the formula =SUM(Table1[@]) sums the entries in row 8 (41+28+49+40), 158.

Of course, all of these formulas are automatically updated if new data is added to the table.

	A	B	C	D	E	F	G	H
1								
2								
3								
4				Product	Q1	Q2	Q3	Q4
5				food1	37	42	24	32
6				mag1	20	23	24	41
7				drug1	47	34	41	28
8		158		drug2	41	28	49	40
9				food2	44	22	46	50
10	=SUM(Table1[@])			drug1	39	25	38	29
11				mag2	26	35	31	30
12				food4	48	49	50	50
13				mag3	65	34	35	43
14				Total	367	292	338	343
15			55	=COUNTA(Table1[#All])				
16			45	=COUNTA(Table1)				
17			45	=COUNTA(Table1[#Data])				
18			5	=COUNTA(Table1[#Headers])				
19			367	=SUM(Table1[Q1])				
20			1340	=SUM(Table1[#Totals])				
21			997	=SUM(Table1[[#Data],[Q1]:[Q3]])				

FIGURE 26-18 Structured references.

Do conditional formats automatically apply to new data added to a table?

Yes, Excel's built-in conditional formats will automatically include new table data. (See Figure 26-19.) As we will see, it is trickier to ensure that conditional formats created by means of the Use A Formula option automatically update when new data is added to a table.

To illustrate, I placed in the worksheet Original of the file Tablestructure.xlsx a conditional format to highlight the three largest Q1 sales in column E. The entries in rows 7, 12, and 13 are highlighted. In the worksheet Add Biggersale, I added the entry 90 in cell E14. This becomes the largest entry in the column and is immediately highlighted. Cell E7 is no longer highlighted because it is no longer one of the three largest numbers in column E of the table.

	D	E	F	G	H
4	Product	Q1	Q2	Q3	Q4
5	food1	37	42	24	32
6	mag1	20	23	24	41
7	drug1	47	34	41	28
8	drug2	41	28	49	40
9	food2	44	22	46	50
10	drug1	39	25	38	29
11	mag2	26	35	31	30
12	food4	48	49	50	50
13	mag3	65	34	35	43
14	drug3	90	45	34	23

FIGURE 26-19 Extending conditional formatting automatically to new table data.

Now suppose you want to highlight the largest number in each column of the file Formattablesfinal.xlsx, shown in Figure 26-20.

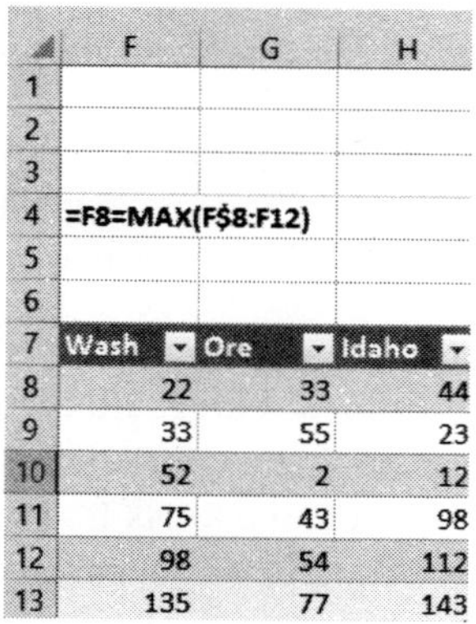

FIGURE 26-20 Highlighting the largest number in each column.

We can create this format easily with the Use A Formula option, but if we want our format to apply to new rows added to the table we need to fill in the New Formatting Rule dialog box (in the Home Tab and Styles group, click Conditional Formatting and then New Rule), as you see in Figure 26-21.

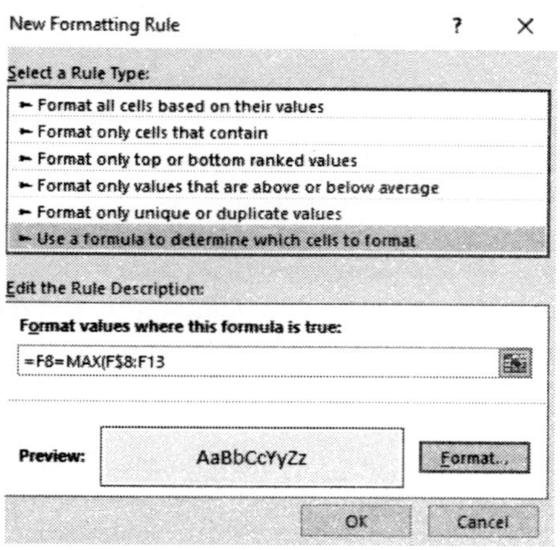

FIGURE 26-21 These settings ensure that when new data is added, Excel highlights the largest number in each column.

When selecting the format values, enter the formula =F8=MAX(F$8:F13). The key here is to not place a $ sign before the 13. If you enter F$13, Excel will lock the format so that it does not extend beyond row 13. Add a new row of data containing large numbers to explore how the format automatically updates to include the new row of data.

Problems

1. The file Singers.xlsx contains a list of songs sung by different singers, as well as the length (in estimated minutes) of each song. Set up your worksheet to compute the total number of songs sung by Eminem and the average length of each song. Of course, if new data is added, your formulas should automatically update.

2. In the file Tableexample.xlsx, set things up so that each salesperson's rank in regard to total revenue and units sold is included in the worksheet. Of course, if new data is included, your ranks should automatically update. You might find it convenient to use the RANK.EQ function. The syntax of the RANK function is =RANK.EQ(number,array,0). This function yields the rank of a number in a range array, with rank=1 being the largest number.

3. The file Lookupdata.xlsx contains product codes and prices. Set up the worksheet so that a product code can be entered and your worksheet will return the product price. Of course, when new products are introduced, your formula should still work.

4. The file Productlookup.xlsx contains the product sales made each day of the week. Set up a formula that returns the sale of any product on any given day. Of course, if new products are added to the data, your formula should be able to include sales for those products.

5. The file Tablepie.xlsx contains sales information for different products sold in a small general store. You want to set up a pie chart to summarize this data. Of course, if new product categories are added, the pie chart should automatically include the new data.

6. The file Tablexnpvdata.xlsx lists cash flows received by a small business. Set up a formula to compute (as of January 5, 2007) the NPV of all cash flows. Assume an annual discount rate of 10 percent. Of course, if new cash flows are entered, your formula should automatically include them.

7. The file Nikedata.xlsx contains quarterly sales revenues for Nike. Create a graph of Nike sales that automatically includes new sales revenue data.

8. For the data in file Tablemakeuptemp.xlsx (from this chapter's Templates folder), determine the total units and revenue for all lip gloss or lipstick sold by Jen or Ashley in the South or East region.

9. The file Closest.xlsx contains people's names and salaries. Set up a worksheet that takes any number and finds the person whose salary is closest to that number. Your worksheet should accomplish this goal even if new names are added or existing names are deleted from the list.

10. The file Adagency.xlsx contains salaries and ages of employees of an ad agency. Set up a spreadsheet that will compute the average salary and age of the agency's employees. Of course, your calculations should automatically update if the agency hires or fires workers.

11. The file Problem11data.xlsx contains statistics on NFL quarterbacks. A QB's name will be entered in cell I2. Set up a format that will highlight the entire row of data for the QB entered in cell I2. Your format should automatically update if new rows of data are added to the worksheet.

CHAPTER 27

Spin buttons, scroll bars, option buttons, check boxes, combo boxes, and group list boxes

Questions answered in this chapter:

- I need to run a sensitivity analysis that has many key inputs, such as Year 1 sales, annual sales growth, Year 1 price, and unit cost. Is there a way I can quickly vary these inputs and see the effect of the variation on the calculation of net present value, for example?
- How do I set up a simple check box that toggles conditional formatting on and off?
- How can I set up my worksheet so that my supply-chain personnel can click a button to choose whether we charge a high, low, or medium price for a product?
- How can I create an easy way for a user of my worksheet to enter a day of the week without having to type any text?

User forms enable a user of Microsoft Excel 2016 to add a variety of cool, useful controls to a worksheet. In this chapter, I show you how easy it is to use spin buttons, scroll bars, option buttons, check boxes, combo boxes, and list boxes. To access user forms, navigate to the Developer tab on the ribbon, and then click Insert in the Controls group to display the forms controls. (These are not to be confused with ActiveX Controls, which are usually used within the Microsoft Visual Basic for Applications [VBA] programming language.)

> **Note** To display the Developer tab, click the File tab, and then click Options. Click Customize Ribbon, select Developer in the Main Tabs list, and then click OK.

The user forms I discuss are shown in Table 27-1. (See also the file Controls.xlsx in the Practice Files folder for this chapter.)

TABLE 27-1 Controls for Excel user forms.

Control name	Image
Spin button	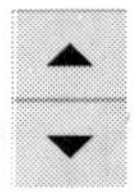
Scroll bar	
Check box	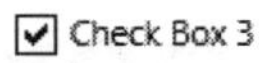
Option button	
Combo box	
List box	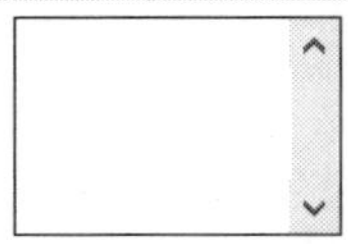

Answers to this chapter's questions

I need to run a sensitivity analysis that has many key inputs, such as Year 1 sales, annual sales growth, Year 1 price, and Year 1 unit cost. Is there a way I can quickly vary these inputs and see the effect of the variation on the calculation of net present value, for example?

As I discussed in Chapter 19, "Using the Scenario Manager for sensitivity analysis," the Scenario Manager (found on the Data tab, in the Forecast group under What-If Analysis) lets you change a group of input cells to see how various outputs change. Unfortunately, the Scenario Manager requires you to enter each scenario individually, which makes creating more than a few scenarios difficult. For example, suppose you believe that four key inputs to a car's net present value (NPV) model are Year1sales, Sales growth, Year1price, and Year1cost. (See the file NPVspinners.xlsx.) You'd like to see how the NPV changes as the inputs change in the following ranges:

Input	Low value	High value
Year 1 sales	$5,000	$30,000
Annual sales growth	0%	50%
Year 1 price	$6	$20
Year 1 cost	$2	$15

Using the Scenario Manager to generate the scenarios in which the input cells vary within the given ranges would be very time-consuming. By using spin buttons, however, a user can quickly generate a host of scenarios that vary each input between its low and high value.

A spin button is a control that is linked to a specific cell. As you click the up or down arrow on the spin button, the value of the linked cell changes. You can see how formulas of interest (such as one that calculates a car's NPV) change in response to changes in the inputs. Explore how spinners change the values by clicking the arrows in D2:D5.

Here's how to create spin buttons that allow you to vary Year1sales, Sales growth, Year1price, and Year1cost within the ranges you want. The Original Model worksheet (see the file NPVspinnerstemp.xlsx in the Templates folder) is shown in Figure 27-1.

	A	B	C	D	E	F
1		taxrate	0.4			
2		Year1sales	10000			
3		Sales growth	0.48		48	
4		Year1price	$ 9.00			
5		Year1cost	$ 6.00			
6		intrate	0.15			
7		costgrowth	0.05			
8		pricegrowth	0.03			
9	Year	1	2	3	4	5
10	Unit Sales	10000	14800	21904	32417.92	47978.5216
11	unit price	$ 9.00	$ 9.27	$ 9.55	$ 9.83	$ 10.13
12	unit cost	$ 6.00	$ 6.30	$ 6.62	$ 6.95	$ 7.29
13	Revenues	$ 90,000.00	$ 137,196.00	$209,141.58	$ 318,815.43	$ 486,002.24
14	Costs	$ 60,000.00	$ 93,240.00	$144,894.96	$ 225,166.77	$ 349,909.16
15	Before Tax Profit	$ 30,000.00	$ 43,956.00	$ 64,246.62	$ 93,648.66	$ 136,093.08
16	Tax	$ 12,000.00	$ 17,582.40	$ 25,698.65	$ 37,459.46	$ 54,437.23
17	Aftertax Profits	$ 18,000.00	$ 26,373.60	$ 38,547.97	$ 56,189.20	$ 81,655.85
18						
19	NPV	$133,664.07				

FIGURE 27-1 The Original Model worksheet, without any spin buttons.

To create the spin buttons, select the rows in which you want to insert spin buttons (I used rows 2–5 in this example), and then increase the height of the rows by right-clicking and selecting Row Height. A row height of 27 is usually enough to accommodate the spin button arrows. Alternatively, hold down the Alt key while you draw the control so that it fits the cell.

Display the User Forms menu by clicking Insert in the Controls group on the Developer tab (recall that we enabled this tab from the Custom Ribbon page of the Excel Options dialog box). Click the spin button form control (shown in Table 27-1). Your cursor will change to a plus sign (+). Clicking the mouse button anchors the spin button where you want it and allows you to draw the shape for the spin button. Draw the button in cell D2. To change the shape of a form control or to move the control, hold down the Ctrl key and click the control to select it. When the pointer turns into a four-headed arrow, drag the control to move it. When the pointer appears as a two-headed arrow, you can drag the control to resize it.

A spin button now appears in cell D2. You can use this spin button to change the value of Year1 sales. Right-click the spin button, and then click Copy. Right-click cell D3, and then click Paste. Also paste the spin button into cells D4 and D5. You should now see four spin buttons as shown in Figure 27-2.

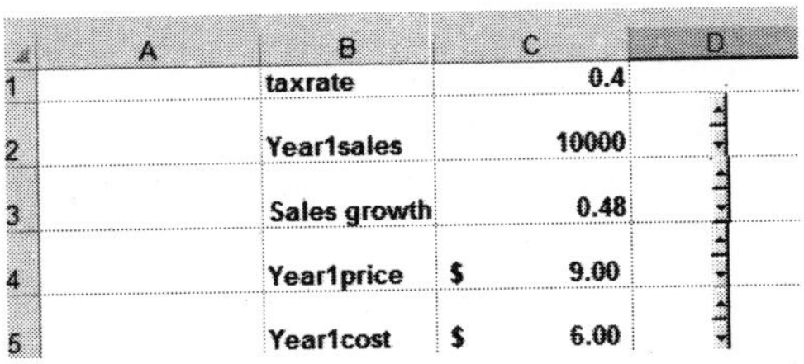

FIGURE 27-2 Placing spin buttons in worksheet cells.

Now you need to link each spin button to an input cell. To link the spin button in D2 to cell C2, right-click the spin button in cell D2, and then click Format Control. Fill in the Format Control dialog box as shown in Figure 27-3: I used 9000 for the current value, 5000 for the minimum value, 30000 for the maximum value, 1000 for the incremental change, and $C$2 as the cell link. I left 3-D Shading selected and clicked OK.

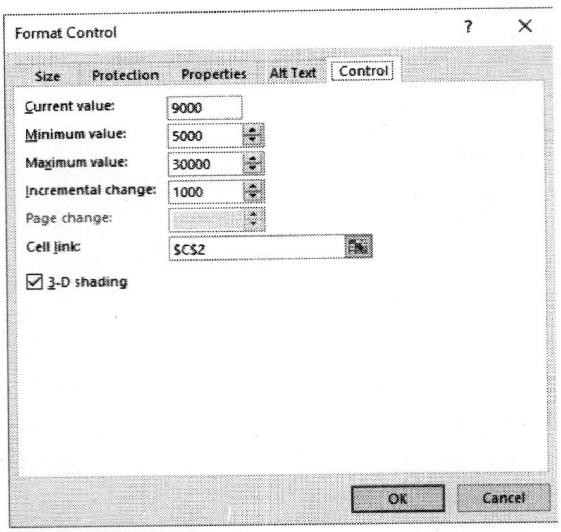

FIGURE 27-3 Using the Format Control dialog box to link Year1 sales to a spin button.

The current value is not as important. The rest of the settings tell Excel that this spin button is linked to the values in cell C2 (Year1 sales), that each click on the up arrow will increase the value in C2 by 1,000, and that each click on the down arrow will decrease the value in C2 by 1,000. When the value in C2 reaches 30,000, clicking the up arrow will not increase it; when the value in C2 reaches 5,000, clicking the down arrow will not decrease the value in cell C2.

Next, use the Format Control dialog box to link the spin button in D4 to Year1 price (cell C4). (We'll cover the spinner in cell D3 last.) For the current value, I used 9. The minimum value is 6, the maximum value is 20, and the incremental change is 1. I linked the spinner to cell C4. Clicking the spin button arrows in cell D4 varies the Year1price value between $6 and $20 in $1 increments.

To link the spin button in cell D5 to Year1cost (cell C5), I used 6 for the current value, 2 for the minimum value, 15 for the maximum value, and 1 as the incremental change. I linked the spinner to cell C5. Clicking the spin button arrows in cell D5 changes Year1cost from $2 to $15 in $1 increments.

Linking the spin button in cell D3 to sales growth is trickier. We want the spin button control to change sales growth to 0 percent, 1 percent, ... 50 percent. The problem is that the minimum increment a spin button value can change is 1. Therefore, you need to link this spin button to a dummy value in cell E3 and place the formula E3/100 in cell C3. Now, as cell E3 varies from 1 to 50, sales growth varies between 1 percent and 50 percent. Figure 26-4 shows how to link this spin button to cell E3: I used 48 for the current value, 0 for the minimum value, 50 for the maximum value, 1 for the incremental change, and linked the spinner to the cell E3. Remember that the sales growth in cell C3 is simply the number in cell E3 divided by 100.

By the way, if the cursor is within the control and you hold down the Ctrl key, you can easily use the handles to resize a control.

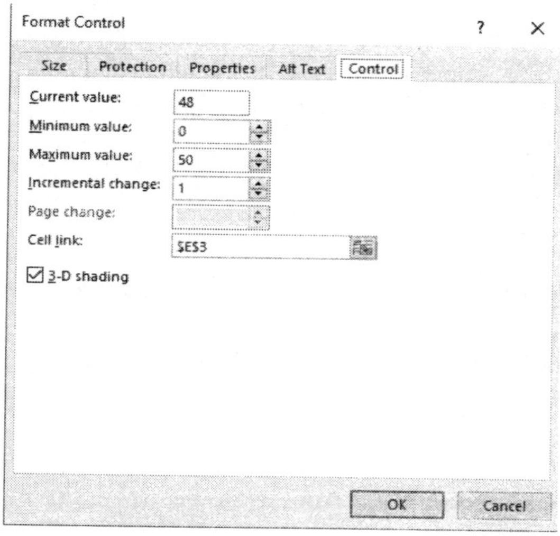

FIGURE 27-4 Using the Format Control dialog box settings to link the spin button in cell D3 to cell E3.

By clicking a spin button arrow, you can easily see how changing a single input cell—given the values for the other inputs listed in the worksheet—changes the car's NPV. To see the effect of the changes, you can select cell F9, click Freeze Panes on the View tab (in the Window group), and then click Freeze Panes again. This command freezes the data above row 9 and to the left of column F. You can now use the scroll bars on the right of the window to arrange it as you see it in Figure 27-5.

	A	B	C	D	E	F
1		taxrate	0.4			
2		Year1sales	10000			
3		Sales growth	0.48		48	
4		Year1price	$ 9.00			
5		Year1cost	$ 6.00			
6		intrate	0.15			
7		costgrowth	0.05			
8		pricegrowth	0.03			
9	Year	1	2	3	4	5
10	Unit Sales	10000	14800	21904	32417.92	47978.5216
11	unit price	$ 9.00	$ 9.27	$ 9.55	$ 9.83	$ 10.13
12	unit cost	$ 6.00	$ 6.30	$ 6.62	$ 6.95	$ 7.29
13	Revenues	$ 90,000.00	$ 137,196.00	$209,141.58	$ 318,815.43	$ 486,002.24
14	Costs	$ 60,000.00	$ 93,240.00	$144,894.96	$ 225,166.77	$ 349,909.16
15	Before Tax Profit	$ 30,000.00	$ 43,956.00	$ 64,246.62	$ 93,648.66	$ 136,093.08
16	Tax	$ 12,000.00	$ 17,582.40	$ 25,698.65	$ 37,459.46	$ 54,437.23
17	Aftertax Profits	$ 18,000.00	$ 26,373.60	$ 38,547.97	$ 56,189.20	$ 81,655.85
18						
19	NPV	$133,664.07				

FIGURE 27-5 Freezing panes to see the results of calculations in other parts of a worksheet.

Given the values of the other inputs, clicking the sales growth spin button arrows shows that a 1 percent increase in sales growth is worth about $2,000. (To return the worksheet to its normal state, click Freeze Panes in the View tab, followed by Unfreeze Panes.)

The scroll bar control is very similar to the spin button. The main difference is that by moving the cursor over the gray area in the middle of the scroll bar, you can cause the linked cell to continuously change in value. By selecting Format Control on the shortcut menu and changing the value under Page Change in the Format Control dialog box, you can control the speed with which the linked cell changes.

How do I set up a simple check box that toggles conditional formatting on and off?

A check box is a form control that specifies a value of *True* in a cell when the box is checked and *False* when the box is clear. Check boxes can be used to create toggle switches that turn a particular feature on or off. As an example, I will show how to use a check box to turn the conditional formatting feature on or off.

Suppose a worksheet contains monthly sales and you want to color the five largest sales in green and the five smallest sales in red. (See the file Checkbox.xlsx, and click the check box to explore how it toggles the formatting.) Enter in cell G4 the formula =LARGE(Sales,5), which computes the fifth-largest sales value. Then, in cell H4, compute the fifth-smallest sales value by entering the formula =SMALL(Sales,5). (See Figure 27-6.)

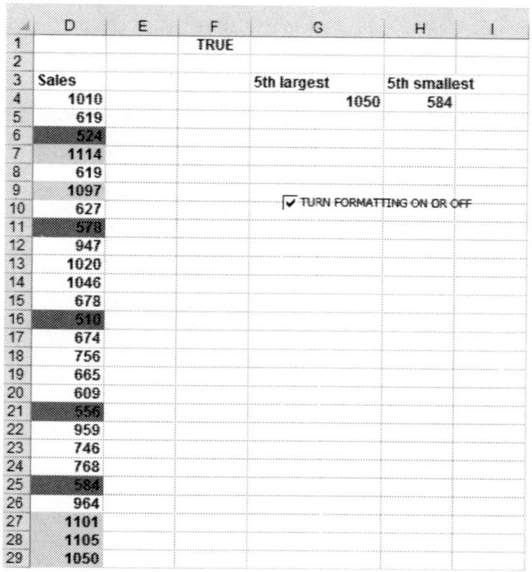

FIGURE 27-6 Using a check box to turn conditional formatting on and off.

Next, you create a check box and configure it to enter True or False in cell F1. Open the file Checkboxtemp.xlsx from this chapter's Templates folder. On the Developer tab, click Insert and select the check box from the Forms Controls palette. Your cursor changes to the cross hairs. Drag the cursor over cell G9, and then change its text (right-click the control and select Edit Text) to read **Turn Formatting On or Off**. You might need to resize the control so that it is wider to see all the text. Then right-click the check box, click Format Control, and fill in the dialog box as shown in Figure 27-7: I selected Checked, linked the check box to cell F1, and clicked OK.

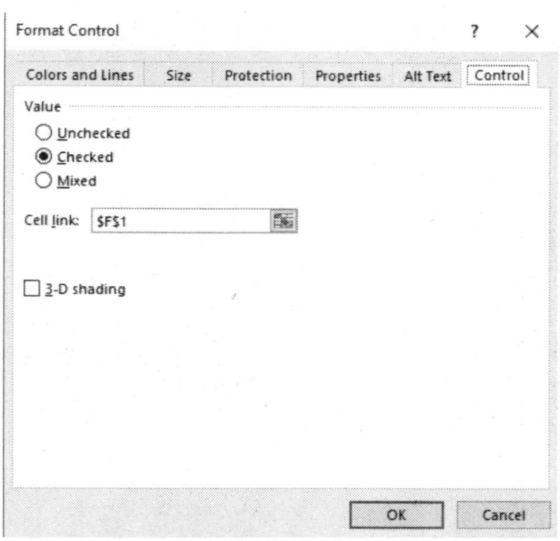

FIGURE 27-7 The Format Control dialog box for a check box.

Now, whenever you select the check box, True is placed in F1, and whenever you clear the check box, False is placed in cell F1.

After selecting the cell range D4:D29, click Conditional Formatting in the Styles group on the Home tab, and then click New Rule. Select Use A Formula To Determine Which Cells To Format, and enter the formula shown in Figure 27-8, =AND($F$1,D4>=$G$4), to color the top five sales green (click Format, click the Fill tab, select a green color, and then click OK). Then enter the formula shown in Figure 27-9, =AND($F$1,D4<=$H$4), to color the bottom five sales red. Note that the AND($F$1) portion of the formula ensures that the formatting can be applied only if cell F1 is True. Of course, the check box determines whether cell F1 is True or False, so if the check box is not selected, the cells will not turn green or red.

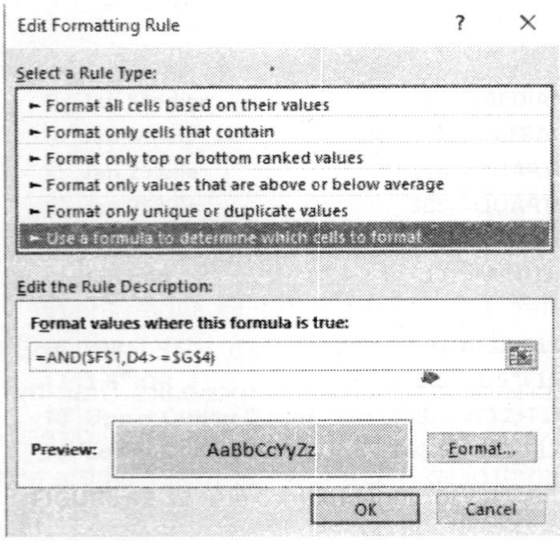

FIGURE 27-8 Changing the format to turn the five largest cells green.

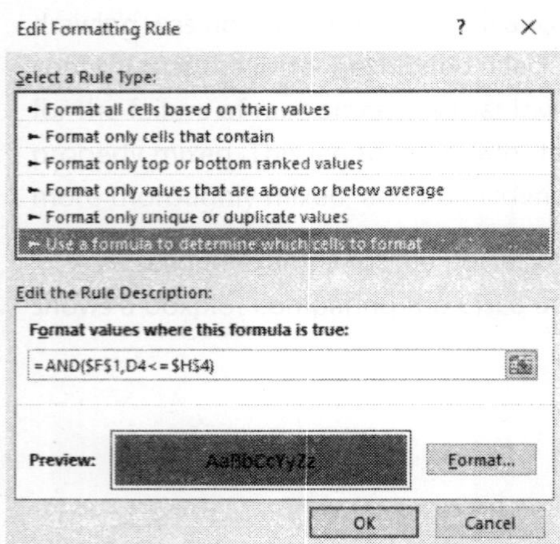

FIGURE 27-9 Changing the format to turn the five smallest cells red.

If you want, you can select cell F1 and change the font color to white to hide True and False.

How can I set up my worksheet so that my supply-chain personnel can check a button to choose whether we charge a high, low, or medium price for a product?

Let's suppose that you can charge one of three prices for a product: high, medium, or low. These prices are listed in cells B7:B9 of the file Optionbuttons.xlsx (try clicking the option buttons). You could easily use a lookup table to print the price if a user typed in **High**, **Medium**, or **Low**. It's a better design, however, if the user can select an option button that says *High Price*, *Medium Price*, or *Low Price* and then have a formula automatically compute the price. (See Figure 27-10.) This button type is also referred to as a *radio button*.

Now open the file Optionbuttonstemp.xlsx from this chapter's Templates folder. To use option buttons, first draw a group box by choosing this control from the User Forms menu on the Developer tab—the ScreenTip for this control is Group Box (Form Control), and it is located at the bottom-left corner of the User Forms list. Drag the control in cells A14:C21. Right-click the group box, click Edit Text, and change the group box text to Select price.

Next, drag an option button for each choice into the group box. Because you have three price levels, you need to drag three option buttons into the group box. In the Developer tab, click Insert, select the option button control (see Table 27-1), and then drag the cursor in cell B16. Right-click each option button, and then use the Format Control command to link each one of the option buttons to a cell. I linked each option button (which I renamed to *High price*, *Medium price*, and *Low price*) to cell E4. All of the option buttons in the group box are now linked to the same cell. Selecting the first option button will enter a **1** in cell E4, selecting the second option button will enter a **2** in cell E4, and selecting the third option button will enter a **3** in cell E4.

Entering the formula = INDEX(A7:A9,E4,1) in cell E7 returns the price description corresponding to the selected option button. In cell F7, entering the formula =VLOOKUP(E7,A7:B9,2,FALSE) computes the price corresponding to the selected option button.

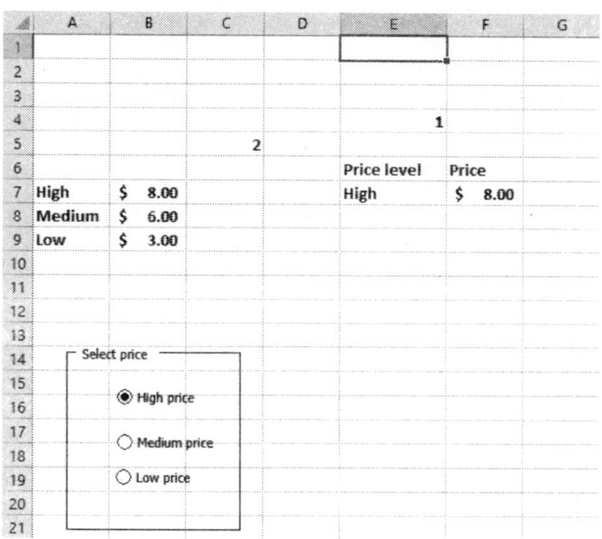

FIGURE 27-10 Using option buttons to select a product price.

How can I create an easy way for a user of my spreadsheet to select a day of the week without having to type any text?

The file Combobox.xlsx shows how to use a combo box or a list box (see Figure 27-11) to allow a user to easily select an item from a list. (Data validation also makes it easy to create drop-down boxes; see Chapter 40, "Validating data.") The goal here is to compute the number of hours an employee worked on a given day. The hours worked each day are listed in cells G9:G15. A combo box or list box allows you to select an entry from a list. If the combo box or list box is linked to a cell (via Format Control), then, if the first entry in the box is selected, a 1 is placed in the linked cell; if the second entry in the list is selected, a 2 is entered in the linked cell, and so on. To set up the worksheet, display the Developer tab, click Insert, select Combo Box from the Form Controls menu (see Table 27-1), and drag a wide rectangle over C5 to set the combo box. Next, add a list box to B14. Right-click the combo box and click Format Control. Select the input range F9:F15 (this contains days of the week) and link it to the cell A8. Now right-click the list box and select Format Control. Select the input range F9:F15 and link it to cell A13. After these steps, if you select *Tuesday* from the combo box and *Friday* from the list box, for example, you see a 2 in A8 and a 5 in A13.

In cell F3, the formula =INDEX(F9:F15,A8,1) lists the day of the week corresponding to the combo box selection. In cell G3, the formula =VLOOKUP(F3,$F$9:$G$15,2,False) locates the number of hours worked for the day selected in the combo box. In a similar fashion, the formulas in F4 and G4 list the day of the week and hours worked for the day selected in the list box.

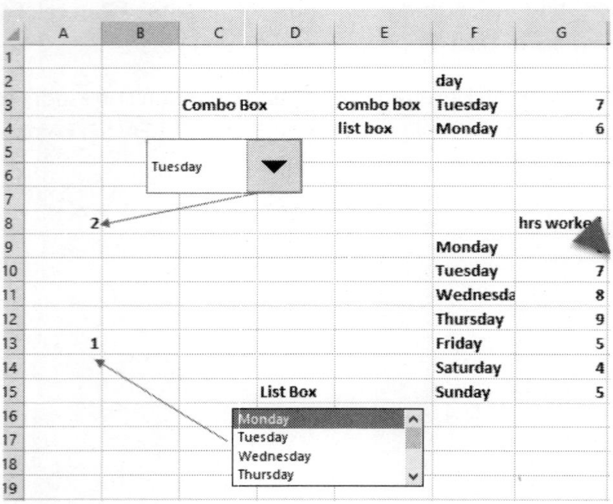

FIGURE 27-11 Using combo boxes and list boxes.

Problems

1. Add a spin button for the car NPV example that allows you to vary the tax rate between 30 percent and 50 percent.

2. Add a spin button for the car NPV example that allows you to vary the interest rate between 5 percent and 20 percent.

3. The Format Control dialog box allows a minimum value of 0. Despite this limitation, can you figure out a way to use a spin button to vary sales growth between –10 percent and 20 percent?

4. Using the lemonade example in Chapter 17, "Sensitivity analysis with data tables," create spin buttons that allow the inputs to vary within the following ranges:

Input	Low value	High value
Price	$2.00	$5.00
Unit cost	$0.20	$1.00
Fixed cost	$20,000.00	$100,000.00

5. Using the mortgage payment example in Chapter 17, create spin buttons that allow inputs to vary within the following ranges:

Input	Low value	High value
Amount borrowed	$270,000	$800,000
Number of months of payments	120	360
Annual interest rate	4%	10%

6. For the weekend example used in Chapter 24, "Conditional formatting," set up a check box that turns conditional formatting on or off.

7. In the financial formulas described in Chapter 10, "More Excel financial functions," I used a last argument of *1* to indicate end of month cash flows and *0* to indicate beginning of month cash flows. Excel recognizes *True* as equivalent to 1 and *False* as equivalent to 0. Set up a worksheet in which a user can enter the number of months in a loan, principal, and annual interest rate to find the monthly payment. Then use a check box to select whether the payments are at the beginning or end of the month.

8. Using the data for Problem 15 in Chapter 22, "The OFFSET function," create a spinner that lets you graph the last few months of sales (ranging from three to eight months).

9. The file Suppliers.xlsx contains the unit price you pay to each of your suppliers and the units purchased. Create a list box that allows you to pick the supplier and that also returns the unit price and units purchased.

CHAPTER 28

The analytics revolution

Questions answered in this chapter:

- What is analytics?
- What is predictive analytics?
- What is prescriptive analytics?
- Why has analytics increased in importance?
- How important is analytics to your organization?
- What do you need to know to do analytics?
- What difficulties can occur when undertaking an analytics implementation?
- What trends will affect future developments in analytics?

Answers to this chapter's questions

What is analytics?

Analytics is the practice of using data to help make decisions that better meet an organization's objectives. Typical objectives include maximizing profit, minimizing cost, reducing financial risk, improving health care and educational outcomes, reducing crime, and so on. Of course, the use of data to make decisions is not a recent phenomenon. For example, the Greek philosopher Thales used options (see Chapter 79, "Pricing stock options") to increase profits and decrease the risk incurred by renting out olive presses. The term analytics became popular after the 2007 publication of Thomas Davenport's book *Competing on Analytics* (Harvard Business Review Press).

What is predictive analytics?

Predictive analytics is simply using data to make accurate predictions about quantities of interest. Some examples include the following:

- Predicting the outcome of presidential elections (see Chapter 58, "Incorporating qualitative factors into multiple regression").
- Predicting the outcome of NFL games (see Chapter 35, "Using Solver to rate sports teams").

- Determining how the placement of a product in a store determines product sales (see Chapter 60, "Analysis of variance: One-way ANOVA).
- Determining how the course of treatment affects the chance of survival from cancer.
- Determining how the marketing mix (advertising, price cuts, putting product on display) affects the daily sales of 3M Scotch tape. This is difficult because seasonality also affects sales, and the prediction model must adjust for the effect of seasonality on sales.
- What is the chance each team wins the NCAA tournament? (See Chapter 77, "Fun and games: Simulating gambling and sporting-event probabilities.")
- Chapters 35, 53–65, and 72 also cover topics in predictive analytics.

What is prescriptive analytics?

Prescriptive analytics involves using mathematical models, usually data driven, to help make decisions that maximize or minimize an appropriate objective. Some examples include the following:

- What product price maximizes profit? (See Chapters 85–88.)
- What product mix maximizes Eli Lilly's monthly profit? (See Chapter 29, "An introduction to optimization with Excel Solver.")
- How can I schedule my workforce to minimize operating costs? (See Chapter 30, "Using Solver to determine the optimal product mix.")
- How can a company minimize the cost of shipping products from plants to customers? (See Chapter 32, "Using Solver to solve transportation or distribution problems.")
- How can an organization choose projects that maximize corporate objectives subject to limited resources? For example, given limited capital and programmers, how can Microsoft maximize the profitability generated from new products? How can your local school board use limited funds to maximize the high school graduation rate? These topics are discussed in Chapter 33, "Using Solver for capital budgeting."
- How much money do I need to save each year to have enough money for retirement? (See Chapter 34, "Using Solver for financial planning.")
- How can bookies set point spreads that ensure they earn a profit? (See Chapter 35, "Using Solver to rate sports teams.")
- Where should warehouses be located to minimize the distance that shipments must travel? (See Chapter 36, "Warehouse location and the GRG Multistart and Evolutionary Solver engines.")
- How should workers be assigned to jobs to make both the bosses and employees happy? (See Chapter 37, "Penalties and the Evolutionary Solver.")
- In what order should your UPS driver drop off packages to minimize the time needed to deliver all the packages? (See Chapter 38, "The traveling salesperson problem.")

- How many Valentine's Day cards should Hallmark print to maximize expected profit? (See Chapter 75, "Calculating an optimal bid.")
- What should a company bid on a construction project to maximize their expected profit? (See Chapter 75, "Calculating an optimal bid.")
- What asset allocation minimizes the risk needed to obtain a desired expected return? (See Chapter 76, "Simulating stock prices and asset-allocation modeling.")

Why has analytics increased in importance?

There are several reasons why analytics has recently become more important. First, there is much more useful data available. For example, Factual is a company that is trying to collect all the data that might be useful. Among its offerings, Factual has databases containing the location of all US gas stations and nutritional information on all items sold by a grocery chain. New sources of useful data are being generated at a rapidly increasing rate. Consider, for instance, the many NBA arenas that have cameras tracking the location of each player and the ball during every second of the game.

In addition to more data available to use, computers and programs are getting faster all the time, making it easier to handle big data sets. For example, Power Pivot (see Chapter 45) makes it easy to create business intelligence reports based on hundreds of millions of rows of data. Alternatives to Excel, such as SAS and HADOOP, make it relatively easy to process and analyze huge data sets.

How important is analytics to your organization?

The importance of analytics in an organization depends on the benefits gained from an analytics approach balanced against the costs of implementation. For example, do the benefits obtained from evaluating teachers via analytics outweigh the costs of examining the data?

Looking at the use of analytics in professional sports sheds a lot of light on the importance of analytics. In baseball (think *Moneyball*), there is lots of readily available data that can be used to evaluate baseball players. Because this data is relatively easy to analyze, almost every major league team has an analytics department. In the past, few NBA teams had analytics departments. At the 2013 Sloan Conference on Sports Analytics, only one team (the Lakers, and we know how they performed) was not represented. On the other hand, not that many NFL teams have analytics departments. I believe this is because many important problems in football analytics are difficult to solve. For example, in baseball and basketball, it is not that difficult to estimate a fair value for a player. In football, this is much more difficult. How can we estimate the value of a great pass blocker when there are few available statistics measuring the performance of offensive linemen?

What do you need to know to do analytics?

Many universities are developing undergraduate, graduate, and online programs to certify analytics professionals. In 2013, the Institute for Operations Research and the Management Sciences (INFORMS) introduced an exam, analogous to the CPA exam, to certify people as Certified Analytics Professionals. At a minimum, the analytics professional should have knowledge of the following topics:

- How to manipulate data in any form. This includes manipulation of nonquantitative data, such as tweets on Twitter.

- How to bring disparate data sets together so that they can be used in an analytics study. For example, a fast-food restaurant may want to reduce employee turnover. This would require collecting for each employee everything known at the time the employee was hired (education, age, test scores, and so on) as well as the employee's performance history. A model can then be developed to predict employee turnover based on what was known about each employee at hire date. Unfortunately, data on employee hires and employee performance resides, at many companies, in separate databases that do not "talk" to each other.
- Having the ability to program in a language such as Java or Python.
- How to analyze and manipulate data in Excel.
- How to analyze big data sets using a statistical package, such as R, SPSS, or SAS.
- Knowledge of statistics, including all forms of predictive analytics and classification algorithms. For example, how can a person be classified as being a likely candidate for a heart attack?
- Knowing how a simulation can be used to model uncertain situations, such as the future value of your 401(k) portfolio or the queue at the hospital emergency room.
- How to use optimization to find the best way to do something. For example, what space allocation to different products maximizes a department store's profits?

What difficulties can occur when undertaking an analytics implementation?

Several problems can arise during an analytics implementation. The following are examples:

- Often, it is difficult to agree on the right metric to evaluate success. For example, until Sabermetrics guru Bill James came along, everyone thought fielders should be evaluated based on fielding percentage (FP), which is the fraction of balls hit near a fielder that are successfully fielded. Clearly this metric does not account for the fact that a slow-footed shortstop allows many balls to go to the outfield and turn into hits. Bill James created *range factor (RF),* which is a much better measure of fielding performance. For a shortstop, for example, range factor is putouts + assists per inning for the player, divided by average putouts + assists per inning for all the shortstops. A range factor exceeding 1 indicates that a player gets to many balls that the average shortstop misses. Ozzie Smith is generally considered one of the greatest fielding shortstops of all time. His career fielding percentage of .966 is not great, but during his best years, his range factor was well above one. Of course, Ozzie played on artificial turf, and this makes his range factor even more amazing. The moral: do not be hesitant to question metrics that you think are not correlated with your organization's performance.
- As previously mentioned, data sources needed for an analytics project often do not communicate with each other. For example, a software company wanted to predict future revenues. They knew that future revenues depended on trial versions that had been sent to potential customers and personal sales calls on potential customers. Unfortunately, the sales data and the customer data were in different databases that did not engage the contents of the other, so the project suffered a huge, unnecessary delay.

- In a predictive analytics study, analysts often do not know what data is needed to make better decisions. I suggest working backwards: After determining what you want to forecast, think about the variables that might help you predict the variable of interest. Here are some examples of situations in which a new set of data needed to be created to complete an analytics project.
  - Noted sports analytics personality Jeff Sagarin and I wanted to determine a method to evaluate the defensive ability of NBA players. Since the NBA box score includes few defensive (steals and blocks) statistics, a new set of data was needed. We reasoned that a good defensive player would cause his team to give up few points when he was in the game and his absence would cause this team to give up more points when the player was out. We created a data set that listed for all minutes of the game the players on the court and the number of points given up. Using this data, we could identify the defensive contributions of great defenders like Ron Artest (now known as Metta World Peace), Kevin Garnett, and Marc Gasol.
  - UnitedHealthcare wanted to reduce health care costs incurred by their employees. They determined that they needed to know whether employees were being treated for conditions that could cause high future health care costs. Diabetes causes large future health care costs (and horrible problems). UnitedHealthcare paid employees $450 to be screened for diabetes and other conditions. Amazingly, 30 percent of employees were diabetic or prediabetic and did not know it! Treating those patients enabled UnitedHealthcare to keep health costs flat and improve future quality of life for UnitedHealthcare employees.

What trends will affect future developments in analytics?

Faster computers and better algorithms for analyzing data and performing optimizations virtually ensure that analytics will become more important in the future. In the future, improvements in visualization will make it easier for the novice analyst to spot patterns in complex data. In Chapter 46, I discuss Excel's exciting Power View capability, which makes it easy to create beautiful, insightful visualizations In Chapter 52, "Charting tricks," you will learn many exciting charting tricks that help you create charts that lead to a better understanding of the data.

Probably the most important trend in analytics in the near future is the fact that many analytics applications will be available anywhere and anytime on mobile devices. In 2011, for example, the city of San Ramon, California, developed a smartphone application to sign up people who know CPR so that they could be contacted to give CPR to a person near them in need of CPR. When a 911 call arrives and an ambulance cannot get there in time, a text message is sent to any registered person giving the location of the stricken person. This enables the stricken person to receive CPR much more quickly.

Another trend in analytics will be an increase in predictions that lead to action in real time. For example, if predictions indicate a Target store will run out of Pepsi by 11 AM, the analytics app will know the location of all the Pepsi trucks, and a message will be sent to the truck in the area telling the driver to restock the Pepsi by 11 AM.

CHAPTER 29

An introduction to optimization with Excel Solver

In many situations, you want to find the best way to do something. More formally, you want to find the values of certain cells in a worksheet that optimize (maximize or minimize) a certain objective. The Microsoft Excel Solver add-in helps you answer optimization problems such as the following:

- How can a large drug company determine the monthly product mix at its Indianapolis plant that maximizes corporate profitability?
- If Microsoft produces Xbox consoles at three different locations, how can it minimize the cost of meeting demand for them?
- What price for Xbox consoles and games will maximize Microsoft's profit from Xbox sales?
- Microsoft would like to undertake 20 strategic initiatives that will tie up money and skilled programmers for the next five years. It does not have enough resources for all 20 projects; which ones should it undertake?
- How do bookmakers find the best set of ratings for NFL teams in order to set accurate point spreads?
- How should I allocate my retirement portfolio among high-tech stocks, value stocks, bonds, cash, and gold?

An optimization model has three parts: the *target cell*, the *changing cells*, and the *constraints*. The target cell represents the objective or goal. You want to either minimize or maximize the quantity in the target cell. In the question about a drug company's product mix given earlier, the plant manager would presumably want to maximize the profitability of the plant during each month. The cell that measures profitability would be the target cell. The target cells for each situation described in the questions at the beginning of the chapter are listed in Table 29-1. Keep in mind, however, that in some situations you might have multiple target cells. For example, Microsoft might have a secondary goal to maximize Xbox market share.

TABLE 29-1 List of target cells.

Model	Maximize or minimize	Target cell
Drug company product mix	Maximize	Monthly profit

Model	Maximize or minimize	Target cell
Xbox shipping	Minimize	Distribution costs
Xbox pricing	Maximize	Profit from Xbox consoles and games
Microsoft project initiatives	Maximize	Net present value (NPV) contributed by selected projects
NFL ratings	Minimize	Difference between scores predicted by ratings and actual game scores
Retirement portfolio	Minimize	Risk factor of portfolio

Changing cells are the worksheet cells that you can change or adjust to optimize the target cell. In the drug company example, the plant manager can adjust the quantity produced for each product during a month. The cells in which these amounts are recorded are the changing cells in this model. Table 29-2 lists the appropriate changing-cell definitions for the models described at the beginning of the chapter, and Table 29-3 lists the problem constraints.

TABLE 29-2 List of changing cells.

Model	Changing cells
Drug company product mix	Quantity of each product produced during the month
Xbox shipping	Quantity produced at each plant each month that is shipped to each customer
Xbox pricing	Console and game prices
Microsoft program initiatives	Which projects are selected
NFL ratings	Team ratings
Retirement portfolio	Fraction of money invested in each asset class

TABLE 29-3 List of problem constraints.

Model	Constraints
Drug company product mix	For product mix, using no more resources than are available Not producing more of a product than can be sold
Xbox shipping	Not shipping more units each month from a plant than plant capacity Ensuring that each customer receives the number of Xbox consoles that they need
Xbox pricing	Keeping prices close to competitors' prices
Microsoft project initiatives	For projects selected, not using more money or skilled programmers than are available
NFL ratings	None
Retirement portfolio	Investing all our money somewhere (cash is a possibility) Obtaining an expected return of at least 10 percent on our investments

The best way to understand how to use Solver is by looking at some detailed examples. In later chapters, you'll learn how to use Solver to address each of the situations described in this chapter, as well as for several other important business problems.

To install Solver, click the File tab, click Options, and then click Add-Ins. In the Manage list box at the bottom of the dialog box, select Excel Add-Ins, and click Go. Select the Solver Add-In check box in the Add-Ins dialog box, and click OK. After Solver is installed, you can run Solver by clicking Solver in the Analyze group on the Data tab. Figure 29-1 shows the Solver Parameters dialog box. In the next few chapters, you'll see how to use this dialog box to identify the target cell, changing cells, and constraints for a Solver model.

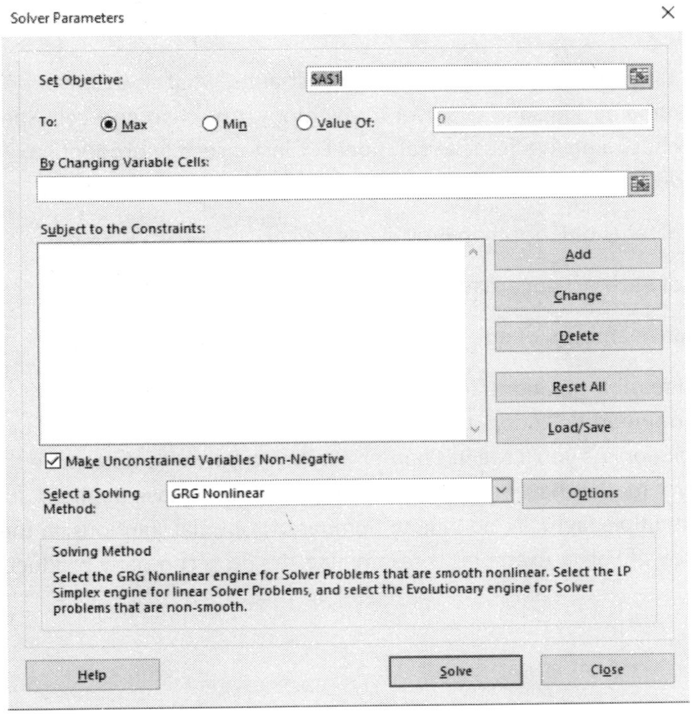

FIGURE 29-1 The Solver Parameters dialog box.

In Figure 29-1, note the Select A Solving Method list. From this list, you must select the appropriate solution engine for your optimization problem.

- The Simplex LP engine is used to solve linear optimization problems. As you will see in Chapters 30–34, a linear optimization problem is one in which the target cell and constraints are all created by adding together terms of the formula (changing cell)*(constant).
- The GRG Nonlinear engine is used to solve optimization problems in which the target cell and/or some of the constraints are not linear and are computed by using common mathematical operations, such as multiplying or dividing changing cells, raising changing cells to a power, exponential or trig functions involving changing cells, and so on. The GRG Nonlinear engine includes a powerful Multistart option that enables you to solve many problems that were solved incorrectly using previous versions of Excel. Chapters 35 and 36 discuss the GRG Nonlinear engine.

- The Evolutionary Solver engine is used when your target cell and/or constraints contain nonsmooth functions that reference changing cells. A *nonsmooth function* is one whose slope abruptly changes. For example, when $x = 0$, the slope of the absolute value of x abruptly changes from -1 to 1. If your target cell and/or constraints contain IF, SUMIF, COUNTIF, SUMIFS, COUNTIFS, AVERAGEIF, AVERAGEIFS, ABS, MAX or MIN functions that reference the changing cells, then you are using nonsmooth functions and the Evolutionary Solver engine probably has the best shot at finding a good solution to your optimization problem. The Evolutionary Solver engine is discussed in Chapters 37 and 38.

After you have identified the target cell, changing cells, and constraints, what does Solver do? To answer this question, you need some background in Solver terminology. Any changing-cells specification that satisfies the model's constraints is a feasible solution. For instance, any product mix that satisfies the following three conditions would be a feasible solution:

- Does not use more raw material or labor than is available.
- Does not produce more of each product than is demanded.
- Does not produce a negative amount of any product.

Essentially, Solver searches all feasible solutions and finds the one that has the "best" target-cell value (the largest value for maximum optimization, the smallest for minimum optimization). Such a solution is called an *optimal solution*. As you'll see in Chapter 30, "Using Solver to determine the optimal product mix," some Solver models have no optimal solution and some have a unique solution. Other Solver models have multiple (actually, an infinite number of) optimal solutions. In the next chapter, we'll begin our study of Solver examples by examining the drug company product-mix problem.

Problems

For each situation described below, identify the target cell, changing cells, and constraints.

1. I am borrowing $100,000 for a 15-year mortgage. The annual rate of interest is 8 percent. How can I determine my monthly mortgage payment?
2. How should an auto company allocate its advertising budget between different advertising formats?
3. How should cities transport students to more distant schools to obtain racial balance?
4. If a city has only one hospital, where should it be located?
5. How should a drug company allocate its sales-force efforts among their products?
6. A drug company has $2 billion allocated to purchasing biotech companies. Which companies should they buy?
7. The tax rate charged to a drug company depends on the country/region in which a product is produced. How can a drug company determine where each drug should be made?

CHAPTER 30

Using Solver to determine the optimal product mix

Questions answered in this chapter:

- How can I determine the monthly product mix that maximizes profitability?
- Does a Solver model always have a solution?
- What does it mean if a Solver model yields the result *Set Values Do Not Converge*?

Answers to this chapter's questions

How can I determine the monthly product mix that maximizes profitability?

Companies often need to determine the quantity of each product to produce on a monthly basis. In its simplest form, the product-mix problem involves how to determine the amount of each product that should be produced during a month to maximize profits. Product mix must usually adhere to the following constraints:

- Product mix can't use more resources than are available.
- There is a limited demand for each product. You don't want to produce more of a product during a month than demand dictates because the excess production is wasted (as in the case of a perishable drug).

Let's now solve the following product-mix problem. You can find a feasible solution to this problem in the Feasible Solution worksheet of the file Prodmix.xlsx, shown in Figure 30-1. Trial values for the amount produced of each drug have been entered in row 2.

	B	C	D	E	F	G	H	I
1								
2		Pounds made	150	160	170	180	190	200
3	Available	Product	1	2	3	4	5	6
4	4500	Labor	6	5	4	3	2.5	1.5
5	1600	Raw Material	3.2	2.6	1.5	0.8	0.7	0.3
6		Unit price	$ 12.50	$ 11.00	$ 9.00	$ 7.00	$ 6.00	$ 3.00
7		Variable cost	$ 6.50	$ 5.70	$ 3.60	$ 2.80	$ 2.20	$ 1.20
8		Demand	960	928	1041	977	1084	1055
9		Unit profit cont.	$ 6.00	$ 5.30	$ 5.40	$ 4.20	$ 3.80	$ 1.80
10								
11								
12		Profit	$ 4,504.00					
13					Available			
14		Labor Used	3695	<=	4500			
15		Raw Material Used	1488	<=	1600			

FIGURE 30-1 A feasible product mix.

Let's say you work for a drug company that produces six different products at its plant. For each product, you need labor and raw material. Row 4 in Figure 30-1 shows the hours of labor needed to produce a pound of each product, and row 5 shows the pounds of raw material needed to produce a pound of each product. For example, producing a pound of Product 1 requires six hours of labor and 3.2 pounds of raw material. For each drug, the price per pound is given in row 6, the unit cost per pound is given in row 7, and the profit contribution per pound is given in row 9. For example, Product 2 sells for $11.00 per pound, incurs a unit cost of $5.70 per pound, and contributes $5.30 profit per pound. The month's demand for each drug is given in row 8. For example, demand for Product 3 is 1,041 pounds. This month, 4,500 hours of labor and 1,600 pounds of raw material are available. How can this company maximize its monthly profit?

If you knew nothing about the Excel Solver, you might attack this problem by constructing a worksheet to track profit and resource usage associated with the product mix. Then you could use trial and error to vary the product mix to optimize profit without using more labor or raw material than is available and without producing any drug in excess of demand. You use Solver in this process only at the trial-and-error stage. Essentially, Solver is an optimization engine that flawlessly performs the trial-and-error search.

A key to solving the product-mix problem is to efficiently compute the resource usage and profit associated with any given product mix. An important tool that you can use to make this computation is the SUMPRODUCT function. The SUMPRODUCT function multiplies corresponding values in cell ranges and returns the sum of those values. Each cell range used in a SUMPRODUCT evaluation must have the same dimensions, which implies that you can use SUMPRODUCT with two rows or two columns but not with one column and one row.

As an example of how you can use the SUMPRODUCT function in the product-mix example, let's try to compute resource usage. Labor usage is calculated by the following formula:

```
(Labor used per pound of drug 1)*(Drug 1 pounds produced)+(Labor used per pound of drug 2)
   *(Drug 2 pounds produced) + ...(Labor used per pound of drug 6)*(Drug 6 pounds produced)
```

You could compute labor usage in a more tedious fashion as D2*D4+E2*E4+F2*F4+G2*G4+H2*H4+I2*I4. Similarly, raw-material usage could be computed as D2*D5+E2*E5+F2*F5+G2*G5+H2*H5+I2*I5. However, entering these formulas in a worksheet for six products is time-consuming. Imagine how long it would take if you were working with a company that produced, for example, 50 products at its plant. A much easier way to compute labor and raw material usage is to copy from D14 to D15 the formula =SUMPRODUCT($D$2:$I$2,D4:I4). This formula computes D2*D4+E2*E4+F2*F4+G2*G4+H2*H4+I2*I4 (which is the labor usage) but is much easier to enter. Notice that I use the $ sign with the range D2:I2 so that when I copy the formula I still capture the product mix from row 2. The formula in cell D15 computes raw-material usage.

In a similar fashion, profit is determined by the following formula:

```
(Drug 1 profit per pound)*(Drug 1 pounds produced) + (Drug 2 profit per pound)
   *(Drug 2 pounds produced) + ...(Drug 6 profit per pound)*(Drug 6 pounds produced)
```

Profit is easily computed in cell D12 with the formula =SUMPRODUCT(D9:I9,$D$2:$I$2).

You now can identify the three components of the product-mix Solver model:

- **Target cell** Maximized profit (computed in cell D12).
- **Changing cells** The number of pounds produced of each product (listed in the cell range D2:I2).
- **Constraints** You have the following constraints:
  - Do not use more labor or raw material than is available. That is, the values in cells D14:D15 (the resources used) must be less than or equal to the values in cells F14:F15 (the available resources).
  - Do not produce more of a drug than is in demand. That is, the values in the cells D2:I2 (pounds produced of each drug) must be less than or equal to the demand for each drug (listed in cells D8:I8).
  - You can't produce a negative amount of any drug.

I'll show you how to enter the target cell, changing cells, and constraints into Solver. Then all you need to do is click the Solve button to find a profit-maximizing product mix.

> **Note** As I explained in Chapter 29, "An introduction to optimization with Excel Solver," Solver is installed by clicking the File tab, then Options, followed by Add-Ins. In the Manage list, click Excel Add-ins and then click Go. In the Add-Ins dialog box, select the Solver Add-In check box, and then click OK.

To begin, click the Data tab, and then in the Analysis group, click Solver. The Solver Parameters dialog box will appear, as shown in Figure 30-2.

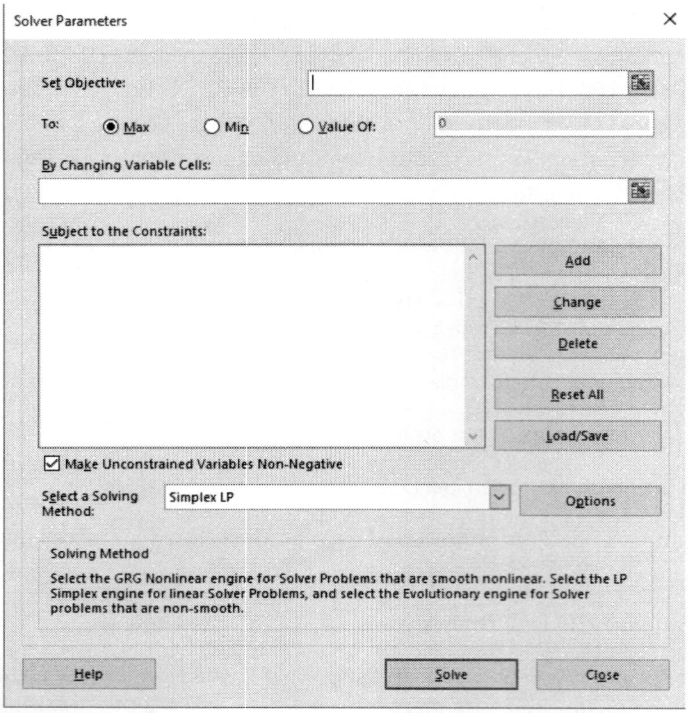

FIGURE 30-2 The Solver Parameters dialog box.

Click the Set Objective box, and then select the profit cell (cell D12). Click the By Changing Variable Cells box, and then point to the range D2:I2, which contains the pounds produced of each drug. The dialog box should now look like it does in Figure 30-3.

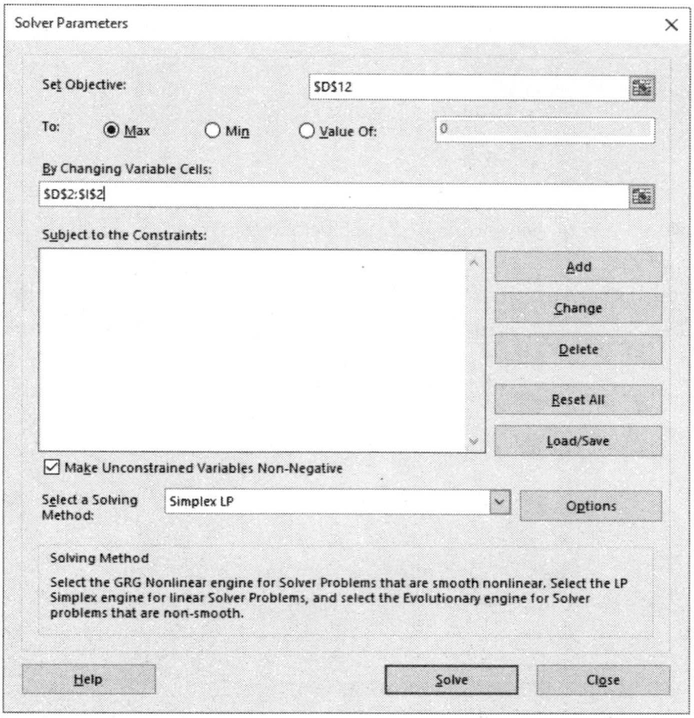

FIGURE 30-3 The Solver Parameters dialog box with the target cell and changing cells defined.

You're now ready to add constraints to the model. Click the Add button. You'll see the Add Constraint dialog box, as shown in Figure 30-4.

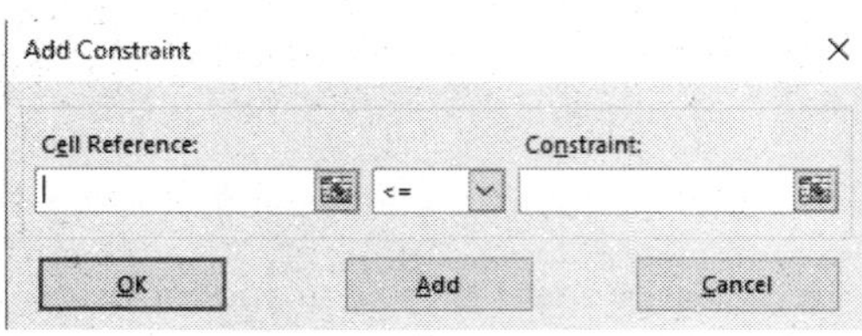

FIGURE 30-4 The Add Constraint dialog box.

To add the resource usage constraints, click the Cell Reference box, and then select the range D14:D15. Next, select **<=** from the middle list. Click the Constraint box, and then select the cell range F14:F15. The Add Constraint dialog box should now look like Figure 30-5.

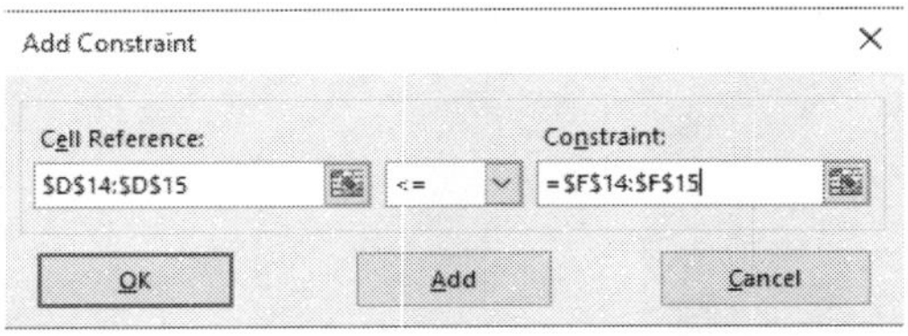

FIGURE 30-5 The Add Constraint dialog box with the resource-usage constraints entered.

You have now ensured that when Solver tries different values for the changing cells, only the combinations that satisfy both D14<=F14 (labor used is less than or equal to labor available) and D15<=F15 (raw material used is less than or equal to raw material available) will be considered. Click Add to enter the demand constraints. Next, fill in the Add Constraint dialog box as shown in Figure 30-6: in the Cell Reference box, select D2:I2, and in the Constraint box, select D8:I8.

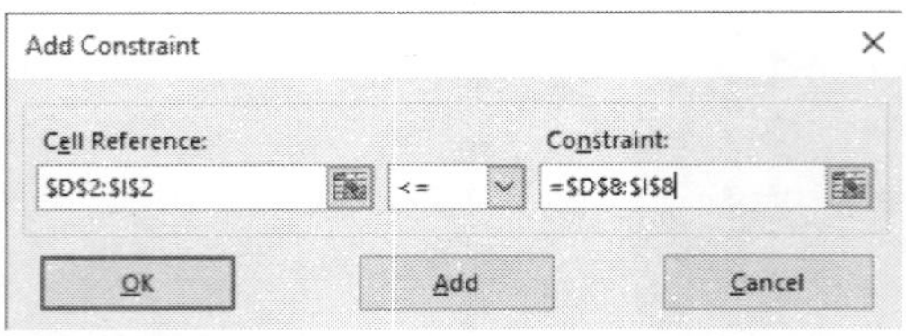

FIGURE 30-6 The Add Constraint dialog box with the demand constraints entered.

Adding these constraints ensures that when Solver tries different combinations for the changing cell values, only combinations that satisfy the following parameters will be considered:

- D2<=D8 (the amount produced of Drug 1 is less than or equal to the demand for Drug 1)
- E2<=E8 (the amount produced of Drug 2 is less than or equal to the demand for Drug 2)
- F2<=F8 (the amount produced of Drug 3 is less than or equal to the demand for Drug 3)
- G2<=G8 (the amount produced of Drug 4 is less than or equal to the demand for Drug 4)
- H2<=H8 (the amount produced of Drug 5 is less than or equal to the demand for Drug 5)
- I2<=I8 (the amount produced of Drug 6 is less than or equal to the demand for Drug 6)

Click OK in the Add Constraint dialog box. The Solver Parameters dialog box should look like Figure 30-7.

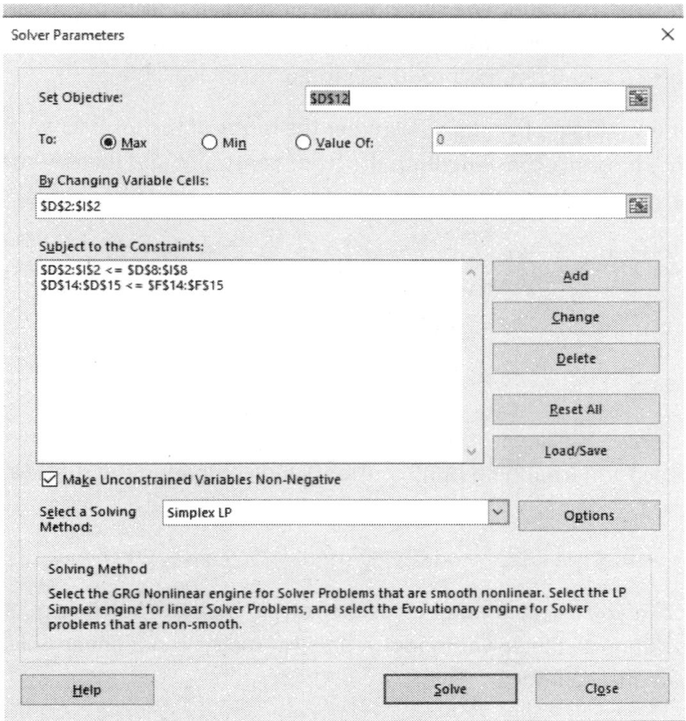

FIGURE 30-7 Final Solver Parameters dialog box for the product-mix problem.

Selecting the Make Unconstrained Variables Non-Negative check box ensures that all the changing cells are forced to be greater than or equal to 0.

Next, choose Simplex LP from the Select A Solving Method list. You choose the Simplex LP engine because the product-mix problem is a special type of Solver problem called a *linear model*. Essentially, a Solver model is linear under the following conditions:

- The target cell is computed by adding together the terms of the form (changing cell)*(constant).
- Each constraint satisfies the linear-model requirement. This means that each constraint is evaluated by adding together the terms of the form (changing cell)*(constant) and comparing the sums to a constant.

Why is this Solver problem linear? Our target cell (profit) is computed as follows:

```
(Drug 1 profit per pound)*(Drug 1 pounds produced) + (Drug 2 profit per pound)
   *(Drug 2 pounds produced) + ...(Drug 6 profit per pound)*(Drug 6 pounds produced)
```

This computation follows a pattern in which the target cell's value is derived by adding together terms of the form (changing cell)*(constant).

Our labor constraint is evaluated by comparing the value derived from (Labor used per pound of Drug 1)*(Drug 1 pounds produced) + (Labor used per pound of Drug 2)*(Drug 2 pounds produced) + ... (Labor used per pound of Drug 6)*(Drug 6 pounds produced) to the labor available.

Therefore, the labor constraint is evaluated by adding together the terms of the form (changing cell)*(constant) and comparing the sums to a constant. Both the labor constraint and the raw-material constraint satisfy the linear model requirement.

The demand constraints take this form:

```
(Drug 1 produced)<=(Drug 1 Demand)
(Drug 2 produced)<=(Drug 2 Demand)
...
(Drug 6 produced)<=(Drug 6 Demand)
```

Each demand constraint also satisfies the linear-model requirement because each is evaluated by adding together the terms of the form (changing cell)*(constant) and comparing the sums to a constant.

Knowing that the product-mix model is a linear model, why should you care?

- If a Solver model is linear and you select Simplex LP as the solving method, Solver is guaranteed to find the optimal solution to the Solver model. If a Solver model is not linear, Solver may or may not find the optimal solution.
- If a Solver model is linear and you select Simplex LP, Solver uses a very efficient algorithm (the simplex method) to find the model's optimal solution. If a Solver model is linear and you do not select Simplex LP, Solver uses a very inefficient algorithm (the GRG2 method) and might have difficulty finding the model's optimal solution.

After you click Solve, Solver calculates an optimal solution (if one exists) for the product-mix model. As I stated in Chapter 29, an optimal solution to the product-mix model would be a set of changing-cell values (pounds produced of each drug) that maximizes profit over the set of all feasible solutions. Again, a feasible solution is a set of changing-cell values satisfying all constraints. The set of changing-cell values shown in Figure 30-8 is a feasible solution because all production levels are nonnegative, production levels do not exceed demand, and resource usage does not exceed available resources. See the worksheet Feasible Solution in the file Prodmix.xlsx.

	B	C	D	E	F	G	H	I
1								
2		Pounds made	150	160	170	180	190	200
3	Available	Product	1	2	3	4	5	6
4	4500	Labor	6	5	4	3	2.5	1.5
5	1600	Raw Material	3.2	2.6	1.5	0.8	0.7	0.3
6		Unit price	$ 12.50	$ 11.00	$ 9.00	$ 7.00	$ 6.00	$ 3.00
7		Variable cost	$ 6.50	$ 5.70	$ 3.60	$ 2.80	$ 2.20	$ 1.20
8		Demand	960	928	1041	977	1084	1055
9		Unit profit cont.	$ 6.00	$ 5.30	$ 5.40	$ 4.20	$ 3.80	$ 1.80
10								
11								
12		Profit	$ 4,504.00					
13					Available			
14		Labor Used	3695	<=	4500			
15		Raw Material Used	1488	<=	1600			

FIGURE 30-8 A feasible solution to the product-mix problem that fits within the constraints.

The changing cell values shown in Figure 30-9 (and in the worksheet Infeasible Solution) represent an infeasible solution for the following reasons:

- You produce more of Drug 5 than the demand for it.
- You use more labor than is available.
- You use more raw material than is available.

	B	C	D	E	F	G	H	I
1								
2		Pounds made	300	0	0	0	1085	1000
3	Available	Product	1	2	3	4	5	6
4	4500	Labor	6	5	4	3	2.5	1.5
5	1600	Raw Material	3.2	2.6	1.5	0.8	0.7	0.3
6		Unit price	$ 12.50	$ 11.00	$ 9.00	$ 7.00	$ 6.00	$ 3.00
7		Variable cost	$ 6.50	$ 5.70	$ 3.60	$ 2.80	$ 2.20	$ 1.20
8		Demand	960	928	1041	977	1084	1055
9		Unit profit cont.	$ 6.00	$ 5.30	$ 5.40	$ 4.20	$ 3.80	$ 1.80
10								
11								
12		Profit	$ 7,723.00					
13					Available			
14		Labor Used	6012.5	<=	4500			
15		Raw Material Used	2019.5	<=	1600			

FIGURE 30-9 An infeasible solution to the product-mix problem that doesn't fit within the defined constraints.

After you click Solve, Solver quickly finds the optimal solution shown in Figure 30-10. You need to select Keep Solver Solution to preserve the optimal solution values in the worksheet.

	B	C	D	E	F	G	H	I
1								
2		Pounds made	0	0	0	596.6667	1084	0
3	Available	Product	1	2	3	4	5	6
4	4500	Labor	6	5	4	3	2.5	1.5
5	1600	Raw Material	3.2	2.6	1.5	0.8	0.7	0.3
6		Unit price	$ 12.50	$ 11.00	$ 9.00	$ 7.00	$ 6.00	$ 3.00
7		Variable cost	$ 6.50	$ 5.70	$ 3.60	$ 2.80	$ 2.20	$ 1.20
8		Demand	960	928	1041	977	1084	1055
9		Unit profit cont.	$ 6.00	$ 5.30	$ 5.40	$ 4.20	$ 3.80	$ 1.80
10								
11								
12		Profit	$ 6,625.20					
13					Available			
14		Labor Used	4500	<=	4500			
15		Raw Material Used	1236.13333	<=	1600			

FIGURE 30-10 The optimal solution to the product-mix problem.

Our drug company can maximize its monthly profit at a level of $6,625.20 by producing 596.67 pounds of Drug 4, 1,084 pounds of Drug 5, and none of the other drugs. You can't determine whether you can achieve the maximum profit of $6,625.20 in other ways. All you can be sure of is that with your limited resources and demand, there is no way to make more than $6,625.20 this month. It is possible that there is more than one optimal solution to a Solver model, but it is not easy to determine whether this is the case.

Does a Solver model always have a solution?

Suppose that demand for each product must be met. (See the No Feasible Solution worksheet in the file Prodmix.xlsx.) You then have to change your demand constraints from D2:I2<=D8:I8 to D2:I2>=D8:I8. To do this, open Solver (from the Data tab, in the Analysis group), select the D2:I2<=D8:I8 constraint, and then click Change. The Change Constraint dialog box, shown in Figure 30-11, appears.

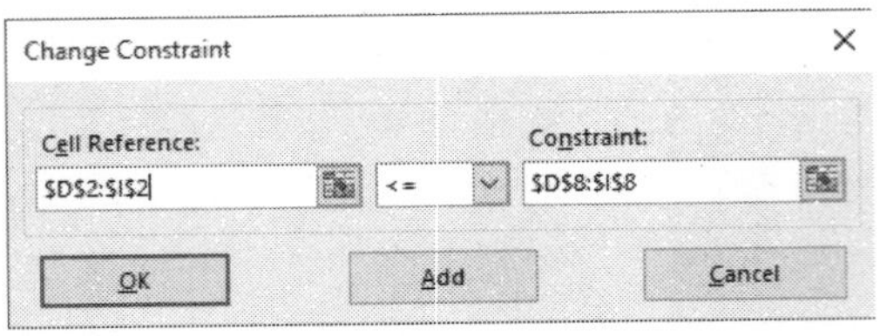

FIGURE 30-11 The Change Constraint dialog box.

Select >=, and then click OK. You've now ensured that Solver will consider changing only cell values that meet all the demands. When you click Solve, you'll see the message *Solver could not find a feasible solution*. This message does not mean that you made a mistake in your model, but rather that with limited resources, you can't meet demand for all products. Solver is simply telling you that if you want to meet demand for each product, you need to add more labor, more raw materials, or more of both.

What does it mean if a Solver model yields the result *Set Values Do Not Converge*?

Let's see what happens if you allow unlimited demand for each product and you allow negative quantities to be produced of each drug. (You can see this Solver problem on the Set Values Do Not Converge worksheet in the file Prodmix.xlsx.) To find the optimal solution for this situation, open Solver and clear the Make Unconstrained Variables Non-Negative check box. In the Solver Parameters dialog box, select the demand constraint D2:I2<=D8:I8, and then click Delete to remove the constraint. When you click Solve, Solver returns the message *Set Cell Values Do Not Converge*. This message means that if the target cell is to be maximized (as in this example), there are feasible solutions with arbitrarily large target cell values. (If the target cell is to be minimized, the message *Set Cell Values Do Not Converge* means there are feasible solutions with arbitrarily small target cell values.) In this situation, by allowing the negative production of a drug, you in effect create resources that can be used to produce arbitrarily large amounts of other drugs. Given your unlimited demand, this allows you to make unlimited profits. In a real situation, you can't make an infinite amount of money. In short, if you see *Set Values Do Not Converge*, your model does have an error.

Problems

1. Suppose our drug company can purchase up to 500 hours of labor at $1 more per hour than its current labor costs. How can it maximize profit?

2. At a chip manufacturing plant, four technicians (A, B, C, and D) produce three products (Products 1, 2, and 3). This month, the chip manufacturer can sell 80 units of Product 1, 50 units of Product 2, and at most 50 units of Product 3. Technician A can make only Products 1 and 3. Technician B can make only Products 1 and 2. Technician C can make only Product 3. Technician D can make only Product 2. For each unit produced, the products contribute the following profit: Product 1, $6; Product 2, $7; and Product 3, $10. The time (in hours) each technician needs to manufacture a product is as follows:

Product	Technician A	Technician B	Technician C	Technician D
1	2	2.5	Cannot do	Cannot do
2	Cannot do	3	Cannot do	3.5
3	3	Cannot do	4	Cannot do

Each technician can work up to 120 hours per month. How can the chip manufacturer maximize its monthly profit? Assume a fractional number of units can be produced.

3. A computer-manufacturing plant produces mice, keyboards, and video-game joysticks. The per-unit profit, per-unit labor usage, monthly demand, and per-unit machine-time usage are given in the following table:

	Mice	Keyboards	Joysticks
Profit/unit	$8	$11	$9
Labor usage/unit	.2 hour	.3 hour	.24 hour
Machine time/unit	.04 hour	.055 hour	.04 hour
Monthly demand	15,000	29,000	11,000

Each month, a total of 13,000 labor hours and 3,000 hours of machine time are available. How can the manufacturer maximize its monthly profit contribution from the plant?

4. Resolve our drug example assuming that a minimum demand of 200 units for each drug must be met.

5. Jason makes diamond bracelets, necklaces, and earrings. He wants to work a maximum of 160 hours per month. He has 800 ounces of diamonds. The profit, labor time, and ounces of diamonds required to produce each product are given in the following table. If demand for each product is unlimited, how can Jason maximize his profit?

Product	Unit profit	Labor hours per unit	Ounces of diamonds per unit
Bracelets	$300	.35	1.2
Necklaces	$200	.15	.75
Earrings	$100	.05	.5

6. In our product-mix example, suppose that whenever you sell more than 400 pounds of any product you must give a $1 per pound discount on each pound above 400 sold. How does this change the answer to the problem?

7. Assuming unlimited demand and unlimited resources, find a solution to our product-mix problem that earns $1 billion.

8. Shoeco manufactures three types of shoes. Demand for shoes is unlimited and 40 hours per week of machine time and labor are available. A pair of shoes yields the following profit and uses the number of minutes of machine time and labor given in the table below. Assuming the number of pairs of shoes made each week must be an integer, how can Shoeco maximize weekly profit? Note that by selecting your changing cells in the constraints, you can use the Int option to ensure that your changing cells assume integer values.

	Shoe 1	**Shoe 2**	**Shoe 3**
Profit	$40	$25	$30
Minutes labor used	40	20	30
Minutes machine time used	45	25	26

9. Woodco produces tables and chairs. The unit profit, wood used (in square feet), and the number of skilled carpentry hours used to produce a pair of shoes are given in the table below.

	Desk	**Chair**
Unit profit	**$250**	**$150**
Wood used	**22**	**18**
Carpentry hours used	**14**	**8**

An integer number of desks and chairs must be made, and demand is unlimited. How can we maximize the weekly profit?

CHAPTER 31

Using Solver to schedule your workforce

Question answered in this chapter:

- How can I efficiently schedule my workforce to meet labor demands?

Many organizations (such as banks, restaurants, and postal service companies) know what their labor requirements are at different times of the day, and they need a method to efficiently schedule their workforce. You can use the Microsoft Excel 2016 Solver to easily solve workforce scheduling problems.

Answers to this chapter's question

How can I efficiently schedule my workforce to meet labor demands?

Bank 24 processes checks seven days a week. The number of workers needed each day to process checks is shown in row 14 of the file Bank24.xlsx, which is shown in Figure 31-1. For example, 13 workers are needed on Tuesday, 15 workers are needed on Wednesday, and so on. All the bank employees work five consecutive days. What is the minimum number of employees Bank 24 can have and still meet its labor requirements?

	A	B	C	D	E	F	G	H	I	J
2	Total				There are multiple solutions all of which use 20 workers.					
3	20		Working?							
4	Number starting	Day worker starts	Monday	Tuesday	Wednesday	Thursday	Friday	Saturday	Sunday	
5	1	Monday	1	1	1	1	1	0	0	
6	3	Tuesday	0	1	1	1	1	1	0	
7	0	Wednesday	0	0	1	1	1	1	1	
8	4	Thursday	1	0	0	1	1	1	1	
9	1	Friday	1	1	0	0	1	1	1	
10	2	Saturday	1	1	1	0	0	1	1	
11	9	Sunday	1	1	1	1	0	0	1	
12		Number working	17	16	15	17	9	10	16	
13			>=	>=	>=	>=	>=	>=	>=	
14		Number needed	17	13	15	17	9	9	12	

FIGURE 31-1 The data we'll use to work through the bank workforce scheduling problem.

You begin by identifying the target cell, changing cells, and constraints for your Solver model, which are described as follows:

- **Target cell** Minimize total number of employees.
- **Changing cells** Number of employees who start work (the first of five consecutive days) each day of the week. Each changing cell must be a nonnegative integer.
- **Constraints** For each day of the week, the number of employees who are working must be greater than or equal to the number of employees required (Number of employees working)>=(Needed employees).

To set up the model for this problem, you need to track the number of employees working each day. I began by entering in the cell range A5:A11 trial values for the number of employees who start their five-day shift each day. For example, in A5, I entered 1, indicating that one employee begins work on Monday and works Monday through Friday. I entered each day's required workers in the range C14:I14.

To track the number of employees working each day, I entered a 1 or a 0 in each cell in the range C5:I11. The value *1* indicates that the employees who started working on the day designated in the cell's row are working on the day associated with the cell's column. For example, the *1* in cell G5 indicates that employees who started working on Monday are working on Friday; the *0* in cell H5 indicates that the employees who started working on Monday are not working on Saturday.

By copying from C12 to D12:I12 the formula =SUMPRODUCT($A$5:$A$11,C5:C11), I compute the number of employees working each day. For example, in cell C12, this formula evaluates to =A5+A8+A9+A10+A11, which equals (Number starting on Monday)+(Number starting on Thursday)+(Number starting on Friday)+(Number starting on Saturday)+(Number starting on Sunday). This total is indeed the number of people working on Monday.

After computing the total number of employees in cell A3 with the formula =SUM(A5:A11), I can enter a model in Solver as shown in Figure 31-2. (To open the Solver Parameters dialog box, click Solver in the Analysis group on the Data tab.)

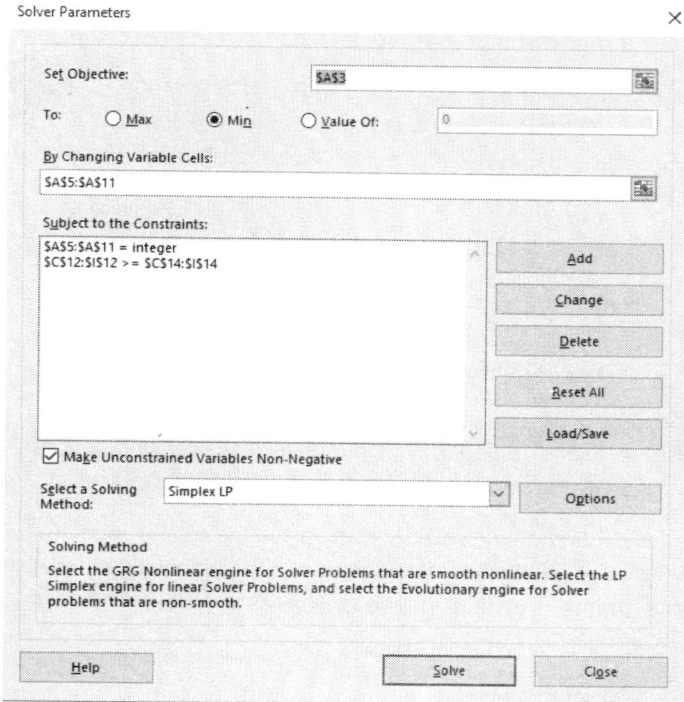

FIGURE 31-2 The Solver Parameters dialog box filled in to solve the workforce problem.

In the target cell (A3), I want to minimize the number of total employees. The constraint C12:I12>=C14:I14 ensures that the number of employees working each day is at least as large as the number needed each day. The constraint A5:A11=integer ensures that the number of employees beginning work each day is an integer. To add this constraint, I clicked Add in the Solver Parameters dialog box and filled in the Add Constraint dialog box as shown in Figure 31-3, by selecting A5:A11 in the Cell Reference box and the comparison int in the middle list, which changed the default constraint to integer.

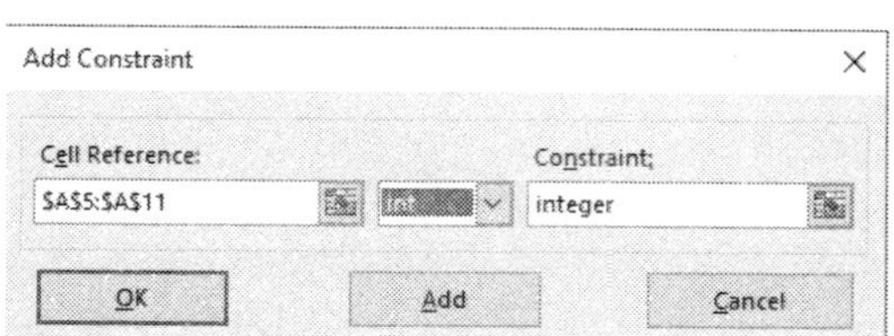

FIGURE 31-3 Adding a constraint to define as an integer the number of workers who start each day.

Note that this model is linear because the target cell is created by adding together changing cells, and the constraint is created by comparing the result obtained by adding together the product of each changing cell times a constant (either *1* or *0*) to the required number of workers. Therefore, I selected the Simplex LP engine. Since you cannot start a negative number of workers on a day,

I checked the Make Unconstrained Variables Non-Negative option. After clicking Solve, I find the optimal solution that's shown earlier in Figure 31-1.

A total of 20 employees is needed. One employee starts on Monday, three start on Tuesday, four start on Thursday, one starts on Friday, two start on Saturday, and nine start on Sunday. Note that this model actually has multiple optimal solutions that use 20 workers. If you run the Solver again, you might very well find one of these alternative optimal solutions.

Problems

1. Suppose Bank 24 has 22 employees and that the goal is to schedule employees so that they have the maximum number of weekend days off. How should the workers be scheduled?
2. Suppose Bank 24 employees are paid $150 per day the first five days they work and can work a day of overtime at a cost of $350. How should the bank schedule its employees?
3. The number of telephone reservation operators needed by an airline during each time of day is shown in the following table. Each operator works one of the following six-hour shifts: midnight–6:00 AM, 6:00 AM–noon, noon–6:00 PM, and 6:00 PM–midnight. What is the minimum number of operators needed?

Time	Operators needed
Midnight–4 AM	12
4 AM–8 AM	16
8 AM–noon	22
Noon–4 PM	30
4 PM–8 PM	31
8 PM–midnight	22

4. You can see in Figure 31-4 the number of people in different demographic groups who watched various TV shows and the cost (in thousands of dollars) of placing a 30-second ad on each show. For example, it cost $160,000 to place a 30-second ad on *Friends*. The show was watched by 6 million males between the ages 18 and 35, 3 million males between 36 and 55, 1 million males over 55, 9 million females between 18 and 35, 4 million females between 36 and 55, and 2 million females over 55. The data also includes the number of people in each group (in millions) to whom you would want to show the ad. For example, the advertiser wanted at least 60 million 18 to 35 year old males to see its ads. What would the cheapest way be to meet these goals?

	D	E	F	G	H	I	J
4	needed	60	60	28	60	60	28
5	Show	M 18-35	M 36-55	M >55	W 18-35	W 36-55	W >55
6	Friends	6	3	1	9	4	2
7	MNF	6	5	3	1	1	1
8	Malcolm	5	2	0	4	2	0
9	Sports Center	0.5	0.5	0.3	0.1	0.1	0
10	MTV	0.7	0.2	0	0.9	0.1	0
11	Lifetime	0.1	0.1	0	0.6	1.3	0.4
12	CNN	0.1	0.2	0.3	0.1	0.2	0.3
13	Jag	1	2	4	1	3	4

FIGURE 31-4 The data for Problem 4.

5. The Pine Valley Credit Union is trying to schedule bank tellers. The credit union is open 8 AM–6 PM and needs the number of tellers each hour as shown in the following table. Full-time tellers can work 8 AM–5 PM (with a noon–1 PM lunch hour) or 9 AM–6 PM (with a 1 PM–2 PM lunch hour). Part-time tellers work 10 AM–2 PM. Full-time tellers receive $300 per day, and part-time tellers receive $60 per day. At most, four part-time tellers can be hired. How can the credit union minimize their daily teller salary cost?

Needed	Time
4	8–9
8	9–10
6	10–11
4	11–12
9	12–1
8	1–2
5	2–3
4	3–4
4	4–5
5	5–6

6. The Houston Credit Union is open weekdays 9 AM to 5 PM. Full-time tellers who work the full day (no lunch break) are paid $200 per day. Part-time tellers working 11 AM–1 PM may be hired for $80 per day. The number of tellers needed each hour is shown in Figure 31-5. Develop a linear Solver model to determine how the credit union can minimize daily labor costs.

	C	D
11	Time	Needed
12	9-10 AM	12
13	10-11 Am	7
14	11 AM- Noo	13
15	Noon-1 PM	15
16	1 PM-2 PM	11
17	2 PM- 3 PM	10
18	3 PM-4 PM	6
19	4 PM-5PM	7

FIGURE 31-5 Data for Problem 6.

CHAPTER 32

Using Solver to solve transportation or distribution problems

Question answered in this chapter:

- How can a drug company determine at which location it should produce drugs and from which location it should ship drugs to customers?

Many companies manufacture products at different locations (often called *supply points*) and ship their products to customers (often called *demand points*). A natural question is, "What is the least expensive way to produce and ship products to customers and still meet demand?" This type of problem is called a *transportation problem*. A transportation problem can be set up as a linear Solver model, with the following specifications:

- **Target cell** Minimize the total production and shipping cost.
- **Changing cells** The amount produced at each supply point that is shipped to each demand point.
- **Constraints** The amount shipped from each supply point can't exceed plant capacity. Each demand point must receive its required demand. Also, each changing cell must be nonnegative.

Answer to this chapter's question

How can a drug company determine at which location it should produce drugs and from which it should ship drugs to customers?

You can follow along with this problem by looking at the file Transport.xlsx. Let's suppose a company produces a certain drug at its Los Angeles, Atlanta, and New York facilities. Each month, the Los Angeles plant can produce up to 10,000 pounds of the drug. Atlanta can produce up to 12,000 pounds, and New York can produce up to 14,000 pounds. Each month, the company must ship the number of pounds listed in cells B2:E2 to the four regions of the United States—East, Midwest, South, and West—as shown in Figure 32-1. For example, the West region must receive at least 13,000 pounds of the drug each month. The cost per pound of producing a drug at each plant and shipping the drug to each region of the country is given in cells B4:E6. For example, it costs $3.50 to produce one pound of the drug in Los Angeles and ship it to the Midwest region. What is the cheapest way to get each region the quantity of the drug it needs?

	A	B	C	D	E	F	G	H
1								
2	DEMAND	9000	6000	6000	13000			
3		EAST	MIDWEST	SOUTH	WEST	CAPACITY		
4	LA	$ 5.00	$ 3.50	$ 4.20	$ 2.20	10000		
5	ATLANTA	$ 3.20	$ 2.60	$ 1.80	$ 4.80	12000		
6	NEW YORK CITY	$ 2.50	$ 3.10	$ 3.30	$ 5.40	14000		
7								
8	Shipments							
9		EAST	MIDWEST	SOUTH	WEST	Sent		Capacity
10	LA	0	0	0	10000	10000	<=	10000
11	ATLANTA	0	3000	6000	3000	12000	<=	12000
12	NEW YORK CITY	9000	3000	0	0	12000	<=	14000
13	Received	9000	6000	6000	13000			
14		>=	>=	>=	>=			
15	Demand	9000	6000	6000	13000			
16								
17								
18	Total Cost	$ 86,800.00						

FIGURE 32-1 Data for a transportation problem.

To express the target cell, you need to track the total shipping cost. After entering in the cell range B10:E12 the trial values for shipments from each supply point to each region, you can compute the total shipping cost, as follows:

```
(Amount sent from LA to East)*(Cost per pound of sending drug from LA to East)
   +(Amount sent from LAto Midwest)*(Cost per pound of sending drug from LA to Midwest)
   +(Amount sent from LA to South)*(Cost per pound of sending drug from LA to South)
   +(Amount sent from LA to West)*(Cost per pound of sending drug from LA to West)
   +...(Amount sent from New York City to West)
   *(Cost per pound of sending drug from New York City to West)
```

The SUMPRODUCT function can multiply corresponding elements in two separate rectangles (as long as the rectangles are the same size) and add together the products. I've named the cell range B4:E6 *costs* and the changing cells range (B10:E12) *shipped*. Therefore, the total shipping and production cost is computed in cell B18 with the formula =SUMPRODUCT(costs,shipped).

To express the problem's constraints, I first compute the total shipped from each supply point. By entering the formula =SUM(B10:E10) in cell F10, I compute the total number of pounds shipped from Los Angeles as (LA shipped to East)+(LA shipped to Midwest)+(LA shipped to South)+(LA shipped to West). Copying this formula to F11:F12 computes the total shipped from Atlanta and New York City. Later I'll add a constraint (called a *supply constraint*) that ensures that the amount shipped from each location does not exceed the plant's capacity.

Next, I compute the total received by each demand point. I begin by entering in cell B13 the formula =SUM(B10:B12). This formula computes the total number of pounds received in the East as (Pounds shipped from LA to East)+(Pounds shipped from Atlanta to East)+(Pounds shipped from New York City to East). By copying this formula from B13 to C13:E13, I compute the pounds of the drug received by the Midwest, South, and West regions. Later, I'll add a constraint (called a *demand constraint*) that ensures that each region receives the amount of the drug it requires.

Now I open the Solver Parameters dialog box (click Solver in the Analyze group on the Data tab) and fill it in, as shown in Figure 32-2.

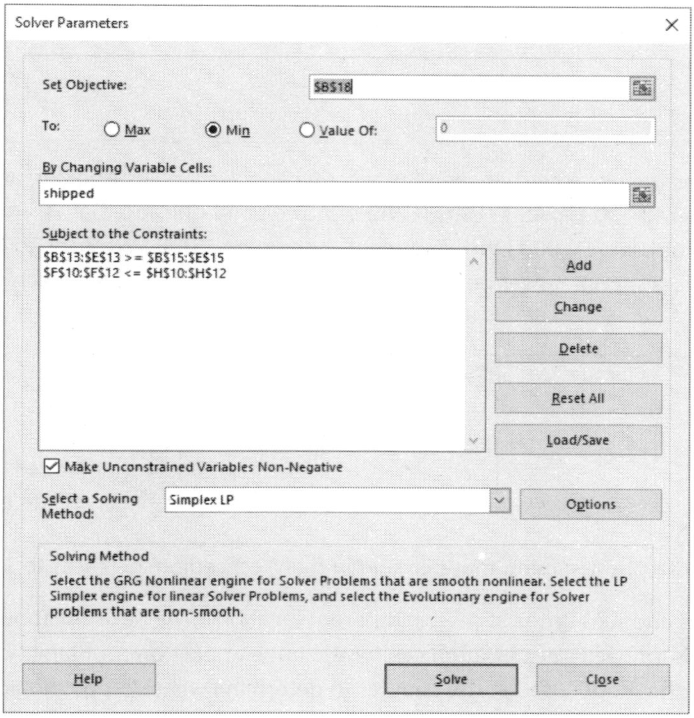

FIGURE 32-2 The Solver set up to solve our transportation problem.

I want to minimize total shipping cost (computed in cell B18). The changing cells are the number of pounds shipped from each plant to each region of the country. (These amounts are listed in the range named *shipped*, consisting of cells B10:E12.) The constraint F10:F12<=H10:H12 (the supply constraint) ensures that the amount sent from each plant does not exceed its capacity. The constraint B13:E13>=B15:E15 (the demand constraint) ensures that each region receives at least the amount of the drug it needs.

This model is a linear Solver model because the target cell is created by adding together the terms of the form (changing cell)*(constant), and both our supply and demand constraints are created by comparing the sum of changing cells to a constant. Because the model is linear, I chose the Simplex LP engine. Clearly, shipments must be nonnegative, so I selected the Make Unconstrained Variables Non-Negative check box.

After clicking Solve in the Solver Parameters dialog box, I am presented with the optimal solution shown earlier in Figure 32-1. The minimum cost of meeting customer demand is $86,800. This minimum cost can be achieved if the company uses the following production and shipping schedule:

- Ship 10,000 pounds from Los Angeles to the West region.
- Ship 3,000 pounds from Atlanta to the West region, and the same amount from Atlanta to the Midwest region. Ship 6,000 pounds from Atlanta to the South region.
- Ship 9,000 pounds from New York City to the East region, and 3,000 pounds from New York City to the Midwest region.

Problems

1. The following table gives the distances between Boston, Chicago, Dallas, Los Angeles, and Miami. Each city requires 40,000 kilowatt hours (kWh) of power, and Chicago, Dallas, and Miami are capable of producing 70,000 kWh. Assume that shipping 1,000 kWh over 100 miles costs $4. From where should power be sent to minimize the cost of meeting each city's demand?

	Boston	**Chicago**	**Dallas**	**Los Angeles**	**Miami**
Chicago	983	0	1205	2112	1390
Dallas	1815	1205	0	801	1332
Miami	1539	1390	1332	2757	0

2. Resolve this chapter's example, assuming that demand in the West region increases to 13,000.
3. Your company produces and sells drugs at several different locations. The decision about where to produce goods for each sales location can have a huge impact on profitability. The model here is similar to the model used in this chapter to determine where drugs should be produced. Use the following assumptions:
   - You produce drugs at six locations and sell to customers in six different areas.
   - The tax rate and variable production cost depend on the location where the drug is produced. For example, any units produced at Location 3 cost $6 per unit to produce; profits from these goods are taxed at 20 percent.
   - The sales price of each drug depends on where the drug is sold. For example, each product sold in Location 2 is sold for $40.

Production location	**1**	**2**	**3**	**4**	**5**	**6**
Sales price	$45	$40	$38	$36	$39	$34
Tax rate	31%	40%	20%	40%	35%	18%
Variable production cost	$8	$7	$6	$9	$7	$7

   - Each of the six plants can produce up to 6 million units per year.

- The annual demand (in millions) for your product in each location is as follows:

Sales location	1	2	3	4	5	6
Demand	1	2	3	4	5	6

- The unit shipping cost depends on the plant where the product is produced and the location where the product is sold, as you see in this table:

	Sold 1	Sold 2	Sold 3	Sold 4	Sold 5	Sold 6
Plant 1	$3	$4	$5	$6	$7	$8
Plant 2	$5	$2	$6	$9	$10	$11
Plant 3	$4	$3	$1	$6	$8	$6
Plant 4	$5	$5	$7	$2	$5	$5
Plant 5	$6	$9	$6	$5	$3	$7
Plant 6	$7	$7	$8	$9	$10	$4

For example, if you produce a unit at Plant 1 and sell it in Location 3, it costs $5 to ship it. How can you maximize the after-tax profit with your limited production capacity?

4. Suppose that each day, Northern, Central, and Southern California each use 100 billion gallons of water. Also assume that Northern California and Central California have available 120 billion gallons of water, whereas Southern California has 40 billion gallons of water available. The cost of shipping 1 billion gallons of water between the three regions is as follows:

	Northern	Central	Southern
Northern	$5,000	$7,000	$10,000
Central	$7,000	$5,000	$6,000
Southern	$10,0000	$6,000	$5,000

You will not be able to meet all the demand for water, so assume that each billion gallons of unmet demand incurs the following shortage costs:

	Northern	Central	Southern
Shortage cost/billion gal-lons short	$6,000	$5,500	$9,000

How should California's water be distributed to minimize the sum of shipping and shortage costs?

5. A hardware store has 50 riding mowers at each of its Houston, Dallas, and San Antonio warehouses. This month, 35 mowers will be sold in Houston, Dallas, San Antonio, and Austin. The costs of shipping a mower from each warehouse to each city are given below. Determine how demand can be met at minimum cost. (See Figure 32-3.)

	C	D	E	F	G
15		Houston	Dallas	San Antonio	Austin
16	Houston	$1.00	$7.00	$5.00	$6.00
17	Dallas	$7.00	$1.50	$10.00	$9.00
18	San Antonio	$8.00	$10.00	$2.00	$4.00

FIGURE 32-3 The data for Problem 5.

6. How can the AutoSum icon be used to help set up transportation problems?

CHAPTER 33

Using Solver for capital budgeting

Question answered in this chapter:

- How can a company use Solver to determine which projects it should undertake?

Each year, a company such as Eli Lilly needs to determine which drugs to develop; a company like Microsoft, which software programs to develop; a company like Proctor & Gamble, which new consumer products to develop. The Solver in Microsoft Excel 2016 can help a company make these decisions.

Answer to this chapter's question

How can a company use Solver to determine which projects it should undertake?

Most corporations want to undertake projects that contribute the greatest net present value (NPV), subject to limited resources (usually capital and labor). Let's say that a software development company is trying to determine which of 20 software projects it should undertake. The NPV (in millions of dollars) contributed by each project as well as the capital (in millions of dollars) and the number of programmers needed during each of the next three years is given on the Basic Model worksheet in the file Capbudget.xlsx, shown in Figure 33-1. For example, Project 2 yields $908 million. It requires $151 million during Year 1, $269 million during Year 2, and $248 million during Year 3. Project 2 requires 139 programmers during Year 1, 86 programmers during Year 2, and 83 programmers during Year 3. Cells E4:G4 show the capital (in millions of dollars) available during each of the three years, and cells H4:J4 indicate how many programmers are available. For example, during Year 1 up to $2.5 billion in capital and 900 programmers are available.

The company must decide whether it should undertake each project. Let's assume that the company can't undertake a fraction of a software project; if 0.5 of the needed resources is allocated, for example, the company would have a nonworking program that would bring in $0 revenue.

The trick in modeling situations in which you either do or don't do something is to use *binary changing cells*. A binary changing cell always equals *0* or *1*. When a binary changing cell that corresponds to a project equals *1*, you do the project. If a binary changing cell that corresponds to a project equals *0*, you don't do the project. You set up Solver to use a range of binary changing cells by adding a constraint: select the changing cells you want to use and then choose Bin from the list in the Add Constraint dialog box.

	A	B	C	D	E	F	G	H	I	J
1		Total NPV								
2		9293		Used	2460	2684	2742	876	895	702
3					<=	<=	<=	<=	<=	<=
4				Available	2500	2800	2900	900	900	900
5	Do IT?		NPV		Cost Year 1	Cost Year 2	Cost Year 3	Labor Year 1	Labor Year 2	Labor Year 3
6	0	Project 1	928		398	180	368	111	108	123
7	1	Project 2	908		151	269	248	139	86	83
8	1	Project 3	801		129	189	308	56	61	23
9	0	Project 4	543		275	218	220	54	70	59
10	0	Project 5	944		291	252	228	123	141	70
11	1	Project 6	848		80	283	285	119	84	37
12	1	Project 7	545		203	220	77	54	44	42
13	1	Project 8	808		150	113	143	67	101	43
14	1	Project 9	638		282	141	160	37	55	64
15	1	Project 10	841		214	254	355	130	72	62
16	0	Project 11	664		224	271	130	51	79	58
17	0	Project 12	546		225	150	33	35	107	63
18	0	Project 13	699		101	218	272	43	90	71
19	1	Project 14	599		255	202	70	3	75	83
20	1	Project 15	903		228	351	240	60	93	80
21	1	Project 16	859		303	173	431	60	90	41
22	0	Project 17	748		133	427	220	59	40	39
23	0	Project 18	668		197	98	214	95	96	74
24	1	Project 19	888		313	278	291	66	75	74
25	1	Project 20	655		152	211	134	85	59	70

FIGURE 33-1 Data we will use with Solver to determine which projects to undertake.

With this background, you're ready to solve the software project selection problem. As always with a Solver model, you should begin by identifying the target cell, the changing cells, and the constraints.

- **Target cell** Maximize the NPV generated by selected projects.
- **Changing cells** Look for a *0* or *1* binary changing cell for each project. I've located these cells in the range A6:A25 (and named the range *doit*). For example, a *1* in cell A6 indicates that you undertake Project 1; a *0* in cell C6 indicates that you don't undertake Project 1.
- **Constraints** You need to ensure that for each Year t (t=1, 2, 3), Year *t* capital used is less than or equal to Year *t* capital available, and Year *t* labor used is less than or equal to Year *t* labor available.

As you can see, the worksheet must compute for any selection of projects the NPV, the capital used annually, and the programmers used each year. In cell B2, I use the formula =SUMPRODUCT(doit,NPV) to compute the total NPV generated by the selected projects. (The range name *NPV* refers to the range C6:C25.) For every project with a *1* in column A, this formula picks up the NPV of the project, and for every project with a *0* in column A, this formula does not pick up the NPV of the project. Therefore, I'm able to compute the NPV of all the projects, and the target cell is linear because it is computed by summing the terms that follow the form (changing cell)*(constant). In a similar fashion, I compute the capital used each year and the labor used each year by copying from E2 to F2:J2 the formula =SUMPRODUCT(doit,E6:E25).

I now fill in the Solver Parameters dialog box as shown in Figure 33-2.

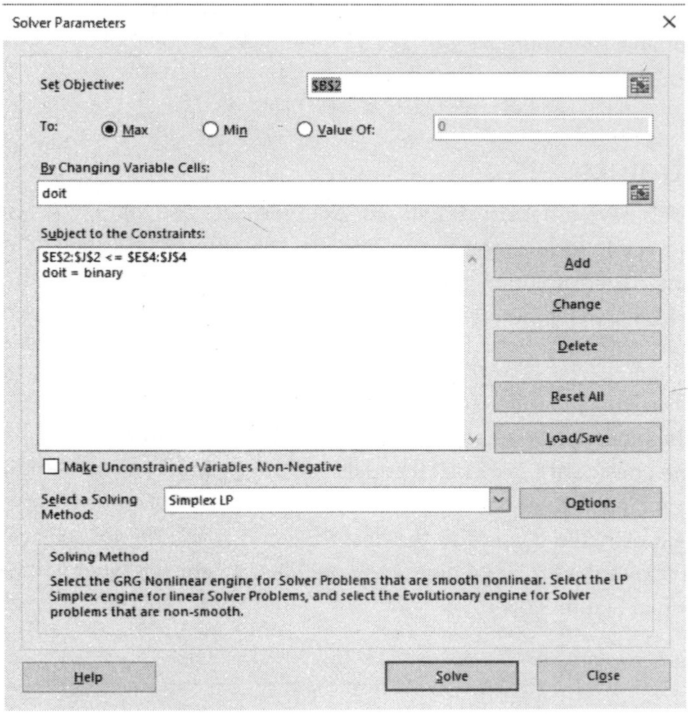

FIGURE 33-2 Solver Parameters dialog box set up for the project selection model.

The goal is to maximize the NPV of selected projects (cell B2). The changing cells (the range named *doit*) are the binary changing cells for each project. The constraint E2:J2<=E4:J4 ensures that during each year, the capital and labor used are less than or equal to the capital and labor available. To add the constraint that makes the changing cells binary, I click Add in the Solver Parameters dialog box and then select Bin from the list in the middle of the Add Constraint dialog box. The Add Constraint dialog box should appear as shown in Figure 33-3.

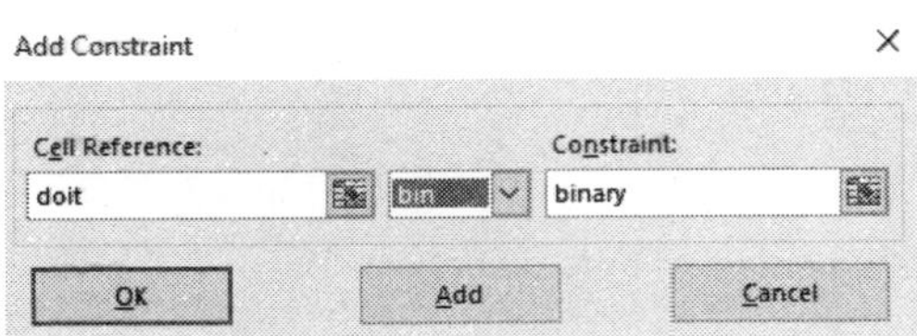

FIGURE 33-3 Using the Bin option in the Add Constraint dialog box to set up binary changing cells: cells that display either a 0 or a 1.

This model is linear because the target cell is computed as the sum of terms that have the form (changing cell)*(constant) and because the resource usage constraints are computed by comparing the sum of (changing cells)*(constants) to a constant. Therefore, I select the Simplex LP engine.

With the Solver Parameters dialog box filled in, I click Solve and get the results shown earlier in Figure 33-1. The company can obtain a maximum NPV of $9,293 million ($9.293 billion) by choosing Projects 2, 3, 6–10, 14–16, 19, and 20.

Handling other constraints

Sometimes project selection models have other constraints. For example, suppose that if you select Project 3, you must also select Project 4. Because the current optimal solution selects Project 3 but not Project 4, this tells you that the current solution can't remain optimal. To solve this problem, simply add the constraint that the binary changing cell for Project 3 is less than or equal to the binary changing cell for Project 4.

You can find this example on the worksheet If 3 Then 4 in the file Capbudget.xlsx, which is shown in Figure 33-4. Cell L9 refers to the binary value related to Project 3, and cell L12 to the binary value related to Project 4. By adding the constraint L9<=L12, L9 equals 1 if you choose Project 3, and this constraint forces L12 (the Project 4 binary) to equal 1. This constraint must also leave the binary value in the changing cell of Project 4 unrestricted if you do not select Project 3. If you do not select Project 3, L9 equals 0 and the constraint allows the Project 4 binary to equal 0 or 1, which is what you want. The new optimal solution is shown in Figure 33-4.

	A	B	C	D	E	F	G	H	I	J	K	L
1		Total NPV										
2		9157		Used	2444	2760	2837	866	895	659		
3					<=	<=	<=	<=	<=	<=		
4				Available	2500	2800	2900	900	900	900		
5	Do IT?		NPV		Cost Year 1	Cost Year 2	Cost Year 3	Labor Year 1	Labor Year 2	Labor Year 3		
6	0	Project 1	928		398	180	368	111	108	123		
7	1	Project 2	908		151	269	248	139	86	83		
8	1	Project 3	801		129	189	308	56	61	23		Proj 3
9	1	Project 4	543		275	218	220	54	70	59		1
10	0	Project 5	944		291	252	228	123	141	70		<=
11	1	Project 6	848		80	283	285	119	84	37		Proj 4
12	1	Project 7	545		203	220	77	54	44	42		1
13	1	Project 8	808		150	113	143	67	101	43		
14	1	Project 9	638		282	141	160	37	55	64		
15	0	Project 10	841		214	254	355	130	72	62		
16	0	Project 11	664		224	271	130	51	79	58		
17	0	Project 12	546		225	150	33	35	107	63		
18	0	Project 13	699		101	218	272	43	90	71		
19	0	Project 14	599		255	202	70	3	75	83		
20	1	Project 15	903		228	351	240	60	93	80		
21	1	Project 16	859		303	173	431	60	90	41		
22	1	Project 17	748		133	427	220	59	40	39		
23	1	Project 18	668		197	98	214	95	96	74		
24	1	Project 19	888		313	278	291	66	75	74		
25	0	Project 20	655		152	211	134	85	59	70		

FIGURE 33-4 The new optimal solution if Project 3's selection requires us to do Project 4.

Now suppose that you can do only four projects from among Projects 1 through 10. (See the worksheet At Most 4 Of P1–P10, shown in Figure 33-5.) In cell L8, you compute the sum of the binary values associated with Projects 1 through 10 with the formula =SUM(A6:A15). Then add the constraint L8<=L10, which ensures that at most, 4 of the first 10 projects are selected. The new optimal solution is shown in Figure 33-5. The NPV has dropped to $9.014 billion.

	A	B	C	D	E	F	G	H	I	J	K	L
1		Total NPV										
2		9014		Used	2378	2734	2755	778	896	702		
3					<=	<=	<=	<=	<=	<=		
4				Available	2500	2800	2900	900	900	900		
5	Do IT?		NPV		Cost Year 1	Cost Year 2	Cost Year 3	Labor Year 1	Labor Year 2	Labor Year 3		
6	0	Project 1	928		398	180	368	111	108	123		
7	0	Project 2	908		151	269	248	139	86	83		At most 4 of Projects 1-10
8	1	Project 3	801		129	189	308	56	61	23		4
9	0	Project 4	543		275	218	220	54	70	59		<=
10	0	Project 5	944		291	252	228	123	141	70		4
11	0	Project 6	848		80	283	285	119	84	37		
12	1	Project 7	545		203	220	77	54	44	42		
13	1	Project 8	808		150	113	143	67	101	43		
14	0	Project 9	638		282	141	160	37	55	64		
15	1	Project 10	841		214	254	355	130	72	62		
21	1	Project 16	859		303	173	431	60	90	41		
22	1	Project 17	748		133	427	220	59	40	39		
23	1	Project 18	668		197	98	214	95	96	74		
24	1	Project 19	888		313	278	291	66	75	74		
25	1	Project 20	655		152	211	134	85	59	70		

FIGURE 33-5 Optimal solution when only four of Projects 1-10 can be selected.

Solving binary and integer programming problems

Linear Solver models in which some or all the changing cells are required to be binary or an integer are usually harder to solve than linear models in which all the changing cells are allowed to be fractions. For this reason, analysts are often satisfied with a near-optimal solution to a binary or integer programming problem. If your Solver model runs for a long time, you may want to consider adjusting the Integer Optimality (formerly called Tolerance) setting in the Solver Options dialog box. (See Figure 33-6.) For example, a Tolerance setting of .5 means that Solver will stop the first time it finds a feasible solution that is within 0.5 percent of the *theoretical optimal target cell value*. (The theoretical optimal target cell value is the optimal target value found when the binary and integer constraints are omitted.) Often, you'll be faced with a choice between finding an answer within 10 percent of optimal in 10 minutes or finding an optimal solution in two weeks of computer time! The default Integer Optimality value is *5%*, which means that Solver stops when it finds a target cell value within 5 percent of the theoretical optimal target cell value. When I first solved the software development example, I had the Integer Optimality set to *5%* and found an optimal target cell value of 9269. When I changed the Integer Optimality value to *0.50%*, I obtained a better target cell value (9293).

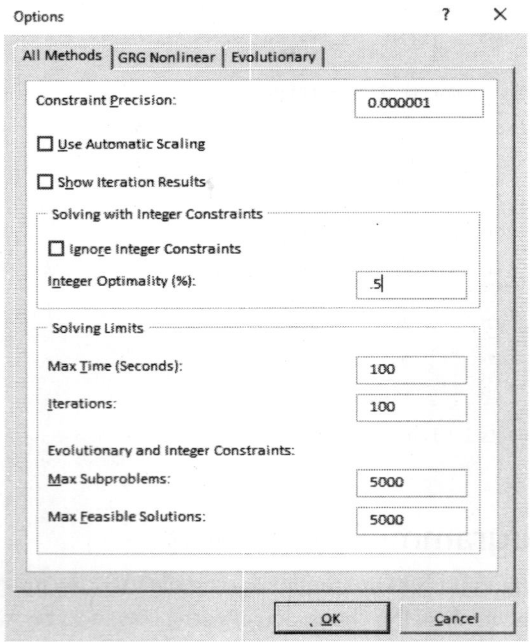

FIGURE 33-6 Adjusting the Integer Optimality option.

Problems

1. A company has nine projects under consideration. The NPV added by each project and the capital required by each project during the next two years is shown in the following table. (All numbers are in millions.) For example, Project 1 will add $14 million in NPV and require expenditures of $12 million during Year 1 and $3 million during Year 2. During Year 1, $50 million in capital is available for projects, and $20 million is available during Year 2.

	NPV	Year 1 expenditure	Year 2 expenditure
Project 1	14	12	3
Project 2	17	54	7
Project 3	17	6	6
Project 4	15	6	2
Project 5	40	32	35
Project 6	12	6	6
Project 7	14	48	4
Project 8	10	36	3
Project 9	12	18	3

- If you can't undertake a fraction of a project but must undertake either all or none of a project, how can you maximize the NPV?
- Suppose that if Project 4 is undertaken, Project 5 must be undertaken. How can you maximize the NPV?

2. A publishing company is trying to determine which of 36 books it should publish this year. The file Pressdata.xlsx gives the following information about each book:

   - Projected revenue and development costs (in thousands of dollars)
   - Pages in each book
   - Whether the book is geared toward an audience of software developers (indicated by a *1* in column E)

   The company can publish books with a total of up to 8,500 pages this year and must publish at least four books geared toward software developers. How can the company maximize its profit?

3. In the equation SEND + MORE = MONEY, each letter represents a different digit from 0–9. Which digit is associated with each letter?

4. Jill is trying to determine her class schedule for the next semester. A semester consists of two seven-week half semesters. Jill must take four courses during each half semester. There are five time slots during each semester. Of course, Jill cannot take the same course twice. Jill has associated a value with each course and time slot. This data is in the file Classdata.xlsx. For example, course 1 during time slot 5 in semester 1 has a value of *5*. Which courses should Jill take during each semester to maximize her total value from the semester's courses?

5. Use conditional formatting to highlight in yellow fill each row corresponding to a selected project.

6. Use Solver to determine the minimum number of coins needed to make change for 92 cents.

7. An oil company is considering 12 drilling projects. The NPV and money needed to complete each project are given in file Problem7.xlsx. $50 million can be spent on completing the projects. What projects should be undertaken?

8. I want to fill a backpack with items that will give me maximum benefit on a hiking trip. The weight in pounds and benefit for each item are given in the file Problem8data.xlsx. The backpack can hold at most 26 pounds. At least one drink (water or Gatorade) and at least one protein (cheese or beef jerky) must be packed. How can I obtain the maximum benefit from items in my backpack?

9. You manufacture expensive necklaces for world royalty. You have enough workers to make three different necklaces. The sales price for each necklace, the available jewels, and the number of jewels needed to make each necklace are given in the file Problem9data.xlsx. Which necklaces maximize your revenue?

CHAPTER 34

Using Solver for financial planning

Questions answered in this chapter:

- Can I use Solver to verify the accuracy of the Excel PMT function or to determine mortgage payments for a variable interest rate?
- Can I use Solver to determine how much money I need to save for retirement?

The Solver feature in Microsoft Excel 2016 can be a powerful tool for analyzing financial planning problems. In many of these types of problems, a quantity such as the unpaid balance on a loan or the amount of money needed for retirement changes over time. For example, consider a situation in which you borrow money. Because only the noninterest portion of each monthly payment reduces the unpaid loan balance, we know that the following equation (which I'll refer to as *Equation 1*) is true.

```
(Unpaid loan balance at end of period t)=(Unpaid loan balance at beginning of period t)
   -[(Month t payment)-(Month t interest paid)]
```

Now suppose that you are saving for retirement. Until you retire, you deposit at the beginning of each period (let's say periods equal years) an amount of money in your retirement account, and during the year, your retirement fund is invested and receives a return of some percentage. During retirement, you withdraw money at the beginning of each year and your retirement fund still receives an investment return. We know that the following equation (*Equation 2*) describes the relationship between contributions, withdrawals, and return.

```
(Retirement savings at end of Year t+1) = (Retirement savings at end of Year t + retirement
   contribution at beginning of Year t+1 - Year t+1 retirement withdrawal)
   *(Investment return earned during Year t+1)
```

Combining basic relationships such as these with Solver enables you to answer a myriad of interesting financial planning problems.

Answers to this chapter's questions

Can I use Solver to verify the accuracy of the Excel PMT function or to determine mortgage payments for a variable interest rate?

Recall that in Chapter 10, "More Excel financial functions," we found the monthly payment (assuming payments occur at the end of a month) on a 10-month loan for $8,000.00, at an annual interest rate of 10 percent, to be $1,037.03. Could we have used Solver to determine our monthly payment? You'll find the answer in the worksheet PMT By Solver in the file Finmathsolver.xlsx, which is shown in Figure 34-1.

	A	B	C	D	E
1			rate	0.00667	
2					
3		From PMT function	$1,037.03		
4	Month	Beginning Balance	Payment	Interest Owed	Ending Balance
5	1	$ 10,000.00	$ 1,037.03	$ 66.67	$ 9,029.63
6	2	$ 9,029.63	$ 1,037.03	$ 60.20	$ 8,052.80
7	3	$ 8,052.80	$ 1,037.03	$ 53.69	$ 7,069.45
8	4	$ 7,069.45	$ 1,037.03	$ 47.13	$ 6,079.55
9	5	$ 6,079.55	$ 1,037.03	$ 40.53	$ 5,083.05
10	6	$ 5,083.05	$ 1,037.03	$ 33.89	$ 4,079.90
11	7	$ 4,079.90	$ 1,037.03	$ 27.20	$ 3,070.07
12	8	$ 3,070.07	$ 1,037.03	$ 20.47	$ 2,053.51
13	9	$ 2,053.51	$ 1,037.03	$ 13.69	$ 1,030.16
14	10	$ 1,030.16	$ 1,037.03	$ 6.87	$ 0.00

FIGURE 34-1 The Solver model for calculating the monthly payment for a loan.

The key to this model is to use Equation 1 to track the monthly beginning balance. The Solver target cell is to minimize the monthly payment. The changing cell is the monthly payment. The only constraint is that the ending balance in Month 10 equals 0.

I entered the beginning balance in cell B5. I entered a trial monthly payment in cell C5. Then I copied the monthly payment to the range C6:C14. Because I've assumed that the payments occur at the end of each month, interest is incurred on the balance at the beginning of the month. The monthly interest rate (I've named cell C1 *rate*) is computed in D1 by dividing the annual rate of 0.08 by 12. The interest paid each month is computed by copying from cell D5 to D6:D14 the formula =rate*B5 (where *rate* is the range name for cell D1). Each month, this formula computes the interest as .006666*(month's beginning balance). By copying the formula =(B5–(Payment–D5)) from cell E5 to E6:E14, I use Equation 1 to compute each month's ending balance. (*Payment* is the range name for cell C5.) Because (Month t+1 beginning balance)=(Month t ending balance), each month's beginning balance is computed by copying from cell B6 to B7:B14 the formula =E5.

I am now ready to use Solver to determine the monthly payment. To see how I've set up the Solver Parameters dialog box, take a look at Figure 34-2. (To open the Solver Parameters dialog box, click Solver in the Analysis group on the Data tab.)

The goal is to minimize the monthly payment (cell C5). Note that the changing cell is the same as the target cell. The only constraint is that the ending balance for Month 10 must equal 0. Adding this constraint ensures that the loan is paid off. After I choose the Simplex LP engine and select the Make Unconstrained Variables Non-Negative option, Solver calculates a payment of $1,037.03, which matches the amount calculated by the Excel PMT function.

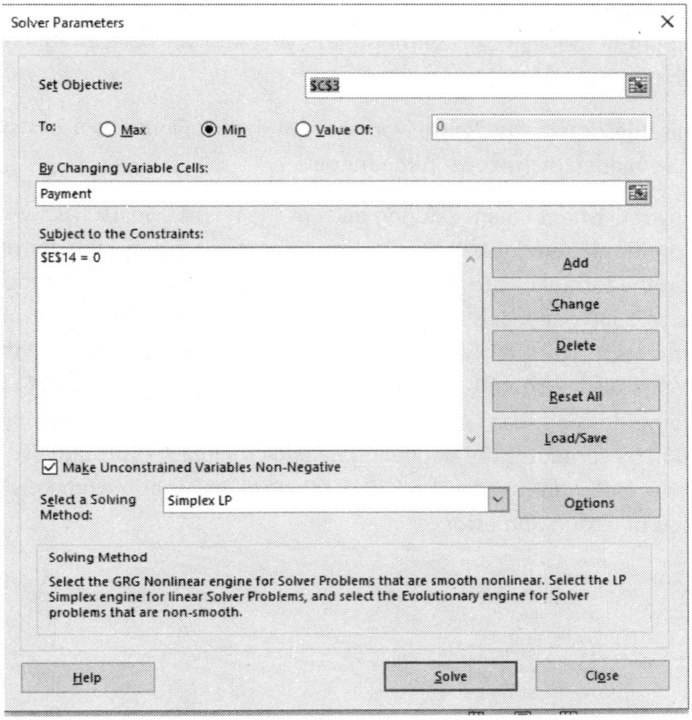

FIGURE 34-2 The Solver Parameters dialog box set up to determine mortgage payments.

This model is linear because the target cell equals the changing cell and the constraint is created by adding multiples of changing cells.

I should mention that when Solver models involve very large and/or very small numbers, Solver sometimes thinks models that are linear are not linear. To avoid this problem, it is good practice to check the Use Automatic Scaling option in the Options dialog box. This should ensure that Solver properly recognizes linear models as being linear.

Can I use Solver to determine how much money I need to save for retirement?

By using Equation 2 (shown earlier in the chapter), you can easily determine how much money a person needs to save for retirement. Here's an example.

I am planning for my retirement, and at the beginning of this year and each of the next 39 years, I'm going to contribute some money to my retirement fund. Each year, I plan to increase my retirement contribution by $500. When I retire in 40 years, I plan to withdraw (at the beginning of each year) $100,000 per year for 20 years. I've made the following assumptions about the yields for my retirement investment portfolio:

- During the first 20 years of my investing, the investments will earn 10 percent per year.
- During all other years, my investments will earn 5 percent per year.

I've assumed that all contributions and withdrawals occur at the beginning of the year. Given these assumptions, what is the least amount of money I can contribute this year and still have enough to make my retirement withdrawals?

You can find the solution to this question on the Retire worksheet in the file Finmathsolver.xlsx, shown in Figure 34-3. Note that I've hidden many rows in the model.

This worksheet simply tracks my retirement balance during each of the next 60 years. Each year, I earn the indicated interest rate on the retirement balance. I begin by entering a trial value for my Year 1 payment in cell C6. Copying the formula =C6+500 from cell C7 to C8:C45 ensures that the retirement contribution increases by $500 per year during Years 2 through 40. I entered in column D the assumed return on my investments for each of the next 60 years. In cells E46:E65, I entered the annual $100,000 withdrawal for Years 41 through 60. Copying the formula =(B6+C6–E6)*(1+D6) from F6 to F7:F65 uses Equation 2 to compute each year's ending retirement account balance. Copying the formula =F6 from cell B7 to B8:B65 computes the beginning balance for Years 2 through 60. Of course, the Year 1 initial balance is 0. Note that the value 6.8704E-07 in cell F65 is approximately 0, with the difference being the result of a rounding error.

	A	B	C	D	E	F
5	Year	Initial balance	Contribution	Return	Withdrawal	Ending Balance
6	1	$0.00	$ 1,387.87	10%	$0.00	$1,526.65
7	2	$1,526.65	$ 1,887.87	10%	$0.00	$3,755.98
8	3	$3,755.98	$ 2,387.87	10%	$0.00	$6,758.23
44	39	$1,146,596.10	$ 20,387.87	5%	$0.00	$1,225,333.17
45	40	$1,225,333.17	$ 20,887.87	5%	$0.00	$1,308,532.09
46	41	$1,308,532.09		5%	$100,000.00	$1,268,958.69
47	42	$1,268,958.69		5%	$100,000.00	$1,227,406.62
62	57	$372,324.80		5%	$100,000.00	$285,941.04
63	58	$285,941.04		5%	$100,000.00	$195,238.10
64	59	$195,238.10		5%	$100,000.00	$100,000.00
65	60	$100,000.00		5%	$100,000.00	$0.00

FIGURE 34-3 Retirement-planning data that can be set up for analysis with Solver.

The Solver Parameters dialog box for this model is shown in Figure 33-4. I want to minimize my Year 1 contribution (cell C6). The changing cell is also my Year 1 contribution (cell C6). I ensure that I never run out of money during retirement by adding the constraint F46:F65>=0 so that the ending balances for Years 41 through 60 are nonnegative.

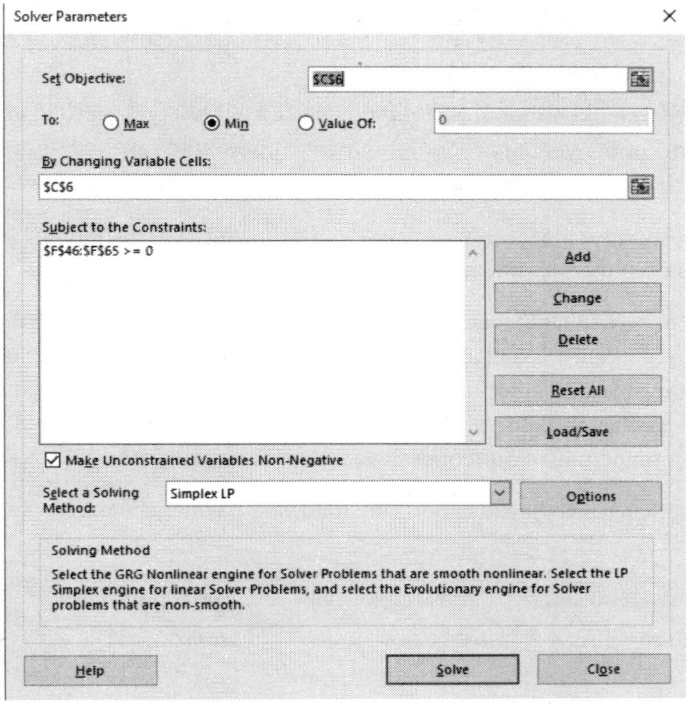

FIGURE 34-4 The Solver Parameters dialog box set up for the retirement problem.

After choosing the Simplex LP engine and selecting the Make Unconstrained Variables Non-Negative option in the Solver Parameters dialog box, I click Solve in the Solver Parameters dialog box and find that the first year's contribution should equal $1,387.87.

This model is linear because the target cell equals the changing cell and the constraint is created by adding multiples of changing cells. Note that because the return on the investments is not the same each year, there is no easy way to use Excel financial functions to solve this problem. Solver provides a general framework that can be used to analyze financial planning problems when mortgage rates or investment returns are not constant.

Problems

1. I am borrowing $15,000 to buy a new car. I am going to make 60 end-of-month payments. The annual interest rate on the loan is 10 percent. The car dealer is a friend of mine, and he will allow me to make the monthly payment for Months 1 through 30 equal to one-half the payment for Months 31 through 60. What is the payment during each month?

2. Solve the retirement-planning problem, assuming that withdrawals occur at the end of each year and contributions occur at the beginning of each year.

3. Solve our mortgage example assuming that payments are made at the beginning of each month.

4. In the retirement-planning example, suppose that during Year 1, your salary is $40,000 and your salary increases 5 percent per year until your retirement. You want to save the same percentage of your salary each year you work. What percentage of your salary should you save?

5. In the mortgage example, suppose that you want your monthly payment to increase by $50 each month. What should each month's payment be?

6. Assume you want to take out a $300,000 loan on a 20-year mortgage with end-of-month payments. The annual rate of interest is 6 percent. Twenty years from now, you need to make an ending balloon payment of $40,000. Because you expect your income to increase, you want to structure the loan so that at the beginning of each year your monthly payments increase by 2 percent. Determine the amount of each year's monthly payment.

7. Blair's mother is saving for Blair's college education. The following payments must be made at the indicated times:

4 years from now	5 years from now	6 years from now	7 years from now
$24,000	$26,000	$28,000	$30,000

The following investments are available:

- Today, one year from now, two years from now, three years from now, and four years from now, she can invest money for one year and receive a 6 percent return.
- Today, two years from now, and four years from now, she can invest money for two years and receive a 14 percent return.
- Three years from now, she can invest money for three years and receive an 18 percent return.
- Today, she can invest money for seven years and receive a 65 percent return.

What is the minimum amount that Blair's mother needs to commit today to Blair's college education that ensures she can pay her college bills?

8. I owe $10,000 on one credit card that charges 18 percent annual interest and $5,000 on another credit card that charges 12 percent annual interest. Interest for the month is based on the month's beginning balance. I can afford to make total payments of $2,000 per month and the minimum monthly payment on each card is 10 percent of the card's unpaid balance at the beginning of the month. My goal is to pay off both cards in two years. What is the minimum amount of interest I need to pay?

9. You have borrowed $50,000 to be repaid in 24 end-of-month payments. The annual rate of interest is 10 percent. In months 7, 13, and 19, the monthly payment increases by $500. How much should you pay each month?

CHAPTER 35

Using Solver to rate sports teams

Question answered in this chapter:

- Can I use Excel to set NFL point spreads?

Many of us follow basketball, football, hockey, or baseball. Odds makers set point spreads on games in all these sports and others. For example, the bookmakers' best guess was that the Carolina Panthers would win the 2016 Super Bowl by five points. Instead, the Denver Broncos won the game. In this chapter, we will learn how the Solver can accurately estimate the relative strength of NFL teams.

Using a simple Solver model, you can generate reasonable point spreads for games based on the scores of the 2015 season (including all the regular season games). The work is in file Nfl2016.xlsx, shown in Figure 35-1. You simply use the score of each game of the 2015 NFL season as input data. The changing cells for the Solver model are a rating for each team and the size of the home-field advantage. For example, if the Indianapolis Colts have a rating of +5 and the New York Jets have a rating of +7, the Jets are considered two points better than the Colts.

With regard to the home-field edge, college and professional football teams, as well as professional basketball teams, tend to win in most years by an average of three points (whereas home college basketball teams tend to win by an average of five points). In our model, however, I will define the home edge as a changing cell and have Solver estimate the home edge. You can define the outcome of an NFL game to be the number of points by which the home team outscores the visitors and predict the outcome of each game by using the following equation (which I'll refer to as *Equation 1*):

```
(Predicted points by which home team outscores visitors)=(Home edge)+(Home team rating)-(Away
Team rating)
```

For example, if the home-field edge equals three points, when the Colts host the Jets, the Colts will be a one-point favorite (3+5–7). If the Jets host the Colts, the Jets will be a five-point favorite (3+7-5).

What target cell will yield reliable ratings? The goal is to find the set of values for team ratings and home-field advantage that best predicts the outcome of all games. In short, you want the prediction for each game to be as close as possible to the outcome of each game. This suggests that you want to minimize the sum over all games of (Actual outcome)–(Predicted outcome). However, the problem with using this target is that positive and negative prediction errors cancel each other out. For example, if you overpredict the home-team margin by 50 points in one game and underpredict the home-team margin by 50 points in another game, the target cell would yield a value of 0, indicating perfect accuracy, when in fact you were off by 50 points a game. You can remedy this problem by minimizing the sum over all the games by using the formula [(Actual Outcome)–(Predicted Outcome)]2. Now positive and negative errors will not cancel each other out.

Answer to this chapter's question

Can I use Excel to set NFL point spreads?

Let's now see how to determine accurate ratings for NFL teams by using the scores from the 2015 regular season. You can find the data for this problem in the file Nfl2016.xlsx, which is shown in Figure 35-1.

	A	B	C	D	E	F	G	H	I
1	homeedge	1.562486							
2									
3		-1.7E-08							SSE
4									32902.9
5	Team	Rating	Home	Away	HomepTs	AwayPts	Home Margin	Home Forecast	Squared Error
6	Arizona Cardinals	12.31	New England Patriots	Pittsburgh Steelers	28	21	7	-0.17	51.47
7	Atlanta Falcons	-3.78	San Diego Chargers	Detroit Lions	33	28	5	-0.86	34.36
8	Baltimore Ravens	-1.95	Buffalo Bills	Indianapolis Colts	27	14	13	8.25	22.60
9	Buffalo Bills	0.03	New York Jets	Cleveland Browns	31	10	21	9.24	138.29
10	Carolina Panthers	8.12	Oakland Raiders	Cincinnati Bengals	13	33	-20	-9.33	113.93
11	Chicago Bears	-1.25	Arizona Cardinals	New Orleans Saints	31	19	12	20.45	71.36
12	Cincinnati Bengals	10.65	Jacksonville Jaguars	Carolina Panthers	9	20	-11	-14.11	9.64
13	Cleveland Browns	-6.15	Denver Broncos	Baltimore Ravens	19	13	6	9.29	10.79
14	Dallas Cowboys	-6.93	Dallas Cowboys	New York Giants	27	26	1	-1.81	7.88
15	Denver Broncos	5.78	St. Louis Rams	Seattle Seahawks	34	31	3	-9.93	167.15
16	Detroit Lions	-0.23	Houston Texans	Kansas City Chiefs	20	27	-7	-8.19	1.41
17	Green Bay Packers	5.30	Chicago Bears	Green Bay Packers	23	31	-8	-4.98	9.10
18	Houston Texans	-0.75	Washington Redskins	Miami Dolphins	10	17	-7	6.45	180.93
19	Indianapolis Colts	-6.65	Tampa Bay Buccaneers	Tennessee Titans	14	42	-28	4.38	1048.63
20	Jacksonville Jaguars	-7.54	San Francisco 49ers	Minnesota Vikings	20	3	17	-9.79	717.59
21	Kansas City Chiefs	9.00	Atlanta Falcons	Philadelphia Eagles	26	24	2	2.40	0.16
22	Miami Dolphins	-6.82	Winner/tie	Loser/tie	PtsW	PtsL			

FIGURE 35-1 Data rating NFL teams that we'll use with Solver.

To begin, I placed a trial home-field advantage value in cell B1 and gave that cell the range name *homeedge*. Also, in B6:B37, we enter trial values (any numbers will do) for each team's rating.

Starting in row 6, columns C and D contain the home and away teams for each game. For example, the first game (listed in row 6) is Pittsburgh playing at New England. Column E contains the home team's score, and column F contains the visiting team's score. As you can see, the Patriots beat the Steelers 28-21. I can now compute the outcome of each game (the number of points by which the home team beats the visiting team) by entering the formula =IFERROR(F6-G6,"") in cell G6. By pointing to the lower-right portion of this cell and double-clicking the left mouse button, you can copy this formula down to the last regular season game, which appears in row 277. (By the way, an easy way to select all the data is to press Ctrl+Shift+Down arow. This key combination takes you to the last row filled with data—row 277 in this case.)

In column H, I use Equation 1 to generate the prediction for each game. The prediction for the first game is computed in cell H6 as follows:

```
=IFERROR(homeedge+VLOOKUP(C6,lookup,2,FALSE)-VLOOKUP(D6,lookup,2,FALSE),"")
```

This formula creates a prediction for the first game by adding the home edge to the home-team rating and then subtracting the visiting-team rating. The term VLOOKUP(C6,lookup,2,FALSE)) locates the home-team rating, and VLOOKUP(D6,,lookup,2,FALSE) looks up the visiting team's rating. (For more information about using lookup functions, see Chapter 3, "Lookup functions."). In column I I compute the squared error (actual score–predicted score)^2 for each game. Our squared error for the first game is computed in cell I6 with the formula =IFERROR((G6-H6)^2,""). After selecting the cell range G6:I6, you can double-click and copy the formulas to row 277.

Next, I compute the target cell in cell I4 by summing all the squared errors with the formula =SUM((I6:I277)

Tip You can enter a formula for a large column of numbers by typing =SUM**(** and then selecting the first cell in the range you want to add together. Press Ctrl+Shift+Down arrow to enter the range from the cell you selected to the bottom row in the column and then add the closing parenthesis.

It is convenient to make the average team rating equal to 0. A team with a positive rating is better than average, and a team with a negative rating is worse than average. I computed the average team rating in cell B3 with the formula =AVERAGE(B6:B37).

I can now fill in the Solver Parameters dialog box, as shown in Figure 35-2.

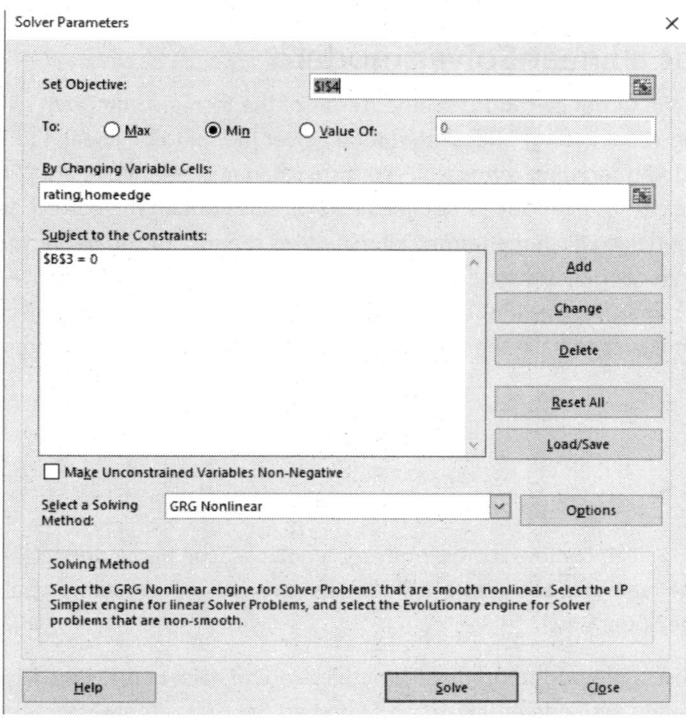

FIGURE 35-2 The Solver Parameters dialog box set up for NFL ratings.

I minimize the sum of the squared prediction errors for all the games (computed in cell I4) by changing each team's rating (listed in cells B6:B37, which I named *rating*) and the home advantage (cell B1). The constraint B3=0 ensures that the average team rating is 0. Figure 35-1 shows the resulting ratings and home edge that results after running Solver. You can see that the home team has an advantage of 1.56 points over the visiting team. The 10 highest-rated teams are shown in Figure 35-3. Remember that the ratings listed in cell range B6:B37 are computed by Solver. In the template file, you can start with any numbers in these cells, and Solver will still find the "best" ratings.

	K	L	M
22	Rank	Team	Rating
23	1	Arizona Cardinals	12.31195
24	2	Seattle Seahawks	11.3338
25	3	Cincinnati Bengals	10.64634
26	4	Kansas City Chiefs	8.99659
27	5	Pittsburgh Steelers	8.703619
28	6	Carolina Panthers	8.124566
29	7	New England Patriots	6.966867
30	8	Minnesota Vikings	5.821125
31	9	Denver Broncos	5.776781
32	10	Green Bay Packers	5.295152

FIGURE 35-3 The top 10 teams for the NFL 2015 season.

These ratings have the Panthers 2.5 points better than the Broncos. The odds makers had Carolina by five points, so we were both wrong!

Why is our model not a linear Solver model?

This model is not linear because the target cell adds together terms of the form (Home Team Rating+Home Field Edge–Visiting Team Rating)^2. Recall that for a Solver model to be linear, the target cell must be created by adding together terms with the form (changing cell)*(constant). That relationship doesn't exist in this case, so the model is not linear. Solver does obtain the correct answer, however, for any sports-rating model in which the target cell minimizes the sum of squared errors. Note that I chose the GRG nonlinear engine because this model is not linear and did not involve nonmathematical or nonsmooth functions, such as IF statements. I did not select the Make Unconstrained Variables Non-Negative option because to have the team ratings average 0, you must allow some of the team ratings to be negative.

Problems

1. The files Nfl0x.xlsx (x = 1, 2, 3, 4) contain scores for every regular season game during the 200x NFL season. Rate the teams for each season. During each season, which teams would you forecast to have made the Super Bowl?

2. For the 2004 season, devise a method to predict the actual score of each game. Hint: Give each team an offensive rating and a defensive rating. Who had the best offense? Who had the best defense?

3. True or False? An NFL team could lose every game and be an above-average team.
4. The file Nba01_02.xlsx contains scores for every game during the 2001–2002 NBA season. Rate the teams.
5. The file Nba02_03.xlsx contains scores for every regular season game during the 2002–2003 NBA season. Rate the teams.
6. The file Worldball.xlsx contains all the scores from the 2006 World Basketball Championships. Rate the teams. Who were the best three teams?
7. Our method of rating teams works fine for football and basketball. What problems arise if you apply these methods to hockey or baseball?
8. The file NflFL2012data.xlsx contains scores of all the NFL 2012 regular season games. Rate the teams. Even though the Colts were 10-6, your ratings have the Colts as well below the average team. Can you explain this anomaly?

CHAPTER 36

Warehouse location and the GRG Multistart and Evolutionary Solver engines

Questions answered in this chapter:

- Where in the United States should an Internet shipping company locate a single warehouse to minimize the total distance that packages are shipped?
- Where in the United States should an Internet shipping company locate two warehouses to minimize the total distance that packages are shipped?

Beginning with Excel 2010, Solver has been blessed with many new exciting capabilities. In this chapter (and Chapters 37 and 38), I will explain how these algorithms can help you solve many important optimization problems.

Understanding the GRG Multistart and Evolutionary Solver engines

As I pointed out in Chapter 29, "An Introduction to optimization with Excel Solver," the Excel 2016 Solver has three engines available to you to solve optimization problems: Simplex LP, GRG Nonlinear, and Evolutionary. In the following sections, I'll provide more details about how the second and third of these engines work to solve optimization problems.

How does Solver solve linear model problems?

As I pointed out in Chapters 30 through 34, a Solver model is linear if all references to changing cells in the target cells and constraints are created by adding together terms of the form (changing cells)*constants. For linear models, you should always select the Simplex LP engine, which is designed to efficiently find solutions to linear Solver models. The Excel 2016 Solver can handle problems with up to 200 changing cells and 100 constraints. Versions of Solver that can handle larger problems are available from the website Solver.com.

How does the GRG Nonlinear engine solve nonlinear optimization models?

If your target cell and/or any of your constraints contain references to changing cells that are not of the form (changing cell)*(constant), you have a nonlinear model. If *x* and *y* are changing cells, references such as the following in the target cell and/or any constraints make your model nonlinear:

- x^2
- x*y
- sin x
- e^x
- $x*e^{2y}$

If your nonlinear formulas involve ordinary math operators like the previous examples, then proper use of the GRG Nonlinear engine should quickly find the optimal solution to your Solver model. To illustrate how the GRG Nonlinear engine works, suppose you want to maximize $-x^2$. This function is graphed in Figure 36-1 (see the file Optimizationexamples.xlsx).

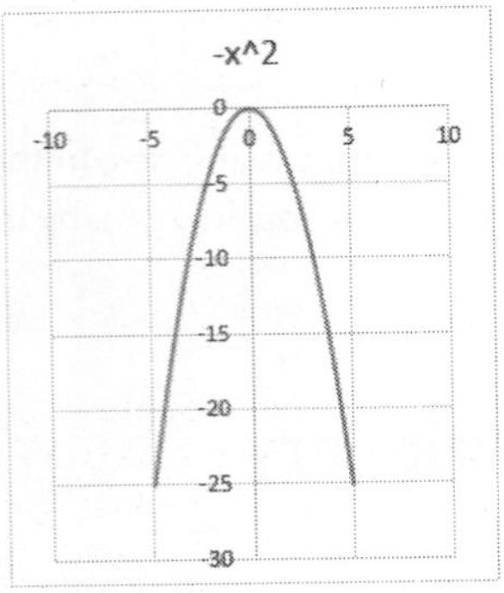

FIGURE 36-1 How the GRG Nonlinear engine maximizes a function.

You can see that this function is maximized for $x = 0$. Notice also that for $x = 0$, the function has a slope of 0. The GRG Nonlinear engine solves this problem by trying to find a point at which the slope of the function is 0. Similarly, if you want to minimize $y = x^2$, the GRG Nonlinear engine solves this problem by determining that the slope of this function is 0 for $x = 0$. See Figure 36-2.

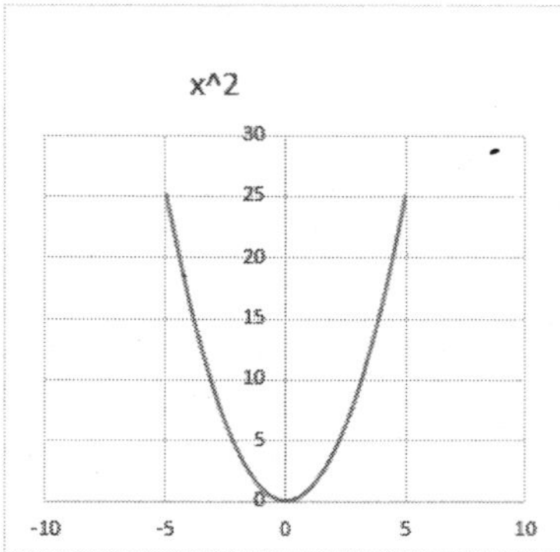

FIGURE 36-2 How the GRG Nonlinear engine minimizes a function.

Unfortunately, there are many functions that cannot be maximized simply by locating a point where the function's slope equals 0. For example, suppose you want to maximize the function shown in Figure 36-3, when *x* ranges between 0 and 12.

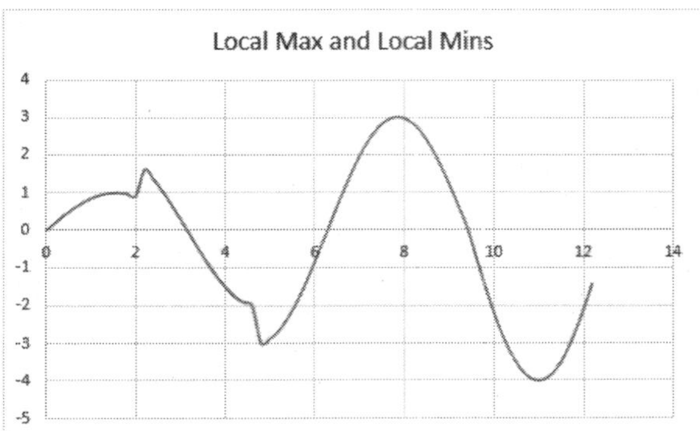

FIGURE 36-3 Maximizing a function with multiple peaks.

You can see that this function has more than one peak. If you start with a value of *x* near 8, you will find the right solution to the problem (*x* a little smaller than 8). If you start near another peak—say near *x* = 2—you will find a solution of *x* a little larger than 2, which is incorrect. Because in most problems (especially those with more than one changing cell) you do not know a good starting point, it appears you have a major hurdle to clear. Fortunately, Excel 2016 has a Multistart option.

To set this option, open the Solver Parameters dialog box by clicking the Data tab, and then clicking Solver in the Analyze group. (If you have not yet installed Solver, refer back to Chapter 29, "An introduction to optimization with Excel Solver".) You can select Multistart by clicking Options to the right of Select A Solving Method and then, in the Options dialog box, selecting the GRG Nonlinear tab. Click Use Multistart in the Multistart section of the dialog box. When the Multistart option is selected, Excel chooses many starting solutions and finds the best answer after beginning with these starting points. This approach usually resolves the multiple peak and valley problem.

By the way, pressing the Esc key stops the Solver. Also, keep in mind that the GRG Multistart option works best when you place reasonable upper and lower bounds on your changing cells. (For example, you do not specify changing cell<100 million.)

The GRG engine also runs into trouble if the target cell and/or constraints use nonsmooth functions like MAX, MIN, ABS, IF, SUMIF, COUNTIF, SUMIFS, COUNTIFS, and others that involve changing cells. These functions create points where there is no uniquely defined slope because the slope changes abruptly. For example, suppose an optimization problem requires you to model the value of a European call option with a $40 exercise price. This call option lets you buy the stock for $40. If the stock price is *s* at expiration of the option, then the value of the call option is max(0, s-40). I graphed this relationship in Figure 36-4. It is clear that when *s* = 40, the option value has no slope, so the GRG engine would break down.

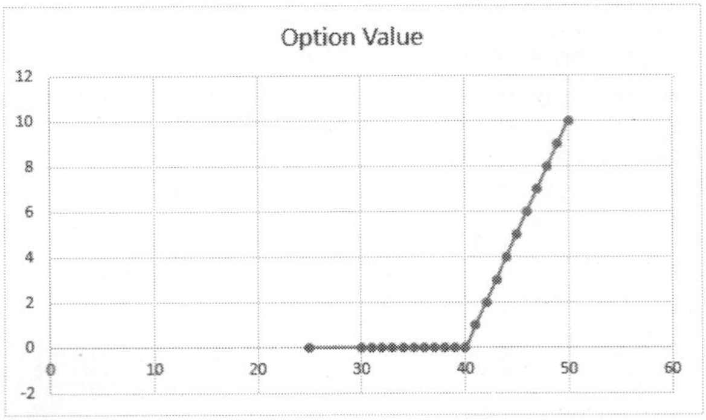

FIGURE 36-4 The option value has no slope for a $40 stock price.

As Figure 36-5 shows, Solver models that include the absolute value function (recall that the absolute value of a number is just the distance of the number from 0) will have no slope for *x*= 0. In Excel, the function ABS(x) returns the absolute value of a number *x*.

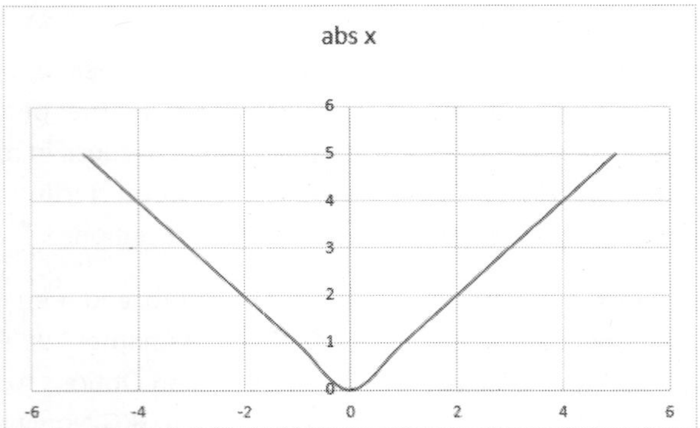

FIGURE 36-5 The absolute value function has no slope for *x* = 0.

Optimization problems in which the target cell and/or any of the constraints have no slope for any changing cell values are called *nonsmooth optimization problems*. Even the GRG Multistart option has difficulty with these types of problems. In these situations, you should apply Solver's Evolutionary engine. For nonlinear solver models, the Solver is limited to 100 changing cells and 100 constraints.

How does the Evolutionary Solver engine tackle nonsmooth optimization problems?

The Evolutionary Solver in Excel 2016 is based on genetic algorithms, a concept discovered by John Holland, a computer science professor at the University of Michigan. To use the Evolutionary Solver, begin by taking 50–100 points in the problem's feasible region (that is, the set of points that meet the constraints). This set of points is called the *population*. Then, the target cell is evaluated for each point. Using the idea of survival of the fittest from the theory of evolution, you change the points in the population in a way that increases the likelihood that future population members are located near previous population members that have a good target cell value. Because this approach is based on target cells values and not on slopes, multiple peaks and valleys pose no problem. Also, functions that do not have slopes (the so-called nonsmooth functions) also become a less important issue. The Evolutionary Solver engine (like the GRG Multistart option) also works best when reasonable upper and lower bounds are placed on your changing cells. After you select the Evolutionary Solver engine (from Select A Solving Method in the Solver Parameters dialog box), it's best to choose Options, display the Evolutionary tab (in the Options dialog box), and change the mutation rate to 0.5. Also select the Required Bounds On Variables check box, and increase the maximum time without improvement to 3,600 **seconds**. Increasing the mutation rate decreases the likelihood that Solver gets stuck near a poor solution. Increasing the maximum time without improvement to 3,600 seconds allows Solver to run until it fails to improve the target cell for 3,600 seconds. That way, Solver keeps running if you leave your computer.

Now let's use Excel 2016 Solver to solve two interesting facility-location problems.

Answer to this chapter's questions

Where in the United States should an Internet shipping company locate a single warehouse to minimize the total distance that packages are shipped?

The number of shipments (in thousands) made each year to various cities is shown in Figure 36-6. (See the worksheet One Warehouse in the file Warehouseloc.xlsx.)

	B	C	D	E	F	G	H	I
3					Lat	Long		Mean
4				1	36.813439	92.48191		1125.827
5						Total	252185.2	
6	City	Lat	Long	Shipments	Distance	Shipped *Dist		
7	New York	40.7	73.9	15	1309.8969	19648.45		
8	Boston	42.3	71	8	1529.8326	12238.66		
9	Philadelphia	40	75.1	10	1219.3395	12193.39		
10	Charlotte	35.2	80.8	6	813.70342	4882.221		
11	Atlanta	33.8	84.4	11	595.15484	6546.703		
12	New Orleans	30	89.9	8	502.75019	4022.002		
13	Miami	25.8	80.2	13	1138.2724	14797.54		
14	Dallas	32.8	96.8	10	406.77005	4067.701		
15	Houston	29.8	95.4	12	524.14383	6289.726		
16	Chicago	41.8	87.7	14	476.71185	6673.966		
17	Detroit	42.4	83.1	11	753.42785	8287.706		
18	Cleveland	41.5	81.7	8	811.19304	6489.544		
19	Indy	39.8	86.1	7	486.18479	3403.294		
20	Denver	39.8	105	8	881.28021	7050.242		
21	Minneapolis	45	93.3	9	567.68613	5109.175		
22	Phoenix	33.5	112	11	1372.8197	15101.02		
23	Salt Lake City	40.8	112	10	1367.7932	13677.93		
24	LA	34.1	118	18	1798.1222	32366.2		
25	SF	37.8	123	12	2079.2628	24951.15		
26	SD	32.8	117	10	1721.0736	17210.74		
27	Seattle	41.6	122	13	2090.6012	27177.82		

FIGURE 36-6 The data for the single warehouse problem.

A key to this model is the following formula, which gives the approximate distance between two US cities having a latitude and longitude given by (Lat1, Long1) and (Lat2 and Long2).

$$Distance = 69 * \sqrt{(Lat1 - Lat2)^2 + (Long1 - Long2)^2}$$

To begin, enter in cells F4:G4 trial values for the latitude and longitude of the warehouse. Next, by copying from F7 to F8:F27 the formula =69*SQRT((C7-$F$4)^2+(D7-$G$4)^2), you compute the approximate distance of each city from the warehouse. Next, by copying from G7 to G8:G27 the formula =E7*F7, you compute the distance traveled by the shipments to each city. In cell H5, the formula =SUM(G7:G27) computes the total distance traveled by all shipments. Our target cell is to minimize H5 by changing F4:G4. After you select the GRG Nonlinear engine, the Solver Parameters dialog box appears as in Figure 36-7.

After you click Solve, you'll find that the warehouse should be located at 36.81 degrees latitude and 92.48 degrees longitude, which is near Springfield, Missouri. (See the coordinates highlighted in cells F4:G5 in Figure 36-6.)

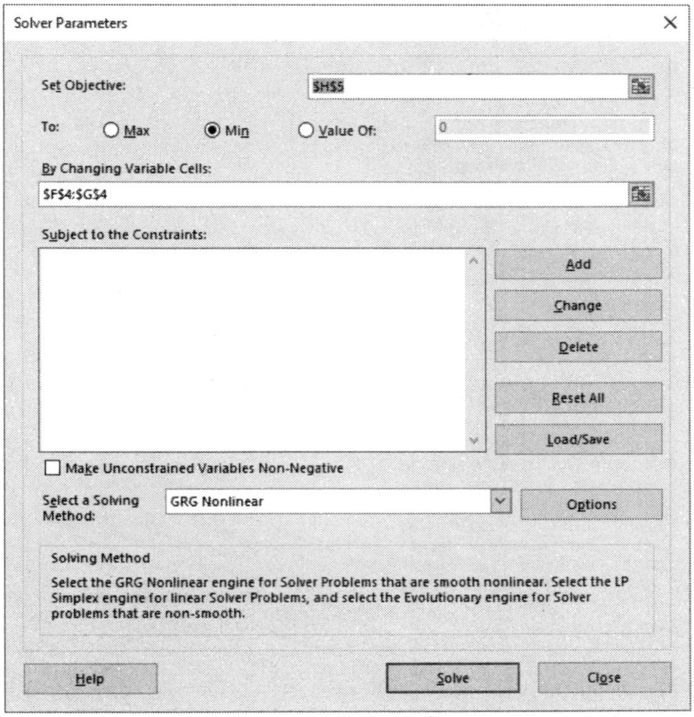

FIGURE 36-7 The Solver Parameters dialog box for the one warehouse problem.

Where in the United States should an Internet shipping company locate two warehouses to minimize the total distance that packages are shipped?

The work for this problem is in the worksheet Two Warehouses in the file Warehouseloc.xlsx, shown in Figure 36-8.

	B	C	D	E	F	G	H	I
2								Mean dis
3					Lat	Long		501.811
4				1	38.1641	84.029		Total
5				2	34.9319	117.792		119676
6	City	Lat	Long	Shipmen	Distance to 1	Distance to 2	Min Distance	Dist*Shipped
7	New York	40.7	73.9	15	720.47	3054.56	720.47	10807.1
8	Boston	42.3	71	8	943.207	3268.4	943.207	7545.66
9	Philadelphia	40	75.1	10	628.987	2966.41	628.987	6289.87
10	Charlotte	35.2	80.8	6	302.436	2552.49	302.436	1814.61
11	Atlanta	33.8	84.4	11	302.206	2305.34	302.206	3324.27
12	New Orleans	30	89.9	8	693.856	1954.38	693.856	5550.85
13	Miami	25.8	80.2	13	893.092	2669.26	893.092	11610.2
14	Dallas	32.8	96.8	10	955.774	1455.87	955.774	9557.74
15	Houston	29.8	95.4	12	973.995	1585.08	973.995	11687.9
16	Chicago	41.8	87.7	14	356.515	2129.72	356.515	4991.2
17	Detroit	42.4	83.1	11	299.226	2448.56	299.226	3291.49
18	Cleveland	41.5	81.7	8	280.726	2531.22	280.726	2245.81
19	Indy	39.8	86.1	7	182.107	2212.37	182.107	1274.75
20	Denver	39.8	104.9	8	1444.52	950.829	950.829	7606.63
21	Minneapolis	45	93.3	9	794.796	1827.14	794.796	7153.16
22	Phoenix	33.5	112.1	11	1963.46	404.958	404.958	4454.54
23	Salt Lake Cit	40.8	111.9	10	1931.68	573.762	573.762	5737.62
24	LA	34.1	118.4	18	2388.12	71.1134	71.1134	1280.04
25	SF	37.8	122.6	12	2661.52	386.318	386.318	4635.82
26	SD	32.8	117.1	10	2311.72	154.647	154.647	1546.47
27	Seattle	41.6	122.4	13	2658.2	559.287	559.287	7270.74

FIGURE 36-8 A model for locating two warehouses.

To begin, enter trial latitudes and longitudes for the warehouses in F4:G5. Next, copy from F7 to F8:F27 the formula =69*SQRT((C7-$F$4)^2+(D7-$G$4)^2) to compute the distance of each city from Warehouse 1. By copying from G7 to G8:G27 the formula =69*SQRT((C7-$F$5)^2+(D7-$G$5)^2), you compute the distance from each city to Warehouse 2. Since the shipments from each city will be sent from the closer warehouse, you now compute the distance of each city to the closer warehouse by copying from H7 to H8:H27 the formula =MIN(F7,G7). In the cells I7:I27, you compute the distance traveled by each city's shipments by copying from I7 to I8:I27 the formula =H7*E7. In cell I5, you compute the total distance traveled by shipments with the formula =SUM(I7:I27).

You're now ready to use Solver to determine the optimal warehouse locations. The setup for the Solver Parameters dialog box is shown in Figure 36-9.

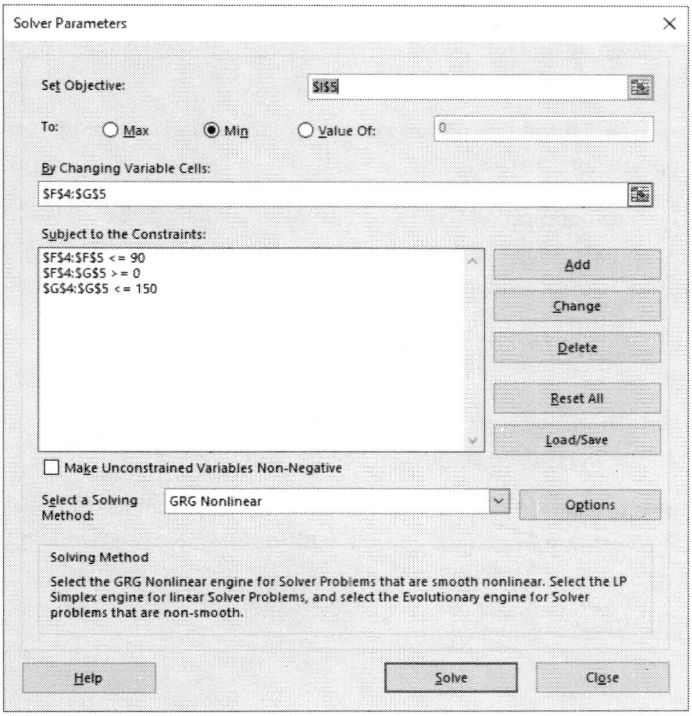

FIGURE 36-9 Solver setup for locating two warehouses.

Begin by selecting the GRG Nonlinear engine in the Select A Solving Method list. Then use the "poor" solution, which places each warehouse at 0 latitude and longitude. This solution is poor for two reasons: It locates the warehouses in Africa and it puts two warehouses in the same place. After running Solver, we find Solver recommends locating both warehouses in the same place. Of course, this is a suboptimal solution. The problem is twofold: The MIN function creates situations with no slopes, and perhaps our target cell, as a function of the four changing cells, has multiple peaks and valleys. If our target cell has multiple peaks and valleys (in four dimensions), our poor starting solution might not be near the lowest valley, which is the true optimal solution. In situations in which you suspect that multiple peaks and valleys exist, it is a good idea to use the GRG Multistart option, which tries multiple starting points and finds the best answer from each starting point. Most of the time, the best of the best solution found by Multistart will be the optimal solution to the problem.

To use Multistart, place bounds on the changing cells and run Solver using the GRG Multistart option. For the bounds on latitude changing cells, I selected 0 and 90 degrees. This ensures that the warehouse is north of the Equator. For the bounds on longitude changing cells, I chose 0 and 150, which ensures that our location is west of Greenwich, England and east of Anchorage, Alaska.

In the results, the average distance traveled per shipment is 502 miles. The locations of the warehouses are shown in cells F4:G5 of Figure 36-8. Warehouse 1 is located near Lexington, Kentucky, while Warehouse 2 is located near Lancaster, California.

To confirm that Solver found the optimal solution, I then ran the Evolutionary Solver engine and found no improvement in the optimal solution.

Suppose I had set an upper bound for longitude of 110 degrees. After running Solver, I would have found that Solver recommends a longitude near 110 degrees. If you place bounds on a changing cell and Solver forces the changing cell to assume a value near a bound, you should relax the bound.

Problems

1. Find the optimal solution to the warehouse problem if three warehouses are allowed.
2. Suppose you want to locate a single restroom so that company employees have to travel the smallest possible distance per day when going to the bathroom. Employees work in four locations within the plant as described in the following table:

X	Y	Number of employees
5	20	6
50	50	12
25	75	23
80	30	15

   Assume that employees always walk in a north-south or east-west direction when going to and from the restroom. Where should the restroom be located?

3. Solve Problem 2 if the company wants to locate two restrooms.
4. A box must enclose four cubic feet of volume. You must choose the height, length, and width of the box. Top and bottom sides of the box costs 30 cents per square foot and the other four sides of the box cost 20 cents per square foot. How would you build the cheapest possible box?
5. Suppose you throw a shotput from a height H with an initial velocity V at an angle θ. If $H = 5$ feet and $V = 100$ feet per second, what angle will cause the shotput to travel the most distance? Assume that after a given time, the y coordinate of the shotput will equal h+v*SIN(theta)*time-0.5*g*(time^2) and the x coordinate will equal v*time*cos(theta).

CHAPTER 37

Penalties and the Evolutionary Solver

Questions answered in this chapter:

- What are the keys to successfully using the Evolutionary Solver?
- How can I use the Evolutionary Solver to assign 80 workers in Microsoft Finance to a job in one of four workgroups?

Answers to this chapter's questions

What are the keys to successfully using the Evolutionary Solver?

Previously, I stated that the Evolutionary Solver should be used to find solutions to optimization problems in which the target cell and/or changing cells involve nonsmooth functions, such as IF, ABS, MAX, MIN, COUNTIF, COUNTIFS, SUMIF, SUMIFS, AVERAGEIF, and AVERAGEIFS. Before solving a problem with Evolutionary Solver, you should do the following in the Solver Parameters dialog box (click Solver in the Analysis group on the Data tab to open the dialog box):

- Click Options, select the Evolutionary tab, and increase the Mutation rate to 0.50.
- Change Maximum Time Without Improvement to 3,600 seconds.
- Place reasonable lower and upper bounds on your changing cells.

Everything in life has an upside and a downside, and the Evolutionary Solver is no exception. The upside of the Evolutionary Solver is that it handles nonsmooth functions well. The downside is that constraints that are not linear functions of the changing cells are not handled very well. To handle most constraints with the Evolutionary Solver, you should penalize the target cell so that violation of a constraint is a bad thing. Then the survival-of-the-fittest rule will get rid of any constraint violators. The chapter's next question shows how to use penalties with the Evolutionary Solver.

How can I use the Evolutionary Solver to assign 80 workers in Microsoft Finance to a job in one of four workgroups?

You need to assign 80 employees to four workgroups. The head of each workgroup has rated each employee's competence on a 0 to 10 scale (10 equals most competent). Each employee has rated his or her satisfaction with each job assignment (again on a 0 to 10 scale). For example, Worker 1 has been given a 9 rating for Workgroup 1 and Worker 1 gives Workgroup 4 a rating of 7.

The work for this question is in the file Assign.xlsx. (See Figure 37-1.) You want to assign between 18 and 22 people to each workgroup. You consider job competence to be twice as important as employee satisfaction. How can you assign employees to workgroups to maximize total satisfaction and ensure that each division has the required number of employees?

	A	B	C	D	E	F	G	H	I	J	K	L	M	N	O
1			Qual				Sat				576	499			
2	Division	Worker	1	2	3	4	1	2	3	4	Quality	Satisfaction			
3	4	1	9	8	6	8	1	2	6	7	8	7			
4	1	2	10	0	5	6	9	6	7	4	10	9			
5	3	3	5	8	10	5	1	7	7	3	10	7	Group	#assigned	penalty
6	1	4	4	0	5	2	9	1	0	3	4	9	1	19	0
7	2	5	9	10	4	5	9	8	8	3	10	8	2	18	0
8	3	6	5	2	7	3	2	8	1	5	7	1	3	22	0
9	1	7	8	3	1	2	1	8	2	2	8	1	4	21	0
10	3	8	2	2	9	2	8	3	1	6	9	1		Total pen	0
11	1	9	8	7	6	3	4	3	4	1	8	4			
12	4	10	7	0	1	8	4	1	5	4	8	4		Total	1651
13	3	11	8	1	6	6	2	0	9	3	6	9			
14	2	12	0	7	1	2	5	2	1	1	7	2			
15	1	13	9	0	5	4	3	0	7	8	9	3			
16	4	14	9	2	2	7	1	1	2	#	7	10			
17	3	15	1	3	8	4	9	8	6	8	8	6			
18	1	16	9	6	4	5	5	7	8	8	9	5			
19	1	17	8	0	5	0	5	7	2	4	8	5			
20	2	18	6	7	6	3	2	4	1	6	7	4			

FIGURE 37-1 The data for the job assignment problem.

In cells A3:A82, I entered trial assignments of workers to workgroups. Assigning each worker to Workgroup 1, for example, is an acceptable starting solution. Copying the formula =HLOOKUP(A3,Qual,B3+1) from cell K3 to the range K3:K82 enables you to look up each employee's qualifications for her assigned job. Note that *Qual* refers to the range C2:F82. Next, copying from L3 to L4:L82 the formula =HLOOKUP(A3,Satis,B3+1) enables you to look up the employee's satisfaction with her assigned job. *Satis* is the range name for G2:J82.

To deal with the fact that each division needs between 18 and 22 employees, you need to count how many employees have been assigned to each workgroup. You can do this in cells N6:N9 by copying from N6 to N7:N9 the formula =COUNTIF($A$3:$A$82,M6). Next, in cells O6:O9, you determine whether a workgroup has the incorrect number of employees by copying from O6 to O7:O9 the formula =IF(OR(N6<18,N6>22),1,0).

Now, I'll show how to work on computing the target cell. In K1:L1, you compute total competence and total job quality by copying from K1 to L1 the formula =SUM(K3:K82). To ensure that each workgroup will have between 18 and 22 workers, you can penalize the target cell. I chose a penalty of 1,000 for each workgroup that has less than 18 or more than 22 workers. There is no hard-and-fast rule to help you determine an appropriate penalty. In this situation, the average rating is 5. This yields a target cell of 2*400 + 400 = 1,200. Therefore, it seems likely that putting the wrong number of people in any division would not benefit the target cell by more than 1,000, so survival of the fittest will kill off any solution for which a workgroup has too many or too few workers. The appropriate penalty should not be too large (100,000) because it sometimes makes Solver ignore the real problem. If the penalty is too small, Solver will not achieve the goal you've set.

In cell O10, I computed the total number of divisions that do not have the correct number of workers by using the formula =SUM(O6:O9). Now we are finally ready to compute the target cell in cell O12 by adding twice the total competence to the total job satisfaction and subtracting a penalty of 1,000 for each group that does not have the correct number of employees. Our final target cell O12 is computed by means of the formula =2*K1+L1-1000*O10.

You now can create the Solver model for this problem You need to use the Evolutionary Solver method because the COUNTIF functions and IF functions are nonsmooth functions of the changing cells. The model is shown in Figure 37-2.

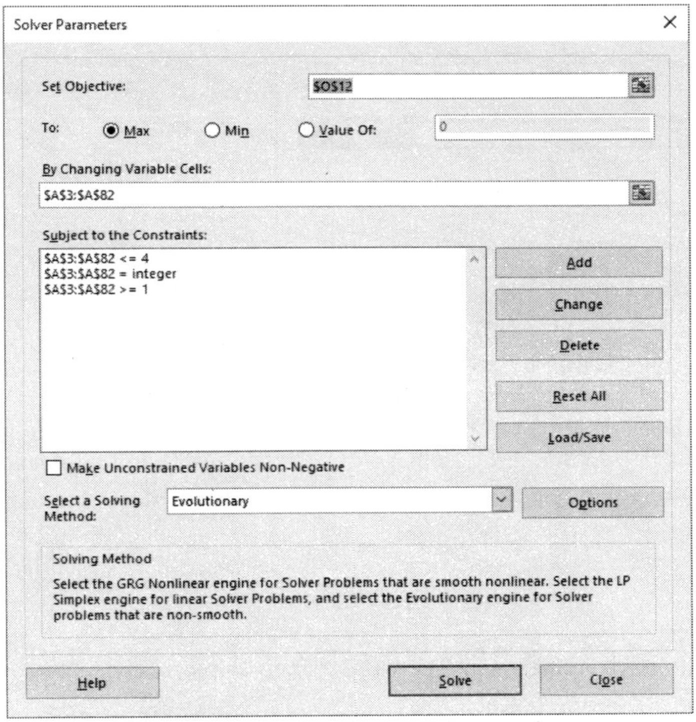

FIGURE 37-2 The Solver model for the worker-assignment problem.

I maximize the weighted sum of workgroup and employee satisfaction, less the penalty for an incorrect number of workers in a workgroup (cell O12). Then I constrain each worker's assignment to be 1, 2, 3, or 4. The solution is shown previously in Figure 37-1. Each group has the right number of workers; the average employee competence is 7.2, while the average employee satisfaction is 6.3. Over all 80 workers, the average of their competence ratings is 4.4, and the overall average for satisfaction ratings is 5, so conditions have improved quite a lot over a random assignment.

If you had tried the GRG Nonlinear engine (even with the Multistart option), Solver would not have found the optimal solution because the model includes nonsmooth functions. Another tip for using Evolutionary method is to use as few changing cells as possible—you will usually be rewarded by having Solver take less time to find an optimal solution.

Using conditional formatting to highlight each employee's ratings

You can use the conditional formatting feature to highlight in red each employee's actual (based on her assignment) competence and satisfaction. Simply go to cell C3 and select the cell range C3:J82. Then, select New Rule from the Conditional Formatting command on the Home tab, select the Use A Formula To Determine Which Cells to Format option, and fill in the dialog box as shown in Figure 37-3.

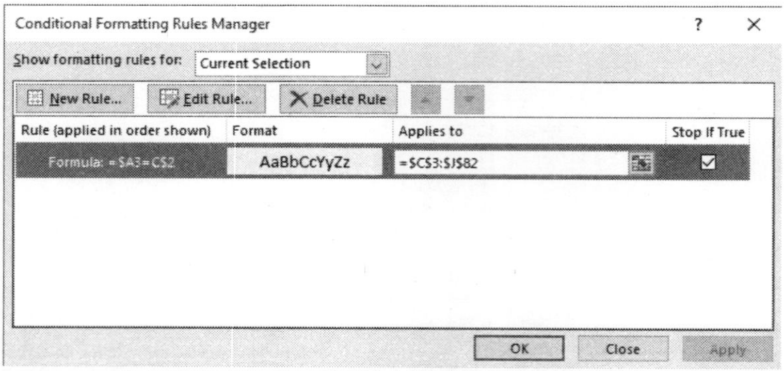

FIGURE 37-3 Using conditional formatting to highlight worker quality and satisfaction.

This formula will enter in cell C3 a red format if and only if the first worker is assigned to Workgroup 1. You can copy this formula across and down so that each worker's quality and satisfaction ratings are highlighted only for the workgroup to which each employee is assigned.

Problems

1. Use Evolutionary Solver to solve Problem 4 in Chapter 33, "Using Solver for capital budgeting."
2. Solve the two warehouse problems in Chapter 36, "Warehouse location and the GRG Multistart and Evolutionary Solver engines," assuming that each warehouse can ship at most 120,000 units.
3. In the fictional state of Politicians Care About the USA, there are eight congressional districts. Each of 15 cities must be assigned to a congressional district, and each district must be assigned between 150,000 and 250,000 voters. The makeup of each district is given below. Assign the cities to districts to maximize the number of districts won by the Democrats. Start with the following data:

City	Republican	Democrat
1	80	34
2	43	61
3	40	44
4	20	24
5	40	114
6	40	64
7	70	34
8	50	44
9	70	54
10	70	64
11	80	45
12	40	50
13	50	60
14	60	65
15	50	70

4. Solve the assignment-of-workers example assuming that worker satisfaction is twice as important as the bosses' ratings.

5. Cook County General Hospital is attempting to schedule work its 20 nurses. Each nurse will work four consecutive days and is assigned to one of the following schedules:

Schedule	Days worked
1	Monday-Thursday
2	Tuesday-Friday
3	Wednesday-Saturday
4	Thursday-Sunday
5	Friday-Monday
6	Saturday-Tuesday
7	Sunday-Wednesday

Each nurse will be assigned for the week to either the ICU or a patient ward. Each nurse's satisfaction with her assignment is given in file Nursejackiedata.xlsx. For example, if Nurse 5 is assigned to the ICU, Nurse 5 gives a perfect 10 rating to work schedule 3.

Each day, the ICU needs six nurses, and the patient wards need five nurses. Schedule the nurses to maximize their satisfaction and meet hospital needs. You will need to know which schedules satisfy the nurse demand for different days. For example, nurses starting on Monday, Friday, Saturday, and Sunday will work on Monday.

CHAPTER 38

The traveling salesperson problem

Questions answered in this chapter:

- How can I use Excel to solve sequencing problems?
- How can I use Excel to solve a traveling salesperson problem (TSP)?

Answers to this chapter's questions

How can I use Excel to solve sequencing problems?

Many business problems involve the choice of an optimal sequence. Here are two examples:

- In what order should a print shop work on 10 jobs to minimize the total time by which jobs fail to meet their due dates? Problems of this type are called *job-shop scheduling problems*.
- A salesperson lives in Boston and wants to visit 10 other cities before returning home. In which order should he visit the cities to minimize the total distance he travels? This is an example of the classic *traveling salesperson problem* (TSP).

Here are two other examples of a TSP:

- A delivery driver needs to make 20 stops today. In which order should she deliver packages to minimize her time on the road?
- A robot must drill 10 holes to produce a single printed circuit board. Which order of drilling the holes minimizes the total time needed to produce a circuit board?

Excel 2016 Solver makes tackling sequencing problems very easy. Navigate to the Solver Parameters dialog box (click Solver in the Analyze group on the Data tab), and then choose Evolutionary from the Select A Solving Method list. Select your changing cells, and then select Dif from the comparison list in the middle of the Add Constraint dialog box when setting up constraints. Setting the AllDifferent option ensures that if you have 10 changing cells, Excel will assign the values 1, 2, . . . 10 to the changing cells with each value occurring exactly once. In general, if you select a range of *n* changing cells to be different, Excel ensures that the changing cells assume the values 1, 2, . . . , *n*, with each possible value occurring exactly once. Let's see how to use the Dif option to easily solve a traveling salesperson problem.

How can I use Excel to solve a traveling salesperson problem (TSP)?

Let's try and solve the following problem.

Willie Lowman is a salesman who lives in Boston. He needs to visit each of the cities listed in Figure 38-1 and then return to Boston. In what order should Willie visit the cities to minimize the total distance he travels? Our work is in the file Tsp.xlsx.

	E	F	G	H	I	J	K	L	M	N	O	P	Q
1													
2													
3			Boston	Chicago	Dallas	Denver	LA	Miami	NY	Phoenix	Pittsburgh	SF	Seattl
4	1	Boston	0	983	1815	1991	3036	1539	213	2664	792	2385	2612
5	2	Chicago	983	0	1205	1050	2112	1390	840	1729	457	2212	2052
6	3	Dallas	1815	1205	0	801	1425	1332	###	1027	1237	1765	2404
7	4	Denver	1991	1050	801	0	1174	1332	###	836	1411	1765	1373
8	5	LA	3036	2112	1425	1174	0	2757	###	398	2456	403	1909
9	6	Miami	1539	1390	1332	1332	2757	0	###	2359	1250	3097	3389
10	7	NY	213	840	1604	1780	2825	1258	0	2442	386	3036	2900
11	8	Phoenix	2664	1729	1027	836	398	2359	###	0	2073	800	1482
12	9	Pittsburgl	792	457	1237	1411	2456	1250	386	2073	0	2653	2517
13	10	SF	2385	2212	1765	1765	403	3097	###	800	2653	0	817
14	11	Seattle	2612	2052	2404	1373	1909	3389	###	1482	2517	817	0
15		Order	Distance	City									
16	1	8	398	Phoenix									
17	2	3	1027	Dallas									
18	3	6	1332	Miami									
19	4	1	1539	Boston									
20	5	7	213	NY									
21	6	9	386	Pittsburgh									
22	7	2	457	Chicago									
23	8	4	1050	Denver									
24	9	11	1373	Seattle									
25	10	10	817	SF									
26	11	5	403	LA									
27		Total	8995										

FIGURE 38-1 The data for the TSP.

To model this problem in a spreadsheet, you should note that any ordering or permutation of the numbers 1 through 11 represents an order for the visiting cities. For example, the ordering 2-4-6-8-10-1-3-5-7-9-11 can be viewed as traveling from Boston (City 1) to Dallas (City 3), to LA (City 5), and finally to SF (City 10) before returning to Boston. Since the ordering is viewed from the location of City 1, there are 10! = 10x9x8x7x6...x2x1 = 3,628,800 possible orderings for Willie to consider.

To begin, you need to determine the total distance traveled for any given order for visiting the cities. The INDEX function is perfect for this situation. Recall from Chapter 4, "The INDEX function," that the syntax of the INDEX function is INDEX(Range,row#,column#). Excel looks in the range of cells named *Range* and picks out the entry specified in *row#* and *column#* of *Range*. In this case, you can use the INDEX function to find the total distance traveled in visiting all cities.

I began by entering in the range F16:F26 an order of the integers 1 through 11. Next, I named the range G4:Q14 *distances* and entered in cell G16 the formula =INDEX(distances,F26,F16). This formula determines the distance between the last city listed (in F26) and the first city listed (in F16). Next, I enter the formula =INDEX(distances,F16,F17) in cell G17 and copy it to the range G18:G26. In G17, the formula computes the distance between the first and second city listed, and so on. Now I can compute the target cell (total distance traveled) in cell G27, with the formula =SUM(G16:G26).

At this point, I'm ready to invoke the Solver. I choose to minimize cell G27 (in the Solver Parameters dialog box, I select G27 in the Set Objective box and select Min), and then I click Add to add a constraint and select the range F16:F26 in the Add Constraint dialog box. Then I select Dif for AllDifferent and click OK to add the constraint. This ensures that Solver always keeps the changing cells in the selected range, assuming the values 1, 2, up to 11. Each value will occur exactly once. The Solver Parameters dialog box is shown in Figure 38-2. Before running Solver, I increased the Mutation rate to 0.5 by clicking Options (to the right of Select A Solving Method) and then, in the Options dialog box, clicking the Evolutionary tab and updating the value in the Mutation Rate box.)

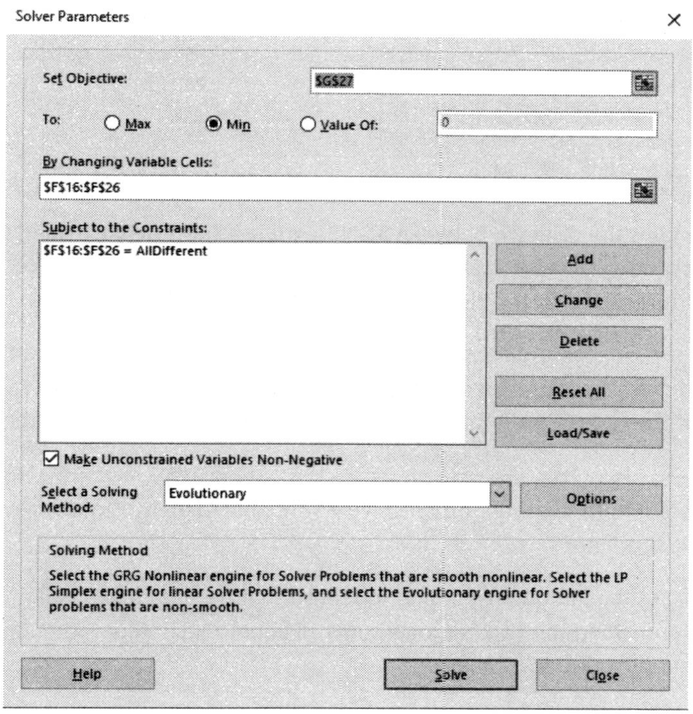

FIGURE 38-2 Solver set up for a traveling salesperson problem.

The minimum possible distance to travel is 8,995 miles. To see the order in which the cities are visited, simply begin in the row with a 1 (corresponding to Willie's home, Boston) and follow the cities in the listed sequence. The cities are visited in the following order: Boston-NY-Pittsburgh-Chicago-Denver-Seattle-SF-LA-Phoenix-Dallas-Miami-Boston. There are many other sequences for visiting the cities that also yield the minimum total travel distance of 8,995 miles.

Problems

1. A small job shop needs to schedule six jobs. The due date and days needed to complete each job are given below. In what order should the jobs be scheduled to minimize the total days the jobs are late?

Job	Processing time	Due date(measured from today)
1	9	32
2	7	29
3	8	22
4	18	21
5	9	37
6	6	28

2. The file Nbamiles.xlsx contains the distance between all NBA arenas. Suppose you live in New York and want to visit each arena once and return to New York. In what order should you visit the cities to minimize the total distance traveled?

3. Suppose now that you live in Atlanta and are driving 29 general managers. Each GM wants to return to his home. Each time you visit an arena, you drop off a GM at his home arena. In what order should you drop off the GMs in order to minimize the total distance traveled by the GMs?

4. In the Willy Lowman problem, suppose you must visit New York immediately after Denver. What is the solution to the problem?

5. A 3-by-3 magic square places the integers 1-9 in the square so that the sum down each column, across each row, and along the two diagonal sums all equal 15. Use the Evolutionary solving method to design a 3-by-3 magic square.

CHAPTER 39

Importing data from a text file or document

Question answered in this chapter:

- How can I import data from a text file into Excel so that I can analyze it?

Jeff Sagarin, the creator of the *USA Today* basketball and football ratings, and I have developed a system to rate NBA players that has been used by several NBA teams, including the Dallas Mavericks and New York Knicks. Every day during the season, Jeff's FORTRAN program produces many bits of information, including ratings for each Dallas Mavericks lineup during each game. Jeff's program produces this data in the form of a text file. In this chapter, I show you how you can import a text file into Microsoft Excel to use it for data analysis.

Answers to this chapter's question

How can I import data from a text file into Excel so that I can analyze it?

You are likely to receive data in a Microsoft Word document or in a text (.txt) file that you often need to import into Excel for numerical analysis. To import a Word document into Excel, you should first save it as a text file (.txt). You can then use the Text Import Wizard to import the file. With the Text Import Wizard, you can break data in a text file into columns by using one of the following approaches:

- If you choose the fixed-width option, Excel guesses where the data should be broken into columns. You can easily modify Excel's assumptions.
- If you choose the delimited option, you pick a character (common choices are a comma, a space, or a plus sign), and Excel breaks the data into columns wherever it encounters the character you choose.

As an example, the file Lineupsch39temp.docx is found in this chapter's Templates folder; it contains the length of time each lineup played for Dallas in several games during the 2002–2003 season. The file also contains the *rating* of the lineup. For example, the first two lines tell you that against Sacramento, the lineup of Bell, Finley, LaFrentz, Nash, and Nowitzki were on the court together for 9.05 minutes and that the lineup played at a level of 19.79 points (per 48 minutes), worse than an average NBA lineup. The following list shows a sample of the data:

```
Bell    Finley   LaFrentz  Nash    Nowitzki   - 19.79   695# 9.05m SAC DAL* Finley   Nash
Nowitzki  Van Exel  Williams   - 11.63   695# 8.86m SAC DAL* Finley   LaFrentz  Nash    Nowitzki
Van Exel   102.98   695# 4.44m SAC DAL* Bradley   Finley   Nash    Nowitzki  Van Exel   - 44.26
695# 4.38m SAC DAL* Bradley   Nash    Nowitzki  Van Exel  Williams    9.71   695# 3.05m SAC DAL*
Bell    Finley   LaFrentz  Nowitzki  Van Exel  - 121.50   695# 2.73m SAC DAL* Bell    LaFrentz
Nowitzki  Van Exel  Williams   39.35   695# 2.70m SAC DAL* Bradley   Finley   Nowitzki  Van Exel
Williams   86.87   695# 2.45m SAC DAL* Bradley   Nash    Van Exel  Williams  Rigaudeau  - 54.55
695# 2.32m SAC DAL*
```

We'd like to import this lineup information into Excel so that, for each lineup, the following information would be listed in different columns:

- Each player's name
- Minutes played by the lineup
- Rating of the lineup

The player Van Exel (his full name is Nick Van Exel) raises a problem. If you choose the delimited option and use a space character to break the data into columns, Van Exel will occupy two columns. For lineups that include Van Exel, the numerical data will be located in a column different from the column in which the data is located for lineups that don't include Van Exel. To remedy this problem, I used the Replace command in Word to change each occurrence of Van Exel to Exel. Now, when Excel breaks up the data where a space occurs, Van Exel will require only one column. The first few rows of our data now look like the following:

```
Bell    Finley   LaFrentz  Nash    Nowitzki   - 19.79  695# 9.05m SAC DAL* Finley   Nash
Nowitzki  Exel  Williams   - 11.63  695# 8.86m SAC DAL* Finley   LaFrentz  Nash    Nowitzki
Exel   102.98  69 5# 4.44m SAC DAL* Bradley   Finley   Nash   Nowitzki  Exel   - 44.26  695#
4.38m SAC DAL* Bradley   Nash    Nowitzki  Exel  Williams    9.71  69 5# 3.05m SAC DAL* Bell
Finley   LaFrentz  Nowitzki  Exel   - 121.50  695# 2.73m SAC DAL* Bell    LaFrentz  Nowitzki
Exel  Williams   39.35  69 5# 2.70m SAC DAL* Bradley   Finley   Nowitzki  Exel  Williams
86.87  69 5# 2.45m SAC DAL* Bradley   Nash    Exel  Williams  Rigaudeau  - 54.55  695# 2.32m SAC
DAL*
```

The trick to importing data from a Word or text file into Excel is to use the Excel Text Import Wizard. As I mentioned earlier, you first need to save the Word file (Lineupsch39temp.docx in this example) as a text file. To do this, simply open the file in Word, click the File tab, click Save As, click Browse, remove the word temp from the title, and then select Plain Text (*.txt) in the Save As Type list. In the File Conversion dialog box, select the Windows (Default) option for Text Encoding, and then click OK. Your file should now be saved with the name *Lineupsch39.txt*. Close the Word document. In Excel, open the file Lineupsch39.txt—click File, then click Open, then click Browse, navigate to the .txt file's folder, select All Files (*.*) from the file type list on the right, select the file, and then click Open. You'll see step 1 of the Text Import Wizard, which is shown in Figure 39-1.

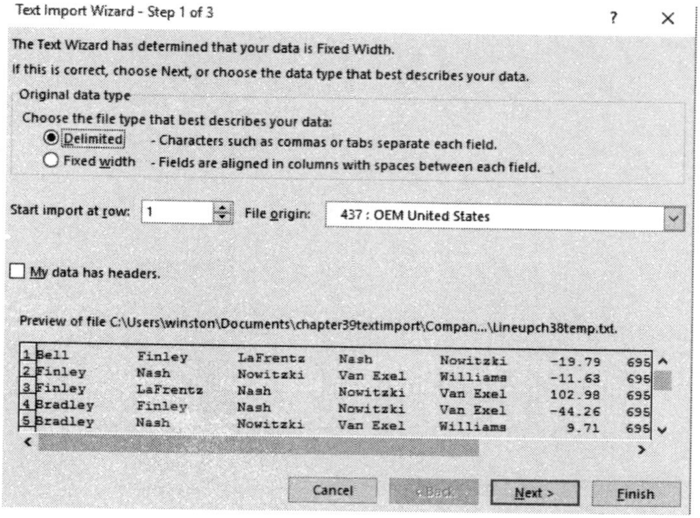

FIGURE 39-1 Step 1 of the Text Import Wizard.

Clearly, in this case you want to select the Delimited option and break the data at each space. However, let's suppose that you choose Fixed Width. Then step 2 of the Text Import Wizard appears, shown in Figure 39-2. As you can see, you can create, move, or delete a break point. For many data import operations, changing column breaks can be a hit-or-miss adventure.

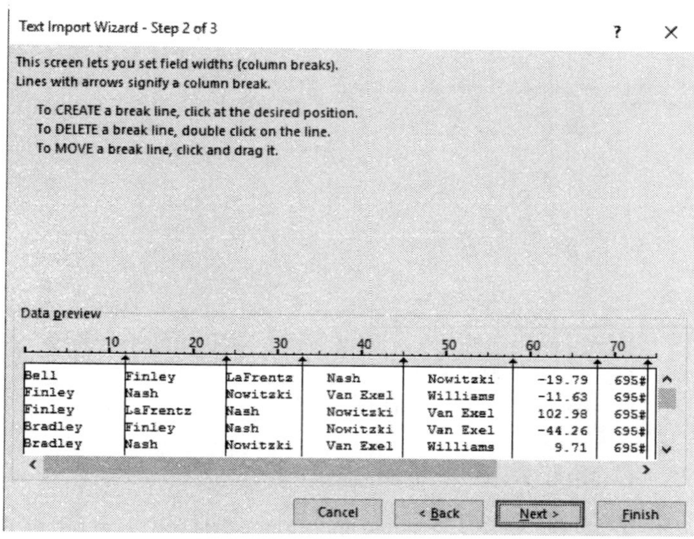

FIGURE 39-2 Step 2 of the Text Import Wizard, after selecting the Fixed Width option.

If you select Delimited in step 1, you'll see the second step of the Text Import Wizard that's shown in Figure 39-3. In this example, I've selected Space as the delimiter. Selecting the Treat Consecutive Delimiters As One option ensures that consecutive spaces result in only a single column break. I recommend keeping Tab selected because many Excel add-ins do not work properly if Tab is cleared.

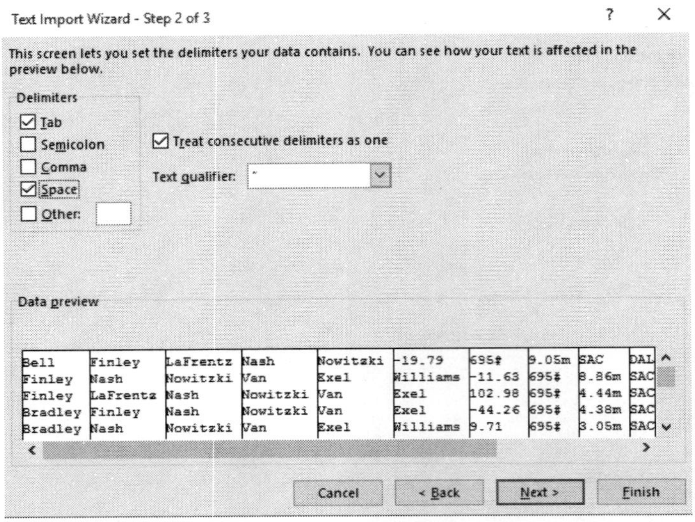

FIGURE 39-3 Step 2 of the Text Import Wizard, after selecting the Delimited option.

When you click Next, you're sent to the third step in the wizard, which is shown in Figure 39-4. By selecting the General option as the format, you direct Excel to treat numerical data as numbers and other values as text.

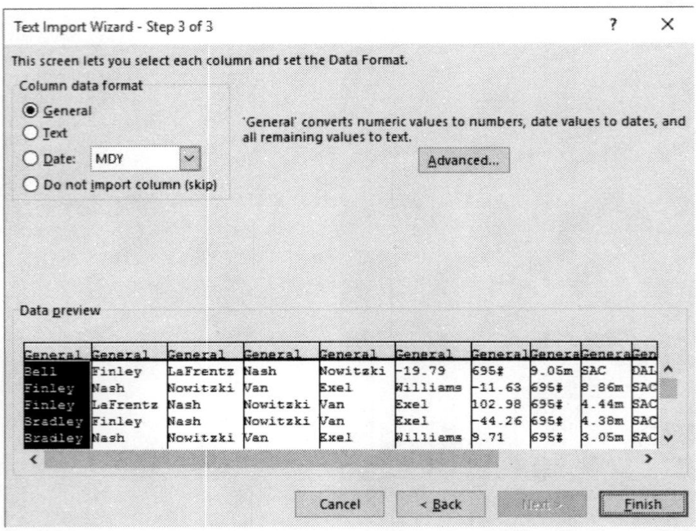

FIGURE 39-4 Step 3 of the wizard, in which you can select a format to apply to the data you're importing.

When you click Finish, the wizard imports the data into Excel, as shown in Figure 39-5.

	A	B	C	D	E	F	G	H	I	J
1	Bell	Finley	LaFrentz	Nash	Nowitzki	-19.79	695#	9.05m	SAC	DAL*
2	Finley	Nash	Nowitzki	Excel	Williams	-11.63	695#	8.86m	SAC	DAL*
3	Finley	LaFrentz	Nash	Nowitzki	Excel	102.98	695#	4.44m	SAC	DAL*
4	Bradley	Finley	Nash	Nowitzki	Excel	-44.26	695#	4.38m	SAC	DAL*
5	Bradley	Nash	Nowitzki	Excel	Williams	9.71	695#	3.05m	SAC	DAL*
6	Bell	Finley	LaFrentz	Nowitzki	Excel	-121.5	695#	2.73m	SAC	DAL*
7	Bell	LaFrentz	Nowitzki	Excel	Williams	39.35	695#	2.70m	SAC	DAL*
8	Bradley	Finley	Nowitzki	Excel	Williams	86.87	695#	2.45m	SAC	DAL*
9	Bradley	Nash	Excel	Williams	Rigaudeau	-54.55	695#	2.32m	SAC	DAL*
10	Finley	LaFrentz	Excel	Williams	Rigaudeau	-26.4	695#	1.73m	SAC	DAL*
11	Bradley	Finley	Nash	Nowitzki	Williams	91.89	695#	1.70m	SAC	DAL*
12	Bell	Finley	Nash	Nowitzki	Excel	34.18	695#	1.05m	SAC	DAL*
13	LaFrentz	Nash	Nowitzki	Excel	Williams	-50.9	695#	1.02m	SAC	DAL*
14	Bell	Bradley	Finley	Nash	Nowitzki	1.42	695#	1.00m	SAC	DAL*
15	Bradley	Finley	Excel	Williams	Rigaudeau	46.75	695#	0.93m	SAC	DAL*
16	Bell	Bradley	Nowitzki	Excel	Williams	-314.43	695#	0.60m	SAC	DAL*

FIGURE 39-5 An Excel file with lineup information.

Each player is listed in a separate column (columns A–E); column F contains the rating of each lineup, column G contains the game number, column H contains the minutes played by each lineup, and columns I and J list the two teams playing in the game. After saving the file as an Excel workbook (.xlsx), you can use all of the analytic capabilities of Excel to analyze the performance of Dallas's line-ups. For example, you could calculate the average performance of the team when Dirk Nowitzki is on or off the court.

Problems

1. The file Kingslineups.docx contains performance ratings for some of the Sacramento Kings lineups. Import this data into Excel.
2. In the example discussed in this chapter, the time each lineup played (column H) ends with an *m*. Modify the file so that the time played by each lineup is an actual number.

CHAPTER 40

Validating data

Questions answered in this chapter:

- I'm entering scores from professional basketball games into Excel. I know that a team scores from 50 to 200 points per game. I once entered 1,000 points instead of 100 points, which messed up my analysis. Is there a way to have Excel prevent me from making this type of error?
- I'm entering the date and amount of my business expenses for a new year. Early in the year, I often enter the previous year in the date field by mistake. Is there a way I can set up Excel to prevent me from making this type of error?
- I'm entering a long list of numbers. Can I have Excel warn me if I enter a nonnumeric value?
- My assistant needs to enter state abbreviations when she enters dozens and dozens of sales transactions. Can we set up a list of state abbreviations to minimize the chance that she'll enter an incorrect abbreviation?

Our work often involves mind-numbing data entry. When you're entering a lot of information into Microsoft Excel, it's easy to make an error. The data validation feature in Excel 2016 can greatly lessen the chances that you'll commit a costly error. To set up data validation, you begin by selecting the cell range that you want to apply data validation to. Click Data Validation on the Data tab of (in the Data Tools group), and then specify the criteria (as you'll see in this chapter's examples) that Excel uses to flag any invalid data that's entered.

Answers to this chapter's questions

I'm entering scores from professional basketball games into Excel. I know that a team scores from 50 to 200 points per game. I once entered 1,000 points instead of 100 points, which messed up my analysis. Is there a way to have Excel prevent me from making this type of error?

Let's suppose that you're going to enter into cells A2:A11 the number of points scored by the home team; in cells B2:B11, you'll enter the number of points scored by the visiting team. (You'll find the work I did to solve this problem in the file Nbadvl.xlsx.) You want to ensure that each value entered in the range A2:B11 is a whole number from 50 through 200.

Begin by selecting the range A2:B11, and then choose Data Validation on the Data tab. Select the Settings tab, select Whole Number from the Allow list, and then fill in the Data Validation dialog box as shown in Figure 40-1.

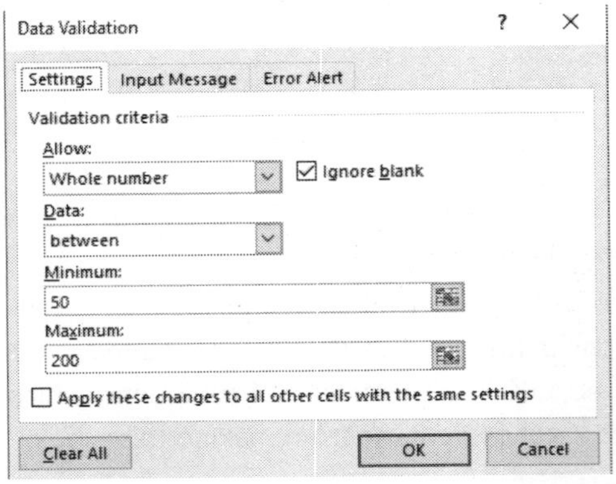

FIGURE 40-1 Use the Settings tab in the Data Validation dialog box to set up the data-validation criteria.

Excel's default response to invalid data (called an *error alert*) is a message stating, "The value entered is not valid. A user has restricted values that can be entered into the cell." You can use the Error Alert tab in the Data Validation dialog box (see Figure 40-2) to change the nature of the error alert, including the icon, the title for the message box, and the text of the message itself. On the Input Message tab, you can create a prompt that informs a user about the type of data that can be safely entered. The message is displayed as a comment in the selected cell. For example, I entered an error alert that states, **Please enter a whole number between 50 and 200.** After typing a number that violates that criteria, say 34, in cell E5, you would then see the message shown in Figure 40-3.

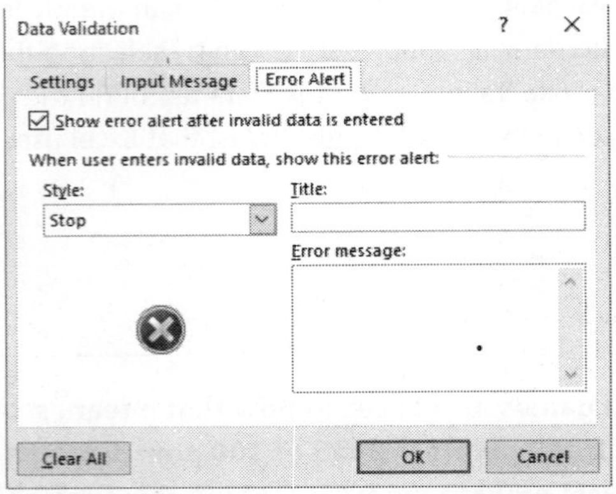

FIGURE 40-2 The Error Alert tab options in the Data Validation dialog box.

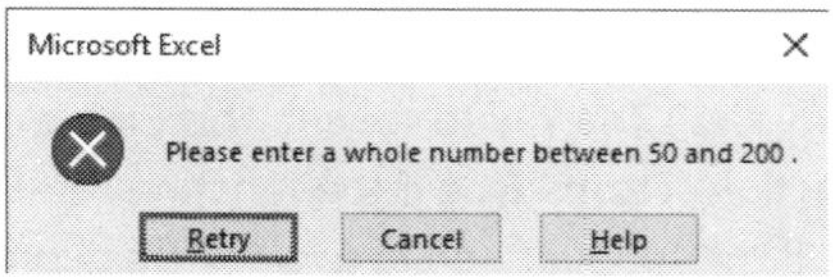

FIGURE 40-3 The error alert for the basketball data-validation example.

I'm entering the date and amount of my business expenses for a new year. Early in the year, I often enter the previous year in the date field by mistake. Is there a way I can set up Excel to prevent me from making this type of error?

Suppose it is early in 2017 and you are entering the date in the cell range A2:A20. (See the file Datedv.xlsx.) Simply select the range A2:A20, and then choose Data Validation from the Data Tools group on the Data tab. Fill in the Settings tab of the Data Validation dialog box as shown in Figure 40-4: I selected Date from the Allow options, selected Greater Than Or Equal To from the Data options list, selected 1/1/2017 as the start date, and clicked OK. Now you will not be allowed to enter any date earlier than 1/1/2017.

FIGURE 40-4 Use settings such as these to ensure the validity of the dates you enter.

If you enter a date in this cell range that occurs earlier than January 1, 2017, you'll be warned about the error. For example, entering **1/15/2016** in cell A3 will bring up the error alert you define.

I'm entering a long list of numbers. Can I have Excel warn me if I enter a nonnumeric value?

To unleash the full power of data validation, you need to use the Custom setting. When you select Custom in the Allow list on the Settings tab of the Data Validation dialog box (see Figure 40-5), you use a formula to define valid data. A formula you enter for data validation works the same way as a formula used for conditional formatting, which is described in Chapter 24, "Conditional formatting." You enter a formula that is true if and only if the content of the first cell in the selected range is valid. When you click OK in the Data Validation dialog box, the formula is copied to the remaining cells in the range. When you enter a value in a cell in the selected range, Excel displays an error alert if the formula you entered returns False for that value.

To illustrate the use of the Custom setting, let's suppose that you want to ensure that each entry in the cell range B2:B20 is a number. (See the file Numberdv.xlsx.) The key to solving this problem is in using the Excel ISNUMBER function. The ISNUMBER function returns True if the function refers to a cell that contains numeric data. The function returns False if the function refers to a cell that contains a nonnumeric value.

After selecting the cell range B2:B20 and placing the cursor in B2, display the Data tab, click Data Validation in the Data Tools group, and then fill in the Settings tab of the Data Validation dialog box as shown in Figure 40-5: I selected Custom from the Allow options and entered in the Formula box =ISNUMBER(B2).

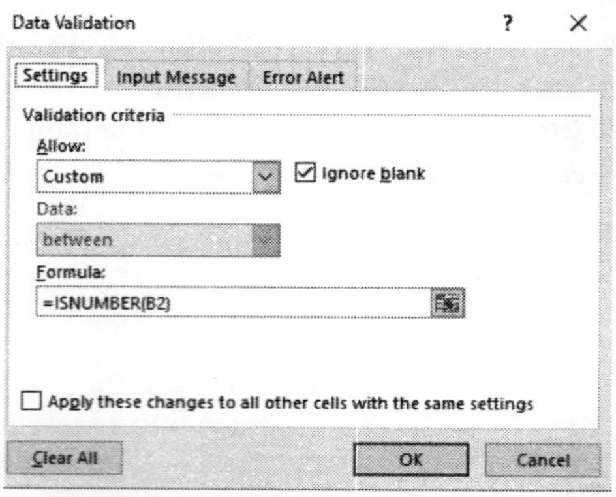

FIGURE 40-5 Using the ISNUMBER function to ensure that the data in a range is numeric.

Now you'll receive an error prompt if you try to enter any nonnumeric value in B2:B20. For example, if you type John in cell B3, you receive an error prompt.

If you click Data Validation while working in cell B3, the formula shown in Figure 40-5 is displayed as =ISNUMBER(B3). This demonstrates that the formula entered in cell B2 is copied in the correct fashion. Entering John in cell B3 causes =ISNUMBER(B3) to return False, so you receive the error alert.

My assistant needs to enter state abbreviations when she enters dozens and dozens of sales transactions. Can we set up a list of state abbreviations to minimize the chance that she'll enter an incorrect abbreviation?

The key to this data validation problem is to use the List validation criteria in the Allow options. Begin by entering a list of state abbreviations. See the file Statedv.xlsx. In this example, I used the range I6:I55 and named the range *abbrev*. Next, select the range in which you'll enter state abbreviations. The example uses D5:D156. After clicking Data Validation on the Data tab, fill in the Data Validation dialog box as shown in Figure 40-6: I selected List from the Allow options, entered =abbrev in the Source box, and clicked OK.

Now, whenever you select a cell in the range D5:D156, clicking the drop-down arrow displays a list of state abbreviations, as shown in Figure 40-7. Only abbreviations that appear on the list are valid values in this range. If you do not use the drop-down list and instead type a state abbreviation, you'll receive an error message if you enter an incorrect abbreviation (such as ALK for Alaska).

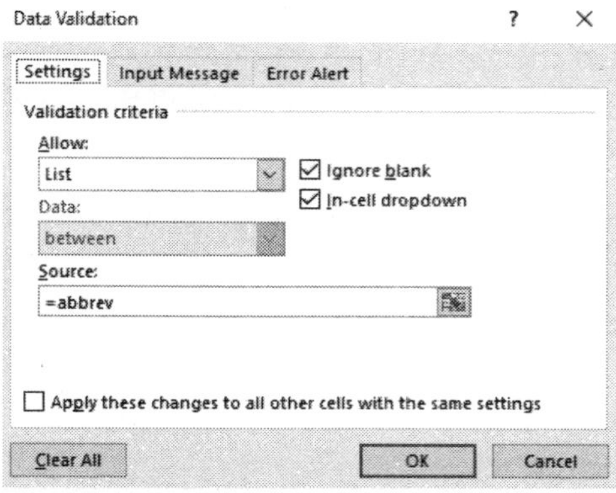

FIGURE 40-6 Using the Data Validation dialog box to define a list of valid values.

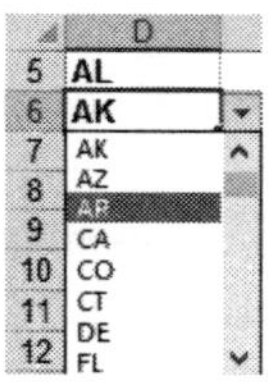

FIGURE 40-7 A drop-down list of state abbreviations.

Remarks

- If you press F5, click Special in the Go To dialog box and then check Data Validation, Excel selects all the cells with data validation settings. You can also use the Go To Special dialog box to select all the cells containing conditional formatting.
- In versions of Excel prior to Excel 2010, if you wanted to use a data validation drop-down list based on a data source list in a different worksheet, you needed to name the list (as I did in this chapter's example) for the drop-down list to work. In Excel 2010 and later, this limitation has been removed.
- If you use the dynamic-range technique described in Chapter 22, "The OFFSET function," changes you make (adding or deleting items) to the data-source list are automatically reflected in the drop-down box. (See Problem 10.) Also, if you name the data-source list as an Excel table (see Chapter 26, "Tables"), changes in the data source are reflected in the drop-down list, as long as you point to the list range and do not try to type the table name.
- Suppose you want to use a drop-down list to select a company you sell candy bars to. You want another drop-down list that you can use to select the list of candy bars you sell at the selected store. The problem is that the same set of candy bars might not be sold at each store. How do you create such a nested-list selection? Suppose the stores are Target and CVS. Suppose you assign a range name of *Target* to the list of candy bars sold at Target and a range name of *CVS* to the list of candy bars sold at CVS. If the drop-down list for store selection is

in, for example, A20, you could create the appropriate drop-down list in cell B20 by clicking Data Validation and filling in, for the list selected, the formula =INDIRECT(A20). As I discussed in Chapter 23, "The INDIRECT function," if A20 contains CVS, the list will key off the range *CVS* that contains all candy bars sold at CVS, and so on. See Problem 11.

- To clear data validation from a range, select the range, choose Data Validation on the Data tab, and then select Clear All.
- If you have a long list, you probably want to invoke Excel's Autocomplete feature. If you start the range for your drop-down list in the cell below the end of the list (no blank cells allowed), then Autocomplete will work. See the file Fruitlist.xlsx.
- You can also use data validation to set up criteria based on the length of text in a cell (see Problem 4) or the time of day (see Problem 15).

Problems

1. You are entering nonnegative whole numbers in the cell range C1:C20. Enter a data-validation setting that ensures that each entry is a nonnegative whole number.
2. You are entering in the cell range C1:C15 the dates of transactions that occurred during July 2004. Enter a data-validation setting that ensures that each date entered occurs in July 2004.
3. With the List option in the group of data-validation settings, you can generate an error message if a value that is not included in a list is entered in the cell range you're validating. Suppose you're entering employee first names in the cell range A1:A10. The only employees of the company are Jen, Greg, Vivian, Jon, and John. Use the List option to ensure that no one misspells a first name.
4. With the Text Length option in the group of data-validation settings, you can generate an error message when the number of characters in a cell does not match the number you define. Use the Text Length option to ensure that each cell in the range C1:C10 will contain at most five characters (including spaces).
5. You are entering employee names in the cell range A1:A10. Use data validation to ensure that no employee's name is entered more than twice. Hint: Use the Custom setting and the COUNTIF function.
6. You are entering product ID codes in the cell range A1:A15. Product ID codes must always end with the characters *xyz*. Use data validation to ensure that each product ID code entered ends with *xyz*. Hint: Use the Custom setting and the RIGHT function.
7. Suppose you want every entry in the cell range B2:B15 to contain text and not a numerical value. Use data validation to ensure that entering a numerical value returns an error. Hint: Use the ISTEXT function.

8. Set up a data-validation procedure that ensures that all numbers typed in column E will contain exactly two decimal places. Hint: Use the LEN and FIND functions.

9. The file Latitude.xlsx contains a formula to compute the distance between two cities using their latitude and longitude. The file also contains the latitude and longitude of various US cities. Set up a drop-down list so that when you select a city in cell P2 and another city in cell Q2, the distance between the cities is computed in Q10.

10. Ensure that if new cities are added to the list of cities in Problem 9, the drop-down list will include the new cities.

11. The file Candybardata.xlsx contains a list of stores where you sell candy bars. The worksheet also contains the types of candy bars you sell at each store and the price charged for each candy bar. Set up your worksheet so that users can enter or select both the store and a candy bar from a drop-down list and have the price show up in D19.

    - Enable users to select a store from the drop-down box in B19.
    - Set up a drop-down list in C13 to let users choose a type of candy bar from a list containing only those candy bars sold at a selected store. Hint: Use the INDIRECT function when defining the list.
    - If you change the store in B19, then C19 might temporarily not list a candy bar sold at the newly selected store. Ensure that in C19, your worksheet says *Make selection above* if this is the case. For example, if B19 contains CVS and C13 contains *gumballs*, then C19 should display *Make selection above.*

12. You have a $100,000 expense budget. In column A, you will enter expenses as they are incurred. Set up a data-validation criterion that ensures that the total expenses listed in column E do not exceed your budget.

13. Set up a data-validation criterion that ensures that a column of numbers is entered in descending order.

14. Set up data-validation criteria that ensures that a person can enter only dates that are on Monday through Friday. Hint: The WEEKDAY function returns a 1 for Sunday, a 2 for Monday, and so on.

15. Set up data-validation criteria that ensures that the time entered in the cell range A1:A20 will be a morning time.

CHAPTER 41

Summarizing data by using histograms and Pareto charts

Questions answered in this chapter:

- People often say that a picture is worth a thousand words. Can I use Excel to create a picture (called a *histogram*) that summarizes the values in a data set?
- What are some common shapes of histograms?
- What can I learn by comparing histograms from different data sets?
- How do I create a Pareto chart?

The ability to summarize a large data set is important. The three tools used most often to summarize data in Microsoft Excel are histograms, descriptive statistics, and PivotTables. In this chapter, I discuss the use of histograms for summarizing data. Prior to Excel 2016, you used the Data Analysis add-in to create histograms. The histograms created by means of the Data Analysis add-in did not update when new data was added. Excel 2016 provides new capabilities to create beautiful histograms that automatically update to include new data. I cover descriptive statistics in Chapter 42, "Summarizing data by using descriptive statistics," and PivotTables in Chapter 43, "Using PivotTables and slicers to describe data."

Answers to this chapter's questions

People often say that a picture is worth a thousand words. Can I use Excel to create a picture (called a *histogram*) that summarizes the values in a data set?

A histogram is a commonly used tool to summarize data. Essentially, a histogram tells you how many *observations* (another term for data points) fall in various ranges of values. For example, a histogram created from monthly Cisco stock returns might show how many monthly returns Cisco had from 0 percent through 10 percent, 11 percent through 20 percent, and so on. The ranges in which you group data are referred to as *bin ranges*.

Let's look at how to construct and interpret histograms that summarize the values of monthly returns for Cisco and GM stock in the years 1990–2000. You'll find this data (and returns for other stocks) in the file Stock.xlsx. Figure 41-1 shows a subset of the data (in the Stockprices worksheet). During March 1990 (row 52), for example, Cisco stock increased in value by 1.075 percent.

	B	C	D	E	F
48					
49			min	-0.24032043	-0.2025
50			max	0.276619107	0.33898
51	Microsoft	GE	Intel	GM	CSCO
52	0.121518984	0.040485829	0.037267081	0.022284122	0.01075
53	0.047404062	-0.00389105	-0.05389221	-0.03542234	0.01064
54	0.258620679	0.083515622	0.221518993	0.115819208	0.04211
55	0.04109589	0.005444646	-0.02590674	-0.02056555	0.07071
56	-0.125	0.034296028	-0.05319149	-0.02099738	-0.0377
57	-0.07518797	-0.13438046	-0.25	-0.1313673	-0.0294
58	0.024390243	-0.11338709	-0.00374532	-0.08805031	-0.0909
59	0.011904762	-0.04587156	0.007518797	0.013793103	0.31111
60	0.13333334	0.052884616	0.119402982	0.013605442	0.33898
61	0.041522492	0.057260275	0.026666667	-0.05821918	0.13608
62	0.303986698	0.115468413	0.188311681	0.054545455	0.30362
63	0.057324842	0.070468754	0.043715846	0.100689657	-0.0427
64	0.022891566	0.023897059	-0.02094241	-0.0443038	-0.1295
65	-0.06713781	0.016157989	0.053475935	-0.05298013	0.22051
66	0.108585857	0.09908127	0.131979689	0.217482507	0.08403
67	-0.06890661	-0.0420712	-0.16591929	-0.05507246	-0.0543
68	0.078899086	-0.01013514	0.010752688	-0.02453988	0.28689
69	0.159863949	0.022184301	0.053191491	-0.03396227	0.15605
70	0.043988269	-0.06664441	-0.14646465	-0.01644737	-0.0964

FIGURE 41-1 Monthly stock returns.

When constructing histograms with Excel, you can let Excel define the bin ranges or you can define the bin ranges yourself. If Excel defines the bin ranges, you could end up with weird-looking bin ranges, such as –12.53 percent to 4.52 percent. For this reason, I prefer to define the ranges myself.

A good way to start defining bin ranges for a histogram (you can think of defining bin ranges as setting boundaries) is to divide the range of values (between the smallest and largest) into 8 to 15 equally spaced categories. All the monthly returns for Cisco are from –30 percent through 40 percent, so I chose bin range boundaries of –30 percent, –20 percent, –10 percent, 0 percent, and so on up to 40 percent.

To create bin ranges, I first enter **CSCO, 0.4, 0.3, 0.2,..., –0.2, –0.3** (the boundaries of the bin ranges) in cells H54:H62. Next, on the Data tab, in the Analysis group, I click Data Analysis to open the Data Analysis dialog box. The dialog box lists the functions of the Analysis ToolPak, which contains many of the statistical capabilities in Excel.

> **Note** If the Data Analysis command doesn't appear on the Data tab, click the File tab, click Options, and then click Add-Ins in the left pane. In the Manage box, click Excel Add-Ins, and then click Go. In the Add-Ins dialog box, select Analysis ToolPak (the first choice, not Analysis ToolPak - VBA), and then click OK. Now you can access the Analysis ToolPak functions by clicking Data Analysis in the Analysis group on the Data tab.

By clicking Histogram in the Data Analysis dialog box (and then clicking OK), you open the Histogram dialog box shown in Figure 41-2.

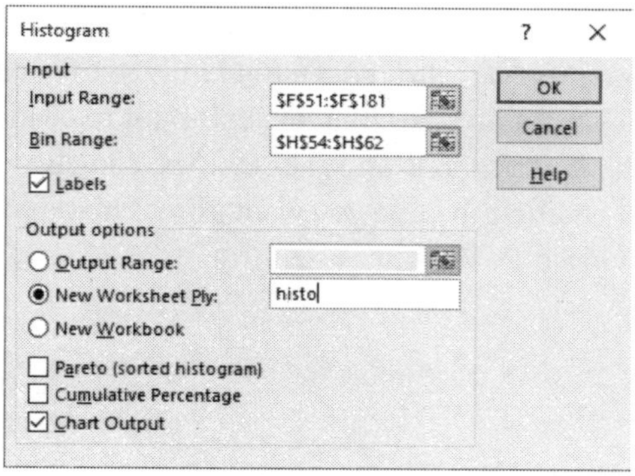

FIGURE 41-2 The Histogram dialog box for the Cisco histogram.

Here's how to fill in the dialog box as it's shown:

- Select the input range (F51:F181). (To select the range F51:F181, you can select cell F51 and then press Ctrl+Shift+Down arrow. This takes you to the bottom of the column.) This range includes all the data you want to use to create the histogram. I included the label *CSCO* from cell F51 because when you do not include a label in the first row, the x-axis of the histogram is often labeled with a number, which can be confusing.
- Select the bin range (H54:H62), which includes the boundaries of the bin ranges. Excel creates bins of –30 percent through –20 percent, –20 percent through –10 percent, and so on up to 30–40 percent.
- Check the Labels option because the first rows of both the bin range and the input range contain labels.
- In the Output Options, select New Worksheet Ply to create the histogram in a new worksheet (named *histo*).
- Select Chart Output, or Excel will not create a histogram.

Click OK in the Histogram dialog box. The Cisco histogram will look like the one shown in Figure 41-3.

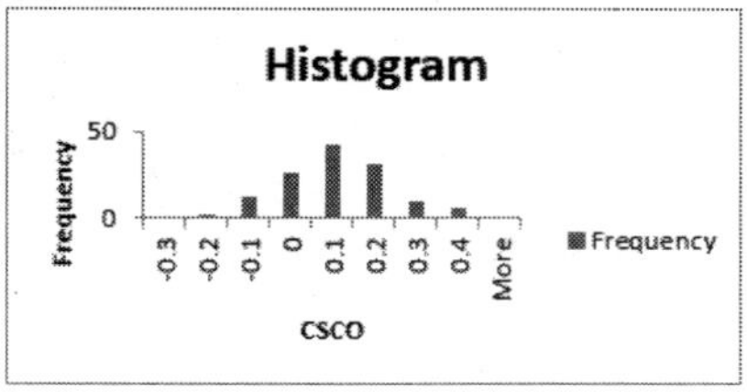

FIGURE 41-3 The Cisco histogram created by using an Excel Analysis ToolPak function.

When you create the histogram, you'll see gaps between the bars. To remove these gaps, right-click any bar on the graph and choose Format Data Series. On the Format Data Series pane, in the Series Options section, drag Gap Width to 0%. You might also see that a label does not appear for each bar. If all the labels do not appear, widen the graph by selecting it and dragging a side handle (circle shape), where your cursor changes to two arrows. You can also reduce the font size to make a hidden label appear. To reduce the font size, right-click the graph axis (the text you want to change), and then click Font. In the Font dialog box, change the font size to 5, and click OK. You can also change the title of the chart by selecting the text and entering the title you want. After I made some of these changes, the histogram appears as its shown in Figure 41-4.

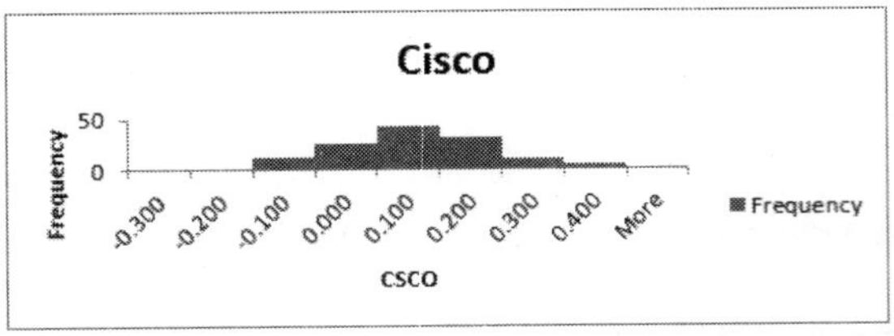

FIGURE 41-4 Changing the format of different elements in the chart.

Notice that Cisco returns are most likely between 0 and 10 percent per month, and the height of the bars drops off as the graph moves away from the tallest bar. When you create the histogram, you also obtain the bin-range frequency summary shown in Figure 41-5.

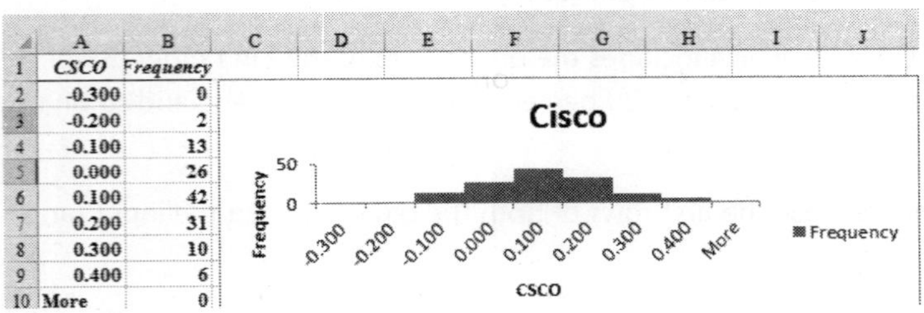

FIGURE 41-5 The Cisco bin-range frequencies.

From the bin-range frequencies, you can learn, for example, that for two months, Cisco's return was greater than –30 percent and less than or equal to –20 percent; for 13 months, the monthly return was greater than –20 percent and less than or equal to –10 percent.

If you add new Cisco monthly returns or even if you just modify the existing monthly returns, your histogram will not change unless you rerun the Data Analysis histogram procedure.

Excel 2016 provides an easy option to create better-looking histograms that automatically update with new data. To illustrate the use of the new Excel 2016 histogram chart, please open the file Iqtemp.xlsx (in this chapter's Templates folder), which contains a sample of 1,083 sixth-grade students' IQs. (See Figure 41-6.)

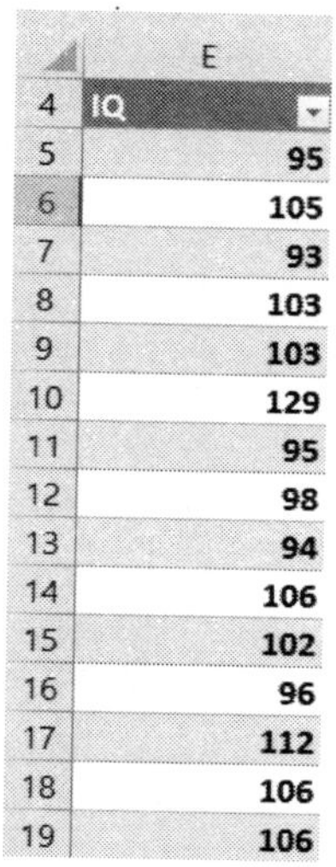

	E
4	IQ
5	95
6	105
7	93
8	103
9	103
10	129
11	95
12	98
13	94
14	106
15	102
16	96
17	112
18	106
19	106

FIGURE 41-6 The IQ data.

After selecting the range E4:E1177, use Ctrl+T to set up the new data as a table (leave My Table Has Headers checked in the Create Table dialog box). This ensures that as we add new data, our histogram changes. Next, select all the data (including cell E4), and then, on the Insert tab, in the Charts group, click the drop-down arrow for the Insert Statistic Chart option (see Figure 41-7), and then select Histogram, as shown in Figure 41-8.

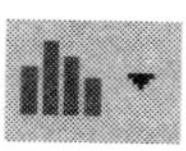

FIGURE 41-7 The Insert Statistic Chart icon.

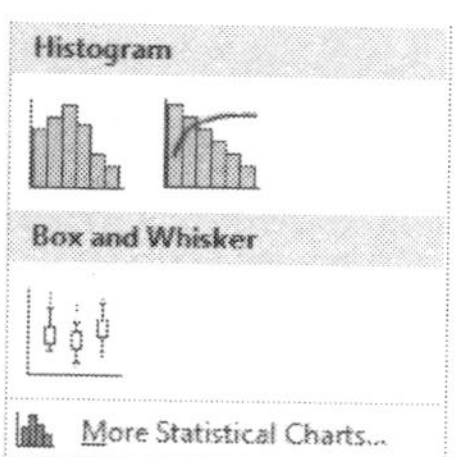

FIGURE 41-8 The statistical chart options.

You now obtain a handsome histogram. From the Design tab, you can choose from several options that change the histogram's appearance. In the Chart Styles group, I made the selection (third from the left) that shows how many data points fall in each range. (See Figure 41-9.)

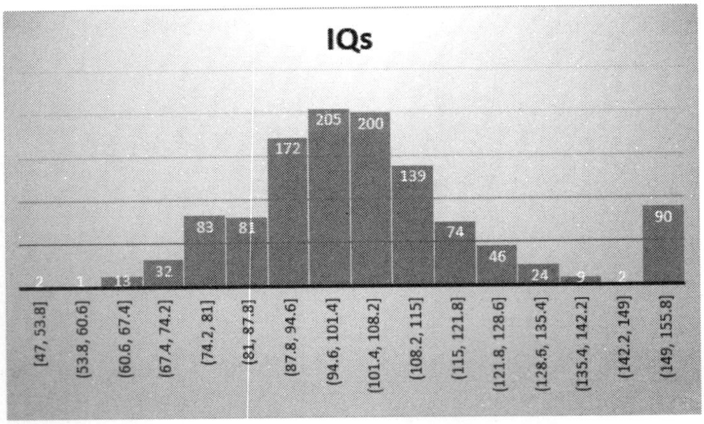

FIGURE 41-9 The IQ histogram.

By right-clicking on the axis and choosing Format Axis, you can change (as shown in Figure 41-10) the definition of the bin ranges and set the lower limit for the first bin and upper limit for the last bin.

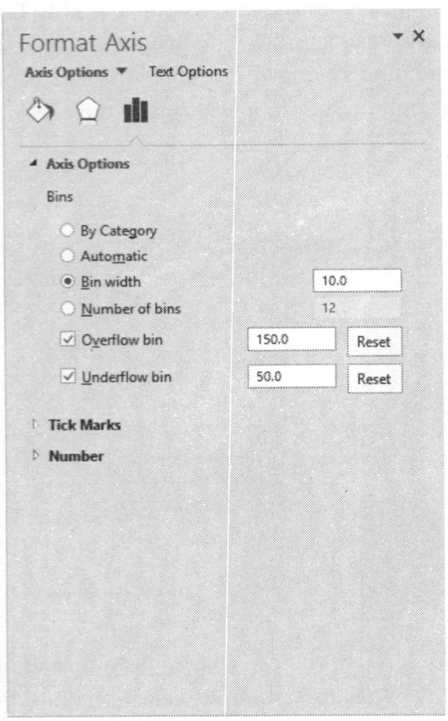

FIGURE 41-10 Changing the bin ranges.

I selected Underflow Bin and set the lower boundary of the first bin at 50. For Overflow Bin, I set the upper boundary of the last bin at 150. I also selected Bin Width and set the width of each bin equal to 10 (you might need to scroll to the right). By clicking Number (to expand that section),

I could have changed the format of the axis (to Currency, for instance, for monetary data.) After making these changes, the histogram appears as shown in Figure 41-11.

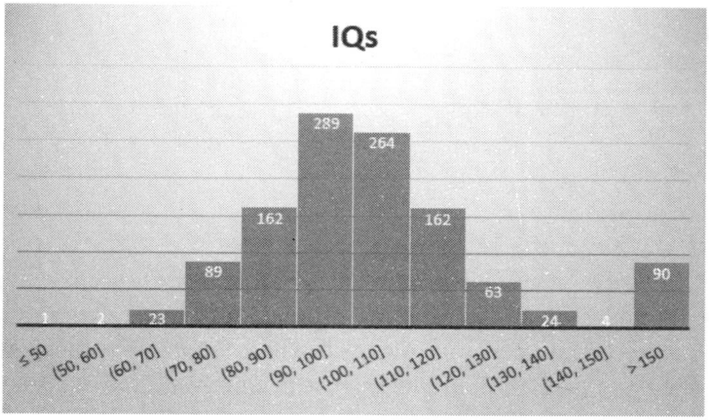

FIGURE 41-11 The histogram with updated bin ranges.

We find, for example, that 90 students have IQs greater than 150. A very smart group indeed! Note that if you add more data (say 20 people with IQs of 55) you will find that the histogram automatically updates to include the new data.

What are some common shapes of histograms?

For most data sets, a histogram created from the data will be classified as one of the following:

- Symmetric
- Skewed right (positively skewed)
- Skewed left (negatively skewed)
- Multiple peaks

Let's look at each type in more detail. See the file Skewexamples.xlsx.

- **Symmetric distribution** A histogram is *symmetric* if it has a single peak and looks approximately the same to the left of the peak as to the right of the peak. Test scores (such as IQ tests) are often symmetric. For example, the histograms of IQs (see cell Z42) might look like Figure 41-12. Notice that the height of the bars one bar away from the peak bar are approximately the same, the height of the bars two bars away from the peak bar are approximately the same, and so on. The bar labeled *105* represents all people with an IQ greater than 95 and less than or equal to 105, the bar labeled *65* represents all people having an IQ less than or equal to 65, and so on. Also note that the Cisco monthly returns are approximately symmetric.

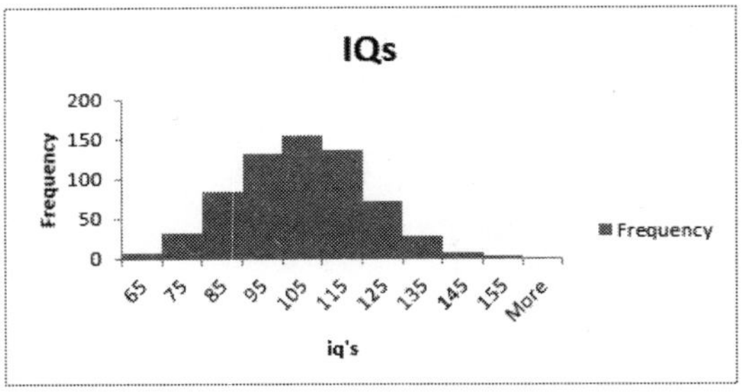

FIGURE 41-12 A symmetric histogram.

- **Skewed right** (positively skewed) A histogram is *skewed right* (positively skewed) if it has a single peak and the values of the data set extend much farther to the right of the peak than to the left of the peak. Many economic data sets (such as family or individual income) exhibit a positive skew. Figure 41-13 (see cell T24) shows an example of a positively skewed histogram created from a sample of family incomes.

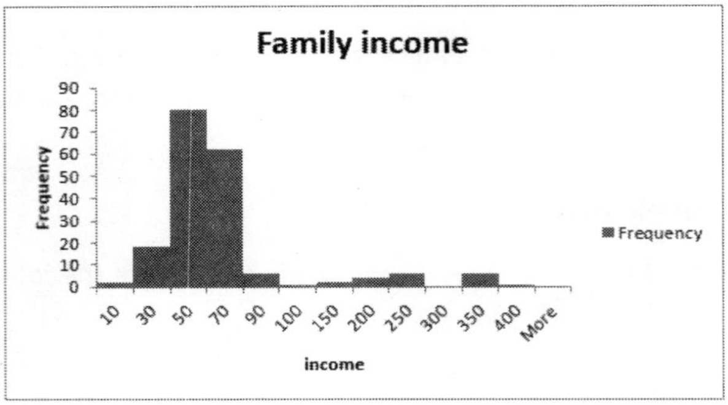

FIGURE 41-13 A positively skewed histogram created from family-income data.

- **Skewed left** (negatively skewed) A histogram is *skewed left* (negatively skewed) if it has a single peak and the values of the data set extend much farther to the left of the peak than to the right of the peak. Days from conception to birth are negatively skewed. An example is shown in cell Q7 and Figure 41-14. The height of each bar represents the number of pregnant women whose time from conception to birth fell in the given bin range. For example, two women gave birth fewer than 180 days after conception.

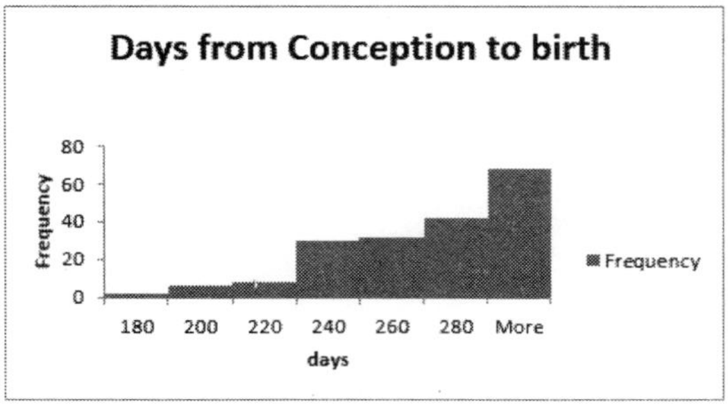

FIGURE 41-14 A negatively skewed histogram of data plotting days from conception to birth.

- **Multiple peaks** When a histogram exhibits *multiple peaks*, it usually means that data from two or more populations are being graphed together. For example, suppose the diameter of elevator rails produced by two machines yields the histogram shown in Figure 41-15. (See cell Q11 in the file Twinpeaks.xlsx.)

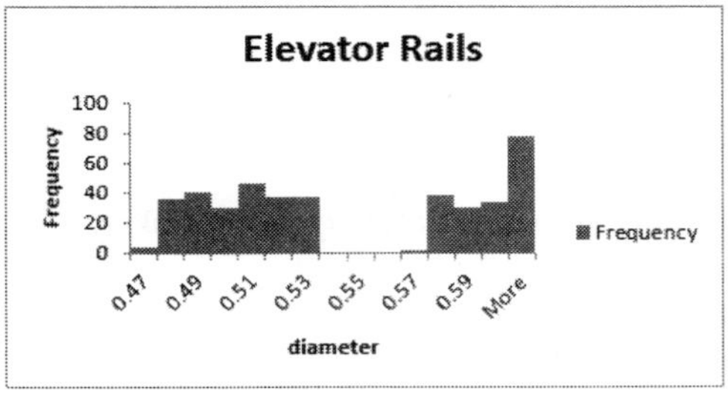

FIGURE 41-15 A multiple-peak histogram.

In this histogram, the data clusters into two separate groups. In all likelihood, each group of data corresponds to the elevator rails produced by one of the machines. If you assume that the diameter you want for an elevator rail is 0.55 inches, you can conclude that one machine is producing elevator rails that are too narrow, whereas the other machine is producing elevator rails that are too wide. You should follow up with your interpretation of this histogram by constructing a histogram that charts the elevator rails produced by each machine. This example shows why histograms are a powerful tool in quality control.

What can I learn by comparing histograms from different data sets?

Analysts are often asked to compare different data sets. For example, you might be asked how the monthly returns on GM and Cisco stock differ. To answer a question such as this, you can construct a histogram for GM by using the same bin ranges as for Cisco and then place one histogram above the other, as shown in Figure 41-16. See the Histograms worksheet of file Stock.xlsx.

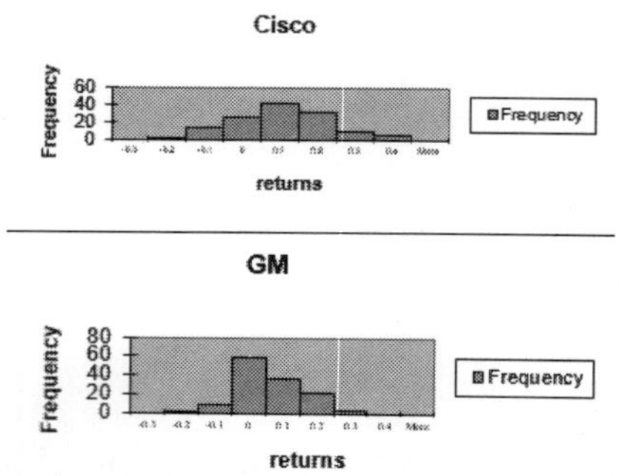

FIGURE 41-16 Using histograms that include the same bin ranges to compare different data sets.

By comparing these two histograms, you can draw two important conclusions:

- Typically, Cisco performed better than GM. You know this because the highest bar for Cisco is one bar to the right of the highest bar for GM. Also, the Cisco bars extend farther to the right than the GM bars.
- Cisco had more *variability*, or spread about the mean, than GM. Note that GM's peak bar contains 59 months, whereas Cisco's peak bar contains only 41 months. This shows that for Cisco, more of the returns are outside the bin that represents the most likely Cisco return. Cisco returns are more spread out than GM returns.

In Chapter 42, we'll use descriptive statistics and Boxplots to look at more details about the differences between the monthly returns on Cisco and GM.

How do I create a Pareto chart?

A *Pareto chart* is a type of chart that contains bars and line graphs. Individual values are portrayed in descending order by bars, and the cumulative total is represented by the line. Pareto charts are often used to illustrate the famous *80-20 rule* that was first discovered by the great Italian economist Vilfredo Pareto (1848–1923). The *Pareto rule* emphasizes the importance of few items in explaining a total. For example:

- 20 percent of products generate 80 percent of profits.
- 20 percent of people have 80 percent of the income.
- 80 percent of all technical support calls result from 20 percent of all possible problems.
- 20 percent of all websites get 80 percent of the hits.

To illustrate the creation of a Pareto chart with Excel 2016, open up the file Paretotemp.xlsx (from this chapter's Templates folder), which gives the revenue from each of a company's 100 products. (See Figure 41-17.)

	E	F
3	**Product**	**Revenue**
4	**Product 1**	**$30.00**
5	**Product 2**	**$340.00**
6	**Product 3**	**$11.60**
7	**Product 4**	**$37.20**
8	**Product 5**	**$25.20**
9	**Product 6**	**$8.40**
10	**Product 7**	**$38.00**
11	**Product 8**	**$38.40**
12	**Product 9**	**$9.60**
13	**Product 10**	**$29.20**
14	**Product 11**	**$14.80**
15	**Product 12**	**$10.00**
16	**Product 13**	**$22.40**
17	**Product 14**	**$29.60**

FIGURE 41-17 Data for a Pareto chart.

After selecting the data (cell range E3:F103), I chose the Insert Statistic Chart icon from the Insert tab (in the Charts group) and then chose Pareto, the second Histogram option. (See Figure 41-8, earlier) We obtain the Pareto chart shown in Figure 41-18. The products are now listed in order of descending sales. The line represents the cumulative percentage of sales generated by the products. We observe that our 10 best-selling products generate about 80 percent of the sales. Of course, if we made the source data a table, then new data would automatically be incorporated in the chart.

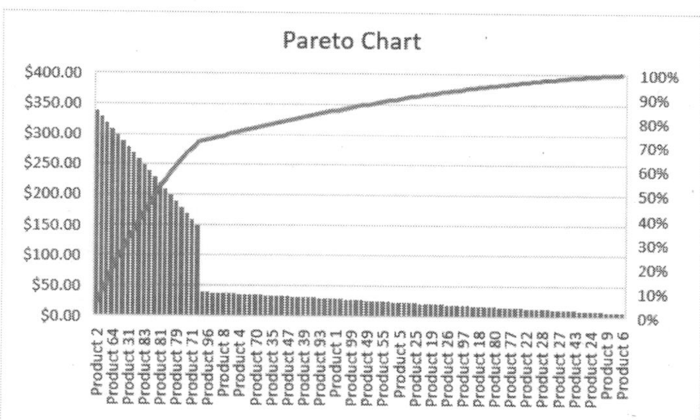

FIGURE 41-18 A Pareto chart.

After clicking the Pareto chart to select it, I chose the fifth option from the Design Tab (in the Chart Styles group) and obtained the chart shown in Figure 41-19.

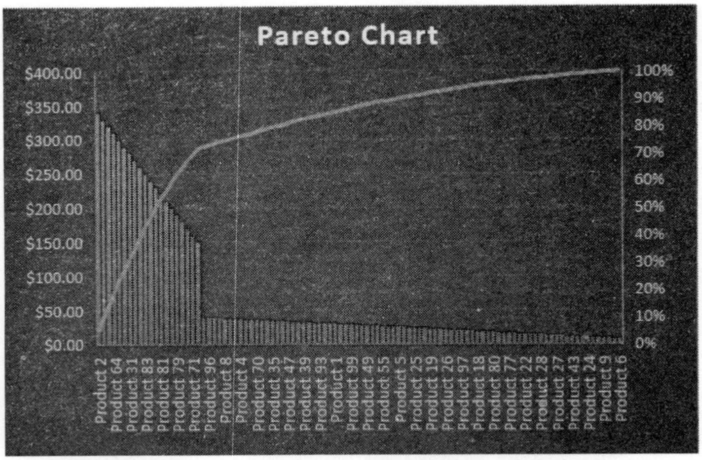

FIGURE 41-19 A Pareto chart created from the Design tab.

Problems

1. Use the data in Stock.xlsx to construct histograms for monthly returns for GE and Intel.
2. Use the data in Historicalinvest2009.xlsx to create histograms for annual returns on stocks and bonds. Then compare the annual returns of these stocks and bonds.
3. You are given (in the file Deming.xlsx) the measured diameter (in inches) for 500 rods produced by Rodco, as reported by the production foreman. A rod is considered acceptable if it is at least 1 inch in diameter. In the past, the diameter of the rods produced by Rodco has followed a symmetric histogram. Do the following:
   - Construct a histogram of these measurements.
   - Comment on any unusual aspects of the histogram.

   Can you guess what might have caused any unusual aspects of the histogram? Hint: One of quality-guru Edwards Deming's 14 points is to "Drive out fear."
4. The file Unemployment.xlsx contains monthly US unemployment rates. Create a histogram. Are the unemployment rates symmetric or skewed?
5. The file Teams.xlsx contains runs scored by major league baseball teams during a season. Create a histogram. Are the runs scored symmetric or skewed?
6. The file NFLpoints.xlsx contains points scored by NFL teams during a season. Create a histogram. Are points scored symmetric or skewed?
7. Using the data in the file Problem7data.xlsx, create a histogram that summarizes the heights of American men.

8. The data in the file Problem8data.xlsx contains the points scored by each Division I NCAA football team during the 2015 season. Create a histogram to summarize this data. Does the data appear to be symmetric?

9. The data in the file Problem9data.xlsx contains income of families in Smalltown, USA. Create a Pareto chart to summarize the family incomes.

CHAPTER 42

Summarizing data by using descriptive statistics

Questions answered in this chapter:

- What defines a typical value for a data set?
- How can I measure how much a data set spreads from its typical value?
- Together, what do the mean and standard deviation of a data set tell me about the data?
- How can I use descriptive statistics to compare data sets?
- For a given data point, can I easily find its percentile ranking within the data set? For example, how can I find the ninetieth percentile of a data set?
- How can I easily find the second largest or second smallest number in a data set?
- How can I rank numbers in a data set?
- What is the trimmed mean of a data set?
- When I select a range of cells, is there an easy way to get a variety of statistics that describe the data in those cells?
- Why do financial analysts often use the geometric mean to summarize the average return on a stock?
- How can I use boxplots to summarize and compare datasets?

In Chapter 41, "Summarizing data by using histograms and Pareto charts," I showed how you can describe data sets by using histograms. In this chapter, I show how to describe a data set by using particular characteristics of the data, such as the *mean*, *median*, *standard deviation*, and *variance*—measures that Microsoft Excel 2016 groups together as descriptive statistics. You can obtain the descriptive statistics for a set of data by clicking Data Analysis in the Analysis group on the Data tab (available as an add-in) and then selecting the Descriptive Statistics option. After you enter the relevant data and click OK, all the descriptive statistics of your data are displayed. You can also obtain descriptive statistics by using Excel functions. At the end of this chapter, I'll show how boxplots can be used to summarize and compare data sets.

Answers to this chapter's questions

What defines a typical value for a data set?

To illustrate the use of descriptive statistics, let's return to the Cisco and GM monthly stock return data in the file Stock.xlsx. To create a set of descriptive statistics for this data, click Data Analysis in the Analysis group on the Data tab, select Descriptive Statistics, and then click OK. Fill in the Descriptive Statistics dialog box as shown in Figure 42-1.

> **Note** If the Data Analysis command doesn't appear on the Data tab, click the File tab, click Options, and then click Add-Ins in the left pane. In the Manage list in the Excel Options dialog box, click Excel Add-Ins, and then click Go. In the Add-Ins dialog box, select Analysis ToolPak (the first choice, not Analysis ToolPak - VBA), and then click OK.

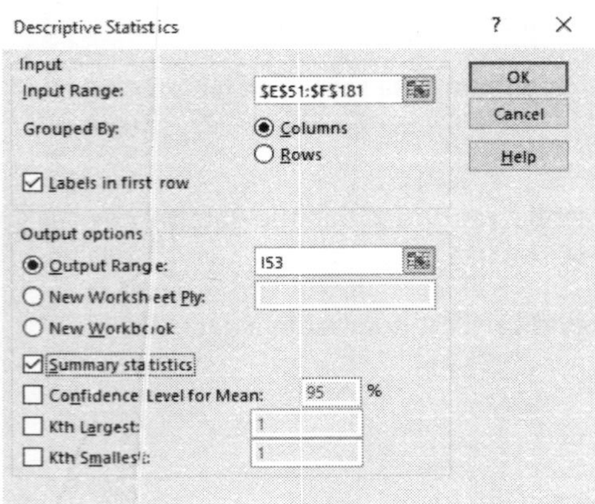

FIGURE 42-1 The Descriptive Statistics dialog box.

The input range I entered is the monthly Cisco and GM returns, located in the range E51:F181 (including the labels in row 51). I filled in the remainder of the Descriptive Statistics dialog box as shown in Figure 42-1 for the following reasons:

- I selected Columns in the Grouped By options because each data set is listed in a different column.
- I selected Labels In First Row because the first row of the data range contains labels and not data.
- I selected Output Range in the Output Options section, and I selected cell I53 of the current worksheet as the first cell in the output range.
- By selecting Summary Statistics, I ensured that I get the most commonly used descriptive-statistics measures for both the GM and Cisco monthly returns.

When you click OK, Excel calculates the descriptive statistics, as shown in Figure 42-2.

	I	J	K	L
53	*GM*		*CSCO*	
54				
55	Mean	0.009	Mean	0.056
56	Standard Error	0.008	Standard Error	0.011
57	Median	-0.005	Median	0.050
58	Mode	#N/A	Mode	0.051
59	Standard Deviation	0.090	Standard Deviation	0.122
60	Sample Variance	0.008	Sample Variance	0.015
61	Kurtosis	0.475	Kurtosis	-0.320
62	Skewness	0.224	Skewness	0.105
63	Range	0.517	Range	0.541
64	Minimum	-0.240	Minimum	-0.203
65	Maximum	0.277	Maximum	0.339
66	Sum	1.206	Sum	7.224
67	Count	130.000	Count	130.000

FIGURE 42-2 The descriptive statistics results for Cisco and GM stocks.

Now let's interpret the descriptive statistics that define a typical value (or a central location) for Cisco's monthly stock returns. The descriptive statistics output contains three measures of central location: *mean* (or *average*), *median*, and *mode*.

- **Mean** The mean of a data set is written as *x* and is simply the average of all observations in the sample. If the data values were $x_1, x_2, \ldots, x_n$, then the following equation calculates the mean:

  $$\bar{x} = \frac{1}{n}\sum \cdot x_i$$

  Here, *n* equals the number of observations in the sample, and x_i is the *i*th observation in the sample. We find that Cisco's mean monthly return is 5.6 percent per month.

  It is always true that the sum of the deviations of all values from the mean equals 0. Thus, you can think of a data set's mean as a *balancing point* for the data. Of course, without using the Descriptive Statistics option, you can obtain a sample's mean in Excel by applying the AVERAGE function to the appropriate cell range.

- **Median** The median of a sample is the *middle* observation when the data is listed from smallest to largest. If a sample contains an odd number of observations, the median is the observation that has as many observations below it as above it. Thus, for a sample of nine, the median would be the fifth smallest (or fifth largest) observation. When a sample includes an even number of observations, you can simply average the two middle observations. Essentially, the median is the fiftieth percentile of the data. For example, the median monthly return on Cisco's stock is 5 percent. You could also obtain this information by using the MEDIAN function.

- **Mode** The mode is the most frequently occurring value in the sample. If no value occurs more than once, the mode does not exist. For GM, no monthly return occurred more than once for the years 1990–2000, so the mode does not exist. For Cisco, the mode was approximately 5.14 percent. In versions of Excel prior to Excel 2010, you could also use the MODE function to compute the mode. If no data value occurred more than once, the MODE function returned #NA.

The problem is that a data set can have more than one mode, and the MODE function simply returned the first mode it found. For this reason, Excel 2010 introduced two functions: MODE.SNGL and MODE.MULT. (See the file Modefunctions.xlsx.)

MODE.SNGL performs exactly as the MODE function performed in earlier Excel versions. Earlier versions of Excel, however, do not recognize the MODE.SNGL function.

MODE.MULT is an *array function*. You'll learn more about array functions in Chapter 88, "Array formulas and functions." To use the MODE.MULT function (or any other array function), you must first select the range of cells to which the function will return values. Next, enter the function or formula. Finally, do not just press Enter; you must hold down the Ctrl key followed by the Shift key and then press Enter. (Or you can press Tab.) The problem with the MODE.MULT function is that you do not know in advance how many modes a data set has, so you do not know the correct size of the range that you need to select.

The file Modefunctions.xlsx (see Figure 42-3) shows the use of all three functions involving modes.

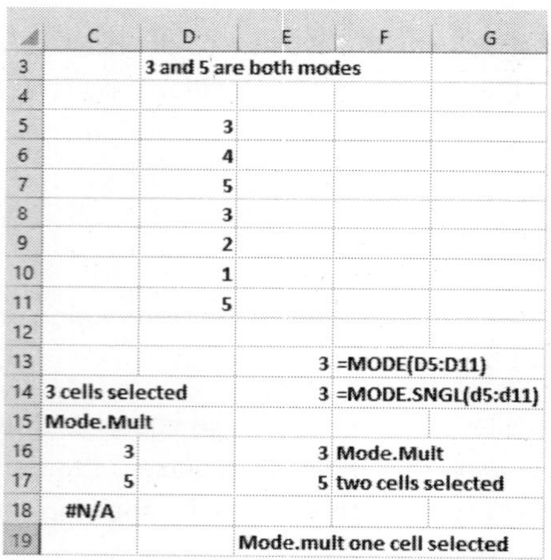

	C	D	E	F	G
3		3 and 5 are both modes			
4					
5		3			
6		4			
7		5			
8		3			
9		2			
10		1			
11		5			
12					
13			3	=MODE(D5:D11)	
14	3 cells selected		3	=MODE.SNGL(d5:d11)	
15	Mode.Mult				
16	3		3	Mode.Mult	
17	5		5	two cells selected	
18	#N/A				
19			Mode.mult one cell selected		

FIGURE 42-3 Examples of Excel's MODE functions.

The data set displayed in Figure 42-3 has two modes (3 and 5). In cell E13, I entered the old-school MODE function with the formula =MODE(D5:D11). Excel returned the first mode it found (3). In cell E14, the formula =MODE.SNGL(D5:D11) duplicates this result.

After selecting the cell range E16:E17, I array-entered the formula =MODE.MULT(D5:D11), and Excel returned both the modes (3 and 5). After selecting the cell range C16:C18 (a three-cell range), I array-entered the same formula, and C18 was filled with an #N/A because the data set had no third mode to fill the cell. Finally, I selected the single cell range E20 and array-entered the same formula. Because I selected a range containing a single cell, Excel returned only the first mode it found (3).

The mode is rarely used as a measure of central location. It is interesting to note, however, that for a symmetric data set, the mean, median, and mode are equal.

A natural question is whether the mean or median is a better measure of central location. Essentially, the mean is the best measure of central location if the data set does not exhibit an excessive skew. Otherwise, you should use the median as the measure of central location. If a data set is highly skewed, extreme values distort the mean. In this case, the median is a better measure of a typical data set value. For example, the US government reports median family income instead of mean family income because family income is highly positively skewed.

The *skewness measure* reported by the descriptive statistics output indicates whether a data set is highly skewed, in the following ways:

- A skew greater than +1 indicates a high degree of positive skew.
- A skew less than –1 indicates a high degree of negative skew.
- A skew between –1 and +1 inclusive indicates a relatively symmetric data set.

Thus, monthly returns of GM and Cisco exhibit a slight degree of positive skewness. Because the skewness measure for each data set is less than +1, the mean is a better measure of a typical return than the median. You can also use the SKEW function to compute the skew of a data set.

By the way, *kurtosis*, which sounds like a disease, is not a very important measure, although you can see that it is one of the descriptive statistics results listed in Figure 42-2. Kurtosis near 0 means a data set exhibits *peakedness* close to the normal (or standard bell-shaped) curve. (I'll discuss the normal curve in Chapter 70, "The normal random variable and Z-scores.") *Positive kurtosis* means that a data set is more peaked than a normal random variable, whereas *negative kurtosis* means that data is less peaked than a normal random variable. GM monthly returns are more peaked than a normal curve, whereas Cisco monthly returns are less peaked than a normal curve.

How can I measure how much a data set spreads from its typical value?

Let's consider two investments. Each yields an average of 20 percent per year. Before deciding which investment you prefer, you'd like to know about the spread, or riskiness, of the investment. The most important measures of the spread (or dispersion) of a data set from its mean are *sample variance*, *sample standard deviation*, and *range*.

We can discuss *sample variance* and *sample standard deviation* together. The sample variance s^2 is defined by the following formula:

$$\frac{1}{n-1}\sum(x_i - \bar{x})^2$$

You can think of the sample variance as the average squared deviation of the data from its mean. Intuitively, it seems like you should divide by *n* to compute a true average squared deviation, but for technical reasons you need to divide by *n–1*.

Dividing the sum of the squared deviations by *n–1* ensures that the sample variance is an unbiased measure of the true variance of the population from which the sampled data is drawn.

The sample standard deviation *s* is just the square root of s^2.

The following is an example of these computations for the three numbers 1, 3, and 5:

$$s^2 = \frac{1}{3-1}\,[(1-3)^2 + (3-3)^2 + (5-3)^2] = 4.$$

We find that these computations yield the following result:

$$s = \sqrt{4} = 2.$$

In the stock example, the sample standard deviation of monthly returns for Cisco is 12.2 percent with a sample variance of *0.015%²*. Naturally, %² is hard to interpret, so you usually look at the sample standard deviation. For GM, the sample standard deviation is 8.97 percent.

In Excel 2007 or earlier, the sample variance of a data set was computed with the VAR function, and the sample standard deviation was computed with the STDEV function. You can still use these functions in Excel 2016, but Excel 2010 added the equivalent functions VAR.S and STDEV.S. (The *S* stands for *sample*.) The relatively new functions VAR.P and STDEV.P compute the population variance and population standard deviation. To compute a population variance or standard deviation, simply replace *n-1* in the denominator of the definition of s^2 by n.

The *range* of a data set is the largest number in the data set minus the smallest number. Here, the range in the monthly Cisco returns is equal to 54 percent, and the range for GM monthly returns is 52 percent.

Together, what do the mean and standard deviation of a data set tell me about the data?

Assuming that a histogram follows a *Gaussian*, or *normal* population, the *rule of thumb* (set of related math rules) tells us the following:

- Approximately 68 percent of all observations are between *x–s* and *x+s*.
- Approximately 95 percent of all observations are between *x–2s* and *x+2s*.
- Approximately 99.7 percent of all observations are between *x–3s* and *x+3s*.

For example, you would expect that approximately 95 percent of all Cisco monthly returns are from –19 percent through 30 percent, as shown here:

Mean–2s = .056-2(.122) = –19% and Mean+2s = .056+2*(.122) = 30%*

Any observation more than two standard deviations away from the mean is called an *outlier*. For the Cisco data, 9 of 130 observations (or roughly 7 percent of all returns) are outliers. In general, the rule of thumb is less accurate for highly skewed data sets but is usually very accurate for relatively symmetric data sets, even if the data does not come from a normal population.

Many valuable insights can be obtained by finding causes of outliers. Companies should try to ensure that the causes of "good outliers" occur more frequently and the causes of "bad outliers" occur less frequently.

Using conditional formatting to highlight outliers

You'll find that it is often useful to highlight all outliers in a data set. An example is shown in Figure 42-4. (See the Stockprices worksheet in the Stock.xlsx file.)

	D	E	F
48			
49	min	-0.240	-0.203
50	max	0.277	0.339
51	INTC	GM	CSCO
52	0.037	0.022	0.011
53	-0.054	-0.035	0.011
54	0.222	0.116	0.042
55	-0.026	-0.021	0.071
56	-0.053	-0.021	-0.038
57	-0.250	-0.131	-0.029
58	-0.004	-0.088	-0.091
59	0.008	0.014	0.311
60	0.119	0.014	0.339
61	0.027	-0.058	0.136
62	0.188	0.055	0.304

FIGURE 42-4 Highlighting the outliers for Cisco with conditional formatting.

For example, to highlight the outliers for the Cisco data, you first compute the lower cutoff for an outlier (*mean–2s*) in cell J69 and the upper cutoff for an outlier (*mean+2s*) in cell J70. Next, select the entire range of Cisco returns (cells F52:F181). Then go to the first cell in the range (F52), select Conditional Formatting on the Home tab (in the Styles group), and select New Rule. In the New Formatting Rule dialog box, select Use A Formula To Determine Which Cells To Format, and then fill in the rest of the dialog box as shown in Figure 42-5: in the Format Values Where This Formula Is True box, enter the formula =OR(F52<$J$69,F52>$J$70).

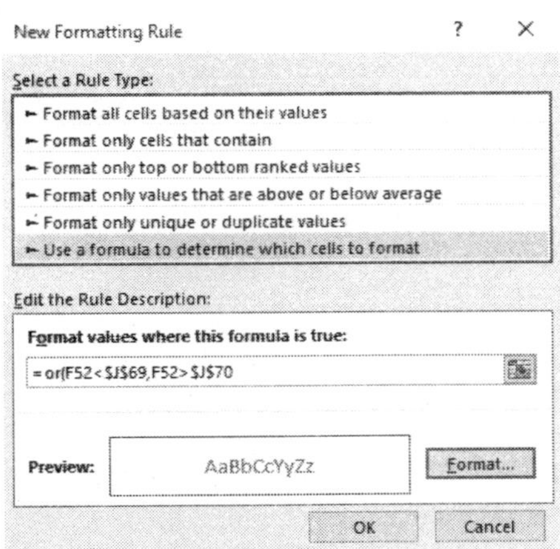

FIGURE 42-5 Conditional formatting rules to select outliers, as shown in the New Formatting Rule dialog box.

This condition ensures that if cell F52 is either more than *2s* above or below the mean monthly Cisco return, the format you select (a red font color in this case) will be applied to cell F52. This formatting condition is automatically copied to the selected range, and all outliers show up in red.

How can I use descriptive statistics to compare data sets?

You can use descriptive statistics to summarize the differences between data sets; for example, between Cisco and GM monthly returns. Looking at the shape and the measures and spread of a typical value, you can conclude the following:

- Typically (looking at either the mean or the median), Cisco monthly returns are higher than GM.
- Cisco monthly returns are more variable (looking at standard deviation, variance, and range) than monthly GM returns.
- Both Cisco and GM monthly returns exhibit slightly positive skews. GM monthly returns are more peaked than a normal curve, whereas Cisco monthly returns are less peaked than a normal curve.

Later in this chapter, I will show how boxplots make it easy to visually compare data sets.

For a given data point, can I easily find its percentile ranking within the data set? For example, how can I find the ninetieth percentile of a data set?

Before Excel 2010, the PERCENTILE and PERCENTRANK functions were useful when you wanted to determine an observation's relative position in a data set. Four related functions were added in Excel 2010: PERCENTILE.INC, PERCENTILE.EXC, PERCENTRANK.INC, and PERCENTRANK.EXC. The functions PERCENTILE.INC and PERCENTRANK.INC give results identical to the old PERCENTILE and PERCENTRANK functions. Take note that previous versions of Excel do not recognize these functions. Examples of how all these functions work are in the file Percentile.xlsx, shown in Figure 42-6.

	C	D	E	F	G	H
2		RANK	RANK			
3	Data	EXC	INC			
4	10	0.062	0	Percentile	EXC	INC
5	20	0.125	0.071	0.1	16	24
6	30	0.187	0.142	0.2	32	38
7	40	0.25	0.214	0.3	48	52
8	50	0.312	0.285	0.4	64	66
9	60	0.375	0.357	0.5	80	80
10	70	0.437	0.428	0.6	96	94
11	80	0.5	0.5	0.7	112	108
12	90	0.562	0.571	0.8	128	122
13	100	0.625	0.642	0.9	204	136
14	110	0.687	0.714			
15	120	0.75	0.785			
16	130	0.812	0.857			
17	140	0.875	0.928			
18	300	0.937	1			

FIGURE 42-6 Examples of the PERCENTILE and PERCENTRANK functions.

The PERCENTILE, PERCENTILE.INC, AND PERCENTILE.EXC functions return the percentile of a data set that you specify. The syntax of the these functions takes the form PERCENTILE.INC(data,k), which returns the *k*th percentile of the information in the cell range specified by data.

Consider a data set consisting of *n* pieces of data. The PERCENTILE and PERCENTILE.INC functions returned the *p*th percentile (0<p<1) as the 1+(n-1)p ranked item in the data set. For example, in H13, the formula PERCENTILE.INC(C4:C18,F13) computes the ninetieth percentile of the data in C4:C18 as 1+(15-1).9, which equals the 13.6 ranked item. That is, assuming the data is sorted in ascending order, Excel computes a number 60 percent of the way between the thirteenth data point (130) and the fourteenth data point (140). This yields 136.

The PERCENTILE.EXC function computes the *k*th percentile as the (n+1)p ranked item in the data set. PERCENTILE.EXC computes the ninetieth percentile of the data as (15+1)(.9), which is the 14.4 ranked item. That is, the ninetieth percentile (assuming again data is sorted in ascending order) is computed to be 40 percent of the way between the fourteenth data point (140) and the fifteenth data point (300). This yields (0.60)(140) + (0.40)(300) =204. You can see that the two functions return drastically different answers. If you consider the data to have been drawn by sampling from a large set of data, you might assume that given the data you've seen, there is much more than a 10 percent chance that a piece of data would be more than 136. After all, two of the 15 data points are more than 130, so it does not seem reasonable to say that the ninetieth percentile of the data is only 136. Therefore, saying the ninetieth percentile is 204 seems more reasonable. I strongly recommend using the .EXC function instead of the .INC function. Note that the .EXC function does not compute a percentile for 0 and 1. The *.EXC* extension stands for the fact that the PERCENTILE.EXC function excludes the zero and one hundredth percentiles.

The PERCENTRANK, PERCENTRANK.INC, and PERCENTRANK.EXC functions return the ranking of an observation relative to all values in a data set. The syntax of the PERCENTRANK.EXC function, for example, is PERCENTRANK.EXC(data,value). The PERCENTRANK and PERCENTRANK.INC functions both calculate the percentile rank of the *k*th smallest number in the data set as (k-1)/(n-1). Thus, as shown in cell E4, the PERCENTILE or PERCENTILE.INC function yields a rank of 0 for 10, because *k* =1 for this data point. The PERCENTRANK.EXC function computes the rank of the *k*th smallest data point as k/(n+1). In cell D4, the PERCENTRANK.EXC function returns a rank of 1/16 = 0.0625. A percentile ranking of 6.25 percent seems more realistic than a ranking of 0 percent, because there is little reason to think that a value of 10 is the smallest data point in a larger data set from which this data was sampled.

Note The PERCENTILE and PERCENTRANK functions are easily confused. To simplify, PERCENTILE yields a possible data value, whereas PERCENTRANK yields a percentage.

How can I easily find the second largest or second smallest number in a data set?

The formula =LARGE(range,k) returns the *k*th largest number in a cell range. The formula =SMALL(range,k) returns the *k*th smallest number in a cell range. For example, in the file Trimmean.xlsx, in cell F1, the formula =LARGE(C4:C62,2) returns the second largest number in the cell range C4:C62 (99), whereas in cell F2, the formula =SMALL(C4:C62,2) returns the second smallest number in the cell range C4:C62 (80). (See Figure 42-7.)

	C	D	E	G	H
1				2nd highest score	99
2				2nd lowest score	80
3	Scores	Rank(ties)	Average Rank	10% trimmed mean	90.04
4	93	20	21.5	5% trimmed mean	90.02
5	84	48	49		
6	88	38	39		
7	100	1	1		
8	86	45	45.5		
9	86	45	45.5	93 is 20th-23rd	
10	95	12	14	94 17th-19th	
11	92	24	24.5		
12	88	38	39		
13	94	17	18		
14	97	5	6.5		
15	91	26	27		
16	92	24	24.5		
17	95	12	14		
18	93	20	21.5		
19	80	56	57.5		
20	89	32	34.5		
21	98	3	3.5		

FIGURE 42-7 Examples of the LARGE and SMALL functions, the RANK and RANK.AVG functions, and the trimmed mean.

How can I rank numbers in a data set?

The RANK function ranks numbers in a data set. The syntax of the RANK function is RANK(number,array,0). Excel 2010 introduced a function, RANK.EQ, which returns results identical to the RANK function. This formula yields the rank of a number in a given array, where the largest number in the array is assigned rank 1, the second largest number is rank 2, and so on. The syntax RANK(number,array,1) or RANK.EQ(number,array,1) results in assigning a rank of 1 to the smallest number in the array, a rank of 2 to the second smallest number, and so on. In the file Trimmean.xlsx (see Figure 42-7), copying the formula =RANK.EQ(C4,$C$4,$C$62,0) from cell D4 to D5:D62 returns the rank of each test score. For example, the score of 100 in cell C7 is the highest score, whereas the scores of 98 in cells C21 and C22 tied for the third highest score. Note that the RANK function returned a 3 for both scores of 98.

The Excel function RANK.AVG has the same syntax as the other RANK functions, but in the case of ties, RANK.AVG returns the average rank for all the tied data points. For example, since the two scores of 98 ranked third and fourth, RANK.AVG returns 3.5 for each. I generated the average ranks by copying the formula =RANK.AVG(C4,$C$4:$C$62,0) from E4 to E5:E62.

What is the trimmed mean of a data set?

Extreme skewness in a data set can distort the mean of the data set. In these situations, people usually use the median as a measure of the data set's typical value. The median, however, is unaffected by many changes in the data. For example, compare the following two data sets:

```
Set 1: -5, -3, 0, 1, 3, 5, 7, 9, 11, 13, 15
```

```
Set 2: -20, -18, -15, -10, -8, 5, 6, 7, 8, 9, 10
```

These data sets have the same median (5), but the second data set should have a lower "typical" value than the first. The *trimmed mean* trims off data points from the top and bottom of the data set.

The Excel TRIMMEAN function is less distorted by extreme values than the AVERAGE function, but it is more influenced by extreme values than the median. The formula =TRIMMEAN(range,percent) computes the mean of a data set, after deleting the data points at the top percent divided by 2 and bottom percent divided by 2. For example, applying the TRIMMEAN function with percent=10% converts the mean after deleting the top 5 percent and bottom 5 percent of the data. In cell H3 of the file Trimmean.xlsx, the formula =TRIMMEAN(C4:C62,0.1) computes the mean of the scores in C4:C62 after deleting the three highest and three lowest scores. (The result is 90.04.) In cell H4, the formula =TRIMMEAN(C4:C62,0.05) computes the mean of the scores in C4:C62 after deleting the top and bottom scores. This calculation occurs because 0.05*59=2.95 would indicate the deletion of 1.48 of the largest observations and 1.48 of the smallest. Rounding off 1.48 results in deleting only the top and bottom observations. (See Figure 42-7.)

When I select a range of cells, is there an easy way to get a variety of statistics that describes the data in those cells?

To see the solution to this question, select the cell range C4:C36 in the file Trimmean.xlsx. In the lower-right corner of your screen, the Excel status bar displays a cornucopia of statistics describing the numbers in the selected cell range. Figure 42-8 shows several of them. If you right-click the status bar, you can change the displayed set of statistics. I selected Minimum and Maximum to see those values in addition to the default statistics shown in Figure 42-8. For the cell range C4:C36, the mean is 90.39, there are 33 numbers, the smallest value is 80, and the largest value is 100.

Average: 90.39393939 Count: 33 Sum: 2983

FIGURE 42-8 The statistics shown on the status bar.

Why do financial analysts often use the geometric mean to summarize the average return on a stock?

The file Geommean.xlsx contains the annual returns of two fictitious stocks. (See Figure 42-9.)

	B	C	D
1			
2			
3			
4		Stock 1	Stock 2
5	Year 1	0.05	-0.5
6	Year 2	0.05	0.7
7	Year 3	0.05	-0.5
8	Year 4	0.05	0.7
9	Average	0.05	0.1
10			
11		1+return	
12		1.05	0.5
13		1.05	1.7
14		1.05	0.5
15		1.05	1.7
16	geometric means	0.05	-0.07805

FIGURE 42-9 A geometric mean.

Cell C9 indicates that the average annual return on Stock 1 is 5 percent and the average annual return on Stock 2 is 10 percent. This would seem to indicate that Stock 2 is a better investment. If you think about it, however, what will probably happen with Stock 2 is that one year you will lose 50 percent and the next gain 70 percent. This means that every two years $1.00 becomes 1(1.7)(.5)=.85. Because Stock 1 never loses money, you know that it is clearly the better investment. Using the geometric mean as a measure of average annual return helps to correctly conclude that Stock 1 is the better investment. The *geometric mean* of *n* numbers is the *n*th root of the product of the numbers (the central number in a geometric progression, where you multiply the numbers together and then take the squared root if there are two numbers, the cubed root if there are three numbers, and so on). For example, the geometric mean of 1 and 4 is the square root of 4 (2), whereas the geometric mean of 1, 2, and 4 is the cubed root of 8 (also 2). To use the geometric mean to calculate an average annual return on an investment, you add 1 to each annual return and take the geometric mean of the resulting numbers. Then subtract 1 from this result to obtain an estimate of the stock's average annual return.

The formula =GEOMMEAN(range) finds the geometric mean of numbers in a range. So, to estimate the average annual return on each stock, you proceed as follows:

1. Compute 1 + each annual return by copying from C12 to C12:D15 the formula =1+C5.
2. Copy from C16 to D16 the formula =GEOMEAN(C12:C15)–1.

The annual average return on Stock 1 is estimated to be 5 percent, and the annual average return on Stock 2 is –7.8 percent. Note that if Stock 2 yields the mean return of –7.8 percent during two consecutive years, $1 becomes $1*(1–0.078)^2=0.85$, which agrees with common sense.

How can I use boxplots to summarize and compare datasets?

Recall from Chapter 41 that a *histogram* is a chart that shows the frequencies of a data set in various ranges. A *boxplot* is a chart that graphically displays five important descriptive values for a data set. These values include the following:

- The minimum value
- The maximum value
- The first quartile (the 25th percentile)
- The median (the 50th percentile)
- The third quartile (the 75th percentile)

An example of a boxplot is shown in Figure 42-11. The length of the box in the boxplot is the *interquartile range* (IQR) = 75th percentile – 25th percentile.

Using the data in the file Boxplottemp.xlsx (in the Templates folder), we create a boxplot to analyze a classic data set: the military draft numbers from the 1969 draft lottery. In the 1969 lottery, a container was filled with the numbers 1–366, which were then supposedly thoroughly mixed. Then a ball was drawn for January 1 (number 305), next a ball was drawn for January 2 (number 159), and so on.

Men with their birth date selected as number 1 were drafted first, then men with draft number 2, and so on. Lower draft numbers made it more likely that a man would be drafted. The cell range A7:B373 contains the draft-lottery number for each birth date (in column B) and the month of the year (in column A). After selecting this range, from the Insert tab, selected Insert Statistic Chart (in the Charts group) and then choose the Box And Whisker option shown in Figure 42-10.

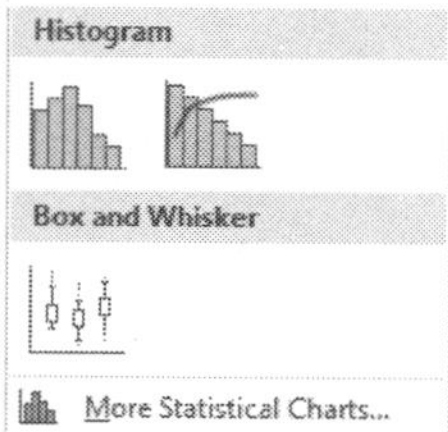

FIGURE 42-10 Selecting a Box And Whisker chart.

To create the boxplot in Figure 42-11, from the Design tab, I chose the fourth option in the Chart Styles group. Then I hovered over the plot area of the chart that shows the diagrams, and when the ScreenTip displayed Series "Number", I right-clicked to select Format Data Series. In the Format Data Series pane, I chose the Show Outlier Points check box because any point more than 1.5*(IQR) from either end of box is declared an outlier. I then chose Show Mean Markers (the Xs on the chart) and Show Mean Line (the line connecting the Xs).

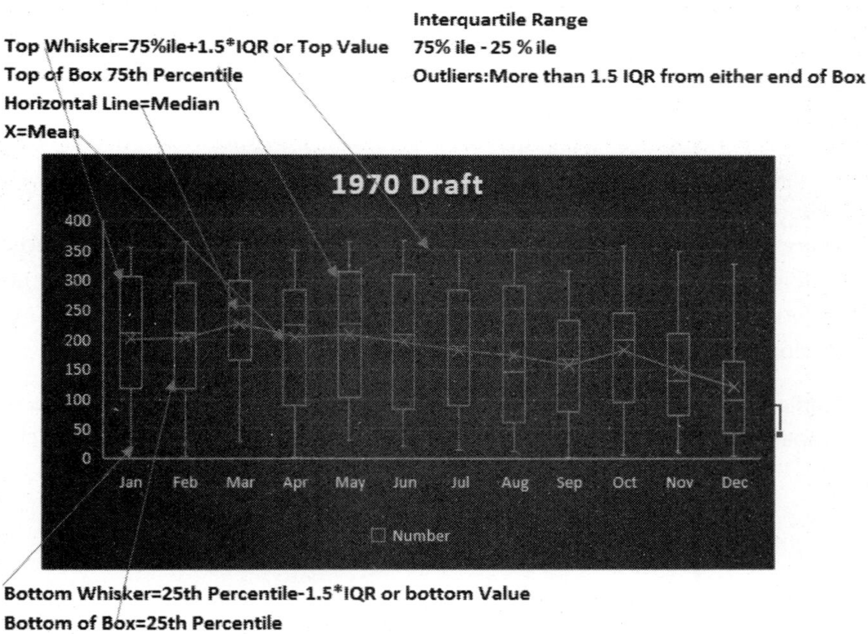

FIGURE 42-11 A boxplot for the draft-lottery data.

For each month's draft numbers, the following information is shown. (Figure 42-12 shows the calculations for January.)

- The top of the box (305) is the 75th percentile.
- The bottom of the box (118) is the 25th percentile.
- The horizontal line (211) is the median, or 50th percentile.
- The top of the upper whisker (355) is the minimum (largest data point, 75th percentile +1.5IQR).
- The bottom of the lower whisker (17) is the maximum (smallest data point, 25th percentile – 1.5*IQR).

	E	F	G
9	Jan Median	211	=MEDIAN(Jan)
10	Jan Mean	201.161	=AVERAGE(Jan)
11	Jan 25%ile	118	=QUARTILE.EXC(Jan,1)
12	Jan 75%ile	305	=QUARTILE.EXC(Jan,3)
13	Jan max	355	=MAX(Jan)
14	Jan min	17	=MIN(Jan)
15			
16	IQR	187	=F12-F11
17	1.5*IQR	280.5	=1.5*F16
18	Upper Outlier Cutoff	585.5	=F12+F17
19	Lower Outlier Cutoff	-162.5	=F11-F17

FIGURE 42-12 The computations for the January boxplot data.

The main takeaway from the boxplot is that the means and medians appear to be decreasing during the calendar year. This indicates that later dates tend to have lower draft numbers, and the drawing was not random. More advanced statistical methods, such as resampling (see Chapter 77) confirm that the lottery exhibited a lack of randomness. The most frequent explanation advanced for the failure of randomness is that lower numbered balls were put in first, and the balls were not properly mixed. This led to later dates tending to have lower draft numbers. In 1970, the balls were more thoroughly mixed, and no evidence of nonrandomness was found.

As a second example of the power of boxplots, Figure 42-13 (see the file Stocksandboxplots.xlsx) shows a boxplot comparing the Cisco and GM stock returns that were discussed earlier in this chapter.

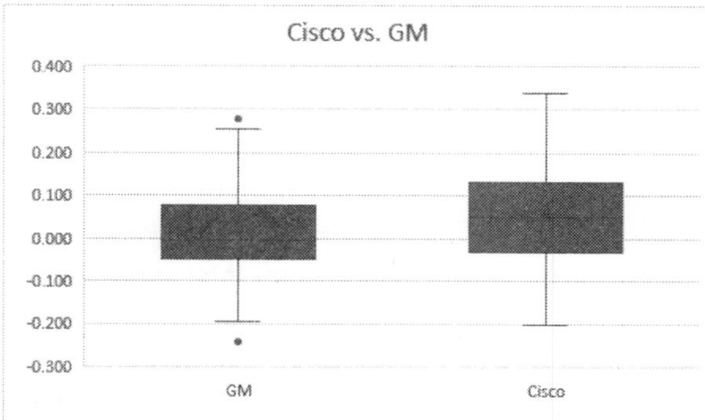

FIGURE 42-13 A boxplot of Cisco and GM monthly returns.

We immediately draw the following three conclusions from the boxplot:

- The Cisco box is higher than the GM box, so on average Cisco did better than GM.
- The Cisco box is longer (taller) than the GM box and the Cisco whiskers are longer than the GM whiskers, so Cisco exhibits more variability than GM.
- The top and bottom whiskers for each stock are roughly of the same length, and for each stock the mean and median are virtually identical. This indicates that the GM and Cisco data sets exhibit symmetry.

In the file Boxplotmultiple.xlsx (see Figure 42-14), you can see how boxplots can be used to compare several populations on multiple variables.

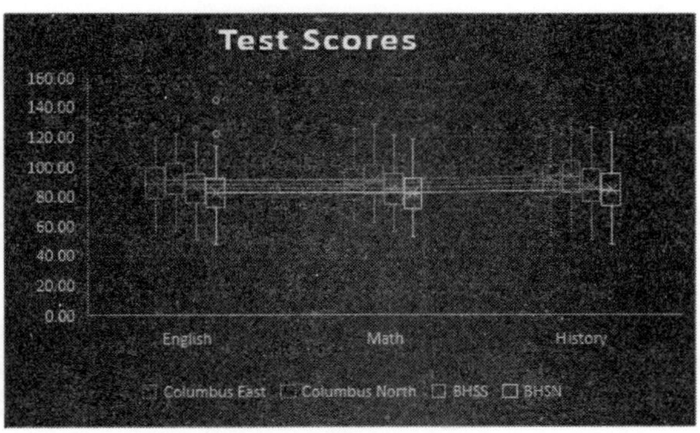

FIGURE 42-14 A boxplot comparing high-school test scores.

For each high school, we are given in a different column English, math, and history test scores. From the boxplot we quickly see the following:

- Each high school had two outliers (on the high side) on English test scores.
- Columbus North students tend to perform the best on each test, and Bloomington North students tend to perform the worst on each test.

- For each test, it appears that all the schools have boxes and whiskers of similar length, indicating the variability of scores on each test is consistent across schools.

Problems

1. Use the data in the file Stock.xlsx to generate descriptive statistics for Intel and GE stock.
2. Use your answer to problem 1 to compare the monthly returns on Intel and GE stock.
3. City Power & Light produces voltage-regulating equipment in New York and ships the equipment to Chicago. A voltage regulator is considered acceptable if it can hold a voltage of 25–75 volts. The voltage held by each unit is measured in New York before each unit is shipped. The voltage is measured again when the unit arrives in Chicago. A sample of voltage measurements from each city is given in the file Citypower.xlsx.
   - Using descriptive statistics, comment on what you have learned about the voltage held by units before and after shipment.
   - What percentage of units is acceptable before and after shipping?
   - Do you have any suggestions about how to improve the quality of City Power & Light's regulators?
   - Ten percent of all New York regulators have a voltage exceeding what value?
   - Five percent of all New York regulators have a voltage less than or equal to what value?
4. In the file Decadeincome.xlsx, you are given a sample of incomes (in thousands of 1980 dollars) for a set of families sampled in 1980 and 1990. Assume that these families are representative of the whole United States. Some Republicans claim that the country was better off in 1990 than in 1980 because the average income increased. Do you agree?
5. Use descriptive statistics to compare the annual returns on stocks, T-bills, and corporate bonds. Use the data contained in the file Historicalinvest.xlsx.
6. In 1969 and 1970, eligibility for the US armed-services draft was determined on the basis of a draft-lottery number. The number was determined by birth date. A total of 366 balls, one for each possible birth date, were placed in a container and shaken. The first ball selected was given the number 1 in the lottery, and so on. Men whose birthdays corresponded to the lowest numbers were drafted first. The file Draftlottery.xlsx contains the actual results of the 1969 and 1970 drawings. For example, in the 1969 drawing, January 1 received the number 305. Use descriptive statistics to demonstrate that the 1969 draft lottery was not random and the 1970 lottery was random. Hint: Use the AVERAGE and MEDIAN functions to compute the mean and median lottery number for each month.
7. The file Jordan.xlsx gives the starting salaries (hypothetical) of all 1984 geography graduates from the University of North Carolina (UNC). What is your best estimate of a "typical" starting salary for a geography major? In reality, the major at UNC with the highest average starting

salary in 1984 was geography, because the great basketball player Michael Jordan was a geography major!

8. Use the LARGE or SMALL function to sort the annual stock returns in the file Historicalinvest.xlsx. What advantage does this method of sorting have over clicking the Sort button?

9. Compare the mean, median, and trimmed mean (trimming 10 percent of the data) of the annual returns on stocks, T-bills, and corporate bonds given in the file Historicalinvest.xlsx.

10. Use the geometric mean to estimate the mean annual return on stocks, bonds, and T-bills in the file Historicalinvest.xlsx.

11. The file Dow.xlsx contains monthly returns on the 30 Dow stocks during the last 20 years. Use this data to determine the three stocks with the largest mean monthly returns.

12. Using the Dow.xlsx data again, determine the three stocks with the most risk or variability.

13. Using the Dow.xlsx data, determine the three stocks with the highest skew.

14. Using the Dow.xlsx data, how do the trimmed-mean returns (trim off 10 percent of the returns) differ from the overall mean returns?

15. The file Incomedata.xlsx contains incomes of a representative sample of Americans in the years 1975, 1985, 1995, and 2005. Describe how US personal income has changed over this time period.

16. The file Coltsdata.xlsx contains yards gained by the 2006 Indianapolis Colts on each rushing and passing play. Describe how the outcomes of rushing plays and passing plays differ.

17. In the file Problem17datat.xlsx, you are given daily returns on Facebook stock. Use this data to answer the following questions:

    - Do Facebook stock returns exhibit significant skewness?
    - Identify all the outliers (using the rule of thumb). Is the number of outliers consistent with the rule of thumb?
    - There is a 1 percent chance that the daily return on Facebook will exceed ____.

18. One theory in brain science states that the level of dopamine in a person's nervous system determines whether someone will exhibit psychotic behavior. In the file Problem18data.xlsx, you are given the dopamine levels for 10 psychotic and 14 nonpsychotic adults. Use descriptive statistics and a boxplot to compare and contrast the distribution of dopamine in psychotic and nonpsychotic people.

19. Participants in a group of 508 people were asked to estimate the percentage of African nations that are members of the United Nations. A wheel of fortune containing the numbers 1–100 was spun before people answered the question. Unknown to the people, the wheel was rigged to show either 25 or 65. In Problem19data.xlsx, you are given the responses of the participants in the experiment. Describe how the wheel result influenced the responses given by the subjects.

CHAPTER 43

Using PivotTables and slicers to describe data

Questions answered in this chapter:

- What is a PivotTable?
- How can I use a PivotTable to summarize grocery sales at several grocery stores?
- What PivotTable layouts are available in Excel 2016?
- Why is a PivotTable called a *PivotTable*?
- How can I easily change the format in a PivotTable?
- How can I collapse and expand fields?
- How do I sort and filter PivotTable fields?
- How do I summarize a PivotTable by using a PivotChart?
- How do I use the Reports Filter section of the PivotTable?
- How do PivotTable slicers work?
- How do I add blank rows or hide subtotals in a PivotTable?
- How do I apply conditional formatting to a PivotTable?
- How can I update my calculations when I add new data?
- I work for a small travel agency for which I need to mass-mail a travel brochure. My funds are limited, so I want to mail the brochure to people who spend the most money on travel. From information in a random sample of 925 people, I know the gender, the age, and the amount these people spent on travel last year. How can I use this data to determine how gender and age influence a person's travel expenditures? What can I conclude about the type of person to whom I should mail the brochure?
- I'm doing market research about station wagons. I need to determine what factors influence the likelihood that a family will purchase a station wagon. From information in a large sample of families, I know the family size (large or small) and the family income (high or low). How can

I determine how family size and income influence the likelihood that a family will purchase a station wagon?

- I work for a manufacturer that sells microchips globally. I'm given monthly actual and predicted sales for Canada, France, and the United States for Chip 1, Chip 2, and Chip 3. I'm also given the variance, or difference, between actual and budgeted revenues. For each month and each combination of country and product, I'd like to display the following data: actual revenue, budgeted revenue, actual variance, actual revenue as a percentage of annual revenue, and variance as a percentage of budgeted revenue. How can I display this information?
- What is a calculated field?
- How do I use a report filter or slicer?
- How do I group items in a PivotTable?
- What is a calculated item?
- What is *drilling down*?
- I often have to use specific data in a PivotTable to determine profit, such as the April sales in France of Chip 1. Unfortunately, this data moves around when new fields are added to my PivotTable. Does Excel have a function that enables me to always extract April's Chip 1 sales in France from the PivotTable?
- How can I use the Timeline feature to summarize data during different time periods?
- How I can use a PivotTable to summarize total sales to date during a year?
- How can I use a PivotTable to summarize sales this month compared to the same month a year earlier?
- How can I create a PivotTable based on data in several different locations?
- How can I create a PivotTable based on an already created PivotTable?
- How can I easily use the report filter to create multiple PivotTables?

Answers to this chapter's questions

What is a PivotTable?

In numerous business situations, you need to analyze, or, as we say, "slice and dice," your data to gain important insights. Imagine that you sell different grocery products in different stores at different points in time. You might have hundreds of thousands of data points to track. PivotTables let you quickly summarize your data in almost any way imaginable. For example, for your grocery-store data, you could use a PivotTable to quickly determine the following:

- Amount spent by customers per year in each store on each product

- Total revenue at each store
- Total revenue for each year

In a travel agency, as another example, you might slice data so that you can determine whether the average amount customers spend on travel is influenced by age or gender or by both factors. In analyzing automobile purchases, you'd like to compare the fraction of your customers who are householders with large families buying station wagons to the fraction of householders with small families purchasing station wagons. If you're a microchip manufacturer, you'd like to determine total Chip 1 sales in France, for example, during April, and so on. A PivotTable is an incredibly powerful tool to use in scenarios like these. The easiest way to understand how a PivotTable works is to walk through some carefully constructed examples, so let's get started! I'll begin with an introductory example and then illustrate many advanced PivotTable features through subsequent examples.

How can I use a PivotTable to summarize grocery sales at several grocery stores?

The Data worksheet in the file Groceriespt.xlsx contains more than 900 rows of sales data. (See Figure 43-1.) Each row contains the number of units sold and revenue for a product at a store, as well as the month and year of the sale. The product group (fruit, milk, cereal, or ice cream) is also included. You would like to see a breakdown of sales during each year of each product group and product at each store. You would also like to be able to show this breakdown during any subset of months in a given year (for example, what the sales were during January–June).

	A	B	C	D	E	F	G
1	Year	Month	Store	Group	Product	Units	Revenue
2	2007	August	south	milk	low fat	805	$ 3,187.80
3	2007	March	south	ice cream	Edies	992	$ 3,412.48
4	2007	January	east	milk	skim	712	$ 1,808.48
5	2006	March	north	ice cream	Edies	904	$ 2,260.00
6	2006	January	south	ice cream	Edies	647	$ 2,076.87
7	2005	September	west	fruit	plums	739	$ 1,707.09
8	2006	March	east	milk	low fat	974	$ 2,181.76
9	2007	June	north	fruit	apples	615	$ 1,894.20
10	2007	July	west	fruit	cherries	714	$ 1,856.40
11	2006	May	south	cereal	Special K	703	$ 1,553.63
12	2005	June	west	ice cream	Edies	528	$ 2,064.48
13	2006	October	east	cereal	Raisin Bran	644	$ 1,809.64
14	2005	June	south	fruit	grapes	919	$ 2,196.41
15	2007	May	west	milk	skim	767	$ 1,932.84
16	2007	June	west	cereal	Raisin Bran	984	$ 1,987.68
17	2005	March	south	cereal	Raisin Bran	744	$ 2,217.12
18	2007	September	east	ice cream	Edies	693	$ 2,189.88
19	2006	October	east	milk	chocolate	658	$ 1,895.04
20	2005	November	east	ice cream	Breyers	878	$ 3,274.94

FIGURE 43-1 The data for the grocery PivotTable example.

Before creating a PivotTable, you must have headings in the first row of your data. Notice that the grocery data contains headings (Year, Month, Store, Group, Product, Units, and Revenue) in row 2. Place your cursor anywhere in the data, and then click PivotTable in the Tables group on the Insert tab. Excel opens the Create PivotTable dialog box, shown in Figure 43-2, and makes an assumption about your data range. (In this case, Excel correctly guessed that the data range was C2:I924.) By selecting Use An External Data Source, you can also refer to a database as a source for a PivotTable. The Data Model option, added in Excel 2013, will be discussed in Chapter 44.

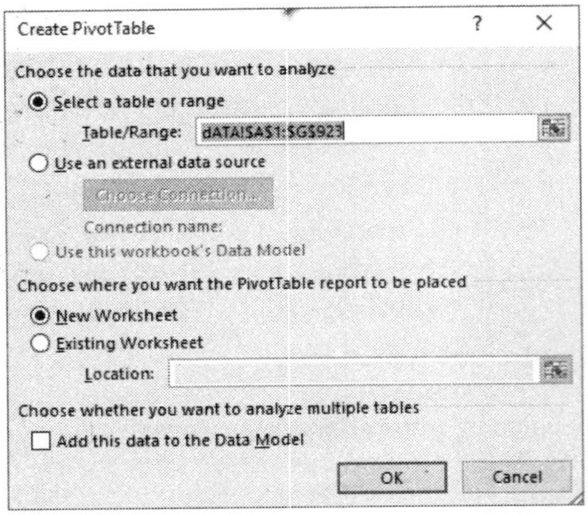

FIGURE 43-2 The Create PivotTable dialog box.

After you click OK, you see the PivotTable Fields pane shown in Figure 43-3.

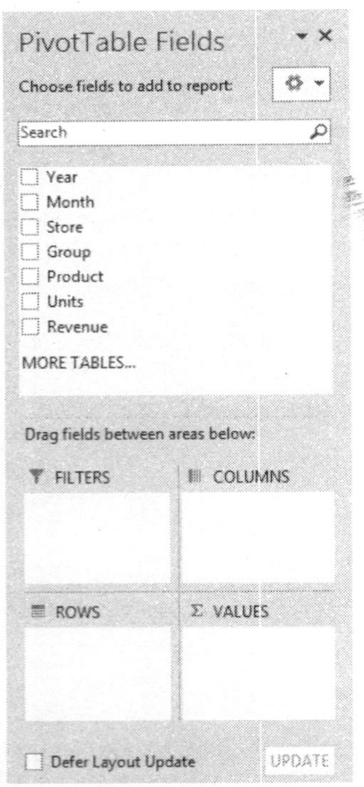

FIGURE 43-3 The PivotTable Fields pane.

You fill in the PivotTable Field pane by dragging PivotTable headings, or fields, into the boxes, or zones. This step is critical to ensuring that the PivotTable will summarize and display the data in the manner you want. The four zones are as follows:

- **Rows** Fields dragged here are listed on the left side of the table in the order in which they are added to the box. For example, I dragged to the Rows box the fields Year, Group, Product, and Store, in that order. This causes Excel to summarize data first by year, then for each product group within a given year, then by product within each group, and finally each product by store. You can drag a field at any time to a different zone or reorder the fields within a zone by dragging a field up or down in a zone or by clicking the arrow to the right of the field label.
- **Columns** Fields dragged here have their values listed across the top row of the PivotTable. As we begin this example, we have no fields in the Columns zone.
- **Values** Fields dragged here are summarized mathematically in the table. I dragged Units and Revenue (in that order) to this zone. Excel tries to guess what kind of calculation you want to perform on a field. In this example, Excel guesses that Revenue and Units should be summed, which happens to be correct. If you want to change the method of calculation for a data field to an average, a count, or something else, simply click the data field and choose Value Field Settings. I give an example of how to use the Value Field Settings command later in the chapter.
- **Filters** For fields dragged to the Filters area, you can easily pick any subset of the field values so that the PivotTable shows calculations based only on that subset. In this example, I dragged Month to the Filters area. That lets me easily select any subset of months, for example January–June, and the calculations are based on only those months. Slicers now make report filters virtually obsolete.

The completed PivotTable Field pane is shown in Figure 43-4. The resulting PivotTable is shown in Figure 43-5 and in the All Row Fields worksheet of the workbook Groceriespt.xlsx. In row 6, you can see that 243,228 units were sold for $728,218.68 in 2005.

Tip Here is some advice about navigating between worksheets:

- Ctrl+Page up moves you back one worksheet
- Ctrl+Page down moves you forward one worksheet
- Right-clicking either of the arrows to the left of the first worksheet name brings up a list of worksheet names from which you can move to any worksheet in the workbook.

Note To see the field list, you need to be in a field in the PivotTable. If you do not see the field list, right-click any cell in the PivotTable and select Show Field List.

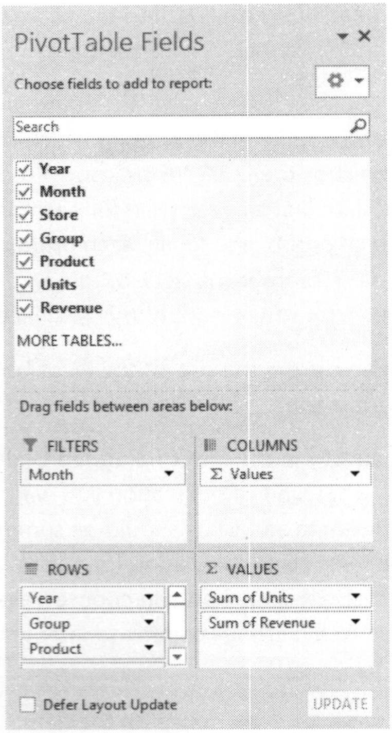

FIGURE 43-4 A completed PivotTable Field List.

	A	B	C
1	Month	(All)	
2			
3		**Values**	
4	**Row Labels**	**Sum of Units**	**Sum of Revenue**
5	**⊖2005**	**243228**	**728218.68**
6	**⊖cereal**	**63689**	**192172.93**
7	⊖Cheerios	11163	32993.1
8	east	1645	5055.8
9	north	1639	4988
10	south	3265	9216.47
11	west	4614	13732.83
12	⊖Raisin Bran	35797	105793.04
13	east	6226	19500.19
14	north	8458	22822.23
15	south	8989	26069.35
16	west	12124	37401.27
17	⊖Special K	16729	53386.79
18	east	2289	5998.21
19	north	4172	14956.36
20	south	3366	11339.47
21	west	6902	21092.75
22	**⊖fruit**	**60047**	**182813.88**
23	⊖apples	14535	48127.74
24	east	1229	3972.44
25	north	3734	13631.83

FIGURE 43-5 The grocery PivotTable in compact form.

What PivotTable layouts are available?

The PivotTable layout shown in Figure 43-5 is called the *compact form*. In the compact form, the row fields are shown one on top of another. To change the layout, first place your cursor anywhere within the table. On the Design tab, in the Layout group, click Report Layout, and choose one of the following: Show In Compact Form (see Figure 43-5), Show In Outline Form (see Figure 43-6 and the Outline Form worksheet), or Show In Tabular Form (Figure 43-7 and the Tabular Form worksheet).

	A	B	C	D	E	F
1	Month	(All)				
2						
3					Values	
4	Year	Group	Product	Store	Sum of Units	Sum of Revenue
5	2005				243228	728218.68
6		cereal			63689	192172.93
7			Cheerios		11163	32993.1
8				east	1645	5055.8
9				north	1639	4988
10				south	3265	9216.47
11				west	4614	13732.83
12			Raisin Bran		35797	105793.04
13				east	6226	19500.19
14				north	8458	22822.23
15				south	8989	26069.35
16				west	12124	37401.27
17			Special K		16729	53386.79
18				east	2289	5998.21
19				north	4172	14956.36
20				south	3366	11339.47
21				west	6902	21092.75
22		fruit			60047	182813.88
23			apples		14535	48127.74
24				east	1229	3972.44
25				north	3734	13631.83
26				south	4317	14763.88
27				west	5255	15759.59

FIGURE 43-6 The outline format.

Month	(All)				
				Values	
Year	**Group**	**Product**	**Store**	**Sum of Units**	**Sum of Revenue**
2005	cereal	Cheerios	east	1645	5055.8
			north	1639	4988
			south	3265	9216.47
			west	4614	13732.83
		Cheerios Total		11163	32993.1
		Raisin Bran	east	6226	19500.19
			north	8458	22822.23
			south	8989	26069.35
			west	12124	37401.27
		Raisin Bran Total		35797	105793.04
		Special K	east	2289	5998.21
			north	4172	14956.36
			south	3366	11339.47
			west	6902	21092.75
		Special K Total		16729	53386.79
	cereal Total			**63689**	**192172.93**
	fruit	apples	east	1229	3972.44
			north	3734	13631.83
			south	4317	14763.88
			west	5255	15759.59
		apples Total		14535	48127.74
		cherries	east	1646	4051.22

FIGURE 43-7 The tabular format.

Why is a PivotTable called a *PivotTable*?

You can easily pivot fields from a row to a column and vice versa to create a different layout. For example, by dragging the Year field to the Columns box, you create the PivotTable layout shown in Figure 43-8. (See the Years Column worksheet.)

Month	(All)							
	Column Labels							
	Sum of Units			**Sum of Revenue**			**Total Sum of Units**	**Total Sum of Revenue**
Row Labels	**2005**	**2006**	**2007**	**2005**	**2006**	**2007**		
cereal	**63689**	**52489**	**58671**	**192172.93**	**150710**	**172828.96**	**174849**	**515711.89**
Cheerios	**11163**	**16142**	**13652**	**32993.1**	**46657.49**	**38617.12**	**40957**	**118267.71**
west	4614	1454	1586	13732.83	4696.16	4633.76	7654	23062.75
south	3265	6424	3064	9216.47	18450.16	8635.3	12753	36301.93
north	1639	3027	4207	4988	10199.31	11409.85	8873	26597.16
east	1645	5237	4795	5055.8	13311.86	13938.21	11677	32305.87
Raisin Bran	**35797**	**24056**	**27715**	**105793.04**	**69391.29**	**81254.09**	**87568**	**256438.42**
west	12124	4515	10115	37401.27	14147.68	27038.27	26754	78587.22
south	8989	6015	5329	26069.35	16593.97	16632.9	20333	59296.22
north	8458	7505	8366	22822.23	23099.35	25008.01	24329	70929.59
east	6226	6021	3905	19500.19	15550.29	12574.91	16152	47625.39
Special K	**16729**	**12291**	**17304**	**53386.79**	**34661.22**	**52957.75**	**46324**	**141005.76**
west	6902	2585	2328	21092.75	7715.78	6860.4	11815	35668.93
south	3366	3436	5826	11339.47	9125.62	17647.74	12628	38112.83
north	4172	2570	3789	14956.36	8665.32	12736.82	10531	36358.5
east	2289	3700	5361	5998.21	9154.5	15712.79	11350	30865.5
fruit	**60047**	**53910**	**61816**	**182813.88**	**157192.37**	**189616.27**	**175773**	**529622.52**
apples	**14535**	**12090**	**13256**	**48127.74**	**34879.74**	**40939.04**	**39881**	**123946.52**
west	5255	3707	5123	15759.59	11024.11	15069.53	14085	41853.23
south	4317	4717	1855	14763.88	14052.05	4829.24	10889	33645.17

FIGURE 43-8 The Year field pivoted to the Column field.

How can I easily change the format in a PivotTable?

If you want to change the format of an entire column field, simply double-click the column heading and select Number Format in the Value Field Settings dialog box. Then apply the format you want in the Format Cells dialog box, and click OK in both dialog boxes. For example, in the Formatted $s worksheet, I formatted the Revenue field as currency by double-clicking the Sum Of Revenue heading and applying a currency format. You can also change the format of a value field by clicking the arrow to the right of the value field in the PivotTable Field pane. Select Value Field Settings to open the field's dialog box, and click Number Format. Then you can reformat the column as you want it.

From any cell in a PivotTable, you can click the Design tab on the ribbon to reveal many PivotTable styles.

How can I collapse and expand fields?

Expanding and collapsing fields (a feature introduced in Excel 2007) is a great advantage in PivotTables. In Figure 43-5, you see minus (–) signs by each year, group, and product. Clicking the minus sign collapses a field and changes the sign to a plus (+) sign. Clicking the plus sign expands the field. For example, if you click the minus sign by *cereal* in any cell in column A, you will find that in each year, *cereal* is reduced to one row, and the various cereals are no longer listed. See Figure 43-9 and the Cerealcollapse worksheet. Clicking the plus sign in cell A6 brings back the detailed or expanded view listing all the cereals.

	A	B	C
1	Month	(All)	
2			
3		Values	
4	Row Labels	Sum of Units	Sum of Revenue
5	⊟2005	243228	728218.68
6	⊞cereal	63689	192172.93
7	⊟fruit	60047	182813.88
8	⊟apples	14535	48127.74
9	east	1229	3972.44
10	north	3734	13631.83
11	south	4317	14763.88
12	west	5255	15759.59
13	⊟cherries	11083	32042.39
14	east	1646	4051.22
15	north	3701	11087.14
16	south	3277	9092.92
17	west	2459	7811.11
18	⊟grapes	20005	60126.15
19	east	4811	13052.68
20	north	4865	14698.63
21	south	6268	20474.65
22	west	4061	11900.19
23	⊟plums	14424	42517.6
24	east	2216	7497.52
25	north	1515	5055.55

FIGURE 43-9 The cereal field collapsed.

You can also expand or collapse an entire field. Go to any row containing a member of that field, and select the Analyze tab on the ribbon. In the Active Field group, click either the Expand Field button (labeled with a green plus sign) or the Collapse Field button (labeled with a red minus sign). (See Figure 43-10.)

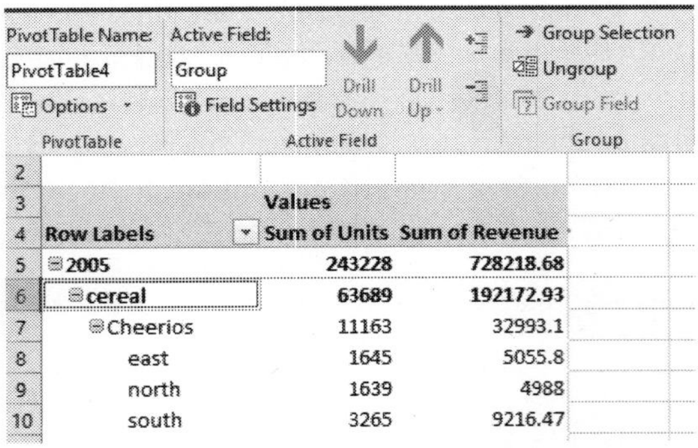

FIGURE 43-10 The Expand Field and Collapse Field buttons.

For example, suppose you simply want to see for each year only the sales by product group. Pick any cell containing a group's name (for example, A6), select the PivotTable Tools Analyze tab on the ribbon, and click the Collapse Field button. You will see the result shown in Figure 43-11 (the Groups Collapsed worksheet). Selecting the Expand Field button brings you back to the original view.

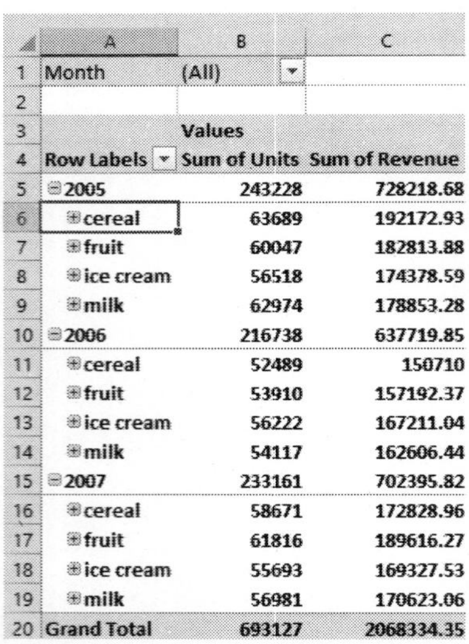

	A	B	C
1	Month	(All)	
2			
3		Values	
4	Row Labels	Sum of Units	Sum of Revenue
5	2005	243228	728218.68
6	cereal	63689	192172.93
7	fruit	60047	182813.88
8	ice cream	56518	174378.59
9	milk	62974	178853.28
10	2006	216738	637719.85
11	cereal	52489	150710
12	fruit	53910	157192.37
13	ice cream	56222	167211.04
14	milk	54117	162606.44
15	2007	233161	702395.82
16	cereal	58671	172828.96
17	fruit	61816	189616.27
18	ice cream	55693	169327.53
19	milk	56981	170623.06
20	Grand Total	693127	2068334.35

FIGURE 43-11 The group fields collapsed.

How do I sort and filter PivotTable fields?

In Figure 43-5, the products are listed alphabetically within each group. For example, Cheerios is the first type of cereal listed. If you want the products to be listed in reverse alphabetical order, simply move the cursor to any cell containing a product (for example, A7, containing Cheerios in the Groups Collapsed worksheet) and click the drop-down arrow to the right of the Row Labels entry in A4. You will see the list of filtering options shown in Figure 43-12. Selecting Sort Z To A, as shown in Figure 43-12, would list Special K first for *cereal*, whole milk first for *milk*, plums for *fruit*, and so on.

Initially, our PivotTable displays results first from 2005, then 2006, and then 2007. If you want to see the data for 2007 first, move the cursor to any cell containing a year (for example, A5), and choose Sort Largest To Smallest from the available options.

At the bottom of the filtering options dialog box, you can also select any subset of products to be displayed. You may want to first clear Select All and then select only the products you want to show.

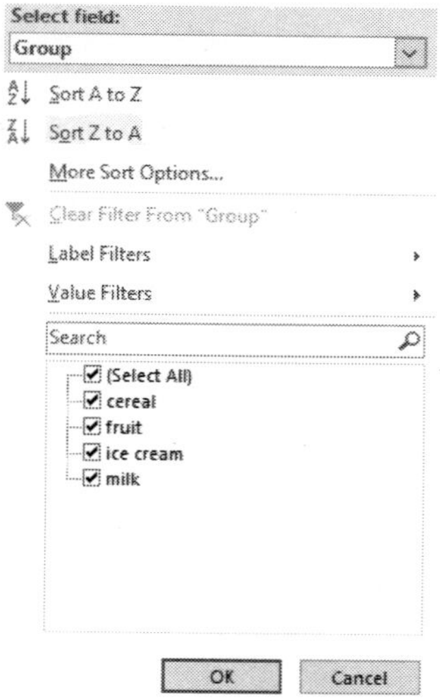

FIGURE 43-12 The PivotTable filtering options for the Product field.

For another example of filtering, look at the Data worksheet in the file Ptcustomers.xlsx, shown in Figure 43-13. The worksheet data contains, for each customer transaction, the customer number, the amount paid, and the quarter of the year in which payment was received. After dragging Customer to the Rows box, Quarter to the Columns box, and Paid to the Values box, the PivotTable shown in Figure 43-14 is displayed. (See the Ptable worksheet in the Ptcustomers.xlsx file.)

	A	B	C	D	E	F
3	Sum of Paid	Column Labels				
4	Row Labels	1	2	3	4	Grand Total
5	1	30965	42039	57790	43417	174211
6	2	96038	121118	59089	45355	321600
7	3	57419	33589	61960	97548	250516
8	4	48947	79352	63052	59520	250871
9	5	57270	86555	69517	33471	246813
10	6	75639	71976	55212	78644	281471
11	7	53130	65768	49064	89018	256980
12	8	33289	74001	45219	43512	196021
13	9	61611	99009	61075	50945	272640
14	10	31785	71213	60417	63835	227250
15	11	59127	35567	62130	107832	264656
16	12	71862	21670	67312	63558	224402
17	13	100626	56058	39500	75109	271293
18	14	74240	63023	36217	77218	250698
19	15	30612	62277	45561	52567	191017
20	16	41870	71490	64909	57120	235389
21	17	61811	85706	46978	40802	235297
22	18	24456	44916	55519	81421	206312
23	19	89591	53157	37558	38247	218553
24	20	68349	104140	35083	69424	276996
25	21	77336	37476	51815	57065	223692

FIGURE 43-13 The Customer PivotTable data.

	A	B	C	D	E	F
3	Sum of Paid	Column Labels				
4	Row Labels	1	2	3	4	Grand Total
5	1	30965	42039	57790	43417	174211
6	2	96038	121118	59089	45355	321600
7	3	57419	33589	61960	97548	250516
8	4	48947	79352	63052	59520	250871
9	5	57270	86555	69517	33471	246813
10	6	75639	71976	55212	78644	281471
11	7	53130	65768	49064	89018	256980
12	8	33289	74001	45219	43512	196021
13	9	61611	99009	61075	50945	272640
14	10	31785	71213	60417	63835	227250
15	11	59127	35567	62130	107832	264656
16	12	71862	21670	67312	63558	224402
17	13	100626	56058	39500	75109	271293
18	14	74240	63023	36217	77218	250698
19	15	30612	62277	45561	52567	191017
20	16	41870	71490	64909	57120	235389
21	17	61811	85706	46978	40802	235297
22	18	24456	44916	55519	81421	206312

FIGURE 43-14 The Customer PivotTable.

Naturally, you might like to show a list of just your top-10 customers. To obtain this layout, simply click the Row Labels arrow and select Value Filters. Then choose Top 10, verify Top 10 Items is selected in the Top 10 Filter dialog box, and then click OK. You obtain the layout shown in Figure 43-15 (see the Top 10 Cus worksheet). Of course, by clicking the arrow again and selecting Clear Filter, you can return to the original layout.

D21

	A	B	C	D	E	F
3	Sum of Paid	Column Labels				
4	Row Labels	1	2	3	4	Grand Total
5	2	96038	121118	59089	45355	321600
6	6	75639	71976	55212	78644	281471
7	9	61611	99009	61075	50945	272640
8	11	59127	35567	62130	107832	264656
9	13	100626	56058	39500	75109	271293
10	20	68349	104140	35083	69424	276996
11	22	31149	77333	104364	65664	278510
12	23	87124	56387	63290	71953	278754
13	27	45214	89826	56302	71285	262627
14	28	53737	69938	73471	69135	266281
15	Grand Total	678614	781352	609516	705346	2774828

FIGURE 43-15 The top-10 customers.

Suppose you simply want to see the top customers that generate 50 percent of your revenue. Click the Row Labels filtering arrow, select Value Filters, click Top 10, and fill in the dialog box as shown in Figure 43-16, updating the Show selection lists to Top 50 Percent.

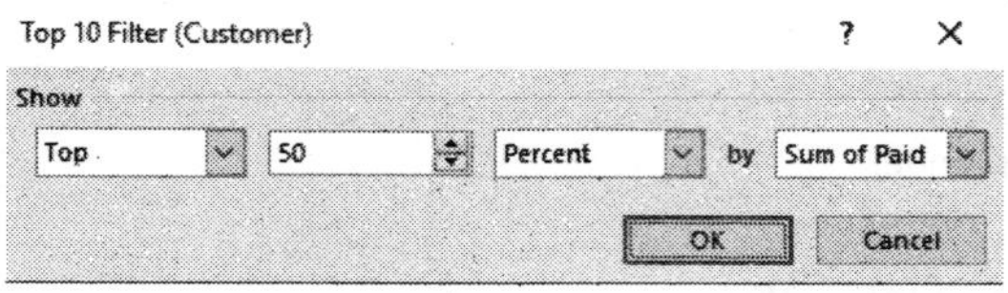

FIGURE 43-16 Configuring the Top 10 Filter dialog box to show customers generating 50 percent of the revenue.

The resulting PivotTable is in the Top Half worksheet and shown in Figure 43-17. As you can see, the top 14 customers generate a little more than half of the revenue.

	A	B	C	D	E	F
3	Sum of Paid	Column Labels				
4	Row Labels	1	2	3	4	Grand Total
5	2	96038	121118	59089	45355	321600
6	3	57419	33589	61960	97548	250516
7	4	48947	79352	63052	59520	250871
8	6	75639	71976	55212	78644	281471
9	7	53130	65768	49064	89018	256980
10	9	61611	99009	61075	50945	272640
11	11	59127	35567	62130	107832	264656
12	13	100626	56058	39500	75109	271293
13	14	74240	63023	36217	77218	250698
14	20	68349	104140	35083	69424	276996
15	22	31149	77333	104364	65664	278510
16	23	87124	56387	63290	71953	278754
17	27	45214	89826	56302	71285	262627
18	28	53737	69938	73471	69135	266281
19	Grand Total	912350	1023084	819809	1028650	3783893

FIGURE 43-17 The top customers generating half of the revenue.

Now, let's suppose you want to sort your customers by Quarter 1 revenue. (See the Sorted Q1 worksheet.) Right-click anywhere in the Quarter 1 column (column B), point to Sort, and then click Sort Largest To Smallest. The resulting PivotTable is shown in Figure 43-18. Note that Customer 13 paid the most in Quarter 1, Customer 2 paid the second most, and so on.

	A	B	C	D	E	F
3	Sum of Paid	Column Labels				
4	Row Labels	1	2	3	4	Grand Total
5	13	100626	56058	39500	75109	271293
6	2	96038	121118	59089	45355	321600
7	19	89591	53157	37558	38247	218553
8	23	87124	56387	63290	71953	278754
9	21	77336	37476	51815	57065	223692
10	6	75639	71976	55212	78644	281471
11	14	74240	63023	36217	77218	250698
12	12	71862	21670	67312	63558	224402
13	20	68349	104140	35083	69424	276996
14	17	61811	85706	46978	40802	235297
15	9	61611	99009	61075	50945	272640
16	26	59994	70594	50446	44050	225084
17	30	59599	64192	44335	42944	211070
18	11	59127	35567	62130	107832	264656
19	3	57419	33589	61960	97548	250516
20	5	57270	86555	69517	33471	246813
21	28	53737	69938	73471	69135	266281
22	7	53130	65768	49064	89018	256980

FIGURE 43-18 Sorting the customers on Quarter 1 revenue.

How do I summarize a PivotTable by using a PivotChart?

Excel makes it easy to visually summarize PivotTables by using PivotCharts. The key to laying out the data the way you want it in a PivotChart is to sort data and collapse or expand fields. In the grocery example, suppose you want to summarize the trend over time of each food group's unit sales. (See the Chart 2 worksheet in the file Groceriespt.xlsx.) You should move the Year field to the Row area and delete Revenue from the Values area. You also need to collapse the entire Group field in the Row Labels zone and move Groups to the Column area. Now, you are ready to create a PivotChart. Simply click anywhere inside the table, and then select PivotChart on the Analyze tab. In the Insert Chart dialog box, pick the chart type you want to create. I chose the first line graph option, which displays the chart in Figure 43-19. The chart shows that milk sales were highest in 2005 and lowest in 2006.

Month	(All)		COMPACT VIEW		
Sum of Units	Column Labels				
Row Labels	milk	ice cream	fruit	cereal	Grand Total
2005	62974	56518	60047	63689	243228
2006	54117	56222	53910	52489	216738
2007	56981	55693	61816	58671	233161
Grand Total	174072	168433	175773	174849	693127

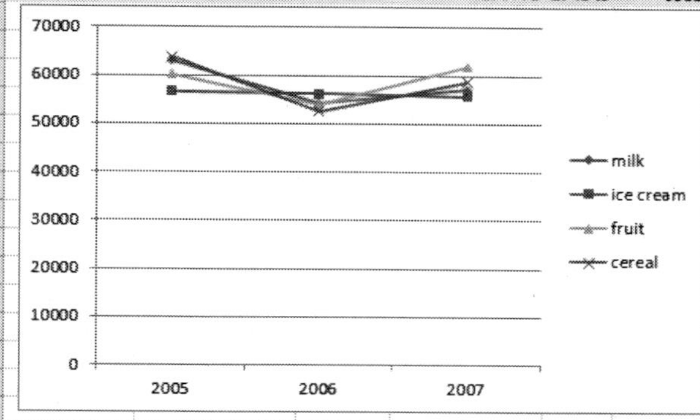

FIGURE 43-19 A PivotChart for the unit group sales trend.

How do I use the Filter section of the PivotTable?

Recall that I placed Month in the Filters section of the table. To see how to use a report filter, suppose that you want to summarize the sales for the months January–June. By clicking the Filter icon in cell B2 of the First 6 Months worksheet, you can select January–June. This results in the PivotTable shown in Figure 43-20, which summarizes the number of units sold by product, group, and year for the months January–June.

Month	(Multiple Ite	
	Values	
Row Labels	Sum of Units	Sum of Revenue
2007	115258	346295.58
milk	30069	89222.68
chocolat	4875	14077.99
west	2014	5839.06
south	736	2141.76
north	1437	4136.37
east	688	1960.8
low fat	9447	27341.25
west	3285	10732.35
south	531	1062
north	3905	10212.44
east	1726	5334.46
skim	10182	30450.57
west	2156	6169.53
south	2778	8881.2
north	2521	7726.56
east	2727	7673.28

FIGURE 43-20 A PivotTable summarizing January–June sales.

How do PivotTable slicers work?

The problem with a report filter is that a viewer of the PivotTable shown in Figure 43-20 cannot easily see that the table summarizes January–June sales. Excel's slicer feature (introduced in Excel 2010) neatly solves this problem. To create a slicer for any of the columns of data used to generate your PivotTable, place your cursor anywhere in the PivotTable, and then click Slicer on the ribbon's Insert tab (in the Filters group). In the worksheet Slicers of the file Groceriespt.xlsx, I selected Slicer from the Insert menu. Then, in the Insert Slicers dialog box, I selected the Month and Product fields to create slicers for Month and Product. Using a given slicer, you can select any subset of possible values to be used in creating your table. In the Month slicer, I selected (one at a time, while holding down the Ctrl key) the months January through June. I did nothing to the Product slicer, so the data is based on all the products in January–June sales. The slicers are shown in Figure 43-21.

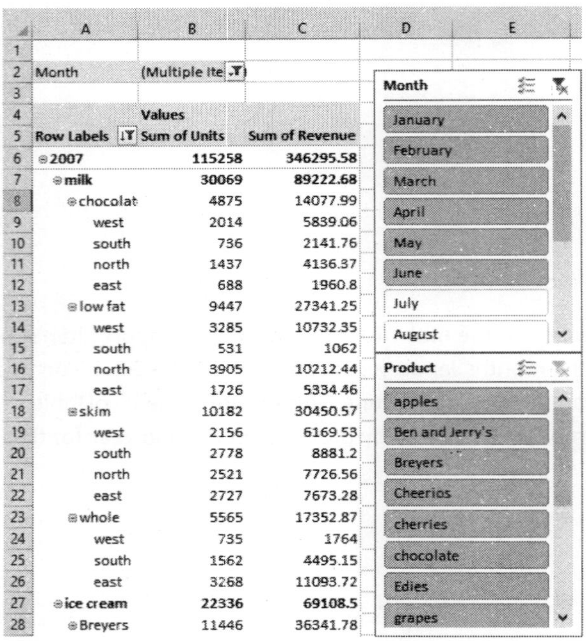

	A	B	C
1			
2	Month	(Multiple Ite	
3			
4		Values	
5	Row Labels	Sum of Units	Sum of Revenue
6	⊖2007	115258	346295.58
7	⊖milk	30069	89222.68
8	⊖chocolat	4875	14077.99
9	west	2014	5839.06
10	south	736	2141.76
11	north	1437	4136.37
12	east	688	1960.8
13	⊖low fat	9447	27341.25
14	west	3285	10732.35
15	south	531	1062
16	north	3905	10212.44
17	east	1726	5334.46
18	⊖skim	10182	30450.57
19	west	2156	6169.53
20	south	2778	8881.2
21	north	2521	7726.56
22	east	2727	7673.28
23	⊖whole	5565	17352.87
24	west	735	1764
25	south	1562	4495.15
26	east	3268	11093.72
27	⊖ice cream	22336	69108.5
28	⊖Breyers	11446	36341.78

FIGURE 43-21 Example of slicers for the Month and Product fields.

If you click a slicer, you see formatting options that allow you to change its appearance. For example, you can change the height and width as well as the number of columns in the slicer. You may also easily resize a slicer if you hold down the Ctrl key.

How do I add blank rows or hide subtotals in a PivotTable?

If you want to add a blank row between each grouped item, click a cell in the PivotTable, select the PivotTable Tools Design tab on the ribbon, click Blank Rows, and then click Insert Blank Line After Each Item. If you want to hide subtotals or grand totals, first select the PivotTable Tools Design tab. Then select Subtotals and click Do Not Show Subtotals, or select Grand Totals and click Off For Rows And Columns. After adding blank rows and hiding all the totals, I obtained the table in the Blank

Rows No Totals worksheet of the workbook Grocerypt.xlsx, shown in Figure 43-22. After right-clicking in any PivotTable cell, you can select PivotTable Options to open the PivotTable Options dialog box. In this dialog box, in the Format section of the Layout & Format tab, you can replace empty cells by entering any character in the For Empty Cells Show box, such as an underscore (_), or by using a 0.

	A	B	C
2	Month	(All)	
3			
4		Values	
5	Row Labels	Sum of Units	Sum of Revenue
6	2007		
7	milk		
8	chocolate		
9	west	4379	12668.95
10	south	1545	4528.31
11	north	2322	7579.02
12	east	2184	5791.1
13			
14	low fat		
15	west	4668	15042.24
16	south	2431	7606.76
17	north	7957	23490.32
18	east	2517	7762.83
19			
20	skim		
21	west	3571	9951.37
22	south	2778	8881.2
23	north	3594	10792.09
24	east	4839	14609.52
25			

FIGURE 43-22 A grocery PivotTable without totals.

How do I apply conditional formatting to a PivotTable?

Suppose you want to apply data bars to the Units column in the grocery PivotTable. One problem you'll encounter is that subtotals and grand totals will have large data bars and also make the other data bars smaller than they should be. It's better to have the data bars apply to all product sales, not the subtotals and grand totals. (See the Cond Form worksheet of the file Groceriespt.xlsx.) To apply the data bars to only the unit sales by product, begin by placing the cursor in a cell containing unit sales for a product (for example, the sales for chocolate milk in B8). On the Home tab, click Conditional Formatting followed by Data Bars, and then choose More Rules. You will see the New Formatting Rule dialog box shown in Figure 43-23.

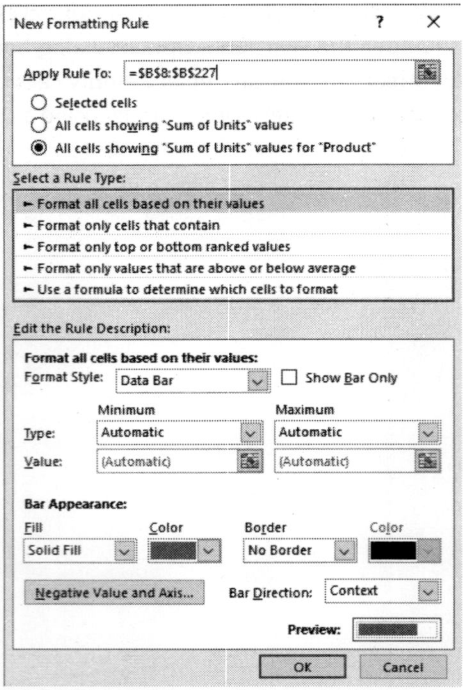

FIGURE 43-23 The New Formatting Rule dialog box for using conditional formatting with PivotTables.

By selecting All Cells Showing "Sum of Units" Values For "Product" and selecting the range $B$8:$B$227, you can ensure that data bars apply only to the cells listing unit sales for products, as you can see in the Cond Form worksheet and Figure 43-24.

	A	B	C
2	Month	(All)	
3			
4		Values	
5	Row Labels	Sum of Units	Sum of Revenue
6	⊟2007	233161	702395.82
7	⊟milk	56981	170623.06
8	⊟chocolate	10430	30567.38
9	west	4379	12668.95
10	south	1545	4528.31
11	north	2322	7579.02
12	east	2184	5791.1
13	⊟low fat	17573	53902.15
14	west	4668	15042.24
15	south	2431	7606.76
16	north	7957	23490.32
17	east	2517	7762.83
18	⊟skim	14782	44234.18
19	west	3571	9951.37
20	south	2778	8881.2
21	north	3594	10792.09
22	east	4839	14609.52
23	⊟whole	14196	41919.35
24	west	3252	8311.84
25	south	1562	4495.15

FIGURE 43-24 Data bars for a PivotTable.

How can I update my calculations when I add new data?

If the data in your original set of rows changes, you can update your PivotTable to include the data changes by right-clicking the table and selecting Refresh. You can also select Refresh from the Analyze tab (in the Data group).

If you want data you add to be automatically included in your PivotTable calculations when you refresh it, you should name your original data set as a table by selecting it with Ctrl+T. (See Chapter 26, "Tables," for more information.)

If you want to change the range of data used to create a PivotTable, you can always select Change Data Source on the Analyze tab (in the Data group). You can also move the table to a different location by selecting Move PivotTable in the Analyze tab's Actions group.

I work for a small travel agency for which I need to mass-mail a travel brochure. My funds are limited, so I want to mail the brochure to people who spend the most money on travel. From information in a random sample of 925 people, I know the gender, the age, and the amount these people spent on travel last year. How can I use this data to determine how gender and age influence a person's travel expenditures? What can I conclude about the type of person to whom I should mail the brochure?

To understand this data, you need to break it down as follows:

- Average amount spent on travel by gender
- Average amount spent on travel for each age group
- Average amount spent on travel by gender for each age group

The data is included on the Data worksheet in the file Traveldata.xlsx, and a sample is shown in Figure 43-25. For example, the first person is a 44-year-old male who spent $997 on travel.

	A	B	C
2	Amount Spent on Travel	Age	Gender
3	997	44	M
4	850	39	F
5	997	43	M
6	951	41	M
7	993	50	F
8	781	39	F
9	912	45	F
10	649	59	M
11	1265	25	M
12	680	38	F
13	800	41	F
14	613	32	F
15	993	46	F
16	1059	38	M
17	939	42	F
18	841	44	F
19	828	38	F
20	1004	50	F
21	983	48	F
22	837	46	M
23	924	42	M
24	852	48	M
25	963	39	M

FIGURE 43-25 The travel agency data showing the amount spent on travel, age, and gender.

Open the file Traveldatatemp.xlsx from this chapter's Templates folder. Let's first get a breakdown of spending by gender. On the Data worksheet, begin by selecting the Insert tab and clicking PivotTable in the Tables group. Excel extracts the range A2:D927 with the option Select A Table Or Range selected. After clicking OK, a new worksheet opens with the PivotTable Fields pane open on the right. Next, drag the Gender column (from the fields list at the top) to the Rows box in the lower left, and drag the field Amount Spent On Travel to the Values box in the lower right. This results in the PivotTable shown in Figure 43-26.

> **Note** The Fields List has changed a little with new versions of Excel. In Excel 2016, it becomes a natural drag-and-drop pane called the PivotTable Fields pane. The names of the areas have also been simplified.

Row Labels	Sum of Amount Spent on Travel
F	413632
M	426387
Grand Total	**840019**

FIGURE 43-26 A PivotTable summarizing the total travel expenditures by gender.

You can tell from the heading Sum Of Amount Spent On Travel that you are summarizing the total amount spent on travel by men and women, but you actually want the average amount spent on travel by men and women. To calculate the averages, double-click the cell showing Sum Of Amount Spent On Travel and then select Average from the Summarize Value Field By list in the Value Field Settings dialog box, shown in Figure 43-27.

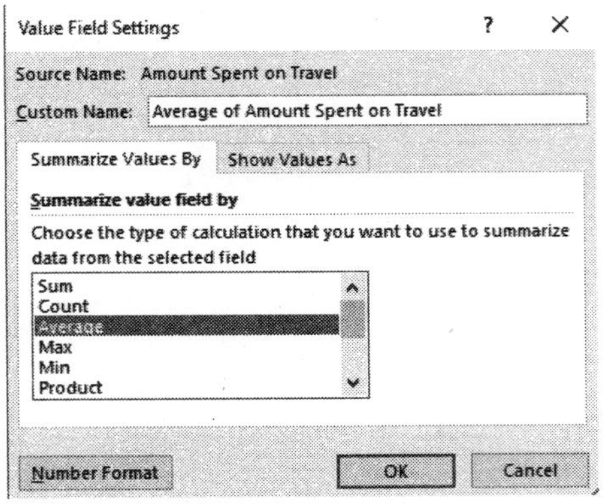

FIGURE 43-27 Selecting a different summary function in the Value Field Settings dialog box.

Click OK. You now see the results shown in Figure 43-28.

Row Labels	Average of Amount Spent on Travel
F	901.1590414
M	914.9935622
Grand Total	**908.1286486**

FIGURE 43-28 The average travel expenditures by gender.

On average, people spend $908.13 on travel (the grand total). Women spend an average of $901.16, whereas men spend $914.99. This PivotTable indicates that gender has little influence on the propensity to travel. By clicking the Row Labels arrow, you can show just male or female results.

Now, you want to see how age influences travel spending. Remove the Gender field from the Rows box (in the PivotTable Fields pane) by clicking it and selecting Remove Field. Then, to break down spending by age, drag Age from the fields list to the Rows area. The PivotTable now appears as it's shown in Figure 43-29.

	A	B	C	D
3	Average of Amount Spent on Travel	Column Labels		
4	Row Labels	F	M	Grand Total
5	25	482.3846154	1305.764706	948.9666667
6	26	526.6923077	1281.583333	889.04
7	27	532.5714286	1266.722222	1061.16
8	28	584	1243.666667	960.952381
9	29	564.5	1229.833333	814
10	30	578	1176.666667	877.3333333
11	31	604.3333333	1212.733333	1038.904762
12	32	636.6153846	1160.818182	876.875
13	33	661.6153846	1146.928571	913.2592593
14	34	674.0909091	1128.615385	920.2916667
15	35	705.5555556	1089.25	886.1176471
16	36	722.4285714	1071.888889	859.173913
17	37	746.9166667	1061.416667	904.1666667
18	38	764.25	1051.846154	913.8

FIGURE 43-29 A PivotTable showing the average travel expenditures by age and gender.

Age seems to have little effect on the travel expenditures. In fact, this PivotTable is pretty useless in its present state. You need to group the data by age to see any trends. To group the results by age, right-click anywhere in the Age column (column A) and choose Group. In the Grouping dialog box (shown in Figure 43-30), you can designate the interval by which to define an age group. By using 10-year increments (in the By box), you obtain the PivotTable shown in Figure 43-31.

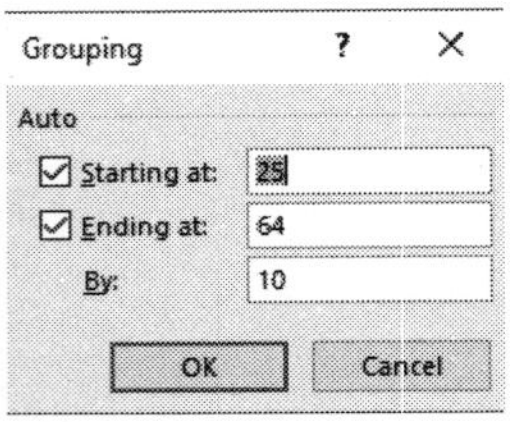

FIGURE 43-30 Using the Group command to group detailed records.

On average, 25–34 year olds spend $935.84 on travel, 55–64 year olds spend $903.57 on travel, and so on. This information is more useful, but it still indicates that people of all ages tend to spend about the same amount on travel (the younger group spends slightly more). This view of the data does not give enough details to help determine to whom you should mail your brochure.

Finally, let's get a breakdown of average travel spending by age, for men and women separately. All you have to do is drag Gender from the field list to the Columns box in the PivotTable Fields pane, resulting in the PivotTable shown in Figure 43-31 (see the Final Table worksheet in the file Traveldata.xlsx).

	A	B	C	D
3	Average of Amount Spent on Travel	Column Labels		
4	Row Labels	F	M	Grand Total
5	25-34	585.4752475	1221.209677	935.8355556
6	35-44	790.1652174	1004.098214	895.7180617
7	45-54	979.4782609	813.5765766	897.9955752
8	55-64	1179.609375	606.6470588	903.5668016
9	**Grand Total**	**901.1590414**	**914.9935622**	**908.1286486**

FIGURE 43-31 Breaking down the age and gender of travel spending.

Now we're cooking! You can see that as age increases, women spend more on travel and men spend less. Now you know who should get the brochure: older women and younger men. As one of my students said, "That would be some kind of cruise!"

A graph provides a nice summary of this analysis. Click the cursor inside the PivotTable, and from the Analyze tab on the ribbon, select PivotChart in the Tools group. A menu of recommended charts appears (the Insert Chart dialog box). Select the first choice in Columns (Clustered Column), and click OK. The result is the chart shown in Figure 43-32. If you want to edit the chart further, with the chart selected, click the Design tab in the PivotChart Tools tabs. Then, for example, if you click Add Chart Element in the Chart Layouts group, you can add titles to the chart and axes and make other changes.

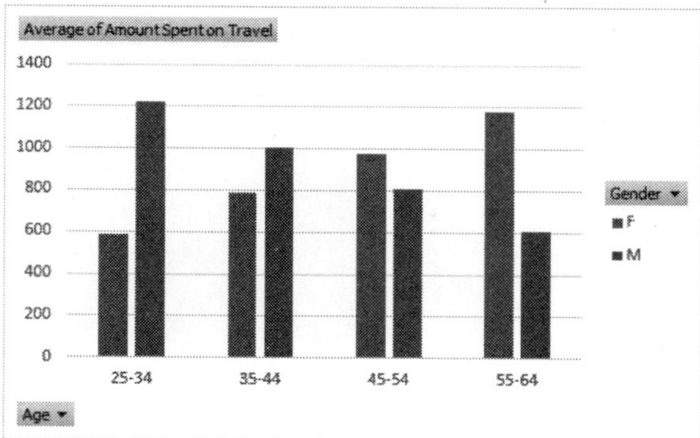

FIGURE 43-32 A PivotChart for the age/gender travel expenditure breakdown.

Each age group spends approximately the same on travel, but as their age increases, women spend more than men. (If you want to use a different type of chart, you can change the chart type by right-clicking the PivotChart and then choosing Change Chart Type. Select a new chart in the Change Chart Type dialog box, and then click OK.)

Notice that the bars showing expenditures by males decrease with age, and the bars representing the amount spent by females increase with age. You can see why the PivotTables that showed only gender and age data failed to unmask this pattern. Because half our sample population is male and half is female, we found that the average amount spent by people does not depend on the age. (Notice that the average height of the two bars for each age is approximately the same.) We also found that the average amount spent by men and women was approximately the same. You can see this because, averaged over all ages, the blue and red bars have approximately equal heights. Slicing and dicing the data simultaneously across age and gender does a much better job of showing you the real information.

Note that by clicking the drop-down arrow (on the PivotChart) that is associated with *Age*, you could filter the graph on age; clicking the drop-down arrow associated with *Gender*, you could filter the graph based on gender.

I'm doing market research about Volvo Cross Country Wagons. I need to determine what factors influence the likelihood that a family will purchase a station wagon. From information in a large sample of families, I know the family size (large or small) and the family income (high or low). How can I determine how family size and income influence the likelihood that a family will purchase a station wagon?

In the file Station.xlsx, you can find the following information:

- Is the family size large or small?
- Is the family's income high or low?
- Did the family buy a station wagon? Yes or no.

A sample of the data is shown in Figure 43-33 (see the Data worksheet). For example, the first family listed is a small, high-income family that did not buy a station wagon.

	A	B	C	D
2		Station Wagon?	Family Siz	Salary
3		No	Small	High
4		Yes	Large	High
5		Yes	Large	High
6		Yes	Large	High
7		Yes	Large	High
8		No	Small	High
9		Yes	Large	High
10		Yes	Large	High
11		Yes	Large	Low
12		Yes	Large	High
13		Yes	Large	Low
14		No	Small	Low
15		No	Small	Low
16		No	Small	High
17		Yes	Large	High
18		Yes	Large	High
19		No	Small	High
20		Yes	Large	High
21		No	Small	High
22		No	Large	Low

FIGURE 43-33 Data collected about income, family size, and the purchase of a station wagon.

You want to determine how family size and income influence the likelihood that a family will purchase a station wagon. The trick is to look at how income affects purchases for each family size and how family size affects purchases for each income level.

To begin, choose the Insert tab and click PivotTable in the Tables group. Then select the data (the cell range B2:D345) and click OK in the Create PivotTable dialog box. Using the PivotTable Fields pane, drag Family Size and Salary to the Rows area, drag Station Wagon? to the Columns area, and drag any of the three fields to the Values area. The result is the PivotTable shown in Figure 43-34 (see the 1st Table worksheet). Notice that Excel has chosen to summarize the data appropriately by counting the number of observations in each category. For example, 34 high-salary, large families did not buy a station wagon, whereas 100 high-salary, large families did buy one.

	A	B	C	D
3	Count of Station Wagon?	Column Labels		
4	Row Labels	No	Yes	Grand Total
5	⊟Large	48	138	186
6	High	34	100	134
7	Low	14	38	52
8	⊟Small	147	10	157
9	High	104	8	112
10	Low	43	2	45
11	Grand Total	195	148	343

FIGURE 43-34 Summary of station wagon ownership by family size and salary.

You would like to know for each row in the PivotTable the percentage of families that purchased a station wagon. To display the data in this format, right-click anywhere in the PivotTable data and then choose Value Field Settings, which displays the Value Field Settings dialog box. In the dialog box, click the Show Values As tab, and then select % Of Row Total in the Show Values As list, and then click OK. You now obtain the PivotTable shown in Figure 43-35. (See the 1st Percent Breakdown worksheet.)

	A	B	C	D
3	Count of Station Wagon?	Column Labels		
4	Row Labels	No	Yes	Grand Total
5	Large	25.81%	74.19%	100.00%
6	High	25.37%	74.63%	100.00%
7	Low	26.92%	73.08%	100.00%
8	Small	93.63%	6.37%	100.00%
9	High	92.86%	7.14%	100.00%
10	Low	95.56%	4.44%	100.00%
11	Grand Total	56.85%	43.15%	100.00%

FIGURE 43-35 Percentage breakdown of station-wagon ownership by income for large and small families.

From Figure 43-35, you learn that for both large and small families, income has little effect on whether the family purchases a station wagon. Now you need to determine how family size affects the propensity to buy a station wagon for high-income and low-income families. To do this, in the PivotTable Fields pane, drag the Salary field above Family Size in the Rows box, resulting in the PivotTable shown in Figure 43-36 (see the Final Percent Breakdown worksheet).

	A	B	C	D
3	Count of Station Wagon?	Column Labels		
4	Row Labels	No	Yes	Grand Total
5	High	56.10%	43.90%	100.00%
6	Large	25.37%	74.63%	100.00%
7	Small	92.86%	7.14%	100.00%
8	Low	58.76%	41.24%	100.00%
9	Large	26.92%	73.08%	100.00%
10	Small	95.56%	4.44%	100.00%
11	Grand Total	56.85%	43.15%	100.00%

FIGURE 43-36 Breakdown of station-wagon ownership by family size for high and low salaries.

From this table, you learn that for high-income families, a large family is much more likely to buy a station wagon than a small family. Similarly, for low-income families, a large family is also more likely to purchase a wagon than a small family. The bottom line is that family size has a much greater effect on the likelihood that a family will purchase a station wagon than income.

I work for a manufacturer that sells microchips globally. I'm given monthly actual and predicted sales for Canada, France, and the United States for Chip 1, Chip 2, and Chip 3. I'm also given the variance, or difference, between actual and budgeted revenues. For each month and each combination of country and product, I'd like to display the following data: actual revenue, budgeted revenue, actual variance, actual revenue as a percentage of annual revenue, and variance as a percentage of budgeted revenue. How can I display this information?

In this scenario, you are a finance manager for a microchip manufacturer. You sell your products in different countries/regions and at different times. PivotTables can help you summarize your data in a format that's easily understood.

The file Ptableexample.xlsx includes monthly actual and predicted sales during 1997 of Chip 1, Chip 2, and Chip 3 in Canada, France, and the United States. The file also contains the variance, or difference, between actual revenues and budgeted revenues. A sample of the data is shown in Figure 43-37 (see the Data worksheet). For example, in the United States in January, sales of Chip 1 totaled $4,000, although sales of $5,454 were predicted. This yielded a variance of –$1,454.

	A	B	C	D	E	F
1	Month	Product	Country	Revenue	Budget	Var
2	January	Chip 1	US	4000	5454	-1454
3	January	Chip 1	Canada	3424	5341	-1917
4	January	Chip 1	US	8324	1232	7092
5	January	Chip 1	France	5555	3424	2131
6	January	Chip 1	Canada	5341	8324	-2983
7	January	Chip 1	US	1232	5555	-4323
8	January	Chip 1	France	3424	5341	-1917
9	January	Chip 1	Canada	8324	1232	7092
10	January	Chip 1	US	5555	3424	2131
11	January	Chip 1	France	5341	8324	-2983
12	January	Chip 1	Canada	1232	5555	-4323
13	January	Chip 1	US	3424	5341	-1917
14	January	Chip 1	Canada	8383	5454	2929
15	January	Chip 1	France	8324	1232	7092
16	January	Chip 1	Canada	5555	3424	2131
17	January	Chip 1	US	5341	8324	-2983
18	January	Chip 1	France	1232	5555	-4323
19	January	Chip 1	France	3523	9295	-5772

FIGURE 43-37 Chip data from different countries/regions for different months, showing actual, budget, and variance revenues.

For each month and each combination of country and product, you would like to display the following data:

- Actual revenue
- Budgeted revenue
- Actual variance
- Actual revenue as a percentage of annual revenue
- Variance as a percentage of budgeted revenue

To begin, select a cell within the range of data you're working with (remember that the first row must include headings), and then select the Insert tab and click PivotTable in the Tables group. Excel automatically determines that your data is in the range A1:F208. Click OK in the Create PivotTable dialog box.

In the PivotTable Fields pane, if you drag the Month field to the Rows area, Country to the Columns area, and Revenue to the Values area, for example, you obtain the total revenue each month by country. A field you add to the Filters area (Product, for example) lets you filter your PivotTable by using values in that field. (Excel adds the Product filter to cells A1:B1.) By adding the Product field to the Filters area, you can filter the PivotTable to view sales of only Chip 1 by month for each country. Given that you want to be able to show data for any combination of country and product, you should drag

Month to the Rows area of the PivotTable Fields pane and both Product and Country to the Filters area. Next, drag Var, Revenue, and Budget (in that order) to the Values area. You have now created the PivotTable that is shown in Figure 43-38. (See the 1st Table worksheet.)

	A	B	C	D
1	Product	(All)		
2	Country	(All)		
3				
4		Values		
5	Row Labels	Sum of Var	Sum of Revenue	Sum of Budget
6	January	-4297	87534	91831
7	February	2843	90377	87534
8	March	-1389	88988	90377
9	April	-2774	84982	87756
10	May	-423	84559	84982
11	June	-548	84011	84559
12	July	2366	86377	84011
13	August	-2843	83534	86377
14	September	1389	84923	83534
15	October	-4318	80605	84923
16	November	3406	84011	80605
17	December	2366	86377	84011
18	Grand Total	-4222	1026278	1030500

FIGURE 43-38 Monthly summary of revenue, budget, and variance.

For example, in January, the total revenue was $87,534 and the total budgeted sales were $91,831, so the actual sales fell $4,297 short of the forecast (the variance).

You want to determine the percentage of revenue earned during each month. Again, drag Revenue from the field list to the Values area of the PivotTable Fields pane (this will show as Sum Of Revenue2). Click this data column, and then choose Value Field Settings. In the Value Field Settings dialog box, click the Show Values As tab. In the Show Values As list, select % Of Column Total and rename this field (in the Custom Name box) as **Sum Of Revenue2**, as shown in Figure 43-39.

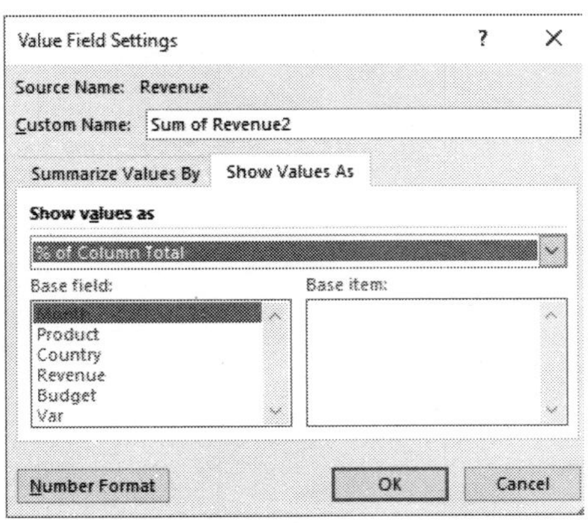

FIGURE 43-39 Creating each month's percentage of annual revenue.

You now obtain the PivotTable shown in Figure 43-40. (See the 2nd Table worksheet.) January sales provided 8.53 percent of the revenue. The total revenue for the year was $1,026,278 (shown in Figure 43-38).

	A	B	C	D
1	Product	(All)		
2	Country	(All)		
3				
4		Values		
5	Row Labels	Sum of Var	Sum of Revenue	Sum of Budget
6	January	-4297	8.53%	91831
7	February	2843	8.81%	87534
8	March	-1389	8.67%	90377
9	April	-2774	8.28%	87756
10	May	-423	8.24%	84982
11	June	-548	8.19%	84559
12	July	2366	8.42%	84011
13	August	-2843	8.14%	86377
14	September	1389	8.27%	83534
15	October	-4318	7.85%	84923
16	November	3406	8.19%	80605
17	December	2366	8.42%	84011
18	Grand Total	-4222	100.00%	1030500

FIGURE 43-40 Monthly revenue breakdown.

What is a calculated field?

Now, you want to determine for each month the variance as a percentage of the average sales. To do this, you can create a *calculated field*. Select a cell anywhere within the data area of the PivotTable, and then choose Fields, Items, & Sets from the Analyze tab (in the Calculations group). Next, choose Calculated Field to display the Insert Calculated Field dialog box. As shown in Figure 43-41, enter a name for your field (I entered **Var Percentage of Budget** in the Name box), and then enter your formula. The formula for this example is =Var/Budget. You can enter the formula yourself or use the list of fields and the Insert Field button to add a field to the formula. After clicking Add and then OK, you see the PivotTable shown in Figure 43-42. (See the Calc Field worksheet of the Ptableexample.xlsx file.)

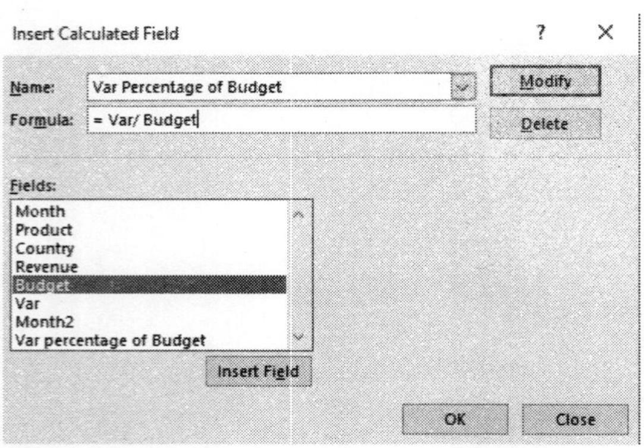

FIGURE 43-41 Creating a calculated field.

	A	B	C	D	E	F
1	Product	(All)				
2	Country	(All)				
3						
4		Values				
5	Row Labels	Sum of Var	Sum of Budget	Sum of Revenue	Sum of Revenue2	Sum of Var percentage of Budget
6	January	-4297	91831	87534	8.53%	-0.046792477
7	February	2843	87534	90377	8.81%	0.032478808
8	March	-1389	90377	88988	8.67%	-0.015368954
9	April	-2774	87756	84982	8.28%	-0.031610374
10	May	-423	84982	84559	8.24%	-0.004977525
11	June	-548	84559	84011	8.19%	-0.006480682
12	July	2366	84011	86377	8.42%	0.028162979
13	August	-2843	86377	83534	8.14%	-0.032913854
14	September	1389	83534	84923	8.27%	0.01662796
15	October	-4318	84923	80605	7.85%	-0.050846061
16	November	3406	80605	84011	8.19%	0.042255443
17	December	2366	84011	86377	8.42%	0.028162979
18	Grand Total	-4222	1030500	1026278	100.00%	-0.00409704

FIGURE 43-42 The PivotTable with a calculated field for variance percentage.

Thus, in January, sales were 4.7 percent lower than budgeted. By displaying the Insert Calculated Field dialog box again, you can modify or delete a calculated field.

How do I use a report filter or slicer?

To see the sales of Chip 2 in France, for example, you can drag the Product and Country fields to the Filters area. With Chip 2 and France selected, you would see the PivotTable shown in Figure 43-43. Figure 43-44 shows how to create the same table with slicers (see the Slicers worksheet).

	A	B	C	D	E
1	Product	Chip 2			
2	Country	France			
3					
4		Values			
5	Row Labels	Sum of Var	Sum of Revenue	Sum of Budget	Sum of Revenue2
6	February	-3846	29108	32954	23.90%
7	May	3318	35363	32045	29.04%
8	August	2769	33432	30663	27.45%
9	November	0	23876	23876	19.61%
10	Grand Total	2241	121779	119538	100.00%

FIGURE 43-43 The sales of Chip 2 in France.

In the worksheet Slicers, I used slicers to create the same table. I clicked the PivotTable and selected Slicer from the Insert tab (in the Filters group). Then I created the slicers shown in Figure 43-44 by selecting the Product and Country fields from the Insert Slicers dialog box. Selecting Chip 2 from the Product slicer and France from the Country slicer yields the relevant computations for all transactions involving Chip 2 in France. If you want to resize a slicer, drag a handle on its border. To resize a slicer while keeping the same proportions, hold down the Ctrl key, and then resize the slicer.

	A	B	C	D	E
1	Product	Chip 2			
2	Country	France			
3					
4		Values			
5	Row Labels	Sum of Var	Sum of Revenue	Sum of Budget	Sum of Revenue2
6	February	-3846	29108	32954	23.90%
7	May	3318	35363	32045	29.04%
8	August	2769	33432	30663	27.45%
9	November	0	23876	23876	19.61%
10	Grand Total	2241	121779	119538	100.00%

Country: Canada, France, US

Product: Chip 1, Chip 2, Chip 3

FIGURE 43-44 The sales of Chip 2 in France with slicers.

How do I group items in a PivotTable?

Often, you want to group headings in a PivotTable. For example, you might want to combine sales for January–March. To create a group, select the items you want to group (press Ctrl and select January, February, and March in cells A6:A8), right-click the selection, and then choose Group. Click Month in the Rows area of the PivotTable Fields pane, and then click Remove Field. After changing the name from Group1 to **Jan-March** in the formula bar, you obtain the PivotTable shown in Figure 43-45.

	A	B	C	D	E
1	Product	(All)			
2	Country	(All)			
3					
4		Values			
5	Row Labels	Sum of Var	Sum of Revenue	Sum of Budget	Sum of Revenue2
6	Jan-March	-2843	266899	269742	26.01%
7	April	-2774	84982	87756	8.28%
8	May	-423	84559	84982	8.24%
9	June	-548	84011	84559	8.19%
10	July	2366	86377	84011	8.42%
11	August	-2843	83534	86377	8.14%
12	September	1389	84923	83534	8.27%
13	October	-4318	80605	84923	7.85%
14	November	3406	84011	80605	8.19%
15	December	2366	86377	84011	8.42%
16	Grand Total	-4222	1026278	1030500	100.00%

FIGURE 43-45 Grouping items together for January, February, and March.

Remarks about grouping

- You can disband a group by right-clicking a grouped cell and then selecting the Ungroup option.
- You can group nonadjacent selections by holding down the Ctrl key while you select nonadjacent rows or columns.

- With numerical values or dates in a row field, you can group by number or dates in arbitrary intervals. For example, you can create groups for age ranges and then find the average income for all 25–34 year olds.

What is a calculated item?

A *calculated item* works just like a calculated field except that you are creating one row rather than a column. To create a calculated item, you should select an item in the row area of the PivotTable, not an item in the body of the PivotTable. Then, on the Analyze tab, in the Calculations group, select Fields, Items, & Sets, followed by Calculated Item.

To illustrate how to create a calculated item, look at the file Calculateditem.xlsx. In the worksheet Data (see Figure 43-46), we have the sales of different car brands. We would like to summarize the total sales by the company's country (Japan, Germany, or United States).

	H	I
8	Brand	Sales
9	Ford	3
10	Nissan	2
11	Ford	6
12	VW	2
13	VW	4
14	Nissan	4
15	Chrysler	2
16	VW	2
17	BMW	6
18	Honda	2
19	VW	4
20	Honda	5
21	BMW	6
22	Honda	4
23	Ford	5
24	Ford	5
25	Ford	2

FIGURE 43-46 Data for creating a calculated item.

To begin, we create a PivotTable listing the total sales by country (see the worksheet PT 1). In the PivotTable Fields pane, drag Brand to the Rows area and Sales to the Values area. After changing Count to Sum (click Count of Sales in the Values area, select Value Field Settings, select Sum in the Summarize Value Field By list, and click OK), I obtain the PivotTable shown in Figure 43-47. (Remember, to open the PivotTable Fields pane, on the Analyze tab, in the Show group, click Field List.)

	A	B
3	Row Labels	Sum of Sales
4	BMW	359
5	Chrysler	286
6	Ford	277
7	GM	239
8	Honda	283
9	Nissan	219
10	VW	323
11	Japan	502
12	Germany	682
13	US	802
14	**Grand Total**	**3972**

FIGURE 43-47 A PivotTable summarizing sales by brand.

Before creating a calculated item, it is a good idea to hide the grand totals by selecting Grand Totals on the Design tab and selecting Off For Rows and Columns. Otherwise, after you create the calculated item, the grand totals will count each car twice.

To create a calculated item for Japan, click anywhere in the Row Labels column and select Fields, Items, & Sets from the Analyze tab (in the Calculations group). After selecting Calculated Item, fill in the dialog box by entering Japan in the Name box, entering the formula =Honda+Nissan in the Formula box, selecting Brand in the Fields list, and selecting Nissan in the Items list. The completed dialog box is shown in Figure 43-48.

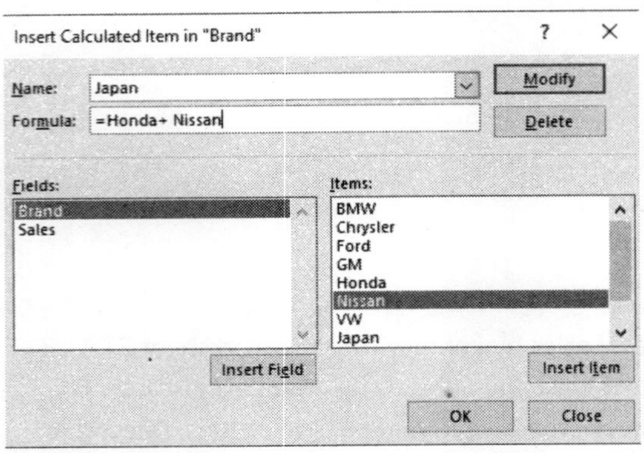

FIGURE 43-48 Calculated-item creation for Japan.

This dialog box creates a calculated item for Japan by adding up Honda and Nissan sales. In a similar fashion, you can create calculated fields that summarize sales in Germany and the United States. The resulting PivotTable is in the worksheet Calc Item and is shown in Figure 43-49.

If you want to delete a calculated item or calculated field, select Calculated Item or Calculated Field from the Fields, Items, & Sets menu (on the Analyze tab). Then, from the Name section of the dialog box, select the field or item you want to delete, and then click Delete.

	A	B
1		
2		
3	Row Labels	Sum of Sales
4	BMW	359
5	Chrysler	286
6	Ford	277
7	GM	239
8	Honda	283
9	Nissan	219
10	VW	323
11	Japan	502
12	Germany	682
13	US	802

FIGURE 43-49 Calculated items.

If you want, you may hide the individual brand sales by filtering on the row labels and selecting just Japan, Germany, and US.

See Problem 11 in the "Problems" section of this chapter for an example of creating a calculated item. In the chip manufacturing PivotTable example, you could not create a calculated item because you had multiple copies of the Revenue field.

What is *drilling down*?

When you double-click a cell in a PivotTable to display all the detailed data that's summarized in that field, you're *drilling down*. For example, double-clicking any March entry in the microchip scenario displays the data that's related to March sales.

I often have to use specific data in a PivotTable, such as the April sales of Chip 1 in France, to determine profit. Unfortunately, this data moves around when new fields are added to my PivotTable. Does Excel have a function that enables me to always extract April's Chip 1 sales in France from the PivotTable?

Yes, there is such a function. The GETPIVOTDATA function fills the bill. Suppose that you want to extract the sales of Chip 1 in France, during April, from the PivotTable contained in the Data worksheet in the file Getpivotdata.xlsx. (See Figure 43-50 and the worksheet Get Pivot Data.) Entering in cell E2 the formula =GETPIVOTDATA(A4,"April France Chip 1 Sum of Revenue") yields the correct value ($37,600), even if additional products, countries/regions, and months are added to the PivotTable later. You can also determine the resulting revenue by pointing to the cell containing Chip 1 April sales in France (cell D24).

The first argument for this function is the cell in the upper-left corner of the PivotTable (cell A4). You enclose in quotation marks (separated by spaces) the PivotTable headings that define the entry you want. The last entry must specify the data field, but other headings can be listed in any order. Thus, the formula here means *For the PivotTable whose upper-left corner is in cell A4, find the Sum of Revenue for Chip 1 in France during April.* This formula returns the correct answer, even if the sales data for Chip 1 in France in April moves to a different location in the PivotTable.

	A	B	C	D	E	F
1					April Chip 2 France	total revenue
2					37600	1026278
3						
4		Values				
5	Row Labels	Sum of Var	Sum of Budget	Sum of Revenue	Sum of Revenue2	Sum of Var percentage of Budget
6	**January**	**-4297**	**91831**	**87534**	**8.53%**	**-0.046792477**
7	**Chip 1**	**-4297**	**91831**	**87534**	**8.53%**	**-0.046792477**
8	Canada	2929	29330	32259	3.14%	0.099863621
9	France	-5772	33171	27399	2.67%	-0.174007416
10	US	-1454	29330	27876	2.72%	-0.049573815
11	**February**	**2843**	**87534**	**90377**	**8.81%**	**0.032478808**
12	**Chip 2**	**2843**	**87534**	**90377**	**8.81%**	**0.032478808**
13	Canada	3318	32045	35363	3.45%	0.103541894
14	France	-3846	32954	29108	2.84%	-0.116708139
15	US	3371	22535	25906	2.52%	0.149589527
16	**March**	**-1389**	**90377**	**88988**	**8.67%**	**-0.015368954**
17	**Chip 3**	**-1389**	**90377**	**88988**	**8.67%**	**-0.015368954**
18	Canada	-10733	35363	24630	2.40%	-0.303509318
19	France	11529	20784	32313	3.15%	0.554705543
20	US	-2185	34230	32045	3.12%	-0.063832895
21	**April**	**-2774**	**87756**	**84982**	**8.28%**	**-0.031610374**
22	**Chip 1**	**-2774**	**87756**	**84982**	**8.28%**	**-0.031610374**
23	Canada	1054	19289	20343	1.98%	0.054642542
24	France	-54	37654	37600	3.66%	-0.001434111
25	US	-3774	30813	27039	2.63%	-0.122480771

FIGURE 43-50 Using the GETPIVOTDATA function to locate April Chip 1 Sales in France.

If you want to simply return the total revenue ($1,026,278), you can enter the formula (see cell F2) =GETPIVOTDATA(A4,"Sum of Revenue").

To see the true power of the GETPIVOTDATA function, suppose you want to summarize the sales of each product, by country, for each month of the year in a nice table, as shown in Figure 43-51.

	I	J	K	L
9	**Month**	**April**		
10				
11				
12		**Chip 1**	**Chip2**	**Chip 3**
13	**Canada**	**20343**	**0**	**0**
14	**France**	**37600**	**0**	**0**
15	**US**	**27039**	**0**	**0**

FIGURE 43-51 Using GETPIVOTDATA to extract the April sales of each product, in each country.

To begin, I created a drop-down box that allows me to enter the month of the year in cell J9. Then we entered the countries in I13:I15 and the products in J12:J12. Now in cell J13, we copied our previous GETPIVOTDATA formula from E2 and edited it to become =IFERROR(GETPIVOTDATA("Sum of Revenue",$A$4,"Month",$J$9,"Product",J$12,"Country",$I13),0). Copying this formula from J13 to J13:L15 pulls the sales of each product during each month from the PivotTable. As we copy the formula across, the product pulled changes; as we copy it down, the country pulled changes. In each cell, the chosen month is pulled from cell J9. The use of the IFERROR function ensures that if no sales of a product occurred in a country during the selected month, we return a 0 instead of an error message. Imagine how useful this trick would be if we sold 1,000 products in 200 countries!

Often, the GETPIVOTDATA function is a nuisance. In these cases, you can turn off the option to use it. Suppose you want to refer to data in cells B5:B11 from a PivotTable elsewhere in your workbook.

You would probably use the formula =B5 and copy it to the range B6:B11. You hope this action would extract B6, B7, ,..., B11 to the cells you want. Unfortunately, if the GETPIVOTDATA option is active, you get a bunch of GETPIVOTDATA functions that refer to the same cell. So if you want to turn off GETPIVOTDATA, click the File tab and then click Options. Select Formulas in the left pane, and under Working With Formulas, clear the option Use GetPivotData Functions For PivotTable References, and then click OK. This ensures that clicking inside a PivotTable yields a formula like =B6, rather than a GETPIVOTDATA function. You can also turn off GETPIVOTDATA in a particular PivotTable by clicking in the PivotTable, and then, in the PivotTable group on the Analyze tab, clicking the Options arrow, and from the drop-down list, clearing Generate GetPivotData.

Finally, note that you can also combine the MATCH and OFFSET functions (explained in Chapter 5, "The MATCH function," and Chapter 22, "The OFFSET function," respectively) to extract various PivotTable entries.

How can I use the Timeline feature to summarize data during different time periods?

Excel 2013 introduced a wonderful new feature, Timeline, which allows you to easily filter your PivotTable based on time periods. You can select any subset of consecutive years, quarters, months, or days in your data, and the Timeline feature ensures that all the PivotTable calculations will include spreadsheet rows only from the selected time period.

To illustrate the use of the Timeline feature, look at the file Makeuptimeline.xlsx. In the worksheet Data, we have listed for 1,900 makeup transactions the following information: Salesperson (the Name column, H), Product (column J), Date (column I), Units (column K), and Revenue (the Dollars column, L). In the worksheet Pivot Table, you see a PivotTable that summarizes the sales of each product by each salesperson. After clicking anywhere in the PivotTable, go to the Insert tab on the ribbon and select Timeline from the Filters group. From the Insert Timelines dialog box, select Date and click OK. You will see the timeline shown in Figure 43-52.

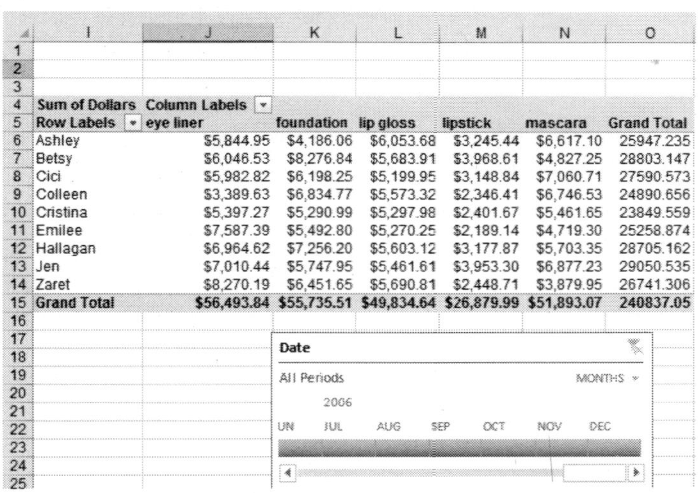

Sum of Dollars	Column Labels					
Row Labels	eye liner	foundation	lip gloss	lipstick	mascara	Grand Total
Ashley	$5,844.95	$4,186.06	$6,053.68	$3,245.44	$6,617.10	25947.235
Betsy	$6,046.53	$8,276.84	$5,683.91	$3,968.61	$4,827.25	28803.147
Cici	$5,982.82	$6,198.25	$5,199.95	$3,148.84	$7,060.71	27590.573
Colleen	$3,389.63	$6,834.77	$5,573.32	$2,346.41	$6,746.53	24890.656
Cristina	$5,397.27	$5,290.99	$5,297.98	$2,401.67	$5,461.65	23849.559
Emilee	$7,587.39	$5,492.80	$5,270.25	$2,189.14	$4,719.30	25258.874
Hallagan	$6,964.62	$7,256.20	$5,603.12	$3,177.87	$5,703.35	28705.162
Jen	$7,010.44	$5,747.95	$5,461.61	$3,953.30	$6,877.23	29050.535
Zaret	$8,270.19	$6,451.65	$5,690.81	$2,448.71	$3,879.95	26741.306
Grand Total	$56,493.84	$55,735.51	$49,834.64	$26,879.99	$51,893.07	240837.05

FIGURE 43-52 The timeline for makeup data.

Using the Shift key, you can select adjacent quarters that can be used to summarize sales. For example, in the worksheet Timeline (see Figure 43-53) we summarized sales during 2004 and the first two quarters of 2005. Clicking the funnel (Clear Filter) restores a PivotTable based on all the data.

	A	B	C	D	E	F	G
1							
2							
3	Sum of Dollars	Column Labels					
4	Row Labels	eye liner	foundation	lip gloss	lipstick	mascara	Grand Total
5	Ashley	$2,259.97	$2,064.62	$3,387.84	$1,191.92	$4,773.72	$13,678.07
6	Betsy	$2,714.91	$4,195.09	$2,862.84	$2,223.66	$2,591.12	$14,587.61
7	Cici	$3,310.71	$3,313.91	$2,076.46	$1,676.03	$3,026.36	$13,403.47
8	Colleen	$2,122.76	$4,064.70	$3,190.32	$1,454.87	$3,163.44	$13,996.09
9	Cristina	$3,890.14	$2,047.07	$2,844.16	$1,531.34	$2,708.86	$13,021.57
10	Emilee	$4,086.75	$2,754.36	$2,808.22	$1,180.96	$2,462.89	$13,293.17
11	Hallagan	$4,195.40	$3,622.60	$2,857.48	$2,133.18	$2,309.15	$15,117.81
12	Jen	$3,364.89	$2,830.40	$1,875.47	$1,762.88	$3,866.27	$13,699.91
13	Zaret	$3,188.38	$2,695.03	$3,040.78	$1,659.86	$1,828.48	$12,412.53
14	Grand Total	29133.89079	27587.77037	24943.58511	14814.69089	26730.28606	123210.2232

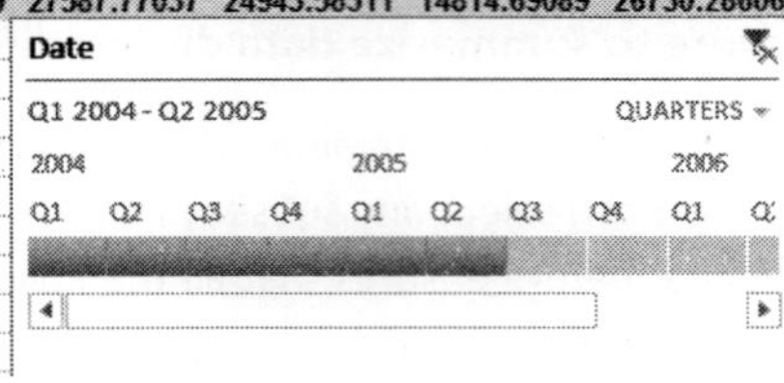

FIGURE 43-53 The timeline that summarizes sales for 2004 and the first two quarters of 2005.

How I can use a PivotTable to summarize total sales to date during a year?

Using Value Field Settings, it is easy to summarize total sales to date during a year. To illustrate how to summarize total sales to date during a year, look at the file Monthtomonth.xlsx. The worksheet Data records the year, month, and revenue for a number of sales transactions. To begin in the worksheet Year To Date, we summarized the monthly sales for each year by dragging Month to the Rows area, Year to the Columns area, and Revenue to the Values area. This yields the PivotTable shown in Figure 43-54.

	A	B	C	D	E
3	Sum of Revenue	Column Labels			
4	Row Labels	2009	2010	2011	Grand Total
5	January		704.15%	-45.73%	
6	February		56.05%	-56.02%	
7	March		-63.15%	-52.46%	
8	April		-13.94%	-33.62%	
9	May		-24.27%	-40.01%	
10	June		-22.73%	44.80%	
11	July		150.55%	-55.59%	
12	August		-35.92%	43.03%	
13	September		-19.52%	-6.95%	
14	October		-57.66%	-15.00%	
15	November		-76.57%	183.40%	
16	December		144.25%	8.66%	
17	Grand Total		-6.94%	-19.88%	

FIGURE 43-54 Summary of sales by month and year.

This figure shows a sales summary, broken down by month and year. From anywhere in cells B5:E17 of the PivotTable, right-click and select Value Field Settings. Then select the Show Values As tab, choose Running Total In from the Show Values As list, and select Month from the Base Field list. Then click OK. The resulting PivotTable, shown in Figure 43-55 (see the worksheet Year To Date), shows for each month the sales for the given year through that month. For example, sales through February of 2009 were $58,449.

	A	B	C	D	E
3	**Sum of Revenue**	**Column Labels**			
4	**Row Labels**	**2009**	**2010**	**2011**	**Grand Total**
5	January	10453	84058	45615	140126
6	February	58449	158954	78558	295961
7	March	171575	200643	98379	470597
8	April	241188	260553	138149	639890
9	May	306343	309898	167749	783990
10	June	361157	352253	229080	942490
11	July	396087	439769	267943	1103799
12	August	447675	472829	315230	1235734
13	September	508510	521792	360789	1391091
14	October	594117	558035	391594	1543746
15	November	666719	575045	439801	1681565
16	December	696762	648426	519534	1864722
17	**Grand Total**				

FIGURE 43-55 The year-to-date sales totals.

How can I use a PivotTable to summarize sales this month compared to the same month a year earlier?

Again, we will use the data in the file Monthtomonth.xlsx. In the worksheet Previous Year, we created a PivotTable by dragging Month to the Rows area, Year to the Columns area, and Revenue to the Values area. After right-clicking anywhere in the range B5:E17 in the PivotTable and selecting Value Field Settings, fill in the dialog box as shown in Figure 43-56 to create the PivotTable shown in Figure 43-57: update the Custom Name box to **Sum of Revenue**, select the Show Values As tab, select % Difference from the Show Value As list, select Year from the Base Field list, select Previous from the Base Item list, and click OK. Here we see how sales during each month compare to the same month in the previous year. For example, January 2010 sales increased 704.15 percent over January 2009 sales.

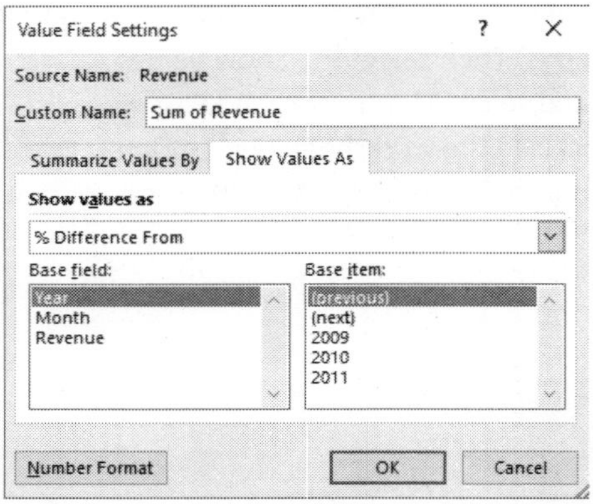

FIGURE 43-56 The settings needed to compare a month to the same month in the previous year.

	A	B	C	D	E
1					
2					
3	**Sum of Revenue**	**Column Labels**			
4	**Row Labels**	**2009**	**2010**	**2011**	**Grand Total**
5	January		704.15%	-45.73%	
6	February		56.05%	-56.02%	
7	March		-63.15%	-52.46%	
8	April		-13.94%	-33.62%	
9	May		-24.27%	-40.01%	
10	June		-22.73%	44.80%	
11	July		150.55%	-55.59%	
12	August		-35.92%	43.03%	
13	September		-19.52%	-6.95%	
14	October		-57.66%	-15.00%	
15	November		-76.57%	183.40%	
16	December		144.25%	8.66%	
17	**Grand Total**		**-6.94%**	**-19.88%**	

FIGURE 43-57 A comparison of sales to the same month during the previous year.

How can I create a PivotTable based on data in several different locations?

Often the data needed to create a PivotTable can lie in different worksheets or different workbooks (files). The key to creating a PivotTable from data in different locations is to press Alt+D+P and bring up the classic PivotTable and PivotChart Wizard, shown in Figure 43-58. (You might need to press Alt+D+P a few times.)

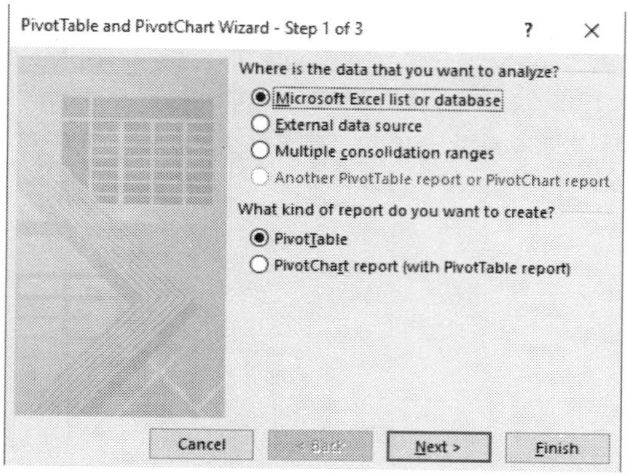

FIGURE 43-58 The classic PivotTable and PivotChart Wizard dialog box.

To illustrate how to create a PivotTable based on data in different ranges, open the files East.xlsx and West.xlsx from this chapter's Templates folder. In the View tab on the ribbon, click Arrange All in the Window group, select Tiled from the Arrange Windows dialog box, and click OK. This displays all the open Excel files side by side or on top of each other as shown in Figure 43-59. (The arrangment depends on your resolution, but most often the windows display side by side.) This data represents the January, February, and March sales in the East and West. We want to produce a PivotTable that summarizes the total sales of each product during each month.

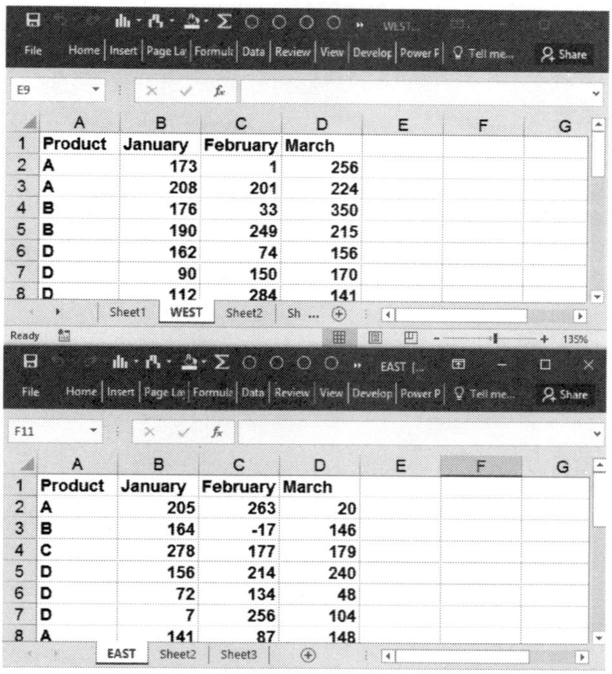

FIGURE 43-59 Two files that will be summarized with a PivotTable.

To begin, press Alt+D+P (to bring up the PivotTable and PivotChart Wizard) and select Multiple Consolidation Ranges in step 1. After selecting Next, choose Create A Single Page Field For Me in step 2a, and then click Next. From step 2b of the PivotTable and PivotChart Wizard, select (as shown in Figure 43-60) the East sales data, EAST!$A$1:$D$18, and click Add to add it to the range of data that will be used to create our PivotTable.

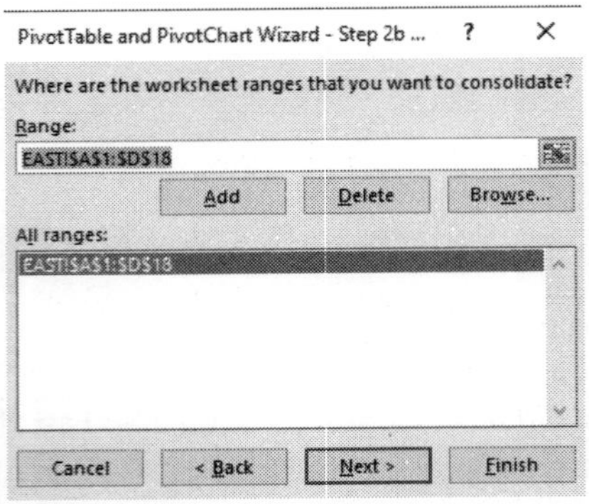

FIGURE 43-60 Adding the East data.

Then clear the East data from the Range portion of the dialog box, and select the West data, WEST!$A$1:$D$24, and then click Add to add this data to the All Ranges section. After clicking Next, you can decide whether to place the final PivotTable in a new worksheet or the current worksheet (step 3). Choose a new worksheet, and after selecting Finish, you obtain the PivotTable (see Figure 43-61) in the worksheet PT of the workbook West.xlsx (in this chapter's Practice Files folder).

	A	B	C	D	E
1	Page1	(All)			
2					
3	Sum of Value	Column			
4	Row	January	February	March	Grand Total
5	A	1323	1317	1445	4085
6	B	890	335	812	2037
7	C	1231	922	843	2996
8	D	767	1424	1199	3390
9	E	579	483	371	1433
10	F	597	577	327	1501
11	G	570	850	811	2231
12	H	131	71	266	468
13	Grand Total	6088	5979	6074	18141

FIGURE 43-61 A PivotTable summarizing the East and West sales.

We find, for example, that total sales of Product A in February were 1,317, and so on. You can filter the products by selecting the drop-down arrow in cell A4; filter the months by using the drop-down arrow in cell B3. The drop-down arrow in cell B1 allows you to filter the PivotTable so that only East or West sales data is used. Refresh updates the PivotTable, showing data changes. The Slicer and Timeline tools do not work with a PivotTable created from multiple ranges.

If you do not like using the Alt+D+P combination, you can add the PivotTable and PivotChart Wizard to the Quick Access Toolbar by selecting File, Options, Quick Access Toolbar, Commands Not In The Ribbon (from the Choose Commands From list), and selecting PivotTable And PivotChart

Wizard. Then click Add to add the command to your customized Quick Access Toolbar, and click OK to close the Excel Options dialog box.

To create a PivotTable from multiple ranges, the headings (in this case January, February, and March) in each range must be identical. In Chapter 44, we will discuss a feature added in Excel 2013, the Data Model, which allows you to create PivotTables even when a heading from one source range occurs in none of the other source ranges.

How can I create a PivotTable based on an already created PivotTable?

Often, we want to create a PivotTable based on an already created PivotTable. This allows us to view several PivotTables based on the same data. For example, in the file Makeuptimeline.xlsx, we created (as shown in Figure 43-53) a summary of makeup sales with a list of salespeople's names going down and a list of products going across. Suppose we also want to create a PivotTable with the list of products going down and names of salespeople going across. After selecting a cell in the worksheet Pivot Table of the file Makeuptimeline.xls, press Alt+D+P to bring up the PivotTable and PivotChart Wizard. Then choose the Another PivotTable Report Or PivotChart Report option in step 1, and click Next. Then, in step 2, choose the PivotTable from which you wish to build your new table. We chose our original PivotTable: PivotTable10. Click Finish. Now the PivotTable Fields pane appears, and you can create a new PivotTable without disturbing your old table. We chose to put Product in the Rows area, Name in the Columns area, and Dollars in the Values area. This creates the PivotTable shown in Figure 43-62.

	H	I	J	K	L	M	N	O	P	Q	R
24	PIVOTTABLE BASED ON ANOTHER PIVOTTABLE										
25											
26	Sum of Dollars	Column Labels									
27	Row Labels	Ashley	Betsy	Cici	Colleen	Cristina	Emilee	Hallagan	Jen	Zaret	Grand Total
28	eye liner	$5,844.95	$6,046.53	$5,982.82	$3,389.63	$5,397.27	$7,587.39	$6,964.62	$7,010.44	$8,270.19	$56,493.84
29	foundation	$4,186.06	$8,276.84	$6,198.25	$6,834.77	$5,290.99	$5,492.80	$7,256.20	$5,747.95	$6,451.65	$55,735.51
30	lip gloss	$6,053.68	$5,683.91	$5,199.95	$5,573.32	$5,297.98	$5,270.25	$5,603.12	$5,461.61	$5,690.81	$49,834.64
31	lipstick	$3,245.44	$3,968.61	$3,148.84	$2,346.41	$2,401.67	$2,189.14	$3,177.87	$3,953.30	$2,448.71	$26,879.99
32	mascara	$6,617.10	$4,827.25	$7,060.71	$6,746.53	$5,461.65	$4,719.30	$5,703.35	$6,877.23	$3,879.95	$51,893.07
33	Grand Total	$25,947.24	$28,803.15	$27,590.57	$24,890.66	$23,849.56	$25,258.87	$28,705.16	$29,050.53	$26,741.31	$240,837.05

FIGURE 43-62 A PivotTable based on another PivotTable.

How can I easily use the report filter to create multiple PivotTables?

In the worksheet Slicers of the file Ptableexample.xlsx, I created filters based on Country and Product. Suppose, for example, you want to create a separate PivotTable for each country. Select a cell within the PivotTable. From the upper left-hand portion of the Analyze tab, select Options in the PivotTable group, as shown in Figure 43-63. Then select the Country field to create a separate PivotTable for each country and select the Product field to create a PivotTable for each product. Figure 43-64 shows, for example, the PivotTable created for sales in France.

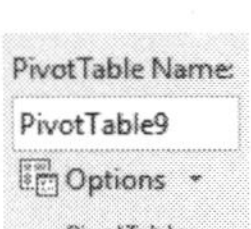

FIGURE 43-63 Selecting Options to create multiple PivotTables based on the report filter.

A1 | Product

	A	B	C	D	E
1	Product	(All)			
2	Country	France			
3					
4		Values			
5	Row Labels	Sum of Var	Sum of Revenue	Sum of Budget	Sum of Revenue2
6	January	-5772	27399	33171	7.43%
7	February	-3846	29108	32954	7.89%
8	March	11529	32313	20784	8.76%
9	April	-54	37600	37654	10.19%
10	May	3318	35363	32045	9.59%
11	June	-3740	32855	36595	8.91%
12	July	-275	27239	27514	7.38%
13	August	2769	33432	30663	9.06%
14	September	-2983	29217	32200	7.92%
15	October	-1917	27300	29217	7.40%
16	November	0	23876	23876	6.47%
17	December	912	33171	32259	8.99%
18	Grand Total	-59	368873	368932	100.00%

FIGURE 43-64 A PivotTable created for France from the Country filter.

Problems

1. Contoso, Ltd. produces microchips. Five types of defects (labeled 1–5) have been known to occur. The chips are manufactured by two operators (A and B) using four machines (1–4). You are given data about a sample of defective chips, including the type of defect, the operator, machine number, and day of the week the defect occurred. Use this data to chart a course of action that would lead, as quickly as possible, to improved product quality. You should use a PivotTable to "stratify" the defects with respect to the type of defect, day of the week, machine used, and operator working. You might even want to break down the data by machine, operator, and so on. Assume that each operator and machine made an equal number of products. You'll find this data in the file Contoso.xlsx.

2. You own a fast-food restaurant and have done some market research in an attempt to better understand your customers. For a random sample of customers, you are given the income, gender, and number of days per week that residents go out for fast food. Use this information to determine how gender and income influence the frequency with which a person goes out to eat fast food. The data is in the file Mcdonalds.xlsx.

3. Students at the School of Fine Art apply to study either English or science. You have been assigned to determine whether the School of Fine Art discriminates against women in admitting students to the school of their choice. You are given the following data for the School of Fine Art's students:

   - Female or male
   - Major applied for: English (Eng) or science (Sci)

- Admit? Yes or No

Assuming that women are as equally qualified for each major as men, does this data indicate that the college discriminates against women? Be sure you use all the available information. The data is in the file Finearts.xlsx.

4. You have been assigned to evaluate the quality of care given to heart-attack patients at Emergency Room (ER) and Chicago Hope (CH). For the last month, you are given the following patient data:

- Hospital (ER or CH).
- Risk category (high or low). High-risk people are less likely to survive than low-risk people.
- Patient outcome (live or die).

Use this data to determine which hospital is doing a better job of caring for heart attack patients. Hint: Use all the data. The data is in the file Hospital.xlsx.

5. You are given the monthly level of the Dow Jones Index for the years 1947 to 1992. Does this data indicate any unusual seasonal patterns in stock returns? Hint: You can extract the month (January, February, and so on) by using the formula =TEXT(A4,"mmm") copied to any column. The data is in the file Dow.xlsx.

6. The file Makeupdb.xlsx contains information about the sales of makeup products. For each transaction, you are given the following information:

- Name of salesperson
- Date of sale
- Product sold
- Units sold
- Transaction revenue

Create a PivotTable to compile the following information:

- The number of sales transactions for each salesperson.
- For each salesperson, the total revenue by product.
- Using your answer to the previous question, create a function that always yields Jen's lipstick sales.
- Total revenue generated by each salesperson, broken down by location.
- Total revenue by salesperson and year. Hint: You need to group the data by year.

7. For the years 1985–1992, you are given monthly interest rates on bonds that pay money one year after the day they're bought. It's often suggested that interest rates are more volatile—

tend to change more—when interest rates are high. Does the data in the file Intratevol-volatility.xlsx support this statement? Hint: PivotTables can display standard deviations.

8. For the grocery example, prepare a chart that summarizes the trend over time of the sales at each store.

9. For the grocery example, create a calculate field that computes an average per-unit price received for each product.

10. For the grocery example, create a PivotChart that summarizes the sales of each product at each store for the years 2005 and 2006.

11. For the data in the file Calcitemdata.xlsx, create calculated fields that summarize the sales of dessert (cakes+puddings) and fruits (apples+grapes).

12. In the chip PivotTable example, create a PivotTable that summarizes the monthly sales of Chips 1 and 3 in France and the United States.

13. In the customer PivotTable example, show the top 15 customers in one table and the bottom 5 customers in another table.

14. The file Ptablepartsdata.xlsx contains sales of various parts. Each part's code begins with either *Part* (for computer part) or *Comp* (for computer). Create a PivotTable that shows only the sales of Parts. Hint: Use a labels filter.

15. For the data in Problem 14, summarize the total sales of parts and computers.

16. The file Cigarettedata.xlsx contains the age of a sample of Americans, whether they smoke cigarettes or cigars, and whether they died during the current year. What can you conclude from this data?

17. The file Collegedata.xlsx tells you the following information about students who applied to graduate school at Kelley University: gender, desired major, and whether they were accepted or rejected. If you construct the appropriate PivotTable, you will find fewer women are accepted than men. Do you think Kelley discriminates against women?

18. The file Analyzesurveydata.xlsx contains answers on a 1–7 scale to various questions on a teaching evaluation survey. Create a PivotChart that charts for each question the fraction of the time each value (1–7) occurs. Then filter the chart to show the breakdown for any set of three questions you choose.

19. Using the data in the file Monthtomonth.xlsx, create a PivotTable that shows for the year 2010 how each month's sales differ from the previous month.

20. More than 1,000 registered voters were asked their political orientation (liberal, moderate, or conservative) and whether or not they favored the Dream Act. Using the data in the file Problem20data.xlsx, construct a PivotTable and PivotChart that show how opinions on the Dream Act depend on political orientation.

21. In the file Problem21data.xlsx, you are given the following information about a representative sample of US residents:

- Do they subscribe to *Garden and Gun Magazine*?
- Income level (low, middle, or upper)
- Location (urban, rural, suburban)

Use a PivotTable to help you determine the type of person who is most likely to subscribe to *Garden and Gun Magazine*.

22. The file Problem22data.xlsx contains information on births during 1995 at Dylan General Hospital. Construct a PivotChart that summarizes the births by day of the week. Then use another PivotTable or PivotChart to help you explain the pattern in births by day of the week.

23. The state of Happyville has nine congressional districts. In the file Problem23data.xlsx, you are given a voter's district and whether the voter is a Democrat or Republican. Construct a PivotTable and PivotChart that show the percentage of Democrats and Republicans in each district. Assuming that the party with the most voters in a district wins the election, how many districts will each party win? Note: this problem illustrates why the Republicans usually control the House of Representatives, even though the Democrats usually receive more total votes nationwide.

CHAPTER 44

The Data Model

Questions answered in this chapter:

- What is the Data Model, and why do I need to learn about it?
- How do I add data to the Data Model?
- How do I remove data from a Data Model?
- How do I create relationships within the Data Model?
- How do I use the Data Model to create PivotTables?
- How does the Quick Explore option work?
- How do I add new data to a Data Model?
- How can I use the Data Model to create a new PivotTable?
- How do I edit or delete relationships?
- How does the DISTINCT COUNT function work?

Answers to this chapter's questions

What is the Data Model, and why do I need to learn about it?

The Data Model feature was added in Excel 2013 (it was originally an add-in for Excel 2010). The Data Model provides an easy way to load data beyond the ordinary capabilities of Excel 2016 (1,048,576 rows of data) and use this data to create PivotTables. The Data Model also enables you to combine data that comes from sources outside Excel (including Access and SQL Server) with data from Excel. Finally, an understanding of the Data Model will make it easier for you to grasp the capabilities of Power Pivot (see Chapter 45).

In Chapter 43, you learned how to use Excel's PivotTable feature to summarize data. I showed you how to create PivotTables based on data in disparate locations, but this approach required the data in each location to have the same column headings. This condition is not often met. For example, the file Datamodeltemp.xlsx (from the Templates folder) contains two worksheets. The worksheet Reps (shown on the left of Figure 44-1) contains a list of salespeople ID numbers and the state where they sell our products. The worksheet Sales (shown on the right of Figure 44-1) shows the unit sales generated by each employee. Naturally, we would like to use a PivotTable to summarize sales by state. The problem is that the data in the Sales worksheet does not include each salesperson's state. Of course, we could add a column using VLOOKUP formulas to insert the states in the Sales worksheet. If we had several hundred thousand rows of data, however, these VLOOKUP's would greatly slow our spreadsheet's performance. The Excel Data Model allows you to work around the VLOOKUPS by easily creating a relationship that tells Excel the state for each salesperson, without the need of the slow VLOOKUPS.

Data must be included in the Data Model to create amazing graphics with Excel Power View (see Chapter 46 for a discussion of Power View). Finally, if you want to mash up data from different sources, such as databases, the web, text files, and Excel spreadsheets, you will want to use Power Pivot (discussed in Chapter 45). Once you understand the Data Model, Power Pivot becomes much easier to understand. Power View and Power Pivot are available in all editions of Excel 2016.

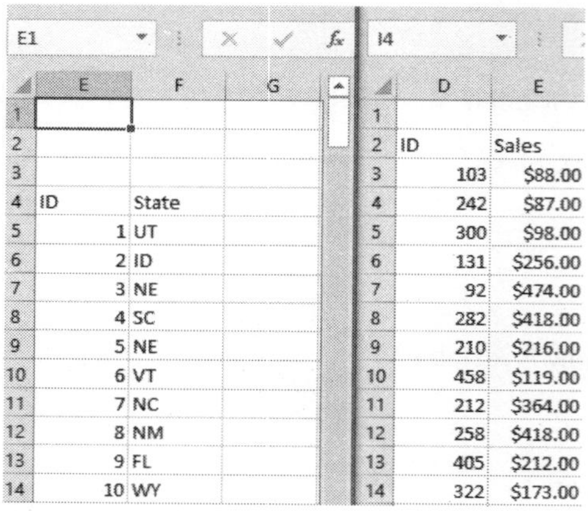

	E	F	G
1			
2			
3			
4	ID	State	
5	1	UT	
6	2	ID	
7	3	NE	
8	4	SC	
9	5	NE	
10	6	VT	
11	7	NC	
12	8	NM	
13	9	FL	
14	10	WY	

	D	E
1		
2	ID	Sales
3	103	$88.00
4	242	$87.00
5	300	$98.00
6	131	$256.00
7	92	$474.00
8	282	$418.00
9	210	$216.00
10	458	$119.00
11	212	$364.00
12	258	$418.00
13	405	$212.00
14	322	$173.00

FIGURE 44-1 The data used in the Data Model example.

How do I add data to the Data Model?

Before adding any data to the Data Model, you should make the data a table (see Chapter 26, "Tables.") I first selected the data in the Reps worksheet and used Ctrl+T to make the data a table. By using the Table Name box in the Properties group on the Table Tools Design tab, I named the table Reps. Then I selected PivotTable from the Insert tab (in the Tables group), and in the Create PivotTable dialog box, shown in Figure 44-2, I checked the Add This Data To The Data Model check box. This ensures that the data in the Reps worksheet is included in the Data Model. In a similar fashion, I selected the data in the Sales worksheet, named the table Sales, and added the Sales table to the Data Model.

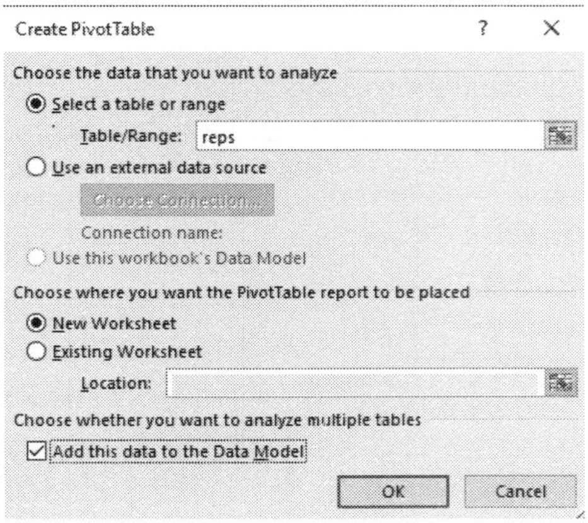

FIGURE 44-2 Adding data from the Reps table to the Data Model.

How do I remove data from the Data Model?

To remove data from the Data Model, you can simply go to the Excel table containing the data and select Convert To Range from the Table Tools Design tab.

How do I create relationships within the Data Model?

If we want to summarize sales by state, we have a problem. At present, there is no way for Excel to know each salesperson's state. Somehow we need to create a relationship that enables Excel to determine the state for each row of data in the Sales worksheet. After adding the Sales worksheet data to the Data Model, we can create the needed relationship by selecting the Relationships option from the Data tab (in the Data Tools group). After clicking Relationships, clicking New brings up the Create Relationship dialog box shown in Figure 44-3. The Primary column must be the column of data that involves a 1-1 relationship, which can be mapped into the Foreign column. Since the Reps worksheet has a state for each sales rep in our example, the Primary column must be the ID column in the Reps worksheet. Then we make the Foreign column be the ID column from the Sales worksheet. These settings are shown in Figure 44-3. Now if we try to create a PivotTable that summarizes sales by state, we will be okay because for each ID number in the Sales worksheet, Excel will know to pull the correct state from the Reps worksheet.

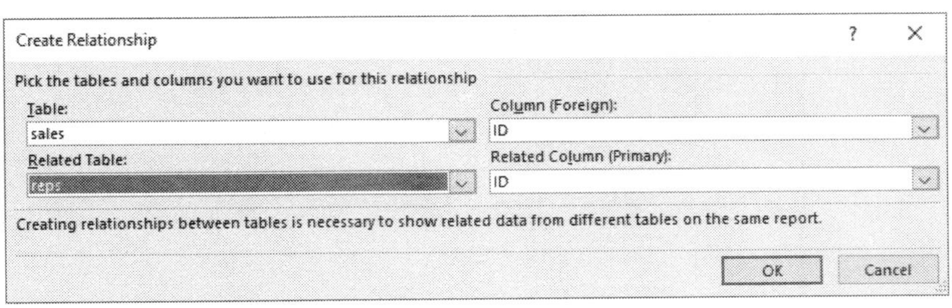

FIGURE 44-3 Creating a relationship between the worksheets.

How do I use the Data Model to create PivotTables?

After adding the Sales table to the Data Model, you will see the PivotTable Fields pane. After selecting the All option at the top, you will see all the tables that were added to the Data Model, as shown in Figure 44-4.

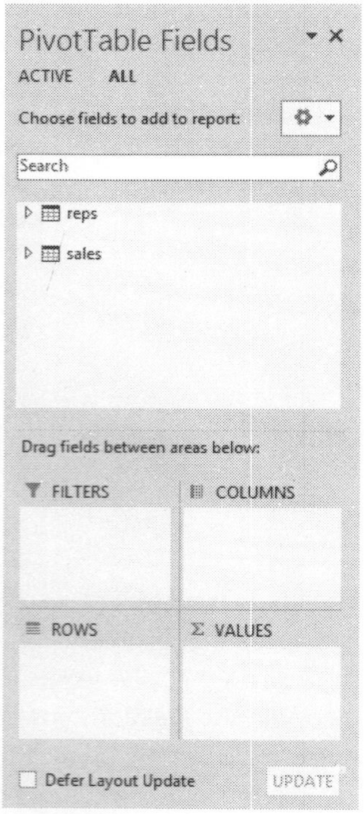

FIGURE 44-4 The Data Model PivotTable Fields pane.

After clicking on the triangles to the left of Reps and Sales, you will see all the table headings from the Reps and Sales worksheets. To create a PivotTable that computes the total sales in each state, drag State to the Rows area and Sales to the Values area, as shown in Figure 44-5. You will obtain the PivotTable shown in Figure 44-6.

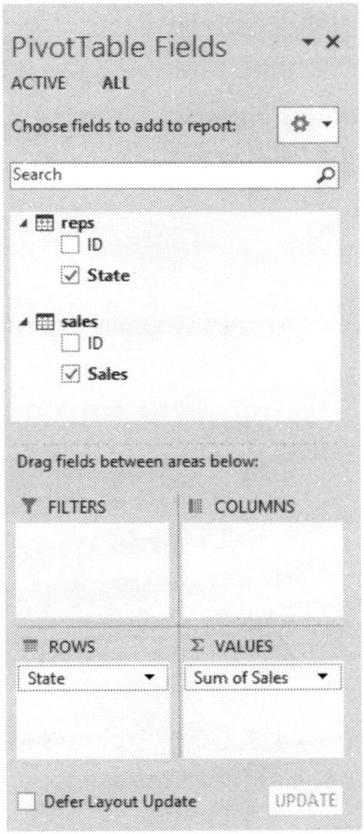

FIGURE 44-5 Creation of a PivotTable to determine the sales in each state.

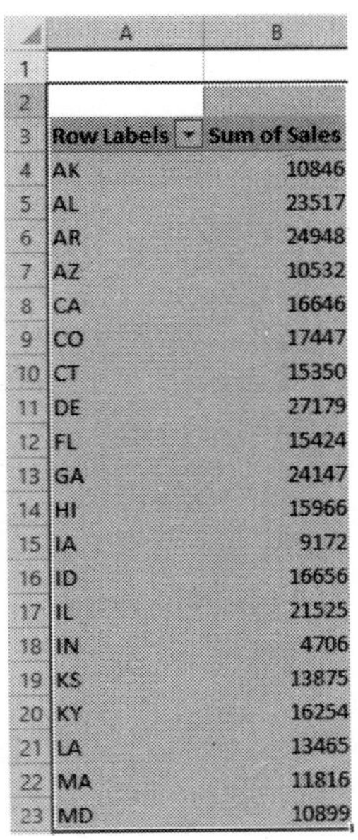

	A	B
1		
2		
3	Row Labels	Sum of Sales
4	AK	10846
5	AL	23517
6	AR	24948
7	AZ	10532
8	CA	16646
9	CO	17447
10	CT	15350
11	DE	27179
12	FL	15424
13	GA	24147
14	HI	15966
15	IA	9172
16	ID	16656
17	IL	21525
18	IN	4706
19	KS	13875
20	KY	16254
21	LA	13465
22	MA	11816
23	MD	10899

FIGURE 44-6 The unit sales in each state.

For example, we find that 10,846 units were sold in Alaska, 24,147 units were sold in Georgia, and so on.

If you had tried to create the PivotTable before creating the relationship shown in Figure 44-3, Excel would have had no way to figure out the state for each row of the Sales worksheet. Excel would have therefore prompted you to create the needed relationship.

How does the Quick Explore option work?

If you click the cell with the total sales for any state (I chose Alaska), you will see the Quick Explore icon shown in Figure 44-7.

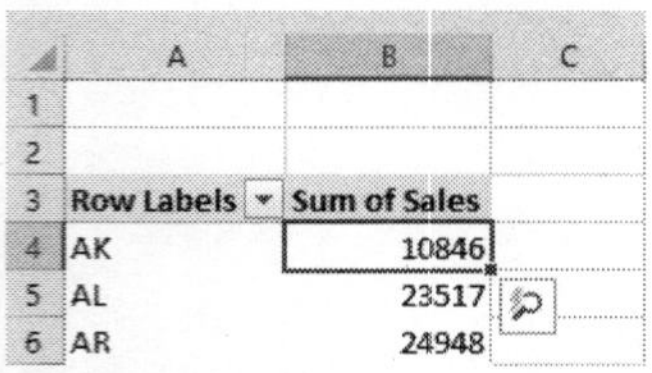

FIGURE 44-7 The Quick Explore icon.

Clicking the magnifying glass icon brings up the box shown in Figure 44-8. Quick Explore suggests drilling down by ID. Clicking Drill To ID shows (in Figure 44-9) the sales for all the salespeople associated with Alaska sales.

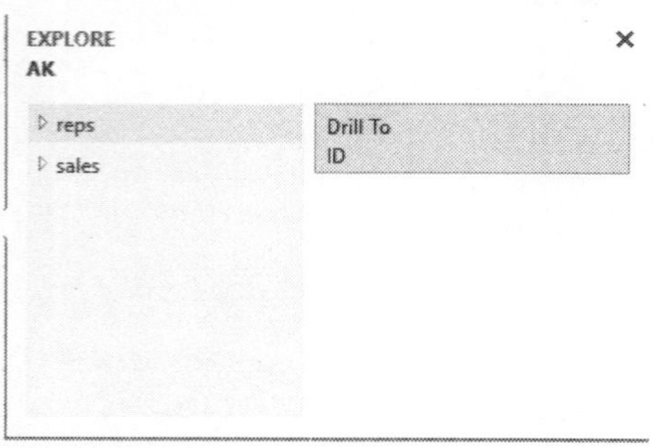

FIGURE 44-8 Quick Explore suggesting to drill down to the salesperson ID.

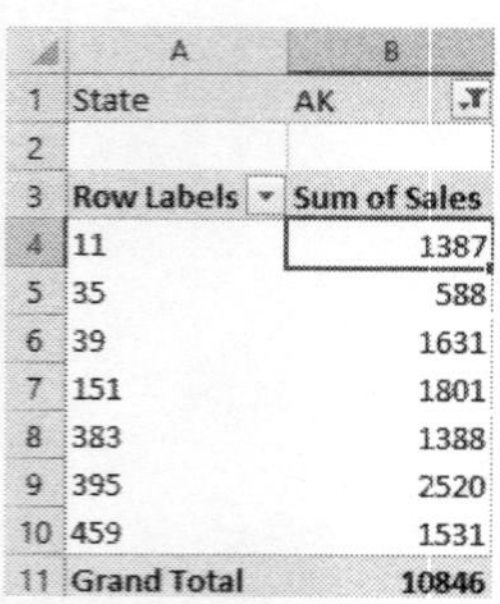

FIGURE 44-9 Alaska salespeople and sales.

How do I add new data to a Data Model?

If you have a new set of data you want to add to the Data Model, simply make the data a table, select the Insert tab, and click PivotTable in the Tables group. Then you can check Add This Data To Data Model; if you select All (instead of Active) in the PivotTable Fields pane, you can now use the new data in your PivotTable.

How can I use the Data Model to create a new PivotTable?

Simply click a cell in a table, select PivotTable from the Insert tab, select Use This Workbook's Data Model in the Create PivotTable dialog box, and click OK. Then select All to bring up everything you have added to the Data Model. Clicking on the triangles shown in Figure 44-5 brings up all the available fields. Now you can create new PivotTables that are consistent with all the relationships you have created.

How do I edit or delete relationships?

To edit or delete relationships, simply select Relationships in the Data Tools group on the Data tab. This displays the Manage Relationships dialog box shown in Figure 44-10. From this dialog box, you can choose the Edit or Deactivate option to manage any current relationships, or you can create new relationships.

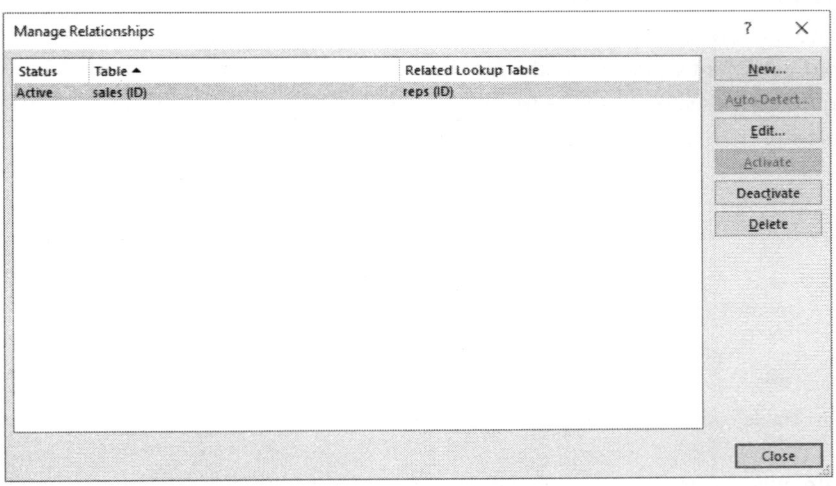

FIGURE 44-10 The Manage Relationships dialog box.

How does the DISTINCT COUNT function work?

In the file Distinctcounttemp.xlsx (in this chapter's Templates folder), you are given a list of athletes (1–100) and salary payments received, as shown in Figure 44-11. Since many athletes received more than one payment, many athletes occur more than once on the list. You are also given the sport each athlete plays.

	E	F	G	H	I	J	K	L
1								
2	Person	Salary						
3	32	6						
4	66	4						
5	15	4						
6	53	7					Person	Sport
7	26	9					1	Basketball
8	56	9					2	Hockey
9	80	7					3	Lacrosse
10	29	7					4	Football
11	63	4					5	Football
12	84	5					6	Lacrosse
13	79	4					7	Lacrosse
14	82	6					8	Baseball
15	69	6					9	Hockey
16	60	8					10	Lacrosse
17	59	8					11	Lacrosse
18	66	4					12	Football
19	6	10					13	Lacrosse
20	91	6					14	Baseball

FIGURE 44-11 The data for the DISTINCT COUNT example.

Suppose you want to determine how many athletes played each sport. First, I made the data in E3:F466 a table named *Money* and the data in the range K6:L106 a table named *Activity*. I made each table part of the Data Model. Then, I created a relationship with the primary column being *Person* in the Activity table and the foreign column being *Person* in the Money table. Next, I created a PivotTable (see the worksheet Count Of Person in the file Distinctcount.xlsx) by dragging Sport to the Rows zone and dragging Count of Person from the Money table to the Values zone. This series of actions yields the PivotTable shown in Figure 44-12.

	A	B
3	Row Labels	Count of Person
4	Baseball	85
5	Basketball	96
6	Football	84
7	Hockey	72
8	Lacrosse	127
9	**Grand Total**	**464**

FIGURE 44-12 This PivotTable counts each athlete multiple times.

Because there are only 100 athletes, we see that each person is counted multiple times. To fix this problem, right-click anywhere in the table and choose Value Field Settings. Scrolling to the bottom, you will find, as shown in Figure 44-13, that the last (but not least!) choice is Distinct Count. This option ensures each athlete is counted at most once and yields the PivotTable shown in Figure 44-14 and the worksheet Distinct Count (in the file Distinctcount.xlsx). This table shows exactly how many athletes play each sport.

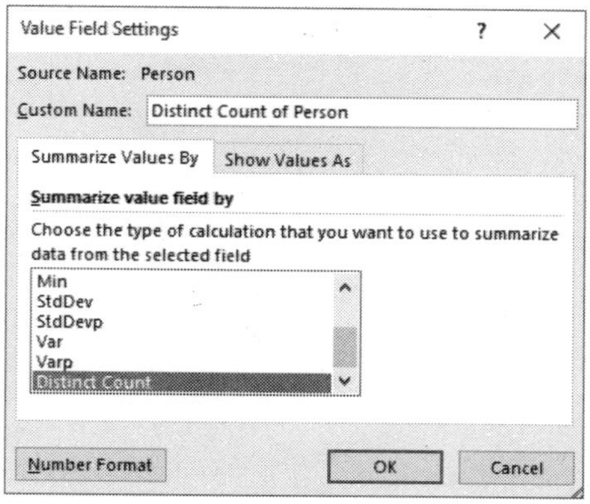

FIGURE 44-13 Choosing Distinct Count to obtain a unique list of number of athletes playing each sport.

	A	B
3	Row Labels	Distinct Count of Person
4	Baseball	21
5	Basketball	19
6	Football	20
7	Hockey	14
8	Lacrosse	26
9	**Grand Total**	**100**

FIGURE 44-14 A distinct count of how many athletes play each sport.

Problems

The file Faberu.xlsx contains salaries, travel expenses, faculty ID, department code, and faculty code for all the business-school faculty. Use this data to answer the following questions. (No VLOOKUPS allowed!)

1. Use the Data Model to create a PivotTable that gives the average salary, broken down by department.
2. Use the Data Model to create a PivotTable that gives the average salary, broken down by the type of faculty member and department.
3. Use the Data Model to create a PivotTable that gives the average travel expenses by departments.

CHAPTER 45

Power Pivot

Questions answered in this chapter:

- How do I read data into Power Pivot?
- How do I use Power Pivot to create a PivotTable?
- How can I use slicers with Power Pivot?
- What are DAX functions?

Power Pivot is available in Office 365 Pro Plus, Office 2016 Pro Plus, and Office 2016 Enterprise. To add Power Pivot, click the File tab, select Options, and then select Add-ins. At the bottom of the Add-ins dialog box, in the Manage list, select COM Add-Ins and then click Go. In the COM Add-Ins dialog box, check Microsoft Power Pivot For Excel, and then click OK. You will now see a Power Pivot tab on the ribbon. Power Pivot is an add-in that enables you to do the following:

- Efficiently store and query large volumes of data (think hundreds of millions of rows) that you can combine from multiple data sources and multiple data formats. For example, some of your data may come from a Microsoft Access database, some from a text file, some from several Excel files, and some from live data imported from a website.
- Create calculated columns (beyond field definitions). For example, if each row of your source data contains revenues and costs, you could create a calculated column to compute Profit = Revenue – Costs. Power Pivot contains many Data Analysis Expressions (DAX) functions that facilitate the creation of calculated columns.
- Create calculated fields that aggregate data from different rows. For example, a calculated field could compute the total profit as the sum of profit from each transaction.
- Create Key Performance Indicators (KPIs) that make it easy for an organization to track performance against targets. For example, a Power Pivot KPI could be used to determine for each year and salesperson, how his actual sales compared to his sales quota.
- Power Pivot can be used as a data source for workbook reports (PivotTables, charts, CUBE functions, Power View, and so on). Power View is covered in Chapter 46.
- Power Pivot reports can be published in Microsoft SharePoint to allow automatic data refreshes, facilitate sharing, and enable IT monitoring. When published, a Power Pivot report

can be used as a data source for other analytic and reporting experiences. (And publishing to SharePoint can be a deployment process.)

Answers to this chapter's questions

How do I read data into Power Pivot?

After you install Power Pivot, you see a Power Pivot tab on the ribbon. Clicking the Power Pivot tab displays the options shown in Figure 45-1. After clicking Manage, the Power Pivot For Excel window opens; you will see the Home tab shown in Figure 45-2.

FIGURE 45-1 The Power Pivot options.

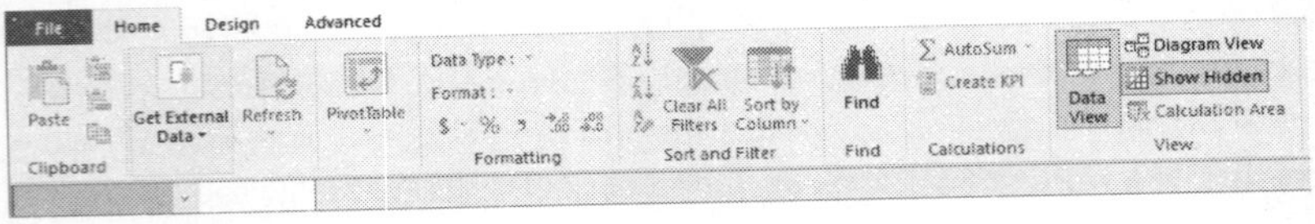

FIGURE 45-2 The Power Pivot Home tab.

If you select Get External Data, you can import data from the multiple sources shown in Figure 45-3.

FIGURE 45-3: The Get External Data command, which offers several data locations from which to choose.

For example, if you select From Database, Power Pivot will accept input from an Access or Microsoft SQL Server database. From Other Sources allows you to read data from the previously described sources as well as from Excel files, text files, and many other types of databases, such as Oracle and Teradata.

After copying the data in Excel, you can select Paste (in the Clipboard group on the Home tab of the Power Pivot window) to insert the data into Power Pivot.

To illustrate how to download data from multiple sources into Power Pivot, I'll use the text file Storesales.txt, in which I've listed sales transactions from 20 stores. A subset of the data is shown in Figure 45-4.

```
storesales - Notepad
File  Edit  Format  View  Help
Store   Product Date      Units    Revenue
20      food    3/15/2011          37       $16.28
10      cds     11/29/2014         70       $19.60
6       dvds    8/11/2010          68       $39.44
4       dvds    5/11/2012          120      $92.40
6       food    7/8/2011           129      $101.91
6       books   9/7/2011           16       $2.24
5       magazines       1/4/2014            101      $72.72
18      cds     9/27/2011          67       $8.04
15      magazines       9/29/2014           132      $105.60
13      food    1/27/2011          38       $23.18
7       books   4/13/2014          103      $17.51
3       books   2/17/2010          127      $21.59
16      food    6/6/2014           129      $29.67
18      dvds    11/30/2011         149      $80.46
17      cds     2/5/2010           64       $9.60
2       books   6/18/2011          147      $26.46
8       toys    6/22/2014          72       $12.24
18      dvds    1/27/2013          85       $66.30
12      food    5/15/2010          32       $15.68
17      dvds    8/20/2012          115      $80.50
12      dvds    8/9/2012           67       $52.93
17      books   11/20/2012         98       $31.36
2       books   7/16/2011          130      $24.70
```

FIGURE 45-4 The sales data to be imported into Power Pivot.

You can see that for each transaction, I am given the store number, the product sold, sale date, units sold, and revenue. I want to summarize this data by state, but the state for each store is listed in a different file, States.xlsx. The location of each store is shown in Figure 45-5.

	F	G
7	Store	State
8	1	IND
9	2	IND
10	3	ILL
11	4	ILL
12	5	ILL
13	6	ILL
14	7	ILL
15	8	ILL
16	9	MICH
17	10	MICH
18	11	MICH
19	12	MICH
20	13	MICH
21	14	MICH
22	15	KY
23	16	KY
24	17	KY
25	18	KY
26	19	IOWA
27	20	IOWA

FIGURE 45-5 The location of each store.

I want to create a PivotTable that lets me slice and dice my data so that I can view how I performed in selling each product in each state. To begin, I select the Power Pivot tab and then click Manage to bring up the Home tab of the Power Pivot window, shown earlier in Figure 45-2. Because I want to import a text file, I click Get External Data, and then click From Other Sources. In the Table Import Wizard dialog box, I select Text File (it is the last choice) and click Next. As shown in Figure 45-6, I can then browse to the file Storesales.txt. The file is automatically given a name, which is optional. Because the first row of data contains column headers, I select the Use First Row As Column Headers option. Above that, in the Column Separator list, I select Tab (t) because the data fields in the text file are not separated by spaces or a character, such as a comma or a semicolon. Clicking Finish and then Close completes the process of importing the text file's data into Power Pivot.

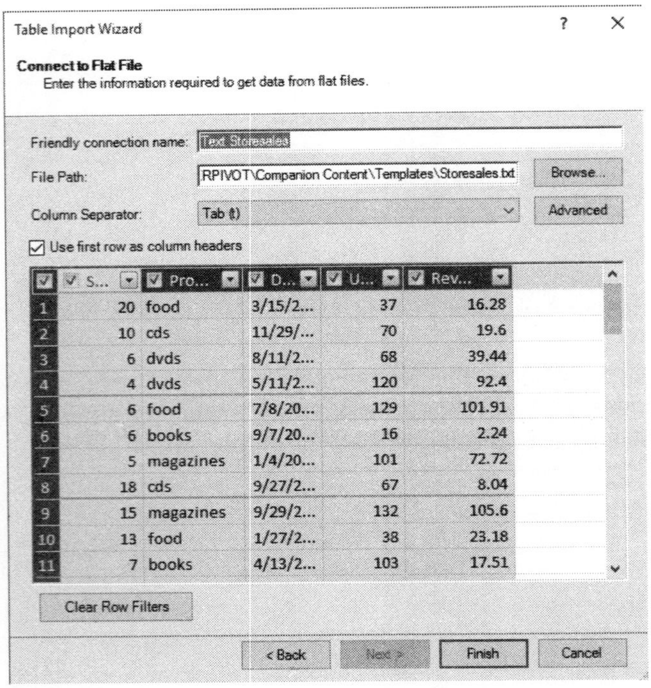

FIGURE 45-6 Setting up a text file import for Power Pivot.

Figure 45-7 shows the result after the text data is imported into Power Pivot. A subset of the data is shown.

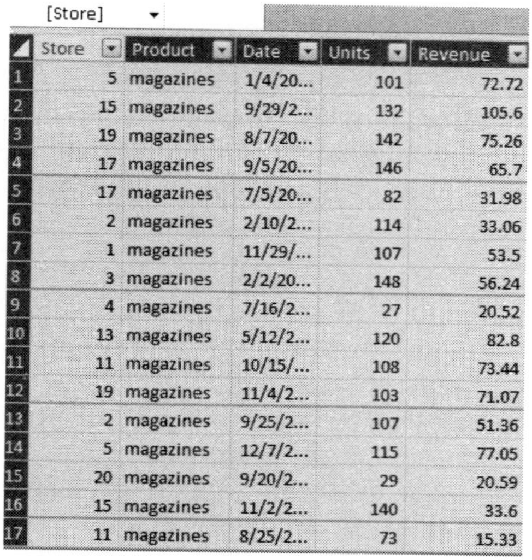

[Store]

	Store	Product	Date	Units	Revenue
1	5	magazines	1/4/20...	101	72.72
2	15	magazines	9/29/2...	132	105.6
3	19	magazines	8/7/20...	142	75.26
4	17	magazines	9/5/20...	146	65.7
5	17	magazines	7/5/20...	82	31.98
6	2	magazines	2/10/2...	114	33.06
7	1	magazines	11/29/...	107	53.5
8	3	magazines	2/2/20...	148	56.24
9	4	magazines	7/16/2...	27	20.52
10	13	magazines	5/12/2...	120	82.8
11	11	magazines	10/15/...	108	73.44
12	19	magazines	11/4/2...	103	71.07
13	2	magazines	9/25/2...	107	51.36
14	5	magazines	12/7/2...	115	77.05
15	20	magazines	9/20/2...	29	20.59
16	15	magazines	11/2/2...	140	33.6
17	11	magazines	8/25/2...	73	15.33

FIGURE 45-7 A subset of the data imported from the file Storesales.txt.

Next, I want to import the file States.xlsx so that Power Pivot will know the state in which each store is located. To import States.xlsx, I return to Excel by clicking the Switch To Workbook Excel icon in the upper-left corner of the Power Pivot ribbon (above the File tab). Then I open the file States.xlsx. Next, I make the data a table, and then I copy the data I need. Now, I select Paste on the Home tab in Power Pivot (see Figure 45-2). The Paste Preview dialog box shown in Figure 45-8 appears.

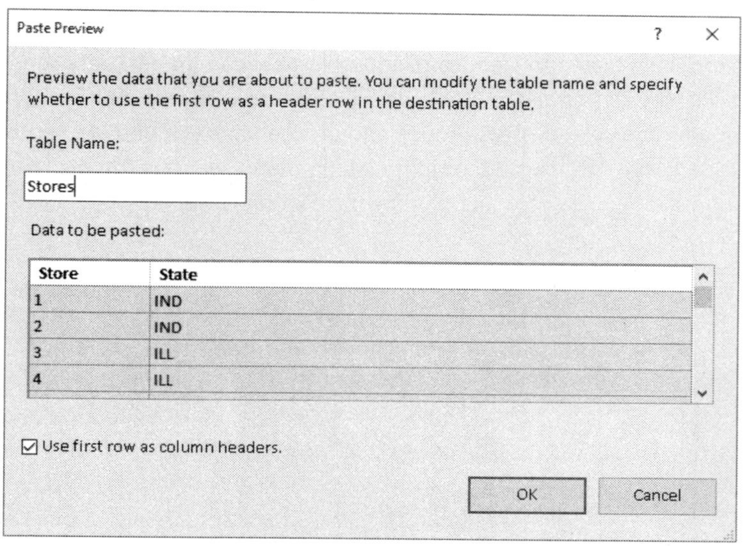

FIGURE 45-8 The Paste Preview dialog box.

I selected Use First Row A's Column Headers and changed the table name to States. After clicking OK, the data from States.xlsx is imported into Power Pivot, as shown in Figure 45-9. Note that at the bottom of the window, a tab appears for each data source used to import data into Power Pivot.

FIGURE 45-9 Importing the data from two sources into Power Pivot.

Recall that I want to analyze sales in different states. The problem is that, at present, Power Pivot does not know that the listing of store locations from States.xlsx corresponds to the stores listed in the text file. To remedy this problem, I need to create a relationship between the two data sources. To create this relationship, I click the Design tab in the Power Pivot window (see Figure 45-10), choose the Create Relationship option (in the Relationships group), and proceed as described in Chapter 44. It is much easier, however, to click Diagram View on the Home tab (in the View group, on the far right) and define the needed relationship by drawing a line, as shown in Figure 45-10.

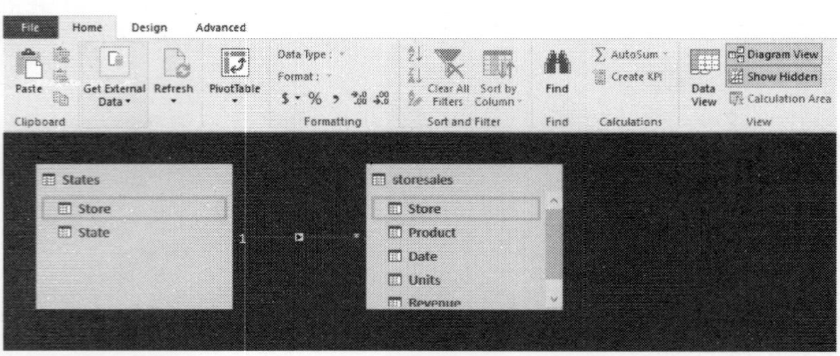

FIGURE 45-10 The relationship diagram allowing us to link stores between data sources.

To return to your Power Pivot data, simply click the Data View icon shown in Figure 45-10, in the View group on the Home tab.

How do I use Power Pivot to create a PivotTable?

Now, I'm ready to use Power Pivot to summarize our company's sales data via a PivotTable. After clicking the Data View icon, select the PivotTable option on the Home tab. The Create PivotTable dialog box appears and prompts me to choose a new worksheet or a location in the current worksheet. I choose a new worksheet. Then the PivotTable Fields pane is displayed, shown in Figure 45-11.

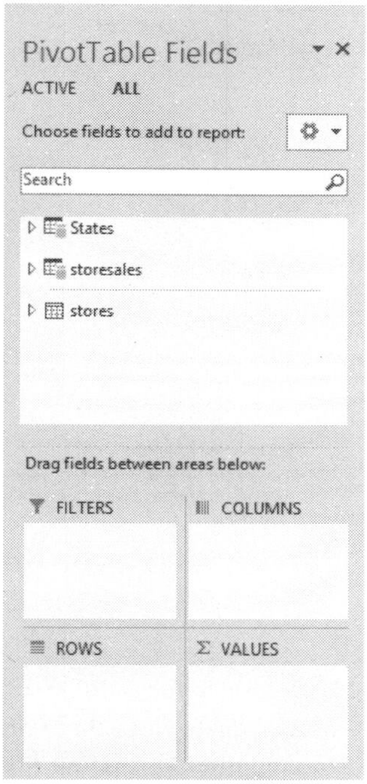

FIGURE 45-11 The PivotTable Fields pane.

After we select All by clicking the triangles to the left of States and Storesales, we have access to all the columns of data in either data source. The goal is to get a breakdown by state and product of the total revenue and units sold. To summarize the revenue and units sold, I drag the Revenue and Units fields to the Values area. Next, I drag State to the Rows area and Product to the Columns area to arrange the PivotTable fields as shown in Figure 45-12. Note that the fields used in the PivotTable are selected.

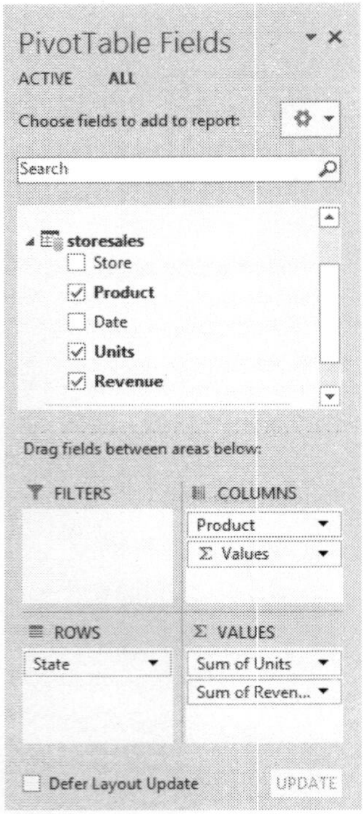

FIGURE 45-12 Assigning fields to create a PivotTable report.

The portion of the PivotTable involving books, CDs, DVDs, and food is shown in Figure 45-13. As you can see, 4,920 DVDs were sold in Illinois (ILL) for a total revenue of $2,295.76. Note that I right-clicked in a Sum of Revenue column, clicked Value Field Settings, clicked Number Format on the lower left, selected Currency from the Format Cells dialog box, and clicked OK in both dialog boxes. This was to ensure that the revenue was formatted as currency.

	B	C	D	E	F	G	H	I
3		Column Labe						
4		books		cds		dvds		food
5	Row Labels	Sum of Units	Sum of Revenue	Sum of Un	Sum of Revenue	Sum of Units	Sum of Revenue	Sum of Units
6	ILL	4063	$1,542.74	3881	$1,880.44	4920	$2,295.76	4658
7	IND	1906	$697.08	1812	$799.09	2009	$874.89	1335
8	IOWA	1341	$518.61	1448	$651.49	787	$480.66	871
9	KY	3329	$1,654.53	2386	$1,051.28	3696	$1,952.70	2461
10	MICH	4384	$2,071.94	4236	$1,680.84	3104	$1,320.06	4620
11	Grand Total	15023	$6,484.90	13763	$6,063.14	14516	$6,924.07	13945

FIGURE 45-13 The PivotTable breaking down the product sales by state.

How can I use slicers with Power Pivot?

In Chapter 43, "Using PivotTables and slicers to describe data," I showed how to use slicers to reveal details and different perspectives in your PivotTable analyses. Slicers look even nicer in Power Pivot PivotTables. Here, I'll create slicers that summarize the data for any subset of products and stores.

To do this, you can click anywhere in your PivotTable and click Insert Slicer on the Analyze tab (in the Filter group). After you select Store (from States) and Product (from Storesales), the resulting slicers are shown in Figure 45-14. (See the file Pivotwithslicers.xlsx.) From the Slicer Tools Options tab, you can modify the appearance of the slicers. For example, I modified the Store slicer to have four columns (using the Columns box in the Buttons group). As described in Chapter 43, you can hold down the Ctrl key as you click to select any subset of products and/or stores. Also the Shift key can be used to select any contiguous range from a slicer. Holding down the Ctrl key also enables you to resize the slicers. The PivotTable shown in Figure 45-14 gives the total revenue and units sold of books and food in stores 7 through 11. Because stores 7 through 11 are in Illinois or Michigan, these are the only states shown in the resulting PivotTable.

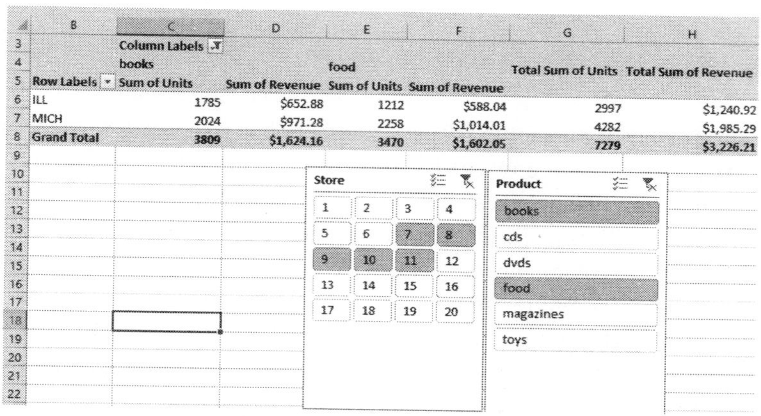

	Column Labels					
	books		food		Total Sum of Units	Total Sum of Revenue
Row Labels	Sum of Units	Sum of Revenue	Sum of Units	Sum of Revenue		
ILL	1785	$652.88	1212	$588.04	2997	$1,240.92
MICH	2024	$971.28	2258	$1,014.01	4282	$1,985.29
Grand Total	3809	$1,624.16	3470	$1,602.05	7279	$3,226.21

FIGURE 45-14 The Product and Store slicers.

What are DAX functions?

Recall from Chapter 43 that you can generate new formulas in a PivotTable by using calculated items or calculated fields. After your data is imported into Power Pivot, you can use the DAX (short for Data Analysis Expressions) formula language to create new calculated columns that make your PivotTables much more meaningful.

To illustrate a DAX formula, I'll show how to place the year, month, and day of the month for each sales transaction in a separate column. To begin, I click the Storesales tab in the Power Pivot window (like a worksheet tab, it's in the lower left) and select the first blank column. Clicking the *fx* button below the Power Pivot ribbon brings up a list of DAX functions. Many of these (such as YEAR, MONTH, and DAY) are virtually identical to ordinary Excel functions. Selecting Date & Time from the Select A Category list in the Insert Function dialog box brings up the list of DAX functions shown in Figure 45-15. The DAX language includes many other powerful functions. For example, the DISTINCT function can return a list of entries in a column that meets a specified criterion.

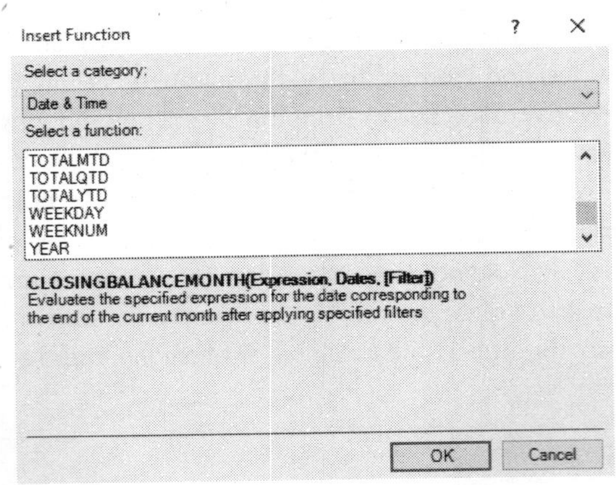

FIGURE 45-15 The list of DAX functions.

To place the year, month, and day of the month for each transaction in a separate column, select the first cell of the first blank column and type **=YEAR(st**. Then you are prompted with the columns from the Power Pivot data sources, to which you can apply the YEAR function. In the first new column, enter the formula **=YEAR(storesales[Date])**. The column is now populated with the year of each sales transaction. By right-clicking the column heading and selecting Rename Column, I can rename the column *Year*. In the next column, I compute the month of the year by entering the formula =MONTH(storesales[Date]). In the next column, I compute the day of the month with the formula =DAY(storesales[Date]). By right-clicking each column heading, I can rename these columns *Month* and *Day Of Month*. The data with the calculated columns is shown in Figure 45-16.

	Store	Product	Date	Units	Revenue	Year	Month	Day of Month
1	5	magazines	1/4/20...	101	72.72	2014	1	4
2	15	magazines	9/29/2...	132	105.6	2014	9	29
3	19	magazines	8/7/20...	142	75.26	2012	8	7
4	17	magazines	9/5/20...	146	65.7	2012	9	5
5	17	magazines	7/5/20...	82	31.98	2013	7	5
6	2	magazines	2/10/2...	114	33.06	2013	2	10
7	1	magazines	11/29/...	107	53.5	2013	11	29
8	3	magazines	2/2/20...	148	56.24	2014	2	2
9	4	magazines	7/16/2...	27	20.52	2012	7	16
10	13	magazines	5/12/2...	120	82.8	2013	5	12
11	11	magazines	10/15/...	108	73.44	2014	10	15
12	19	magazines	11/4/2...	103	71.07	2014	11	4
13	2	magazines	9/25/2...	107	51.36	2012	9	25
14	5	magazines	12/7/2...	115	77.05	2012	12	7
15	20	magazines	9/20/2...	29	20.59	2013	9	20
16	15	magazines	11/2/2...	140	33.6	2014	11	2
17	11	magazines	8/25/2...	73	15.33	2012	8	25

FIGURE 45-16 The Year, Month, and Day Of Month columns, created with DAX formulas.

Now I can create a variety of informative PivotTables. For example, I can summarize sales in each state by year. (See Problem 1.)

Problems

1. Using the file States.xlsx, summarize the total sales in each state by year.
2. Using the file Storesales.txt, summarize the total revenue by store, and create a slicer for the Store field.

CHAPTER 46

Power View and 3D Maps

Questions answered in this chapter:

- How do I prepare data for Power View?
- What kind of charts can I create with Power View?
- How do I filter Power View charts?
- How do I display sales data by state or country/region?
- How do I turn a time-series scatter chart into an animated movie?
- How do I use the Multiples feature to easily create many charts?
- How do I use 3D Maps?

If you have Excel 2016, Power View for Excel and 3D Maps are available to you. In this chapter, you will learn the basics of how to use Power View to create amazing charts and graphics. Basically, Power View creates a new sheet in your workbook that acts like a blank canvas on which you can create several charts. You can map sales onto a US or world map. You can even turn a scatter chart of US crimes over time into a movie that animates the evolution of US crimes.

To add in Power View, select File from the ribbon. Next, select Options followed by Add-ins. At the bottom of the Excel Options dialog box, in the Manage list, select COM Add-ins and then click Go. In the COM Add-ins dialog box, check Microsoft Office Power View for Excel and click OK. Then Power View can be added to the ribbon, and it is up to you where it goes. I proceeded as follows:

- From the File tab, select Options, and then choose Customize Ribbon.
- Double-click Insert in the Main Tabs list on the right, and then click New Group. Rename the custom group Reports.
- On the upper left, in the Choose Commands From list, select Commands Not In The Ribbon, and select Insert A Power View Report.
- Click Add to add Insert A Power View Report to the Reports group on the Insert tab.

Now, on the Insert tab, you will see the Power View icon on the far right of the ribbon, as shown in Figure 46-1.

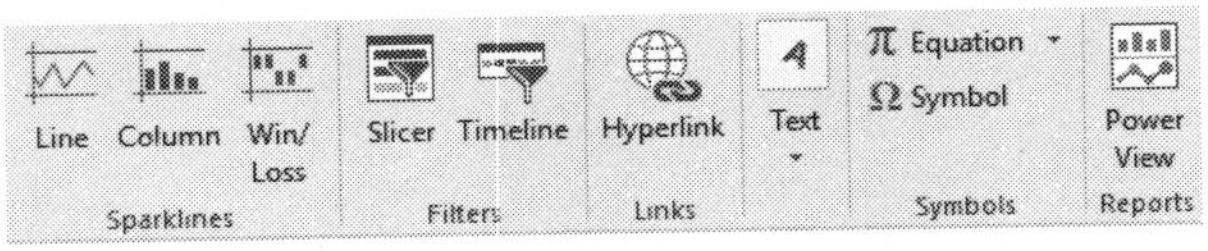

FIGURE 46-1 A view of the ribbon after selecting the Insert tab, including the Power View icon.

Questions answered in this chapter

How do I prepare data for Power View?

To prepare data for use in Power View, simply make the data a table (see Chapter 26) and add the table to the Data Model (see Chapter 44). Figure 46-2 shows sales data for an iced-tea company. (See the file Teasalestemp.xlsx in the Templates folder.) Each row gives the year, state, product sold, and units sold. The data has been converted to a table (named *teasales*) and has been added to the Data Model.

	C	D	E	F
4	Year	State	Units	Product
5	2010	MO	415	black tea
6	2013	NC	462	black tea
7	2008	IL	662	peach tea
8	2010	AL	279	white tea
9	2012	VA	309	black tea
10	2013	ID	495	black tea
11	2010	MS	645	black tea
12	2008	ND	202	black tea
13	2009	MT	605	black tea
14	2014	NJ	668	white tea
15	2012	WV	667	white tea
16	2009	VT	543	white tea
17	2013	ID	634	peach tea
18	2011	OR	609	white tea
19	2014	SC	603	lemon tea
20	2012	SC	550	black tea

FIGURE 46-2 The tea-sales data used to illustrate Power View.

To get ready to create charts from this data, select Power View from the Insert tab (in the Reports group). A blank sheet appears (see Figure 46-3) with the Power View Fields pane (based on the Teasales table) appearing on the right side of the screen. In the Power View Fields pane, clicking the triangle to the left of Teasales displays all the fields in the Teasales table.

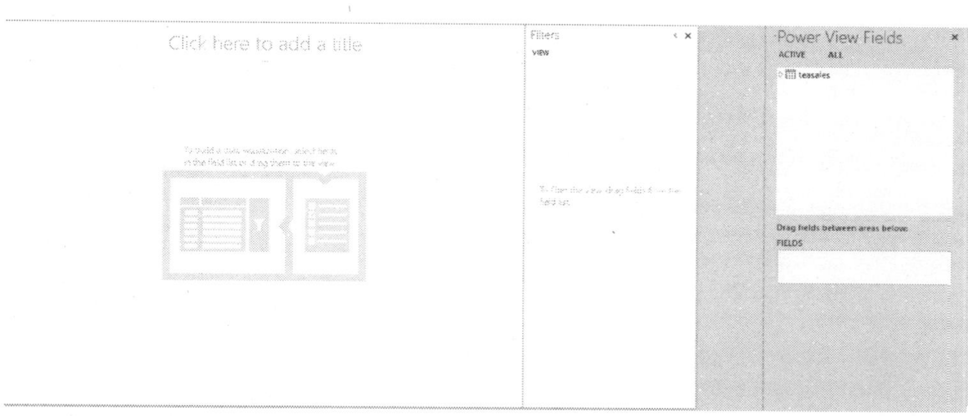

FIGURE 46-3 A blank Power View sheet.

Let's suppose you want create charts based on the year, units sold, and product sold. After checking Year and Units (as shown in Figure 46-4), these fields are added to the Fields area at the bottom of the Power View Fields pane. I changed the method of calculation for Year to Do Not Summarize. (In the Fields area at the bottom, I clicked the down arrow to the right of Year, and then I selected Do Not Summarize.) Otherwise, all the rows that have the same year will be summed to obtain the entry in the Year column. Then I typed in a title (**Teasales**) by clicking Click Here To Add A Title on the top of the Power View canvas. Now I have a table (see Figure 46-5) that contains the total units sold each year. Now this data can be used to create charts.

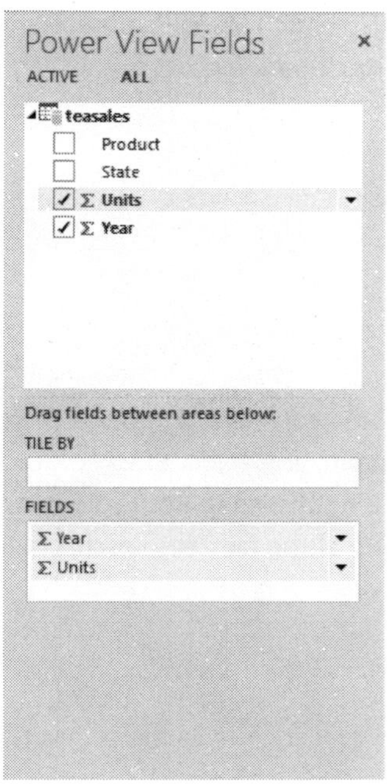

FIGURE 46-4 Year and Units are added to the Fields area.

Teasales

Year	Units
2008	88714
2009	89254
2010	85339
2011	77059
2012	96854
2013	90668
2014	82893
2015	85233
Total	**696014**

FIGURE 46-5 The year and units table.

What kind of charts can I create with Power View?

If you click the Design tab, which appears when you click a table on the Power View canvas, you see on the left side of the ribbon the Power View arsenal of charts (in the Switch Visualization group), shown in Figure 46-6. Under Other Chart, you will see the line, scatter, and pie chart entries. The Map option will be explained later in the chapter.

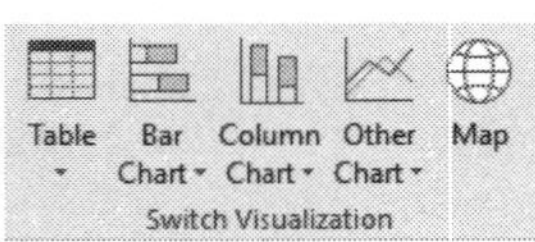

FIGURE 46-6 The available Power View charts.

I begin by creating a stacked-column chart showing total units sold each year. Simply click in the table, switch to the Design tab, click Column Chart to display the menu, and select Stacked Column. To resize the chart, hover over it, and drag the middle sizing handle on the right, until your chart looks like the chart in Figure 46-7 and in the worksheet Power View1 of the file Teasalescharts.xlsx.

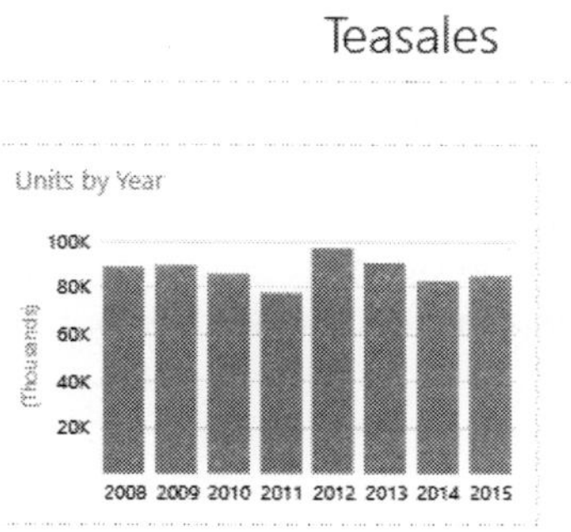

FIGURE 46-7 The tea sales, by year.

Now let's add another chart to our canvas. Suppose you want to create a line chart that shows the units sold each year of each product. Click a blank portion of the canvas and, in the Power View Fields pane, check Year (click the arrow to the right of Year in the Fields list at the bottom, and check Do Not Summarize), Units, and Product to create a table involving these three fields. After clicking inside the table, I click the Design tab, and in the Switch Visualization group, I choose the line chart from the Other Chart menu. Then I hover over the chart and drag the middle sizing handle on the right until it yields the chart shown on the right of Figure 46-8, as well as in the worksheet Power View1 in the file Teasalescharts1.xlsx.

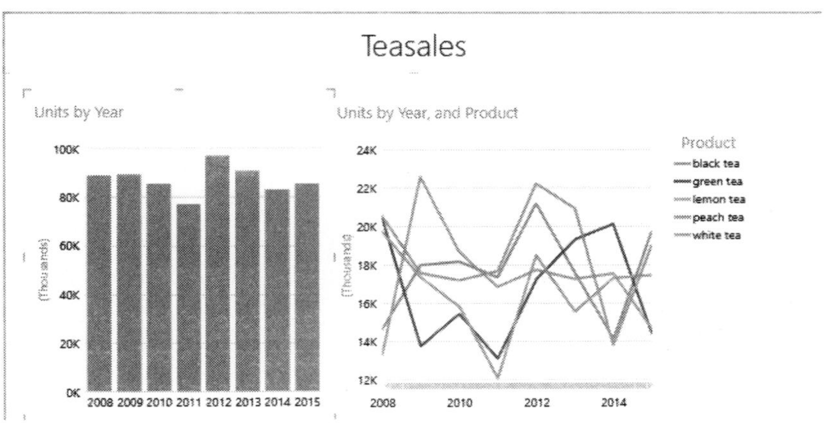

FIGURE 46-8 Two charts of tea-sales data.

How do I filter Power View charts?

In Chapter 44, you learned how to filter PivotTables. In Chapter 45, you learned how to filter with slicers in Power Pivot. You will now learn four ways to filter in Power View:

- Filters
- Slicers

- Filtering by chart
- Tiles

If you hover inside a chart or table, you will see the Show Filters (the funnel) icon and the Pop Out (or Pop In) icon (the arrow to the right of the Filter icon), as you see in Figure 46-9. Clicking the Pop Out icon makes the chart or table go full screen. Clicking the icon again makes the chart or table pop in to its previous size.

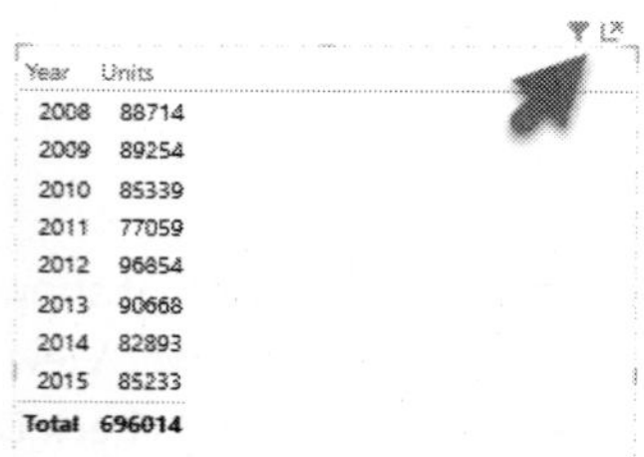

FIGURE 46-9 The Show Filters and Pop Out icons in the upper-right portion of the table or chart.

After hovering inside the chart in the worksheet Power View2 of the file Teasalescharts1.xlsx, I click the Show Filters icon. Then, on the right of the screen (see Figure 46-10), I filter the chart to show only the sales through 2012. (To change the year filter, click the arrow to the left of the filter Year, and then drag the sliders.)

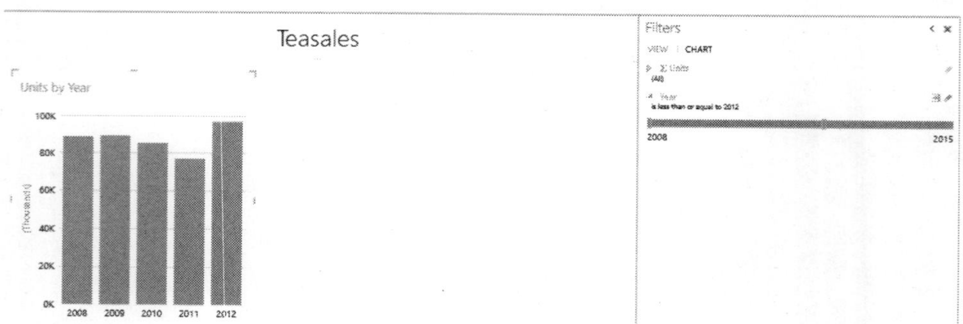

FIGURE 46-10 The sales filtered through 2012.

A wonderful feature of Power View is the fact that one chart can be used to filter all the charts on a Power View worksheet. In the worksheet Power View1 of the file Teasalesfilterbycharts.xlsx, I selected 2008, 2010, and 2012 on the Units By Year chart (hold Ctrl while clicking the columns). As shown in Figure 46-11, the Units By Year And Product line chart automatically filters as you select the columns; it shows only the sales in 2008, 2010, and 2012. If you select a highlighted column or anywhere off the columns in the Units By Year chart, then you restore the unfiltered charts.

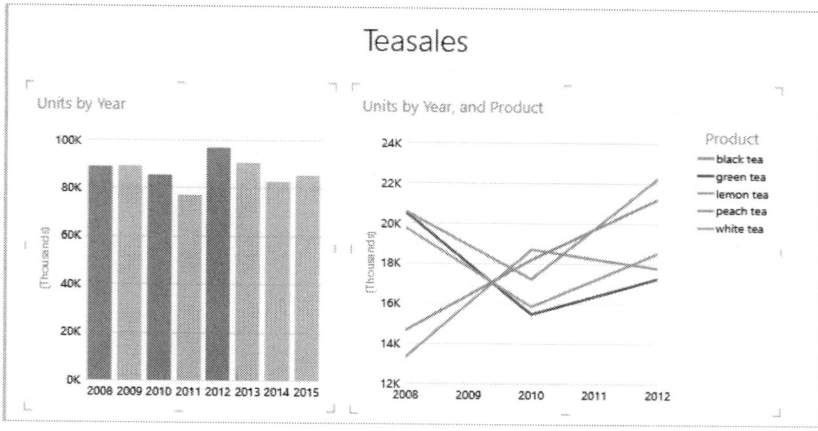

FIGURE 46-11 Selecting 2008, 2010, and 2012 on Units By Year to filter another chart.

You can also filter a Power View chart via a slicer. In the worksheet Power View1 of the file Teasalesslicer.xlsx (see Figure 46-12), I used a slicer to filter the annual units sales by product to show only black-tea and peach-tea sales. To begin, move to a blank part of the canvas and select the Product field to move it to the Fields list at the bottom of the Power View Fields pane. You will see a list of products appear as a table. Click in the table, and then select the Slicer option from the Design tab to create the slicer. Holding the Ctrl key, I select Black Tea and Peach Tea. To clear the filter, hover within the slicer and click the Clear Filter (eraser) icon.

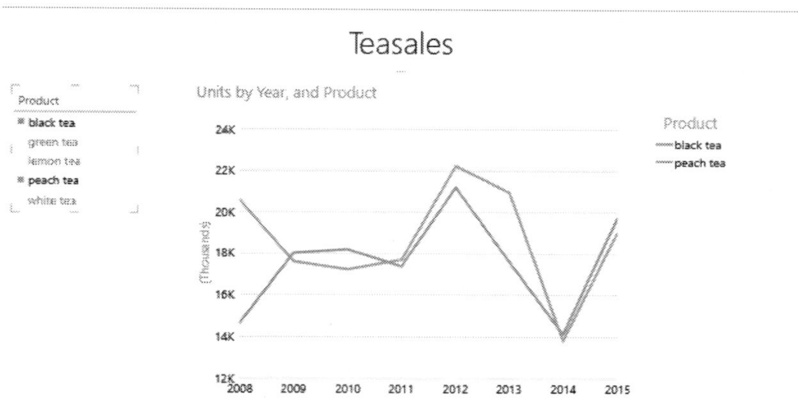

FIGURE 46-12 A slicer showing only black-tea and peach-tea sales.

Finally, you can use the Tiles option to filter one item of a field at a time. In the worksheet Power View1 of the fileTeasalestiles.xlsx, I create a tile that allows us to zero in on each individual state. To begin, I create a table showing Years (Not Summarized), States, and Units. Then I create a line chart that shows sales in each state during each year. This chart is too busy, so I add a tile for states by dragging State from the Legend area to the Tile By area. Now select any state and see the total sales for that state from 2008 through 2015. The chart filtered by means of the California tile is shown in Figure 46-13.

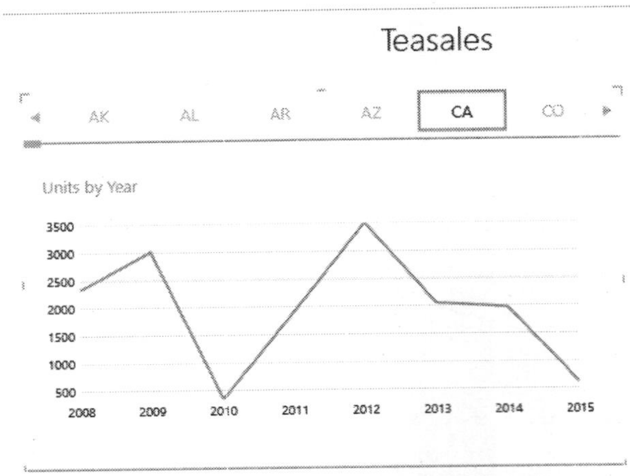

FIGURE 46-13 The tile used to show the annual California sales.

Any chart that is between the blue lines is filtered by the tile, so you can use the tile to filter more than one chart.

How do I display sales data by state or country/region?

In the file Teasalesmap.xlsx, I want to summarize the total sales by state on a US map. To begin, I select State and Units (from the Power View Fields pane) to add them to the Fields area. This creates the table shown in Figure 46-14.

State	Units
AK	14022
AL	16061
AR	15118
AZ	16484
CA	15696
CO	13128
CT	16664
DE	11874
FL	11279
GA	15833
HI	13244
IA	11461
ID	17028
IL	18825
IN	13024
KS	19196
KY	10522
LA	12486
MA	8523
MD	10304

FIGURE 46-14 Summarizing the total tea sales by state.

After clicking within the table, switch to the Design tab and click the Map option in the Switch Visualization group. If this is your first map, you will be prompted to enable Bing Maps. After you enable Bing Maps, you will see the amazing sales summary shown in Figure 46-15. For each state, you will see a bubble for which size represents the state's sales. You can hover your cursor over a bubble to reveal statistics for that state.

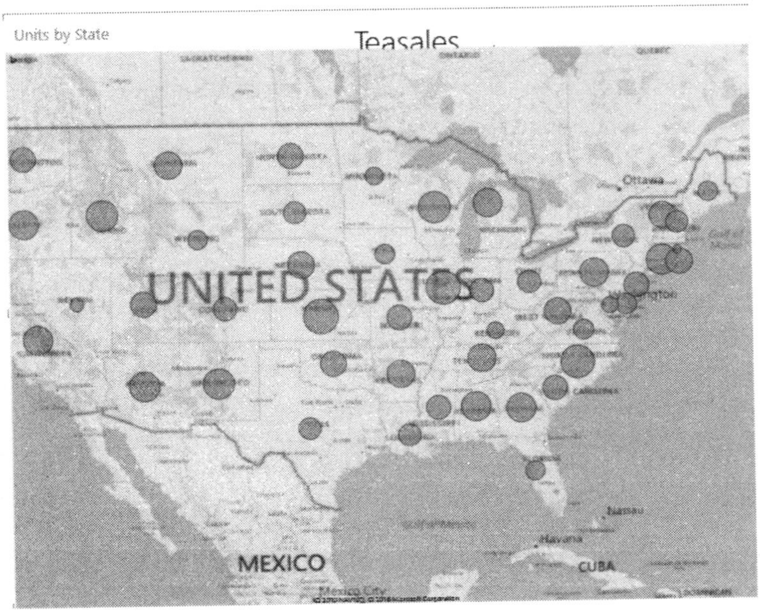

FIGURE 46-15 The unit sales summarized by state.

How do I turn a time-series scatter chart into an animated movie?

In 2006, German statistician Hans Rosling gave a TED Talk (*https://www.ted.com/talks/hans_rosling_shows_the_best_stats_you_ve_ever_seen*) in which he used amazing graphics to summarize the evolution of world economic development. Now Power View empowers you to create similarly amazing graphics, which display the evolution of three different variables.

I will illustrate the process with US crimes between 1960 and 2009. The file Crimedata.xlsx (from the Templates folder) contains the columns Year (that tracks the crimes), Violent (the number of violent crimes), Property (property crimes), and Murder during each of these years. I want to create a movie showing how these numbers change over time. To begin, I make the data a table (already done in the file), and after clicking and selecting a cell outside the table in the worksheet Sheet1, I select the Insert tab and click Power View to create the worksheet Power View1. In the Power View Fields pane, I select the Violent field, I click the Design tab, and I select Scatter from the Other Chart options. I then fill in the field areas as shown in Figure 46-16. Notice the following conditions:

- Placing the Violent field in the X Value area ensures that violent crimes are represented by the X-axis value.
- Placing Property in the Y Value area ensures that property crimes are represented by the Y-axis value.
- Placing Murder in the Size area ensures that murders are represented by the size of a bubble.
- Dragging Year into the Details area (or clicking the down arrow to the right of the Year field, and selecting Add To Details) ensures that one point is displayed for each year.

- I leave the optional Color area blank. If the Color area is filled in, it colors each point.
- The key is to drag the Year field into the Play Axis area. This causes a Play button and time line to appear at the bottom of the chart. Clicking the Play button cycles through all the years. You can use the time line to begin your animation during any year.

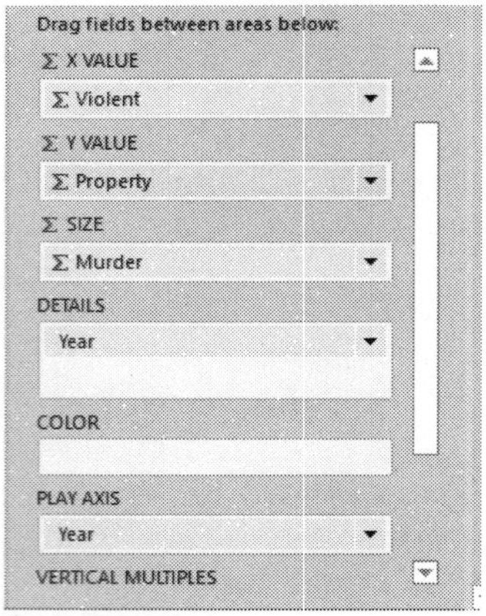

FIGURE 46-16 The settings used to create a crime-data movie.

I add the title **USA Crime Movie** in the canvas area, by updating Click Here To Add A Title. Figure 46-17 shows the final chart. Warning: These charts are addictive!

FIGURE 46-17 An animated summary of crime data.

If you play the animation shown in Figure 46-17, you will see crimes increase for a while and then, to our relief, decline. There is great debate whether the primary cause of this crime decline is improvement in policy strategies or simply demographics. (Young males commit most crimes, and the number of young males eventually drop.)

How do I use the Multiples feature to easily create many charts?

Suppose you want to summarize the annual sales of each product in a separate chart. Power View's Multiples feature makes this a snap. To see how, look at worksheet Power View1 in the file Teasalesmultiples.xlsx. I begin with the summary of unit sales shown back in Figure 46-7. Then I simply drag Product to either the Vertical or Horizontal Multiples section of the Fields area. I chose Vertical Multiples and obtain the following set of charts for each product, as shown in Figure 46-18. The Layout tab (in the ribbon) allows you to change the appearance of these charts.

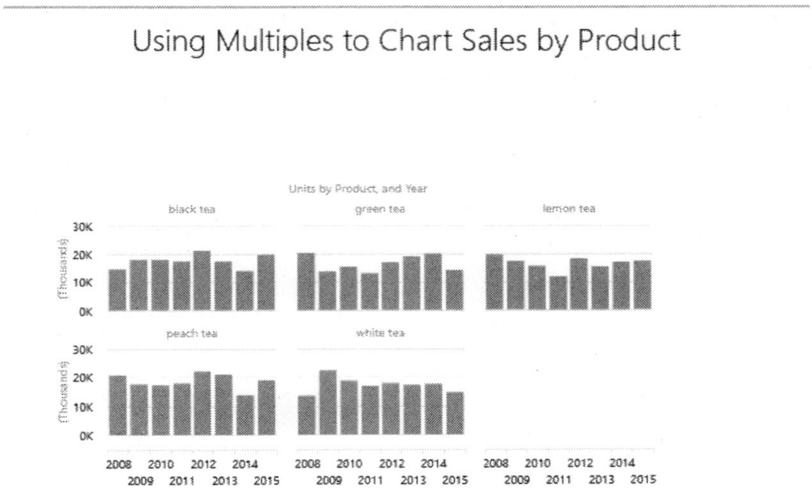

FIGURE 46-18 Product charts created by means of the Multiples feature.

How do I use 3D Maps?

We have already used Power View to create a map. Excel 2016's 3D Maps feature allows you to create truly amazing maps, based on the following geographic formats:

- Street address
- City
- State/Province
- Zip Code/Postal Code
- Country/Region

In this section, I give a quick introduction to the 3D Maps feature. As shown in Figure 46-19, the 3D Map option can be opened from the middle of the Insert tab, in the Tours group.

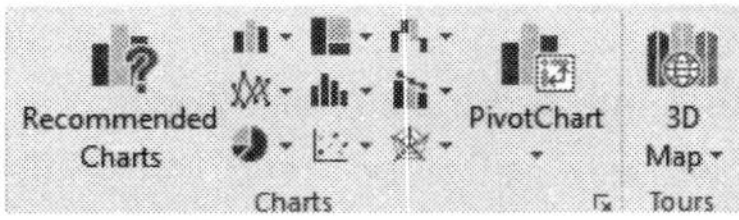

FIGURE 46-19 The location of 3D Map on the ribbon.

To illustrate the use of the 3D Map option, open the file Powercapacitytemp.xlsx. This file contains information on US power-generation capacity. The state, county, plant capacity, and energy-description columns will provide the basis for our first 3D Map. Suppose you would like to graph, with a stacked-column chart, the amount of capacity for each state by energy type. Begin by making the data a table and add it to the Data Model. After clicking 3D Map and choosing Open 3D Maps, fill in the Layer pane as shown in Figure 46-20.

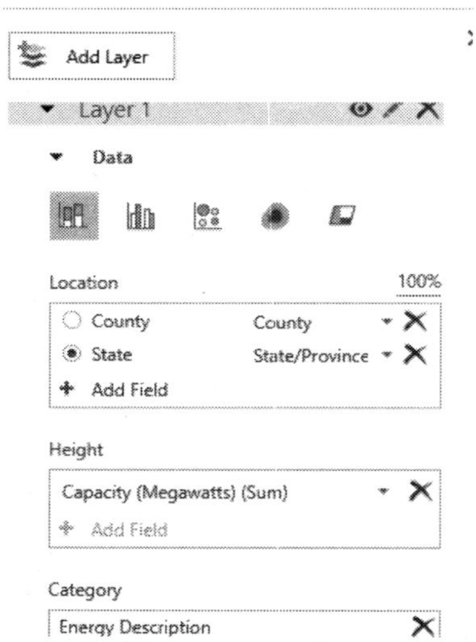

FIGURE 46-20 The settings to create a stacked-column map.

- In the location portion of the pane, you select the geographic data (in this case, select State) that provides the basis for the area mapped.
- I selected Capacity (Sum) to control the height of our 3D map. Thus, the height of a state's column represents the total generating capacity for a state.
- By selecting Energy Description as our Category and choosing the stacked-column chart (the first chart option, at the top of the pane in the Data section), the energy capacity for each state is summarized by category. You may also choose a clustered Column map, heat map, bubble map, or region map. (The map options are displayed in the Data section at the top of the Layer pane.)

Our resulting 3D map is shown in Figure 46-21. You can click the + button (or double-click the map, or press the + key) to enlarge the map. Clicking the – button (or pressing the – key) shrinks the map. The up and down arrows (clicking the buttons and pressing the keys) move the globe up or down while the left and right arrows rotate the map. You can also use a mouse wheel to zoom in and out, and you can click and drag on the map to spin the globe. Your map is saved as a Tour, which can be played back. If you want to, you can choose to open a new tour. Clicking the X in the upper-right corner of the ribbon will close the map and return you to Excel. Clicking Map Labels on the 3D Maps ribbon (in the Map group) adds labels (such as the country/region and states) to your map.

Clicking the 3D column for any state provides useful insights into where a state gets its power. For example, Texas gets a large percentage of its power from natural gas, the state of Washington gets a large fraction of its power from water or hydroelectric power, and Indiana gets a large fraction of its power from coal.

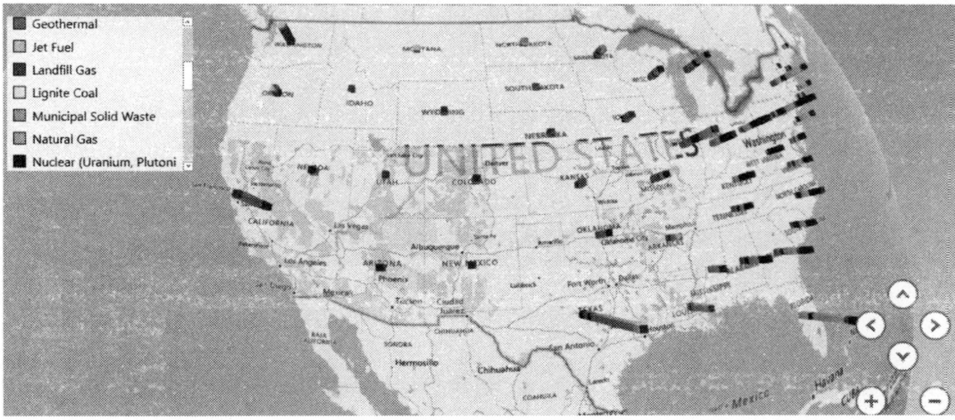

FIGURE 46-21 A 3D map of power-generation capacity, by state and type of power.

Figure 46-22 shows a column map that summarizes the average food-inspection scores for cities in the state of Washington. I leave the creation of this chart as a homework problem (see Problem 7). Note that I clicked on Issaquah and found the average food-inspection score was 14.16.

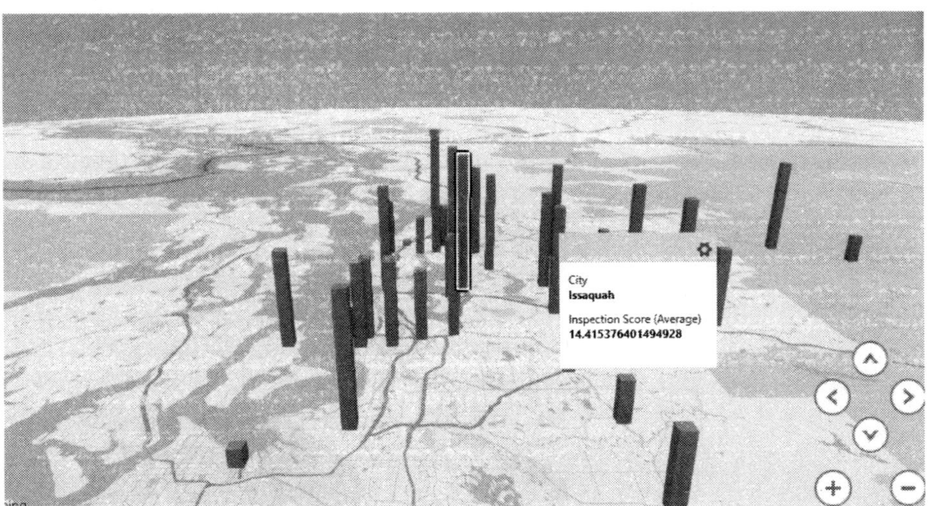

FIGURE 46-22 The average food inspection score by city.

Problems

The file Cellphonedata.xlsx contains the population and number of cell phones for the 20 countries/regions having the most cell phones. Use this data in Problems 1–5.

1. Create a column chart that summarizes cell phones by country/region.
2. Create a scatter chart that plots cell phones vs. population.
3. Set up a slicer to filter a clustered column graph of cell phones by country/region.
4. Set up a tile to filter a column chart that summarizes cell phones by country/region.
5. Summarize the population data on a map.
6. The file Returns.xlsx contains annual returns on US stocks, T-bills, and bonds for the period 1928–2012. Create an animation to show the evolution of investment returns over time.
7. Use the data in the file Seattle.xlsx to create the map shown in Figure 46-23. The height of each column represents the average inspection score in each area.

FIGURE 46-23 A map depicting average inspection scores in the Seattle area.

8. The file Stateincome.xlsx contains median income by state for the year 2010. Create a map that summarizes this data.

CHAPTER 47

Sparklines

Questions answered in this chapter:

- How can you graphically summarize daily customer counts for each of a bank's branches in a single cell?
- How can you modify sparklines?
- How can you summarize an NFL team's sequence of wins or losses in a single cell?
- Do sparklines automatically update when new data is included?

Sparklines are exciting graphics that can summarize a row or column of data in a single cell. The term sparkline was first used by Edward Tufte, a famous expert on the visual presentation of data and its analysis. Tufte described sparklines as "data-intense, design-simple, word-sized graphics." Microsoft Excel 2016 makes it a snap to create amazing graphics that reside in a single cell.

Answers to this chapter's questions

How can you graphically summarize daily customer counts for each of a bank's branches in a single cell?

The file Sparklines.xlsx contains daily customer counts at several branches of a New York state bank. Some of the data is shown in Figure 47-1.

	C	D	E	F	G	H
7		Monday	Tuesday	Wednesday	Thursday	Friday
8	New York	1176	768	808	864	1235
9	Rochester	475	323	333	356	515
10	Utica	360	250	228	275	378
11	Syracuse	594	412	408	459	618
12	Buffalo	698	475	504	551	803
13	Ossining	306	208	204	234	322
14	Ithaca	437	288	294	299	450

FIGURE 47-1 The data for sparklines.

Let's say that you want to summarize the weekly customer counts by graphing the daily counts for each branch in a single cell. Simply select the range where you want your sparklines to go (I chose

I8:I14), and then, on the Insert tab, select Line from the Sparklines group, which is shown in Figure 47-2.

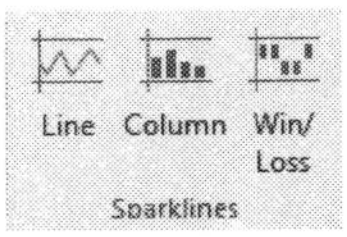

FIGURE 47-2 The sparkline choices.

Then fill in the Create Sparklines dialog box, shown in Figure 47-3, with the data on which the sparklines are based, by entering D8:H14 in the Data Range box.

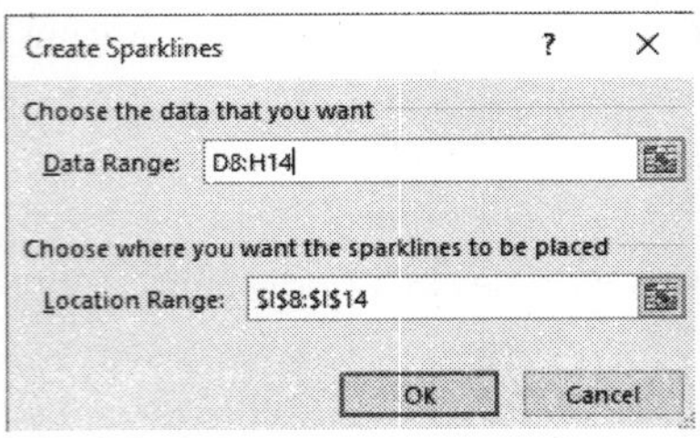

FIGURE 47-3 Creating line sparklines.

You now see a line graph (Figure 47-4) that summarizes the customer traffic for each branch. You can see this in the worksheet Line Sparkline in the file Sparklines.xlsx.

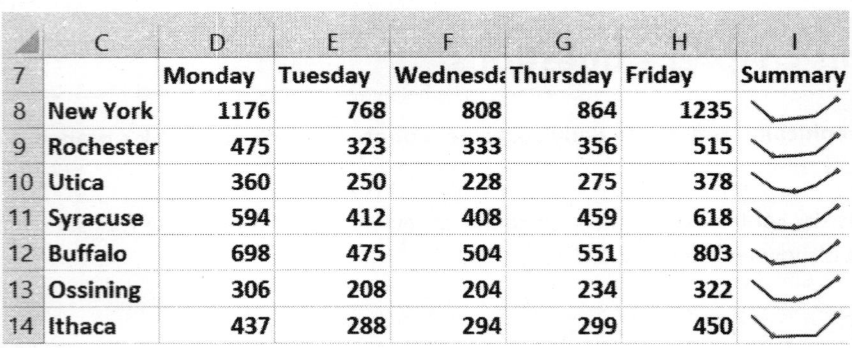

	C	D	E	F	G	H	I
7		Monday	Tuesday	Wednesda	Thursday	Friday	Summary
8	New York	1176	768	808	864	1235	
9	Rochester	475	323	333	356	515	
10	Utica	360	250	228	275	378	
11	Syracuse	594	412	408	459	618	
12	Buffalo	698	475	504	551	803	
13	Ossining	306	208	204	234	322	
14	Ithaca	437	288	294	299	450	

FIGURE 47-4 Line sparklines summarizing the branch traffic.

You can see that for each branch, Monday and Friday are clearly the busiest days.

How can you modify sparklines?

If you click any cell containing a sparkline, the Sparkline Tools Design tab appears. After selecting the Design tab, you can make many changes to your sparklines. For example, as shown in Figure 47-5, I selected the high and low points to be marked.

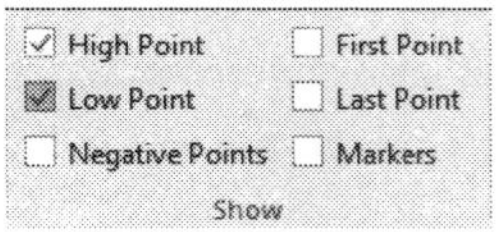

FIGURE 47-5 Selecting high and low points to mark on sparklines.

The resulting sparklines are shown in Figure 47-6 and in the worksheet High Low in the file Sparklines.xlsx.

	C	D	E	F	G	H	I
7		Monday	Tuesday	Wednesd	Thursday	Friday	Summary
8	New York	1176	768	808	864	1235	
9	Rochester	475	323	333	356	515	
10	Utica	360	250	228	275	378	
11	Syracuse	594	412	408	459	618	
12	Buffalo	698	475	504	551	803	
13	Ossining	306	208	204	234	322	
14	Ithaca	437	288	294	299	450	

FIGURE 47-6 High and low points marked on sparklines.

These sparklines make it clear that Friday is the busiest day for each branch (the high points) and Tuesday or Wednesday is the least busy day (the low points).

From the Design tab, you can make the following changes to your sparklines:

- Change the type of sparkline (select Line, Column, or Win/Loss). I discuss column and win/loss sparklines later in the chapter.
- Use the Edit Data options to change the data used to create the sparklines. You can also change the default setting so that hidden data is included in your sparklines.
- Select any combination of the high point, low point, negative points, first point, or last point to be marked.
- Change the style or color associated with the sparklines and/or sparkline markers.
- By selecting Axis (in the Group group), you can change the way the axes are set for each sparkline. For example, you can make the x-axis or y-axis scale the same for each sparkline. The default is to base the scale for each axis on the data for the individual sparkline. This is the scaling used previously in Figure 47-4. The Custom option allows you to pick an upper and lower limit for each axis.
- When data points occur at irregularly spaced dates, you can select Date Axis Type from the Axis options so that the graphed points are separated by an amount of space proportional to the differences in dates. Figure 47-7 shows company sales at irregularly spaced dates. (See the worksheet Date Axis in the file Sparklines.xlsx.) In cell F12, the sparkline is graphed as

though the dates are spaced at regular intervals. In cell F10, I click Axis and Date Axis Type on the Design tab, choose the range C10:C13 to use as the data axis, and then click OK in the Sparkline Date Range dialog box. The sparkline in cell F10 (as shown in Figure 47-7) reflects the irregular date spacing.

	C	D	E	F	G
9	Date	Sales			
10	1/1/2010	1000			Date axis
11	6/1/2010	1200			
12	9/1/2012	1400			No date axis
13	1/1/2015	1900			

FIGURE 47-7 Sparklines with a date axis.

You can also change line sparklines to column sparklines by clicking any sparkline and then selecting Column in the Type group on the Sparklines Tools Design tab. (See Figure 47-8 and the worksheet Column Sparkline in the file Sparklines.xlsx.)

	C	D	E	F	G	H	I
7		Monday	Tuesday	Wednesda	Thursday	Friday	Summary
8	New York	1176	768	808	864	1235	
9	Rochester	475	323	333	356	515	
10	Utica	360	250	228	275	378	
11	Syracuse	594	412	408	459	618	
12	Buffalo	698	475	504	551	803	
13	Ossining	306	208	204	234	322	
14	Ithaca	437	288	294	299	450	

FIGURE 47-8 A column sparkline graph.

How can you summarize an NFL team's sequence of wins or losses in a single cell?

The file Nflwinslosses.xlsx contains the game-by-game performance for each NFL team during the 2009 regular season. A subset of this data is shown in Figure 47-9. (See the Win Loss worksheet.)

	C	D	E	F	G	H	I	J	K	L	M	N	O	P	Q	R	S	T
6			Game															
7		Team	1	2	3	4	5	6	7	8	9	10	11	12	13	14	15	16
8		Arizona Cardinals	-1	1	-1	1	1	1	-1	1	1	1	-1	1	-1	1	1	-1
18		Detroit Lions	-1	-1	1	-1	-1	-1	-1	-1	-1	1	-1	-1	-1	-1	-1	-1
19		Green Bay Packers	1	-1	1	-1	1	1	-1	-1	1	1	1	1	1	-1	1	1
20		Houston Texans	-1	1	-1	1	-1	1	1	1	-1	-1	-1	-1	1	1	1	1
21		Indianapolis Colts	1	1	1	1	1	1	1	1	1	1	1	1	1	1	-1	-1
22		Jacksonville Jaguars	-1	-1	1	1	-1	1	-1	1	1	1	-1	1	-1	-1	-1	-1
23		Kansas City Chiefs	-1	-1	-1	-1	-1	1	-1	-1	1	1	-1	-1	-1	-1	-1	1
24		Miami Dolphins	-1	-1	-1	1	1	-1	1	-1	1	1	-1	1	1	-1	-1	-1
25		Minnesota Vikings	1	1	1	1	1	1	-1	1	1	1	1	-1	1	-1	-1	1
26		New England Patriots	1	-1	1	1	-1	1	1	1	-1	1	-1	-1	1	1	1	-1
27		New Orleans Saints	1	1	1	1	1	1	1	1	1	1	1	1	1	-1	-1	-1
28		New York Giants	1	1	1	1	1	-1	-1	-1	-1	1	-1	1	-1	1	-1	-1
29		New York Jets	1	1	1	-1	-1	-1	1	-1	-1	-1	1	1	1	-1	1	1
30		Oakland Raiders	-1	1	-1	-1	-1	1	-1	-1	-1	1	-1	1	-1	1	-1	-1
31		Philadelphia Eagles	1	-1	1	1	-1	1	1	-1	-1	1	1	1	1	1	1	-1
32		Pittsburgh Steelers	1	-1	-1	1	1	1	1	1	-1	-1	-1	-1	-1	1	1	1
33		San Diego Chargers	1	-1	1	-1	-1	1	1	1	1	1	1	1	1	1	1	1

FIGURE 47-9 Sparklines summarizing wins and losses for NFL teams.

A *1* denotes a win, and a *–1* a loss. Each win/loss sparkline treats any positive number as an *up block* and any negative number as a *down block*. Any *0*s are graphed as a gap. To create the win/loss sparklines, select the range in which the sparklines should be placed (cell range C8:C39), and then select Win/Loss from the Sparklines group on the Insert tab. Next, in the Create Sparklines dialog box, choose the data range E8:T39, and click OK. The sparklines make the 2009 NFL season come alive. You can see the amazing starts of the Indianapolis Colts and the New Orleans Saints. You can see that the Tennessee Titans started poorly and then got red hot. The New York Giants started well and then hit a rough patch. Win/loss sparklines are great for tracking an organization's progress toward meeting quotas or goals. See Problem 4 at the end of this chapter.

Do sparklines automatically update when new data is included?

If you want your sparklines to automatically update to include new data, you should make the data a table (see Chapter 26, "Tables") or convert the data into a dynamic range (see Chapter 22, "The OFFSET function").

Problems

1. For the bank branch data, make your line sparklines use the same scale for each branch.
2. The data Dow.xlsx contains the values of the Dow Jones Index for January 2–August 10, 2010. Create a line sparkline to show the ups and downs of the market.
3. Use win/loss sparklines to capture the market's ups and downs. Again use the file Dow.xlsx.
4. The file Goals.xlsx shows the percentage amount by which bank branches met or failed to meet their goals each month. Summarize this data with win/loss sparklines.

CHAPTER 48

Summarizing data with database statistical functions

Questions answered in this chapter:

- Joolas is a small makeup company that tracks each sales transaction in a Microsoft Excel worksheet. Often, they want to answer questions such as these:
  - How many dollars' worth of lip gloss did Jen sell?
  - What was the average number of lipstick units sold each time Jen made a sale in the East region?
  - What was the total dollar amount of all the makeup sold by Emilee or sold in the East region?
  - How many dollars' worth of lipstick were sold by Colleen or Zaret in the East region?
  - How many lipstick transactions were not in the East region?
  - How many dollars' worth of lipstick did Jen sell during 2004?
  - How many units of makeup were sold for a price of at least $3.20?
  - What is the total dollar amount each salesperson sold of each makeup product?
- What helpful tricks can I use to set up criteria ranges?
- I have a database that lists for each sales transaction the revenue, the date sold, and the product-ID code. Given the date sold and the ID code for a transaction, is there an easy way to extract the transaction's revenue?

As you saw in Chapter 43, "Using PivotTables and slicers to describe data," Excel PivotTables are a great tool for summarizing data. Often, however, a PivotTable gives you much more information than you need. Database statistical functions make it easy to answer any reporting question without having to create a PivotTable.

You are already familiar with functions such as SUM, AVERAGE, COUNT, MAX, and MIN. By prefixing a *D* (which stands for *database*) to these and other functions, you create *database statistical functions*. But what does the DSUM function do, for example, that the SUM function can't? Whereas the SUM function adds up every cell in a cell range, the DSUM function enables you to specify (by using criteria) a subset of rows to add together in a cell range. For example, suppose you have a sales database for a small makeup company that contains the following information about each sales transaction:

- Name of salesperson
- Transaction date
- Product sold
- Units sold
- Dollars of revenue generated per transaction
- Region of the country where the transaction took place

You can find this data in the file Makeupdb.xlsx, which is shown in Figure 48-1.

	G	H	I	J	K	L	M
4	Trans Number	Name	Date	Product	Units	Dollars	Location
5	1	Betsy	4/1/2004	lip gloss	45	$ 137.20	south
6	2	Hallagan	3/10/2004	foundatio	50	$ 152.01	midwest
7	3	Ashley	2/25/2005	lipstick	9	$ 28.72	midwest
8	4	Hallagan	5/22/2006	lip gloss	55	$ 167.08	west
9	5	Zaret	6/17/2004	lip gloss	43	$ 130.60	midwest
10	6	Colleen	11/27/2005	eye liner	58	$ 175.99	midwest
11	7	Cristina	3/21/2004	eye liner	8	$ 25.80	midwest
12	8	Colleen	12/17/2006	lip gloss	72	$ 217.84	midwest
13	9	Ashley	7/5/2006	eye liner	75	$ 226.64	south
14	10	Betsy	8/7/2006	lip gloss	24	$ 73.50	east
15	11	Ashley	11/29/2004	mascara	43	$ 130.84	east
16	12	Ashley	11/18/2004	lip gloss	23	$ 71.03	west
17	13	Emilee	8/31/2005	lip gloss	49	$ 149.59	west
18	14	Hallagan	1/1/2005	eye liner	18	$ 56.47	south
19	15	Zaret	9/20/2006	foundatio	-8	$ (21.99)	east
20	16	Emilee	4/12/2004	mascara	45	$ 137.39	east
21	17	Colleen	4/30/2006	mascara	66	$ 199.65	south
22	18	Jen	8/31/2005	lip gloss	88	$ 265.19	midwest
23	19	Jen	10/27/2004	eye liner	78	$ 236.15	south
24	20	Zaret	11/27/2005	lip gloss	57	$ 173.12	midwest

FIGURE 48-1 Data for working with database statistical functions.

Using the DSUM function with the appropriate criteria, you could, for example, add up the revenue generated only by transactions involving lip gloss sales in the East during 2004. Essentially, the criteria you set up flags those rows that you want to include in the total sum. Within these rows, the DSUM function acts like the ordinary SUM function.

The syntax of the DSUM function is DSUM(database,field,criteria). The arguments are as follows:

- *Database* is the cell range that makes up the database. The first row of the list contains labels for each column.
- *Field* is the column containing the values you want the function to add. You can define the field by enclosing the column label in quotation marks. For example, you would designate the Dollars column by entering "Dollars". The field can also be specified by using the position of the column in the database, measured from left to right. For example, the makeup transaction

database would use columns H through M. (I did not include the Transactions column as part of the database.) You could specify column H as field 1 and column M as field 6.

- *Criteria* refers to the cell ranges that specify the rows on which the function should operate. The first row of a criteria range must include one or more column labels. (The only exception to this rule is *computed criteria*, which I'll discuss in the last two examples in this chapter.) As the examples illustrate, the key to creating a criteria range is to understand that multiple criteria in the same row are joined by AND, whereas criteria in different rows are joined by OR.

Answers to this chapter's questions

Now let's go on to some examples that illustrate the power and versatility of database statistical functions. These examples are shown in Figure 48-2.

How many dollars' worth of lip gloss did Jen sell?

In this example, you want to apply DSUM to column 5 of the database. Column 5 contains the dollar volume for each transaction. (I gave the name *data* to the database, which consists of the range H4:M1895.) The criteria range in O4:P5 flags all the rows in the database in which Name equals *Jen* and Product equals *lip gloss*. Thus, entering in cell N5 the formula =DSUM(data,5,O4:P5) calculates the total dollar amount of lip gloss sold by Jen. You could have also entered the formula as =DSUM(data,"Dollars",O4:P5). Jen sold $5,461.61 worth of lip gloss. In cell N6, you can find the same answer by using the SUMIFS function (see Chapter 21, "The SUMIF, AVERAGEIF, SUMIFS, and AVERAGEIFS functions") with the formula =SUMIFS(Dollars,Name,"Jen",Product,"lip gloss").

	N	O	P	Q	R
4	Jen lip gloss $	Name	Product		
5	$ 5,461.61	Jen	lip gloss		
6	5461.61479				
7	Jen avg.units lipstick in east	Name	Product	Location	
8	42.25	Jen	lipstick	east	
9	42.25				
10	$s Emilee or east	Name	Location		
11	$ 76,156.48	Emilee			
12			east		
13	$s lipstick by Colleen or Zaret in east	Name	Location	Product	
14	$ 1,073.20	Colleen	east	lipstick	
15	1073.203709	Zaret	east	lipstick	
16	Number of lipstick transactions not in ea	Product	Location		
17	164	lipstick	<>east	164	
18	total $s jen lipstick in 2004	Name	Product	Date	Date
19	$ 1,690.79	Jen	lipstick	>=1/1/2004	<1/1/2005
20	1690.793115				
21	Units sold for >=$3.20	Big price			
22	1127	FALSE			

FIGURE 48-2 Database statistical functions at work.

What was the average number of lipstick units sold each time Jen had a sale in the East region?

You can compute this number by entering in cell N8 the formula =DAVERAGE(data,4,O7:Q8). Using 4 as the value for *field* specifies the Units column, and the criteria range O7:Q8 flags all the rows in the database in which Name equals *Jen*, Product equals *lipstick*, and Location equals *East*. Using DAVERAGE ensures that you average the units sold for the flagged rows. You can see that on average, Jen sold 42.25 units of lipstick in transactions in the East region. In cell N9, you can calculate the same answer by using the formula =AVERAGEIFS(Units,Name,"Jen",Product,"Lipstick",Location,"east").

What was the total dollar amount of all the makeup sold by Emilee or sold in the East region?

In cell N11, you can compute the total dollars ($76,156.48) of sales made by Emilee or made in the East by using the formula =DSUM(data,5,O10:P12). The criteria in O10:P12 flags sales in the East or by Emilee because criteria in different rows are treated as an OR operation. The great programmers at Microsoft have ensured that this formula does not double-count Emilee's sales in the East. Here, you cannot use SUMIFS to easily find the answer.

How many dollars' worth of lipstick were sold by Colleen or Zaret in the East region?

The formula =DSUM(data,5,O13:Q15) in cell N14 computes the total lipstick revenue generated through Colleen and Zaret's sales ($1,073.20) in the East. Notice that O14:Q14 specifies criteria that selects Colleen's lipstick sales in the East, and O15:Q15 specifies criteria that selects Zaret's lipstick sales in the East. Remember that criteria in different rows are joined by OR. In cell N15, the answer to this question is calculated with the following formula:

```
=SUMIFS(Dollars,Name,"Colleen",Product,"lipstick",Location,"east")
   +SUMIFS(Dollars,Name,"Zaret",Product,"lipstick",Location,"east")
```

How many lipstick transactions were not in the East region?

In cell N17, you can compute the total number of lipstick transactions (164) outside the East region with the formula =DCOUNT(data,4,O16:P17). You use DCOUNT in this problem because you want to specify criteria by which the function will count the number of rows involving lipstick sales and regions other than the East. Excel treats the expression <>East in the criteria range as "not East." For this problem, using SUMIFS would require that you have a SUMIFS function for each region.

Because the COUNT function counts numbers, you need to refer to a column containing numerical values. Column 4, the Units column, contains numbers, so I designated that column in the formula. The formula DCOUNT(data,3,O16:P17) would return *0* because there are no numbers in the database's third column (which is column J in the worksheet). Of course, the formula =DCOUNTA(data,3,O16:P17) would return the correct answer because COUNTA counts text as well as numbers.

How many dollars' worth of lipstick did Jen sell during 2004?

The trick here is knowing how to flag only sales that occurred in 2004. By including in one row of your criteria range a reference to the Date field, using the expressions >=1/1/2004 and <1/1/2005 captures only the 2004 sales. Thus, entering in cell N19 the formula =DSUM(data,5,O18:R19) computes the total lipstick sales by Jen ($1,690.79) after January 1, 2004, and before January 1, 2005. In cell N20, the answer to this problem is calculated by means of the following formula:

```
=SUMIFS(Dollars,Date,">=1/1/2004",Date,"<=12/31/2004",Product,"lipstick",Name,"Jen").
```

How many units of makeup were sold for a price of at least $3.20?

This example involves computed criteria. Basically, computed criteria flags rows of the database on the basis of whether a computed condition is true or false for that row. For this question, you want to flag each row that contains Dollars/Units>=$3.20. When setting up a computed criterion (see Figure 48-3), the label in the first row above the computed criteria must not be a column label. For example, you can't use Name, Product, or another label from row 4 of this worksheet. The computed criteria is set up to be a formula that returns True based on the first row of information in the database. Thus, to specify rows in which the average price is greater than or equal to $3.20, you need to enter =(L5/K5)>=3.2 in your criteria range below a heading that is not a column label. If the first row of data does not satisfy this condition, you will see FALSE in the worksheet, but Excel will still flag all the rows having a unit price that's greater than or equal to $3.20. Entering in N22 the formula =DSUM(data,4,O21:O22) computes the total number of units of makeup sold (1,127) in orders for which the unit price was greater than or equal to $3.20. Note that cell O22 contains the formula =(L5/K5)>=3.2.

	N	O
21	Units sold for >=$3.20	Big price
22	1127	FALSE

FIGURE 48-3 Computed criteria.

What is the total dollar amount each salesperson sold of each makeup product?

For this problem, I'd like to use a DSUM function whose criteria range is based on both the Name and Product columns. Using a data table, I can easily loop through all the possible combinations of ame and product in the criteria range and compute the total revenue for each name and product combination.

I begin by entering any name in cell X26 and any product in cell Y26. Then I enter in cell Q25 the formula =DSUM(data,5,X25:Y26), which computes the total sales revenue for (in this case) Betsy and eye liner. Next, I enter each salesperson's name in the cell range Q26:Q33 and each product in the cell range R25:V25. Now I select the data table range (Q25:V33). On the Data tab, in the Forecast group, click What-If Analysis, and then click Data Table. Choose cell X26 as the column input cell and Y26 as the row input cell. You then obtain the results shown in Figure 48-4. Each entry in the data table computes the revenue generated for a different name/product combination because the data table causes the names to be placed in cell X26 and the products to be placed in cell Y26. For example, Ashley sold $3,245.44 worth of lipstick.

	Q	R	S	T	U	V	W	X	Y
25	6046.53428	lip gloss	foundatio	lipstick	mascara	eye liner		Name	Product
26	Betsy	5675.65005	8043.486	3968.605	4827.254	6046.534		Betsy	eye liner
27	Hallagan	5603.11938	6985.734	3177.871	5703.347	6964.621			
28	Zaret	5670.32933	6451.65	2448.707	3879.95	8166.749			
29	Colleen	5573.32373	6834.768	2346.414	6746.525	3389.625			
30	Cristina	5297.97981	5290.99	2401.668	5461.647	5397.274			
31	Jen	5461.61479	5628.648	3953.3	6887.175	7010.441			
32	Ashley	6053.68456	4186.059	3245.443	6617.1	5844.949			
33	Emilee	5270.25031	5313.788	2189.138	4719.3	7587.389			
34									
35									
36		lip gloss	foundatio	lipstick	mascara	eye liner			
37	Betsy	5675.65005	8043.486	3968.605	4827.254	6046.534			
38	Hallagan	5603.11938	6985.734	3177.871	5703.347	6964.621			
39	Zaret	5670.32933	6451.65	2448.707	3879.95	8166.749			
40	Colleen	5573.32373	6834.768	2346.414	6746.525	3389.625			
41	Cristina	5297.97981	5290.99	2401.668	5461.647	5397.274			
42	Jen	5461.61479	5628.648	3953.3	6887.175	7010.441			
43	Ashley	6053.68456	4186.059	3245.443	6617.1	5844.949			
44	Emilee	5270.25031	5313.788	2189.138	4719.3	7587.389			

FIGURE 48-4 Combining data tables with a DSUM function.

This example shows how combining data tables with database statistical functions can quickly generate many statistics of interest. Note that I also solved this problem by copying from cell R37 to R37:V44 the formula =SUMIFS(Dollars,Name,$Q37,Product,R$36).

What helpful tricks can I use to set up criteria ranges?

Here are some examples of little tricks that might help you set up an appropriate criteria range. Suppose the column label in the first row of the criteria range refers to a column containing text (for example, column H).

- ***Allie*** will flag records containing the text string Allie in column H.
- **A?X** will flag a record if the record's column H entry begins with *A* and contains *X* as its third character. (The second character can be anything!)
- **<>*B*** will flag a record if column H's entry does not contain any *B*s.

Suppose a column (for example, column I) contains numerical values.

- **>100** will flag a record if column I contains a value greater than 100.
- **<>100** will flag a record if column I contains a value not equal to 100.
- **>=1000** will flag a record if column I contains a value greater than or equal to 1,000.
- You can refer to another cell in a criterion by using the **&** sign. For example, as shown in Figure 48-5 (see file Makeupdb.xlsx), using the formula =">"&T10 allows us to create a cutoff for dollars in our conditional sum that is based on the contents of cell T10. Then, the formula =DSUM(data,5,S6:T7) calculates the total dollars sold by Betsy in transactions where the dollar amount was greater than whatever number is in cell T10.

	S	T	U	V	W
1					
2					
3					
4					
5					
6	Name	Dollars			
7	Betsy	>160	=">"&T10		
8					
9					
10	Cutoff	160			
11					
12		18212.1	=DSUM(data,5,S6:T7)		

FIGURE 48-5 Using the & sign to create a criterion.

I have a database that lists for each sales transaction the revenue, the date sold, and the product-ID code. Given the date sold and the ID code for a transaction, is there an easy way to capture the transaction's revenue?

The file Dget.xlsx (see Figure 48-6) contains a database that lists revenues, dates, and product-ID codes for a series of sales transactions. If you know the date and the product-ID code for a transaction, how can you find the transaction's revenue? With the DGET function, it's simple. The syntax of the DGET function is DGET(database,field#,criteria). Given a cell range for *database* and a value for *field#* in the database (counting columns from left to right across the range), the DGET function returns the entry in the column *field#* from the database record satisfying the criteria. If no record satisfies the criteria, the DGET function returns the #VALUE error message. If more than one record satisfies the criteria, the DGET function returns the #NUM! error message.

Suppose that you want to know the revenue for a transaction involving product-ID code 62426 that occurred on 1/9/2006. Assuming that the transaction involving this product on the given date is unique, the formula =DGET(B7:D28,1,G5:H6), entered in cell G9, yields the transaction's revenue of $169. Note that I used *1* for the *field#* argument because revenue is listed in the first column of the database (which is contained in the cell range B7:D28). The criteria range G5:H6 ensures that you find a transaction involving product 62426 on 1/9/2006.

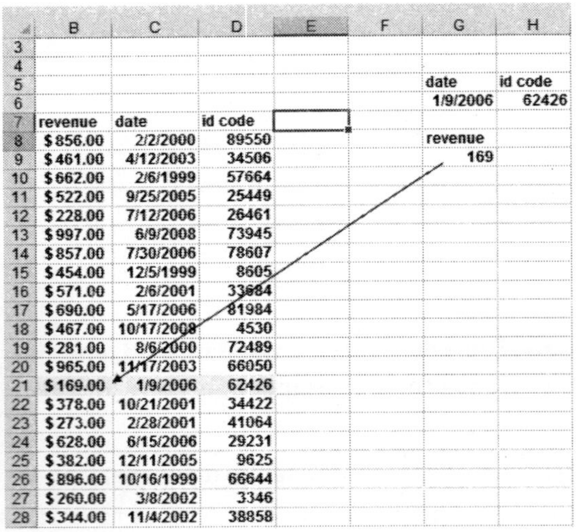

	B	C	D	E	F	G	H
3							
4							
5						date	id code
6						1/9/2006	62426
7	revenue	date	id code				
8	$856.00	2/2/2000	89550			revenue	
9	$461.00	4/12/2003	34506			169	
10	$662.00	2/6/1999	57664				
11	$522.00	9/25/2005	25449				
12	$228.00	7/12/2006	26461				
13	$997.00	6/9/2008	73945				
14	$857.00	7/30/2006	78607				
15	$454.00	12/5/1999	8605				
16	$571.00	2/6/2001	33684				
17	$690.00	5/17/2006	81984				
18	$467.00	10/17/2008	4530				
19	$281.00	8/6/2000	72489				
20	$965.00	11/17/2003	66050				
21	$169.00	1/9/2006	62426				
22	$378.00	10/21/2001	34422				
23	$273.00	2/28/2001	41064				
24	$628.00	6/15/2006	29231				
25	$382.00	12/11/2005	9625				
26	$896.00	10/16/1999	66644				
27	$260.00	3/8/2002	3346				
28	$344.00	11/4/2002	38858				

FIGURE 48-6 Using the DGET function.

Problems

1. Using the data in the file Makeupdb.xlsx, how many units of lip gloss did Zaret sell during 2004 and 2005?
2. Create a data table that contains each person's total revenue and units sold.
3. How many units of lip gloss did Colleen sell outside the West region?
4. Using the data in the file Makeupdb.xlsx, create a data table that shows the average per-unit revenue generated by each person for sales in which the average per-unit price exceeded $3.30.
5. Use the data in the file Sales.xlsx to determine the following:
   - Total dollar sales in the Midwest
   - Total dollars that Heather sold in the East
   - Total dollars that Heather sold or that were sold in the East
   - Total dollars sold in the East by Heather or John
   - Number of transactions in the East region
   - Number of transactions with greater than average sales
   - Total sales not in the Midwest

6. The file Housepricedata.xlsx contains the following information for selected homes:

- Square footage
- Price
- Number of bathrooms
- Number of bedrooms

Use this information to answer the following questions:

- What is the average price of all homes having a total number of bathrooms and bedrooms greater than or equal to six?
- How many homes sell for more than $300,000 and have a total number of bedrooms and bathrooms less than or equal to five?
- How many homes have at least three bathrooms but the total number of bedrooms and bathrooms is less than or equal to six?
- What is the highest price of a home having at most 3,000 square feet and a total number of bedrooms and bathrooms less than or equal to six? Hint: Use the DMAX function to solve this problem.

7. The file Deciles.xlsx contains the unpaid balance for 20 accounts. Use DBASE functions to compute the total unpaid balances in each decile.

CHAPTER 49

Filtering data and removing duplicates

Questions answered in this chapter:

- Joolas is a small company that manufactures makeup. Its managers track each sales transaction in a Microsoft Excel worksheet. Sometimes they want to extract, or filter out, a subset of their sales data. For example, they might want to identify sales transactions that answer the following questions:
  - How can I identify all the transactions in which Jen sold lipstick in the East region?
  - How can I identify all the transactions in which Cici or Colleen sold lipstick or mascara in the East or South region?
  - How can I copy all the transactions in which Cici or Colleen sold lipstick or mascara in the East or South region to a different worksheet?
  - How do I clear filters from a column or database?
  - How can I identify all the transactions that involved sales greater than $280 and greater than 90 units?
  - How can I identify all the sales occurring in 2005 or 2006?
  - How can I identify all the transactions in the last three months of 2005 or the first three months of 2006?
  - How can I identify all the transactions for which the salesperson's first name starts with *C*?
  - How can I identify all the transactions for which the cell containing the product name is colored in red?
  - How can I identify all the transactions in the top 30 revenue values for which Hallagan or Jen was the salesperson?
  - How can I easily obtain a complete list of salespeople?
  - How can I view every combination of salesperson, product, and location that occurs in the database?

- If my data changes, how can I reapply the same filter?
- How can I extract all the foundation transactions in the first six months of 2005 for which Emilee or Jen was the salesperson and the average per-unit price was more than $3.20?

Microsoft Excel 2016 has filtering capabilities that make identifying any subset of data a snap. Excel also makes it easy to remove duplicate records from a list. You'll find the data for this example in the file Makeupfiltertemp.xlsx in this chapter's Templates folder. For the 1,891 sales transactions listed in this file, you have the following information. Figure 49-1 shows a subset of the data.

- Transaction number
- Name of the salesperson
- Date of the transaction
- Product sold
- Units sold
- Dollar amount of the transaction
- Transaction location

	C	D	E	F	G	H	I
3	Transaction number	Name	Date	Product	Units	Dollars	Location
4	1	Betsy	4/1/2004	lip gloss	45	$ 137.20	south
5	2	Hallagan	3/10/2004	foundatio	50	$ 152.01	midwest
6	3	Ashley	2/25/2005	lipstick	9	$ 28.72	midwest
7	4	Hallagan	5/22/2006	lip gloss	55	$ 167.08	west
8	5	Zaret	6/17/2004	lip gloss	43	$ 130.60	midwest
9	6	Colleen	11/27/2005	eye liner	58	$ 175.99	midwest
10	7	Cristina	3/21/2004	eye liner	8	$ 25.80	midwest
11	8	Colleen	12/17/2006	lip gloss	72	$ 217.84	midwest
12	9	Ashley	7/5/2006	eye liner	75	$ 226.64	south
13	10	Betsy	8/7/2006	lip gloss	24	$ 73.50	east
14	11	Ashley	11/29/2004	mascara	43	$ 130.84	east
15	12	Ashley	11/18/2004	lip gloss	23	$ 71.03	west
16	13	Emilee	8/31/2005	lip gloss	49	$ 149.59	west
17	14	Hallagan	1/1/2005	eye liner	18	$ 56.47	south
18	15	Zaret	9/20/2006	foundatio	-8	$ (21.99)	east
19	16	Emilee	4/12/2004	mascara	45	$ 137.39	east
20	17	Colleen	4/30/2006	mascara	66	$ 199.65	south
21	18	Jen	8/31/2005	lip gloss	88	$ 265.19	midwest
22	19	Jen	10/27/2004	eye liner	78	$ 236.15	south

FIGURE 49-1 Makeup sales data.

Each column (C through I) of our database (cell range C4:I1894) is called a *field*. Each row of the database that contains data is called a *record*. (Thus, the records in our database are contained in the cell range C4:I1894.) The first row of each field must contain a field name. For example, the name of the field in column F is *Product*. By using the Excel AutoFilter, you can query the database using the AND criteria to identify a subset of records. This means that you can use queries of the form "Find all records where Field 1 satisfies certain conditions, Field 2 satisfies certain conditions, and Field 3 satisfies certain conditions." This chapter's examples illustrate the capabilities of the Excel AutoFilter.

Answers to this chapter's questions

How can I identify all the transactions in which Jen sold lipstick in the East region?

To begin, click anywhere in the database and select Filter in the Sort & Filter group on the Data tab. As shown in Figure 49-2, each column of the database now has an arrow in the heading row (see the Data worksheet).

	C	D	E	F	G	H	I
3	Transaction number	Name	Date	Product	Units	Dollars	Location
4	1	Betsy	4/1/2004	lip gloss	45	$ 137.20	south
5	2	Hallagan	3/10/2004	foundatior	50	$ 152.01	midwest
6	3	Ashley	2/25/2005	lipstick	9	$ 28.72	midwest
7	4	Hallagan	5/22/2006	lip gloss	55	$ 167.08	west
8	5	Zaret	6/17/2004	lip gloss	43	$ 130.60	midwest
9	6	Colleen	11/27/2005	eye liner	58	$ 175.99	midwest
10	7	Cristina	3/21/2004	eye liner	8	$ 25.80	midwest
11	8	Colleen	12/17/2006	lip gloss	72	$ 217.84	midwest
12	9	Ashley	7/5/2006	eye liner	75	$ 226.64	south
13	10	Betsy	8/7/2006	lip gloss	24	$ 73.50	east
14	11	Ashley	11/29/2004	mascara	43	$ 130.84	east
15	12	Ashley	11/18/2004	lip gloss	23	$ 71.03	west
16	13	Emilee	8/31/2005	lip gloss	49	$ 149.59	west
17	14	Hallagan	1/1/2005	eye liner	18	$ 56.47	south
18	15	Zaret	9/20/2006	foundatior	-8	$ (21.99)	east
19	16	Emilee	4/12/2004	mascara	45	$ 137.39	east
20	17	Colleen	4/30/2005	mascara	66	$ 199.65	south
21	18	Jen	8/31/2005	lip gloss	88	$ 265.19	midwest
22	19	Jen	10/27/2004	eye liner	78	$ 236.15	south

FIGURE 49-2 AutoFilter adds drop-down arrows to the heading row.

After clicking the arrow for the Name column, you will see the choices shown in Figure 49-3. You could choose Text Filters, which allows you to filter based on characteristics of the person's name (more on this later). For now, you just want to work with the data for Jen, so first clear the Select All check box, then select the check box for Jen, and then click OK.

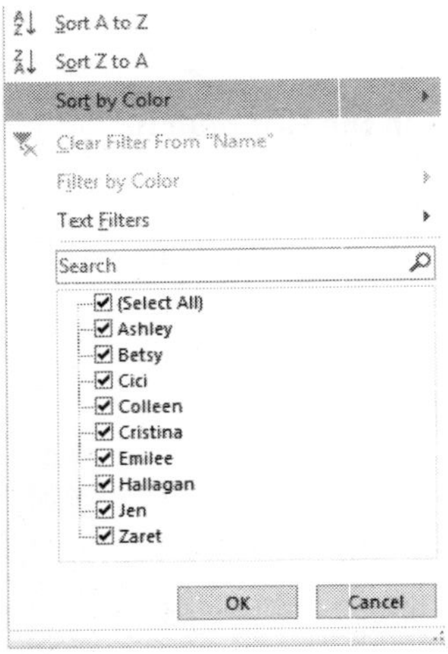

FIGURE 49-3 The choices for filtering or sorting the Name column.

You now see only those records for which Jen was the salesperson. Next, click the arrow for the Product column and select only the Lipstick check box. Then click the arrow for the Location column, and select only the East check box. You now see only those transactions for which Jen sold lipstick in the East region. (See Figure 49-4 and the Lipstick Jen East worksheet from the file Makeupfilter.xlsx.) Notice that the arrow has changed to a funnel symbol in the columns in which you set up filtering criteria.

	C	D	E	F	G	H	I
3	Transaction number	Name	Date	Product	Units	Dollars	Location
503	500	Jen	3/19/2005	lipstick	6	$ 20.04	east
509	506	Jen	2/17/2004	lipstick	67	$ 202.62	east
691	688	Jen	3/6/2006	lipstick	36	$ 110.26	east
763	760	Jen	1/23/2005	lipstick	12	$ 37.85	east
846	843	Jen	7/27/2006	lipstick	34	$ 103.40	east
232	1229	Jen	9/24/2004	lipstick	92	$ 277.63	east
781	1778	Jen	8/31/2005	lipstick	24	$ 74.61	east
815	1812	Jen	5/22/2006	lipstick	67	$ 203.18	east

FIGURE 49-4 The lipstick Jen sold in the East region.

How can I identify all the transactions in which Cici or Colleen sold lipstick or mascara in the East or South region?

You simply select Cici and Colleen from the Name column list, lipstick and mascara from the Product column list, and East and South from the Location column list. The records meeting this filtering criteria are shown in Figure 49-5 and in the Cici Colleen Lipstick And Masc worksheet.

	C	D	E	F	G	H	I
3	Transaction number	Name	Date	Product	Units	Dollars	Location
20	17	Colleen	4/30/2006	mascara	66	$ 199.65	south
84	81	Cici	6/13/2006	lipstick	-3	$ (7.62)	south
106	103	Cici	11/18/2004	mascara	38	$ 115.86	south
139	136	Cici	9/24/2004	mascara	89	$ 269.40	east
143	140	Cici	3/8/2005	lipstick	37	$ 113.65	east
174	171	Colleen	5/26/2004	lipstick	60	$ 182.02	east
191	188	Colleen	2/6/2004	mascara	-5	$ (12.90)	east
201	198	Colleen	2/6/2004	mascara	60	$ 181.94	east
237	234	Colleen	7/9/2004	lipstick	-3	$ (7.40)	south
239	236	Cici	7/9/2004	mascara	5	$ 17.20	east
244	241	Colleen	11/3/2006	mascara	64	$ 194.25	east
253	250	Colleen	2/14/2005	lipstick	65	$ 196.49	south
255	252	Cici	7/16/2006	mascara	-1	$ (1.93)	south
317	314	Colleen	3/17/2006	lipstick	43	$ 130.95	south
337	334	Colleen	2/14/2005	lipstick	15	$ 46.64	east
339	336	Cici	7/18/2005	mascara	85	$ 257.29	south
400	397	Colleen	2/17/2004	mascara	91	$ 274.81	south
435	432	Cici	3/19/2005	mascara	27	$ 83.00	south

FIGURE 49-5 The transactions in which Cici or Colleen sold lipstick or mascara in the East or South region.

How can I copy all the transactions in which Cici or Colleen sold lipstick or mascara in the East or South region to a different worksheet?

Select all the filtered cells in the worksheet (Cici, Colleen, lipstick, and mascara) and paste them into a blank worksheet. (In the new worksheet, you lose the filter settings on the column headers, and you might need to widen column E to display the dates.) You can create a blank worksheet in your workbook by right-clicking any worksheet tab, clicking Insert, selecting Worksheet, and then clicking OK (or click the + symbol to the right of the worksheet). The worksheet Visible Cells Copied contains the records where Cici or Colleen sold lipstick or mascara in the East.

How do I clear filters from a column or database?

Clicking Filter on the Data tab removes all the filters. Clicking the funnel for any column for which you created a filter displays the Clear Filter From option to clear the filter from that column (it clears the filter results but does not remove the filter button).

How can I identify all the transactions that involved sales greater than $280 and greater than 90 units?

After clicking Filter on the Data tab, first click the Units column filter arrow to display the options shown in Figure 49-6.

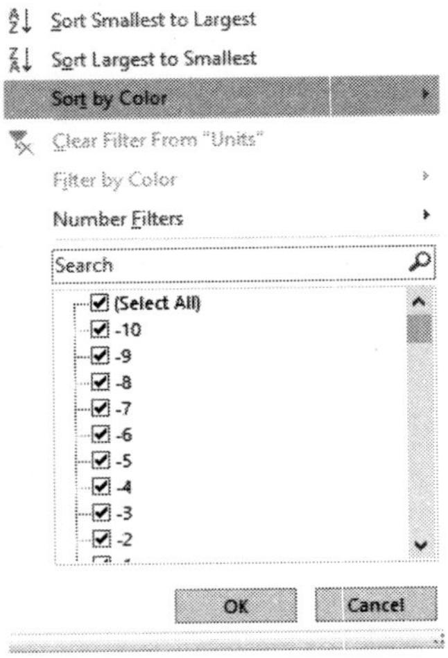

FIGURE 49-6 The filtering options for a numerical column.

You can check any subset of numerical unit values (for example, all the transactions for which sales were –10 or –8 units). I clicked Number Filters to display the choices in Figure 49-7.

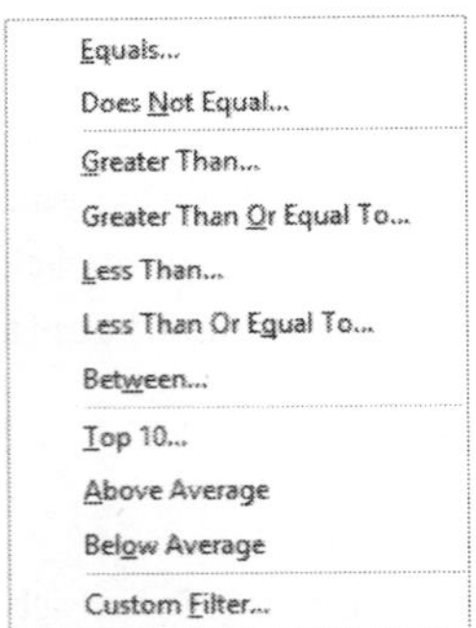

FIGURE 49-7 The Number Filters options.

Most of the options you see in the figure are self-explanatory. Here, you choose the Greater Than option and then fill in the Custom AutoFilter dialog box as shown in Figure 49-8, by entering 90 in the upper-right Units box.

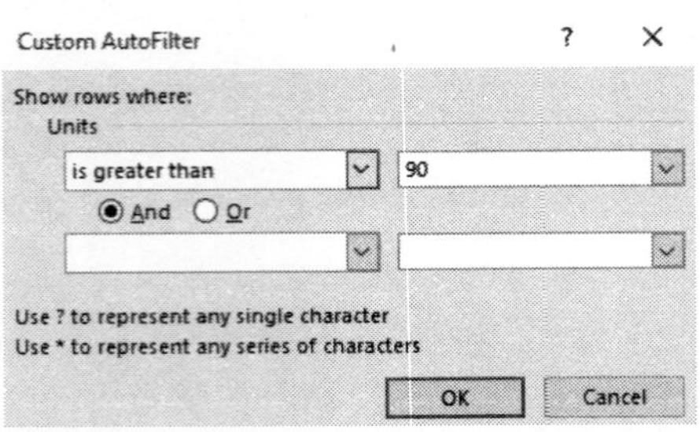

FIGURE 49-8 Selecting all the records where the number of units sold is greater than 90.

Next, go to the Dollars column and click the arrow to include only the records for which the dollar amount is greater than $280. Click Number Filters, Greater Than, enter 280, and then click OK. You obtain the records shown in Figure 49-9. (See the worksheet Sales > 90 units dollars > $280.) Note that all the selected records have both the number of units greater than 90 and the dollars greater than $280.

	C	D	E	F	G	H	I
3	Transaction number	Name	Date	Product	Units	Dollars	Location
40	37	Ashley	8/9/2005	mascara	93	$ 280.69	east
57	54	Cici	6/17/2004	eye liner	95	$ 287.76	midwest
64	61	Emilee	12/21/2004	eye liner	95	$ 287.05	midwest
65	62	Ashley	11/16/2005	lipstick	93	$ 280.77	west
165	162	Betsy	10/14/2005	foundatior	93	$ 280.17	west
217	214	Betsy	9/13/2004	foundatior	94	$ 283.74	west
284	281	Emilee	11/16/2005	foundatior	94	$ 283.85	midwest
289	286	Betsy	7/27/2006	mascara	94	$ 284.14	west
314	311	Jen	5/15/2004	eye liner	94	$ 283.88	east
338	335	Ashley	5/26/2004	mascara	94	$ 283.62	midwest
340	337	Colleen	11/18/2004	lip gloss	95	$ 286.86	west
406	403	Jen	6/4/2005	mascara	93	$ 281.17	south
450	447	Cici	10/1/2006	mascara	94	$ 283.45	west
545	542	Ashley	4/19/2006	foundatior	93	$ 281.17	midwest
579	576	Emilee	4/10/2005	lipstick	93	$ 280.80	midwest

FIGURE 49-9 The transactions where more than 90 units were sold for a total of more than $280.

How can I identify all the sales occurring in 2005 or 2006?

After clicking Filter on the Data tab, click the arrow for the Date column to display the choices in Figure 49-10.

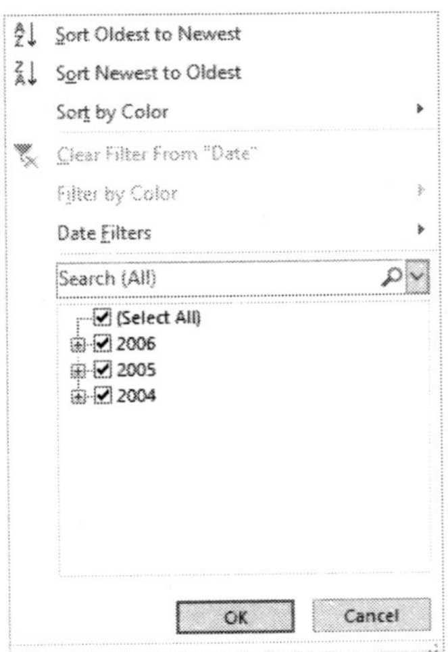

FIGURE 49-10 The filtering options for the Date column.

After selecting 2005 and 2006, you see only those records involving sales in 2005 or 2006, as shown in Figure 49-11. (See the Sales In 2005 And 2006 worksheet to the left of the previous worksheets.)

	C	D	E	F	G	H	I
3	Transaction number	Name	Date	Produc	Units	Dollars	Locatio
6	3	Ashley	2/25/2005	lipstick	9	$ 28.72	midwest
7	4	Hallagan	5/22/2006	lip gloss	55	$ 167.08	west
9	6	Colleen	11/27/2005	eye liner	58	$ 175.99	midwest
11	8	Colleen	12/17/2006	lip gloss	72	$ 217.84	midwest
12	9	Ashley	7/5/2006	eye liner	75	$ 226.64	south
13	10	Betsy	8/7/2006	lip gloss	24	$ 73.50	east
16	13	Emilee	8/31/2005	lip gloss	49	$ 149.59	west
17	14	Hallagan	1/1/2005	eye liner	18	$ 56.47	south
18	15	Zaret	9/20/2006	foundatio	-8	$ (21.99)	east
20	17	Colleen	4/30/2006	mascara	66	$ 199.65	south
21	18	Jen	8/31/2005	lip gloss	88	$ 265.19	midwest
23	20	Zaret	11/27/2005	lip gloss	57	$ 173.12	midwest
24	21	Zaret	6/2/2006	mascara	12	$ 38.08	west
26	23	Colleen	2/1/2006	mascara	25	$ 77.31	midwest
27	24	Emilee	12/6/2006	lip gloss	24	$ 74.62	west
29	26	Cristina	9/22/2005	foundatio	77	$ 233.05	midwest
30	27	Cristina	3/28/2006	lip gloss	53	$ 161.46	midwest
32	29	Zaret	9/9/2006	mascara	19	$ 59.15	west

FIGURE 49-11 Sales during 2005 and 2006.

Note that you could also have selected Date Filters to display the options shown in Figure 49-12.

- Equals...
- Before...
- After...
- Between...
- Tomorrow
- Today
- Yesterday
- Next Week
- This Week
- Last Week
- Next Month
- This Month
- Last Month
- Next Quarter
- This Quarter
- Last Quarter
- Next Year
- This Year
- Last Year
- Year to Date
- All Dates in the Period ▸
- Custom Filter...

FIGURE 49-12 The Date filtering options.

Most of these options are self-explanatory as well. The Custom Filter option allows you to select any range of dates as your filtering criteria.

How can I identify all the transactions in the last three months of 2005 or the first three months of 2006?

After clicking the filter arrow for the Date column, you see the list of years shown earlier in Figure 49-10. Click the + sign to the left of the year to display a list of months. You can check October through December of 2005 and then January through March of 2006 to show all the sales during those months. (See Figure 49-13 and the Filter By Months worksheet, to the right of the previous worksheets.)

	C	D	E	F	G	H	I
3	Transaction number	Name	Date	Product	Units	Dollars	Location
9	6	Colleen	11/27/2005	eye liner	58	$ 175.99	midwest
23	20	Zaret	11/27/2005	lip gloss	57	$ 173.12	midwest
26	23	Colleen	2/1/2006	mascara	25	$ 77.31	midwest
30	27	Cristina	3/28/2006	lip gloss	53	$ 161.46	midwest
33	30	Cici	2/23/2006	foundation	-9	$ (24.63)	west
53	50	Cristina	12/8/2005	lip gloss	8	$ 26.24	midwest
55	52	Colleen	11/16/2005	foundation	62	$ 189.25	midwest
61	58	Hallagan	11/5/2005	foundation	63	$ 191.37	south
65	62	Ashley	11/16/2005	lipstick	93	$ 280.77	west
70	67	Colleen	3/6/2006	foundation	-2	$ (3.94)	west
75	72	Jen	1/10/2006	lip gloss	69	$ 208.69	east
82	79	Zaret	12/19/2005	eye liner	26	$ 80.30	south
93	90	Colleen	1/21/2006	lip gloss	75	$ 226.74	south
94	91	Betsy	10/3/2005	eye liner	74	$ 224.23	west
98	95	Jen	3/17/2006	lipstick	-8	$ (22.11)	west
109	106	Emilee	1/21/2006	foundation	39	$ 118.63	south

FIGURE 49-13 All the sales during October 2005–March 2006.

How can I identify all the transactions for which the salesperson's first name starts with *C*?

Simply click the Name column arrow, and then choose Text Filters. Next, select Begins With, and in the Custom AutoFilter dialog box shown in Figure 49-14, choose Begins With C, and then click OK.

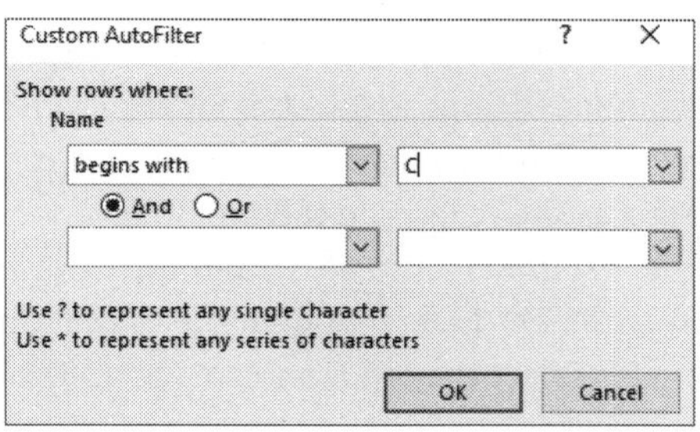

FIGURE 49-14 The Custom AutoFilter dialog box set up to select all the records for which the salesperson's name begins with *C*.

How can I identify all the transactions for which the cell containing the product name is colored in red?

Click the Product column arrow, and then choose Filter By Color. You can now select the color to use as a filter. As shown in Figure 49-15, I chose to include only the rows for which the product is colored in red. Figure 49-16 shows the resulting records. (See the Filter By Color worksheet.)

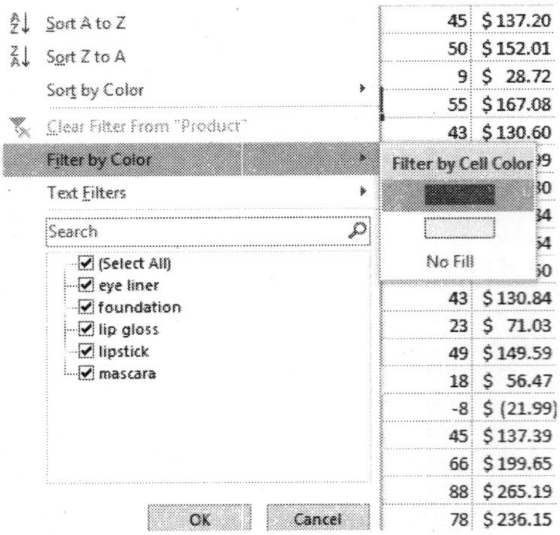

FIGURE 49-15 The dialog box for filtering by cell color.

	C	D	E	F	G	H	I
3	Transaction number	Name	Date	Product	Units	Dollars	Location
11	8	Colleen	12/17/2006	lip gloss	72	$ 217.84	midwest
247	244	Ashley	9/24/2004	foundation	84	$ 253.29	east
292	289	Zaret	5/26/2004	lipstick	56	$ 169.19	south

FIGURE 49-16 All the records in which the product cell color is red.

How can I identify all the transactions in the top 30 revenue values for which Hallagan or Jen was the salesperson?

After clicking Filter on the Data tab, click the Name column arrow and then select the check boxes for Hallagan and Jen. Then click the arrow for the Dollars column and choose Number Filters. From the Number Filters list, select the Top 10 option, and then fill in the Top 10 AutoFilter dialog box as shown in Figure 49-17, replacing 10 with 30. You have now filtered all the records in the top 30 revenue values in which Jen or Hallagan is the salesperson. See the results in Figure 46-18 and the worksheet Top 30 $s With Hallagan Or Jen to the left of the other worksheets. Note that only five of the top 30 sales had Hallagan or Jen as the salesperson. You can also select the top 5 percent, bottom 20 percent, and so on, for any numerical column.

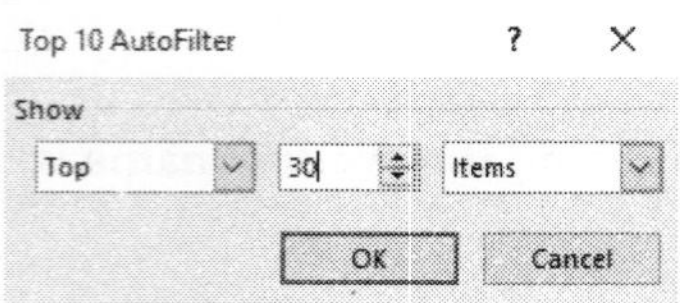

FIGURE 49-17 The dialog box to select the top 30 records by dollar value.

	D	E	F	G	H	I
3	Name	Date	Produc	Units	Dollars	Locatio
314	Jen	5/15/2004	eye liner	94	$ 283.88	east
722	Hallagan	6/13/2006	lip gloss	95	$ 286.68	midwest
797	Hallagan	8/18/2006	foundatio	95	$ 287.80	midwest
1259	Hallagan	4/8/2006	lip gloss	95	$ 286.76	midwest
1619	Hallagan	7/29/2005	eye liner	95	$ 287.15	west

FIGURE 49-18 The top 30 records by dollar value for which Jen or Hallagan was the salesperson.

How can I easily obtain a complete list of salespeople?

Here we want a list of all the salespeople, without anybody's name repeated. Begin by selecting Remove Duplicates on the Data tab (in the Data Tools group) to display the Remove Duplicates dialog box shown in Figure 49-19. After choosing Unselect All, select only the Name check box, and then click OK. This setting shows the data for only the first record involving each salesperson's name (it permanently removes the other rows). See the results in Figure 49-20 and in the Name Duplicates Removed worksheet to the right of the other worksheets.

Important Because selecting Remove Duplicates removes some of your data, I recommend making a copy of your data before selecting Remove Duplicates.

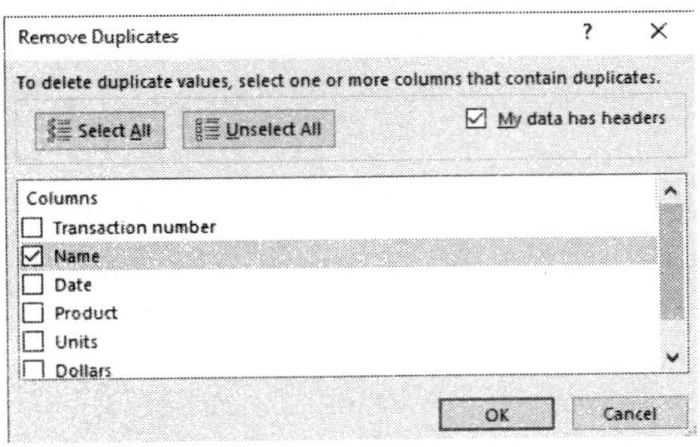

FIGURE 49-19 The Remove Duplicates dialog box with the Name column selected.

	C	D	E	F	G	H	I
3	Transaction number	Name	Date	Product	Units	Dollars	Location
4	1	Betsy	4/1/2004	lip gloss	45	$ 137.20	south
5	2	Hallagan	3/10/2004	foundatio	50	$ 152.01	midwest
6	3	Ashley	2/25/2005	lipstick	9	$ 28.72	midwest
7	5	Zaret	6/17/2004	lip gloss	43	$ 130.60	midwest
8	6	Colleen	11/27/2005	eye liner	58	$ 175.99	midwest
9	7	Cristina	3/21/2004	eye liner	8	$ 25.80	midwest
10	13	Emilee	8/31/2005	lip gloss	49	$ 149.59	west
11	18	Jen	8/31/2005	lip gloss	88	$ 265.19	midwest
12	28	Cici	6/17/2004	mascara	41	$ 125.27	west

FIGURE 49-20 A list of the salesperson names.

How can I view every combination of salesperson, product, and location that occurs in the database?

Here again, you need to click Remove Duplicates on the Data tab to begin. In the Remove Duplicates dialog box, shown in Figure 49-21, click Unselect All; select Name, Product, and Location; and then click OK.

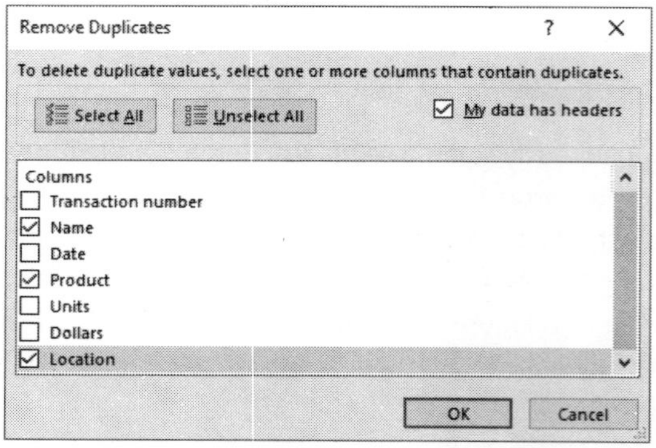

FIGURE 49-21 Finding unique salesperson, product, and location combinations.

Figure 49-22 lists the first record for each combination of person, product, and location occurring in the database. (See the Unique Name Product Location worksheet.) A total of 180 unique combinations occurred. Note that the twentieth record was omitted because it included Zaret selling lip gloss in the Midwest and the fifth record had already picked up this combination.

	C	D	E	F	G	H	I
3	Transaction number	Name	Date	Product	Units	Dollars	Location
4	1	Betsy	4/1/2004	lip gloss	45	$ 137.20	south
5	2	Hallagan	3/10/2004	foundation	50	$ 152.01	midwest
6	3	Ashley	2/25/2005	lipstick	9	$ 28.72	midwest
7	4	Hallagan	5/22/2006	lip gloss	55	$ 167.08	west
8	5	Zaret	6/17/2004	lip gloss	43	$ 130.60	midwest
9	6	Colleen	11/27/2005	eye liner	58	$ 175.99	midwest
10	7	Cristina	3/21/2004	eye liner	8	$ 25.80	midwest
11	8	Colleen	12/17/2006	lip gloss	72	$ 217.84	midwest
12	9	Ashley	7/5/2006	eye liner	75	$ 226.64	south
13	10	Betsy	8/7/2006	lip gloss	24	$ 73.50	east
14	11	Ashley	11/29/2004	mascara	43	$ 130.84	east
15	12	Ashley	11/18/2004	lip gloss	23	$ 71.03	west
16	13	Emilee	8/31/2005	lip gloss	49	$ 149.59	west
17	14	Hallagan	1/1/2005	eye liner	18	$ 56.47	south
18	15	Zaret	9/20/2006	foundation	-8	$ (21.99)	east
19	16	Emilee	4/12/2004	mascara	45	$ 137.39	east
20	17	Colleen	4/30/2006	mascara	66	$ 199.65	south
21	18	Jen	8/31/2005	lip gloss	88	$ 265.19	midwest
22	19	Jen	10/27/2004	eye liner	78	$ 236.15	south
23	21	Zaret	6/2/2006	mascara	12	$ 38.08	west

FIGURE 49-22 A list of unique salesperson, product, and location combinations.

If my data changes, how can I reapply the same filter?

Simply right-click any cell in your filtered results, point to Filter, and then click Reapply. Any changes to your data are reflected in the filtered data.

How can I extract all the foundation transactions in the first six months of 2005 for which Emilee or Jen was the salesperson and the average per-unit price was more than $3.20?

The AutoFilter feature (even with the Custom option) is limited to AND queries across columns. This means, for example, that you cannot find all the transactions for lipstick sales by Jen during 2005 or the foundation sales by Zaret during 2004. To perform more complex queries such as this one, you need to use the Advanced Filter feature. To use Advanced Filter, you set up a criteria range that specifies the records you want to extract. (This process is described in detail in Chapter 48, "Summarizing data with database statistical functions.") After specifying the criteria range, you tell Excel whether you want the records extracted to the current location or to a different location. To identify all the foundation transactions in the first six months of 2005 for which Emilee or Jen was the salesperson and for which the average per-unit price was more than $3.20, you can use the criteria range shown in the range O4:S6 in Figure 49-23. (See the Jen + Emilee worksheet in the file Advancedfilter.xlsx.)

	O	P	Q	R	S
4	Name	Date	Date	Price	Product
5	Jen	>=1/1/2005	<=6/30/2005	FALSE	Foundation
6	Emilee	>=1/1/2005	<=6/30/2005	FALSE	Foundation

FIGURE 49-23 Setting up a criteria range to use with an advanced filter.

In cells R5 and R6, I entered the formula =(L5/K5)>3.2. Recall from Chapter 48 that this formula creates computed criteria that flag each row in which the per-unit price is more than $3.20. Also remember that your heading for an instance of computed criteria must not be a field name. I used *Price* as the field heading here. The criteria in O5:S5 flag all the records in which Jen is the salesperson, the date is between 1/1/2005 and 6/30/2005, the product sold is foundation, and the per-unit price is more than $3.20. The criteria in O6:S6 flag all the records in which Emilee is the salesperson, the date is between 1/1/2005 and 6/30/2005, the product sold is foundation, and the per-unit price is more than $3.20. The criteria range O4:S6 flags exactly the records you want. Remember that criteria in different rows are joined by OR.

You can now select any cell within the database range and then select Advanced (the funnel symbol with the pencil) in the Sort & Filter group on the Data tab. Then fill in the Advanced Filter dialog box as shown in Figure 49-24, and click OK.

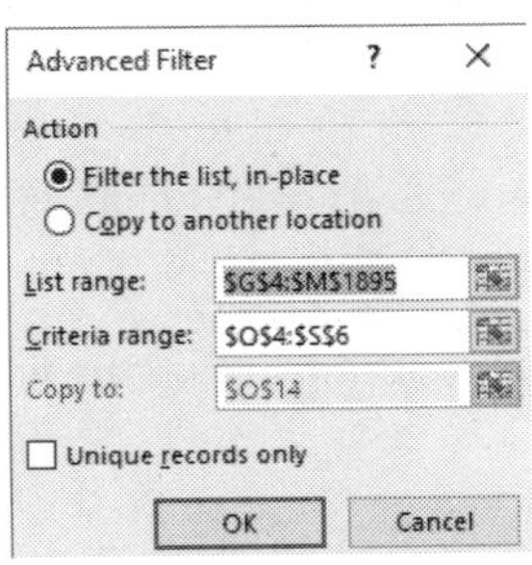

FIGURE 49-24 The Advanced Filter dialog box settings.

With these settings, you are telling Excel to extract all the records in the database (the cell range G4:M1895) that satisfy the criteria specified in O4:S6. These records should be copied to a range whose upper-left corner is cell O14. The records extracted are shown in the cell range O14:U18. Only the four records shown in Figure 49-25 meet the defined criteria. (See the Jen + Emilee worksheet again.)

	O	P	Q	R	S	T	U
14	Trans Number	Name	Date	Product	Units	Dollars	Location
15	392	Jen	2/25/2005	foundation	8	$ 26.31	south
16	479	Emilee	5/24/2005	foundation	2	$ 7.68	east
17	1035	Emilee	4/10/2005	foundation	8	$ 26.40	east
18	1067	Jen	3/19/2005	foundation	1	$ 4.86	east

FIGURE 49-25 The Advanced Filter results.

If you select Unique Records Only at the bottom of the Advanced Filter dialog box, no duplicate records are returned. For example, if Jen had another foundation transaction in the East region on 3/19/2005 for one unit for $4.88, only one of those transactions would be extracted.

Problems

1. Using the file Makeupfiltertemp.xlsx (for this problem and all the following problems), find all the transactions in which Hallagan sold eyeliner in the West region.
2. Find all the transactions that rank in the top 5 percent with regard to units sold.
3. Find the top 20 revenue-generating transactions that involve foundation sales.
4. Find all the transactions involving sales of at least 60 units during 2004 for which the per-unit price was a maximum of $3.10
5. Find all the foundation transactions during the first three months of 2004 for which the per-unit price was larger than the average price received for foundation during the entire time period.
6. Find all the transactions in which Zaret or Betsy sold either lipstick or foundation.
7. Find all the unique combinations of the product and salesperson's name.
8. Find all of the top-30 sales (by units) occurring in 2005 that involved lip gloss or mascara.
9. Find all the sales by Jen between August 10 and September 15, 2005.
10. Find all the sales of lipstick sold by Colleen for which the number of units sold is higher than the average number of units in a lipstick transaction.
11. Find all the unique combinations of name, product, and location occurring during the first three months of 2006.
12. Find all the records in which the product cell is colored yellow.

CHAPTER 50

Consolidating data

Question answered in this chapter:

- My company sells products in several regions of the United States. Each region keeps records of the number of units of each product sold during the months of January, February, and March. Is there an easy way to create a master workbook that always combines each region's sales and gives a tally of the total amount of each product sold during each month?

A business analyst often receives worksheets that tally the same information (such as monthly product sales) from different affiliates or regions. To determine the company's overall profitability, the analyst usually needs to combine or consolidate this information into a single Microsoft Excel workbook. PivotTables built from multiple consolidation ranges can be used to accomplish this goal, but the little-known Consolidate command (on the Data tab, in the Data Tools group) is another way to accomplish this goal. With Consolidate, you can ensure that changes in the individual worksheets are automatically reflected in the consolidated worksheet.

Answer to this chapter's question

My company sells products in several regions of the United States. Each region keeps records of the number of units of each product sold during the months of January, February, and March. Is there an easy way to create a master workbook that always combines each region's sales and gives a tally of the total amount of each product sold during each month?

The file East.xlsx (shown in Figure 50-1) displays the monthly unit sales of Products A–H in the eastern US during January, February, and March. Similarly, the file West.xlsx (shown in Figure 50-2) displays monthly unit sales of Products A–H in the western US from January through March. You need to create a consolidated worksheet that tabulates each product's total sales by month.

	A	B	C	D	E	F
1	Product	January	February	March		East Sales
2	A	205	263	20		
3	B	164	-17	146		
4	C	278	177	179		
5	D	156	214	240		
6	D	72	134	48		
7	D	7	256	104		
8	A	141	87	148		
9	A	2	-15	135		
10	A	-44	47	72		
11	B	7	-81	2		
12	E	25	120	171		
13	E	197	90	124		
14	E	221	121	48		
15	A	84	103	134		
16	G	-13	250	51		
17	D	-5	159	70		
18	E	136	152	28		

FIGURE 50-1 East region sales during January–March.

	A	B	C	D
1	Product	January	February	March
2	A	173	1	256
3	A	208	201	224
4	B	176	33	350
5	B	190	249	215
6	D	162	74	156
7	D	90	150	170
8	D	112	284	141
9	G	154	217	113
10	G	152	200	275
11	G	277	183	372
12	H	131	71	266
13	F	294	211	249
14	F	146	125	5
15	A	115	214	141
16	F	157	241	73
17	A	125	227	135
18	A	314	189	180
19	C	189	154	101
20	C	313	182	68
21	C	389	247	257
22	B	353	151	99
23	C	62	162	238
24	D	173	153	270

FIGURE 50-2 West region sales during January–March.

Before you use the Consolidate command, it's helpful to see both worksheets together on the screen. To do this, open both workbooks, click Arrange All in the Window group on the View tab, select the Tiled option in the Arrange Windows dialog box, and click OK. Your screen should look like Figure 50-3.

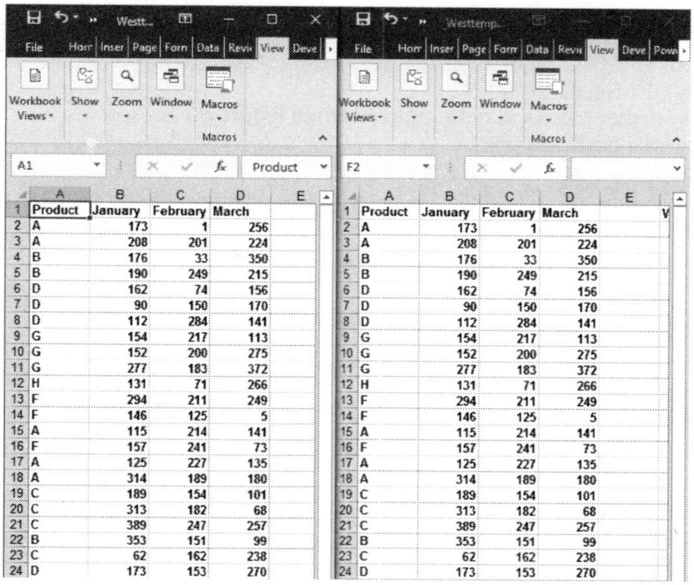

FIGURE 50-3 East and West sales arranged on the same screen.

Now open a blank worksheet in a new workbook, click Arrange All, and select Tiled again. In the blank worksheet, click Consolidate in the Data Tools group on the Data tab, and you'll see the Consolidate dialog box, shown in Figure 50-4.

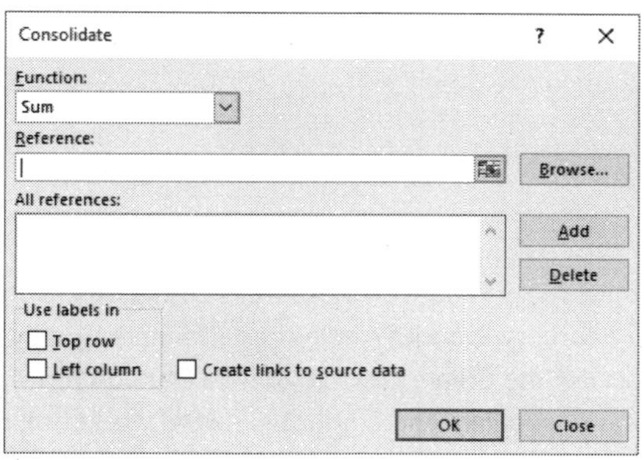

FIGURE 50-4 The Consolidate dialog box.

To consolidate the data from the East and West regions into your new worksheet, enter the ranges you want to consolidate in the Reference box of the Consolidate dialog box, clicking Add after selecting each range. By selecting the Top Row and Left Column check boxes in the Use Labels In area, you ensure that Excel consolidates the selected ranges by looking at labels in the top row and left column of each range. The Create Links To Source Data option enables changes in the selected ranges to be reflected in the consolidated worksheet. Select Sum in the Function list at the top because you want Excel to add up the total sales of each product by month. Selecting Count, for instance, would count the number of transactions for each product during each month; selecting Max would compute the largest sales transaction for each product during each month. The Consolidate dialog box should be filled out as shown in Figure 50-5.

After you click OK, the new worksheet looks like the one shown in Figure 50-6. (See the file Eastandwestconsolidated.xlsx.) You can see, for example, that 1,317 units of Product A were sold in February, 597 units of Product F were sold in January, and so on.

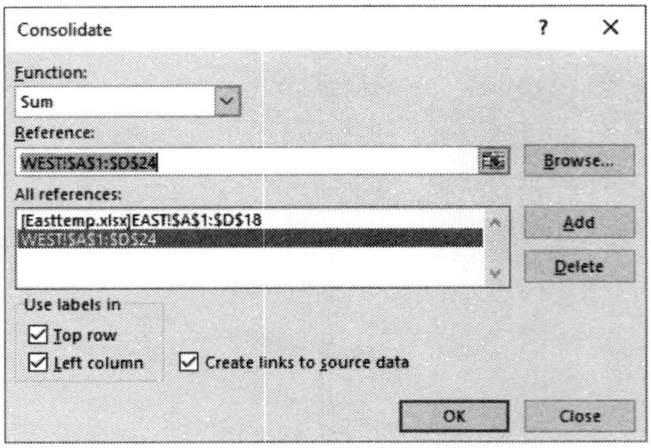

FIGURE 50-5 The completed Consolidate dialog box.

	A	B	C	D	E	F
3				January	February	March
5		H		131	71	266
9		F		597	577	327
20		A		1323	1317	1445
26		B		890	335	812
32		C		1231	922	843
41		D		767	1424	1199
46		E		579	483	371
51		G		570	850	811

FIGURE 50-6 The total sales after consolidation.

Now go to cell C2 of East.xlsx and change the February Product A sales from 263 to 363. Notice that in the consolidated worksheet, the entry for February Product A sales has also increased by 100 (from 1,317 to 1,417). This change occurs because the Create Links To Source Data option was selected in the Consolidate dialog box. (By the way, if you click the 2 right below the workbook name in the consolidated worksheet, you'll see how Excel grouped the data to perform the consolidation.) The final result is contained in the file Eastandwestconsolidated.xlsx. Of course, you could also summarize data from different worksheets by using PivotTables with the Multiple Consolidation Ranges option (see Chapter 43) or the Data Model (see Chapter 44).

If you frequently download new data to your source workbooks (in this case, East.xlsx and West.xlsx), it's a good idea to name the ranges including your data as a table. Then new data is automatically included in the consolidation. You might also choose to select some blank rows below the current data set. When you populate the blank rows with new data, Excel picks up the new data when it performs the consolidation. A third choice is to make each data range a dynamic range. (See Chapter 22, "The OFFSET function," for more information.)

Problems

The following problems refer to the data in files Jancon.xlsx and Febcon.xlsx. Each file contains the unit sales, dollar revenues, and product sold for each transaction during the month.

1. Create a consolidated worksheet that gives the total unit sales and dollar revenue for each product by region.
2. Create a consolidated worksheet that gives the largest first-quarter transaction for each product by region from the standpoint of revenue and units sold.

CHAPTER 51

Creating subtotals

Questions answered in this chapter:

- Is there an easy way to set up a worksheet to calculate the total revenue and units sold by region?
- Can I also obtain a breakdown by salesperson of the sales in each region?

Joolas is a small company that manufactures makeup. For each transaction, it tracks the name of the salesperson, the location of the transaction, the product sold, the units sold, and the revenue. The managers want answers to the questions above.

PivotTables can be used to slice and dice data in Microsoft Excel. Often, however, you'd like an easier way to summarize a list or a database within a list. In a sales database, for example, you might want to create a summary of sales revenue by region, a summary of sales revenue by product, and a summary of sales revenue by salesperson. If you sort a list by the column in which specific data is listed, the Subtotal command allows you to create a subtotal in a list on the basis of the values in the column. For example, if you sort the makeup database by location, you can calculate the total revenue and units sold for each region and place the totals just below the last row for that region. As another example, after sorting the database by product, you can use the Subtotal command to calculate the total revenue and units sold for each product and then display the totals below the row in which the product changes. In the next section, we'll look at some specific examples.

Answers to this chapter's questions

Is there an easy way to set up a worksheet to calculate the total revenue and units sold by region?

The data for this question is in the file Makeupsubtotals.xlsx. In Figure 51-1, you can see a subset of the data as it appears after sorting the list by the Location column.

	A	B	C	D	E	F	G
4	Trans Number	Name	Date	Product	Units	Dollars	Location
5	10	Betsy	8/7/2006	lip gloss	24	$ 73.50	east
6	11	Ashley	11/29/2004	mascara	43	$ 130.84	east
7	15	Zaret	9/20/2006	foundatio	-8	$ (21.99)	east
8	16	Emilee	4/12/2004	mascara	45	$ 137.39	east
9	45	Emilee	9/20/2006	lip gloss	2	$ 7.85	east
10	46	Ashley	8/9/2005	mascara	93	$ 280.69	east
11	58	Cristina	4/12/2004	foundatio	34	$ 104.09	east
12	60	Jen	10/27/2004	mascara	89	$ 269.09	east
13	69	Cristina	1/23/2005	eye liner	73	$ 221.41	east
14	77	Cristina	1/15/2004	mascara	27	$ 83.29	east
15	81	Jen	1/10/2006	lip gloss	69	$ 208.69	east
16	86	Jen	8/9/2005	eye liner	-2	$ (4.24)	east
17	87	Emilee	8/31/2005	eye liner	5	$ 17.03	east
18	98	Jen	4/12/2004	lip gloss	92	$ 277.54	east
19	108	Cici	8/31/2005	lip gloss	-10	$ (28.41)	east
20	114	Betsy	9/22/2005	lipstick	77	$ 233.33	east
21	116	Zaret	6/24/2006	eye liner	22	$ 68.07	east
22	119	Colleen	5/22/2006	eye liner	20	$ 62.37	east
23	131	Jen	11/29/2004	mascara	56	$ 168.87	east
24	133	Betsy	7/9/2004	mascara	11	$ 34.42	east

FIGURE 51-1 Sorting a list by the values in a specific column, and then creating subtotals for that data.

To calculate the revenue and units sold by region, place the cursor anywhere in the database, and then click Subtotal in the Outline group on the Data tab. In the Subtotal dialog box, fill in the values as shown in Figure 51-2.

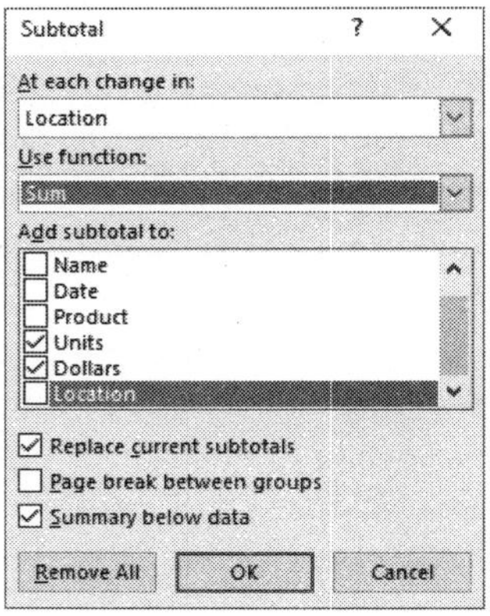

FIGURE 51-2 The Subtotal dialog box.

By selecting Location from the At Each Change In list, you ensure that the subtotals are created at each point at which the value in the Location column changes. This corresponds to the different regions. Selecting Sum from the Use Function list tells Excel to total the units and dollars for each different region. By selecting the Units and Dollars options in the Add Subtotal To area, you indicate that subtotals should be created on the basis of the values in these columns. The Replace Current Subtotals option causes Excel to remove any previously computed subtotals. Because you haven't created any subtotals, it doesn't matter whether this option is selected for this example. If the Page Break Between Groups option is selected, Excel inserts a page break after each subtotal. Selecting the Summary Below Data check box causes Excel to place subtotals below the data. If this option is not selected, the subtotals are created above the data used for the computation. Clicking Remove All removes the subtotals from the list.

A sample of the subtotal results is shown in Figure 51-3. You can see that 18,818 units were sold in the East region, earning revenue of $57,372.09.

	A	B	C	D	E	F	G
446	1849	Zaret	7/29/2005	lip gloss	12	$ 37.85	east
447	1853	Cici	4/23/2004	lip gloss	87	$ 262.81	east
448	1855	Emilee	7/18/2005	lip gloss	50	$ 152.13	east
449	1860	Emilee	8/11/2004	lip gloss	-9	$ (24.76)	east
450	1863	Zaret	3/6/2006	eye liner	73	$ 220.67	east
451	1867	Cristina	8/18/2006	mascara	73	$ 220.77	east
452	1869	Betsy	10/3/2005	lipstick	18	$ 56.08	east
453	1877	Cici	9/13/2004	eye liner	66	$ 199.36	east
454	1881	Emilee	10/3/2005	foundatio	0	$ 2.66	east
455	1883	Betsy	7/20/2004	lip gloss	-6	$ (15.74)	east
456	1890	Cici	6/15/2005	foundatio	16	$ 49.75	east
457	1891	Betsy	4/10/2005	foundatio	39	$ 119.19	east
458	1894	Colleen	5/15/2004	lip gloss	60	$ 181.87	east
459	1895	Emilee	11/27/2005	eye liner	15	$ 47.16	east
460	1896	Ashley	2/14/2005	foundatio	36	$ 109.84	east
461					18818	$ 57,372.09	east Total

FIGURE 51-3 The subtotals for the East region.

Notice that in the upper-left corner of the window, below the Name box, buttons labeled 1, 2, and 3 appear. Clicking the largest number (in this case 3) yields the data and subtotals. If you click button 2, you see just the subtotals by region, as shown in Figure 51-4. Clicking button 1 yields the Grand Total, as shown in Figure 51-5. In short, clicking a lower number reduces the level of detail shown.

	E	F	G
4	Units	Dollars	Location
461	18818	$ 57,372.09	east Total
886	17985	$ 54,805.41	midwest Total
1408	21083	$ 64,296.35	south Total
1899	20821	$ 63,438.82	west Total
1900	78707	$ 239,912.67	Grand Total

FIGURE 51-4 When you create subtotals, Excel adds buttons that you can click to display only subtotals or both subtotals and details.

	E	F	G
4	Units	Dollars	Location
1900	78707	$ 239,912.67	Grand Total

FIGURE 51-5 Displaying the overall total without any detail.

Can I also obtain a breakdown by salesperson of the sales in each region?

If you want to, you can nest subtotals. In other words, you can obtain a breakdown of sales by each salesperson in each region, or you can even get a breakdown of how much each salesperson sold of each product in each region. (See the file Nestedsubtotals.xlsx.) To demonstrate the creation of nested subtotals, let's create a breakdown of sales by each salesperson in each region.

To begin, you must sort your data first by Location and then by Name. This gives you a breakdown for each salesperson of units sold and revenue within each region. If you sort first by Name and then by Location, you would get a breakdown of units sold and revenue for each salesperson by region. After sorting the data, you proceed as before and create the subtotals by region. Then you click Subtotal again and fill in the dialog box as shown in Figure 51-6.

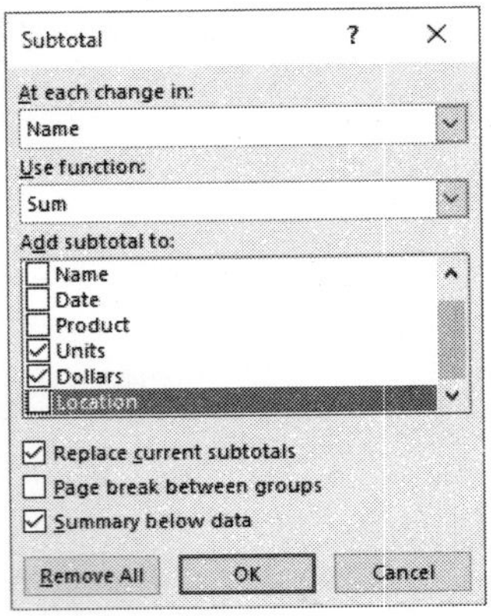

FIGURE 51-6 Creating nested subtotals.

You now want a breakdown by Name. Clearing the Replace Current Subtotals box ensures that you will not replace your regional breakdown. You can now see the breakdown of sales by each salesperson in each region, as shown in Figure 51-7.

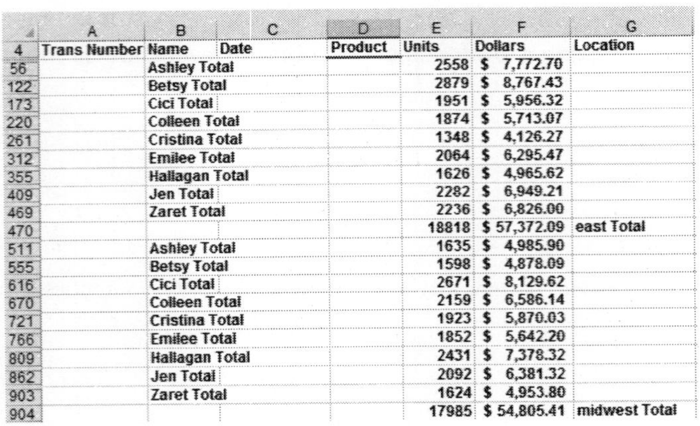

	A	B	C	D	E	F	G
4	Trans Number	Name	Date	Product	Units	Dollars	Location
56		Ashley Total			2558	$ 7,772.70	
122		Betsy Total			2879	$ 8,767.43	
173		Cici Total			1951	$ 5,956.32	
220		Colleen Total			1874	$ 5,713.07	
261		Cristina Total			1348	$ 4,126.27	
312		Emilee Total			2064	$ 6,295.47	
355		Hallagan Total			1626	$ 4,965.62	
409		Jen Total			2282	$ 6,949.21	
469		Zaret Total			2236	$ 6,826.00	
470					18818	$ 57,372.09	east Total
511		Ashley Total			1635	$ 4,985.90	
555		Betsy Total			1598	$ 4,878.09	
616		Cici Total			2671	$ 8,129.62	
670		Colleen Total			2159	$ 6,586.14	
721		Cristina Total			1923	$ 5,870.03	
766		Emilee Total			1852	$ 5,642.20	
809		Hallagan Total			2431	$ 7,378.32	
862		Jen Total			2092	$ 6,381.32	
903		Zaret Total			1624	$ 4,953.80	
904					17985	$ 54,805.41	midwest Total

FIGURE 51-7 Nested subtotals.

Problems

You can find the data for this chapter's problems in the file Makeupsubtotals.xlsx. Use the Subtotal command for the following computations:

1. Find the units sold and revenue for each salesperson.
2. Find the number of sales transactions for each product.
3. Find the largest transaction (in terms of revenue) for each product.
4. Find the average dollar amount per transaction by region.
5. For each salesperson, display a breakdown of units sold as well as revenue, showing the results for each product by region.

CHAPTER 52

Charting tricks

Questions answered in this chapter:

- How do I create combination charts?
- How do I create a secondary axis?
- How can I handle missing data?
- How can I handle the appearance of hidden data?
- How can I use pictures to add bling to my column graphs?
- I charted annual sales data in a column graph, but the years do not show up as column labels. What did I do wrong?
- How can I include data labels and data tables in my charts?
- How can I use Excel 2016 to place data labels on a chart based on the contents of cells?
- How can I track sales-force performance over time?
- How can I create a band chart to check whether inventory is within acceptable levels?
- How can I store a chart as a template?
- How can I use a thermometer chart to portray progress against a target?
- How can I create dynamic chart labels?
- How can I use check boxes to control which series are charted?
- How can I use a list box to choose the series to be charted?
- How do I create a Gantt chart?
- How do I create a chart based on sorted data?
- How can I create a histogram that automatically updates when I include new data?
- How can I add conditional colors to a chart?
- How can I use waterfall charts to track progress toward a sales target or to break down the components of a sales price?

- How can I use the GETPIVOT data function and Excel's table feature to create dynamic dashboards?
- How can I insert a vertical line in a chart to separate pre- and post-merger performance?
- How can I use a radar chart to portray how basketball team members differ in strength, speed, and jumping ability?
- I know I can use a scatter chart to display how two variables change. How can I use a bubble chart to summarize the variation of three variables?
- How do I create waterfall charts with Excel 2016?
- How do I use an Excel 2016 treemap and sunburst chart to summarize hierarchical data?

An old Chinese proverb says a picture is worth a thousand words. Excel can create many amazing charts, and in this chapter I will show you many examples of charting tips and tricks. Be aware that charting in Excel has changed a lot (for the better!) from previous versions of Excel.

Answers to this chapter's questions

How do I create combination charts?

The file Combinationstemp.xlsx contains actual and target sales for January through July. You would like to create a chart that shows each month's actual and target sales. First, I select the range F5:H12 and, from the Insert tab, I select Insert Column Or Bar Chart. I choose the first chart in the 2D Column Chart options (the clustered column chart) to create the chart shown in Figure 52-1.

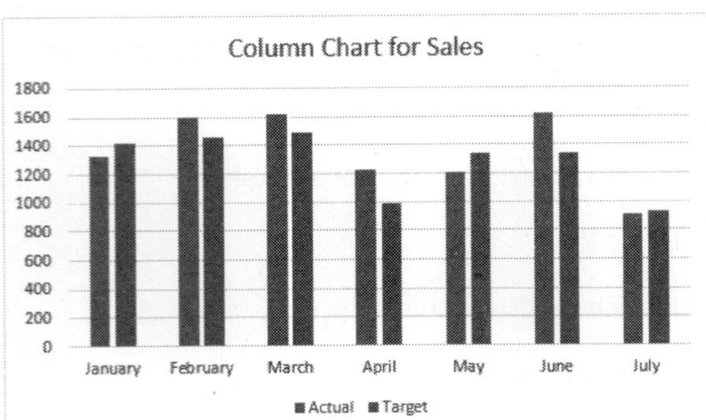

FIGURE 52-1 A column chart for the actual sales and sales target.

Using two columns makes it difficult to see the contrast between the actual and target sales, so I prefer a combination chart in which one series is charted as a line and the other as a column. To create this chart, right-click on either series and select Change Chart Type. After clicking Combo in the left pane to see the options, I chose the first Clustered Column - Line choice, shown in Figure 52-2, and I obtained the combination chart shown in Figure 52-3.

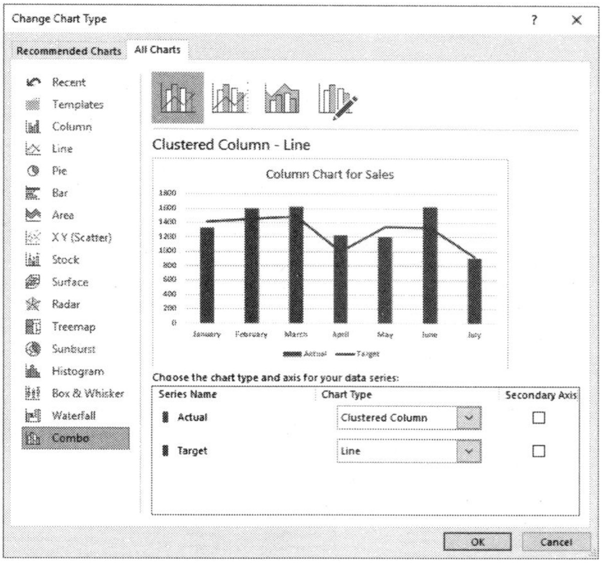

FIGURE 52-2 Selecting the combo-chart type.

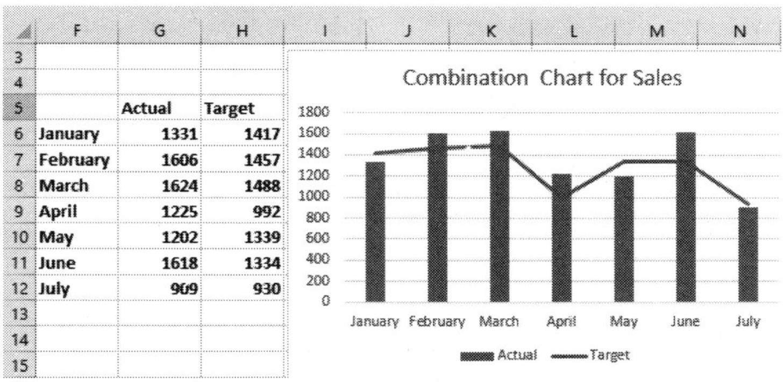

FIGURE 52-3 A combination chart.

How do I create a secondary axis?

When charting two quantities of differing magnitude, a secondary axis is often needed to make sense of the chart. To illustrate the idea, Figure 52-6 (see the file Secondaryaxis.xlsx) shows the monthly revenues and units sold. If I show this data on a single y-axis, monthly revenues will be hardly visible. To remedy this problem, I begin by selecting the range (D7:F16) that I want to chart. Then, from the Insert tab, I select the Combo chart icon (shown in Figure 52-4) and then select Create Custom Combo Chart. I filled in the Insert Chart dialog box as shown in Figure 52-5: in addition to the default settings, select the Secondary Axis check box for the Revenue series, and then click OK.

FIGURE 52-4 The combo chart icon.

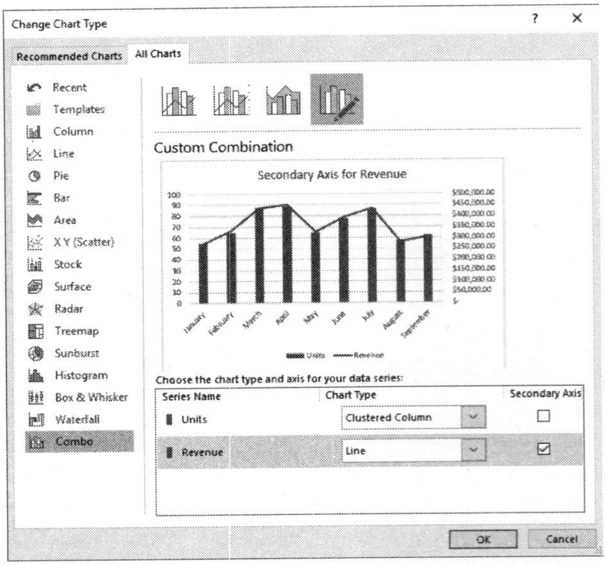

FIGURE 52-5 Creating a combo chart with a secondary axis.

The resulting chart (see Figure 52-6) has revenue summarized on a secondary axis with a line chart and clearly shows that monthly revenues and units sold change in a virtual lockstep fashion.

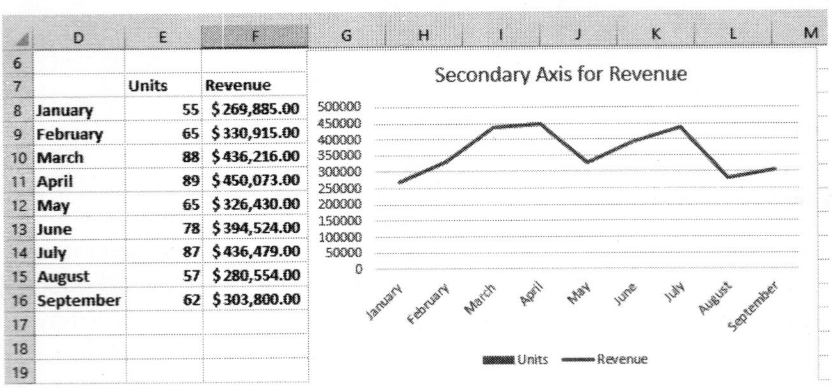

FIGURE 52-6 The secondary axis is used to summarize revenue.

How can I handle missing data?

Often, some rows of a spreadsheet have missing data. Excel gives you the following three ways to chart missing data:

- Show the data as zeroes.
- Show the data as blank.
- Replace a missing data point by a line joining adjacent data points.

To illustrate how you can handle missing data, look at the file Misssingdata.xlsx. This file contains hourly temperatures, but several values are missing. After plotting the data as a line chart, I right-click the data and choose Select Data. In the Select Data Source dialog box, click Hidden And Empty Cells in the lower right. This brings up the Hidden And Empty Cell Settings dialog box shown in Figure 52-7.

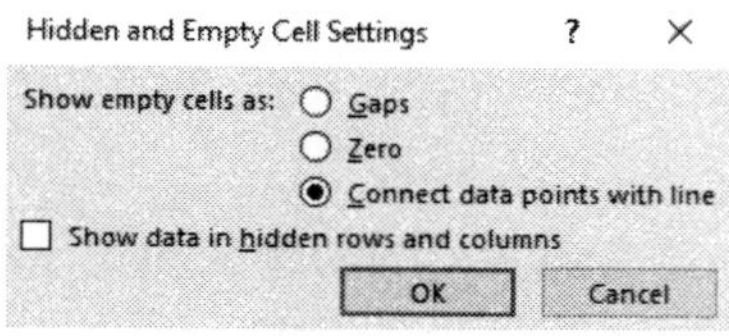

FIGURE 52-7 The Hidden And Empty Cell Settings dialog box.

After selecting the Connect Data Points With Line option, I obtain the graph shown in Figure 52-8. Note that I chose the line graph choice with dots and lines so that I identify the missing data: the missing data points have no dots.

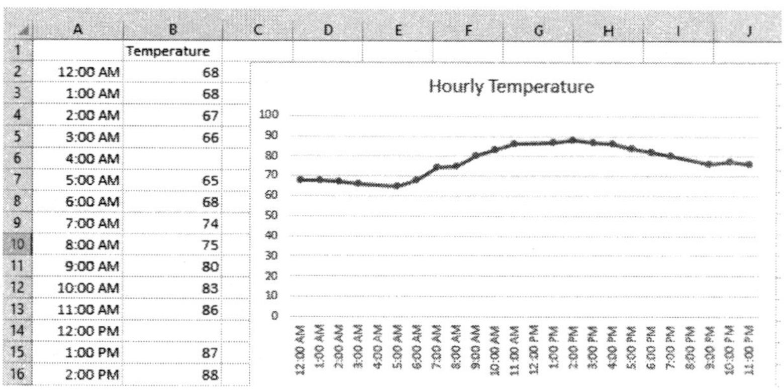

FIGURE 52-8 Replacing the missing data by lines.

How can I handle the appearance of hidden data?

Often, we plot data, such as daily sales, and filter the data in the spreadsheet. In this situation, Excel gives us a choice to either continue showing all the data in the chart or to just show the filtered data in the chart. The file Hidden.xlsx contains the daily sales of a product for a year. If I graph the data as a line chart, I see the chart shown in Figure 52-9.

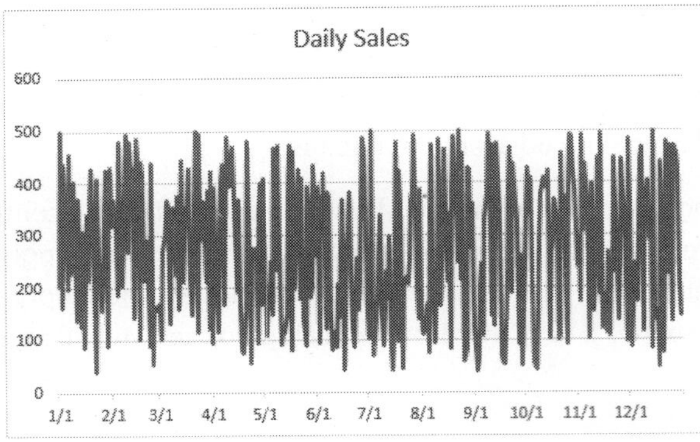

FIGURE 52-9 Daily product sales.

Right-click the chart and click Select Data, click Hidden And Empty Cells from the Select Data Source dialog box, and then select the Show Data In Hidden Rows And Columns check box at the bottom of the Hidden And Empty Cell Settings dialog box shown earlier in Figure 52-7. Then, even if I filter the data, all the data points will still show in the chart. For example, as shown in Figure 52-10, the data is filtered to show only the December sales, but the chart still shows all the daily sales for the entire year. If I did not check the Show Data In Hidden Rows And Columns check box, only December sales would be visible in the chart.

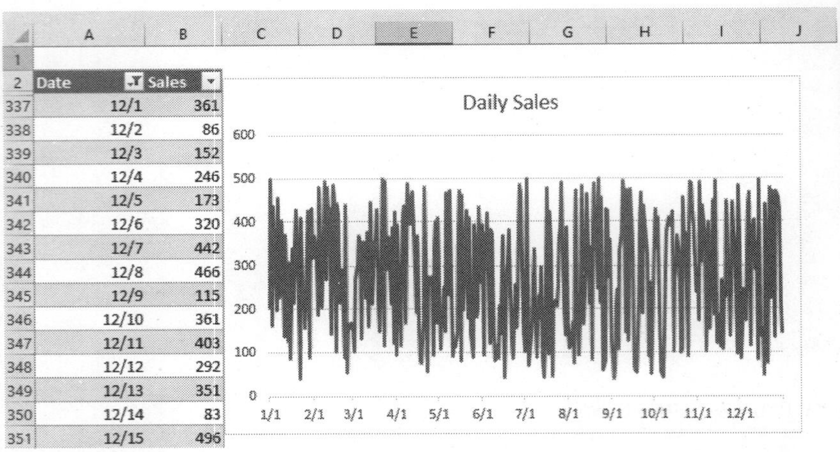

	A	B
1		
2	Date	Sales
337	12/1	361
338	12/2	86
339	12/3	152
340	12/4	246
341	12/5	173
342	12/6	320
343	12/7	442
344	12/8	466
345	12/9	115
346	12/10	361
347	12/11	403
348	12/12	292
349	12/13	351
350	12/14	83
351	12/15	496

FIGURE 52-10 Filtering the data but not the chart.

How can I use pictures to add bling to my column graphs?

The magnitude of product sales is usually summarized by means of boring columns or bars in which the height of the column or width of the bar is proportional to the product sales. Wouldn't it be more fun to summarize a product's sales with a picture of your product, scaled proportionally to the actual sales? To illustrate the idea, check out the file Picturegraph.xlsx and the chart shown in Figure 52-11. Let's assume you sell books.

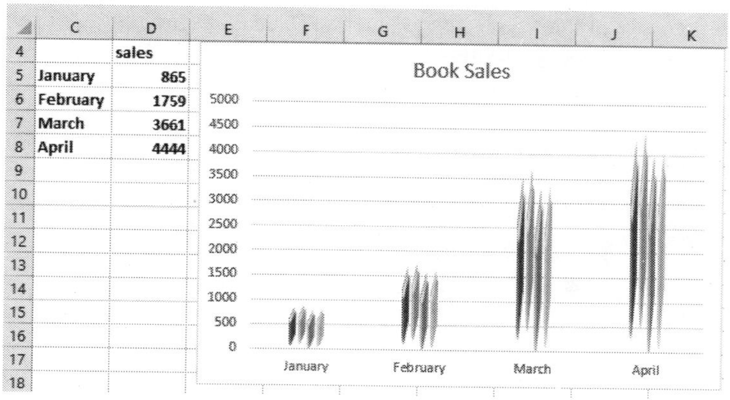

FIGURE 52-11 Book sales summarized with book images.

To begin, select the range C5:D8. On the Insert tab, click Insert Column Or Bar Chart and select the first chart in the 2D Column options (clustered column.) Then right-click any column. Select Fill (above the context menu) and then click Picture; you will see the window shown in Figure 52-12. After typing Books in Bing Image Search and pressing Enter, you are presented with many pictures of books. After selecting the book image you want and clicking Insert, your picture is inserted into the graph, as shown previously in Figure 52-11, with the size of the books proportional to the actual sales.

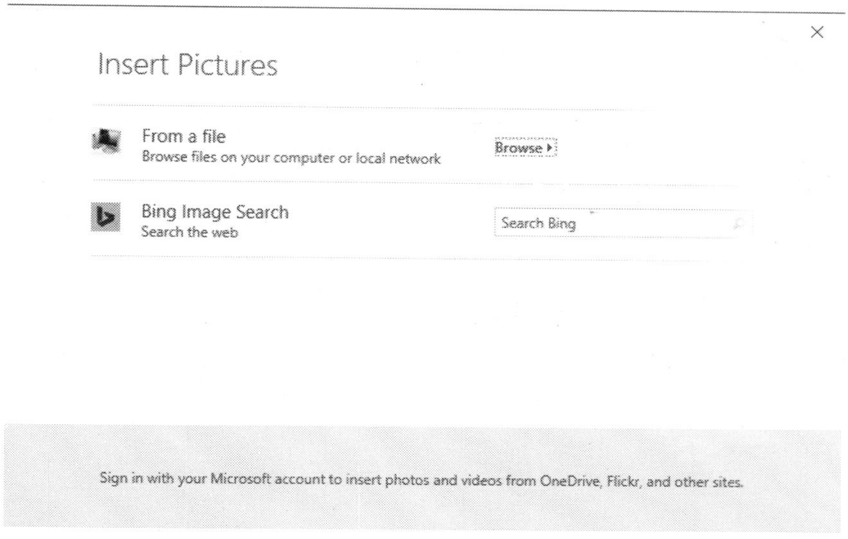

FIGURE 52-12 The Insert Pictures dialog box.

I charted annual sales data in a column graph, but the years do not show up as column labels. What did I do wrong?

The file Categorylabels.xlsx (see Figure 52-13) contains the annual product sales for the years 2007–2010. When I create a column graph with the chart data source being D5:E9, the chart fails to show the year on the x-axis because Excel thinks I want the year charted as a series. If I omit the Year category label in the upper-left corner of the source range and use D20:E24 as the range for the chart, my chart shows the year on the x-axis, as desired.

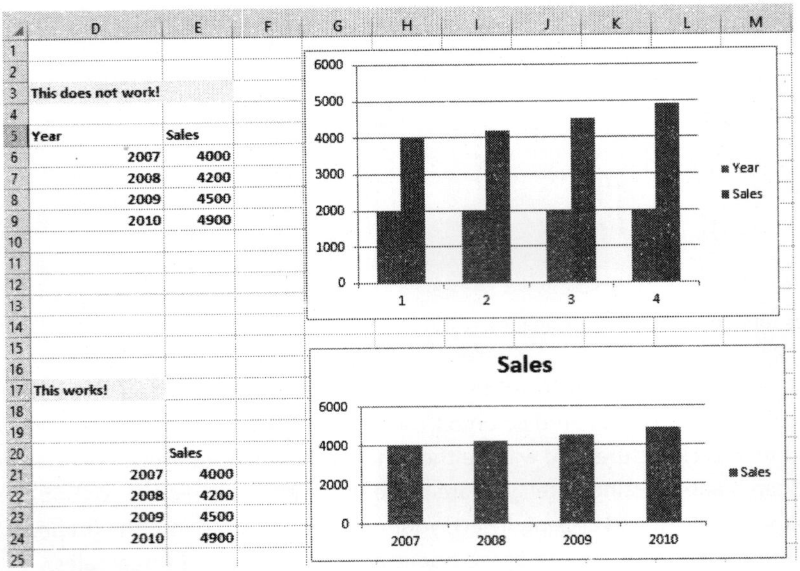

FIGURE 52-13 Omitting the category label to graph column charts correctly.

How can I include data labels and data tables in my charts?

Often, we want to insert data labels next to our columns or bars or perhaps show a nice table below our chart. To illustrate this process, look at the file Labelsandtables.xlsx. In this file, you are given sales of four product categories during the current month. To begin, I summarize this data in a column graph and place a label containing the product name and actual sales above the column. After creating a column graph in the usual fashion, select the column series in the chart and click the + sign to the right of the chart. Then click the arrow to the right of Data Labels and click More Options. In the Format Data Labels pane, after filling in the Label Options section as shown in Figure 52-14, you will now see the chart shown in Figure 52-15.

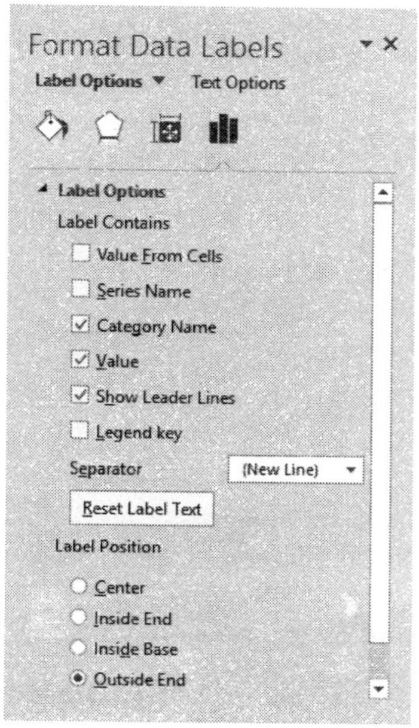

FIGURE 52-14 The settings needed to show the sales and series name on separate lines.

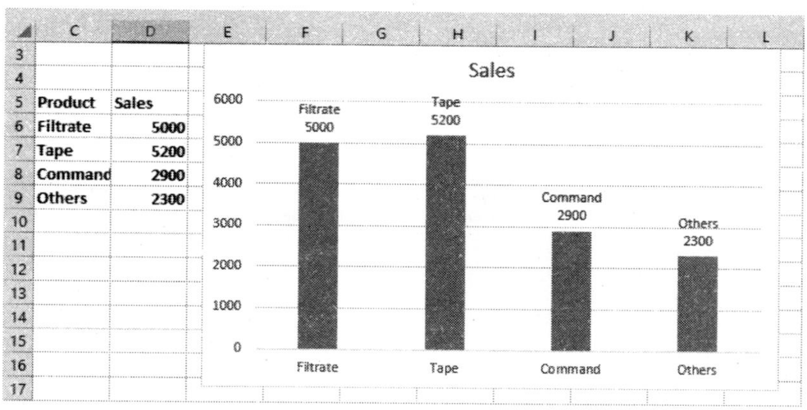

FIGURE 52-15 The category names and sales included in charts.

I will now show how to place a data table summarizing the sales below the chart. Simply select the category axis and click the + sign to the right of the chart. After clicking Data Table, you will see the data table shown in Figure 52-16.

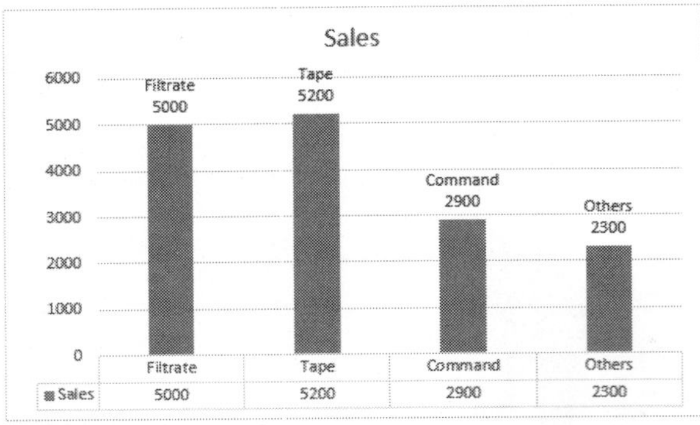

FIGURE 52-16 The sales summarized with a data table.

If you want to see more data table options, simply select the triangle to the right of the Data Table item.

How can I use Excel 2016 to place data labels on a chart based on the contents of cells?

Beginning with Excel 2013, Excel made it possible to place data labels from cells directly on charts. To illustrate the idea, examine the file Labelsfromcells.xlsx shown in Figure 52-17.

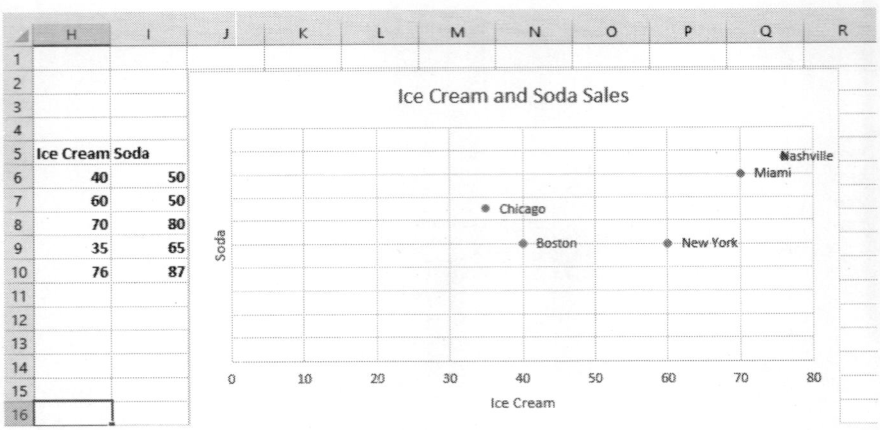

FIGURE 52-17 A scatter chart with labels from cells.

To begin creating this graph, select the cell range H5:I10 and choose the first scatter chart option that's displayed when you select Insert Scatter (X, Y) Or Bubble Chart (the icon with the dots, to the right of the pie chart icon). This creates the scatter chart that you see in Figure 52-17, without the city labels. To create the city labels, first select the chart. On the Chart Tools Design tab, select Add Chart Element, select Data Labels, and then More Data Label Options. In the Format Data Labels pane, check Value From Cells, and clear Y Value. Now you can select the cell range G6:G10 to insert the city labels in the chart, as shown in Figure 52-17.

How can I track sales-force performance over time?

The file Salestracker.xlsx lists the monthly sales by your crack sales force during January through May (see Figure 52-18).

	D	E	F	G	H	I
1	p	h	up			
2	q	i	down			
3	u	g	flat			
4						
5		January	February	March	April	May
6	Lebron	85	66	81	61	56
7	Wade	82	63	74	78	75
8	Dirk	45	100	115	127	150
9	Manning	75	88	89	76	83
10	Brady	96	90	98	76	93
11	Halliday	75	73	79	91	95
12	Britney	98	91	109	99	84
13	Lindsay	83	84	97	81	98
14	Paris	106	98	84	93	82
15	JLO	104	88	109	101	115
16	Emma	115	94	105	101	107
17	Melo	118	98	128	126	108
18	KD	100	114	104	116	131
19	Vick	112	122	102	124	107
20	Rodgers	127	114	116	139	108

FIGURE 52-18 The monthly sales data.

You want to use icons (up, down, or right arrow) to track during each month whether a salesperson's ranking has improved, declined, or stayed the same. You could use Excel's icons sets (described in Chapter 24, "Conditional formatting"), but then you would have to insert a set of icons for each month, which is a tedious task. A more efficient (although not as aesthetically pleasing) way to create these icons is to enter an *h* when you want an up arrow, enter an *I* when you want a down arrow, and enter a *g* when you want a flat arrow. Then, if you change the font to Wingdings 3, you will see the arrows you want. This is because the letters of the alphabet correspond in Wingdings 3 to the symbols shown in Figure 52-19.

	J	K	L
22	Letter	Wingdings 3	
23	a	⇨	
24	b	⇦	
25	c	⇨	
26	d	⇦	
27	e	⇨	
28	f	←	
29	g	→	
30	h	↑	
31	i	↓	
32	j	↖	
33	k	↗	
34	l	↙	
35	m	↘	
36	n	↔	
37	o	↕	
38	p	▲	
39	q	▼	
40	r	△	
41	s	▽	
42	t	◀	
43	u	▶	
44	v	◁	
45	w	▷	
46	x	◣	
47	y	◢	
48	z	◤	

FIGURE 52-19 Correspondence between letters and Wingdings 3 symbols.

To create the icons shown in Figure 52-20, I proceed as follows:

- Copying from J6 to J6:N20 the formula =RANK(E6,E$6:E20,0) computes each person's sales rank during each month.
- Copying from O6 to O7:R20 the formula =IF(K6<J6,"h",IF(K6>J6,"I","g")) creates an *h* if the person's rank has improved, an *I* if the person's rank has declined, and a *g* if the salesperson's rank has stayed the same.
- After changing the font in the range O6:R20 to Wingdings 3, I see the icons shown in Figure 52-20.

	D	E	F	G	H	I	J	K	L	M	N	O	P	Q	R
1	p	h	up												
2	q	i	down												
3	u	g	flat												
4							rank	rank	rank	rank	rank	trend	trend	trend	trend
5		January	February	March	April	May	January	February	March	April	May	Feb	March	April	May
6	Lebron	85	66	81	61	56	10	14	13	15	15	↓	↑	↓	→
7	Wade	82	63	74	78	75	12	15	15	12	14	↓	→	↑	↓
8	Dirk	45	100	115	127	150	15	4	3	2	1	↑	↑	↑	↑
9	Manning	75	88	89	76	83	13	10	11	13	12	↑	↓	↓	↑
10	Brady	96	90	98	76	93	9	9	9	13	10	→	→	↓	↑
11	Halliday	75	73	79	91	95	13	13	14	10	9	→	↓	↑	↑
12	Britney	98	91	109	99	84	8	8	4	8	11	→	↑	↓	↓
13	Lindsay	83	84	97	81	98	11	12	10	11	8	↓	↑	↓	↑
14	Paris	106	98	84	93	82	5	5	12	9	13	→	↓	↑	↓
15	JLO	104	88	109	101	115	6	10	4	6	3	↓	↑	↓	↑
16	Emma	115	94	105	101	107	3	7	6	6	6	↓	↑	→	→
17	Melo	118	98	128	126	108	2	5	1	3	4	↓	↑	↓	↓
18	KD	100	114	104	116	131	7	2	7	5	2	↑	↓	↑	↑
19	Vick	112	122	102	124	107	4	1	8	4	6	↑	↓	↑	↓
20	Rodgers	127	114	116	139	108	1	2	2	1	4	↓	→	↑	↓

FIGURE 52-20 Icons used to track change in salesperson performance.

The advantage of this approach is that you can use IF statements to easily customize the conditions that define the icons.

How can I create a band chart to check whether inventory is within acceptable levels?

Often, we need to track a quantity (such as inventory, cash on hand, or number of accidents) and want to track whether the quantity remains between historical upper and lower limits. A band chart provides a useful tool to monitor how a process changes over time. Figure 52-21 shows an example of a band chart (see the file Bandchart.xlsx).

	A	B	C	D	E	F	G
1	Limits						
2	Lower Limit	5					
3	Upper Limit	25					
4		Jan	Feb	Mar	Apr	May	Jun
5	Lower Limit	5	5	5	5	5	5
6	Upper Limit	20	20	20	20	20	20
7	Values	25	33	27	4	26	29

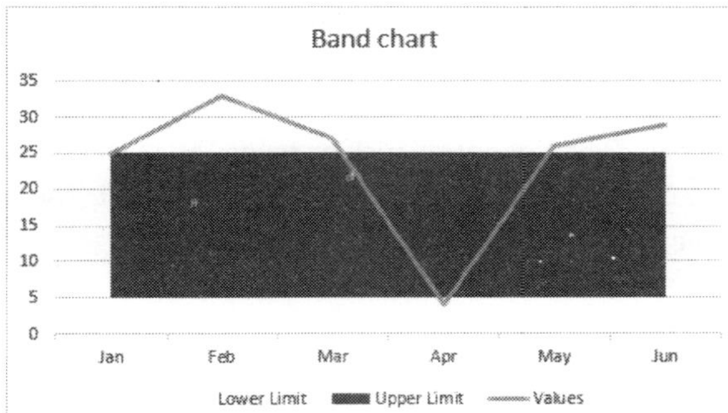

FIGURE 52-21 A band chart summarizing the inventory levels.

To create the band chart, proceed as follows:

- Enter in B2 your lower limit on inventory (5) and in B3 your upper limit (25) on inventory.
- In row 5, enter the lower limit for each month by copying from B5 to C5:G5 the formula =$B$2.
- Copying from B6 to C6:G6 the formula = $B$3-$B$2 computes Upper Limit-Lower Limit. You label this row *Upper Limit* because this row will be used to generate the line representing your upper inventory limit of 25 units.
- Select the range A4:G7, and on the Insert tab, select Insert Line Or Area Chart, and click Stacked Column (the second option in the 2-D Column section). Change the chart title to Band chart.
- Right-click the Value series (the green bar), and select Change Series Chart Type. In the Change Chart Type dialog box, under Choose The Chart Type And Axis For Your Data Series, for the Upper Limit series, select Area (the first option from the Area section), and for the Values series, select the Line chart (the first chart option in the Line section). Click OK.

- Right-click the Lower Limit series in the chart (a blue bar) and select Fill. From the Fill menu, select No Fill.

My band chart shows that I am having great difficulty maintaining inventory levels between the desired lower and upper limits.

How can I store a chart as a template?

I just created a beautiful band chart. You might think that each time you want to create a band chart, you need to repeat the previously described steps. This is not the case. You can save the band chart (or any other chart) as a template and pull up the chart settings whenever you need them. To illustrate the idea, open the file Bandchart.xlsx, right-click the chart, select Save As Template, and give the chart any name you want. (I chose *Band*.) Now suppose you want a band chart just for the months January–March. Simply select the data range A4:D7, and then, in the Charts group on the Insert tab, select the dialog box launcher in the lower-right corner of the Charts group. Select the All Charts tab, and then select Templates in the left pane. Then browse to the chart template you want, click OK, and you are finished!

How can I use a thermometer chart to portray progress against a target?

A thermometer chart shows the actual values of a quantity, such as revenues, stacked within a column that shows a target value. The resulting chart (shown in Figure 52-22 and in the file Thermometer.xlsx) resembles a thermometer, hence the name, *thermometer chart*.

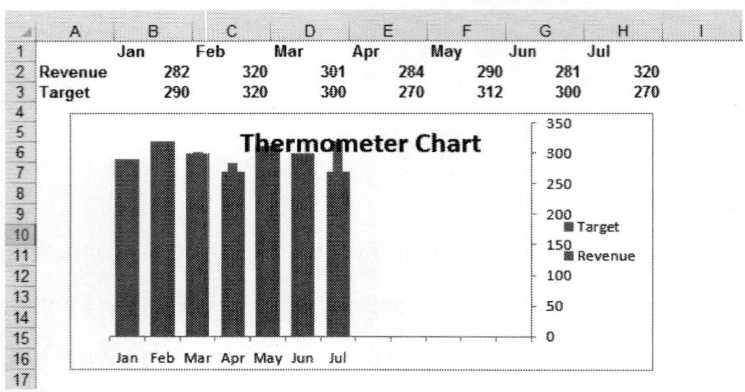

FIGURE 52-22 A thermometer chart.

To create a thermometer chart, proceed as follows:

- Select the range A1:H3, click Insert Column Or Bar Chart on the Insert tab, and select Clustered Column chart (first icon) from the 2-D Column options.
- Right-click the revenue series (a blue bar) in the chart, and then select Format Data Series. In the Format Data Series pane, select Secondary Axis.
- In the Format Data Series pane, with the revenue series still selected, set Series Overlap to 0% and Gap Width to 261%.

- Click the target series (a red bar), and then set Series Overlap to 0% and Gap Width to 48%.

You will now see the chart shown in Figure 52-22. You might have to adjust the gap widths to obtain a chart you like. Making the gap width for the target series smaller, for example, makes the red bars wider; making the gap width for revenue larger, makes the blue bars narrower.

How can I create dynamic chart labels?

You have probably encountered workbooks with charts in which you change a worksheet input and the chart labels do not change in response to the worksheet inputs. This situation often causes confusion. You will now learn how to link series labels and chart titles to worksheet cells. To illustrate the idea (see the file Dynamiclabels.xlsx and Figure 52-23), suppose you want to chart the future GDP in the United States and China. You want the chart title to contain the year in which China's GDP passes the US GDP, and you want the series label to contain the annual growth rate for each nation. In C5 and C8, you can change the estimated growth rates from their current values of 3 percent for the US and 10 percent for China.

	B	C	D	E	F	G	H	I	J	K	L	M	N	O	P	Q	R
2		0	1	2	3	4	5	6	7	8	9	10	11	12	13	14	15
3	GDP																
4	US GDP	500	515.0	530.5	546.4	562.8	579.6	597.0	614.9	633.4	652.4	672.0	692.1	712.9	734.3	756.3	779.0
5	Growth (%)	3.0%	3.0%	3.0%	3.0%	3.0%	3.0%	3.0%	3.0%	3.0%	3.0%	3.0%	3.0%	3.0%	3.0%	3.0%	3.0%
7	China GDP	250	275.0	302.5	332.8	366.0	402.6	442.9	487.2	535.9	589.5	648.4	713.3	784.6	863.1	949.4	1044.3
8	Growth (%)	10.0%	10.0%	10.0%	10.0%	10.0%	10.0%	10.0%	10.0%	10.0%	10.0%	10.0%	10.0%	10.0%	10.0%	10.0%	10.0%
10	China>US?		0	0	0	0	0	0	0	0	0	0	1	1	1	1	1
14	First year that China	11															
17	Title	Chinese GDP to pass US GDP in Y															
18	US Label	USA (3.0% annual growth)															
19	China Label	China (10.0% annual growth)															

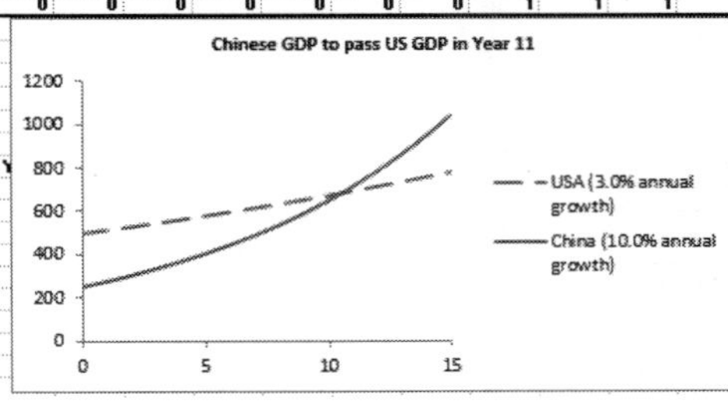

FIGURE 52-23 Creating dynamic labels.

The key idea is to link your chart title and labels to cells that change when the growth rates change. Proceed as follows:

- Copying from D10 to E10:R10 the formula =IF(D7>=D4,1,0), enters a 1 if the GDP for China is at least as big as the US GDP.

- In cell C14, determine the year in which China passes the US with the formula =IFERROR(MATCH(1,D10:R10,0),"none"). Note that if China never passes the US, this formula enters None.

- In cell C17, the formula =IF(C14="none", "US stays on top","Chinese GDP to pass US GDP in Year "&TEXT(C14,"0")) creates the chart title you want. Note if China never passes the US, your chart title will be **US stays on top**. Otherwise, your chart title is linked to C14, so the chart title will contain the year in which China passes the US. The *"0"* in the TEXT function ensures that the year is formatted as an integer.

- In cell C18, the formula ="USA ("&TEXT(C5,"0.0%")&" annual growth)" creates the chart title for the US series. The *"0.0%"* portion of the TEXT function ensures that the growth rate is formatted as a percentage.
- In cell C19, the formula ="China ("&TEXT(C8,"0.0%")&" annual growth)" creates the chart title for the China series.

Now you are ready to create the chart with dynamic labels, proceeding as follows:

- Using the Ctrl key, select the noncontiguous range C2:R2, C4:R4, C7:R7, and then create a scatter chart with smooth lines: click the Insert tab, click Insert Scatter (X, Y) Or Bubble Chart, and then click Scatter With Smooth Lines (the third option) in the Scatter section.
- On the Design tab, select Add Chart Element in the Chart Layouts group, select Chart Title, and then select Centered Overlay. In the formula bar, type an equal sign, click cell C17, and press the Enter key. You now have a dynamic chart label.
- Right-click Series 1 in the chart (the USA GDP series blue line), and choose Select Data. Then click Edit in the Legend Entries (Series) area on the left, and fill in the Edit Series dialog box, as shown in Figure 52-24: Enter the Series Name as ='Dynamic labels'!$C$18, leave the other defaults, and click OK in both dialog boxes.

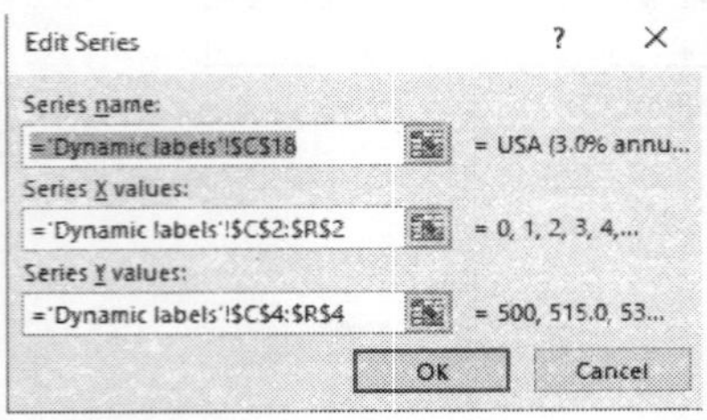

FIGURE 52-24 Creating the dynamic USA series label.

This links the USA series label to cell C18, which contains the annual growth rate. In a similar fashion, you link the China series label to cell C19. You now have the completed chart with dynamic labels.

How can I use check boxes to control which series are charted?

You may recall from Chapter 27 that a check box can be used to toggle the contents of a cell between True and False. It turns out that if Excel sees an #N/A error in a cell, the cell will not generate a point appearing in the chart. Therefore, if you do not want to chart a series, you simply use an IF formula to make the charted series #N/A when the check box puts a False in a cell. You can see an example of this in Figure 52-25.

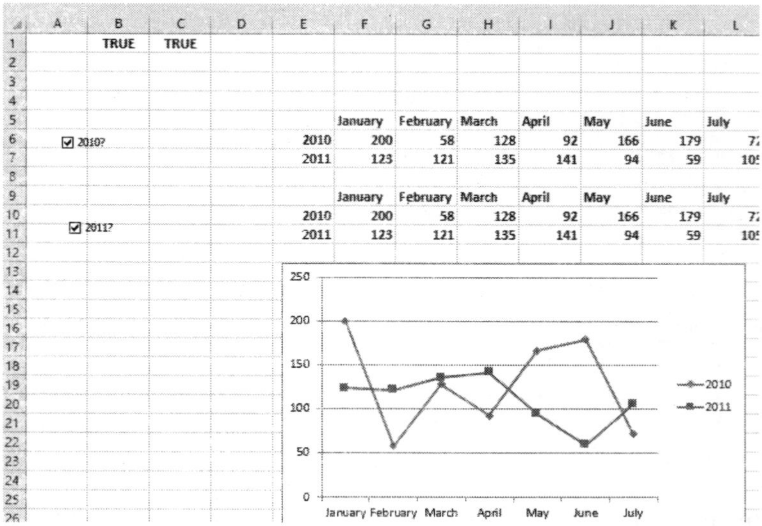

FIGURE 52-25 Using check boxes to control the series appearing in a chart.

Open the file Checkbox.xlsx. To begin, you use the methods described in Chapter 27 to create two check boxes: one to control the 2010 series and another to control the 2011 series. The 2010 check box controls whether cell B1 is True or False, and the 2011 check box controls cell C1. The original data is in E6:L7. Copying the formula =IF($B$1,F6,NA()) from F10 to F11:L11 simply copies the original data for the year if the year's check box is checked, and it enters an #N/A if the year's check box is unchecked. Now select the cell range E9:L11 as the source data for a Line With Markers chart (click the Insert tab, click Insert Line Or Area Chart, and select the Line With Markers chart, the fourth chart in the 2-D Line section). Unchecking a year's check box will hide a year's data in the chart; checking the check box will reinsert the year's data in the chart.

How can I use a list box to choose the series to be charted?

Suppose your spreadsheet (see Listbox.xlsx) contains 2007–2011 sales in the East, West, Midwest, and South regions. You want an easy way to control which series is charted. A list box (see Chapter 27) provides an easy way to control the charted series. To begin, go the Developer tab on the ribbon, and in the Controls group, click Insert, and then select the List Box option from the Form Controls section. Add a list box to the spreadsheet, right-click it, and select Format Control. In the Format Control dialog box, select $A$14:$A$17 as the Input Range and select $H$2 as the Cell Link. Click OK. Now, with an intelligent use of the INDEX function, you can use cell H2 to control the charted series, as shown in Figure 52-26.

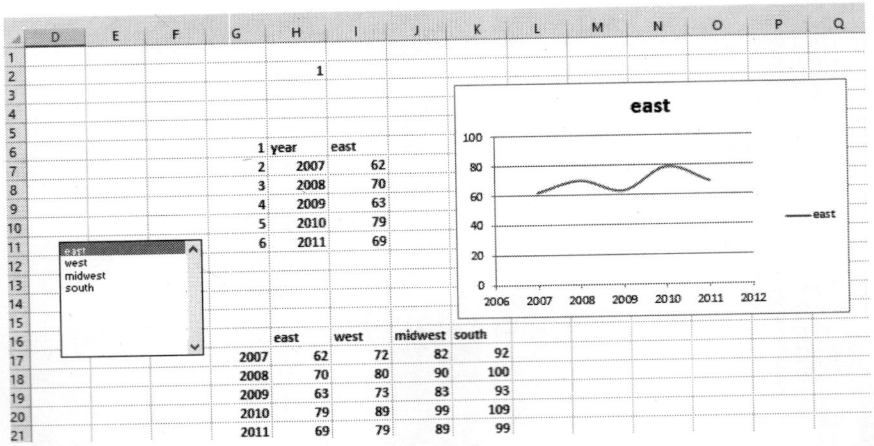

FIGURE 52-26 Using a list box to control the charted series.

Copying from I7 to I8:I10 the formula =INDEX($H$16:$K$21,G7,$H$2) pulls the correct series. For example, in the list box shown in Figure 52-26, the East region was selected. This places a 1 in cell H2. Then my INDEX function pulls the first column (column H) of data as desired. Now, select the range H7:Y11 and create a scatter chart by clicking Insert Scatter (X, Y) Or Bubble Chart, and then selecting the Scatter chart) option. You will see that when you click a region in the list box, the correct series is displayed on all the charts.

How do I create a Gantt chart?

Often, a project requires that a number of projects be completed. A Gantt chart portrays the time each project begins. Shown in Figure 52-27 (see file Gantt.xlsx) is a Gantt chart for a project consisting of five tasks. To create this chart, proceed as follows:

- Select the cell range F3:H8, and create a stacked 2D bar chart (click Insert Column Or Bar Chart, and select Stacked Bar, the second option in the 2-D Bar section).
- Right-click the Start series (a blue bar), and after selecting Fill, choose No Fill to hide the Start series.
- Right-click the vertical axis (the tasks on the left), select Format Axis, and then, in the Format Axis pane, select the check box Categories In Reverse Order to ensure that Task 1 is listed first instead of last.

	C	F	G	H
3	Gantt Chart		Start	Duration
4	1. Graph with stacked bar	Task 1	0	2
5	2. Select first series and	Task 2	2	6
6	then Choose No Fill	Task 3	8	9
7	3. Select Axis and reverse categories	Task 4	17	3
8		Task 5	20	5

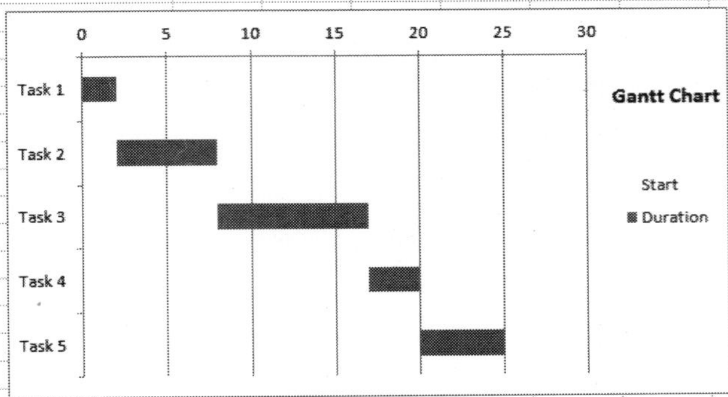

FIGURE 52-27 A Gantt chart.

How do I create a chart based on sorted data?

Suppose you have sales in a number of states (see Figure 52-28 and the file Sortedgraph.xlsx), and you want the graph to list the states in descending order of sales, as shown in Figure 52-29. To create this chart, you need to reorganize the data in columns J–L so that the sales data is sorted in descending order.

	E	F	G	H	I	J	K	L
8	State	Sales	Original rank	Revised		Rank	State	Sales
9	NJ	40	1	1		1	NJ	40
10	NY	18	6	6		2	Wva	20
11	Ind	14	10	10		3	Min	19
12	Cal	15	9	9		4	Mic	19
13	KY	10	13	13		5	Fla	19
14	Ari	10	13	14		6	NY	18
15	Ala	10	13	15		7	Va	17
16	Min	19	3	3		8	Mo	16
17	Ill	13	11	11		9	Cal	15
18	Mic	19	3	4		10	Ind	14
19	Mo	16	8	8		11	Ill	13
20	Fla	19	3	5		12	Pa	13
21	Pa	13	11	12		13	KY	10
22	Wva	20	2	2		14	Ari	10
23	Va	17	7	7		15	Ala	10

FIGURE 52-28 The sales data for a sorted graph.

To accomplish this goal, I proceed as follows:

- Copying from G9 to G10:G23 the formula =RANK(F9,$F$9:$F$23,0), I compute the rank of each state's sales. For example, New York ranks sixth. Note, however, that Kentucky, Alabama, and Arizon have the same level of sales. To sort the states in descending order of sales, I need to associate a unique rank with each state.
- Copying from H9 to H10:H23 the formula =G9+COUNTIF($G$8:G8,G9) creates a unique rank for each state by increasing the rank of a state with a tied rank each time a tied rank occurs.
- Copying from K9 to K10:L23 the formula =INDEX(E$9:E$23,MATCH($J9,$H$9:$H$23,0),1) sorts the states and sales based on descending sales.
- Now, creating a column graph based on K9:L23 (select Clustered Column in the Charts group) yields the graph shown in Figure 52-29.

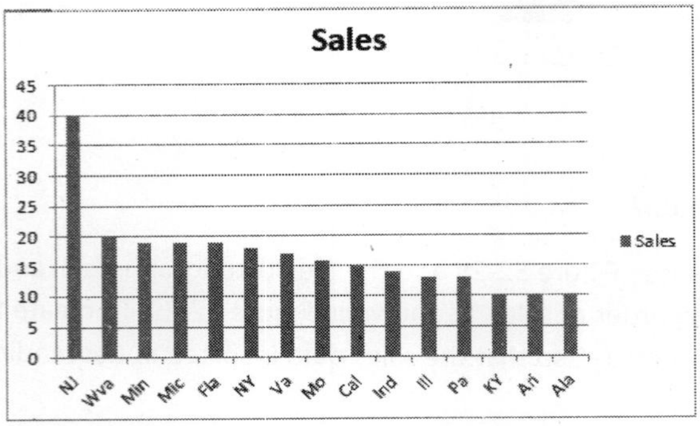

FIGURE 52-29 The sales sorted in descending order.

How can I create a histogram that automatically updates when I include new data?

In Chapter 41, you learned how to use the Data Analysis template to create a histogram, Unfortunately, histograms created with the Analysis ToolPak will not update if the existing data is changed or if new data is added. Using the Excel table feature, you can easily create histograms that automatically adjust to changes in the source data. The file Dynamichistograms.xlsx illustrates the idea. (See Figure 52-30.)

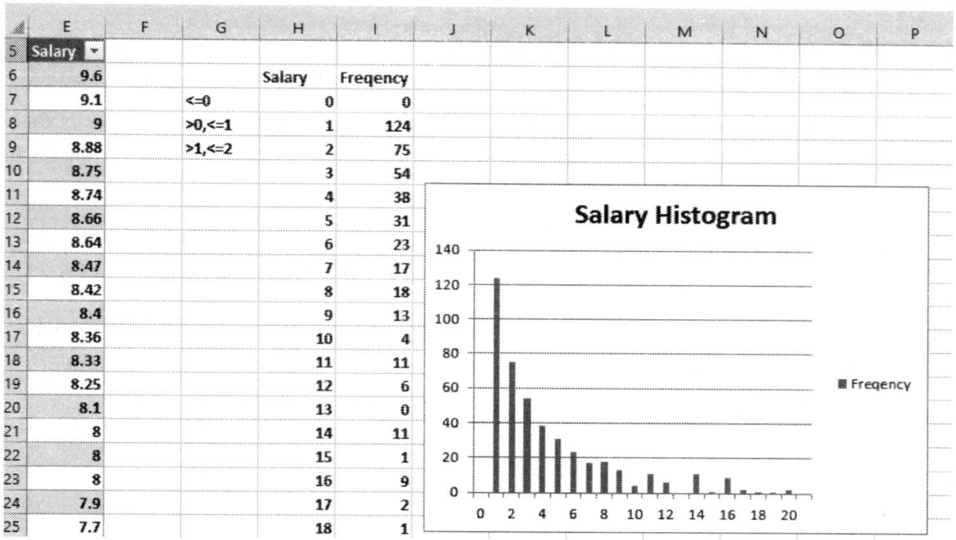

	E	F	G	H	I
5	Salary				
6	9.6			Salary	Freqency
7	9.1		<=0	0	0
8	9		>0,<=1	1	124
9	8.88		>1,<=2	2	75
10	8.75			3	54
11	8.74			4	38
12	8.66			5	31
13	8.64			6	23
14	8.47			7	17
15	8.42			8	18
16	8.4			9	13
17	8.36			10	4
18	8.33			11	11
19	8.25			12	6
20	8.1			13	0
21	8			14	11
22	8			15	1
23	8			16	9
24	7.9			17	2
25	7.7			18	1

FIGURE 52-30 A dynamic histogram.

Column E contains NBA player salaries in millions of dollars for the 2003–2004 season. To begin, I selected the range E5:E446 and made that range a table. Then I entered the bin ranges for my histogram in the range H7:H28. Note that row 28 will calculate the number of salaries that are larger than $20 million. Now I will use the FREQUENCY function to count how many salaries fall into each bin range. The FREQUENCY function (see Chapter 89) is an *array function*. To use this function, you need to first select the range the function populates (in this case I7:I28), then enter the function syntax, and then press Ctrl+Shift+Enter. Here, after selecting I7:I28, type in the formula **=FREQUENCY(E6:E446,H7:H27)** and press Ctrl+Shift+Enter. Excel now enters in cell I7 the number of players (0) with a salary less than or equal to 0, in cell I8 it enters the number of salaries >0 and <=1 million (124), and so on to cell I27, where Excel enters the number of players with salaries >19 and <=20 million (2), and finally in cell I28 it enters the number of players with a salary >20 million (0). To create the dynamic histogram, simply select the cell range H7:I28 and create a column graph (select Clustered Column in the Charts group). You now have a dynamic histogram, which will automatically update to account for changes in the source data. To prove that the histogram updates, add a few salaries of $30 million in column E (rows 447 and higher). You will now see a new column appear on the right side of the graph.

How can I add conditional colors to a chart?

Suppose you are charting for each month actual and targeted sales and you want months in which you perform at 90 percent of target or better to be graphed in blue; 75 percent of target or worse in green, and other months in red. The file Condcolors.xlsx (Figure 52-31) shows how this is done. The trick to create this chart is to put the data for each color in a different row (see rows 19–21). To begin, I place sales I want colored blue in row 19 by copying from F19 to G19:M19 the formula =IF(F13/F14>F15,F13/F14," "). Then, I place the sales I want colored red in row 20 by copying from F20 to G20:M20 the formula =IF(AND(F13/F14>F16,F13/F14<=F15), F13/F14," "). Finally, I place the sales for months that should appear in green in row 20 by copying from F21 to G21:M21 the formula =IF(COUNT(F19:F20)=0,F13/F14," "). Now, select the range E18:M21 and create a column chart (select Clustered Column in the Charts group). If you want to change the color for any series, select the series/column and click the paintbrush icon to the right of the chart; then select Color, and choose the color theme you want to to use. You can select a new combination of colors that apply to all your series.

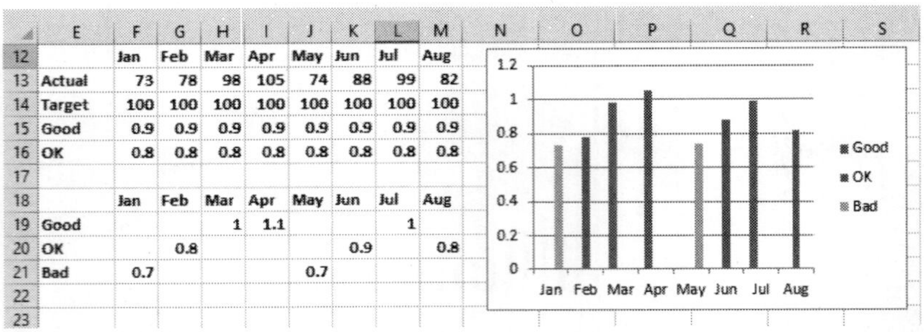

FIGURE 52-31 Showing how blue indicates a good month, green a bad month, and red a so-so month.

How can I use waterfall charts to track progress toward a sales target or to break down the components of a sales price?

Waterfall charts, originally developed by the McKinsey consulting firm, are often used to show progress toward a final cash position or to break down a company's total revenue into cost components and profit. In this section, I show how to use Excel 2013 or earlier versions to create waterfall charts. Late in the chapter, I show how Excel 2016 makes it much easier to create waterfall charts. The file Waterfallcharts.xlsx contains several examples of waterfall charts.

In the worksheet All Positive (see Figure 52-32), I create a waterfall chart for a situation in which all the cash flows are positive. I want the chart to show the monthly progress toward my cash flow goal of $3,270. After entering my cash flows in column C, I need to simply track in column B my cumulative cash flow. Copying it from B3 to B4:B7, the formula =B2+C2 computes the cumulative cash flow through the end of each month. Next, I select the cell range A1:C7 and create a stacked column chart (the second choice in the 2-D Column section). Change the chart title to Waterfall Chart: All Amounts Positive. Right-click the Base series (blue bar), and choose No Fill from the Fill menu; this yields the waterfall chart shown in Figure 52-32.

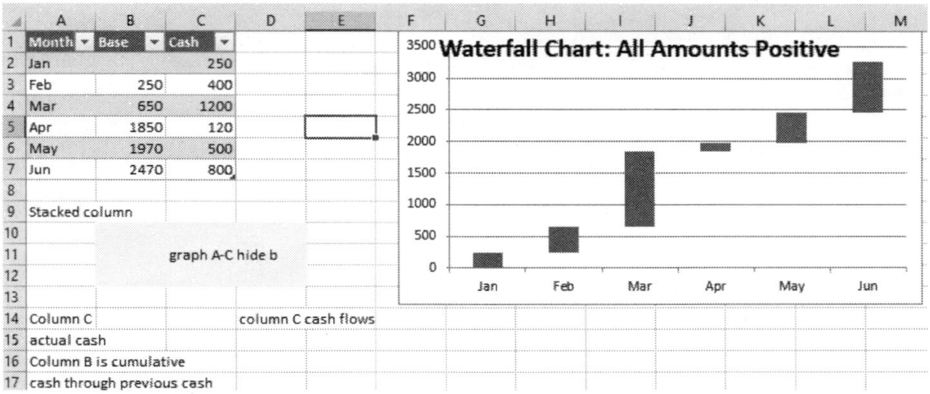

FIGURE 52-32 A waterfall chart where all the cash flows are positive.

Figure 52-33 (see the worksheet Positive And Negative) shows a waterfall chart in a situation for which some cash flows are negative.

After entering the positive cash flows in column C and negative cash flows in column D, I compute the total cash flow through the end of each month by copying from E2 to E3:E7 the formula =E1+C2-D2. Next, by copying from B2 to B3:B7 the formula =E1-D2, I compute in column B the cumulative cash flow through the last month, adjusted by the current month's negative cash flow. After selecting the range A1:D7 and creating a stacked column chart (the Clustered Column option), all I have to do is hide column B (the Base series), and then I have the waterfall chart shown in Figure 52-33. (To hide the column, right-click a blue bar, and then select No Fill from the Fill menu.) Also, I changed the chart title to **Waterfall Chart Positive and Negative Value**.

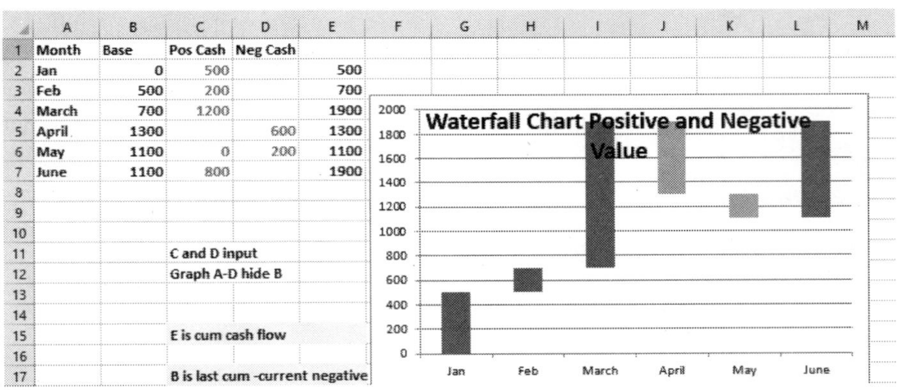

FIGURE 52-33 A waterfall chart where some cash flows are negative.

By following the method used in the Positive And Negative worksheet, you can easily break down a company's revenue into its cost components (including profit). See the worksheet Profitability Waterfall and Figure 52-34.

	A	B	C	D	E
1	Month	Base	Pos Cash	Neg Cash	
2	Sales	0	450000		450000
3	COGS	230000		220000	230000
4	Wages	150000		80000	150000
5	Property	100000		50000	100000
6	Overhead	75000		25000	75000
7	Profit	0		75000	0
8					
9					
10				input c and d	
11				graph a-d hide b	
12					
13					
14					
15					

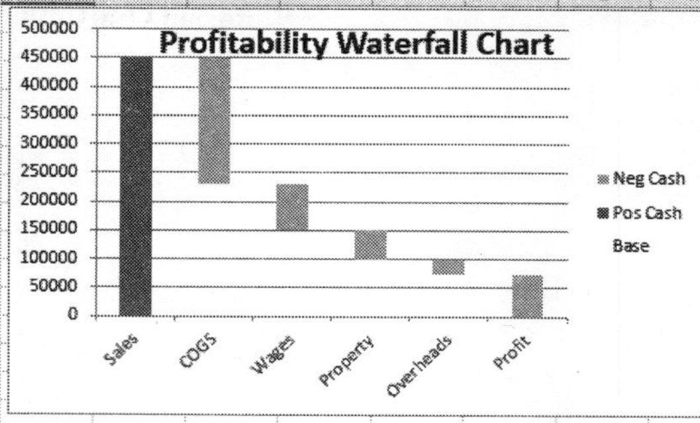

FIGURE 52-34 A profitability waterfall chart.

How can I use the GETPIVOT data function and Excel's table feature to create dynamic dashboards?

Often, we download monthly, quarterly, or weekly sales data and want to summarize the sales data in charts that will automatically update to include new data. Knowledge of Excel's GETPIVOTDATA function (see Chapter 43) and Excel's table feature (see Chapter 26) makes this relatively straightforward (see the file Randy.xlsx.) Let's suppose you download weekly sales data for four product categories (filtrate, tape, command, and abrasives) at four stores (Menard's, Target, Lowes, and Home Depot). Your goal is to set up a dashboard that allows you to quickly chart the weekly sales data at a given store and control which product categories appear in the chart. As shown in Figure 52-35, your data is downloaded in columns D–G. I made the range D4:G243 a table. This action will ensure that a PivotTable based on this data will automatically update to include new data when you refresh the table.

	D	E	F	G
4	WEEK	Category	Store	Revenue
5	3	Abrasives	Lowes	2043
6	12	Safety	Menards	2343
7	3	Tape	Home Depot	1414
8	12	Command	Target	1820
9	9	Tape	Home Depot	943
10	7	Tape	Target	1219
11	7	Command	Menards	1156
12	11	Abrasives	Lowes	2127
13	12	Safety	Menards	1315
14	3	Tape	Target	1580
15	10	Abrasives	Home Depot	1598
16	4	Command	Lowes	1000
17	7	Tape	Menards	1087
18	7	Abrasives	Menards	1728
19	1	Abrasives	Target	1911
20	7	Abrasives	Menards	1563
21	2	Tape	Target	2482
22	7	Safety	Lowes	1534
23	12	Safety	Menards	1471
24	2	Abrasives	Lowes	990
25	11	Tape	Lowes	1580
26	1	Safety	Target	2389
27	2	Safety	Menards	2263

FIGURE 52-35 The sales data.

I now create a PivotTable by clicking the Insert tab and then PivotTable in the Tables group. In the PivotTable Fields pane, I drag the Week field to the Rows area, Store and Category to the Columns area, and Revenue to the Values area. This PivotTable (shown in Figure 52-36) summarizes the weekly sales for each category in each store.

	I	J	K	L	M	N	O	P	Q	R	S	T
9												
10												
11	Sum of Revenue	Column Labels										
12		⊟ Lowes				Lowes Total	⊟ Menards				Menards Total	Home ⊟ Depot
13	Row Labels	Abrasives	Safety	Tape	Command		Abrasives	Safety	Tape	Command		Abrasive
14	1		1065		1247	2312	3772	526	3466		7764	3272
15	2	2349	4510			6859	6220	3296	2159		11675	1921
16	3	2797	1233	2046	6335	12411	3472		959	2369	6800	
17	4	1501	3822	1180	1000	7503	6018	2212			8230	
18	5	1940		833	2945	5718	708		501	597	1806	1758
19	6			1918	6494	8412	4145	6205	4653		15003	
20	7	3049	3228			6277	3291	2303	6472	1156	13222	3580
21	8	4208	2890	1873		8971	910		1494	3776	6180	2445
22	9			2052	2825	4877	6265		1888		8153	
23	10	6117		1875		7992			2138		2138	4807
24	11	2127	1971	4461	2394	10953	3596	1169			4765	
25	12		1542	4786	850	7178	1124	7565	7264	2431	18384	2471
26	13				1196	1196				3400	3400	
27	14	1455				1455						
28	Grand Total	25543	20261	21024	25286	92114	39521	23276	####	13729	107520	20254

FIGURE 52-36 A PivotTable summarizing the category sales by store.

Now I am ready to use the GETPIVOTDATA function to extract the data needed to create the charts I want. To begin, I create a drop-down list (see Chapter 40) in cell AG8 (still in the Model worksheet), which can be used to select a store. Then I create check boxes (see Chapter 27) for each category that can be used to control the range AH9:AK9. These cells control which categories appear in my chart. Then I copy from AH11 to the range AH11:AK24 the formula =IF(AH$9=FALSE,NA(),IFERROR(GETPIVOTDATA("Revenue",$I$11,"WEEK",$AG11,"Category",AH$10,"Store",$AG$8)," ")). If I select the check box for a category, this formula extracts the weekly sales for the category; if the category is unchecked, then an #N/A is entered in the cell. Also, if 0 sales occurred, the IFERROR portion of the formulas ensures that sales of 0 are entered. Next, I make the range AG10:AK24 a table so that any charts based on this range will update automatically to include the new data. Figure 52-37 shows how the source data for my chart appears if I want to summarize abrasives, safety equipment, and tape sales at Lowes.

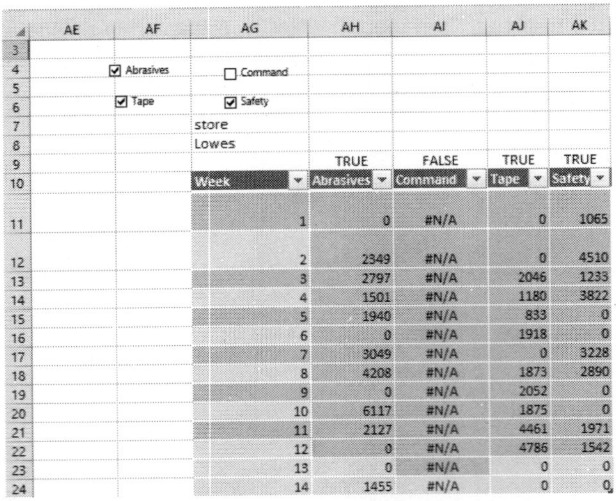

	AE	AF	AG	AH	AI	AJ	AK
3							
4		☑ Abrasives	☐ Command				
5							
6		☑ Tape	☑ Safety				
7			store				
8			Lowes				
9				TRUE	FALSE	TRUE	TRUE
10			Week	Abrasives	Command	Tape	Safety
11			1	0	#N/A	0	1065
12			2	2349	#N/A	0	4510
13			3	2797	#N/A	2046	1233
14			4	1501	#N/A	1180	3822
15			5	1940	#N/A	833	0
16			6	0	#N/A	1918	0
17			7	3049	#N/A	0	3228
18			8	4208	#N/A	1873	2890
19			9	0	#N/A	2052	0
20			10	6117	#N/A	1875	0
21			11	2127	#N/A	4461	1971
22			12	0	#N/A	4786	1542
23			13	0	#N/A	0	0
24			14	1455	#N/A	0	0

FIGURE 52-37 The source data for the chart.

Now it is time for the payoff! Select the range AG10:AK24 and create a scatter chart with smooth lines by selecting Insert Scatter (X, Y) Or Bubble Chart in the Charts group, and then Scatter With Smooth Lines from the Scatter section. The finished product is shown in Figure 52-38. This chart can show sales at any store of any category combination and will update when new data is downloaded.

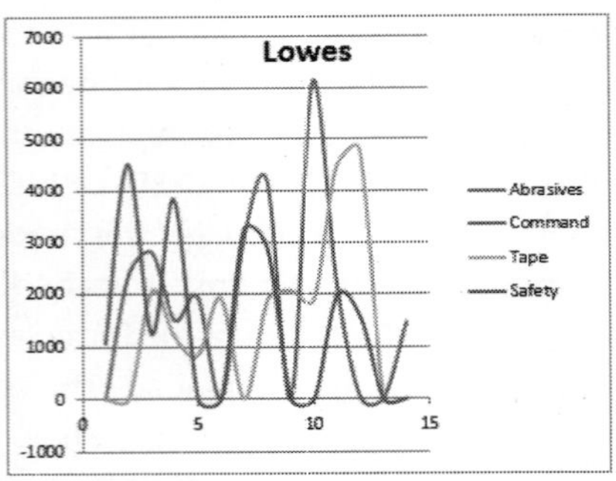

FIGURE 52-38 A dynamic dashboard summarizing the sales at Lowes of abrasives, tape, and safety equipment.

How can I insert a vertical line in a chart to separate pre- and post-merger performance?

Suppose your company was merged with another company on January 10, 2011 (see the file Verticalline.xlsx and Figure 52-39), and you are charting the daily sales. You might want to insert a vertical line in your graph to indicate the date of the merger. If you draw the vertical line with the Excel shapes feature, and the chart is moved, the line will be in the wrong place. To remedy this problem, I begin by selecting the range E10:F32 and creating a scatter chart with lines (the third option in the Scatter section). In the range B15:C16, I enter the date of the merger and the lower and upper limits on the y coordinates for my vertical line. (In this case, lower limit = 0 and upper limit =120.) Next, I copy the range B15:C16 and then right-click the chart. Clicking the Paste icon inserts the vertical line on the January 10 date.

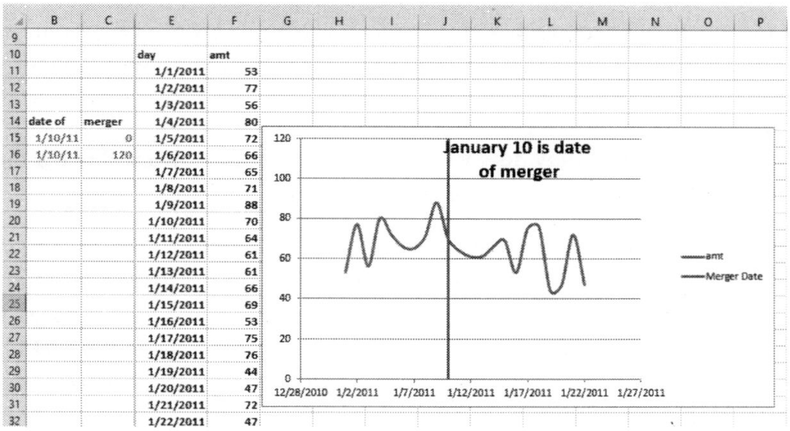

day	amt
1/1/2011	53
1/2/2011	77
1/3/2011	56
1/4/2011	80
1/5/2011	72
1/6/2011	66
1/7/2011	65
1/8/2011	71
1/9/2011	88
1/10/2011	70
1/11/2011	64
1/12/2011	61
1/13/2011	61
1/14/2011	66
1/15/2011	69
1/16/2011	53
1/17/2011	75
1/18/2011	76
1/19/2011	44
1/20/2011	47
1/21/2011	72
1/22/2011	47

date of	merger
1/10/11	0
1/10/11	120

FIGURE 52-39 Using a vertical line to indicate January 10, 2011 was the merger date.

How can I use a radar chart to portray how basketball team members differ in strength, speed, and jumping ability?

The file Radar.xlsx summarizes data for four athletes on the dimensions of speed, strength, and agility. First, select the range C2:F6. On the Insert tab, select the radar chart icon (Insert Surface Or Radar Chart; shown in Figure 52-40). From the options displayed, select Radar With Markers (the second option in the Radar section), and you will have the radar chart shown in Figure 52-41.

FIGURE 52-40 The radar chart icon.

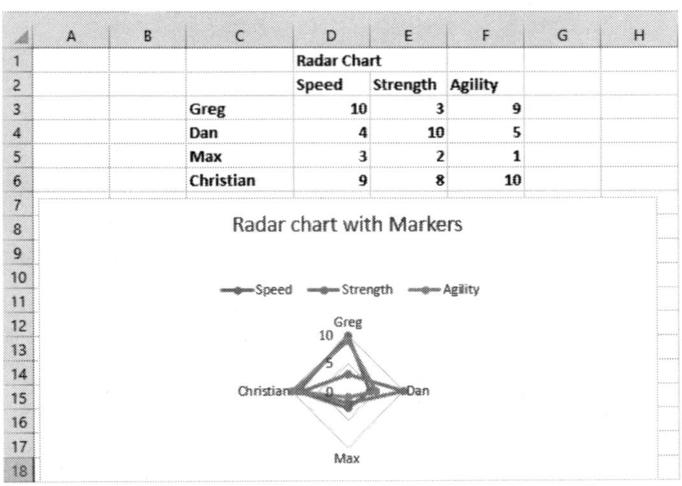

Radar Chart

	Speed	Strength	Agility
Greg	10	3	9
Dan	4	10	5
Max	3	2	1
Christian	9	8	10

FIGURE 52-41 A radar chart with markers.

The center of the radar chart indicates a score of 0; the farther a marker is from the center, the better the score. The chart makes it easy to see, for example, that Max scores poorly on all measures, while Christian scores well on all three measures.

I know I can use a scatter chart to display how two variables change. How can I use a bubble chart to summarize the variation of three variables?

While a scatter chart allows you to see how two variables vary, a bubble chart allows you to visually summarize three variables. The file Bubble.xlsx (see Figure 52-42) contains for several countries/regions the percentage variance in sales relative to the budget, the annual growth in sales, and each country/region's market size. To summarize this data in a bubble chart, select the range D9:F14, click the drop-down arrow by the scatter chart icon, and choose Bubble (the first bubble-chart option). Change the title of the chart to Area Bubble Chart. After adding (as described earlier in the chapter) a data label for each bubble, based on the country/region (cell range C10:C14), and placing the labels above each bubble, I obtain the bubble chart shown in Figure 52-42. (To add the labels, in the Format Data Labels pane, under Label Options, check the first choice, Value From Cells, and uncheck Y Value. Now you can select the cell range C10:C14 to insert the labels for the countries/regions in the chart. Under Label Position, select Above.) The areas of the bubbles are proportional to the market size of each country/region. For example, the US bubble contains 50 percent more area than the bubble for China.

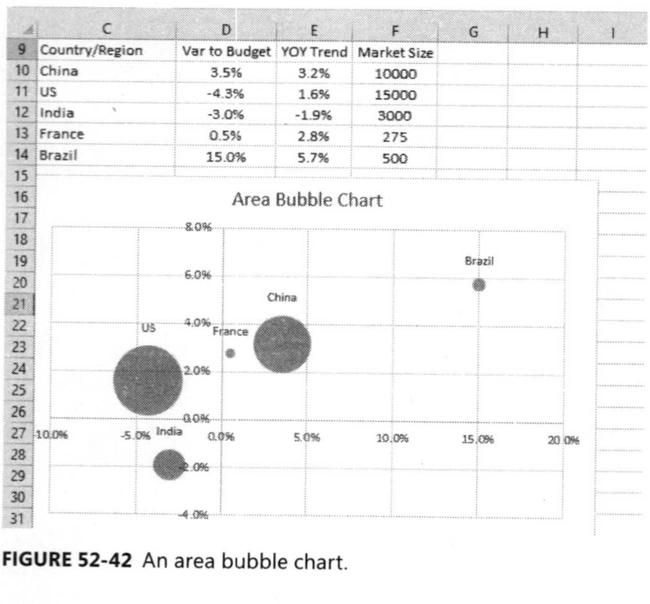

FIGURE 52-42 An area bubble chart.

How do I create waterfall charts with Excel 2016?

Earlier in the chapter, I showed you how versions of Excel preceding Excel 2016 could be tricked into creating waterfall charts. Here, I show you how easy it is to create waterfall charts using Excel 2016. In the workbook Watefallpandltemp.xlsx (see Figure 52-43), you are given data for a company's revenue; cost of goods sold (COGS); selling, general, and administrative expenses (SG&A); and profit. You want to create a waterfall chart that shows the progress from a revenue of $25,000 to a profit of $16,000. Gross margin and profit are totals and not *changes*, so they will need to be treated differently.

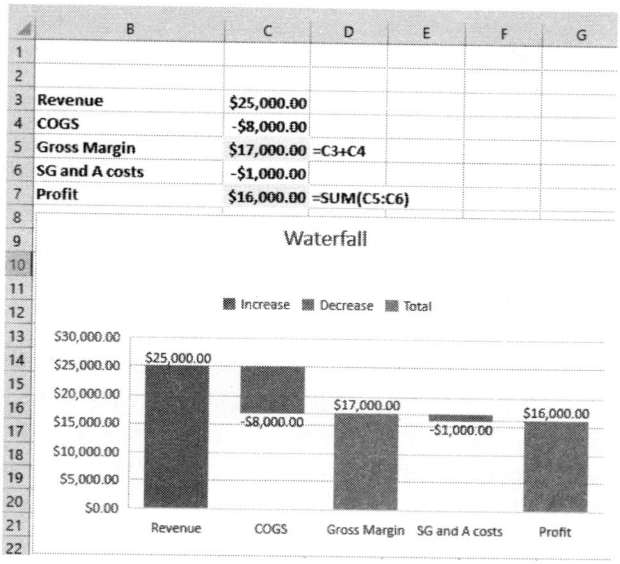

FIGURE 52-43 A waterfall chart that captures revenue, costs, and profit.

To begin, select the cell range B3:C7. On the Insert tab, select the Insert Waterfall Or Stock Chart option shown in Figure 52-44.

FIGURE 52-44 The Insert Waterfall Or Stock Chart icon.

Next, as shown in Figure 52-45, I select the Waterfall chart option.

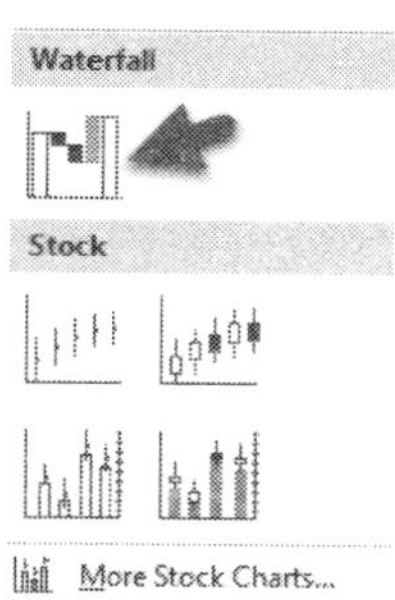

FIGURE 52-45 Selecting the Waterfall chart option.

You will obtain the waterfall chart shown in Figure 52-46.

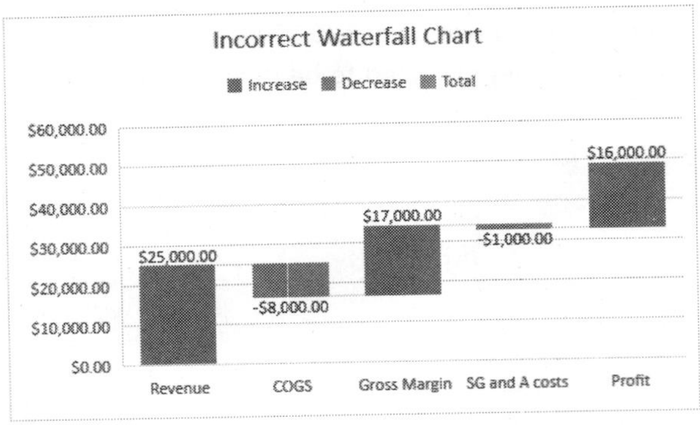

FIGURE 52-46 An incorrect waterfall chart.

The problem with this chart is that the Gross Margin and Profit columns should be anchored to the x-axis. To accomplish this goal, click the Gross Margin column twice, right-click the column, and choose Format Data Point; in the Format Data Point pane, select Set As Total, and then click the Profit column and select Set As Total for that column as well. You now obtain the correct waterfall chart shown earlier in Figure 52-43, which shows the total columns highlighted in gray. You now clearly see the path from a revenue of $25,000 to a profit of $16,000.

As another example of a waterfall chart, consider the data in the file Waterfallcashtemp.xlsx from this chapter's Templates folder (see Figure 52-47), which gives the opening cash balance at the beginning of the year, the monthly changes in cash balance, and the end-of-year cash balance.

	A	B	C	D
1	**Opening**	**110000**		
2	**Jan**	**-15000**		
3	**Feb**	**25000**		
4	**Mar**	**-100000**		
5	**Apr**	**-50000**		
6	**May**	**25000**		
7	**Jun**	**38000**		
8	**Jul**	**25000**		
9	**Aug**	**-15000**		
10	**Sep**	**25000**		
11	**Oct**	**50000**		
12	**Nov**	**75000**		
13	**Dec**	**-25000**		
14	**Closing**	**168000**	**=B1+SUM(B2:B13)**	

FIGURE 52-47 The cash flow for one year.

After selecting the cell range A1:B14 and creating a waterfall chart, I again find that the first and last points need to be changed to a total (click the Opening column twice, then right-click it, select Format Data Point, and select Set As Total; then select the Closing column and select Set As Total for that column as well.) You now obtain the waterfall chart shown in Figure 52-48.

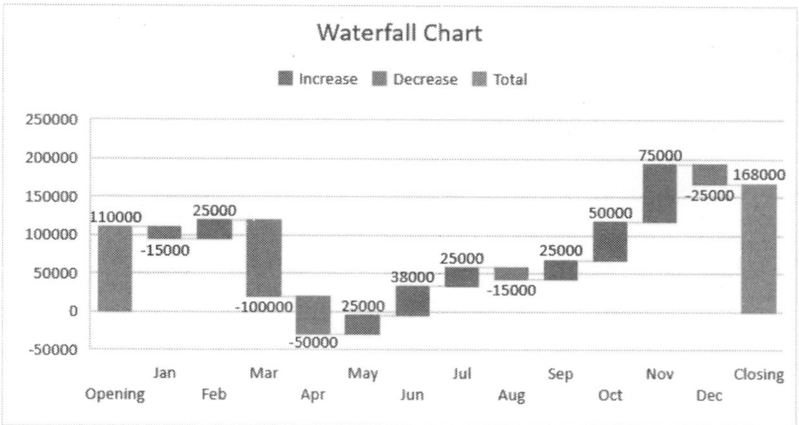

FIGURE 52-48 A cash-flow waterfall chart.

How do I use an Excel 2016 treemap and sunburst chart to summarize hierarchical data?

Treemap charts (also known as *mosaic* charts) and sunburst charts enable you to visualize hierarchical data. Hierarchical data is a way to organize data with multiple one-to-many relationships. The structure is based on the rule that one parent can have many children, but children can have only one parent. For example, if I look at the sales of a product based on *quarter of year, month of year,* and *week of month*, then the *quarter* is the parent with three children (the months in the quarter), and each month has either four or five children, corresponding to the weeks in the month.

As another example, consider a small bookstore. The parents in this case might be types of books (like children's books, art and photography books, and so on). The children of the art and photography category might be crafts and coffee-table books. For children's books, the children might be books in categories such as Age 3–5 and Age 6–8. Age 3–5 books might have subcategories of first-readers, ABCs, and Tolstoy for Tots.

Based on the Microsoft Office blog post entitled "Breaking down hierarchical data with treemap and sunburst charts" (*https://blogs.office.com/2015/08/11/breaking-down-hierarchical-data-with-treemap-and-sunburst-charts/*), let's create examples of treemap and sunburst charts. In the file Treemapbookstoretemp.xlsx from this chapter's Templates folder (see Figure 52-49), I have the revenue for different book categories at a small bookstore.

	A	B	C	D
1	GENRE	SUB-GENRE	TOPIC	REVENUE
2	Arts & Photogra	How-to Crafts		$ 2,711
3		Coffee-table	Photography	$ 2,309
4	Children's Book	Baby Books		$ 16,092
5		Age 3-5	1st Readers	$ 24,514
6			ABCs	$ 17,771
7			Tolstoy for Tot	$ 13,295
8		Age 6-8		$ 14,046
9		Pre-Teen & Teen		$ 18,046
10	Computers & In	Troubleshooting		$ 4,527
11	Mystery	Crime	Fiction	$ 11,186
12			True Crime	$ 8,790
13		Spy		$ 6,516
14			True Spy	$ 3,809
15	Nonfiction	Health	Diet	$ 3,293
16			Fitness	$ 6,891
17		History		$ 1,131
18	Magazine	Fashion	Women's	$ 7,315
19			Men's	$ 2,222
20		Home		$ 2,612
21		Other		$ 3,140
22		Sports	Sport's Illustra	$ 8,009
23			MMA	$ 4,257
24	Romance	Break up	Teen	$ 6,205
25			Young Adult	$ 25,193
26			Audiobooks	$ 3,045
27		Make Up		$ 15,050
28	Science Fiction	Apocalyptic		$ 10,200
29		Comics		$ 3,456

FIGURE 52-49 The data for treemap and sunburst charts.

To create a treemap chart, begin by selecting the cell range A1:D29. Then, on the Insert tab, select Insert Hierarchy Chart, the treemap icon shown in Figure 52-50.

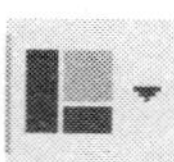

FIGURE 52-50 The treemap icon.

From the set of options shown in Figure 52-51, I choose the Treemap option and obtain the chart shown in Figure 52-52.

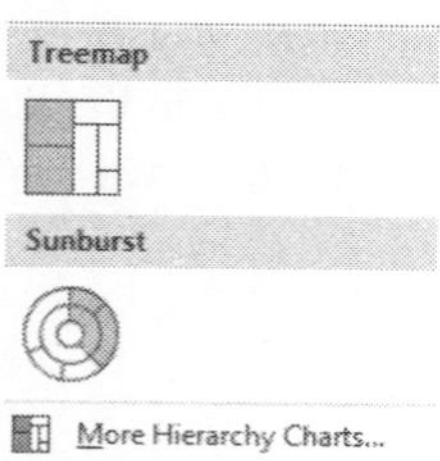

FIGURE 52-51 Options for selecting a treemap or sunburst chart.

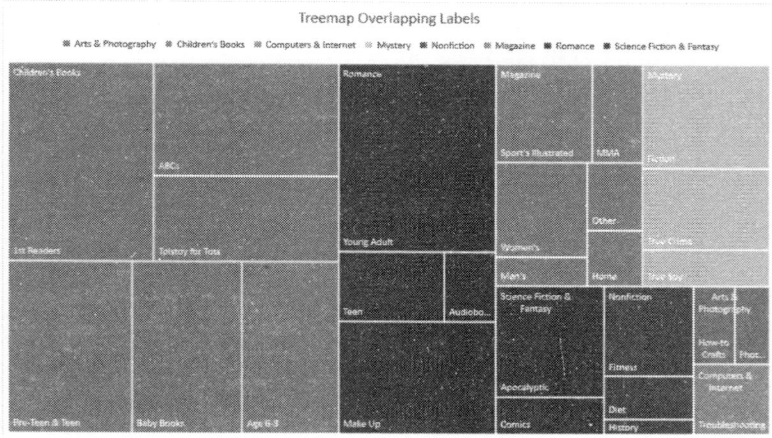

FIGURE 52-52 A treemap chart with overlapping labels.

This treemap chart shows the fraction of total sales belonging to each type of book. Notice that all book types with the same parent are portrayed with the same color. This chart shows, for example, that a little less than half your sales (actually 42 percent) come from children's books. You can hover over a rectangle to get the data. If you right-click any rectangle, you can select Format Data Series and change the labels to banner labels, which places the labels for each parent alone in its own rectangle.

Note that because of a lack of space, your treemap chart does not show the Age 3–5 label. A sunburst chart solves this problem. If I again select the cell range A1:D29 and choose the Sunburst chart option, I obtain the sunburst chart shown in Figure 52-53. (See the file Sunburstfinal.xlsx.)

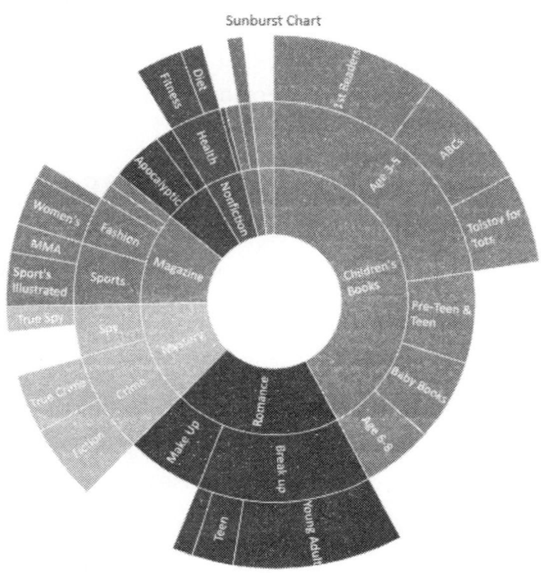

FIGURE 52-53 A sunburst chart for the bookstore.

Note that I now see the breakdown of Age 3–5 books into its three subcategories. Of course, in the sunburst chart, it is more difficult to determine the fraction of all sales derived from each type of book.

Problems

The file Cakes.xlsx contains for each month the number of salespeople and revenue for a bakery. Use this data for Problems 1–4.

1. Create a combination chart with a secondary axis to summarize the monthly number of salespeople and revenues.
2. Graph monthly revenue and insert data labels on the chart.
3. Graph the number of salespeople and insert a data table below the chart.
4. Plot monthly sales using a cake image for the columns, rather than a column chart.

The file Hiddenpivot.xlsx contains the sales of candy between 2009 and 2017. Use this data for Problems 5 and 6.

5. Filter the data so that only 2013 sales appear in the spreadsheet but all the data appears in the chart.
6. Summarize each year's sales in a PivotTable, and also show the percentage improvement in sales from year to year.
7. Using the data in the file Salestracker.xlsx, highlight the top two salespeople each month with an up arrow, the bottom two with a down arrow, and the others with a flat (right) arrow.
8. The Indiana University basketball team considers at least 50 deflections per game a good performance and 30 or fewer deflections a poor performance. In the last six games, Indiana had 25, 55, 45, 43, 59, and 39 deflections. Plot this data on a band chart.
9. Plot the data of Problem 8 on a column chart in which good defensive games are highlighted in green, bad games in red, and other games in orange.
10. During its first year of operation, a firm's revenue was $5 million and expenses were $6 million. For different assumed growth rates in expenses and revenues, plot 10 years of revenues and expenses; ensure that the graph title shows the year that the revenue first exceeds expenses.

The file Crimedata.xlsx contains annual violent crimes, property crimes, and murders in the United States. Use this data for Problems 11–12.

11. Create a graph showing the number of crimes each year. Use check boxes to control which series are plotted.
12. Create a histogram that summarizes murders that updates automatically when new data is included.

13. The following table contains performance reviews for five employees. Use a radar chart to summarize the performance reviews.

Person	Hard working	Collegial	Completes tasks on time	Punctual
Wayne	1	2	3	4
Vivian	5	6	7	8
Greg	10	9.5	9	8.5
Jen	9	2	9	4
Wanda	1	1.5	2	2.5

14. A project consists of five activities. The start time and duration of each activity are given below. Summarize this data in a Gantt chart.

Activity	Start time	Duration
A	0	4
B	3	6
C	5	7
D	6	8
E	3	6

15. A company's profit, revenue, and cost breakdown for a year are given below. Summarize this data in a waterfall chart.

Item	Amount
Revenue	$300,000
Profit	$65,000
Labor Costs	$100.000
Material Costs	$80,000
Overhead Costs	$55,000

16. The file Problem16data.xlsx contains information about lunch and breakfast sales at Mel's Diner. Create a treemap chart to summarize this sales data. Hint: You will need to aggregate the data,

17. Use the data in the file Problem16data.xlsx to create a sunburst chart that summarizes restaurant sales.

CHAPTER 53

Estimating straight-line relationships

Questions answered in this chapter:

- How can I determine the relationship between monthly production and monthly operating costs?
- How accurately does this relationship explain the monthly variation in plant-operating costs?
- How accurate are my predictions likely to be?
- When estimating a straight-line relationship, which functions can I use to get the slope and intercept of the line that best fits the data?

Suppose you manage a plant that manufactures small refrigerators. National headquarters tells you how many refrigerators to produce each month. For budgeting purposes, you want to forecast your monthly operating costs, and you need answers to the questions that are the focus of this chapter.

Every business analyst should have the ability to estimate the relationship between important business variables. In Microsoft Excel, the *trend curve*, which I'll discuss in this chapter as well as in Chapter 54, "Modeling exponential growth," and in Chapter 55, "The power curve," is often helpful in determining the relationship between two variables. The variable that analysts try to predict is called the *dependent variable*. The variable you use for prediction is called the *independent variable*. The following table demonstrates some examples of business relationships you might want to estimate:

Independent variable	Dependent variable
Units produced by plant in a month	Monthly cost of operating plant
Dollars spent on advertising in a month	Monthly sales
Number of employees	Annual travel expenses
Company revenue	Number of employees (headcount)
Monthly return on the stock market	Monthly return on a stock (for example, Dell)
Square feet in home	Value of home

The first step in determining how two variables are related is to graph the data points (by using the Scatter Chart option on the Insert tab) so that the independent variable is on the x-axis and the dependent variable is on the y-axis. With the chart selected, you click a data point (all data points are then displayed in blue), and on the Chart Tools Design tab, click Add Chart Element in the Chart Layouts group, select Trendline, and then click More Trendline Options (or right-click and select Add Trendline). You'll see the Format Trendline pane, which is shown in Figure 53-1.

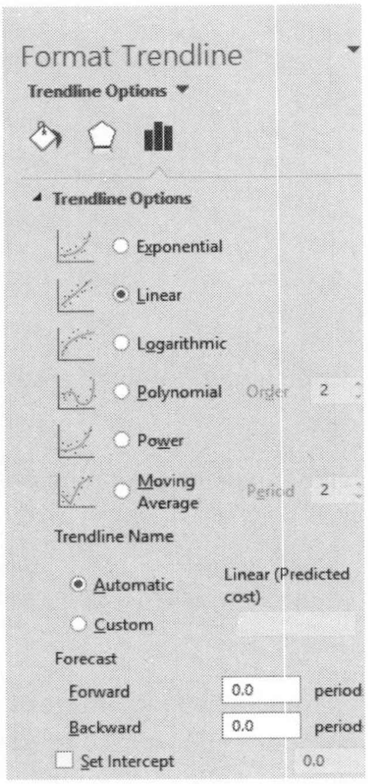

FIGURE 53-1 The Format Trendline options.

If your graph indicates that a straight line is a reasonable fit for the points, choose the Linear option. If the graph indicates that the dependent variable increases at an accelerating rate, the Exponential (and perhaps Power) option probably fits the relationship. If the graph shows that the dependent variable increases at a decreasing rate or that the dependent variable decreases at a decreasing rate, the Power option is probably the most relevant.

In this chapter, I'll focus on the Linear option. In Chapter 54, I'll discuss the Exponential option, and in Chapter 55, I'll cover the Power option. In Chapter 62, "Using moving averages to understand time series," I'll discuss the moving average curve, and in Chapter 86, "Pricing products by using subjectively determined demand," I'll discuss the polynomial curve. (The logarithmic curve is of little value in this discussion, so I won't address it.)

Answers to this chapter's questions

How can I determine the relationship between monthly production and monthly operating costs?

The file Costestimate.xlsx, shown in Figure 53-2, contains data about the units produced and the monthly plant-operating cost for a 14-month period. You are interested in predicting monthly operating costs from units produced, which helps the plant manager determine the operating budget and better understand the cost of producing refrigerators.

	B	C	D	E	F
1				sum errors	-0.0304
2	Month	Units Produced	Monthly Plant cost	Predicted cost	Error
3	1	1260	123118	118872.66	4245.342
4	2	1007	99601	102612.68	-3011.68
5	3	1296	132000	121186.33	10813.67
6	4	873	80000	94000.671	-14000.7
7	5	532	52000	72085.044	-20085
8	6	476	58625	68485.997	-9861
9	7	482	74624	68871.609	5752.391
10	8	1273	110000	119708.15	-9708.15
11	9	692	81000	82368.036	-1368.04
12	10	690	73507	82239.499	-8732.5
13	11	564	95024	74141.642	20882.36
14	12	470	88004	68100.385	19903.62
15	13	675	70000	81275.468	-11275.5
16	14	870	110253	93807.865	16445.14
17	15	1100		108589.67	

FIGURE 53-2 The plant operating data.

Begin by creating an XY chart (or a scatter chart) that displays the independent variable (units produced) on the x-axis and the dependent variable (monthly plant cost) on the y-axis. The column of data that you want to display on the x-axis must be located to the left of the column of data you want to display on the y-axis. To create the graph, select the data in the range C2:D16 (including the labels in cells C2 and D2). Then click Insert Scatter (X, Y) Or Bubble Chart in the Charts group on the Insert tab, and select the first option, Scatter (with only markers) as the chart type. You'll see the graph shown in Figure 53-3.

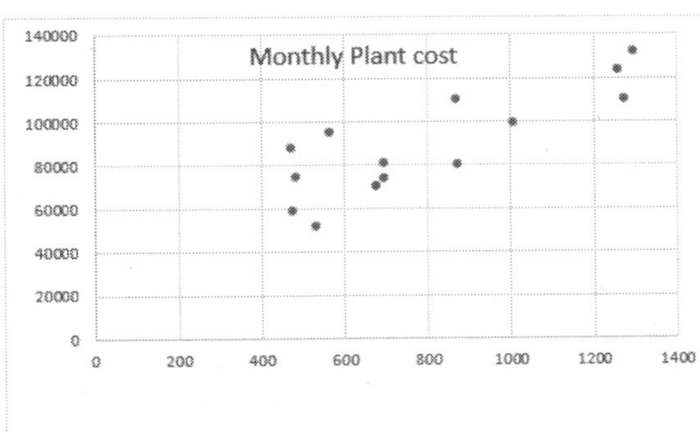

FIGURE 53-3 A scatter chart of the operating cost versus the units produced.

Looking at the scatter chart, it seems reasonable that a straight line (or linear relationship) exists between the units produced and the monthly operating costs. You can see the straight line that best fits the points by adding a trendline to the chart. Click within the chart to select it, and then click a data point. All the data points are displayed in blue, with an X covering each point. Right-click a point, and then click Add Trendline. In the Format Trendline pane, select the Linear option, and then select the Display Equation On Chart and the Display R-Squared Value On Chart check boxes, as shown in Figure 53-4.

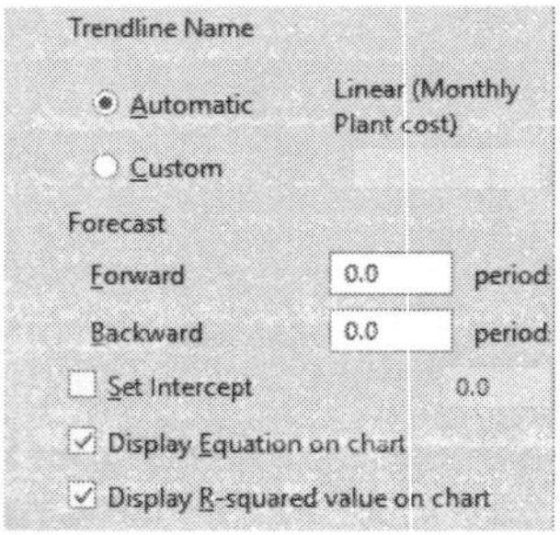

FIGURE 53-4 Selecting trendline options.

After closing the Format Trendline pane and adding axis labels and a chart title, you'll see the results shown in Figure 53-5. Notice that I added a title to the chart and labels for the x-axis and y-axis by selecting Add Chart Element from the Chart Tools Design tab, and then Axis Titles and Chart Title.

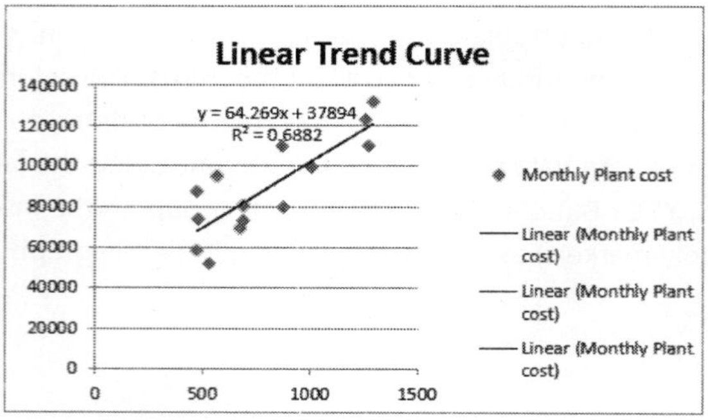

FIGURE 53-5 A completed trendline.

If you want to add more decimal points to the values in the equation, select the trendline equation, and then choose Format Selection from the Current Selection group on the Chart Tools Format tab. Select Number, and the Number section opens in the Format Trendline pane. Select Number from the Category list, and then update the Decimal Places box.

How does Excel determine the best-fitting line? Excel chooses the line that minimizes (over all lines that could be drawn) the sum of the squared vertical distance from each point to the line. The vertical distance from each point to the line is called an *error*, or *residual*. The line created by Excel is called the *least-squares line*. You minimize the sum of squared errors rather than the sum of the errors because in simply summing the errors, positive and negative errors can cancel each other out. For example, a point 100 units above the line and a point 100 units below the line cancel each other out if you add errors. If you square errors, however, the fact that your predictions for each point are wrong is used by Excel to find the best-fitting line.

Thus, Excel calculates that the best-fitting straight line for predicting the monthly operating costs from the monthly units produced, as follows:

```
(Monthly operating cost)=37,894.0956+64.2687(Units produced)
```

By copying the formula =64.2687*C3+37894.0956 from cell E3 to the cell range E4:E17, you compute the predicted cost for each observed data point. For example, when 1,260 units are produced, the predicted cost is $123,118. (See Figure 53-2.)

You should not use a least-squares line to predict values of an independent variable that lie outside the range for which you have data. The line in this example should be used only to predict monthly plant operating costs during months in which production is between approximately 450 and 1,300 units.

The intercept of this line is $37,894.10, which can be interpreted as the monthly fixed cost. So, even if the plant does not produce any refrigerators during a month, this graph estimates that the plant will still incur costs of $37,894.10. The slope of this line (64.2687) indicates that each extra refrigerator produced increases monthly costs by $64.27. Thus, the variable cost of producing a refrigerator is estimated to be $64.27.

In cells F3:F16, I computed the errors (or residuals) for each data point. I defined the error for each data point as the amount by which the point varies from the least-squares line. For each month, the error equals the observed cost minus the predicted cost. Copying from F3 to F4:F16 the formula =D3-E3 computes the error for each data point. A positive error indicates a point is above the least-squares line, and a negative error indicates that the point is below the least-squares line. In cell F1, I computed the sum of the errors with the formula =SUM(F3:F16) and obtained –0.0304. In reality, for any least-squares line, the sum of the errors should equal 0. (I obtained –0.0304 because I rounded the equation to four decimal points.) The fact that the errors sum to 0 implies that the least-squares line has the intuitively satisfying property of splitting the points in half.

How accurately does this relationship explain the monthly variation in plant-operating cost?

Clearly, each month both the operating cost and the units produced vary. A natural question is, "What percentage of the monthly variation in operating costs is explained by the monthly variation in units produced?" The answer to this question is the *R-squared value* (0.69, shown earlier in Figure 53-5). You can state that the linear relationship explains 69 percent of the variation in monthly operating costs. This implies that 31 percent of the variation in monthly operating costs is explained by other factors. Using multiple regression (see Chapters 57 through 59), you can try to determine other factors that influence operating costs.

People always ask, what is a good R-squared value? There is really no definitive answer to this question. With one independent variable, of course, a larger R-squared value indicates a better fit of the data than a smaller R-squared value. A better measure of the accuracy of your predictions is the standard error of the regression, which I'll describe in the next section.

How accurate are my predictions likely to be?

When you fit a line to points, you obtain a standard error of the regression that measures the *spread* of the points around the least-squares line. The standard error associated with a least-squares line can be computed with the STEYX function. The syntax of this function is STEYX(yrange,xrange), where *yrange* contains the values of the dependent variable, and *xrange* contains the values of the independent variable. In cell K1, I computed the standard error of the cost-estimate line in the file Costestimate.xlsx, using the formula =STEYX(D3:D16,C3:C16). The result is shown in Figure 53-6.

Approximately 68 percent of the points should be within one standard error of regression (SER) of the least-squares line, and about 95 percent of the points should be within two SER of the least-squares line. These measures are reminiscent of the descriptive statistics rule of thumb that I described in Chapter 42, "Summarizing data by using descriptive statistics." In this example, the absolute value of around 68 percent of the errors should be $13,772 or smaller, and the absolute value of around 95 percent of the errors should be $27,544 (or 2*13,772) or smaller. Looking at the errors in column F, you can see that 10 out of 14, or 71 percent, of the points are within one SER of the least-squares line and all (100 percent) of the points are within two standard SER of the least-squares line. Any point that is more than two SER from the least-squares line is called an *outlier.* Looking for causes of outliers can often help you improve the operation of your business. For example, a month in which the actual operating costs are $30,000 higher than anticipated would be a cost outlier on the high side. If you could ascertain the cause of this high cost outlier and prevent it from recurring, you would clearly improve your plant's efficiency. Similarly, consider a month in which the actual costs are $30,000 less than expected. If you could ascertain the cause of this low-cost outlier and ensure it occurred more often, you would improve the plant's efficiency.

	H	I	J	K
1	slope	64.2687	std err	13771.85
2	intercept	37894.1		
3	RSq	0.688203		
4				

FIGURE 53-6 The computation of slope, intercept, RSQ, and standard error of regression.

When estimating a straight-line relationship, which functions can I use to get the slope and intercept of the line that best fits the data?

The Excel SLOPE(yrange,xrange) and INTERCEPT(yrange,xrange) functions return the slope and intercept, respectively, of the least-squares line. Thus, entering in cell I1 the formula SLOPE(D3:D16,C3:C16) returns the slope (64.27) of the least-squares line, as you can see in Figure 53-6. Entering in cell I2 the formula INTERCEPT(D3:D16,C3:C16) returns the intercept (37,894.1) of the least-squares line. By the way, the RSQ(yrange,xrange) function returns the R-squared value associated with a least-squares line. So, entering in cell I3 the formula RSQ(D3:D16,C3:C16) returns the R-squared value of 0.6882 for the least-squares line.

Problems

The file Delldata.xlsx contains monthly returns for the Standard & Poor's stock index and for Dell stock. The *beta* of a stock is defined as the slope of the least-squares line used to predict the monthly return for a stock from the monthly return for the market. Use this file for Problems 1–4.

1. Estimate the beta of Dell.

2. Interpret the meaning of Dell's beta.

3. If you believe a recession is coming, would you rather invest in a high-beta or a low-beta stock?

4. During a month in which the market goes up 5 percent, you are 95 percent sure that Dell's stock price will increase between which range of values?

The file Housedata.xlsx gives the square footage and sales prices for several houses in Bellevue, Washington. Use this file for Problems 5–7.

5. You are going to build a 500-square-foot addition to your house. How much do you think your home value will increase as a result?

6. What percentage of the variation in home value is explained by variation in house size?

7. A 3,000-square-foot house is selling for $500,000. Is this price out of line with typical real-estate values in Bellevue? What might cause this discrepancy?

8. We know that 32 degrees Fahrenheit is equivalent to 0 degrees Celsius, and that 212 degrees Fahrenheit is equivalent to 100 degrees Celsius. Use the trend curve to determine the relationship between Fahrenheit and Celsius temperatures. When you create your initial chart, before clicking Finish, you must indicate that the data is in columns and not rows, because with only two data points, Excel assumes different variables are in different rows.

9. The file Betadata.xlsx contains the monthly returns on the Standard & Poor's index, as well as the monthly returns on Cinergy, Dell, Intel, Microsoft, Nortel, and Pfizer. Estimate the beta of each stock.

10. The file Electiondata.xlsx contains, for several elections, the percentage of votes Republicans gained from voting machines (counted on Election Day) and the percentage Republicans gained from absentee ballots (counted after Election Day). Suppose that during an election, Republicans obtained 49 percent of the votes on Election Day and 62 percent of the absentee ballot votes. The Democratic candidate cried "Fraud." What do you think?

11. The file Oldfaithful.xlsx gives the duration between eruptions of the Old Faithful Geyser and the length of the next eruption. Suppose it has been four minutes since the last eruption. You are 95 percent sure that the length of the next eruption is between _____ and ____ minutes.

12. The file Dailydow.xlsx gives daily values for the Dow Jones index during the period 1996–2010. What is the R-squared value when you predict tomorrow's Dow Jones from today's values? Does this high R-squared value mean that the market is easy to predict?

13. In the Problem13data.xlsx file are listed the size (in square feet) and appraised value for several homes in the River Oaks area of Houston. Estimate the relationship between house size and price. What percentage of variation in home price is explained by house size? You would estimate that an extra square foot of home size increases home price by how much?

CHAPTER 54

Modeling exponential growth

Question answered in this chapter:

- How can I model the growth of a company's revenue over time?

If you want to value a company, it's important to have some idea about its future revenues. Although the future might not be like the past, you often begin a valuation analysis of a corporation by studying the company's revenue growth during the recent past. Many analysts like to fit a trend curve to recent revenue growth. To fit a trend curve, you plot the year on the x-axis (for example, the first year of data is Year 1, the second year of data is Year 2, and so on), and on the y-axis, you plot the company's revenue.

Usually, the relationship between time and revenue is not a straight line. Recall that a straight line always has the same slope, which implies that when the independent variable (in this case, the year) is increased by 1, the prediction for the dependent variable (revenue) increases by the same amount. For most companies, revenue grows by a fairly constant percentage each year. If this is the case, as revenue increases, the annual increase in revenue also increases. After all, revenue growth of 10 percent of $1 million means revenue grows by $100,000. Revenue growth of 10 percent of $100 million means revenue grows by $10 million. This analysis implies that a trend curve for forecasting revenue should grow more steeply and have an increasing slope. The exponential function has the property that as the independent variable increases by 1, the dependent variable increases by the same percentage. This relationship is exactly what you need to model revenue growth.

The equation for the exponential function is $y=ae^{bx}$. Here, *x* is the value of the independent variable (in this example, the year), whereas *y* is the value of the dependent variable (in this case, the annual revenue). The value *e* (approximately 2.7182) is the base of natural logarithms. If you select Exponential from Excel's trendline options, Excel calculates the values of *a* and *b* that best fit the data. Let's look at an example.

Answers to this chapter's question

How can I model the growth of a company's revenue over time?

The file Ciscoexpo.xlsx, shown in Figure 54-1, contains the revenues for Cisco for the years 1990 through 1999. All the revenues are in millions of dollars. In 1990, for example, Cisco's revenues were $103.47 million.

	A	B	C	D
1		Year 1=1990		
2				
3	Year	Sales	Prediction	Ratio
4	1	70	103.471229	
5	2	183	182.848984	1.767148
6	3	340	323.121233	1.767148
7	4	649	571.003071	1.767148
8	5	1243	1009.04699	1.767148
9	6	1979	1783.13546	1.767148
10	7	4096	3151.06443	1.767148
11	8	6440	5568.39749	1.767148
12	9	8459	9840.18301	1.767148
13	10	12154	17389.0606	1.767148
14				
15	16		529558.325	

FIGURE 54-1 Cisco's annual revenues for the years 1990 through 1999.

To fit an exponential curve to this data, begin by selecting the cell range A3:B13. Next, on the Insert tab, in the Charts group, click Insert Scatter. Selecting the first chart option (Scatter, with only markers) creates the chart shown in Figure 54-2.

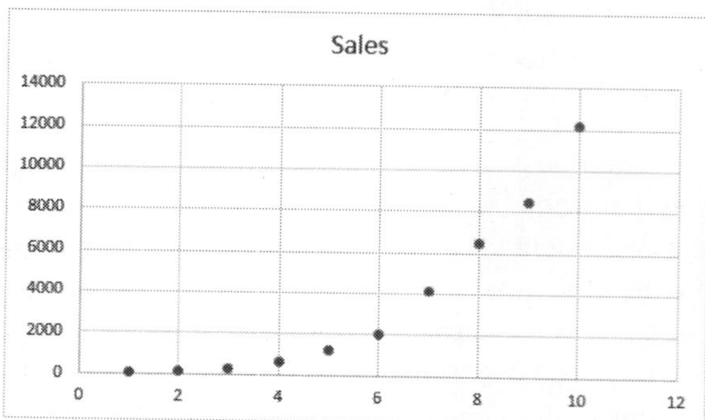

FIGURE 54-2 A scatter chart for the Cisco trend curve.

Since the slope of a straight line is constant, fitting a straight line to this data would be ridiculous. When a graph's slope is rapidly increasing, as in this example, an exponential growth will usually provide a good fit for the data.

To obtain the exponential curve that best fits this data, right-click a data point (all the points turn blue), and then click Add Trendline. In the Format Trendline pane, select the Exponential option in the Trendline Options area, and also select the Display Equation On Chart and Display R-Squared Value On Chart check boxes. You'll see the trend curve shown in Figure 54-3.

The estimate of Cisco's revenue in year *x* (remember that *x*=1 is the year 1990) is computed from the following formula:

```
Estimated Revenue=58.552664e.569367x
```

I computed estimated revenue in the cell range C4:C13 by copying from C4 to C5:C13 the formula =58.552664*EXP(0.569367*A4). For example, the estimate of Cisco's revenue in 1999 (year 10) is $17.389 billion.

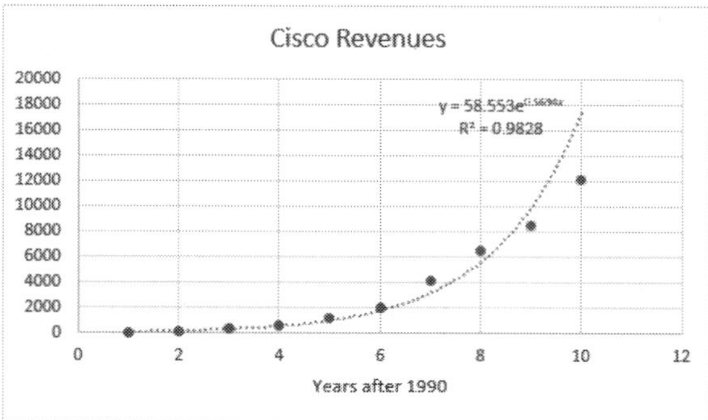

FIGURE 54-3 An exponential trend curve for Cisco's revenues.

Notice that most of the data points are very close to the fitted exponential curve. This pattern indicates that exponential growth does a good job of explaining Cisco's revenue growth during the 1990s. The fact that the R-squared value (0.98) is very close to 1 is also consistent with the visual evidence of a good fit.

Remember that whenever *x* increases by 1, the estimate from an exponential curve increases by the same percentage. You can verify this fact by computing the ratio of each year's estimated revenue to the previous year's estimated revenue. To compute this ratio, copy from D5 to D6:D13 the formula =C5/C4. You'll find that the estimate of Cisco's growth rate is 76.7 percent per year, which is the best estimate of Cisco's annual growth rate for the years 1990 through 1999. This estimate of a company's annual growth rate over a period is known as *Compound Annual Growth Rate* (or CAGR.)

Of course, to use the CAGR in valuation analysis, you need to ask yourself whether it's likely that this growth rate can be maintained. Be forewarned that exponential growth cannot continue forever. For example, if you use the exponential trend curve to forecast revenues for 2005 (year 16), Cisco's 2005 predicted revenues would be $530 billion. If this estimate were realized, Cisco's revenues would have tripled the 2005 revenues of the world's largest company (Walmart). This seems highly unrealistic. The moral is that during its early years, the revenue growth for a technology company follows exponential growth. After a while, the growth rate slows down. If Wall Street analysts had understood this fact during the late 1990s, the Internet stock bubble might have been avoided. Note that during 1999, Cisco's actual revenue fell well short of the trend curve's estimated revenue. This fact may well have indicated the start of the technology slowdown, which began during late 2000.

Often the Gompertz or Logistic curve (commonly called *S curve*) fits the annual growth of revenue for new companies better than exponential growth. This is because S curves capture the eventual slowdown in revenue growth. My book *Marketing Analytics: Data-Driven Techniques with Microsoft Excel* (Wiley, 2014) contains an extensive discussion of S curves.

By the way, why must you use *x*=1 instead of *x*=1990? If you used *x*=1990, Excel would have to juggle numbers around the size of e^{1990}. A number this large causes Excel a great deal of difficulty.

Problems

The file Exponentialdata.xlsx contains the annual sales revenue for Staples, Walmart, and Intel. Use this data to work through the first five problems for this chapter.

1. For each company, fit an exponential-trend curve to its sales data.
2. For which company does exponential growth have the best fit with its revenue growth?
3. For which company does exponential growth have the worst fit with its revenue growth?
4. For each company, estimate the annual percentage growth rate for revenues.
5. For each company, use your trend curve to predict the 2003 revenues.
6. The file Impalas.xlxs contains the prices of 2009, 2008, 2007, and 2006 Impalas during 2010. From this data, what can you conclude about how a new car loses its value as it grows older?
7. The file Problem7data.xlsx contains Google's annual revenues during the years 2005–2013. Use this data to estimate Google's CAGR and predict Google's 2014 revenue.

CHAPTER 55

The power curve

Question answered in this chapter:

- As my company produces more of a product, it learns how to make the product more efficiently. Can I model the relationship between units produced and the time needed to produce a unit?

A *power curve* is calculated by means of the equation $y = ax^b$. In the equation, *a* and *b* are constants. Using a trend curve, you can determine the values of *a* and *b* that make the power curve best fit a scatter chart. In most situations, *a* is greater than 0. When this is the case, the slope of the power curve depends on the value of *b*, as follows:

- For $b>1$, *y* increases as *x* increases, and the slope of the power curve increases as *x* increases.
- For $0<b<1$, *y* increases as *x* increases, and the slope of the power curve decreases as *x* increases.
- For $b=1$, the power curve is a straight line.
- For $b<0$, *y* decreases as *x* increases, and the power curve flattens out as *x* increases.

Next, I'll cover examples of different relationships that can be modeled by a power curve. These examples are contained in the file Powerexamples.xlsx.

If you are trying to predict the total production cost as a function of units produced, you might find a relationship similar to that shown in Figure 55-1. Notice that *b* equals 2. As I mentioned previously, with this value of *b*, the cost of production increases with the number of units produced. The slope becomes steeper, which indicates that each additional unit costs more to produce. This relationship might occur because increased production requires more overtime labor, which costs more than regular labor.

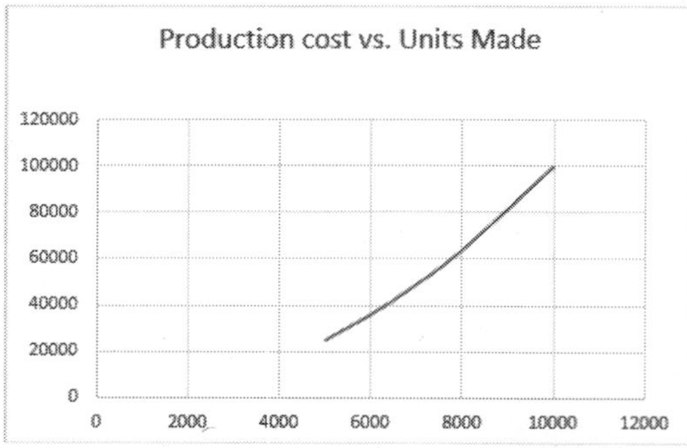

FIGURE 55-1 Predicting cost as a function of the number of units produced.

If you are trying to predict sales as a function of advertising expenditures, you might find a curve similar to that shown in Figure 55-2.

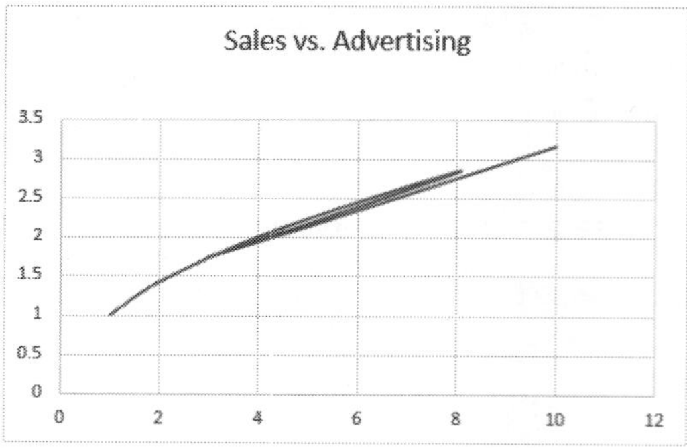

FIGURE 55-2 Plotting sales as a function of advertising.

Here, *b* equals 0.5, which is between 0 and 1. When *b* has a value in this range, sales increase with increased advertising but at a decreasing rate. Thus, the power curve allows you to model the idea of diminishing return—that each additional dollar spent on advertising will provide less benefit.

If you are trying to predict the time needed to produce the last unit of a product, based on the number of units produced to date, you often find a scatter chart is useful, similar to that shown in Figure 55-3.

Here you find that *b* equals –0.1. Because *b* is less than 0, the time needed to produce each unit decreases, but the rate of decrease—that is, the rate of "learning"—slows down. This relationship means that during the early stages of a product's life cycle, huge savings in labor time occur as learning accrues. As the process continues and you make more of a product, however, savings in labor time occur at a slower rate. The relationship between cumulative units produced and time needed to produce the last unit is called the *learning* or *experience curve*.

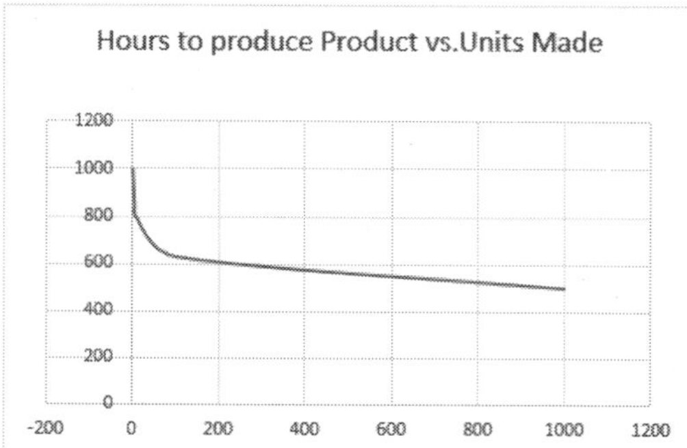

FIGURE 55-3 Plotting the time needed to build a unit based on cumulative production.

A power curve has the following properties:

- **Property 1** If *x* increases by 1 percent, *y* increases by approximately *b* percent.
- **Property 2** Whenever *x* doubles, *y* increases by the same percentage.

Suppose that demand for a product as a function of price can be modeled as $1000(\text{Price})^{-2}$. Property 1 then implies that a 1 percent increase in price will lower demand (regardless of price) by 2 percent. In this case, the exponent *b* (without the negative sign) is called the *elasticity*. I will discuss elasticity further in Chapter 84, "Estimating a demand curve." With this background, let's take a look at how to fit a power curve to data.

Answer to this chapter's question

As my company produces more of a product, it learns how to make the product more efficiently. Can I model the relationship between units produced and the time needed to produce a unit?

The file Fax.xlsx contains data about the number of fax machines produced and the unit cost (in 1982 dollars) of producing the "last" fax machine made during each year. In 1983, for example, 70,000 fax machines were produced, and the cost of producing the last fax machine was $3,416. The data is shown in Figure 55-4.

	A	B	C	D	E	F	G
1	Learning curve FAX data						
2							
3	Year	Production	Cumulative Production	Unit Cost	Forecast		
4	1982	64000	64000	$3,700.00	3955.81		
5	1983	70000	134000	$3,416.00	3280.54		
6	1984	100000	234000	$3,125.00	2848.51		
7	1985	150000	384000	$2,583.00	2512.63		
8	1986	175000	559000	$2,166.00	2284.66		
9	1987	400000	959000	$1,833.00	1992.72		
10	1988	785000	1744000	$1,788.00	1712.60		
11	1989	1000000	2744000		1526.85		learning
12		double	3488000		1436.83		percentage
13		cumulative production					0.838975
14							

FIGURE 55-4 The data used to plot the learning curve for producing fax machines.

Because a learning curve tries to predict either the cost or the time needed to produce a unit from the data about cumulative production, I've calculated in column C the cumulative number of fax machines produced by the end of each year. In cell C4, I refer to cell B4 to show the number of fax machines produced in 1982. By copying from C5 to C6:C10 the formula =SUM($B$4:B4), I compute the cumulative fax-machine production for the end of each year.

You can now create a scatter chart that shows the cumulative units produced on the x-axis and the unit cost on the y-axis. After creating the chart, click one of the data points to select them (the data points will be displayed in blue), then right-click and select the Add Trendline option. In the Format Trendline pane, select the Power option (under Trendline Options) and then select the Display Equation On Chart and the Display R-Squared Value On Chart check boxes, at the bottom of the pane. With these settings, you obtain the chart shown in Figure 55-5. The curve drawn represents the power curve that best fits the data.

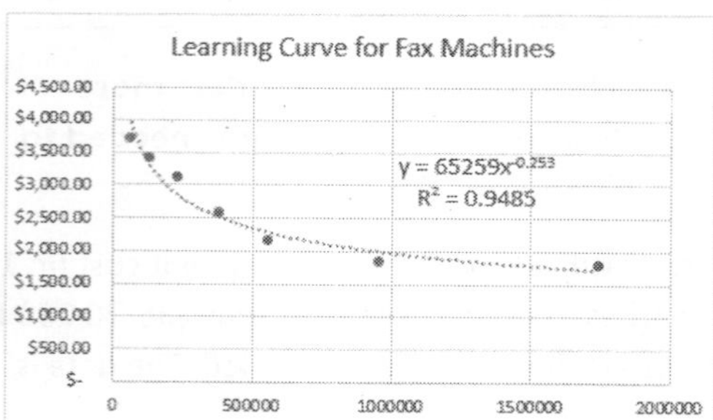

FIGURE 55-5 The learning curve for producing fax machines.

The power curve predicts the cost of producing a fax machine, as follows:

```
Cost of producing fax machine=65,259(cumulative units produced)^-0.2533
```

Notice that most data points are near the fitted power curve and that the R-squared value is nearly 1, indicating that the power curve fits the data well.

By copying from cell E4 to E5:E10 the formula =65259*C4^–0.2533, you compute the predicted cost for the last fax machine produced during each year. (The carat symbol [^], which is located over the 6 key, is used to raise a number to a power.)

If you estimated that 1,000,000 fax machines were produced in 1989, after computing the total 1989 production (2,744,000) in cell C11, you can copy the forecast equation to cell E11 to predict that the last fax machine produced in 1989 cost $1,526.85.

Remember that Property 2 of the power curve states that whenever *x* doubles, *y* increases by the same percentage. By entering twice the cumulative 1988 production in cell C12 and copying your forecast formula in E10 to cell E12, you'll find that doubling the cumulative units produced reduces the predicted cost to 83.8 percent of its previous value (1,516.83/1,712.60). For this reason, the current learning curve is known as an 84-percent learning curve. Each time you double the units produced, the labor required to make a fax machine drops by 16.2 percent.

If a curve gets steeper, the exponential curve might fit the data as well as the power curve does. A natural question is, then, which curve fits the data better? In most cases, this question can be answered simply by eyeballing the curves and choosing the one that looks like it's a better fit. More precisely, you could compute the *sum of squared errors* (SSE) for each curve (obtained by adding up for each data point the square of the curve value minus the actual value) and then choose the curve with the smaller SSE.

The learning curve was discovered in 1936 at Wright-Patterson Air Force Base in Dayton, Ohio. It was found that whenever the cumulative number of airplanes produced doubled, the time required to make each airplane dropped by around 15 percent.

Wikipedia gives the following learning curve estimates for various industries:

- Aerospace: 85 percent
- Shipbuilding: 80–85 percent
- Complex machine tools for new models: 75–85 percent
- Repetitive electronics manufacturing: 90–95 percent
- Repetitive machining or punch-press operations: 90–95 percent
- Repetitive electrical operations: 75–85 percent
- Repetitive welding operations: 90 percent
- Raw materials: 93–96 percent
- Purchased parts: 85–88 percent

Problems

1. Use the fax-machine data to model the relationship between the cumulative fax machines produced and the total production cost.
2. Use the fax-machine data to model the relationship between the cumulative fax machines produced and the average production cost per machine.

3. A marketing director estimates that the total sales of a product as a function of price will be as shown in the following table. Estimate the relationship between the price and the demand, and predict the demand for a $46 price. A 1 percent increase in price will reduce the demand by what percentage?

Price	Demand
$30.00	300
$40.00	200
$50.00	110
$60.00	60

4. The brand manager for a new drug believes that the annual sales of the drug, as a function of the number of sales calls on doctors, will be as shown in the following table. Estimate the sales of the drug if 80,000 sales calls are made on doctors.

Sales calls	Units sold
50,000	25,000
100,000	52,000
150,000	68,000
200,000	77,000

5. For an airplane manufacturer, the time needed to produce each of the first 10 airplanes in a year is as follows:

Unit	Hours
1	1,000
2	800
3	730
4	630
5	600
6	560
7	560
8	500
9	510
10	510

Estimate the total number of hours needed to produce the next 10 airplanes.

CHAPTER 56

Using correlations to summarize relationships

Question answered in this chapter:

- How are monthly stock returns for Microsoft, GE, Intel, GM, and Cisco related?

Trend curves are a great help in understanding how two variables are related. Often, however, you need to understand how more than two variables are related. Looking at the correlation between any pair of variables can provide insights into how multiple variables move up and down in value together.

The correlation (usually denoted by *r*) between two variables (call them *x* and *y*) is a unit-free measure of the strength of the linear relationship between *x* and *y*. The correlation between any two variables is always between –1 and +1. Although the exact formula used to compute the correlation between two variables isn't very important, being able to interpret the correlation between the variables is.

A correlation near +1 means that *x* and *y* have a strong positive linear relationship. That is, when *x* is larger than average, *y* tends to be larger than average, and when *x* is smaller than average, *y* also tends to be smaller than average. When a straight line is applied to the data, there will be a straight line with a positive slope that does a good job of fitting the points. As an example, for the data shown in Figure 56-1 (*x* = units produced and *y* = monthly production cost), *x* and *y* have a correlation of +0.95. (See the file Correlationexamples.xlsx for Figures 56-1 through 56-3.)

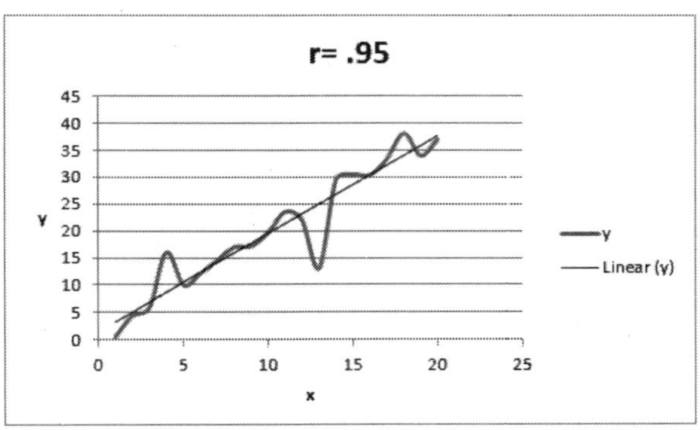

FIGURE 56-1 A correlation near +1, indicating that two variables have a strong positive linear relationship.

On the other hand, a correlation near –1 means that there is a strong negative linear relationship between *x* and *y*. That is, when *x* is larger than average, *y* tends to be smaller than average, and when *x* is smaller than average, *y* tends to be larger than average. When a straight line is applied to the data, the line has a negative slope that does a good job of fitting the points. As an example, for the data shown in Figure 52-2, *x* and *y* have a correlation of –0.90.

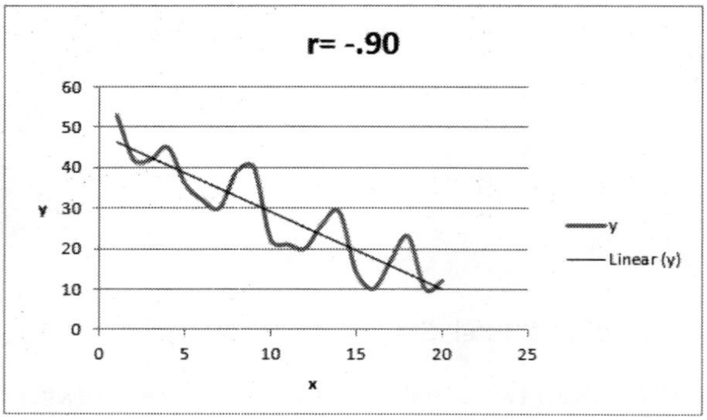

FIGURE 56-2 A correlation near –1, indicating that two variables have a strong negative linear relationship.

A correlation near 0 means that *x* and *y* have a weak linear relationship. That is, knowing whether *x* is larger or smaller than its mean tells you little about whether *y* will be larger or smaller than its mean. Figure 56-3 shows a graph of the dependence of unit sales (*y*) on years of sales experience (*x*). Years of experience and unit sales have a correlation of 0.003. In this data set, the average experience is 10 years. You can see that when a person has more than 10 years of sales experience, his or her sales can be either low or high. You can also see that when a person has fewer than 10 years of sales experience, sales can be low or high. Although experience and sales have little or no linear relationship, there is a strong nonlinear relationship (see the fitted curve) between years of experience and sales. Correlation does not measure the strength of nonlinear relationships.

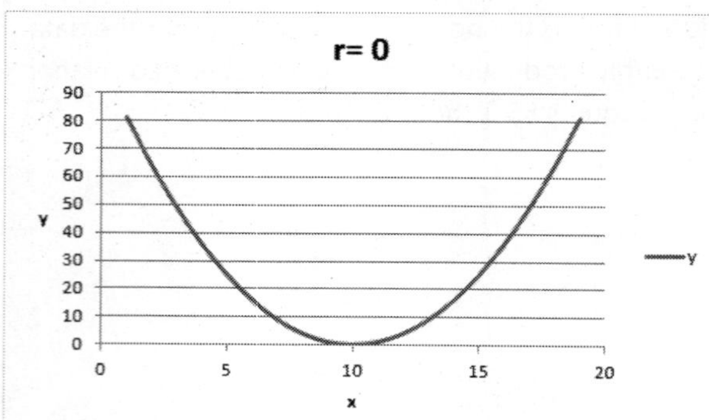

FIGURE 56-3 A correlation of 0, indicating a weak linear relationship between two variables.

Answer to this chapter's question

How are monthly stock returns for Microsoft, GE, Intel, GM, and Cisco related?

The file Stockcorrel.xlsx (see Figure 56-4) shows monthly stock returns for Microsoft, GE, Intel, GM, and Cisco during the 1990s. You can use correlations to try to understand how movements in these stocks are related.

To find the correlations between each pair of stocks (in the Initial Correlation Matrix worksheet), click Data Analysis in the Analysis group on the Data tab. (Before you can use this feature, you must install the Analysis ToolPak. To install it, click the File tab, click Options, and then click Add-Ins. Select Excel Add-Ins in the Manage list, click Go, select Analysis ToolPak, and then click OK. For examples and detailed instructions, see Chapters 41 and 42.) In the Data Analysis dialog box, select the Correlation option, click OK, and then fill in the Correlation dialog box as shown in Figure 56-5.

	A	B	C	D	E	F
51	Date	MSFT	GE	INTC	GM	CSCO
52	3/30/1990	0.122	0.040	0.037	0.022	0.011
53	4/30/1990	0.047	-0.004	-0.054	-0.035	0.011
54	5/31/1990	0.259	0.084	0.222	0.116	0.042
55	6/29/1990	0.041	0.005	-0.026	-0.021	0.071
56	7/31/1990	-0.125	0.034	-0.053	-0.021	-0.038
57	8/31/1990	-0.075	-0.134	-0.250	-0.131	-0.029
58	9/28/1990	0.024	-0.113	-0.004	-0.088	-0.091
59	10/31/1990	0.012	-0.046	0.008	0.014	0.311
60	11/30/1990	0.133	0.053	0.119	0.014	0.339
61	12/31/1990	0.042	0.057	0.027	-0.058	0.136
62	1/31/1991	0.304	0.115	0.188	0.055	0.304
63	2/28/1991	0.057	0.070	0.044	0.101	-0.043
64	3/28/1991	0.023	0.024	-0.021	-0.044	-0.129
65	4/30/1991	-0.067	0.016	0.053	-0.053	0.221
66	5/31/1991	0.109	0.099	0.132	0.217	0.084
67	6/28/1991	-0.069	-0.042	-0.166	-0.055	-0.054
68	7/31/1991	0.079	-0.010	0.011	-0.025	0.287
69	8/30/1991	0.160	0.022	0.053	-0.034	0.156
70	9/30/1991	0.044	-0.067	-0.146	-0.016	-0.096
71	10/31/1991	0.055	-0.005	-0.038	-0.060	0.189
72	11/29/1991	0.036	-0.062	0.009	-0.113	0.015
73	12/31/1991	0.144	0.190	0.195	-0.061	0.338

FIGURE 56-4 Monthly stock returns during the 1990s.

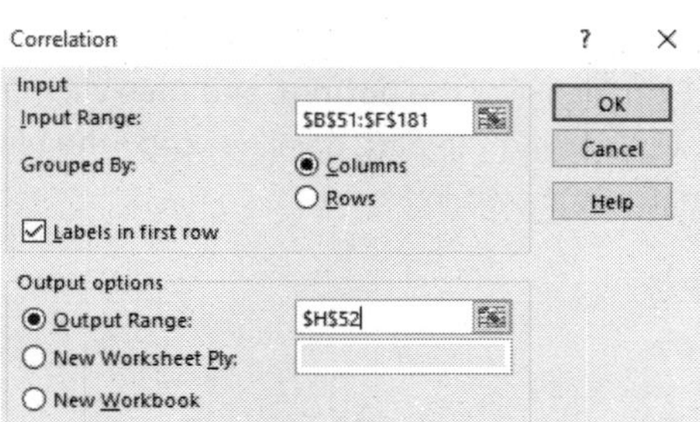

FIGURE 56-5 The Correlation dialog box.

The easiest way to enter the input range is to select the upper-left cell of the range (B51) and then press Ctrl+Shift+Right arrow, followed by the Down arrow. Select the Labels In First Row option because the first row of the input range contains labels. I entered cell H52 as the upper-left cell of the output range. After clicking OK, I got the results shown in Figure 56-6.

	H	I	J	K	L	M	N
51			Full correlation matrix				
52		*Date*	*MSFT*	*GE*	*INTC*	*GM*	*CSCO*
53	Date	1.000	-0.101	0.073	-0.019	0.011	-0.126
54	MSFT	-0.101	1.000	0.445	0.517	0.069	0.513
55	GE	0.073	0.445	1.000	0.324	0.380	0.376
56	INTC	-0.019	0.517	0.324	1.000	0.317	0.488
57	GM	0.011	0.069	0.380	0.317	1.000	0.159
58	CSCO	-0.126	0.513	0.376	0.488	0.159	1.000

FIGURE 56-6 The stock-return correlations.

The correlation between Cisco and Microsoft is 0.513, for example, whereas the correlation between GM and Microsoft is 0.069. The analysis shows that returns of Cisco, Intel, and Microsoft are most closely tied together. Because the correlation between each pair of these stocks is around 0.5, these stocks exhibit a moderate positive relationship. In other words, if one stock does better than average, it is likely (but not certain) that the other stocks will do better than average. Because Cisco, Intel, and Microsoft stock returns are closely tied to technology spending, their fairly strong correlation is not surprising. You can also see that the monthly returns on Microsoft and GM are virtually uncorrelated. This relationship indicates that when Microsoft stock does better than average, you really can't tell whether GM stock will do better or worse than average. Again, this trend is not surprising because GM is not really a high-tech company and is more susceptible to the vagaries of the business cycle.

Filling in the correlation matrix

As you can see in this example, Excel left some entries in the correlation matrix blank. For example, the correlation between Microsoft and GE (which is equal to the correlation between GE and Microsoft) is omitted. If you want to fill in the entire correlation matrix, right-click the matrix, and then click Copy. Then, right-click a blank portion of the worksheet and select Paste Special. In the Paste Special dialog box, select Transpose at the bottom. This flips the data on its side. Now right-click the flipped data, and click Copy. Right-click the original correlation matrix, and then click Paste Special again. In the Paste Special dialog box, select Skip Blanks at the bottom, and then click OK. The transposed data is copied to the original matrix, but pasting the data does not copy the blank cells from the transposed data. The full correlation matrix is shown in Figure 56-7.

	H	I	J	K	L	M	N
48		correl function					
49		0.159					
50							
51			Full correlation matrix				
52		*Date*	*MSFT*	*GE*	*INTC*	*GM*	*CSCO*
53	Date	1.000	-0.101	0.073	-0.019	0.011	-0.126
54	MSFT	-0.101	1.000	0.445	0.517	0.069	0.513
55	GE	0.073	0.445	1.000	0.324	0.380	0.376
56	INTC	-0.019	0.517	0.324	1.000	0.317	0.488
57	GM	0.011	0.069	0.380	0.317	1.000	0.159
58	CSCO	-0.126	0.513	0.376	0.488	0.159	1.000
59							
60							
61		1.000	-0.101	0.073	-0.019	0.011	-0.126
62			1.000	0.445	0.517	0.069	0.513
63				1.000	0.324	0.380	0.376
64					1.000	0.317	0.488
65						1.000	0.159
66							1.000
67							
68			Transposed correlations				

FIGURE 56-7 The complete correlation matrix.

Using the CORREL function

As an alternative to using the Correlation option in the Analysis ToolPak, you can use the CORREL function. For example, entering in cell I49 (in the Complete Matrix worksheet) the formula =CORREL(CSCO,E52:E181) confirms that the correlation between the monthly returns on Cisco (shown in column F) and GM (shown in column E) is 0.159.

Relationship between correlation and R-squared

In Chapter 53, "Estimating straight-line relationships," you found an R-squared value of 0.688 for the units produced and the monthly operating cost. How is this value related to the correlation between units produced and monthly operating costs? The correlation between the two sets of data is simply the following formula for the trendline:

$$\sqrt{R^2 \text{value}}$$

In this formula, you choose the sign for the square root to be the same as the sign of the slope of the trendline. Thus, the correlation between the units produced and the monthly operating cost for the data in Chapter 53 is the following equation:

$$+\sqrt{.688} = +.829$$

Correlation and regression toward the mean

You have probably heard the phrase, *regression toward the mean*. Essentially, this statement means that the predicted value of a dependent variable will be in some sense closer to its average value than the independent variable. More precisely, suppose you try to predict a dependent variable *y* from an independent variable *x*. If *x* is *k* standard deviations above average, then your prediction for *y* will be *rk* standard deviations above average. (Here, *r*=correlation between *x* and *y*.) Because *r* is between -1 and +1, this means that *y* is fewer standard deviations away from the mean than *x*. This is the real definition of *regression toward the mean*. See Problem 5 for an interesting application of the concept of regression toward the mean.

Problems

The data for the following problems is in the file Ch56data.xlsx.

1. The Problem 1 worksheet contains the number of cars parked each day both in the outdoor lot and in the parking garage near the Indiana University Kelley School of Business. Find and interpret the correlation between the number of cars parked in the outdoor lot and in the parking garage.

2. The Problem 2 worksheet contains the daily sales volume (in dollars) of laser printers, printer cartridges, and school supplies. Find and interpret the correlations between each pair of these quantities.

3. The Problem 3 worksheet contains annual returns on stocks, T-bills, and T-bonds. Find and interpret the correlations between each pair of the annual returns on these three classes of investments.

Here are two more problems:

4. The file Dow.xlsx contains the monthly returns of the 30 stocks comprising the Dow Jones Index. Find the correlations between each pair of stocks. Then, for each stock, use conditional formatting to highlight the three stocks most correlated with that stock. (Of course, you should not highlight a stock as correlated with itself.)

5. NFL teams play 16 games during the regular season. Suppose the standard deviation of the number of games won by all teams is 2, and the correlation between each pair of the numbers of games a team wins in two consecutive seasons is 0.5. If a team goes 12 and 4 during a season, what is your best prediction for how many games that team will win next season?

CHAPTER 57

Introduction to multiple regression

Questions answered in this chapter:

- Our factory manufactures three products. How can I predict the cost of running the factory, based on the number of units produced?
- How accurate are my forecasts for predicting the monthly cost, based on the units produced?
- I know how to use the Data Analysis command to run a multiple regression. Is there a way to run the regression without using this command and place the regression's results in the same worksheet as the data?

Answers to this chapter's questions

Our factory manufactures three products. How can I predict the cost of running the factory, based on the number of units produced?

In Chapters 53 through 55, I described how to use the trend curve in Microsoft Excel 2016 to predict one variable (called *y*, or the dependent variable) from another variable (called *x*, or the independent variable). However, you often want to use more than one independent variable (called the independent variables *x*1, *x*2, ... *xn*) to predict the value of a dependent variable. In these cases, you can use either the multiple-regression option in the Excel Data Analysis feature or the LINEST function to estimate the relationship you want.

Multiple regression assumes that the relationship between *y* and *x*1, *x*2, ... *xn* has the following form:

```
Y=Constant+B1X1+B2X2+...BnXn
```

Excel calculates the values of *Constant*, *B*1, *B*2, ... *Bn* to make the predictions from this equation as accurate (in the sense of minimizing the sum of squared errors) as possible. The following example illustrates how multiple regression works.

The Data worksheet in the file Mrcostest.xlsx (see Figure 57-1) contains the cost of running a plant over 19 months, as well as the number of units of Product A, Product B, and Product C produced during each month.

	A	B	C	D	E
3	Month	Cost	A Made	B Made	C Made
4	1	44439	515	541	928
5	2	43936	929	692	711
6	3	44464	800	710	824
7	4	41533	979	675	758
8	5	46343	1165	1147	635
9	6	44922	651	939	901
10	7	43203	847	755	580
11	8	43000	942	908	589
12	9	40967	630	738	682
13	10	48582	1113	1175	1050
14	11	45003	1086	1075	984
15	12	44303	843	640	828
16	13	42070	500	752	708
17	14	44353	813	989	804
18	15	45968	1190	823	904
19	16	47781	1200	1108	1120
20	17	43202	731	590	1065
21	18	44074	1089	607	1132
22	19	44610	786	513	839

FIGURE 57-1 The data for predicting the monthly operating costs.

You would like to find the best forecast for the monthly operating cost that has the following form (which I'll refer to as *Form 1*):

```
Monthly operating cost=Constant+B1*(Units A produced)+B2*(Units B produced)
   +B3*(Units C produced)
```

The Excel Data Analysis feature can find for this form the equation that best fits your data. Click Data Analysis in the Analysis group on the Data tab, and then select Regression. Fill in the Regression dialog box as shown in Figure 57-2.

> **Note** If you haven't previously installed the Analysis ToolPak, click the File tab, click Options, and then click Add-Ins. With Excel Add-ins selected in the Manage box, click Go, select the Analysis ToolPak check box, and then click OK.

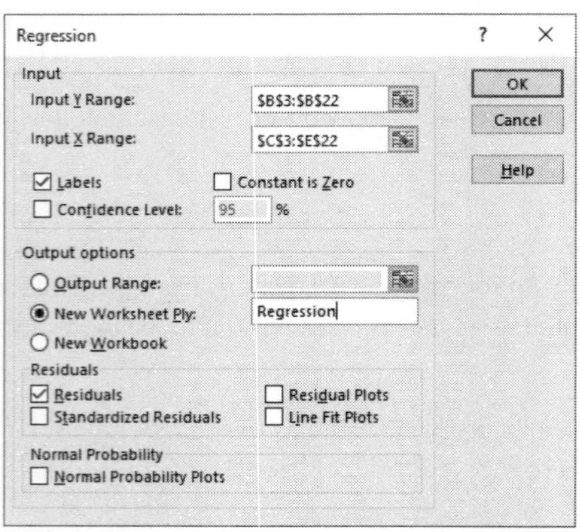

FIGURE 57-2 The Regression dialog box.

- Input Y Range (B3:B22 in this example) contains the dependent variable or data (including the Cost label) that you want to predict.
- Input X Range (C3:E22) contains the data or independent variables (including the labels A Made, B Made, and C Made) that you want to use in the prediction. Excel has a limit of 15 independent variables, which must be in adjacent columns.
- Because both Input X Range and Input Y Range include labels, I've checked the Labels option.
- I chose to place the output in a new worksheet titled Regression.
- Selecting the Residuals check box causes Excel to list, for each observation, the prediction from Form 1 and the residual, which equals the observed cost minus the predicted cost.

After clicking OK in the Regression dialog box, you obtain the output shown in Figures 57-3 and 57-4. (See the Regression worksheet.)

	A	B	C	D	E	F	G	H	I
1	SUMMARY OUTPUT								
2									
3	*Regression Statistics*								
4	Multiple R	0.803398744							
5	R Square	0.645449542							
6	Adjusted R Square	0.57453945							
7	Standard Error	1252.763898							
8	Observations	19							
9									
10	ANOVA								
11		*df*	*SS*	*MS*	*F*	*Significance F*			
12	Regression	3	42856229.89	1.4E+07	9.1024	0.001126532			
13	Residual	15	23541260.74	1569417					
14	Total	18	66397490.63						
15									
16		*Coefficients*	*Standard Error*	*t Stat*	*P-value*	*Lower 95%*	*Upper 95%*	*Lower 95.0%*	*Upper 95.0%*
17	Intercept	35102.90045	1837.226911	19.1065	6E-12	31186.94158	39018.8593	31186.94158	39018.8593
18	A Made	2.065953296	1.664981779	1.24083	0.2337	-1.482873542	5.61478013	-1.48287354	5.61478013
19	B Made	4.176355531	1.681252566	2.48407	0.0253	0.592848311	7.75986275	0.592848311	7.75986275
20	C Made	4.790641037	1.789316107	2.67736	0.0172	0.97680169	8.60448038	0.97680169	8.60448038

FIGURE 57-3 The original multiple-regression output.

	A	B	C
24	RESIDUAL OUTPUT		
25			
26	*Observation*	*Predicted Cost*	*Residuals*
27	1	42871.99	1567.01
28	2	43318.35	617.65
29	3	43668.36	795.64
30	4	43575.81	-2042.81
31	5	45342.07	1000.93
32	6	44685.80	236.20
33	7	42784.48	418.52
34	8	43662.85	-662.85
35	9	42753.82	-1786.82
36	10	47339.70	1242.30
37	11	46550.10	-1547.10
38	12	43484.02	818.98
39	13	42668.27	-598.27
40	14	44764.61	-411.61
41	15	45329.26	638.74
42	16	47574.96	206.04
43	17	44179.19	-977.19
44	18	45310.78	-1236.78
45	19	42888.56	1721.44

FIGURE 57-4 The original multiple-regression residual output.

What is the best prediction equation? You'll find in the Coefficients column (cells B16:B20 of the summary output) that the best equation for Form 1 that can be used to predict monthly cost is the following:

```
Predicted monthly cost=35,102.90+2.07(AMade)+4.18(BMade)+4.79(CMade)
```

A natural question is, then, which of the independent variables are useful for predicting the monthly cost? After all, if you choose the number of games won by the Seattle Mariners during a one-month period as an independent variable, you would expect that this variable would have little effect on predicting monthly operating cost. When you run a regression, each independent variable has a *p*-value between 0 and 1. Any independent variable with a *p*-value (see cells E16:E20) of less than or equal to 0.05 is considered to be useful for predicting the dependent variable. Thus, the smaller the *p*-value, the higher the predictive power of the independent variable. The three independent variables have *p*-values of 0.23 (for A Made), 0.025 (for B Made), and 0.017 (for C Made). These *p*-values can be interpreted as follows:

- When you use B Made and C Made to predict the monthly operating cost, you have a 77 percent chance (1–0.23) that A Made adds predictive power.
- When you use A Made and C Made to predict the monthly operating cost, there is a 97.5 percent chance (1–0.025) that B Made adds predictive power.
- When you use A Made and B Made to predict the monthly operating cost, there is a 98.3 percent chance (1–0.017) that C Made adds predictive power.

The *p*-values indicate that A Made does not add much predictive power to B Made and C Made, which means that if you know B Made and C Made, you can predict the monthly operating cost about as well as you can if you include A Made as an independent variable. Therefore, you can opt to delete A Made as an independent variable and use just B Made and C Made for your prediction. I copied the data to the worksheet titled A Removed and deleted the A Made column (it was column C in the Data worksheet). I then adjusted the input *x* range to be C3:D22. In the worksheet titled NoA, you can see the regression output shown in Figure 57-5 and Figure 57-6.

	A	B	C	D	E	F	G	H	I
1	SUMMARY OUTPUT								
2									
3	*Regression Statistics*								
4	Multiple R	0.780421232							
5	R Square	0.609057299							
6	Adjusted R Square	0.560189461							
7	Standard Error	1273.715391							
8	Observations	19							
9									
10	ANOVA								
11		*df*	*SS*	*MS*	*F*	*Significance F*			
12	Regression	2	40439876.29	2E+07	12.463	0.0005456			
13	Residual	16	25957614.34	2E+06					
14	Total	18	66397490.63						
15									
16		*Coefficients*	*Standard Error*	*t Stat*	*P-value*	*Lower 95%*	*Upper 95%*	*Lower 95.0%*	*Upper 95.0%*
17	Intercept	35475.30255	1842.860853	19.25	2E-12	31568.613	39381.992	31568.613	39381.992
18	B Made	5.320968077	1.429095476	3.723	0.0018	2.2914217	8.3505145	2.2914217	8.3505145
19	C Made	5.417137848	1.745311646	3.104	0.0068	1.7172433	9.1170324	1.7172433	9.1170324

FIGURE 57-5 A multiple-regression output with A Made data removed as an independent variable.

	A	B	C
25	*Observation*	*Predicted Cost*	*Residuals*
26	1	43381.05021	1057.949794
27	2	43008.99747	927.002527
28	3	43716.91148	747.0885248
29	4	43173.14649	-1640.146495
30	5	45018.33547	1324.664528
31	6	45352.53278	-430.5327792
32	7	42634.5734	568.4265963
33	8	43497.43576	-497.4357601
34	9	43096.66501	-2129.665007
35	10	47415.43478	1166.565215
36	11	46525.80688	-1522.806879
37	12	43366.11226	936.8877388
38	13	43312.00414	-1242.004144
39	14	45093.11881	-740.1188117
40	15	44751.5519	1216.448104
41	16	47438.12957	342.8704271
42	17	44383.92553	-1181.925527
43	18	44837.33022	-763.3302206
44	19	42749.93783	1860.062168

FIGURE 57-6 The residual output calculated when the A Made data is removed as an independent variable.

You can see that B Made and C Made each have very low *p*-values (0.002 and 0.007, respectively). These values indicate that both these independent variables have useful predictive power. Using the new coefficients in column B, you can now predict the monthly operating cost using the following equation:

```
Predicted monthly operating cost=35,475.3+5.32(BMade)+5.42(CMade)
```

How accurate are my forecasts for predicting the monthly cost, based on the units produced?

In the regression output in cell B5 of the NoA worksheet (see Figure 53-5), *R*-squared equals 0.61. An R-squared value such as this one means that together, B Made and C Made explain 61 percent of the variation in the monthly operating costs. Notice that in the original regression, which included A Made as an independent variable, R-squared equals 0.65. This indicates that the addition of A Made as an independent variable explains only 4 percent more variation in monthly operating costs. Having such a minor difference is consistent with the decision to delete A Made as an independent variable.

In the regression output in cell B7 in the NoA worksheet, the standard error for the regression with B Made and C Made as independent variables is 1,274. You would expect about 68 percent of your multiple-regression forecasts to be accurate within one standard error, and 95 percent to be accurate within two standard errors. Any forecast that differs from the actual value by more than two standard errors is considered an outlier. Thus, if your forecasted operating cost is in error by more than $2,548 (2*1274), you consider that observation to be an outlier.

In the Residual portion of the output, shown earlier in Figure 57-6, you are given for each observation the predicted cost and the residual, which equals the actual cost less the predicted cost. For the first observation, for example, the predicted cost is $43,381.05. The residual of $1,057.95 indicates that the prediction of actual cost was too low by $1,057.95.

I know how to use the Data Analysis command to run a multiple regression. Is there a way to run the regression without using this command and place the regression's results in the same worksheet as the data?

The Excel LINEST function can be used to insert the results of a regression analysis directly into a workbook. To use the LINEST function when there are *m* independent variables, begin by selecting a blank cell range consisting of five rows and *m*+1 columns, where you want LINEST to deposit the results. In the A Removed worksheet, I used the range F5:H9.

The syntax of the LINEST function is LINEST(KnownYs,KnownXs,True,True). If the third argument is changed to False, Excel estimates the equation without a constant term. Changing the fourth argument to False causes the LINEST function to omit many regression computations and return only the multiple-regression equation.

With the upper-left cell of the target range selected (F5 in this example), select the range of the size you want (in this case, the cell range F5:H9), and then enter the formula =LINEST(B4:B22,C4:D22 ,True,True). At this point, do not press Enter. LINEST is an array function, so you must first hold down Ctrl+Shift and then press Enter for the function to work correctly. (See Chapter 88, "Array formulas and functions," for further discussion of array functions.) After using this key combination, you obtain the results shown in Figure 57-7. (See the A Removed worksheet.)

	F	G	H	I	J
4				LINEST OUTPUT	
5	5.417137848	5.320968077	35475.30255		
6	1.745311646	1.429095476	1842.860853		
7	0.609057299	1273.715391	#N/A		
8	12.46335684	16	#N/A		
9	40439876.29	25957614.34	#N/A		
10					
11	Cmadecoef	Bmadecoef	Const		
12	Std err C	Std Err B	Std err const		
13	rsq	std err est			
14	F	df			
15	ssreg	ssresid			

FIGURE 57-7 Using the LINEST function to calculate a multiple regression.

In row 5, you find the prediction equation (coefficients read right to left, starting with the intercept) of Predicted monthly cost=35,475.3+5.32(B Made)+5.43(C Made). Row 6 contains standard errors for each coefficient estimate, but these are not extremely relevant. Cell F7 contains the

R-squared value of 0.61, and cell G7 contains the regression standard error of 1,274. Rows 8 and 9 contain information (F statistic, degrees of freedom, sum of squares regression, and sum of squares residual) that is less important.

Note Problems that you can work with to learn more about multiple regression are available at the end of Chapter 59.

CHAPTER 58

Incorporating qualitative factors into multiple regression

Questions answered in this chapter:

- How can I predict quarterly US auto sales?
- How can I predict US presidential elections?
- Is there an Excel function I can use to easily make forecasts from a multiple-regression equation?

In the first example of multiple regression in Chapter 57, "Introduction to multiple regression," I forecasted the monthly cost of plant operations by using the number of units of each product manufactured at the plant. Because you can quantify exactly the amount of a product produced at a plant, you can refer to the units produced of Product A, Product B, and Product C as *quantitative independent variables*. In many situations, however, independent variables can't be easily quantified. In this chapter, we'll look at ways to incorporate qualitative factors such as seasonality, gender, or the party of a presidential candidate into a multiple-regression analysis.

Answers to this chapter's questions

How can I predict quarterly US auto sales?

Suppose you want to predict quarterly US auto sales to determine whether the quarter of the year impacts auto sales. We'll use the data in the Data worksheet in the file Auto.xlsx, shown in Figure 58-1. Sales are listed in thousands of cars, and GNP is in billions of dollars.

	A	B	C	D	E	F
9	Historical data					
10	Year	Quarter	Sales	GNP	Unemp	Int
11	79	1	Sales	2541	5.9	9.4
12	79	2	2910	2640	5.7	9.4
13	79	3	2562	2595	5.9	9.7
14	79	4	2385	2701	6	12
15	80	1	2520	2785	6.2	13
16	80	2	2142	2509	7.3	9.6
17	80	3	2130	2570	7.7	9.2
18	80	4	2190	2667	7.4	14
19	81	1	2370	2878	7.4	14
20	81	2	2208	2835	7.4	15
21	81	3	2196	2897	7.4	15
22	81	4	1758	2744	8.3	12
23	82	1	1944	2582	8.8	13
24	82	2	2094	2613	9.4	12
25	82	3	1911	2529	10	9.3
26	82	4	2031	2544	10.7	7.9
27	83	1	2046	2633	10.4	7.8
28	83	2	2502	2878	10.1	8.4
29	83	3	2238	3051	9.4	9.1
30	83	4	2394	3274	8.5	8.8
31	84	1	2586	3594	7.9	9.2
32	84	2	2898	3774	7.5	9.8

FIGURE 58-1 The auto-sales data.

You might be tempted to define an independent variable that equals 1 during the first quarter, 2 during the second quarter, and so on. Unfortunately, this approach would force the fourth quarter to have four times the effect of the first quarter, which might not be true. The quarter of the year is a *qualitative independent variable*. To model a qualitative independent variable, you create an independent variable called a *dummy variable* for all but one of the qualitative variable's possible values. (It is arbitrary which value you leave out. In this example, I chose to omit Quarter 4.) The dummy variables tell you which value of the qualitative variable occurs. Thus, we'll have a dummy variable for Quarter 1, Quarter 2, and Quarter 3, with the following properties:

- The Quarter 1 dummy variable equals 1 if the quarter is Quarter 1 or 0 if otherwise.
- The Quarter 2 dummy variable equals 1 if the quarter is Quarter 2 or 0 if otherwise.
- The Quarter 3 dummy variable equals 1 if the quarter is Quarter 3 or 0 if otherwise.

A Quarter 4 observation will be identified by the fact that the dummy variables for Quarter 1 through Quarter 3 equal 0. You can see why you don't need a dummy variable for Quarter 4. In fact, if you include a dummy variable for Quarter 4 as an independent variable in the regression, Excel returns an error message. The error arises because if an exact linear relationship exists between any set of independent variables, Excel must perform the mathematical equivalent of dividing by 0 (an impossibility) when running a multiple regression. In this example, if you include a Quarter 4 dummy variable, every data point satisfies the following exact linear relationship:

```
(Quarter 1 Dummy)+(Quarter 2 Dummy)+(Quarter 3 Dummy)+(Quarter 4 Dummy)=1
```

> **Note** An exact linear relationship occurs if there exist constants c0, c1, ... cN, so that for each data point c0 + c1x1 + c2x2 + ... cNxN = 0. Here, *x1* through *xN* are the values of the independent variables.

To create the dummy variable for Quarter 1, I copied from G12 to G13:G42 the formula =IF(B12=1,1,0). This formula places a 1 in column G whenever a quarter is the first quarter or a 0 in column G whenever the quarter is not the first quarter. In a similar fashion, I created dummy variables for Quarter 2 (in H12:H42) and Quarter 3 (in I12:I42). You can see the results of the formulas in Figure 58-2.

	G	H	I	J	K	L
10	Q1	Q2	Q3	LagGNP	LagUnemp	LagInt
11	Q1	Q2	Q3	LagGNP	LagUnemp	LagInt
12	0	1	0	2541	5.9	9.4
13	0	0	1	2640	5.7	9.4
14	0	0	0	2595	5.9	9.7
15	1	0	0	2701	6	11.9
16	0	1	0	2785	6.2	13.4
17	0	0	1	2509	7.3	9.6
18	0	0	0	2570	7.7	9.2
19	1	0	0	2667	7.4	13.6
20	0	1	0	2878	7.4	14.4
21	0	0	1	2835	7.4	15.3
22	0	0	0	2897	7.4	15.1
23	1	0	0	2744	8.3	11.8
24	0	1	0	2582	8.8	12.8
25	0	0	1	2613	9.4	12.4
26	0	0	0	2529	10	9.3
27	1	0	0	2544	10.7	7.9
28	0	1	0	2633	10.4	7.8
29	0	0	1	2878	10.1	8.4
30	0	0	0	3051	9.4	9.1
31	1	0	0	3274	8.5	8.8
32	0	1	0	3594	7.9	9.2

FIGURE 58-2 Using dummy variables to track the quarter in which a sale occurs.

In addition to seasonality, we'd like to use macroeconomic variables, such as gross national product (GNP, in billions of 1986 dollars), interest rates, and unemployment rates to predict car sales. Suppose, for example, that you are trying to estimate the sales for the second quarter of 1979. Because values for GNP, interest rate, and unemployment rate aren't known at the beginning of the second quarter in 1979, you can't use second quarter 1979 GNP, interest rate, and unemployment rate to predict Quarter 2 1979 auto sales. Instead, you use the values for GNP, interest rate, and unemployment rate lagged one quarter to forecast auto sales. By copying from J12 to J12:L42 the formula =D11, you create the lagged value for GNP, the first of your macroeconomic independent variables. For example, the range J12:L12 contains GNP, unemployment rate, and interest rate for the first quarter of 1979. (When past values of an independent variable or variables are used to predict a dependent variable, we refer to the independent variables as *lagged independent variables*.)

You can now run the multiple regression by clicking Data Analysis on the Data tab in the Analysis group. (You must install the Analysis TookPak. See Chapter 42 for instructions.) Select Regression in the Data Analysis dialog box, and then click OK. In the Regression dialog box, use C11:C42 as the Input Y Range, G11:L42 as the Input X Range, select the Labels check box (row 11 contains labels), and also select the Residuals check box. After clicking OK, you obtain the output, which you can see in the Regression worksheet and in Figures 58-3 through 58-5.

	A	B	C	D	E	F
1	SUMMARY OUTPUT					
2						
3	*Regression Statistics*					
4	Multiple R	0.884139126				
5	R Square	0.781701994				
6	Adjusted R Squar	0.727127492				
7	Standard Error	190.5240756				
8	Observations	31				
9						
10	ANOVA					
11		*df*	*SS*	*MS*	*F*	*Significance F*
12	Regression	6	3119625.193	519937.5322	14.324	6.79746E-07
13	Residual	24	871186.1616	36299.4234		
14	Total	30	3990811.355			

FIGURE 58-3 A summary output and ANOVA table for auto-sales data.

In Figure 58-4, you can see that the equation (equation 1) used to predict quarterly auto sales is as follows:

```
Predicted quarterly sales=3154.7+156.833Q1+379.784Q2+203.03Q3+0.174(LAGGNP in billions)
   -93.83(LAGUNEMP)-73.91(LAGINT)
```

Also in Figure 58-4, you see that each independent variable has a *p*-value less than or equal to 0.15. You can conclude that all the independent variables have a significant effect on quarterly auto sales. You interpret all the coefficients in a regression equation *ceteris paribus* (which means that each coefficient gives the effect of the independent variable after adjusting for the effects of all the other variables in the regression).

	A	B	C	D	E
16		*Coefficients*	*Standard Erroi*	*t Stat*	*P-value*
17	Intercept	3154.700285	462.6530922	6.818716525	5E-07
18	Q1	156.833091	98.87110703	1.586237838	0.1258
19	Q2	379.7835116	96.08921514	3.95240518	0.0006
20	Q3	203.035501	95.40891864	2.128055783	0.0438
21	LagGNP	0.174156906	0.05842	2.981117865	0.0065
22	LagUnemp	-93.83233214	28.32328716	-3.312904029	0.0029
23	LagInt	-73.9167147	17.78851573	-4.155305356	0.0004

FIGURE 58-4 The coefficient information for an auto-sales regression.

An interpretation of each coefficient is as follows:

- A $1 billion increase in last quarter's GNP increases the quarterly car sales by 174.
- An increase of 1 percent in last quarter's unemployment rate decreases the quarterly car sales by 93,832.
- An increase of 1 percent in last quarter's interest rate decreases the quarterly car sales by 73,917.

To interpret the coefficients of the dummy variables, you must realize that they tell you the effect of seasonality relative to the value left out of the qualitative variables. The data you see in Figure 58-4 can be expressed the following way:

- In Quarter 1, the car sales exceed the Quarter 4 car sales by 156,833.
- In Quarter 2, the car sales exceed the Quarter 4 car sales by 379,784.
- In Quarter 3, the car sales exceed the Quarter 4 car sales by 203,036.

Therefore, you find that car sales are highest during the second quarter (April through June; because tax refunds and summer are coming) and lowest during the third quarter (October through December); why buy a new car when winter salting will ruin it?

From the Summary Output shown earlier in Figure 58-3, you can learn the following:

- The variation in the independent variables (macroeconomic factors and seasonality) explains 78 percent of the variation in the dependent variable (quarterly car sales).
- The standard error of regression is 190,524 cars. You can expect around 68 percent of your forecasts to be accurate within 190,524 cars, and about 95 percent of your forecasts to be accurate within 381,048 cars (2*190,524).
- There are 31 observations used to fit the regression.

The only quantity of interest in the ANOVA table in Figure 58-3 is the significance (0.00000068). This measure implies that there are only 6.8 chances in 10,000,000 that, when taken together, all of the independent variables are useless in forecasting the car sales. Thus, you can be quite sure that the independent variables are useful in predicting the quarterly auto sales. (You will learn more about ANOVA—analysis of variance—in Chapters 60 and 61.)

Figure 58-5 shows, for each observation, the predicted sales and residual. For example, for the second quarter of 1979 (observation 1), the predicted sales from equation 1 are 2,728.6 thousand and the residual is 181,400 cars (2910–2728.6). Note that no residual exceeds 381,000 in absolute value, so you have no outliers.

	A	B	C
27	RESIDUAL OUTPUT		
28			
29	*Observation*	*Predicted Sales*	*Residuals*
30	1	2728.588616	181.4113836
31	2	2587.848606	-25.84860587
32	3	2336.034563	48.96543676
33	4	2339.328281	180.6717193
34	5	2447.266343	-305.2663429
35	6	2400.118977	-270.1189769
36	7	2199.7408	-9.740800106
37	8	2076.383266	293.6167341
38	9	2276.947422	-68.94742189
39	10	2026.185621	169.8143789
40	11	1848.731191	-90.73119119
41	12	2138.394335	-194.3943352
42	13	2212.298456	-118.2984563
43	14	2014.216596	-103.2165964
44	15	1969.394332	61.60566841
45	16	2166.640544	-120.6405443
46	17	2440.632301	61.3676994
47	18	2290.352403	-52.35240272
48	19	2131.386979	262.6130214
49	20	2433.681173	152.3188271
50	21	2739.094517	158.9054833
51	22	2586.877653	-138.8776532
52	23	2362.035446	97.96455439
53	24	2667.994409	-21.99440885
54	25	2937.601377	50.39862257
55	26	2838.174893	128.8251074
56	27	2713.079218	-274.0792178
57	28	2887.577992	-289.5779921
58	29	3004.570968	40.42903226
59	30	2921.225251	291.7747488
60	31	2781.597472	-96.59747188

FIGURE 58-5 The residuals for the auto-sales data.

How can I predict the US presidential elections?

When asked which factors drive presidential elections, former presidential advisor James Carville said, "It's the economy, stupid." Yale economist Ray Fair showed that Carville was correct in thinking that the state of the economy has a large influence on the results of presidential elections. Fair's dependent variable (see the Data worksheet in the file President16.xlsx, shown in Figure 58-6) for each election (1916 through 2012) was the percentage of the two-party vote (ignoring votes received by third-party candidates) that went to the incumbent party. For the 2016 election, I listed the data given by Fair on his website as of July 2, 2016. Fair tried to predict the incumbent party's percentage of the two-party vote by using independent variables such as the following:

- The party in power. In my data, I use 1 to denote when the Republican Party was in power and 0 to denote when the Democratic Party was in power.
- The percentage growth in GNP during the first nine months of the election year.
- The absolute value of the inflation rate during the first nine months of the election year. You use the absolute value because either a positive or a negative inflation rate is bad.
- The number of quarters during the last four years in which economic growth was strong. Strong economic growth is defined as growth at an annual level of 3.2 percent or more.
- The length of time an incumbent party has been in office. Fair used 0 to denote one term in office, 1 for two terms, 1.25 for three terms, 1.5 for four terms, and 1.75 for five terms or more.

This definition implies that each term after the first term in office has less influence on the election results than the first term in office.

- The elections during wartime. The elections in 1920 (World War I), 1944 (World War II), and 1948 (World War II was still underway in 1945) were defined as wartime elections. (Elections held during the Vietnam War were not considered to be wartime elections.) During wartime years, the variables related to quarters of good growth and inflation were deemed irrelevant and were set to 0.
- The current president running for reelection. If this is the case, this variable is set to 1; otherwise, this variable is set to 0. In 1976, Gerald Ford was not considered a president running for reelection because he was not elected either as president or as vice president.

	A	B	C	D	E	F	G	H	I	J	K
6	Candidates	Year	Incumbent Share	Party in Power	Growth rate in election year	Abs. Value Inflation rate in election year	Quarters Growth>3.2 %	Time Incumbent in Office	Incumbent Party 1 = Republican	War	President Running?
7	Wilson-Hughes	1916	51.7	D	2.2	4.3	3	0	0	0	1
8	Harding-Cox	1920	36.1	D	-11.5	0	0	1	0	1	0
9	Coolidge-Davis	1924	58.3	R	-3.9	5.2	10	0	1	0	1
10	Hoover-Smith	1928	58.8	R	4.6	0.2	7	1	1	0	0
11	Hoover-FDR	1932	40.9	R	-14.9	7.1	4	1.25	1	0	1
12	FDR-Landon	1936	62.2	D	11.9	2.5	9	0	0	0	1
13	FDR-Wilkie	1940	55	D	3.7	0	8	1	0	0	1
14	FDR-Dewey	1944	53.8	D	4.1	0	0	1.25	0	1	1
15	Truman-Dewey	1948	52.3	D	1.8	0	0	1.5	0	1	1
16	Ike-Stevenson	1952	44.7	D	0.6	2.3	7	1.75	0	0	0
17	Ike-Stevenson	1956	57.1	R	-1.5	1.9	5	0	1	0	1
18	Kennedy-Nixon	1960	49.9	R	0.1	1.9	5	1	1	0	0
19	Johnson-Goldwater	1964	61.2	D	5.1	1.3	9	0	0	0	1
20	Nixon-Humphrey	1968	49.4	D	4.8	3.1	7	1	0	0	0
21	Nixon-McCgovern	1972	61.8	R	6.3	4.8	4	0	1	0	1
22	Ford-Carter	1976	49	R	3.7	7.6	5	1	1	0	0
23	Carter-Reagan	1980	44.8	D	-3.8	7.9	5	0	0	0	1
24	Reagan-Mondale	1984	59.1	R	5.4	5.2	8	0	1	0	1
25	Bush-Dukakis	1988	53.8	R	2.1	3	5	1	1	0	0
26	Bush-Clinton	1992	46.4	R	2.3	3.3	3	1.25	1	0	1
27	Clinton-Dole	1996	54.7	D	2.9	2	4	0	0	0	1
28	Gore Bush	2000	50.3	D	2.2	1.6	7	0	0	0	0
29	Bush Kerry	2004	51.2	R	2	2.2	2	0	1	0	1
30	Obama McCain	2008	46.3	R	-2.3	3.1	2	1	1	0	0
31	Obama Romney	2012	51.9	D	1.57	1.03	1	0	0	0	1
32	Clinton Trump	2016		D	2.16	1.28	3	1	0	0	0

FIGURE 58-6 The presidential-election data.

I've attempted to use the data from the elections from 1916 through 2004 to develop a multiple-regression equation that can be used to forecast future presidential elections. I saved the 2008 through 2016 elections as validation points. When fitting a regression to data, it's always a good idea to hold back some of your data for use in validating your regression equation. Holding back data allows you to determine whether your regression equation can do a good job of forecasting data it hasn't seen. Any forecasting tool that poorly forecasts data it hasn't seen should not be used to predict the future.

To run the regression, click Data Analysis in the Analysis group on the Data tab, select the Regression tool in the Data Analysis dialog box, and then click OK. In the Regression dialog box, I used C6:C29 as the Input Y Range and E6:L29 as the Input X Range. I also selected the Labels option (row 6 contains labels). I placed the output to the right of the data in the Data worksheet, which you can see in Figure 58-7 (starting on cell N14).

	N	O	P	Q	R	S	T
12							
13							
14	SUMMARY OUTPUT						
15							
16	*Regression Statistics*						
17	Multiple R	0.943094					
18	R Square	0.889425					
19	Adjusted R Square	0.837824					
20	Standard Error	2.721034					
21	Observations	23					
22							
23	ANOVA						
24		*df*	*SS*	*MS*	*F*	*gnificance F*	
25	Regression	7	893.3326	127.6189	17.23643	4.05E-06	
26	Residual	15	111.0604	7.404026			
27	Total	22	1004.393				
28							
29		*Coefficient*	*andard Err*	*t Stat*	*P-value*	*Lower 95%*	*Upper 95*
30	Intercept	43.36238	2.798678	15.49388	1.23E-10	37.39714	49.32762
31	Growth rate in election year	0.687368	0.118827	5.784599	3.6E-05	0.434094	0.940642
32	Abs. Value Inflation rate in electi	-0.57147	0.308857	-1.85026	0.084073	-1.22978	0.086848
33	Quarters Growth>3.2%	1.102468	0.298506	3.693286	0.002169	0.466218	1.738719
34	Time Incumbent in Office	-2.91359	1.194638	-2.43889	0.027638	-5.45991	-0.36728
35	Incumbent Party 1 = Republican	5.162856	1.321898	3.905638	0.001405	2.345296	7.980416
36	War	6.344981	2.998314	2.116183	0.051462	-0.04577	12.73574
37	President Running?	3.926576	1.38939	2.826116	0.012768	0.965162	6.887991

FIGURE 58-7 The regression output for predicting presidential elections.

In Figure 58-7, you can see that all the independent variables (if you round down the war coefficient to 0.10) have *p*-values less than or equal to 0.10 and should all be used in the prediction. From the coefficients section in Figure 58-7, you can determine that the best equation to predict elections is given by the following (equation 2):

```
Predicted presidential election percentage= 43.36+.69*GROWTH-0.57*ABSINF+1.1*QTRSGOODGROWTH-
2.91*TIMEINOFFICE+5.16*REP+6.34*WAR+3.93*PRESRUNNING.
```

The coefficients of the independent variables can be interpreted as follows (after adjusting for all other independent variables):

- A 1 percent increase in the annual GNP growth rate during an election year is worth 0.69 percent to the incumbent party.
- A 1 percent deviation from the ideal (0 percent inflation) costs the incumbent party 0.57 percent of the vote.
- Every good quarter of growth during an incumbent's term increases his (maybe her someday soon) vote by 1.1 percent.
- Relative to having one term in office, the second term in office decreases the incumbent's vote by 2.91 percent, and each later term decreases the incumbent's vote by 0.25*(2.91 percent)=0.73 percent.
- A Republican has a 5.16 percent edge over a Democrat.
- The United States being at war adds 6.34 percent to the prediction for the incumbent vote share.

- If the incumbent president is running, you should add 3.93 percent to the prediction for the incumbent vote share.

You can see the residual output for the presidential-election equation in Figure 58-8.

	M	N	O	P
41		RESIDUAL OUTPUT		
42				
43	Year	*Observation*	*d Incumbe*	*Residuals*
44	1916	1	49.65127	2.048729
45	1920	2	38.88904	-2.78904
46	1924	3	57.82414	0.475856
47	1928	4	56.37652	2.423479
48	1932	5	38.92051	1.97949
49	1936	6	63.96219	-1.76219
50	1940	7	55.73837	-0.73837
51	1944	8	52.81015	0.989847
52	1948	9	50.50081	1.799191
53	1952	10	45.07892	-0.37892
54	1956	11	55.84732	1.25268
55	1960	12	50.10694	-0.20694
56	1964	13	59.97384	1.226156
57	1968	14	49.69389	-0.29389
58	1972	15	58.44907	3.350929
59	1976	16	49.32411	-0.32411
60	1980	17	45.67473	-0.87473
61	1984	18	62.01173	-2.91173
62	1988	19	50.85306	2.946939
63	1992	20	51.81234	-5.41234
64	1996	21	52.54927	2.150733
65	2000	22	51.67752	-1.37752
66	2004	23	54.77426	-3.57426

FIGURE 58-8 The residuals from the presidential-election equation.

From cell O18, you see that your regression explains 88.9 percent of the variation in the incumbent's vote share. From the standard error of 2.72 percent, you learn that approximately 95 percent of your forecasts should be accurate within 2*2.72 = 5.44 percent. Since the margin of error in presidential polls the day of the election is around 3 percent, it is amazing that your model, which does not account for the quality of the candidates, does so well! Looking at Figure 58-8, you see that the only (borderline) outlier was the 1992 Bush-Clinton election, in which Clinton performed 5.41 percent better than expected. I personally attribute this to the fact that Clinton was a great campaigner.

Is there an Excel function I can use to easily make forecasts from a multiple regression equation?

It's tedious to make forecasts using an equation such as equation 2, but the Excel TREND function makes it easy to generate forecasts from a multiple regression. You don't even have to run a regression with the Data Analysis command.

To illustrate the use of the TREND function, I'll describe how to generate forecasts for the 1916 through 2016 elections, using data from only the 1916 through 2004 elections. See the worksheet Trend Function and Figure 58-9. Begin by selecting the cell range (in this example, L7:L32) in which you want your forecasts to go. With the pointer in the first cell of this range (cell L7), enter the formula =TREND(C7:C29,E7:K29,E7:K32). Next, press Ctrl+Shift+Enter. Note by selecting rows 7–29 in the first two arguments of the TREND function, you ensured that your regression equation will be fit based on data from 1916–2004.

You'll now see, in Figure 58-9, the forecast for each election, generated in cells L7:L32. Note that in 2008, the party in power (the Republicans) performed 1.8 percent worse than expected; in 2012, the incumbent Democrats performed 3.0 percent better than expected. So for the two elections in your validation set, your average absolute error was 2.4 percent. For the 1916–2004 elections that were used to fit your regression equation, you found an average absolute error of 1.8 percent. Thus your validation set performance was not much worse than the in-sample performance.

	A	B	L	M
6	Candidates	Year	Prediction	Abs error
7	Wilson-Hughes	1916	49.65127	2.048729
8	Harding-Cox	1920	38.88904	2.789038
9	Coolidge-Davis	1924	57.82414	0.475856
10	Hoover-Smith	1928	56.37652	2.423479
11	Hoover-FDR	1932	38.92051	1.97949
12	FDR-Landon	1936	63.96219	1.762187
13	FDR-Wilkie	1940	55.73837	0.738371
14	FDR-Dewey	1944	52.81015	0.989847
15	Truman-Dewey	1948	50.50081	1.799191
16	Ike-Stevenson	1952	45.07892	0.37892
17	Ike-Stevenson	1956	55.84732	1.25268
18	Kennedy-Nixon	1960	50.10694	0.206938
19	Johnson-Goldwater	1964	59.97384	1.226156
20	Nixon-Humphrey	1968	49.69389	0.293889
21	Nixon-McCgovern	1972	58.44907	3.350929
22	Ford-Carter	1976	49.32411	0.32411
23	Carter-Reagan	1980	45.67473	0.874726
24	Reagan-Mondale	1984	62.01173	2.911728
25	Bush-Dukakis	1988	50.85306	2.946939
26	Bush-Clinton	1992	51.81234	5.412336
27	Clinton-Dole	1996	52.54927	2.150733
28	Gore Bush	2000	51.67752	1.377525
29	Bush Kerry	2004	54.77426	3.574262
30	Obama McCain	2008	44.46409	1.835909
31	Obama Romney	2012	48.88198	3.018016
32	Clinton Trump	2016	44.50943	

FIGURE 58-9 The forecast for each election.

The TREND function is an example of an array function. I'll provide a more complete discussion of array functions in Chapter 88, "Array formulas and functions." For now, the following is some background information about array functions:

- Before entering an array function, you must always select the cell range in which you want the results of the array function to be located.
- Instead of pressing Enter to perform the calculation, you must press Ctrl+Shift+Enter to complete the entry of an array function.
- After entering an array function, you'll see a curly bracket in the formula bar when you select a cell in which the array function's results are located. This bracket indicates that the results in the cell were computed by means of an array function.
- You can't modify the data in any part of a range created by an array function.

Problems that you can work with to learn more about multiple regression are available at the end of Chapter 59.

CHAPTER 59

Modeling nonlinearities and interactions

Questions answered in this chapter:

- What does it mean when we say that an independent variable has a nonlinear effect on a dependent variable?
- What does it mean when we say that the effects of two independent variables on a dependent variable interact?
- How can I test for the presence of nonlinearity and interaction in a regression?

Answers to this chapter's questions

What does it mean when we say that an independent variable has a nonlinear effect on a dependent variable?

An independent variable often influences a dependent variable through a nonlinear relationship. For example, if you try to predict your product sales using an equation such as Sales=500–10*Price, the price influences sales *linearly*. This equation indicates that a unit increase in the price will (at any price level) reduce sales by 10 units. If the relationship between the sales and price were governed by an equation such as Sales=500+4*Price–.40*Price^2, the price and sales would be related *nonlinearly*. As shown in Figure 59-1, larger increases in price result in larger decreases in demand (see the Nonlinearity worksheet in the file Interactions.xlsx). In short, if the change in the dependent variable caused by a unit change in the independent variable is not constant, there is a nonlinear relationship between the independent and dependent variables.

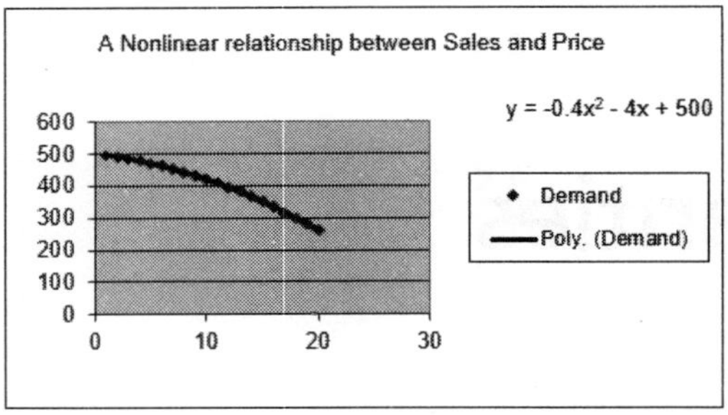

FIGURE 59-1 A nonlinear relationship between demand and price.

What does it mean when we say that the effects of two independent variables on a dependent variable interact?

If the effect of one independent variable on a dependent variable depends on the value of another independent variable, you can say that the two independent variables exhibit *interaction*. For example, suppose you try to predict your sales using the price and the amount spent on advertising. If the effect of changing the level of advertising dollars is large when the price is small and small when the price is high, then the price and advertising exhibit interaction. If the effect of changing the level of advertising dollars is the same for any price level, the sales and price do not exhibit any interaction.

How can I test for the presence of nonlinearity and interaction in a regression?

To see whether an independent variable has a nonlinear effect on a dependent variable, you simply add an independent variable to the regression that equals the square of the independent variable. If the squared term has a low *p*-value (less than 0.15), you have evidence of a nonlinear relationship.

To check whether two independent variables exhibit interaction, you simply add a term to the regression that equals the product of the independent variables. If the term has a low *p*-value (less than 0.15), you have evidence of interaction.

To illustrate, I'll try to determine how gender and experience influence the salaries at a small manufacturing company. For each employee, you are given the following set of data. You can find the following information in the Data worksheet in the file Interactions.xlsx, shown in Figure 59-2:

- Annual salary (in thousands of dollars)
- Years of experience working in the manufacturing business
- Gender (1=female, 0=male)

	A	B	C	D	E
1	Salary	Exp	Gender	Exp^2	Exp*Gender
2	55.92199	5	1	25	5
3	62.39869	15	0	225	0
4	67.84753	12	0	144	0
5	64.80815	19	0	361	0
6	58.29632	9	0	81	0
7	51.93969	3	0	9	0
8	36.34266	12	1	144	12
9	28.38828	15	1	225	15
10	73.57633	8	0	64	0
11	44.16733	12	1	144	12
12	57.03224	1	1	1	1
13	61.58797	5	0	25	0
14	63.21908	14	0	196	0
15	58.15548	1	1	1	1
16	47.4811	3	1	9	3
17	44.43084	6	1	36	6
18	59.10713	4	0	16	0
19	64.55505	9	0	81	0
20	64.65747	18	0	324	0
21	49.09593	7	1	49	7
22	69.01037	14	0	196	0
23	64.99559	16	0	256	0

FIGURE 59-2 The data for predicting a salary, based on gender and experience.

We'll use this data to predict the salary (the dependent variable), based on years of experience and gender. To test whether the length of experience has a nonlinear effect on salary, I added the term *Exp^2* by copying from D2 to D3:D98 the formula =B2^2. In the Data worksheet, replace D2 with the formula =B2^2. Then copy D2 to D3:D98. To test whether experience and gender have a significant interaction, I added the term *Exp*Gender* by copying from E2 to E3:E98 the formula =B2*C2. Replace E2 with the formula =B2*C2. I ran a regression with an Input Y Range of A1:A98 and an Input X Range of B1:E98. After selecting the labels option in the Regression dialog box and clicking OK, I got the results shown in Figure 59-3.

	H	I	J	K	L	M
1						
2	SUMMARY OUTPUT					
3						
4	*Regression Statistics*					
5	Multiple R	0.930645916				
6	R Square	0.866101822				
7	Adjusted R Square	0.860280162				
8	Standard Error	4.530277908				
9	Observations	97				
10						
11	ANOVA					
12		*df*	*SS*	*MS*	*F*	*Significance F*
13	Regression	4	12213.26555	3053.316	148.7723146	2.77158E-39
14	Residual	92	1888.154449	20.52342		
15	Total	96	14101.42			
16						
17		*Coefficients*	*Standard Error*	*t Stat*	*P-value*	*Lower 95%*
18	Intercept	58.30311924	1.960660525	29.73647	5.6775E-49	54.40907819
19	Exp	0.860472831	0.381574828	2.255057	0.02650141	0.102632286
20	Gender	1.119399728	1.94092596	0.576735	0.565527049	-2.735446764
21	Exp^2	-0.035148705	0.017761027	-1.978979	0.050808362	-0.070423637
22	Exp*Gender	-2.164501713	0.180872223	-11.96702	1.86636E-20	-2.523729559

FIGURE 59-3 The regression results that test for nonlinearity and interaction.

You can see that gender is insignificant (its *p*-value is greater than 0.15). All other independent variables are significant (meaning they have a *p*-value less than or equal to 0.15). You can delete the insignificant gender variable as an independent variable. To do this, I copied the data into a new worksheet called Finalregression (right-click any worksheet tab, click Move Or Copy, and then select the Create A Copy check box, and click OK.) After deleting the Gender column, you obtain the regression results included in the Finalregression worksheet and shown in Figure 59-4.

	H	I	J	K	L	M
1						
2	SUMMARY OUTPUT					
3						
4	*Regression Statistics*					
5	Multiple R	0.9303858				
6	R Square	0.8656177				
7	Adjusted R Square	0.8612828				
8	Standard Error	4.5139938				
9	Observations	97				
10						
11	ANOVA					
12		*df*	*SS*	*MS*	*F*	*Significance F*
13	Regression	3	12206.43899	4068.813	199.6852	2.12292E-40
14	Residual	93	1894.981012	20.37614		
15	Total	96	14101.42			
16						
17		*Coefficients*	*Standard Error*	*t Stat*	*P-value*	*Lower 95%*
18	Intercept	59.057442	1.455412135	40.57781	6.06E-61	56.16728518
19	Exp	0.7811172	0.354623849	2.202664	0.03009	0.076905191
20	Exp^2	-0.0335942	0.017492209	-1.92052	0.057856	-0.06833021
21	Exp*Gender	-2.0733945	0.087774433	-23.6219	4.49E-41	-2.247696986

FIGURE 59-4 Your regression results after deleting the insignificant gender variable.

All the independent variables are now significant (they have a *p*-value less than or equal to 0.15). Therefore, you can predict the salary (in thousands of dollars) by using the following equation (equation 1):

```
Predicted salary=59.06+0.78(EXP)-0.033EXP²-2.07(EXP*GENDER)
```

The negative EXP^2 term indicates that each additional year of experience has less impact on salary, which means that experience has a nonlinear effect on salary. In fact, this model shows that after 13 years of experience, each additional year of experience actually reduces salary.

Remember that gender equals 1 for a woman and 0 for a man. After substituting 1 for gender in equation 1, a woman's salary can be predicted as follows:

```
Predicted salary=59.06+78EXP-0.033EXP²-2.07(EXP*1)=59.06-0.033EXP²-1.29EXP
```

For a man (substituting gender=0), the following equation can be used:

```
Predicted salary=59.06+0.78EXP-0.033EXP²-2.07(EXP*0)=59.06+0.78EXP-0.033EXP²
```

Thus, the interaction between gender and experience shows that each additional year of experience benefits a woman an average of 0.78–(–1.29) = $2,070 less than a man. This indicates that women are not being treated fairly.

Problems for Chapters 57 through 59

Fizzy Drugs wants to optimize the yield from an important chemical process. The company thinks that the number of pounds produced each time the process is run depends on the size of the container used, the pressure, and the temperature. The scientists involved believe the effect of changing one variable might depend on the values of the other variables. The size of the process container must be between 1.3 and 1.5 cubic meters, the pressure must be between 4 and 4.5 mm, and the temperature must be between 22 and 30 degrees Celsius. The scientists patiently set up experiments at the lower and upper levels of the three control variables and obtain the data shown in the file Fizzy.xlsx. Use the data from this file to answer the Problems 1-3:

1. Determine the relationship between yield, size, temperature, and pressure.
2. Discuss the interactions between pressure, size, and temperature.
3. What settings for temperature, size, and pressure would you recommend?

Here are additional multiple regression problems:

4. For 12 straight weeks, you have observed the sales (in the number of cases) of canned tomatoes at Mr. D's Supermarket. (See the file Grocery.xlsx.) Each week, you keep track of the following:

   - Was a promotional notice for canned tomatoes placed in all the shopping carts?
   - Was a coupon for canned tomatoes given to each customer?
   - Was a price reduction (none, 1, or 2 cents off) given?

   Use this data to determine how the preceding factors influence sales. Predict the sales of canned tomatoes during a week in which you use a shopping cart notice, a coupon, and reduce the price by 1 cent.

5. The file Countryregion.xlsx contains the following data for several underdeveloped countries/regions:

   - Infant mortality rate
   - Adult literacy rate
   - Percentage of students finishing primary school
   - Per capita GNP

   Use this data to develop an equation that can be used to predict infant mortality. Are there any outliers in this set of data? Interpret the coefficients in your equation. Within what value should 95 percent of your predictions for infant mortality be accurate?

6. The file Baseball96.xlsx gives the runs scored, singles, doubles, triples, home runs, and bases stolen for each major league baseball team during the 1996 season. Use this data to determine the effects of singles, doubles, and other activities on run production.

7. The file Cardata.xlsx provides the following information for 392 different car models:

- Cylinders
- Displacement
- Horsepower
- Weight
- Acceleration
- Miles per gallon (MPG)

Determine an equation that can be used to predict MPG. Why do you think all the independent variables are not significant?

8. The file Priceads.xlsx contains weekly unit sales of a product as well as the product price and advertising expenditures. Explain how advertising and product price influence unit sales.

9. The file Teams.xlsx contains the runs scored, hit-by-pitcher, walks, singles, doubles, triples, and home runs for major league baseball teams during the 2000–2006 seasons. Answer the following problems:

- Use this data to build a model that predicts how many runs a team will score based on the team's hitting statistics.
- How accurate is this model for predicting how many runs a team will score during a season?
- Suppose a team had a positive residual exceeding three times the regression's standard error. What might cause such a result?

10. A hitter's on-base percentage (OPS) is calculated as hit-by-pitcher + walks + hits / (at bats + hit-by-pitcher + walks + sacrifice flies). A hitter's slugging percentage (SLG) is the total bases (home runs gets credit for four bases, triples get three, doubles, two, and singles, 1) divided by at bats. The file OPSslug.xlsx contains hitting data for major league teams during the 2000–2006 seasons.

Use this data to build a model that can be used to predict runs scored by a team from a team's OPS and SLG.

- Would you recommend a team use this model or the model from Problem 9 to predict runs scored?
- How could this model be used to evaluate an individual player's hitting abilities?
- Why might you be skeptical if this model were used to evaluate the hitting ability of a truly great hitter, like Albert Pujols (who was then playing for the St. Louis Cardinals)?

11. The file NFLinfo.xlsx contains the following data for NFL teams during the 2003–2006 seasons:

- Margin = Number of points by which a team outscores their opponent.
- NYP/A = Yards gained passing per pass attempt.
- YR/A = Yard gained per rushing attempt.
- DNYP/A = Yards gained passing by opponents per pass attempt.
- DYR/A = Yards gained rushing by opponents per attempt.
- TO = Turnovers by team.
- DTO = Turnovers by a team's opponents.

Answer the following questions:

a. Does this data indicate that passing or rushing effectiveness has more impact on team success?

b. Around how many points does a turnover cost a team?

c. Many football fans believe you need a good rushing attack to set up the passing game. Does this data give any support to that view?

12. The file Qbinfo.xlsx lists the famous quarterback ratings for NFL quarterbacks during the 2009 season. The quarterback rating is based on the quarterback's completion percentage, the percentage of passes that result in a touchdown, the yards made per pass attempt, and the percentage of passes that are intercepted.

- Develop a formula to predict a quarterback's rating, based on his season statistics.
- How accurate are your predictions?

13. In the file Problem13data.xlsx, you are given weekly cookie sales at a supermarket. You are also told for each week whether there was a price cut and/or whether the product was on display. Explain how the price and display affect cookie sales. During a week in which the product is on display and the price is cut, you are 95 percent sure weekly sales will be between _____ and _____.

14. A drug company is trying to determine how pressure, temperature, and container size influence product yield for a new drug. You are given the yield on several batches of the new drug, as well as the pressure, temperature, and product yield for each batch. Determine an equation that explains how these factors affect yield. If the process is run with high pressure, low temperature, and a large container, you are 95 percent sure the yield of the process will be between _____ and _____ You may ignore nonlinearities and interactions.

15. In the file Problem15data.xsls, you are given the number of greeting cards sold by a drugstore during several quarters and the average price charged for cards during the quarter. Determine how price and seasonality affect card sales. If you charge $4 per card in a fourth quarter, you are 95 percent sure between _____ and _____ cards will be sold.

16. In the file Problem16data.xlsx, you are given the number of almond-cream croissants sold each day by a bakery. For each day, you are given whether the day was sunny or cloudy. Develop an equation to forecast the daily croissant sales. Explain how weather and the day of the week affect sales. On a cloudy weekend day, you are 95 percent sure sales will be between _____ and _____.

CHAPTER 60

Analysis of variance: One-way ANOVA

Questions answered in this chapter:

- The owner of my company, which publishes computer books, wants to know whether the position of our books in the computer book section of bookstores influences sales. More specifically, does it really matter whether the books are placed in the front, back, or middle of the computer-book section?
- If I am determining whether populations have significantly different means, why is the technique called *analysis of variance*?
- How can I use the results of a one-way ANOVA for forecasting?

Data analysts often have data about several different groups of people or items and want to determine whether the data about the groups differs significantly. Here are some examples:

- Is there a significant difference in the length of time that four doctors keep mothers in the hospital after they give birth?
- Does the production yield for a new drug depend on whether the size of the container in which the drug is produced is large, small, or medium?
- Does the drop in blood pressure attained after taking one of four drugs depend on the drug taken?

When you're trying to determine whether the means in several sets of data that depend on one factor are significantly different, *one-way analysis of variance*, or ANOVA, is the correct tool to use. In the examples given above, the factors are the doctors, the container size, and the drug, respectively. In analyzing the data, you can choose between the following two hypotheses:

- Null hypothesis, which indicates that the means of all groups are identical.
- Alternative hypothesis, which indicates that there is a statistically significant difference among the groups' means.

To test these hypotheses in Microsoft Excel, you can use the Anova: Single Factor option in the Data Analysis dialog box. (Click Data Analysis on the Data tab, which is available after you install the Analysis ToolPack add-in.) If the *p*-value computed by Excel is small (usually less than or equal to 0.15), you can conclude that the alternative hypothesis is true (the means are significantly different). If the *p*-value is greater than 0.15, the null hypothesis is true (the populations have identical means). Let's look at an example.

Answers to this chapter's questions

The owner of my company, which publishes computer books, wants to know whether the position of our books in the computer book section of bookstores influences sales. More specifically, does it really matter whether the books are placed in the front, back, or middle of the computer-book section?

The publishing company wants to know whether its books sell better when a display is set up in the front, back, or middle of the computer book section. The weekly sales (in hundreds) were monitored at 12 different stores. At five stores, the books were placed in the front; at four stores, in the back; and at three stores, in the middle. The resulting sales are contained in the Data worksheet in the file Onewayanovatemp.xlsx, which is shown in Figure 60-1. Does the data indicate that the location of the books has a significant effect on sales?

	A	B	C	D
1	One-Way ANOVA			
2				
3		Front	Back	Middle
4		7	12	10
5		10	13	11
6		8	15	12
7		9	16	
8		11		

FIGURE 60-1 The book-sales data.

You can assume that the 12 stores have similar sales patterns and are approximately the same size. This assumption allows you to use one-way ANOVA because you believe that, at most, one factor (the position of the display in the computer book section) is affecting the sales. (If the stores were different sizes, you would need to analyze the data with two-way ANOVA, which I'll discuss in Chapter 61, "Randomized blocks and two-way ANOVA.")

To analyze the data, on the Data tab, click Data Analysis (in the Analysis group), and then select Anova: Single Factor. Fill in the dialog box as shown in Figure 60-2.

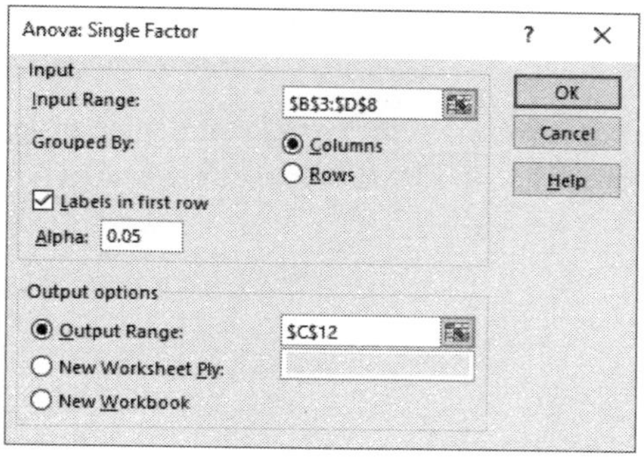

FIGURE 60-2 The Anova: Single Factor dialog box.

I used the following configurations:

- The data for the input range, including labels, is in cells B3:D9.
- Select the Labels In First Row option because the first row of the input range contains labels.
- I selected the Columns option because the data is organized in columns.
- I selected Output Range and C12 as the upper-left cell of the output range.
- The selected alpha value is not important. You can use the default value.

After clicking OK, you obtain the results shown in Figure 60-3.

	C	D	E	F	G	H	I
11							
12	Anova: Single Factor						
13							
14	SUMMARY						
15	*Groups*	*Count*	*Sum*	*Average*	*Variance*		
16	Front	5	45	9	2.5		
17	Back	4	56	14	3.333333		
18	Middle	3	33	11	1		
19							
20							
21	ANOVA						
22	*Source of Variation*	*SS*	*df*	*MS*	*F*	*P-value*	*F crit*
23	Between Groups	55.66667	2	27.83333	11.38636	0.00343	4.25649
24	Within Groups	22	9	2.444444			
25							
26	Total	77.66667	11				
27							
28	est std error	1.563472					

FIGURE 60-3 The one-way ANOVA results.

In cells F16:F18, you see the average sales depending on the location of the display. When the display is at the front of the computer book section, the average sales are 900; when the display is at the back of the section, the sales average 1,400; and when the display is in the middle, the sales average 1,100. Because the *p*-value of 0.003 (in cell H23) is less than 0.15, you can conclude that these means are significantly different.

If I am determining whether populations have significantly different means, why is the technique called *analysis of variance*?

Suppose that the data in your book sales study is the data shown in the worksheet named Insig, shown in Figure 60-4 (and also in the file Onewayanovatemp.xlsx). If you run a one-way ANOVA on this data, you obtain the results shown in Figure 60-5.

	B	C	D
3	Front	Back	Middle
4	7	2	3
5	20	16	19
6	8	25	11
7	8	13	
8	2		

FIGURE 60-4 The bookstore data for which the null hypothesis is accepted.

Note that the mean sales for each part of the store are exactly as before, yet the *p*-value of 0.66 indicates that you should accept the null hypothesis and conclude that the position of the display in the computer book section doesn't affect sales. The reason for this strange result is that in the second data set, you have much more variation in sales when the display is at each position in the computer book section. In the first data set, for example, the variation in sales when the display is at the front is between 700 and 1,100, whereas in the second data set, the variation in sales is between 200 and 2,000. The variation of sales within each store position is measured by the sum of the squares of data within a group. This measure is shown in cell D24 in the first data set and in cell F24 in the second. In the first data set, the sum of squares of data within groups is only 22, whereas in the second data set, the sum of squares within groups is 574! This large variation, within the data points at each store position, masks the variation between the groups (store positions) themselves and makes it impossible to conclude for the second data set that the difference between sales in different store positions is significant.

	E	F	G	H	I	J	K
12	Anova: Single Factor		Overall mean				
13			11.1666667				
14	SUMMARY						
15	*Groups*	*Count*	*Sum*	*Average*	*Variance*		
16	Front	5	45	9	44		
17	Back	4	56	14	90		
18	Middle	3	33	11	64		
19							
20							
21	ANOVA						
22	*Source of Variation*	*SS*	*df*	*MS*	*F*	*P-value*	*F crit*
23	Between Groups	55.66667	2	27.83333	0.436411	0.659334	4.25649
24	Within Groups	574	9	63.77778			
25							
26	Total	629.6667	11				
27							
28	est std err	7.986099					

FIGURE 60-5 The ANOVA results accepting the null hypothesis.

How can I use the results of a one-way ANOVA for forecasting?

If there is a significant difference between group means, the best forecast for each group is simply the group's mean. Therefore, in the first data set, you predict the following:

- Sales, when the display is at the front of the computer book section, will be 900 books per week.
- Sales, when the display is at the back, will be 1,400 books per week.
- Sales, when the display is in the middle, will be 1,100 books per week.

If there is no significant difference within the group means, your best forecast for each observation is simply the overall mean. Thus, in the second data set, you predict the weekly sales of 1,117, independent of where the books are placed.

You can also estimate the accuracy of your forecasts. The square root of the Within Groups MS (mean square) is the standard deviation of the forecasts from a one-way ANOVA. As shown earlier in Figure 60-3, the standard deviation of forecasts for the first data set is 1.56 (see cell D28 in the Signif worksheet again). By the rule of thumb, this means that you would expect, for example, the following results:

- During 68 percent of all the weeks in which books are placed at the front of the computer section, the sales will be between 900–156=744 and 900+156=1,056 books.
- During 95 percent of all weeks in which books are placed at the front of the computer book section, the sales will be between 900–2(156)=588 books and 900+2(156) =1,212 books.

Problems

You can find the data for the following problems in the file Chapter60data.xlsx:

1. For patients of four cardiologists, you are given the number of days the patients stayed in the hospital after open-heart surgery. Answer the following questions:
   - Is there evidence that the doctors have different discharge policies?
   - You are 95 percent sure that a patient of Doctor 1 will stay in the hospital between what range of days?
2. A drug can be produced by using a 400-degree, 300-degree, or 200-degree oven. You are given the pounds of the drug yielded when various batches are baked at different temperatures. Answer the following questions:
   - Does the temperature appear to influence the process yield?
   - What is the range of pounds of the product that you are 95 percent sure will be produced with a 200-degree oven?
   - If you believe that pressure within the container also influences the process yield, does this analysis remain valid?

CHAPTER 61

Randomized blocks and two-way ANOVA

Questions answered in this chapter:

- I am trying to analyze the effectiveness of my sales force. The problem is that in addition to a sales representative's own effectiveness, the amount that a representative sells depends on the district to which he or she is assigned. How can I incorporate the district assignments of my representatives into my analysis?
- Based on my knowledge of sales representatives and districts, how can I forecast sales? How accurate are my sales forecasts?
- How can I determine whether varying the price and the amount of advertising affects the sales of a video game? How can I determine whether the price and advertising interact significantly?
- How can I interpret the effects of price and advertising on sales in the absence of significant interaction between the price and advertising?

In many sets of data, two factors can influence a dependent variable. The following table shows some examples:

Factors	Dependent variable
Sales representative and district assignment	Sales
Product price and advertising expenditure	Sales
Temperature and pressure	Production yield
Surgeon and brand of stent used	Health of patient after open-heart surgery

When two factors might influence a dependent variable, you can use either the method *randomized blocks* or the method *two-way analysis of variance* (ANOVA) to determine which, if any, of the factors have a significant influence on the dependent variable. With two-way ANOVA, you can also determine whether the two factors exhibit a significant interaction. For example, suppose you are trying to predict sales by using the product price and advertising budget. Price and advertising interact significantly if the effect of advertising depends on the product price.

In a randomized block model, you observe each possible combination of factors exactly once. You can't test for interactions in a randomized block design. In a two-way ANOVA model, you observe each combination of factors the same number of times (call it *k*). In this case, *k* must be greater than 1. In a two-way ANOVA model, you can easily test for interactions.

Answers to this chapter's questions

I am trying to analyze the effectiveness of my sales force. The problem is that in addition to a sales representative's own effectiveness, the amount that a representative sells depends on the district to which he or she is assigned. How can I incorporate the district assignments of my representatives into my analysis?

Suppose you want to determine how a sales representative, and the sales district to which the representative is assigned, influence product sales. To answer the question in this example, you can have each of four sales reps spend a month selling in each of five sales districts. The resulting sales are given in the Randomized Blocks worksheet in the file Twowayanova.xlsx and shown in Figure 61-1. For example, Rep 1 sold 20 units during the month she was assigned to District 4.

	C	D	E	F	G
5		Rep 1	Rep 2	Rep 3	Rep 4
6	Dist 1	1	3	10	12
7	Dist 2	17	12	16	14
8	Dist 3	17	21	22	25
9	Dist 4	20	10	17	23
10	Dist 5	22	21	37	32

FIGURE 61-1 Data for the randomized-blocks example.

This model is called a *two-way ANOVA without replication* because two factors (district and sales representative) can potentially influence sales, and you have only a single instance pairing each representative with each district. This model is also called a *randomized blocks design* because you'd like to randomize (chronologically) the assignment of representatives to districts. In other words, you'd like to ensure that the month during which Rep 1 is assigned to District 1 is equally likely to be the first, second, third, fourth, or fifth month. You hope this randomization lessens the effect of time (a representative presumably becomes better over time) on your analysis; in a sense, you are "blocking" the effect of districts when you try to compare sales representatives.

To analyze this data in Microsoft Excel, click Data Analysis on the Data tab (in the Analysis group), and then select the Anova: Two-Factor Without Replication option. (You need to install the Analysis ToolPak add-in. See Chapter 42 for instructions.) Then fill in the dialog box as shown in Figure 61-2.

I used the following information to set up this analysis:

- The input range data is in cells C5:G10.
- I selected Labels because the first row of the input range contains labels.
- I entered B12 as the upper-left cell of the output range.
- The alpha value is not important. You can use the default value.

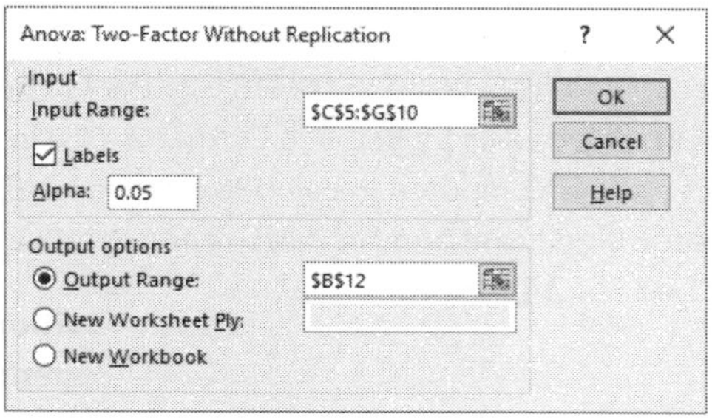

FIGURE 61-2 The Anova: Two-Factor Without Replication dialog box, for setting up a randomized-blocks model.

The output you obtain is shown in Figure 61-3. (The results in cells G12:G24 were not created by the Excel Data Analysis feature. I entered formulas in those cells, as I'll explain later in the chapter.)

	B	C	D	E	F	G	H
12	Anova: Two-Factor Without Replication					17.6	
13							
14	*SUMMARY*	*Count*	*Sum*	*Average*	*Variance*		
15	Dist 1	4	26	6.5	28.3333	-11.1	
16	Dist 2	4	59	14.75	4.91667	-2.85	
17	Dist 3	4	85	21.25	10.9167	3.65	
18	Dist 4	4	70	17.5	31	-0.1	
19	Dist 5	4	112	28	60.6667	10.4	
20						-17.6	
21	Rep 1	5	77	15.4	69.3	-2.2	
22	Rep 2	5	67	13.4	59.3	-4.2	
23	Rep 3	5	102	20.4	104.3	2.8	
24	Rep 4	5	106	21.2	67.7	3.6	
25							
26							
27	ANOVA						
28	*Source of Variation*	*SS*	*df*	*MS*	*F*	*P-value*	*F crit*
29	Rows	1011	4	252.825	15.876	9.7E-05	3.2592
30	Columns	216.4	3	72.1333	4.52957	0.0241	3.4903
31	Error	191.1	12	15.925			
32			stdev	3.99061			
33	Total	1419	19				

FIGURE 61-3 Randomized-blocks output.

To determine whether the row factor (districts) or column factor (sales representatives) has a significant effect on sales, just look at the *p*-value. If the *p*-value for a factor is low (less than 0.15), the factor has a significant effect on sales. The row *p*-value (0.0000974) and column *p*-value (0.024) are both less than 0.15, so both the district and the representative have a significant effect on sales.

Based on my knowledge of sales representatives and districts, how can I forecast sales? How accurate are my sales forecasts?

How should you predict product sales? You can predict sales during a month by using the following equation 1:

```
Predicted sales=Overall average+(Rep effect)+(District effect)
```

In this equation, *Rep effect* equals 0 if the sales-rep factor is not significant. If the sales-rep factor is significant, *Rep effect* equals the mean for the given rep minus the overall average. Likewise, *District effect* equals 0 if the district factor is not significant. If the district factor is significant, *District effect* equals the mean for the given district minus the overall average.

I computed the overall average (17.6) in cell G12 by using the formula =AVERAGE(D6:G10). The representative and district effects are computed by copying from cell G15 to G16:G24 the formula =E15–$G$12. As an example, you can compute the predicted sales by Rep 4 in District 2 (*Dist* in the file abbreviates *District*) as 17.6–2.85+3.6=18.35. This value is computed in cell D38 (see Figure 61-4) with the formula =G12+G16+G24. If the district effect is significant and the sales-representative effect is not, the predicted sales for Rep 4 in Dist 2 would be 17.6–2.85=14.75.

	C	D
36	District 2	
37	Rep 4 Forecast	
38	Mean	18.35
39	Lower	10.3688
40	Upper	26.3312

FIGURE 61-4 The forecast for the sales in District 2 by Rep 4.

As in one-way ANOVA, the standard deviation of the forecast errors is the square root of the mean square error shown in cell E31. I computed this standard deviation in cell E32 with the formula =SQRT(E31). Thus, you can be 95 percent sure that if Rep 4 is assigned to District 2, monthly sales will be between 18.35–2(3.99)=10.37 and 18.35+2(3.99)=26.33. These limits are computed in cell D39 and D40 with the formulas =$D$38–2*$E$32 and =$D$38+2*$E$32, respectively.

How can I determine whether varying the price and the amount of advertising affects the sales of a video game? How can I determine whether price and advertising interact significantly?

When you have more than one observation for each combination of the row and column factors, you have a two-factor ANOVA with replication. To perform this sort of analysis, Excel requires that you have the same number of observations for each row-and-column combination.

In addition to testing for the significance of the row and column factors, you can also test for significant interaction between them. For example, if you want to understand how price and advertising affect sales, an interaction between price and advertising would indicate that the effect of an advertising change would depend on the price level (or equivalently, the effect of a price change would depend on the advertising level). A lack of interaction between price and advertising would mean that the effect of a price change would not depend on the level of advertising.

As an example of two-factor ANOVA with replication, suppose you want to determine how the price and advertising level affect the monthly sales of a video game. In the Two Way ANOVA No Interaction worksheet in the file Twowayanova.xlsx, you can find the data shown in Figure 61-5. For example, during the three months in which advertising was low and the price was medium, 21, 20, and 16 units were sold.

	B	C	D	E	F	G
1		Average	25.04			
2			Price			
3			Low	Medium	High	Effect
4		Low	41	21	10	-5.5926
5	Adv		25	20	11	
6			23	16	8	
7		Medium	28	28	11	-1.8148
8			30	22	22	
9			32	18	18	
10		High	35	26	21	7.4074
11			45	40	26	
12			47	32	20	
13		Effect	8.963	-0.2593	-8.7	

FIGURE 61-5 The video-game sales data; no interaction.

Notice that for each price/advertising combination, there are exactly three observations. In cell D1, I computed the overall average (25.037) of all the observations with the formula =AVERAGE(D4:F12). In cells G4, G7, and G10, I computed the effect for each level of advertising. For example, the effect of having a low level of advertising equals the average for low advertising minus the overall average. In cell G4, I computed the low advertising effect of –5.59 with the formula =AVERAGE(D4:F6)–$D$1. In a similar fashion, I computed the effect of each price level by copying from D13 to E13:F13 the formula =AVERAGE(D4:D12)–$D$1.

To analyze this data, click Data Analysis on the Data tab, and then select Anova: Two-Factor With Replication in the Data Analysis dialog box. Fill in the dialog box as shown in Figure 61-6.

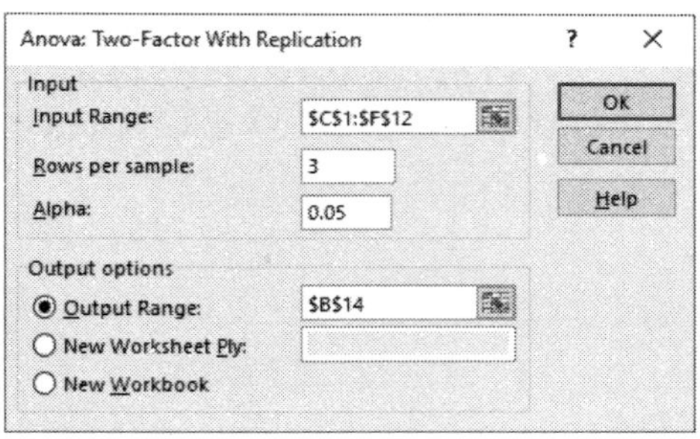

FIGURE 61-6 The Anova: Two-Factor With Replication dialog box for running a two-factor ANOVA with replication.

I used the following information to set up the analysis:

- The input range data, including labels, is in C3:F12. In two-way ANOVA with replication, Excel requires a label for each level of the column effect in the first row of each column in the input range. Thus, I entered **Low**, **Medium**, and **High** in cells D3:F3 to indicate the possible price levels. Excel also requires a label for each level of the row effect in the first column of the input range. These labels must appear in the row that marks the beginning of the data for each level. Thus, I placed labels corresponding to low, medium, and high levels of advertising in cells C4, C7, and C10.

- In the Rows Per Sample box, I entered 3 because we have three replications for each combination of the price and advertising level.
- The upper-left cell of our output range is B14.

I then click OK. The only important portion of the output is the ANOVA table, which is shown in Figure 61-7.

	B	C	D	E	F	G	H	I
42	ANOVA							
43	*Source of Variation*	*SS*	*df*	*MS*	*F*	*P-value*	*F crit*	*F crit*
44	Sample	804.96296	2	402.481	13.52	0.0003	3.5546	3.55456109
45	Columns	1405.4074	2	702.704	23.6	9E-06	3.5546	3.55456109
46	Interaction	50.592593	4	12.6481	0.425	0.7888	2.9277	2.92774871
47	Within	536	18	29.7778				
48								
49	Total	2796.963	26					

FIGURE 61-7 A two-way ANOVA with replication output; no interaction.

As with randomized blocks, an effect (including interactions) is significant if it has a *p*-value that's less than 0.15. Here, Sample (this is the row for advertising effect) and Price (shown in the row labeled Columns) are highly significant, and also, there is no significant interaction. (The interaction *p*-value is 0.79!) Therefore, you can conclude that price and advertising influence sales and that the effect of advertising on sales does not depend on the price level. Figure 61-8 graphically demonstrates the fact that price and advertising do not exhibit a significant interaction. (See the Graph No Interaction worksheet to the right of the worksheets in the file Twowayanova.xlsx.)

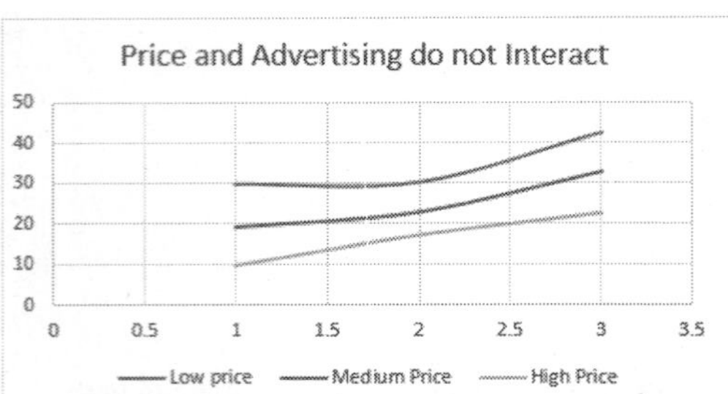

FIGURE 61-8 Showing how the price and advertising do not interact in this data set.

Notice that as advertising increases, sales increase at roughly the same rate, whether the price level is low, medium, or high. Basically, we can recognize *no interaction* by the fact that the series for each price level are nearly parallel.

How can I interpret the effects of price and advertising on sales in the absence of significant interaction between price and advertising?

In the absence of a significant interaction, you can forecast sales in a two-factor ANOVA with replication in the same way that you do in a two-factor ANOVA without replication. Use the following equation 2:

```
Predicted sales=Overall average+[Row or advertising effect(if significant)]
   +[Column or price effect(if significant)]
```

This analysis assumes that price and advertising are the only factors that affect sales. If sales are highly seasonal, seasonality would need to be incorporated into the analysis. (I'll discuss seasonality in Chapter 63, "Winters method," and Chapter 65, "Forecasting in the presence of special events.") For example, when price is high and advertising is medium, the predicted sales are given by 25.037+(–1.814)+(–8.704)=14.52. (See cell E54 in Figure 61-9, which shows the Two Way ANOVA No Interaction worksheet again.) In Figure 61-5, shown earlier, you can see that the overall average is equal to 25.037, the medium advertising effect equals –1.814, and the high price effect =–8.704.

	B	C	D	E	F	G	H	I
42	ANOVA							
43	*Source of Variation*	*SS*	*df*	*MS*	*F*	*P-value*	*F crit*	*F crit*
44	Sample	804.96296	2	402.481	13.52	0.0003	3.5546	3.55456109
45	Columns	1405.4074	2	702.704	23.6	9E-06	3.5546	3.55456109
46	Interaction	50.592593	4	12.6481	0.425	0.7888	2.9277	2.92774871
47	Within	536	18	29.7778				
48								
49	Total	2796.963	26					
50								
51			Stdev	5.4569				
52			Medium Ad					
53			High Price					
54			Mean	14.5185				
55			Lower	3.60471				
56			Upper	25.4323				
57								

FIGURE 61-9 The forecasts for sales with high price and medium advertising.

The standard deviation of the forecast errors equals the square root of our mean squared within error, demonstrated by the following example:

$$\sqrt{29.78}=5.46$$

You can be about 95 percent sure that the forecast is accurate within 10.92 units. In other words, you are 95 percent sure that sales during a month with a high price and medium advertising will be between 3.60 and 25.43 units.

In the Two Way ANOVA with Interaction worksheet, I changed the data from the previous example to the data shown in Figure 61-10. After running the analysis for a two-factor ANOVA with replication, I obtained the results shown in Figure 61-11.

	D	E	F	G
2			Price	
3				
4		Low	Medium	High
5	Low	41	21	15
6		25	20	14
7		23	16	13
8	Medium	28	28	14
9		30	22	13
10		32	18	12
11	High	50	34	13
12		51	40	13
13		52	32	13

FIGURE 61-10 The sales data with interaction between the price and advertising.

	C	D	E	F	G	H	I
43	ANOVA						
44	*Source of Variation*	*SS*	*df*	*MS*	*F*	*P-value*	*F crit*
45	Sample	828.963	2	414.481	24.22	7.86E-06	3.55456
46	Columns	2498.74	2	1249.37	73.02	2.31E-09	3.55456
47	Interaction	509.926	4	127.481	7.45	0.001006	2.92775
48	Within	308	18	17.1111			
49							
50	Total	4145.63	26				
51		Std dev	4.137				

FIGURE 61-11 The output for the two-factor ANOVA with interaction.

In this data set, the *p*-value for interaction is 0.001. When you see a low *p*-value (less than 0.15) for interaction, you do not even check *p*-values for row and column factors. You simply forecast the sales for any price and advertising combination to equal the mean of the three observations involving that price and advertising combination. For example, the following forecast is best for sales during a month with high advertising and medium price:

$$\frac{34+40+32}{4}=\frac{106}{3}=35.555 \text{units}$$

The standard deviation of forecast errors is again the square root of the mean square error, as demonstrated by the following equation:

$$\left(\sqrt{17.11}=4.14\right)$$

Thus, you can be 95 percent sure that the sales forecast is accurate within 8.26 units.

Figure 61-12 illustrates why this data exhibits a significant interaction between price and advertising. For a low and medium price, increased advertising increases sales, but if price is high, increased advertising has no effect on sales. This explains why you cannot use equation 2 to forecast sales when a significant interaction is present. After all, how can you talk about an advertising effect when the effect of advertising depends on the price?

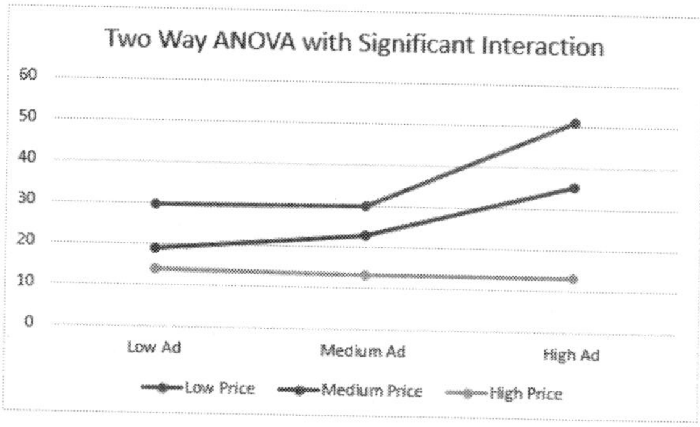

FIGURE 61-12 Showing how price and advertising exhibit a significant interaction in this set of data.

The key thing to notice about this graph is that the different series are not parallel. This detail tells us that at different price levels, changes in advertising have different effects on sales.

Problems

The data for the following Problems 1–3 is in the file Ch61.xlsx:

1. You believe that pressure (high, medium, or low) and temperature (high, medium, or low) influence the yield of a production process. Given this theory, determine the answers to the following problems:

   - Use the data in the Problem 1 worksheet to determine how temperature and/or pressure influence the yield of the process.

   - With high pressure and low temperature, you're 95 percent sure that process yield will be in what range?

2. You are trying to determine how the particular sales representative and the number of sales calls (one, three, or five) made to a doctor influence the amount (in thousands of dollars) that each doctor prescribes of your drug. Use the data in the Problem 2 worksheet to determine the answers to the following problems:

   - How do the representative and number of sales calls influence the sales volume?

   - If Rep 3 makes five sales calls to a doctor, you're 95 percent sure she will generate prescriptions within what range of dollars?

3. Answer the questions in Problem 2, but use the new data in the Problem 3 worksheet.

4. The file Coupondata.xlsx contains information on the sales of peanut butter for weeks when a coupon was given out (or not) and advertising was done (or not) in the Sunday paper. Describe how the coupon and advertising influence peanut-butter sales.

CHAPTER 62

Using moving averages to understand time series

Question answered in this chapter:

- I'm trying to analyze the upward trend in quarterly revenues of Amazon.com since 1996. Fourth quarter sales in the United States are usually larger (because of Christmas) than sales during the first quarter of the following year. This pattern obscures the upward trend in sales. Is there any way that I can graphically show the upward trend in revenues?

Answers to this chapter's question

Time-series data simply displays the same quantity measured at different points in time. For example, the data in the file Amazon.com.xlsx, a subset of which is shown in Figure 62-1, displays the time series for quarterly revenues in millions of dollars for Amazon.com. The data covers the time interval from the fourth quarter of 1995 through the fourth quarter of 2015.

	A	B	C	D
4	FiscalYear	FiscalQuarter	Quarter#	Revenue
5	1995	4	1	0.511
6	1996	1	2	0.875
7	1996	2	3	2.23
8	1996	3	4	4.173
9	1996	4	5	8.468
10	1997	1	6	16.005
11	1997	2	7	27.855
12	1997	3	8	37.887
13	1997	4	9	66.04
14	1998	1	10	87.361
15	1998	2	11	115.982
16	1998	3	12	153.649
17	1998	4	13	252.893
18	1999	1	14	293.643
19	1999	2	15	314.376
20	1999	3	16	355.778
21	1999	4	17	676.042
22	2000	1	18	573.889
23	2000	2	19	577.876
24	2000	3	20	637.858
25	2000	4	21	972.36

FIGURE 62-1 The quarterly revenues for Amazon.com sales.

To graph this time series, select the range C4:D85, which contains the quarter number (the first quarter is Quarter 1, and the last is Quarter 81) and Amazon quarterly revenues (in millions of dollars). Then, in the Charts group on the Insert tab, select Insert Scatter (X, Y) Or Bubble Chart, and choose the second option under the Scatter chart type (Scatter With Smooth Lines And Markers). The time-series plot is shown in Figure 62-2.

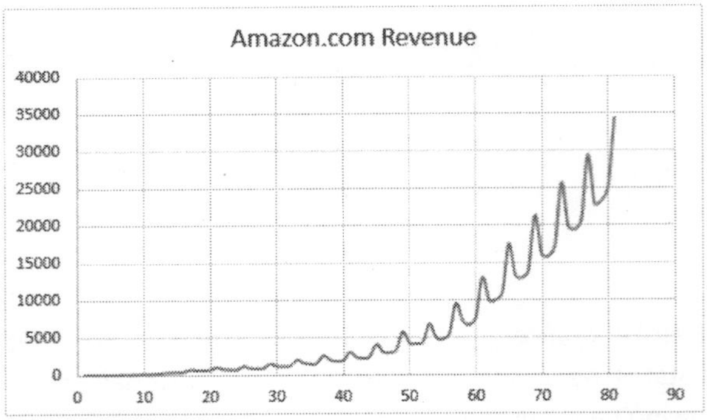

FIGURE 62-2 The time series plot of quarterly Amazon.com revenues.

There is an upward trend in revenues, but the fact that the fourth quarter revenues dwarf the revenues during the first three quarters of each year makes it hard to spot the trend. Because there are four quarters per year, it would be nice to graph the average revenues during the last four quarters. This is called a *four-period moving average*. Using a four-quarter moving average smooths out the seasonal influence because each average will contain one data point for each quarter. Such a graph is called a *moving-average graph* because the plotted average "moves" over time. Moving-average graphs also smooth out random variation, which helps you get a better idea of what is going on with your data.

To create a moving-average graph of quarterly revenues, you can modify the chart. Select the graph, and then click a data point until all the data points are displayed in blue. Right-click any point, click Add Trendline, and then select the Moving Average option in the Format Trendline pane. Set the Period list (to the right of Moving Average) equal to 4. Excel now creates the four-quarter moving average trend curve that's shown in Figure 62-3. (See the file Amazon.com.xlsx.)

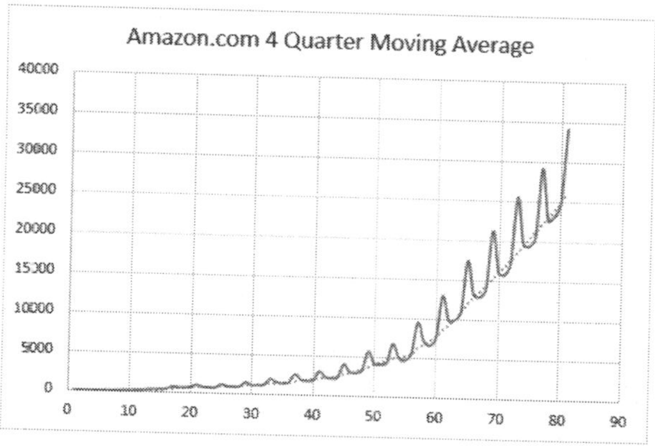

FIGURE 62-3 A four-quarter moving average trend curve.

For each quarter, Excel plots the average of the current quarter and the last three quarters. Of course, for a four-quarter moving average, the moving-average curve starts with the fourth data point. The moving-average curve makes it clear that Amazon.com's revenues had a steady upward trend. In fact, the slope of the four-quarter moving average appears to be increasing. In all likelihood, the slope of this moving average graph will eventually level off, resulting in a graph that looks like an *S curve*. The Excel trend curve feature cannot fit S curves, but the Excel 2016 Solver can be used to fit S curves to data. See my book *Marketing Analytics* (Wiley, 2014) for an explanation of how to fit S curves to data.

Problem

- The file Ch62data.xlsx contains quarterly revenues for GM, Ford, and GE. Construct a four-quarter moving average trend curve for each company's revenues. Describe what you learn from each trend curve.

CHAPTER 63

Winters method

You often need to predict future values of a time series, such as monthly costs or monthly product revenues. This is usually difficult because the characteristics of any time series are constantly changing. Exponential smoothing or adaptive methods are usually best suited for forecasting the future values of a time series. In this chapter, I describe the most powerful smoothing method: *Winters method* (attributed to Peter Winters and Charles Holt). To help you understand how Winters method works, I'll use it to forecast monthly housing starts in the United States. Housing starts are simply the number of new homes whose construction begins during a month. I'll begin by describing the three key characteristics of a time series.

Time-series characteristics

The behavior of most time series can be explained by understanding the following three characteristics (*base*, *trend*, and *seasonality*):

- The *base* of a series describes the series' current level in the absence of any seasonality. For example, suppose the base level for US housing starts is 160,000. In this case, you can believe that if the current month were an average month relative to other months of the year, 160,000 housing starts would occur.
- The *trend* of a time series is the percentage increase, per period, in the base. Thus, a trend of 1.02 means that you estimate that housing starts are increasing by 2 percent each month. A trend of 0.97 means that you estimate that housing starts are decreasing by 3 percent per month.
- The *seasonality* (seasonal index) for a period tells you how far above or below a typical month you can expect housing starts to be. For example, if the December seasonal index is 0.8, then December housing starts are 20 percent below a typical month. If the June seasonal index is 1.3, then June housing starts are 30 percent higher than a typical month.

Parameter definitions

After observing month t, you will have used all the data observed through the end of month t to estimate the following quantities of interest:

- L_t=Level of the series
- T_t=Trend of the series
- S_t=Seasonal index for the current month

The key to Winters method is in the following three equations, which are used to update L_t, T_t, and S_t. In the following formulas, *alp*, *bet*, and *gam* represent *alpha*, *beta*, and *gamma* and are called *smoothing parameters*. You choose the values of these parameters to optimize forecasts. In the following formulas, *c* equals the number of periods in a seasonal cycle (*c*=12 months, for example) and x_t equals the observed value of the time series at time *t*:

- Formula 1: $L_t = alp(x_t/s_{t-c}) + (1-alp)(L_{t-1}*T_{t-1})$
- Formula 2: $T_t = bet(L_t/L_{t-1}) + (1-bet)T_{t-1}$
- Formula 3: $S_t = gam(x_t/L_t) + (1-gam)s_{t-c}$

Formula 1 indicates that the new base estimate is a weighted average of the current observation (*deseasonalized*), and the last period's base is updated by the last trend estimate. Formula 2 indicates that the new trend estimate is a weighted average of the ratio of the current base to the last period's base (this is a current estimate of the trend) and the last period's trend. Formula 3 indicates that you update your seasonal index estimate as a weighted average of the estimate of the seasonal index based on the current period and the previous estimate. Note that the larger values of the smoothing parameters correspond to putting more weight on the current observation.

You can define $F_{t,k}$ as your forecast (*F*), after period *t* for the period *t+k*. This results in the formula $F_{t,k} = L_t*(T_t)^k s_{t+k-c}$. (I refer to this as Formula 4.)

This formula first uses the current trend estimate to update the base *k* periods forward. Then the resulting base estimate for period *t+k* is adjusted by the appropriate seasonal index.

Initializing Winters method

To start Winters method, you must have the initial estimates for the series base, trend, and seasonal indexes. I used monthly housing starts for the years 1986 and 1987 to initialize my use of Winters method. Then I chose smoothing parameters to optimize one-month-ahead forecasts for the years 1988 through 1996. See Figure 63-1 and the file House2.xlsx.

E10

	A	B	C	D	E	F	G	H	I	J
1	DATE	HS							1987 mean	150.45
2	Jan-86	105.4							1986 mean	145.142
3	Feb-86	95.4							Trend	1.003
4	Mar-86	145								
5	Apr-86	175.8								
6	May-86	170.2								
7	Jun-86	163.2								
8	Jul-86	160.7								
9	Aug-86	160.7								
10	Sep-86	147.7					alp	bet	gam	
11	Oct-86	173					0.493579	0.01481	0.2724162	
12	Nov-86	124.1								
13		120.5					seasonal indices			
14	Jan-87	115.6					0.747653			
15	Feb-87	107.2					0.685405			
16	Mar-87	151					1.001381			
17	Apr-87	188.2					1.231428			
18	May-87	186.6					1.207071			
19	Jun-87	183.6					1.17324			
20	Jul-87	172					1.125539			
21	Aug-87	163.8			MAPE	0.0731	1.097798			
22	Sep-87	154					1.020665			
23	Oct-87	154.8					1.108962			
24	Nov-87	115.6	Base	Trend	Forecast	APE	0.810916			
25	Dec-87	113	143	1.003			0.789941			
26	Jan-88	105.1	142	1.003	107.271	0.0207	0.745544			
27	Feb-88	102.8	146.2	1.003	97.6351	0.0502	0.69028			
28	Mar-88	141.2	143.9	1.003	146.844	0.04	0.995969			
29	Apr-88	159.3	136.9	1.002	177.676	0.1154	1.212913			
30	May-88	158	134.1	1.002	165.634	0.0483	1.199217			

FIGURE 63-1 Initializing Winters method.

I used the following steps:

1. I estimated, for example, the January seasonal index as the average of the January housing starts for 1986 and 1987, divided by the average monthly starts for 1986 and 1987. Therefore, copying from G14 to G15:G25 the formula =AVERAGE(B2,B14)/AVERAGE($B$2:$B$25) generates the estimates of the seasonal indexes. For example, the January estimate is 0.75 and the June estimate is 1.17.

2. To estimate the average monthly trend, I took the twelfth root of the 1987 mean starts, divided by the 1986 mean starts. I computed this in cell J3 (and copied it to cell D25) with the formula =(J1/J2)^(1/12).

3. Going into January 1987, I estimated the base of the series as the deseasonalized December 1987 value. This was computed in C25 with the formula =(B25/G25).

Estimating the smoothing constants

Now I'm ready to estimate the smoothing constants. In column C, I will update the series base; in column D, the series trend; and in column G, the seasonal indexes. In column E, I compute the forecast for next month, and in column F, I compute the absolute percentage error for each month. Finally, I use Solver to choose values for the smoothing constants that minimize the sum of the absolute percentage errors. The following steps reveal the process:

1. In G11:I11, I enter trial values (between 0 and 1) for the smoothing constants.

2. In C26:C119, I compute the updated series level with Formula 1 by copying from C26 to C27:C119 the formula =alp*(B26/G14)+(1–alp)*(C25*D25).
3. In D26:D119, I use Formula 2 to update the series trend, copying from D26 to D27:D119 the formula =bet*(C26/C25)+(1–bet)*D25.
4. In G26:G119, I use Formula 3 to update the seasonal indexes, copying from G26 to G27:G119 the formula =gam*(B26/C26)+(1–gam)*G14.
5. In E26:E119, I use Formula 4 to compute the forecast for the current month by copying from E26 to E27:E119 the formula =(C25*D25)*G14.
6. In F26:F119, I compute the absolute percentage error for each month by copying from F26 to F27:F119 the formula =ABS(B26-E26)/B26.
7. I compute the average absolute percentage error for the years 1988 through 1996 in F21 with the formula =AVERAGE(F26:F119).
8. Now I click the Data tab and click Solver in the Analyze group. I use Solver to determine smoothing parameter values that minimize the average absolute percentage error. The Solver Parameters dialog box is shown in Figure 63-2. Solver is discussed in Chapters 29-38.

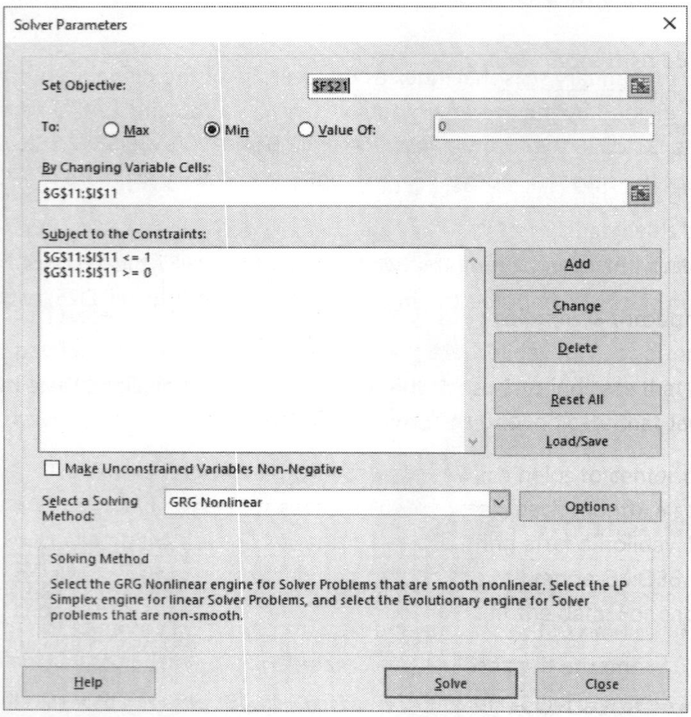

FIGURE 63-2 The Solver Parameters dialog box for Winters method.

Note To install the Solver add-in, click the File tab, click Options, and then click Add-Ins on the left pane of the Excel Options dialog box. With the default Excel Add-Ins selected, click Go to the right of the Manage button, select Solver Add-In in the Add-Ins dialog box, and click OK. The Solver button appears on the Data tab, in the Analyze group. For more information, see Chapter 29, "An introduction to optimization with Excel Solver."

I used smoothing parameters (G11:I11) to minimize the average absolute percentage error (cell F21). Solver ensures that you find the best combination of smoothing constants. Smoothing constants must be between 0 and 1. Here, *alp*=0.50, *bet*=0.01, and *gam*=0.27 minimizes the average absolute percentage error. You might find slightly different values for the smoothing constants, but you should obtain a mean absolute percentage error (MAPE) close to 7.3 percent. In this example, there are many combinations of the smoothing constants that give forecasts, having approximately the same MAPE. My one-month-ahead forecasts are off by an average of 7.3 percent.

Remarks

- Instead of choosing smoothing parameters to optimize one-period forecast errors, you could, for example, choose to optimize the average absolute percentage error incurred in forecasting the total housing starts for the next six months.
- If at the end of month *t*, you want to forecast sales for the next four quarters, you would simply add $f_{t,1}+f_{t,2}+f_{t,3}+f_{t,4}$. If you want, you could choose smoothing parameters to minimize the absolute percentage error incurred in estimating the sales for the next year.

Problems

All the data for the following problems is in the file Quarterly.xlsx:

1. Use Winters method to forecast one-quarter-ahead revenues for Apple.
2. Use Winters method to forecast one-quarter-ahead revenues for Amazon.com.
3. Use Winters method to forecast one-quarter-ahead revenues for Home Depot.
4. Use Winters method to forecast total revenues for the next two quarters for Home Depot.

CHAPTER 64

Ratio-to-moving-average forecast method

Questions answered in this chapter:

- What is the trend of a time series?
- How do I define seasonal indexes for a time series?
- Is there an easy way to incorporate trend and seasonality into forecasting future product sales?

Often you need a simple, accurate method to predict the future quarterly revenues of a corporation or future monthly sales of a product. The *ratio-to-moving-average method* provides an accurate, easy-to-use forecasting method for these situations.

In the file Ratioma.xlsx, you are given the sales of a product during 20 quarters (shown later in Figure 64-1 in rows 5 through 28), and you want to predict the sales during the next four quarters (Quarters 21-24). This time series has both a trend and seasonality.

Answers to this chapter's questions

What is the trend of a time series?

A trend of 10 units per quarter means, for example, that sales are increasing by 10 units per quarter, while a trend of -5 units per quarter means that sales tend to decrease 5 units per quarter.

How do I define seasonal indexes for a time series?

We know that Walmart sees a large increase in its sales during the fourth quarter (because of the holiday season.) If you do not recognize this, you would have trouble coming up with good forecasts of quarterly Walmart revenues. The concept of *seasonal indexes* helps you better understand a company's sales pattern. The quarterly seasonal indexes for Walmart revenues are as follows:

- Quarter 1 (January through March): 0.90
- Quarter 2 (April through June): 0.98
- Quarter 3 (July through September): 0.96

- Quarter 4 (October through December): 1.16

These indexes imply, for example, that sales during a fourth quarter are typically 16 percent higher than sales during an average quarter. Seasonal indexes must average out to 1.

To see whether you understand seasonal indexes, try to answer the following question: Suppose that during Quarter 4 of 2013, Walmart has sales of $200 billion, and during Quarter 1 of 2014, Walmart has sales of $180 billion. Are things getting better or worse for Walmart? The key idea here is to deseasonalize the sales and express each quarter's sales in terms of an average quarter. For example, the Quarter 4 2013 sales are equivalent to selling 200/1.16 = $172.4 billion in an average quarter, and the Quarter 1 2014 sales are equivalent to selling 180/0.9 = $200 billion in an average quarter. Thus, even though Walmart's actual sales decreased 10 percent, sales appear to be increasing by (200/172.4) – 1 = 16 percent per quarter. This simple example shows how important it is to understand the seasonal indexes of your company or product.

Is there an easy way to incorporate trend and seasonality into forecasting future product sales?

Now let's turn to the simple *ratio-to-moving-average forecasting method*. This technique enables you to easily estimate a time series' trend and seasonal indexes and makes it easy to generate the forecasts of future values of the time series. The work I did for this question is shown in Figure 64-1 and the file Ratioma.xlsx.

	B	C	D	E	F	G	H	I	J	K	L
1				slope	6.93879						
2				intercep	30.1662				quarter	season al index	normalized
3									1	0.8185	0.813736785
4	Quarter	Yea	Quarte	Sales	4 period M	Centered M	Actual/CM	Forecas	2	0.9393	0.933819599
5	1	1	1	24					3	1.0674	1.06109143
6	2	1	2	44	52				4	1.1984	1.191352187
7	3	1	3	61	58	55.00	1.11				
8	4	1	4	79	63.5	60.75	1.30				
9	5	2	1	48	71	67.25	0.71				
10	6	2	2	66	77.5	74.25	0.89				
11	7	2	3	91	82.5	80.00	1.14				
12	8	2	4	105	87.25	84.88	1.24				
13	9	3	1	68	89.5	88.38	0.77				
14	10	3	2	85	94.5	92.00	0.92				
15	11	3	3	100	104.25	99.38	1.01				
16	12	3	4	125	114.25	109.25	1.14				
17	13	4	1	107	123.75	119.00	0.90				
18	14	4	2	125	132.25	128.00	0.98				
19	15	4	3	138	139.25	135.75	1.02				
20	16	4	4	159	146.75	143.00	1.11				
21	17	5	1	135	156	151.38	0.89				
22	18	5	2	155	164.25	160.13	0.97				
23	19	5	3	175							
24	20	5	4	192							
25	21	6	1			175.881		143.1			
26	22	6	2			182.819		170.7			
27	23	6	3			189.758		201.4			
28	24	6	4			196.697		234.3			

FIGURE 64-1 The data for the ratio-to-moving-average example.

You begin by trying to estimate the deseasonalized level of the series during each period (using *centered moving averages*). Then you can fit a trend line to your deseasonalized estimates (in column G). Next you determine the seasonal index for each quarter. Finally, you estimate the future level of the series by extrapolating the trend line, and then you predict the future sales by reseasonalizing the trend-line estimate. The following steps break down each task:

- **Calculating moving averages** To begin, compute a four-quarter moving average (having four quarters eliminates seasonality) for each quarter by averaging the prior quarter, the current quarter, and the next two quarters. To do this, copy from F6 to F7:F22 the formula =AVERAGE(E5:E8). For example, for Quarter 2, the moving average is 0.25*(24+44+61+79)=52.
- **Calculating centered moving averages** The moving average for Quarter 2 is centered at Quarter 2.5, while the moving average for Quarter 3 is centered at Quarter 3.5. Averaging these two moving averages gives a *centered moving average*, which estimates the level of the process at the end of Quarter 3. Copying from cell G7 the formula =AVERAGE(F6:F7) gives you an estimate of the level of the series during each series—without seasonality!
- **Fitting a trend line to the centered moving averages** You use the centered moving averages to fit a trend line that can be used to estimate the future level of the series.

  In F1, I use the formula =SLOPE(G7:G22,B7:B22) to find the *slope* of the trend line, and in cell F2 I use the formula =INTERCEPT(G7:G22,B7:B22) to find the *intercept* of the trend line. You can now estimate the level of the series during Quarter t to be 6.94t+30.17. Copying from G25 to G26:G28 the formula =Intercept+Slope*B23 computes the estimated level of the series from Quarter 21 onward.
- **Computing the seasonal indexes** Recall that a seasonal index of, say, 2 for a quarter, means the sales in that quarter are twice the sales during an average quarter, and a seasonal index of 0.5 for a quarter means that the sales during that quarter are half of an average quarter. To determine the seasonal indexes, begin by calculating for each quarter for which you have the sales that are actual sales/centered moving average. To do this, copy from cell H7 to H8:H22 the formula =E7/G7. You'll see, for example, that during each first quarter, the sales were 77, 71, 90, and 89 percent of the average, so you can estimate the seasonal index for Quarter 1 as the average of these four numbers (82 percent). To calculate the initial seasonal index estimates, copy from cell K3 to K4:K6 the formula =AVERAGEIF($D$7:$D$22,J3,$H$7:$H$22). This formula averages the four estimates you have for the Quarter 1 seasonality.

  Unfortunately, the seasonal indexes do not average exactly to 1. To ensure that the final seasonal indexes average to 1, copy from L3 to L4:L6 the formula =K3/AVERAGE($K$3:$K$6).
- **Forecasting sales during Quarters 21–24** To create the sales forecast for each future quarter, you simply multiply the trend-line estimate for the quarter's level (from column G) by the appropriate seasonal index. Copying from cell I25 to I26:I28 the formula =VLOOKUP(D25,season,3)*G25 computes the final forecast for Quarters 21–24.

If you think the trend of the series has changed recently, you can estimate the series' trend based on more recent data. For example, you could use the centered moving averages for Quarters 13–18 to get a more recent trend estimate with the formula =SLOPE(G17:G22,B17:B22). This yields an estimated trend of 8.09 units per quarter. If you want to forecast Quarter 22 sales, for example, you would take the last centered moving average you have (from Quarter 18) of 160.13 and add 4(8.09) to estimate the level of the series in Quarter 22. Then multiplying by the Quarter 2 seasonal index of 0.933 yields a final forecast for the Quarter 22 sales of (160.13+4(8.09))*(0.933) = 179.6 units.

Problem

1. The file Walmartdata.xlsx (in the Practice Files folder) contains the quarterly revenues of Walmart during the years 1994–2009. Use the ratio-to-moving-average method to forecast the revenues for Quarters 3 and 4 in 2009 and Quarters 1 and 2 of 2010. Use Quarters 53–60 to create a trend estimate that you use in your forecasts.

CHAPTER 65

Forecasting in the presence of special events

Questions answered in this chapter:

- How can I determine whether specific factors influence customer traffic?
- How can I evaluate my forecast accuracy?
- How can I check whether my forecast errors are random?

For a student project in the early 1990s (before direct deposit!), a class and I attempted to forecast the number of customers visiting the Eastland Plaza Branch of the Indiana University (IU) Credit Union each day. Interviews with the branch manager made it clear that the following factors affected the number of customers:

- Month of the year
- Day of the week
- Whether the day was a faculty or staff payday
- Whether the day before or the day after was a holiday

Answers to this chapter's questions

How can I determine whether specific factors influence customer traffic?

The data collected is contained in the Original worksheet in the file Creditunion.xlsx, shown in Figure 65-1. If you try to run a regression on this data by using dummy variables (as described in Chapter 58, "Incorporating qualitative factors into multiple regression"), the dependent variable would be the number of customers arriving each day (the data in column E). You would need 19 independent variables:

- Eleven to account for the month (12 months minus 1)
- Four to account for the day of the week (5 business days minus 1)
- Two to account for the types of paydays that occur each month

- Two to account for whether a particular day follows or precedes a holiday

Microsoft Excel allows only 15 independent variables, so it appears that you're in trouble.

	B	C	D	E	F	G	H	I	J
1								RSQ	0.7712
2									
3	MONTH	DAYMON	DAYWEEK	CUST	SPECIAL	SP	FAC	BH	AH
4	1	2	2	1825	SP,FAC,AI	1	1	0	1
5	1	3	3	1257	0	0	0	0	0
6	1	4	4	969	0	0	0	0	0
7	1	5	5	1672	SP	1	0	0	0
8	1	8	1	1098	0	0	0	0	0
9	1	9	2	691	0	0	0	0	0
10	1	10	3	672	0	0	0	0	0
11	1	11	4	754	0	0	0	0	0
12	1	12	5	972	0	0	0	0	0
13	1	15	1	816	0	0	0	0	0
14	1	16	2	717	0	0	0	0	0
15	1	17	3	728	0	0	0	0	0
16	1	18	4	711	0	0	0	0	0
17	1	19	5	1545	SP	1	0	0	0
18	1	22	1	873	0	0	0	0	0
19	1	23	2	713	0	0	0	0	0
20	1	24	3	626	0	0	0	0	0
21	1	25	4	653	0	0	0	0	0
22	1	26	5	1080	0	0	0	0	0
23	1	29	1	650	0	0	0	0	0
24	1	30	2	644	0	0	0	0	0
25	1	31	3	803	0	0	0	0	0
26	2	1	4	1282	FAC	0	1	0	0

FIGURE 65-1 The data used to predict credit-union customer traffic.

When a regression forecasting model requires more than 15 independent variables, you can use Solver to estimate the coefficients of the independent variables. You can also use Excel to compute the R-squared values between the forecasts and actual customer traffic and the standard deviation for the forecast errors. To analyze this data (see Figure 65-2), I created a forecasting equation by using a lookup table to locate the day of the week, the month, and other factors. Then I used Solver to choose the coefficients for each level of each factor that yields the minimum sum of squared errors. (Each day's error equals actual customers minus forecasted customers.) Here are the particulars.

I began by creating indicator variables (in columns G through J) for whether the day is a staff payday (SP), faculty payday (FAC), before a holiday (BH), or after a holiday (AH). (See Figure 65-1.) For example, in cells G4, H4, and J4, I entered 1 to indicate that January 2 was a staff payday, faculty payday, and after a holiday. Cell I4 contains 0 to indicate that January 2 was not before a holiday.

The forecast is defined by a constant (which helps to center the forecasts so that they will be more accurate) and effects for each day of the week, each month, a staff payday, a faculty payday, a day occurring before a holiday, and a day occurring after a holiday. I inserted trial values for all these parameters (the Solver changing cells) in the cell range O4:O26, shown in Figure 65-2. Solver will then choose the values that make the model best fit the data. For each day, the forecast of customer count will be generated by the following equation:

```
Predicted customer count=Constant+(Month effect)+(Day of week effect)
   +(Staff payday effect, if any)+(Faculty payday effect, if any)+
   (Before holiday effect, if any)+(After holiday effect, if any)
```

Using this model, you can compute a forecast for each day's customer count by copying from K4 to K5:K257 the following formula:

```
=$O$26+VLOOKUP(B4,$N$14:$O$25,2)+VLOOKUP(D4,$N$4:$O$8,2)+G4*$O$9+H4*$O$10+I4*$O$11+J4*$O$12
```

Cell O26 picks up the constant term. VLOOKUP(B4,$N$14:$O$25,2) picks up the month coefficient for the current month, and VLOOKUP(D4,$N$4:$O$8,2) picks up the day of the week coefficient for the current week. G4*$O$9+H4*$O$10+I4*$O$11+J4*$O$12 picks up the effects (if any) when the current day is coded as SP, FAC, BH, or AH.

By copying from L4 to L5:L257 the formula =(E4-K4)^2, I compute the squared error for each day. Then, in cell L2, I compute the sum of squared errors with the formula =SUM(L4:L257).

	G	H	I	J	K	L	M	N	O	P	Q	R
1			RSQ	0.7712		stdeverr	163.1772					
2					SSE	6736582						
3	SP	FAC	BH	AH	Forecast	Sq Err	Error	Day of Week			average	
4	1	1	0	1	1766.78	3389.56	58.21993	1	103.357		dayweek	0
5	0	0	0	0	709.603	299643	547.3965	2	-139.19		month	-4E-09
6	0	0	0	0	745.698	49863.78	223.302	3	-150.34			
7	1	0	0	0	1557.22	13174.18	114.7788	4	-114.25			
8	0	0	0	0	963.303	18143.29	134.697	5	300.424			
9	0	0	0	0	720.753	885.2568	-29.7533	SP	396.851			
10	0	0	0	0	709.603	1414.02	-37.6035	FAC	394.894			
11	0	0	0	0	745.698	68.92317	8.301998	BH	205.293			
12	0	0	0	0	1160.37	35483.19	-188.37	AH	254.281			
13	0	0	0	0	963.303	21698.16	-147.303	Month				
14	0	0	0	0	720.753	14.08701	-3.75327	1	-110.69			
15	0	0	0	0	709.603	338.4326	18.39654	2	-75.715			
16	0	0	0	0	745.698	1203.951	-34.698	3	-40.341			
17	1	0	0	0	1557.22	149.3565	-12.2212	4	0.02839			
18	0	0	0	0	963.303	8154.623	-90.303	5	87.8157			
19	0	0	0	0	720.753	60.11313	-7.75327	6	133.341			
20	0	0	0	0	709.603	6989.539	-83.6035	7	115.803			
21	0	0	0	0	745.698	8592.92	-92.698	8	28.7743			
22	0	0	0	0	1160.37	6459.308	-80.3698	9	-87.563			
23	0	0	0	0	963.303	98158.74	-313.303	10	-53.002			
24	0	0	0	0	720.753	5891.064	-76.7533	11	-42.761			
25	0	0	0	0	709.603	8722.913	93.39654	12	44.3091			
26	0	1	0	0	1175.57	11328.02	106.4332	constant	970.635			

FIGURE 65-2 Changing cells and customer forecasts.

In cell R4, I average the day of the week changing cells with the formula =AVERAGE(O4:O8), and in cell R5, I average the month changing cells with the formula =AVERAGE(O14:O25). Later, I'll constrain the average month and day of the week effects to equal 0, which ensures that a month or day of the week with a positive effect has a higher-than-average customer count, and a month or day of the week with a negative effect has a lower-than-average customer count.

You can use the Solver settings shown in Figure 65-3 to choose the forecast parameters to minimize the sum of squared errors. To run Solver, click the Data tab on the ribbon, and then click Solver in the Analyze group.

> **Note** To install the Solver add-in, click the File tab, click Options on the left pane, and then click Add-Ins on the left pane of the Excel Options dialog box. With the default Excel Add-Ins selected, click Go to the right of the Manage list, select Solver Add-In in the Add-Ins dialog box, and click OK. The Solver button appears on the Data tab, in the Analyze group. For more information, see Chapter 29, "An introduction to optimization with Excel Solver."

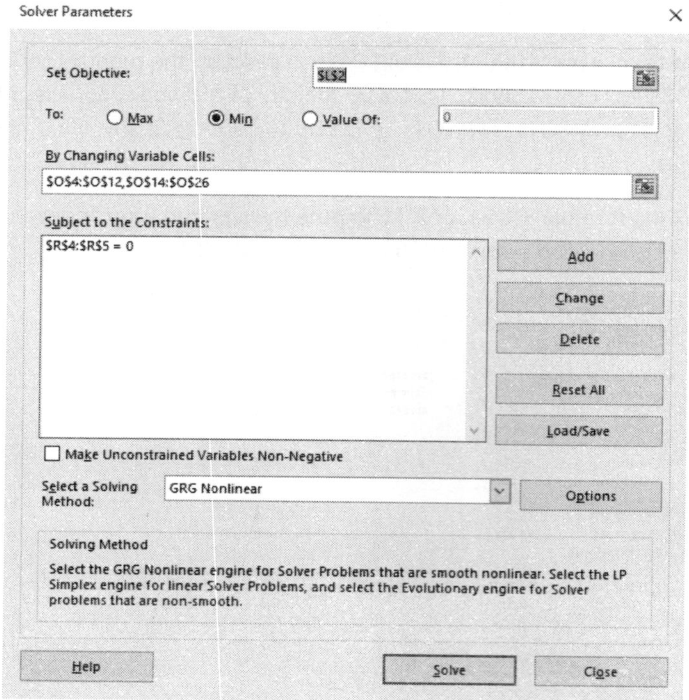

FIGURE 65-3 The Solver Parameters dialog box, for determining forecast parameters.

The Solver model changes the coefficients for the month, day of the week, BH, AH, SP, FAC, and the constant to minimize the sum of square errors. I also constrained the average day of the week and month effect to equal 0. Using Solver, the results shown earlier in Figure 65-2 are obtained. For example, Friday is the busiest day of the week and June is the busiest month. A staff payday raises the forecast (all else being equal—in the Latin, *ceteris paribus*) by 397 customers.

How can I evaluate my forecast accuracy?

To evaluate the accuracy of the forecast, you compute the R-squared value between the forecasts and the actual customer count in cell J1. The formula you use is =RSQ(E4:E257,K4:K257). This formula computes the percentage of the actual variation in customer count that is explained by the forecasting model. Here, the independent variables explain 77 percent of the daily variation in customer count.

You compute the error for each day in column M by copying from M4 to M5:M257 the formula E4–K4. A close approximation to the standard error of the forecast is given by the standard deviation of the errors. This value is computed in cell M1 by using the formula =STDEVS(M4:M257). Thus, approximately 68 percent of the forecasts should be accurate within 163 customers, 95 percent accurate within 326 customers, and so on.

Let's try and spot any outliers. Recall that an observation is an outlier if the absolute value of a forecast error exceeds two times the standard error of the regression. Select the range M4:M257 (select the cell M4 and press Ctrl+Shift+Down arrow), and then click Conditional Formatting on the

Home tab, in the Styles group. Next, select New Rule, and in the New Formatting Rule dialog box, in the Select A Rule Type list, choose Use A Formula To Determine Which Cells To Format. Fill in the rule description in the dialog box as shown in Figure 65-4. (For more information about conditional formatting, see Chapter 24, "Conditional formatting.")

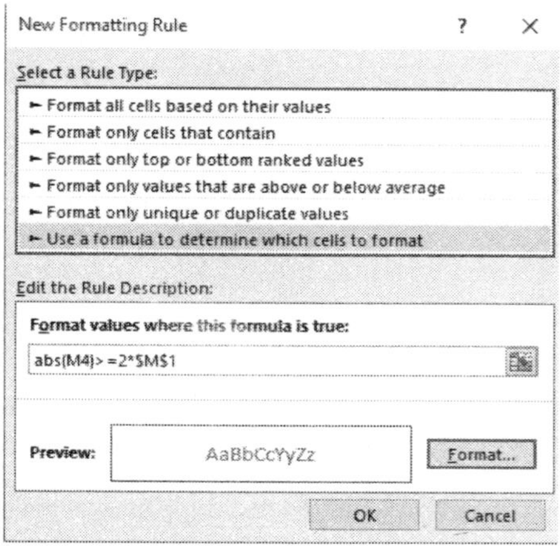

FIGURE 65-4 Using conditional formatting to spot forecast outliers.

After you choose a format with a red font, the conditional formatting settings will display in red any error that exceeds 2*(standard deviation of errors) in absolute error. Looking at the outliers, you can see that the model often underforecasts the customer count for the first three days of the month. Also, during the second week in March (spring break), the model overforecasts, and the day before spring break, it greatly underforecasts.

To remedy this problem, I added in the 1st Three Days worksheet (of the file Creditunion.xlsx) changing cells for each of the first three days of the month, for spring break, and the day before spring break. I added trial values for these new effects in cells O26:O30. I included the effects of the first three days of the month by copying from K4 to K5:K257 the following formula:

```
=$O$25+VLOOKUP(B4,$N$13:$O$24,2)+VLOOKUP(D4,$N$4:$O$8,2)+G4*$O$9+H4*$O$10+I4*$O$11+J4*$O$12
   +IF(C4=1,$O$26,IF(C4=2,$O$27,IF(C4=3,$O$28,0)))
```

The term IF(C4=1,$O$26,IF(C4=2,$O$27,IF(C4=3,$O$28,0))) picks up the effect of the first three days of the month. I manually entered the spring break coefficients in cells K52:K57. For example, in cell K52 I added +O29 to the formula, and in cells K53:K57, I added +O30.

After including the new changing cells in the Solver dialog box, I get the results shown in Figure 65-5. Notice that the first three days of the month greatly increase customer count (probably because of government support and Social Security checks), and that spring break reduces customer count. Figure 65-5 also shows the improvement in the forecasting accuracy. The R-squared value (using RSQ in cell J1) has improved to 87 percent, and the standard error is reduced to 122 customers.

	I	J	K	L	M	N	O	P	Q	R
1	RSQ	0.871		stdeverr	122.285					
2			SSE	3783269						
3	BH	AH	Forecast	Sq Err	Error	Day of Week			average	
4	0	1	1879.63	2984.54	-54.631	1	107.706		dayweek	0
5	0	0	995.4	68434.5	261.6	2	-138.93		month	2.5E-14
6	0	0	722.934	60548.4	246.066	3	-153.32			
7	0	0	1554.45	13818.2	117.551	4	-115.08			
8	0	0	945.724	23188.1	152.276	5	299.624			
9	0	0	699.086	65.3826	-8.08595	SP	416.808			
10	0	0	684.701	161.326	-12.7014	FAC	96.6442			
11	0	0	722.934	965.091	31.0659	BH	196.457			
12	0	0	1137.64	27436.9	-165.641	AH	299.116			
13	0	0	945.724	16828.2	-129.724	1	-105.51			
14	0	0	699.086	320.913	17.9141	2	-81.763			
15	0	0	684.701	1874.77	43.2986	3	-27.856			
16	0	0	722.934	142.422	-11.9341	4	-7.2892			
17	0	0	1554.45	89.2902	-9.44935	5	83.8453			
18	0	0	945.724	5288.71	-72.7235	6	130.672			
19	0	0	699.086	193.601	13.9141	7	106.616			
20	0	0	684.701	3445.86	-58.7014	8	13.2601			
21	0	0	722.934	4890.78	-69.9341	9	-64.687			
22	0	0	1137.64	3322.49	-57.641	10	-68.305			
23	0	0	945.724	87452.4	-295.724	11	-33.753			

FIGURE 65-5 The forecast parameters and forecasts, including spring break and the first three days of the month.

By looking at the forecast errors for the week 12/24 through 12/31 (see Figure 65-6), you can see that the model has greatly overforecasted the customer counts for the days in this week. It also underforecasted the customer counts for the week before Christmas. Further examination of the forecast errors (often called residuals), also shows the following:

- Thanksgiving is different from a normal holiday in that the credit union is far less busy than expected the day after Thanksgiving.
- The day before Good Friday is really busy because people leave town for Easter.
- Tax day (April 16) is also busier than expected.
- The week before Indiana University starts fall classes (last week in August) was not busy, probably because many staff and faculty take a summer-fling vacation before the hectic onrush of the fall semester.

	B	C	D	K	L	M
3	MONTH	DAYMON	DAYWEEI	Forecast	Sq Err	Error
253	12	24	1	1302.46	130656	-361.463
254	12	26	3	1144.1	21054.1	-145.1
255	12	27	4	883.217	69810.6	-264.217
256	12	28	5	1297.92	130266	-360.924
257	12	31	1	1302.46	24480.7	-156.463

FIGURE 65-6 The errors for Christmas week.

In the Christmas Week worksheet, I added changing cells to incorporate the effects of these factors. After adding the new parameters as changing cells, I ran Solver again. The results are shown in Figure 65-7. The R-squared value is up to 92 percent, and the standard error is down to 98.61 customers! Note that the post-Christmas week effect reduced the daily customer count by 359, the day before Thanksgiving added 607 customers, the day after Thanksgiving reduced the customer count by 161, and so on.

	I	J	K	L	M	N	O	P	Q	R
1	RSQ	0.916		stdeverr	98.61		cutoff	110.56262		
2			SSE	2460390			actual	125		
3	BH	AH	Foreca	Sq Err	Error	Day of Week		sign change	average	
4	0	1	1981	24363.99	-156	1	108		dayweek	-0
5	0	0	976	78914.97	280.9	2	-155	1	month	0
6	0	0	718	63163.6	251.3	3	-165	0		
7	0	0	1539	17577.99	132.6	4	-121	0		
8	0	0	947	22839.22	151.1	5	332	0		
9	0	0	684	46.55953	6.823	SP	368	0		
10	0	0	674	3.925658	-1.98	FAC	97.1	1		
11	0	0	718	1319.41	36.32	BH	273	1		
12	0	0	1171	39631.63	-199	AH	478	1		
13	0	0	947	17127.87	-131	1	-111	0		
14	0	0	684	1077.379	32.82	2	-82.1	1		
15	0	0	674	2918.017	54.02	3	-26.4	0		
16	0	0	718	44.57311	-6.68	4	-34.8	1		
17	0	0	1539	31.15878	5.582	5	71	1		
18	0	0	947	5457.293	-73.9	6	127	1		
19	0	0	684	830.7915	28.82	7	94	1		
20	0	0	674	2302.208	-48	8	60.9	1		
21	0	0	718	4183.025	-64.7	9	-75.3	0		
22	0	0	1171	8295.008	-91.1	10	-67.9	0		
23	0	0	947	88133.87	-297	11	-35.9	0		
24	0	0	684	1614.155	-40.2	12	80.3	0		
25	0	0	674	16645.82	129	constant	950	1		
26	0	0	1388	11207.14	-106	d1	544	1		
27	0	0	1922	14631.65	121	d2	354	1		
28	0	0	976	28935.87	170.1	d3	302	0		
29	0	0	713	718.3699	26.8	day before sp break	183	0		
30	0	0	703	25.02358	-5	sp break	-55.2	1		
31	0	0	747	2672.615	-51.7	christmas week	-359	0		
32	0	0	1200	1689.043	-41.1	before xmas week	183	0		
33	0	0	976	9004.971	-94.9	before thanks	607	0		
34	0	0	713	3003.306	54.8	after thanks	-161	1		
35	0	0	703	2401.231	-49	good thurday	320	1		
36	0	0	747	12388.28	111.3	summerfling	-165	1		
37	0	0	1568	6171.827	78.56	tax day	244	0		

FIGURE 65-7 The final forecast parameters.

Notice also how the forecasting model is improved by using outliers. If your outliers have something in common (like being the first three days of the month), include the common factor as an independent variable, and your forecasting error will drop.

How can I check whether my forecast errors are random?

A good forecasting method should create forecast errors or residuals that are random. By *random errors*, I mean that your errors exhibit no discernible pattern. If your forecast errors are random, the sign of your errors should change (from plus to minus or minus to plus) approximately half the time. Therefore, a commonly used test to evaluate the randomness of forecast errors is to look at the number of sign changes in the errors. If you have *n* observations, the nonrandomness of the errors is indicated if you find fewer changes in sign than the results of the following equation:

$$\frac{n-1}{2} - \sqrt{n}$$

Your forecast errors are also nonrandom if you find more changes in sign than the following equation:

$$\frac{n-1}{2} + \sqrt{n}$$

In the Christmas Week worksheet, shown earlier in Figure 65-7, I determined the number of sign changes in the residuals by copying from cell P5 to P6:P257 the formula =IF(M5*M4<0,1,0). A sign change in the residuals occurs if and only if the product of two consecutive residuals is negative. Therefore, this formula yields 1 whenever a change in the sign of the residuals occurs. There were 125 changes in sign. In cell P1, I computed the following equation to determine the changes in sign as the cutoff for nonrandom residuals:

$$\frac{254-1}{2} - \sqrt{254} = 110.6$$

Therefore, we have random residuals.

I performed a similar analysis to predict the daily customer counts for dinner at a major restaurant chain. The special factors corresponded to holidays. The study found that Super Sunday (the day of the NFL's Super Bowl) was the least busy day and Valentine's Day and Mother's Day were the busiest. Also, Saturday was the busiest day of the week for dinner and Friday was the busiest day of the week for lunch.

Problems

1. How can you use the techniques outlined in this chapter to predict the daily sales of pens at Staples?
2. If you had several years of data, how would you incorporate a trend in the analysis?

CHAPTER 66

An introduction to probability

Questions answered in this chapter:

- What are the definitions of an experiment, a sample space, and an event?
- What are some axioms that event probabilities must satisfy?
- What is the Law of Complements?
- What are mutually exclusive events?
- What is the Additive Rule for Computing Probabilities?
- What are independent events?
- What is conditional probability?
- What is the Law of Total Probability?
- What is Bayes' theorem?

Just about the only thing we can be certain of is that we live in an uncertain world. To be an intelligent consumer of the barrage of statistics and probabilities that we see every day, you must have an understanding of basic probability.

Answers to this chapter's questions

What are the definitions of an experiment, a sample space, and an event?

An *experiment* is any procedure that can be repeated many times and has a well-defined set of outcomes. The set of all possible outcomes for an experiment is the *sample space*. Here are some examples of experiments and sample spaces:

You toss two fair dice. Each die is equally likely to show 1, 2, 3, 4, 5, or 6 dots. The sample space would consist of the following 36 points. The first number for each point is the number of dots showing on the first die, and the second number is the number of dots showing on the second die:

```
(1,1) (1,2) (1,3) (1,4) (1,5) (1,6) (2,1) (2,2) (2,3) (2,4) (2,5) (2,6) (3,1) (3,2) (3,3) (3,4)
(3,5) (3,6)
```

```
(4,1) (4,2) (4,3) (4,4) (4,5) (4,6) (5,1) (5,2) (5,3) (5,4) (5,5) (5,6) (6,1) (6,2) (6,3) (6,4)
(6,5) (6,6)
```

You toss two coins. The sample space consists of four equally likely points:

```
(H, H) (H, T) (T, H) (T, T)
```

An *event* is any subset of points in a sample space. The following are two examples of events:

- The total number of dots showing on two dice is eight.
- When two coins are tossed, a total of one head is observed.

What are some axioms that event probabilities must satisfy?

Event probabilities (we use *P* to denote probability) must satisfy the following axioms:

- **Axiom 1**: For any event *E* 0<=P(E)<=1.
- **Axiom 2**: If the event *E* consists of all the points in the sample space, then P(E) = 1.

If we assume that two fair dice are tossed, then each of the points in the sample space has the same probability *x*. Therefore, Axiom 2 implies 36x = 1 or x = 1/36.

Using this fact, you can determine the probability of throwing a total of 8 with two dice. The following five points in the sample space yield a total of 8: (2, 6), (3,5), (4,4), (5,3) and (6,2). Therefore, the chance of tossing a total of 8 with two dice is 5/36. This means that if you tossed two dice many times, on average you would expect 5/36 of the tosses to result in a total of 8.

What is the Law of Complements?

The Law of Complements is also known as the Complement Rule of Probability. For any event *A*, the event *Not A* consists of all points in the sample space not in *A*. The Law of Complements then states the following:

```
P(Not A) = 1 - P(A)
```

As an example of the Law of Complements, suppose you throw two dice. What is the chance that you do not throw a total of 2? Define *A* = Probability of throwing a total of 2. Since the only point in the sample space yielding a 2 is (1,1), then P(A) = 1/36. The event Not A = Total with two dice is not a 2. The Law of Complements then tells us the following:

```
P(Total not 2) = 1 - P(Total is 2) = 1 - 1/36 = 35/36
```

The importance of the Law of Complements is that once you compute the "easier" element of P(A) or P(Not A), then you know the other probability.

What are mutually exclusive events?

If two events cannot occur simultaneously, the events are *mutually exclusive*. Observe the following two examples:

- If event A = Total with two dice is 4 and event B = Total with two dice is 8, then the events A and B are mutually exclusive.
- If Event A = Dow Jones Index goes up by at least 10 percent in 2020 and Event B = Dow Jones Index goes up by at least 15 percent in 2020, then Events A and B are not mutually exclusive.

What is the Additive Rule for Computing Probabilities?

In general, for two events *A* and *B,* the Additive Rule for Computing Probabilities states the following:

```
P(A or B) = P(A) + P(B) - P(A and B)
```

You need to subtract P(A and B) or else you double-count the probability of points in the sample space that are common to events A and B. As a special case, if *A* and *B* are mutually exclusive, then P(A and B) = 0 and the Additive Rule reduces to the following:

```
P(A or B) = P(A) + P(B)
```

The following are two examples of the Additive Rule in action:

- If there is a 50 percent chance it rains on Saturday and there is a 50 percent chance it rains on Sunday, is there a 100 percent chance of rain during the weekend?

  If we let *A* = event it rains on Saturday and *B* = event it rains on Sunday, then we see the following:

  ```
  P(Rain during weekend) = P(Rain on Saturday) + P(Rain on Sunday) - P(Rain on both Saturday and Sunday = 0.5 + 0.5 - P(Rain on both Saturday and Sunday) = 1 - P(Rain on both Saturday and Sunday)
  ```

  Since *P*(Rain on both Saturday and Sunday) > 0, we find that the *P*(Rain during weekend) < 1, so it is not sure whether it rains on the weekend (except in Seattle).

As a second example of the Additive Rule, suppose you toss two dice. What is the chance that you get at least one 4? If we let *A* = event first die is 4 and *B* = event second die is 4, we have P(A) = 1/6, P(B) = 1/6, and P(A and B) = 1/36. Then you see the following:

```
P(1st die or 2nd die shows 4) = (1/6) + (1/6) - (1/36) = 11/36
```

What are independent events?

Two events, *A* and *B*, are *independent* if knowing that one event has occurred does not change your estimate of the probability of the other event occurring. Therefore, the two events *A* and *B* are independent if and only if P(A and B) = P(A)*P(B). For more than two events, the rigorous definition of independent events is beyond our scope, but if *n* events *A1, A2,* ... *An* are independent, then the following is true:

```
P(A1 and A2, and ,... An) = P(A1)*P(A2),... *P(An-1)*P(An)
```

The following are two "intuitive" examples that should clarify the definition of independent events:

- Let *A* = Event that the Dow Jones Index increases in 2018 and *B* = Event that the Houston Texans win the 2018 Super Bowl. Knowing that one of these events happened should not change your estimate of the probability of the other event, so these events are independent.

- Let *A* = Event the Chicago Cubs (please!) win the 2017 World Series and *B* = Event the Houston Astros win the 2017 World Series. Clearly if *A* happens, then the chance of event *B* drops to 0, so events *A* and *B* are not independent. Clearly, events *A* and *B* cannot be both mutually exclusive and independent (see Problem 6).

- The following examples should cement your understanding of the concept of independent events:

- Suppose you toss a fair coin and throw a fair die. What is the probability that the coin comes up heads and you throw a 6 on the die? If we define *A* = event coin comes up heads and *B* = Event a 6 is thrown, then it is clear that *A* and *B* are independent. Since P(A) = 1/2 and P(B) = 1/6, then P(Coin comes up Heads and a 6 is thrown) = (1/2)*(1/6) = 1/12.

  Suppose a randomly chosen card is drawn from a deck of cards. You draw a single card. Are the events you draw a spade *and* draw an ace independent events? Let *A* = Event card is a spade and *B* = Event card is an ace. Since there are 13 spades and 4 aces in a deck of 52 cards, P(A) = 13/52 and P(B) = 4/52. Also, the only card in the deck that is an ace and a spade is the ace of spades, so P(Spade and Ace) = 1/52. Since P(Spade)*P(Ace) = (13/52)*(4/52) = 1/52, we find that events *A* and *B* are independent.

  Now suppose that before drawing the card, we remove the 2 of spades from the deck. Are the events *A* and *B* still independent? Now P(A) = 12/51, P(B) = 4/51, and P(A and B) = 1/51. Since (12/51)*(4/51) is not (1/51), events *A* and *B* are independent.

- Finally, suppose you throw three dice. What is the chance you throw at least one 6? Let *Ai* = event die *i* does not show a 6. Then P(Ai) = 1 – (1/6) = 5/6. By the Law of Complements, we see the following:

  ```
  P(At least 1 six) = 1 - P(0 sixes)
  ```

  Since successive die rolls are independent, P(0 sixes) = P(A1)*P(A2)*P(A3) = $(5/6)^3$ = 125/216. Therefore, we see the following:

  ```
  P(At least 1 six) = 1 - (125/216) = 91/216 = 0.42
  ```

What is conditional probability?

Often, we want to know how knowledge that one event has occurred changes the probability of another event. More formally, we define the *conditional probability* of event *B* occurring, given that event *A* has occurred as P(B|A). You read this as Probability Event *B* occurs, given that event *A* has occurred. P(B|A) may be computed by the following equation:

$$P(B|A) = \frac{P(A \text{ and } B)}{P(A)}$$

We often rewrite this equation as P(A and B) = P(A)*P(B|A) or P(A and B) = P(B)*P(A|B).

Events *A* and *B* are independent if and only if P(B|A) = P(B).

The following are two examples to help you understand conditional probability:

- Suppose you toss two dice. Define *A* = Event you get at least one 6 and *B* = Event total of the two dice is 10. What is P(B|A)? P(A and B) = 2/36 and P(A) = 1-P(No sixes) = 1-$(5/6)^2$ = 11/36. Therefore, you see the following:

  ```
  P(B|A) = (2/36)/(11/36) = 2/11
  ```

- Suppose we draw an ace from a deck of cards. If we then draw a second card, what is the chance the card is an ace? If we let event *A* = Event first card is an ace and *B* = Event second card is an ace, after we take the first card (an ace) out of the deck, the deck contains 51 cards and 3 aces, so P(B|A) = 3/51 = 1/17.

What is the law of total probability?

The *law of total probability* refers to computing the probability of an event by adding together the probabilities of several mutually exclusive events. Sometimes we can compute the probability of an event by conditioning it on other events. For example, suppose 5 percent of used cars have flood damage and 80 percent of those cars later develop engine problems. Also suppose that 10 percent of cars that are not flood damaged later develop engine problems. What is the chance that a randomly chosen car will have engine problems?

To solve this problem, let *EP* = Event car has engine problems later, *FL* = Event car has flood damage. Then the event *EP* can be decomposed into the following two mutually exclusive events: A car with flood damage has problems and a car without flood damage has problems, as you see in this formulation:

```
P(EP) = P(EP and FL) + P(EP and  no FL) = P(EP|FL)*P(FL) + P(EP|No FL)*P(No FL) = (0.80)*(.05)
+(0.10)*(0.95) = 0.135
```

You can also create a *contingency table*, which shows all the possibilities. The following is an example of a contingency table:

	Engine problem	**No engine problem**
FL	0.04	0.01
No FL	0.095	0.855

The numbers in the No Engine Problem column are included to show how the first row should add to 0.05 and the second row should add to 0.95.

What is Bayes' theorem?

Once you understand conditional probability and the law of total probability, *Bayes theorem* is easy to understand. In many situations, we are trying to estimate the probabilities of various states of the world. Then we receive information that we use to change our probability estimates. For example, consider a 40-year-old woman with no risk factors for breast cancer. The states of the world can be defined by the events *C* = Event woman has cancer and *NC* = Event woman does not have cancer. Given no other information, the probabilities of these events (known as *prior* or *a priori* probabilities) are given by P(C) = 0.004 and P(NC) = 0.996.

Now we receive more information (results of a mammogram) that change our estimates of prior probabilities. Suppose a mammogram yields a positive (+) test result. To update our probability estimates, we need to know the likelihood of a positive test result for each state of the world. The likelihoods for a positive test result are known to be P(+|C) = 0.80 and P((+|NC) = 0.10. Now we want to update our prior probability (0.004) of cancer after receiving the positive test result. This new probability (P(C|+) is called a *posterior* or *a posteriori* probability. Applying the definitions of conditional probability and the law of total probability, we find the following:

$$P(C|+) = \frac{P(C\cap +)}{P(+)} = \frac{P(+|C)P(C)}{P(+|C)*P(C)+P(+|NC)*P(NC)} = \frac{.80*.004}{.80*.004+.996(.10)} = 0.031$$

Perhaps surprisingly, even after a positive test result, there is a small chance (thankfully!) that the woman has cancer. This is because of the fact that most women do not have breast cancer, so many of their mammograms will result in false positives. Another way to see this is to look at a typical sample of 10,000 women. Then a contingency table would show that the 10,000 women would be classified as follows:

	E	F	G
7		+ Test	- Test
8	Cancer	10,000*(.004)*(.8) = 32	10000*(.004)*(1-.8)= 8
9	No Cancer	10,000*(.996)*(.1) = 996	10,000*(.996)*(.8)=8964

Given a positive test result, we are working with the 1,028 women in column F. Therefore, after a positive test result, the chance the woman has cancer is 32/1028 = 0.031.

As a final example of Bayes' theorem, consider the classic Let's Make a Deal problem popularized by Marilyn Vos Savant in her "Ask Marilyn" column in *Parade Magazine.*

A car is behind one of three doors, and there is a goat behind the other two doors. I choose a door (let's say door 1). Now Monty Hall (the host of *Let's Make a Deal*) chooses to open a door (door 2 or door 3) and reveals a goat. You are now allowed to switch doors. Should you?

Let's assume Monty opens door 2. The following are the relevant events:

- The states of the world are *D1, D2, D3*, which are the events that the car is behind door *i.*
- Define S1, S2, S3 to be events that Monty says the car is behind door *i.*
- We know P(D1) = P(D2) = P(D3) = 1/3 are the prior probabilities.
- The likelihoods are P(S3|D1) = 1/2, P(S2|D1) = 1/2, P(S3|D2) = 1, and P(S2|D3)=1.

Now we know the car is behind either door 3 or door 1. By means of Bayes' theorem, we calculate the following:

$$P(D3|S2) = \frac{P(D3 \text{ and } S2)}{P(D3 \text{ and } S2)+P(D1 \text{ and } S2)} = \frac{\left(\frac{1}{3}\right)*1}{\left(\frac{1}{3}\right)*1+\left(\frac{1}{3}\right)*\frac{1}{2}} = \frac{2}{3}$$

Therefore, we find that P(D1|S2) = 1 - (2/3) = 1/3. Thus, we should switch our guess to door 3!

> **Note**: The answers to this chapter's problems are in a Word file, not an Excel file.

Problems

1. If you toss two dice, find the probability of each possible total.
2. If you throw three dice, what is the chance the total is 9?
3. Of Carver High School students, 20 percent play baseball and 15 percent play basketball. Five percent play both. What fraction of students play baseball or basketball?
4. Let *A* = Event a die comes up even and *B* = Event die shows one or two dots. Are events *A* and *B* independent?
5. Are the events *A* and *Not A* mutually exclusive?
6. Can mutually exclusive events be independent?
7. In the game of craps, you roll two dice. A total of 7 or 11 on the first roll wins. What is the chance you win a game on the first roll?
8. If you draw two cards (without replacement) from a deck of cards, what is the chance that both are clubs?
9. A roulette wheel contains the numbers 0, 00, 1, 2,..., 36. Suppose you bet on each of 25 spins that 00 will show. After 25 spins, what is chance you have won at least once?
10. Suppose that 10 percent of all adults watch *The Bachelor.* Assume that 80 percent of *The Bachelor*'s viewers are women and half of all adults are men. Compute the probability that a given woman or man is a viewer of *The Bachelor.*
11. What fraction of men and women watch *The Bachelor*?
12. In our flood-engine example, you are told that an engine had problems. What is the probability the engine had prior flood damage?
13. A chest has two drawers. Each drawer contains two coins; you know one drawer has two gold coins, and the other drawer has one gold and one silver coin. You randomly pick a drawer and a coin; the selected coin is gold. What is the chance that the other coin in the drawer is also gold?
14. Of all the cabs, 85 percent are blue and the rest are green. A cab identified in a hit-and-run accident is identified as green. People can correctly identify the color of a cab 80 percent of

the time. When surveyed, most Stanford students thought there was an 80 percent chance the cab is actually green. Do you agree?

15. An urn contains nine balls. Each ball has one of the numbers 1, 2, ..., 9 painted on the ball. Draw two balls (with replacement). What is the chance the two numbers are the same?

16. Toss a die and let A = Event you roll an odd number and B = Event you roll a number >=4. Find P(A|B).

17. Two engines each have a 0.9 chance of working. The success or failure of the engines is independent. If the engines are in a series, both engines need to work for the system to work. If the engines are in parallel, the system works if at least one engine works. What is the probability that a series or parallel system works?

18. The following table shows admission statistics for men and women at a large US university. The total number applying for admittance is in parentheses, and the number admitted is not in parentheses. You can see the percentage of men admitted is more than the percentage of women admitted. Using statistics, do you think the university discriminated against women?

	Men	Women
Easy major	864 (1386)	106 (133)
Difficult major	334 (1306)	451 (1702)

19. A company has a plant in Houston and in Dallas. Seventy percent of the employees work in Houston, and 30 percent work in Dallas. Each year, 3 percent of the Houston employees are involved in an accident; 5 percent of the Dallas employees are involved in an accident. If you randomly choose an employee who had an accident last year, what is the chance he or she works in Houston?

20. An MBA student is studying finance and marketing. Assume the student has a 90 percent chance of getting an A in finance and an 80 percent chance of getting an A in marketing. If her performance in each of the two courses is independent of the other, what is the probability that she gets at least one A?

21. A bowl contains four red balls and six blue balls. Two balls are drawn (without replacement) from the bowl. Given that the second ball is blue, what is the chance the first ball is blue?

22. Suppose you toss two dice. Let A = Event first die shows a 3 and B = Event total of the two dice is 8. Are events A and B independent?

23. Of an insurance company's policyholders, 80 percent are high risk and 20 percent are low risk. Assume nobody has more than one accident in a year. Also assume 10 percent of high-risk people have an accident during a year and 3 percent of low-risk people have an accident during a year. If you randomly choose a policyholder who had an accident last year, what is the chance he or she is a high-risk policyholder?

24. In each year's NCAA basketball tournament, there are four teams with a 3 percent chance of beating a #1 seed. Before the tournament started, what is the chance that at least one #16-seed team beats a #1-seed team?

25. Assume one in every 1,000 people is a liar (incapable of telling the truth). Also suppose a lie-detector test is 98 percent accurate. That is, if a person is lying, there is a 98 percent chance the test will indicate that person is lying. Also, if the person is not lying, there is a 98 percent chance the test will indicate the person is not lying. If the lie-detector test indicates the person is lying, what is the chance the person is lying?

26. After throwing two dice, define event A = Total of the dice is even and B = First die shows a five. Are events A and B independent?

27. During 40 percent of all weeks, a supermarket cuts the price on macaroni and cheese. During 20 percent of all weeks, the supermarket puts macaroni and cheese on display, and during 15 percent of all weeks, the supermarket cuts the price of macaroni and cheese and puts macaroni and cheese on display. During what fraction of weeks is macaroni and cheese sold at a discount or on display?

28. You are told two cards have been drawn from a deck of cards, and both are hearts. What is the probability that the first card was the two of hearts?

29. In a drawer, there are two normal quarters and one quarter with two heads. With your eyes closed, you choose one of the coins; your friend flips the coin and reports the coin came up heads. What is the probability you selected the two-headed coin?

30. You toss two dice. Let event A = Total is 10 and B = Event first die shows an odd number. Are the events A and B independent?

31. Of an insurance company's policyholders, 20 percent are high risk, 40 percent are low risk, and 40 percent are intermediate risk. Of the low-risk policyholders, 2 percent have an accident during a year, 4 percent of intermediate-risk policyholders have an accident during a year, and 20 percent of high-risk policyholders have an accident during a year. If a policyholder has an accident, what is the chance he or she was a high-risk policyholder?

CHAPTER 67

An introduction to random variables

Questions answered in this chapter:

- What is a random variable?
- What is a discrete random variable?
- What are the mean, variance, and standard deviation of a random variable?
- What is a continuous random variable?
- What is a probability density function?
- What are independent random variables?

In today's world, the only thing that's certain is uncertainty. In the next nine chapters, I'll give you some powerful techniques that you can use to incorporate uncertainty in business models. The key building block in modeling uncertainty is understanding how to use *random variables*.

Answers to this chapter's questions

What is a random variable?

Any situation whose outcome is uncertain is called an *experiment*. The value of a random variable emerges from the (uncertain) outcome of an experiment. For example, tossing a pair of dice is an experiment, and a random variable might be defined as the sum of the values shown on each die. In this case, the random variable could assume any of the values 2, 3, and so on, up to 12. As another example, consider the experiment of selling a new video-game console, for which a random variable might be defined as the market share for this new product.

What is a discrete random variable?

A random variable is *discrete* if it can assume a countable (but usually finite) number of possible values. Here are some examples of discrete random variables:

- Number of potential competitors for your product

- Number of aces drawn in a five-card poker hand
- Number of car accidents you have (hopefully zero!) in a year
- Number of dots showing on a die
- Number of free throws out of 12 that Kevin Durant makes during a basketball game

What are the mean, variance, and standard deviation of a random variable?

In Chapter 42, "Summarizing data by using descriptive statistics," I discussed the *mean*, *variance*, and *standard deviation* for a data set. In essence, the mean of a random variable (often denoted by μ) is the average value of the random variable you would expect if you performed an experiment many times. The mean of a random variable is often referred to as the random variable's *expected value*. The variance of a random variable (often denoted by s^2) is the average value of the squared deviation from the mean of a random variable that you would expect if you performed an experiment many times. The standard deviation of a random variable (often denoted by σ) is simply the square root of its variance. As with data sets, the mean of a random variable is a summary measure for a typical value of the random variable, whereas the variance and standard deviation measure the spread of the random variable about its mean.

As an example of how to compute the mean, variance, and standard deviation of a random variable, suppose you believe that the return on the stock market during the next year is governed by the following probabilities:

Probability	Market return
0.40	+20 percent
0.30	0 percent
0.30	-20 percent

Hand calculations show the following:

$$\mu=0.40*(0.20)+0.30*(0.00)+0.30*(-0.20)=0.02 \text{ or } 2 \text{ percent}$$
$$s^2=0.4*(0.20-0.02)^2+0.30*(0.0-0.02)^2+0.30*(-0.20-0.02)^2=0.0276$$

Then σ=0.166 or 16.6 percent.

In the file Meanvariance.xlsx (shown in Figure 67-1), I verified these computations.

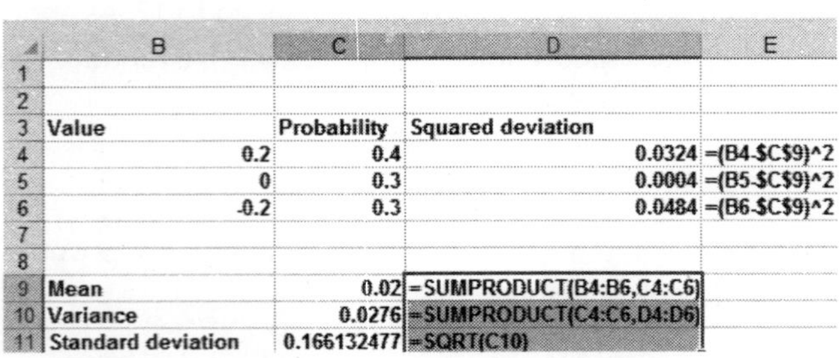

	B	C	D	E
1				
2				
3	Value	Probability	Squared deviation	
4	0.2	0.4	0.0324	=(B4-$C$9)^2
5	0	0.3	0.0004	=(B5-$C$9)^2
6	-0.2	0.3	0.0484	=(B6-$C$9)^2
7				
8				
9	Mean	0.02	=SUMPRODUCT(B4:B6,C4:C6)	
10	Variance	0.0276	=SUMPRODUCT(C4:C6,D4:D6)	
11	Standard deviation	0.166132477	=SQRT(C10)	

FIGURE 67-1 Computing the mean, standard deviation, and variance of a random variable.

I computed the mean of the market return in cell C9 with the formula SUMPRODUCT(B4:B6,C4:C6). This formula multiplies each value of the random variable by its probability, and then it sums the products.

To compute the variance of the market return, I determined the squared deviation of each value of the random variable from its mean by copying from D4 to D5:D6 the formula =(B4–$C$9)^2. Then, in cell C10, I computed the variance of the market return as the average squared deviation from the mean by using the formula =SUMPRODUCT(C4:C6,D4:D6). Finally, in cell C11, I computed the standard deviation of the market return with the formula =SQRT(C10).

What is a continuous random variable?

A *continuous random variable* is a random variable that can assume a very large number or, to all intents and purposes, an infinite number of values, including all values on some interval. The following are some examples of continuous random variables:

- Price of Microsoft stock one year from now
- Market share for a new product
- Market size for a new product
- Cost of developing a new product
- Newborn baby's weight
- Person's IQ
- Dirk Nowitzki's three-point shooting percentage during next season

What is a probability density function?

A *discrete random variable* can be specified by a list of values and the probability of occurrence for each value of the random variable. Because a continuous random variable can assume an infinite number of values, you can't list the probability of occurrence for each value of a continuous random variable. A continuous random variable is completely described by its *probability density function*. For example, the probability density function for a randomly chosen person's IQ is shown in Figure 67-2.

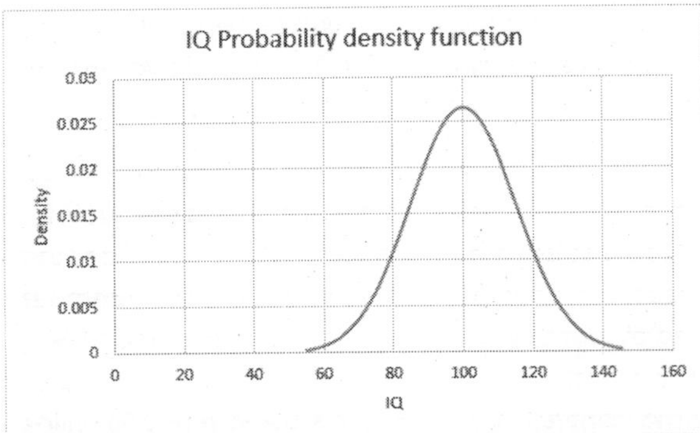

FIGURE 67-2 The probability density function for IQs.

A probability density function (PDF) has the following properties:

- The value of the PDF is always greater than or equal to 0.
- The area under the PDF equals 1.
- The height of the PDF for a value *x* of a random variable is proportional to the likelihood that the random variable assumes a value near *x*. For example, the height of the density for an IQ of 83 is roughly half the height of the density for an IQ of 100. This tells you that IQs near 83 are approximately half as likely as IQs around 100. Also, because the density peaks at 100, IQs around 100 are most likely.
- The probability that a continuous random variable assumes a range of values equals the corresponding area under the PDF. For example, the fraction of people having IQs from 80 through 100 is simply the area under the density from 80 through 100.
- Note that a discrete random variable that assumes many values is often modeled as a *continuous random variable*. (See Chapter 70, "The normal random variable and Z-scores.") For example, while the number of half gallons of milk sold in a single day by a small grocery store is discrete, it proves more convenient to model this discrete random variable as a continuous random variable.

What are independent random variables?

A set of random variables is *independent* if knowledge of the value of any of their subsets tells you nothing about the values of the other random variables. For example, the number of games won by the Indiana University football team during a year is independent of the percentage return on Microsoft during the same year. Knowing that Indiana did very well would not change your view of how Microsoft stock did during the year.

On the other hand, the returns on Microsoft stock and Intel stock are not independent. If you are told that Microsoft stock had a high return in one year, in all likelihood, computer sales were high, which tells you that Intel probably had a good year as well.

Problems

1. Identify the following random variables as discrete or continuous:
   - Number of games the Seattle Seahawks win next season
   - Number that comes up when spinning a roulette wheel
   - Unit sales of tablet PCs next year
   - Length of time that a light bulb lasts before it burns out
2. Compute the mean, variance, and standard deviation of the number of dots showing when a die is tossed.
3. Determine whether the following random variables are independent:
   - Daily temperature and sales at an ice-cream store
   - Suit and number of a card drawn from a deck of playing cards
   - Inflation and return on the stock market
   - Price charged for each and the number of units sold of a car
4. The current price of a company's stock is $20. The company is a takeover target. If the takeover is successful, the company's stock price will increase to $30. If the takeover is unsuccessful, the stock price will drop to $12. Determine the range of values for the probability of a successful takeover that would make it worthwhile to purchase the stock today. Assume your goal is to maximize your expected profit. Hint: Use the Goal Seek command, which is discussed in detail in Chapter 18, "The Goal Seek command."
5. When a roulette wheel is spun, the possible outcomes are 0, 00, 1, 2, ..., 36. If you bet on a number coming up, you win $35 if your number comes up and you lose $1 otherwise. What is the mean and standard deviation of your winnings on a single play of the game?
6. A stock currently sells for $40. In the next month, there is a 60 percent chance the stock price will double and a 40 percent chance the stock will drop 50 percent. In a month, you will sell the stock. Find the mean and standard deviation of your profit (in dollars).
7. Suppose you bet on an odd number coming up in roulette. If an odd number comes up, you win $1, and if an odd number does not come up, you lose $1. Find the mean and standard deviation of your profit.

CHAPTER 68

The binomial, hypergeometric, and negative binomial random variables

Questions answered in this chapter:

- What is a binomial random variable?
- How do I use the BINOM.DIST and BINOM.DIST.RANGE functions to compute binomial probabilities?
- If equal numbers of people prefer Coke to Pepsi and Pepsi to Coke, and I ask 100 people whether they prefer Coke to Pepsi, what is the probability that exactly 60 people prefer Coke to Pepsi and the probability that between 40 and 60 people prefer Coke to Pepsi?
- Of all the elevator rails my company produces, 3 percent are considered defective. We are about to ship a batch of 10,000 elevator rails to a customer. To determine whether the batch is acceptable, the customer will randomly choose a sample of 100 rails and check whether each sampled rail is defective. If two or fewer sampled rails are defective, the customer will accept the batch. How can I determine the probability that the batch will be accepted?
- Airlines do not like flights with empty seats. Suppose that, on average, 95 percent of all ticket purchasers show up for a flight. If the airline sells 105 tickets for a 100-seat flight, what is the probability that the flight will be overbooked?
- The local Village Deli knows that 1,000 customers come for lunch each day. On average, 20 percent order the specialty vegetarian sandwich. These sandwiches are made in advance. How many should the deli make if they want to have a 5 percent chance of running out of vegetarian sandwiches?
- What is the hypergeometric random variable?
- What is the negative binomial random variable?

Answers to this chapter's questions

What is a binomial random variable?

A *binomial random variable* is a discrete random variable used to calculate probabilities in a situation in which all three of the following apply:

- *n* independent trials occur.
- Each trial results in one of two outcomes: success or failure.
- In each trial, the probability of success (*p*) remains constant.

In such a situation, the binomial random variable can be used to calculate probabilities related to the number of successes in a given number of trials. I let *x* be the random variable denoting the number of successes occurring in *n* independent trials, when the probability of success on each trial is *p*. Here are some examples in which the binomial random variable is relevant.

Coke or Pepsi Assume that equal numbers of people prefer Coke to Pepsi and Pepsi to Coke. You ask 100 people whether they prefer Coke to Pepsi. You're interested in the probability that exactly 60 people prefer Coke to Pepsi and the probability that from 40 through 60 people prefer Coke to Pepsi. In this situation, you have a binomial random variable defined by the following:

- Trial: Survey individuals
- Success: Prefer Coke
- *p* equals 0.50
- *n* equals 100

Let *x* equal the number of people sampled who prefer Coke. You want to determine the probability that $x=60$ and also the probability that $40 \le x \le 60$.

Elevator rails Of all the elevator rails you produce, 3 percent are considered defective. You are about to ship a batch of 10,000 elevator rails to a customer. To determine whether the batch is acceptable, the customer will randomly choose a sample of 100 rails and check whether each sampled rail is defective. If two or fewer sampled rails are defective, the customer will accept the batch. You want to determine the probability that the batch will be accepted.

You have a binomial random variable defined by the following:

- Trial: Look at a sampled rail
- Success: Rail is defective
- *p* equals 0.03
- *n* equals 100

Let *x* equal the number of defective rails in the sample. You want to find the probability that $x \le 2$.

Airline overbooking Airlines don't like flights with empty seats. Suppose that, on average, 95 percent of all ticket purchasers show up for a flight. If the airline sells 105 tickets for a 100-seat flight, what is the probability that the flight will be overbooked?

You have a binomial random variable defined by the following:

- Trial: Individual ticket holders
- Success: Ticket holder shows up
- *p* equals 0.95
- *n* equals 105

Let *x* equal the number of ticket holders who show up. Then you want to find the probability that $x \geq 101$.

How do I use the BINOM.DIST and BINOM.DIST.RANGE functions to compute binomial probabilities?

Microsoft Excel 2016 includes the BINOM.DIST and BINOM.DIST.RANGE functions, which you can use to compute binomial probabilities. If you want to compute the probability of *x* or fewer successes, for a binomial random variable having *n* trials with probability of success *p*, simply enter BINOM.DIST(x,n, p,1). If you want to compute the probability of exactly *x* successes for a binomial random variable having *n* trials with probability of success of *p*, enter BINOM.DIST(*x*,*n*,*p*,0). Entering 1 as the last argument of BINOM.DIST yields a "cumulative" probability; entering 0 yields the "probability mass function" for any particular value. (Note that a last argument of True can be used instead of a 1, and a last argument of False can be used instead of a 0.)

The function BINOM.DIST.RANGE(n,p,s1,s2) gives the probability of obtaining between *s1* and *s2* successes (inclusive) in *n* independent trials with probability of success *p* on each trial.

Here are a few examples of using the BINOM.DIST function to calculate probabilities of interest. You'll find the data and analysis in the file Binomialexamples.xlsx, which is shown in Figure 68-1.

	B	C	D	E	F
2					
3	Coke vs. Pepsi	Binom.dist			
4	Probability exactly 60 people prefer Coke to Pepsi	0.010843867	=BINOM.DIST(60,100,0.5,0)	BINOM.DIST.RANGE	
5	Probability from 40 through 60 people prefer Coke to Pepsi	0.9647998	=BINOM.DIST(60,100,0.5,1)-BINOM.DIST(39,100,0.5,1)	0.9647998	=BINOM.DIST.RANGE(100,0.5,40,60)
6					
7	Elevator Rails				
8	Probability 2 or fewer of 100 rails are defective	0.419775083	=BINOM.DIST(2,100,0.03,1)	0.419775083	=BINOM.DIST.RANGE(100,0.03,0,2)
9	Airline Overbooking				
10	Probability flight is overbooked if 105 tickets are sold	0.392433721	=1-BINOM.DIST(100,105,0.95,1)	0.392433721	=BINOM.DIST.RANGE(105,0.95,101,105)

FIGURE 68-1 Using the binomial random variable.

If equal numbers of people prefer Coke to Pepsi and Pepsi to Coke, and I ask 100 people whether they prefer Coke to Pepsi, what is the probability that exactly 60 people prefer Coke to Pepsi and the probability that between 40 and 60 people prefer Coke to Pepsi?

You have n=100 and p=0.5. You seek the probability that x=60 and the probability that $40 \le x \le 60$, where x equals the number of people who prefer Coke to Pepsi. First, you find the probability that x=60 by entering in cell C4 the formula =BINOM.DIST(60,100,0.5,0). Excel returns the value 0.011.

To use the BINOM.DIST function to compute the probability that $40 \le x \le 60$, you can note that the probability that $40 \le x \le 60$ equals the probability that $x \le 60$ minus the probability that $x \le 39$. Thus, you can obtain the probability that from 40 through 60 people prefer Coke by entering in cell C5 the formula =BINOM.DIST(60,100,0.5,1)–BINOM.DIST(39,100,0.5,1). Excel returns the value 0.9648. So, if Coke and Pepsi are equally preferred, it is very unlikely that in a sample of 100 people, Coke or Pepsi would be more than 10 percent ahead. If a sample of 100 people shows Coke or Pepsi to be more than 10 percent ahead, you should probably doubt that Coke and Pepsi are equally preferred. Alternatively, in cell E5 I used the formula =BINOM.DIST.RANGE(100,0.5,40,60) to compute the same probability.

Of all the elevator rails my company produces, 3 percent are considered defective. We are about to ship a batch of 10,000 elevator rails to a customer. To determine whether the batch is acceptable, the customer will randomly choose a sample of 100 rails and check whether each sampled rail is defective. If two or fewer sampled rails are defective, the customer will accept the batch. How can I determine the probability that the batch will be accepted?

If you let x equal the number of defective rails in a batch, you have a binomial random variable with n=100 and p=0.03. You seek the probability that $x \le 2$. Simply enter in cell C8 the formula =BINOM.DIST(2,100,0.03,1). Excel returns the value 0.42 Thus, the batch will be accepted 42 percent of the time. Alternatively, in cell E7 I used the formula =BINOM.DIST.RANGE(100,0.03,0,2) to compute the same probability.

Really, your chance of success is not exactly 3 percent on each trial. For example, if the first 10 rails are defective, the chance the next rail is defective has dropped to 290/9,990; if the first 10 rails are not defective, the chance the next rail is defective is 300/9,990. Therefore, the probability of success on the eleventh trial is not independent of the probability of success on one of the first 10 trials. Despite this fact, the binomial random variable can be used as an approximation when a sample is drawn and the sample size is less than 10 percent of the total population. Here, the population equals 10,000, and the sample size is 100. Exact probabilities involving sampling from a finite population can be calculated with the *hypergeometric random variable*, which I'll discuss later in this chapter.

Airlines do not like flights with empty seats. Suppose that, on average, 95 percent of all ticket purchasers show up for a flight. If the airline sells 105 tickets for a 100-seat flight, what is the probability that the flight will be overbooked?

Let x equal the number of ticket holders who show up for the flight. You have n=105 and p=0.95. You seek the probability that $x \ge 101$. Note that the probability that $x \le 101$ equals 1 minus the probability that $x \le 100$. So, to compute the probability that the flight is overbooked, you enter in cell C10 the formula =1–BINOM.DIST(100,105,0.95,1). Excel yields 0.392, which means there is a 39.2 percent chance that the flight will be overbooked. Alternatively, in cell E10 I computed the same probability by using the following formula:

```
=BINOM.DIST.RANGE(105,0.95,101,105)
```

The local Village Deli knows that 1,000 customers come for lunch each day. On average, 20 percent order the specialty vegetarian sandwich. These sandwiches are made in advance. How many should the deli make if they want to have a 5 percent chance of running out of vegetarian sandwiches?

In Excel 2016, the function BINOM.INV, with the syntax BINOM.INV(trials, probability of success, *alpha*), determines the smallest number *x*, for which the probability of less than or equal to *x* successes is at least *alpha*. In earlier versions of Excel, the function CRITBINOM(trials, probability of success, *alpha*) yielded the same results as BINOM.INV. In this example, *trials* equals 1,000, *probability of success* equals 0.2, and *alpha* equals 0.95. As shown in Figure 68-2, if the deli orders 221 sandwiches, the probability that demand will be less than or equal to 221 is at least 0.95. Also, the probability that 220 or fewer sandwiches will be demanded is less than 0.95.

	G	H
4	Customers	1000
5	fraction wanting veggie	0.2
6	prob of filling demand	0.95
7		
8	221	=BINOM.INV(H4,H5,H6)

FIGURE 68-2 An example of the BINOM.INV function.

What is the hypergeometric random variable?

The *hypergeometric random variable* governs a situation such as the following:

- A bowl contains *N* balls.
- Each ball is one of two types (called *success* or *failure*).
- There are *s* successes in the bowl.
- A sample of size *n* is drawn from the bowl.

Let's look at an example in the file Hypergeom.dist.xlsx, which is shown in Figure 68-3. The Excel 2016 formula HYPERGEOM.DIST(x,n,s,N,0) gives the probability of *x* successes if *n* balls are drawn from a bowl containing *N* balls, of which *s* are marked as *success*. The Excel 2016 formula HYPERGEOM.DIST(x,n,s,N,1) gives the probability of less than or equal to *x* successes if *n* balls are drawn from a bowl containing *N* balls, of which *s* are marked as *success*. (As with the BINOM.DIST function, True can be used to replace 1 and False to replace 0.)

For example, suppose that 40 of the Fortune 500 companies have a woman CEO. The 500 CEOs are analogous to the balls in the bowl (*N*=500) and the 40 women are representative of the *s* successes in the bowl. Then, copying from D8 to D9:D18 the formula =HYPERGEOM.DIST(C8, Sample_size,Population_women,Population_size,FALSE) gives the probability that a sample of 10 Fortune 500 companies will have 0, 1, 2,..., 10 women CEOs. Here *Sample_size* equals 10, *Population_women* equals 40, and *Population_size* equals 500. You can substitute FALSE for *0* in the formula.

Finding a woman CEO is a success. In the sample of 10, for example, there's a probability of 0.431 that no women CEOs will be in the sample. By the way, you could have approximated this probability with the formula BINOMDIST(0,10,0.08,0), yielding 0.434, which is very close to the true probability of 0.431. In cell F10, I computed the probability that at most 2 of the 10 people in the sample would be women with the formula =HYPGEOM.DIST(2,Sample_Size,Population_women,Population_size,TRUE). Thus there is a 96.2 percent chance that at most two people in the sample will be women. Of course, I also could have obtained this answer by adding together the highlighted cells (D8:D10).

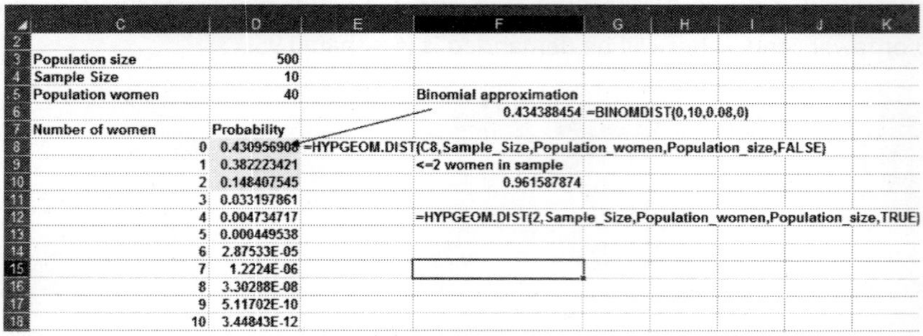

FIGURE 68-3 Using the hypergeometric random variable.

What is the negative binomial random variable?

The *negative binomial random variable* applies to the same situation as the binomial random variable, but the negative binomial random variable gives the probability of *f* failures occurring before the *s*th success. Thus =NEGBINOM.DIST(f,s,p,0) gives the probability that exactly *f* failures will occur before the *s*th success when the probability of success is *p* for each trial, and =NEGBINOM.DIST(f,s,p,1) gives the probability that at most *f* failures will occur before the *s*th success when the probability of success is *p* for each trial. For example, consider a baseball team that wins 40 percent of their games (see the file Negbinom.dist.xlsx and Figure 68-4). Copying from E9 to E34 the formula =NEGBINOM.DIST(D9,2,.4,False) gives the probability of 0, 1, 2,..., 25 losses occurring before the second win. Note here that success equals a game won. For example, there is a 19.2 percent chance the team will lose exactly one game before winning two games. In cell G10, I used the formula =NEGBINOM.DIST(3,2,0.4,TRUE) to compute the chance that at most three losses will occur before the team wins two games (0.663). Of course, I could have obtained this answer by simply adding up the shaded cells (E9:E12).

	D	E	F	G	H	I
4	40% chance of success					
5						
6						
7						
8	Losses before 2nd win	prob		Probability <=3 failures		
9	0	0.16	=NEGBINOM.DIST(D9,2,0.4,FALSE)	before 2nd win		
10	1	0.192	=NEGBINOM.DIST(D10,2,0.4,FALSE)	0.66304		
11	2	0.1728	=NEGBINOM.DIST(D11,2,0.4,FALSE)			
12	3	0.13824	=NEGBINOM.DIST(D12,2,0.4,FALSE)			
13	4	0.10368				
14	5	0.07465				
15	6	0.05225				
16	7	0.03583				
17	8	0.02419				
18	9	0.01612				
19	10	0.01064				
20	11	0.00697				

FIGURE 68-4 Using the negative binomial random variable.

Problems

1. Suppose that, on average, 4 percent of all CD drives received by a computer company are defective. The company has adopted the following policy: Sample 50 CD drives in each shipment, and accept the shipment if none are defective. Using this information, determine the following:

   - What fraction of shipments will be accepted?
   - If the policy changes so that a shipment is accepted if only one CD drive in the sample is defective, what fraction of shipments will be accepted?
   - What is the probability that a sample size of 50 will contain at least 10 defective CD drives?

2. Use the airline overbooking data to do the following:

   - Determine how the probability of overbooking varies as the number of tickets sold varies from 100 through 115. Hint: Use a one-way data table.
   - Show how the probability of overbooking varies as the number of tickets sold varies from 100 through 115 and the probability that a ticket holder shows up varies from 80 percent through 95 percent. Hint: Use a two-way data table.

3. Suppose that during each year, a given mutual fund has a 50 percent chance of beating the Standard & Poor's 500 Stock Index (S&P Index). In a group of 100 mutual funds, what is the probability that at least 10 funds will beat the S&P Index during at least 8 out of 10 years?

4. Professional basketball player Steve Nash is a 90 percent foul shooter. Answer the following questions:

   - If he shoots 100 free throws, what is the probability that he will miss more than 15 shots?

- How good a foul shooter would Steve Nash be if he had only a 5 percent chance of making fewer than 90 free throws out of 100 attempts? Hint: Use Goal Seek in the What-If Analysis options.

5. When tested for extra sensory perception (ESP), participants are asked to identify the shape of a card from a 25-card deck. The deck consists of five cards, of each of five shapes. If a person identifies 12 cards correctly, what would you conclude?

6. Suppose that in a group of 100 people, 20 have the flu and 80 do not. If you randomly select 30 people, what is the chance that at least 10 people have the flu?

7. A student is selling magazines for a school fundraiser. There is a 20 percent chance that a given house will buy a magazine. He needs to sell five magazines. Determine the probability that he will need to visit 5, 6, 7,..., 100 houses to sell five magazines.

8. Use the BINOM.DIST function to verify that the BINOM.INV function yields the correct answer to my Village Deli example.

9. In the seventeenth century, French mathematicians Pierre de Fermat and Blaise Pascal were inspired to formulate the modern probability theory after trying to solve the *problem of points*. Here is a simple example: Pascal and Fermat take turns tossing coins. Fermat wins a point if a head is tossed, and Pascal wins a point if a tail is tossed. If Pascal is ahead 8-7 and the first player with 10 points wins, what is the chance that Pascal will win?

10. Suppose that each time the Houston Astros play the New York Yankees, the Astros have a 35 percent chance of winning the game. If the Astros play the Yankees 10 times, what is the chance the Astros win at least half the games?

11. I make 55 percent of my free throws. If I shoot 400 free throws, what is the chance that I make between 200 and 300 free throws inclusive?

12. Suppose 10 percent of all staplers are defective. If 60 staplers are sold, what is the chance that at least 10 staplers are defective?

13. A factory has five assembly lines. Each assembly line is down (not working) *p* percent of the time. What must *p* equal so that there is a 95 percent chance that at least one assembly line is working?

CHAPTER 69

The Poisson and exponential random variable

Questions answered in this chapter:

- What is the Poisson random variable?
- How do I compute probabilities for the Poisson random variable?
- If the number of customers arriving at a bank is governed by a Poisson random variable, what random variable governs the time between arrivals?

Answers to this chapter's questions

What is the Poisson random variable?

The *Poisson random variable* is a discrete random variable that is useful for describing probabilities for situations in which events (such as customer arrivals at a bank or orders placed for a product) have a small probability of occurring during a short time interval. More specifically, during a short time interval, denoted as t, either zero or one event will occur, and the probability of one event occurring during a short interval of length t is (for some λ) given by λt. Here, λ (*lambda*) is the mean number of occurrences per time unit.

Situations in which the Poisson random variable can be applied include the following:

- Number of units of a product demanded during a month.
- Number of deaths per year by horse kick in the Prussian army.
- Number of car accidents you have during a year.
- Number of copies of *The Seat of the Soul* ordered today at Amazon.com.
- Number of workers' compensation claims filed at a company this month.
- Number of defects in 100 yards of string. (Here, 1 yard of string plays the role of time.)

How do I compute probabilities for the Poisson random variable?

You can use the Microsoft Excel 2016 POISSON.DIST function to compute probabilities involving the Poisson random variable. In versions of Excel prior to Excel 2013, the POISSON function yielded POISSON probabilities. Just remember that in a length of time *t*, the mean of a Poisson random variable is *t*. The syntax of the POISSON function is as follows:

- POISSON.DIST(x,λ,True or 1) calculates the probability that a Poisson random variable with a mean equal to λ is less than or equal to *x*.
- POISSON.DIST(x,λ,False or 0) calculates the probability that a Poisson random variable with a mean equal to λ is equal to *x*.

Here are some examples of how to compute probabilities for Poisson random variables. You can find these examples in the file Poisson.xlsx, shown in Figure 69-1.

	B	C	D
1	Calls per hour	30	
2	Mean	60	
3			
4	Prob 60 calls in two hours	0.05143	=POISSON.DIST(60,C2,FALSE)
5	Prob<= 60 calls in two hours	0.53426	=POISSON.DIST(60,C2,1)
6	Prob between 50 and 100 calls(inclusive) in two hour	0.91559	=POISSON.DIST(100,C2,TRUE)-POISSON.DIST(49,C2,TRUE)

FIGURE 69-1 Using the Poisson random variable.

Suppose that my consulting business receives an average of 30 phone calls per hour. During a two-hour period, I want to determine the following:

- The probability that exactly 60 calls will be received in the next two hours
- The probability that the number of calls received in the next two hours will be fewer than or equal to 60
- The probability that from 50 through 100 calls will be received in the next two hours

During a two-hour period, the mean number of calls is 60. In cell C4, I find the probability (0.05) that exactly 60 calls will be received in the next two hours, by using the formula =POISSON.DIST(60,C2,False). In cell C5, I find the probability (0.534) that at most 60 calls will be received in two hours by using the formula =POISSON.DIST(60,C2,1). (I use 1 as the alternate value for True.) In cell C6, I find the probability (0.916) that from 50 through 100 calls will be received in two hours by using the formula =POISSON.DIST(100,C2,True)–POISSON.DIST(49,C2,True).

> **Note** You can always use 1 instead of True as an argument in any Excel function.

If the number of customers arriving at a bank is governed by a Poisson random variable, what random variable governs the time between arrivals?

The time between arrivals can be any value, which means that the time between arrivals is a continuous random variable. If an average of λ arrivals occur per time unit, the time between arrivals follows an exponential random variable having for *t*>=0 the probability density function (PDF) of $f(t)= \lambda e^{-\lambda t}$.

This random variable has a mean, or average, value equal to *1/λ*. For *λ=30*, a graph of the exponential PDF is shown in Figure 69-2. You can find this chart and the data for this example in the Density worksheet in the file Exponentialdist.xlsx.

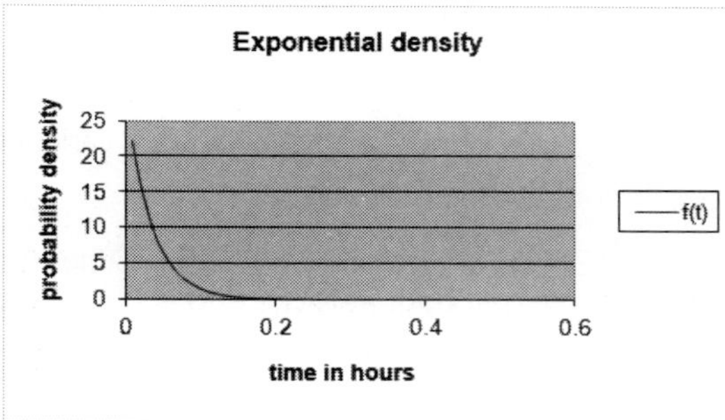

FIGURE 69-2 An exponential probability density function.

Recall from Chapter 67, "An Introduction to random variables," that for a continuous random variable, the height of the PDF for a number *x* reflects the likelihood that the random variable assumes a value near *x*. You can see in Figure 69-2 that extremely short times between customer arrivals at a bank (for example, less than 0.05 hours) are very likely, but that for longer times, the PDF drops off sharply.

Even though the average time between arrivals is 1/30=0.033 hours, there's a reasonable chance that the time between arrivals will be as much as 0.20 hours. The formula EXPON.DIST(x,1/mean,True or 1) will give the probability that an exponential random variable with a given mean will assume a value less than or equal to *x*. Thus, the second argument to the EXPON.DIST function is the rate per time unit at which events occur. For example, in the Computation worksheet, to compute the probability that the time between arrivals is at least 5, 10, or 15 minutes, I copied from cell D5 to D7 the formula =1–EXPON.DIST(C5,$D$2,True). In earlier versions of Excel, the EXPONDIST function yields the same results as EXPON.DIST.

Note that I first converted minutes to hours (5 minutes equals 1/12 hour, and so on). Also, the mean time between arrivals is 0.033 hours, so I entered the formula **1/Mean=1/0.033=30**. In short, I entered the arrival rate per time unit, as you can see in Figure 69-3 and in the Computation worksheet.

	B	C	D	E
1		mean	0.033333333	
2		1/mean	30	
3				
4		x = Time between arrivals	Prob time >=x	
5	5 minutes	0.08333333	0.082084999	=1-EXPON.DIST(C5,$D$2,TRUE)
6	10 minutes	0.16666667	0.006737947	=1-EXPON.DIST(C6,$D$2,TRUE)
7	15 minutes	0.25	0.000553084	=1-EXPON.DIST(C7,$D$2,TRUE)

FIGURE 69-3 Computations of exponential probabilities.

Problems

1. Beer drinkers order an average of 40 pitchers of beer per hour at Nick's Pub in Bloomington, Indiana. Answer the following questions:
   - What is the probability that at least 100 pitchers are ordered in a two-hour period?
   - What is the chance that the time between ordered pitchers will be 30 seconds or less?
2. Suppose that teenage drivers have an average of 0.3 accidents per year. Answer the following questions:
   - What is the probability that a teenager will have no more than one accident during a year?
   - What is the probability that the time between accidents will be six months or less?
3. I am next in line at a fast-food restaurant in which customers wait in a single line, and the time to serve a customer follows an exponential distribution with a mean of three minutes. What is the chance that I will have to wait at least five minutes to be served?
4. Since 1900, a fraction (0.00124) of all major league baseball games have resulted in no-hitters. A team plays 162 games in a season. What is the chance that a team pitches two or more no-hitters during a season?
5. An average of 80 customers arrive each hour at the Central Forest Coffee Shop. What is the probability that at least 150 customers arrive in a two-hour period?
6. What hourly arrival rate would ensure that the chance that at least 150 customers arrive at Central Forest in three hours would equal 0.5?

CHAPTER 70

The normal random variable and Z-scores

Questions answered in this chapter:

- What are the properties of the normal random variable?
- How do I use Excel to find the probabilities for the normal random variable?
- Can I use Excel to find the percentiles for normal random variables?
- Why is the normal random variable appropriate in many real-world situations?
- What are Z-scores?

Answers to this chapter's questions

What are the properties of the normal random variable?

In Chapter 67, "An introduction to random variables," you learned that continuous random variables can be used to model quantities such as the following:

- The price of Microsoft stock one year from now
- The market share for a new product
- The market size for a new product
- The cost of developing a new product
- A newborn baby's weight
- A person's IQ

Remember that if a discrete random variable (such as the sales of Big Macs during 2018) can assume many possible values, you can approximate the value by using a continuous random variable as well. As I described in Chapter 67, any continuous random variable X has a probability density function (PDF). The PDF for a continuous random variable is a nonnegative function with the following properties (a and b are arbitrary numbers):

- The area under the PDF is 1.
- The probability that $X<a$ equals the probability that $X\leq a$. This probability is represented by the area under the PDF, to the left of a.
- The probability that $X>b$ equals the probability that $X\geq b$. This probability is given by the area under the PDF to the right of b.
- The probability that $a<X<b$ equals the probability that $a\leq X\leq b$. This probability is the area under the PDF between a and b.

Thus, the area under a continuous random variable's PDF represents probability. Also, the larger the value of the density function at X, the more likely the random variable will take on a value near X. For example, if the density function of a random variable at 20 is twice the density function of the random variable at 5, then the random variable is twice as likely to take on a value near 20 than a value near 5.

For a continuous random variable, the probability that X equals a will always equal 0. For example, some people are from 5.99999 feet through 6.00001 feet tall, but no person can be exactly 6 feet tall. This explains why you can replace the less-than sign (<) with the less-than-or-equal-to sign (≤) in the probability statements.

Figure 70-1 displays the PDF for X=IQ of a randomly chosen person. The area under this PDF is 1. If you want to find the probability that a person's IQ is less than or equal to 90 (0.252), you simply find the area to the left of 90. If you want to find the probability that a person's IQ is between 90 and 120 (0..656), you find the area under the PDF between 90 and 120. If you want to find the probability that a person's IQ is more than 120 (0.091), you find the area under the density function to the right of 120.

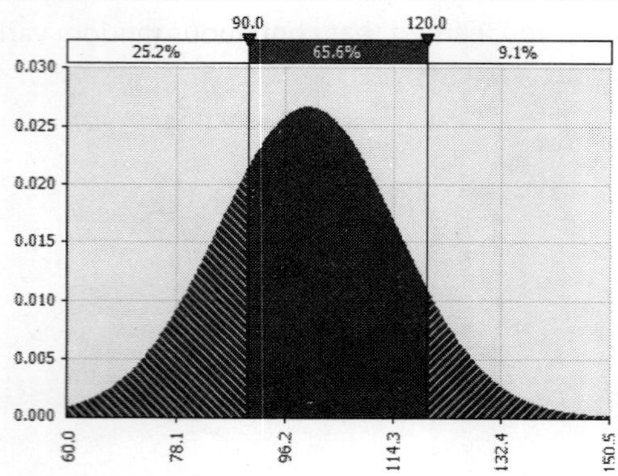

FIGURE 70-1 The probability density function for IQs.

Actually, the density plotted in Figure 70-1 is an example of the *normal random variable*. The normal random variable is specified by its mean and standard deviation. IQs follow a normal random variable with μ=100 and σ=15. This is the PDF displayed in Figure 70-1. The normal random variable has the following properties:

- The most likely value of a normal random variable is μ (as indicated by the PDF peaking at 100 in Figure 70-1).
- As the value x of the random variable moves away from μ, the probability that the random variable is near x sharply decreases.
- The normal random variable is symmetric about its mean. For example, IQs near 80 are as likely as IQs near 120.
- A normal random variable has 68 percent of its probability within σ (sigma, representing the standard deviation) of its mean, 95 percent within 2σ of its mean, and 99.7 percent within 3σ of its mean. These measures should remind you of the rule of thumb I described in Chapter 42, "Summarizing data by using descriptive statistics." In fact, the rule of thumb is based on the assumption that data is "sampled" from a normal distribution, which explains why the rule of thumb does not work as well when the data fails to exhibit a symmetric histogram.

For a larger σ, a normal random variable is more spread out about its mean. This pattern is illustrated in Figures 70-2 and 70-3. (See the worksheet Sigma Of 5 And 15 in the file Normalexamples.xlsx.)

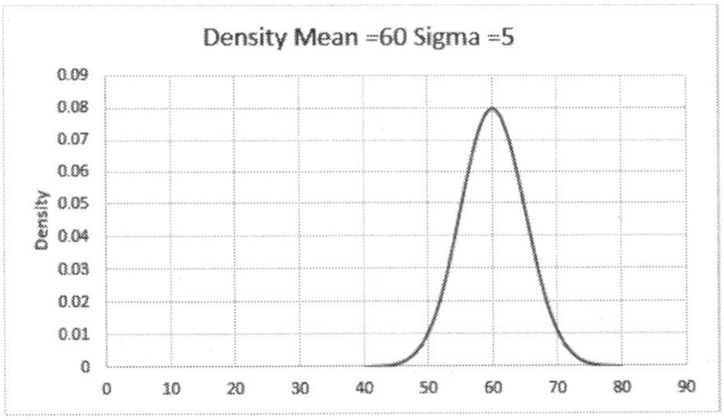

FIGURE 70-2 A normal random variable PDF, with a mean equal to 60 and a standard deviation equal to 5.

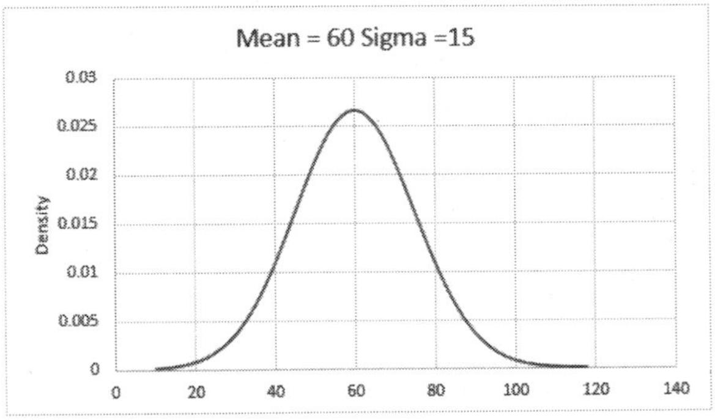

FIGURE 70-3 A normal random variable PDF, with a mean equal to 60 and a standard deviation equal to 15.

How do I use Excel to find the probabilities for the normal random variable?

Consider a normal random variable *X* with a mean μ and standard deviation σ. Suppose for any number *x*, you want to find the probability that $X \le x$, which is called the *normal cumulative function*. To use Microsoft Excel 2016 to find the probability that $X \le x$, enter the formula =NORM.DIST(x,μ,σ,1). Of course, the fourth argument of *1* could be replaced by *True*.

The argument *1* tells Excel to compute the normal cumulative. If the last argument of the function is *0*, Excel returns the actual value of the normal random variable PDF. Beginning with Excel 2010, statistical functions (like NORM.DIST) have been modified or redesigned completely to provide better accuracy than their counterparts (like NORMDIST) in previous versions of Excel.

You can use the NORM.DIST function to answer many questions concerning normal probabilities. You can find examples in the Normal worksheet in the file Normalexamples.xlsx, which is shown in Figure 70-4, and in the following three scenarios.

	B	C	D
2		Prob	
3	IQ<90	0.25249254	=NORM.DIST(90,100,15,1)
4	90<IQ<120	0.65629624	=NORM.DIST(120,100,15,1)-NORMDIST(90,100,15,1)
5	IQ>120	0.09121122	=1-NORM.DIST(120,100,15,1)
6			
7	99 %ile Prozac	71.6317394	=NORM.INV(0.99,60,5)
8	10% Bloomington income	19747.5875	=NORM.INV(0.1,30000,8000)

FIGURE 70-4 Calculating the normal probability.

- **What fraction of people have an IQ of less than 90?** Let *X* equal the IQ of a randomly chosen person. Then you seek the probability that $X<90$, which is equal to the probability that $X \le 90$. Therefore, you can enter into cell C3 of the Normal worksheet the formula =**NORM.DIST(90,100,15,1)**, and Excel returns 0.252. Thus, 25.2 percent of all people have an IQ less than 90.

- **What fraction of all people have IQs between 90 and 120?** When finding the probability that $a \le X \le b$, you use the form (area under the normal density function to the left of *b*)–(area under normal density function to the left of *a*). Thus, you can find the probability that $a \le X \le b$ by entering the formula =**NORM.DIST(b,μ,s,1)–NORM.DIST(a,μ,s,1)**. You can answer the question about IQs from 90 through 120 by entering into cell C4 of the worksheet Normal the formula =**NORM.DIST(120,100,15,1)–NORM.DIST(90,100,15,1)**. Excel returns the probability 0.656, so 65.6 percent of all people have an IQ from 90 through 120.

- **What fraction of all people have IQs of at least 120**? To find the probability that $X \ge b$, note that the probability that $X \ge b$ equals 1–probability $X<b$. You can compute the probability that $X \ge b$ by entering the formula 1–NORM.DIST(b,μ,σ,1). You seek the probability that $X \ge 120$. This equals 1–probability $X<120$. You enter in cell C5 of the worksheet Normal the formula =1–NORM.DIST(120,100,15,1). Excel returns 0.091, so you know that 9.1 percent of people have an IQ of at least 120.

Can I use Excel to find the percentiles for normal random variables?

Consider a given normal random variable *X* with mean (μ) and standard deviation (σ). In many situations, you want to answer questions such as the following:

- A drug manufacturer believes that next year's demand for its popular antidepressant will be normally distributed, with a mean equal to 60 million days of therapy (DOT) and σ (standard deviation) equal to 5 million DOT. How many units of the drug should be produced this year if the company wants to have only a 1 percent chance of running out of the drug?
- Family income in Bloomington, Indiana, is normally distributed, with a mean equal to $30,000 and σ equal to $8,000. The poorest 10 percent of all families in Bloomington are eligible for federal aid. What should the aid cutoff be?

In the first example, you want to determine the ninety-ninth percentile of demand for the antidepressant. That is, you seek the number *x* so that there is only a 1 percent chance that demand will exceed *x* and a 99 percent chance that demand will be less than *x*. In the second example, you want the tenth percentile of family income in Bloomington. That is, you seek the number *x* so that there is only a 10 percent chance that the family income will be less than *x* and a 90 percent chance that the family income will exceed *x*.

Suppose you want to find the *p*th percentile (expressed as a decimal) of a normal random variable *X* with a mean (μ) and a standard deviation (σ). Simply enter the formula =**NORM.INV(p,μ,σ)**. This formula returns a number *x* so that the probability that $X \leq x$ equals the specified percentile. You now can solve the examples. You'll find these exercises on the Normal worksheet in the file Normalexamples.xlsx.

For the drug manufacturing example, let *X* equal the annual demand for the drug. You want a value *x* so that the probability that $X \geq x$ equals 0.01 or the probability that $X < x$ equals 0.99. Again, you seek the ninety-ninth percentile of demand, which you find (in millions) by entering in cell C7 the formula =**NORM.INV(0.99,60,5)**. Excel returns 71.63, so the company must produce 71,630,000 DOT. This assumes, of course, that the company begins the year with no supply of the drug on hand. If, for example, they had a beginning inventory of 10 million DOT, they would need to produce 61,630,000 DOT during the current year.

To determine the cutoff for federal aid, if *X* equals the income of a Bloomington family, you seek a value of *x* so that the probability that $X \leq x$ equals 0.10, or the tenth percentile of Bloomington family income. You find this value with the formula NORM.INV(0.10,30000,8000). Excel returns $19,747.59, so aid should be given to all families with incomes less than $19,749.59.

Why is the normal random variable appropriate in many real-world situations?

A well-known mathematical result called the *central limit theorem (CLT)* indicates that if you add together many (usually at least 30 is sufficient) independent random variables, their sum is normally distributed. This result holds true even if the individual random variables are not normally distributed. Many quantities (such as measurement errors) are created by adding together many independent random variables, which explains why the normal random variable occurs often in the real world. The following are some other situations in which you can use the CLT.

- The total demand for pizzas during a month at a supermarket is normally distributed, even if the daily demand for pizzas is not.
- The amount of money you win if you play craps 1,000 times is normally distributed, even though the amount of money you win on each individual play is not.

Another important mathematical result shows how to find the mean, variance, and standard deviations of sums of independent random variables. If you are adding together independent random variables $X_1, X_2,..., Xn$ where the mean $X_i = \mu_i$, and the standard deviation $X_i = \sigma_i$, then the following are true:

1. Mean $(X_1+X_2+...X_n)=\mu_1+\mu_2+...\mu_n$
2. Variance $(X_1+X_2+...X_n)= \sigma_1^2+\sigma_2^2+...+\sigma_n^2$
3. Standard deviation $(X_1+X_2+...X_n)= \sqrt{\sigma_1^2+\sigma_2^2+\cdots+\sigma_n^2}$

Note that 1 is true even when the random variables are not independent. By combining 1 through 3 by means of the central limit theorem, you can solve many complex probability problems, such as modeling the demand for pizza over a 30-day period.

As an example of the central limit theorem, suppose daily demand for pizza at your local pizza parlor is not normally distributed but has a mean of 45 and standard deviation of 12. Suppose demand on different days is independent. What is the chance during a 30-day period that you will sell at least 1,400 pizzas? If you order pizza dough at the beginning of the 30-day period, how much dough should you order to ensure you have a 1 percent chance of running out of pizza dough? See the example in Figure 70-5 and the Central Limit worksheet of the file Normalexamples.xlsx.

	C	D	E
2	Daily frozen pizza demand		
3	mean	45	
4	sigma	12	
5			
6	30 day		
7	mean	1350	=D3*30
8	variance	4320	=30*D4^2
9	sigma	65.7267069	=SQRT(D8)
10			
11	Probability more than 1400 sold	0.22568935	=1-NORM.DIST(1399.5,D7,D9,TRUE)
12	1% chance of running out	1502.90318	=NORM.INV(0.99,D7,D9)

FIGURE 70-5 Using the central limit theorem.

Even though the daily demand for frozen pizzas is not normally distributed, you know from the CLT that the 30-day demand for frozen pizzas is normally distributed. Given this, 1 through 3 above imply the following:

- From 1, the mean of a 30-day demand equals 30(45)=1,350.
- From 2, the variance of a 30-day demand equals $30(12)^2$=4,320.
- From 3, the standard deviation of a 30-day demand equals $\sqrt{4320}$=65.73

Thus, the 30-day demand for pizzas can be modeled following a normal random variable with a mean of 1,350 and a standard deviation of 65.73. In cell D11, I compute the probability that at least 1,400 pizzas are sold as the probability that the normal approximation is at least 1,399.5, with the formula =1–NORM.DIST(1399.5,D7,D9,TRUE). (Note that a demand of 1,399.6, for example, would round up to 1,400.) I find the probability that demand in a 30-day period for at least 1,400 pizzas is 22.6 percent.

The number of pizzas that you must stock to have only a 1 percent chance of running out of pizzas is just the ninety-ninth percentile of the demand distribution. You determine the ninety-ninth percentile of the demand distribution (1,503) in cell D12 by using the formula =NORM.INV(0.99,D7,D9). Therefore, at the beginning of a month, you should bring your stock of pizzas up to 1,503 if you want only a 1 percent chance of running out of pizzas.

What are Z-scores?

When given a data set, you want to quickly determine how unusual a data point is. The most common approach is to standardize each data point by computing a *Z-score* the following way:

```
(Data value - Mean of data)/(Standard deviation of data)
```

Essentially a Z-score measures the number of standard deviations the data point differs from average. Since 95 percent of observations from a normal random variable are within two standard deviations of average, any data point with a Z-score exceeding 2 in absolute value is deemed an outlier.

As an example of the computation of Z-scores, the file Superbowlspreads.xlsx (see Figure 70-6) contains for the years 1967–2016 the Las Vegas prediction for the number of points by which the favorite would win the game and the number of points by which the favorite won. For example, in 2016 the Carolina Panthers were favored by 5 and lost by 14, so they performed -14 – 5 = -19 points relative to the point spread. We call the difference between the point spread and actual game outcome the *residual* or error for the game. You can compute Z-scores for the residuals as a measure for each game of how unexpected or unusual the game's outcome was. Proceed as follows:

- Compute the residual for each game by copying from cell C6 to C7:C55 the formula =E6-D6.
- In cell C4, compute the mean residual (-0.39) with the formula =AVERAGE(C6:C55).
- In cell I4, compute the standard deviation (16.10) of the errors with the formula =STDEV(C6:C55).

To compute the Z-score for each observation, copy from G6 to G7:G55 the formula =(C6-$C$4)/$I$4.

	C	D	E	F	G	H	I
2					Z Score		
3	Mean				Mean	2.9E-17	Stdev
4	-0.39				Sigma	1	16.1043
5	residual or error	Favorite	Result	Year	Z Score		
6	-19	5	-14	2016	-1.155588822		
7	4	0	4	2015	0.272597256		
8	-37.5	2.5	-35	2014	-2.30434719		
9	-7.5	4.5	-3	2013	-0.441495783		
10	-6.5	2.5	-4	2012	-0.379400736		
11	3	3	6	2011	0.210502209		
12	-19	5	-14	2010	-1.155588822		
13	-3	7	4	2009	-0.162068072		
14	-15	12	-3	2008	-0.907208635		
15	5	7	12	2007	0.334692303		
16	7	4	11	2006	0.458882396		
17	-4	7	3	2005	-0.224163119		

FIGURE 70-6 The Z-scores for the Super Bowl outcomes.

You find, for example, that in 2014, the favored Denver Broncos performed 2.3 standard deviations below average (the largest outlier in Super Bowl history!), while in 1990 the favored San Francisco 49ers performed 2.07 standard deviations better than average. I used conditional formatting to highlight both these outliers.

For any data set, the mean Z-score will be 0, and the standard deviation of the Z-scores will equal 1. As shown in cells H3 and H4, the mean Z-score is 0, and the standard deviation of the Z-scores is 1.

Problems

1. Suppose you can set the mean number of ounces of soda that is put into a can. The actual number of ounces has a standard deviation of 0.05 ounces. Answer the following questions:
   - If you set the mean at 12.03 ounces, and a soda can is acceptable if it contains at least 12 ounces, what fraction of cans are acceptable?
   - What fraction of cans have less than 12.1 ounces?
   - To what should you set the mean if you want at most 1 percent of your cans to contain at most 12 ounces? Hint: Use the Goal Seek command.
2. The annual demand for a drug is normally distributed with a mean of 40,000 units and a standard deviation of 10,000 units. Answer the following questions:
   - What is the probability that annual demand is from 35,000 through 49,000 units?
   - If you want to have only a 5 percent chance of running out of the drug, at what level should you set annual production?

3. The probability of winning a game of craps is 0.493. If I play 10,000 games of craps and bet the same amount on each game, what is the probability that I'm ahead? Begin by determining the mean and standard deviation of the profit in one game of craps. Then use the central limit theorem.

4. The weekly sales of Volvo's Cross Country station wagons are normally distributed with a mean of 1,000 and standard deviation of 250. Answer the following questions:

   - What is the probability that from 400 through 1,100 station wagons are sold during one week?
   - There is a 1 percent chance that fewer than what number of station wagons is sold during a week?

5. My time for swimming 100 yards follows a normal random variable with a mean that equals 51 seconds and a standard deviation of 1.5 seconds. If I swim the race in under 49 seconds, I will win the race. What is the chance I win the race?

6. The federal government wants to charge a Medicare surcharge to Americans 65 or older whose income ranks in the top 2 percent of all American family incomes. If the American family incomes follow a normal random variable with a mean that equals $60,000 and a standard deviation that equals $20,000, what should be the cutoff for the surcharge?

7. The voltage held by a voltage regulator follows a normal random variable with a mean that equals 200 volts and a standard deviation that equals 5 volts. A regulator meets the specifications if the regulator can hold a voltage between 185 and 210 volts. What fraction of the regulators meet the specifications?

8. Texas wants to give welfare checks to the 5 percent poorest of all Texas families. If the family income in Texas follows a normal random variable with a mean that equals $50,000 and a standard deviation that equals $15,000, what income level should be the cutoff for welfare?

9. A rod meets its specifications if its diameter is between 0.98 and 1.02 inches. The mean diameter of a rod is 1 inch. What should the standard deviation of rods equal for 99 percent of rods to meet the specifications?

10. The file Problem10data.xlsx gives the number of touchdown passes thrown by each quarterback in 2014. Determine the Z-score for each quarterback, and use conditional formatting to highlight all the outliers.

11. The number of bottles of ice tea sold by a supermarket on a Monday follows a normal random variable with a mean that equals 100 and a standard deviation that equals 12. On a given Monday, what is the chance that the supermarket will sell at least 105 bottles of ice tea? Fill in the blank: There is a 10 percent chance that _____ or fewer bottles of ice tea will be sold on a Monday.

12. Assume the mean daily percentage change in the Dow Jones Index is 1 percent, with a standard deviation of 1.5 percent. Assume there are 252 trading days in a year. What is the chance the Dow Jones Index increases by 20 percent or more during a year?

13. I have 500 potential customers who come to my candy store each day. Seventy percent of the customers buy no pieces of candy, 15 percent buy one piece, 10 percent buy two pieces, and 5 percent buy three pieces. What is the chance that I sell at least 280 pieces of candy in a day?

CHAPTER 71

Weibull and beta distributions: Modeling machine life and duration of a project

Questions answered in this chapter:

- How can I estimate the probability that a machine will work without failing for at least 20 hours?
- How can I estimate the probability that installing drywall in a building will take more than 200 hours?

The *Weibull random variable* is a continuous random variable that is often used to model the lifetime of a machine. If you have data about how long similar machines have lasted in the past, you can estimate the two parameters (*alpha* and *beta*) that define a Weibull random variable. You can then use the WEIBULL.DIST function in Microsoft Excel 2016 to determine the probabilities of interest, such as an estimate of how long a machine will run without failing.

The *beta random variable* is a continuous random variable that's often used to model the duration of an activity. Given estimates of the minimum duration, maximum duration, mean duration, and the standard deviation of the duration, you can use the BETA.DIST function to determine the probabilities of interest.

Answers to this chapter's questions

How can I estimate the probability that a machine will work without failing for at least 20 hours?

Suppose you have observed the lifetime of seven similar machines. The data collected about the machines is contained in the file Weibullest.xlsx, shown in Figure 71-1.

	B	C
16	Machine 1	8.5
17	Machine 2	12.54
18	Machine 3	13.75
19	Machine 4	19.75
20	Machine 5	21.46
21	Machine 6	26.34
22	Machine 7	28.45

FIGURE 71-1 Machine-lifetime data.

Reliability engineers have found that the Weibull random variable is usually appropriate for modeling machine lifetimes. The Weibull random variable is specified by two parameters: *alpha* and *beta*. Based on the data, you can determine (using the AVERAGE and STDEV.S functions in cells B13 and B14) that, on average, a machine lasts 18.68 hours, with a standard deviation of 7.40 hours. By copying these values to cells G6 and G11 and running Solver with the settings shown in Figure 71-2, you can find estimates of *alpha* and *beta* that ensure that the Weibull random variable will have a mean and standard deviation matching the data.

> **Note** To run the Solver add-in, you need to activate it. Click the File tab, and click Options. On the Add-Ins page, with Excel Add-Ins selected in the Manage list, click Go, select Solver Add-In, and then click OK. Solver appears on the Data tab, in the Analyze group. For more information, see Chapter 29, "An introduction to optimization with Excel Solver."

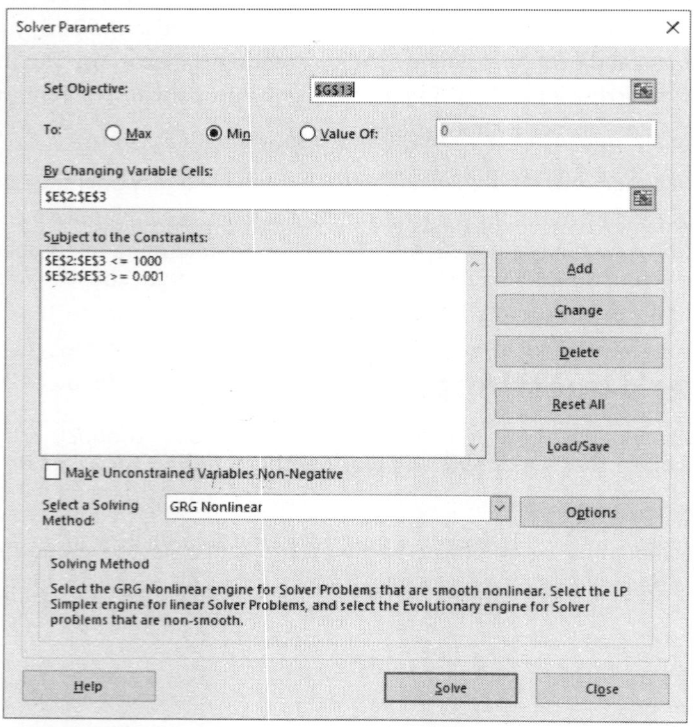

FIGURE 71-2 The Solver settings for determining the parameters for a Weibull random variable.

In this case, *alpha* equals 2.725 and *beta* equals 21.003, as you can see in Figure 71-3. Any value you enter for *alpha* and *beta* in cells E2 and E3 for a Weibull random variable yields a mean (computed in cell E6) and standard deviation (computed in cell E11). The Solver model varies *alpha* and *beta* until the mean and standard deviation of the Weibull distribution equal the mean and standard deviation of the machine lifetime computed from your data. I recommend using the Multistart option for the GRG Nonlinear engine. The Multistart engine works best with upper and lower bounds on the changing cells. A lower bound of 0.010 on *alpha* and *beta* will always work. I tried an upper bound of 1,000 for *alpha* and *beta*. If Solver makes *alpha* or *beta* bump up against your upper bound, you should relax the bound.

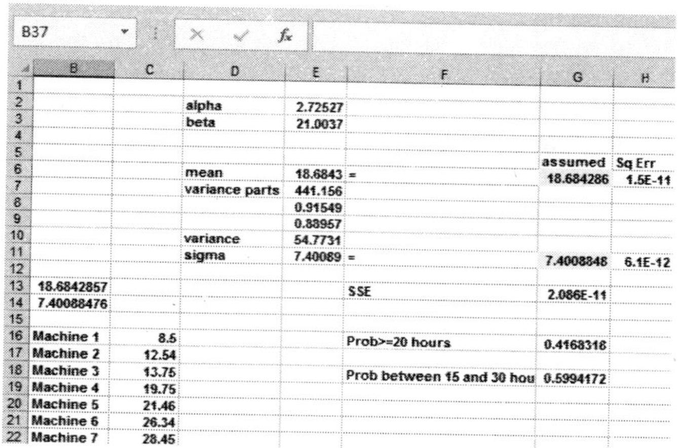

B37

	B	C	D	E	F	G	H
1							
2			alpha	2.72527			
3			beta	21.0037			
4							
5						assumed	Sq Err
6			mean	18.6843 =		18.684286	1.5E-11
7			variance parts	441.156			
8				0.91549			
9				0.88957			
10			variance	54.7731			
11			sigma	7.40089 =		7.4008848	6.1E-12
12							
13	18.6842857				SSE	2.086E-11	
14	7.40088476						
15							
16	Machine 1	8.5			Prob>=20 hours	0.4168318	
17	Machine 2	12.54					
18	Machine 3	13.75			Prob between 15 and 30 hou	0.5994172	
19	Machine 4	19.75					
20	Machine 5	21.46					
21	Machine 6	26.34					
22	Machine 7	28.45					

FIGURE 71-3 The estimates of *alpha* and *beta* for a Weibull random variable.

The following is the syntax of the WEIBULL.DIST function:

```
WEIBULL.DIST(x,alpha,beta,Cumulative)
```

When *Cumulative* equals True, this formula results in the probability that a Weibull random variable with the parameters *alpha* and *beta* is less than or equal to *x*. Changing True to False yields the height of the Weibull probability density function (PDF). Remember from Chapter 67, "An introduction to random variables," that the height of a PDF, for any value *x* of a continuous random variable, indicates the likelihood that the random variable assumes a value near *x*. Thus, if the Weibull density for 20 hours were twice the Weibull density for 10 hours, you would know that a machine is twice as likely to work for 20 hours before failing than to work for 10 hours before failing. Before answering some questions involving probabilities of interest, I'll note that in prior versions of Excel, the WEIBULLDIST function yields the same results as WEIBULL.DIST.

- **What is the probability that a machine will last at least 20 hours?** This probability (41.7 percent) is computed in cell G16 (of the file Weibullest.xlsx) with the formula =1–WEIBULL.DIST(20,alpha,beta,1). Essentially, this formula computes the area under the Weibull PDF to the right of 20 hours by subtracting from 1 the area to the left of 20 hours.

- **What is the probability that a machine will last between 15 and 30 hours?** This probability (59.9 percent) is computed in cell G18 with the formula =WEIBULL.DISTL(30,alpha,beta,True)–WEIBULL.DIST(15,alpha,beta,True). This formula finds the area under the Weibull PDF from 15 to 30 hours by computing the area to the left of 30 hours minus the area to the left of 15 hours. After you subtract the probability of a machine working without failure for less than 15 hours from the probability of a machine working without failure for less than or equal to 30 hours, you are left with the probability that a machine will work without failure from 15 to 30 hours.

How can I estimate the probability that installing drywall in a building will take more than 200 hours?

Since the development of the Polaris missile in the 1950s, project managers have modeled activity durations with the *beta random variable*. To specify a beta random variable, you need to specify a minimum value, a maximum value, and two parameters (*alpha* and *beta*). The data in the file Beta.xlsx (see Figure 71-4) can be used to estimate the parameters of a beta distribution.

	B	C	D	E	F
3	Fit a beta				
4					
5	alpha	2.196262		mean	78.486
6	beta	14.59335		sigma	47.967
7	lower	0			Data
8	upper	600			26.257
9	mean	78.48647			91.840
10	sigma	47.96749			66.543
11	transformed mean	0.130811			53.893
12	transformed var	0.006391			222.437
13					72.054
14					75.357
15	Probability>=200 hours	0.020502			78.274
16	Probability <=80 hours	0.583238			99.044
17	Probability between 30 and 150 hours	0.771058			90.476
18					47.000
19					16.215
20					117.277
21					69.935
22					50.694

FIGURE 71-4 Determining probabilities with the beta random variable.

Suppose that you believe that the time needed to install drywall in a building is sure to be between 0 and 600 hours. These are your minimum and maximum values, entered in cells C7 and C8. The cell range F8:F22 contains the lengths of time needed to install drywall in 15 buildings of a similar size. In cell F5, I used the AVERAGE function to compute the mean time (78.49 hours) needed to install drywall in these 15 buildings. In cell F6, I used the STDEV.S function to determine the standard deviation (47.97 hours) of the time needed to install drywall in these buildings. Any choice of values of *alpha* and *beta* determine the shape of the beta distribution's PDF and the mean and standard deviation for the corresponding beta random variable. If you can choose the *alpha* and *beta* values to match the mean and standard deviation of the drywall installation times computed from this data, it seems reasonable that these *alpha* and *beta* values will yield probabilities that are consistent with the observed data. After you enter the mean and standard deviation for the drywall installation data in cells C9 and C10, the worksheet computes values for *alpha* (2.20) in cell C5 and *beta* (14.59) in cell C6 that ensure that the mean and standard deviation of the beta random variable match the mean and standard deviation of the data.

The function BETA.DIST(x,alpha,beta,True or 1,lower,upper) determines the probability that a beta random variable ranging from lower to upper, with the parameters *alpha* and *beta*, assumes a value less than or equal to *x*. The last two parameters are optional, and if they are omitted, Excel assumes *lower* equals 0 and *upper* equals 1. The function BETA.DIST(x,alpha,beta,False or 0,lower,upper) returns the PDF for a random variable following a beta distribution. You can now use the BETA.DIST function to determine the probabilities of interest.

To compute the probability that installing drywall will take at least 200 hours, you can use the formula in cell C15, =1–BETA.DIST(200,alpha,beta,True,lower,upper). The result is 2.1 percent. This formula simply computes the probability that installing drywall will take at least 200 hours as 1–probability drywalling takes less than or equal to 200 hours.

The probability that installing drywall will take at most 80 hours (58.3 percent) can be computed with the formula in cell C16, =BETA.DIST(80,alpha,beta,True,lower,upper). And to compute the probability that the task will take between 30 and 150 hours (77.1 percent), I used the formula =BETA.DIST(150,alpha,beta,True,lower,upper)–BETA.DIST(30,alpha,beta,True,lower,upper) in cell C17. This formula computes the probability that installing drywall takes between 30 and 150 hours as the probability that drywalling takes less than or equal to 150 hours, minus the probability that drywalling takes less than or equal to 30 hours. The difference between these probabilities counts only the instances when dry walling takes from 30 to 150 hours.

Problems

The data for this chapter's problems is contained in the file Ch71data.xlsx.

1. In the Problem 1 worksheet, you are given data about the duration of a machine's lifetime. Answer the following questions:
   - What is the probability that the machine will last at least 10 hours?
   - What is the probability that the machine will last from 1 to 5 hours?
   - What is the probability that the machine will fail within 6 hours?
2. You need to clean your house today. In the Problem 2 worksheet, you are given data about how long it has taken to clean your house in the past. If you start cleaning at noon, what are the chances that you'll be finished in time to leave at 7:00 PM for a movie?

CHAPTER 72

Making probability statements from forecasts

Questions answered in this chapter:

- On what basis do we evaluate forecasts?
- If a drug company forecasts that it will sell 60 million units of a drug next year, what is the chance that it will sell more than 65 million units of that drug next year?

Every day, we are inundated by forecasts. Here are some examples:

- The government predicts the GNP will grow by 4 percent during the next year.
- The Eli Lilly marketing department predicts that during the next year, demand for a given drug will be 400,000,000 DOT (days of therapy).
- A Wall Street guru predicts the Dow will go up 20 percent during the next 12 months.
- The bookmakers forecast that the Indiana Pacers will beat the Houston Rockets by six points in the opening game of the 2017 NBA season.

Although the forecasts you receive may be the best available, they are almost sure to be incorrect. For example, the bookmaker's prediction that the Pacers will win by six points is incorrect unless the Pacers win by exactly six points. In short, any single value (or point forecast) implies a distribution for the quantity being forecasted. How can you take a point forecast and find a random variable that correctly models the uncertainty inherent in the point forecast? The key to putting a distribution around a point forecast is to have some historical data about the accuracy of past forecasts of the quantity of interest. For example, with regard to the forecast for the Dow Jones Industrial Average, you might have for the last 10 years the forecast made in January of each year for the percentage change in the Dow and the actual change in the Dow for each of the 10 years.

Answers to this chapter's questions

On what basis do we evaluate forecasts?

You can begin by seeing whether past forecasts exhibit any bias. For each past forecast, you determine the actual value and forecasted values. Then you average these ratios. If your forecasts are unbiased, this average should be around 1. Any significant deviation from 1 indicates a significant bias. For example, if the average of the actual and forecasted values is 2, the actual results tend to be around twice the forecast. To correct for a bias, you should automatically double your forecast. If the average of the actual and forecasted values is 0.5, then the actual results tend to be around half the actual forecast, so to eliminate a bias you should automatically halve your forecast. After you eliminate the forecast bias, you look at the standard deviation of the percentage errors of the unbiased forecast and use the following normal random variable to model the quantity being forecasted:

- Mean = the unbiased forecast
- Standard deviation = (unbiased forecast)*(standard deviation of the percentage errors associated with the unbiased forecasts)

The standard deviation of the percentage errors measures the accuracy of the past forecasts. Clearly, a smaller standard deviation of percentage forecast errors is preferred to a larger standard deviation.

The file Drugfore.xlsx (see Figure 72-1) illustrates the ideas of forecast bias and forecast accuracy. The file contains the actual and forecasted sales (in millions of DOT) for the years 2005–2012. I'll first show that these forecasts are biased and then correct the bias.

	C	D	E	F	G	H	I
1						mean	std dev
2			mean	0.91803		5E-17	0.11375
3							
4	Year	Actual Sales	Forecast	A/F	Unbiased forecast	%age error	
5	2005	17	22	0.77273	20.19668	-16%	
6	2006	59	61	0.96721	55.9999	5%	
7	2007	46	51	0.90196	46.81959	-2%	
8	2008	85	86	0.98837	78.95067	8%	
9	2009	98	103	0.95146	94.5572	4%	
10	2010	94	118	0.79661	108.3277	-13%	
11	2011	24	22	1.09091	20.19668	19%	
12	2012	14	16	0.875	14.6885	-5%	

FIGURE 72-1 Correcting for forecast bias and measuring forecast accuracy.

To begin, in cells F5:F12 I check for bias by computing for each year actual sales and forecasted sales. To do this, I copy from F5 to F6:F12 the formula =D5/E5.

Next, in cell F2, I compute the bias of the original forecasts by averaging each year's actual and forecasted value with the formula =AVERAGE(F5:F12). I find that the actual sales tend to come in 8 percent under the forecast. To correct past biased forecasts, I multiply them by 0.92 by copying from G5 to G6:G12 the formula =$F$2*E5. In H5:H12, I compute each year's percentage error for the unbiased forecast by copying from H5 to H6:H12 the formula =(D5-G5)/G5. As you can see, for example, 2005 actual sales were 16 percent less than the unbiased forecast, while in 2011 actual sales were 19 percent larger than the unbiased forecast.

Now I evaluate the accuracy of the forecast errors in cell I2 by computing the standard deviation of the percentage errors with the formula =STDEV.S(H5:H12). I find the standard deviation of past unbiased forecasts has been around 11.4 percent of the unbiased forecast.

If a drug company forecasts that it will sell 60 million units of a drug next year, what is the chance that it will sell more than 65 million units of the drug next year?

Forecast errors often follow a normal random variable. Therefore, after correcting for bias, you can assume the forecast errors follow a normal random variable with the following conditions:

- Mean = the unbiased forecast
- Standard deviation = (unbiased forecast)*(standard deviation of the percentage errors associated with the unbiased forecasts)

In my example, this means that you should model drug sales next year as a normal random variable, where the mean = 60(0.918) = 55.08 million, and the standard deviation = (0.11375)*55.08 = 6.27 million. You can now use the Excel NORM.DIST function to compute in cell E18 (see Figure 72-2) the chance of selling at least 65 million units next year by using the formula =1-NORM.DIST(65,F15,F16,True). There is a 5.7 percent chance of selling more than 65 million units of the drug.

	D	E	F	G	H
15		Mean 2013	55.0819		
16		Sigma 2013	6.2657		
17					
18	Probability	0.05671928			
19	we sell >65 million	1-NORM.DIST(65,F15,F16,TRUE)			
20	units				

FIGURE 72-2 The chance of selling more than 65 million units of the drug.

Problems

1. In Game 7 of the Boston Celtics-Los Angeles Lakers 2010 NBA finals, the Lakers were favored by seven points. Looking at past NBA games, you will find that bookmakers' forecasts are unbiased. Also, the standard deviation of bookmaker forecasts in past NBA games is 12 points. Before the game, what would you have estimated as the probability that the Lakers would win the game?

2. A leading cell-phone company forecasts that next year it will sell 3 million units of its best-selling phone. In the past, actual sales have been unbiased, with the forecast errors having a standard deviation equal to 10 percent of the forecasted sales. What are the chances that less than 2.5 million phones will be sold next year?

3. The file USC.xlsx contains the USC football team's margins of victory for the years 2005–2009 and the bookmaker's forecast (before the game) for the USC margin of victory. Does this data indicate that the bookmaker's forecasts are unbiased? If USC is favored by 10 points, estimate the chance that USC wins the game.

CHAPTER 73

Using the lognormal random variable to model stock prices

Questions answered in this chapter:

- What is the lognormal random variable?
- Is there a reason stock prices might follow a lognormal random variable?
- How can I model the future price of any stock as a lognormal random variable?
- How can I compute the probability that Microsoft's stock price will exceed $60 six months from now?
- How can I compute the probability that Microsoft's stock price will be less than or equal to $40 in six months?
- How can I compute the median stock price for Microsoft in six months?

Many people are interested in modeling the future price of a stock, a commodity such as oil or wheat, or a future exchange rate. For the last 40 years, the lognormal random variable has been the random variable most often used to model stock prices. In this chapter, you will learn why the lognormal random variable is a reasonable model for stock prices and how to determine the appropriate lognormal parameters for any stock. I'll close the chapter by showing how the Excel LOGNORM.DIST and LOGNORM.INV functions can be used to calculate the probabilities that involve the future price of a stock.

Answers to this chapter's questions

What is a lognormal random variable?

A random variable *Y* follows a lognormal random variable if the natural logarithm of *Y* (written as *ln Y*) follows a normal random variable. When using the Excel LOGNORM.DIST and LOGNORM.INV functions, a lognormal random variable *Y* is characterized by two parameters: a mean *Mu* is equal to the expected value of *ln Y*, and a standard deviation *Sigma* is equal to the standard deviation of *ln Y*.

Is there a reason stock prices might follow a lognormal random variable?

Let *Y* equal the price of a stock *n* days from now, *P* equal the stock's price today, and *Xt* equals the percentage change in the stock's price during day *t*. Then $Y = P*X_1*X_2*...X_n$. Because the logarithm of a product is the sum of the logarithms, it's true that $ln\ Y = ln\ P + ln\ X_1 + ln\ X_2 +... ln\ X_n$. Suppose the changes in prices on different days are independent random variables. Recall from Chapter 70, "The normal random variable and Z-scores," that the central limit theorem implies that the sum of many independent random variables will be a normal random variable even if the individual random variables are not normally distributed. This explains why *ln Y* is likely to be a normal random variable, and this implies that *Y* is a lognormal random variable.

How can I model the future price of any stock as a lognormal random variable?

At the close of trading on July 7, 2016, the price of Microsoft stock was $51.78. Suppose you are interested in modeling the price of Microsoft stock in six months as a lognormal random variable. How can you estimate *Mu* and *Sigma*? Luckily, information is easily available on the Internet to help you model the future price of a stock. The website (see Figure 73-1) IVolatility.com provides an estimate of a stock's annual volatility (call it *Sigma_*). The annual volatility is a surrogate for a stock's riskiness or variability. At the close of trading on July 7, 2016, the website IVolatility.com indicated that Microsoft's *implied volatility* was 17.38 percent. To represent *Sigma_* as a decimal, you write Sigma_ = 0.1738. (The method used to compute the implied volatility is discussed in Chapter 79, "Pricing stock options.")

	Current	1 WK AGO	1 MO AGO	52 wk Hi/Date	52 wk Low/Date
			HISTORICAL VOLATILITY		
10 days	33.04%	35.16%	21.35%	57.72% - 02-Sep	10.63% - 19-Oct
20 days	26.81%	26.83%	20.74%	44.22% - 16-Sep	13.21% - 09-Jul
30 days	24.63%	24.91%	20.00%	37.46% - 09-Sep	13.81% - 09-Jul
			IMPLIED VOLATILITY		
IV Index call	27.83%	28.74%	18.65%	40.33% - 20-Jan	17.41% - 27-May
IV Index put	27.66%	28.73%	17.77%	39.05% - 20-Jan	16.65% - 31-Jul
IV Index mean	27.74%	28.73%	18.21%	39.69% - 20-Jan	17.38% - 31-Jul

FIGURE 73-1 The implied volatility of Microsoft stock on July 7, 2016.

From the Investment section of *finance.yahoo.com*, you can find the consensus opinion of analysts for the price of Microsoft in a year, shown in Figure 73-2.

Price Target Summary	
Mean Target:	58.13
Median Target:	60.00
High Target:	70.00
Low Target:	36.00
No. of Brokers:	34

FIGURE 73-2 The estimates for Microsoft's stock price on July 7, 2017.

Let S_0 equal today's stock price, and S_1 equal the estimated mean price in one year. Then *Mu_*, a surrogate for the annual mean return on the stock, can be estimated by $Mu\_= ln\ (S_1/S_0)$.

From Yahoo.com, I found that at the close of trading on July 7, 2016, S_0 equals $51.78 and S_1 equals $58.13. Therefore, *Mu_* = *ln* (58.13/51.78) = 0.115678, as computed in cell F7 of the file Lognormal.xlsx. (See Figure 73-3.)

	E	F	G
1			
2	**Microsoft July 7, 2016**		
3			
4	Price today	$ 51.78	
5	Forecast in a year	$ 58.13	
6	sigma_	0.2227	
7	Mu_	0.115678	=LN(Forecast_in_a_year/Price_today)
8	time(years)	0.5	
9	Mu for t	3.992444	=LN(Price_today)+(Mu_-0.5*sigma_^2)*time_years
10	Sigma for t	0.1738	
11			
12	**In 6 months**		
13	Chance price >=$60	0.278834	=1-LOGNORM.DIST(60,Mu_for_t,Sigma_for_t,TRUE)
14	Chance price <=$40	0.040351	=LOGNORM.DIST(40,Mu_for_t,Sigma_for_t,TRUE)
15	Median Price	54.18717	=LOGNORM.INV(0.5,Mu_for_t,Sigma_for_t)

FIGURE 73-3 Using the Lognormal variable to model the price of Microsoft stock in six months.

If you want to model the price of Microsoft stock *t* years in the future, you need to know Mu_t equals the mean of *ln* of Microsoft stock price in *t* years, and $Sigma_t$ equals the standard deviation of *ln* of Microsoft's stock price in *t* years. I found the following:

Mu_t = *ln S0+t(Mu_-0.5*Sigma_^2)* and $Sigma_t$ = *Sigma*sqrt(t)*

For six months, *t* =0.5 years. In cell E9, I computed $Mu_{.5}$ as *ln*(51.78)+0.5*(0.115678)-0.5*(0.1738^2) = 3.992444. In cell E10, I computed the following:

$$Sigma_{.5} = .227 * \sqrt{.5} = 0.1738$$

Therefore, you can model the price of Microsoft stock in six months as a lognormal random variable with *Mu* = 3.99244 and *Sigma* = 0.1738.

How can I compute the probability that Microsoft's stock price will exceed $60 six months from now?

The Excel 2016 function LOGNORM.DIST(x, Mean, Sigma, True or 1) computes the probability that a lognormal random variable with the parameters *Mean* and *Sigma* is less than or equal to *x*. Changing *True* or 1 to *False* or 0 returns the height of the lognormal probability density function (PDF) at *x*.

In versions of Excel preceding Excel 2013, the function LOGNORMDIST returns the same results as LOGNORM.DIST. In cell F13, I determine the chance that the price of a share of Microsoft will exceed $60. This is calculated by 1 – Probability that share is <$60, so I use the formula =1-LOGNORM.DIST(60,*Mu_for_t*,*Sigma_for_t*,True). (In the file Lognormal.xlsx, I use range names in the formulas rather than the cells, where the range name *Mu_for_t* is cell F9 and *Sigma_for_t* is cell F10.) There is a 27.9 percent chance that a share of Microsoft will sell for more than $60 in six months.

How can I determine the chance that in six months Microsoft will sell for $40 or less?

In cell F14, I determine the chance that a share of Microsoft will sell for less than or equal to $40 in six months by means of the formula =LOGNORM.DIST(40,*Mu_for_t*,*Sigma_for_t*,True). There is a 4 percent chance that a share of Microsoft will sell for $40 or less in six months.

How can I determine the median price of Microsoft stock in six months?

Suppose you want to determine the median price of Microsoft stock in six months. This is a price $*x* so that there is a 50 percent chance that the Microsoft stock price in six months will be less than or equal to $*x*. In cell F15, I find the median price in six months using the formula =LOGNORM.INV(0.5,*Mu_for_t*,*Sigma_for_t*). The median price in six months is $54.19.

Remarks

- In Chapter 79, I discuss the famous Black-Scholes option-pricing formula. The Black-Scholes formula assumes that the price of a stock follows a lognormal random variable.
- In recent years, it has become apparent that for many stocks, future stock prices take on extremely high or low values more often than the lognormal random variable predicts. This has caused analysts to search for other random variables with "fat tails" that can be used to model future stock prices. For more details on this topic, see Nassim Nicholas Taleb's best-selling book *The Black Swan*. Also, in Chapter 76, "Simulating stock prices and asset-allocation modeling," I discuss an alternative method for modeling stock prices that does not assume that future stock prices follow a lognormal random variable.

Problems

Suppose a stock sells for $30 today. The annual volatility of the stock is 35 percent, and analysts predict the expected price of the stock in a year will be $35. Use this information to answer questions 1 through 3:

1. What is the probability that in two years the stock will sell for more than $45?
2. What is the probability that in two years the stock will sell for less than $25?
3. You are 95 percent sure that the price of the stock in two years will be between what two values? Hint: Use 0.025 and 0.975 as the first arguments in the LOGNORM.INV function.

CHAPTER 74

Introduction to Monte Carlo simulation

Questions answered in this chapter:

- Who uses Monte Carlo simulation?
- What happens when I type =RAND() in a cell?
- How can I simulate values of a discrete random variable?
- How can I simulate values of a normal random variable?
- How can a greeting-card company determine how many cards to produce?

Data analysts would like to accurately estimate the probabilities of uncertain events. For example, what is the probability that a new product's cash flows will have a positive net present value (NPV)? What is the risk factor of an investment portfolio? Monte Carlo simulation enables you to model situations that present uncertainty and then play them out on a computer thousands of times.

Note The term *Monte Carlo simulation* comes from the computer simulations performed during the 1930s and 1940s to estimate the probability that the chain reaction needed for an atom bomb to detonate would work successfully. The physicists involved in this work were big fans of gambling, so they gave the simulations the code name *Monte Carlo*.

In the next five chapters, I provide some examples of how you can use Microsoft Excel 2016 to perform Monte Carlo simulations.

Answers to this chapter's questions

Who uses Monte Carlo simulation?

Many companies use Monte Carlo simulation as an important part of their decision-making process. Here are some examples.

- General Motors (GM), Procter & Gamble, Pfizer, Bristol-Myers Squibb, and Eli Lilly use simulation to estimate both the average return and the risk factor of new products. At these companies, this information is used to determine which products come to market.
- GM uses simulation for activities such as forecasting the net income for the corporation, predicting the structural and purchasing costs, and determining its susceptibility to different kinds of risk (such as interest-rate changes and exchange-rate fluctuations).
- Eli Lilly uses the simulation to determine the optimal plant capacity for each drug.
- Procter & Gamble uses the simulation to model and optimally hedge foreign-exchange risk.
- Sears uses the simulation to determine how many units of each product line should be ordered from suppliers—for example, the number of pairs of Dockers trousers that should be ordered this year.
- Oil and drug companies use the simulation to value *real options*, such as the value of an option to expand, contract, or postpone a project.
- Financial planners use Monte Carlo simulation to determine optimal investment strategies for their clients' retirement.

What happens when I type =RAND() in a cell?

When you type the formula =RAND() in a cell, you get a number that is equally likely to assume any value between 0 and 1. Thus, around 25 percent of the time, you should get a number less than or equal to 0.25; around 10 percent of the time you should get a number that is at least 0.90, and so on. To demonstrate how the RAND function works, take a look at the file Randdemo.xlsx, shown in Figure 74-1.

	B	C	D	E	F
1					
2	Trial			mean	0.495952
3	1	0.813262			
4	2	0.288988		Fraction	
5	3	0.939361		0-.25	0.2575
6	4	0.786287		.25-.50	0.2425
7	5	0.91443		.50-.75	0.2475
8	6	0.26157		.75-1	0.2525
9	7	0.336107			
10	8	0.503733			
11	9	0.105186			
12	10	0.956549			
13	11	0.857657			
14	12	0.126325			
15	13	0.558723			
16	14	0.351238			
17	15	0.856488			
18	16	0.77694			
19	17	0.626955			
20	18	0.552412			

FIGURE 74-1 Demonstrating the RAND function.

Note When you open the Sheet1 worksheet in the file Randdemo.xlsx, you will not see the same random numbers shown in Figure 74-1. The RAND function always recalculates the numbers it generates when a worksheet is opened or when new information is entered in the worksheet. The Frozen worksheet has its values fixed to correspond to the preceding figure.

In the Sheet1 worksheet, I copied from cell C3 to C4:C402 the formula =RAND(). I named the range C3:C402 *data*. Then, in column F, I tracked the average of the 400 random numbers (cell F2) and used the COUNTIF function to determine the fractions that are between 0 and 0.25, 0.25 and 0.50, 0.50 and 0.75, and 0.75 and 1. When you press the F9 key, the random numbers are recalculated. Notice that the average of the 400 numbers (cell F2) is always approximately 0.5, and that around 25 percent of the results are in intervals of 0.25. These results are consistent with the definition of a random number. Also note that the values generated by RAND in different cells are independent. For example, if the random number generated in cell C3 is a large number (for example, 0.99), that tells you nothing about the values of the other random numbers generated.

How can I simulate values of a discrete random variable?

Suppose the demand for a calendar is governed by the following discrete random variable:

Demand	Probability
10,000	0.10
20,000	0.35
40,000	0.3
69,000	0.25

How can you have Excel play out, or simulate, this demand for calendars many times? The trick is to associate each possible value of the RAND function with a possible demand for calendars. The following assignment ensures that a demand of 10,000 will occur 10 percent of the time, and so on:

Demand	Random number assigned
10,000	Less than 0.10
20,000	Greater than or equal to 0.10, and less than 0.45
40,000	Greater than or equal to 0.45, and less than 0.75
69,000	Greater than or equal to 0.75

To demonstrate the simulation of demand, look at the Sim worksheet in the file Discretesim.xlsx (or its Frozen version shown in Figure 74-2).

	A	B	C	D	E	F	G
1						Cutoffs	Demand
2	Trial		rand			0	10000
3	1	60000	0.855			0.1	20000
4	2	60000	0.794			0.45	40000
5	3	10000	0.058			0.75	60000
6	4	40000	0.524				
7	5	20000	0.14		Demand	Fraction of time	
8	6	40000	0.611		10000	0.1	
9	7	60000	0.966		20000	0.345	
10	8	20000	0.416		40000	0.305	
11	9	20000	0.379		60000	0.25	
12	10	20000	0.282				
13	11	40000	0.563				
14	12	60000	0.871				

FIGURE 74-2 Simulating a discrete random variable.

The key to this simulation is to use a random number to initiate a lookup from the table range F2:G5 (named *lookup*). Random numbers greater than or equal to 0 and less than 0.10 will yield a demand of 10,000; random numbers greater than or equal to 0.10 and less than 0.45 will yield a demand of 20,000; random numbers greater than or equal to 0.45 and less than 0.75 will yield a demand of 40,000; and random numbers greater than or equal to 0.75 will yield a demand of 69,000. I generated 400 random numbers by copying from C3 to C4:C402 the formula =RAND(). I then generated 400 trials, or iterations, of calendar demand by copying from B3 to B4:B402 the formula =VLOOKUP(C3,lookup,2). This formula ensures that any random number less than 0.10 generates a demand of 10,000, any random number between 0.10 and 0.45 generates a demand of 20,000, and so on. In the cell range F8:F11, I used the COUNTIF function to determine the fraction of the 400 iterations yielding each demand. When I press F9 to recalculate the random numbers, the simulated probabilities are close to the assumed demand probabilities.

How can I simulate values of a normal random variable?

If you type in any cell the formula =NORM.INV(rand(),mu,sigma), you will generate a simulated value of a normal random variable having a mean *Mu* and a standard deviation *Sigma*. I've illustrated this procedure in the Sim worksheet in the file Normalsim.xlsx (see Figure 74-3 for the Frozen version).

	A	B	C	D	E	F	G
1				mean	40000		
2				sigma	10000		
3	Trial	Normal Rv	Rand				
4	1	51474.28518	0.8744			sim mean	39917.206
5	2	47174.57061	0.76345			sim sigma	10090.233
6	3	28679.63394	0.12881				
7	4	38347.61662	0.43438				
8	5	35589.45315	0.32959				
9	6	21426.72175	0.03163				
10	7	45611.61787	0.71266				
11	8	49758.08713	0.83542				
12	9	74377.58134	0.99971				
13	10	43021.64238	0.61874				
14	11	52902.32552	0.90152				

FIGURE 74-3 Simulating a normal random variable.

Let's suppose you want to simulate 400 trials for a normal random variable with a mean of 40,000 and a standard deviation of 10,000. (I typed these values in cells E1 and E2, and named these cells *mean* and *sigma*, respectively.) Copying the formula =RAND() from C4 to C5:C403 generates 400 different random numbers. Copying from B4 to B5:B403 the formula =NORM.INV(C4,mean,sigma) generates 400 different trial values from a normal random variable with a mean of 40,000 and a standard deviation of 10,000. When I press the F9 key to recalculate the random numbers, the mean remains close to 40,000 and the standard deviation close to 10,000.

Essentially, for a random number *p*, the formula =NORMINV(p,mean,sigma) generates the *p*th percentile of a normal random variable, with a mean *Mu* and a standard deviation *Sigma*. For example, the random number 0.87 in cell C4 (see Figure 73-3 earlier) generates in cell B4 approximately the eighty-seventh percentile of a normal random variable with a mean of 40,000 and a standard deviation of 10,000.

How can a greeting-card company determine how many cards to produce?

In this section, I'll demonstrate how Monte Carlo simulation can be used as a decision-making tool. Suppose that the demand for a Valentine's Day card is governed by the following discrete random variable:

Demand	Probability
10,000	0.10
20,000	0.35
40,000	0.3
69,000	0.25

The greeting card sells for $4.00, and the variable cost of producing each card is $1.50. Leftover cards must be disposed of at a cost of $0.20 per card. How many cards should be printed?

Basically, you simulate each possible production quantity (10,000, 20,000, 40,000, or 69,000) many times (for example, 1,000 iterations). Then you determine which order quantity yields the maximum average profit over the 1,000 iterations. You can find the data for this section in the Sim worksheet in the file Valentine.xlsx. (The Frozen version is shown in Figure 74-4.) I assigned the range names in cells B1:B11 to cells C1:C11. I assigned the cell range G3:H6 the name *lookup*. The sales price and cost parameters are entered in cells C4:C6.

	B	C	G	H
1	produced	40000		
2	rand#	0.216599428		
3	demand	20000	0	10000
4	unit prod cost	$ 1.50	0.1	20000
5	unit price	$ 4.00	0.45	40000
6	unit disp cost	$ 0.20	0.75	60000
7				
8	revenue	$ 80,000.00		
9	total var cost	$ 60,000.00		
10	total disposing cost	$ 4,000.00		
11	profit	$ 16,000.00		

FIGURE 74-4 A Valentine's Day card simulation.

I then enter a trial production quantity (40,000 in this example) in cell C1. Next I create a random number in cell C2 with the formula =RAND(). As previously described, I simulate demand for the card in cell C3 with the formula =VLOOKUP(rand,lookup,2). (In the VLOOKUP formula, *rand* is the cell name assigned to cell C3, not the RAND function.)

The number of units sold is the smaller of the production quantity and demand. In cell C8, I compute the revenue with the formula =MIN(produced,demand)*unit_price. In cell C9, I compute the total production cost with the formula =produced*unit_prod_cost.

If more cards are produced than are in demand, the number of units left over equals the production minus demand; otherwise, no units are left over. I compute the disposal cost in cell C10 with the formula =unit_disp_cost*IF(produced>demand,produced–demand,0). Finally, in cell C11, I compute the profit with the formula =revenue–total_var_cost-total_disposing_cost.

It would be nice to have an efficient way to press F9 many times (for example, 1,000) for each production quantity and tally the expected profit for each quantity. This situation is one in which a two-way data table comes to the rescue. (See Chapter 17, "Sensitivity analysis with data tables," for details about data tables.) The data table I used in this example is shown in Figure 74-5.

	A	B	C	D	E	F
13	mean	25000	46094	57958	45000	
14	st dev	0	12204.26598	47634.1	73193.8	
15	100000	10000	20000	40000	60000	production quantity
16	1	25000	50000	100000	-18000	
17	2	25000	50000	100000	66000	
18	3	25000	50000	16000	66000	
19	4	25000	50000	-26000	-18000	
20	5	25000	50000	100000	-60000	
21	6	25000	50000	100000	-18000	
22	7	25000	50000	100000	-18000	
23	8	25000	50000	16000	-18000	
24	9	25000	50000	16000	-18000	
25	10	25000	50000	-26000	66000	
26	11	25000	50000	16000	66000	
27	12	25000	50000	100000	150000	
28	13	25000	50000	100000	66000	
29	14	25000	8000	16000	66000	
30	15	25000	50000	16000	150000	

FIGURE 74-5 A two-way data table for a greeting-card simulation.

In the cell range A16:A1015, I entered the numbers 1 to 1,000 (corresponding to the 1,000 trials). One easy way to create these values is to start by entering 1 in cell A16. Select the cell, and then on the Home tab in the Editing group, click Fill (the icon with the down arrow), and select Series to display the Series dialog box. In the Series dialog box, shown in Figure 74-6, enter the Step Value of 1 and the Stop Value of 1,000. In the Series In area, select the Columns option. The numbers 1 through 1,000 will be entered in column A starting in cell A16.

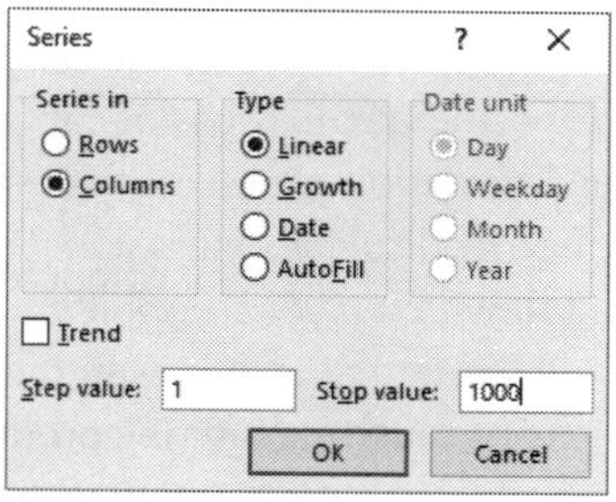

FIGURE 74-6 Using the Series dialog box to fill in the trial numbers 1 through 1,000.

Next, I enter the possible production quantities (10,000, 20,000, 40,000, 69,000) in cells B15:E15. I want to calculate the profit for each trial number (1 through 1,000) and each production quantity. I refer to the formula for profit (calculated in cell C11) in the upper-left cell of the data table (A15) by entering =profit (since I assigned cell C11 the name *profit*).

You can now trick Excel into simulating 1,000 iterations of demand for each production quantity. Select the table range (A15:E1015), and then, in the Forecast group on the Data tab, click What If Analysis, and then select Data Table. The Data Table diaolog box opens. To set up a two-way data table, choose the production quantity (cell C1) as the Row Input Cell and select any blank cell (I chose cell I14) as the Column Input Cell. After you click OK, Excel simulates 1,000 demand values for each order quantity.

To understand why this works, consider the values placed by the data table in the cell range C16:C1015. For each of these cells, Excel uses a value of 20,000 in cell C1. In C16, the column input cell value of 1 is placed in a blank cell, and the random number in cell C2 recalculates. The corresponding profit is then recorded in cell C16. Then the column input cell value of 2 is placed in a blank cell, and the random number in C2 again recalculates. The corresponding profit is entered in cell C17.

By copying from cell B13 to C13:E13 the formula =AVERAGE(B16:B1015), you can compute the average simulated profit for each production quantity. By copying from cell B14 to C14:E14 the formula =STDEV.S(B16:B1015), you can compute the standard deviation of the simulated profits for each order quantity. Each time you press F9, 1,000 iterations of demand are simulated for each order quantity. Producing 40,000 cards always yields the largest expected profit, so producing 40,000 cards appears to be the proper decision.

The impact of risk on your decision

If you produce 20,000 instead of 40,000 cards, the expected profit drops approximately 22 percent, but the risk (as measured by the standard deviation of profit) drops almost 73 percent. Therefore, if you are extremely averse to risk, producing 20,000 cards might be the right decision. Incidentally, producing 10,000 cards always has a standard deviation of 0 cards, because if you produce 10,000 cards, you will always sell all of them without any leftovers.

Note In the file Valentine.xlsx, I set the Calculation option to Automatic Except For Tables. (This option is found in the Calculation Options menu in the Calculation group on the Formulas tab.) This setting ensures that the data table does not recalculate unless you press F9, which is a good idea because a large data table will slow down your work if it recalculates every time you type something in your worksheet. Note that in this example, whenever you press F9, the mean profit changes. This happens because each time you press F9, a different sequence of 1,000 random numbers is used to generate demands for each order quantity.

Confidence interval for mean profit

A natural question to ask in this situation is, "Into what interval will I be 95 percent sure that the true mean profit will fall?" This interval is called *the 95 percent confidence interval for mean profit*. A 95 percent confidence interval for the mean of any simulation output is computed by the following formula:

$$\mathit{Mean\ Profit} \pm \frac{1.96 * \mathit{profitst.dev}}{\sqrt{\mathit{number\ iterations}}}$$

In cell J11, I computed the lower limit for the 95 percent confidence interval on mean profit when 40,000 calendars are produced, with the formula =D13–1.96*D14/SQRT(1000). In cell J12, I computed the upper limit for the 95 percent confidence interval with the formula =D13+1.96*D14/SQRT(1000). These calculations are shown in Figure 74-7.

	I	J	K	L	M
9	95% CI for mean profit				
10	ordering 40,000 calendars				
11	Lower	55282.47	=D13-1.96*D14/SQRT(1000)		
12	Upper	61221.53	=D13+1.96*D14/SQRT(1000)		

FIGURE 74-7 A 95 percent confidence interval for mean profit, when 40,000 calendars are ordered.

You can be 95 percent sure that your mean profit, when 40,000 calendars are ordered, is between \$55,076 and \$61,008.

Problems

1. An auto dealer believes that the demand for 2015 model cars will be normally distributed with a mean of 200 and a standard deviation of 30. His cost of receiving an Envoy is \$25,000, and he sells an Envoy for \$40,000. Half of all the Envoys not sold at full price can be sold for \$30,000. He is considering ordering 200, 220, 240, 269, 280, or 300 Envoys. How many should he order?

2. A small supermarket is trying to determine how many copies of *People* magazine it should order each week. The owner believes the demand for *People* is governed by the following discrete random variable:

Demand	Probability
15	0.10
20	0.20
25	0.30
30	0.25
35	0.15

The supermarket pays $1.00 for each copy of *People* and assumes a copy sells at the store for $1.95. Each unsold copy can be returned for $0.50. How many copies of People should the store order?

3. Your supermarket is trying to determine how many meatloaf dinners should be produced on Monday. The Monday demand for meatloaf dinners is normally distributed with a mean of 100 and a standard deviation of 20. The cost of producing a meatloaf dinner is $2.00, and the dinner sells for $7.00. It costs $0.60 at the end of the day to dispose of each unsold dinner. If the only possible production quantities are 100, 110, 120, and 130, what production quantity would you recommend?

4. The Monday demand for almond croissants is normally distributed with a mean of 100 and a standard deviation of 25. It costs $1.00 to produce a croissant, which sells for $4.00. Leftover croissants must be disposed of at a cost of $0.40 each. The bakery is considering producing 80, 100, 120, or 140 croissants. Use Monte Carlo simulation to determine the order quantity that maximizes the bakery's expected profit.

5. The demand in pounds for kale salad on Sunday is normally distributed with a mean of 500 and a standard deviation of 100. Kale salad costs $3.00 per pound to produce and sells for $8.00 per pound. At the end of the day, the leftover kale salad has no value. Considering the production levels of 500, 520, 540, 560, 580, and 600 pounds, determine the production quantity that maximizes your expected profit,

6. A greeting-card company is trying to determine how many Valentine's Day greeting cards to produce. The cost of printing x cards is $2 million +0.70$x$. For example, printing 1 million cards costs $2.7 million. Demand for cards follows a normal random variable with a mean of 2 million and a standard deviation of 400,000. The cards are sold for $4.00, and leftover cards have a value of $0.05. Among the production quantities of 2.4, 2.6, 2.8, 3 or 3.2 million, which production quantity maximizes the company's expected profit?

CHAPTER 75

Calculating an optimal bid

Questions answered in this chapter:

- How do I simulate a binomial random variable?
- How can I determine whether a continuous random variable should be modeled as a normal random variable?
- How can I use a simulation to determine the optimal bid for a construction project?

When you're bidding against competitors on a project, the two major sources of uncertainty are the number of competitors and the bids submitted by each competitor. If your bids are high, you'll make a lot of money on each project, but you'll get very few projects. If your bids are low, you'll work on lots of projects but make very little money on each one. The optimal bid is somewhere in the middle. Monte Carlo simulation is a useful tool for determining the bid that maximizes expected profit.

Answers to this chapter's questions

How do I simulate a binomial random variable?

The formula BINOM.INV(n,p,rand()) simulates the number of successes in *n* independent trials, each of which has a probability of success equal to *p*. As explained in Chapter 74, "Introduction to Monte Carlo simulation," the RAND function generates a number equally likely to assume any value between 0 and 1. As shown in the file Binomialsim.xlsx (see Figure 75-1), when you press F9, the formula =BINOM.INV(100,0.9,D3) entered in cell C3 simulates the number of free throws that Steve Nash (a now-retired 90 percent foul shooter in the NBA) makes in 100 attempts. The formula =BINOM.INV(100,0.5,D4) in cell C4 simulates the number of heads tossed in 100 tosses of a fair coin. In cell C5, the formula =BINOM.INV(3,0.4,D5) simulates the number of competitors entering the market during a year in which there are three possible entrants and each competitor is assumed to have a 40 percent chance of entering the market. Of course, in D3:D5, I entered the formula =RAND().

	B	C	D	E
2			Rand#	
3	Number of free throws Steve Nash makes out of 100	92	0.717266	=BINOM.INV(100,0.9,D3
4	Number of heads in 100 tosses	50	0.483365	=BINOM.INV(100,0.5,D4
5	Number of competitors entering market; p =4 n= 3	2	0.864771	=BINOM.INV(3,0.4,D5)

FIGURE 75-1 Simulating a binomial random variable.

How can I determine whether a continuous random variable should be modeled as a normal random variable?

Let's suppose that you think the most likely bid by a competitor is \$50,000. Recall that the normal probability density function (PDF) is symmetric about its mean. Therefore, to determine whether a normal random variable can be used to model a competitor's bid, you need to test for symmetry about the bid's mean. If the competitor's bid exhibits symmetry about the mean of \$50,000, bids of \$40,000 and \$60,000, \$45,000 and \$55,000, and so on should be approximately equally likely. If the symmetry assumption seems reasonable, you can then model each competitor's bid as a normal random variable with a mean of \$50,000.

How can you estimate the standard deviation of each competitor's bid? Recall from the rule of thumb discussed in Chapter 42, "Summarizing data by using descriptive statistics," that data sets with symmetric histograms have roughly 95 percent of their data within two standard deviations of the mean. Similarly, a normal random variable has a 95 percent probability of being within two standard deviations of its mean. Suppose that you are 95 percent sure that a competitor's bid will be between \$30,000 and \$70,000. This implies that 2*(standard deviation of competitor's bid) equals \$20,000, or the standard deviation of a competitor's bid equals \$10,000.

If the symmetry assumption is reasonable, you can now simulate a competitor's bid with the formula =NORM.INV(rand(),50000,10000). (See Chapter 74 for details about how to model normal random variables using the NORM.INV function.)

Also, a normal random variable has a *skewness* and *kurtosis* of 0. Assuming that you have a fairly large sample, if you find that the skewness and/or kurtosis is greater than 1 in its absolute value, then it is unlikely that the data comes from a normal random variable.

How can I use a simulation to determine the optimal bid for a construction project?

Let's assume that you're bidding on a construction project that will cost you \$25,000 to complete. It costs \$1,000 to prepare your bid. You have six potential competitors, and you estimate that there is a 50 percent chance that each competitor will bid on the project. If a competitor places a bid, its bid is assumed to follow a normal random variable with a mean equal to \$50,000 and a standard deviation equal to \$10,000. Also suppose you are preparing bids that are exact multiples of \$5,000. What should you bid to maximize your expected profit? Remember, the low bid wins! You'll find the work for this question in the file Bidsim.xlsx, shown in Figures 75-2 and 75-3.

	D	E	F	G
1	costproject	25000		
2	cost bid	1000	rand#	
3	Number bidders	5	0.96126	
4	mybid	40000		
5				
6				
7				
8	Bidder #	In	Bid	rand#
9	1	yes	73012.31	0.989311
10	2	yes	52686.65	0.605906
11	3	yes	70296.25	0.978803
12	4	yes	38241.56	0.119829
13	5	yes	57651.38	0.777905
14	6	no	100000	0.582284
15				
16	Do I win?			
17	no			
18	Profit			
19	-1000			

FIGURE 75-2 A bidding simulation model.

	D	E	F	G	H	I	J	K
21	mean	3630	7290	8240	5680	3175	2120	225
22	-1000	30000	35000	40000	45000	50000	55000	60000
23	1	4000	9000	-1000	19000	-1000	-1000	-1000
24	2	4000	9000	-1000	19000	-1000	-1000	-1000
25	3	-1000	9000	-1000	-1000	-1000	-1000	-1000
26	4	4000	9000	14000	-1000	24000	-1000	-1000
27	5	4000	9000	14000	19000	-1000	-1000	-1000
28	6	4000	-1000	-1000	-1000	24000	-1000	-1000
29	7	4000	9000	14000	-1000	-1000	-1000	-1000
30	8	4000	9000	-1000	-1000	-1000	-1000	-1000
31	9	4000	9000	14000	-1000	-1000	-1000	-1000
32	10	4000	9000	-1000	19000	24000	-1000	-1000
33	11	4000	9000	14000	-1000	-1000	-1000	-1000
34	12	4000	-1000	-1000	-1000	-1000	29000	-1000
35	13	4000	9000	-1000	-1000	24000	-1000	-1000
36	14	4000	9000	14000	-1000	-1000	-1000	-1000
37	15	4000	9000	14000	-1000	24000	-1000	-1000
38	16	4000	-1000	14000	-1000	-1000	-1000	-1000
39	17	4000	9000	14000	-1000	-1000	-1000	34000
40	18	4000	9000	14000	-1000	-1000	-1000	-1000
41	19	4000	9000	14000	-1000	24000	-1000	-1000
42	20	4000	9000	14000	-1000	-1000	-1000	-1000

FIGURE 75-3 A bidding simulation data table.

Your strategy should be as follows:

- Generate the number of bidders.
- For each potential bidder who actually bids, use the normal random variable to model the bid. If a potential bidder does not bid, you assign a large bid (for example, $100,000) to ensure that they do not win the bidding.
- Determine whether you are the low bidder.
- If you are the low bidder, you earn a profit equal to your bid, less project cost, less $1,000 (the cost of making the bid). If you are not the low bidder, you lose the $1,000 cost of the bid.

- Use a two-way data table to simulate each possible bid (for example, $30,000, $35,000, ... $60,000) 1,000 times, and then choose the bid with the largest expected profit.

To begin, I assigned the names in the cell range D1:D4 to the range E1:E4. I determine in cell E3 the number of bidders with the formula =BINOM.INV(6,0.5,F3). Cell F3 contains the formula =RAND(). Next I determine which of the potential bidders actually bid by copying from E9 to E10:E14 the formula =IF(D9<=Number_bidders,"yes","no").

I then generate a bid for each bidder (nonbidders are assigned a bid of $100,000) by copying from cell F9 to F10:F14 the formula =IF(E9="yes",NORM.INV(G9,50000,10000),100000). Each cell in the cell range G9:G14 contains the RAND function. In cell D17, I determine whether I am the low bidder and win the project with the formula =IF(mybid<=MIN(F9:F14),"yes","no"). In cell D19, I compute the profit with the formula =IF(D17="yes",mybid–costproject–cost_bid,–cost_bid), recognizing that I receive only the amount of the bid and pay the project costs if I win the bid.

Now I can use a two-way data table (shown earlier in Figure 74-3) to simulate 1,000 bids between $30,000 and $60,000. I copy the profit to cell D22 by entering the formula =D19. Then I select the table range D22:K1022. On the Data tab, in the Forecast group, I click What-If Analysis and then click Data Table to specify the input values for the data table. The column input cell is any blank cell in the worksheet, and I enter E4 (the location of the bid) in the Row Input Cell box. Then I click OK in the Data Table dialog box to simulate the profit from each bid 1,000 times.

Copying from E21 to F21:K21 the formula =AVERAGE(E23:E1022) calculates the mean profit for each bid. Each time I press F9, I see that the mean profit for 1,000 trials is maximized by bidding $40,000.

Problems

1. How would the optimal bid change if you had 12 competitors?
2. Suppose you are bidding for an oil well that you believe will yield $40 million (including the cost of developing and mining the oil) in profits. Three competitors are bidding against you, and each competitor's bid is assumed to follow a normal random variable, with a mean of $30 million and a standard deviation of $4 million. What should you bid (within $1 million)?
3. A commonly used continuous random variable is the *uniform random variable*. A uniform random variable—written as *U(a,b)*—is equally likely to assume any value between two given numbers *a* and *b*. Explain why the formula =a+(b–a)*RAND() can be used to simulate *U(a,b)*.
4. Investor Peter Fischer is bidding to take over a biotech company. The company is equally likely to be worth any amount between $0 and $200 per share. Only the company itself knows its true value. Peter is such a good investor that the market will immediately estimate the firm's value at 50 percent more than its true value. What should Peter bid per share for this company?

5. Seattle Mariner baseball player Robinson Cano is asking for salary arbitration on his contract. Salary arbitration in Major League Baseball works as follows: The player submits a salary that he thinks he should be paid, as does the team. The arbitrator (without seeing the salaries submitted by the player or the team) estimates a fair salary. The player is then paid the submitted salary that is closer to the arbitrator's estimate. For example, suppose Cano submits a $12 million offer, and the Seattle Mariners submit a $7 million offer. If the arbitrator says a fair salary is $10 million, Cano will be paid $12 million, whereas if the arbitrator says a fair salary is $9 million, Cano will be paid $7 million. Assume that the arbitrator's estimate is equally likely to be anywhere between $8 and $11 million, and the team's offer is equally likely to be anywhere between $6 million and $9 million. Within $1 million, what salary should Cano submit?

6. Two beverage companies are bidding on the exclusive rights for selling soda at the University of Houston for the next 10 years. Company 1 will earn 50 cents profit per bottle sold (exclusive of the payment to the university) and believes the number of bottles sold during the next 10 years will be normally distributed, with a mean of 6 million and a standard deviation of 1.5 million. Company 1 believes that Company 2's bid is equally likely to be any amount between $1 million and $2.5 million. What should Company 1 bid to maximize their expected profit? You may find it helpful to know that for any two integers *n*1 and *n*2, the Excel function =RANDBETWEEN(n1,n2) is equally likely to return any integers between *n*1 and *n*2 inclusive. Considering bids of $1, $1.5, $2, $2.5, and $3 million, which bid maximizes the expected profit?

7. You are bidding on a project to fix all the potholes on Westheimer Road in Houston. (Good luck!) You estimate the cost of fixing the potholes is $4 million. Four competitors are going to bid against you. Each competitor's bid is normally distributed, with a mean of $6 million and a standard deviation of 0.5 million. Considering bids of $4.5, $5, $5.5, and $6 million, which bid maximizes the expected profit?

CHAPTER 76

Simulating stock prices and asset-allocation modeling

Questions answered in this chapter:

- I recently bought 100 shares of GE stock. What is the probability that during the next year this investment will return more than 10 percent?
- I'm trying to determine how to allocate my investment portfolio between stocks, T-bills, and bonds. What asset allocation over a five-year planning horizon will yield an expected return of at least 8 percent and minimize my risk?

The last few years have shown that future returns on investments are highly uncertain. In Chapter 73, I showed how to use the lognormal random variable to model stock prices. Many financial experts have been critical of using the lognormal random variable to model stock prices because the lognormal underestimates the probability of extreme events (often called *black swans*). In this chapter, I'll explain a relatively simple approach to assessing uncertainty in future investment returns. This approach is based on the idea of *bootstrapping*. Essentially, bootstrapping simulates future investment returns by assuming that the future will be similar to the past. For example, if you want to simulate the stock price of GE in one year, you can assume that each month's percentage change in price is equally likely to be one of, for example, the percentage changes for the previous 60 months. This method allows you to easily generate thousands of scenarios for the future value of your investments. In addition to scenarios that assume that future variability and average returns will be similar to the recent past, you can easily adjust bootstrapping to reflect a view that future returns on investments will be less or more favorable than in the recent past.

After you've generated future scenarios for investment returns, it's a simple matter to use Microsoft Excel Solver to work out the asset-allocation problem—that is, how you should allocate your investments to attain the level of expected return you want but with minimum risk.

The following two examples demonstrate the simplicity and power of the bootstrapping approach.

Answers to this chapter's questions

I recently bought 100 shares of GE stock. What is the probability that during the next year this investment will return more than 10 percent?

Let's suppose that GE stock is currently selling for $28.50 per share. Data for the monthly returns on GE (as well as for Microsoft and Intel) for the months between August 1997 and July 2002 is included in the file GEsim.xlsx, shown in Figure 76-1. For example, in the month ending on August 2, 2002 (basically, the data from July 2002), GE lost 12.1 percent. These returns include dividends (if any) paid by each company.

	C	D	E	F
3	mean	0.014746	0.006237	0.008828
4		MSFT	INTC	GE
5	8/2/2002	-0.08316	-0.15397	-0.12112
6	7/2/2002	-0.12285	0.028493	0.108434
7	6/2/2002	0.074445	-0.33853	-0.06139
8	5/2/2002	-0.02583	-0.03464	-0.01276
9	4/2/2002	-0.13348	-0.05894	-0.15658
10	3/2/2002	0.033768	0.064867	-0.02849
11	2/2/2002	-0.08429	-0.18514	0.041088
12	1/2/2002	-0.03834	0.114295	-0.07314
13	12/1/2001	0.031771	-0.03709	0.045898
14	11/1/2001	0.104213	0.337433	0.057167
15	10/1/2001	0.136408	0.194417	-0.02102
16	9/1/2001	-0.10307	-0.26889	-0.08653
17	8/1/2001	-0.13809	-0.06181	-0.05957
18	7/1/2001	-0.09329	0.019172	-0.10944
19	6/1/2001	0.055218	0.082654	0
20	5/1/2001	0.021107	-0.12601	0.009701
21	4/1/2001	0.238801	0.174658	0.159413
22	3/1/2001	-0.07305	-0.07886	-0.09653
23	2/1/2001	-0.03374	-0.22808	0.011168

FIGURE 76-1 The GE, Microsoft, and Intel stock data.

The price of GE stock in one year is uncertain, so how can you get an idea about the range of variation in the price of GE stock one year from now? The bootstrapping approach simply estimates a return on GE during each of the next 12 months by assuming that the return during each month is equally likely to be any of the returns for the 60 months listed. In other words, the return on GE next month is equally likely to be any of the numbers in the cell range F5:F64. To implement this idea, you use the formula =RANDBETWEEN(1,60) to choose a scenario for each of the next 12 months. For example, if this function returns 7 for next month, you use the return for GE in cell F11 (4.1 percent), which is the seventh cell in the range, as next month's return. The results are shown in Figure 76-2. (You'll see different values because the RANDBETWEEN function automatically recalculates random values when you open the worksheet.)

To begin, you enter GE's current price per share ($28.50) in cell J6. Then, you generate a scenario for each of the next 12 months by copying from K6 to K7:K17 the formula =RANDBETWEEN(1,60). Next, you use a lookup table to obtain the GE return based on your scenario. To do this, you simply copy from L6 to L7:L17 the formula =VLOOKUP(K6,lookup,5). As the formula indicates, the range B5:F64 is named *Lookup*, with the returns for GE in the fifth column of the lookup range. In the scenarios shown in Figure 76-2, you can see, for example, that the return for GE six months into the future is equal to the 11/1/2001 data point—that is, a 5.7 percent return. (Remember that each time you open the file, you will see a different set of scenarios.)

	I	J	K	L	M
4	GE				
5	Month	Start price	Scenario	Return	End price
6	1	28.5	35	0.142670499	32.56611
7	2	32.5661092	11	-0.021021021	31.88154
8	3	31.8815364	10	0.05716676	33.7041
9	4	33.7041005	56	0.056165541	35.59711
10	5	35.5971095	36	0.055724138	37.58073
11	6	37.5807278	10	0.05716676	39.7291
12	7	39.7290962	37	0.030415009	40.93746
13	8	40.937457	1	-0.121118012	35.97919
14	9	35.9791936	53	-0.01186197	35.55241
15	10	35.5524095	28	0.003940887	35.69252
16	11	35.6925175	34	-0.039560942	34.28049
17	12	34.2804879	32	-0.133960753	29.68825

FIGURE 76-2 Simulating the GE stock price in one year.

Copying from M6 to M7:M17 the formula =(1+L6)*J6 determines each month's ending GE price. The formula takes the form (1+ month's return)*(GE's beginning price). Finally, copying from J7 to J8:J17 the formula =M6 computes the beginning price for each month as equal to the previous month's ending price.

You can now use a data table to generate 1,000 scenarios for GE's price in one year and the one-year percentage return on your investment. The data table is shown in Figure 76-3. In cell J19, you copy the ending price with the formula =M17. In cell K19, you enter the formula =(M17–$J$6)/$J$6 to compute the one-year return as (Ending GE price–Beginning GE price)/Beginning GE price.

	I	J	K	L	M
18		End Price	End Return		
19		29.6882479	0.04169291	Mean	0.106679
20	1	23.7177891	-0.167796874	Prob lose money	0.403
21	2	25.8389085	-0.093371631	Prob make more than 10	0.451
22	3	26.3086531	-0.076889363	Make between 0 and 10%	0.146
23	4	28.6928527	0.00676676	Lose between 0 and 10%	0.121
24	5	26.582571	-0.06727821	Lose More than 10%	0.282
25	6	51.0550021	0.791403584		
26	7	18.7384374	-0.342510967		
27	8	24.4760342	-0.141191781		
28	9	48.0968093	0.687607345		
29	10	37.2935418	0.308545327		
30	11	20.4767428	-0.281517797		
31	12	32.3495125	0.135070615		
32	13	24.4546509	-0.141942075		
33	14	36.8287092	0.292235411		
34	15	25.4360206	-0.107508048		

FIGURE 76-3 The data table for the GE simulation.

Next, select the table range (J19:K1019), click What-If Analysis in the Forecast group on the Data tab, and then select Data Table. You set up a one-way data table by selecting a blank cell in the Column Input Cell box. After you click OK in the Data Table dialog box, Excel generates 1,000 scenarios for GE's stock price in one year. (I set the calculation option for this workbook by clicking the Formulas tab, clicking Calculation Options in the Calculation group, and selecting Automatic Except For Tables. You need to press F9 if you want to see the simulated prices change.)

In cells M20:M24, I used the COUNTIF function (see Chapter 20, "The COUNTIF, COUNTIFS, COUNT, COUNTA, and COUNTBLANK functions") to summarize the range of returns that can occur in one year. For example, in cell M20, I computed the probability of losing money in one year with the formula =COUNTIF(returns,"<0")/1000. (I named the range containing the 1,000 simulated returns as *Returns*.) The simulation indicates that, based on the data for 1997–2002, there is roughly a 39 percent chance that your GE investment will lose money during the next year. You can also see that for the 1,000 simulated returns generated in the data tale the following are true:

- There is a 46 percent probability that returns will be more than 10 percent.
- There is a 15 percent probability that returns will be between 0 and 10 percent.
- There is a 12 percent chance that the investment will lose between 0 and 10 percent.
- There is a 28 percent chance that the investment will lose more than 10 percent.
- The average return for the next year will be approximately 10.7 percent.

Many pundits believe that future stock returns will not be as good as in the recent past. Suppose you feel that in the next year, GE will perform on average 5 percent worse per year than it performed during the 1997–2002 period for which you have data. You can easily incorporate this assumption into a simulation by changing the final price formula for GE in cell M17 to =(1+L17)*J17–0.05*J6. This appends –0.05*J6 and simply reduces the ending GE price by 5 percent of its initial price, which reduces your returns for the next year by 5 percent. You can see these results in the file GEsimless5.xlsx, shown in Figure 76-4.

	L	M
19	Mean	0.062461
20	Prob lose money	0.496
21	Prob make more than 10	0.391
22	Make between 0 and 10%	0.113
23	Lose between 0 and 10%	0.147
24	Lose More than 10%	0.349

FIGURE 76-4 A more pessimistic view of the future of the GE stock.

Note that the estimate shows now a 50 percent chance that the price of GE stock will decrease during the next year. The average is not exactly 5 percent lower than the previous simulation because each time you run 1,000 iterations, the simulated values change. Therefore, when you open the file you will see slightly different values than those shown in Figure 76-4.

I'm trying to determine how to allocate my investment portfolio between stocks, T-bills, and bonds. What asset allocation over a five-year planning horizon will yield an annual expected return of at least 8 percent and minimize my risk?

A key decision made by individuals, mutual fund managers, and other investors is how to allocate assets among different asset classes, given the future uncertainty about returns for these asset classes. A reasonable approach to asset allocation is to use bootstrapping to generate 1,000 simulated values for the future values of each asset class, and then use Excel Solver to determine an asset allocation that yields an expected return yet minimizes risk. As an example, suppose you are given annual returns on stocks, T-bills, and bonds during the period 1973–2012. You are investing for a five-year planning horizon, and based on the historical data, you want to know which asset allocation yields a minimum risk (as measured by standard deviation) of annual returns and yields an annual expected return of at least 8 percent. You can see this data in the file Assetallsim.xlsx, shown in Figure 76-5. (Not all the data is shown.)

	A	B	C	D
7	Year	Stocks	T.Bills	T.Bonds
8	1973	-14.31%	5.07%	3.66%
9	1974	-25.90%	7.45%	1.99%
10	1975	37.00%	7.15%	3.61%
11	1976	23.83%	5.44%	15.98%
12	1977	-6.98%	4.35%	1.29%
13	1978	6.51%	6.07%	-0.78%
14	1979	18.52%	9.08%	0.67%
15	1980	31.74%	12.04%	-2.99%
16	1981	-4.70%	15.49%	8.20%
17	1982	20.42%	10.85%	32.81%
18	1983	22.34%	7.94%	3.20%
19	1984	6.15%	9.00%	13.73%
39	2004	10.88%	8.51%	1.02%
40	2005	4.91%	7.81%	1.20%
41	2006	15.79%	1.19%	2.98%
42	2007	5.49%	9.88%	4.66%
43	2008	-37.00%	25.87%	1.60%
44	2009	26.46%	-14.90%	0.10%
45	2010	14.82%	0.13%	8.46%
46	2011	2.07%	0.03%	16.04%
47	2012	15.83%	0.05%	2.97%

FIGURE 76-5 The historical returns on stocks, T-bills, and bonds.

To begin, you use bootstrapping to generate 1,000 simulated values for stocks, T-bills, and bonds in five years. Assume that each asset class has a current price of $1. (See Figure 76-6.)

For each asset class, you enter an initial unit price of $1 in the cell range H10:J10. Next, by copying from K10 to K11:K14 the formula =RANDBETWEEN(1973,2012), you generate a scenario for each of the next five years. For example, for the data shown in Figure 76-6, next year will be similar to 1989; the following year will be similar to 1995, and so on. Copying from L10 to L10:N14 the formula =H10*(1+VLOOKUP($K10,lookup,L$8)) generates each year's ending value for each asset class. For stocks, for example, this formula computes the following:

```
(Ending5 year t stock value)=(Beginning year t stock value)*(1+Year t stock return)
```

AB61

	G	H	I	J	K	L	M	N
8						2	3	4
9	Year	Stock value	Bill value	Bond value	Scenario	End stock	End bill	End bond
10	1	1	1	1	1989	1.3148	1.0807	1.1769
11	2	1.3148	1.0807	1.1769	1995	1.80391	1.14122	1.45324
12	3	1.80391	1.1412192	1.45324	1976	2.23378	1.2033	1.68546
13	4	2.23378	1.20330152	1.68546	1976	2.76609	1.26876	1.9548
14	5	2.76609	1.26876113	1.9548	1979	3.27836	1.38396	1.9679
15			5 yr stock	5 year bill	5 yr bond			
16			3.27836418	1.38396	1.9679			
17		1	1.55773242	1.34121	1.43355			
18		2	1.46563567	1.51332	1.36851			
19		3	1.83888295	1.34003	1.34805			
39		23	1.69391631	1.08681	1.33715			
40		24	1.34290885	1.08479	1.86996			
41		25	1.56318891	1.40887	1.45032			
42		26	1.5611624	1.12008	0.95405			
43		27	2.02287627	1.44102	1.48345			
44		28	1.27765393	1.60323	1.36872			
45		29	1.5152309	1.2509	1.24045			
46		30	1.75041279	1.2581	1.44209			

FIGURE 76-6 Simulating five-year returns on stocks, T-bills, and bonds.

Copying from H11 to H11:J14 the formula =L10 computes the value for each asset class at the beginning of each successive year.

You can now use a one-way data table to generate 1,000 scenarios of the value of stocks, T-bills, and bonds in five years. Begin by copying the Year 5 ending value for each asset class to cells I16:K16. Next, select the table range (H16:K1015), click What If Analysis on the Data tab (in the Forecast group), and then click Data Table. Use any blank cell in the Column Input Cell box to set up a one-way data table. After clicking OK in the Data Table dialog box, you obtain 1,000 simulated values for the value of stocks, T-bills, and bonds over five years. It is important to note that this approach models the fact that stocks, T-bills, and bonds do not move independently. In each of the five years, the stock, T-bill, and bond returns are always chosen from the same row of data. This enables the bootstrapping approach to reflect the interdependence of returns on these asset classes that has been exhibited during the recent past. (See Problem 7 at the end of this chapter for concrete evidence that bootstrapping appropriately models the interdependence between the returns on the three asset classes.)

With this setup, you're ready to find the optimal asset allocation, which I calculated in the file Assetallocationopt.xlsx, shown in Figure 76-7. To start, I copy the 1,000 simulated five-year asset values and paste them into a blank worksheet. (I used the cell range C4:E1003.) In cells C2:E2, I enter trial fractions of the assets allocated to stocks, T-bills, and bonds, respectively. In cell F2, I add these asset-allocation fractions, with the formula =SUM(C2:E2). Later, I'll add the constraint F2=1 to the Solver model, which ensures that I invest 100 percent of the money in one of the three asset classes.

	B	C	D	E	F	G	H	I
1		stock	bill	bond	total			
2		0.336592	0.60655	0.056858	1			
3	Iteration#	5 yr stock	5 yr bill	5 yr bond	final value	annual return	mean	0.08
4	1	2.013289	1.27984	1.361632	1.5313642	0.088969449	stdev	0.029121
5	2	1.697591	1.34639	1.300374	1.4619844	0.078918264		
6	3	0.64513	1.99583	1.359452	1.505012	0.085195517		
7	4	2.498326	1.15132	1.510334	1.6251227	0.101988926		
8	5	1.733605	1.25654	1.189519	1.4133082	0.071636204		
9	6	1.554756	1.5456	1.590621	1.5512388	0.0917815		
10	7	1.597563	1.25608	1.514132	1.3856958	0.067415679		
11	8	1.7993	1.26951	1.237904	1.4460352	0.076553888		
12	9	1.802803	1.31441	1.677732	1.4994544	0.084392874		
13	10	2.877351	1.42034	1.616723	1.9219261	0.139586609		
14	11	2.806566	1.10423	1.300825	1.6884038	0.11044043		
15	12	2.784766	1.43937	1.61732	1.9023383	0.137254208		
16	13	1.651119	1.4176	1.35738	1.4927782	0.083425516		
17	14	2.743893	1.24369	1.845042	1.7828353	0.12259278		

FIGURE 76-7 The optimal asset-allocation model.

Next, I want to determine the final portfolio value for each scenario. To make this calculation, I can use a formula such as (Final portfolio value)=(Final value of stocks)+(Final value of T-bills)+(Final value of bonds). Copying from cell F4 to F5:F1003 the formula =SUMPRODUCT(C4:E4,$C$2:$E$2) determines the final asset position for each scenario.

The next step is to determine the annual return over the five-year simulated period for each scenario that Excel generated. Note that (1+ Annual return)^5 = (Final portfolio value)/(Initial portfolio value). Because the initial portfolio value is just $1, this tells you that Annual return = (Final portfolio value)$^{1/5}$–1.

By copying from cell G4 to G5:G1003 the formula =(F4/1)^(1/5)–1, I compute the annual return for each scenario during the five-year simulated period. After naming the range G4:G1003 (which contains the simulated annual returns) as *Returns*, I compute the average annual return in cell I3 with the formula =AVERAGE(returns) and the standard deviation of the annual returns in cell I4 with the formula =STDEV.S(returns).

Now I'm ready to use Solver to determine the set of allocation weights that yields an expected annual return of at least 8 percent, yet minimizes the standard deviation of the annual returns. The Solver Parameters dialog box set up to perform this calculation is shown in Figure 76-8.

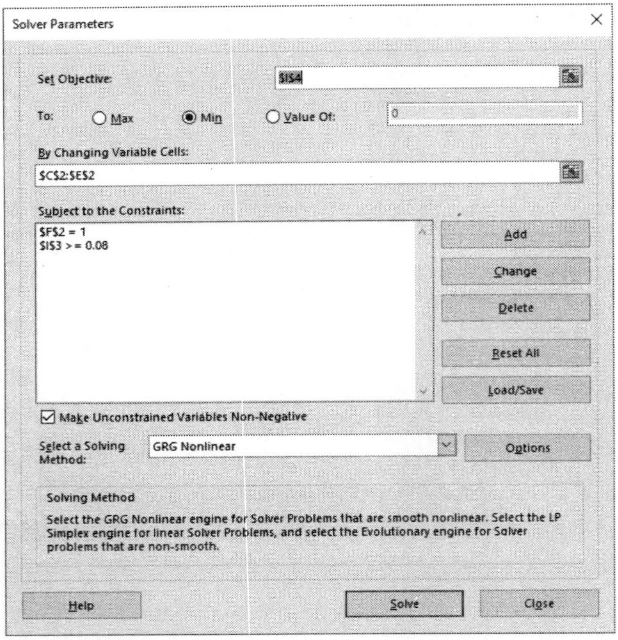

FIGURE 76-8 The Solver Parameters dialog box set up for the asset-allocation model.

In the Analyze group on the Data tab, I click Solver and specify the following settings in the Solver Parameters dialog box:

- I try to minimize the standard deviation of the annual portfolio return (cell I4).
- The changing cells are the asset-allocation weights (cells C2:E2).
- I must allocate 100 percent of the money I have to the three asset classes (F2=1).
- The expected annual return must be at least 8 percent (I3>=0.08).
- I assume that no short sales are allowed, which is modeled by forcing the fraction of the money in each asset class to be nonnegative. To implement this, I selected the Make Unconstrained Variables Non-Negative check box.
- The minimum risk asset allocation is 33.7 percent stocks, 60.7 percent T-bills, and 5.7 percent bonds. This portfolio yields an expected annual return of 8 percent and an annual standard deviation of 2.9 percent.

> **Note** If the Solver option isn't available on the Data tab, you need to activate it. To activate the Solver add-in, click the File tab, click Options, and then click Add-Ins. On the Add-Ins page, click the Go button, select Solver Add-In, and click OK. For more information, see Chapter 29, "An introduction to optimization with Excel Solver."

Suppose you believe that the next five years will, on average, produce returns for stocks that are 5 percent worse than they've been for the last 30 years. It is easy to incorporate these expectations into the simulation. (See Problem 4 at the end of the chapter.)

Problems

Problems 1 through 3 use data in the file GEsim.xlsx:

1. Assume that the current price of Microsoft stock is $28 per share. What is the probability that in two years the price of Microsoft stock will be at least $35?

2. Solve Problem 1 again, but this time with the assumption that during the next two years, Microsoft will on average perform 6 percent better per year than it performed during the 1997–2002 period for which you have data.

3. Assume that the current price of Intel is $20 per share. What is the probability that during the next three years, you will earn at least a 30 percent return (for the three-year period) on a purchase of Intel stock?

Problems 4 through 7 use data in the file Assetallsim.xlsx:

4. Suppose you believe that over the next five years, stocks will produce returns that are 5 percent worse per year, on average, than the 1973–2012 data. Find an asset allocation among stocks, T-bills, and bonds that yields an expected annual return of at least 6 percent yet minimizes risk.

5. Suppose you believe that it is two times more likely that investment returns for each of the next five years will be more like the period 1992–2001 than the period 1972–1991. For example, the chance that next year will be like 1993 has twice the probability that next year will be like 1980. This belief causes your bootstrapping analysis to give more weight to the recent past. How would you factor this belief into your portfolio optimization model?

6. Many mutual funds and investors hedge the risk that stocks will go down by purchasing put options. (See Chapter 79, "Pricing stock options," for more discussion of put options.) How could an asset-allocation model be used to determine an optimal hedging strategy that uses puts?

7. Determine the correlations (based on the 1973–2012 data) among annual returns on stocks, T-bills, and bonds. Then determine the correlations (based on the 1,000 scenarios created by bootstrapping) among the final values for stocks, T-bills, and bonds. Does it appear that the bootstrapping approach picks up the interdependence among the returns on stocks, T-bills, and bonds?

CHAPTER 77

Fun and games: Simulating gambling and sporting-event probabilities

Questions answered in this chapter:

- What is the probability of winning at craps?
- In five-card draw poker, what is the probability of getting three of a kind?
- Going into the 2003 NCAA men's basketball Final Four, what was the probability of each team winning the tournament?

Gambling and following sporting events are popular pastimes. I think gambling and sports are exciting because you never know what's going to happen. Monte Carlo simulation is a powerful tool that you can use to approximate gambling and sporting-event probabilities. Essentially, you estimate the probability by playing out a gambling or sporting-event situation multiple times. If, for example, you have Microsoft Excel play out the game of craps 10,000 times, and you win 4,900 times, you would estimate the probability of winning at craps to equal 4,900/10,000, or 49 percent. If you play out the 2003 NCAA men's Final Four 1,000 times and Syracuse wins 300 of the iterations, you would estimate Syracuse's probability of winning the championship as 300/1,000, or 30 percent.

Answers to this chapter's questions

What is the probability of winning at craps?

In the game of craps, a player rolls two dice. If the combination is 2, 3, or 12, the player loses. If the combination is 7 or 11, the player wins. If the combination is a different number, the player continues rolling the dice until he or she either matches the number thrown on the first roll (called the *point*) or rolls 7. If the player rolls the point before rolling 7, the player wins. If the player rolls 7 before rolling the point, the player loses. By complex calculations, you can show that the probability of a player winning at craps is 0.493. You can use Excel to simulate the game of craps many times (I chose 2,000) to approximate this probability.

In this example, it is crucial to keep in mind that you don't know how many rolls the game will take. I will show that the chance of a game requiring more than 50 rolls of the dice is highly unlikely, so we'll play out 50 rolls of the dice. After each roll, the game status is tracked as follows:

- 0 equals the game is lost.
- 1 equals the game is won.
- 2 equals the game continues.

The output cell keeps track of the status of the game after the fiftieth roll by recording 1 to indicate a win and 0 to indicate a loss. You can review the work I did in the file Craps.xlsx, shown in Figure 77-1.

C22

	A	B	C	D	E	F	G	H	AX	AY
1	TOSS#	1	2	3	4	5	6	7	49	50
2	Die Toss 1	5	3	1	2	4	2	5	5	2
3	Die Toss 2	3	5	3	4	5	5	4	4	1
4	Total	8	8	4	6	9	7	9	9	3
5	GAME STATUS	2	1	1	1	1	1	1	1	1
6		WIN??	1							
7										
8				prob win	0.49					
9					1					
10				1	1					
11				2	0					
12				3	0					
13				4	1					
14				5	1					
15				6	0					
16				7	0					
17				8	1					

FIGURE 77-1 Simulating a game of craps.

In cell B2, I used the RANDBETWEEN function to generate the number on the first die on the first roll by using the formula =RANDBETWEEN(1,6). The RANDBETWEEN function ensures that each of its arguments is equally likely, so each die has an equal (1/6) chance of yielding 1, 2, 3, 4, 5, or 6. Copying this formula to the range B2:AY3 generates 50 rolls of the dice. (In Figure 77-1, I hid rolls 8 through 48 on columns I through AW.)

In the cell range B4:AY4, I compute the total dice combination for each of the 50 rolls by copying from B4 to C4:AY4 the formula =SUM(B2:B3). In cell B5, I determine the game status after the first roll with the formula =IF(OR(B4=2,B4=3,B4=12),0,IF(OR(B4=7,B4=11),1,2)). Remember that a roll of 2, 3, or 12 results in a loss (entering 0 in the cell); a roll of 7 or 11 results in a win (1); and any other roll results in the game continuing (2).

In cell C5, I compute the status of the game after the second roll with the formula =IF(OR(B5=0,B5=1),B5,IF(C4=$B4,1,IF(C4=7,0,2))). If the game ends on the first roll, I maintain the status of the game. If a roll makes the point, I record a win with 1. If a roll is a 7, I record a loss. Otherwise, the game continues. I added a dollar sign in the reference to column B ($B4) in this formula to ensure that each roll tries to match the point thrown on the first roll. Copying this formula from C5 to D5:AY5 records the game status after rolls 2 through 50.

The game result is in cell AY5, which is copied to C6 so that you can easily see it. I then use a one-way data table to play out the game of craps 2,000 times. In cell E9, I enter the formula =C6, which tracks the final outcome of the game (0 if a loss or 1 if a win). Next, I select the table range (D9:E2009), click What-If Analysis in the Forecast group on the Data tab, and then click Data Table. I choose a one-way table with any blank cell selected in the Column Input Cell box. After clicking OK in the Data Table dialog box, I press F9, and Excel simulates the game of craps 2,000 times.

In cell E8, I can compute the fraction of the simulations that result in wins, with the formula =AVERAGE(E10:E2009). For the 2,000 iterations, I won 49 percent of the time. If I had run more trials (for example, 10,000 iterations), I would have come closer to the true probability of winning at craps (49.3 percent). For information about using a one-way data table, see Chapter 17, "Sensitivity analysis with data tables."

In five-card draw poker, what is the probability of getting three of a kind?

An ordinary deck of cards contains four cards of each type—four aces, four deuces, and so on, up to four kings. To estimate the probability of getting a particular poker hand, you can assign the value 1 to an ace, 2 to a deuce, and on up through the deck so that a jack is assigned the value 11, a queen is assigned 12, and a king is assigned 13.

In five-card draw poker, you are dealt five cards. Many probabilities are of interest, but let's use a simulation to estimate the probability of getting three of a kind, which requires that you have three of one type of card and no pairs. (If you have a pair and three of a kind, the hand is a full house.) To simulate the five cards drawn, you proceed as follows. (See the file Poker.xlsx, shown in Figure 77-2.)

- Associate a random number with each card in the deck.
- The five cards chosen will be the five cards associated with the five smallest random numbers, which gives each card an equal chance of being chosen.
- Count how many of each card (ace through king) are drawn.

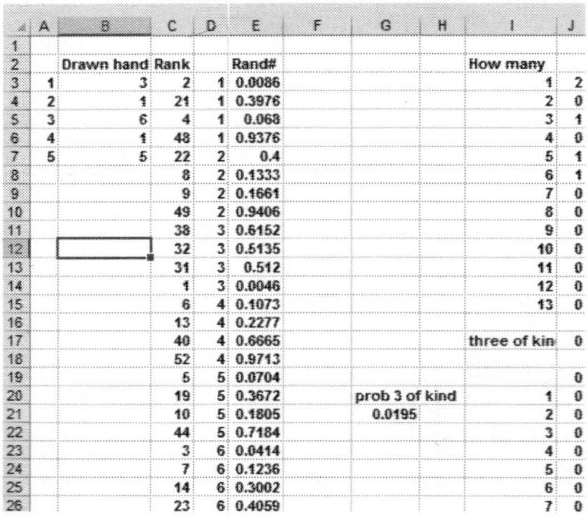

	A	B	C	D	E	F	G	H	I	J
1										
2		Drawn hand	Rank		Rand#				How many	
3	1	3	2	1	0.0086				1	2
4	2	1	21	1	0.3976				2	0
5	3	6	4	1	0.068				3	1
6	4	1	48	1	0.9376				4	0
7	5	5	22	2	0.4				5	1
8			8	2	0.1333				6	1
9			9	2	0.1661				7	0
10			49	2	0.9406				8	0
11			38	3	0.6152				9	0
12			32	3	0.5135				10	0
13			31	3	0.512				11	0
14			1	3	0.0046				12	0
15			6	4	0.1073				13	0
16			13	4	0.2277					
17			40	4	0.6665				three of kin	0
18			52	4	0.9713					
19			5	5	0.0704					0
20			19	5	0.3672		prob 3 of kind		1	0
21			10	5	0.1805		0.0195		2	0
22			44	5	0.7184				3	0
23			3	6	0.0414				4	0
24			7	6	0.1236				5	0
25			14	6	0.3002				6	0
26			23	6	0.4059				7	0

FIGURE 77-2 Estimating the probability that you'll draw three of a kind in a poker game.

To begin, I list in cells D3:D54 all the cards in the deck: four 1s (representing aces), four 2s, and so on up to four 13s (representing kings). Then, I copy from cell E3 to E4:E54 the RAND function to associate a random number with each card in the deck. Copying from C3 to C4:C54 the formula =RANK.EQ(E3,$E$3:$E$54,1) gives the rank (ordered from smallest to largest) of each random number. For example, in Figure 77-2, you can see that the first 3 in the deck (row 11) is associated with the 38th-smallest random number. (You will see different results in the worksheet because the random numbers are automatically recalculated when you open the worksheet.)

The syntax of the RANK.EQ function is RANK.EQ(number,array,1 or 0). If the last argument of the RANK.EQ function is *1*, the function returns the rank of the number in the array with the smallest number receiving a rank of 1, the second-smallest number a rank of 2, and so on. If the last argument of the RANK.EQ function is *0*, the function returns the rank of the number in the array with the largest number receiving a rank of 1, the second-largest number receiving a rank of 2, and so on.

In ranking random numbers, no ties can occur (because the random numbers would have to match 16 digits).

Suppose, for example, that you are ranking the numbers 1, 3, 3, and 4 and that the last argument of the RANK.EQ function was *1*. Excel would return the following ranks:

Number	Rank (smallest number has rank of 1)
1	1
3	2
3	2
4	4

Because 3 is the second smallest number, 3 would be assigned a rank of 2. The other 3 would also be assigned a rank of 2. Because 4 is the fourth-smallest number, it would be assigned a rank of 4.

Understanding the treatment of ties by the RANK.EQ function will help you complete Problem 1 at the end of the chapter.

By copying from cell B3 to B4:B7 the formula =VLOOKUP(A3,lookup,2,FALSE), you can draw five cards from the deck. This formula draws the five cards corresponding to the five smallest random numbers. (The lookup table range C3:D54 has been named *Lookup*.) I used FALSE in the VLOOKUP function because the ranks need not be in ascending order.

Having assigned the range name *Drawn* to the drawn cards (the range B3:B7), copying from J3 to J4:J15 the formula =COUNTIF(drawn,I3) counts how many of each card number are in the hand drawn. In cell J17, I determine whether the hand includes three of a kind with the formula =IF(AND(MAX(J3:J15)=3,COUNTIF(J3:J15,2)=0),1,0). This formula returns a 1 if and only if the hand has three of one kind and no pairs.

I now use a one-way data table to simulate 4,000 poker hands. In cell J19, I recopy the results of cell J17 with the formula =J17. Next, I select the table range (I19:J4019). After clicking What-If Analysis in the Forecast group on the Data tab and then clicking Data Table, I set up a one-way data table by selecting any blank cell as the column input cell. After I click OK, Excel simulates 4,000 poker hands. In cell G21, I record the estimated probability of three of a kind with the formula =AVERAGE(J20:J4019). I estimate the chance of three of a kind at 2.0 percent. (Using basic probability theory, you can show that the true probability of drawing three of a kind is 2.1 percent.)

Going into the 2003 NCAA men's basketball Final Four, what was the probability of each team winning the tournament?

You can rate college basketball teams using the methodology described in Chapter 35, "Using Solver to rate sports teams," but it is difficult to get the scores of all the past games. The highly respected Sagarin ratings (available at Sagarin.com) always gives up-to-date ratings for all college basketball teams. On the eve of the 2003 men's Final Four, the Sagarin ratings of the four teams were Syracuse (led by Carmelo Anthony), 91.03; Kansas, 92.76; Marquette (led by Dwayne Wade), 89.01; and Texas, 90.66. Given this information, you can play out the Final Four several thousand times to estimate the chance that each team will win.

The mean prediction for the number of points by which the home team wins is (favorite rating) – (underdog rating). In the Final Four, there is no home team, but if there were one, you would add four points to the home team's rating. (In professional basketball, the home edge is three points, and in college and professional football, the home edge is three points.) Then you can use the NORM.INV function to simulate the outcome of each game. (See Chapter 70, "The normal random variable and Z-scores," for a discussion of using the NORM.INV function to simulate a normal random variable.)

I calculated the likely outcome of the 2003 Final Four in the file Final4sim.xlsx, shown in Figure 77-3. The semifinals pitted Kansas against Marquette and Syracuse against Texas.

	C	D	E	F	G	H	I	J	K	L	M
1											
2			Semifinals								
3		Rating	Outcome	rand#							
4	KU	92.76	-2.739418	0.258188	Final	rand#	Forecast	Outcome	Winner		
5	MARQ	89.01			MARQ	0.1037	89.01	-14.2591	TEX		
6					TEX		90.66				
7											
8	SYR	91.03	-0.913007	0.448955							
9	TEX	90.66									
10											
11							odds		PROB WIN		TEX
12							1.717391	KU	0.368	1	SYR
13							3.319654	TEX	0.2315	2	KU
14							2.952569	SYR	0.253	3	TEX
15							5.779661	MARQ	0.1475	4	KU
16										5	KU
17										6	TEX
18										7	SYR
19										8	SYR
20										9	KU

FIGURE 77-3 Simulating the outcome of the NCAA 2003 Final Four.

To begin, I enter each team's name and rating in the cell range C4:D5 and C8:D9. In cell F4, I use the RAND function to enter a random number for the Marquette-Kansas game, and in cell F8 I enter a random number for the Syracuse-Texas game. The simulated outcome is always relative to the top team listed.

In cell E4, I determine the outcome of the Kansas-Marquette game (from the standpoint of Kansas) with the formula =NORM.INV(F4,D4–D5,10). Note that Kansas is favored by D4–D5 points. In cell E8, I determine the outcome of the Texas-Syracuse game (from the standpoint of Syracuse) with the formula =NORM.INV(F8,D8–D9,10). (The standard deviation for the winning margin of college basketball games about the point spread is 10 points.)

In cells G5 and G6, I ensure that the winner of each semifinal game moves on to the finals. A semifinal outcome of greater than 0 causes the top-listed team to win; otherwise, the bottom-listed team wins. Thus, in cell G5, I enter the winner of the first game by using the formula =IF(E4>0,"KU", "MARQ"). In cell G6, I enter the winner of the second game by using the formula =IF(E8>0,"SYR","TEX").

In cell H5, I enter a random number that is used to simulate the outcome of the championship game. Copying from I5 to I6 the formula =VLOOKUP(G5,$C$4:$D$9,2,FALSE) obtains the rating for each team in the championship game. Next, in cell J5, I compute the outcome of the championship game (from the reference point of the top-listed team in cell G5) with the formula =NORM.INV(H5, I5–I6,10). Finally, in cell K5, I determine the actual champion with the formula =IF(J5>0,G5,G6).

Now I can use a one-way data table in the usual fashion to play out the Final Four 2,000 times. The simulated winners are in the cell range M12:M2011. Copying from K12 to K13:K15 the formula = COUNTIF($M$12:$M$2011,J12)/2000 computes the predicted probability for each team winning: 37 percent for Kansas, 25 percent for Syracuse, 23 percent for Texas, and 15 percent for Marquette. These probabilities can be translated to odds, using the following formula:

```
Odds against team winning = Probability team loses/Probability team wins
```

For example, the odds against Kansas are 1.63 to 1:

```
(1 - 0.37)/0.37 = 1.70
```

This means that if you placed $1 on Kansas to win and a bookmaker paid you $1.70 for a Kansas championship, the bet is fair. Of course, the bookie will lower these odds slightly to ensure that he makes money. (See Problem 6 at the end of this chapter for a related exercise.)

This methodology can easily be extended to simulate the entire NCAA tournament. Just use IF statements to ensure that each winner advances, and use VLOOKUP functions to find each team's rating. See the file Ncaa2003.xlsx for a simulation of the 2003 tournament. The analysis gave Syracuse (the eventual winner) a four percent chance to win at the start of tournament.

In this worksheet, I used comments to explain my work, which you can see in Figure 77-4. The following is some background about using comments:

- To insert a comment in a cell, first select the cell. On the Review tab, in the Comments group, click New Comment, and then type your comment text. You will see a small, red mark in the upper-right corner of any cell containing a comment.
- To edit a comment, right-click the cell containing the comment, and click Edit Comment. Or, when you select a cell with a comment, on the Review tab in the Comments group, click Edit Comment (the New Comment button changes to Edit Comment).
- To make a comment always visible (when the comment is hidden), right-click the cell, and click Show/Hide Comments. Clicking Hide Comment when the comment is displayed hides the comment unless the pointer is hovering over the cell containing the comment.
- If you want to print your comments, click the Page Layout tab on the ribbon, and in the Page Setup group, click the Page Setup dialog box launcher (the small arrow in the bottom-right corner of the group) to display the Page Setup dialog box. In the Comments box on the Sheet tab (in the Print section), you can indicate whether you want comments printed as displayed on the sheet or at the end of the sheet. Click OK to save your preference.

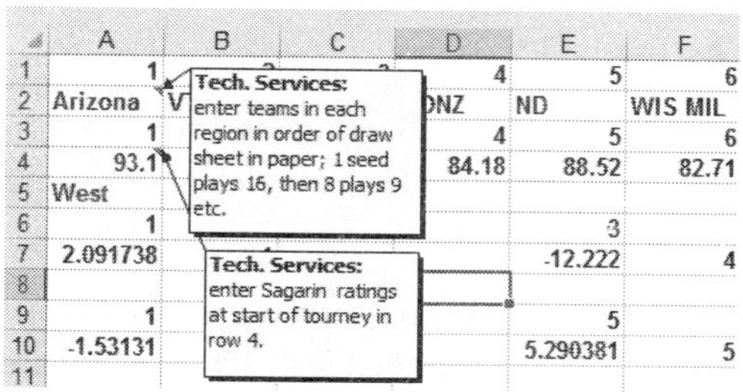

FIGURE 77-4 Showing comments in a worksheet.

Problems

1. Suppose 30 people are in a room. What is the probability that at least two of them have the same birthday?
2. What is the probability of getting dealt one pair in five-card draw poker?

3. What is the probability of getting dealt two pairs in five-card draw poker?

4. In the game of keno, 80 balls (numbered 1 through 80) are mixed up, and then 20 balls are randomly drawn. Before the 20 balls are drawn, a player chooses 10 different numbers. If at least five of the numbers are drawn, the player wins. What is the probability of winning?

5. Going into the 2003 NBA finals, the rating system described in Chapter 35 rated the San Antonio Spurs three points higher than the New Jersey Nets. Teams play until one team wins four games. The first two games were at San Antonio, the next three at New Jersey, and the final two games were scheduled for San Antonio. What is the probability that San Antonio will win the series?

6. What odds should the bookmaker give on Kansas winning the Final Four if the bookmaker wants to earn an average of 10 cents per dollar bet?

7. What is the probability of getting dealt a flush in five-card draw poker?

8. If you break a one-inch stick in two places that are randomly chosen, you have three smaller sticks. What are the chances that the three sticks form a triangle?

9. Suppose each hitter on a baseball team has a 50 percent chance of hitting a home run and a 50 percent chance of striking out. On average, how many runs will this team score in an inning?

10. Katy and Taylor toss a coin 100 times. Each time heads comes up, Katy pays Taylor $1; each time tails comes up, Taylor pays Katy $2. What is the chance that Taylor is never ahead?

11. You toss a fair coin 20 times. Estimate the chance you throw at least four consecutive heads.

12. At the beginning of 2015, you have $100 invested in a stock. Each year there is a 60 percent chance that the stock increases 50 percent; a 20 percent chance the stock goes up 10 percent, and a 20 percent chance the stock drops 50 percent. What is the chance that by the beginning of 2065, your cash level will (at least once) have reached $10,000?

13. In the game blackjack, the dealer draws cards until her total is 16 or higher. Then she stops. Assume an ace counts as 1 and a jack, queen, or king counts as 10. If the dealer draws cards with replacement, what is the chance her final total will be 19, 20, and 21?

14. You are going to roll a fair die 50 times. If the die comes up even, you are paid the number of dots showing on the die. If the die comes up odd, you lose $1. What is the chance you are ever at least $75 ahead?

15. Consider three decks of cards. Deck 1 contains 10 cards: 3 twos, 4 fives, and 3 nines. Deck 2 contains four cards that are numbered 1 through 4. Deck 3 contains 6 cards numbered 1 through 6. Gregory draws one card from Deck 1; Taylor draws one card from Deck 2 and one card from Deck 3. What is the chance that Gregory's card shows a larger number than the total of Taylor's two cards?

CHAPTER 78

Using resampling to analyze data

Question answered in this chapter:

- I produced nine batches of a product by using a high temperature and seven batches by using a low temperature. What is the probability that the product yield is better at the high temperature?

Data analysts often need to address questions such as these:

- What is the probability that a new teaching technique improves student learning?
- What is the probability that aspirin reduces the incidence of heart attacks?
- What is the probability that Machine 1 is the most productive of our three machines?

You can use a simple yet powerful technique known as *resampling* to make inferences from data. To make statistical inferences by using resampling, you regenerate data many times by sampling with replacement from your data. Sampling with replacement from data means that the same data point can be chosen more than once. You then make inferences based on the results of this repeated sampling. A key tool in implementing resampling is the RANDBETWEEN function. Entering the function RANDBETWEEN(*a*,*b*) yields with equal probability any integer between *a* and *b*, inclusive. For example, the formula =RANDBETWEEN(1,9) is equally likely to yield one of the numbers 1 through 9, inclusive.

Answer to this chapter's question

I produced nine batches of a product by using a high temperature and seven batches by using a low temperature. What is the probability that the product yield is better at the high temperature?

The file Resampleyield.xlsx, shown in Figure 78-1, contains the product yield from nine batches of a product manufactured at a high temperature and seven batches manufactured at a low temperature.

The mean yield at a high temperature is 39.74, and the mean yield at a low temperature is 32.27. This difference does not prove, however, that the mean yield at a high temperature is better than the mean yield at a low temperature. You want to know, based on your sample data, the probability that a yield at a high temperature is better than at a low temperature. To answer this question, you can randomly generate nine integers between 1 and 9, which creates a resampling of the high-temperature yields. For example, if you generate the random number 4, the resampled data for high-temperature yields will include a yield of 41.40, and so on. Next, you randomly generate seven integers between 1 and 7, which creates a resampling of the low-temperature yields. You can then check the resampled data to see whether the high-temperature mean is larger than the low-temperature mean, and then use a data table to repeat this process several hundred times. (I repeated the process 400 times in this example.) In the resampled data, the fraction of the time that the high-temperature mean is larger than the low-temperature mean estimates the probability that the high-temperature process is superior to the low-temperature process.

	C	D	E
3	mean	39.74	32.27
4	Number	High Temp	Low Temp
5	1	17.55	37.37
6	2	39.93	43.20
7	3	48.98	34.85
8	4	41.40	31.22
9	5	35.70	26.59
10	6	42.24	42.67
11	7	54.75	10.00
12	8	46.96	
13	9	30.19	

FIGURE 78-1 The product yields at high and low temperature.

To begin, you generate a resampling of the high-temperature data by copying from cell C16 to C17:C24 the formula =RANDBETWEEN(1,9), as shown in Figure 78-2. A given observation can be chosen more than once or not chosen at all. Copying from cell D16 to D17:D24 the formula =VLOOKUP(C16,lookup,2)—the range C4:E13 has been named *Lookup*—generates the yields corresponding to the random resampling of the data. Next, you generate a resampling from the low-temperature yields. Copying from E16 to E17:E22 the formula =RANDBETWEEN(1,7) generates a resampling of seven observations from the original low-temperature data. Copying from F16 to F17:F22 the formula =VLOOKUP(E16,lookup,3) generates the seven actual, resampled low-temperature yields.

	C	D	E	F
15	Resampled	High Temp	Resampled	Low Temp
16	4	41.40	3	34.85
17	5	35.70	4	31.22
18	5	35.70	3	34.85
19	8	46.96	7	10.00
20	5	35.70	6	42.67
21	1	17.55	7	10.00
22	1	17.55	3	34.85
23	4	41.40		
24	8	46.96		
25				
26	Average	35.44		28.35
27				
28				
29	High better	1		
30				Prob high better
31		1		0.94
32	1	0		
33	2	1		
34	3	1		
35	4	1		
36	5	1		
37	6	1		

FIGURE 78-2 An implementation of resampling.

In cell D26, I compute the mean of the resampled high-temperature yields with the formula =AVERAGE(D16:D24). Similarly, in cell F26 I compute the mean of the resampled low-temperature yields with the formula =AVERAGE(F16:F22). In cell D29, I determine whether the resampled mean for high temperature is larger than the resampled mean for low temperature with the formula =IF(D26>F26,1,0).

To replay the resampling 400 times, you can use a one-way data table. I put iteration numbers 1 through 400 in the cell range C32:431. (See Chapter 74, "Introduction to Monte Carlo simulation," for an explanation of how to use the Fill Series command to easily create a list of iteration values.) By typing =D29 in cell D31, I create the formula that records whether a high-temperature mean is larger than a low-temperature mean in the output cell for the data table. After selecting the table range (C31:D431) and then selecting Data Table from the What-If Analysis menu in the Forecast group on the Data tab, choose any blank cell in the worksheet as the column input cell. You have now set up Microsoft Excel to play out the resampling 400 times. Each iteration with a value of 1 indicates a resampling in which the high temperature has the larger mean. Each iteration with a value of 0 indicates a resampling for which the low temperature has a larger mean. In cell F31, I determine the fraction of time that the high-temperature yield has a larger mean by using the formula =AVERAGE(D32:D431). In Figure 78-2, the resampling indicates a 94 percent chance that the high temperature has a larger mean than the low temperature. Of course, pressing F9 will generate a different set of 400 resamplings and give you a slightly different estimate of the probability that high-temperature yield is superior to low-temperature yield.

Problems

1. You are testing a new flu drug. Of the 24 flu victims who were given the drug, 20 felt better and 4 felt worse. Of the 9 flu victims who were given a placebo, 6 felt better and 3 felt worse. What is the probability that the drug is more effective than the placebo?

2. A talk on the dangers of high cholesterol was given to eight workers. Each worker's cholesterol was tested both before and after the talk, with the results given below. What is the probability that the talk caused the workers to undertake lifestyle changes that reduced their cholesterol?

Cholesterol before	Cholesterol after
220	210
195	198
250	210
200	199
220	224
260	212
175	179
198	184

3. The *beta* of a stock is simply the slope of the best-fitting line used to predict the monthly return on the stock from the monthly return given in the Standard & Poor's (S&P) 500 index. A beta that is larger than 1 indicates that a stock is more cyclical than the market, whereas a beta of less than 1 indicates that a stock is less cyclical than the market. The file Betaresampling.xlsx contains more than 12 years of monthly returns on Microsoft (MSFT), Pfizer (PFE), other stocks, and the S&P index. Use this data to determine the probability that Microsoft has a lower beta than Pfizer. You will need to use the Excel SLOPE function to estimate the beta for each iteration of resampling.

4. The file Lawdata.xlsx gives the LSAT scores and law school GPA for 15 law-school students. Based on this data, you are 95 percent sure the correlation between LSAT score and GPA is between which two values?

CHAPTER 79

Pricing stock options

Questions answered in this chapter:

- What are call and put options?
- What is the difference between American and European options?
- As a function of the stock price on the exercise date, what do the payoffs look like for European calls and puts?
- What parameters determine the value of an option?
- How can I estimate the volatility of a stock based on historical data?
- How can I use Excel to implement the Black-Scholes formula?
- How do changes in key parameters change the value of a call or put option?
- How can I use the Black-Scholes formula to estimate a stock's volatility?
- I don't want somebody changing my neat option-pricing formulas. How can I protect the formulas in my worksheet so that nobody can change them?
- How can I use option pricing to help my company make better investment decisions?

During the early 1970s, economists Fischer Black, Myron Scholes, and Robert Merton derived the *Black-Scholes option-pricing formula*, which enables you to derive values for European call or put options. Scholes and Merton were awarded the 1997 Nobel Prize in Economics for their efforts. (Black died before 1997, and Nobel prizes are not awarded posthumously.) The work of these economists revolutionized corporate finance. In this chapter, I'll introduce you to their important work.

> **Note** For an excellent technical discussion of options, see David G. Luenberger's book, *Investment Science*, 2nd ed. (Oxford University Press, 2013).

Answers to this chapter's questions

What are call and put options?

A *call option* gives the owner of the option the right to buy a share of stock for a price called the *exercise* price. A *put option* gives the owner of the option the right to sell a share of stock for the exercise price.

What is the difference between American and European options?

American options can be exercised on or before a date known as the *exercise date* (often referred to as the *expiration date*). *European options* can be exercised only on the exercise date.

As a function of the stock price on the exercise date, what do the payoffs look like for European calls and puts?

Let's look at cash flows from a six-month European call option on shares of IBM with an exercise price of $110. Let *P* equal the price of IBM stock in six months. The payoff from a call option on these shares is $0 if P≤110 and P–110 if P>110. With a value of *P* below $110, you would not exercise the option. If *P* is greater than $110, you would exercise the option to buy stock for $110 and immediately sell the stock for *P*, thereby earning a profit of P–110. Figure 79-1 shows the payoff from this call option. In short, a call option pays $1 for every dollar by which the stock price exceeds the exercise price. The payoff for this call option can be written as Max(0,P–110). Notice that the call-option graph in Figure 79-1 has a slope 0 for a value of *P* smaller than the exercise price. (See the Call worksheet in the file Optionfigures.xlsx.) Its slope is 1 for a value of *P* greater than the exercise price.

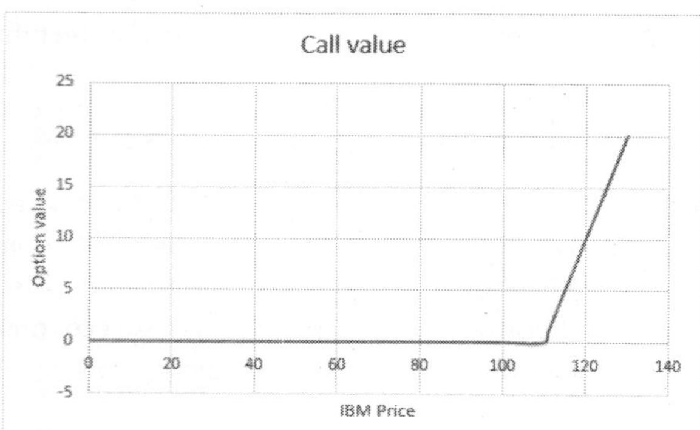

FIGURE 79-1 The cash flows from a call option.

You can show that if a stock pays no dividends, it is never optimal to exercise an American call option early. Therefore, for stock that does not pay a dividend, American and European call options both have the same value.

Now let's look at cash flows from a six-month European put option on shares of IBM with an exercise price of $110. Let *P* equal the price of IBM in six months. The payoff from the put option is $0 if P≥110 and 110–P if P<110. For a value of *P* below $110, you would buy a share of stock for *P* and immediately sell the stock for \$110. This yields a profit of 110–P. If *P* is larger than \$110, it would not be profitable to buy the stock for *P* and sell it for \$110, so you would not exercise the option to sell the stock for \$110.

Figure 79-2 displays the payoff from this put option. (See the Put worksheet in the file Optionfigures.xlsx.) In short, a put option pays \$1 for each dollar by which the stock price is below the exercise price. A put payoff can be written as Max(0,110–P). Note that the slope of the put payoff is –1 for a value of *P* less than the exercise price, and the slope of the put payoff is 0 for a value of *P* greater than the exercise price.

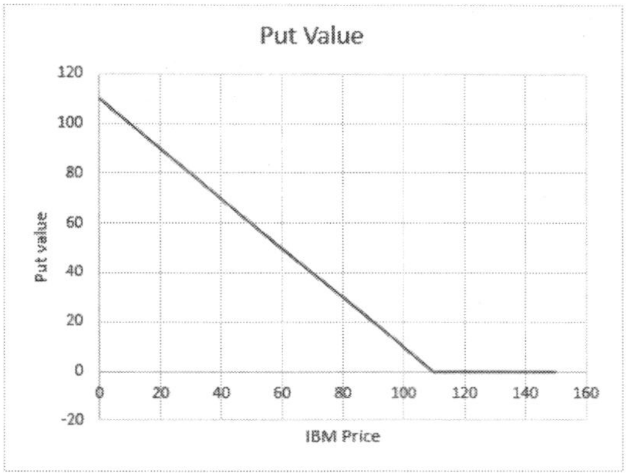

FIGURE 79-2 The cash flows from a put option.

An American put option can be exercised early, so the cash flows from an American put option cannot be determined without knowledge of the stock price at times before the expiration date.

What parameters determine the value of an option?

In their derivation of the Black-Scholes option-pricing model, Black, Scholes, and Merton showed that the value of a call or put option depends on the following parameters:

- Current stock price.
- The option's exercise price.
- Time (in years) until the option expires (referred to as the option's *duration*).
- Interest rate (per year on a compounded basis) on a risk-free investment (usually T-bills) throughout the duration of the investment. This rate is called the *risk-free rate*. For example, if three-month T-bills are paying 5 percent, the risk-free rate is computed as ln(1+0.05). (Calculating the logarithm transforms a simple interest rate into a compounded rate.) Compound interest simply means that at every instant, you are earning interest on your interest.
- Annual rate (as a percentage of the stock price) at which dividends are paid. If a stock pays 2 percent of its value each year in dividends, the dividend rate is 0.02.

- Stock volatility (measured on an annual basis). An annual volatility of, for example, 30 percent means that (approximately) the standard deviation of the annual percentage changes in the stock's price is expected to be around 30 percent. During the Internet bubble of the late 1990s, the volatility of many Internet stocks exceeded 100 percent. I'll show you two ways to estimate this important parameter.

The Black-Scholes pricing formula requires that the price of the stock follows a lognormal random variable. See Chapter 73, "Using the lognormal random variable to model stock prices," for further discussion of the lognormal random variable.

How can I estimate the volatility of a stock based on historical data?

To estimate the volatility of a stock based on data about the stock's monthly returns, you can proceed as follows:

- Determine the monthly return on the stock for a period of several years.
- Determine for each month ln(1+monthly return).
- Determine the standard deviation of ln(1+monthly return). This calculation gives you the monthly volatility.
- Multiply the monthly volatility by the square root of 12 to convert the monthly volatility to an annual volatility.

This procedure is illustrated in the file Dellvol.xlsx, in which I estimate the annual volatility of Dell stock using monthly prices from the period August 1988 through May 2001. (See Figure 79-3, in which I've hidden several rows of data.)

	A	B	C	D	E	F	G	H
1	Date	Dell Price	Return	1+Return	ln(1+Return)			
2	5/1/01	24.36	-0.0716	0.92835	-0.074342521			
3	4/1/01	26.24	0.02151	1.02151	0.021280472		monthly vol	0.1669
4	3/1/01	25.6875	0.17429	1.17429	0.16066006		annual vol	0.5781
5	2/1/01	21.875	-0.1627	0.83732	-0.177548278			
148	3/1/89	0.0742	-0.0951	0.90488	-0.099955097			
149	2/1/89	0.082	-0.1717	0.82828	-0.188400603			
150	1/1/89	0.099	-0.0499	0.9501	-0.051192279			
151	12/1/88	0.1042	-0.0803	0.91968	-0.083727039			
152	11/1/88	0.1133	-0.0841	0.91593	-0.087820111			
153	10/1/88	0.1237	0.15824	1.15824	0.146901353			
154	9/1/88	0.1068	0.28211	1.28211	0.248509377			
155	8/1/88	0.0833						

FIGURE 79-3 Computing the historical volatility for Dell's stock.

Copying from cell C2 to C3:C154 the formula =(B2–B3)/B3 computes each month's return on Dell stock. Then copying from D2 to D3:D154 the formula =1+C2 computes for each month, 1+month's return. Next I compute ln(1+ month's return) for each month by copying from E2 to E3:E154 the formula =LN(D2), and I compute the monthly volatility in cell H3 with the formula =STDEV.S(E2:E154). Finally, I compute an estimate of Dell's annual volatility in cell H4 with the formula =SQRT(12)*H3. Dell's annual volatility is estimated to be 57.8 percent.

How can I use Excel to implement the Black-Scholes formula?

To apply the Black-Scholes formula in Microsoft Excel, you need input values for the following parameters:

- *S*=Today's stock price
- *t*=Duration of the option (in years)
- *X*=Exercise price
- *r*=Annual risk-free rate (This rate is assumed to be continuously compounded.)
- σ=Annual volatility of stock
- *y*=Percentage of stock value paid annually in dividends

Given these input values, the Black-Scholes price for a European call option can be computed using the following equations. First, define d1 as follows:

$$d_1 = \frac{Ln(\frac{S}{X}) + (r - y + \frac{\sigma^2}{2})t}{\sigma\sqrt{t}}$$

Next, define d2 as follows:

$$d_2 = d_1 - \sigma\sqrt{t}$$

Then, the call price *C* is given by the following:

$$C = Se^{-yt}N(d_1) - Xe^{-rt}N(d_2)$$

Here, *N(x)* is the probability that a normal random variable with a mean of 0 and a σ equal to 1 is less than or equal to *x*. For example, N(–1)=0.16, N(0)=0.5, N(1)=0.84, and N(1.96)=0.975. A normal random variable with a mean of 0 and a standard deviation of 1 is called a *standard normal.* The cumulative normal probability can be computed in Excel with the NORM.S.DIST function. Entering NORM.S.DIST(x,True or 1) returns the probability that a standard normal random variable is less than or equal to *x*. For example, entering the formula =NORM.S.DIST(–1,True) in a cell will yield 0.16, which indicates that a normal random variable with a mean of 0 and a standard deviation of 1 has a 16 percent chance of assuming a value less than –1.

The price of a European put *P* can be written the following way:

$$P = Se^{-yt}(N(d_1) - 1) - Xe^{-rt}(N(d_2) - 1)$$

In the file Bstemp.xlsx (see Figure 79-4), I created a template that computes the value for a European call or put option. Enter the parameter values in B5:B10, and read the value of the European call in D13 and the European put in D14.

	A	B	C	D	E
4	Input data				
5	Stock price	20			
6	Exercise price	24			
7	Duration	7			
8	Interest rate	0.04879			
9	dividend rate	0			
10	volatility	0.5			
11					
12				Predicted	
13	Call price			$10.64	
14	put			$7.69	
15					
16					
17	Other quantities for option price				
18	d1	0.781789		N(d1)	0.7828
19	d2	-0.54109		N(d2)	0.2942

FIGURE 79-4 Valuing European calls and puts.

> **Note** Valuing American options is beyond the scope of this book. Interested readers should refer to Luenberger's book, *Investment Science*.

As an example, suppose that Cisco stock sells for $20 today and that you've been issued a seven-year European call option. Assume that the annual volatility of Cisco stock is 50 percent, and the risk-free rate during the seven-year period is estimated at 5 percent per year. Compounded, this translates to ln(1+0.05)=0.04879. Cisco does not pay dividends, so the annual dividend rate is 0. The value of the call option is calculated to be $10.64. A seven-year put option with an exercise price of $24 would be worth $7.69.

How do changes in key parameters change the value of a call or put option?

Observe the following value changes:

- In general, the effect of changing an input parameter on the value of a call or put is given in the following table:

Parameter	European call	European put	American call	American put
Stock price	+	-	+	-
Exercise price	-	+	-	+
Time to expiration	?	?	+	+
Volatility	+	+	+	+
Risk-free rate	+	-	+	-
Dividends	-	+	-	+

An increase in today's stock price always increases the value of a call and decreases the value of a put.

- An increase in the exercise price always increases the value of a put and decreases the value of a call.
- An increase in the duration of an option always increases the value of an American option. In the presence of dividends, an increase in the duration of an option can either increase or decrease the value of a European option.
- An increase in volatility always increases the option value.
- An increase in the risk-free rate increases the value of a call because higher rates tend to increase the growth rate of the stock price (which is good for the call). This situation more than cancels out the fact that the option payoff is worth less as a result of the higher interest rate. An increase in the risk-free rate always decreases the value of a put because the higher growth rate of the stock tends to hurt the put, as does the fact that future payoffs from the put are worth less.
- Dividends tend to reduce the growth rate of a stock price, so increased dividends reduce the value of a call and increase the value of a put.

Using one-way and two-way data tables (see Chapter 17, "Sensitivity analysis with data tables," for details about how to work with data tables), you can, if you want, explore the specific effects of parameter changes on the value of calls and puts.

How can I use the Black-Scholes formula to estimate a stock's volatility?

Earlier in this chapter, I showed how to use historical data to estimate a stock's annual volatility. The problem with historical volatility estimates is that the analysis looks backward. What you really want is an estimate of a stock's volatility looking forward. The implied volatility approach simply estimates a stock's volatility as the volatility value that will make the Black-Scholes price match the option's market price. In short, implied volatility extracts the volatility value implied by the option's market price.

You can easily use the Goal Seek command and the input parameters we've been using to compute an implied volatility. On July 22, 2003, Cisco was selling for $18.43. An October 2003 call option with a $17.50 exercise price was selling for $1.85. This option expired on October 18 (89 days later). Thus, the option had a duration of 89/365=0.2438 years. Cisco did not expect to pay dividends, and I've assumed a T-bill rate of 5 percent and a corresponding risk-free rate of ln(1+.05)=0.04879. To determine the volatility for Cisco implied by this option price, you can enter the relevant parameters in cells B5:B10 of the file Ciscoimpvol.xlsx, which is shown in Figure 79-5.

	A	B	C	D	E
4	Input data				
5	Stock price	18.43			
6	Exercise price	17.5			
7	Duration	0.24384			
8	Interest rate	0.04879			
9	dividend rate	0			
10	volatility	0.34036			
11					
12				Predicted	
13	Call price			$1.85	
14	put			$0.71	
15					
16					
17	Other quantities for option price				
18	d1	0.4629		N(d1)	0.678281
19	d2	0.29483		N(d2)	0.615937

FIGURE 79-5 Using implied volatility to estimate the volatility of Cisco stock.

Next, you use the Goal Seek dialog box (see Figure 79-6) to determine the volatility (the value in cell B10) that makes the call price (the formula in D13) hit a value of $1.85. On the Data tab, in the Forecast group, click What-If Analysis and select Goal Seek.

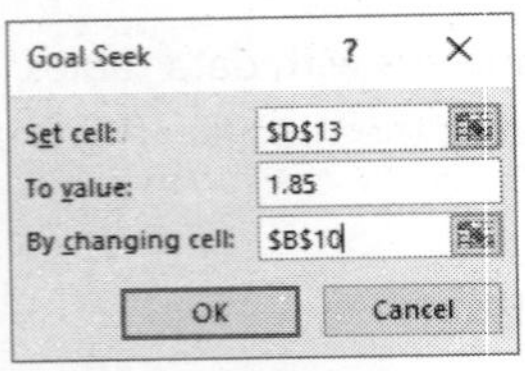

FIGURE 79-6 The Goal Seek settings to find implied volatility.

This option implies an annual volatility for Cisco of 34 percent, as you can see in Figure 79-5.

> **Note** The website IVolatility.com provides an estimate of the volatility of any stock, either historical or implied.

I don't want somebody changing my neat option-pricing formulas. How can I protect the formulas in my worksheet so that nobody can change them?

I'm sure that you have sent a worksheet to someone who then changed your carefully constructed formulas. Sometimes you want to protect a worksheet so that another user can enter only input data but not modify the worksheet's formulas. As an example, I'll show you how to protect all the formulas in the Black-Scholes template. (See the files Bstemp.xlsx and Bstempprotected.xlsx.)

I begin by unlocking all the cells in the worksheet. Then, I will lock the cells I want to protect. First, in the file Bstemp.xlsx, click the gray box with the dark-gray triangle, in the upper-left corner of the worksheet, where the row and column headings intersect. After you click this box, any format changes you make affect the entire worksheet. For example, if you select a bold format after clicking this box, all the cells in the worksheet will use the bold format.

After selecting the entire worksheet, click the Font dialog box launcher (the small arrow) in the Font group on the Home tab. This displays the Format Cells dialog box, shown in Figure 79-7. On the Protection tab, clear the Locked check box, as shown in Figure 79-7, and then click OK. Now all the cells in the worksheet are unlocked, which means that even if the worksheet is protected, you can still access these cells.

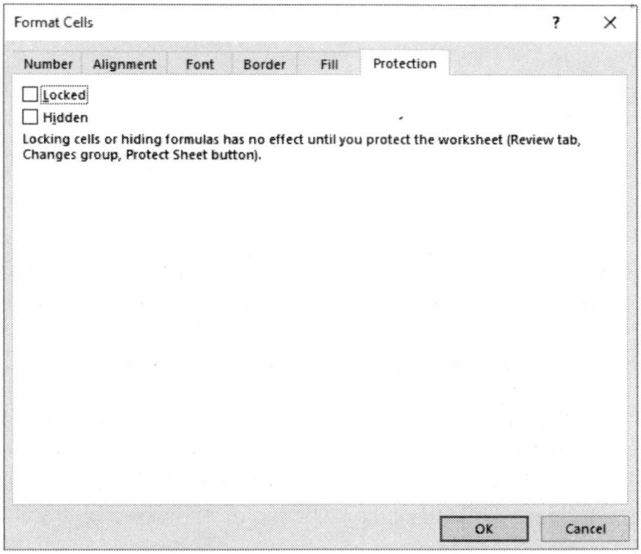

FIGURE 79-7 The Format Cells dialog box.

Next, select all the formulas in the worksheet. To do this, press F5, which opens the Go To dialog box. Click Special, select Formulas, and click OK. Click the Font dialog box launcher again (to open the Format Cells dialog box), and on the Protection tab, select the Locked check box. Selecting this box locks all the formulas.

Now, you can protect the worksheet, which will prevent a user from changing your formulas. On the Review tab, in the Changes group, click Protect Sheet. In the Protect Sheet dialog box, select the Select Unlocked Cells check box, as shown in Figure 79-8, and then click OK. This option allows users of a template to select unlocked cells, but the formulas will be off-limits.

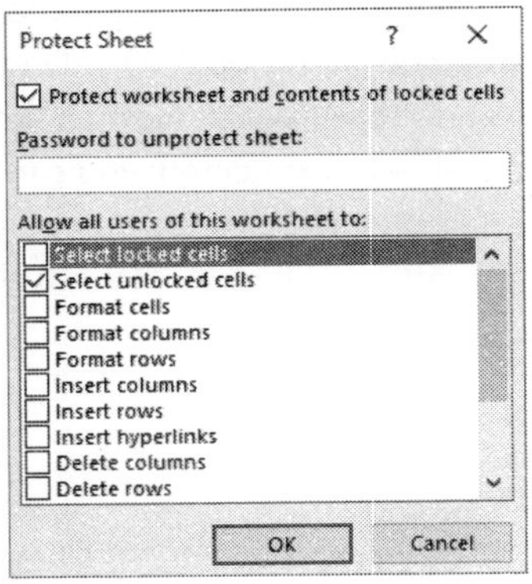

FIGURE 79-8 Allowing users to access unlocked cells.

Now, when you click any formula, you cannot see or change its contents. Go ahead and try to mess up a formula! The final result of protecting this workbook is saved in the file Bstempprotected.xlsx.

How can I use option pricing to help my company make better investment decisions?

Option pricing can be used to improve a company's capital budgeting or financial decision-making process. The use of option pricing to evaluate actual investment projects is called *real options*. The idea of real options is credited to Judy Lewent, the former chief financial officer of Merck. Essentially, real options let you put an explicit value on managerial flexibility, which is often missed by traditional capital budgeting. The following two examples illustrate the concepts of real options.

> **Note** Refer to David Luenberger's book for a more detailed discussion of real options.

Let's say that you own an oil well. Today, your best guess is that the oil in the well is worth $50 million. In five years (if you own the well), you will make a decision to develop the oil well, at a cost of $70 million. A wildcatter is willing to buy the well today for $10 million. Should you sell the well?

Of course, the value of the oil in five years might increase. Even if you assume that the value of the oil would increase by 5 percent a year, the oil would be worth only $63.81 million in five years. Traditional capital budgeting says that the well is worthless because the cost to develop it is more than the value of the oil in the well. But wait; in five years' time, the value of the oil in the well will be different because many things (such as the global oil price) might change. There's a chance that the oil will be worth at least $70 million in five years. If the oil is worth $80 million in five years, developing the well in five years would return $10 million.

Essentially, you own a five-year European call option on this well, because the payoff from the well in five years is the same as the payoff on a European call option with a stock price of $50 million, an exercise price of $70 million, and a duration of five years. You can assume an annual volatility similar to the volatility of a typical oil-company stock (for example, 30 percent). If you use a T-bill rate of 5 percent, corresponding to a risk-free rate of 4.879 percent, in the file Oilwell.xlsx (see Figure 79-9), you can determine that the value of this call option is $11.47 million, which means that you should not sell the well for $10 million.

Of course, you do not know the actual volatility for this oil well. Therefore, you can use a one-way data table to determine how the value of the option depends on a volatility estimate. (See Figure 79-9.) From the data table, you can see that as long as the oil well's volatility is at least 27 percent, your oil well "option" is worth more than $10 million.

E31

	A	B	C	D	E	F	G	H
4	Input data							
5	Stock price	50						
6	Exercise price	70						
7	Duration	5						
8	Interest rate	0.05						
9	dividend rate	0					Volatility	$11.47
10	volatility	0.3					0.1	2.635248
11							0.11	3.064456
12				Predicted			0.12	3.498668
13	Call price			$11.47			0.13	3.936575
14	put			$16.32			0.14	4.377212
15							0.15	4.819845
16							0.16	5.263906
17	Other quantities for option price						0.17	5.708942
18	d1	0.2		N(d1)	0.5783		0.18	6.15459
19	d2	-0.47		N(d2)	0.318		0.19	6.600548
20							0.2	7.046562
21							0.21	7.492419
22							0.22	7.937931
23							0.23	8.382936
24							0.24	8.82729
25							0.25	9.270862
26							0.26	9.713537
27							0.27	10.15521
28							0.28	10.59577
29							0.29	11.03514
30							0.3	11.47322

FIGURE 79-9 The oil-well real options.

As a second example, consider a biotech drug company that is developing a drug for a pharmaceutical firm. The biotech company currently believes the value of the drug is $50 million. Of course, the value of the drug might drop over time. To protect against a price drop, the biotech company wants the drug to have a guaranteed value of $50 million in five years. If an insurance company wants to underwrite this liability, what is a fair price to charge?

Essentially, the biotech company is asking for a payment of $1 million in five years for each $1 million by which the value of the drug in five years is below $50 million. This is equivalent to a five-year put option on the value of the drug. Assuming a T-bill rate is 5 percent, and the annual volatility on comparable drug stocks is 40 percent (see the file Drugabandon.xlsx, shown in Figure 79-10), the value of this option is $10.51 million. This type of option is often referred to as an *abandonment option*, but it is equivalent to a put option. (I also included a one-way data table, shown in Figure 79-10, to show how the value of the abandonment option depends on the assumed volatility, ranging from 30 to 45 percent of the drug's value.)

	A	B	C	D	E	F	G	H
1	**Call with dividends**							
2								
3								
4	Input data							
5	Stock price	50						
6	Exercise price	50						
7	Duration	5						
8	Interest rate	0.049						
9	dividend rate	0					Volatility	$10.51
10	volatility	0.4					0.3	7.03399
11							0.31	7.383411
12				Predicted			0.32	7.732875
13	Call price			$21.34			0.33	8.082211
14	put			$10.51			0.34	8.431265
15							0.35	8.779894
16							0.36	9.127966
17	Other quantities for option price						0.37	9.475362
18	d1	0.72		N(d1)	0.764		0.38	9.821968
19	d2	-0.174		N(d2)	0.431		0.39	10.16768
20							0.4	10.51241
21							0.41	10.85605
22							0.42	11.19853
23							0.43	11.53976
24							0.44	11.87967
25							0.45	12.21819

FIGURE 79-10 Calculating an abandonment option.

Problems

1. Use the monthly stock returns in the file Volatility.xlsx to determine estimates of annual volatility for Intel, Microsoft, and GE.

2. A stock is selling today for $42. The stock has an annual volatility of 40 percent, and the annual risk-free rate is 10 percent. Answer the following questions:

   - What is a fair price for a six-month European call option with an exercise price of $40?
   - How much does the current stock price have to increase for the purchaser of the call option to break even in six months?
   - What is a fair price for a six-month European put option with an exercise price of $40?
   - How much does the current stock price have to decrease for the purchaser of the put option to break even in six months?
   - What level of volatility would make the $40 call option sell for $6? Hint: Use the Goal Seek command.

3. On September 25, 2000, JDS Uniphase stock sold for $106.81 per share. On the same day, a $100 European put expiring on January 20, 2001, sold for $11.875. Compute an implied volatility for JDS Uniphase stock based on this information. Use a T-bill rate of 5 percent.

4. On August 9, 2002, Microsoft stock was selling for $48.58 per share. A $35 European call option, expiring on January 17, 2003, was selling for $13.85. Use this information to estimate the implied volatility for Microsoft stock. Use a T-bill rate of 4 percent.

5. You have an option to buy a new plane in three years for $25 million. Your current estimate of the value of the plane is $21 million. The annual volatility for the change in the plane's value is 25 percent, and the risk-free rate is 5 percent. What is the option to buy the plane worth?

6. The current price of copper is 95 cents per pound. The annual volatility for copper prices is 20 percent, and the risk-free rate is 5 percent. In one year, you have the option (if you want it) to spend $1.25 million to mine 8 million pounds of copper. The copper can be sold at whatever the copper price is in one year. It costs 85 cents to extract a pound of copper from the ground. What is the value of this situation to you?

7. You own the rights to a biotech drug. Your best estimate is that the current value of these rights is $50 million. Assuming that the annual volatility of biotech companies is 90 percent and the risk-free rate is 5 percent, what is the value of an option to sell the rights to the drug five years from now for $40 million?

8. Merck is debating whether to invest in a pioneer biotech project. The company estimates that the worth of the project is –$56 million. Investing in the pioneer project gives Merck the option to own, if it wants to, a much bigger technology that will be available in four years. If Merck does not participate in the pioneer project, it cannot own the bigger project. The bigger project will require $1.5 billion in cash four years from now. Currently, Merck estimates the net present value (NPV) of the cash flows from the bigger project to be $597 million. Assuming a risk-free rate of 10 percent and that the annual volatility for the bigger project is 35 percent, what should Merck do? (This is the problem that started the whole field of real options!)

9. Develop a worksheet that uses the following inputs to compute an annual profit:

   - Annual fixed cost
   - Unit cost
   - Unit price
   - Annual demand=10,000–100*(price)

   Protect the cells used to compute the annual demand and annual profit.

CHAPTER 80

Determining customer value

Questions answered in this chapter:

- A credit-card company currently has an 80 percent retention rate. How will the company's profitability improve if the retention rate increases to 90 percent or higher?
- A long-distance phone company gives the competition's customers an incentive to switch. How large of an incentive should it give?

Many companies undervalue their customers. When valuing a customer, a company should look at the net present value (NPV) of the long-term profits that the company earns from the customer. (For detailed information about net present value, see Chapter 8, "Evaluating investments by using net present value criteria.") Failure to look at the long-term value of a customer often causes a company to make poor decisions. For example, a company might cut its customer-service staff by 10 percent to save $1 million, but the resulting decrease in service quality might cause the company to lose much more than $1 million in *customer value* when customers take their business elsewhere. This would, of course, result in the company being less profitable. The following two examples show how to compute customer value.

Answers to this chapter's questions

A credit-card company currently has an 80 percent retention rate. How will the company's profitability improve if the retention rate increases to 90 percent or higher?

This example is based on a discussion in Frederick Reichheld's excellent book *The Loyalty Effect* (Harvard Business School Press, 2001). You can find the sample data I'll use in the file Loyalty.xlsx, shown in Figure 80-1. Reichheld estimates the profitability of a credit-card customer based on the number of years the customer has held a card. For example, during the first year a customer has the credit card, the cardholder generates –$40 profit, which is the result of customer acquisition costs and the cost of setting up the customer's account. During each successive year, the profit generated by the customer increases until a customer who has owned a card for 20 or more years generates $161 per year in profits.

The credit-card company wants to determine how the value of a customer depends on the company's retention rate. Currently, the company has an 80 percent retention rate, which means that at the end of each year, 20 percent (1–0.80) of all customers do not renew their card. (I refer to the

20 percent of customers who don't renew as the *annual churn rate*.) The credit-card company wants to determine the long-term value of a customer for retention rates of 80 percent, 85 percent, 90 percent, 95 percent, and 99 percent.

	A	B	C	D	E	F	G
4				npv per customer	141.718		
5							
6		retention rate	0.8				
7		Interest rate	0.15				
8	Year	Mean Profit(if still here)	Number	Profit		retention rate	141.718
9	1	($40.00)	100	($4,000.00)		0.8	141.718
10	2	$66.00	80	$5,280.00		0.85	193.15
11	3	$72.00	64	$4,608.00		0.9	269.347
12	4	$79.00	51.2	$4,044.80		0.95	390.713
13	5	$87.00	40.96	$3,563.52		0.99	548.577
14	6	$92.00	32.768	$3,014.66			
15	7	$96.00	26.2144	$2,516.58			
16	8	$99.00	20.9715	$2,076.18			
17	9	$103.00	16.7772	$1,728.05			
18	10	$106.00	13.4218	$1,422.71			
19	11	$111.00	10.7374	$1,191.85			
20	12	$116.00	8.58993	$996.43			
21	13	$120.00	6.87195	$824.63			
22	14	$124.00	5.49756	$681.70			
23	15	$130.00	4.39805	$571.75			
24	16	$137.00	3.51844	$482.03			
25	17	$142.00	2.81475	$399.69			
26	18	$148.00	2.2518	$333.27			

FIGURE 80-1 The value of a credit-card customer.

To determine the long-term value of a customer, you start with a cohort of, say, 100 customers. (A *cohort* is a group of individuals who have a statistical factor in common. The size 100 is arbitrary here, but round numbers make it easier to follow the analysis.) Then, you determine how many of these customers are still around each year with the formula (Customers around for year t+1)=(Retention rate)*(Customers around for year t). You can assume that customers quit only at the end of each year. Then you use the NPV function to determine the total NPV (assuming a 15 percent discount rate) generated by the original cohort of 100 customers. The 15 percent discount rate implies that $1 earned one year from now is worth the same as $1.00/$1.15 of profit earned now. Dividing this number by the number of customers in the original cohort (100) gives you the value of an individual customer.

I first assign the names in the cell range B6:B7 to the cell range C6:C7. Then I enter the number of original customers (100) in cell C9. Copying from cell C10 to the range C11:C38 the formula =retention_rate*C9 generates the number of customers present for each year. For example, 80 customers will be present in Year 2.

I compute the profit earned each year by multiplying the number of remaining customers by each customer's profit. To make this calculation, copy from cell D9 to D10:D38 the formula =C9*B9. In cell E4, I compute the average NPV generated by an individual customer with the formula =(1+Interest_rate)*NPV(Interest_rate,D9:D38)/100. I am assuming the cash flows are at the beginning of the year and a 15 percent annual discount rate. The portion of the formula that reads NPV(Interest_rate,D9:D38) computes the average NPV generated by an individual customer, assuming end-of-year cash flows. Multiplying by (1+Interest_rate) converts the end-of-year cash flow NPV to a beginning-of-year NPV.

With an 80 percent retention rate, the average customer is worth $141.72. To determine how the value of an individual customer varies with a change in the annual retention rate, I use a one-way data table. I enter the relevant annual retention rates in the cell range F9:F13. In cell G8, I enter the formula I want the data table to calculate (NPV per customer) with the formula =E4. Next, I select the table range (F8:G13) and then choose Data Table from the What-If Analysis command on the Data tab. After entering a column input cell of C6, I obtain the profit calculations shown earlier in Figure 80-1. Notice that increasing the retention rate from 80 percent to 90 percent nearly doubles the value of each customer, which strongly argues for being nice to these customers and against pinching pennies on activities related to customer service. Understanding the value of a customer gives most companies a crucial lever that can be used to increase their profitability.

A long-distance phone company gives the competition's customers an incentive to switch. How large of an incentive should it give?

Let's say that you work for a phone company in which the average long-distance customer spends $400 per year, and the company generates a 10 percent profit margin on each dollar spent. At the end of each year, 50 percent of your company's customers switch to competitors, and without any incentives, 30 percent of your competitors' customers switch to your company. You're considering giving your competitors' customers a one-time incentive to switch companies. How large of an incentive can you give and still break even?

The key to analyzing this problem (which you can find in the file Phoneloyalty.xlsx, shown in Figure 80-2) is to look at the NPV for the following two situations:

- Situation 1: 100 customers begin with the competition.
- Situation 2: You pay the 100 customers who are with the competition a certain amount to switch to your company.

Following through each situation for a period of time (for example, 20 years), you can use the Goal Seek command to determine the dollar amount *x* paid to a person switching to your company that makes you indifferent about the following two situations:

- Situation 1: You have just paid 100 disloyal customers $*x* each to switch to your company.
- Situation 2: The market consists of 100 disloyal customers.

Assume that the analysis begins on June 30, 2014, and that customers switch companies at most once per year. I assigned the range names in cells A2:A6 to cells B2:B6. The key step in the analysis is to realize the following:

```
(year t+1 customers with us)=0.3*(year t competitor customers)+0.5*(year t your customers)
```

Similarly,

```
(year t+1 customers with competition)=0.7*(year t competition customers)+0.5*(year t your
customers)
```

	A	B	C	D	E	F	G	H	I
2	switch fee	34.22193			pay-no pay	0			
3	probleave	0.5							
4	probcome	0.3							
5	annrevenue	400	NPV	13674.36			13674.36		
6	profitmargin	0.1		Pay them			Do not pay them		
7		Date	Year	Number with us	Number with them	Profit	Number with us	Number with them	Profit
8		initial							
9		6/30/2014	1	100	0	577.81	30	70	1200
10		6/30/2015	2	50	50	2000	36	64	1440
11		6/30/2016	3	40	60	1600	37.2	62.8	1488
12		6/30/2017	4	38	62	1520	37.44	62.56	1498
13		6/30/2018	5	37.6	62.4	1504	37.488	62.512	1500
14		6/30/2019	6	37.52	62.48	1500.8	37.4976	62.5024	1500
15		6/30/2020	7	37.504	62.496	1500.2	37.49952	62.5005	1500
16		6/30/2021	8	37.5008	62.4992	1500	37.4999	62.5001	1500
25		6/30/2030	17	37.5	62.5	1500	37.5	62.5	1500
26		6/30/2031	18	37.5	62.5	1500	37.5	62.5	1500
27		6/30/2032	19	37.5	62.5	1500	37.5	62.5	1500
28		6/30/2033	20	37.5	62.5	1500	37.5	62.5	1500

FIGURE 80-2 A phone company incentive analysis.

Next, I enter 100 in cell D9 (customers with your company) and 0 in cell E9 (customers with your competitors). This customer alignment corresponds to the situation right after the incentive is offered to 100 customers. I'm assuming that customers who receive the incentive must stay with the company for at least one year. Copying from D10 to D11:D28 the formula =(1–probleave)*D9+probcome*E9 generates the number of customers during each year. (Years 2022 through 2029 are hidden rows in Figure 80-2.) Copying from E10 to E11:E28 the formula =probleave*D9+(1–probcome)*E9 calculates the number of customers with the competition during each year.

In cell F9, I generate the profit earned during the first year with the formula =D9*annrevenue*profitmargin–switch_fee*100. Note that I have subtracted the cost of paying the 100 competitor customers to switch. Copying from F10 to F11:F28 the formula =D10*annrevenue*profitmargin generates profit during later years. In cell D5, I compute the NPV of the profits associated with the incentive by using the formula =XNPV(0.1,F9:F28,B9:B28). (See Chapter 8 for a discussion of the XNPV function.)

In a similar fashion, in the cell range G8:I28 I generate the profits earned each year from 100 customers who were originally with the competition. On June 30, 2014, 30 of these 100 customers switched (even without incentives). In cell F2, I compute the difference between the NPV with the incentive and the NPV without the incentive.

Finally, I use the Goal Seek command to vary the size of the incentive (cell B2) to set F2 equal to 0. That is, in the Goal Seek dialog box, specify the Set Cell as F2, set To Value to 0, select By Changing Cell as B2, and then click OK. The Goal Seek dialog box is shown in Figure 80-3. An incentive of $34.22 makes the NPV of the two situations identical. Therefore, you could give incentives of up to $34.22 for a customer to switch and still have increased profitability.

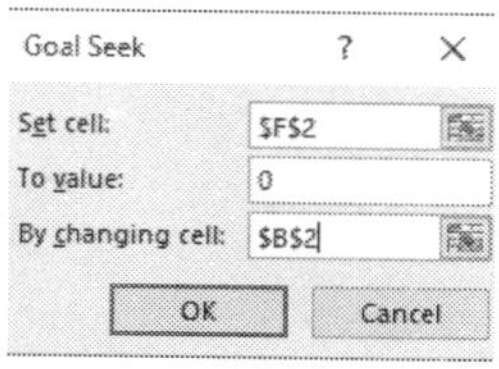

FIGURE 80-3 The Goal Seek settings to determine the maximum incentive that increases profitability.

Problems

1. Whirlswim Appliance is considering giving each of its customers free maintenance on each VCR purchased. (A VCR was a videocassette recorder, and they used to burn the movies onto tape, before movies became digital files.) The company estimated that this proposal would require it to pay an average of $2.50 for each VCR sold (the cost in dollars). The market consisted of 72,000 consumers whose last purchase was from Whirlswim and 86,000 consumers whose last purchase was from a competitor. In one year, 40 percent of all consumers purchased a VCR. If their last purchase was a Whirlswim, there is a 60 percent chance that their next purchase will be a Whirlswim. If their last purchase was not a Whirlswim, there is a 30 percent chance that their next purchase will be a Whirlswim. A purchase during the year led to a $20 profit. The contribution to profit (and maintenance cost per purchaser) from a purchaser grew 5 percent per year. Profits (over a 30-year horizon) were discounted 10 percent per year.

   Suppose that you provided free maintenance on the VCRs. If the customer's last purchase was a Whirlswim, the probability that the customer's next purchase will be a Whirlswim will increase by an unknown amount between 0 percent and 10 percent. Similarly, if you give free maintenance and the customer's last purchase was not a Whirlswim, the probability that the next purchase is a Whirlswim will increase by an unknown amount between 0 percent and 10 percent. Do you recommend that Whirlswim adopt the free maintenance policy?

2. Mr. D's Supermarket is determined to please its customers with a customer-advantage card. Currently, 30 percent of all their shoppers are loyal to Mr. D's. A loyal Mr. D's customer shops at Mr. D's 80 percent of the time. A disloyal Mr. D's customer shops at Mr. D's 10 percent of the time. A typical customer spends $150 per week, and Mr. D's is running on a 4 percent profit margin.

   The customer-advantage card will cost Mr. D's an average of $0.01 per dollar spent. You believe Mr. D's share of loyal customers will increase by an unknown amount between 2 percent and 10 percent. You also believe that the fraction of the time a loyal customer shops at Mr. D's will increase by an unknown amount between 2 percent and 12 percent. Should Mr. D's adopt a customer-advantage card? Should Mr. D's adopt the card if its profit margin is 8 percent instead of 4 percent?

CHAPTER 81

The economic order quantity inventory model

Questions answered in this chapter:

- An electronics store sells 10,000 cell phones per year. Each time an order is placed for a supply of cell phones, the store incurs an order cost of $10. The store pays $100 for each cell phone, and the cost of holding a cell phone in inventory for a year is assumed to be $20. When the store orders cell phones, how large an order should it make?
- A computer-manufacturing plant produces 10,000 servers per year. The cost to produce each server is $2,000. The cost to set up a production run of servers is $200, and the cost to hold a server in inventory for a year is $500. The plant can produce 25,000 servers per year if it wants to. When the plant produces servers, how large a batch should it produce?

When a store orders an item repeatedly, a natural question soon arises: what quantity should the store order each time? If the store orders too many items, it incurs excessive inventory or holding costs. If the store orders too few items, it incurs excessive reordering costs. Somewhere, there must be a happy medium that minimizes the sum of annual inventory and order costs.

Similarly, consider a manufacturing plant that produces batches of a product. What batch size minimizes the sum of annual inventory and setup costs? The two examples in this chapter show how to use the *economic order quantity formula* (developed in 1913 by F. Harris of Westinghouse Corporation) to answer these questions.

Answers to this chapter's questions

An electronics store sells 10,000 cell phones per year. Each time an order is placed for a supply of cell phones, an order cost of $10 is incurred. The store pays $100 for each cell phone, and the cost of holding a cell phone in inventory for a year is assumed to be $20. When the store orders cell phones, how large an order should it make?

The size of an order that minimizes the sum of the annual inventory and ordering costs can be determined after the following parameters are known:

- K=Cost per order

- *h*=Cost of holding one unit in inventory for a year
- *D*=Annual demand for product

You can follow an example of how to work with these parameters by using the EOQ worksheet in the file Eoq.xlsx, which is shown in Figure 81-1.

	A	B	C	D
2	cost/order	K	10	
3	annual holding cost per unit	h	20	
4	annual demand	D	10000	
5	order quantity	EOQ	100	=SQRT(2*K*D/h)
6	holding cost per year	annhc	$1,000.00	
7	order cost per year	annoc	$1,000.00	
8	total annual cost (excluding purchasin	anncost	$2,000.00	=annhc+annoc
9	orders per year	annorder:	100	=D/EOQ

FIGURE 81-1 An EOQ template.

If *q* equals the order size, the annual inventory cost equals 0.5qh. (Throughout this example, I refer to this equation as *Equation 1*.) We derive Equation 1 because the average inventory level (0.5q) will be half the maximum inventory level. To see why the average inventory level is 0.5*q*, note that you can compute the average inventory level for a cycle (the time between the arrival of orders). At the beginning of a cycle, an order arrives, and the inventory level is *q*. At the end of the cycle, you are out of stock, and the inventory level is 0. Because demand occurs at a constant rate, the average inventory level during a cycle is simply the average of 0 and *q* or 0.5*q*. The maximum inventory level will equal *q* because orders are assumed to arrive at the instant that the inventory level is reduced to 0.

Because *D/q* orders are placed per year, the annual ordering cost equals (D/q)*K. (I refer to this equation as *Equation 2*.) Using calculus or Excel Solver, you can show that the annual sum of inventory and ordering costs is minimized for a value of *q* that is equal to the economic order quantity (EOQ), which is calculated using the following formula. (I refer to this equation as *Equation 3*.)

$$\mathrm{EOQ} = \sqrt{\frac{2KD}{h}}$$

From this formula, you can see the following:

- An increase in demand or ordering cost will increase the EOQ.
- An increase in holding cost will decrease the EOQ.

In the file Eoq.xlsx, in cell C5, I use Equation 3 to determine the EOQ by using the formula =SQRT(2*K*D/h). I determine the annual holding cost in cell C6 by using Equation 1, with the formula = 0.5*EOQ*h. I determine the annual ordering cost in cell C7 with Equation 2, using the formula =K*annorders. Notice that for EOQ, the annual ordering cost equals the annual holding cost, which will always be the case. In cell C8, I determine the total annual cost (ignoring the purchasing cost, which does not depend on my ordering strategy), with the formula =annhc+annoc, which is the same as C6+C7.

Of course, you can use one-way and two-way data tables to determine the sensitivity of the EOQ and various costs to variations in *K*, *h*, and *D*. In this example, *K*=$10, *D*=10,000 cell phones per year, and *h*=$20 per cell phone. By inserting these values in cells C2:C4, I find the following:

- Each order should be for 100 cell phones.
- The annual holding and ordering costs each equal $1,000. The EOQ always sets the annual holding costs equal to the annual ordering costs.
- The total annual costs (exclusive of purchasing costs) equal $2,000.

When you are working with EOQ, keep the following in mind:

- The presence of quantity discounts invalidates the EOQ because the annual purchase cost then depends on the order size.
- The EOQ assumes that demand occurs at a relatively constant rate throughout the year. The EOQ should not be used for products for which there is seasonal demand.
- An annual holding cost is usually assumed to be between 10 percent and 40 percent of a product's unit purchasing cost.
- I've included (in the EOQ Protected worksheet in the file Eoq.xlsx) a version of the EOQ worksheet in which all the formulas are protected. When the sheet is protected, nobody can change the formulas. See Chapter 79, "Pricing stock options," for instructions about how to protect a worksheet.

> **Note** For more information about inventory modeling, interested readers can refer to my book *Operations Research: Applications and Algorithms* (Duxbury Press, 2007).

A computer-manufacturing plant produces 10,000 servers per year. The cost to produce each server is $2,000. The cost to set up a production run of servers is $200, and the cost to hold a server in inventory for a year is $500. The plant can produce 25,000 servers per year if it wants to. When the plant produces servers, how large a batch should it produce?

With the EOQ model, you assume an order arrives the instant the order is placed. When a company manufactures a product instead of ordering it, an order must be produced and cannot arrive instantaneously. In such situations, instead of computing the cost-minimizing order quantity, you need to determine the cost-minimizing batch size. When a company produces a product internally instead of purchasing the product externally, the batch size that minimizes costs depends on the following parameters:

- *K*=Cost of setting up a batch for production
- *h*=Cost of holding each unit in inventory for a year
- *D*=Annual demand for the product

- *R*=Annual rate at which the product can be produced. For example, IBM might have the capacity to produce 25,000 servers per year.

If *q* equals the size of each production batch, the annual holding cost equals 0.5*(q/R)*(R–D)*h. (I refer to this equation as *Equation 4*.) Equation 4 follows because each batch takes *q/R* years to produce, and during a production cycle, the inventory increases at a rate of *R–D*. The maximum inventory level, which occurs at the completion of a batch, can be calculated as (q/R)*(R–D). The average inventory level will thus equal 0.5*(q/R)*(R–D).

Because *D/q* batches are produced per year, the annual setup cost equals *KD/q* (which I refer to as *Equation 5*). Using calculus or Excel Solver, you can show that the batch size that minimizes the sum of annual setup and production-run costs is given by the following (which I refer to as *Equation 6*). The following model is called the economic order batch (EOB) size:

$$\text{EOB}=\sqrt{\frac{2KDR}{h\,(R-D)}}$$

From this formula, you can determine the following:

- An increase in *K* or *D* will increase the EOB.
- An increase in *h* or *R* will decrease the EOB.

In the Cont Rate EOQ worksheet in the file Contrateeoq.xlsx, I constructed a template to determine the EOB, annual setup, and holding costs. The worksheet is shown in Figure 81-2.

	A	B	C	D
2	cost per batch	K	$ 200.00	
3	annual holding cost per unit	h	$ 500.00	
4	annual demand	D	10000	
5	annual production rate	rate	25000	
6	batch size	EOB	115.470054	=SQRT(2*K*D*rate/(h*(rate-D)))
7	holding cost per year	annhc	$17,320.51	=(EOB/rate)*(rate-D)*0.5*h
8	order cost per year	annoc	$17,320.51	=annbatches*K
9	total annual cost (excluding purchasin	anncost	$34,641.02	=annhc+annoc
10	batches per year	annbatches	86.6025404	=D/EOB

FIGURE 81-2 A template for computing the EOB.

For this example, *K*=$200, *h*=$500, *D*=10,000 units per year, and *R*=25,000 units per year. After entering these parameter values in the cell range C2:C5, I find the following:

- The batch size that minimizes costs is 115.47 servers. Thus, the company should produce 115 or 116 servers in each batch.
- The annual holding cost and setup costs equal $17,320.51. Again, the EOB will always set the annual holding cost equal to the annual setup cost.
- The total annual cost (exclusive of variable production costs) is $34,641.02.
- 86.6 batches per year will be produced.

When you are working with the EOB model, keep the following in mind:

- If the unit variable cost of producing a product depends on the batch size, the EOB model is invalid.
- The EOB assumes that demand occurs at a relatively constant rate throughout the year. The EOB should not be used for products for which there is seasonal demand.
- The annual holding cost is usually assumed to be between 10 percent and 40 percent of a product's unit purchasing cost.
- I've included (in the Protected worksheet in the file Contrateeoq.xlsx) a version of the EOB worksheet in which all the formulas are protected. See Chapter 79 for instructions about how to protect a worksheet.

Problems

1. An appliance store sells plasma TVs. The annual demand is estimated at 1,000 units. The cost to carry a TV in inventory for one year is $500, and the cost to place an order for plasma TVs is $400. Answer the following questions:
   - How many TVs should be ordered each time an order is placed?
   - How many orders per year should be placed?
   - What are the annual inventory and ordering costs?
2. Suppose that the Waterford Crystal company can produce up to 100 iced-tea pitchers per day. Further suppose that the plant is open 250 days per year, and that the annual demand is for 20,000 pitchers. The cost to hold a pitcher in inventory for a year might be $10, and the cost to set up the facility to produce iced-tea pitchers might be $40. Answer the following questions:
   - What batch size would you recommend for iced-tea pitchers?
   - How many batches per year should be produced?
   - What are the annual setup and inventory costs for iced-tea pitchers?

CHAPTER 82

Inventory modeling with uncertain demand

Questions answered in this chapter:

- At what inventory level should I place an order if my goal is to minimize the annual holding, ordering, and shortage costs?
- What does the term 95 percent service level mean?

In Chapter 81, "The economic order quantity inventory model," I showed you how to use the economic order quantity (EOQ) to determine an optimal order quantity and production batch size. The examples assumed that demand occurred at a constant rate. Thus, if annual demand occurred at a rate of, for example, 1,200 units per year, monthly demand would equal 100 units. As long as demand occurs at a relatively constant rate, the EOQ is a good approximation of the cost-minimizing order quantity.

In reality, demand during any time period is uncertain. When demand is uncertain, a natural question is how low to let the inventory level go before placing an order. The inventory level at which an order should be placed is called the *reorder point.* Clearly, a high reorder point will decrease shortage costs and increase holding costs. Similarly, a low reorder point will increase shortage costs and decrease holding costs. At some intermediate reorder point, the sum of shortage and holding costs is minimized. The first example in this chapter shows you how to determine a reorder point that minimizes the expected ordering, shortage, and holding costs, based on the following two assumptions:

- Each unit you are short is back-ordered by a customer, and you incur the shortage cost c_B. This cost is primarily a measure of the customer's dissatisfaction caused by the late receipt of an ordered item.
- Each unit you are short results in a lost sale, and you incur the shortage cost $c_{LS}>c_B$. The lost sales cost includes the profit lost from the lost sale as well as the shortage cost included in c_B.

The second example shows how to determine the optimal reorder point based on a service-level approach. For example, a *95 percent service level* means that you set the reorder point at a level ensuring that, on average, 95 percent of all demand is met on time. It is usually difficult to determine the cost of a shortage in either the back-ordered case or the lost-sales case. For that reason, most companies set reorder points by using the service-level approach.

Answers to this chapter's questions

At what inventory level should I place an order if my goal is to minimize the annual holding, ordering, and shortage costs?

As I indicated in Chapter 81, the EOQ depends on the following parameters:

- *K*=Cost per order .
- *h*=Cost of holding one unit in inventory for a year.
- *D*=Annual demand for the product. Because demand is now uncertain, you let D stand for the expected annual demand for the product.

The back-order case

See the file Reorderpoint_backorder.xlsx, shown in Figure 82-1, for the data I'm using in this example. Let's first suppose that each shortage results in the back-ordered units. In other words, a shortage does not result in any lost demand. Also assume that each unit you are short incurs a cost c_B.

	A	B	C
2	cost/order	K	$ 50.00
3	annual holding cost per unit	h	$ 10.00
4	mean annual demand	D	1000
5	order quantity	EOQ	100
6	orders per year	annorders	10
7	unit stockout cost	SOC	$ 20.00
8	annual sigma	annsig	40.8
9	mean lead time	meanLT	0.0384615
10	sigma lead time	sigmaLT	0
11	mean lead time demand	meanLTD	38.461538
12	sigma lead time demand	sigmaLTD	8.0015383
13	probability of stockout	probout	0.05
14	reorder point	RP	51.622898
15	safety stock	SS	13.161359

FIGURE 82-1 Determining the reorder point when shortages are back-ordered.

In this case, the reorder point depends on the following quantities:

- *EOQ* is the economic order quantity (the quantity ordered each time an order is placed)
- *K* is the cost per order
- *h* is the annual holding cost per unit
- *D* is the mean annual demand
- *SOC* is the cost per unit short
- *annsig* is the standard deviation of annual demand
- *meanLT* is the average lead time; that is, the average time between placing an order and the time the order is received

- *sigmaLT* is the standard deviation of lead time

Say that a department store wants to determine an optimal inventory policy for ordering electric mixers. They have the following information:

- It costs $50 to place an order for mixers.
- It costs $10 to hold a mixer in inventory for a year.
- On average, the store sells 1,000 mixers per year.
- All the customers who try to purchase a mixer when the store is sold out of them return at a later date and buy a mixer when the mixer is in stock. The store incurs a penalty of $20 for each unit it is short.
- The annual demand for mixers (based on historical data) has a standard deviation of 40.8.
- Lead time is always two weeks (0.038 years), with a standard deviation of 0.

After you enter *K*, *h*, and *D* in cells C2:C4, the spreadsheet computes the EOQ (100 mixers) in C5. After you enter *SOC*, *annsig*, *meanLT*, and *sigmaLT* in cells C7:C10, the spreadsheet computes in cell C14 the reorder point that minimizes the sum of expected annual holding and shortage costs (51.63 mixers). Thus, the department store should order 100 mixers whenever its stock decreases to 51.62 (or 52) mixers.

The safety-stock level associated with a given reorder point is (reorder point)–(mean lead-time demand). The department store maintains a safety-stock level of 51.62–38.46=13.16 mixers, computed in cell C15. Essentially, the safety stock is always in inventory, resulting in extra holding costs. A higher level of safety stock will, of course, reduce shortages.

The lost-sales case

Now suppose that each shortage results in a lost sale. The cost associated with a lost sale is usually estimated as the back-order penalty plus the profit associated with a unit sold. Suppose that the department store earns a $20 profit on each mixer it sells. The unit-shortage cost for the lost-sales case is then $40 ($20 lost profit+$20 back-order penalty).

In the file Reorderpoint_lostsales.xlsx, shown in Figure 82-2, you can see the work I did to estimate the reorder point for the lost-sales case. After entering in cell C7 of the spreadsheet the lost-sales cost of $40, I find that the optimal inventory policy is to order 100 mixers and place an order when the inventory is down to 54.23 mixers. My safety-stock level is 15.77 mixers, and 2.4 percent of the store's demand for mixers will be unmet. Notice that the assumption of a lost sale has increased the reorder point and reduced the probability of a shortage. This happens because the increased cost of a shortage (from $20 to $40) makes the store more eager to avoid shortages.

	A	B	C
2	cost/order	K	$ 50.00
3	annual holding cost per unit	h	$ 10.00
4	mean annual demand	D	1000
5	order quantity	EOQ	100
6	orders per year	annorders	10
7	lost sales cost	LSC	$ 40.00
8	annual sigma	annsig	40.8
9	mean lead time	meanLT	0.038461538
10	sigma lead time	sigmaLT	0
11	mean lead time demand	meanLTD	38.46153846
12	sigma lead time demand	sigmaLTD	8.001538314
13	probability of stockout	probout	0.024390244
14	reorder point	RP	54.22861214
15	safety stock	SS	15.76707368

FIGURE 82-2 Determining the reorder point when sales will be lost.

Increased uncertainty greatly increases the reorder point. For example, in the lost-sales case, if the standard deviation for lead time is one week (0.019 years) rather than 0, the reorder point increases to 79.50 mixers, and the safety stock more than doubles from the case in which the lead time was known with certainty.

What does the term 95 percent service level mean?

As stated earlier in the chapter, a 95 percent service level simply means that you want 95 percent of your demand to be met on time. Because estimating the back-order penalty and/or the penalty that results from a lost sale is often difficult, many companies set safety-stock levels for products by setting a service level. Using the file Servicelevelreorder.xlsx (shown in Figure 82-3), you can determine the reorder point corresponding to any service level you want.

	A	B	C	D	E	F
1	Service level	SL	0.95			
2	cost/order	K	$ 50.00			
3	annual holding cost per unit	h	$ 10.00			
4	mean annual demand	D	1000			
5	order quantity	EOQ	100			
6	orders per year	annorders	10			
7	annual sigma	annsig	69.28			
8	mean lead time	meanLT	0.0833			
9	sigma lead time	sigmaLT	0			
10	mean lead time demand	meanLTD	83.333			
11	sigma lead time demand	sigmaLTD	19.999			
12	reorder point	ROP	90.23			
13	standardized reorder point	SROP	0.3448			DIFF
14	normal loss for stand. ROP	NLSTANDROP	0.25	=	0.25	6E-08
15	safety stock	SS	6.8967			

FIGURE 82-3 Determining the reorder point using the service-level approach.

As an example, consider a pharmacy that is trying to determine an optimal inventory policy for a drug it stocks. The pharmacy would like to meet 95 percent of the demand for the drug on time. The following parameters are relevant:

- Each order for the drug costs $50.
- The cost to hold a unit of the drug in inventory for a year is $10.
- The average demand per year for the drug is 1,000 units.
- The standard deviation of the annual demand is 69.28 units.

- The time required to receive a shipment of the drug always takes exactly one month (0.083 years).

You enter the service level you want (0.95) in cell C1 and all the other parameters in cells C2:C4 and C7:C9 (the cells highlighted in Figure 82-3). To determine the reorder point yielding the service level you want, click Solver in the Analysis group on the Data tab.

> **Note** To activate the Solver add-in, click the File tab, click Options, and then click Add-Ins. Click the Go button at the bottom of the Excel Options dialog box, select Solver Add-In, and then click OK.

The Solver model (see Figure 82-4) adjusts the reorder point until the percentage of demand met on time matches the service level you want. Click the Options button, and then choose the Multistart setting in the GRG Nonlinear tab. (See Chapter 36, "Warehouse location and the GRG Multistart and Evolutionary Solver engines.") Then you put a lower bound of 0.001 on the reorder point (to keep Solver from trying a negative reorder point) and an upper bound of 10,000 (fairly arbitrary) on the reorder point. If Solver bumps up against your upper bound, you should relax the bound. As you can see in Figure 82-3, the pharmacy should order 100 units of the drug whenever its inventory level drops to 90.23 units. This reorder point corresponds to a safety-stock level of 6.90 units.

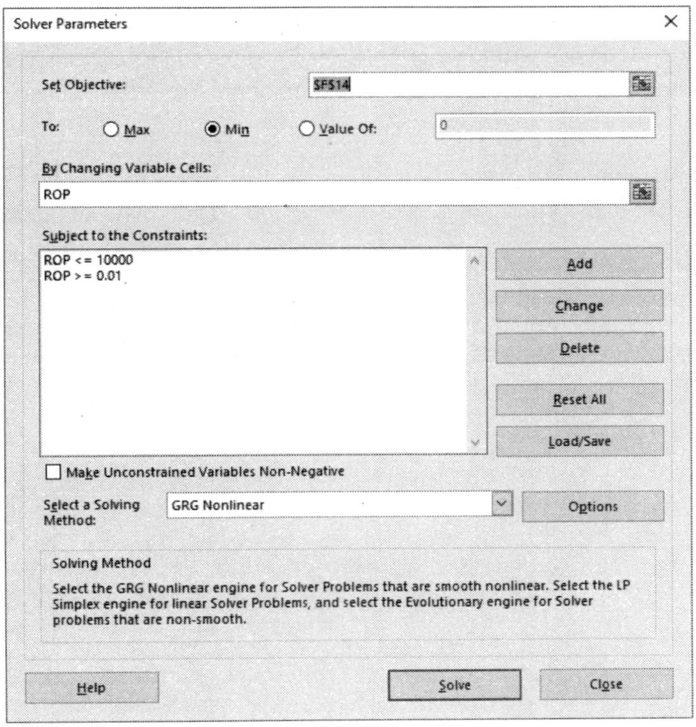

FIGURE 82-4 The Solver Parameters dialog box for determining the reorder point for a 95 percent service level.

In the following table, I've listed the reorder point and safety-stock levels corresponding to service levels between 80 percent and 99 percent:

Service-level percentage	Reorder point/units	Safety stock/units
80	65.34	-17.99
85	71.85	-11.48
90	79.57	-3.76
95	90.23	6.90
99	108.44	25.11

Notice that moving from an 80 percent service level to a 99 percent service level increases the reorder point by almost 67 percent! Also note that you can attain a 90 percent service level with a reorder point less than the mean lead-time demand (refer back to cell C10 in Figure 82-3). A 90 percent service level results in a negative safety-stock level, which is possible because shortages occur only during the lead time and lead times usually cover a small portion of a year.

Problems

When working with Problems 1 and 2, assume that a restaurant serves an average of 5,000 bottles of wine per year. The standard deviation of the annual demand for wine is 1,000 bottles. The annual holding cost for a bottle of wine is $1. It costs $10 to place an order for wine, and it takes an average of three weeks (with a standard deviation of one week) for the wine to arrive. Solve the following problems:

1. Assume that when the restaurant is out of wine, it incurs a penalty of $5 as the result of lost goodwill. Also, the restaurant earns a profit of $2 per bottle of wine. Determine an optimal ordering policy for the wine.
2. Determine an inventory policy for wine that yields a 99 percent service level.
3. A reorder-point policy is often referred to as a *two-bin policy*. How can a reorder-point policy be implemented in a situation in which two bins are used to store inventory?

CHAPTER 83

Queuing theory: The mathematics of waiting in line

Questions answered in this chapter:

- What factors affect the number of people and the time we spend waiting in line?
- What conditions should be met before analyzing the average number of people present or the average time spent in a queuing system?
- Why does variability degrade the performance of a queuing system?
- Can I easily determine the average time a person spends at airport security or waiting in line at a bank?

We have all spent a lot of time waiting in lines (Mickey Mouse demands it), and you'll soon see that a slight increase in service capacity can often greatly reduce the size of the lines you encounter. If you run a business, ensuring that your customers do not spend too much time waiting is important. Therefore, business people need to understand the mathematics of wait time, usually referred to as *queuing theory*. In this chapter, I'll show you how to determine the service capacity needed to provide adequate service.

Answers to this chapter's questions

What factors affect the number of people and the time we spend waiting in line?

In this chapter, I'll address queuing problems in which all arriving customers wait in one line for the first available service person. (To keep things simple, I'll refer to service people as servers.) This model is a fairly accurate representation of the situations you face when you wait at a bank, at an airport security line, or at the post office. By the way, the idea of having customers wait in one line started in about 1970, when banks and post-office branches realized that although waiting in one line does not reduce the average time customers spend waiting, it does reduce the variability of the time they spend in line, thereby creating an apparently fairer system.

Three main factors influence the time you spend in a queuing system:

- **The number of servers** Clearly, the more servers, the less time on average customers spend in line, and fewer people on average will be present in the line.
- **The mean and the standard deviation of the time between arrivals** The time between arrivals is called *interarrival time*. If the average interarrival time increases, the number of arrivals decreases, which results in shorter lines and less time spent in a queuing system. As you'll soon see, an increase in the standard deviation of interarrival times increases the average time a customer spends in a queuing system and the average number of customers present.
- **The mean and the standard deviation of the time needed to complete the service** If the average service time increases, you will see an increase in the average time a customer spends in the system and in the number of customers present. As you'll see, an increase in the standard deviation of service times increases the average time a customer spends in a queuing system and the average number of customers present.

What conditions should be met before analyzing the average number of people present or the average time spent in a queuing system?

When analyzing the time people spend waiting in lines, mathematicians talk about *steady-state characteristics* of a system. Essentially, steady state means that a system has operated for a long time. More specifically, analysts would like to know the value of the following quantities in the steady state:

- W=Average time a customer spends in the system
- W_q=Average time a customer spends waiting in line before the customer is served
- L=Average number of customers present in the system
- L_q=Average number of customers waiting in line

By the way, it is always true that L=(1/mean interarrival time)*W and L_q=(1/mean interarrival time)*W_q.

To discuss the steady state of a queuing system meaningfully, the following must be the case:

- The mean and standard deviation of both the interarrival times and the service times change little over time. The technical phrase is that the distribution of interarrival and service times is stationary over time.
- (1/mean service time)*(number of servers)>(1/(mean interarrival time)). I'll refer to this equation as *Equation 1*.

Essentially, if Equation 1 is true, you can serve more people per hour than are arriving. For example, if the mean service time equals 2 minutes (or 1/30 of an hour), and the mean interarrival time equals 1 minute (or 1/60 of an hour), Equation 1 tells you that 30*(number of servers)>60 or that the number of servers must be greater than or equal to three for a steady state to exist. If you cannot serve customers faster than they arrive, eventually you fall behind and never catch up, resulting in an infinite line.

Why does variability degrade the performance of a queuing system?

To see why variability degrades the performance of a queuing system, consider a one-server system in which customers arrive every 2 minutes and service times always equal 2 minutes. There will never be more than one customer in the system. Now suppose that customers arrive every 2 minutes, but half of all service times are 0.5 minutes and half are 3.5 minutes. Even though arrivals are totally predictable, the uncertainty in service time means that eventually the server falls behind and a line forms. For example, if the first four customers have 3.5 minute service times, after 12 minutes, four customers are waiting, which is illustrated in the following table:

Time	Event	Present after event
0 minutes	Arrival	1 person
2 minutes	Arrival	2 people
3.5 minutes	Service completed	1 person
4 minutes	Arrival	2 people
6 minutes	Arrival	3 people
7 minutes	Service completed	2 people
8 minutes	Arrival	3 people
10 minutes	Arrival	4 people
10.5 minutes	Service completed	3 people
12 minutes	Arrival	4 people

Can I easily determine the average time a person spends at airport security or waiting in line at a bank?

The Model worksheet in the file Queuingtemplate.xlsx contains a template that you can use to determine the approximate values for *L*, *W*, L_q, and W_q (usually within 10 percent of their true value). The worksheet is shown in Figure 83-1.

	A	B	C
3	Arrival rate	0.077734	per minute
4	Service rate	0.01297	per minute
5	s(servers)	6	
6	Mean interarrival time	12.864	
7	Mean service time	77.102	
8	Standard deviation of interarrival times	4.43908	
9	Standard deviation of service times	48.05051	
10	CV arrive	0.119079	
11	CV service	0.388387	
12	u	5.993412	
13	ro	0.998902	
14	R(s,mu)	0.73554	
15	Ec(s,mu)	0.996956	
16	W_q	2960.658	
17	L_q	230.1434	
18	W	3037.76	
19	L	236.1368	

FIGURE 83-1 A queuing template.

After you enter the following data, the template computes W_q, L_q, W, and L. The parameters in cells B6:B9 can easily be estimated by using the following past data:

- Number of servers (cell B5)
- Mean interarrival time (cell B6)
- Mean service time (cell B7)
- Standard deviation of interarrival times (cell B8)
- Standard deviation of service times (cell B9)

Here's an example of the template in action. You want to determine how the operating characteristics of an airline security line during the 9:00 AM to 5:00 PM shift depend on the number of agents working. In the Queuing Data worksheet in the file Queuingtemplate.xlsx, shown in Figure 83-2, I've tabulated interarrival times and service times. (Some rows have been hidden.)

	A	B	C	D
1	mean	12.86440678	77.10169492	seconds!
2	sigma	4.43908047	48.05051039	
3		Interarrival tim	Service Time	
4		5	95	
5		17	240	
6		12	71	
7		18	68	
8		9	90	
9		16	117	
10		15	291	
11		15	116	
12		10	107	
13		11	100	
14		9	28	
15		15	119	
16		19	98	
17		9	72	
18		16	127	
57		13	74	
58		11	27	
59		13	84	
60		19	90	
61		11	42	
62		18	74	

FIGURE 83-2 Airline interarrival and service times.

By copying from cell B1 to C1 the formula =AVERAGE(B4:B62), you find the mean interarrival time is 12.864 seconds, and the mean service time is 77.102 seconds. Because the mean service time is almost six times as large as mean interarrival time, you need at least six agents to guarantee a steady state. Copying from cell B2 to C2 the formula =STDEV.S(B4:B62) tells you that the standard deviation of the interarrival times is 4.439 seconds, and the standard deviation of the service times is 48.051 seconds.

Returning to the queuing template in the Model worksheet, if you enter these values in cells B6:B9 and enter six servers in cell B5, you find that disaster ensues. In the steady state, nearly 236 people will be in line (cell B19). You've probably been at the airport in this situation.

I used a one-way data table (shown in Figure 83-3) to determine how changing the number of agents affects the system's performance. In cells F10:F14, I entered the number of agents to consider (6 through 10). In cell G9, I enter the formula to compute L (=B19), and in H9, I enter the formula to compute W (=B18). Next, I select the table range (F8:H14) and then click Data Table on the What-If Analysis menu on the Data tab (in the Forecast group). After choosing cell B5 (the number of servers) for the Row Input Cell box, I obtain the data table shown in Figure 83-3. Notice that adding just one ticket agent to the original six agents reduces the expected number of customers present in line from 236 to fewer than 7. Adding the seventh agent reduces a customer's average time in the system from 3,038 seconds (50.6 minutes) to 89 seconds (1.5 minutes). This example shows that a small increase in service capacity can greatly improve the performance of a queuing system.

	E	F	G	H	I	J	K
7			L	W			
8		Servers	236.1368	3037.76			
9		6	236.1368	3037.76			
10		7	6.917396	88.9882			
11		8	6.262791	80.56709			
12		9	6.092038	78.37046			
13		10	6.031636	77.59342			
14							
15					servers		
16		3037.76	6	7	8	9	10
17		40	2342.086	86.1952	79.75282	78.07234	77.47788
18	service time	50	3225.354	89.74136	80.78666	78.45085	77.62457
19	sigma	60	4304.905	94.07556	82.05026	78.91348	77.80387
20		70	5580.737	99.1978	83.54359	79.46023	78.01577
21		80	7052.851	105.1081	85.26668	80.09109	78.26027
22		90	8721.247	111.8064	87.2195	80.80607	78.53736

FIGURE 83-3 A sensitivity analysis for an airport security line.

In cells F16:K22, I used a two-way data table to examine the sensitivity of the average time in the system (*W*) to changes in the number of servers and standard deviation of service times. The row input cell is B5, and the column input cell is B9. When seven agents are working, an increase in the standard deviation of service times from 40 seconds to 90 seconds results in a 29 percent increase in the mean time in the system (from 86.2 seconds to 111.8 seconds).

Note Readers who are interested in a more extensive discussion of the queuing theory should refer to my book *Operations Research: Applications and Algorithms* (Duxbury Press, 2007).

Problems

A bank has six tellers. Use the following information to answer Problems 1 through 4:

- Mean service time equals 1 minute.
- Mean interarrival time equals 25 seconds.
- Standard deviation of service times equals 1 minute.

- Standard deviation of interarrival times equals 10 seconds.

Solve the following problems:

1. Determine the average time a customer waits in line.
2. On average, how many customers are present in the bank line?
3. Would you recommend adding more tellers?
4. Suppose it costs $20 per hour to have a teller working, and you value a customer's time at $15 per hour. How many tellers should you have working?
5. Thirty women work on the fifth floor of a business school. Assume that each woman uses the restroom three times a day. (The office is open from 8 AM to 5 PM.) Each visit takes 180 seconds on average, with a standard deviation of 90 seconds. Assume the standard deviation of time between arrivals to the restroom is 5 minutes. How many toilets would you recommend for the women's restroom?

CHAPTER 84

Estimating a demand curve

Questions answered in this chapter:

- What do I need to know to price a product?
- What is the meaning of elasticity of demand?
- Is there any easy way to estimate a demand curve?
- What does a demand curve tell us about a customer's willingness to pay for our product?

Every business must determine a price for each of its products. Pricing a product properly is difficult. In Chapter 85, "Pricing products by using tie-ins," and Chapter 86, "Pricing products by using subjectively determined demand," I'll describe some simple models that might aid you in pricing a product to maximize profitability. For further insights into pricing, refer to the excellent book *Power Pricing,* by Robert J. Dolan and Hermann Simon (Free Press, 1996).

Answers to this chapter's questions

What do I need to know to price a product?

Let's consider a product such as a candy bar. To determine a profit-maximizing price, you need to know two things:

- The variable cost of producing each unit of the product (I'll call this *UC*).
- The product's demand curve. Simply put, a *demand curve* tells you the number of units of a product a customer will demand at each price. In short, if you charge a price of $*p* per unit, the demand curve gives you a number *D(p)*, which equals the number of units of the product that will be demanded at price $*p*. Of course, a firm's demand curve is constantly changing and often depends on factors beyond the firm's control (such as the state of the economy and a competitor's price).

After you know *UC* and the demand curve, the profit corresponding to a price of $*p* is simply (p–UC)*D(p). After you have an equation for *D(p)*, which gives the quantity of the product demanded for each price, you can use Microsoft Excel Solver to find the profit-maximizing price, which I'll show you how to do in Chapters 85 and 86.

What is the meaning of elasticity of demand?

Given a demand curve, the price elasticity for demand is the percentage decrease in demand resulting from a 1 percent increase in price. When elasticity is larger than 1 percent, the demand is price elastic. When the demand is price elastic, a price cut increases your revenue. When elasticity is less than 1 percent, the demand is price inelastic. When the demand is price inelastic, a price cut decreases revenue. The following are some observed estimates of elasticities:

- Salt, 0.1 (very inelastic)
- Coffee, 0.25 (inelastic)
- Legal fees, 0.4 (inelastic)
- TV sets, 1.2 (slightly elastic)
- Restaurant meals, 2.3 (elastic)
- Foreign travel, 4.0 (very elastic)

A 1 percent decrease in the cost of foreign travel, for example, will result in a 4 percent increase in demand for foreign travel.

Is there any easy way to estimate a demand curve?

Using *q* to represent the quantity demanded of a product, the two most commonly used forms for estimating demand curves are as follows:

- **Linear demand curve** In this case, the demand follows a straight line relationship of the form $q=a-bp$. For example, $q=10-p$ is a linear demand curve. (Here *a* and *b* can be determined by using a method that I'll describe later in the chapter.) When the demand curve is linear, the elasticity is constantly changing.
- **Power demand curve** In this situation, the demand curve is described by a power curve of the form $q=ap^b$, $b<0$. (See Chapter 55, "The power curve," for more information.) Again, *a* and *b* can be determined by the method I'll describe later in the chapter. The equation $q=100p^{-2}$ is an example of a power demand curve. If the demand follows a power curve, for any price, the elasticity equals $-b$. Thus, for the demand curve $q=100p^{-2}$, the price elasticity of demand always equals 2.

Suppose that a product's demand curve follows a linear or power demand curve. If you know the current price and demand for a product and the product's price elasticity of demand, determining the product's demand curve is a simple matter. Here are two examples.

A product is currently selling for $100, and the demand equals 500 units. The product's price elasticity for demand is 2. Assuming the demand curve is linear, you want to determine the equation of the demand curve. The solution is in the file Linearfit.xlsx, which is shown in Figure 84-1.

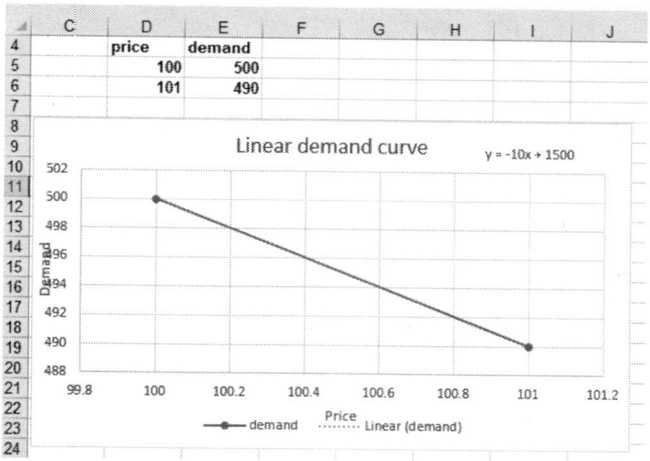

FIGURE 84-1 Fitting a linear demand curve.

Given two points, you know that a unique straight line passes through those two points, and you actually know the two points on the demand curve. One point is p=100 and q=500. Because the elasticity of demand equals 2, a 1 percent increase in the price results in a 2 percent decrease in the demand. Thus, if p=101 (a 1 percent increase), the demand drops by 2 percent of 500 (10 units) to 490. Thus p=101 and q=490 is a second point on the demand curve. You can now use the Excel trendline feature to find the straight line that passes through the points (100,500) and (101,490).

You begin by entering these points in the worksheet in the cell range D5:E6, as shown in Figure 84-1. Then you select the range D4:E6, and on the ribbon, in the Charts group on the Insert tab, click the Insert Scatter (X, Y) Or Bubble Chart option, and choose Scatter With Straight Lines (the last entry in the Scatter section). After selecting this option for a scatter chart, you see that the graph has a positive slope. This implies that higher prices lead to higher demand, which isn't correct. The problem is that with only two data points, Excel assumes that the data points you want to graph are in separate columns, not separate rows. To be sure that Excel understands that the individual points are in separate rows, click inside the graph, and on the ribbon, click the Design tab in the Chart Tools section, and then click Switch Row/Column in the Data group. (Note that by clicking the Select Data button, you can change the source data that generates your chart.) Now you right-click one of the points, click Add Trendline, and then select the Linear option and the Display Equation On Chart check box. Now you will see the straight line plot, complete with the equation (in the upper right of the chart) shown in Figure 84-1. Because x is the price and y is the demand, the equation for the demand curve is q=1500–10p. This equation means that each $1 increase in price costs you 10 units of demand. Of course, demand cannot be linear for all the values of p because for large values of p, a linear demand curve will yield a negative demand. For the prices near the current price, however, the linear demand curve is usually a good approximation of the product's true demand curve.

As a second example, let's again assume that a product is currently selling for $100 and the demand equals 500 units. The product's price elasticity for demand is 2. Now let's fit a power demand curve to this information. See the file Powerfit.xlsx, shown in Figure 84-2.

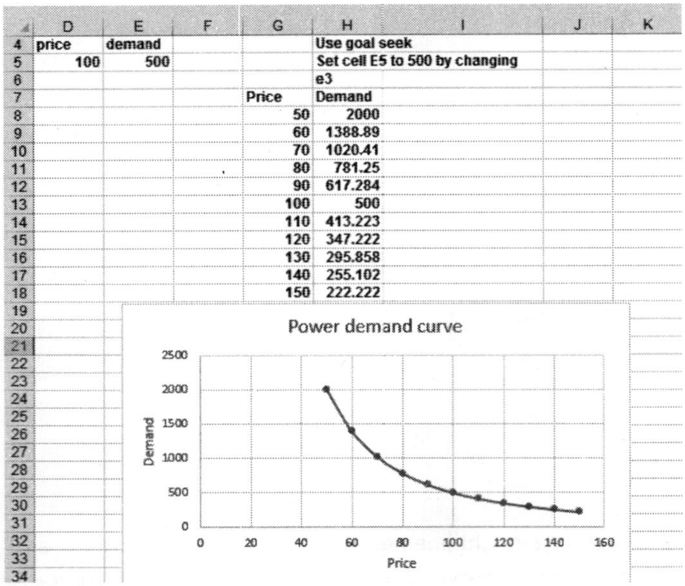

FIGURE 84-2 A power demand curve.

In cell E3, I enter a trial value for *a*. Then, in cell D5, I enter the current price of $100. Because the elasticity of demand equals 2, I know that the demand curve has the form $q=ap^{-2}$, where *a* is unknown. In cell E5, I enter the demand for a price of $100, corresponding to the value of *a* in cell E3, with the formula =a*D5^-2. Now I can use the Goal Seek command (for details, see Chapter 18, "The Goal Seek command") to determine the value of *a* that makes the demand for the price $100 equal to 500 units. I simply set cell E5 to the value 500 by changing cell E3. I find that a value for *a* of 5 million yields a demand of 500 at a price of $100. Thus, the demand curve (graphed in Figure 84-2) is given by $q=5{,}000{,}000p^{-2}$. For any price, the price elasticity of demand on this demand curve equals 2.

What does a demand curve tell us about a customer's willingness to pay for our product?

Let's suppose you are trying to sell a software program to a Fortune 500 company. Let *q* equal the number of copies of the program the company demands, and let *p* equal the price charged for the software. Suppose you have estimated that the demand curve for the software is given by q=400–p. Clearly, your customer is willing to pay less for each additional unit of the software program. Locked inside this demand curve is information about how much the company is willing to pay for each unit of the program. This information is crucial for maximizing your profitability of sales.

Let's rewrite the demand curve as p=400–q. Thus, when q=1, then p=$399, and so on. Now let's try to figure out the value the customer attaches to each of the first two units of the program. Assuming that the customer is rational, the customer will buy a unit if and only if the value of the unit exceeds your price. At a price of $400, the demand equals 0, so the first unit cannot be worth $400. At a price of $399, however, demand equals 1 unit. Therefore, the first unit must be worth something between $399 and $400. Similarly, at a price of $399, the customer does not purchase the second unit. At a price of $398, however, the customer is purchasing two units, so the customer does purchase the second unit. Therefore, the customer values the second unit somewhere between \$399 and \$398.

It can be shown that the best approximation of the value of the *i*th unit purchased by the customer is the price that makes the demand equal to i–0.5. For example, by setting q equal to 0.5, the value of the first unit is 400–0.5=\$399.50. Similarly, by setting q=1.5, the value of the second unit is 400–1.5=\$398.50.

Problems

1. Suppose you are charging \$60 for a board game you invented, and you have sold 3,000 copies during the last year. The elasticity for board games is known to equal 3. Use this information to determine a linear and power demand curve.
2. For each of your answers in Problem 1, determine the value consumers place on the 2,000th unit purchased of your game.

CHAPTER 85

Pricing products by using tie-ins

Question answered in this chapter:

- How does the fact that customers buy razor blades as well as razors affect the profit-maximizing price of razors?

Certain consumer-product purchases frequently result in the purchase of related products, or tie-ins. The following table shows some examples:

Original purchase	Tie-in product
Razor	Razor blades
Men's suit	Shirt and/or tie
Personal computer	Software training manual
Video game console	Video game

Using the techniques I described in Chapter 84, "Estimating a demand curve," it's easy to determine a demand curve for the product that's originally purchased. You can then use Microsoft Excel Solver to determine the original product price that maximizes the sum of the profit earned from the original and the tie-in products. The following example shows how this analysis is done.

Answer to this chapter's question

How does the fact that customers buy razor blades as well as razors affect the profit-maximizing price of razors?

Suppose that you're currently charging $5.00 for a razor and you're selling six million razors. Assume that the variable cost of producing a razor is $2.00. Finally, suppose that the price elasticity of demand for razors is 2. What price should you charge for razors?

Let's assume (incorrectly) that no purchasers of razors buy blades. You determine the demand curve (assuming a linear demand curve), as shown in Figure 85-1. (You can find this data and the chart on the No Blades worksheet in the file Razorsandblades.xlsx.) Two points on the demand curve are price=$5.00, demand=six million razors and price=$5.05 (an increase of 1 percent), demand=5.88 million (2 percent less than six million). After drawing a chart and inserting a linear trendline, as described in Chapter 84, you find the demand curve equation is y=18–2.4x. Because *x* equals price and *y* equals demand, you can write the demand curve for razors as follows: demand (in millions)=18–2.4(price).

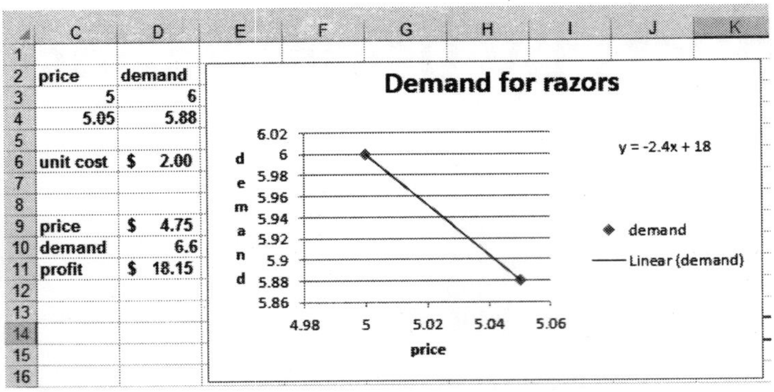

FIGURE 85-1 Determining the profit-maximizing price for razors.

I associate the names in cell C6 and the range C9:C11 with cells D6 and D9:D11. Next, I enter a trial price in D9 and determine the demand for that price in cell D10 with the formula =18-2.4*price. Then, I determine in cell D11 the profit for razors by using the formula =demand*(price–unit_cost).

Next, I use Solver to determine the profit-maximizing price. On the Data tab, click Solver in the Analyze group. The Solver Parameters dialog box is shown in Figure 85-2.

> **Note** If you haven't activated the Solver add-in, click the File tab, click Options, and then click Add-Ins. In the Excel Options dialog box, click the Go button (at the bottom), select Solver Add-In, and then click OK.

I maximize the profit cell (cell D11) by changing the price (cell D9). The model is not linear because the target cell multiplies together two quantities—demand and (price–cost)—each depending on the changing cell. Solver finds that charging $4.75 for a razor maximizes profit. (The maximum profit is $18.15 million.)

Now let's suppose that the average purchaser of a razor buys 50 blades and that you earn $0.15 of profit per blade purchased. How does this change the price you should charge for a razor? Assume that the price of a blade is fixed. (In Problem 3 at the end of the chapter, the blade price changes.) The analysis is in the Blades worksheet, which is shown in Figure 85-3.

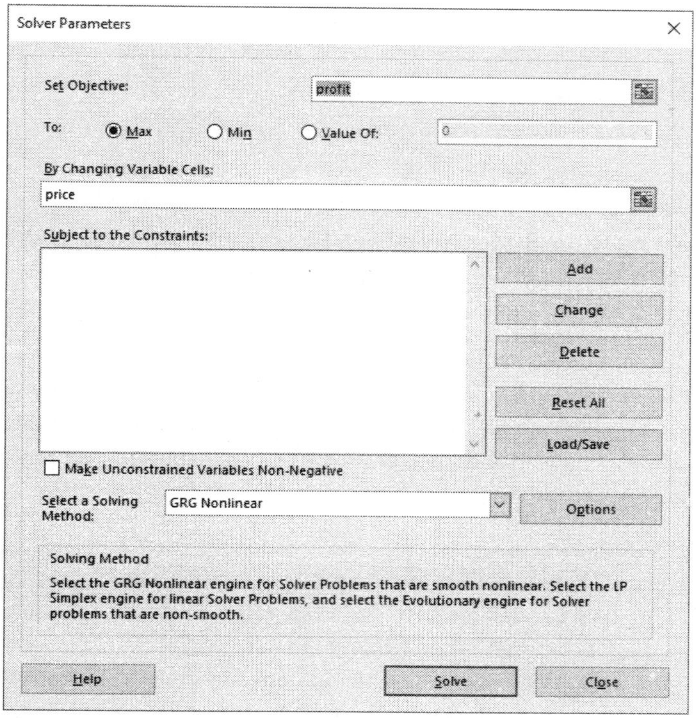

FIGURE 85-2 The Solver Parameters dialog box set up for maximizing your razor profit.

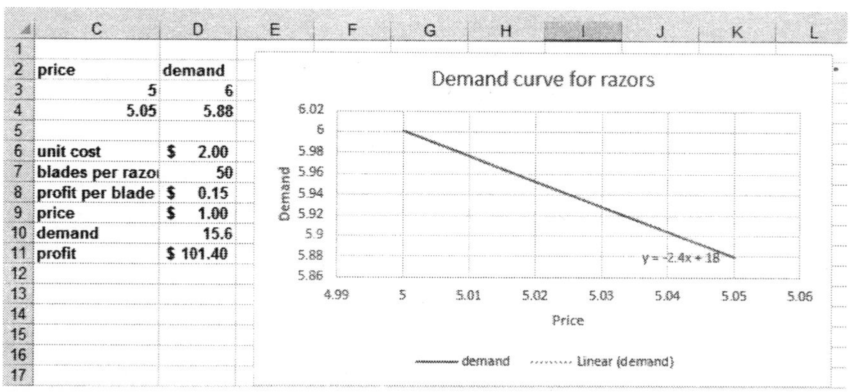

FIGURE 85-3 The price for razors with the blade profit included.

I used the Create From Selection command in the Defined Names group on the Formulas tab to associate the names in cells C6:C11 with cells D6:D11. (For example, cell D10 is named *Demand*.)

> **Note** Astute readers will recall that I also named cell D10 of the No Blades worksheet *Demand*. What does Excel do when you use the range name *Demand* in a formula? Excel simply refers to the cell named *Demand* in the current worksheet. In other words, when you use the range name *Demand* in the Blades worksheet, Excel refers to cell D10 of that worksheet and not to cell D10 in the No Blades worksheet.

In cells D7 and D8 of the Blades worksheet, I entered the relevant information about blades. In D9, I entered a trial price for the razors, and in cell D10 I computed the demand with the formula =18-2.4*price. Next, in cell D11, I computed the total profit from the razors and blades with the formula =demand*(price–unit_cost)+demand*blades_per_razor*profit_per_blade. Notice that demand*blades_per_razor*profit_per_blade is the profit from blades.

The Solver setup is exactly as shown earlier in Figure 85-2: change the price to maximize the profit. Of course, now the profit formula includes the profit earned from blades. Excel shows that the profit is maximized by charging only $1.00 (half the variable cost!) for a razor. This price results from making so much money from blades. You are much better off ensuring that many people have razors, even though you lose $1.00 on each razor sold. Many companies do not understand the importance of the profit from tie-in products. This leads them to overprice their primary product and not maximize their total profit.

Problems

In all the following problems, assume a linear demand curve:

1. You are trying to determine the profit-maximizing price for a video-game console. Currently, you are charging $180 and selling two million consoles per year. It costs $150 to produce a console, and the price elasticity of demand for consoles is 3. What price should you charge for a console?
2. Now, assume that a purchaser of your video-game console buys, on average, 10 video games and you earn $10 profit on each video game. What is the correct price for consoles?
3. In the razor and blade example, suppose the cost to produce a blade is $0.20. If you charge $0.35 for a blade, a customer buys an average of 50 blades. Assume the price elasticity of demand for blades is 3. What price should you charge for a razor and for a blade?
4. You are managing a movie theater that can handle up to 8,000 patrons per week. The current demand, price, and elasticity for ticket sales, popcorn, soda, and candy are given in Figure 85-4. The theater keeps 45 percent of the ticket revenues. The unit cost per ticket, popcorn sales, candy sales, and soda sales are also given. Assuming linear demand curves, how can the

theater maximize profits? Demand for foods is the fraction of patrons who purchase the given food. See Figure 85-4 for the data.

	B	C	D	E	F	G	H	I
2								
3			elasticity	current price	demand	cost	ticket percentage	
4	keep 45%	ticket	3	8	3000	0	0.45	
5		popcorn	1.3	3.5	0.5	0.4		
6		soda	1.5	3	0.6	0.6		
7		candy	2.5	2.5	0.2	1		

FIGURE 85-4 The movie-problem data.

5. A prescription drug is produced in the United States and sold internationally. Each unit of the drug costs $60 to produce. In the German market, you are selling the drug for 150 euros per unit. The current exchange rate is 0.667 US dollars per euro. Current demand for the drug is 100 units, and the estimated elasticity is 2.5. Assuming a linear demand curve, determine the appropriate sales price (in euros) for the drug.

6. Assume the demand for suits at a men's clothing store is linear with a price elasticity of 5. At the current price of $500, 60 suits per week are sold. The cost per suit is $200. Assume that with each suit, a man buys two ties and one shirt. The profit per tie is $15 and the profit per shirt is $25. What price should the store set for a suit?

7. Currently, your local sports-car dealer sells 200 cars per year at a price of $150,000. The dealer's cost of purchasing a car is $60,000. Assume that during a car's lifetime, the dealer makes $25,000 in profits from repair. The annual demand for cars follows a linear demand curve with an elasticity of 4. What price should the dealer charge to maximize the profit from sales and repairs?

CHAPTER 86

Pricing products by using subjectively determined demand

Questions answered in this chapter:

- Sometimes, I don't know the price elasticity for a product. In other situations, I don't believe a linear or power demand curve is relevant. Can I still estimate a demand curve and use Solver to determine a profit-maximizing price?
- How can a small drugstore determine the profit-maximizing price for lipstick?

Answer to this chapter's questions

Sometimes, I don't know the price elasticity for a product. In other situations, I don't believe a linear or power demand curve is relevant. Can I still estimate a demand curve and use Solver to determine a profit-maximizing price?

When you don't know the price elasticity for a product or don't think you can rely on a linear or power demand curve, a good way to determine a product's demand curve is to identify the lowest price and the highest price that seem reasonable. You can then try to estimate the product's demand with the high price, the low price, and a price midway between the high and low prices. Given these three points on the product's demand curve, you can use the Microsoft Excel trendline feature to fit a quadratic demand curve with the following formula (which I'll call *Equation 1*):

$$Demand=a(price)^2+b(price)+c$$

For any three specified points on the demand curve, values of *a*, *b*, and *c* exist that will make Equation 1 exactly fit the three specified points. Because Equation 1 fits three points on the demand curve, it seems reasonable to believe that the equation will give an accurate representation of demand at the other prices. You can then use Equation 1 and Solver to determine the maximum profit, which is given by the formula =(price–unit cost)*demand. The following example shows how this process works.

How can a small drugstore determine the profit-maximizing price for lipstick?

Let's suppose that a drugstore pays $0.90 for each unit of lipstick it orders. The store is considering charging from $1.50 through $2.50 for a unit of lipstick. The store thinks that at a price of $1.50, it will sell 60 units per week. (See Figure 86-1 and the file Lipstickprice.xlsx.) At a price of $2.00, the store thinks it will sell 51 units per week, and at a price of $2.50, 20 units per week. What price should the store charge for lipstick?

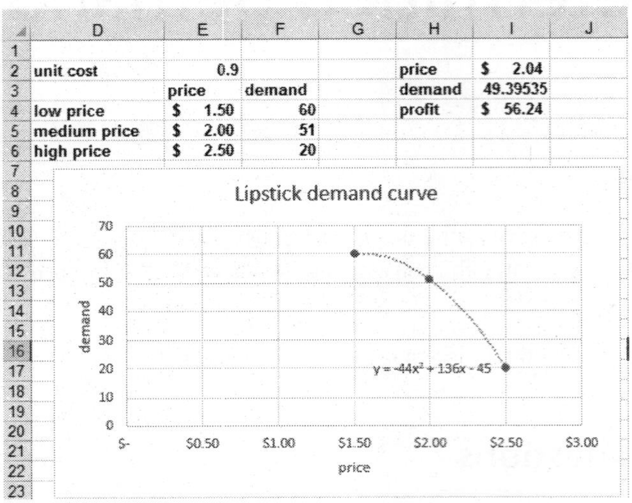

FIGURE 86-1 The lipstick-pricing model.

You begin by entering in the cell range E3:F6 the three points with which you'll chart the demand curve. After selecting E3:F6, in the Charts group on the ribbon's Insert tab, click Insert Scatter (X, Y) Or Bubble Chart, and then select the first option for a scatter chart. You can then right-click a data point and select Add Trendline. In the Format Trendline pane (see Figure 86-2), choose Polynomial and select 2 in the Order box (to obtain a quadratic curve of the form of Equation 1). Then select the option Display Equation On Chart.

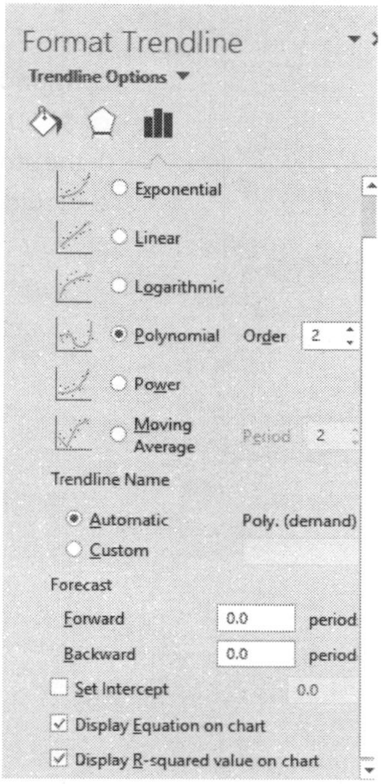

FIGURE 86-2 Configuring the Format Trendline pane for selecting the Polynomial demand curve option.

Excel creates the chart shown earlier in Figure 86-1. The estimated demand curve (*Equation 2*) is Demand=–44*Price^2+136*Price–45.

Next, you insert a trial price in cell I2. You compute the product demand by using Equation 2 in cell I3, with the formula =–44*price^2+136*price–45. (I named cell I2 *Price*.) Then, you compute the weekly profit from lipstick sales in cell I4, with the formula =demand*(price–unit_cost). (Cell E2 is named *Unit_Cost*, and cell I3 is named *Demand*.) Then you use Solver to determine the price that maximizes profit. The Solver Parameters dialog box is shown in Figure 86-3. Note that I constrain the price to be from the lowest through the highest specified prices ($1.50 through $2.50). If you allow Solver to consider prices outside this range, the quadratic demand curve might slope upward, which implies that a higher price would result in larger demand. This result is unreasonable, which is why you should constrain the price.

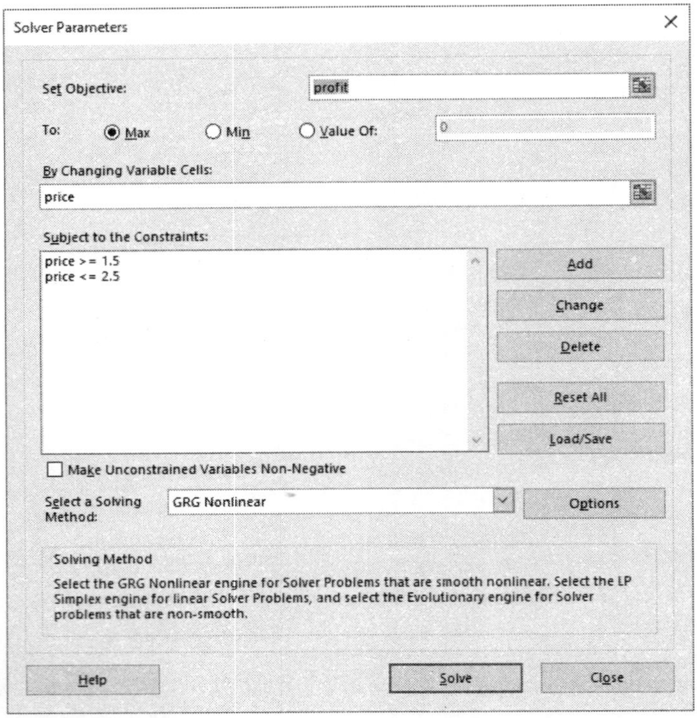

FIGURE 86-3 Configuring the Solver Parameters dialog box to calculate lipstick pricing.

The result is that the drugstore should charge $2.04 for a unit of lipstick. This yields sales of 49.4 units per week and a weekly profit of $56.24.

The approach to pricing outlined in this chapter requires no knowledge of the concept of price elasticity. Inherently, the Solver considers the elasticity for each price when it determines the profit-maximizing price. This approach can easily be applied by organizations that sell thousands of different products. The only data that needs to be specified for each product is its variable cost and the three given points on the demand curve.

Problems

1. Suppose it costs $250 to produce a video-game console. A price from $200 through $400 is under consideration. The estimated demand for the game console is shown in the following table:

Price	Demand (in millions)
$200	2
$300	0.9
$400	0.2

What price should you charge for a game console?

2. This problem uses the demand information given in Problem 1. Each game owner buys an average of 10 video games. You earn $10 profit per video game. What price should you charge for the game console?

3. You are trying to determine the correct price for a new weekly magazine. The variable cost of printing and distributing a copy of the magazine is $0.50. You are thinking of charging from $0.50 through $1.30 per copy. The estimated weekly sales of the magazine are shown in the following table:

Price	Demand (in millions)
$0.50	2
$0.90	1.2
$1.30	0.3

In addition to sales revenue from the magazine, you can charge $30 per 1,000 copies sold for each of the 20 pages of advertising in each week's magazine. What price should you charge for the magazine?

4. A drugstore is trying to determine what price to charge for a candy bar. The drugstore pays 60 cents for each candy bar and is considering charging between $1 and $2 for a candy bar. The estimated weekly demand for three prices is given in the following table. What price should be charged for a candy bar?

Price	Demand
$1.00	88
$1.50	72
$2.00	40

5. Your local women's clothing store pays $200 for a suit. The weekly demand for suits is estimated as follows:

Price	Demand
$250	32
$300	25
$350	23

Assume each woman who buys a suit purchases $80 of additional garments, on which the store earns a 50 percent profit margin. What price should the store set for a suit?

6. Subscribers to my recommendation service get access to recommendations about local workers, such as doctors, plumbers, and so on. I believe the number of new subscribers I obtain each month depends on price, as follows:

Price	Demand
$10	20,000
$20	15,000
$30	6,000

Assume each subscriber remains a subscriber for a year. In addition to subscription fees, I make money when a subscriber clicks an ad. The average subscriber views 10 ads per year. What price will maximize my total revenue?

7. The number of ink-jet printers sold in a week by your local electronics store is estimated to have the following dependence on price:

Price	Demand
$70	128
$100	90
$130	20

The store pays $50 for each ink-jet printer. On average, each person who buys a printer buys 10 cartridges and the store earns $8 profit per cartridge. What printer price maximizes total profit?

CHAPTER 87

Nonlinear pricing

Questions answered in this chapter:

- What is linear pricing?
- What is nonlinear pricing?
- What is bundling, and how can it increase profitability?
- How can I find a profit-maximizing nonlinear pricing plan?

Answers to this chapter's questions

What is linear pricing?

In Chapter 85, "Pricing products by using tie-ins," and Chapter 86, "Pricing products by using subjectively determined demand," I show how to determine a profit-maximizing price for a product. In those chapters' examples, however, I make the implicit assumption that no matter how many units a customer purchases, the customer is charged the same amount per unit. This model is known as linear pricing because the cost of buying *x* units is a straight line function of *x*; namely, cost of *x* units=(unit price)**x*. You will see in this chapter that nonlinear pricing can often greatly increase a company's profit.

What is nonlinear pricing?

A *nonlinear pricing scheme* simply means that the cost of buying *x* units is not a straight-line function of *x*. We have all encountered nonlinear pricing strategies. Here are two examples:

- **Quantity discounts** The first five units might cost $20 each, and the remaining units cost $12 each. Quantity discounts are commonly used by companies selling software and computers. An example of the cost of purchasing *x* units is shown in the Nonlinear Pricing Examples worksheet in the file Nlp.xlsx, which is shown in Figure 87-1. Notice that the graph has a slope of 20 for five or fewer units purchased and a slope of 12 for more than five units purchased.

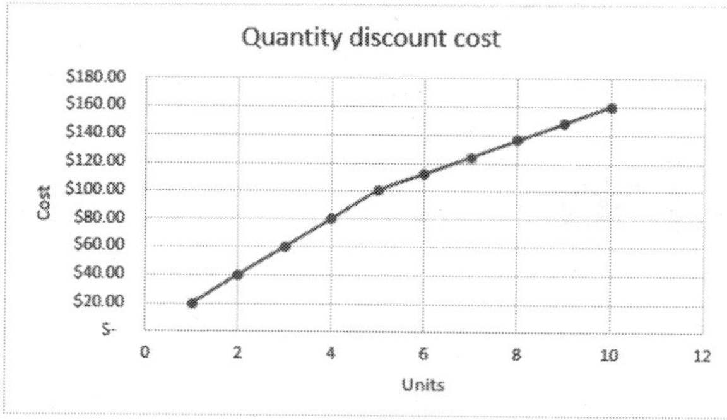

FIGURE 87-1 The cost of a quantity-discount plan.

- **Two-part tariff** When you join a country club, you usually pay a fixed fee for joining the club and then a fee for each round of golf you play. Suppose that your country club charges a membership fee of $500 per year and charges $20 per round of golf. This type of pricing strategy is called a two-part tariff. For this pricing policy, the cost of purchasing a given number of rounds of golf is shown in Figure 87-2. Again, look at the Nonlinear Pricing Examples worksheet in the file Nlp.xlsx. Note that the graph has a slope of 520 from zero through one unit purchased and a slope of 20 for more than one unit purchased. Because a straight line must always have the same slope, you can see that a two-part tariff is highly nonlinear.

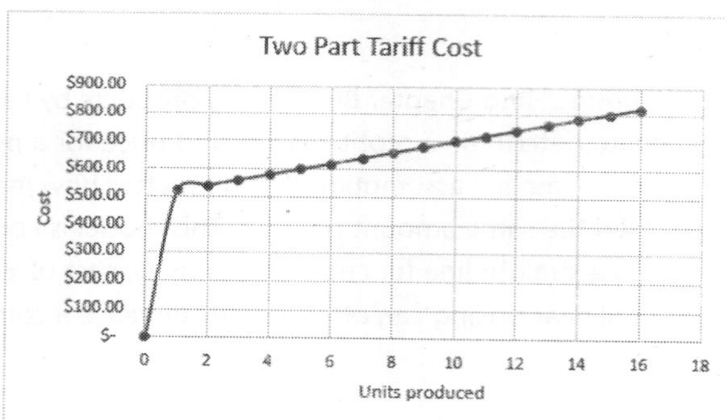

FIGURE 87-2 The cost of a two-part tariff.

What is bundling, and how can it increase profitability?

Price bundling involves offering a customer a set of products for a price less than the sum of the products' individual prices. To analyze why bundling works, you need to understand how a rational consumer makes decisions. For each product combination available, a rational consumer looks at the value of what you are selling and subtracts the cost to purchase it. This yields the *consumer surplus* of the purchase. A rational consumer buys nothing if the consumer surplus of each available option is negative. Otherwise, the consumer purchases the product combination having the largest consumer surplus.

So how can bundling increase your profitability? Suppose that you sell computers and printers and have two customers. The values each customer attaches to a computer and a printer are shown in the following table:

Customer	Computer value	Printer value
1	$1,000	$500
2	$500	$1,000

You offer the computer and printer for sale only separately. By charging $1,000 each for a printer and for a computer, you will sell one printer and one computer and receive $2,000 in revenue. Now suppose that you offer the printer and computer in combination for $1,500. Each customer buys both the computer and the printer, and you receive $3,000 in revenue. By bundling the computer and printer, you can extract more of the consumer's total valuation. Bundling works best if the customer valuations for the bundled products are negatively correlated. In this example, the negative correlation between the values for the bundled products results because the customer who places a high value on a printer places a low value on a computer, and the customer who places a low value on a printer places a high value on a computer.

When you go to a theme park such as Disneyland, you don't buy a ticket for each ride. You buy a ticket to enter the theme park, or you don't go. This is an example of pure bundling because the consumer does not have the option of paying for a subset of the offered products. This approach reduces lines (imagine the longest line at every ride) and also results in more profit.

To see why this bundling approach increases profitability, suppose there is only one customer and that the number of rides the customer wants to go on is governed by a demand curve that is calculated as (Number of rides)=20–2*(Price of ride). From the discussion of demand curves in Chapter 84, "Estimating a demand curve," you know that the value the consumer gives to the *i*th ride is the price that makes demand equal to *i*–0.5. Thus, you know that i–0.5=20–2*(value of ride i) or, solving for the value of ride *i*, that (value of ride i)=10.25–(i/2). The first ride is worth $9.75, the second ride is worth $9.25, and so on to the twentieth ride, which is worth $0.25.

Assume you charge a constant price per ride and that it costs $2 in variable costs per ride. You seek the profit-maximizing linear pricing scheme. In the OnePrice worksheet in the file Nlp.xlsx, shown in Figure 87-3, I show how to determine the profit-maximizing price per ride.

	B	C	D
6	Linear		
7	Pricing		
8		price	$ 6.00
9		Demand	$ 8.00
10		unit cost	$ 2.00
11			
12		profit	$ 32.00

FIGURE 87-3 The profit-maximizing linear pricing scheme.

I associate the range names in C8:C10 with cells D8:D10. I enter a trial price in cell D8 and compute the number of ride tickets purchased in cell D9 with the formula =20–(2*D8). Then I compute profit in cell D12 with the formula =Demand*(price–unit_cost). I can now use Solver to maximize the value in

D12 (profit) by changing cell D8 (price). A price of $6 results in eight ride tickets being purchased, and I earn a maximum profit of $32.

Now let's pretend that you're like Disneyland and offer only a bundle of 20 rides to the customer. You set a price equal to the sum of the customer's valuations for each ride ($9.75+$9.25+...$0.75+$0.25=$100.00). The customer values all 20 rides at $100.00, so the customer will buy a park entry ticket for $100.00. You earn a profit of $100.00–$2.00(20) = $60.00, which almost doubles your profit from linear pricing.

How can I find a profit-maximizing nonlinear pricing plan?

In this section, I'll show how you can determine a profit-maximizing, two-part tariff-pricing plan for the amusement-park example. I'll proceed as follows:

- Hypothesize trial values for the fixed fee and the price per ride.
- Determine the value the customer associates with each ride: Value of ride i=10.5–0.5i.
- Determine the cumulative value associated with buying *i* rides.
- Determine the price charged for *i* rides: Fixed fee + i*(price per ride).
- Determine the consumer surplus for buying *i* rides: Value of i rides–price of i rides.
- Determine the maximum consumer surplus.
- Determine the number of units purchased. If the maximum consumer surplus is negative, no units are purchased. Otherwise, I'll use the MATCH function to find the number of units yielding the maximum surplus.
- Use a VLOOKUP function to look up revenue corresponding to the number of units purchased.
- Compute profit as revenue–costs.
- Use a two-way data table to determine a profit-maximizing fixed fee and price per ride.

See the Two-Part Tariff worksheet in the file Nlp.xlsx, shown in Figure 87-4.

To begin, I named cell F2 *Fixed* and cell F3 *LP*. I entered trial values for the fixed fee and the price per ride in cells F2 and F3. Next, I determine the value the consumer places on each ride by copying from cell E6 to E7:E25 the formula =10.25–(D6/2). I find that the customer places a value of $9.75 on the first ride, $9.25 on the second ride, and so on.

	C	D	E	F	G	H	I	J
1						Units bought	15	
2	cost		fixed fee	$ 56.00		Revenue	$ 93.50	
3	$ 2.00		price per ride	$ 2.50		Prod Cost	$ 30.00	
4					Max surplus	0.25		
5		Unit	Value	Cum Value	Price paid	Surplus		Profit
6		1	9.75	9.75	58.5	-48.75		$ 63.50
7		2	9.25	19	61	-42		
8		3	8.75	27.75	63.5	-35.75		
9		4	8.25	36	66	-30		
10		5	7.75	43.75	68.5	-24.75		
11		6	7.25	51	71	-20		
12		7	6.75	57.75	73.5	-15.75		
13		8	6.25	64	76	-12		
14		9	5.75	69.75	78.5	-8.75		
15		10	5.25	75	81	-6		
16		11	4.75	79.75	83.5	-3.75		
17		12	4.25	84	86	-2		
18		13	3.75	87.75	88.5	-0.75		
19		14	3.25	91	91	0		
20		15	2.75	93.75	93.5	0.25		
21		16	2.25	96	96	0		
22		17	1.75	97.75	98.5	-0.75		
23		18	1.25	99	101	-2		
24		19	0.75	99.75	103.5	-3.75		
25		20	0.25	100	106	-6		

FIGURE 87-4 The determination of an optimal two-part tariff.

To compute the cumulative value of the first *i* rides, I copy from F6 to F7:F25 the formula =SUM($E$6:E6). This formula adds up all values in column E that are in or above the current row. By copying from G6 to G7:G25 the formula =fixed_fee+price_per_ride*D6, I compute the cost of *i* rides. For example, the cost of five rides is $68.50.

Recall that the consumer surplus for *i* rides equals (Value of i rides)–(Cost of i rides). By copying from cell H6 to the range H7:H25 the formula =F6–G6, I compute the consumer's surplus for purchasing any number of rides. For example, the consumer surplus for purchasing five rides is –$24.75, which is the result of the large fixed fee.

In cell H4, I compute the maximum consumer surplus with the formula =MAX(H6:H25). Remember that if the maximum consumer surplus is negative, no units are purchased. Otherwise, the consumer will purchase the number of units yielding the maximum consumer surplus. Therefore, entering in cell I1 the formula =IF(H4>=0,MATCH(H4,H6:H24,0),0), I determine the number of units purchased (in this case, 15). Notice that the MATCH function finds the number of rows I need to move down in the range H6:H24 to find the first match to the maximum surplus.

I now give the range D5:G25 the name *Lookup*. I can then look up the total revenue in the fourth column of this range, based on the number of units purchased (which is already computed in cell I1). The total revenue is computed in cell I2 with the formula =IF(I1=0,0,VLOOKUP(I1,lookup,4)). Notice that if no rides are purchased, I earn no revenue. I compute total production cost for rides purchased in cell I3 with the formula =I1*C3. In cell J6, I compute profit as revenues less costs with the formula =I2–I3.

Now I can use a two-way data table to determine the profit-maximizing combination of fixed fee and price per ride. The data table is shown in Figure 87-5. (Many rows and columns are hidden.) In setting up the data table, I vary the fixed fee between $10.00 and $60.00 (the values in the range K10:K60), and I vary the price per ride between $0.50 and $5.00 (the values in L9:BE9). I recomputed the profit in cell K9 with the formula =J6.

I select the table range (cells K9:BE60), and then on the Data tab, in the Forecast group, I click What-If Analysis and then select Data Table. In the Column Input Cell box, select F2 (the fixed fee), and in the Row Input Cell box, select F3 (the price per ride). Clicking OK in the Data Table dialog box computes the profit for each fixed fee and the price per ride combination represented in the data table.

	J	K	L	M	N	AE	AF	BB	BC	BD	BE
5	Profit				Max Profit						
6	$ 63.50				$ 63.50						
7											
8			Unit	cost							
9		$ 63.50	0.5	0.6	0.7	2.4	2.5	4.7	4.8	4.9	5
10		10	-18.5	-17	-14.7	16	17.5	39.7	38	39	40
11		11	-17.5	-16	-13.7	17	18.5	40.7	39	40	41
12		12	-16.5	-15	-12.7	18	19.5	41.7	40	41	42
13		13	-15.5	-14	-11.7	19	20.5	42.7	41	42	43
14		14	-14.5	-13	-10.7	20	21.5	43.7	42	43	44
15		15	-13.5	-12	-9.7	21	22.5	44.7	43	44	45
16		16	-12.5	-11	-8.7	22	23.5	45.7	44	45	46
17		17	-11.5	-9.6	-7.7	23	24.5	46.7	45	46	47
18		18	-10.5	-8.6	-6.7	24	25.5	47.7	46	47	48
19		19	-9.5	-7.6	-5.7	25	26.5	48.7	47	48	49
20		20	-8.5	-6.6	-4.7	26	27.5	49.7	48	49	50
21		21	-7.5	-5.6	-3.7	27	28.5	50.7	49	50	51
22		22	-6.5	-4.6	-2.7	28	29.5	51.7	50	51	52
23		23	-5.5	-3.6	-1.7	29	30.5	52.7	51	52	53
24		24	-4.5	-2.6	-0.7	30	31.5	53.7	52	53	54
25		25	-3.5	-1.6	0.3	31	32.5	54.7	53	54	55
49	Fixed	49	20.5	22.4	24.3	55	56.5	0	0	0	0
50	cost	50	21.5	23.4	25.3	56	57.5	0	0	0	0
51		51	22.5	24.4	26.3	57	58.5	0	0	0	0
52		52	23.5	25.4	27.3	58	59.5	0	0	0	0
53		53	24.5	26.4	28.3	59	60.5	0	0	0	0
54		54	25.5	27.4	29.3	60	61.5	0	0	0	0
55		55	26.5	28.4	30.3	61	62.5	0	0	0	0
56		56	27.5	29.4	31.3	62	63.5	0	0	0	0
57		57	28.5	30.4	32.3	63	0	0	0	0	0
58		58	29.5	31.4	33.3	0	0	0	0	0	0
59		59	30.5	32.4	34.3	0	0	0	0	0	0
60		60	31.5	33.4	35.3	0	0	0	0	0	0

FIGURE 87-5 A two-way data table computing an optimal two-part tariff.

To highlight the profit-maximizing two-part tariff, I used conditional formatting, selecting the range L10:BE60. Click Conditional Formatting on the Home tab (in the Styles group), click Top/Bottom Rules, and then click Top 10 Items**.** Then, change the 10 in the dialog box to a 1 so that only the largest profit is formatted. Here, a fixed fee of $56.00 and a price per ride of $2.50 earns a profit of $63.50, which almost doubles the profit from linear pricing. A fixed fee of $59.00 and a price per ride of $2.30 also yields a profit of $63.50.

Because a quantity-discount plan involves selecting three variables (cutoff, high price, and low price), you cannot use a data table to determine a profit-maximizing quantity-discount plan. You might think you could use a Solver model (with changing cells set to cutoff, high price, and low price) to determine a profit-maximizing quantity-discount strategy. Before Excel 2010, Solver often had difficulty determining optimal solutions when the target cell is computed by using formulas containing IF statements. Excel 2016 Solver handles the quantity-discount problem with ease, even with the use of IF statements. In the file Qd.xlsx (see Figure 87-6), I used the Evolutionary Solver engine to find the profit-maximizing quantity-discount plan. I assumed that all units bought up to a cutoff (called *CUT*) are sold at a high price (called *HP*) and that the remaining items are sold at a low price (called *LP*).

The only change in the spreadsheet setup is in column G. After giving cells F1:F3 the names in E1:E3, I compute the amount a person would pay to buy any number of units by copying from G6 to G7:G25 the formula =IF(D6<=Cut,D6*HP,HP*Cut+(D6-Cut)*LP). The Solver Parameters dialog box setup is shown in Figure 87-7. As I described in Chapter 36, "Warehouse location and the GRG Multistart and Evolutionary Solver engines," I use Evolutionary Solver here because the model uses IF statements that involve changing cells. I also changed the Mutation Rate under the Evolutionary Solver options to 0.5. Note that I constrained the cutoff point to be an integer and used an upper bound of $20 for all the changing cells. Of course, if Solver had chosen a price near $20, I would have relaxed the upper bound on the price-changing cells.

Solver found a maximum profit of $63.97, obtained by charging $18.48 for the first four units purchased and $1.84 for the remaining units. The customers will buy 16 units. If I had run Solver longer, it would have found the true maximum profit, which is $64.00.

	C	D	E	F	G	H	I	J
1			Cut	4		Units bought	16	
2	cost		HP	$ 18.48		Revenue	$ 95.97	
3	$ 2.00		LP	$ 1.84		Prod Cost	$ 32.00	
4					Max surplus	0.03156491		
5		Unit	Value	Cum Value	Price paid	Surplus		Profit
6		1	9.75	9.75	18.48110027	-8.731100274		$ 63.97
7		2	9.25	19	36.96220055	-17.96220055		
8		3	8.75	27.75	55.44330082	-27.69330082		
9		4	8.25	36	73.9244011	-37.9244011		
10		5	7.75	43.75	75.76140393	-32.01140393		
11		6	7.25	51	77.59840676	-26.59840676		
12		7	6.75	57.75	79.4354096	-21.6854096		
13		8	6.25	64	81.27241243	-17.27241243		
14		9	5.75	69.75	83.10941526	-13.35941526		
15		10	5.25	75	84.94641809	-9.946418094		
16		11	4.75	79.75	86.78342093	-7.033420926		
17		12	4.25	84	88.62042376	-4.620423759		
18		13	3.75	87.75	90.45742659	-2.707426592		
19		14	3.25	91	92.29442942	-1.294429425		
20		15	2.75	93.75	94.13143226	-0.381432257		
21		16	2.25	96	95.96843509	0.03156491		
22		17	1.75	97.75	97.80543792	-0.055437923		
23		18	1.25	99	99.64244076	-0.642440755		
24		19	0.75	99.75	101.4794436	-1.729443588		
25		20	0.25	100	103.3164464	-3.316446421		

FIGURE 87-6 Using Solver to find the profit-maximizing quantity-discount plan.

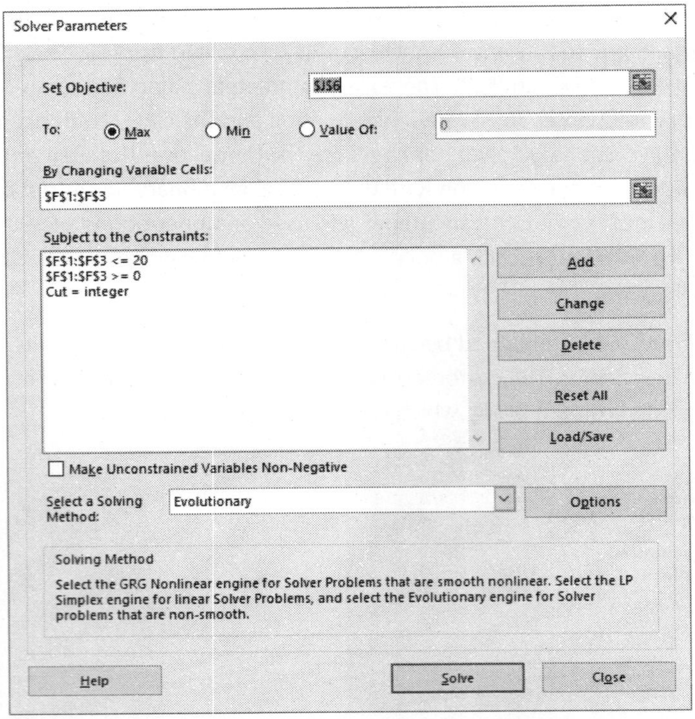

FIGURE 87-7 The Solver settings for maximizing a quantity-discount plan.

Problems

You own a small country club and have three types of customers who value each round of golf they play during a month as shown in the following table:

Round no.	Customer type 1	Customer type 2	Customer type 3
1	$60	$50	$40
2	$50	$45	$30
3	$40	$30	$20
4	$30	$15	$10
5	$20	$0	$0
6	$10	$0	$0

1. Find a profit-maximizing two-part tariff.
2. Suppose you are going to offer a pure bundle. For example, a member can play up to five rounds of golf for $60 per month. The member has no option to choose from other than the pure bundle. What pure bundle maximizes your profit?

CHAPTER 88

Array formulas and functions

Questions answered in this chapter:

- What is an array formula?
- How do I interpret formulas such as (D2:D7)*(E2:E7) and SUM(D2:D7*E2:E7)?
- I have a list of names in one column. These names change often. Is there an easy way to transpose the listed names to one row so that changes in the original column of names are reflected in the new row?
- I have a list of monthly stock returns. Is there a way to determine the number of returns from –30 percent through –20 percent, –10 percent through 0 percent, and so on that will automatically update if I change the original data?
- Can I write one formula that will sum the second digit of a list of integers?
- Is there a way to look at two lists of names and determine which names occur on both lists?
- Can I write a formula that averages all numbers in a list that are greater than or equal to the list's median value?
- I have a sales database for a small makeup company that lists the salesperson, product, units sold, and dollar amount for every transaction. I know I can use database statistical functions or COUNTIFS, SUMIFS, and AVERAGEIFS to summarize this data, but can I also use array functions to summarize the data and answer questions such as how many units of makeup a salesperson sold, how many units of lipstick were sold, and how many units were sold by a specific salesperson?
- What are array constants, and how can I use them?
- How do I edit array formulas?
- Given quarterly revenues for a toy store, can I estimate the trend and seasonality of the store's revenues?
- Given a list of transactions in different countries/regions, how can I calculate the median size of a transaction in each country/region?
- Given unit sales transactions broken down by person, product, and location, can I determine the standard deviation of units sold for each person-product-location combination?

Answers to this chapter's questions

What is an array formula?

Array formulas often provide a shortcut or more efficient approach to performing complex calculations with Microsoft Excel. An array formula can return a result in either one cell or in a range of cells. Array formulas perform operations on two or more sets of values, called *array arguments*. Each array argument used in an array formula must contain exactly the same number of rows and columns.

When you enter an array formula, you must first select the range in which you want Excel to place the array formula's results. Then, after entering the formula in the first cell of the selected range, you must press Ctrl+Shift+Enter. If you fail to press Ctrl+Shift+Enter, you'll obtain incorrect or nonsensical results. I refer to the process of entering an array formula and then pressing Ctrl+Shift+Enter as *array-entering* a formula.

Excel also contains a variety of array functions. In Chapter 42, "Summarizing data by using descriptive statistics," I discuss the array function MODE.MULT. You met two array functions (LINEST and TREND) in Chapter 57, "Introduction to multiple regression," and Chapter 58, "Incorporating qualitative factors into multiple regression." As with an array formula, to use an array function you must first select the range in which you want the function's results placed. Then, after entering the function in the first cell of the selected range, you must press Ctrl+Shift+Enter. In this chapter, I'll introduce you to three other useful array functions: TRANSPOSE, FREQUENCY, and LOGEST.

As you'll see, you cannot delete any part of a cell range that contains results computed with an array formula. Also, you cannot paste an array formula into a range that contains both blank cells and array formulas. For example, if you have an array formula in cell C10 and you want to copy it to the cell range C10:J15, you cannot simply copy the formula to this range because the range contains both blank cells and the array formula in cell C10. To work around this difficulty, copy the formula from C10 to the cells D10:J10 on row 10, and then copy the contents of C10:J10 to C11:J15. (You create the top row of data first.)

The best way to learn how array formulas and functions work is by looking at some examples, so let's get started.

How do I interpret formulas such as (D2:D7)*(E2:E7) and SUM(D2:D7*E2:E7)?

In the Total Wages worksheet in the file Arrays.xlsx, I list the number of hours worked and the hourly wage rates for six employees, as you can see in Figure 88-1.

	C	D	E	F	G
1		Hours	wage rate	total owed each person	grand total owed
2	John	3	$ 6.00	$ 18.00	$ 295.00
3	Jack	4	$ 7.00	$ 28.00	
4	Jill	5	$ 8.00	$ 40.00	
5	Jane	8	$ 9.00	$ 72.00	
6	Jean	6	$ 10.00	$ 60.00	
7	Jocelyn	7	$ 11.00	$ 77.00	

FIGURE 88-1 Using array formulas to compute hourly wages.

If you want to compute each person's total wages, you could simply copy from F2 to F3:F7 the formula =D3*E3. There is certainly nothing wrong with that approach, but using an array formula provides a more elegant solution. Begin by selecting the range F2:F7, where you want to compute each person's total earnings. Then enter the formula =(D2:D7*E2:E7) and press Ctrl+Shift+Enter. You will see that each person's total wages are correctly computed. Also, if you look at the Formula bar, you'll see that the formula appears as {=(D2:D7*E2:E7)}. The curly brackets are the way Excel tells you that you've created an array formula. (You don't enter the curly brackets that show up at the beginning and end of an array formula; they are created automatically by Excel. But to indicate that a formula is an array formula in this chapter, I'll show the curly brackets.)

To see how this formula works, click in the Formula bar, highlight D2:D7 in the formula, and then press F9. You will see {3;4;5;8;6;7}, which is the way Excel creates the cell range D2:D7 as an array. Now select E2:E7 in the Formula bar, and then press F9 again. You will see {6;7;8;9;10;11}, which is the way Excel creates an array corresponding to the range E2:E7. The inclusion of the asterisk (*) tells Excel to multiply the corresponding elements in each array. Because the cell ranges being multiplied include six cells each, Excel creates arrays with six items, and because you selected a range of six cells, each person's total wage is displayed in its own cell. Had you selected a range of only five cells, the sixth item in the array would not be displayed.

Suppose you want to compute the total wages earned by all employees. One approach is to use the formula =SUMPRODUCT(D2:D7,E2:E7). Again, however, let's try to create an array formula to compute total wages. Begin by selecting one cell (I choose cell G2) in which to place the result. Then enter in cell G2 the formula {=SUM(D2:D7*E2:E7)}. After pressing Ctrl+Shift+Enter, you obtain (3)(6)+(4)(7)+(5)(8)+(8)(9)+(6)(10)+(7)(11)=295. To see how this formula works, select the D2:D7*E2:E7 portion in the Formula bar, and then press F9. You will see =SUM({18;28;40;72;60;77}), which shows that Excel created a six-element array whose first element is 3*6(18), whose second element is 4*7(28), and so on, until the last element, which is 7*11 (77). (After you press F9, the curly brackets are only around the selected section and no longer around the entire formula.) Excel then adds up the values in the array to obtain the total of $295.00.

I have a list of names in one column. These names change often. Is there an easy way to transpose the listed names to one row so that changes in the original column of names are reflected in the new row?

In the Transpose worksheet in the file Arrays.xlsx, shown in Figure 88-2, I've listed a set of names in cells A4:A8. The goal is to list these names in one row (the cell range C3:G3). If you knew that the original list of names would never change, you could accomplish this goal by copying the cell range and then using the Transpose option in the Paste Special dialog box. (See Chapter 14, "The Paste Special command," for details.) Unfortunately, if the names in column A change, the names in row 3 would not reflect those changes if you use Paste Special, Transpose. What you need in this situation is the TRANSPOSE function.

	A	B	C	D	E	F	G
3			Julie	Jason	Jack	Jill	Jane
4	Julie						
5	Jason						
6	Jack						
7	Jill						
8	Jane						

FIGURE 88-2 Using the TRANSPOSE function.

The TRANSPOSE function is an array function that changes the rows of a selected range into columns, and vice versa. To begin using TRANSPOSE in this example, you select the range C3:G3, where you want the transposed list of names to be placed. Then, in cell C3, you array-enter the formula {=TRANSPOSE(A4:A8)}. The list of names is now displayed in one row. More important, if you change any of the names in A4:A8, the corresponding name will change in the transposed range.

I have a list of monthly stock returns. Is there a way to determine the number of returns from –30 percent through –20 percent, –10 percent through 0 percent, and so on that will automatically update if I change the original data?

This problem is a job for the FREQUENCY array function. The FREQUENCY function counts how many values in an array (called the *data array*) occur within given value ranges (specified by a *bin array*). The syntax of the FREQUENCY function is FREQUENCY(data array,bin array).

To illustrate the use of the FREQUENCY function, look at the Frequency worksheet in the Arrays.xlsx file, shown in Figure 88-3. I list monthly stock returns for a fictitious stock in the cell range A4:A77.

I find in cells A1:B1 and A2:B2 (using the MIN and MAX functions) that all returns are from –44 percent through 53 percent. Based on this information, I set up bin value boundaries in cells C7:C17, starting at –0.4 and ending at 0.6. Now I select the range D7:D18, where I want the results of the FREQUENCY function to be placed. In this range, cell D7 counts the number of data points less than or equal to –0.4, D8 counts the number of data points greater than –0.4 and less than or equal to –0.3, and so on. Cell D17 counts all data points greater than 0.5 and less than or equal to 0.6, and cell D18 counts all the data points that are greater than 0.6.

	A	B	C	D
1	min	-43.84%		
2	max	52.56%		
3	Returns			
4	43.81%			Total
5	-8.30%			74
6	-25.12%		Bin values	
7	-43.84%		-0.4	1
8	-8.64%		-0.3	1
9	49.98%		-0.2	2
10	-1.19%		-0.1	5
11	46.74%		0	13
12	31.94%		0.1	11
13	-35.34%		0.2	13
14	29.28%		0.3	12
15	-1.10%		0.4	11
16	-10.67%		0.5	4
17	-12.77%		0.6	1
18	19.17%			0

FIGURE 88-3 Using the FREQUENCY function.

In cell D7, I enter the formula {=FREQUENCY(A4:A77,C7:C17)} and then press Ctrl+Shift+Enter. This formula tells Excel to count the number of data points in A4:A77 (the data array) that lie in each of the bin ranges defined in C7:C17. The results show that one return is greater than −0.4 and less than or equal to −0.3. Thirteen returns are greater than 0.1 and less than or equal to 0.2. If you change any of the data points in the data array, the results generated by the FREQUENCY function in cells D7:D17 will reflect the changes in your data. If you had made the source data for the FREQUENCY function into a table, then the FREQUENCY function would have picked up any new data added to the table.

Can I write one formula that will sum the second digit of a list of integers?

In the cell range A4:A10 in the Sum Up 2nd Digit worksheet in the file Arrays.xlsx, I listed seven integers. (See Figure 88-4.) I would like to write one formula that sums the second digit of each number. I could obtain this sum by copying from B4 to B5:B10 the formula =VALUE(MID(A4,2,1)). This formula returns (as a numerical value) the second character in cell A4. Then I could add up the range B4:B10 and obtain the total of 27.

C7 | {=SUM(VALUE(MID

	A	B	C	D	E
1		Total			
2		27			
3					
4	140	4			
5	85	5			
6	76	6			
7	1610	6	27		Error trapped
8	302	0			27
9	434	3			
10	13	3			
11	1	#VALUE!			

FIGURE 88-4 Summing the second digits in a set of integers.

An array function makes this process much easier. Simply select cell C7 and array-enter the formula {=SUM(VALUE(MID(A4:A10,2,1)))}. Your array formula will return the correct answer, 27.

To see what this formula does, highlight MID(A4:A10,2,1) in the Formula bar, and then press F9. You will see {"4";"5";"6";"6";"0";"3";"3"}. This string of values shows that Excel has created an array consisting of the second digit (viewed as text) in the cell range A4:A10. The VALUE portion of the formula changes these text strings into numerical values, which are added up by the SUM portion of the formula.

Notice that in cell A11, I enter a number with one digit (1). Because this number has no second digit, the MID portion of my formula returns #VALUE. How can you modify this array formula to account for the possible inclusion of one-digit integers? Simply array-enter in cell E8 the formula {=SUM(IF(LEN(A4:A11)>=2,VALUE(MID(A4:A11,2,1)),0))}. This formula replaces any one-digit integer with a 0, so you still obtain the correct sum.

Is there a way to look at two lists of names and determine which names occur on both lists?

In the Matching Names worksheet (on the far left) in the file Arrays.xlsx file, I include two lists of names (in columns D and E), as you can see in Figure 88-5. Here, you want to determine which names on List 1 also appear on List 2. To accomplish this, you select the range C5:C28 and array-enter in cell C5 the formula {=MATCH(D5:D28,E5:E28,0)}. This formula loops through the cells C5:C28. In cell C5, the formula verifies whether the name in D5 has a match in column E. If a match exists, the formula returns the position of the first match in E5:E28. If no match exists, the formula returns #NA (for not available). Similarly, in cell C6, the formula verifies whether the second name on List 1 has a match. You see, for example, that Artest does not appear on the second list but Harrington does. (It is first matched in the second cell in the range E5:E28.)

	B	C	D	E
4			List 1	List 2
5	NO	#N/A	Artest	BMiller
6	NO	#N/A	Artest	Harrington
7	YES	2	Harrington	BMiller
8	NO	#N/A	Artest	Harrington
9	NO	#N/A	Artest	Harrington
10	NO	#N/A	Artest	BMiller
11	YES	2	Harrington	BMiller
12	NO	#N/A	Artest	Mercer
13	NO	#N/A	Artest	Harrington
14	NO	#N/A	Artest	Harrington
15	YES	8	Mercer	BMiller
16	NO	#N/A	Artest	Mercer
17	NO	#N/A	O'Neal	RMiller
18	NO	#N/A	O'Neal	BMiller
19	NO	#N/A	O'Neal	RMiller
20	NO	#N/A	O'Neal	RMiller
21	YES	13	RMiller	BMiller
22	NO	#N/A	O'Neal	RMiller
23	NO	#N/A	O'Neal	RMiller
24	YES	13	RMiller	BMiller
25	NO	#N/A	O'Neal	Mercer
26	NO	#N/A	O'Neal	BMiller
27	NO	#N/A	O'Neal	RMiller
28	NO	#N/A	O'Neal	BMiller

FIGURE 88-5 Finding duplicates in two lists.

To enter *Yes* for each name in List 1 with a match in List 2, and *No* for each List 1 name without a match, select the cell range B5:B28 and array-enter the formula {IF(ISERROR(C5:C28),"No","Yes")} in cell B5. This formula displays No in column B, for each cell in C5:C28 containing the #NA message and Yes for all cells in column C that return a numerical value. Note that the formula =ISERROR(x) yields True if the formula *x* evaluates to an error, and it yields False otherwise.

Can I write a formula that averages all numbers in a list that are greater than or equal to the list's median value?

In the Average Those > Median worksheet in the Arrays.xlsx file, shown in Figure 88-6, the range D5:D785 (named *Prices*) contains a list of prices. I'd like to average all prices that are at least as large as the median price. In cell F2, I compute the median with the formula =MEDIAN(prices). In cell F3, I compute the average of numbers greater than or equal to the median by entering the formula =SUMIF(prices,">="&F2,prices)/COUNTIF(prices,">="&F2). This formula adds up all prices that are at least as large as the median value (243), and then it divides by the number of prices that are at least as large as the median. The average of all prices at least as large as the median price is $324.30.

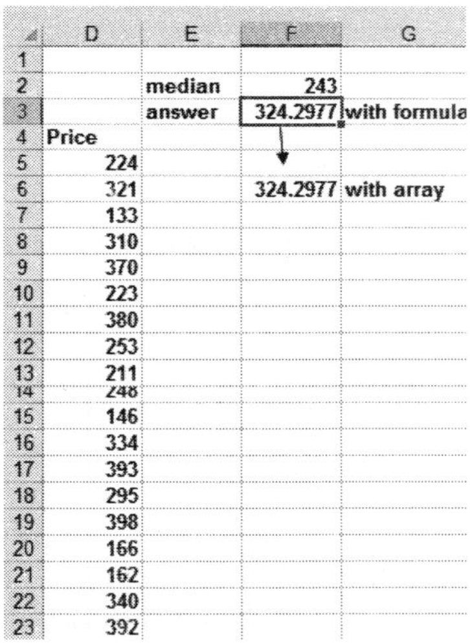

	D	E	F	G
1				
2		median	243	
3		answer	324.2977	with formula
4	Price			
5	224			
6	321		324.2977	with array
7	133			
8	310			
9	370			
10	223			
11	380			
12	253			
13	211			
14	248			
15	146			
16	334			
17	393			
18	295			
19	398			
20	166			
21	162			
22	340			
23	392			

FIGURE 88-6 Averaging prices that are at least as large as the median price.

An easier approach is to select cell F6 and array-enter the following formula:

```
{=AVERAGE(IF(prices>=MEDIAN(prices),prices,""))}
```

This formula creates an array that contains the row's price if the row's price is greater than or equal to the median price or a space otherwise. Averaging this array gives you the results you want.

I have a sales database for a small makeup company that lists the salesperson, product, units sold, and dollar amount for every transaction. I know I can use database statistical functions or COUNTIFS, SUMIFS, and AVERAGEIFS to summarize this data, but can I also use array functions to summarize the data and answer questions such as how many units of makeup a salesperson sold, how many units of lipstick were sold, and how many units were sold by a specific salesperson?

The Makeuparray.xlsx file contains a list of 1,900 sales transactions made by a makeup company. For each transaction, the transaction number, salesperson, transaction date, product sold, units sold, and dollar volume are listed. You can see some of the data in Figure 88-7.

	I	J	K	L	M	N
4	Trans Number	Name	Date	Product	Units	Dollars
5	1	Betsy	4/1/2004	lip gloss	45	$ 137.20
6	2	Hallagan	3/10/2004	foundation	50	$ 152.01
7	3	Ashley	2/25/2005	lipstick	9	$ 28.72
8	4	Hallagan	5/22/2006	lip gloss	55	$ 167.08
9	5	Zaret	6/17/2004	lip gloss	43	$ 130.60
10	6	Colleen	11/27/2005	eye liner	58	$ 175.99
11	7	Cristina	3/21/2004	eye liner	8	$ 25.80
12	8	Colleen	12/17/2006	lip gloss	72	$ 217.84
13	9	Ashley	7/5/2006	eye liner	75	$ 226.64
14	10	Betsy	8/7/2006	lip gloss	24	$ 73.50
15	11	Ashley	11/29/2004	mascara	43	$ 130.84
16	12	Ashley	11/18/2004	lip gloss	23	$ 71.03
17	13	Emilee	8/31/2005	lip gloss	49	$ 149.59
18	14	Hallagan	1/1/2005	eye liner	18	$ 56.47
19	15	Zaret	9/20/2006	foundation	-8	$ (21.99
20	16	Emilee	4/12/2004	mascara	45	$ 137.39
21	17	Colleen	4/30/2006	mascara	66	$ 199.65
22	18	Jen	8/31/2005	lip gloss	88	$ 265.19
23	19	Jen	10/27/2004	eye liner	78	$ 236.15
24	20	Zaret	11/27/2005	lip gloss	57	$ 173.12
25	21	Zaret	6/2/2006	mascara	12	$ 38.08
26	22	Betsy	9/24/2004	eye liner	28	$ 86.51

FIGURE 88-7 The makeup database.

This data can easily be summarized by using database statistical functions, as I described in Chapter 48, "Summarizing data with database statistical functions," or by using the COUNTIFS and SUMIFS functions. (See Chapter 20, "The COUNTIF, COUNTIFS, COUNT, COUNTA, and COUNTBLANK functions," and Chapter 21, "The SUMIF, AVERAGEIF, SUMIFS, and AVERAGEIFS functions"). As you'll see in this section, array functions provide an easy, powerful alternative to these functions. The following questions explain the data:

- **How many units of makeup did Jen sell?** You can easily answer this question by using the SUMIF function. In this worksheet, I name the cell range J5:J1904 *Name* and the cell range M5:M1904 *Units*. I enter in cell E7 the formula SUMIF(Name,"Jen",Units) to sum up all the units sold by Jen. The total is 9,537 units. You can also answer this question by array-entering in cell E6 the formula {=SUM(IF(J5:J1904="Jen",M5:M1904,0))}. This formula creates an array that contains the units sold for a transaction made by Jen and a 0 for all other transactions. Therefore, summing this array also yields the number of units sold by Jen, which is 9,537, as you can see in Figure 88-8.

	A	B	C	D	E	F	G
4							
5					units sold by jen	units lipstick sold by jen	units sold by Jen or lipstick
6				Array function	9537	1299	17061
7				other functions	9537	1299	17061
8							
9					Name	Product	
10					Jen	lipstick	
11							
12					Name	Product	
13					Jen		
14						lipstick	
15							
16		eye liner	foundation	lip gloss	lipstick	mascara	
17	Ashley	1920	1373	1985	1066	2172	
18	Betsy	1987	2726	1857	1305	1582	
19	Cici	1960	2031	1701	1035	2317	
20	Colleen	1107	2242	1831	765	2215	
21	Cristina	1770	1729	1734	788	1790	
22	Emilee	2490	1803	1725	720	1545	
23	Hallagan	2288	2387	1840	1045	1873	
24	Jen	2302	1883	1792	1299	2261	
25	Zaret	2715	2117	1868	800	1268	

FIGURE 88-8 Summarizing data with array formulas.

- **How many units of lipstick did Jen sell?** This question requires a criterion that uses two columns (Name and Product). You can answer this question by using the database statistical function formula =DSUM(J4:N1904,4,E9:F10), which is entered in cell F7. This formula shows that Jen sold 1,299 units of lipstick. You can also obtain this answer by using the array-entered formula in cell F6, {=SUM((J5:J1904="jen")*(L5:L1904="lipstick")*M5:M1904)}.

  To understand this formula, you need to know a bit about Boolean arrays. The portion of this formula that reads (J5:J1904="jen") creates a Boolean array. For each entry in J5:J1904 that equals Jen, the array includes the value True, and for each entry in J5:J1904 that does not equal Jen, the array contains False. Similarly, the portion of this formula (L5:L1904="lipstick") creates a Boolean array with a True corresponding to each cell in the range that contains the word *lipstick* and a False corresponding to each cell in the range that does not. When Boolean arrays are multiplied, another array is created using the following rules:

  - True*True=1
  - True*False=0
  - False*True=0
  - False*False=0

  In short, multiplying the Boolean arrays mimics the AND operator. Multiplying the product of the Boolean arrays by the values in the range M5:M1904 creates a new array. In any row in which Jen sold lipstick, this array contains the units sold. In all other rows, this array contains a 0. Summing this array yields Jen's total lipstick sales (1,299).

- **How many units were sold by Jen or were lipstick?** In cell G7, I use the database statistical function =DSUM(J4:N1904,4,E12:F14) to find that all units that were sold by Jen or that were lipstick total 17,061. In cell G6, I compute the number of units that were sold by Jen or that were lipstick by array-entering the formula {=SUM(IF((J5:J1904="jen")+(L5:L1904="lipstick"),1,0)*M5:M1904)}.

Again, the portion of this formula that reads (J5:J1904="jen")+(L5:L1904="lipstick") creates two Boolean arrays. The first array contains True if and only if Jen (the formula is not case sensitive) is the salesperson. The second array contains True if and only if the product sold is lipstick. When Boolean arrays are added, the following rules are used:

- False+True=1
- True+True=1
- True+False=1
- False+False=0

In short, adding Boolean arrays mimics the OR operator. Therefore, this formula creates an array in which each row where Jen is the salesperson or lipstick is the product sold has the number of units sold multiplied by 1. In any other row, the number of units sold is multiplied by 0. The same result is obtained as with the database statistical formula (17,061).

- **Can I summarize the number of units of each product sold by each salesperson?** Array formulas make it easy to answer this question. You begin by listing each salesperson's name in the cell range A17:A25 and each product name in the cell range B16:F16. Now you array-enter in cell B17 the formula {=SUM(($J$5:$J$1904=$A17)*($L$5:$L$1904=B$16)*$M$5:$M$1904)}.

  This formula counts only units of eyeliner sold by Ashley (1,920 units). By copying this formula to the cell range C17:F17, I compute the units of each product sold by Ashley. Next, I copy the formulas in B17:F17 to B18:F25 and compute the number of units of each product sold by each salesperson. Notice that I add a dollar sign to *A* in the reference to cell A17 so that I always pull the person's name, and I add a dollar sign to the 16 in the reference to cell B16 so that I always pull the product.

> **Note** Astute readers might ask why I simply don't select the formula in cell B17 and try to copy it in one step to fill in the table. Remember that you cannot paste an array formula into a range that contains both blank cells and array formulas, which is why I first copy the formula in cell B17 to the cell range C17:F17 and then drag it down to complete the table.

What are array constants, and how can I use them?

You can create your own arrays and use them in array formulas. Simply enclose the array values in curly brackets, { }. You need to enclose text in double quotation marks (" ") as well. You can also include the logical values *True* and *False* as entries in the array. Formulas or symbols, such as dollar signs or commas, are not allowed in array constants.

As an example of how an array constant might be used, look at the Creating Powers worksheet in the Arrays.xlsx file, shown in Figure 88-9.

	C	D	E	F
3	Sales	Sales^2	Sales^3	Sales^4
4	2	4	8	16
5	4	16	64	256
6	8	64	512	4096
7	10	100	1000	10000
8	14	196	2744	38416
9	20	400	8000	160000

FIGURE 88-9 Creating second and fourth powers of sales.

In this worksheet, you're given a product's sales during six months, and you want to create for each month the second, third, and fourth power of sales. Simply select the range D4:F9, which is where you want the resulting computation to be placed. Array-enter in cell D4 the formula {=C4:C9^{2,3,4}}. In the cell range D4:D9, this formula loops through and squares each number in C4:C9. In the cell range E4:E9, the formula loops through and cubes each number in C4:C9. Finally, in the cell range F4:F9, the formula loops through and raises each number in C4:C9 to the fourth power. The array constant {2,3,4} is required to let you loop through different power values.

How do I edit array formulas?

Suppose you have an array formula that creates results in multiple cells, and you want to edit, move, or delete the results. You cannot edit a single element of the array. To edit an array formula, however, you can begin by selecting all cells in the array range. Then pick one cell in the array. By pressing F2 to edit a cell in the array, you can make changes in that cell. After making the changes, press Ctrl+Shift+Enter to enter your changes. Now, the entire selected array will reflect your changes.

Given quarterly revenues for a toy store, can I estimate the trend and seasonality of the store's revenues?

The Toysrustrend.xlsx file, shown in Figure 88-10, contains quarterly revenues (in millions of dollars) for a toy store during the years 1997–2002. I would like to estimate the quarterly trend in revenues as well as the seasonality associated with each quarter (the first quarter equals January–March; the second quarter equals April–June; the third quarter equals July–September; the fourth quarter equals October–December). A trend of 1 percent per quarter, for example, means that sales are increasing at 1 percent per quarter. A seasonal index for the first quarter of 0.80, for example, means that sales during Quarter 1 are approximately 80 percent of an average quarter.

The trick to solving this problem is to use the LOGEST function. Suppose that you are trying to predict a variable *y* from independent variables *x1, x2,..., xn*, and you believe that for some values of *a, b1, b2,..., bn*, the relationship between *y* and *x1, x2,..., xn* is given by $y=a(b1)^{x1}(b2)^{x2}(bn)^{xn}$. (I'll call this *Equation 1*.)

	C	D	E	F	G	H	I	J	K	L	M	N	O
1													
2								mean quarter	0.5822	q4	172%		
3													
4					1	2	3	index	80%	73%	75%		
5	Year	Quarter	Sales	Quarter#	Q1 dummy	Q2 dummy	Q3 dummy	Forecast	q3	q2	q1	trend	const
6	1997	1	1646	1	1	0	0	1853.104665	0.46777	0.43	0.435	1.009	4219.6
7	1997	2	1738	2	0	1	0	1826.702203					
8	1997	3	1883	3	0	0	1	2025.018084					
9	1997	4	4868	4	0	0	0	4366.196216					
10	1998	1	1924	5	1	0	0	1917.500329					
11	1998	2	1989	6	0	1	0	1890.180377					
12	1998	3	2142	7	0	0	1	2095.387765					
13	1998	4	4383	8	0	0	0	4517.922188					
14	1999	1	2043	9	1	0	0	1984.133752					
15	1999	2	2020	10	0	1	0	1955.864428					
16	1999	3	2171	11	0	0	1	2168.202803					
17	1999	4	4338	12	0	0	0	4674.920659					
18	2000	1	2186	13	1	0	0	2053.082697					
19	2000	2	2204	14	0	1	0	2023.83101					
20	2000	3	2465	15	0	0	1	2243.548175					
21	2000	4	5027	16	0	0	0	4837.374851					
22	2001	1	2319	17	1	0	0	2124.427627					
23	2001	2	1994	18	0	1	0	2094.15944					
24	2001	3	2220	19	0	0	1	2321.51181					
25	2001	4	4799	20	0	0	0	5005.474351					
26	2002	1	2061	21	1	0	0	2198.251805					
27	2002	2	2021	22	0	1	0	2166.931793					

FIGURE 88-10 The toy-revenue trend and seasonality estimation.

The LOGEST function is used to determine the values of *a*, *b*1, *b*2,..., *bn* that best fit this equation to the observed data. To use the LOGEST function to estimate trend and seasonality, note the following:

- *y* equals quarterly revenues.
- *x*1 equals the quarter number (listed in chronological order; the current quarter is Quarter 1, the next quarter is Quarter 2, and so on).
- *x*2 equals 1 if the quarter is the first quarter of the year, and 0 otherwise.
- *x*3 equals 1 if the quarter is the second quarter of the year, and 0 otherwise.
- *x*4 equals 1 if the quarter is the third quarter of the year, and 0 otherwise.

You need to choose one quarter to leave out of the model. (I arbitrarily chose the fourth quarter.) This approach is similar to the one used with dummy variables in Chapter 58. The model you choose to estimate is then $y=a(b1)^{x1}(b2)^{x2}(b3)^{x3}(b4)^{x4}$. When the LOGEST function determines the values of *a*, *b*1, *b*2, *b*3, and *b*4 that best fit the data, the values are interpreted as follows:

- *a* is a constant used to scale the forecasts.
- *b*1 is a constant that represents the average per-quarter percentage increase in toy-store sales.
- *b*2 is a constant that measures the ratio of first-quarter sales to the omitted quarter's (fourth quarter) sales.
- *b*3 is a constant that measures the ratio of second-quarter sales to the omitted quarter's sales.
- *b*4 is a constant that measures the ratio of third-quarter sales to the omitted quarter's sales.

To begin, I create the dummy variables for Quarters 1–3 in the cell range G6:I27 by copying from G6 to G6:I27 the formula =IF($D6=G$4,1,0). Remember that a fourth quarter is known to Excel because all three dummy variables equal 0 during the fourth quarter, which is why you can leave out the dummy variable for this quarter.

I now select the cell range K6:O6, where I want LOGEST to place the estimated coefficients. The constant *a* will be placed in the right-most cell, followed by the coefficients corresponding to the ordering of the independent variables. Thus, the trend coefficient will be next to the constant, then the Quarter 1 coefficient, and so on.

The syntax I use for the LOGEST function is LOGEST(y range,x range,True,True). After array-entering in cell K6 the formula {=LOGEST(E6:E27,F6:I27,True,True)}, I obtain the coefficient estimates shown earlier in Figure 88-10. The equation to predict quarterly revenues (in millions) is as follows:

$$4219.57*(1.0086)^{\text{quarter number}}*(0.435)^{\text{Q1dummy}}*(0.426)^{\text{Q2dummy}}*(0.468)^{\text{Q3dummy}}$$

During the first quarter, the Q1 dummy equals 1, and the Q2 and Q3 dummies equal 0. (Recall that any number raised to the power 0 equals 1.) Thus, during a first quarter, quarterly revenues are predicted to equal $4219.57*(1.0086)^{\text{quarter number}}*(0.435)$.

During a second quarter, the Q1 dummy and the Q3 dummy equal 0, and the Q2 dummy equals 1. During this quarter, the quarterly revenues are predicted to equal $4219.57*(1.0086)^{\text{quarter number}}*(0.426)$. During a third quarter, the Q1 dummy and the Q2 dummy equal 0, and the Q3 dummy equals 1. The quarterly revenues during this quarter are predicted to equal $4219.57*(1.0086)^{\text{quarter number}}*(0.468)$. Finally, during a fourth quarter, the Q1, Q2, and Q3 dummies equal 0. During this quarter, the quarterly revenues are predicted to equal $4219.57*(1.0086)^{\text{quarter number}}$.

In summary, I estimate a quarterly upward trend in revenues of 0.9 percent (around 3.6 percent annually). After adjusting for the trend, I find the following:

- Quarter 1 revenues average 43.5 percent of Quarter 4 revenues.
- Quarter 2 revenues average 42.6 percent of Quarter 4 revenues.
- Quarter 3 revenues average 46.8 percent of Quarter 4 revenues.

To create a seasonal index for each quarter, you give the omitted quarter (Quarter 4) a value of 1 and find that an average quarter has a weight equal to the following (see cell K2 in Figure 88-10, shown previously):

$$\frac{.435+.426+.468+1}{4}=.582$$

Then, you can compute the relative seasonal index for Quarters 1–3 by copying from K4 to L4:M4 the formula =K6/$K$2. The Quarter 4 seasonality is computed in cell M2 with the formula =1/K2. After adjusting for the trend, I can conclude the following:

- Quarter 1 sales are 75 percent of a typical quarter.
- Quarter 2 sales are 73 percent of a typical quarter.
- Quarter 3 sales are 80 percent of a typical quarter.
- Quarter 4 sales are 172 percent of a typical quarter.

Suppose you want to generate the forecast for each quarter corresponding to the fitted equation (Equation 1). You can use the Excel GROWTH function to create this forecast. The GROWTH function is an array function with the syntax GROWTH(known ys,known xs,new xs,True). This formula gives the predictions for the new *xs* when Equation 1 is fitted to the data contained in the ranges specified by known *ys* and known *xs*. Thus, selecting the range J6:J27 and array-entering in cell J6 the formula {=GROWTH(E6:E27,F6:I27,F6:I27,TRUE)} generates forecasts from Equation 1 for each quarter's revenue. For example, the forecast for Quarter 4 of 1997 using Equation 1 is $4.366 billion.

Given a list of transactions in different countries/regions, how can I calculate the median size of a transaction in each country/region?

The file Medians.xlsx (see Figure 88-11) contains the revenue generated by a company's transactions in France, the United States, and Canada. Here, you want to calculate the median size of the transactions in each country/region. Suppose, for example, you want to compute the median size of a transaction in the US. An easy way to do this is to create an array that contains only the US revenues and replaces other revenues by a blank space. Then you can have Excel compute the median of this new array. After naming the data in column C *Country* and naming the data in column D *Revenue*, you can array-enter the formula {=MEDIAN(IF(Country=F5,Revenue,""))} in cell G5 to replace the revenue in each row containing a non-US transaction by a blank space, and then calculate the median size of the US transactions ($6,376.50). Copying this formula from G5 to G6:G7 computes the median transaction size for Canada and France.

S17

	C	D	E	F	G
1	Country	Revenue			
2	US	5919			
3	Canada	4005			Median
4	US	6456			Revenue
5	France	8328		US	6376.5
6	Canada	9426		Canada	6326
7	US	5929		France	7403
8	France	7746			
9	Canada	9292			
10	US	8839			
11	France	7403			
12	Canada	3911			
13	US	7458			
14	Canada	8094			
15	France	4727			
16	Canada	5675			

FIGURE 88-11 Finding the median transaction size in each country/region.

Given unit sales transactions broken down by person, product, and location, can I determine the standard deviation of units sold for each person-product-location combination?

The file Stdevif.xlsx contains 456 makeup sales transactions. (See Figure 88-12.) For each transaction, you are given the salesperson, units sold, product, and location. You want to determine for each salesperson-product-location combination the standard deviation of the units sold for the relevant transactions. First, I use Create From Selection on the Formulas tab (in the Defined Names group) to name each column of data. Next, I copy the data to a new worksheet (Sheet2) and use Remove Duplicates (on the Data tab, in the Data Tools group) to create each unique salesperson-product-location combination. Then I paste these combinations to the cell range L6:N51 (back in the worksheet Sheet1). Then I array-enter the formula {=STDEV(IF(Name=L7,IF(Product=M7,IF(Location=N7,Units))))} in cell O7 and copy the formulas to O8:O51. This formula first creates an array of ones (if *Name* in the cell is Ashley) and of zeros (if *Name* is not Ashley). Then an array of ones and zeros is created based on whether the product is mascara, and finally an array of ones and zeros is created based on whether the location is East. Then these arrays are multiplied, yielding a one for only the rows in which Ashley sold mascara in the East. When this final array of ones and zeros is multiplied by the Units column, you have an array of all units sold in transactions where Ashley sold mascara in the East. Then the STDEV function returns the standard deviation (29.2) of units sold in all transactions involving Ashley selling mascara in the East. Copying this formula to O8:O51 yields the needed standard deviations. To better understand this cool formula, you can apply Evaluate Formula from the Formulas tab (in the Formula Auditing group).

	G	H	I	J	K	L	M	N	O
1									
2									
3									
4	Name	Product	Units	Location					
5	Ashley	mascara	43	east					
6	Ashley	mascara	93	east		Name	Product	Location	Std dev
7	Ashley	lip gloss	63	east		Ashley	mascara	east	29.20046
8	Ashley	mascara	19	east		Ashley	lip gloss	east	26.32319
9	Ashley	eye liner	41	east		Ashley	eye liner	east	23.8838
10	Ashley	foundation	84	east		Ashley	foundatio	east	28.5482
11	Ashley	lipstick	-8	east		Ashley	lipstick	east	28.74022
12	Ashley	eye liner	76	east		Betsy	lip gloss	east	26.83129
13	Ashley	lip gloss	31	east		Betsy	lipstick	east	26.21341
14	Ashley	foundation	8	east		Betsy	mascara	east	22.94559
15	Ashley	eye liner	81	east		Betsy	foundatio	east	28.26438
16	Ashley	foundation	12	east		Betsy	eye liner	east	36.03074
17	Ashley	lip gloss	50	east		Cici	lip gloss	east	35.35887
18	Ashley	eye liner	39	east		Cici	mascara	east	34.82632
19	Ashley	mascara	17	east		Cici	lipstick	east	25.92939
20	Ashley	lip gloss	32	east		Cici	eye liner	east	19.77361
21	Ashley	lipstick	71	east		Cici	foundatio	east	22.94816
22	Ashley	lip gloss	40	east		Colleen	eye liner	east	39.11266
23	Ashley	eye liner	92	east		Colleen	lipstick	east	23.16679

FIGURE 88-12 Computing standard deviations when you slice and dice your data.

Problems

All data for Problems 1 through 5 is in the Chapter88data.xlsx file.

1. The Duplicate worksheet contains two lists of names. Use an array formula to count the number of names appearing on both lists.

2. The Find Errors worksheet contains some calculations. Use an array formula to count the number of cells containing errors. Hint: Use the ISERROR function in your array formula.

3. The Sales worksheet contains 48 months of sales at a toy store. Create an array formula to add (beginning with Month 3) every fifth month of sales. Hint: You might want to use the Excel MOD function. MOD(number,divisor) yields the remainder after the number is divided by the divisor. For example, MOD(7,5) yields 2.

4. Also in the Sales worksheet, use an array function to compute the third, fifth, and seventh power of each month's sales.

5. The Product worksheet contains sales during April through August of Products 1 through 7. Sales for each product are listed in the same column as each month. Rearrange the data so that sales for each month are listed in the same row and any changes to the original data are reflected in the new arrangement you have created.

6. Use the data in the file Historicalinvest.xlsx to create a count of the number of years in which stock, bond, and T-bill returns are from –20 percent through –15 percent, –15 percent through –10 percent, and so on.

7. An *m*-by-*n* matrix is a rectangular array of numbers containing *m* rows and *n* columns. The following, for example, is a 3-by-3 matrix:

$$\begin{bmatrix} 1 & 2 & 3 \\ 4 & 5 & 6 \\ 7 & 8 & 9 \end{bmatrix}$$

Consider two matrices, *A* and *B*. Suppose that the number of columns in matrix *A* equals the number of rows in matrix *B*. Then you can multiply matrix *A* by matrix *B*. (The product is written as *AB*.) The entry in row I and column J of *AB* is computed by applying the SUMPRODUCT function to row I of *A* and column J of *B*. *AB* will have as many rows as *A* and as many columns as *B*. The Excel MMULT function is an array function with which you can multiply matrices. Use the MMULT function to multiply the following matrices:

$$A = \begin{bmatrix} 1 & 2 & 3 \\ 4 & 5 & 6 \\ 7 & 7 & 0 \end{bmatrix} \text{ and } B = \begin{bmatrix} 1 & 2 & 3 \\ 1 & 2 & 0 \\ 3 & 3 & 0 \end{bmatrix}$$

8. A square matrix has the same number of rows and columns. Given a square matrix *A*, suppose there exists a matrix *B* whereby *AB* equals a matrix in which each diagonal entry equals 1, and

all other entries equal 0. You can then say that *B* is the inverse of *A*. The Excel array function MINVERSE finds the inverse of a square matrix. Use the MINVERSE function to find the inverse for matrices *A* and *B* in Problem 7.

9. Suppose you have invested a fraction *fi* of your money in investment *i* (*i*=1,2,...,*n*). Also, suppose the standard deviation of the annual percentage return on investment *i* is *si* and the correlation between the annual percentage return on investment *i* and investment *j* is *ñij*. You would like to know the variance and standard deviation of the annual percentage return on your portfolio. This can easily be computed by using matrix multiplication. Create the following three matrices:

- Matrix 1 equals a 1-by-*n* matrix whose *i*th entry is *sifi*.
- Matrix 2 equals an *n*-by-*n* matrix whose entry in row *i* and column *j* is *ñij*.
- Matrix 3 is a *n*-by-1 matrix whose *i*th entry is *sifi*.

The variance of the annual percentage return on your portfolio is simply (Matrix 1)*(Matrix 2)*(Matrix 3). The data in the file Historicalinvest.xlsx gives annual returns on stocks, bonds, and T-bills. Use the MMULT and TRANSPOSE functions to estimate (based on the given historical data) the variance and standard deviation of a portfolio that invests 50 percent in stocks, 25 percent in bonds, and 25 percent in T-bills.

Problems 10 through 13 use the data in the Makeupdb.xlsx file.

10. How many dollars' worth of lip gloss did Jen sell?

11. What was the average number of lipstick units sold by Jen in the East region?

12. How many dollars of sales were made by Emilee or in the East region?

13. How many dollars' worth of lipstick were sold by Colleen or Zaret in the East region?

14. Use the data in the file Chapter88data.xlsx to estimate the trend and seasonal components of the quarterly revenues of Ford and GM.

15. In the toy-store example (using the file Toysrustrend.xlsx), use the data for 1999–2001 to forecast the quarterly revenues for 2002.

16. The Lillydata.xlsx file contains information from a market-research survey that was used to gather insights to aid in designing a new blood-pressure drug. Fifteen experts (six from Lilly and nine from other companies—see column N) were asked to compare five sets of four potential Lilly products. The fifth choice in each scenario is that a competitor's drug is chosen over the four listed Lilly drugs.

For example, in the first scenario, the second option considered would be a Lilly drug that reduced blood pressure 18 points, resulted in 14 percent of side effects, and sold for $16.

The range I6:N21 contains the choices each expert made for each of the five scenarios. For example, the first expert (who worked for Lilly) chose a competitor's drug when faced with Scenario 1 and chose the first listed drug when faced with Scenario 2.

Use this information to do the following:

- Enter a formula that can be copied from I2 to I2:M5 that calculates the price for each scenario and option in I2:M5.

- Enter an array formula in I23 that can be copied to I23:I32 and then to J23:M32 that calculates for each question the frequency of each response (1–5), broken down by Lilly and non-Lilly experts. Thus for Question 1, one Lilly expert responded 1, three responded 2, and two responded 5.

17. The file Arrayexam1data.xlsx contains sales data by company and date. Your job is to break the sales down on a quarterly basis by using array formulas. Summarize the data (using only array formulas) by company and by quarter, as shown in Figure 88-13.

	C	D	E	F	G	H	I
1							
2	Date	Num	Name	Memo	Clr	Split	Amount
3	01/01/2004	1053544-03	ACS			2000 · Accounts Payable	54.63
4	01/01/2004	1052976-01	ACS			2000 · Accounts Payable	98.75
5	01/01/2004	1053544-01	ACS			2000 · Accounts Payable	224.96
6	01/01/2004	1053544-02	ACS			2000 · Accounts Payable	224.94
7	01/02/2004	4818189	Cardinal Health	67210		2000 · Accounts Payable	135.00
8	01/03/2004	4820762	Cardinal Health	67210		2000 · Accounts Payable	55,817.37
9	01/03/2004	4820860	Cardinal Health	67210		2000 · Accounts Payable	78.35
10	01/05/2004	47786	ActSys Medical, Inc.	INT014		2000 · Accounts Payable	3,455.00
11	01/05/2004	4822189	Cardinal Health	67210		2000 · Accounts Payable	650.81
12	01/05/2004	4822835	Cardinal Health	67210		2000 · Accounts Payable	6,950.36
13	02/26/2004	49426	ActSys Medical, Inc.	INT014		2000 · Accounts Payable	1,596.00
14	02/27/2004	4936605	Cardinal Health	67210		2000 · Accounts Payable	18,879.05
15	02/27/2004	4936809	Cardinal Health	67210		2000 · Accounts Payable	741,427.08
16	02/27/2004	1056106-02	ACS			2000 · Accounts Payable	55.69
17	02/28/2004	4938525	Cardinal Health	67210		2000 · Accounts Payable	35,812.86
18	04/30/2004	5063491	Cardinal Health	67210		2000 · Accounts Payable	13,466.25
19	04/30/2004	5063060	Cardinal Health	67210		2000 · Accounts Payable	24,092.33
20	05/01/2004	5065649	Cardinal Health	67210		2000 · Accounts Payable	25,148.30
21	05/04/2004	90021858	BioMed Plus, Inc.			2000 · Accounts Payable	1,107.00
22	05/05/2004	5073200	Cardinal Health	67210		2000 · Accounts Payable	47,485.66
23	05/05/2004	451499-0	Cardinal Health	67210		2000 · Accounts Payable	(2,336.24)
24	05/05/2004	5072364	Cardinal Health	67210		2000 · Accounts Payable	3,764.50
25	05/05/2004	1881410 RI	Briggs Corporation	200977		2000 · Accounts Payable	147.49
26	05/06/2004	5076324	Cardinal Health	67210		2000 · Accounts Payable	51,598.62

FIGURE 88-13 The format for the Problem 17 answer.

For example, L7 should contain Quarter 1 (January 1 through March 31) ACS sales, and so on. Verify your answer with a PivotTable.

18. Explain why array-entering the formula {=SUM(1/COUNTIF(Info,Info))} will yield the number of unique entries in the range *Info*. Apply this formula to the data in the file Unique.xlsx, and verify that it returns the number of unique entries.

19. The file Salaries.xlsx contains the salaries of NBA players. Write an array formula that adds the four largest player salaries. Hint: Use the array constant {1,2,3,4} in conjunction with the LARGE function.

20. Then generalize your formula so that you can enter any positive integer *n* and your formula will add the *n* largest salaries. Hint: If cell G9 contains an integer *n*, when you array-enter a formula ROW(Indirect("1:"&G9)), Excel will create an array constant {1,2,...,*n*}.

CHAPTER 89

Recording macros

Questions to be answered in this chapter:

- What is a macro?
- What role does the Developer tab play in recording and running macros?
- How do I record a macro?
- How can I record a macro that applies a desired format to any range of cells?
- How can I run a macro?
- How do I use relative references to record macros?
- How can I record a macro that filters a PivotTable to show only data from my top-20 customers?

Answers to this chapter's questions

What is a macro?

Macros enable you to easily automate many repetitive Excel tasks. For example, if you often apply a particular format to a range of cells, you can create a macro that performs this formatting task with the click of a button. Perhaps there is a set of headings you often use in your worksheets. Again, after creating the appropriate macro, a click of a button will insert these headings anywhere in your workbook. In this chapter, you will learn how easy it is to record macros. Although you can accomplish a lot with recorded macros, many macros cannot be recorded and must be created using the Excel VBA (Visual Basic for Applications) programming language. I refer the reader interested in VBA to the book *Excel 2016 Power Programming with VBA* (Wiley, 2016).

What role does the Developer tab play in recording and running macros?

To create macros (by either recording or writing your own macros in VBA) or to run macros, you will need to see the Developer tab on the ribbon. To place the Developer tab on the ribbon (if it is not yet on the ribbon), go to the File tab and choose Options. Then, after choosing Customize Ribbon in the left pane, select the check box for the Developer tab in the area on the right, as shown in Figure 89-1. Then click OK in the Excel Options dialog box.

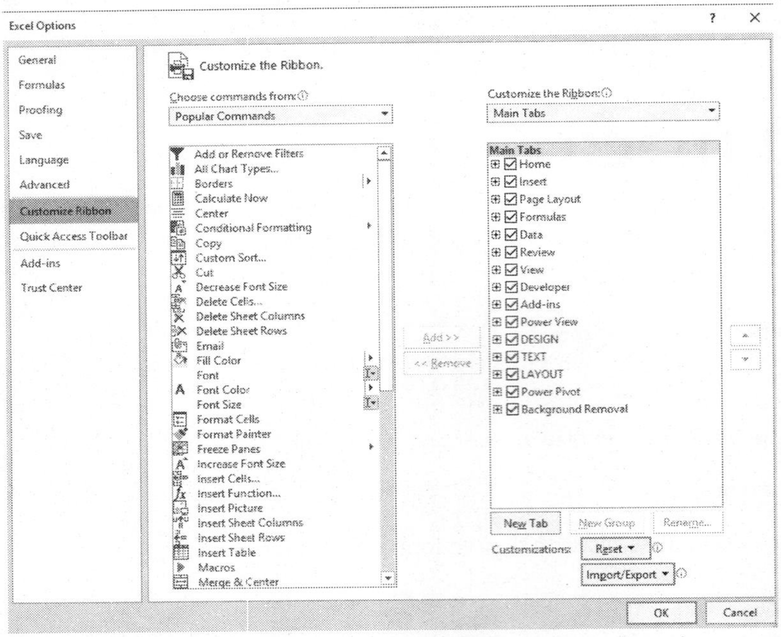

FIGURE 89-1 Placing the Developer tab on the ribbon.

How do I record a macro?

To record a macro, begin by displaying the Developer tab. Then you will see the options displayed in Figure 89-2.

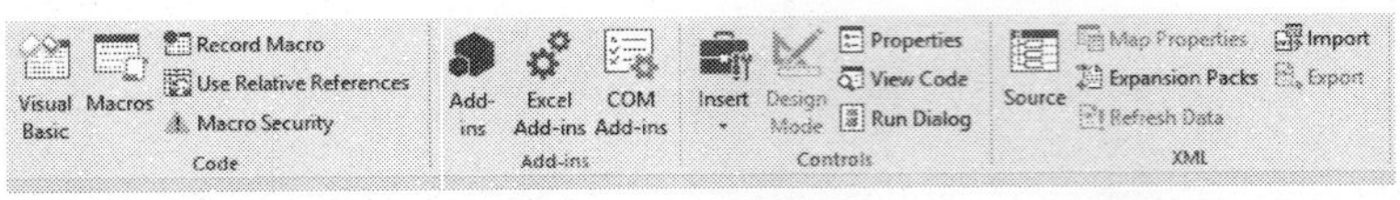

FIGURE 89-2 The Developer tab in Excel.

To begin recording a macro, simply click Record Macro in the Code group. You will then see the Record Macro dialog box shown in Figure 89-3.

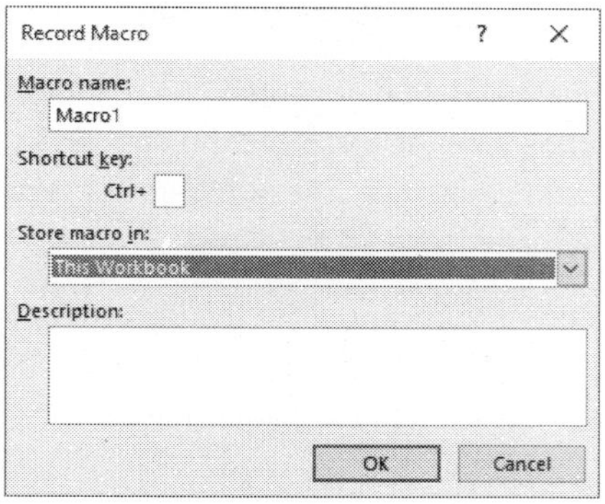

FIGURE 89-3 The Record Macro dialog box.

Let's now look in more detail at the following four parts of the Record Macro dialog box:

- **Macro Name** Excel gives a default name (such as *Macro1*) to a macro. You will probably want to create a more informative name for your macro. For example, if your macro boldfaces and changes the font to red for selected cells, you might name the macro *redbold*.
- **Shortcut Key** As you will soon learn, there are many ways that you can run a macro. By creating a *shortcut key*, you define a sequence of keystrokes that can be used to run the macro. For example, entering Shift+F ensures that the Ctrl+Shift+F key sequence will cause your macro to run. You have to be careful in assigning a shortcut-key sequence. For example, since Ctrl+B boldfaces a selection, you cannot simply use Ctrl+B as your shortcut key. The creation of a shortcut key is optional.
- **Store Macro In** The default choice is to store the macro in the current workbook. Then the macro is available to run whenever the workbook is open. If you want your macro to always be available, you can choose to store the macro in the Personal Macro Workbook.
- **Description** Filling in this field is optional, but you might want to enter a description of the macro, especially if you're sharing the Excel file.

After you have filled in the Record Macro dialog box, you are ready to record your macro. Click OK, and then performing the tasks you want to be repeated when the macro runs. When you're finished, select Stop Recording on the Developer tab in the Code group. (The Record Macro option changes to Stop Recording.) To stop recording, you can also click the small gray rectangle that appears in the lower-left portion of your screen (under the worksheet tabs).

How can I record a macro that applies a desired format to a selected range of cells?

Let's suppose that your work often requires you to have numerical data highlighted in a boldfaced, red font. You can easily create a macro to automate this routine task. (You can see the final result in the file Redbold.xlsm.) Before recording the macro, enter some data (say, the numbers in the cell range F3:F6) that you want to format. Select the range of cells, and proceed as follows:

1. On the Developer tab, select Record Macro (in the Code group) and fill in the Record Macro dialog box as shown in Figure 89-4. Note you will use Ctrl+Shift+R as the keystroke combination that runs the macro. Click OK when you're ready to start recording your macro.

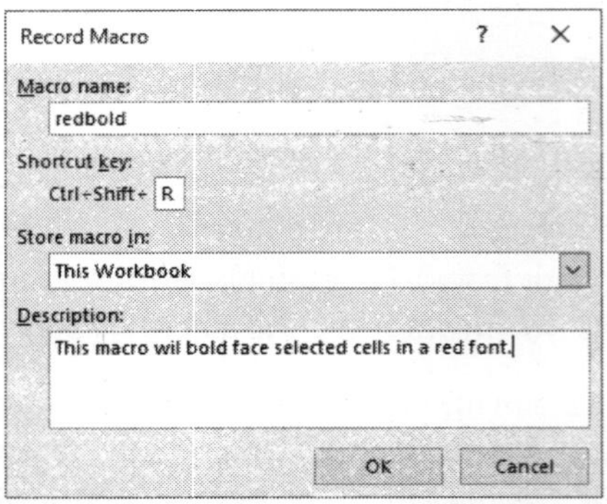

FIGURE 89-4 The settings for the macro named *redbold.*

2. Press Ctrl+1 (or right-click and select Format Cells) to bring up the Format Cells dialog box. Select the Font tab in the dialog box, and choose Bold in the Font Style list and a red font under Color.
3. Click Stop Recording.
4. Since the workbook contains a macro, save the file as an Excel Macro-Enabled workbook. The final name of the workbook is Redbold.xlsm. The suffix *.xlsm* indicates the file is a macro-enabled workbook.
5. To run the macro, you can use the keystroke combination Ctrl+Shift+R.
6. You can further test the macro by entering data in J5:J7, for example, selecting those cells, and running the macro again. Cells J5:J7 are now formatted in a boldfaced, red font. You can repeat this text in other cell ranges.

A macro can also be run by selecting the Developer tab and clicking Macros in the Code group. This brings up the list of available macros, shown in Figure 89-5. Selecting the redbold macro and clicking Run will run the macro.

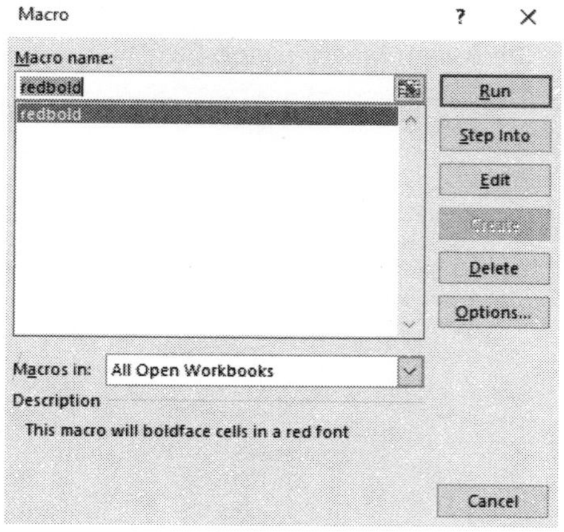

FIGURE 89-5 The list of available macros in the open workbooks.

When you record a macro, you are recording VBA code. Clicking Edit in the Macro dialog box shows you the VBA code. (See Figure 89-6.)

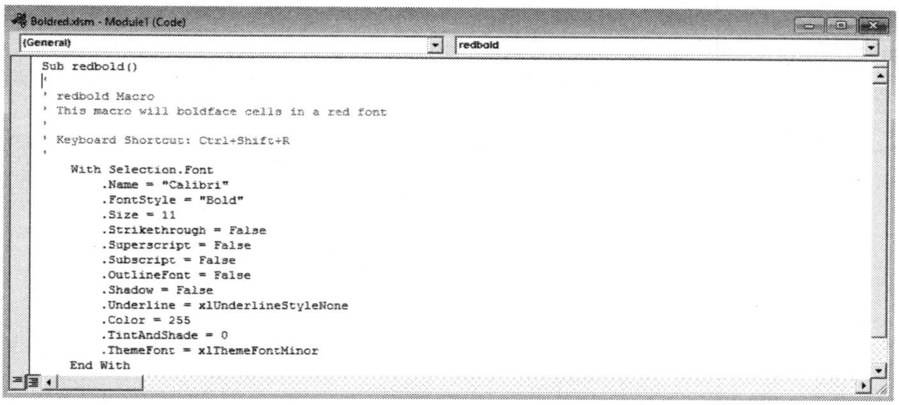

FIGURE 89-6 The recorded macro code for the redbold macro.

Observe that all I wanted to do was select a red font (see the statement `.Color=255`) and choose a bold font (see the statement `.FontStyle="Bold"`). The recorded macro code is inefficient because it includes many extraneous statements. Later, I will show how to edit a macro,

How can I run a macro?

You have already seen how to run a macro by using a keystroke combination or by selecting a macro in the Macro dialog box. In this section, I discuss how you can run a macro by using a form control such as a button (see Chapter 27) or by placing a macro on the Quick Access Toolbar (which is in the upper left of the ribbon).

To run a macro from a button, simply select Insert on the Developer tab (in the Controls group) and choose the Button option (the first choice) from the Form Controls section. Draw a button, and the dialog box shown in Figure 89-7 appears. From this dialog box, you can assign the button to the redbold macro. Select the macro, and then click OK in the Assign Macro dialog box.

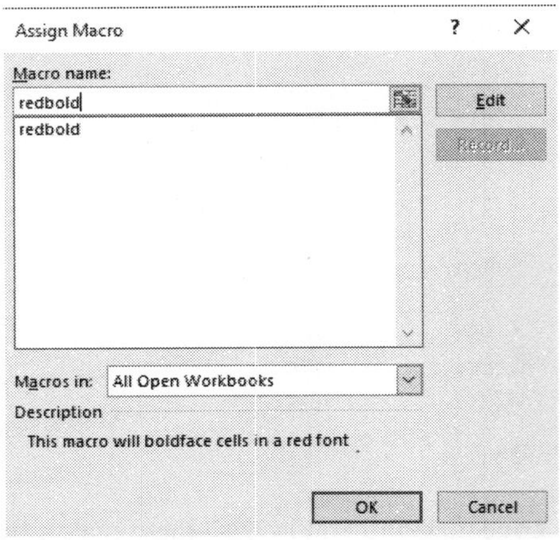

FIGURE 89-7 Assigning a macro to a button.

To change the name of the button to redbold, right-click the button and click Edit Text. Replace the text with **redbold**. Click a cell in the worksheet to complete your change. (See Figure 89-8.) Try out the button by entering some new data, selecting the data, and then clicking the button. The new data will be boldfaced and in a red font.

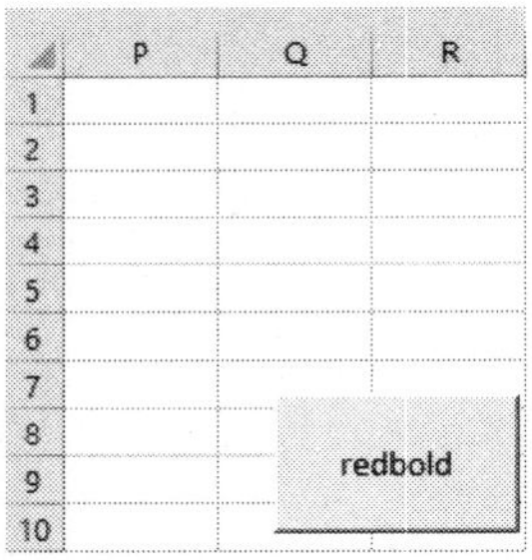

FIGURE 89-8 The button for running the redbold macro.

To place a macro on the Quick Access Toolbar, proceed as follows:

1. Right-click the Quick Access Toolbar, and choose Customize Quick Access Toolbar.
2. In the Excel Options dialog box, shown in Figure 89-9, select Macros from the Choose Commands From drop-down list.
3. Select the redbold macro, and then click the Add button.
4. By clicking Modify (in the lower right), you can modify the icon used to run the macro to be the last icon shown on the Quick Access Toolbar. Click OK in the Modify Button dialog box and again in the Excel Options dialog box.

5. After you select a range of cells, clicking the icon you added to the Quick Access Toolbar will run the redbold macro.

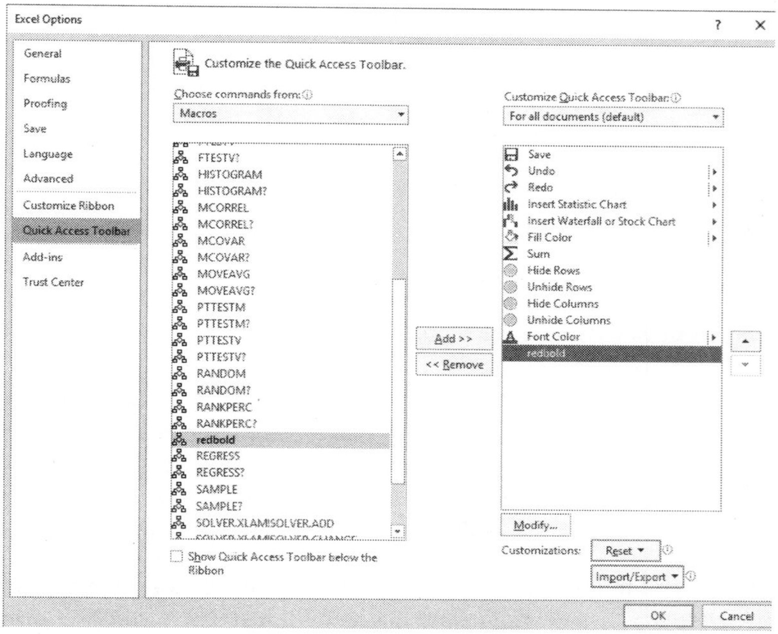

FIGURE 89-9 Selecting the macro redbold to add it to the Quick Access Toolbar.

How do I use relative references to record macros?

Let's suppose you want to enter your name in a given cell, and you want to enter the current date in the cell directly to the right of your name.

To begin, let's create a macro that always puts your name in cell A1 and the current date in cell B1. (See the file Namedatemacro.xlsm.)

1. On the Developer tab, select Record Macro, name the macro *Namedatea1*, and assign the shortcut key Ctrl+Shift+A. Click OK to close the Record Macro dialog box.
2. Move to cell A1 and type your name, and then move to cell B1 and enter the formula =TODAY(), which always enters today's date in a cell.
3. Click Stop Recording.
4. To test the macro, go to any cell and enter the keystroke sequence Ctrl+Shift+A. You will see the name you typed entered in cell A1 and today's date entered in cell B1.

Now click Edit in the Macro dialog box to see the VBA code displayed in Figure 89-10.

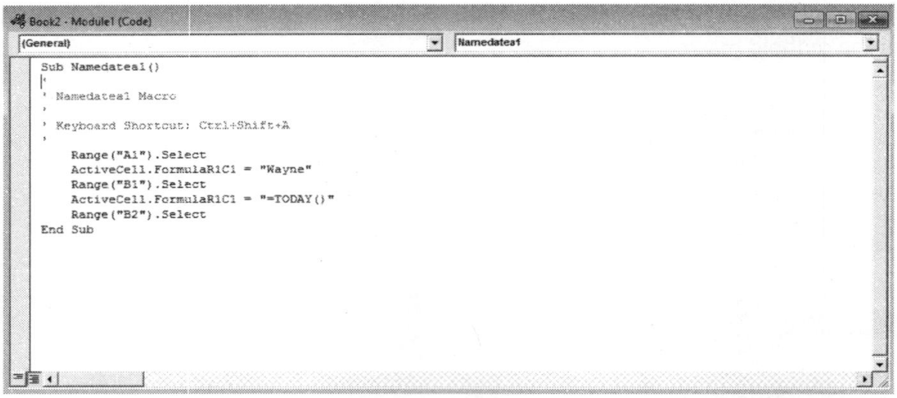

FIGURE 89-10 A macro that puts a name in cell A1 and today's date in cell B1.

Looking at the code, you can see that Excel first selects cell A1. This is now the active cell, and Excel enters *Wayne* in the current active cell (A1). Then it moves to cell B1 and enters the formula =TODAY(). Since I did not change the cursor movement, Excel moved down one cell to cell B2. If you simply delete the line `Range("B2").Select` from the macro and rerun the macro, you will find that the macro ends in cell B1, not cell B2. This simple example shows how you can edit the code of a macro.

Now suppose you want to be able to select any cell and enter your name in that cell and enter today's date one cell to the right of your name. This requires that you record your macro with relative references. To do this, select the Use Relative References option in the Code group on the Developer tab, shown in Figure 89-11.

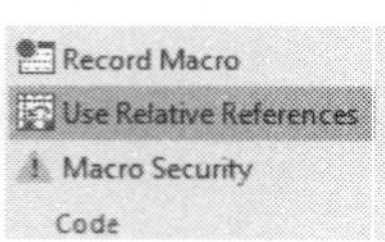

FIGURE 89-11 Turning on the Use Relative References option.

When Use Relative References is turned on, the macro will contain no explicit references to any cell other than the cell you selected before recording the macro. During the execution of the macro, all the keystrokes will be executed relative to the currently active cell. To create a macro that records your name in the selected cell and then puts the current date one cell to the right of the current cell, proceed as follows. (See the file Namedaterelative.xlsm.)

1. Open up a new workbook and move to any cell (I chose cell H5.)
2. After clicking the Developer tab, turn on the Use Relative References option (in the Code group).
3. Select Record Macro, and give the macro the name *Namedaterelative*. Click OK.
4. Type your name in the active cell (mine is H5).
5. Move one cell to the right, to cell I5, and enter the formula =TODAY().

6. Double-click the column I heading to widen the column to match the width of today's date.

7. Click Stop Recording.

8. As previously described, create a button to run the macro.

9. Go to any cell in the workbook and run the macro. You will see your name in the selected cell and the current date one cell to the right. At the end of the macro, the cursor moves one cell below the date. If you do not like that, you can easily edit the macro by deleting the statement that moves your cursor one cell below the date.

The VBA code for your macro is shown in Figure 89-12.

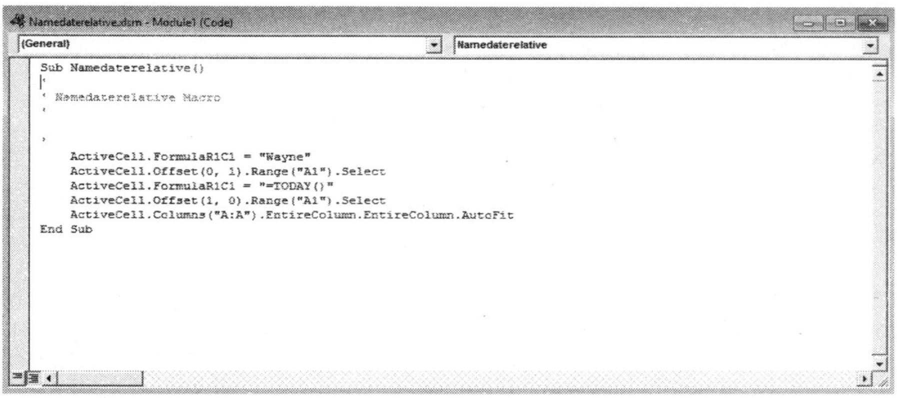

FIGURE 89-12 The VBA code to put your name and the current date in a cell.

The following descriptions explain the meaning of each statement in the macro:

- **Sub Namedaterelative()** Macros start with a Sub statement that contains the name of the macro.

- **' Namedaterelative Macro** Statements that begin with a single straight quotation mark (') are comments and are not executed. This statement is simply a comment that identifies the name of the macro.

- **ActiveCell.FormulaR1C1 = "Wayne"** This statement inserts the text *Wayne* in the cell you have selected before running the macro.

- **ActiveCell.Offset(0, 1).Range("A1").Select** This statement moves one cell to the right of the current cell. Note the use of `Offset`, which is similar to the use of the OFFSET function discussed in Chapter 22.

- **ActiveCell.FormulaR1C1 = "=TODAY()"** This statement enters the current date in the active cell, which is now one column to the right of the cell containing your name.

- **ActiveCell.Offset(1, 0).Range("A1").Select** This statement moves one cell below the cell containing the current date. If you delete this statement from the macro, the active cell at the completion of the macro will be the cell containing the current date.

- **ActiveCell.Columns("A:A").EntireColumn.EntireColumn.AutoFit** This statement widens the column containing the date to match the width of the date.
- **End Sub** An End Sub statement marks the end of a macro.

How can I record a macro that filters a PivotTable to show only the data from my top-20 customers?

The file Ptcustomerstemp.xlsx (in this chapter's Template folder) contains a PivotTable I created in Chapter 43 to summarize the sales for 100 customers. Now you will create a macro that allows you to click a button to filter the PivotTable and show the data from the top-20 customers. Complete the following steps:

1. On the Developer tab (in the Code group), select Record Macro. In the Record Macro dialog box, name the *Topcustomers*. Click OK to start recording.
2. Go to cell A4, and from the drop-down arrow, select Value filters.
3. Select Top 10. Then, in the Top 10 Filter (Customer) dialog box, change the 10 to 20 so that you have filtered to show only the top-20 customers. Click OK.
4. Click Stop Recording.
5. Create a button to run the macro. When you run the macro, only the top-20 customers' data will be shown. To try the macro on my completed file, open the file Ptcustomers.xlsm in this chapter's Practice Files folder, clear the filter on cell A4, and then click the Top20 button.

You can, if you want, record a macro to restore the original PivotTable. (See Problem 4.)

Problems

1. Your MBA team members are Wayne, Taylor, Britney, and Katy. Create a macro that enters the team members in cells A1:D1.
2. Modify your Problem 1 macro to enter the team members in a single row, starting in any cell you want.
3. Create a macro that will place a red border (boldfaced) around any set of selected cells.
4. For the PivotTable example in the file Ptcustomers.xlsm, create a macro that clears any filter on customers.
5. Create a macro that will format any selected range in bold italics.
6. Ctrl+A selects all cells in the current worksheet. Use this fact to create a macro that will ensure that each cell in a worksheet is formatted in boldfaced italics.

7. Often I want to freeze the results of a range resulting from formulas, and then change the formulas to values. Create a macro that will find, based on the selected cell, the largest range of cells containing the current cell and turn all formulas into values. Hint: Ctrl+Shift+* will select the desired range. Test your macro by entering a bunch of =RAND() functions in your workbook.

8. Create a macro that will highlight an entire column of data in yellow. Your macro should work no matter how many rows of data are in the column. Hint: Remember to use Ctrl+Shift+Down arrow!

Index

Symbols

\# All, AutoComplete, 244
& operator, 42
* (asterisk)
  in array formulas, 787
  as COUNTIF wildcard, 166
  as MATCH wildcard, 34
  as multiplication symbol, 6, 787
^ (caret), 65
: (colon), to indicate time, 114
{ } (curly brackets), array formulas, 787, 794
#Data, AutoComplete, 244
#DIV/0! error, 107
$ (dollar sign)
  cell range names, 18
  conditional formatting, formulas, 216, 217, 219
  demand curve, 7–8
  use in formulas, 5–6
! (exclamation point), in ranges, 16
>= (greater than or equal to), 166
#Headers, AutoComplete, 244
λ (lambda), Poisson random variable, 656–658
\- (minus sign), in PivotTable fields, 391
#N/A (Not Available)
  array formula ranges, 368
  charts, check-box controls and, 522–523, 531
  MATCH function and, 34
  replacing with blanks, 105–107
  Trace Error and, 133
  VLOOKUP, 22
#NAME? error, 107
<> (not equal to), 166
#NUM! error, 107
( ) parentheses, order of operations, 6–7
. (period), in ranges, 19
\+ (plus sign), in PivotTable fields, 391
" " (quotation marks)
  COUNTIF text values, 165–166
  IF statements, 100
  MATCH text values, 34
#REF! error, 107
@/#This Row, AutoComplete, 245
#Totals, AutoComplete, 245
_ (underscore), in ranges, 18–19
#VALUE error, 48–49
#VALUE! error, 107

A

A Date Occurring, Highlight Cell Rules, 203
abandonment option, 731–732
abbreviations, data validation, 346–347
ABS function, GRG Multistart and, 320
accounts payable, payments to suppliers, 2–4
Add Constraint, Solver Parameters, 277–278
Add Level, Sort, 230
Add-ins
  Analysis ToolPak, 352, 563
  Data Analysis, 352, 366
  Power Pivot, 439
  Power View, 451
  Solver installation, 271–272, 617
addition, order of operation, 6–7
Additive Rule for Computing Probabilities, 633
address, 3D Maps, 462–463
AGGREGATE function, 106–107
  table slicers, use of, 244
aggregation, Power Pivot and, 439
#All, AutoComplete, 244
Allow list, Data Validation, 345–346
Amazon.com.xlsx, 609–611
Amazon.xlsx, 215–217
American stock options, 722. *See also* stock options
amusement parks, two-part tariff pricing, 780–783
Analysis ToolPak, 352–353, 366. *See also* descriptive statistics
  installing, 563
analytics
  challenges and trends in, 266–267
  defined, 263
  predictive analytics, defined, 263–264

analytics , *continued*
  prescriptive analytics, defined, 264–265
  skills needed for, 265–266
  value of, 265
AND, Boolean arrays, 793
AND, use in formulas, 215
and (&) operator, 42
animation, Power View, 459–460
annual average return, 376
annuity values
  FV function, future value, 77–78
  PV function, 75–77
ANOVA (analysis of variance)
  one-way ANOVA, 593–597
  two-way ANOVA, 599–607
Applynames.xlsx, 16–17
array arguments, 786
array constants, 794–795
array formulas
  average of numbers on list compared to median, 791
  bin arrays, 788–789
  data arrays, 788–789
  defined, 786
  duplicates in two lists, finding, 790–791
  editing of, 795
  interpretation of, 786–787
  median transaction by country, 798
  sales by person-product-location, 799
  sales summaries by employee, 794
  summing second digits in integer set, 789–790
  Worksheet ranges, 197
array functions
  FREQUENCY, 527, 788–789
  GROWTH, 798
  interpreting formulas, 786–787
  LOGEST, 795–798
  MODE.MULT, 368
  sales data by employee, and units sold, 792–794
  seasonal trend analysis, 795–798
  tips for use, 584
  TRANSPOSE, 788
  TREND, 583–584
Arrays.xlsx, 786–788, 790–791, 795
Asiansales.xlsx, 179–180
asset allocation decisions, 702–707
Assetallocationopt.xlsx, 704–707
Assign.xlsx, 328–329
asterisk (*)
  in array formulas, 787
  as COUNTIF wildcard, 166
  as MATCH wildcard, 34
  as multiplication symbol, 6, 787
auditing tool, 131–137
Audittwosheets.xlsx, 137
AutoComplete, 15
  table formulas, 236–237
  table specifiers, 244–245
Automatic, calculation options, 143
Automatic Axis, data bars, 207
Auto.xlsx, 575–580
AVERAGE
  average salary, 2, 105–107
  circular references, resolving, 92
  descriptive statistics, 367, 370
  name ranges, use of, 14–15
  of numbers on list compared to median, 791
  sports point spreads, 313–314
  Z-scores, 665–666
average (mean), descriptive statistics, 367, 369, 370
  Z-scores, 665–666
average annual return, 376
average rank, RANK.AVG, 374
average units sold, 174–175
AVERAGEIF, 171–175
AVERAGEIFS, 171–175
averages, moving, 609–611
  centered moving averages, 621
  ratio-to-moving averages method, 619–621

B

back-order penalty, 749–752
Bakery1temp.xlsx, 2–4
balance sheet, pro forma statements, 101–105
band charts, 519–520
Bandchart.xlsx, 520
Banded Columns, Table Tools, 238
Banded Rows, Table Tools, 238
Bank24.xlsx, 285–288
base, time series, 613
Baseball.xlsx, 35–36
Basketball.xlsx, 219–220
Bayes' theorem, 635–637
before tax profits, 135–136
beta random variable, 669, 672–673
BETA.DIST, 669, 672–673
Bezos.xlsx, 144–146
bids, optimal, 693–696
bin array, 788–789
bin ranges, defining, 351. *See also* histograms
binary programming problems, Solver, 301
BINOM.DIST, 649–653
BINOM.DIST.RANGE, 649–653
binomial random variables, 647–653
  negative binomial random variable, 652–653
  simulation of, 693–694
Binomialexamples.xlsx, 649–653
Binomialsim.xlsx, 693–694
BINOM.INV, 650–653, 693–694
Black, Fischer, 721

black swans, 699
Black-Scholes option-pricing formula, 682, 721–732
book value, depreciation and, 82–83
Boolean arrays, 793–794
bootstrapping, 699–707
Borders, conditional formatting, 213–214
Box And Whisker chart option, 377
Boxplotmultiple.xlsx, 379
boxplots, 376–380
Boxplottemp.xlsx, 376–380
breakeven analysis, 144–146, 151–152
Bstempprotected.xlsx, 728–730
Bstemp.xlsx, 725–726, 728–730
bubble charts, 534
Bubble.xlsx, 534
budgets
  capital budgeting, Solver, 297–302
  operating cost trends, charting of, 544–548
  option pricing, use of, 730–732
  revenue by location, PivotTable, 407–410
buttons, for macros, 807–809
buttons, radio, 259
buttons, spin, 251–256
By Changing Variable Cells, Solver Parameters, 276

C

Calculated Field, PivotTable, 410–411
Calculateditem.xlsx, 413–415
calculations. *See also* formulas; sales calculations; specific function names
  Automatic, options for, 143
  calculated items, PivotTable, 413–415
  OFFSET, data from variable cell locations, 179–180
  OFFSET, use in formulas, 178–181
  PivotTable, new data and, 401
  results, moving of, 119–120
  subtotals, creation of, 501–504
  table slicers, 242–244
call options, 721–723
Capbudget.xlsx, 297–302
capital budgeting
  option pricing and, 730–732
  Solver, 297–302
capital investments
  depreciation calculations, 82–83
  PV function, annuity value, 75–77
caret (^), 65
cash flows
  internal rate of return (IRR), 66–67, 70–73
  MIRR, modified IRR, 72–73
  net present value (NPV) calculations, 64–67
  PV function, annuity value, 75–77
  waterfall charts, 536–537
  XIRR, irregular cash flow dates, 72
Categorylabels.xlsx, 513–514
Cell Icon, Sort, 231
cells
  AutoComplete options, 244–245
  color, sorting by, 230–231
  locking and unlocking, 728–730
  OFFSET, extracting data from cells, 181–183
  OFFSET function, uses of, 177–178
  radio buttons, linking, 259
  select all cells in sheet, 728
  spin buttons, linking of, 253–255
centered moving averages, 621
central limit theory (CLT), 663–665
Cerealcollapse.xlsx, 391–392
ceteris paribus, 578
Change Table Name, 238
changing cells, optimization models, 269–270. *See also* Solver
Chapter1customer.xlsx, 4–6
CHAR function, 42
  #VALUE error handling, 48–49
Chart Styles, 355–357, 377
charts and graphs. *See also* 3D Maps; Power View
  band chart, inventory tracking, 519–520
  boxplots, 376–380
  bubble charts, 534
  category labels, 513–514
  check boxes, data selection, 522–523
  combination charts, 508–510
  conditional colors, adding, 527–528
  data labels and tables, inclusion of, 514–516
  dynamic labels, 520–521
  Gantt charts, 524–525
  GETPIVOT, dynamic dashboards and, 530–532
  hidden data, handling of, 511–512
  histograms, 353–359
  histograms, data updates and, 526–527
  Insert Statistic Chart, 355
  list boxes, data selection, 523–524
  missing data, handling of, 510–511
  moving averages and time series, 609–611
  one-way ANOVA graphs, 604
  Pareto charts, 360–361
  pictures, adding of, 512–513
  PivotChart, 396–397
  pre- and post-merger distinctions, 532–533
  radar chart, 533–534
  for salesforce performance over time, 517–519
  scatter charts, 532, 534
  secondary axis, 509–510
  sorted data and, 525–526
  sparklines, 465–469
  storing as templates, 520
  straight-line relationships, 543–548

charts and graphs, *continued*
sunburst charts, 537–540
table data updates, 239–240
thermometer chart, 520–521
treemaps, 537–540
two-way ANOVA graphs, 607
waterfall charts, 528–530, 534–537
check boxes, user forms, 251–252
for conditional formatting, 256–258
Checkboxtemp.xlsx, 256–258
Checkbox.xlsx, 256–258, 523
churn rate, 4–6
circular references
AVERAGE, 15
defined, 89–90
Formula Auditing group, 132–133
pro forma financial statements, 104–105
resolving, 90–92
Circular.xlsx, 89–92
Ciscoexpo.xlsx, 551–553
Ciscoimpvol.xlsx, 727–728
city, 3D Maps, 462–463
CLEAN function, 43
#VALUE error handling, 48–49
Cleanexample.xlsx, 48
Clear Rules, conditional formatting, 200–201, 214
coefficients, regression equations
ceteris paribus, 578
of dummy variables, 578–579
election result predictions, 582–583
cohort, defined, 736
Collapse Field, PivotTable, 391–392
colon (:), to indicate time, 114
Color Scales
conditional formatting, 200–201
Highlight Cells and, 203
stock returns, color coding, 207–209, 212–214
temperature trend data, 201–202
use of, 207–209
colors
charts, conditional colors, 527–528
filtering by, 489–490
sorting by, 230–231
Colorscales2016.xlsx, 207–209
column charts, combination charts, 508–510
column index, VLOOKUP, 21–22
columns
array formulas and functions, 786
Banded Columns, Table Tools, 238
calculated columns, Power Pivot, 439
changing column data into row data, 120–121
column references, tables, 245
Convert Text to Columns Wizard, 47–51
Design, Table Tools, 238
first and last, tables, 238
OFFSET function, uses of, 177–178
PivotTable creation, 387
table slicers and, 243–244
TRANSPOSE, 788
COM Add-Ins, Power Pivot, 439
combination charts, 508–510
Combinationstemp.xlsx, 508–510
combo boxes, user forms, 251–252
day of week selection, 260
Combobox.xlsx, 260
compact form, PivotTable, 389–390
Complement Rule of Probability, 632
Compound Annual Growth Rate (CAGR), 553
CONCATENATE function, 42
extracting product descriptions, 44–45
Condcolors.xlsx, 527–528
conditional formatting
AND, OR, NOT, use in formulas, 215–216
Borders, 213–214
charts, conditional colors, 527–528
check box, on/off toggle, 256–258
checking or customizing rules, 203–205
Clear Rules, 214
Color Scales, 207–209, 258
Data Bars, 205–207
Data Bars, Color Scales, Icon Sets, 200–201
Delete Rule, 214
duplicate data, highlighting, 203
editing rules, 214
Fill, 213–214, 258
Format Painter, 221–222
Highlight Cell Rules, 200, 203
Icon Sets, 209–212
icons, Wingdings 3 conversion, 517–519
New Formatting Rule dialog box, 206–207
new table data and, 246–247
PivotTable, 399–400
quarterly revenue data, 214–217
ranking players and positions, 218–220
rule precedence, 214
statistical outliers, 371
stock returns, color coding of, 212–214
Stop If True, 220–221
temperature trend data, 201–202
Top/Bottom Rules, 200, 201–202
uses of, 199–201
weekend dates, color coding, 217–218
workgroup assignments, 330
Conditional Formatting Rules Manager, 204–205
rule precedence, 214
Use A Formula, 215–217
conditional probability, 634–635
confidence interval for mean profit, 690
Consolidate command, 495–498
constraints, optimization models, 269–270. *See also* Solver

consumer surplus, 778–780
contingency table, 635
continuous random variables, 643
  beta random variable, 669, 672–673
  optimal bid calculations, 694
Contrateeoq.xlsx, 744–745
Convert Text to Columns Wizard, 47–51, 182–183
Convert to Range, Table Tools, 238
Copy Level, Sort, 230
copying formulas
  dollar sign ($) and, 5–6
  GETPIVOTDATA and, 416
  methods for, 2
CORREL function, 565
Correlationexamples.xlsx, 561–566
cost calculations
  back-order penalty, 749–752
  demand curve estimation and, 759
  economic order quantity, 741–745
  multiple regression and, 567–573
  OFFSET, costs per location, 180–181
  OFFSET, drug development cost per phase, 180–181
  optimal product mix decisions and, 274–282
  power curve, 555–559
  reorder point decisions, 747–752
  trends, charting of, 544–548
  waterfall charts, 534–537
Costestimate.xlsx, 545–548
COUNT, 163–168
  automatic updates, monthly sales, 186–187
COUNTA, 163–168
  OFFSET, extracting data from cells, 182–183
COUNTBLANK, 163–168
COUNTIF, 163–168
  GRG Multistart and, 320
  workgroup assignments, 328–329
COUNTIFS, 163–168
  GRG Multistart and, 320
country, 3D Maps, 462–463
craps, probability of winning, 709–711
Create From Selection
  named ranges, 11–12
Create PivotTable dialog box, 385–386
Creditunion.xlsx, 623–626, 627
Crimedata.xlsx, 459–460
CRITBINOM, 650–653
criteria
  COUNT, COUNTIF, COUNTA, COUNTBLANK, 164–168
  multiple criteria, row flags for, 172
  SUMIF, 172
CUMIPMT (cumulative interest payment)
function, 80–83
CUMPRINC (cumulative principal) function, 80–83
curly brackets ({ }), array formulas, 787, 794
Custom, Data Validation, 345–346
Custom Lists, Sort, 231–232
  Import List From Cells, 233–234
customer data
  marketing decisions, PivotTable, 401–407
  revenue by location, PivotTable, 407–410
  text data extraction, Flash Fill, 49–50
customer estimation model, 4–6
customer retention rate, 735–737
customer value, determination of, 735–739

D

data, resampling of, 717–719
Data Analysis, 352–353. *See also* descriptive statistics
Data Analysis Expressions (DAX)
  overview of, 447–448
  Power Pivot and, 439
data array, 788–789
Data Bars
  conditional formatting, 200–201
  conditional formatting, PivotTable, 399–400
  use of, 205–207
data displays. *See* charts and graphs
Data Model
  adding and removing data, 430–431
  adding new data sets, 435
  creating PivotTables, 431–434, 435
  creating relationships, 431
  DISTINCT COUNT, 435–437
  overview of, 429–430
  Power View, preparing data for, 452–454
  Quick Explore, 434
  relationships, creating or deleting, 435
data tables
  calculation options, 143
  sensitivity, price and unit cost, 140–143
  sensitivity analysis, 139–140
Data Validation, 343–348
Databars.xlsx, 205–207
database statistical functions. *See also* descriptive statistics; specific statistic names
  sales by employee, region, and product, 473–476
  syntax, 472–473
  tips for criteria ranges, 476
  transaction revenue by date sold and product ID, 477–478
  uses for, 471–473
databases, external data, 440–444
#Data, AutoComplete, 244
Datamodeltemp.xlsx, 429–430
date sold
  price lookup, 24–25
  transaction summaries by employee, 240–242

dates and date functions
- actual date, recovery of, 60
- combo (list) box, day of week selection, 260
- data validation, 345
- date formats, 55–57
- DATEIF, 60
- DATEIF function, 60
- DATEVALUE function, 55–57
- extracting month, year, day information, 59
- filtering for specific time period, 487–489
- highlighting specific dates, 203
- macros and, 810–812
- monthly sales *vs.* previous year, 419–420
- moving averages and time series, 609–611
- NETWORKDAYS, 59
- sorting by month, 231–232
- static dates, 60
- Timeline, PivotTable, 417–418
- today's date, display of, 57
- total sales to date, PivotTable, 418–419
- weekend dates, conditional formatting, 217–218
- workdays calculations, 57–58

Dates.xlsx, 56–60
DAVERAGE, 473–474
DAX. *See* Data Analysis Expressions (DAX)
DCOUNT, 474
DCOUNTA, 474
Define Name
- applying name ranges, 16–17
- dynamic ranges, creating, 184–185
- name range creation, 12–13
- worksheet names, listing of, 196–198

Delete Level, Sort, 230
Delete Rule, conditional formatting, 214
Delimited, Convert Text to Columns, 182–183
delimited text files, importing of, 337–341
demand curve, 7–8
- elasticity of demand, 760, 774
- estimation of, 759–763
- linear demand curve, 760–762
- power demand curve, 760–762
- product tie-ins, pricing effects, 765–768
- quadratic demand curve, 772–774
- subjectively determined demand, 771–774

demand points, 291–294
dependent variables
- ANOVA, two-way, 599–607
- interactions, modeling of, 585–588
- multiple regression, overview of, 567–573
- nonlinearities, modeling of, 585–588
- straight-line relationships, 543–548

dependents, 133
depreciation calculations, 82–83
descriptive statistics. *See also* database statistical functions; specific statistic names
- boxplots, 376–380
- comparing data sets, 371–372
- conditional formatting, 371
- geometric mean, 375–376
- kurtosis, 369
- mean (average), 367, 369, 370
- median, 367, 369
- mode, 367–369
- outliers, 370, 371
- percentile ranking, 372–373
- range, 369–370
- ranking numbers in data sets, 374
- rule of thumb, 370
- sample variance, 369–370
- second largest or smallest number, 373–374
- of selected range, 375
- skewness measure, 369
- standard deviation, 369–370
- standard error of regression, 548
- trimmed mean, 374–375
- typical values for data sets, 366–369

Design tab, PivotTable, 391
Design tab, Table Tools
- formatting tables, 236–238
- options, overview of, 238

Developer tab. *See also* user forms
- macros and, 803–804

discounts, quantity, 777
discrete random variables, 641–642
distance, story problems, 153–154
- traveling-salesperson problem (TSP), 333–335

distance between cities, INDEX, 29–31
DISTINCT COUNT, 435–437
Distinctcounttemp.xlsx, 435–437
distribution decisions, Solver, 291–294
#DIV/0! error, 107
Divide, Paste Special command, 121–123
dividend rate, stock options and, 723–726, 727
division, order of operation, 6–7
Dolan, Robert J., 759
dollar sign ($)
- cell range names, 18
- conditional formatting, formulas, 216, 217, 219
- demand curve, 7–8
- use in formulas, 5–6

double-declining-balance depreciation (DDB), 82–83
drilling down, PivotTable, 415
drilling down, Quick Explore, 434
drop-down boxes, user forms
- data validation and, 347–348
- day of week selection, 260

drug development phase costs, 180–181
Drugabandon.xlsx, 731–732
Drugfore.xlsx, 676–677
DSUM

as array function, 793–794
overview of, 471–473
sales by employee, region, and product, 473
dummy variable, 576–577
duplicates
Design tab, Table Tools, 238
Highlight Cells formatting for, 203
removing, tables, 238
in two lists, finding of, 790–791
duration, stock options, 723–726, 727
dynamic dashboards, creation of, 530–532
dynamic ranges
automatic updates, monthly sales, 185–187
data validation, 347–348
expanding on data entry, 236–237
retrieving new (updated) data, 184–185
Dynamichistograms.xlsx, 526–527
Dynamiclabels.xlsx, 520–521
Dynamicrange.xlsx, 184–185

E

East.xlsx, 420–423, 495–498
economic order quantity (EOQ), 741–745
Edit Formatting Rule dialog box
Color Scales, 208–209
Data Bars, 206–207
Edit Name dialog box, 13–14
Edit Rule, conditional formatting, 214
elasticity, 557
of demand, 760, 774
election result predictions, 580–583
email lists, text data extraction (Flash Fill), 49–50
employees. *See also* labor; wage calculations
employee ratings, 327–329
workgroup assignments, 327–329
Enable Iterative Calculation, 89, 91
Eoq.xlsx, 742–745
Error Checking, Formula Auditing group, 132–133
error messages, invalid data, 344
error values, 106–107
errors, random, 628–630
errors, trendlines, 546–547
Errortrap.xlsx, 105–107, 132–133
Esc key, Solver and, 320
European stock options, 722
Evaluate Formula, 183
event probabilities, 632
event, defined, 631–632
independent events, 633–634
mutually exclusive events, 632–633
Evolutionary Solver engine, 271–272
conditional formatting results, 330
keys to success, 327
overview of, 317–321
two-part tariff calculations, 783–784
warehouse location decisions, 326
workgroup assignments, 327–329
Excel Solver. *See* Solver
Excelfinfunctions.xlsx, 76–83
exclamation point (!), in ranges, 16
exercise date, stock options, 722–723
Expand Field, PivotTable, 391–392
expenses. *See also* cost calculations
expense projections, sensitivity analysis, 144–146
expense tracking, waterfall charts, 534–537
experience curve, 556
experiment, defined, 631–632
exponential growth, modeling of, 551–553
Exponentialdist.xlsx, 658
external data, Power Pivot, 440–444

F

Fax.xlsx, 557–559
field list, PivotTable, 387
Fill, conditional formatting, 213–214
Filter By Color, 489–490
filters
by cell color, 489–490
clearing filters, 485
for combinations of people, products, and location, 492–493
for number of units, 485–487
for specific time period, 487–489
list of salespeople, 491
overview of, 481–482
PivotTable, 392–396, 397
Power View chart filters, 455–458
Remove Duplicates, 491
reports and, 411–412
revenue by location, 408–410
slicers and, 398
table design and, 236
table slicers, 242–244
text, Begins With, 489
top sales by employee, 490–491
for total sales amount, 485–487
transactions by employee, product, and location, 483–485
transactions by employee and price, 493–494
Filters, PivotTable creation, 387
Final Four performance probabilities, 713–715
Final4sim.xlsx, 713–715
financial functions. *See also* investments
CUMIPMT (cumulative interest payment) function, 80–83
CUMPRINC (cumulative principal) function, 80–83

financial functions, *continued*
depreciation calculations, 82–83
FV function, future value, 77–78
mortgage decisions, 143–144, 152–153, 306–307
NPER (number of periods) function, 81
PMT function, 78–80
PV function, annuity value, 75–77
RATE function, 81
retirement savings, Solver, 307–309
FIND, 41
extracting regional sales data, 45–46
#VALUE error handling, 48–49
worksheet name, 197
Find and Select command, 46
Finmathsolver.xlsx, 306–309
First Column, Table Tools, 238
first quartile, boxplots, 376–380
Flash Fill
disabling, 50
extracting data from cells, 182–183
text data extraction, 49–50
Flashfill.xlsx, 49–51
font. *See also* formatting
color, sorting by, 230–231
histograms, formatting of, 353–354
football point spreads, 311–314
forecasts. *See also* analytics; probability; Solver
accuracy of, 626–629
ANOVA, one-way, 593–597
ANOVA, two-way, 599–607
asset allocation decisions, 702–707
bias in, 675–677
correlations, 561–566
exponential growth, modeling of, 551–553
Forecast group, Data tab
breakeven analysis, units sold, 151–152
mortgage decisions, 143–144
Scenario Manager, 157–161
sensitivity, price and unit cost, 141–143
forecast errors, 628–630
LINEST function, 572–573
LOGEST array function, 795–798
Monte Carlo simulation, 683–690
moving averages and time series, 609–611
multiple regressions, 567–573
election results, 580–583
forecasting with, 583–584
quarterly US auto sales, 575–580
nonlinearities and interactions, 585–588
number of customers over time, 4–6
power curve, 555--559
probability statements, 675–677
randomized blocks, 599–601
ratio-to-moving average method, 619–621
revenue by location, PivotTable, 407–410
seasonal trend analysis, 795–798
special events and, 623–630
stock price modeling, 699–702
straight-line relationships, estimating, 543–548
TREND function, 583–584
Winters method, 613–617
Form Controls. *See also* user forms
check box, chart data selection, 522–523
list box, chart data selection, 523–524
for macros, 807–809
Format Axis, 356
Format Control, spin button linking, 254–255
Format Data Labels, 534
Format Data Series
boxplots, 377
histograms, 353–357
Format Only Cells That Contain, 213–214
Format Painter, conditional formatting and, 221–222
formatting. *See also* conditional formatting
applying to new data, 235–238
conditional formatting and new data, 246–247
histograms, 353–357
icons, Wingdings 3 conversion, 517–519
macros, use of, 806–807
PivotTable, 391
Table Tools, Design tab options, 238
Formula Auditing group, 131–137
before tax profits, 135–136
data from multiple worksheets, 136–137
net present value calculations, 134–135
Formula AutoComplete, 236–237
formulas. *See also* array formulas; AVERAGE; IF statements; SUM
AND, use of, 215–216
applying name ranges, 16–17
AutoComplete, 236–237, 245
copying of, 2
Data Analysis Expressions (DAX), 447–448
dollar sign ($), 5–6
GETPIVOTDATA and, 415–417
INDIRECT, formula evaluation and, 192–193
input and output value placement in sheets, 5
maintaining ranges, row additions and, 193–195
named ranges, 11
NOT, use of, 215–216
OFFSET, use of, 178–181
OR, use of, 215–216
order of evaluation, IF statements, 97
order of operation (PEDMAS), 6–7
protecting in worksheet, 728–730
range name lookups, INDIRECT and, 195
three-dimensional formulas, 125–128
Use A Formula, New Formatting Rule dialog box, 215–217
FORMULATEXT function, 2, 131–133

Freeze Panes , 99
    spin buttons and, 255–256
FREQUENCY, 527, 788–789
Fruitlist.xlsx, 347–348
functions. *See* array functions; specific function names
FV function, future value, 77–78

G

gambling, probability and, 709–713
Gantt charts, 524–525
Gantt.xlsx, 524–525
Gasprices507.xlsx, 239–240
Gaussian population, 370
gender wage gap, 586–588
geographic formats, 3D Maps, 462–463
geometric mean, 375–376
GEOMMEAN, 375–376
Geommean.xlsx, 375–376
GEsimless5.xlsx, 702
Get External Data, Power Pivot, 440–444
GETPIVOTDATA, 415–417
    dynamic dashboards, creation of, 530–532
Getpivotdata.xlsx, 415–417
GET.WORKBOOK, 197
Globalwarming2016.xlsx, 201–202
Goal Seek
    break even analysis, units sold, 151–152
    incentive offers, customer loyalty and, 737–739
    mortgage decisions, 152–153
    power demand curve, 762
    stock volatility estimates, 727–728
    story problems, 153–154
    uses for, 151
Gompertz curve, 553
graphs. *See* 3D Maps; charts and graphs; Power View
greater than or equal to (>=), 166
GRG Multistart
    overview of, 317–321
    warehouse location decisions, 321–326
    workgroup assignments, 329
GRG Nonlinear engine, Solver, 271–272
    Weibull random variable, 671–672
Groceriespt.xlsx, 385–388, 396–397, 398
grocery store sales, PivotTable and, 385–388
Grocerypt.xlsx, 399
gross national product (GNP), as variable, 577
Group Box (Form Control), 259
group list boxes, user forms, 251–252
GROWTH function, 798
guess argument, internal rate of return, 70

H

Harris, F., 741
header row, AutoComplete options, 244–245
Header Row, Table Tools, 238
#Headers, AutoComplete, 244
height, OFFSET function, 178, 181
Hidden.xlsx, 511–512
hierarchical data, charting of, 537–540
Highlight Cell Rules, 200, 203
    temperature trend data, 201–202
Highlightcells.xlsx, 203
histograms
    common shapes for, 357–359
    comparisons of, interpreting, 359–360
    constructing and interpreting, 351–359
    data updates (dynamic histograms), 526–527
Historicalinvest.xlsx, 211–212
HLOOKUP
    syntax, 22
    workgroup assignments, 328–329
holidays, workday calculations, 57–58
Holland, John, 321
HOUR function, 116
hours worked, start and end times, 116–117
House2.xlsx, 614–615
HYPERGEOM.DIST, 650–652
hypergeometric random variables, 650–652
hyperlink navigation, 127–128
Hyperlinks.xlsx, 127–128
hypotheses testing, ANOVA, 593–594

I

Icon sets
    conditional formatting, 200–201
    sorting by icon, 231
    use of, 209–212
icons, Wingdings 3 conversion, 517–519
IF function, GRG Multistart and, 320
IF statements, 96–97
    break even analysis, 145–146
    craps rolls, modeling, 101
    maximum number per cell, 108
    moving-average trading, stocks, 98–100
    #N/A errors, replacing with blanks, 105–107
    nested IF formula, 97
    order of evaluation, 97
    pro forma financial statements, 101–105
    purchase cost as function of unit number, 96–97
    sales revenues, 107–108
    Solver and, 782–783
    stock hedges, 97–98
    workgroup assignments, 328–329
IFERROR function, 105–107

IFERROR function, *continued*
GETPIVOTDATA and, 416
sports point spreads, 312
IFstatement.xlsx, 96
Import List From Cells, Custom Lists, 233–234
importing text data, Word documents, 337–341
incentive offers, customer loyalty, 737–739
income statement, pro forma statements, 101–105
Income.xlsx, 220–221
independent events, probability, 633–634
independent random variables, 644
independent variables
ANOVA, two-way, 599–607
interactions, modeling of, 585–588
multiple regression, overview of, 567–573
nonlinearities, modeling of, 585–588
qualitative independent variables, 576
quantitative independent variables, 575
straight-line relationships, 543–548
INDEX
combo (list) box, day of week, 260
distance between cities, 29–31
radio button, price charged options, 259
syntax, 29
INDEX.xlsx, 29–31
INDIRECT
compiling data, multiple worksheets, 193
consolidating data from multiple worksheets, 196
formula evaluation and, 192–193
formula ranges, row additions and, 193–195
range name lookups, 195
uses of, 191–192
worksheets, list of names, 196–198
Indirectconsolidate.xlsx, 196
Indirectinsertrow.xlsx, 193–195
Indirectmultiplesheet.xlsx, 193
Input Message, 344
inputs
placement in spreadsheet, 5
for predictions, 4–6
Insert Line Or Area Chart, table data updates, 239–240
Insert Statistic Chart, 353–359
Box And Whisker option, 377
INT, table slicers and, 243–244
Integer Optimality, Solver, 301
integer programming problems, Solver, 301
interactions, modeling of, 585–588
interarrival time, 754
INTERCEPT function, 548
interest
CUMIPMT (cumulative interest payment) function, 80–83
IPMT function, loans, 79–80
mortgage decisions, 143–144, 152–153, 306–307
PPMT function, loans, 79–80
RATE function, 81
stock options and interest rate, 723–726
internal rate of return (IRR), 66–67
of cash flows, 70
guess argument, 70
MIRR, modified IRR, 72–73
overview of, 69
unique IRRs, 70–72
XIRR, irregular dates, 72
international sales data, 179–180
interquartile range (IQR), 376–380
inventory decisions
95 percent service level, 750–752
economic order quantity, 741–745
reorder point, 747–752
uncertain demand, modeling with, 747–752
inventory tracking, 519–520
investments. *See also* descriptive statistics
asset allocation decisions, 702–707
automatic updates, new data, 788–789
bootstrapping, 699–707
conditional formatting, color scales, 208–209, 212–214
depreciation calculations, 82–83
FV function, future value, 77–78
geometric mean, 375–376
histograms, constructing and interpreting, 351–359
Icon Sets, conditional formatting, 211–212
internal rate of return (IRR), 66–67
lognormal random variable, modeling with, 679–682
moving-average trading, stocks, 98–100
net present value (NPV) calculations, 64–67
payback periods, 36–38
pricing stock options, 721–732
American and European, 722
call and put options, 721–722
decision-making and, 730–732
parameter changes, effects of, 726–727
protecting sheet formulas, 728–730
stock price on exercise date, 722–723
value, parameters for, 723–724
volatility and, 724, 727–728
PV function, annuity value, 75–77
retirement savings, Solver, 307–309
stock hedges, 97–98
stock price modeling, 699–702
stock return correlations, 563–566
IPMT function, loan payments, 79–80
IRR.xlsx, 70–73
ISERROR, 791
ISFORMULATEXT.xlsx, 131
ISNUMBER (), 346
IVolatility.com, 680

J

James, Bill, 266
job-shop scheduling problems, 333–335

K

Key Performance Indicators (KPIs), 439
kurtosis, 369, 694

L

Labelsandtables.xlsx, 514–516
labor. *See also* wage calculations
  capital budgeting decisions, 297–302
  optimal product mix decisions, 274–282
  traveling-salesperson problem (TSP), 333–335
  workforce schedule, optimal, 285–288
  workgroup assignments, 327–329
lagged variables, 577
lambda *(λ)*, Poisson random variable, 656–658
LARGE, 36, 373–374
Last Column, Table Tools, 238
Lastyear.xlsx, 17–18
Law of Complements, 632
Law of Total Probability, 635
learning curve, 556
least-squares line, 546–547
LEFT function, 41
  extracting product descriptions, 44–45
  extracting regional sales data, 45–46
Lefthandlookup.xlsx, 179
Lemonadegs.xlsx, 151–152
LEN function, 41
  extracting product descriptions, 44–45
  extracting regional sales data, 45–46
Lewent, Judy, 730
line graphs. *See also* charts and graphs
  combination charts, 508–510
  sparklines, 465
  table data updates and, 239–240
linear demand curve, 760–762
linear functions, Solver and, 271–272, 279–280, 301, 307
linear pricing, 777
linear relationships, correlations, 561–566
Linearfit.xlsx, 760–761
LINEST function, 572–573
Lineupsch39temp.xlsx, 337–341
Lipstickprice.xlsx, 772–774
list boxes, chart data selection and, 523–524
Listbox.xlsx, 523–524
lists
  changing column data into row data, 120–121
  combo (list) box, user forms, 260
Listtemp.xlsx, 233–234
loans
  CUMIPMT (cumulative interest payment) function, 80–83
  CUMPRINC (cumulative principal) function, 80–83
  mortgage decisions, 143–144, 152–153, 306–307
  NPER (number of periods) function, 81
  PMT function, payments, 78–80
  RATE function, 81
location, 3D Maps, 462–463
LOGEST, 795–798
Logicalexamples.xlsx, 215
Logistic curve, 553
logistics
  inventory tracking, 519–520
  transportation problems, Solver, 291–294
  traveling-salesperson problem (TSP), 333–335
  warehouse location decisions, 317–326
lognormal random variable, 679–682
  optimal bid calculations, 694
Lognormal.xlsx, 680–681
LOGNORM.DIST, 679–682
LOGNORM.INV, 679–682
lookup range, MATCH, 33–35
lookup value, 21–22, 33–35
Lookup.xlsx, 22–25
LOWER function, 42
Loyalty.xlsx, 735–737
lqtemp.xlsx, 354–355

M

machine life, Weibull random variable, 669
macroeconomic variables, 577
macros
  applying formatting to range of cells, 806–807
  defined, 803
  Developer tab, role of, 803–804
  GET.WORKBOOK, 197
  PivotTable filters, 812
  recording of, 804–805
  relative references, use in recording, 809–812
  running of, 807–809
Make Unconstrained Variables Non-Negative, 279
Makeup2007.xlsx, 172–173
Makeuparray.xlsx, 792–794
Makeupdb.xlsx, 472–476
Makeupfiltertemp.xlsx, 481–482
Makeupsorttemp.xlsx, 227–233
Makeupsubtotals.xlsx, 501–504
Makeuptimeline.xlsx, 417–418, 423
Manage Rules, conditional formatting, 200–201
  checking or customizing rules, 203–205
  Edit Rule, 214

Manage Rules, conditional formatting, *continued*
  Format Only Cells That Contain, 213–214
Maps, 3D, 462–463
margin of error, polls, 583
Maria.xlsx, 153–154
marketing decisions
  one-way ANOVA, 594–595
  PivotTable and, 401–407
  two-way ANOVA, 602–607
MATCH
  baseball player salaries, 35–36
  finding duplicates in two lists, 790–791
  investments, payback period, 36–38
  monthly product sales, 35
  with OFFSET, left-hand lookup, 179
  syntax, 33–35
Matchex.xlsx, 34–35
Matradingrule.xlsx, 98–100
MAX
  GRG Multistart and, 320
  highest salary, finding, 35–36
maximum value, boxplots, 376–380
mean
  descriptive statistics, 367, 369, 370
  group mean square, 597
  lognormal random variable, 679–682
  of random variables, 642–643
  regression toward, 566
  trimmed, 374–375
Meanvariance.xlsx, 642–643
measures of central location, 367–369
MEDIAN, 367
  average of numbers on list compared to median, 791
median, descriptive statistics, 367, 369
  boxplots, 376–380
  trimmed mean, 375
Medians.xlsx, 798
Merge, Scenario Manager, 161
Merton, Robert, 721
Microsoft Word, importing text from, 337–341
MID function, 41
  extracting product descriptions, 44–45
  extracting regional sales data, 45–46
MIN function, GRG Multistart and, 320
minimum value, boxplots, 376–380
minus sign (-), in PivotTable fields, 391
MINUTE function, 116
Missingdata.xlsx, 511
MODE, 367
mode, descriptive statistics, 367–369
Modefunctions.xlsx, 368
MODE.MULT, 368
MODE.SNGL, 368
Monte Carlo simulation, 683–690
monthly sales *vs.* previous year, 419–420
months, sorting by, 231–232
Monthtomonth.xlsx, 418–419
More Rules, Color Scales, 208–209
mortgage decisions, 143–144
  Goal Seek, 152–153
  variable interest and payments, 306–307
Mortgagedt.xlsx, 143–144
mosaic charts, 537–540
Mostrecent.xlsx, 184
Move Or Copy Sheet, 240
Movies.xlsx, 181–183
moving averages, 609–611
  centered moving averages, 621
moving-average trading, stocks, 98–100
Mrcostest.xlsx, 567–573
Mu, lognormal random variable, 679–682, 686–687
Multiple Consolidation Ranges, PivotTable, 421
multiple peaks, histograms, 359
multiple regression
  accuracy of, 571–572
  election result predictions, 580–583
  forecasting with, 583–584
  LINEST function, 572–573
  nonlinearities and interactions, 585–588
  overview of, 567–573
  qualitative factors, overview, 575
  quarterly US auto sales predictions, 575–580
Multiples, Power View, 461
multiplication, order of operation, 6–7
Multistart
  overview of, 317–321
  Weibull random variable, 671–672
mutually exclusive events, 632–633
My Table Has Headers, 236

N

#N/A (Not Available)
  array formula ranges, 368
  charts, check-box controls and, 522–523, 531
  MATCH function and, 34
  replacing with blanks, 105–107
  Trace Error and, 133
  VLOOKUP, 22
Name box, named range creation, 10–11
#NAME? error, 107
Name Manager, name range creation, 13–14
name ranges
  applying to formulas, 16–17
  creating, 9–14
  deleting, 14
  displaying defined range names, 10
  editing of, 13–14
  noncontiguous cells, 10–11

- for revenue projections, 17–18
- rules for naming, 18
- sales calculations, 14–15
- workbook *vs.* worksheet scope, 15–16

Namedatemacro.xlsx, 809–812
natural gas price tracking, 239–240
navigation tips, worksheets, 387
Nbadvl.xlsx, 343
negative binomial random variable, 652–653
Negative Values and Axis, data bars, 207
Negativedatabars.xlsx, 207
negatively skewed histograms, 358
NEGBINOM.DIST, 652–653
Nestedsubtotals.xlsx, 503–504
net present value. *See* NPV (net present value)
NETWORKDAYS function, 59
New Formatting Rules dialog box, 206–207
- Icon Sets, 209–212
- statistical outliers, formatting for, 371
- Use A Formula, 215–217

New Name dialog box, 12–13
New Rule, conditional formatting, 200–201
NFL point spreads, 311–314
Nfl2016.xlsx, 311–314
NFLwinslosses.xlsx, 468–469
95 percent service level, 750–752
Nlp.xlsx, 779
noncontiguous cells, named ranges, 10–11
nonlinear functions, Solver and, 271–272
- GRG Multistart, overview of, 317–321

nonlinear pricing, 777–784
nonlinear relationships, correlations, 561–566
nonlinearities, modeling of, 585–588
nonnumeric values, data validation, 345–346
nonsmooth functions, Solver and, 271–272, 327. *See also* Evolutionary Solver engine; GRG Multistart
normal cumulative function, 662
normal population, 370
normal random variables, 659–665
- central limit theory (CLT), 664–665
- optimal bid calculations, 694
- percentiles and, 663
- simulating values for, 686–687
- standard normal, 725

Normalexamples.xlsx, 661, 662, 664–665
Normalsim.xlsx, 686–687
NORM.DIST, 662
NORM.INV, 663, 686–687
NOT, use in formulas, 215–216
not equal to (<>), 166
NPER (number of periods) function, 81
NPV (net present value), 64–67
- capital budgeting decisions, 297–302
- customer value, determining, 735–739
- Formula Auditing, 134–135
- PV function, annuity value, 75–77
- Scenario Manager and, 157–161
- spin buttons, sensitivity analysis and, 252–256

NPVauditscenario.xlsx, 157–161
NPVaudit.xlsx, 134–135
NPVspinners.xlsx, 252–256
null hypothesis, defined, 593
#NUM! error, 107
Number Format, PivotTable, 391
Numberdv.xlsx, 346

O

OFFSET function, 177–187
- automatic updates, monthly sales, 185–187
- data from variable cell locations, 179–180
- drug development cost per phase, 180–181
- dynamic ranges, creating, 184–185
- extracting data from cells, 181–183
- with MATCH, left-hand lookup, 179
- retrieving most recent data, 184
- retrieving new (updated) data, 184–185
- uses of, 177–178

Offsetcost.xlsx, 180–181
Offsetexample.xlsx, 178–178, 180–181
one-time incentive offers, 737–739
one-way ANOVA, 593–597
Onewayanovatemp.xlsx, 594–596
operating costs. *See* cost calculations
optimal bid, calculation of, 693–696
optimal product mix decisions, 273–282
optimal solution, Solver, 269–272. *See also* Solver
option buttons, user forms, 251–252
option pricing, 721–732
Optionbuttons.xlsx, 259
Optionfigures.xlsx, 722–723
Optionsbuttonstemp.xlsx, 259
OR, Boolean arrays, 794
OR, use in formulas, 215
order of operation
- formulas, 6–7
- IF statements, 97

outliers, 370–371, 548
outputs, placement in spreadsheet, 5

P

parentheses, order of operations, 6–7
Pareto charts, 360–361
Paretotemp.xlsx, 360–361
Paste List, 17
Paste Name, 17
Paste Special command, 788
- calculation results, moving of, 119–120

Paste Special command, *continued*
- Divide option, 121–123
- lists, changing column data into rows, 120–121
- Transpose, 120–121
- uses for, 119
- Values, 120

Pastespecial.xlsx, 119–120
payback period, investments, 36–38
Payback.xlsx, 36–37
payment on principal, 79–80
Paymentgs.xlsx, 152–153
payments, mortgage decisions, 143–144
PEDMAS, order of operations, 6–7
percentage
- order of operation, 7
- revenue by location, PivotTable, 407–410

PERCENTILE, 372–373
PERCENTILE.EXC, 372–373
PERCENTILE.INC, 372–373
PERCENTILERANK.EXC, 372–373
PERCENTILERANK.INC, 372–373
percentiles, normal random variables, 663
Percentile.xlsx, 372–373
PERCENTRANK, 372–373
period (.), in ranges, 19
Phoneloyalty.xlsx, 737–739
Picturegraph.xlsx, 512–513
PivotChart, 396–397
PivotChart Wizard, 420–423
PivotTable
- adding blank rows, 398–399
- calculated field, 410–411
- calculated items, 413–415
- charts, dynamic dashboards and, 530–532
- collapsing and expanding fields, 391–392
- conditional formatting, 399–400
- creating from previous table, 423
- creating with Data Model, 431–434, 435
- creating with Power Pivot, 445–446
- drilling down, 415 field lists, 387
- format changes, 391
- GETPIVOTDATA, 415–417
- grouping items, 412–413
- hiding subtotals, 398–399
- layout options, 389–390
- macros, use of, 812
- for marketing decisions, 401–407
- monthly sales *vs.* previous year, 419–420
- from multiple sheets or workbooks, 420–423
- new data, calculations and, 401
- new fields, calculations and, 415–417
- overview of use, 384–385
- PivotChart and, 396–397
- report filter, creating multiple tables, 423–424
- report filters and slicers, 411–412
- retrieving new (updated) data, 184–185
- for revenue by location, 407–410
- slicers, 398
- sorting and filtering, 392–396, 397
- store sale summaries, 385–388
- Timeline, 417–418
- total sales to date, 418–419

PivotTable Fields pane, 386–387
- grouping items, 412–413

PivotTable Options, 399
Pivotwithslicers.xlsx, 447
players and positions, ranking of, 218–220
plus sign (+), in PivotTable fields, 391
PMT function, 78–80
- mortgage decisions, 143–144, 152–153, 306–307

point spreads, NFL, 311–314
Poisson random variables, 655–658
POISSON.DIST, 656–658
Poisson.xlsx, 657–658
poker hands, probability and, 711–713
populations, descriptive statistics, 370
populations, Evolutionary Solver and, 321
portfolio insurance, 97–98
positively skewed histograms, 358
postal code, 3D Maps, 462–463
power curve, 555–559
power demand curve, 760–762
Power Pivot. *See also* Data Model
- creating PivotTables, 445–446
- Data Analysis Expression (DAX), 447–448
- overview of, 430
- reading data into, 440–444
- slicers, use of, 446–447
- uses for, 439–440

Power View
- 3D Maps and, 461–463
- animated movie, from chart, 459–460
- charts, filtering of, 455–458
- charts, types available, 454–455
- Multiples, 461
- preparing data for, 452–454
- as ribbon add-in, 451
- sales data by country, 458–459
- uses for, 451–452

Powercapacitytemp.xlsx, 462–463
Powerexamples.xlsx, 555–559
Powerfit.xlsx, 761–762
PPMT function, loan payments, 79–80
precedents, 133
predictions. *See* forecasts
predictive analytics, 263–264. *See also* analytics
prescriptive analytics, 264–265. *See also* analytics
President16.xlsx, 580–583
price
- breakeven analysis, 151–152

demand curve estimation, 759–763
effect on profits, 7–8
elasticity of demand, 760, 774
linear pricing, 777
lookup by date sold, 24–25
natural gas price tracking, 239–240
nonlinear pricing, 777–784
price bundling, 778–780
product tie-ins and, 765–768
quantity discounts, 777
radio buttons, price charged options, 259
sensitivity analysis, 140–143
subjectively determined demand, 771–774
two-part tariff, 778, 780–783
two-way ANOVA, 602–607
VLOOKUP and, 24
principal, mortgage decisions, 143–144
pro forma financial statements, 101–105
probability. *See also* forecasts
Additive Rule for Computing Probabilities, 633
asset allocation decisions, 702–707
Bayes' theorem, 635–637
beta random variable, 669, 672–673
binomial random variables, 647–653, 693–694
central limit theory (CLT), 663–665
conditional probability, 634–635
confidence interval for mean profit, 690
contingency table, 635
event, defined, 631–632
event probability, axioms of, 632
experiment, defined, 631–632
Final Four performance, 713–715
forecast bias, 675–677
hypergeometric random variables, 650–652
independent events, 633–634
Law of Complements, 632
Law of Total Probability, 635
lognormal random variable, 679–682
Monte Carlo simulation, 683–690
mutually exclusive events, 632–633
negative binomial random variable, 652–653
normal random variables, 659–665
Poisson random variables, 655–658
poker hands, 711–713
probability density function, 643–644, 671–672
probability statements, 675–677
project management decisions, 672–673
random variables, 641–644
resampling data, 717–719
sample space, defined, 631–632
stock price modeling, 699–702
Weibull random variable, 669–672
of winning at craps, 709–711
Z-scores, 665–666
Prodmix.xlsx, 273–282
product descriptions, extracting, 44–45
product ID
price lookups, 24
price lookups by date sold, 24–25
product mix decisions, 273–282
product sales summaries, Power View
sales by country, 458–459
product sales summaries, PivotTable, 385–388
calculated items, 413–415
creating with Data Model, 431–434
monthly sales *vs.* previous year, 419–420
multiple workbooks or worksheets, 420–423
revenue by location, 407–410
sales by location, 413–415
Timeline, 417–418
total sales to date, 418–419
product sales summaries, subtotals, 501–504
product tie-ins, pricing and, 765–768
production decisions
economic order quantity, 741–745
Monte Carlo simulation, 687–689
Productlookup.xlsx, 35
profit
before tax profits, 135–136
customer value, determining, 735–739
demand curve estimation, 759–763
linear pricing and, 777
nonlinear pricing and, 777–784
optimal product mix decisions, 273–282
price bundling and, 778–780
price changes, effect of, 7–8
product tie-ins, pricing of, 765–768
revenue and expense projections, 144–146
Scenario Manager, sensitivity analysis and, 160–161
subjectively determined demand, pricing and, 771–774
two-part tariff pricing plan, 780–783
waterfall charts, 534–537
Proforma.xlsx, 101–105
progress tracking, waterfall charts, 528–530
project management, beta random variable, 672–673
projected annual revenues, 17–18
PROPER function, 42
protected formulas, 728–730
Ptableexample.xlsx, 407–411, 423
Ptcustomerstemp.xlsx, 812
Ptcustomers.xlsx, 393–396
purchasing decisions
purchase cost as function of unit number, 96–97
PV function, annuity value, 75–77
put options, 721–723
PV function, 75–77
p-value
multiple regression, 570–571, 578
one-way ANOVA, 593–594, 595
two-way ANOVA, 606

Q

quadratic demand curve, 772–774
qualitative independent variables, 576
quantitative independent variables, 575
quantity discounts, 777
quarterly revenue
  conditional formatting, 214–217
  seasonal trend analysis, LOGEST, 795–798
quarterly sales predictions, multiple regression, 575–580
quartiles, boxplots, 376–380
? (wildcard), 167
queuing theory, 753–757
Queuingtemplate.xlsx, 755–757
Quick Access Toolbar, 421–422
  macros, placing button on, 808–809
Quick Explore, Data Model, 434
quotation marks (" ")
  COUNTIF text values, 165–166
  IF statements, 100
  MATCH text values, 34

R

radar charts, 533–534
Radar.xlsx, 533–534
radio buttons, 259
RAND(), 684–685
RANDBETWEEN, 700, 703
  probability of winning at craps, 710–711
  resampling data, 717–719
Randdemo.xlsx, 684–685
random errors, 628–630
random variables
  beta random variable, 669, 672–673
  binomial random variables, 647–653, 693–694
  continuous random variables, 643, 694
  defined, 641
  discrete random variables, 641–642
  hypergeometric random variables, 650–652
  independent random variables, 644
  lognormal, simulating values for, 686–687, 694
  lognormal random variable, 679–682
  mean, variance, and standard deviation of, 642–643
  negative binomial random variable, 652–653
  Poisson random variables, 655–658
  probability density function, 643–644
  standard normal, defined, 725
  Weibull random variable, 669–672
randomized blocks, 599–601
Randy.xlsx, 530–532
range factor (RF), 266
range lookup
  MATCH, 33–35
  sum range, 172
  VLOOKUP, 21–22
ranges
  applying to formulas, 16–17
  array formulas and functions, 786
  automatic updates, monthly sales, 185–187
  bin ranges, defining, 351–353
  check boxes, chart data selection, 522–523
  conditional formatting, uses of, 199–201
  creating named ranges, 9–14
  data validation, 347–348
  database statistical functions, 476
  deleting name ranges, 14
  descriptive statistics, sample range, 369–370
  descriptive statistics of, 375
  Design, Table Tools, 238
  displaying defined range names, 10
  dynamic charts labels and, 520–521
  dynamic ranges, automatic updates, 185–187
  dynamic ranges, creating, 184–185
  editing of, 13–14
  expanding on data entry, 236–237
  formula ranges and row additions, 193–195
  geometric mean, 376
  INDIRECT, range name lookups, 195
  interquartile range (IQR), boxplots, 376
  LINEST function, 572–573
  list boxes, chart data selection, 523–524
  macros, use of, 806–807
  multiple regressions, 568–569
  noncontiguous cells, 10–11
  OFFSET and MATCH, lookups, 179
  OFFSET function, uses of, 177–178
  PivotTable, grouping items, 412–413
  PivotTable, multiple worksheets, 420–423
  retrieving new (updated) data, 184–185
  for revenue projections, 17–18
  RSQ (yrange, xrange), 548
  rules for naming, 18
  STEYX, standard error of regression, 548
  two-way ANOVA, 603–604
  workbook *vs.* worksheet scope, 15–16
  worksheet names, listing of, 196–198
RANK, 374
RANK.AVG, 374
RANK.EQ, 374, 712–713
ranking players and positions, 218–220
RATE function, 81
Ratioma.xlsx, 619–621
ratio-to-moving average forecasts, 619–621
raw materials, optimal product mix decisions, 274–282
Razorsandblades.xlsx, 765–768
real options, 730
#REF! error, 107
references, OFFSET function, 177–178
region, 3D Maps, 462–463

regional sales data, extracting from totals, 45–46
regression, multiple, 567–573
Regression dialog box, 568–569
regression toward the mean, 566
Reichheld, Frederick, 735
Relationships, Data Model, 431
  creating or deleting relationships, 435
relationships between variables. *See also* multiple regression
  correlations, 561–566
  interactions, modeling of, 585–588
  nonlinearities, modeling of, 585–588
  power curve, 555–559
  straight-line relationships, 543–548
relative references, macro recording and, 809–812
Remove Duplicates, filters, 491
Remove Duplicates, Table Tools, 238
reorder point decisions, 747–752
Reorderpoint_backorder.xlsx, 748–752
Repeatedhisto.xlsx, 47
Replace command, 46
REPLACE function, 42
Report Layout, PivotTable, 389–390
REPT function, 41
Required Bounds On Variables, 321
Resampleyield.xlsx, 717–719
resampling data, 717–719
residuals, trendlines, 546–547
Resize Table, 238
retention rate, customer, 735–737
retirement savings decisions, Solver, 307–309
return on investment, payback period, 36–38
revenue. *See also* sales calculations
  database statistical functions, 473–478
  demand curve estimation, 759–763
  exponential growth, modeling of, 551–553
  linear pricing, 777
  median transaction by country, 798
  moving averages and time series, 609–611
  name ranges, use of, 17–18
  nonlinear pricing and, 777–784
  price bundling and, 778–780
  product tie-ins, pricing and, 765–768
  projections, sensitivity analysis, 144–146
  quarterly revenue data, conditional formatting, 214–217
  subjectively determined demand, pricing and, 771–774
  subtotals, creation of, 501–504
  total sales to date, PivotTable, 418–419
  two-part tariff, 780–783
  waterfall charts, 534–537
Reverse Icon Order, 211–212
RIGHT function, 41
  extracting product descriptions, 44–45
risk-free rate, stock options, 723, 727
Rock.xlsx, 164–168
Rosling, Hans, 459
rows
  array formulas and functions, 786
  AutoComplete options, 244–245
  banded rows, 238
  Banded Rows, Table Tools, 238
  changing column data into row data, 120–121
  Design, Table Tools, 238
  formula ranges and row additions, 193–195
  new table rows, formulas and format, 236–238
  OFFSET function, uses of, 177–178
  PivotTable
    adding rows, 398–399
    creation of, 387
    hiding subtotals, 398–399
    layout options, 389–390
  table slicers and, 243–244
  TRANSPOSE, 788
RSQ (yrange, xrange), 548
R-squared value, 547, 565
rule of thumb, 370

S

S curve, 553
Sabermetrics, 266
safety-stock level, 749, 750–752
salary
  array formulas, use of, 786–787
  average salary calculations, 105–107
  baseball player salaries, MATCH, 35–36
  gender wage gap, 586–588
  name ranges, use of, 18
  wage calculations, 1–2
sales calculations
  array formulas and, 794
  array functions and, 792–794
  automatic updates, monthly sales, 185–187
  calculated items, PivotTable, 413–415
  charts, sorted data and, 525–526
  compiling data from multiple worksheets, 193
  consolidating data from multiple worksheets, 196
  COUNT sales transactions, 164
  database statistical functions and, 473–478
  extracting regional sales data, 45–46
  IF statements for, 107–108
  INDIRECT, formula evaluation and, 192–193
  by location, PivotTable and, 385–388, 413–415
  median transaction by country, 798
  monthly product sale, 35
  monthly sales *vs.* previous year, 419–420
  moving averages and time series, 609–611
  multiple worksheets, PivotTable, 420–423
  name ranges, use of, 14–15
  OFFSET, data from variable cell locations, 179–180

sales calculations, *continued*
- optimal product mix decisions, 274–282
- PivotTable, creating with Data Model, 431–434
- Power Pivot, reading data into, 440–444
- Power View, sales by location, 458–459
- quarterly revenue, conditional formatting, 214–217
- quarterly sales predictions, multiple regression, 575–580
- ratio-to-moving average forecasts, 619–621
- retrieving most recent data, 184
- revenue by location, PivotTable, 407–410
- sales by person-product-location, 799
- salesforce performance analysis, 517–519, 600–602
- Scenario Manager, sensitivity analysis and, 157–161
- seasonal trend analysis, 795–798
- sorting transaction data, 227–230
- spin buttons, sensitivity analysis and, 252–256
- subtotals, creation of, 501–504
- SUMIF, AVERAGEIF, 172–175
- table formatting, new data and, 235–238
- table slicers, data subsets and, 243–244
- Timeline, PivotTable, 417–418
- total sales to date, PivotTable, 418–419
- transaction summaries, by employee, 240–242
- transactions by employee, 174–175
- transactions by total dollar amount, 174–175
- waterfall charts, progress tracking, 528–530

Salesstripping.xlsx, 45–47
Salestracker.xlsx, 517–519
sample space, defined, 631–632
sample standard deviation, 369–370
sample variance, 369–370
Sandp.xlsx, 212–214
Saragin, Jeff, 267
Scalesiconsdatabars.xlsx, 205–207, 209–212
scatter charts, 532, 534
- exponential growth, modeling of, 552–553
- linear demand curve, 761
- power curve, 555–559
- subjectively determined demand, 772–774
- trends, charting of, 545–548

Scenario Manager, sensitivity analysis and, 157–161
Scenario PivotTable Report, 161
Scenario Summary, 160–161
schedule, workforce, 285–288
scroll bars, user forms, 251–252, 256
SEARCH function, 41
seasonal index
- defining for time series, 619–621
- Winters method, 613

seasonal trend analysis, 795–798
SECOND function, 116
Secondaryaxis.xlsx, 509–510
Select A Solving Method list, 271–272
sensitivity analysis, 139–140
- mortgage decisions, 143–144
- price and unit cost, 140–143
- revenue and expense projections, 144–146
- Scenario Manager and, 157–161
- spin buttons, user forms, 252–256

service time, queuing theory, 753–757
Servicelevelreorder.xlsx, 750–752
Set Cell, story problems, 153–154
Set Objective, Solver Parameters, 276
Set Values Do Not Converge message, 282
SharePoint, 439–440
SHEET() formula, 197
SHEET() function, 197–198
Sheetnames.xlsx, 15–16
shipping decisions, Solver, 291–294
- warehouse location decisions, 317–326

Sholes, Myron, 721
Show Bar Only, 206–207
Show Field List, PivotTable, 387
Show Mean Line, 377
Show Mean Markers, 377
Show Values As, PivotTable, 419
Sigma, lognormal random variable, 679–682, 686–687
Simon, Hermann, 759
Simplex LP engine, Solver, 271–272, 279, 309
- capital budgeting decisions, 299–302

skewed left histograms, 358
skewed right histograms, 358
skewness measure, 369, 694
Slicers, 242–244
- PivotTable filters and, 387, 398
- PivotTable reports, 411–412
- in Power Pivot, 446–447
- Power View charts, 455–458

SLOPE function, 548
SMALL, 36, 373–374
smoothing constants, Winters method, 615–617
smoothing parameters, Winters method, 614
Solver. *See also* Evolutionary Solver engine; GRG Multistart
- asset allocation decisions, 702, 705–707
- capital budgeting, 297–302
- distribution decisions, 291–294
- Esc key, stop, 320
- forecasting with special events, 623–626
- IF statements, use of, 782–783
- installation, 271–272, 617
- Integer Optimality (Tolerance), 301
- introduction to, 269–272
- job-shop scheduling problems, 333
- mortgage payment, variable interest, 306–307
- 95 percent service level, 751–752
- no solution found message, 282
- optimal product mix decisions, 273–282
- profit-maximizing price, 766–768
- quadratic demand curve, 773–774
- retirement savings decisions, 307–309

Set Values Do Not Converge, 282
sports team ratings, 311–314
transportation decisions, 291–294
traveling-salesperson problem (TSP), 333–335
two-part tariff calculations, 782–784
warehouse location decisions, 317–326
Weibull random variable, 669–672
Winters method, 615–617
workforce scheduling, 285–288
Solver Parameters dialog box, 276–279. *See also* Solver
Sort & Filter group, Data, 228–230, 233
Sortedgraph.xlsx, 525–526
sorting
by cell or font color, 230–231
by icon, 231
lists, auto fill and, 233–234
by month, 231–232
PivotTable, 392–396
sales transaction data, options for, 227–230
without Sort dialog box, 232–233
Space, Delimiters, 182–183
sparklines, 465–469
Sparklines.xlsx, 465–469
spin buttons, user forms, 251–252
creation of, 253–255
sensitivity analysis, 252–256
sports performance, probability and, 713–715
sports team ratings, Solver, 311–314
spread, trendlines, 548
square root, order of operation, 7
standard deviation, 369–370
forecast bias and, 675–677
lognormal random variable, 679–682
one-way ANOVA, 597
queuing theory, 754–757
of random variables, 642–643
regression toward the mean, 566
sales by person-product-location, 799
standard normal and, 725
two-way ANOVA, 605
Z-scores, 665–666
standard error of regression (SER), 548
multiple regression, 571–572, 579
standard normal, 725
state abbreviations, data validation, 346–347
Statedv.xlsx, 346–347
States.xlsx, 14–15, 443–444
static dates, 60
Station.xlsx, 405–407
statistics. *See* database statistical functions; descriptive statistics; specific statistic names
STDEV, 370, 799
Z-scores, 665–666
Stdevif.xlsx, 799
STDEV.P, 370
STDEV.S, 370
steady-state characteristics, defined, 754
STEYX function, 548
stock options
abandonment option, 731–732
call and put options, 721–722
decision-making and, 730–732
parameter changes, effects of, 726–727
stock price and exercise date, 722–723
value of, parameters of, 723–724
volatility and, 724, 727–728
Stockcorrel.xlsx, 563–566
stocks. *See* investments
Stocksandboxplots.xlsx, 378–379
Stock.xlsx, 352, 366–369, 371–372
Stop If True, conditional formatting, 220–221
Storesales.txt, 440–444
story problems, Goal Seek and, 153–154
straight-line depreciation (SLN), 82–83
straight-line relationships, 543–548
structured references, tables, 244–246
styles, tables, 238
SUBSTITUTE function, 43
#VALUE error handling, 48–49
Subtotal dialog box, 502
subtotals
creation of, 501–504
hiding in PivotTable, 398–399
subtraction, order of operation, 6–7
SUM
array functions and, 792–794
formula ranges and row additions, 193–195
selecting data range, 3–4
summing second digits in integer set, 789–790
total hours worked, 2
workgroup assignments, 328–329
sum of squared errors (SSE), 559
SUMIF, 171–175
as array function, 792–794
database statistical functions, 474
GRG Multistart and, 320
SUMIFS, 171–175, 320
Sumindirect.xlsx, 192–193
summarizing data, multiple worksheets, 196
Summary Statistics, 366. *See also* descriptive statistics
sum-of-years' digits depreciation (SYD), 82–83
SUMPRODUCT, 274–275, 292
capital budgeting decisions, 298
Sumwithslicerstemp.xlsx, 243–244
sunburst charts, 537–540
suppliers, payment calculations, 2–4
supply points, 291–294
symbols, Icon Sets, 200–201
symmetric distributions, 357–358, 368

T

Table Import Wizard, 442
Table Name, AutoComplete, 244
table range, VLOOKUP, 21–22. *See also* ranges
Table Styles, 238
Table Tools Design tab, 238
Tablemakeuptemp.xlsx, 240–242
tables
  banded rows, 238
  column references, 245
  columns, first and last, 238
  conditional formatting and, 246–247
  duplicates, removing, 238
  dynamic ranges, 236–237
  formatting, applying to new data, 235–238
  Formula AutoComplete, 236–238
  formulas, automatic updates, 235–238
  header row, 238
  natural gas price tracking, 239–240
  ranges, converting, 238
  resizing, 238
  structured references, 244–246
  styles for, 238
  table slicers, 242–244
  total row, 238
  transaction summaries by employee, 240–242
Tablestructure.xlsx, 244–246, 245
target cells, optimization models, 269–270, 301. *See also* Solver
tax rate computations, 22–24
teacher evaluation data, 47–48
Teasalescharts.xlsx, 454–456
Teasalesfilterbycharts.xlsx, 456–458
Teasalesslicer.xlsx, 457
Teasalestemp.xlsx, 452–454
Teasalestiles.xlsx, 457
temperature trend data, formatting, 201–202
templates, charts, 520
text (.txt) files, 337–341
text functions
  CHAR, 42
  CLEAN, 43
  CONCATENATE, 42
  conditional formatting, uses of, 200–201
  Convert Text To Columns Wizard, 47–51
  data validation, 346–347
  duplicate data, highlighting, 203
  extracting product descriptions, 44–45
  extracting regional sales data, 45–46
  filters, Begins With, 489
  FIND and SEARCH, 41
  Flash Fill as option, 49–50
  importing text data into Excel, 337–341
  LEFT, 41
  LEN, 41
  MID, 41
  OFFSET, extracting data from cells, 181–183
  REPLACE, 42
  REPT, 41
  RIGHT, 41
  SUBSTITUTE, 43
  syntax, 40–41
  teacher evaluation data, 47–48
  TRIM, 41
  Unicode character sets, 51
  UPPER, LOWER, and PROPER, 42
  VALUE, 42
  #VALUE error, 48–49
  worksheet names, extracting, 197–198
Text Import Wizard, 337–341
Text To Columns, 182–183
Textfunctions.xlsx, 40
theoretical optimal target cell value, 301
thermometer chart, 520–521
Thermometer.xlsx, 520–521
third quartile, boxplots, 376–380
@/#This Row, AutoComplete, 245
3D Maps, 451–452, 461–463
three-dimensional formulas, 125–128
Tiles, Power View, 457–458
time and time functions
  computations with times, 114–115
  creating time in formulas, 115
  current time, displaying, 115
  entering times in cells, 114
  extracting hour, minute, or second, 116
  hours worked, start and end times, 116–117
  sequence of time intervals, 117
  serial numbers, 113
  static time, inserting in cell, 117
  time story problems, 153–154
  Timeline, PivotTable, 417–418
  TIMEVALUE function, 116
  wait time, queuing theory, 753–757
time-series data
  moving averages, 609–611
  trends and seasonality, 619–621
  Winters method, 613–617
Time.xlsx, 114
TODAY() function, 57, 60, 810–812
Tolerance, Solver, 301
toolbars
  macros, placing button on, 808–809
  Quick Access Toolbar, 421–422
Top/Bottom Rules, formatting, 200, 201–202
#Totals, AutoComplete, 245
Trace Dependents, 133, 134–135
Trace Error, 132–133
Trace Precedents, 133, 135–136

transactions. *See also* sales calculations
database statistical functions, 473–478
by employee, 174–175
sorting sales transaction data, 227–230
summary by employee, 240–242
by total dollar amount, 174–175
transportation decisions, Solver, 291–294
Transport.xlsx, 291–294
TRANSPOSE, 788
Transpose, Paste Special command, 120–121
Traveldata.xlsx, 401–405
traveling-salesperson problem (TSP), 333–335
treemap charts, 537–540
Treemapbookstoretemp.xlsx, 537–540
TREND function, 583–584
trends. *See also* forecasts
ANOVA, one-way, 593–597
ANOVA, two-way, 599–607
correlations, 561–566
exponential growth, modeling of, 552–553
linear demand curve, 761
LINEST function, 572–573
moving averages and time series, 609–611
multiple regressions, 567–573
election result predictions, 580–583
forecasting with, 583–584
quarterly US auto sales, 575–580
nonlinearities and interactions, 585–588
power curve, 555–559
randomized blocks, 599–601
seasonal trend analysis, LOGEST, 795–798
slope intercept, best fit of line, 548
straight-line relationships, estimating, 543–548
subjectively determined demand, 771–774
time-series and seasonality, 619–621
Winters method, 613
TRIM function, 41
extracting product descriptions, 44–45
TRIMMEAN, 374–375
Trimmean.xlsx, 375
trimmed mean, 374–375
Tsp.xlsx, 333–335
Tufte, Edward, 465
two-part tariff, 778, 780–783
two-way ANOVA, 599–607
two-way data table, profit-maximizing combinations, 780–783
Twowayanova.xlsx, 600

U

underscore (_), in ranges, 18–19
UNICHAR function, 51
Unicode character sets, 51
UNICODE function, 51
unit cost. *See also* sales calculations
effect on profit, 7–8
purchase cost as function of unit number, 96–97
sensitivity analysis, 140–143
units sold. *See also* sales calculations
break even analysis, 151–152
transactions summary by employee, 240–242
UPPER function, 42
Use A Formula, conditional formatting, 215–217, 247
Use An External Data Source, 386
user forms
check box, chart data selection, 522–523
check box for conditional formatting, 256–258
combo (list) box, day of week selection, 260
controls for, 251–252
list box, chart data selection, 523–524
macros, form controls and, 807–809
radio button, price charged options, 259
scroll bar, 256
spin buttons, creation of, 253–255
spin buttons and sensitivity analysis, 252–256

V

validating data, 343–348
VALUE, 42
extracting product descriptions, 44–45
summing second digits in integer set, 789–790
Value Field Settings, PivotTable, 391
Values, PivotTable creation, 387
#VALUE error, 48–49
#VALUE! error, 107
variables
ANOVA, two-way, 599–607
beta random variable, 669, 672–673
binomial random variables, 647–653, 693–694
continuous random variables, 643, 694
correlations, 561–566
dummy variable, 576–577
lagged variables, 577
LINEST function, 572–573
lognormal random variable, 679–682
macroeconomic variables, 577
multiple regressions, 567–573
nonlinearities and interactions, modeling of, 585–588
normal random variables, 659–665, 686–687
Poisson random variables, 655–658
qualitative independent variables, 576
quantitative independent variables, 575
random variables, 641–644
randomized blocks, 599–601
regression toward the mean, 566
straight-line relationships, 543–548

variables, *continued*
  Weibull random variable, 669–672
variance
  of random variables, 642–643
  revenue by location, PivotTable, 407–410
VAR.P, 370
VAR.S, 370
VLOOKUP
  combo (list) box, day of week, 260
  Data Model and, 430
  #N/A errors, replacing with blanks, 105–107
  price lookup, 24
  price lookup by date sold, 24–25
  radio button, price charged options, 259
  random variables, 686
  range name lookups, INDIRECT and, 195
  sports point spreads, 313
  syntax for, 21–22
  tax rate computations, 22–24
volatility, stock, 723–728

W

wage calculations, 1–2
  array formulas, use of, 786–787
  average salary calculations, 105–107
  baseball player salaries, MATCH, 35–36
  gender wage gap, 586–588
  name ranges, use of, 18
Wagestemp.xlsx, 1–2
wait time, queuing theory, 753–757
Walmartrev.xlsx, 107–108
warehouse location decisions, 317–326
Warehouseloc.xlsx, 321–326
waterfall charts, 534–537
Waterfallcashtemp.xlsx, 536–537
Waterfallcharts.xlsx, 528–530
Waterfallpandltemp.xlsx, 534–537
Weekendformatting.xlsx, 217–218
Weibull random variable, 669–672
WEIBULL.DIST, 669–672
West.xlsx, 420–423, 495–498
What-If Analysis
  break even analysis, units sold, 151–152
  mortgage decisions, 143–144
  Scenario Manager, 157–161
  sensitivity, price and unit cost, 141–143
width, OFFSET function, 178, 181
wildcard (?), 167
Winters method, 613–617
Within Groups MS (mean square), 597
wizards
  Convert Text To Columns Wizard, 47–51
  PivotChart Wizard, 420–423
  Table Import Wizard, 442
Word documents, importing text data, 337–341
workbooks
  auditing data across worksheets, 136–137
  compiling data from multiple worksheets, 193
  consolidating data from multiple worksheets, 196, 495–498
  hyperlink navigation, 127–128
  list of worksheet names, 196–198
  name ranges, scope of, 15–16
  OFFSET, data from variable cell locations, 179–180
  PivotTable, multiple workbooks, 420–423
  protecting formulas in, 728–730
  three-dimensional formulas, 125–128
  worksheet navigation tips, 387
WORKDAY function, 57–58
WORKDAY.INTL, 58
workforce scheduling, 285–288
workgroup assignments, Evolutionary Solver, 327–329
Worksheet, array formula, 197
Worksheetnames.xlsx, 196–198
worksheets
  auditing data across worksheets, 136–137
  compiling data from multiple worksheets, 193
  consolidating data from multiple worksheets, 196, 495–498
  copying of, 240
  hyperlink navigation, 127–128
  list of worksheet names in workbook, 196–198
  name ranges, scope of, 15–16
  navigation tips, 387
  OFFSET, data from variable cell locations, 179–180
  PivotTable, multiple worksheets, 420–423
  protecting formulas in, 728–730
  select all cells, 728
  three-dimensional formulas, 125–128

X

XNPV.xlsx, 66

Z

zip code, 3D Maps, 462–463
Z-scores, 665–666

About the author

WAYNE L. WINSTON is Professor Emeritus of Decision Sciences at Indiana University's Kelley School of Business and Visiting Professor of Decision and Information Sciences at University of Houston Bauer College of Business. He has earned numerous MBA teaching awards. For more than 20 years, he has taught clients at Fortune 500 companies, various accounting groups, the US Navy, and the US Army how to use Excel to make smarter business decisions. Wayne and his business partner Jeff Sagarin developed the player-statistics tracking and rating system used by the Dallas Mavericks professional basketball team. He is also a two time *Jeopardy!* champion.